AF898208

The Supreme Court, Federal and State Taxation, and the Constitution

Second Edition

By Jasper L. Cummings, Jr.

Studies in Taxation

AMERICAN BAR ASSOCIATION
Tax Section

The views and opinions expressed herein are entirely those of the author. Nothing contained herein is to be considered as the rendering of legal advice, nor should it be construed as representing the opinions, views, or actions of the American Bar Association or the Section of Taxation, unless duly approved by the Association or the Section. This book is intended for educational and informational purposes only.

The views expressed herein have not been approved by the House of Delegates nor the Board of Governors, nor the Section of Taxation of the American Bar Association and, accordingly, should not be construed as representing the policy of the American Bar Association.

Printed in the United States of America.

Published by the American Bar Association Section of Taxation.
1050 Connecticut Ave., N.W., Washington, DC 20036; www.americanbar.org/tax.

13-Digit ISBN: 978-1-64105-764-6 (Print)
13-Digit ISBN: 978-1-64105-765-3 (E-book)

For more information or to order additional copies, visit www.ShopABA.org or contact the ABA Service Center at (800) 285-2221 and request product code 5470835.

Table of Contents

Preface

Like my earlier book, *The Supreme Court's Federal Tax Jurisprudence* (2010, 2016),[1] this is a hornbook on a subject never treated by a hornbook (although hornbooks usually are not limited to Supreme Court decisions). As a hornbook, it is intended to be useful in practice. However, due to the somewhat limited application of constitutional law in everyday tax practice, this hornbook also attempts to be generally entertaining and informative on the general subjects of constitutional and American history. The principal exception to the limited use in practice is state and local taxation, which commonly involves federal constitutional claims. The new Chapter IX added in this second edition treats the Supreme Court's SALT rulings.

Hornbooks fit in the array of legal writing like this:

- *Litigators* brief arguments designed to win the case at hand, without much regard to whether the argument fits into the larger logic of the law.
- *Courts* decide those cases with opinions usually (but not always) designed to state just enough law to decide the case at hand.
- *Hornbooks* attempt to take the courts' opinions to the next level by weaving them into categories designed to make them more accessible for use by the litigators, other practitioners, and judges, thus helping those lawyers to advance the cycle of law making. Hornbooks make a modest attempt to

[1] Jasper L. Cummings, Jr., The Supreme Court's Federal Tax Jurisprudence (2d ed. 2016) (available on Westlaw at ABA-SCTTAX). Also the first edition is available on HeinOnline.

provide integrating frameworks, if not theories, in the law, which is a task that courts usually (but not always[2]) eschew.

- *Academic* articles tend either to spin what courts actually do into ever deepening insights that may outrun matters normally considered by courts, or to ignore what courts actually do and instead suggest alternate systems that are preferable to the actual systems of law applied in the courts.[3]

This hornbook addresses the one area of the Supreme Court's federal tax jurisprudence not addressed by my earlier book: the Court's federal tax opinions that have involved the application of the Constitution of the United States. And this second edition adds the only major group of constitutional tax cases left out of the first edition: state tax decisions. The two books together address all federal tax rulings of the Court, plus the Court's state tax rulings involving the Constitution, which comprise essentially all of its tax rulings.

Although *The Supreme Court's Federal Tax Jurisprudence* delved into a matter of substantial current academic interest—statutory construction—this one trenches on the much more vast subject of constitutional law, which has an even larger academic following, but relatively little practitioner following. Perhaps a general constitutional law expert should have written a book on the intersection of the Constitution and federal taxation, but none has.[4] Therefore, I am attempting to bring the Mohammed of tax to the mountain of constitutional law. The result may be imperfect from the constitutional expert's viewpoint, but should be an improvement for tax folk over cursing the darkness. This book identifies some academic treatments of the subjects addressed, usually older ones, but does not simply build on other secondary writings; instead it works principally from the original sources, the Supreme Court's own opinions. Some would find it shortsighted to ignore the academic literature; I consider it extremely practical, because the Supreme Court also will ignore the academic literature and will rely

---

[2] The Supreme Court, more frequently than other courts, sometimes attempts to create frameworks for analysis. A notable failure was Frank Lyon Co. v. United States, 435 U.S. 561 (1978), which listed 26 or 27 factors that might be considered in determining if a lessor actually owned the property, which has been read by lower courts as an all-purpose framework of uncertain meaning for disentangling substance from form. A classic example of a more successful opinion that describes a framework of analysis picking a path through disparate authorities is Justice Jackson's concurring opinion in Youngstown Sheet & Tube Co. v. Sawyer, 343 U.S. 579, 634 (1952), which created a way to analyze the constitutionality of exercises of executive power. Justice Jackson had a penchant for organization and his opinion in Miller Bros. Co. v. Maryland, 347 U.S. 340 (1954) contains the best and only compendium of Supreme Court SALT decisions to that date (and later).

[3] A prime example in the income tax area is the penchant of academic articles to begin discussions of income with citations to the Haig-Simons definition of income, with no regard to the fact that the Supreme Court has never relied on it to define income as that term is used in the Sixteenth Amendment and the Code.

[4] *Cf.* Staff of the Joint Committee on Taxation, The Taxing Power of the Federal and State Governments (1936) (available on Joint Committee website) (effectively discusses federal tax constitutional issues as of 1936, with a slant toward conservative views like those in United States v. Butler, 297 U.S. 1 (1936), which it cites).

heavily on its own prior rulings, except when it suits them, which is a political, not academic, choice. The book's goal is to attempt to know what the law is, not what academics might wish it to be.

Researching and writing this book began with and worked from the Supreme Court opinions, and employed a number of methodologies (including trial and error) to capture all opinions addressing federal and state tax constitutional issues. The opinions themselves have primarily informed my analysis. Although the Court has the luxury and power of rejecting its own prior rulings, we do not; and it can be said with confidence that the Court does not usually exercise that power,[5] absent either (1) a fairly lengthy process of disenchantment with a wrong turn it has taken (for example, the intergovernmental tax immunity cases), or (2) a fairly abrupt political jog to the left or right, which is the Court's prerogative (for example, the anti-tax rulings from 1922 to 1936 and their rejection in 1937).

Obviously there is much more constitutional case law in relation to taxes than can be found in the Supreme Court's opinions. The lower federal courts have been busy in the area of federal (but not state) taxation for nearly 100 years in the case of the income tax, and longer as to other federal taxes, and they provide the last word on many issues the Supreme Court has not chosen to review. And state court opinions on state taxes commonly address constitutional issues. Nevertheless, this book focuses entirely on the Supreme Court's opinions for four reasons:

- The lower federal and state court rulings tend to be all over the lot, and tend to sow more confusion than understanding of many subjects (as illustrated by the fact that the most effective way to obtain review of appellate rulings on federal tax is to develop a conflict among the circuits).
- While the litigator will assiduously seek out the lower court ruling that is on "all fours" with his case, or that can be analogized, or whose dictum can be pirated in any way, shape, or form, an on point (or even not so on point), Supreme Court opinion usually will trump all lower court authority.
- Many of the numerous "old" tax decisions of the Supreme Court tend to be overlooked by practitioners and the lower courts, but generally the Court does not overlook them; rather it feels compelled to deal with them, if not to follow them, when they are implicated by a current case. And, of course, electronic research and searching has made it easier to locate all possibly related authorities.

---

[5] *See, e.g.*, United States v. Home Concrete & Supply, LLC, 566 U.S. 478 (2012), following under the principle of stare decisis its earlier decision in Colony, Inc. v. Commissioner, 357 U.S. 28 (1958), somewhat to the surprise and dismay of many commentators. Congress.gov contains a Table of Supreme Court Decisions Overruled by Subsequent Decisions as well as annotations of the Constitution.

- Perhaps most important, the Court's opinions "are not final because [they] are infallible, but [they] are infallible only because [they] are final."[6] Consequently, the lower courts must follow the Supreme Court's federal tax constitutional law precedents, but the Supreme Court usually gives no credence to the views of the lower courts.

At various points this book addresses several major aspects of constitutional law that are not specifically related to tax but that bear on the tax subject (for example, "substantive due process").[7] Not only should these discussions aid in fully explaining the constitutional tax decisions, but also they aim to help the tax specialists to recall subjects they once learned in law school but may not have used since, and to see the connection between those subjects and federal taxation.

This book devotes much space to topics that may not have current prominence, because nothing said in Supreme Court opinions ever dies. Chapter II overemphasizes the Court's statements supporting the vast scope of the federal taxing power because it is so commonly questioned today. Chapter III rehearses the seemingly outmoded *Child Labor Tax Case* and *Butler* decisions and too carefully reviews the fractured *Sebelius* opinions, because they will be resurrected and new commentators will purport to find new meanings. Chapter IV perhaps is too repetitive in differentiating taxes and user fees and regulatory charges and special assessments, but the subject will grow in importance and confusion abounds. Chapter V beats the dead horse of direct taxation because tax avoiders will try to breathe life into it. Chapter VIII is briefer than it needs to be because using personal rights (which corporations increasingly possess) to attack taxes will be a growth area. And Chapter IX completes the entire set of Supreme Court constitutional law tax rulings with the state tax cases. It does not contain exhaustive analyses of subtopics like the infinite applications of the *Complete Auto Transit* test for tax discrimination against interstate commerce, but rather states what the law is known to be based solely on holdings in Supreme Court opinions.

Finally, the reader may notice that this book contains an abundance of quotations from and about the Court. They appear not entirely due to the author's laziness, but (1) to prove the sometimes surprising force with which the Court has protected the federal taxing power, and (2) to show the great trove of pithy (and sometimes not so pithy) statements from the past, which make points that we sometimes think we have just discovered.

I thank the Section of Taxation for publishing this and my first book (twice each). Fortunately it publishes to serve practitioners, who might actually need to know what the law is.

Jasper L. Cummings, Jr.
Raleigh, North Carolina
October, 2021

---

[6] Justice Robert H. Jackson, concurring in Brown v. Allen, 344 U.S. 443, 540 (1953).
[7] *See* Ch. V.D.3(b)(7).

Ch. I. The Constitutional Law of Federal Taxation

A. Summary of Book

Taxation is an inherently constitutional subject because sovereign states, which now generally operate under constitutions authorizing taxation, cannot exist without it. The constitutional law of taxation by the United States is deep and complex. The Constitution of the United States principally deals with the allocation of power among the three branches of government and with the states, and how power is limited, prominently including the taxing power.

Two important tax scholars of different eras, Thomas Reed Powell (in 1921) and Boris Bittker (in 1987), observed that there are essentially no, or no important, limits on the federal taxing power, which observation might cause a student to abandon the subject.[1] Moreover, in between those two statements another eminent tax expert, Randolph Paul, said one need not accept Powell's cavalier

---

[1] Thomas Reed Powell, Constitutional Aspects of Federal Income Taxation, in The Federal Income Tax, edited by Robert M. Haig, p. 51 (1921) ("The constitutional aspects of federal income taxation are relatively unimportant."); Boris I. Bittker, *Constitutional Limits on the Taxing Power of the Federal Government*, 41 Tax Law. 3 (1987) [hereinafter Bittker] (". . . my inspection of these two standard works indicated that there are no limits to the federal taxing power."). *See also* Tracy A. Kaye and Stephen W. Mazza, *United States—National Report: Constitutional Limitations on the Legislative Power to Tax in the United States*, 15 Mich. St. J. Int'l Law 481 (2007) ("constitutional law has played a relatively minor role in the development of tax laws in the United States.").

remark, but in truth Congress is free to enact pretty much any tax law it wants.[2] However, Powell managed to write over 40 pages about the constitutionality of the income tax, and Bittker stated that federal taxation has been "unusually prominent" in our constitutional history.[3] As this book shows, there is considerably more to the subject than meets the eye.[4]

The subject can seem obscure to the general practitioner and to the expert in federal taxation, because it rarely comes up in federal tax practice. That contrasts sharply with state taxation, in which constitutional issues abound in everyday state tax practice, particularly involving multistate taxpayers. When constitutional issues do arise in the federal taxation, their appearance tends to occur in cycles so lengthy that they escape the attention of the busy practitioner. For example, a federal tax constitutional issue arose in 2010 (and resolved in 2012) in the form of constitutional attacks on the tax adopted to enforce the so called "individual mandate" in the Patient Protection and Affordable Care Act (P. L. 111-148), requiring that individuals buy health insurance.[5] The arguments made in those attacks are direct descendants of arguments made in constitutional tax cases dating back to the *License Tax Cases* of 1867,[6] *Pollock* in 1895,[7] the *Child Labor Tax Case* in 1922,[8] but last seen in the Supreme Court in attacks on New Deal legislation.

When such federal tax constitutional issues arise, they tend to present challenges for research and even understanding, due to the relative lack of contemporary writing about them and to the incremental and changing nature of the constitutional precedents. The casual observer faces the dangers both of inadvertently plucking a precedent from the past that the Court no longer follows, and of overlooking ancient precedents that are still viable.[9]

In contrast, the constitutional law of state taxation is robust, largely because state taxation is constrained by a frequently litigated limitation that does not

---

[2] RANDOLPH E. PAUL, TAXATION FOR PROSPERITY 211 (1947).

[3] Bittker, at 3.

[4] *See, e.g.*, JAMES M. GRAY, LIMITATIONS OF THE TAXING POWER (1906) [hereinafter GRAY] (a 1316 page book principally devoted to constitutional limitations on taxation, mainly at the state level; chapter VIII focuses on federal tax limitations); Thomas M. Cooley and Alexis C. Angell, TREATISE ON THE CONSTITUTIONAL LIMITATIONS WHICH REST UPON THE LEGISLATIVE POWER OF THE STATES OF THE AMERICAN UNION Ch. XIV (6th ed.) ("The power [of states] to impose taxes is one so unlimited in force and so searching in extent, that the courts scarcely venture to declare that it is subject to any restrictions whatever . . .").

[5] *See* Ch. III.E.2.c.

[6] License Tax Cases, 72 U.S. 462 (1867).

[7] Pollock v. Farmers' Loan & Trust Co., 157 U.S. 429 (1895), *confirmed and expanded*, 158 U.S. 601 (1895).

[8] J.W. Bailey v. Drexel Furn. Co., 259 U.S. 20 (1922).

[9] Sometimes the errors are not limited to casual observers. In a case of statutory construction, Justice Thomas cited United States v. Merriam, 263 U.S. 179 (1923) in a concurrence in United Dominion Indus. v. United States, 532 U.S. 822, 839 (2001) for the discarded doctrine that ambiguous tax statutes are construed in favor of the taxpayer. *See* JASPER L. CUMMINGS, JR., THE SUPREME COURT'S FEDERAL TAX JURISPRUDENCE (2d ed. 2016) [hereinafter CUMMINGS], at ch. II.B.2.c(1).

apply to the United States, the Commerce Clause, which has produced a huge jurisprudence governing the taxation of interstate transactions. Moreover, once the state tax practitioner begins to think about constitutional objections other possibilities came to mind, encouraged by railroads, telegraph companies, and chain stores in the early days that did not like paying state taxes and saw discriminations against them in every state and local tax. Up to now, such constitutional sensitivity has been largely absent from federal tax disputes, although that could be changing, particularly in areas of individual rights.

This book addresses state tax issues under the federal Constitution in Chapter IX, although it does cite some state tax opinions of the Supreme Court in the context of discussing principles such as equal protection, due process and intergovernmental immunity, which can apply to both state and federal taxes. State tax cases cannot be excluded because it is the more important issue; as Justice Holmes said:

> I do not think that the United States would come to an end if we lost our power to declare an act of Congress void. I do think the Union would be imperiled if we could not make that declaration as to the laws of the several states.[10]

Constitutional law is in theory the law of measuring statutes and other actions of all three branches of the federal government, and of the states, against the standards of the Constitution. In the federal tax area most constitutional attacks question statutes, although questions about administrative actions can arise (such as search and seizure, self-incrimination, and other enforcement actions). Based on the activities of the Court receiving the most attention since the 1950s, many may tend to think of constitutional disputes in terms of individual civil rights.[11] But it has not always been so. The far more pervasive and recurrent theme in constitutional litigation has been the protection of property rights,[12] and the parties claiming those rights tended to be corporations, including particularly railroads, which pioneered the genre after the Civil War.

Therefore the constitutional federal tax history of the United States is largely a history of (certain types of) taxpayers' search for constitutional reasons not to pay taxes. In turn that history is an important window on the history of the United States itself, given the seminal roles of issues related to property—first and foremost slavery, state versus federal sovereignties, and laissez faire economics, to name just three general historical subjects—that strongly shaped both the nation and federal taxation.

It is well understood that the theories of constitutional law differ markedly from its practice generally, and that is true also as to the constitutional federal tax issues. While the Court might like the public to think that it is simply "calling balls and strikes," since the early days of the Court even semi-knowledgeable

---

[10] Oliver Wendell Holmes, Collected Legal Papers 295-296 (1920).

[11] *See* The Oxford Guide to the Supreme Court Court of the United States 458-465 (2005) ("Rights Consciousness in Contemporary Society").

[12] Beginning most prominently with Charles A. Beard, An Economic Interpretation of the Constitution of the United States 52 (1921).

observers have discerned it making policy, making law, and following the ballot box (though sometimes by decades).[13] For that reason the history of the Court's rulings and membership has frequently served as a handy template for many histories of the United States. This book participates in that conjoining of the Court's history with the nation's history by attempting at various points to explain how the tax issue of the moment might be fitted into the nation's history at that time.

This book can be summarized as follows. By far the substantial majority of the numerous Supreme Court opinions applying the Constitution to federal taxes deal with one, and sometimes two (and rarely all three—see *Veazie Bank v. Fenno*) of these three issues that have overshadowed the constitutional history of federal taxation: (1) intergovernmental tax immunity/federal supremacy, (2) Commerce Clause/Tenth Amendment/taxing power intersection, and (3) direct versus indirect taxation.

Issues (1) and (3) are largely resolved and have been for the last 75-100 years, but periodically reappear. For example, when presidential candidates advocated a wealth tax in 2019-2020, opponents complained that it would be an unconstitutional direct tax.[14]

Issue (2) is an aspect of the most contentious political issue in the entire history of the United States, which will never be wholly resolved, because the federal-state tug of war will never end. It is not so much that states as entities are necessarily concerned with their relationship with the federal government, as that individuals and corporations can assert the rights of states in the person's own defense to undo or prevent a federal action adversely affecting them. The last major movement on issue (2), during the New Deal era, not unexpectedly was toward the federal taxing power and away from Tenth Amendment or other limits based on states' rights. The health insurance tax dispute was resolved in 2012 consistently with the post 1936 rulings, at least as to the taxing power.[15]

The states' rights theme runs throughout these three issues: They all involve the pitting of federal power against state authority. The proponents of the states' rights in the vast majority of the litigated cases have not been states or individuals acting on behalf of their state in any real sense, but rather have been taxpayers

---

[13] Finley Peter Dunne's Mr. Dooley said in 1901 that the Supreme Court "follows th' illiction returns." Quoted in Young and Blondel, *Does the Supreme Court Follow the Economic Returns? A Response to a Macrotheory of the Court*, 58 Duke L. J. 1759 (2009) (accepting some statistical results of the Staudt, et al., studies but questioning broader conclusions). *Cf.* Nancy Staudt, Lee Epstein, Peter Wiedenbeck, *The Ideological Component of Judging in the Taxation Context*, 84 Wash. U. L. Rev. 1797 (2006) (concluding from empirical studies that no correlation is possible between "liberal" and "conservative" labels of the judges and their tendency to rule for or against taxpayers in statutory construction cases; but liberals do tend to rule against corporations and conservatives to rule in favor of corporations; the study did not address constitutional cases). *See also* Cummings, *Tax Myths and Ideologies*, 157 Tax Notes 1803 (Dec. 18, 2017).

[14] *See* Cummings, *Wealth Tax Constitutionality*, 166 Tax Notes Federal 947 (Feb. 10, 2020).

[15] *See* Ch. III.E.2.c.

seeking to reduce their own tax liabilities.[16] Therefore, to a substantial degree constitutional federal tax law is the law of federal tax avoidance. The Constitution is the last refuge of the tax avoider, to which he turns after trying politics (to avoid the adoption of the tax) and statutory interpretation (to limit the meaning of the statute, either by favorable regulatory interpretation or court ruling).

The exception that proves the rule is the Supreme Court's decision that ultimately launched almost all of the litigation involving the three core federal tax issues: *McCulloch v. Maryland*.[17] It was a case that was not pursued by Maryland for private tax reduction but for a similar private aim: the protection of local banks from competition by the Bank of the United States; the Court ruled that Maryland could not tax the notes of the Bank of the United States. From that decision flowed a century of misdirected tax immunity rulings, mostly benefiting individuals and businesses,[18] as well as the mantra that the power to tax involves the power to destroy, which has been the cry of every tax "patriot" objecting to being taxed.

In addition to these grand constitutional tax issues, there is a surprisingly large number of lesser issues arising under the Constitution, as listed in the Table of Contents. They all tend to arise only infrequently; examples include the tax status of the Territories, or of Native American Tribes, or taxation in the District of Columbia, which issues were largely established, if not totally clarified, decades or centuries ago. But, again, it only takes one disgruntled taxpayer who can afford to wonder why a certain tax can be applied in a certain way to generate anew a constitutional challenge in any of these areas.

B. Constitutional Law Generally

The Constitution of the United States best exemplifies the adjective, protean. It is versatile, capable of being nearly all things to all people. But it also is first in importance in the law of the United States. Therefore, it has attracted more study, and more astute and careful study, than any other area of American law.[19] Most of those studies try to group or categorize their subjects, around either chronological periods, subjects of interest to which the Constitution can be ap-

---

[16] *See* ROBERT H. JACKSON, THE STRUGGLE FOR JUDICIAL SUPREMACY 21-22 (1941) ("Thus 'states' rights' have tended to become a vested private interest in federal impotency rather than a positive privilege of the states themselves.").

[17] *See* Ch. II.A.1 and II.C.2.

[18] *See* Ch. II.C.8.

[19] Books on the Constitution (not to speak of articles) are too numerous to list; they include surveys of cases, general works of analysis, and discussions of targeted subjects or defined period. Each generation of scholars brings forth a new set of writings in each category. Prof. Bernard Swartz, for example, wrote a number of excellent books on the Court and most recently BARRY FRIEDMAN, THE WILL OF THE PEOPLE (2009) [hereinafter FRIEDMAN], cogently portrays the entirety of the Court's important decisions in relation to "the will of the people." *See also* KELLY, HARBISON AND BELZ, THE AMERICAN CONSTITUTION: ITS ORIGIN AND DEVELOPMENT, Two Vols. (7th ed.); THE OXFORD GUIDE TO THE SUPREME COURT COURT OF THE UNITED STATES (2005). For one recent article on important Supreme Court decisions generally, *see* Frank B. Cross and James F. Sprigg II, *The Most Important (and Best) Supreme Court Opinions and Justices*, 60 EMORY L. J. 407 (2011) (no federal tax cases are on the list).

plied, or legal concepts inherent in the Constitution itself. A popular set of concepts includes judicial supremacy, judicial restraint in exercising that supremacy, judicial protection of property rights, and judicial protection of individual liberties. The first three find a variety of important applications in the federal tax constitutional law cases; the latter is largely limited to the First Amendment tax cases.

The approach of this book is to organize and summarize the whole body of the Supreme Court's constitutional federal tax opinions, not focusing solely on what the Court has said lately, though being advertent to the current state of the law of the Court. This approach reveals that the Court has had an expansive view of the federal taxing power from the early days to the present, has exercised unusual judicial restraint against efforts to limit the federal taxing power, and has subjected property rights to the taxing power in ways that seem more forceful than in cases outside the taxing power. It should be noted, however, that a small group of academic writings about the Constitution and taxation have disagreed with the Court's expansive reading of the taxing power.[20]

The best tradition of the Supreme Court is one of judicial restraint in the area of constitutional attacks on statutes of economic regulation and taxation. The exponents of this tradition have ranged most prominently from Justice Holmes[21] to Chief Justice Taney. For example, in *Luther v. Borden*, Chief Justice Taney properly decided to leave a political issue to the politicians (enforcement of the Guarantee Clause: the guarantee of a republican form of government).[22] In the *Dred Scott* decision he failed to do so.[23] It decided that slaves were property under the Constitution and could not be or become citizens (the political question), and so Congress could not pass a law prohibiting slavery in the Territories

---

[20] *See, e.g.*, Gale Ann Norton, *The Limitless Federal Taxing Power*, 8 Harv. J. L. & Pub. Pol'y 591, 592 (1985); Richard Epstein, *Taxation, Regulation and Confiscation*, 20 Osgoode Hall Law J. 433 (1982).

[21] *See* Felix Frankfurter, *Mr. Justice Holmes and the Constitution: A Review of His Twenty five Years on the Supreme Court*, 41 Harv. L. Rev. 121, 147 (1928) ("[he] allows no finicky or textual arguments to interpose the Constitution as a barrier to the states' taxing power").

[22] Luther v. Borden, 48 U.S. 1 (1849). *See also* Chief Justice Taney's opinion in Proprietors of Charles River Bridge v. Proprietors of Warren Bridge, 36 U.S. 420 (1837). Due to the unwillingness of some states to provide even an approximation of equal representation of voters, the Court had to address the political question in Baker v. Carr, 369 U.S. 186 (1962) and related voting rights decisions.

[23] Dred Scott v. Sandford, 60 U.S. 393 (1857). President Lincoln said of the *Dred Scott* opinion: ". . . the decision was made in a sort of way. I mean it was made in a divided Court, by a bare majority of the judges, and they not quite agreeing with one another in the reasons for making it, that it is so made as that its avowed supporters disagree with one another about its meaning, and that it was mainly based upon a mistaken statement of fact—the statement in the opinion that 'the right of property in a slave is distinctly and expressly affirmed in the Constitution. . . .'" Abraham Lincoln, *Address at Cooper Institute*, New York, New York, Feb. 27, 1860. Justice Jackson cogently explained how that failed decision brought about the Civil War that led the Supreme Court's power to its lowest ebb, when President Lincoln would not respond to its writ of habeas corpus. Robert H. Jackson, The Struggle for Judicial Supremacy 325-327 (1941), discussing Ex Parte Merryman, 17 Fed. Cas. 144 (1861), and stating "one such precedent is enough!"

(the Missouri Compromise). History proved that judicial restraint likely would have been the wiser choice in that case.

Judicial review of statutes began with the most prominent exception that proves the rule of judicial restraint, *Marbury v. Madison*, which Chief Justice Marshall used to establish judicial supremacy.[24] The next decision of the Court to rule a federal statute unconstitutional was the *Dred Scott* decision, 54 years later. Once judicial supremacy was established and after *Dred Scott* and the Civil War, the Court's decisions ruling statutes, both state and federal, unconstitutional proliferated, and can be parsed in many ways. One trend line finds government power prevailing over property rights for a limited period (*Charles River Bridge*, *Munn*),[25] but then government power lost out in a series of decisions first striking down state economic regulations and then federal economic regulations, such as *Lochner*[26] and *Hammer v. Dagenhart*,[27] continuing through the rulings against New Deal legislation, which finally ended in 1936.[28] When the trend turned back to support governmental power over property rights in 1937 in decisions upholding New Deal legislation, it seemed unstoppable, until the Court began to find limits on federal Commerce Clause powers in 1995,[29] which reappeared in the split decision on The Affordable Care Act, finding Congress had the taxing power but not upholding the act under the Commerce Clause.[30]

But in the interim a new trend was developing (after a false start in the failure of the Reconstruction Era amendments to protect civil rights): judicial activism striking down statutes in order to protect individual liberties, such as protection against racial discrimination (*e.g.*, *Brown v. Board of Education*),[31] criminal due process (*e.g.*, *Miranda*),[32] privacy (*e.g.*, *Griswold v. Connecticut*),[33] and free speech (*e.g.*, *Button*).[34] This trend presented problems of consistency for some, such as Justice Frankfurter, because it seemed to apply a double standard to legislative action: stricter scrutiny when individual liberties and civil rights were at stake and laissez faire in testing economic regulations (and taxation), at least after the about face of the Supreme Court in 1937 on economic legislation.[35]

---

[24] Marbury v. Madison, 5 U.S. 137 (1803). However, the Court had earlier considered the constitutionality of federal statutes.

[25] Proprietors of Charles River Bridge v. Proprietors of Warren Bridge, 36 U.S. 420 (1837) (city could authorize a new bridge despite charter granted to existing bridge company); Munn v. Illinois, 94 U.S. 113 (1877) (state could regulate grain elevators).

[26] Lochner v. New York, 198 U.S. 45 (1905).

[27] Hammer v. Dagenhart, 247 U.S. 251 (1918).

[28] *See* Ch. III.F.2.

[29] *Id.*

[30] Nat'l Fed'n of Indep. Bus. v. Sebelius, 567 U.S. 519 (2012).

[31] Brown v. Board of Education, 347 U.S. 483 (1954).

[32] Miranda v. Arizona, 384 U.S. 436 (1966).

[33] Griswold v. Connecticut, 381 U.S. 479 (1965).

[34] NAACP v. Button, 371 U.S. 415 (1963). This trend peaked in the Warren Court but began earlier in the 20th Century with the reading of most of the Bill of Rights into the Fourteenth Amendment. *See* KELLY, HARBISON AND BELZ, THE AMERICAN CONSTITUTION: ITS ORIGIN AND DEVELOPMENT, Vol. II 516-523 (7th ed.).

[35] FRIEDMAN, at 238-239; NOAH FELDMAN, SCORPIONS ch. 16 (2010) [hereinafter FELDMAN].

The new trend and the exception to judicial restraint for judicial action to protect individual liberties usually is traced at least symbolically to Justice Stone's footnote 4 in *Carolene Products*.[36] Most recently the Court has begun to apply that new trend to protect unlimited spending in political campaigns, as speech, and dubiously applied the Equal Protection Clause to stop vote counting in the Bush-Gore election.[37] Such adaptions of Justice Stone's footnote are somewhat reminiscent of the perversion of the Fourteenth Amendment away from a protection for the former slaves and into a protection for capital (*i.e.*, substantive due process[38]). It reflects the fact that one person's individual liberty violation is another person's appropriate economic regulation. In another development this tool was not turned against the hitherto unstoppable federal taxing power in the 2012 *Sebelius* decision, although Chief Justice Roberts' dictum applied the more fundamental approach of limiting the enumerated Commerce Clause power on its own terms, rather than finding an exercise of a power invaded individual rights.[39]

Many of the Supreme Court's decisions that ruled statutes unconstitutional to protect property rights were later reversed in the public mind, if not in fact:

- *Dred Scott* (slaves are property and Congress could not change that status by legislation in the Missouri Compromise); it took the Civil War to reverse *Dred Scott*.[40]
- *Pollock* (income taxes are direct taxes and so unconstitutional because not apportioned);[41] the Court did not wait for the Sixteenth Amendment to reverse *Pollock*, because *Stone Tracy* effectively did so in 1911 by calling the 1909 corporate income tax an excise tax (as all income taxes are).[42]
- *Lochner* (thought by lawyers to be the worst example of judges imposing their own views on the Constitution's meaning);[43] this decision based the inability of the state to impose maximum hour laws on "liberty of contract."[44]

---

[36] United States v. Carolene Prod. Co., 304 U.S. 144, 152 n. 4 (1938) (distinguishes between the rational basis test for economic regulation and heightened scrutiny for Bill of Rights issues, and interference with the political process, though the subjects of heightened scrutiny are vaguely identified).

[37] Citizens United v. FEC, 558 U.S. 310 (2010); FRIEDMAN, at 334, *discussing* Bush v. Gore, 531 U.S. 98 (2000). Also, free speech was applied to protect commercial rights to mine data about private prescriptions Sorrell v. IMS Health Inc., 564 U.S. 552 (2011).

[38] *See* Ch. V.D.3.b(7).

[39] *See* Ch. III.E.2.c.

[40] Dred Scott v. Sandford, 60 U.S. 393 (1857).

[41] Pollock v. Farmers' Loan & Trust Co., 157 U.S. 429 (1895), *confirmed and expanded*, 158 U.S. 601 (1895). *See* Ch. V.D.2.c.

[42] Flint v. Stone Tracy Co., 220 U.S. 107 (1911).

[43] Lochner v. New York, 198 U.S. 45 (1905). *See* FRIEDMAN, at 167.

[44] *Id.* at 56.

But the Court ruled there was no such inviolable constitutional right to contract in *Nebbia*, and later upheld various similar laws.[45]

- *Child Labor Tax Case* (the United States tried to enforce the child labor laws stricken down in *Hammer v. Dagenhart* through a tax, which the Court also struck down);[46] subsequently federal child labor laws were upheld generally in *Darby* without a tax.[47]
- *Adkins* (struck down minimum wage legislation);[48] overruled in the first of the Court's decisions that turned the tide in favor of New Deal legislation (although the case involved state law).[49] *Adkins* is the case that was viewed as the leading symbol of the conservative resurgence of the Court, based on "liberty of contract" and *Lochner*.[50]
- *Butler* (struck down the New Deal AAA processing tax);[51] subsequently the AAA was upheld in *Wickard v. Filburn*,[52] although *Butler* has never been overruled. Justice Jackson thought its opinion was the best example of conservative opposition to government action, which is probably why it is the poster child for anti-tax and anti-regulatory arguments to this day.[53] However, the resistance to the AAA persisted, and finally in 2015 the Court struck down part of it as a taking (a new line of attack on tax-like impositions).[54]

---

[45] Nebbia v. New York, 291 U.S. 502, 523 (1934); West Coast Hotel Co. v. Parrish, 300 U.S. 379, 391 (1937).

[46] *See* Ch. III.E.2.c; Hammer v. Dagenhart, 247 U.S. 251 (1918).

[47] United States v. Darby, 312 U.S. 100 (1941).

[48] Adkins v. Children's Hospital, 261 U.S. 525 (1923). Justice Holmes said in dissent: "Pretty much all law consists in forbidding men to do some things that they want to do, and contract is no more exempt from law than other acts." 261 U.S. at 568.

[49] West Coast Hotel Co. v. Parrish, 300 U.S. 379 (1937).

[50] Russell Galloway, The Rich and the Poor in Supreme Court History 119 (1982).

[51] United States v. Butler, 297 U.S. 61 (1936). Professor Leuchtenburg called the *Butler* opinion "wretchedly argued," and noted that Senator Bankhead called it a "political stump speech," and the Governor of Pennsylvania said the six member majority was "committed to the policies of the Liberty League." William E. Leuchtenburg, Franklin D. Roosevelt and the New Deal 170-171 (1963).

[52] Wickard v. Filburn, 317 U.S. 111 (1942) (upholding the Agricultural Adjustment Act of 1938 as a proper regulation of intrastate commerce that affected interstate commerce), as explained in Maneja v. Waialua Agricultural Co., 349 U.S. 254, 259 (1955) (effectively rejecting *Butler*). *See also* Mulford v. Smith, 307 U.S. 38 (1939) (similar to *Wickard*, upholding regulation of flue-cured tobacco market). The program at issue in *Wickard* did not involve a tax but only a subsidy and accompanying regulations that the farmer could comply with or not, on pain of losing the subsidy. The opinion contained the important line: "It is hardly lack of due process for the Government to regulate that which it subsidizes." 317 U.S. at 131. *See also* Gonzales v. Raich, 545 U.S. 1 (2005) (reaffirming *Wickard*).

[53] Robert H. Jackson, The Struggle for Judicial Supremacy 312 (1941).

[54] Horne v. Department of Agriculture, 576 U.S. 351 (2015).

- *Carter Coal* (struck down the New Deal Coal Code);[55] subsequently called an echo from a bygone era.[56]

Similarly, the individual rights cases have proceeded from a broad failure to enforce individual rights, beginning before the Civil War with the *Dred Scott* case, through the Reconstruction period when the Thirteenth and Fourteenth Amendments were not enforced to protect the freed blacks, as in *Plessy v. Ferguson*,[57] to its overruling in *Brown v. Board of Education*. It is noteworthy that *Dred Scott* falls in both the groups of cases protecting capital and those failing to protect individuals.

C. The Constitution's Tax Rules

David Waldstreicher's important 2009 book, *Slavery's Constitution: From Revolution to Ratification*, patiently explains how so much of the Constitution can be traced to slavery concerns, and not just the obvious clauses.[58] Similarly, much of the Constitution relates to the core power of taxation, as amplified by the fact that the taxing powers of two sets of sovereigns had to be accommodated. The provisions of the Constitution that address or have come to be related to taxation, state and federal, are as follows.

Article I, Section 2, clause 3:

> Representatives and direct Taxes shall be apportioned among the several States which may be included within this Union, according to their respective Numbers, which shall be determined by adding to the whole Number of free Persons, including those bound to Service for a Term of Years, and excluding Indians not taxed, three fifths of all other Persons [Modified by Amendment XIV as to representatives only; Amendment XIII abolished slavery]. The actual Enumeration shall be made within three Years after the first Meeting of the Congress of the United States, and within every subsequent Term of ten Years, in such Manner as they shall by Law direct. The Number of Representatives shall not exceed one for every thirty Thousand, but each State shall have at Least one Representative; and until such enumeration shall be made, the State of New Hampshire shall be entitled to chuse three, Massachusetts eight, Rhode-Island and Providence Plantations one, Connecticut five, New-York six, New Jersey four, Pennsylvania eight, Delaware one, Maryland six, Virginia ten, North Carolina five, South Carolina five, and Georgia three.[59]

Article I, Section 7, clause 1:

> All Bills for raising Revenue shall originate in the House of Representatives; but the Senate may propose or concur with Amendments as on other Bills.[60]

---

[55] Carter v. Carter Coal Co., 298 U.S. 238 (1936).

[56] Wickard v. Filburn, 317 U.S. 111, 122 n. 21 (1942).

[57] Plessy v. Ferguson, 163 U.S. 537 (1896).

[58] As to the obvious clauses, the Joint Committee on Taxation identified eight in a 1936 report, THE TAXING POWER OF THE FEDERAL AND STATE GOVERNMENTS, vii (1936) (available on Joint Committee website).

[59] *See* Ch. V.C.; II.C.11.

[60] *See* Ch. VIII.C.

Article I, Section 7, clause 2:

> Every Bill which shall have passed the House of Representatives and the Senate, shall, before it become a Law, be presented to the President of the United States: If he approve he shall sign it, but if not he shall return it, with his Objections to that House in which it shall have originated, who shall enter the Objections at large on their Journal, and proceed to reconsider it.[61]

Article I, Section 8, clause 1 (the first enumerated power of Congress):

> The Congress shall have Power To lay and collect Taxes, Duties, Imposts and Excises, to pay the Debts and provide for the common Defence and general Welfare of the United States; but all Duties, Imposts and Excises shall be uniform throughout the United States; . . .[62]

Article I, Section 8, clause 2:

> To borrow money on the credit of the United States;[63]

Article I, Section 8, clause 3:

> To regulate commerce with foreign nations, and among the several states, and with Indian Tribes;[64]

Article I, Section 8, clause 5:

> To coin Money, regulate the Value thereof, and of foreign Coin, . . .[65]

Article I, Section 8, clause 17:

> To exercise exclusive Legislation in all Cases whatsoever, over such District (not exceeding ten Miles square) as may, by Cession of particular States, and the Acceptance of Congress, become the Seat of the Government of the United States, and to exercise like Authority over all Places purchased by the Consent of the Legislature of the State in which the Same shall be, for the Erection of Forts, Magazines, Arsenals, dock-Yards, and other needful Buildings;[66]

Article I, Section 8, clause 18:

> To make all Laws which shall be necessary and proper for carrying into Execution the foregoing Powers, and all other Powers vested by this Constitution in the Government of the United States, or in any Department or Officer thereof.[67]

Article I, Section 9, clause 1:

> The Migration or Importation of such Persons as any of the States now existing shall think proper to admit, shall not be prohibited by the Congress prior to

---

[61] *Id.*
[62] *See* Ch. V.
[63] *See* Ch. III.D.6.
[64] *See* Ch. III; II.C.11.
[65] *See* Ch. II.C.2.
[66] *See* Ch. V.D.3.a(3).
[67] *See* Ch. III.E.4.a.

the Year one thousand eight hundred and eight, but a Tax or duty may be imposed on such Importation, not exceeding ten dollars for each Person.[68]

Article I, Section 9, clause 3:

No Bill of Attainder or ex post Facto law shall be passed.[69]

Article I, Section 9, clause 4:

No capitation, or other direct, Tax shall be laid, unless in Proportion to the Census or Enumeration herein before directed to be taken.[70]

Article I, Section 9, clause 5:

No Tax or Duty shall be laid on Articles exported from any State.[71]

Article I, Section 9, clause 6:

No Preference shall be given by any Regulation of Commerce or Revenue to the Ports of one State over those of another; nor shall Vessels bound to, or from, one State, be obliged to enter, clear, or pay Duties in another.[72]

Article I, Section 9, clause 7:

No Money shall be drawn from the Treasury, but in Consequence of Appropriations made by Law; and a regular Statement and Account of the Receipts and Expenditures of all public Money shall be published from time to time.[73]

Article I, Section 10, clause 1:

No State shall . . . pass any . . . Law impairing the Obligation of Contracts . . .;[74]

Article I, Section 10, clause 2:

No State shall, without the Consent of the Congress, lay any Imposts or Duties on Imports or Exports, except what may be absolutely necessary for executing it's inspection Laws: and the net Produce of all Duties and Imposts, laid by any State on Imports or Exports, shall be for the Use of the Treasury of the United States; and all such Laws shall be subject to the Revision and Controul of the Congress.[75]

Article I, Section 10, clause 3:

No State shall, without the Consent of Congress, lay any Duty of Tonnage . . . .[76]

---

[68] *See* Ch. V.C.4.i.

[69] *See* Ch. V.D.3.b(4).

[70] *See* Ch. V.C.

[71] *See* Ch. VI.D.

[72] *See* Ch. VI.C. The distinction between a regulation of commerce and a tax was highly important to the Founders who were willing to allow the British to regulate commerce in the Colonies but not to tax. *See* Robert G. Natelson, *What the Constitution Means by 'Duties, Imposts, and Excises' - and 'Taxes' (Direct or Otherwise)*, 66 Case W. Res. L. Rev. 297 (2015).

[73] *See* Ch. III.D.5.

[74] *See* Ch. V.D.3.b(4).

[75] *See* Ch. VI.E.

[76] *See* Ch. VI.F.

Article II, Section 2, clause 2:

'[The President] . . . shall nominate, and by and with the Advice and Consent of the Senate, shall appoint . . . and all other Officers of the United States, whose Appointments are not herein otherwise provided for, and which shall be established by Law: but the Congress may by Law vest the Appointment of such inferior Officers, as they think proper, in the President alone, in the Courts of Law, or in the Heads of Departments.[77]

Article III, Section 1:

The Judges . . . Compensation . . . shall not be diminished during their Continuance in Office.[78]

Article IV, Section 2:

The Citizens of each State shall be entitled to all Privileges and Immunities of Citizens in the several States.[79]

Article IV, Section 3, clause 2:

The Congress shall have Power to dispose of and make all needful Rules and Regulations respecting the Territory or other Property belonging to the United States; and nothing in this Constitution shall be so construed as to Prejudice any Claims of the United States, or of any particular State.[80]

Article VI, clause 2:

This Constitution, and the Laws of the United States which shall be made in Pursuance thereof; and all Treaties made, or which shall be made, under the Authority of the United States, shall be the supreme Law of the Land; . . .[81]

Amendment I:

Congress shall make no law respecting an establishment of religion, or prohibiting the free exercise thereof; or abridging the freedom of speech, or of the press; or the right of the people peaceably to assemble, and to petition the Government for a redress of grievances.[82]

Amendment IV:

The right of the people to be secure in their persons, houses, papers, and effects, against unreasonable searches and seizures, shall not be violated, . . .[83]

Amendment V:

. . . ; nor shall any person be subject for the same offence to be twice put in jeopardy of life or limb; nor shall be compelled in any criminal case to be a

[77] *See* Ch. VIII.E.3.b.
[78] *See* Ch. VIII.F.
[79] *See* Ch. V.D.3.b(2)(c).
[80] *See* Ch. V.D.3.a(4).
[81] *See* Ch. II.B.1; II.C.2.
[82] *See* Ch. VIII.D.
[83] *See* Ch. VII.D.

witness against himself, nor be deprived of life, liberty, or property, without due process of law; nor shall private property be taken for public use, without just compensation.[84]

Amendment VI:

In all criminal prosecutions, the accused shall enjoy the right to a speedy and public trial, by an impartial jury . . . to be confronted with the witnesses against him; . . .[85]

Amendment VII:

In Suits at common law, where the value in controversy shall exceed twenty dollars, the right of trial by jury shall be preserved, and no fact tried by a jury, shall be otherwise re-examined in any Court of the United States, than according to the rules of the common law.[86]

Amendment VIII:

. . . nor excessive fines imposed, nor cruel and unusual punishments inflicted.[87]

Amendment IX:

The enumeration in the Constitution, of certain rights, shall not be construed to deny or disparage others retained by the people.[88]

Amendment X:

The powers not delegated to the United States by the Constitution, nor prohibited by it to the States, are reserved to the States respectively, or to the people.[89] [The Supreme Court usually refers to the Tenth Amendment to encompass any "implied constitutional limitation on Congress' authority to regulate state activities, whether grounded in the Tenth Amendment itself or in principles of federalism derived generally from the Constitution."[90]]

Amendment XIII, Section 1:

Neither slavery nor involuntary servitude, except as a punishment for crime whereof the party shall have been duly convicted, shall exist within the United States, or any place subject to their jurisdiction.[91]

Amendment XIV, Section 1:

All persons born or naturalized in the United States, and subject to the jurisdiction thereof, are citizens of the United States and of the State wherein they reside. No State shall make or enforce any law which shall abridge the privileges

---

[84] *See* Ch. VII.E; V.D.3.b(8)(b).
[85] *See* Ch. VII.B and G.
[86] *See* Ch. VIII.E.3.b.
[87] *See* Ch. VII.F.
[88] *See* Ch. VIII.D.2.b.
[89] *See* Ch. III.F.3.
[90] South Carolina v. Baker, 485 U.S. 505, 511 n. 5 (1988).
[91] *See* Ch. I.E.2.a.

> or immunities of citizens of the United States; nor shall any State deprive any person of life, liberty, or property, without due process of law; nor deny to any person within its jurisdiction the equal protection of the laws.[92]

Amendment XIV, Section 2:

> Representatives shall be apportioned among the several States according to their respective numbers, counting the whole number of persons in each State, excluding Indians not taxed . . .[93]

Amendment XVI:

> The Congress shall have power to lay and collect taxes on incomes, from whatever source derived, without apportionment among the several States, and without regard to any census or enumeration.[94]

Amendment XVIII:

> After one year from the ratification of this article the manufacture, sale, or transportation of intoxicating liquors within, the importation thereof into, or the exportation thereof from the United States and all territory subject to the jurisdiction thereof for beverage purposes is hereby prohibited. [Repealed by Amendment XXI][95]

Amendment XVIV:

> The right of citizens of the United States to vote in any primary or other election for President or Vice President, for electors for President or Vice President, or for Senator or Representative in Congress, shall not be denied or abridged by the United States or any State by reason of failure to pay poll tax or other tax.[96]

Amendment XXVII:

> No law, varying the compensation for the services of the Senators and Representatives, shall take effect, until an election of representatives shall have intervened.[97]

Chapter IX addresses state and local tax constitutional rulings of the Supreme Court.

D. Types of Taxes

The issues of the proper categorization of a tax, either in contrast to some other type of governmental levy or in distinguishing among various types of taxes, recur in constitutional tax cases. For further discussion in connection with the

---

[92] *See* Ch. V.D.3.b.
[93] *See* Ch. II.C.11.
[94] *See* Ch. V.D.2.e.
[95] *See* Ch. III.E.4.c.
[96] *See* Ch. III.E.6. *See generally* Nancy C. Staudt, *Taxation Without Representation*, 55 TAX L. REV. 555 (2002).
[97] *See* Ch. I.E.2.b.

direct tax question, see Chapter V.B; in connection with regulations versus taxes, see Chapter III.C and IX.C.4; in connection with user fees and other charges see Chapter IV; and in connection with the purposes of taxation, see Chapter III.D. Chapter IX on state taxes also addresses state tax classifications.

The Constitution categorizes taxes as direct taxes (which must be apportioned among the states according to census population), and all other "duties, imposts and excises" (which are taxes that must be geographically uniform). The Constitution's context and studies of contemporaneous usage show that duties were taxes generally, including taxes on imports and exports; excises were taxes or duties, generally imposed inland on trade in goods; and imposts were mostly taxes on imports.[98] The Constitution also imposes requirements on state tonnage duties, which are taxes.[99] One potential confusion has long been made clear: Justice Cardozo in *Steward Machine* explained that tax in the constitutional sense "includes every form of tax appropriate to sovereignty . . . taxes, duties, imposts and excises."[100] Therefore, duties, imposts and excises are also taxes, but all taxes are not duties, imposts or excises.[101]

Although the terminology of tax types is confusing and inconsistent, the most fundamental generic classifications for taxes are three:[102]

- head or capitation taxes, i.e., so many dollars per person;
- property taxes levied on value of property owned by the taxpayer (sometimes called capital taxes when levied on an entity such as a corporation, and may include income taxes not directly levied on value, according to *Pollock*, prior to the Sixteenth Amendment); and
- excise taxes (including imposts and duties, which are types of excise taxes, franchise[103] and license taxes,[104] income taxes, as in the case of the 1864 income tax,[105] the 1909 corporate excise tax, and income taxes under the

---

[98] United States Constitution Art. I, sec. 9, cl. 5; and Art. I, sec. 10, cl. 2. *See* Robert G. Natelson, *What the Constitution Means by 'Duties, Imposts, and Excises' - and 'Taxes' (Direct or Otherwise)*, 66 Case W. Res. L. Rev. 297 (2015) (a reference to duties and imposts generally meant duties on exports and imposts on imports).

[99] *See* Ch. IX.

[100] Steward Machine Co. v. Davis, 301 U.S. 548, 581 (1937).

[101] United States v. IBM, 517 U.S. 843, 857 (1996) ("impost and duty are narrower terms than tax.").

[102] Many economic writers and earlier students of taxation generally essayed various categorizations for other than constitutional purposes. *See, e.g.*, E.R.A. Seligman, Essays in Taxation (1895) [hereinafter Seligman]; Stephen Dowell, A History of Taxation and Taxes in England (1888).

[103] *See* Werner Machine Co. v. Director, 350 U.S. 492 (1956) ("bona fide" state franchise tax was not a tax on property and so could include federal obligations in tax base).

[104] *See* Binns v. United States, 194 U.S. 486 (1904) (Court assumed tax for license to sell liquor was an excise tax in the constitutional sense).

[105] Pacific Ins. Co. v. Soule, 74 U.S. 433, 446 (1869) (the opinion concluded the tax was an excise tax without reliance on such a statement in the taxing statute).

Sixteenth Amendment, which must be viewed as levied on the income received and not on the underlying property so as not to be property taxes[106]).

Head taxes and property taxes. Head taxes are extinct for practical purposes due to the 24th Amendment (literally limited to poll taxes for the right to vote). The United States rarely has imposed property taxes other than the handful of affirmatively direct apportioned taxes imposed during the War of 1812 and the Civil War.[107] Of course *Pollock* held the 1894 income tax to be a direct tax on real and personal property that produced the taxed income, although it could not be characterized as an ad valorem tax.[108]

Excise taxes. The predominant type of regularly collected federal tax up to the advent of the income tax of 1913 was the excise tax, which included most importantly imposts or tariffs on imports,[109] as well as manufacturing and consumption taxes, license taxes, estate and gift taxes, other sales taxes, and the Civil War income/excise tax. Because excise taxes per se avoided the direct tax prohibition, which was thought to be limited to property and head taxes (see Chapter V.B and C), and tried to avoid even the uncertainty about direct taxation by an income tax (resolved one way in *Pollock* and reversed by the Sixteenth Amendment, as discussed in Chapter V.D.2), the excise category has been an attractive one for the United States. Moreover, it was most compatible with the range of taxing subjects practically available in the first century and a quarter of the nation's life. Indeed the Constitution was engineered to tilt towards federal consumption taxes, which excise taxes (not levied on the receipt of income) primarily are, because of the difficulties involved with trying to levy an apportioned property tax.[110]

Federal excise taxes in the form of consumption taxes declined in importance after the late 19th and early 20th Century through a combination of factors, including: (1) Prohibition, which removed a major type of consumption transaction that was heavily taxed by the United States,[111] (2) the populist objection to high tariffs and the declining need to use tariffs to build up at least the original industries of the nation (textiles, etc.), (3) the rise in political interest in

---

[106] *See* Ch. V.D.2.e.

[107] *See* Ch. V.C.

[108] *See* Ch. V.D.2.c.

[109] *See* Jackson Turner Main, The Anti-Federalists ch. IV "The Impost" (1961) (Explaining that imposts (tariffs or excise taxes imposed on imports) were the primary type of tax contemplated for the federal government at the time of the Confederation and the debating of the Constitution.).

[110] *See* Ch. V.C.3.h.

[111] *See* Daniel Okrent, Last Call 54-55 (2010) (71% of all internal revenue and over 30% of total federal revenue came from alcohol taxes by 1910; prohibitionists recognized that a replacement tax would be needed and linked the adoption of an income tax to prohibition); Sidney Ratner, American Taxation 398 (1942) [hereinafter Ratner] (the ratification of the Eighteenth Amendment reduced the expected revenues from liquor excise taxes from $1 billion to $75 million. Only through the substantial tax increases of the 1918 Revenue Act, of which the Child Labor Tax the Court struck down in *Drexel Furn. Co.* was a part, could the government fund itself during the War).

income taxation as a more appropriate tool for raising the increasing amounts of revenues needed from sources other than indirect consumption taxes,[112] and (4) the need for more federal revenue than excises could produce, largely due to the First World War.[113]

An excise tax is most commonly related to a business transaction or occupation,[114] although the person taxed may be a consumer (as in sales taxes) and the ultimate burden of excises on business usually falls on the consumer. A classic nonbusiness excise tax is the inheritance or estate tax, which the Court defined as a tax on transmission of property on the event of death and thus an excise and not a direct tax.[115]

The fundamental definition of an excise tax is what it is not: it is not a tax on the ownership of property, usually measured by value. *Patton v. Brady* canvassed the law books and dictionaries and found definitions of excise taxes that emphasized the inland tax (internal revenue) as opposed to import imposts or duties, and included what we would call sales taxes and other consumption taxes, but also taxes on manufacturing as an early stage of the sales process as well as on all occupations and businesses (usually in the form of licenses).[116] Like many other opinions, *Patton v. Brady* suggests that an impetus for the both amorphous and expansive definition of excise was that it was thought not be a direct tax in the direct v. indirect constitutional dichotomy.

License and occupation taxes that relate to a certain occupation or transaction being regulated sometimes have been improperly viewed as exercises of the police power rather than the taxing power, when levied by states,[117] because they are in fact regulatory. However, taxes can regulate (Ch. III) and license and franchise taxes have always been viewed as taxes because sovereigns charge them for a right that only the sovereign can grant. See Ch. IV.C., and IX.C.4.g.

---

[112] *See* Ajay K. Mehrotra, *Edwin R.A. Seligman and the Beginnings of the U.S. Income Tax*, 109 Tax Notes (TA) 933 (Nov. 15, 2005). The income tax was a major plank of the Populist movement of the 1890s.

[113] *See* George Soule, Prosperity Decade 48-49 (1947) (listing increased income taxes, excess profits taxes and excise taxes as sources for financing the War, in addition to borrowing).

[114] *See* Pollock v. Farmers' Loan & Trust Co., 157 U.S. 429, 637 (1895) ("excise taxes on business, privileges, employments and vocations."). Justice Field's concurrence stated: "Excise taxes are a species of tax consisting generally of duties laid upon the manufacture, sale, or consumption of commodities within the country, or upon certain callings and occupations, often taking the form of exactions for licenses to pursue them." 157 U.S. at 592.

[115] Knowlton v. Moore, 178 U.S. 41 (1900).

[116] Patton v. Brady, 184 U.S. 608, 617-618 (1902).

[117] Robert Eugene Cushman, *The National Police Power under the Taxing Clause of the Constitution*, 4 Minn. L. Rev. 253 (1920). As to the definition of police power, see Bell's Gap R. Co. v. Pennsylvania, 134 U.S. 232, 238 (1890) (". . . neither the amendment—broad and comprehensive as it is—nor any other amendment, was designed to interfere with the power of the State, sometimes termed its police power, to prescribe regulations to promote the health, peace, morals, education and good order of the people, and to legislate so as to increase the industries of the State, develop its resources and add to its wealth and prosperity. . . .," quoting Barbier v. Connolly, 113 U.S. 27, 31 (1885)).

A related area of label confusion is the state "franchise tax."[118] This is another tax charged for a sovereign grant, which can function as an excise tax.[119] See Ch. IV.C. and IX.C.4.g. By labeling a tax an excise tax on franchises the Court was able at an early date to rule that state franchise taxes alone did not burden interstate commerce, because the states had an interest in and right to tax the franchise privilege they had granted,[120] although a franchise tax may now have to be apportioned for Commerce Clause purposes.

The ability of the Court to categorize a tax as an excise tax has proved repeatedly helpful to findings of constitutionality, as reflected in the following decisions.

- Property tax versus excise tax: *Flint v. Stone Tracy* upheld the 1909 tax on corporate income, which was effectively the same as the 1894 income tax ruled unconstitutional by *Pollock*, by calling it an excise tax.[121] The 1909 excise tax was not a tax on the property that produced the income that measures the excise tax base.[122]

- United States debt obligations: The Court early allowed states to collect an excise tax on corporations holding and receiving income from United States debt, even though the states could not tax the debt itself or its income.[123] However, since 1959 31 U.S.C. section 3124 has provided that state and local governments cannot impose a tax that would require the value of or interest on federal debt obligations to be considered in computing the tax, with the exception of a nondiscriminatory franchise tax or another non-property tax instead of a franchise tax, imposed on a corporation, and an estate or inheritance tax.

- State debt obligations: Similarly, the United States could tax state-granted franchises on the basis of state debt held by the corporation, through an excise tax measured by municipal bond interest but not imposed on it.[124]

---

[118] *See, e.g.*, SELIGMAN, at 186-187 (struggling with the meaning of franchise tax and pointing out that the categorization was so important because of the different limitations imposed on property taxes and franchise taxes, as imposed by states).

[119] *See, e.g.*, Complete Auto Transit, Inc. v. Brady, 430 U.S. 274 (1977) (both); First Agricultural National Bank v. State Tax Comm'n, 392 U.S. 339 (1968) (federal law allowed states to levy franchise or excise tax on national banks); Helvering v. Gerhardt, 304 U.S. 405 (1938) (explaining that *Stone Tracy* approved the levying of federal excise tax on the privilege of exercising state corporate franchises). However, another complication is caused by sometimes treating franchise taxes as taxes on property. *See* Case of State Freight Tax, 82 U.S. 232 (1873) (ruling that franchise tax was actually a tax on property rather than the business of the railroads); Gulf & Ship Is. Ry. Co. v. Hewes, 183 U.S. 66 (1901) (treating privilege license tax as property tax).

[120] *See* Maine v. Grand Trunk R. Co., 142 U.S. 217 (1891) (the Court refused to be swayed by the fact that the tax was measured like an income tax on receipts from interstate commerce). But the formalism came to be abandoned, as explained in Okla. Tax Comm'n v. Jefferson Lines, 514 U.S. 175 (1995).

[121] Flint v. Stone Tracy Co., 220 U.S. 107 (1911).

[122] McCoach v. Minehill & S. H. R. Co., 228 U.S. 295 (1913).

[123] Society for Savings v. Coite, 73 U.S. 594 (1868); Provident Inst. v. Mass., 73 U.S. 611 (1868); Werner Machine Co. v. Director, 350 U.S. 492 (1956).

[124] Flint v. Stone Tracy Co., 220 U.S. 107, 162, 171 (1911).

This application of the arbitrary distinction between excise and income or property taxes is not subject to a rule like that in 31 U.S.C. section 3124.

- Sales tax versus excise tax: Whereas the federal tax on motorcycle sales in *Indian Motorcycles* was unconstitutional when levied on a local government, the flat rate tobacco tax was constitutional because Congress deemed it an excise tax on manufacture.[125]
- Estate tax: The transmission of property is a classic subject for an excise tax and thus helps avoid claims that the states solely could tax inheritance.[126]

Commentators have over the centuries proposed other categorizations of taxes.[127]

E. The Supreme Court's Constitutional Tax Jurisprudence

1. *Overview*

Just as taxation is at the heart of the Constitution, taxation is at the heart of the Court's constitutional jurisprudence, and so should the Constitution be at the heart of the Court's federal tax jurisprudence. The first reported decision in which the Court considered the constitutionality of a federal statute was *Hylton v. United States*, rejecting the charge that the first federal taxing statute (taxing carriages) was unconstitutional because it was an unapportioned direct tax.[128] Thus *Hylton* prepared the way for *Marbury v. Madison*, which asserted most famously the Court's supreme power to interpret the Constitution.[129] An even more important early decision on state taxes and federal supremacy, *McCulloch v. Maryland*, ruled a state tax on the notes of the Bank of the United States to be unconstitutional.[130] *McCulloch* established the role of the Necessary and Proper Clause, the supremacy of the United States vis à vis the states in matters within its powers, and the doctrine of intergovernmental immunity, which expanded for a century to apply also to federal taxation of state entities, until scaled back in the 1930s. And the large group of constitutional tax decisions that this book does not addressed in Chapter IX—the state tax Commerce Clause, Due Process Clause and Privilege and Immunities decisions—also are at the center of that great constitutional conflict between federal and state power. Once again

---

[125] Indian Motorcycle Co. v. United States, 283 U.S. 570 (1931); Liggett & Myers Tobacco Co. v. United States, 299 U.S. 383 (1937).

[126] Knowlton v. Moore, 178 U.S. 41, 60 (1900); United States v. Mfrs. National Bank, 363 U.S. 194 (1960).

[127] Seligman, at 302 (identified the categories of receipts by governments as follows: Gratuitous, Contractual, Compulsory, Eminent domain, Penal power, Taxing power [Fees, Special assessments, Taxes]).

[128] Hylton v. United States, 3 U.S. 171 (1796). It is possible that United States v. Yale Todd was an earlier decision that actually held a federal statute unconstitutional. *See* United States v. Ferreira, 54 U.S. 40 (1852).

[129] Marbury v. Madison, 5 U.S. 1 (1803).

[130] McCulloch v. Maryland, 17 U.S. 316 (1819). As to intergovernmental tax immunity, see Ch. II.C.

in 2012 the Court was found at the center of a great constitutional and public policy and political debate concerning the health insurance tax.[131]

As in areas of the Court's jurisprudence not involving the Constitution,[132] sensitivity to the Court's peculiar powers and constraints as a court is essential. Justices themselves have remarked on their relative inability to shed useful light on federal taxation, with the rare and important exception of constitutional tax issues.[133] In addition to being "final" but not necessarily "infallible,"[134] the Court's opinions have other particular characteristics including: (1) they generally can be counted on to contain logical, sequential, analyses of the issues, albeit dealing with an echelon of considerations higher than that to which lower courts usually limit themselves, but (2) they also can depart from logic, or even from seemingly controlling precedent, without explanation, or with dubious explanation, with much more ease than can a lower court.[135]

Although they can be intensely logical and generally are superbly footnoted, Supreme Court opinions tend to carry another particular attribute reflecting the fact that the Supreme Court is a political actor in the constitutional scheme. The degree to which the Court is viewed as overtly political has varied throughout its history. Early on some Justices, particularly Justice Samuel Chase, exhibited substantial partisanship on the bench. After a failed attempt to impeach Justice Chase, who had been a vocal Federalist supporter, the Justices somewhat got the message and tried to appear non-partisan, and hence were accorded a measure of independence.[136] However, the stakes are just too high in Supreme Court decision making, and the presidential appointment power too central to the life of the Court, for politics not to emerge in its decisions, at least at critical junctures.[137]

---

[131] *See* Ch. III.E.2.c.

[132] *See generally* CUMMINGS.

[133] Justice Douglas dissenting in United States v. Skelly Oil Co., 394 U.S. 678, 690-691 (1969) ("If we were trained in the art and science of taxation, we might serve a useful function. But taxation is a specialty in which we have only sporadic and no continuous experience. It has been said that one of our decisions is like a 'lightning bolt' that 'illuminates only a very small portion of the landscape,' leaving a darkness that later decisions do not remove. R. PAUL, STUDIES IN FEDERAL TAXATION 249-250 (3d series 1940). Our contributions, if such they can be called, are dubious indeed, for the Joint Committee can and does rewrite the Code frequently. It is therefore the rare tax case we should consider, except the even rarer constitutional case. The present case has no constitutional overtones . . .").

"I still think the Tax Court is a more competent and steady influence toward a systematic body of tax law than our sporadic omnipotence in a field beset with invisible boomerangs." Arrowsmith v. Commissioner, 344 U.S. 6 (1952) (dissent of Justice Jackson).

[134] Justice Robert H. Jackson, concurring in Brown v. Allen, 344 U.S. 443, 540 (1953).

[135] For example, when Chief Justice Taft ruled the Child Labor Tax unconstitutional in 1922 he effectively rejected 135 years of nearly uniform expansion of the federal taxing power (the prior exception being *Pollock*, which involved a different issue) by exclaiming that he just could not shut his eyes to the obvious motive to regulate behind Congress' tax (which Congress had never tried to hide, but which should not have been relevant to deciding the case). J.W. Bailey v. Drexel Furn. Co., 259 U.S. 20 (1922).

[136] FRIEDMAN, at 64-71.

[137] *See generally* JAMES MACGREGOR BURNS, PACKING THE COURT (2009) [hereinafter BURNS].

Indeed, the "determined bar" and their clients, discussed in Chapter I.E.3, viewed the Court as the last resort for protection from populist assaults on property.[138] However, the Court has fulfilled that role as to federal taxation only in the income tax case in 1895, *Pollock*, and in the period of 1922 through 1936 when the Court ruled unconstitutional five tax provisions in four acts of Congress on the ground that they were not taxes but unconstitutional regulation. The relatively disappointing response of the Court to the defenders of property from taxation is partly explained by (1) the strong momentum of the early Federalist support for taxation and the federal government, evidenced first in the *Hylton* decision in 1796, which was based on (2) the inescapable fact that taxes are the life blood of government.

This book attempts to show what the Court has done, as contrasted with cataloguing "doctrines" of constitutional tax adjudication that some may attribute to it.[139] This distinction is appropriate because the Court is intensely practical, though its members understand the value (or danger) of the mythology of doctrine.[140] The most practical approach to disentangling the cases is to identify categories, or clusters, to which practical problems can be assigned; only after classifying the problem at hand does the standard for decision need to be addressed; and then the standard can be stated where known (sometimes called doctrines) and the unknown areas can be corralled.

Justice Jackson best illustrated how analyzing the Court's precedents and constitutional decision making can be done in his opinion in *Youngstown Sheet & Tube*, albeit not a tax case.[141] The Court enjoined President Truman's seizure of the steel mills. Justice Jackson reasoned as follows:

- First, identify and focus on the fundamental constitutional principle at stake (which was the balance of powers), rather than the needs of the moment;
- Second, recognize that the authorities are confused and establish no clear method of analysis;
- Third, identify groupings or clusters of practical cases that have arisen and try to place them in a framework that reflects the fundamental constitution-

---

[138] Arnold M. Paul, Conservative Crisis And The Rule Of Law 159 (1960, 1976 reprint) [hereinafter Paul].

[139] A doctrine is a general principle that the Court has developed in any one of several ways and used in deciding cases other than by literal application of the words of the Constitution, or in the absence of directly governing words of the Constitution. The Court employs various ways of creating doctrine, including most importantly text, structure of the Constitution, and prior Constitutional doctrine. *See* The Oxford Guide to the Supreme Court of the United States 211-218 (2005) (discussing modalities of constitutional interpretation generally).

[140] *See, e.g.*, dissenting opinion of Justice Jackson in Korematsu v. United States, 323 U.S. 214, 246 (1944) ("A military commander may overstep the bounds of constitutionality, and it is an incident. But if we review and approve, that passing incident becomes the doctrine of the Constitution. There it has a generative power of its own, and all that it creates will be in its own image. Nothing better illustrates this danger than does the Court's opinion in this case.").

[141] Youngstown Sheet & Tube Co. v. Sawyer, 343 U.S. 579, 634 (1952). *See* Feldman, at 365 (the three part test became "standardized as the law of the land").

al principle of the balance of powers; that framework logically will depend on the various types of interactions between the power of the two competing departments, the President and the Congress (in cases testing executive power);

- Fourth (defining a three part test), those groupings are cases in which the President has acted (a) in accord with congressional direction (in which case the President's action can be unconstitutional only if the entire federal government lacks the power to act), (b) in a vacuum of congressional direction ("any actual test of power is likely to depend on the imperatives of events and contemporary imponderables rather than on abstract theories of law"), or (c) contrary to congressional direction ("Courts can sustain exclusive presidential control in such a case only by disabling the Congress from acting upon the subject.").

A similar but more pithy statement was made by Justice Holmes in his dissent in *Lochner*: "General propositions [*i.e.*, doctrines] do not decide concrete cases."[142] An orderly approach (like that suggested in *Youngstown*) might have protected the Court (if it wanted to be protected) from its creation of doctrines, such as "liberty of contract," which originated outside the tax area in cases like *Lochner*,[143] and spread into the tax area in cases like *Drexel Furniture*,[144] only to be discarded when it was noted that "the Constitution does not speak of freedom of contract."[145]

Finally, the Court has shown in its constitutional federal tax decisions, as it has in other areas of the law, that the Constitution and its meaning are not static. The best example is the century long expansion and then contraction of the doctrine of intergovernmental tax immunity, discussed in Chapter II.C. Fortunately, the ability to fit the Constitution to the times is a method with a distinguished pedigree. Thomas Jefferson said toward the end of his life:

> Some men look at constitutions with sanctimonious reverence, and deem them like the ark of the covenant, too sacred to be touched. . . . I am certainly not an advocate for frequent and untried changes in laws and institutions . . . But I know also that laws and institutions must go hand in hand with the progress of the human mind. As that becomes more developed, more enlightened, as new discoveries are made, new truths disclosed, and manners and opinions change with the change of circumstances, institutions must advance also, and keep pace with the times. We might as well require a man to wear still the coat which

---

[142] Lochner v. New York, 198 U.S. 45, 76 (1905).

[143] *Id.* at 56 ("Of course the liberty of contract relating to labor includes both parties to it. The one has as much right to purchase as the other to sell labor.").

[144] J.W. Bailey v. Drexel Furn. Co., 259 U.S. 20 (1922) ("Although Congress does not invalidate the contract of employment or expressly declare that the employment within the mentioned ages is illegal, it does exhibit its intent practically to achieve the latter result by adopting the criteria of wrongdoing and imposing its principal consequence on those who transgress its standard.").

[145] West Coast Hotel Co. v. Parrish, 300 U.S. 379, 391 (1937).

> fitted him when a boy, as civilized society to remain ever under their barbarous ancestors[146] [referring to the Founding Fathers, of which he was one].

This book relies on the Court's opinions, not denials of certiorari, for which see Justice Stevens' chastisement of Justice Blackmun for dissenting to a denial of certiorari (in a federal tax case).[147]

2. *Federal Tax Provisions Ruled Unconstitutional by the Supreme Court*

a. *Summary*

The Supreme Court has ruled unconstitutional 25 federal tax provisions, either in general or as applied, and invalidated one tax based on finding a related non-tax statute unconstitutional (*Windsor*).[148] It is a commonplace observation that from the creation of the nation to 1857 the Supreme Court ruled only two federal statutes unconstitutional, a jurisdictional statute in *Marbury v. Madison* and the Missouri Compromise in the *Dred Scott* decision (in dictum).[149] In the 1870s it ruled two federal taxes unconstitutional as applied on the grounds of intergovernmental immunity stemming from *McCulloch v. Maryland*.[150] But it was not until 1895 in *Pollock* that the Supreme Court ruled a federal tax to be unconstitutional for any other reason, thereby thwarting a major initiative of Congress.

In retrospect *Pollock* has been viewed with almost as much disdain as the *Dred Scott* decision, and its close rival, *Lochner*.[151] The Court distinguished *Pollock* on the most artificial of grounds in upholding the 1909 corporate excise tax (levied on income) in 1911, and Congress and the people rejected *Pollock* in the Sixteenth Amendment, somewhat as the Thirteenth Amendment rejected *Dred Scott*.

As suggested by a statement of Justice Jackson, however numerous these 25 rulings (not counting *Windsor* for this purpose) may seem, they are relatively unimportant in comparison with the larger point about money and taxes:

---

[146] Letter to Samuel Kercheval, June 12, 1816, inscribed on the rotunda of the Jefferson Memorial in Washington, DC.; National Archives, Founders Online.

[147] Singleton v. Commissioner, 439 U.S. 940 (1978).

[148] *See* Henry W. Edgerton, *Incidence of Judicial Control over Congress*, 22 CORN. L. Q. 299 (1937) [hereinafter Edgerton] (compiled tax and nontax rulings of unconstitutionality by the Supreme Court as of 1936, based on Library of Congress survey through 1936). This book has updated and added to Edgerton's list.

[149] Marbury v. Madison, 5 U.S. 1 (1803) (first decision to hold a federal statute unconstitutional, the statute purporting to grant the court jurisdiction to hear this appeal); Dred Scott v. Sandford, 60 U.S. 393 (1857). *See also* Hylton v. United States, 3 U.S. 171 (1796) (Justice Chase considered declaring the act of Congress unconstitutional but stated "I will never exercise it, but in a very clear case.").

[150] McCulloch v. Maryland, 17 U.S. 316, 425 (1819); *see* Ch. II.A.1 and II.C.2.

[151] *See* BERNARD SCHWARTZ, A HISTORY OF THE SUPREME COURT 184, 190 (1993) [hereinafter SCHWARTZ] (*Pollock* was Justice Fuller's most criticized opinion; *Lochner*, second only to *Dred Scott* as the most discredited case in the Court's history).

> Two of the greatest powers possessed by the political branches, which seem to me the disaster-potentials in our system, are utterly beyond judicial reach. They are the war power and the money, taxing, and spending power, which is the power of inflation. The improvident use of these powers can destroy the conditions for the existence of liberty, because either can set up great currents of strife within the population which might carry down constitutional forms and limitations before them.[152]

Similarly, Chief Justice Charles Evans Hughes stated:

> . . . far more important for the development of the country, than the decisions holding acts of Congress to be invalid, have been those in which the authority of Congress has been sustained and adequate national power to meet the necessities of a growing country has been found to exist within constitutional limitations.[153]

b. *The 25 Federal Tax Provisions Ruled Unconstitutional*

The decisions of the Supreme Court ruling unconstitutional the 25 federal tax provisions (and one general rule applied to a federal tax) are listed chronologically and briefly described below. All are discussed further in this book as indicated in the footnotes, in addition to the general analysis in the next Chapter.

1. *Intergovernmental immunity*: *Collector v. Day*, 78 U.S. 113 (1871).[154] The United States could not tax the income of a state judge. This decision was thought to be required by analogy to *McCulloch v. Maryland* (holding unconstitutional a state tax on the Bank of the United States). *Collector v. Day* was overruled by *Graves v. New York* in 1939.[155]

2. *Intergovernmental immunity*: *United States v. R.R. Co.*, 84 U.S. 322 (1873).[156] The United States could not require a debtor (the railroad) to withhold the federal Civil War income tax on interest paid to a municipality because a municipality shares in the immunity of the state (established in *Collector v. Day*).

3. *Direct tax and intergovernmental immunity*: *Pollock v. Farmers' Loan & Trust Co.*, 157 U.S. 429 (1895), *confirmed and expanded*, 158 U.S. 601 (1895).[157] The United States could not tax income from property, real or personal, because the tax on income was a direct tax, and also could not tax interest on state bonds under the rule of *Collector v. Day*. *Pollock* was rendered moot as

---

[152] Robert H. Jackson, The Supreme Court in the American System of Government, 59 (1963 Harper Ed.).

[153] Charles Evans Hughes, The Supreme Court of the United States 96 (1928).

[154] Justice Bradley dissented. *See* Ch. II.C.7.a.

[155] Graves v. New York, 306 U.S. 466 (1939).

[156] Justices Clifford and Miller dissented. *See* Ch. II.C.8.

[157] Justices White and Harlan dissented from the first opinion; Justices Harlan, Brown, Jackson and White dissented from the second opinion. *See* Ch. V.D.2.c.; II.C.7. For the full briefs and other materials see House of Representatives Print, Decisions of the United States Supreme Court in the Corporate Tax Cases and the Income Tax Cases (1912).

to direct taxation though an income tax by the Sixteenth Amendment and was overruled by *South Carolina v. Baker* as to nondiscriminatory federal taxation of state bond interest.[158]

4. *Export tax*: *Fairbank v. United States*, 181 U.S. 283 (1901).[159] The United States could not impose a stamp tax on a foreign bill of lading under the clause forbidding taxation of exports by the United States.
5. *Export tax*: *United States v. Hvoslef*, 237 U.S. 1 (1915).[160] The United States could not impose a stamp tax on charter parties to foreign countries, because the stamp requirement had the effect of a tax on exports.
6. *Export tax*: *Thames & Mersey Ins. Co. v. United States*, 237 U.S. 19 (1915).[161] The United States could not impose a tax on insurance for marine risks issued to insure export transportation, because insurance is a necessity for exportation.
7. *Direct tax*: *Eisner v. Macomber*, 252 U.S. 189 (1920).[162] The United States could not tax "true stock dividends" even under the Sixteenth Amendment. Although not directly overruled, the Court has since adopted a broader definition of income,[163] and distinguished *Macomber* when the shareholder received a different interest in the corporation.[164]

---

[158] South Carolina v. Baker, 485 U.S. 505, 522-524 (1988) ("That this Court has yet to overrule *Pollock* explicitly, however, is explained not by any distinction between the income derived from government bonds and the income derived from other government contracts, but by the historical fact that Congress has always exempted state bond interest from taxation by statute, beginning with the very first federal income tax statute. Act of Oct. 3, 1913, ch. 16, § II(B), 38 Stat. 168. . . . We thus confirm that subsequent case law has overruled the holding in *Pollock* that state bond interest is immune from a nondiscriminatory federal tax."). *Baker* was unusual because it was heard under the original jurisdiction of the Supreme Court, with findings of fact made by a Special Master. 485 U.S. at 510.

[159] Justices Harlan, Gray, White and McKenna dissented. *See* Ch. VI.D. *Cf.* United States v. Cuba Mail Steamship Co., 200 U.S. 488 (1906) (tax on exports upheld because it was paid voluntarily).

[160] *See* Ch. VI.D.

[161] *See Id.*

[162] Justices Holmes, Brandeis and Clarke dissented. *See* Ch. V.D.2.f. An earlier similar decision did not purport to be on constitutional grounds, and the statute did not then attempt to include stock dividends in income. Towne v. Eisner, 245 U.S. 418 (1918), as explained in Koshland v. Helvering, 298 U.S. 441 (1936).

[163] *See* Commissioner v. Glenshaw Glass Co., 348 U.S. 426 (1955). Other early decisions found items not to be income under the Sixteenth Amendment, but they should probably be viewed as cases of statutory construction that have been superseded by decisions like *Glenshaw Glass*. *See, e.g.*, Edwards v. Cuba R. Co., 268 U.S. 628 (1925) (contribution to capital by government not income under statute; opinion also stated not income under Sixteenth Amendment.); Weiss v. Stearn, 265 U.S. 242 (1924) (a nonrealization case).

[164] *See* Koshland v. Helvering, 298 U.S. 441 (1936).

8. *Federal judge's salary*: *Evans v. Gore*, 253 U.S. 245 (1920).[165] The United States could not apply a nondiscriminatory tax to the salary of a federal judge because the tax diminishes the compensation. In effect the Court denied the ability of the Sixteenth Amendment to affect its reading of Article III, section 1. *Evans v. Gore* was overruled in part by *United States v. Hatter*, which approved a generally applicable, nondiscriminatory tax on federal judges.[166]

9. *Tenth Amendment*: *J.W. Bailey v. Drexel Furn. Co.*, 259 U.S. 20 (1922) (*Child Labor Tax Case*).[167] A federal exaction that was labeled a tax on the employment of child labor was not a tax but was a regulatory penalty imposed to achieve a purpose solely within the power of the state and so was unconstitutional. The Court viewed this tax as a direct challenge to its ruling in *Hammer v. Dagenhart*, which struck down a similar regulatory scheme without a tax shortly before.[168] Chief Justice Taft's opinion in *Drexel* is often cited for this explanation of judicial vision, which is the fundamental conclusion in the case: "In the light of these features of the act, a court must be blind not to see that the so called tax is imposed to stop the employment of children within the age limits prescribed. Its prohibitory and regulatory effect and purpose are palpable. All others can see and understand this. How can we properly shut our minds to it?"[169] The government did not defend the law at issue in the *Child Labor Tax Case* as a regulation of interstate commerce, which defense would have been possible under the subsequent holding of *United States v. Darby*, overruling *Hammer v. Dagenhart*, which was the pure regulatory version of the *Child Labor Tax Case*.[170] *Hammer* and

---

[165] Justices Holmes and Brandeis dissented. *See* Ch. VIII.F. Chief Justice Taney had objected to a tax increase on federal judges in 1863, the collection of the Civil War income tax, but felt he could not sit on a case deciding the issue. The Treasury ultimately agreed and refunded the taxes paid by federal judges. CARL B. SWISHER, ROGER B. TANEY 568-569 (1935).

[166] United States v. Hatter, 532 U.S. 557 (2001). *See also* Amendment XXVII as to senators and representatives' compensation.

[167] Justice Clarke dissented. *See* Ch. III.E.2 and III.F. This case was a repeat of the result in Hammer v. Dagenhart, 247 U.S. 251 (1918), involving essentially the same restrictions, but imposed without a tax. Henry W. Edgerton stated with respect to *Drexel*: "Few decisions have had more serious consequences. Available data indicate that the employment of children increased markedly after this law was invalidated. The effects of child labor in mechanical industries on children, on the wage level, and on society generally, and the impossibility of dealing effectively with the matter by states are only too well known." Edgerton, at 331. *See also* Bailey v. George, 259 U.S. 16 (1922) (a companion case seeking an injunction; dismissed under the Anti-Injunction Act, as not sufficiently extraordinary to warrant avoidance of refund remedy).

[168] 259 U.S. at 39 ("The case before us cannot be distinguished from *Hammer v. Dagenhart*.").

[169] *Id.* at 37. *See, e.g.*, Watts v. Indiana, 338 U.S. 49, 52 (1949). *See also*, Stephen B. Wood, Constitutional Politics in the Progressive Era 278-279 (1964) (identifying this sentence as the fundamental conclusion, by which Taft attempted to explain why he was not examining the motives of Congress).

[170] United States v. Darby, 312 U.S. 100 (1941), overruling Hammer v. Dagenhart, 247 U.S. 251 (1918). *See* Western Union Tel. Co. v. Lenroot, 323 U.S. 490, 497 (1945) (explaining *Drexel* as not involving a statute purporting to regulate interstate commerce).

Drexel effectively made employment regulations impossible in the United States, because if the federal government could not impose such regulation, states would hardly be able to do so due to the interstate competition to loosen or eliminate labor regulations that would ensue to attract business into the state. Although the *Child Labor Tax Case* was never overruled, the 1937 about face by the Supreme Court on New Deal legislation cast doubt on the factual finding that the child labor tax was not a tax.[171] Other majority opinions of the Court subsequently stated that the Court abandoned the distinction between regulatory and revenue raising taxes,[172] and otherwise cast doubt on the decision's viability,[173] as unduly based on the Court's view of Congress' motives,[174] and as reflecting the earlier Court's "belief" that the United States had no interest in the child labor issue.[175] Later decisions have cited *Drexel* mostly for Chief Justice Taft's vision statement, or in dissent. However, Chief Justice Roberts' opinion for the Court in *Sebelius* purported to apply the test used in *Drexel* to the 2010 health insurance tax, though he likewise cast doubt on *Drexel*'s viability.[176] Even though the decision of the *Drexel* court was unanimous, the private papers of Justice Brandeis reveal that he believed the tax to be constitutional.[177] See Ch. III.E.2.c(4) discussing the reliance on this decision in *Sebelius* (2012), the health insurance tax case.

---

[171] *See* Steward Machine Co. v. Davis, 301 U.S. 548 U.S. 591 (1937) (the Court earlier "believed" that the tax was unrelated to the fiscal need). The *Sebelius* (2012) opinion also cast doubt on it, as discussed in Ch. III.E.2.c.

[172] Bob Jones Univ. v. Simon, 416 U.S. 725, 741 n. 12 (1974) (citing Sonzinsky v. United States, 300 U.S. 506, 513 (1937), which did not so clearly abandon the distinction, although it did uphold a firearms tax that was fairly clearly regulatory). *See* Ch. III.E.2 and III.F.

[173] *See* Daniel v. Family Sec. Life Ins. Co., 336 U.S. 220, 224 (1949) (contrasted *Drexel* and *Constantine*, case 20, as cases in which the Court improperly relied on evidence of congressional motive in holding a statute unconstitutional).

[174] *Id.*

[175] Steward Machine Co. v. Davis, 301 U.S. 548 (1937).

[176] Nat'l Fed'n of Indep. Bus. v. Sebelius, 567 U.S. 519 (2012). *See* Ch. III.E.2.c

[177] A.M. Bickel, The Unpublished Opinions of Mr. Justice Brandeis 16-19 (1957).

10. *Tenth Amendment*: *Hill v. Wallace*, 259 U.S. 44 (1922).[178] On the same day the Court ruled in the *Child Labor Tax Case*, it held unconstitutional on the same grounds the Future Trading Act, which the Republican Congress adopted in 1921, presumably to aid Midwest farmers (then a major constituency of the party); indeed the *Wallace* opinion referred to the *Child Labor Tax Case* opinion for its reasoning and reliance on the Tenth Amendment.[179] *Wallace* was in reality a suit by some members of the Chicago Board of Trade against the Board itself, as well as the Treasury and the Department of Agriculture, to enjoin the Board from complying with the Act, which plaintiffs believed would end their monopoly control of trading in agricultural commodities for future delivery, by allowing farmers acting on a cooperative basis to sell commodity futures without paying the Board's commissions. The Act imposed a 20 cents per bushel tax on commodity futures trades on the Exchange if the Board did not comply with the Act's anti-monopoly rules; the tax was in addition to a two percent general tax on commodity trades. The new tax was to be in the range of 15-50% (or more) of the price per bushel of various commodity futures, which tax the plaintiffs said was high enough to effectively coerce the Board into compliance with the Act's regulations and requirements for membership on the Exchange. Therefore, the ruling for the plaintiffs was a victory for the monopoly power of the Board's members (the futures traders) over the farmers. *Wallace* found the tax in sections 4 and 10 of the Act to be not a tax but a regulation of intrastate commerce that Congress could not regulate, because it was a subordinate part of the scheme of section 4, which had a purely regulatory purpose. The Court's either-or approach to characterization meant that the features of the Act that were admittedly related to tax collection (*e.g.*, record keeping) could not determine the tax's character, because of the "real purpose" of Congress to regulate that which it could not regulate.[180] There is evidence that the Court was at one time 5 to 3 in favor of the tax, but decided to coordinate it with the decision in the *Child Labor Tax Case* by finding to be a penalty

[178] *See* Ch. III.D.2. Justice Brandeis wrote a strange concurrence in *Hill v. Wallace* in which he presumably agreed with the ruling on constitutionality for unstated reasons, but said the plaintiffs did not have standing to raise the question. He made these observations about the duty of a taxpayer to resist, or not, unconstitutional taxes: "Nothing is better settled than that an individual may acquiesce in or waive an admitted infringement of a constitutional right; and I am not aware of any rule of law which requires a corporation, upon request of a minority stockholder, to play the knight-errant and tilt at every statute affecting it, which he believes to be invalid. A corporation, like an individual, may refrain from embarking in litigation to enforce even a clear right of action if litigation is deemed inadvisable; and it is immaterial, in this respect, whether the right of action arises at common law or under a statute or under a constitutional provision. Nor do I know of any reason why the disadvantages which may flow from 'antagonizing public officials' may not properly be considered by directors and managing officers of a corporation in determining whether to embark in litigation. The fear of antagonizing customers or other business connections or the public is a motive which quite commonly and properly influences the conduct of men." 259 U.S. at 74.

[179] 259 U.S. at 67.

[180] 269 U.S. at 480.

the tax that was labeled as a tax, at the suggestion of Justice Brandeis; thus the two cases can be viewed as one in terms of holding.[181] Although never overruled, the Supreme Court subsequently lumped *Wallace* with a group of decisions such as *Hammer v. Dagenhart* from a prior era of limited view of the Commerce Clause,[182] and also stated that it had abandoned the distinction between regulatory and revenue raising taxes.[183] *Hill v. Wallace* was also unusual because it invoked the seldom-cited opinion in *Dodge v. Woolsey* to justify taking equity jurisdiction of a suit by members of the Board of Trade to enjoin the organization from paying the tax.[184] *Hill* did not rely on due process even though the plaintiffs argued it.

11. *Export tax*: *Spalding & Bros. v. Edwards*, 262 U.S. 66 (1923).[185] The Court held unconstitutional a general tax on the sale of baseball bats, as applied to sales to a commission agent buying for export to the ultimate purchaser.

12. *Federal judge's salary*: *Miles v. Graham*, 268 U.S. 501 (1925).[186] This decision extended the result of *Evans v. Gore* (1920) to a judge appointed after the 1913 income tax became effective. It was overruled in part by *O'Malley v. Woodrough*.[187]

13. *Tenth Amendment*: *Trusler v. Crooks*, 269 U.S. 475 (1926) [This decision is treated here separately from *Hill v. Wallace* (1922) and thus increases the number of Supreme Court rulings against federal tax provisions of the 1922 to 1936 period from four to five, even though it involves the same Act at issue in *Hill* and was decided on the same grounds, without any separate reasoning. In reality, the two rulings could count as one.] *Hill v. Wallace*

---

[181] ALPHEUS T. MASON, WILLIAM HOWARD TAFT CHIEF JUSTICE 207 (1964) [hereinafter MASON] (Mason's reference to a May 1923 decision is confusing. Evidently he is referring to Graham v. Du Pont, 262 U.S. 234 (1923), which distinguished Hill v. Wallace as involving a tax that was really a penalty, which explained why the Anti-Injunction Act was not applicable).

[182] Wickard v. Filburn, 317 U.S. 111, 122 n. 21 (1942). *See also* Gonzales v. Raich, 545 U.S. 1 (2005) (reaffirming *Wickard*).

[183] Bob Jones Univ. v. Simon, 416 U.S. 725, 741 n. 12 (1974) (citing Sonzinsky v. United States, 300 U.S. 506, 513 (1937), which did not so clearly abandon the distinction, although it did uphold a firearms tax that was fairly clearly regulatory). *See* Ch. III.E.2 and III.F. *See also* Steward Machine Co. v. Davis, 301 U.S. 548, 591 (1937) (indicating disagreement with the prior "belief" of the Court as to the lack of relationship of the tax to the fiscal need).

[184] Dodge v. Woolsey, 59 U.S. 331 (1856) (ruled state tax could not be collected because it impaired the obligation of contract that was the corporate charter; plaintiff was a stockholder who invoked the Court's equity jurisdiction). Something like that also occurred in *Pollock*, which was a shareholder's suit against its corporation to prevent payment of the tax. *Hill v. Wallace* is one of the rare exceptions to the Anti-Injunction Act; the Court decided the case outside the normal procedure for contesting taxes. *See* Bob Jones University v. Simon, 416 U.S. 725, 743 (1974). *Dodge* was an important decision in the early disputes over the inviolability of contracts and charters granted by states. *See* CHARLES WARREN, THE SUPREME COURT IN UNITED STATES HISTORY Vol. II, 254 (1926).

[185] *See* Ch. VI.D.

[186] Justice Brandeis dissented. *See* Ch. VIII.F.

[187] O'Malley v. Woodrough, 307 U.S. 277 (1939).

(written by Chief Justice Taft) had not decided the constitutionality of a separate tax in section 3 of the Future Trading Act, although it indicated it was constitutional because it was not part of the regulatory regime that section 4 attempted to enforce with a tax.[188] But when a case testing the section 3 tax came before the Court in 1926, the Court ruled that tax unconstitutional as well in a unanimous opinion by Justice McReynolds. The tax was imposed on all commodity futures contracts that were options rather than absolute agreements of sale for future delivery. Congress thought these to be "gambling" contracts. Taxpayer sold for $1 (the typical price) an option on 1,000 bushels for future delivery at a fixed price, and refused to pay the 20 cents per bushel tax of $200 (not the same 20 cents per bushel tax at issue in *Hill v. Wallace*). The opinion did not cite any constitutional ground, but rather (a) said the tax fell because it had the same purpose as the section 4 tax and so had to share its invalidity (contrary to the indication in the earlier opinion[189]), and (b) said the purpose and effect of the tax were not to raise revenue and thus it was not a tax. Between *Wallace* and *Trusler* Congress reenacted the regulatory part of the Act ruled unconstitutional in *Wallace* and Chief Justice Taft wrote an opinion finding that reenactment to be constitutional in 1923 simply because Congress had made a finding that manipulation of the local markets interfered with interstate commerce.[190] The ruling in *Trusler* is not surprising in light of the fact that the Lawyers' Edition summary of the Attorney General's argument shows that he stated his personal opinion that the tax was unconstitutional![191]

14. *Due process: Nichols v. Coolidge*, 274 U.S. 531 (1927).[192] The Court applied the Due Process Clause to rule unconstitutional due to retroactivity the application of an estate tax rule requiring the inclusion of a gift made before the enactment of the tax law, which gift was to take effect at death (which

---

[188] 259 U.S. at 71.

[189] The invalidation of the tax seemed directly contrary to Nicol v. Ames, 173 U.S. 509 (1899), as the Court stated in leaving the question of the tax to another day in the *Hill* opinion: "This is the imposition of an excise tax upon certain transactions of a unilateral character in grain markets which approximate gambling or offer full opportunity for it and does not seem to be associated with § 4. Such a tax without more would seem to be within the congressional power." 259 U.S. at 71-72. *Nicol v. Ames* had upheld a one cent per hundred dollars value stamp tax on futures contracts. Presumably the small amount of the tax did not attract the opposition that the later tax did. Also the *Nicol* tax was a war revenue tax, which may have limited its life.

[190] Bd. of Trade v. Olsen, 262 U.S. 1, 31 (1923) (upholding the new solely regulatory act). Thus, presumably the "prohibitive" tax under the original act would have been constitutional if Congress had previously "found" the interstate commerce effect. Note, however, that the regulatory act carried a $10,000 fine and a one year imprisonment as punishment for violation. *See* Edgerton, at 336 n. 207.

[191] ". . . [W]e feel under no obligation to conceal our opinion that in this case Congress under the guise of a revenue measure which cannot produce a dollar of revenue (except that paid to make a test case) has attempted to completely prohibit transactions which it has no power under the Constitution to deal with." 70 L. Ed. 365.

[192] Justices Holmes, Brandeis, Sanford and Stone concurred without joining the opinion. See Ch. V.D.3.b(4).

was after the enactment). The result was said to be arbitrary and capricious so as to amount to a confiscation of property. The Court later cast serious doubt on the viability of the decision.[193]

15. *Due process*: *Blodgett v. Holden*, 275 U.S. 142 (1927)[194] and Untermeyer v. Anderson, 276 U.S. 440 (1928).[195] These retroactivity decisions also ruled unconstitutional the application of a newly enacted gift tax to gifts made earlier in the same year, and were based on *Nichols v. Coolidge*. The Court later cast serious doubt on the viability of the decisions.[196]

16. *Intergovernmental immunity*: *National Life Ins. Co. v. United States*, 277 U.S. 508 (1928).[197] The United States could not define an insurance company's income tax base in a way that gave no benefit to the exclusion of interest received on state, local and United States bonds. Several later decisions distinguished somewhat similar schemes.[198] Because there is no longer any constitutional restriction on taxing state bond interest in a nondiscriminatory manner, the authority of the *National Life Ins. Co.* decision is questionable.[199]

17. *Intergovernmental immunity*: *Indian Motorcycle Co. v. United States*, 283 U.S. 570 (1931).[200] The United States could not impose an excise (sales) tax on motorcycles purchased by a local police force.[201] The holding has been limited to its facts and other cases make every effort to find the tax to be levied on the seller.[202]

---

[193] United States v. Carlton, 512 U.S. 26, 34 (1994) ("long since been discarded" and limited to wholly new tax).

[194] Justices Holmes, Brandeis, Sanford and Stone concurred without joining the opinion. *See* Ch. V.D.3.b(4). The opinion was modified at 276 U.S. 594 (1928).

[195] Justices Holmes, Brandeis and Stone dissented and Sanford concurred in the result. *Untermeyer* differed from *Blodgett* in that the statutory change had already been introduced as a bill. *See* Ch. V.D.3.b(4).

[196] United States v. Carlton, 512 U.S. 26, 34 (1994) ("long since been discarded" and limited to wholly new tax).

[197] Justices Brandeis, Stone and Holmes dissented. *See* Ch. II.C.3 and 7.

[198] Helvering v. Indep. Life Ins. Co., 292 U.S. 371 (1934); Denman v. Slayton, 282 U.S. 514 (1931).

[199] South Carolina v. Baker, 485 U.S. 505, 522-524 (1988).

[200] Justices Stone and Brandeis dissented. *See* Ch. II.C.7.

[201] *Cf.* Lash's Prod. Co. v. United States, 278 U.S. 175 (1929) (federal excise tax on soft drink sales was levied on the sale price to the consumer even though the vendor claimed it included the tax in the sale price and wanted the tax base reduced; based on the fact that the vendor was the taxpayer, not the buyer).

[202] *See* James v. Dravo Contracting Co., 302 U.S. 134, 151 (1937); Helvering v. Gerhardt, 304 U.S. 405, 423 (1938); Massachusetts v. United States, 435 U.S. 444, 455 (1978) (stating that later cases had confined its scope and holding constitutional a user fee called a tax, designed to pay for federal services). The *Motorcycles* opinion ruled that the excise tax was levied on the sale and not on the manufacture. The last time it was cited by the Court was in 1988 in an opinion indicating that it was the product of an era when state and federal exemptions proceeded in tandem, which they no longer do. South Carolina v. Baker, 485 U.S. 505, 517-518 (1988).

18. *Due process*: *Heiner v. Donnan*, 285 U.S. 312 (1932).[203] The United States could not conclusively presume that a gift within two years of death was in contemplation of death for estate tax purposes. Generally the due process objection to certain irrebuttable presumptions is still part of constitutional jurisprudence.[204]

19. *Intergovernmental immunity*: *Burnet v. Coronado Oil & Gas Co.*, 285 U.S. 393 (1932).[205] The United States could not tax the production of an oil lease obtained from a state.[206] This decision was overruled by *Helvering v. Mountain Producers Corp.*[207]

20. *Tenth Amendment*: *United States v. Constantine*, 296 U.S. 287 (1935).[208] The Court reversed a conviction for selling alcohol illegally under Alabama law after the repeal of national Prohibition, without payment of $1,000 denominated a "special excise tax." The Court found the $1,000 to be a penalty

---

[203] Justices Stone and Brandeis dissented. Handy v. Delaware Trust Co., 285 U.S. 352 (1932) is to the same effect. *See* Ch. V.D.3.b(5).

[204] *See* Vlandis v. Kline, 412 U.S. 441 (1973); Michael H. v. Gerald D., 491 U.S. 110 (1989).

[205] Justices Stone, Roberts, Brandeis and Cardozo dissented. *See* Ch. II.C.7. The dissent of Justice Brandeis in *Coronado* is one of the most frequently cited statements of how and when the Court should reconsider its prior rulings: "The doctrine of res judicata demands that a decision made by the highest court, whether it be a determination of a fact or a declaration of a rule of law, shall be accepted as a final disposition of the particular controversy, even if confessedly wrong. But the decision of the Court, if, in essence, merely the determination of a fact, is not entitled, in later controversies between other parties, to that sanction which, under the policy of stare decisis, is accorded to the decision of a proposition purely of law. For not only may the decision of the fact have been rendered upon an inadequate presentation of then existing conditions, but the conditions may have changed meanwhile. . . . Moreover, the judgment of the Court in the earlier decision may have been influenced by prevailing views as to economic or social policy, which have since been abandoned. In cases involving constitutional issues of the character discussed, this Court must, in order to reach sound conclusions, feel free to bring its opinions into agreement with experience and with facts newly ascertained, so that its judicial authority may, as Mr. Chief Justice Taney said, 'depend altogether on the force of the reasoning by which it is supported.'" 285 U.S. at 412-413.

[206] *See also* Gillespie v. Oklahoma, 257 U.S. 501 (1922) (federal immunity), *overruled by* Oklahoma Tax Comm'n v. Texas Co., 336 U.S. 342 (1949).

[207] Helvering v. Mountain Producers Corp., 303 U.S. 376 (1938).

[208] Justices Cardozo, Brandeis and Stone dissented, stating: "The judgment of the court rests upon the ruling that another purpose, not professed, may be read beneath the surface, and by the purpose so imputed the statute is destroyed. Thus the process of psychoanalysis has spread to unaccustomed fields." 296 U.S. at 298-299. *See* Ch. III.E.2 and III.F. *See also* United States v. Kesterson, 296 U.S. 299 (1935) (similar case).

for something the United States could not penalize, and not a tax.[209] The opinion cited as evidence of penalty: it was conditioned on commission of state law crime; it was exorbitant in amount in relation to the normal $20 tax levied by the United States on the same conduct, and there was already a $20 tax; the amount was not related in amount to the business carried on.[210] Professor McKay pointed out that the Court reached the opposite result the next year in an almost identical case involving a firearms tax, with the difference that the firearms tax fell on both the legal and the illegal acts of the taxpayers.[211] As discussed in Chapter III.A, *Constantine* is the proverbial hard case that makes bad law.[212]

21. *Tenth Amendment: United States v. Butler*, 297 U.S. 1 (1936).[213] The United States could not tax cotton processors as part of the Agricultural Adjustment Act because the exaction was not a tax under Article I, section 8, clause 1, but rather was part of an attempt to regulate local agriculture, which was outside its power to regulate. Unlike some taxes objected to on grounds of being regulations, the tax on cotton processors clearly produced revenues, which were appropriated in the Act to pay price supports to farmers. However, the government amazingly did not try to justify the regulation of agriculture under the Commerce Clause and its power to do so was not

---

[209] The opinion did not question the power of the United States to impose an excise tax on purely local dealing in alcohol. Indeed, Constantine had paid the $25 or $20 excise tax that had been in place since 1864, despite being in violation of Alabama law when selling alcohol. 26 U.S.C. § 1394 (1926 ed.). The opinion also affirmed the power of the United States to tax an activity that was illegal under federal law, citing United States v. Yuginovich, 256 U.S. 450 (1921) (but finding an implied repeal of pre-Prohibition penalty); United States v. Stafoff, 260 U.S. 477 (1923) (same); United States v. One Ford Coupe Auto, 272 U.S. 321 (1926) (forfeiture affirmed); and also that was illegal under state law, citing License Tax Cases, 72 U.S. 462 (1867). Later opinions limiting the *Child Labor Tax Case* and *Hill v. Wallace*, distinguished *Constantine* from those cases with a "cf." Steward Machine Co. v. Davis, 301 U.S. 548, 591 (1937); Sonzinsky v. United States, 300 U.S. 506, 513 (1937); United States v. Miller, 307 U.S. 174 (1939).

[210] The opinion improperly relied on Helwig v. United States, 188 U.S. 605 (1903), which involved a penalty for not properly paying a tax, a custom duty, not a tax that was deemed to be a penalty; also the issue was one of construction of a jurisdictional statute, not one of constitutional power to tax.

[211] *See* Robert B. McKay, *Taxing and Spending for the General Welfare: A Reply to Mr. Nillson*, 48 A.B.A. J. 38, 41 (1962).

[212] *See* dissent of Justice Stevens in Hudson v. United States, 522 U.S. 93, 106 (1997) (explaining *La Franca*, which with *Lipke* were cited by *Constantine* and created the background for the hard case; Justice Stevens applied the maxim to the case at hand). *See also* Dep't of Revenue v. Kurth Ranch, 511 U.S. 767 n. 15 (1994) ("Notably, in reaching that conclusion we relied in part on an earlier case recognizing that a tax statute might be considered punitive in character for double jeopardy purposes. . . . That case, *United States v. La Franca* . . .").

[213] Justices Stone, Brandeis and Cardozo dissented. *See* Ch. III.D.2. Evidently Congress was so unhappy with *Butler* that it changed the refund statute to make it practically impossible for a company that paid the processing tax to recover it. *See* Wilson & Co. v. United States, 311 U.S. 104 (1940). *Butler* was preceded in the line of anti-New Deal decisions by A. L. A. Schechter Poultry Corp. v. United States, 295 U.S. 495 (1935).

decided in *Butler*, which reserved that issue,[214] but later was decided in favor of such regulation in *Wickard v. Filburn*.[215] *Butler* appears to have been chosen over *Drexel* as the stalking horse for taxpayers and sympathetic Justices bent on striking down taxes and regulations, because it has been principally and frequently cited in Supreme Court opinions in dissent,[216] although the 2012 opinion in *Sebelius* focused on the *Child Labor Tax Case* as a precedent rather than *Butler*.[217] Its most prominent use in majority opinions is for the interpretation of the Constitution's General Welfare Clause: "It results that the power of Congress to authorize expenditure of public money for public purposes is not limited by the direct grants of legislative power found in the Constitution."[218] Immediately after the Court's switch to upholding New Deal legislation in 1937, Justice Sutherland characterized *Butler* as a case in which the "sole aim" of the statute was regulation that was beyond the power of the United States, and in which there was a "naked taking" of property of one group and giving it to another.[219] *Butler* specifically did not consider the due process/takings arguments;[220] it also did not label the tax a penalty, as did the other four decisions striking down taxes as not being taxes.[221] One of the dissenters in *Butler* pointed out in the first subsequent opinion upholding a New Deal law that *Butler* had been decided by a divided court

---

214 297 U.S. at 64 ("Indeed, the Government does not attempt to uphold the validity of the act on the basis of the commerce clause, which, for the purpose of the present case, may be put aside as irrelevant.").

215 Wickard v. Filburn, 317 U.S. 111 (1942) (upholding the Agricultural Adjustment Act of 1938 as a proper regulation of intrastate commerce that affected interstate commerce), as explained in Maneja v. Waialua Agricultural Co., 349 U.S. 254, 259 (1955). *See also* Mulford v. Smith, 307 U.S. 38 (1939) (similar to *Wickard*, upholding regulation of flue-cured tobacco market). The program at issue in *Wickard* did not involve a tax but only a subsidy and accompanying regulations that the farmer could comply with or not, on pain of losing the subsidy. The opinion contained the important line: "It is hardly lack of due process for the Government to regulate that which it subsidizes." 317 U.S. at 131. *See also* Gonzales v. Raich, 545 U.S. 1 (2005) (reaffirming *Wickard*).

216 *But see* New York v. United States, 505 U.S. 144, 158 (1992) (*Butler* was cited by Justice O'Connor in ruling unconstitutional part of a federal statute designed to force states to deal with radioactive waste; the citation implied that it was an example of a prior more limited notion of the proper objects of government spending that has been expanded over the years, but still not enough to justify the regulation at issue; this statement by Justice O'Connor refutes the usual conservative view that the Constitution does not change).

217 *See* Ch. III.E.2.c.

218 297 U.S. at 66. But as discussed in Ch. III.D.2, this was not as liberal a view as it might seem.

219 Cincinnati Soap Co. v. United States, 301 U.S. 308 (1937).

220 297 U.S. at 62 n. 8.

221 There are at least two different groupings for these five decisions: *Hill*, *Trusler*, *Drexel*, and *Constantine* viewed the tax as not a tax because it was a regulatory penalty; *Butler* could not very well say the tax was penal because it was actually producing about $1 billion in revenue, and so it obviously was not preventing anything. Rather it was raising money for an improper spending purpose. *See* dissent of Justice Stone in *Butler*, arguing that the distinction with the other four decisions, which he also labeled as as involving penal taxes, should lead to a different result for a non-penal tax. 297 U.S. at 80.

and it relied on the earmarking of the funds and on the lack of regulatory power.[222] Subsequent majority opinions cast doubt on *Butler*.[223]

22. *Tenth Amendment/Commerce Clause*: *Carter v. Carter Coal Co.*, 298 U.S. 238 (1936).[224] The United States could not enforce cooperation with the New Deal Coal Code by penalty of a "tax" that would be forgiven to the extent of 90% if the taxpayer cooperated with the Code. The case is not literally a tax case because the United States did not defend the nominal tax under the taxing power, but rather defended it under the Commerce Clause (evidently over learning the lesson of *Butler*).[225] The Court ruled the regulation to be outside the Commerce Clause and the tax to be a penalty. Although never overruled, the Supreme Court subsequently lumped it with a group of decisions such as *Hammer v. Dagenhart* from a prior era of limited view of the Commerce Clause.[226] This was the last time the Court ruled a federal statute unconstitutional until 1946.[227]

23. *Intergovernmental immunity*: *Brush v. Commissioner*, 300 U.S. 352 (1937).[228] The Court ruled that the United States could not tax the salary of a state official. *Brush* was implicitly overruled by *Helvering v. Gerhardt*.[229]

24. *Export Clause*: *United States v. IBM*, 517 U.S. 843 (1996).[230] The Court applied stare decisis and followed *Thames & Mersey Marine Ins.* to strike down an excise tax on insurance on export transportation, despite the fact that it was nondiscriminatory.

25. *Export Clause*: *United States v. United States Shoe Corp.*, 523 U.S. 360 (1998).[231] The Court ruled the Harbor Maintenance Tax unconstitutional

---

[222] Steward Machine Co. v. Davis, 301 U.S. 548, 593 (1937).

[223] Cleveland v. United States, 323 U.S. 329, 333 (1945) (citing *Butler* in stating Congress had the power to erect local low income housing); Daniel v. Family Sec. Life Ins. Co., 336 U.S. 220 (1949) (indicating that *Butler* relied improperly on investigation of Congress' motive); New York v. United States, 505 U.S. 144, 158 (1992) (the Court's view of Congress' spending powers have evolved, citing *Butler* as an earlier constricted example).

[224] Justices Cardozo, Brandeis and Stone dissented. *See* Ch. III.E.2.b and III.F.

[225] 298 U.S. at 289.

[226] Wickard v. Filburn, 317 U.S. 111, 122 n. 21 (1942). *See also* concurrence of Justice Kennedy in United States v. Lopez, 514 U.S. 549, 573 (1995) (observing that shortly after *Carter Coal* the Court ruled effectively the other way, without even attempting to distinguish *Carter Coal*, in NLRB v. Jones & Laughlin Steel Corp., 301 U.S. 1 (1937)). *Carter Coal* was decided immediately before the first decision to break the string of rulings against regulatory legislation, in this case a state minimum wage law for women and children, West Coast Hotel Co. v. Parrish, 300 U.S. 379 (1937).

[227] United States v. Lovett, 328 U.S. 303 (1946).

[228] *See* Ch. II.C.7.

[229] Helvering v. Gerhardt, 304 U.S. 405 (1938), *as stated in* Garcia v. San Antonio Metro. Transit Authority, 469 U.S. 528 (1985).

[230] *See* Ch. VI.D.

[231] *See* Ch. VI.D.

as a tax on exports and not a fee by applying an especially strict distinction between a user fee and tax.

26. *Defense of Marriage Act*: *United States v. Windsor*, 570 U.S. 744 (2013). The Court held section 3 of DOMA unconstitutional under the Equal Protection Clause, thus allowing the plaintiff to recover estate taxes that were refundable because her same-sex marriage to the decedent was respected by the decedent's state of residence and her inheritance was therefore subject to the marital deduction.

As noted above, the list treats *Hill v. Wallace* and *Trusler v. Crooks* as two separate decisions, even though they involved the same Act and *Trusler* was clearly the second chapter of the *Hill* decision. This list does not include other cases decided under statutes outside Title 26, though related to taxes.[232] It also does not include *Dewitt*, which held unconstitutional a crime created under the revenue statute for an act that was not taxed.[233] It does not include a decision ruling unconstitutional as violating a contract, a statute that reneged on a tax exemption granted to certain Native American Tribes.[234] It does not include *Lipke v. Lederer*, a Prohibition case, because the fine at issue was not defended as a tax and the Court ruled that whatever it was, the defendant did not receive due process.[235]

c. *Analysis of the 25 Decisions*

The constitutional grounds for rulings in the 25 decisions listed in the preceding Chapter rank, from most to least (totaling 27 because two decisions rested on two grounds):

- Intergovernmental immunity: 7
- Export Clause: 6
- Tenth Amendment: 6
- Due Process Clause/retroactivity: 3
- Direct tax: 2
- Federal judge's salary: 2
- Commerce Clause: 1

---

[232] *See, e.g.*, Leary v. United States, 395 U.S. 6 (1969) (ruling a presumption in a criminal statute unconstitutional; related to Marijuana Tax Act).

[233] United States v. Dewitt, 76 U.S. 41 (1869).

[234] Choate v. Trapp, 224 U.S. 665 (1912).

[235] Lipke v. Lederer, 259 U.S. 557 (1922). *See* Ch. III.F.2. *Cf.* CHARLES WARREN, CONGRESS, THE CONSTITUTION AND THE SUPREME COURT 299 (1930) (treating it as holding a federal "tax" unconstitutional as a penalty). It is remarkable that *Lipke* is the only one of the 101 Supreme Court opinions on Prohibition Acts to even come close to the list. *See* TREASURY DEPARTMENT, DEPARTMENT OF PROHIBITION, DIGEST OF SUPREME COURT DECISIONS INTERPRETING THE NATIONAL PROHIBITION ACT AND WILLIS-CAMPBELL ACT (USGPO 1929).

In terms of current significance, the cases rank very differently, with the most significant first:

- Tenth Amendment defenses to taxation continue to be asserted when a federal tax is claimed not to be a tax but a regulation outside Congress' Commerce Clause or other powers, as in the *Sebelius* case considering the health insurance tax (although only the dissent discussed the Tenth Amendment).[236] However, the Tenth Amendment rulings in the list above fall within a narrow date range from 1922 to 1936. The Tenth Amendment cases are examined in Chapter III.F.3.
- The one Commerce Clause decision, *Carter Coal*, involved a tax that was not defended as a tax. After 1936 the Court removed technical limitations on Congress' Commerce Clause powers up to 1995, when for the first time since 1936, the Court ruled a federal statute to exceed Congress' Commerce Clause powers.[237] The new view of the Commerce Clause may not be limited to noneconomic regulations because Chief Justice Roberts' sole opinion, and the four dissenters, in *Sebelius*, would have struck down the health insurance tax under the Commerce Clause.[238]
- Export Clause cases can still arise, as evidenced by the last two decisions in the list above.
- In theory Due Process Clause/retroactivity cases can arise, but the last case in the list above was decided in 1932, and all of the cases won by taxpayers on this ground related to the estate tax. If Congress adopts a new taxing system, such as a value added tax, then retroactivity claims may be seen again.
- Even less likely today are claims by federal judges of compensation reduction through taxation, and claims based on intergovernmental immunity. Chapter II.C examines the progression of the intergovernmental immunity cases. The Court reversed itself in part in this line of cases, with the help of Congress, illustrating the view that stare decisis should not be an inexorable rule in cases of constitutional decisions because Congress cannot act to change the Constitution.[239]
- Hopefully, the Sixteenth Amendment resolved the direct tax questions and Congress will not try to impose an unapportioned tax on property, although that is always in the eye of the beholder (for example, a wealth tax).

Several other observations can be made about the list:

---

[236] *See* Ch. III.E.2.c.

[237] United States v. Lopez, 514 U.S. 549 (1995) (reasoning that because carrying guns around schools was not economic activity, as to which the Commerce Clause has broader reach, it did not have "substantial effect" on interstate commerce; and that deference to Congress' determinations has limits). *See also* United States v. Morrison, 529 U. S. 598 (2000).

[238] *See* Ch. III.E.2.c.

[239] James v. United States, 366 U.S. 213, 233 (1961) (Black and Douglas concurrence and dissent).

- Every successful lawsuit was brought by a taxpayer (or proxies for a taxpayer) that did not want to pay a federal tax, as contrasted with a state (as in the case of *South Carolina v. Baker*[240]), or a person complaining about use of tax funds (as in *Frothingham v. Mellon*[241]), or a congressperson or any other category or interested parties.[242]
- The majority of the decisions ruled a particular tax unconstitutional as applied to a particular taxpayer. The major exception that resulted in destruction of an entire tax schedule is *Pollock* (1894 income tax). In other cases a particular tax that was not part of a larger taxing act was effectively invalidated: for example, *Child Labor Tax Case* (the child labor regulation scheme using taxation as a penalty), the commodity trading taxes (*Hill v. Wallace* and *Trusler v. Crooks*), the Agricultural Adjustment Act tax (*Butler*), the coal producer's tax (*Carter v. Carter Coal*), and the Harbor Maintenance Tax (*United States Shoe Corp.*). Of course, the government will cease collecting a tax from similarly situated taxpayers when the Court has allowed one taxpayer a refund or prevented an assessment.[243]
- The first five of the six taxes cited in the prior bullet were pursued by coordinated and intensive anti-tax litigation efforts, two of the five were anti-New Deal tax rulings, another two of the five were in opposition to taxes improbably enacted under a Republican administration, and the first of the five was the prototype of the battle between agrarian populist elements, which spurred the 1894 federal income tax and the business community of the Gilded Age.[244]
- With the exception of the Export Clause cases, most of the decisions can reasonably be assessed in hindsight as real stretches of legal reasoning. *Pollock* was contrary to the entire history of federal taxation.[245] *Eisner v. Macomber* is the sole exception to the rule that the meaning of income is all inclusive.[246] The state tax immunity cases went too far, as the Court itself had to admit in reining in the intergovernmental immunity doctrine.[247] The due process cases were limited to a narrow period of time and a similar set of estate tax issues. The Tenth Amendment cases clearly were ideologically driven (as was *Pollock*).

---

240 South Carolina v. Baker, 485 U.S. 505, 513 (1988) (attack on federal requirement that state bonds be registered in order for holders to claim income tax exemption for interest received).

241 Frothingham v. Mellon, 262 U.S. 447 (1923).

242 *See, e.g.*, Raines v. Byrd, 521 U.S. 811 (1997) (ruling that Senator Byrd and other congresspersons did not have a personal stake in the constitutionality of the line item veto law and dismissed their suit against the OMB to have the law declared unconstitutional).

243 *E.g.*, United States v. Butler, 297 U.S. 1 (1936) simply ordered a refund but as a result the tax was no longer collected and others were refunded. *See* discussion of *Butler* in Ch.I.E.7.

244 *See Burns*, at ch. 6 "*A Court for the Gilded Age*"; Arnold M. Paul, Conservative Crisis And The Rule Of Law Chs. 8 and 9 (1960, 1976 reprint).

245 *See* Ch.V.D.2.c

246 *See* Ch. V.D.2.f.

247 *See* Ch. II.C. 4 and 7.

- The timing of the rulings somewhat correlates with the amount of time on the Court's hands. The Court was first able to reduce its circuit riding duties substantially as a result of legislation in 1891. Then the "Judge's Bill" gave the Court complete control over its calendar in 1925 (except for cases from state supreme courts).[248] Only two of the decisions predate 1895 and 15 post-date 1925.
- The five taxes that were defended as taxes (*Carter v. Carter Coal* was not defended under the taxing power), and rejected as not taxes, were rejected on two different types of reasoning: *Hill*, *Trusler*, *Drexel Furniture* and *Constantine* found the taxes to be regulations of a subject the United States could not regulate in part because they were penal in nature and therefore regulated by effectively banning certain behavior; *Butler* found the tax to be a regulation of a matter the United States did not have the power to regulate not because it was penal, but because it was part of an Act whose spending purpose was outside the spending powers of the United States. In *Hill*, *Trusler*, *Drexel Furniture*, and *Constantine* the taxes were sufficiently heavy that they could have had the result of stopping the conduct taxed entirely (commodities futures speculation, child labor in manufacturing, selling liquor after Prohibition had been repealed). In *Butler*, the cotton processing tax was being paid and collected (except from the processors who obtained injunctions) and apparently not stopping cotton processing. For that reason the tax could not be categorized as penal and an even more arbitrary method of stopping the tax had to be devised: it was not a tax at all because it was part of an Act whose "sole object" was a "prohibited end."[249]
- The interplay between federal reliance on the taxing power and the Commerce Clause in the five cases referred to above and in other related decisions reflects shifts in views of those powers over time, with the taxing power starting strong and finishing strong and the Commerce Clause powers building over time. Congress early experienced great power in regulating through the taxing power, as reflected for example in *McCray*.[250] Nevertheless, it first tried to regulate child labor directly under the Commerce Clause and lost in *Hammer v. Dagenhart*.[251] Congress reenacted essentially the same regulation in reliance on the taxing power and lost in *Drexel*.[252] Congress then tried to regulate commodity markets and lost under both the taxing power and the Commerce Clause in *Hill v. Wallace* and under the taxing power in *Trusler v. Crooks*, but reenacted a very similar law without a tax that was upheld in *Board v. Olsen* under the Commerce Clause.[253] Then the first

---

[248] Judiciary Act of 1925, 43 Stat. 936.

[249] 297 U.S. at 58, 68, 77. *See* Ch. III.D.2 and E.

[250] McCray v. United States, 195 U.S. 27 (1904).

[251] Hammer v. Dagenhart, 247 U.S. 251 (1918).

[252] J.W. Bailey v. Drexel Furn. Co., 259 U.S. 20 (1922).

[253] Hill v. Wallace, 259 U.S. 44 (1922); Trusler v. Crooks, 269 U.S. 475 (1926); Bd. of Trade v. Olsen, 262 U.S. 1 (1923).

New Deal regulation involving a tax was defended solely as a tax and lost in *Butler*,[254] while the second was defended under the Commerce Clause alone and lost in *Carter Coal*.[255] After the Court's switch in 1937, *Steward* ruled the federal unemployment tax constitutional solely under the taxing power,[256] as did *Davis* for the social security tax.[257] *Darby* (1941) marked the expansion of the Commerce Clause.[258] So the taxing power led the way in reversing the loss of New Deal programs, probably because the restricted view of the taxing power between 1922 and 1936 was so out of step with prior decisions, and then the expansion of the Commerce Clause power was actually the new development of the Roosevelt Court.

- The 2012 *Sebelius* decision continued to support the strength of the federal taxing power, but five of the Justices would have ruled that the Commerce Clause did not authorize the health insurance tax.[259] This suggests a retrenchment as to the Commerce Clause in tax cases, similar to the 1922-1936 retrenchment as to the taxing power.

3. *The Determined Bar*

An astonishing number of the most important reported attacks on federal and state taxes and regulations during the period from the 1890s through the 1920s when so many were ruled unconstitutionality were litigated by a handful of prominent attorneys on behalf of the tax and regulation protesters.[260] The most prolific of these, William D. Guthrie, provides a useful insight into the determined efforts of both business interests and their attorneys against all taxation. Guthrie had a clear ideological bent.[261] Guthrie, who was born in 1859 and died in 1935 and was associated with the predecessor of Cravath, Swaine and Moore, litigated over 70 appeals to the Supreme Court of the United States, almost all

---

[254] United States v. Butler, 297 U.S. 1 (1936).

[255] Carter v. Carter Coal Co., 298 U.S. 238 (1936).

[256] Steward Machine Co. v. Davis, 301 U.S. 548 (1937).

[257] Helvering v. Davis, 301 U.S. 619 (1937).

[258] United States v. Darby, 312 U.S. 100 (1941).

[259] *See* Ch. III.E.2.c.

[260] Others included John W. Davis of Davis Polk, Joseph Choate and Elihu Root.

[261] Roger K. Newman, The Yale Biographical Dictionary of American Law 242 (2009) (Guthrie's ideological anchors were judicial review, the Catholic Church and the Republican Party). A review of a collection of Guthrie's speeches said: "[His] . . . marked characteristic seems to be a distrust of new ideas. . . . [He] . . . refuses with Podsnapian gesture to recognize the force of current opinion. . . . Perhaps the value of Mr. Guthrie's views on the legal and governmental problems that he discusses can be best gauged by reading his addresses on Catholic Parochial Schools, in which he argues in favor of granting to denominational schools moneys out of the public funds because such schools are rendering a public service. He does not seems to be conscious of the fact that the public service rendered by such schools is questionable, since, unlike free, undenominational public schools, they are teaching and perpetuating that dogmatism which has in all times past stood in the way of that more perfect union which it is the aim of humanitarian and undenominational philosophy to secure." *Book Review*, 67 U. of Pa. L. Rev. 103 (1919). The review writer, David Werner Amram, was later a prominent lawyer and an early Zionist. Guthrie also wanted all nominations to be by conventions so as to avoid primary elections.

of which raised constitutional issues, including these cases, many of which are quite prominent in discussions elsewhere in this book:

- *Pollock v. Farmers' Loan & Trust Co.* (1895) ruled the federal income tax adopted in 1894 unconstitutional both as a direct tax on land and personal property and an impermissible tax on state bond interest.[262]
- *Magoun v. Illinois Trust* (1898) rejected attack on progressive state inheritance taxes.[263]
- *Collins v. New Hampshire* (1898) agreed that the state could not force a oleomargarine manufacturer to color the product pink because that would amount to a prohibition of the product that the state could not constitutionally prohibit.[264]
- *Cotting v. Kansas City Stock Yards Co.* (1901) enjoined state regulation of stock yards as violating the Equal Protection Clause.[265]
- *Champion v. Ames* (1903), a very important Commerce Clause decision, rejected an attack on federal regulation of lotteries.[266]
- *McCray v. United States* (1904) rejected an attack on a federal tax on colored margarine.[267] *Champion* and *McCray* were major exceptions to the conservative era of the Court from 1890 to 1937.

---

[262] Pollock v. Farmers' Loan & Trust Co., 157 U.S. 429 (1895), *confirmed and expanded*, 158 U.S. 601 (1895). *See* Ch. V.D.2.c.

[263] Magoun v. Illinois Trust & Savings Bank, 170 U.S. 283 (1898).

[264] Collins v. New Hampshire, 171 U.S. 30 (1898). *See also* Schollenberger v. Pennsylvania, 171 U.S. 1 (1898) (similar).

[265] Cotting v. Kansas City Stock Yards Co., 183 U.S. 79 (1901).

[266] Champion v. Ames, 188 U.S. 321 (1903) (also known as the *Lottery Case*). *See* Herbert F. Margulies, *Pioneering the Federal Police Power: Champion v. Ames and the Anti-Lottery Act of 1895*, 4 J. S. Legal Hist. 45 (1995). Margulies' article explains that Guthrie was one of several high-powered lawyers representing the indictee for violating the federal anti-lottery act. Express companies had a great interest in the matter because they wanted to transport the tickets in interstate commerce. The five to four opinion of the Court written by Justice Harlan relied on *Gibbons v. Ogden* and the Commerce Clause. Therefore, in effect Congress exercised a federal police power to the extent it could shelter that power under the Commerce Clause. However, the ability of Congress to use the Commerce Clause in that way remained in heavy dispute up to *United States v. Darby*, 312 U.S. 100 (1941), which overruled *Hammer v. Dagenhart*, which had ignored *Champion v. Ames*. The employment of the Commerce Clause in this way was not objected to in 1894 when the bill was passed because of the general dislike of the Louisiana Lottery, which had dominated the national lottery scene, and then decamped to Honduras, when things got hot.

[267] McCray v. United States, 195 U.S. 27 (1904). *See also* Cliff v. United States, 195 U.S. 159 (1904) (similar); Schick v. United States, 195 U.S. 65 (1904) (similar). *See* Ch. III.E.2.a and III.F. The tax on colored margarine at issue in *McCray* was mostly supported by Republicans who had many dairy farmer adherents. *See* Herbert F. Margulies, *Federal Police Power by Taxation*, 5 J. S. Legal Hist. 1, 6 (1997).

- *Metropolitan Street Railway v. New York* (1905) rejected an attack on a tax on street railroads that differed in amount from the tax imposed on underground railroads.[268]
- *Flint v. Stone Tracy Co.* (1911) rejected an attack on the 1909 federal corporate excise tax.[269]
- *Stratton's Independence, Ltd. v. Howbert* (1913) rejected the argument that the 1909 corporate excise tax could not apply to a mining business.[270]
- *United States v. Billings* (1914) rejected an attack on a federal excise tax on foreign built yachts.[271]
- *Dodge v. Osborn* (1916) rejected an attempt to enjoin the allegedly unconstitutional federal income tax of 1913.[272]
- *National Prohibition Cases* (1920) rejected an attack on the constitutionality of the Eighteenth Amendment.[273]
- *United States v. Standard Brewery, Inc.* (1920) agreed with a brewer that "near beer" was not so obviously intoxicating that its production should be criminal under the Prohibition Act, based on the principle that a statute should be construed to be constitutional if possible.[274]
- *Marcus Brown Holding Co., Inc. v. Feldman* (1921) rejected the argument that a law requiring a landlord to furnish water, etc. to tenants violated the landlord's Thirteenth Amendment rights.[275]
- *La Belle Iron Works v. United States* (1921) rejected a Fifth Amendment challenge to the federal excess profits tax.[276]
- *Walsh v. Brewster* (1921) rejected an attack on a tax on capital gain under the Sixteenth Amendment, but affirmed that value in 1913 established the property's tax basis.[277]

---

[268] New York ex rel. Metropolitan Street Ry. Co. v. New York State Bd., 199 U.S. 1 (1905).

[269] Flint v. Stone Tracy Co., 220 U.S. 107 (1911). *See* Ch. V.D.2.d.

[270] Stratton's Independence v. Howbert, 231 U.S. 399 (1913).

[271] United States v. Billings, 232 U.S. 261(1914). *See* Ch. II.B.1 and V.D.3.b.

[272] Dodge v. Osborn, 240 U.S. 118 (1916). *See also* Dodge v. Brady, 240 U.S. 122 (1916) (same claim).

[273] National Prohibition Cases, 253 U.S. 350 (1920).

[274] United States v. Standard Brewery, Inc., 251 U.S. 210 (1920).

[275] Marcus Brown Holding Co., Inc. v. Feldman, 256 U.S. 170 (1921).

[276] La Belle Iron Works v. United States, 256 U.S. 377 (1921) (the taxpayer claimed that a deduction for invested capital should be based on current fair market value rather than historical cost).

[277] Walsh v. Brewster, 255 U.S. 536 (1921). *See also* Goodrich v. Edwards, 255 U.S. 527 (1921) (same).

- *United States v. L. Cohen Grocery Co.* (1921) held unconstitutional a portion of the Lever Act on the grounds that it was void for vagueness.[278]
- *Edgar A. Levy Leasing Co., Inc. v. Siegel* (1922) rejected a Fifth Amendment challenge to a New York emergency housing law.[279]
- *Meyer v. Nebraska* (1923) (amicus) agreed with plaintiff in rejecting state requirement of English-only education.[280]
- *Pierce v. Society of Sisters* (1925) agreed with plaintiff in striking down a requirement of public school attendance.[281] This opinion, written by the conservative Justice McReynolds, is an indirect cause of the discovery of the equal protection component of the Fifth Amendment. It and *Meyer v. Nebraska*, were cited in the draft of the opinion in *Bolling v. Sharpe*, for applying the result of *Brown v. Board of Education* to the District of Columbia in 1954. Evidently Justice Black, in particular, did not want to give credence to those due process opinions and so *Bolling v. Sharpe* effectively incorporated the Equal Protection Clause into the Fifth Amendment, without really viewing it as a major shift.[282]

Obviously Guthrie was not alone. Other important lawyers in the tax fray included Joseph Choate, William Evarts, and George Wharton Pepper, as explained in detail in Dr. Benjamin R. Twiss' fascinating book, *Lawyers and the Constitution: How Laissez Faire Came to the Supreme Court* (1942).[283] Although Guthrie lost more cases than he won in the Supreme Court, his biggest win, *Pollock*, was a landmark. Moreover, Guthrie's arguments were credited with the later conservative victories in *Hammer v. Dagenhart* (1918) and the *Child Labor Tax Case* (1922).[284] And, of course, these attorneys were not contributing their services (at least outside of the church cases); paying clients obviously highly prized the anti-government zealotry of at least Guthrie, as well as their perceived expertise.

---

[278] United States v. L. Cohen Grocery Co., 255 U.S. 81 (1921) (it dismissed the criminal charge for selling sugar for excessive prices).

[279] Edgar A. Levy Leasing Co., Inc. v. Siegel, 258 U.S. 242 (1922).

[280] Meyer v. Nebraska, 262 U.S. 390 (1923). *See also* Bartels v. Iowa, 262 U.S. 404 (1922) (similar). Guthrie was an ardent protector of and lawyer for the Catholic Church, which presumably had an interest in protecting foreign born non English speaking Catholics in the United States.

[281] Pierce v. Society of Sisters, 268 U.S. 510 (1925). A cite to this opinion appeared in Espinoza v. Mont. Dep't of Revenue, 140 S. Ct. 2246 (2020), forcing a state to continue a state private school scholarship tax deduction so as not to impact the free exercise of religion.

[282] For discussion of these cases, see Ch. V.D.3.b(2). *See* Bernard Schwartz, Super Chief 98-100 (1983).

[283] Dr. Benjamin R. Twiss, Lawyers and the Constitution: How Laissez Faire Came to the Supreme Court (1942). Pepper argued *Butler* and stated: "I pray almighty God, that not in my time 'the land of the regimented' be accepted as a worthy substitute for 'the land of the free.'" United States v. Butler, 297 U.S. 1, 44 (1936). Pepper's autobiography explains his antipathy for the New Deal. George Wharton Pepper, Philadelphia Lawyer 239-244 (1944).

[284] *See also* Stephen B. Wood, Constitutional Politics in the Progressive Era 235 (1964).

On the other side of these cases, the party wanting a tax paid was represented at least once by the private bar too, most notably in *Pollock*, in which the anti-tax party was the shareholder seeking to enjoin his corporation from paying the 1894 income tax. James C. Carter, an eminent leader of the bar of the day, ably defended the corporation, which desired to pay the tax, stating:

> I appear here for the Continental Trust Company. This is one of the companies which, it might be supposed, represent interests which would be the especial subjects of income taxation, and yet I am instructed by it to defend and maintain to the best of my ability the validity of the law. I am glad that there is at least one great corporation subjected to the tax, which avows its readiness to submit itself without controversy or contention to the law of the country, and to discharge the burdens which that law imposed upon it. . . . Nothing could be more unwise and dangerous—nothing more foreign to the spirit of the Constitution—than an attempt to baffle and defeat a popular determination by a judgment in a lawsuit. When the opposing forces of sixty millions of people have become arrayed in hostile political ranks upon a question which all men feel is not a question of law, but of legislation, the only path of safety is to accept the voice of the majority as final. The American people can be trusted not to commit permanent injustice; nor has history yet recorded an instance in which governments have been destroyed by attempts of the many to lay undue burdens of taxation on the few. The teachings of history have all been in the other direction.[285]

As the disputes moved into the later 1920s a broader variety of counsel appeared. The breadth of the bar interested in opposing the New Deal on legal grounds is reflected in the activities of the National Lawyers' Committee of the American Liberty League.[286] The League was a successor to an organization that had lobbied for the repeal of Prohibition, principally on the hope that renewed excise taxes on alcohol would supplant the hated income tax.[287]

4. *A Methodology for Judging the Constitutionality of Federal Taxes*

a. *Presumptions*

The Court has used a cluster of overlapping principles of statutory construction and presumptions in evaluating the constitutionality of federal and state

---

[285] Brief of James C. Carter, 39 L. Ed. 759 (1895).

[286] *See* Note, *The Activities of the National Lawyers' Committee of the American Liberty League*, 14 TENN. L. REV. 101 (1936) (reprinting an ABA ethics ruling on the Committee's solicitation of clients to receive free services in opposing New Deal measures; the ABA ruled the solicitation was not unethical). An author who studied lawyers opposing to the New Deal concluded that they were a "rather limited circle of law firms that were tightly related to each other through an extensive system of mutual activities in the American Bar Association and the American Liberty League." RONEN SHAMIR, MANAGING LEGAL UNCERTAINTY 92 (Duke Press 1995).

[287] GEORGE WOLFSKILL, THE REVOLT OF THE CONSERVATIVES; A HISTORY OF THE AMERICAN LIBERTY LEAGUE 1934-1940, 47-49 (1962). The Committee's attorney members included John W. Davis, George W. Wickersham, James M. Beck (Solicitor General who argued the *Child Labor Tax Case*). *Id.* at 71-72.

statutes generally, with emphasis here on their application to federal and state taxing statutes.[288] Most of these principles have the purpose or effect of retarding the exercise of judicial power to rule a statute unconstitutional.

One of the great debates of American constitutional history concerns the proper role of the courts, and particularly the Supreme Court, in judicial review under the Constitution. The Court has been viewed as too activist in striking down government economic regulation in the 1920s and 1930s and as too activist in striking down limits on individual rights in the 1950s and 1960s. The caution that the Constitution should not be used as the cure for all perceived ills of democratic legislation has come from both more liberal Justices and more conservative Justices.[289] The subject has become much more important to the Supreme Court lately as it has pursued a literalist approach to statutory interpretation, leading Justices to believe they can always interpret the statute. When combined with a presumption for constitutionality, that approach could lead to forced interpretations. But at the same time, some Justices are less enthusiastic about their powers being fettered by canons of construction, including a presumption of constitutionality. Therefore this subject is likely to shift and change outside of tax cases, but a brief outline follows.

First, if reasonably possible a court should avoid in construing an act of Congress any construction that would render it unconstitutional, or raise grave doubts as to its constitutionality.[290] This principle is an application of Justice Brandeis' more complete set of guidelines for deciding a case on statutory grounds if possible, stated in his concurrence in *Ashwander*.[291] It was applied most prominently by Justice Jackson in refusing to extend *Eisner v. Macomber* in *Helvering v. Griffiths*: ". . . we do not decide whether a tax may constitutionally be laid until we find that Congress has laid it."[292] The principal practical circumstance that facilitates avoidance of an unconstitutional reading is the possibility

---

[288] *Cf.* Cummings, at ch. VI (such rules outside the constitutional area).

[289] Chief Justice Stone stated that before 1937 the Court was in danger of becoming "a legislative and Constitution making body, enacting into law its own predilictions." Alpheus T. Masin, Harlan Fiske Stone: Pillar of the Law, 779 (1956). Justice Jackson stated that it was not possible to find in a "4000 word Eighteenth Century document . . . some clear bulwark against all dangers and evils that today beset us internally." Robert H. Jackson, The Supreme Court in the American System of Government, 57-58 (1955). John Marshall Harlan III stated, "The Constitution is not a panacea for every blot upon the public welfare. . . ." Reynolds v. Simms, 377 U.S. 533, 620 (1954).

[290] United States v. Jin Fuey Moy, 241 U.S. 394, 401 (1916); United States v. Standard Brewery, Inc., 251 U.S. 210, 220 (1920); United States v. La Franca, 282 U.S. 568 (1931); Bingham v. United States, 296 U.S. 211 (1935); George Moore Ice Cream Co. v. Rose, 289 U.S. 373 (1933); Skilling v. United States, 561 U.S. 358 (2010) (not a tax case; the Court should try to construe rather than invalidate).

[291] Ashwander v. TVA, 297 U. S. 288, 347 (1936); *cited in* United States v. Wells Fargo Bank, 485 U.S. 351, 354 (1988).

[292] Helvering v. Griffiths, 318 U.S. 371, 394 (1943).

of two constructions of the statute, only one of which is unconstitutional.[293] But the principle has limits:

> The foundation of this rule is the possibility of two constructions and the existence of the grave doubt as to constitutionality. To apply the rule in a case like this, where neither of such conditions exists would be to cause an imaginary doubt as to the constitutionality of a statute to render it necessary to give to the statute a wholly fictitious and unauthorized meaning, that is to say, the effect of adopting the contention would be but to declare that in every case where the construction of a statute was in issue its misconstruction would become necessary if only it was asserted that if rightly construed repugnancy to the Constitution would result.[294]

Applying this principle is not simply a matter of construction of the law directly in issue. The Court also will search for other ways to rule against the complaining taxpayers, so as to totally avoid even construing the statute complained about; such other include finding procedural footfaults, and choosing to address issues not presented by the parties.[295]

Second, separate and apart from the initial construction of the statute and finding other ways out of ruling, statutes are presumed to be constitutional.[296] At least several Justices view the presumption as being two "canons of avoidance": (1) the traditional presumption of constitutionality, which looks like promoting interpretation to reach a different meaning, and (2) another approach that perhaps ignores the unconstitutional reading if any alternate can be found.[297] Without resolving the nuances, some presumptive weight inevitably will be used, except when the Justices really want to rule the statute unconstitutional.

The procedural consequence of the presumption is that the party challenging constitutionality must prove the invalidity.[298] But as to the interpretation of the Constitution, there obviously is no burden of proof.

Third, to find a statute unconstitutional its status must not be just doubtful but must be clearly over the constitutional line:

---

[293] *See* opinion of Chief Justice Roberts in Nat'l Fed'n of Indep. Bus. v. Sebelius, 567 U.S. 519 (2012). Chief Justice Roberts' opinion (joined by no other Justice) implied that there is a two step process: first determine if the alternate construction is "fairly possible," and then determine if the court can render a judgment that that is what the statute means, which presumably requires more than "fairly possible."

[294] United States v. Bennett, 232 U.S. 299, 304 (1914). The same point could be made if a court were to decline to attempt to construe a statute because it was ambiguous on its face; that would create the possibility of two constructions under the *Chevron* doctrine, although proper construction using interpretive tools beyond the face of the statute might leave only one unambiguous meaning. *See* Ch. VIII.E.2.

[295] United States v. Wells Fargo Bank, 485 U.S. 351 (1988) (taxpayer was complaining that an exemption was taken away, but the Court found the property was never exempt).

[296] *See, e.g.*, Ogden v. Saunders, 25 U.S. 213 (1827); United States v. Butler, 297 U.S. 1, 67 (1936) ("Every presumption is to be indulged in favor of faithful compliance by Congress with the mandates of the fundamental law.").

[297] United States v. Davis, 139 S. Ct. 2319 (2019) at fn. 6.

[298] Binns v. United States, 194 U.S. 486 (1904).

> It is not enough that a statute goes to the verge of constitutional power. We must be able to see clearly that it goes beyond that power. In case of real doubt a law must be sustained.[299]

Fourth, the presumption of constitutionality has some sort of extra force in cases of federal taxing statutes:

> The presumption, as has frequently been said, is in favor of the validity of the act, and it is only when the question is free from any reasonable doubt that the court should hold an act of the lawmaking power of the nation to be in violation of that fundamental instrument upon which all the powers of the Government rest. This is particularly true of a revenue act of Congress. The provisions of such an act should not be lightly or unadvisedly set aside, although if they be plainly antagonistic to the Constitution it is the duty of the court to so declare. The power to tax is the one great power upon which the whole national fabric is based. It is as necessary to the existence and prosperity of a nation as is the air he breathes to the natural man. It is not only the power to destroy, but it is also the power to keep alive.[300]

Fifth (and related to the fourth step), the preeminence of the taxing power strongly colors the Court's disfavor of attacks on it:

> The constitutionality of an exercise of the taxing power of Congress is not to be determined by such shadowy and intricate distinctions of common law property concepts and ancient fictions. The Constitution grants Congress the "Power To lay and collect Taxes, Duties, Imposts, and Excises, to pay the Debts and provide for the common Defence and general Welfare." No more essential or important power has been conferred upon the Congress and the presumption that an Act of Congress is valid applies with added force and weight to a levy of public revenue.[301]

b. *Bill of Rights and Political Process Challenges: Strict Scrutiny*

Even equal protection attacks on statutes are met by a presumption that the classification is rationally related to a legitimate state interest.[302] However, there is a sixth principle of constitutional analysis, in addition to the five presumptions or processes discussed in the preceding Chapter, which in theory restricts the presumptions against unconstitutionality when certain types of interests are at risk in federal taxation. This principle would apply to federal taxation strict

---

[299] Interstate C.S.R. Co. v. Mass., 207 U.S. 79 (1907). *See also* United States v. Harris, 106 U.S. 629, 635 (1883), cited for this point by Nat'l Fed'n of Indep. Bus. v. Sebelius, 567 U.S. 519 (2012).

[300] Nicol v. Ames, 173 U.S. 509, 514-515 (1899). The author improbably was Justice Peckham, not generally a supporter of taxes.

[301] United States v. Jacobs, 306 U.S. 363, 369-370 (1939). *See also* Nicol v. Ames, 173 U.S. 509, 515-516 (1899).

[302] *See* concurrence of Justice O'Connor in Lawrence v. Texas, 539 U.S. 558, 579-580 (2003). For equal protection, *see* Ch. V.D.3.b(2).

or heightened scrutiny,[303] which the Court has come to apply to several types of equal protection claims, which are based either on a suspect category, a protected right or the inability of the party discriminated against to protect herself in the political process.

However, the Court has never stated that the equal protection strict scrutiny standard for such distinctions can apply to federal taxes. The Court once entertained the argument that strict scrutiny applied to tax exemptions for lobbying organizations, but concluded strict scrutiny did not apply because it ruled Congress was not required to spend to subsidize free speech and so was not required to supply a tax exemption for the same purpose.[304] Therefore, while it is generally true that a discrimination that appears to affect a specially protected class or interest is likely to receive strict scrutiny and therefore more likely to be found unconstitutional, it remains to be seen to what extent that approach applies to federal taxation, which long has enjoyed an effective freedom from discrimination claims even though many such claims have been asserted.[305] No federal tax has ever been ruled unconstitutional on grounds of discrimination (although DOMA was ruled unconstitutional in *Windsor*).

One of the categories for strict scrutiny is certainly racial discrimination and another is First Amendment free speech and freedom of the press claims.[306] The Court has applied strict scrutiny to state taxes, stating:

> A statute is presumptively inconsistent with the First Amendment if it imposes a financial burden on speakers because of the content of their speech. Leathers v. Medlock, 499 U.S. 439, 447 (1991). As we emphasized in invalidating a content-based magazine tax: "Official scrutiny of the content of publications as the basis for imposing a tax is entirely incompatible with the First Amendment's guarantee of freedom of the press.'"[307]

Although the famous footnote 4 of *Carolene Products*,[308] referenced in Chapter I.B, is the usual citation for the suspect categories or protected interests, it is not the origin of skepticism about regulatory discrimination based on suspect categories of differentiation. The progress of the theory of special scrutiny of certain types of discrimination for constitutional purposes is confusing, with the

---

[303] There is a considerable body of law on the difference between strict and heightened scrunity that will not be explored here. *See, e.g.*, United States v. Am. Library Ass'n, 539 U.S. 194, 217 (2003) (Breyer, J., concurring in judgment).

[304] Regan v. Taxation with Representation, 461 U.S. 540, 547-549 (1983). *See also* South Carolina v. Baker, 485 U.S. 505, 513 (1988) (rejected South Carolina's argument under *Carolene Products*).

[305] *See* Ch. V.D.3.b(2) on equal protection in federal taxation.

[306] *See* Ch. VIII.D.

[307] Simon & Schuster, Inc. v. Members of the N.Y. State Crime Victims Bd., 502 U.S. 105, 115 (1991). *See also* South Carolina v. Baker, 485 U.S. 505, 513 (1988) (citing footnote 4 of *Carolene Products*, the opinion in *South Carolina v. Baker* suggested that heightened scrutiny might be appropriate in Tenth Amendment cases if a state could show Congress had "singled [it] out in a way that left it politically isolated and powerless").

[308] United States v. Carolene Prod. Co., 304 U.S. 144, 152 n. 4 (1938).

following major landmarks, including pertinent tax authorities, most of which involve state taxes:

- 1868: The Fourteenth Amendment is the starting point for discrimination analysis: "nor [shall any state] deny to any person within its jurisdiction the equal protection of the laws." When butchers complained about a city monopoly on butchering, the Court rebuffed them in the *Slaughter-House Cases*, stating that only a discrimination based on race would rise to the level of a constitutional violation.[309] This reflected a straightforward analysis of the Amendment based on its primary purpose. But the dissenters announced their intent to broaden the Amendment to economic protection, which blossomed eventually into substantive due process.[310] That doctrine would identify "fundamental rights," of indeterminate scope,[311] to be protected by a judicial evaluation of the reasonableness of any legislation employing classifications.[312] The *Slaughter-House Cases*' majority's approach in the area of equal protection has been called the model of impermissible classification and the dissenters' approach has been called the model of unjustifiable classification.[313] The latter became the norm.
- 1879: The Court expanded impermissible classifications to ethnic groups generally.[314]
- But under the pressure of the dissenters the Court imperceptibly shifted toward the unjustifiable classifications model, which may have facilitated the expansion of the suspect classifications as stated in 1900 in *American Sugar Refining*: "The act in question does undoubtedly discriminate in favor of a certain class of refiners, but this discrimination, if founded upon a reasonable distinction in principle, is valid. Of course, if such discrimination were purely arbitrary, oppressive or capricious, and made to depend upon differences of color, race, nativity, religious opinions, political affiliations or other considerations having no possible connection with the duties of citizens as taxpayers, such exemption would be pure favoritism, and a denial of the equal protection of the laws to the less favored classes."[315] Thus this statement did not identify political or religious affiliations as per se improper bases of discrimination but rather as potentially arbitrary and thus unjus-

---

[309] Slaughter-House Cases, 83 U.S. 36 (1873). *See* Richard S. Kay, *The Equal Protection Clause in the Supreme Court: 1873-1903*, 29 BUFF. L. REV. 667 (1980) [hereinafter Kay].

[310] *See* Ch. V.D.3.b.(7).

[311] 83 U.S. at 95, 98 (dissent of Justice Field).

[312] *See* Kay, at 679-680.

[313] *Id.* at 678-679.

[314] Strauder v. West Virginia, 100 U.S. 303, 308 (1879) (white men); Yick Wo v. Hopkins, 118 U.S. 356 (1886) (statute as applied to Chinese; the import of the ruling was that a police power regulation would be constitutional unless it served no legitimate police power purpose and so fell outside that category). *See* Kay, at 694, arguing that *Yick Wo* was not decided primarily on the basis of racial discrimination but absence of police power.

[315] American Sugar Refining Co. v. Louisiana, 179 U.S. 89, 93 (1900) (written by Justice Brown, the author of *Plessy v. Ferguson*).

tifiable if found to be arbitrary on the facts of the case.[316] In fact even racial classifications, the paradigm impermissible classification, came under the unjustifiable classifications method, with the unfortunate result of finding of no discrimination despite a clear distinction based on race, in decisions like *Plessy v. Ferguson*.[317]

- Justice Holmes in dissent to the decisions relying on substantive due process outlined the preferred method, which would require merely a rational basis when passing on economic legislation, but would impose a higher standard for limitations on free speech.[318]
- 1926: The Court ruled unconstitutional under the Constitution of the Philippines the Chinese Bookkeeping Act by which the Philippines forbade Chinese merchants from keeping a set of books in Chinese.[319] The case does not literally fit into this grouping because it was a criminal case to which special scrutiny would apply for other reasons.
- 1926: But Professor Thomas Reed Powell surveyed the entire field of state tax discrimination, even citing the *American Sugar Refining* opinion, and did not discuss tax discrimination based on race, religion or such factors, or perceive any special significance in the *American Sugar* dictum.[320]
- 1938: In *Carolene Products* Justice Stone upheld a federal prohibition of interstate shipment of filled milk under the Commerce Clause.[321] The milk problem addressed was remarkably similar to the butter problem addressed by an earlier tax on colored margarine, upheld under the taxing power in *McCray* in 1904 in perhaps the broadest statement ever made supporting the taxing power.[322] *Carolene Products* stated it need not investigate Congress' purposes for regulatory legislation affecting ordinary commercial transactions where "the existence of facts supporting the legislative judgment is to be presumed, . . . [and] is not to be pronounced unconstitutional

---

[316] Professor Kay explained the fundamental difference between the two models: the impermissible classification model restricts the power of the courts and the unjustifiable classification model expands it. The fundamental problem with the unjustifiable classification model is that it expands judicial discretion without providing a standard: "That problem was the need to review the suitability of classifications to the work of government with no external a priori guidelines as to what that work properly was or what in any case was a reasonable pursuit of it. *See* Kay, at 715.

[317] *Id.* at 717. In contrast, Justice Harlan's dissent restated impermissible classification.

[318] *See* Lochner v. New York, 198 U.S. 45, 76 (1905); Abrams v. United States, 250 U.S. 616, 627 (1919).

[319] Yu Cong Eng v. Trinidad, 271 U.S. 500 (1926).

[320] Thomas Reed Powell, *Supreme Court Condonations and Condemnations of Discriminatory State Taxation 1922-1925*, 12 Va. L. Rev. 441 (1926). Other articles cited the *Sugar* opinion in the context of discrimination but did not see it as groundbreaking. *See, e.g.*, Susan Minot Woody, *The Legal Classification of Persons: A Search for Standards*, 18 Am. J. Juris 18, 25 (1973).

[321] United States v. Carolene Prod. Co., 304 U.S. 144, 152 n. 4 (1938). The approach of this opinion can be sourced to McCulloch v. Maryland, 4 U.S. 316 (1819) (referring to the political inability of the people of the United States to obtain redress within a single state).

[322] 304 U.S. at 151 (*cf. McCray*).

unless in the light of the facts made known or generally assumed it is of such a character as to preclude the assumption that it rests upon some rational basis within the knowledge and experience of the legislators." The accompanying footnote 4 suggests, but does not firmly define, three areas in which the normal presumption might not apply: (1) when a law appears to violate a specific constitutional prohibition; (2) when the democratic process may be obstructed, as by restrictions upon the right to vote, restraints upon the dissemination of information, interferences with political organizations, prohibition of peaceable assembly; and (3) when the statute affects particular religious, national,[323] racial or other discrete and insular minorities. No such category was involved in *Carolene Products*. That religious issues were included is not surprising, given the unique treatment later given to taxpayer standing to question spending for religion in *Flast v. Cohen*.[324]

- 1966: The Court ruled that a state poll tax levied as a prerequisite for voting discriminates on the basis of affluence in violation of the Equal Protection Clause.[325] The ruling is based on the fundamental nature of the right to vote.[326] It is more of a voting case than a tax case. The Twenty-Fourth Amendment, ratified in 1964, prohibited the poll tax.
- 1973: The Court stated that "[a] bare congressional desire to harm a politically unpopular group cannot constitute a legitimate governmental interest."[327]
- 1974: Gender based discrimination is suspect, although in the first state tax decision after the Court's move to more strictly scrutinize gender based discrimination it upheld a differentiation in state taxation based on gender.[328] Later nontax opinions state that "gender-based discriminations must serve important governmental objectives and that the discriminatory means employed must be substantially related to the achievement of those objectives."[329] Discriminations based on gender receive heightened scrutiny.[330]

---

[323] Aliens as a class are a discrete and insular minority. Graham v. Richardson, 403 U.S. 365, 372 (1971).

[324] Flast v. Cohen, 392 U.S. 83 (1968).

[325] Harper v. Virginia State Bd. of Elections, 383 U.S. 663 (1966).

[326] "We have long been mindful that where fundamental rights and liberties are asserted under the Equal Protection Clause, classifications which might invade or restrain them must be closely scrutinized and carefully confined." 383 U.S. at 670.

[327] U.S.D.A. v. Moreno, 413 U.S. 528, 534 (1973) (plaintiffs were unrelated persons in a group seeking food stamps). This is sometimes referred to as a "suspect category," such as race. *See* Gratz v. Bollinger, 539 U.S. 244 (2003).

[328] Kahn v. Shevin, 416 U.S. 351 (1974) (state income tax could exempt widows and not widowers). *See* Reed v. Reed, 404 U.S. 71 (1971) (identified as the first decision recognizing the need to more substantially justify a gender based discrimination).

[329] Wengler v. Druggists Mut. Ins. Co., 446 U.S. 142, 150 (1980).

[330] Sessions v. Morales-Santana, 137 S. Ct. 1678 (2017).

- 1983: The Court struck down under the First and Fourteenth Amendments a use tax on paper and ink that singled out newspapers, and a particular group of newspapers, without any reasonable explanation.[331]
- 1983: The Court refused to apply strict scrutiny to different treatment of lobbying expenses, on the theory that the Constitution did not require that Congress subsidize lobbying or free speech, and by analogizing Congress' choice to spend or not with the similarly permitted choice to subsidize or not; only if the tax treatment was based on the content of the speech was it subject to strict scrutiny.[332]
- 1987: The Court struck down under the First Amendment a state sales tax that differentiated on the basis of content of magazines.[333]
- 1988: The Court failed to find any *Carolene Products* problem with the requirement that state bonds be registered to pay tax exempt interest.[334]
- 1992: The Court stated that strict scrutiny may be required if a state tax impinges on the right to travel.[335]
- 1993: The Religious Freedom Restoration Act of 1993 requires that strict scrutiny be applied in determining whether the Free Exercise Clause has been violated.[336]
- 2003: A state tax opinion lists the discrimination bases that are not subject to the normal tests:[337] race, gender (*cf. Muller* and *Kahn v. Shevin*), interstate commerce and recent arrivals in the state (*cf. Allegheny*).[338]

See also Chapter VIII.D for substantive discussion of First Amendment issues and Chapter V.D.3.b for discussion of discrimination in taxation. For additional discussion of these issues in the context of state taxation see Chapter IX.

c. *Practicable Construction*

Generally the Supreme Court makes every effort not to impose on the nation an impracticable construction of the Constitution. For example, the important federal tax decision *Knowlton v. Moore* rejected the extension of intergovernmental immunity to embrace the theory argued by the executors that a federal estate tax was "on" the state power to regulate transmission of property at death and

---

331 Minneapolis Star & Tribune Co. v. Minn. Comm'r of Revenue, 460 U.S. 575 (1983). *See* Ch. VIII.D.3 on First Amendment issues generally.

332 Regan v. Taxation with Representation, 461 U.S. 540, 548 (1983). *See* Ch. VIII.D.2.b.

333 Arkansas Writers' Project, Inc. v. Ragland, 481 U.S. 221 (1987). But the Court rejected a First Amendment claim by cable TV operators. Leathers v. Medlock, 499 U.S. 439 (1991).

334 South Carolina v. Baker, 485 U.S. 505 (1988).

335 *See* Nordlinger v. Hahn, 505 U.S. 1 (1992) (not finding that claim applicable to plaintiff).

336 42 U.S.C. § 2000bb through 42 U.S.C. § 2000bb-4. *See* Ch. VIII.D.5.

337 Fitzgerald v. Racing Ass'n, 539 U.S. 103 (2003). *See also* Armour v. City of Indianapolis, 566 U.S. 673 (2012) (citing *Fitzgerald* and not applying strict scrutiny).

338 *Id.* at 107. It is perhaps significant that the opinion cited a different case for the recent arrival point: Hooper v. Bernalillo County Assessor, 472 U.S. 612 (1985).

thus unconstitutional.[339] The opinion stated that to rely on such a theory would spell "the end of all taxation," because almost all events and transactions are regulated by some government, frequently exclusively (i.e., under the states' police powers). Therefore, it found that the tax was on the transmission of property and not "on" the state power.

Another example is the Court's ruling that the Constitution is not self-defeating,[340] which precludes the Eminent Domain Clause from taking away what the taxing power grants. Also the Constitution does not conflict with itself, meaning that the Due Process Clause does not take away from the taxing power.[341]

As the exception that proves the rule the *Pollock* opinion expressed no concern with the practical result of its ruling, which was that no federal tax could be levied on capital income, though it could be levied on the wage earnings of individuals and possibly on business income through an excise tax (as in *Flint v. Stone Tracy*[342]). Moreover, while the court found it impossible to sever the tax on dividends from the rest of the income tax, it had no trouble severing the tariffs. At least *Pollock* was right about the impracticality of an apportioned tax on incomes, much less capital incomes.[343]

5. *Statutory Construction Generally and the Constitution*

The Court's constitutional federal tax opinions addressed in this book well illustrate that the origin of most methods of statutory construction as practiced by American courts can be traced to the methods of construction of the Constitution of the United States used by the Supreme Court. Except for religious texts, there is probably no other document that has received such careful scrutiny in the United States, weighing all of its interactions, and studying its authors' views. The Court's scrutiny of the Constitution has at various points emphasized text, intent, the integrated meaning of the document as a whole, presumptions, historical context, maxims, historical understanding of the Constitution since its adoption, in sum all of the methods applied in statutory construction generally.[344]

To pick out just one method, it is useful to observe that no matter how much solicitude might be shown for the intent of the Constitution's authors, the Court has had no trouble applying the Constitution in just the way many taxpayers like to apply the Internal Revenue Code: as written, though perhaps not as intended. For example:

---

339 Knowlton v. Moore, 178 U.S. 41, 60 (1904).

340 Billings v. United States, 232 U.S. 261, 282 (1914) "not self destructive"); Brushaber v. Union Pacific R. Co., 240 U.S. 1, 24 (1916 ("does not conflict with itself" by conferring the taxing power in one clause and taking it away in the Due Process Clause).

341 Brushaber v. Union Pacific R. Co., 240 U.S. 1, 24 (1916 ("does not conflict with itself" by conferring the taxing power in one clause and taking it away in the Due Process Clause).

342 Flint v. Stone Tracy Co., 220 U.S. 107 (1911).

343 *See* Edward A. Harriman, *Original Power to Levy Income Tax*, 7 A.B.A.J. 303-304 (1921) (explaining that Congress could have imposed an excise tax on business income and wages and an apportioned tax on capital income, in theory, but not in practice).

344 *See* CUMMINGS.

- Chief Justice Marshall in *Loughborough v. Blake* carefully read Article I, section 2, clause 3 to say that a state with 59,000 persons counted in the census might be allowed only one representative, but for direct tax apportionment purposes that state would be taxed based on the actual enumeration.[345]
- Article I, section 7, the Origination Clause, which requires that a revenue bill must originate in the House, however receives a very lenient reading from the Court, and is largely left to the Houses of Congress to interpret.[346]
- Article I, section 8, clause 1 and section 9, clause 4 are read together so that "duties, imposts and excises" must be uniform but the taxes that are direct taxes need not be uniform but most be apportioned among the states.[347] "Throughout" the United States imports geographical uniformity.
- Article I, section 9, clause 2 says that states cannot levy import or export duties except as necessary for inspection laws, leading the Court to conclude that the Founders intended for such inspection duties to be considered to be taxes (even though not usually so considered).[348]
- The most stark example of a constitutional provision being applied as written and not as intended is the application of the Fifth Amendment and the Fourteenth Amendment, which received their initial and heavy use not in defense of individual rights but in arguments by businesses, mostly railroads, for protection of their property from regulation and taxation.[349]
- In *Brushaber* Justice White accomplished a signal feat of construing the Sixteenth Amendment to require a form over substance evaluation of taxes. He agreed that the 1913 income tax was a direct tax (under *Pollock*'s view).[350] He rejected the argument that the Sixteenth Amendment authorized an income tax by creating some third category of taxes never before allowed to the United States,[351] because the exhaustive nature of the taxing power surely encompassed an income tax and the Sixteenth Amendment did not for the first time authorize an income tax. Moreover, it did not exempt the income tax as a direct tax from the apportionment rule. Rather it directed that the source of the income not be the basis of categorizing the income tax as direct or indirect ("from whatever source derived"), and thus it would be

---

345 Loughborough v. Blake, 18 U.S. 317 (1820). *See* Ch. V.D.3.a(3) and V.C.4.h.
346 *See* Ch. VIII.C.
347 *See* Ch. V.D.3.a.
348 *See* Ch. IV.A.4 (*Brown v. Maryland*).
349 *See* Ch. V.D.3.b(7).
350 Brushaber v. Union Pacific R. Co., 240 U.S. 1 (1916).
351 *Id.* at 12.

an indirect tax based on the event of income and not a direct tax based on the ownership of property that produced income.[352]

This ability and even tendency of the Court to literally apply the Constitution and taxing laws, despite obeisance to substance over form, is examined further in Chapter I.E.8.

6. *Reliance on History of Taxation*

The relevance of legislative history for statutory construction is a large and contentious subject,[353] that is all the more contentious when the history of the Constitution's adoption is resorted to in its construction.[354] This Chapter focuses on a different sort of history: the history showing what Congress and the Court have always thought the Constitution to mean, reflected by the tax laws Congress consistently has enacted and the type of taxes the Court consistently has approved. Certainly the Court has felt free to ignore decades of contrary views of Congress, as occurred most prominently (and erroneously) in the *Pollock* case concerning the meaning of a direct tax,[355] and in its own about-face on intergovernmental immunity in the 1930s.[356] However, when one reads all of the Court's federal tax opinions cited in this book, one cannot help but notice the significant number of times the Court has stated that the long history of a tax or type of tax indicates it must be constitutional.

Frequently the Court points out that various types of taxes have been imposed without objections.[357] *Steward Machine* found the federal unemployment compensation tax constitutional as an excise by observing the long history of excises based on other events.[358] The *License Tax Cases* recounted the history of license

---

[352] *Id.* at 18-19. Stanton v. Baltic Mining Co., 240 U.S. 103 (1916) decided a month later and also written by Justice White states somewhat more forcefully that income taxes inherently belonged in the not direct category, but then reasserted the function of the Sixteenth Amendment as explained above: " . . . we are here dealing solely with the restriction imposed by the Sixteenth Amendment on the right to resort to the source whence an income is derived in a case where there is power to tax for the purpose of taking the income tax out of the class of indirect, to which it generically belongs, and putting it in the class of direct, to which it would not otherwise belong, in order to subject it to the regulation of apportionment."

[353] *See* CUMMINGS, at ch. VI.B.3.

[354] *See, e.g.*, Pollock v. Farmers' Loan & Trust Co., 157 U.S. 429 (1895), *confirmed and expanded*, 158 U.S. 601 (1895); Home Building and Loan Assoc. v. Blaisdell, 290 U.S. 398 (1934) (an important early break from the anti-regulation slant of the Court during the first third of the century, holding that a state could exempt property from foreclosure for a period despite the argument that the law impaired the obligation of contracts; Chief Justice Hughes' opinion quoted Chief Justice Marshall's statement that "it is a constitution we are expounding," in rejoinder to the dissent's otherwise convincing argument that the history of the Constitution's enactment did not support the ruling). For an extended discussion of *Blaisdell*, see JOEL FRANCIS PASCHAL, MR. JUSTICE SUTHERLAND A MAN AGAINST THE STATE 167 et seq. (1951).

[355] *See* Ch. V.D.2.c.

[356] *See* Ch. II.C.9.

[357] *See, e.g.*, Brushaber v. Union Pacific R. Co., 240 U.S. 1, 25 (1916) (progressive tax and various distinctions among taxpayers); Knowlton v. Moore, 178 U.S. at 55-56, 68-69, 90-92 (1900).

[358] Steward Machine Co. v. Davis, 301 U.S. 548, 580 (1937) ("Our colonial forbears knew more about ways of taxing than some of their descendants seem to be willing to concede.").

taxes dating back to 1794 to justify its ruling.[359] In *Veazie Bank* Chief Justice Chase concluded that a tax on state bank notes was not a direct tax by reviewing the five direct taxes laid previously by Congress and finding only taxes on land and slaves and houses.[360] More recently, *Comm. for Pub. Educ. and Relig. Liberty v. Nyquist* explained that while property tax exemptions for churches went back to at least 1802, income tax credits for attending church and other non public schools were of recent origin.[361] *Walz* stated in approving an exemption for religious organizations: "But historical acceptance without more would not alone have sufficed, as . . . no one acquires a vested or protected right in violation of the Constitution by long use. . . . It was the reason underlying that long history of tolerance of tax exemptions for religion that proved controlling."[362] *American Sugar Refining* justified a tax discrimination by explaining that similar discriminations in federal taxation had been used since 1813.[363]

In contrast, *Pollock* ignored the fact that the Court had found a tax on personal property to be a constitutional indirect tax in 1796 in *Hylton*,[364] and had rejected all challenges to federal taxes as direct taxes, including a challenge to the Civil War income tax.[365]

However, it has been noted that reliance on the typicality of a tax rule, usually coupled with suspicion of any novel approach, is consistent with substantive due process, as contrasted with an equal protection rule applying heightened scrutiny only to limited suspect categories.[366]

7. *Severability and Remedy*

The decision made by a court whether to sever an unconstitutional taxing provision from the rest of the statute or act of which it may be a part and allow the rest to continue in force is not presented in every constitutional tax case but when it is presented it raises a huge constitutional question of its own: who will write the law going forward? There can be no more basic constitutional issue than the role of the courts versus Congress in lawmaking and a decision to sever or not is clearly lawmaking. Hence there has been an explosion of writing in

---

[359] License Tax Cases, 72 U.S. 462 (1867).
[360] Veazie Bank v. Fenno, 75 U.S. 533 (1869).
[361] Comm. for Pub. Educ. and Relig. Liberty v. Nyquist, 413 U.S. 756, 792 (1973).
[362] Walz v. Tax Com. of New York, 397 U.S. 664, 678 (1970).
[363] American Sugar Refining Co. v. Louisiana, 179 U.S. 89, 93 (1900).
[364] Hylton v. United States, 3 U.S. 171 (1796).
[365] Springer v. United States, 102 U.S. 586 (1881).
[366] *See* Kay, at 708 (the "unjustifiable classification" model of equal protection analysis espoused by Justice Field and leading to substantive due process, can be contrasted with the "impermissible classification" model that would treat a more limited set of discriminations, such as those based on race, as per se invalid; also substantive due process is particularly malleable in that the degree to which a distinction is novel can change with the way it is described).

recent years about the severability issue,[367] as well as considerable variability in the Court's approaches.

In the majority of cases when a taxpayer wins a federal tax dispute due to a constitutional violation, it has either recovered the taxes paid, avoided a deficiency assessment, or obtained reversal of a criminal conviction. Frequently the taxing provision at issue is unconstitutional as applied to the particular taxpayer: for example, an estate tax applied to a transfer that predated the enactment of the tax,[368] or a general income tax imposed on a federal judge who claimed that his compensation could not be diminished by taxation,[369] or a general income tax imposed on a government contractor who claimed intergovernmental immunity.[370] Because in practice the government will not apply the same tax provision to similarly situated taxpayers after the Court has so ruled in favor of a taxpayer on constitutional grounds, the effect of the Court's rulings in the "as applied" cases is to amend the statute judicially to exempt that class of taxpayers. Congress may or may not follow suit and formally amend the statute.

Beyond the "as applied" cases, a second group of decisions ruling taxes unconstitutional can render a taxing provision that is unconstitutional unenforceable as to all taxpayers due to the nature of the grounds of the holding. That occurred in *Butler*, which ruled unconstitutional the tax on agricultural commodity processors that was used in part to fund price supports for farmers.[371]

Butler also illustrates a third type of case in which striking down a tax also has the de facto effect of invalidating a regulatory scheme of which the tax was a part. The *Butler* opinion did not literally void the part of the Agricultural Adjustment Act that imposed quotas and paid price supports to farmers, but because the government defend the processing tax only under the taxing power and not the Commerce Clause, and the opinion purported to find the spending of the taxes raised also unconstitutional, the Agricultural Adjustment Act of 1933 fell as a result of the ruling. Shortly thereafter in 1938 another Agricultural Adjustment Act with similar quotas and price supports but no processor tax was enacted, and it later was ruled constitutional;[372] similar regulatory schemes for agriculture also were found constitutional.[373] But the attack on the "individual mandate" tax failed; if it had not, the Affordable Care Act likely would have been entirely stricken in 2012.

In a fourth group of cases the Court ruled unconstitutional a taxing provision that was part of a larger act, tax or regulatory, and specifically addressed the

---

[367] *See, e.g.*, Kenneth A. Klukowski, *Severability Doctrine, How Much of a Statute Should Federal Courts Invalidate?*, 16 TEX. REV. L. & POL. 1 (2011) (also tracing the history of the law's movements).

[368] *See, e.g.*, Nichols v. Coolidge, 274 U.S. 531 (1927).

[369] Evans v. Gore, 253 U.S. 245 (1920).

[370] *See, e.g.*, Collector v. Day, 78 U.S. 113 (1871).

[371] United States v. Butler, 297 U.S. 1 (1936).

[372] Maneja v. Waialua Agricultural Co., 349 U.S. 254, 259 (1955). *See* Neil Brooks and Donald A. Campbell, *Marketing Quotas Under the Agricultural Adjustment Act of 1938*, 26 GEO. WASH. L. REV. 255 (1957-1958).

[373] Wickard v. Filburn, 317 U.S. 111, 131 (1942).

severability of the illegal tax from the rest of the act. Sometimes the Court pronounced the entire taxing statute or a major part thereof unconstitutional generally, with the most prominent examples being *Pollock* and the 1894 income tax, *Drexel Furniture* and the Child Labor Tax Act, *Hill/Trusler* and the Commodity Futures Act taxes, and *Carter Coal* and the Guffy Coal Conservation Act. *Hill v. Wallace* ruled a securities markets tax unconstitutional,[374] but Chief Justice Taft shortly thereafter found an identical securities markets regulatory scheme without a tax to be constitutional.[375] *Pollock* could have ruled on the income tax on an "as applied" basis, carving out taxes on rents, dividends and interest. However, it struck down the entire income tax system, eliminating taxes on compensatory income too. It did not, however, strike down the major tariff system, which was the second part of the same act that included the 1894 income tax. *Drexel Furniture* was an unlikely candidate for allowing the regulatory scheme to go forward without the illegal tax because the act at issue had been adopted with a tax to try to circumvent the Court's earlier ruling against the regulatory scheme in *Hammer v. Dagenhart*.[376]

The Court's unwillingness to sever an offending taxing provision from the rest of the statute, be it regulatory or tax, appears to correlate well with the political opposition of the Court to federal taxes and more importantly regulation, in the 1895-1936 period, which also encompassed twenty of the twenty-five rulings against federal taxes. Alternately, *Pollock* may have reflected the general trend of nonseverability of its era, which was said to give way to greater severability later.[377] The current law of severability was rehearsed in the briefs in the cases attacking the 2010 healthcare act.[378] The remedies in the 25 cases listed in Chapter I.E.2 in which the Court ruled for the federal taxpayer on the basis of the Constitution are as follows:

1. *Intergovernmental immunity*: *Collector v. Day*, 78 U.S. 113 (1871). The decision ordered refund of the small tax involved, $61.50.[379] However, it set in motion wide-spread exemption of state officers from federal taxes as a practical effect.

2. *Intergovernmental immunity*: *United States v. R.R. Co.*, 84 U.S. 322 (1873). The decision dismissed the tax collector's suit for taxes to be withheld on interest paid to a state government.

3. *Direct tax and intergovernmental immunity*: *Pollock v. Farmers' Loan & Trust Co.*, 157 U.S. 429 (1895), confirmed and expanded, 158 U.S. 601 (1895). The decision ruled invalid sections 27-37 of the Tariff Act of 1894, 28 Stat.

---

[374] Hill v. Wallace, 259 U.S. 44 (1922).

[375] Bd. of Trade v. Olsen, 262 U.S. 1, 31 (1923) (upholding the new solely regulatory act).

[376] Hammer v. Dagenhart, 247 U.S. 251 (1918).

[377] John Copeland Nagle, *Severability*, 72 N.C.L. Rev. 203, 218-219 (1993).

[378] Brief for Respondents in Nos. 11-393 and 11-400 dated January 2012; Brief for State Petitioners on Severability dated January 6, 2012; Brief for Court-Appointed Amicus Curiae Supporting Complete Severability dated Feb. 17, 2012 (available at www.supremecourtpreview.org).

[379] Day v. Buffinton, 7 F. Cas. 222 (1871).

509, 553 et seq. These were all of the income tax provisions (including procedures and collection). The invalidation did not touch, however, the tariff provisions and several other taxes including the next section, section 38, levying a tax on playing cards, which might appear to be more "direct" than an income tax. The Court literally ruled unconstitutional only the tax on income from property, but Joseph Choate persuasively argued for the plaintiffs that it would be unfair to leave the tax in place only upon income from occupations and labor; hence the entire income tax was voided.[380]

4. *Export tax*: *Fairbank v. United States*, 181 U.S. 283 (1901). The defendant had been convicted of the crime of not affixing the stamp to an export bill of lading and so presumably on remand his conviction was reversed. The stamp tax was generally applicable and so presumably it continued to be applied, but not to export bills of lading.

5. *Export tax*: *United States v. Hvoslef*, 237 U.S. 1 (1915). The decision ordered the refund of a tax on a charter party, which it viewed as a bill of lading on exports, and thus the case was controlled by *Fairbank*.

6. *Export tax*: *Thames & Mersey Ins. Co. v. United States*, 237 U.S. 19 (1915). The decision reversed the dismissal of the tax refund suit with respect to a tax on insurance of exports, also an extension of *Fairbank*.

7. *Direct tax*: *Eisner v. Macomber*, 252 U.S. 189 (1920). "The Revenue Act of 1916, in so far as it imposes a tax upon the stockholder because of such dividend, contravenes the provisions of Article I, § cl. 3, and Article I, § 9, cl. 4, of the Constitution, and to this extent is invalid notwithstanding the Sixteenth Amendment."

8. *Federal judge's salary*: *Evans v. Gore*, 253 U.S. 245 (1920). The decision allowed the tax refund, and in practice the result was applied to the category of judges generally. The tax was authorized for the first time in the Revenue Act of 1918 and the complaining judge had been appointed before that date.

9. *Tenth Amendment*: *J. W. Bailey v. Drexel Furn. Co.*, 259 U.S. 20 (1922) (*Child Labor Tax Case*). In this tax refund action the Court ruled unconstitutional the entire Child Labor Tax Act, Title XII of the Revenue Act of 1918, 40 Stat. 1138, entitled "Tax on Employment of Child Labor."

10. *Tenth Amendment*: *Hill v. Wallace*, 259 U.S. 44 (1922). The decision enjoined enforcement of all regulatory portions of the Act and the tax that would have enforced them, despite a severability clause. The opinion stated: "Section 4 with its penalty to secure compliance with the regulations of Boards of Trade is so interwoven with those regulations that they cannot be separated. None of them can stand. Section 11 did not intend the court to dissect an unconstitutional measure and reframe a valid one out of it by inserting limitations

[380] PAUL, at 210.

it does not contain. This is legislative work beyond the power and function of the court."[381] This was the first time that the Court limited a severability clause.[382] The opinion did not invalidate the section 3 tax, which was not dependent on complying with the regulations, and indicated that it might be valid, but left that to another day (see *Trusler v. Crooks*, below).

11. *Export tax*: *Spalding & Bros. v. Edwards*, 262 U.S. 66 (1923). The decision allowed the refund of tax on a sale to a commission agent because it was a sale in the process of exportation.

12. *Judge's salary*: *Miles v. Graham*, 268 U.S. 501 (1925). This case involved the application to a federal judge appointed after the enactment of the Revenue Act of 1918 of the provision therein taxing federal judges' salaries, which *Evans v. Gore* held unconstitutional in the case of a judge appointed before 1918. The government argued that the 1918 provision could still apply to the after appointed judge, because the Act had a section directing that portions other than one held invalid would continue in effect. The Court refused to parse between earlier appointments and later appointments and just said federal judges' salaries were not subject to the income tax. However, the opinion did affirm the lower court, which had considered the severability issue.[383] It ruled that the type of severability clause in the 1918 Act did not literally apply because the portion held invalid was the portion levying tax on a judge and there was no way to parse it between judges based on when they were appointed because Congress had not written it with such distinctions stated. Compare the severability clause of a later act applied in *National Life Ins. Co.*, below. The Court refused to rewrite the statute to draw a distinction that Congress had not drawn.

13. *Tenth Amendment*: *Trusler v. Crooks*, 269 U.S. 475 (1926). The decision rejected the assessment and effectively prevented any further enforcement of the tax. Even though the Act had a severability clause the opinion stated that the section 3 tax at issue was infected with the same error as the section 4 tax, despite the fact that it was not part of the enforcement of the regulatory scheme found unconstitutional in *Hill*, and had been left standing by *Hill*, apparently due to the severability clause.

14. *Due process*: *Nichols v. Coolidge*, 274 U.S. 531 (1927). The decision allowed refund of tax paid on a gift in contemplation of death made before the statute's enactment and left undecided the application of the statute to a later gift. Therefore the law was only unconstitutional as applied.

15. *Due process*: *Blodgett v. Holden*, 275 U.S. 142 (1927) and *Untermeyer v. Anderson*, 276 U.S. 440 (1928). In invalidating a subsequent contemplation of

---

[381] 259 U.S. at 70.

[382] Michael D. Shumsky, *Severability, Inseverability, and the Rule of Law*, 41 HARV. J. ON LEGIS. 227, 234 (2004) [hereinafter Shumsky].

[383] Graham v. Miles, 284 F. 878 (D. Md. 1922).

death statute the Court stated in *Blodgett*: "So far as the Revenue Act of 1924 undertakes to impose a tax because of the gifts made during January, 1924, it is arbitrary and invalid under the Due Process Clause of the Fifth Amendment." The tax refund was allowed. The *Untermeyer* decision extended the ruling to gifts made between the introduction of the bill and its enactment, stating: "the gift tax provisions of the Act of 1924 here challenged must be construed as applicable to gifts made during the entire calendar year 1924. And, further, that so far as applicable to bona fide gifts not made in anticipation of death and fully consummated prior to June 2, 1924, those provisions are arbitrary and invalid under the Due Process Clause of the Fifth Amendment."

16. *Intergovernmental immunity*: *National Life Ins. Co. v. United States*, 277 U.S. 508 (1928). This taxpayer refund action confronted the savings clause of the 1921 Revenue Act that had not been applicable in *Miles v. Graham*: ""That if any provision of this Act, or the application thereof to any person or circumstances, is held invalid, the remainder of the Act, and the application of such provision to other persons or circumstances, shall not be affected thereby." Therefore, the Court could say that this taxpayer's tax should be refunded, but did not invalidate the offending section generally.

17. *Intergovernmental immunity*: *Indian Motorcycle Co. v. United States*, 283 U.S. 570 (1931). This was a refund action in which the Court did not have to address the remedy because it only answered a question on the merits on certificate from the Claims Court.

18. *Due process*: *Heiner v. Donnan*, 285 U.S. 312 (1932). In this refund action on certificate from the court of appeals the Court ruled the tax was unconstitutional as applied to the taxpayer due to retroactivity.

19. *Intergovernmental immunity*: *Burnet v. Coronado Oil & Gas Co.*, 285 U.S. 393 (1932). The decision reversed the tax assessment on intergovernmental immunity grounds.

20. *Tenth Amendment*: *United States v. Constantine*, 296 U.S. 287 (1935). The decision reversed the criminal conviction, stating the statute was invalid, but presumably only as to acts occurring after repeal of Prohibition.

21. *Tenth Amendment*: *United States v. Butler*, 297 U.S. 1 (1936). The Court denied the enforcement of the tax against a taxpayer and stated there was no power in Congress to impose the tax or to spend the proceeds and the entire act "does not affect the rights of the parties."[384] Much confusion ensued as to how to deal with the illegally collected taxes. Congress approved refunds to the processors if they could prove that they had not passed on the burden of the taxes. The Court approved that approach.[385] However, that result was not as tough as it looks, because many processors had never paid the tax at

[384] 297 U.S. at 78.
[385] Anniston Mfg. Co. v. Davis, 301 U.S. 337 (1937).

all. Earlier the federal district courts had broadly disregarded the tax Anti-Injunction Act and issued 1,600 injunctions preventing collection of the tax under the Agricultural Adjustment Act, denying only 167 such requests. Those 1,600 taxpayers did not have to seek refunds because they never paid; and the Court approved the injunctions.[386]

22. *Tenth Amendment/Commerce Clause*: *Carter v. Carter Coal Co.*, 298 U.S. 238 (1936). The Court ruled that the shareholders' suit to enjoin corporate compliance with the Coal Code under the Guffy Coal Conservation Act was not a violation of the tax Anti-Injunction Act because the Court found the tax not to be a tax but a 13½% penalty for failure to comply with the Code. The opinion stated: "These two sets of requirements are not like a collection of bricks, some of which may be taken away without disturbing the others, but rather are like the interwoven threads constituting the warp and woof of a fabric, one set of which cannot be removed without fatal consequences to the whole."[387]

23. *Intergovernmental immunity*: *Brush v. Commissioner*, 300 U.S. 352 (1937). The decision reversed the deficiency assessment against the city employee in the last intergovernmental immunity decision.

24. *Export Clause*: *United States v. IBM*, 517 U.S. 843 (1996). The decision ordered refund of tax as applied to the export contract of insurance of the taxpayer.

25. *Export Clause*: *United States v. United States Shoe Corp.*, 523 U.S. 360 (1998). The Harbor Maintenance Tax, section 4461, referred separately to imports and exports and the decision held the tax unconstitutional as imposed on exports. It was easy under the severability clause of section 7852(a) to continue to apply the tax to imports while striking down the tax on exports. Congress eliminated the export subsection in 2005.

---

[386] Rickert Rice Mills v. Fontenot, 297 U.S. 100 (1936), as explained in Robert H. Jackson, The Struggle for Judicial Supremacy 140-141 (1941).

[387] And the quotation continued: "Paraphrasing the words of this court in Butts v. Merchants Transportation Co., 230 U.S. 126, 133, we inquire—What authority has this court, by construction, to convert the manifest purpose of Congress to regulate production by the mutual operation and interaction of fixed wages and fixed prices into a purpose to regulate the subject by the operation of the latter alone? Are we at liberty to say from the fact that Congress has adopted an entire integrated system that it probably would have enacted a doubtfully-effective fraction of the system? The words of the concurring opinion in the Schechter case, 295 U.S. at pages 554-555, are pertinent in reply. 'To take from this code the provisions as to wages and the hours of labor is to destroy it altogether. . . . Wages and the hours of labor are essential features of the plan, its very bone and sinew. There is no opportunity in such circumstances for the severance of the infected parts in the hope of saving the remainder.' The conclusion is unavoidable that the price-fixing provisions of the code are so related to and dependent upon the labor provisions as conditions, considerations or compensations, as to make it clearly probable that the latter being held bad, the former would not have been passed. The fall of the latter, therefore, carries down with it the former." 298 U.S. at 316.

26. *Fifth Amendment*: *United States v. Windsor*, 570 U.S. 744 (2013). The Court ruled DOMA unconstitutional and affirmed the order of refund of the estate tax paid because the surviving spouse could not claim the marital deduction.

As it turns out, two of the cases above are considered to be important decisions of the Court in the history of its varying approaches to statute severability. *Carter Coal* was a milestone in the Court's severability jurisprudence, said to revert to a prior presumption of non-severability traceable to *Hill v. Wallace* and *Williams v. Standard Oil Co.*[388] For a season the Court took the opposite view that there is a presumption of severability, with or without a severability clause.[389] But the current majority on the Court is prone to be unable to sever when it does not like the federal statute.[390]

One of the most reasonable analyses of severance was written by the first Justice Harlan in a federal tax case concerning the invalidation of a tax within an act that also contains a wholly separate provision that might be unconstitutional.[391] The Tariff Act of 1890 contained the usual numerous tariff schedules and also contained a section providing for "bounties" to be paid to sugar producers under certain conditions. Without deciding whether the bounties were constitutional, the opinion stated:

> "It is an elementary principle," this court has said, "that the same statute may be in part constitutional and in part unconstitutional, and that if the parts are wholly independent of each other, that which is constitutional may stand while that which is unconstitutional will be rejected." . . . Mr. Justice Field, speaking for the court, said: "It is only when different clauses of an act are so dependent upon each other that it is evident the legislature would not have enacted one of them without the other—as when the two things provided are necessary parts of one system—that the whole act will fall with the invalidity of one clause. When there is no such connection and dependency, the act will stand, though different parts of it are rejected." It cannot be said to be evident that the provisions imposing duties on imported articles are so connected with or dependent upon those giving bounties upon the production of sugars in this country that the former would not have been adopted except in connection with the latter. Undoubtedly, the object of the act was not only to raise revenue for the support of the government, but to so exert the power of laying and collecting taxes and duties as to encourage domestic manufactures and industries of different kinds, upon the success of which, the promoters of the act claimed, materially depended the national prosperity and the national safety. But it cannot be assumed, nor can it be made to appear from the act, that the provisions imposing

[388] 278 U.S. 235 (1928). *See* Shumsky, at 227, 234-237.

[389] *See* Alaska Airlines v. Brock, 480 U.S. 678 (1987). It appears that the Court still follows the *Alaska Airlines* approach. Free Enter. Fund v. Pub. Co. Accounting Oversight Bd., 561 U.S. 477 (2010).

[390] Murphy v. NCAA, 138 S. Ct. 1461 (2018).

[391] Marshall Field & Co. v. Clark, 143 U.S. 649 (1892). Justice Jackson in dissent in *Pollock* cited this and other state tax cases for the general principle that severability should be pursued if at all possible. Pollock v. Farmers' Loan & Trust Co., 158 U.S. 601, 697-698 (1895).

> duties on imported articles would not have been adopted except in connection with the clause giving bounties on the production of sugar in this country. These different parts of the act, in respect to their operation, have no legal connection whatever with each other. They are entirely separable in their nature, and, in law, are wholly independent of each other. One relates to the imposition of duties upon imported articles; the other, to the appropriation of money from the Treasury for bounties on articles produced in this country. While, in a general sense, both may be said to be parts of a system, neither the words nor the general scope of the act justifies the belief that Congress intended they should operate as a whole, and not separately for the purpose of accomplishing the objects for which they were respectively designed. Unless it be impossible to avoid it, a general revenue statute should never be declared inoperative in all its parts because a particular part relating to a distinct subject may be invalid. A different rule might be disastrous to the financial operations of the government, and produce the utmost confusion in the business of the entire country.[392]

8. *The Great Issues: From Substance to Form*

So far there have been three great constitutional issues in federal taxation and a fourth complementary issue in state taxation: (1) direct versus indirect federal taxes, (2) intergovernmental tax immunity, (3) taxation versus regulation, and (4) state taxation of interstate commerce. As with many other tax issues these frequently involve the substance versus form debate, asking what is being taxed, and whether the nominal subject of tax or event causing tax liability is the ultimate object of the tax. These inquiries frequently ask whether tax shifting has occurred either between different property or transactions or taxpayers, or whether tax has been avoided entirely by misuse of labels. The substance versus form inquiry has many potential applications in constitutional tax jurisprudence, including most importantly:

- Does the tax fall on imports or exports?
- Does the tax fall on another sovereign?
- Is the tax a direct tax on property or an indirect tax?
- Does a tax that relates to intrastate commerce inhibit interstate or foreign commerce?
- Is a tax really a tax or a regulation?

Both of the direct versus indirect tax issue and the intergovernmental immunity issue evolved from being resolved largely on the basis of substance to being resolved largely on the basis of form. Furthermore, since 1937 the fourth issue, tax versus regulation, has generally been resolved based on form, as it was before 1922 (see *McCray*).[393] Only the identification of federal taxes on exports has continued to be actively pursued on a substance over form basis, perhaps because

[392] 143 U.S. at 696-697.

[393] McCray v. United States, 195 U.S. 27 (1904). *See* Ch. III.E.2 and III.F.

Congress has persisted in ignoring earlier rulings of the Court.[394] The direct tax issue provides the starkest example of substance and form analysis. Up to 1895 the Court identified direct taxes based on the form in which Congress had chosen to cast the tax: if Congress did not apportion a tax, and particularly if Congress called it an excise tax, the Court uniformly ruled it was not a direct tax that had to be apportioned. But *Pollock* applied a substance over form analysis to find that a tax on rent was a tax on land.[395] The Sixteenth Amendment reversed *Pollock* by stating, in effect, that substance over form analysis was not to be used to classify income taxes as direct.[396] It stated that income can be taxed "from whatever source derived," meaning that no economic investigation of the income's ultimate source is needed because the tax is levied on the receipt of the income, not on the property that may have produced the income.[397] The Sixteenth Amendment mandates cessation of searches for the ultimate burden of income taxation: if the tax nominally falls on income, it is on the income and not on the property that may have produced the income.[398] And the Sixteenth Amendment followed the lead of the Court, which two years earlier in 1911 had ruled the 1909 corporate excise tax on income to be constitutional, distinguishing it from *Pollock* using the form over substance approach that a corporate excise tax is not a tax on property.[399]

Likewise, due to the Court's evolving dissatisfaction with having to look for the substance of indirect impacts of taxes on states and on the United States,[400] the Court limited intergovernmental immunity to taxes that are fairly clearly imposed on the sovereign and not on third parties that deal with the sovereign.[401] The refusal to look through the immediate event to an ultimate infringement of state power began in *Knowlton v. Moore* when the Court refused to view a federal estate tax as falling "on" the state power to regulate the transmission of property at death.[402] In 1939 the Court announced (without citation to *Pollock* that "The theory . . . that a tax on income is is legally or economically a tax on its source, is no longer tenable."[403] Thus the law now applies a formalistic approach and has largely abandoned a search for where the ultimate economic burden of taxation comes to rest. Today

---

[394] Fairbank v. United States, 181 U.S. 283 (1901) (tax on bill of lading was tax on export); United States v. Hvoslef, 237 U.S. 1 (1915) (tax on charter party was tax on bill of lading); Thames & Mersey Ins. Co. v. United States, 237 U.S. 19 (1915) (tax on insurance was tax on export); Spalding & Bros. v. Edwards, 262 U.S. 66 (1923) (sale to commission merchant was in process of exportation); United States v. IBM, 517 U.S. 843 (1996) (tax on insurance was tax on exportation); United States v. United States Shoe Corp., 523 U.S. 360 (1998) (Harbor Maintenance Tax was effectively tax on exports).

[395] Pollock v. Farmers' Loan & Trust Co., 157 U.S. 429, 579-582 (1895), *confirmed and expanded*, 158 U.S. 601 (1895).

[396] *See* Ch. V.D.2.e.

[397] *See id.*

[398] Brushaber v. Union Pacific R. Co., 240 U.S. 1 (1916).

[399] Flint v. Stone Tracy Co., 220 U.S. 107 (1911). *See* Ch. V.D.2.d.

[400] Indeed, *Pollock* relied on the substance over form approach of the intergovernmental immunity cases to support its ruling as to the income tax. 157 U.S. at 581-582.

[401] *See* Ch. II.C.4.

[402] Knowlton v. Moore, 178 U.S. 41, 60 (1904).

[403] Graves v. New York ex rel. O'Keefe, 306 U.S. 466, 480 (1939).

a tax on another sovereign can be unconstitutional only if it is "real, not imaginary; substantial, not negligible."[404] For example, in the case of federal bonds, the state tax must be "on" the bond as property or "on" its interest as income and not on a distinct transaction or for a distinct right like a franchise (*e.g.*, the market sale of the bond producing market gain).[405] There must be some proof by evidence of the adverse impact on the governmental issue, not resort wholly to judicial notice, of which the Court found none in a state tax on gains on federal bonds.[406]

The Commerce Clause case law in state taxation (see Ch. IX) also has evolved tremendously, but it has gone both ways on the substance-form continuum. On the one hand, the principal commentators state that it has shifted towards substance, based on the *Complete Auto Transit* standard for discrimination against interstate commerce, which is filled with discretionary fact finding tests.[407] And on a related issue the "physical presence" requirement for sales tax nexus was finally replaced by economic nexus in 2018.[408] But the earlier rulings that seemed to be formalistic (e.g., the "original package doctrine") were so because of the Court's ironclad refusal to allow any state tax to impinge on interstate commerce. The Court itself viewed those earlier cases as based on analysis of substance.[409] And yet the supposedly freer analysis today can most readily lead to invalidating a tax when it facially discriminates, meaning it states any formal rule in terms that relate to interstate commerce, whether there is a substantive effect or not.[410] However, the expansion of the federal Commerce Clause powers beginning in the New Deal Era ushered in a willingness to search for indirect impacts of state and even private activity on interstate commerce, outside the tax area, and thus to apply a substance over form approach.[411]

As discussed in Chapter III.E, the issue of regulation versus taxation is the least settled, although there has been a truce based on the ability of a tax to produce some revenue, which is a formalistic test. Support for reliance on form in identifying a tax also may be found in an unexpected place: Chief Justice Marshall's opinion in *Weston v. Charleston*.[412] The City of Charleston imposed

---

404 Willcuts v. Bunn, 282 U.S. 216 (1931) (tax on bond sale gain that was not original issue discount); Plummer v. Coler, 178 U.S. 115 (1900) (estate tax on bonds not a burden).

405 282 U.S. 216.

406 *Id.*

407 *See* HELLERSTEIN & HELLERSTEIN, STATE TAXATION ¶ 4.12.

408 South Dakota v. Wayfair, Inc., 138 S. Ct. 2080 (2018).

409 *See Pollock*, 157 U.S. at 582. *See also* Brown v. Maryland, 25 U.S. 419 (1827) (Chief Justice Marshall created the "original package doctrine" providing that a state tax on goods still in the original package in which they were imported was indirectly a tax on the import and thus in violation of Article I, section 10; the Court moved away from this indirect burden approach, culminating in Michelin Tire Corp. v. Wages, 423 U.S. 276 (1976) (upholding property tax on imported tires stored in warehouse).

410 Fulton Corp. v. Faulkner, 516 U.S. 325 (1996).

411 *See* ALPHEUS T. MASON, THE SUPREME COURT FROM TAFT TO WARREN 90-112 (1968). A classic example would be the civil rights laws that reach private conduct based on presumed indirect impacts on interstate travel. *See, e.g.*, Katzenbach v. McClung, 379 U.S. 294 (1964) (local restaurant subject to civil rights laws).

412 Weston v. Charleston, 27 U.S. 449, 466 (1829).

a nondiscriminatory tax on notes, including federal government notes. Chief Justice Marshall saw that to be a tax on the United States just as plainly as Maryland's tax on the Bank of the United States was a tax on the United States. Justice Johnson in dissent, pleaded on behalf of his home city that Charleston had no intent to attack the United States, in contrast with the Maryland tax, which was not a tax at all.[413] Thus rather than examining the evidence to see that there was no intent to regulate the United States, Chief Justice Marshall based his ruling on the form of the tax and the rule of *McCulloch* that a tax could not be laid on the United States by a state.

Outside the core issues discussed above, the Court also has tended to allow form to control substance in other constitutional tax issues, including:

- The corporate form: The local taxpayer, shareholder of a national bank, argued that by taxing his shares the city was taxing the federal bonds that the bank held and was required to hold as a major part of its capital. The Court rejected that argument, citing an English decision holding that the shareholders of a corporation do not own the ship owned by the corporation.[414] A major recent regression in this area is the *Hobby Lobby* ruling, which invested an S corporation with the religious interests of its shareholders.[415]
- Double Jeopardy Clause: As discussed in Chapter VII.E, the Court's *Hudson* opinion rejected its prior *Halper* test that measured whether a civil penalty was a criminal punishment by assessing substantively how severe the penalty appeared to be, as opposed to the new test (which was a reversion to the old test adopted in a tax case, *Mitchell*) based primarily on the indicia of civil versus criminal punishment that Congress put in the statute.
- Standing in taxpayer suits and Establishment Clause cases: As explained in Chapter VIII.D.4.b, the Court has moved away from the relative flexibility of *Flast v. Cohen* in finding taxpayer standing to challenge unconstitutional federal spending, and has moved toward a formalistic test for establishment of religion.
- Equal Protection Clause: The Court has never ruled a federal tax rule unconstitutional because it discriminated against a taxpayer that was taxed more heavily than another (except for the retroactivity decisions and the suspect category in *Windsor*), despite the fact that the Code is filled with instances of discrimination, many of which are hard to explain.[416] In effect the Court has reasoned that because there is in fact a difference between butter and cheese (assuming, which is entirely possible, that a customs duty is imposed on one and not the other), then they can be taxed differently.

Whether these examples evidence a trend is in the eye of the beholder, but they seem to, when added to the trends in the core constitutional tax issues discussed

---

[413] *See* Donald G. Morgan, Justice William Johnson 249-250 (1954).
[414] Van Allen v. Assessors, 70 U.S. 573 (1866).
[415] Burwell v. Hobby Lobby Stores, Inc., 573 U.S. 682 (2014).
[416] *See* Ch. V.D.3.b(2).

above. However, the major exception that either will prove the rule or mark a departure generally back toward alleged substance of taxation is the hovering possibility that a tax labeled as such will be ruled to be an unconstitutional regulation of something Congress cannot regulate. The Court held the line for reliance on objective factors, if not pure form as a tax, in the 2012 health care tax decision.[417]

9. *Economics Versus Law*

The Supreme Court's general tendency to shift away from even a modest focus on economic effects of taxation to rely more on form, as discussed in the preceding Chapter, can be explained in many ways: perhaps the Court is more willing to defer to the creators of the formal rules, Congress, in matters of taxation; perhaps the Court saw the error of its earlier ways; perhaps the Court wearied of contending with economic distinctions that were basically irresolvable. Another explanation is that at the end of the day the Court is a court of law and not a legislature or an economics department.

The Court saw the error of its ways rather quickly with respect to its 1895 decisions in *Pollock*.[418] The majority opinion in the first *Pollock* decision relied heavily on economics. Counsel for the plaintiff cited to the Court the works of Adam Smith and the French economist Turgot as to the meaning of direct taxes.[419] The government rejected the relevance of the works of economists, stating that "economic definitions are inapplicable."[420] Chief Justice Fuller began his explanation why a tax on income from land was a direct tax by stating as a given the definition that direct taxes cannot be "shifted," which derived from the economic writings, and was by no means a generally accepted definition.[421] Sixteen years later the Court unanimously upheld the corporate income/excise tax of 1909 against a direct tax attacked based on *Pollock*.[422] This time the plaintiff's counsel did not argue economics, but rather argued the Fourth Amendment, the Fifth Amendment, the Fourteenth Amendment, and the Commerce Clause, among others. The Court's opinion relied principally on the form of the tax as an excise tax, which precluded finding that land was taxed indirectly by a tax on its income.

The Court's disregard of economics greatly discommodes the numerous academic writers who insist on beginning discussions of the income tax with a citation to the Haig-Simons definition of income, a concept the Court has never relied upon.[423] Instead a statement made by an early student of the Court's

---

[417] *See* Ch. III.E.2.c.

[418] Pollock v. Farmers' Loan & Trust Co., 157 U.S. 429 (1895), *confirmed and expanded*, 158 U.S. 601 (1895).

[419] Argument of Clarence A. Seward, reported in Lawyer's Edition. Pollock v. Farmers' Loan & Trust Co., 39 L. Ed. 759 (1895).

[420] Argument of Assistant Attorney General Whitney, reported in Lawyer's Edition.

[421] 157 U.S. at 558. His conclusion that indirect taxes can be shifted (hence they indirectly tax another person) whereas direct taxes could not be shifted is rather odd, given the facts that a consumer's sales tax is agreed by all not to be a direct tax but cannot be shifted, and an ad valorem tax on land that is rented is surely a direct tax and can usually be shifted to the tenants.

[422] Flint v. Stone Tracy Co., 220 U.S. 107 (1911).

[423] *See* CUMMINGS, at ch. VI.A.

constitutional tax decisions in 1925 remains equally true today. Agreeing with Justice White's dissents in *Pollock*, she stated:

> A court is not dealing with an academic question, but is laying down principles for the guidance of legislatures and citizens. To vacillate for the sake of gradually perfecting a theory is to cause inconvenience or actual injustice. It is not necessarily advisable for the judiciary to accept the conclusions of leading economists. Although the Supreme Court discusses the incidence and effects of taxation, its tax decisions are rendered, not as economics, but as law.[424]

When *Lochner* struck down a state law imposing maximum hours for labor on the basis of Fourteenth Amendment "freedom of contract," also known as "substantive due process,"[425] Justice Holmes said in dissent:

> This case is decided upon an economic theory which a large part of the country does not entertain. . . . [and the Fourteenth Amendment does not] enact Mr. Herbert Spencer's Social Statics. . . . a constitution is not intended to embody a particular economic theory, whether of paternalism and the organic relation of the citizen to the state or of laissez faire.[426]

Nicol v. Ames stated:

> . . . [I]t is no part of the duty of this court to lessen, impede or obstruct the exercise of the taxing power by merely abstruse and subtle distinctions as to the particular nature of a specified tax, where such distinction rests more upon the differing theories of political economists than upon the practical nature of the tax itself. In deciding upon the validity of a tax with reference to these requirements, no microscopic examination as to the purely economic or theoretical nature of the tax should be indulged in for the purpose of placing it in a category which would invalidate the tax.[427]

Weiss v. Wiener stated:

> The income tax laws do not profess to embody perfect economic theory. They ignore some things that either a theorist or a business man would take into account in determining the pecuniary condition of the taxpayer.[428]

The Court's relative unwillingness to investigate the economic incidence of taxation is part of a broader and more important constitutional principle: taxes are levied by a coordinate branch of government, the Congress; Congress is properly motivated by many considerations in taxation, and generally the courts do not concern themselves with those motivations; at the most fundamental level Congress makes judgments about the economic theories on which it will tax—income

---

[424] MARGARET SPAHR, THE SUPREME COURT ON THE INCIDENCE AND EFFECTS OF TAXATION: AN ANALYSIS OF ECONOMIC THEORY EMBEDDED IN THE CONSTITUTIONAL LAW DERIVED FROM THE EXPLICIT TAX CLAUSES, SMITH COLLEGE STUDIES IN HISTORY, Vol. X, Nos. 2, 3, and 4, pp. 257-258 (Jan.-July, 1925) (reprinted by Making of the Modern Law, Legal Treatises, 1800-1926).

[425] *See* Ch. V.D.3.b(7).

[426] Lochner v. New York, 198 U.S. 45, 75 (1905).

[427] Nicol v. Ames, 173 U.S. 509, 515-516 (1899).

[428] Weiss v. Wiener, 279 U.S. 333, 335 (1929).

versus consumption, capital versus labor, etc.—and those choices are fundamentally political and not legal.[429] If the people do not like the economic theory reflected in a tax, their redress lies in the political branches, not the courts.[430]

In answering the very basic question what is a tax, confusion arises due to conflation of economic and legal definitions. From an economic viewpoint a tax may be a compulsory payment for public benefits received.[431] But as applied, under the Constitution, taxes need not be compulsory nor for benefits received.[432] A privilege license tax, for example, is not compulsory; the taxpayer can choose not to seek the privilege that is taxed. Moreover the hallmark of taxes is recognized to be that they *are not* charged for specific benefits received from the government. For all these reasons, this book and the Court's constitutional federal tax opinions do not concern themselves with economics.

10. *The Justices Themselves*

a. *Individual Justices*

Part of the attraction of studying Supreme Court decisions issued throughout the life of the Court is gaining some insight into the Justices who wrote the important opinions in tax.[433] Those insights can help the subject matter come alive, as perhaps will the knowledge that key practitioners influenced federal tax decision, as discussed in Chapter I above. Some of the more interesting Justices who have connections to important tax cases include:

- Chief Justice Marshall, who wrote *McCulloch v. Maryland*,[434] the starting point for the majority of all federal constitutional tax issues. He is by universal agreement The Great Chief Justice.
- Chief Justice Salmon P. Chase, who wrote *Veazie Bank v. Fenno*,[435] upholding the federal taxing power, but then voted against federal power in the *Legal Tender Cases*,[436] despite being Secretary of the Treasury when the federal law was enacted. Chase wanted to be President.[437]

---

429 An often forgotten statement about the relative merits of labor and capital was made by President Lincoln in his First State of the Union Address (Dec. 3, 1861): "Labor is prior to and independent of capital. Capital is only the fruit of labor, and could never have existed if labor had not first existed. Labor is the superior of capital, and deserves much the higher consideration." Quoted in RATNER, at 92.

430 *See* GRAY, at 14-15.

431 *Id.* at 27.

432 *See* Ch. IV.

433 *See generally* THE OXFORD GUIDE TO THE SUPREME COURT (2005) (containing brief biographies of the Justices); LEON FRIEDMAN AND FRED ISRAEL, THE JUSTICES OF THE UNITED STATES SUPREME COURT (1789-1978) (1980); and the numerous biographies of the Justices.

434 *See* Ch. II.C.2.

435 Veazie Bank v. Fenno, 75 U.S. 533 (1869). *See* Ch. III.E.4.

436 Hepburn v. Griswold, 75 U.S. 603 (1870), *reversed*, Knox v. Lee, 79 U.S. 457 (1871) (together, the *Legal Tender Cases*).

437 As to Chief Justice Chase's somewhat peculiar jurisprudence, see G. Edward White, *Reconstructing the Constitutional Jurisprudence of Salmon P. Chase*, 21 N. KY. L. REV. 41 (1993).

- Chief Justice Fuller, who wrote the Court's opinion in both of the *Pollock* decisions.[438] One Supreme Court scholar described him as "the prime example of that luckiest of all persons known to the law—the innocent third party without notice."[439] On the other hand, he was thought to be an effective Chief Justice, of whom Justice Frankfurter said: "He had gentle firmness, courtesy and charm."[440]
- Justice Field was a surprisingly prescient 19th Century Tea Partier who almost single handedly created the liberty of contract theory and substantive due process and contributed to the Court's ability to reason as it did in the *Child Labor Tax Case*.[441] He wrote a stinging concurrence in *Pollock*.[442] One of Field's brothers was David Dudley Field, the father of the civil procedure reforms, and another was Cyrus Field, the inventor and investor. Justice Field was once involved in a murder trial of his own bodyguard, who killed someone attempting to kill Justice Field.[443] He was influenced by former Justice Campbell's losing argument in the *Slaughter-House Cases*,[444] based on natural rights to liberty and on the writings of Mark Hopkins (1802-1887) espousing inalienable rights of individuals and limited government.[445]
- Justice Peckham wrote some of the Court's state tax opinions but is best known for his opinion in *Lochner*, enshrining the liberty of contract to strike down maximum hour laws.[446] *Lochner* led to the *Child Labor Tax Case*. When a law clerk asked Justice Holmes what Justice Peckham was like intellectually, Holmes said: "I never thought of him in that connection. His major premise was 'God damn it!'"[447]
- The first Justice Harlan wrote a strong dissent to *Pollock*. Justice Holmes said he was the "last of the tobacco-spittin' judges" and the press called his dissent "the most violent political tirade ever heard in a court of last resort."[448]

---

[438] Pollock v. Farmers' Loan & Trust Co., 157 U.S. 429 (1895); Pollock v. Farmers' Loan & Trust Co., 158 U.S. 601 (1895).

[439] Schwartz, at 175.

[440] William L. King, Mellville Weston Fuller 476-477 (1950) [hereinafter King].

[441] The Oxford Guide to the Supreme Court 236-338 (2005); Ted Nace, Gangs of America, ch. 9, "The Judge" (2003); Carl Brent Swisher, Stephen J. Field Craftsman of the Law 424-425 (1930).

[442] "The present assault upon capital is but the beginning." 157 U.S. at 607.

[443] *In re* Neagle, 135 U.S. 1 (1890).

[444] *See* Ch. V.D.3.b(7)(a).

[445] Ralph H. Gabriel, The Course of American Democratic Thought 216-233 (1940) (containing many other fascinating details about Justice Field, including that he started his own town in California, he could shoot from the hip, and he went bankrupt but paid off all of his debts).

[446] Lochner v. New York, 198 U.S. 45 (1905). His opinion in Allgeyer v. Louisiana, 165 U.S. 578 (1897) established the liberty of contract theory. The Oxford Guide to the Supreme Court 725-726 (2005).

[447] Dean Acheson, Morning and Noon 65 (1965).

[448] Frank B. Latham, The Great Dissenter: John Marshall Harlan 114 (1970); King, at 216.

Justice Harlan is perhaps better known for his lone dissents in the *Civil Rights Cases*[449] (holding the Civil Rights Act of 1875 unconstitutional) and *Plessy v. Ferguson*.[450]

- Justice White wrote the opinion in *McCray*, the high water mark of Congress' power to tax, basically saying that if Congress calls it a tax it is a tax and may have the effect of regulating that which Congress cannot regulate, so long as any "free government" can regulate it.[451] He also wrote *Knowlton v. Moore*, upholding the federal inheritance tax and stating many foundational principles of federal taxing power.[452] White forecast his broad view of the federal taxing power in his dissent in *Pollock*. He was an unlikely candidate for a strong-government man, being from a wealthy sugar business family in Louisiana.[453]
- Chief Justice Taft wrote the *Child Labor Tax Case* and made the infamous remark that he could not shut his eyes to that which all men see (that Congress' motive was to regulate child labor and not tax).[454] Theodore Roosevelt tapped Taft for the presidential nomination and later regretted it. Had Roosevelt run instead, or tapped Charles Evans Hughes, who also had presidential ambitions, the history of the Court might have been very different. As it turned out, Taft got the job he most liked when appointed Chief Justice by President Harding, eight years after ending his one term as President.
- The Four Horsemen, as were called, Justices Sutherland, Van Devanter, McReynolds, and Butler, are remembered for their strongly conservative rulings, but they surprisingly supported the taxing power in many decisions.[455]
- Justice Holmes made his mark on tax cases as in all other areas, but excelled at pithy interpretation of the tax laws.[456]
- Justice Brandeis clearly occupied the tax chair on the Court, if there is one, and is sometimes said to have worn its "tax wreath."[457] He wrote a detailed economic analysis of the *Eisner v. Macomber* stock dividend in dissent. It is largely forgotten that his nomination process was even more contentious than that for Justice Thomas and that the American Bar Association and ex-pres-

---

[449] Civil Rights Cases, 109 U.S. 3 (1883).

[450] Plessy v. Ferguson, 163 U.S. 537 (1896).

[451] McCray v. United States, 195 U.S. 27 (1904).

[452] Knowlton v. Moore, 178 U.S. 41 (1900).

[453] The Oxford Guide to the Supreme Court 1086 (2005); Sister Marie Carolyn Klinkhamer, Edward Douglas White, Chief Justice of the United States 156-177 (1943) (discussing the tax decisions).

[454] J.W. Bailey v. Drexel Furn. Co., 259 U.S. 20 (1922).

[455] Barry Cushman, *Secret Lives of the Four Horsemen*, 83 Va. L. Rev. 559 (1997). *See also* Cummings, *The Four Horsemen and Estate Taxation*, 42 ACTEC Law Journal 5 (2016).

[456] Perlie P. Fallon, *Justice Holmes' Influence on Current Tax Law*, 24 Taxes 168 (1946).

[457] Kirk J. Stark, *The Unfulfilled Tax Legacy of Justice Robert H. Jackson*, 54 Tax L. Rev. 171, 214 (2001) [hereinafter Stark]. *See also* Mason, at 206 (stating that Taft viewed Brandeis as a tax expert and assigned tax cases to him).

ident and Chief Justice Taft wrote an unprecedented letter in opposition, stating that he "is not a fit person to be a member of the Supreme Court."[458]

- Chief Justice Hughes provided a swing vote that was instrumental in engineering the so called switch in time that saved nine in 1937. He wrote *James v. Dravo*, a pivotal opinion in reversing the spread of intergovernmental tax immunity.[459] He was 68 when he was appointed and was thought to be the master of guiding the Justices.[460] However, he tried to obscure his switch from opposing regulation to supporting regulation in garbled opinions: "Determination to hold fast the appearance of stability even while shifting decisions is the key to [his] constitutional jurisprudence."[461]

- Justice Jackson had more knowledge of federal taxation than any Justice that ever served on the Court, having been Chief Counsel of the IRS, Assistant Attorney General for the Tax Division, Solicitor General and Attorney General. Justice Brandeis said he should have been Solicitor General for life.[462] He prosecuted the tax case of the century: the civil fraud case against Andrew Mellon.[463] But his tax opinions were not as significant as others, and tended to be in the area of statutory construction.[464] An exception was *Helvering v. Griffiths*, which declined to overrule *Eisner v. Macomber*.[465] Justice Jackson left his hospital bed to attend court the day Chief Justice Warren announced the unanimous opinion in *Brown v. Board of Education*, and died shortly thereafter.[466] That opinion played a leading role in Justice Rehnquist's appointment to the Court because of a memo that either he or Justice Jackson wrote taking the other side of the *Brown* decision.[467] In addition his *Miller Bros.* opinion surveyed the entirety of the state tax constitutional rulings to that date, shortly before his death.[468]

- Justice Stone (later Chief Justice) joined either or some of Justices Brandeis, Cardozo and Holmes in dissenting to several of the decisions of the Court

---

458 Mason, at 74.

459 James v. Dravo Contracting Co., 302 U.S. 134 (1937). *See also* Helvering v. Mountain Producers Corp., 303 U.S. 376 (1938) (similar). *See* Ch. II.C.9.

460 Schwartz, at 226-228, 235-236.

461 Mason, at 116. Many believe that a change of heart had occurred before the Court packing plan was proposed by the Roosevelt Administration, at least on the part of Justice Roberts. *See, e.g.*, Kelly, Harbison and Belz, The American Constitution: Its Origin and Development, Vol. II 487-488 (7th ed.).

462 Felix Frankfurter, *Mr. Justice Jackson*, 68 Harv. L. Rev. 937, 939 (1954-1955).

463 Mellon v. Commissioner, 36 B.T.A. 977 (1937).

464 *See generally* Stark.

465 Helvering v. Griffiths, 318 U.S. 371 (1943).

466 Schwartz, *supra* note 436, at 304.

467 John W. Dean, The Untold Story of The Nixon Appointment that Redefined the Supreme Court (2002); John Q. Barrett and Brad Snyder, *Rehnquist's Missing Letter: A Former Law Clerk's 1955 Thoughts on Justice Jackson and Brown*, 53 B. C. L. Rev. 631 (March 2012).

468 Miller Bros. Co. v. Maryland, 347 U.S. 340 (1954).

holding federal taxes unconstitutional.[469] He also wrote important opinions limiting intergovernmental tax immunity.[470] Footnote 4 in his *Carolene Products* opinion set the stage for "strict scrutiny" of infringements of individual liberties, while supposedly leaving economic regulation (and taxation) to a rational basis scrutiny.[471] Karl Llewellyn predicted that Justice Stone would be (and he was) the one who carried the Holmes-Brandeis tradition to fulfillment and consolidated its gains.[472] Stone also wrote many opinions interpreting federal tax laws without constitutional issues.

- More recently, Justices Black, Douglas, Blackmun,[473] Marshall, Suiter, Breyer, Thomas and Ginsburg have written many tax opinions, but not necessarily ones that were important constitutional decisions due to the decline of disputed federal tax constitutional issues after 1937.[474]

b. *The Court's Use of Its "Old" Decisions*

This book does not discount the Court's "old" constitutional tax decisions and statements made in it "old" opinions unless the Court has stated it has passed them by or overruled them, or further development of the law renders an early opinion an incomplete statement of today's law. Rather than ignoring the early opinions, this book generally undertakes to present them in the sequence of their chronology for a fuller understanding of the current law. Some observers may doubt whether the Court gives full stare decisis effect to "old" tax constitutional decisions,[475] although in 2012 it gave proof of the power of stare decisis in a case of tax statutory construction.[476]

This book finds no evidence to support such doubt, although the matter is somewhat hard to prove given the recent rarity of federal tax constitutional decisions. The bottom line seems to be that federal tax constitutional issues come up to the Court only episodically, but when they do the Court is likely to begin its analysis with its prior rulings in the area, no matter how old. Of course, stare decisis is by definition a rule of stability but not rigidity; it arose out of the common law in which case law had to be followed because it was the only law, but because it was the only law it also had to be malleable.[477]

---

[469] *See* Ch. I.E.2.

[470] *See* Graves v. New York, 306 U.S. 466 (1939).

[471] United States v. Carolene Prod. Co., 304 U.S. 144, 152 n. 4 (1938).

[472] Mason, at 142-143.

[473] Robert A. Green, *Justice Blackmun's Federal Tax Jurisprudence*, 26 Hastings Const. L.Q. 109 (1998).

[474] Justice Thomas wrote United States v. IBM, 517 U.S. 843 (1996), to which Justice Ginsburg dissented. Justice Ginsburg wrote the unanimous opinion in United States v. United States Shoe Corp., 523 U.S. 360 (1998). Her now deceased husband, Martin D. Ginsburg, was a prominent corporate tax expert.

[475] *Cf.* Nancy Staudt, et al., *Judging Statutes: Interpretive Regimes*, 38 Loy. L. A. L. Rev. 1909, 1960 (2005).

[476] United States v. Home Concrete & Supply, LLC, 566 U.S. 478 (2012), *affirming*, 634 F.3d 249 (4th Cir. 2011), decided on the basis of Colony, Inc. v. Commissioner, 357 U.S. 28 (1958).

[477] *See* The Oxford Guide to the Supreme Court of the United States 198 (2005).

The following are some examples of uses of "old" federal tax constitutional decisions in "modern" opinions of the Court, both in tax and other cases:

- Justice Thomas seems particularly fond of relying on early federal tax constitutional case law, and of doing so in a way that would cause the constitutional wheel to turn back to the 1920s and 1930s. For example in 1995 he harkened back to "as recently as 1936" when the Court still thought the federal government was one of limited powers, citing *Carter v. Carter Coal.*[478] He reasoned by analogy that the word commerce was limited to sale and/or transport rather than business generally, a theory thought (by many) to have been rejected in 1937.
- Citations of the 1936 *Butler* case tend to show up in dissents, which may refer to either the majority or the dissenting opinions in *Butler*; for example a dissent in *Bush v. Gore* cited Justice Stone's dissent in *Butler*,[479] and several dissents have cited the majority as an unfortunately by-passed way of looking at federal taxation and regulation.[480]
- Of course "famous" old tax cases are cited all the time: for example *Eisner v. Macomber*, even though its view of the scope of income has been bypassed.[481]
- And then there are the "old" cases that might not be familiar to most tax professionals, but were very important in their day, and either are must-cites for any discussion of an area of the law, or are sources of good quotes, as in the case of *Boyd*, a self-incrimination tax case from 1886.[482]

Some empirical studies seem to show that the Court currently relies less on its own prior rulings in cases of statutory construction than in the earlier part of the 20th Century.[483] That is unlikely to be true of prior federal tax constitutional decisions relevant to a current case.

---

[478] United States v. Lopez, 514 U.S. 549, 599 (1995) (concurrence by Justice Thomas in the opinion striking down the Gun-Free School Zone Act of 1990).

[479] Bush v. Gore, 531 U.S. 98, 158 (2000) (dissent of Justice Breyer).

[480] United States v. Comstock, 560 U.S. 126 (2010) (dissent of Justice Thomas).

[481] Cottage Sav. Ass'n v. Commissioner, 499 U.S. 554, 562 (1991).

[482] Boyd v. United States, 116 U.S. 616, 617 (1886), *cited in* Stern v. Marshall, 564 U.S. 462 (2011) ("Although '[i]t may be that it is the obnoxious thing in its mildest and least repulsive form,' we cannot overlook the intrusion: 'illegitimate and unconstitutional practices get their first footing in that way, namely, by silent approaches and slight deviations from legal modes of procedure.'").

[483] *See* CUMMINGS, at Ch. III.C.2.

Ch. II. The Power to Tax

A. Taxation and Sovereignty

1. *Taxation Is the Essential Feature of Sovereignty*

The power of a government to tax is a matter of self-preservation that has not, in practice, awaited a constitutional grant. It is a necessary feature of a government's exercise of power over a geographic area, which can be called sovereignty.[1] The geographical extent of sovereignty may be disputed, as discussed in Chapter III.A.3; that occurred between the American Colonies and Great Britain, but those are not the common disputes about the sovereign power to tax that have arisen under the Constitution of the United States. Rather the extent of the taxing power in terms of amount has been the more contentious issue, as discussed in Chapter III.A.2. But, again, the sovereignty concept answers the question of amount, as pointed out by Alexander Hamilton, who used the word sovereign as an adjective to describe a type of unlimited power (a sovereign power).[2] Taxation

---

[1] *See* DAN PHILPOTT, SOVEREIGNTY, THE STANFORD ENCYCLOPEDIA OF PHILOSOPHY (Summer 2010). *See also* Ch. IX.C.1.

[2] JACOB E. COOKE EDITOR, THE REPORTS OF ALEXANDER HAMILTON, *Opinion on the Constitutionality of the Bank* 84 (1964) [hereinafter COOKE] ("every power vested in a government is in its nature sovereign, and includes by force of the term, a right to employ all the means requisite, and fairly applicable to the attainment of the ends of such power; [and therefore the United States had the power to charter a corporation to achieve federal purposes even though it did not generally have the power to charter corporations].").

is of first importance because it is the common means by which the sovereign (or state) sustains itself, which initially meant providing for the costs of its defense.[3] The Colonists were willing for Britain to regulate trade with the Colonies (which may have involved a regulatory tax), but not to tax them for revenue. Therefore, taxation is a fundamental attribute of sovereignty, which is itself the essential defining feature of a government or state.[4]

However, the power to tax is not before the United States Constitution; it is in and subject to the Constitution.[5] Nevertheless, it is the first stated power and many Supreme Court opinions reflect the importance of the taxing power:

- "Taxation is a sacred right, essential to the existence of government; an incident of sovereignty."[6]
- *Chisolm v. Georgia*, which ruled that a state had given up its sovereignty to the extent that it could be sued in federal courts by citizens of other states, listed taxation as an attribute of sovereignty (albeit ruling that states' sovereignty had been severely curtailed by the Constitution).[7]
- The power to tax has its foundations "in society itself."[8]
- The absolute necessity of the power to tax is reflected in the principle that an exemption from tax will not be implied.[9]
- Chief Justice Marshall said in *McCulloch v. Maryland* that "the power of taxing the people and their property is essential to the very existence of government . . . ."[10]
- The Court has repeatedly stated that the taxing power resides in the government as part of itself and is never presumed to be relinquished.[11]

---

[3] ADAM SMITH, AN INQUIRY INTO THE NATURE AND CAUSE OF THE WEALTH OF NATIONS, Books V.1. and V.2 (1776, Harvard Classics ed. 1909).

[4] *Staff of the Joint Committee on Taxation, The Taxing Power of the Federal and State Governments* 1 (1936) (available on Joint Committee website).

[5] McCulloch v. Maryland, 17 U.S. 316, 425 (1819) ("But, such is the paramount character of the constitution, that its capacity to withdraw any subject from the action of even this power, is admitted.").

[6] Dobbins v. The Commissioners of Erie, 41 U.S. 435, 447 (1842).

[7] Chisolm v. Georgia, 2 U.S. 419 (1793).

[8] Providence Bank v. Billings, 29 U.S. 514, 563 (1830).

[9] *Id.* at 562-563 (the bank argued that because the state chartered it, an obligation of contract would be violated if the state taxed it; the opinion reasoned that anything could be taxed into destruction and that principle was not inconsistent with the initial authorization of the thing taxed). This principle has become part of the "unmistakability doctrine," under which the United States cannot be held to have bargained away its sovereign powers except by unmistakably clear language. *See* United States v. Winstar Corp., 518 U.S. 839 (1996).

[10] McCulloch v. Maryland, 17 U.S. 316, 428 (1819). *See generally* Daniel A. Farber, *The Story of McCulloch: Banking on National Power*, 20 CONSTITUTIONAL COMMENTARY 679 (2004).

[11] *See, e.g.*, Society for Savings v. Coite, 73 U.S. 594, 606 (1867).

- Chief Justice Taney likened the taxing power to the power to grant public charters at issue in the important *Charles River Bridge* case, as a power that the whole community has an interest in preserving, undiminished.[12]
- "A government that cannot by self-administered methods, collect from its subjects the means necessary to support and maintain itself in the execution of its functions is a government merely in name."[13]
- In addition to being the highest attribute of sovereignty, the second major aspect of federal taxation is that it can be levied only by Congress; the Court cannot order a tax to be levied.[14]
- But the placement of the taxing power first in the Constitution does not cause different rules to apply to the degree to which Congress can delegate functions in taxation.[15]

Chief Justice Marshall further elucidated the taxing power in *McCulloch v. Maryland* in the context of a state taxing the Bank of the United States, which was considered to be a federal instrumentality:

> The people of a State, therefore, give to their Government a right of taxing themselves and their property, and as the exigencies of Government cannot be limited, they prescribe no limits to the exercise of this right, resting confidently on the interest of the legislator and on the influence of the constituent over their representative to guard them against its abuse. But the means employed by the Government of the Union have no such security [against over taxation by the states], nor is the right of a State to tax them sustained by the same theory. Those means are not given by the people of a particular State, not given by the constituents of the legislature which claim the right to tax them, but by the people of all the States. They are given by all, for the benefit of all—and, upon theory, should be subjected to that Government only which belongs to all. It may be objected to this definition that the power of taxation is not confined to the people and property of a State. It may be exercised upon every object brought within its jurisdiction. This is true. But to what source do we trace this right? It is obvious that it is an incident of sovereignty, and is coextensive with that to which it is an incident. All subjects over which the sovereign power of a State extends are objects of taxation, but those over which it does not extend are, upon the soundest principles, exempt from taxation. This proposition may almost be pronounced self-evident. The sovereignty of a State extends to everything which exists by its own authority or is introduced by its permission, but does it extend to those means which are employed by Congress to carry into execution powers conferred on that body by the people of the United States? We think it demonstrable that it does not. Those powers are not given by the people of a single State. They are given by the people of the United States, to a Government whose laws, made in pursuance of the Constitution, are declared

---

[12] Proprietors of Charles River Bridge v. Proprietors of Warren Bridge, 36 U.S. 420, 547-548 (1837).

[13] United States v. Snyder, 149 U.S. 210, 214 (1893).

[14] Rees v. Watertown, 86 U.S. 107 (1874).

[15] Skinner v. Mid-America Pipeline Co., 490 U.S. 212, 220 (1989).

> to be supreme. Consequently, the people of a single State cannot confer a sovereignty which will extend over them.[16]

The linkage of taxation and sovereignty was well understood during the period of the Confederation and while the Constitution was being debated.[17] Opponents of a strong central government principally opposed the desires of Federalists for the Confederation to impose a five percent impost on imports. They well understood that the issue was not primarily one of money but of power.[18] They wanted power to reside in the states, which controlled the purse strings of the Confederation, rather than in a central government. But it was not that they liked state governments; rather they feared concentrations of power and well understood that the power to tax could be exercised arbitrarily to any extent, as discussed in the next Chapter.[19]

2. *The Extent of the Sovereign's Taxing Power*

Once the power of a government to tax is recognized, the next most important issues are the amount of taxes that can be levied and on whom? Recently Chief Justice Roberts explained the limitless reach of taxation by quoting Benjamin Franklin's statement in reference to the Constitution that "nothing can be said to be certain, except death and taxes."[20] The most famous of all statements of the Supreme Court about taxes affirmed that there is no limit in amount that can be enforced in court; taxpayers are remitted to the political process.[21] Chief Justice Marshall stated in *McCulloch v. Maryland*:

> That the power of taxing it [the Bank of the United States] by the States may be exercised so as to destroy it, is too obvious to be denied,[22] . . . the power to tax involves the power to destroy. . . .[23]

Sometimes this statement is quoted in opposition to taxation in general or in some particular case. Obviously that was not the meaning intended by Chief Justice Marshall, and the Court has expressed just the opposite view in many opinions quoted below. It has embraced the federal government's power to tax as a positive and nearly limitless governing tool, not to be allowed grudgingly or stingily, but to be recognized as robust. One practical reason for the early embrace of the federal taxing power by the American moneyed classes (in contrast with later lack of enthusiasm for the progressive income tax) is that federal tax revenues were needed to pay federal and state debts. Alexander Hamilton's program for fiscal stability for the new United States included funding at 100 cents on the dollar not only the federal debts incurred to fight the Revolutionary War,

---

[16] McCulloch v. Maryland, 17 U.S. 316, 435-436 (1818).
[17] *See* Jackson Turner Main, The Anti-Federalists ch. IV "The Impost" (1961).
[18] *Id.* at 77.
[19] *Id.* at 78-79.
[20] Nat'l Fed'n of Indep. Bus. v. Sebelius, 567 U.S. 519 (2012).
[21] United States v. Kahriger, 345 U.S. 22, 28 (1953).
[22] McCulloch v. Maryland, 17 U.S. 316, 427 (1818).
[23] *Id.* at 431.

but also assuming and paying in full the war debts incurred by the states. Most of this debt had been bought up by financial speculators, who were happy to see the federal government tax and spend in this manner.[24]

The statement in *McCulloch v. Maryland* originated in the argument made by Daniel Webster, representing the Bank of the United States (through its officer McCulloch). He made the argument not because the tax actually levied was so onerous, but because the hostility it reflected against the Bank of the United States went to the core of the federal government's power to utilize the Bank, which was the real matter in dispute. The statement means that once the camel's nose is under the tent—once states are allowed to tax the United States as it goes about governing—the amount of the tax that may be imposed is limitless and hence the imposition on federal supremacy is limitless. Chief Justice Marshall went on to identify the only true brake on taxation, once jurisdiction to tax was allowed:

> . . . [Taxation] may be legitimately exercised on the objects to which it is applicable, to the utmost extent to which the government may chuse to carry it. The only security against the abuse of this power, is found in the structure of the government itself. In imposing a tax the legislature acts upon its constituents. This is in general a sufficient security against erroneous and oppressive taxation. . . . and as the exigencies of government cannot be limited, they prescribe no limits to the exercise of this right, resting confidently on the interest of the legislator, and on the influence of the constituents over their representative, to guard then against its abuse.[25]

That the Constitution itself contemplated, and the Founders understood, the destructive power of taxation is illustrated by its peculiar requirement for apportioning direct taxes based on the census, but subject to the Three Fifths Clause, which counted slaves as three fifths of a person. The apportionment requirement had the effect of preventing the national taxes from falling more heavily on the larger, more sparsely populated southern and western states, relative to the northeast, and the three fifths limit had the effect of diluting the apportionment of direct taxes to the southern states by undercounting the slaves.[26] The effect, in part, was to ameliorate the otherwise potentially destructive power to tax land.[27]

But the people of the whole United States lacked that brake insofar as state taxation was concerned; they could not rely on the "magic of confidence" that a state would not abuse the power of taxation to destroy the federal government, but rather could only repose confidence in the United States not to exercise its taxing power destructively, because all were represented by it.[28] For that reason the State of Maryland could not be allowed to tax the instrumentality of the United States, the Bank of the United States. Chief Justice Marshall used the

---

[24] Carl Brent Swisher, American Constitutional Development 65 (1954).

[25] 17 U.S. at 428.

[26] *See* Ch. V.C.4.b.

[27] Sidney Rattner, American Taxation 20 (1942) [hereinafter Ratner].

[28] 17 U.S. at 431.

same argument to strike down the state tax on United States debt instruments, stating: "If the right to impose the tax exists, it is a right which in its nature acknowledges no limits."[29] In *Providence Bank v. Billings* Chief Justice Marshall returned to the point that taxation may be exorbitant and still not prevented by the Constitution, but rather the taxpayer is remitted to the political process for protection.[30]

Veazie Bank v. Fenno approved a Civil War measure to tax bank notes issued by state banks in order to drive them out of competition with national banks, which Congress employed to aid in creating a national currency.[31] It was understood that the tax aimed to destroy the ability of state banks to issue currency and so the tax was based in part on the separate power of Congress to regulate the currency as well as the power to tax.[32]

Moving forward almost a century, the same sentiments continued to appear in Supreme Court opinions, in this example eschewing economic theory in favor of practicality:

> The power to tax is the one great power upon which the whole national fabric is based. It is as necessary to the existence and prosperity of a nation as is the air he breathes to the natural man. It is not only the power to destroy, but it is also the power to keep alive. . . . it is no part of the duty of this court to lessen, impede or obstruct the exercise of the taxing power by merely abstruse and subtle distinctions as to the particular nature of a specified tax, where such distinction rests more upon the differing theories of political economists than upon the practical nature of the tax itself. In deciding upon the validity of a tax with reference to these requirements, no microscopic examination as to the

---

[29] Weston v. Charleston, 27 U.S. 449, 466 (1829).

[30] Providence Bank v. Billings, 29 U.S. 514, 563 (1830) (referring in this case to state taxation: "This vital power may be abused; but the constitution of the United States was not intended to furnish the corrective for every abuse of power which may be committed by the state governments. The interest, wisdom, and justice of the representative body, and its relations with its constituents furnish the only security, where there is no express contract, against unjust and excessive taxation; as well as against unwise legislation generally.").

[31] Veazie Bank v. Fenno, 75 U.S. 533 (1869). The story of the creation of currency threads throughout the story of federal taxation. As discussed in Ch. II.C.2, the effort of the United States to create national currency through the Bank of the United States was at issue in *McCulloch v. Maryland.* When President Jackson prevented renewal of the Second Bank's charter, currency reverted to gold and silver and local banks' emissions of notes. But the strain of the Civil War proved too great and Congress authorized a limited but relatively large issuance of "greenbacks." That was viewed as unfortunate monetary policy by some advocates of hard money, and so then Congress authorized national banks, which would issue bank notes, and *Veazie* affirmed the federal law that taxed state bank notes that might try to compete with the national bank notes. *See generally* James Grant, Mr. Speaker 98-107 (2011).

[32] 75 U.S. at 540, 547. *See* Margulies, 5 J. S. Legal Hist. at 10.

> purely economic or theoretical nature of the tax should be indulged in for the purpose of placing it in a category which would invalidate the tax.[33]

In *Flint v. Stone Tracy*, upholding the 1909 corporate excise tax, the Court said:

> The Constitution contains only two limitations on the right of Congress to levy excise taxes; they must be levied for the public welfare and are required to be uniform throughout the United States. As Mr. Chief Justice Chase said, speaking for the court in *License Tax Cases*, 5 Wall. 462, 471: "Congress cannot tax exports, and it must impose direct taxes by the rule of apportionment, and indirect taxes by the rule of uniformity. Thus limited and thus only, it reaches every subject and may be exercised at discretion." The limitations to which the Chief Justice refers were the only ones imposed in the Constitution upon the taxing power.[34]

And in the same opinion:

> It is urged that this power can be so exercised by Congress as to practically destroy the right of the States to create corporations, and for that reason it ought not to be sustained, and reference is made to the declaration of Chief Justice Marshall in *McCulloch v. Maryland* that the power to tax involves the power to destroy. This argument has not been infrequently addressed to this court with respect to the exercise of the powers of Congress. Of such contention this court said in *Knowlton v. Moore, supra.* "This principle is pertinent only when there is no power to tax a particular subject, and has no relation to a case where such right exists. In other words, the power to destroy which may be the consequence of taxation is a reason why the right to tax should be confined to subjects which may be lawfully embraced therein, even although it happens that in some particular instance no great harm may be caused by the exercise of the taxing authority as to a subject which is beyond its scope. But this reasoning has no application to a lawful tax, for if it had there would be an end of all taxation; that is to say, if a lawful tax can be defeated because the power which is manifested by its imposition may when further exercised be destructive, it

---

[33] Nicol v. Ames, 173 U.S. 509, 515-516 (1899) (unanimous opinion by Justice Peckham, who generally was a quite conservative Justice, best known as the author of *Lochner v. New York*, striking down a state law limiting hours of bakers, relying on substantive due process and liberty of contract, constitutional theories that have subsequently been diminished or discarded, even by conservatives). *See also* Weiss v. Wiener, 279 U.S. 333, 335 (1929) ("The income tax laws do not profess to embody perfect economic theory. They ignore some things that either a theorist or a business man would take into account in determining the pecuniary condition of the taxpayer.").

[34] Flint v. Stone Tracy Co., 220 U.S. 107, 153-154 (1911).

would follow that every lawful tax would become unlawful, and therefore no taxation whatever could be levied."[35]

Justice White in *McCray*, upholding a tax on oleomargarine that had been colored to look like butter, in 1904 stated:

> The proposition that where a tax is imposed which is within the grant of powers, and which does not conflict with any express constitutional limitation, the courts may hold the tax to be void because it is deemed that the tax is too high, is absolutely disposed of by the opinions in the cases hitherto cited, and which expressly hold, to repeat again the language of one of the cases (*Spencer v. Merchant*[36]) that "The judicial department cannot prescribe to the legislative department limitations upon the exercise of its acknowledged powers. The power to tax may be exercised oppressively upon persons; but the responsibility of the legislature is not to the courts, but to the people by whom its members are elected."[37] . . . It hence results, that even although it be true that the effect of the tax in question is to repress the manufacture of artificially colored oleomargarine, it cannot be said that such repression destroys rights which no free government could destroy, and, therefore, no ground exists to sustain the proposition that the judiciary may invoke an implied prohibition, upon the theory that to do so is essential to save such rights from destruction.[38]

Justice Holmes, evaluating in 1921 a state tax designed to discourage the use of herring for manure, in favor of uses the state considered more appropriate, opined that the fact that the tax might destroy the taxed business was not a ground for constitutional objection, analogizing the century long tradition of

---

[35] *Id.* at 168. *See also* concurrence of Justice Iredell in Calder v. Bull, 3 U.S. 386, 400 (1798) ("It is not sufficient to urge, that the power [to take private property] may be abused, for, such is the nature of all power,—such is the tendency of every human institution: and, it might as fairly be said, that the power of taxation, which is only circumscribed by the discretion of the Body, in which it is vested, ought not to be grounded, because the Legislature, disregarding its true objects, might, for visionary and useless projects, impose a tax to the amount of nineteen shillings in the pound. We must be content to limit power where we can, and where we cannot, consistently with its use, we must be content to repose a salutary confidence. It is our consolation that there never existed a Government, in ancient or modern times, more free from danger in this respect, than the Governments of America.").

[36] Spencer v. Merchant, 125 U.S. 345 (1888) (a special assessment was held void by the state court due to lack of any opportunity for hearing as to the apportionment of the tax; the legislature reimposed the unpaid assessments with a method of hearing; ruled constitutional, even though obviously retrospective).

[37] McCray v. United States, 195 U.S. 27, 60 (1904).

[38] *Id.* at 63.

destroying import businesses through the protective tariff.[39] In a different but analogous context, the Court ruled that a municipality must pay its debts even if it meant the debtor would have to levy a tax so heavy that it could not be collected; to deny the judgment on the debt would be to impair the obligation of contract.[40] *Sanchez* ruled that $100 per ounce tax on marijuana in 1950 was still a tax permitted by the Constitution, in part because Congress said it was raising revenue.[41] In 1932 in dissent to a ruling that a city could not limit the number of ice houses in the city, Justice Brandeis argued that the city could have entered the ice business and taxed competitors to limit then, and so it should be able to achieve the same purpose of providing ice to the public by limiting entry into the business.[42]

In 1933 Chief Justice Hughes stated in ruling on an estate tax:

> As a nation with all the attributes of sovereignty, the United States is vested with all the powers of government necessary to maintain an effective control of international relations. . . ." We should hesitate long," we said in Mackenzie v. Hare, 239 U.S. 299, 311, "before limiting or embarrassing such powers."[43]

In 1978 Justice Brennan defined taxes as those levies for the support of the government: (a) that did not have to bear any relationship to benefits received, (b) but instead were normally levied based on ability to pay, and (c) could become so heavy as to eliminate the thing being taxed.[44] He cited both *McCulloch* and *Weston v. Charleston* for the principle that the power to tax acknowledges no limits and so explained the immunity of states from federal taxation, lest the constitutional arrangement of states within the federal system be destroyed.

---

[39] Alaska Fish Salting & By-Products Co. v. Smith, 255 U.S. 44, 48 (1921) (The taxpayer alleged that the tax "will prohibit and confiscate" its business; the United States demurred to the complaint; the ruling affirmed dismissal of the complaint). State tax opinions with similar language include Tanner v. Little, 240 U.S. 369, 380 (1916) (which affirmed convictions of merchants who failed to pay a $6,000 license fee to give trading stamps to customers, stating "The power of taxation rests upon necessity and is inherent in every independent State. It is as extensive as the range of subjects over which the government extends; it is absolute and unlimited, in the absence of constitutional limitations and restraints, and carries with it the power to embarrass and destroy."); A. Magnano Co. v. Hamilton, 292 U.S. 40 (1934) (observing that if the tax had been one third the actual rate, likely no one would have objected, and that the absolute amount of the tax could not be the determinant of constitutionality). *Cf.* Henneford v. Silas Mason Co., 300 U.S. 577 (1937) (distinguishing between a revenue tariff and a protective tariff and restating that either can burden interstate commerce, in the context of state taxation). However, conservative writers strive to convert even protective tariffs into nontax regulations. *See* Robert Eugene Cushman, *The National Police Power under the Taxing Clause of the Constitution*, 4 MINN. L. REV. 247, 257 (1920) [hereinafter CUSHMAN] (citing Cooley).

[40] Wolff v. New Orleans, 103 U.S. 358 (1881).

[41] United States v. Sanchez, 340 U.S. 42 (1950).

[42] New State Ice Co. v. Liebmann, 285 U.S. 262, 304-305 (1932).

[43] Burnet v. Brooks, 288 U.S. 378, 396 (1933).

[44] Massachusetts v. United States, 435 U.S. 444, 455 (1978). *See also* National Cable Television Ass'n v. United States, 415 U.S. 336, 340 (1974) ("Taxation is a legislative function, and Congress, which is the sole organ for levying taxes, may act arbitrarily and disregard benefits bestowed by the Government on a taxpayer and go solely on ability to pay, based on property or income.").

To a taxpayer the amount of the tax need not be destructive to provoke objections. One objection to the amount of taxation that in theory might be made is that a government is taxing just to lay up riches, without any public need, as Thomas Jefferson feared.[45] But that state of affairs will never exist in the United States because paying debts is a constitutionally sanctioned purpose of taxation, and the United States will never run out of debts it could pay with tax revenues.

Despite all of these statements, both in dictum and in holding, that a tax properly can have the effect of destroying the subject of taxation, such as the business of turning herring into manure, objections will continue to be made to taxes on the grounds that they appear to be confiscatory and mean spirited and for no purposes other than to regulate or harm, despite the availability of good uses for all taxes collected; some members of each new generation will not have received the message about the vast scope of the taxing power. Because there is no limit on the degree of taxation, these objections usually must turn into Tenth Amendment disputes in which the taxpayer's victory depends not on proving the tax to be excessive, but on moving the tax out of the tax category and solely into the category of a regulatory penalty that is meddling in a matter outside the purview of Congress, as discussed in Chapter III.E and F. For example, *United States v. Constantine* invalidated as a penalty, and not a tax, a $1,000 levy on liquor dealing only when it was illegal under state law.[46] However, the real ground of the ruling was that the trigger for the tax was violation of state law; nevertheless, the opinion made reference to the "highly exorbitant" amount of the fine, without fixing that as the ground of the ruling.[47]

The way in which a tax is "exorbitant" informs its analysis and can lead to a finding of unconstitutionality on a ground other than that the tax is "too high." Taxes can be imposed as (1) a fixed percentage of something valued in dollars; (2) an escalating percentage of something valued in dollars; (3) an absolute dollar amount per person, per transaction, per piece or value of property; or (4) an escalating dollar amount per person, per transaction, per piece or value of property. Then any of those categories can be limited to a relatively small number of taxpayers.

In 1944 the highest individual income tax rate was 94% on income over $250,000; in 1952 that rate was 92%. Assuming a 100% tax rate would be wholly confiscatory, rates above 90% seem confiscatory in practice, whether one thinks they are excessive or not. Likewise, estate tax rates went up to 77% from 1941 to 1977. And yet this author cannot find any Supreme Court decision

---

[45] *See* statement of Thomas Jefferson, quoted in Cushman, at 250 n. 16 ("Congress are not to lay taxes ad libitum."). Alexander Hamilton addressed this statement in his legal opinion on the Bank of the United States, noting that the Secretary of State (Jefferson) had made the statement and agreeing with it but defining it to mean that Congress could not tax for "purely local" purposes. COOKE, at 109.

[46] United States v. Constantine, 296 U.S. 287 (1935).

[47] *Id.* at 295. *See* Ch. III.E.8 and III.F; *see also* Ch. III.E.2.c, discussing the 2012 health insurance tax case, which considered arguments about the amount and penal nature of the tax.

considering an attack on those high tax rates.[48] Perhaps the saving feature of these rates was that they kicked in only at high levels of income or estate value. The taxpayer could not argue that the entire income or the entire estate was confiscated.

If the high tax is limited to a relatively small number of taxpayers, the taxpayers may complain of a violation of the Equal Protection Clause or Due Process Clause, based on arbitrariness of the category, particularly if a suspect category is involved.[49] But the Court has never found a federal tax to be unconstitutional on such grounds (although it found DOMA to be unconstitutional in *Windsor*). Finally, the expansive scope of the taxing power brings expansive enforcement and collection powers. For example, the Court has found a common law power to sue on a tax debt owed to the United States despite absence of specific authority for such suit, citing the royal prerogatives of the British crown.[50]

It is important to contrast the constitutional power of a tax to destroy a business or the value of property with the very different constraint the Supreme Court early chose to place on rate regulation at the request of the railroads. In 1890 in a railroad state rate making case the Court established (1) the ultimate control of the courts over regulatory rate making, and (2) the principle that rates must be set so as to allow the carrier to make a reasonable profit.[51] If that principle were applied to taxation, then the power of taxation would be drastically diminished.

3. *The Subjects of the Sovereign's Taxing Power*

Once the federal power to tax, and to tax in unlimited amounts, is recognized as constitutional, the question of the potential subjects of that taxation must be addressed: what persons will be taxed directly, or indirectly by withholding from or levying upon their property?[52] Conceptually, the taxing power is coextensive with the sovereignty that underlies it. It extends to persons and property within the sovereign's jurisdiction, meaning both its legal and practical ability to reach persons and their property. The issue is much more acute for state taxation, addressed by Ch. IX.

---

[48] Neither can the author find any court of appeals cases. District court opinions mention the high rates, usually in the context of capital gains planning, but the taxpayer did not attack the rate. *E.g.*, Fields v. Granquist, 134 F. Supp. 624 (D. Or. 1955).

[49] *See* Ch. I.E.4.b and V.D.3.b(3).

[50] United States v. Chamberlin, 219 U.S. 250, 261 (1911), *citing*, Dollar Sav. Bank v. United States, 86 U.S. 227, 238-240 (1874). *See* Ch. VIII.E.

[51] Chicago, M. & St. P. Ry. v. Minnesota, 134 U.S. 418, 458 (1890). *See also* Swift & Co. v. Wickham, 382 U.S. 111, 117 (1965) (the most recent opinion to cite the 1890 decision, favorably); Smyth v. Ames, 169 U.S. 466 (1898) (to the same effect).

[52] The practice of requiring the payor to withhold first arose in connection with taxes on shares, interest and dividends paid by corporations, as to which the corporation was required to pay a tax. The Court stated that the corporation could withhold from what was paid over to the shareholder or creditor, or not, but so far as tax liability was concerned, the corporation was liable to the treasury for the tax. *See* Barnes v. R.R., 84 U.S. 294, 305 (1873).

While not dictated by the Constitution, the United States has chosen as the subjects of income taxation: (1) citizens (which reflects a legal jurisdiction to tax), (2) resident aliens (which reflects practical ability to tax), and (3) property within the jurisdiction (including outbound payments and property rights generated by local activities), whether owned by nonresident aliens or residents (based on practical ability to collect, and including intangible property deemed to be found in the jurisdiction). This tripartite categorization is so well accepted in the United States that the Court states it in an off-hand way like this: "And where the bondholder was subject to congressional legislation, by reason of citizenship, residence, or situs of the property taxed, it was within the lawful power of Congress to do so."[53]

This intuitive classification reflects Congress' intent to push to the practical limits on the nation's means of getting at tax dollars; recall that Article I, section 8 grants to Congress the powers to lay and collect taxes, which are distinct undertakings. If Congress cannot collect a tax, the laying of the tax is meaningless.[54] Therefore, in practice, jurisdiction to tax is defined by the practical ability to reach the revenue, meaning those areas where the nation can exert its legal power through physical coercion, that is, distraint (seizure of property to collect an amount due) and arrest (of the taxpayer). For the United States this area of jurisdiction has always extended beyond the physical boundaries of the states, to include the Territories and other areas as discussed in Chapter V.D.3.a(3) and (4).

Obviously the legal implications of the practical ability of a nation's taxing power to reach aliens and foreign source income and even foreign sitused property can involve international relations and international law generally.[55] International taxation has its own terminologies for the choices nations make in defining tax jurisdiction; it usually collapses the three categories used above into two: taxation based on territoriality (source) and on nationality (residence).[56] Another terminology differentiates global systems (*i.e.*, nationality) and schedular systems (meaning taxing various types of income classified by type, according to source).[57] And frequently the choices are called source based taxation and residence based taxation, which is somewhat of a misnomer as applied to the

---

[53] R.R. Co. v. Collector, 100 U.S. 595, 598 (1880).

[54] *See* Dodge v. Woolsey, 59 U.S. 331, 353 (1856) (noting the distinct importance of collection and stating that Congress could not collect a tax if a state court or state legislature had the unreviewable power to nullify a federal tax levied within its bounds, in the context of discussing a direct tax).

[55] *See id.*; Reuven S. Avi-Yonah, *International Tax as International Law*, 57 Tax L. Rev. 483 (2004) [hereinafter Avi-Yonah].

[56] *See* Michael S. Kirsch, *Tax Code as Nationality Law*, 49 Harv. J. on Leg. 375, 390-391 (2006) [hereinafter Kirsch]; Avi-Yonah, at 484.

[57] Martin Norr, *Jurisdiction to Tax and International Income*, 17 Tax L. Rev. 431, 433-434 (1962) [hereinafter Norr].

United States because citizens need not be residents of the United States to be subject to residence based taxation.[58]

The United States' attempts to accommodate other countries' interests and to avoid double taxation are reflected in the use of tax credits and the system of tax treaties in which the United States engages. But because income tax conventions (tax treaties) are subject to congressional approval, under the Constitution a subsequent tax law can override a treaty and vice versa,[59] which shows the fragility of the hold of international law over federal taxation.

In 1962 Martin Norr concluded: "No rules of international law exist to limit the extent of any country's tax jurisdiction."[60] The Court has not subsequently identified any such rules and the current Court is not likely to do so. Nevertheless, academic writers are prolific in discussing international norms of taxation, which, again, focus on source and residence, with a minority interest in citizenship.[61] It has been argued that the Court finds the jurisdictional limits of the United States' taxing power in the Court's notions of sovereignty and not the taxing power.[62] But it is more likely that the Court feels more constrained by practicality than by international norms. For example when the British retook a port in a Territory during the War of 1812, imports during the time of British occupation could not be taxed because Justice Story said in an unusually brief opinion that the United States had lost its sovereignty for that period and so its laws could not be enforced.[63] At least in early years the Court viewed this rule entirely in practical terms: did a conqueror control a Territory?[64] However, the Court sometimes tried to harmonize physical control with principles of in-

---

[58] *See generally* Jeffrey M. Colon, *Changing U.S. Tax Jurisdiction: Expatriates, Immigrants and the Need for a Coherent Tax Policy*, 34 San Diego L. Rev. 4 (1997). The United States' practice of taxing citizens as opposed to residents only is rare among nations. *See* Norr, at 436.

[59] Constitution Article VI, paragraph 2. *See, e.g.*, Whitney v. Robertson, 124 U.S. 190 (1888); Cook v. United States, 288 U.S. 102 (1933); Breard v. Greene, 523 U.S. 371 (1998); Rainey v. United States, 232 U.S. 310, 316 (1914); Missouri v. Holland, 252 U.S. 416 (1920) (a rather remarkable holding that a treaty properly adopted under the power of the United States is not subject to the limitations that otherwise would apply to a mere act of Congress, in particular, the Tenth Amendment). *See also* Bittker & Lokken, Federal Taxation of Income, Estates and Gifts ¶ 65.4 [hereinafter Bittker & Lokken].

[60] Norr.

[61] *See, e.g.*, Nancy H. Kaufman, *Fairness and the Taxation of International Income*, 29 Law and Pol'y Int'l Bus., 145, 148 (1998).

[62] *See* Kirsch, at 413.

[63] United States v. Rice, 17 U.S. 246 (1819). The same analysis applied to the Confederacy. Thorington v. Smith, 75 U.S. 1 (1869). *See also* Pearcy v. Stranahan, 205 U.S. 257 (1907) (Isle of Pines remained under the control of Cuba during the Spanish-American War and so was treated as a foreign country for import duty purposes; "There has been no change of nationality for revenue purposes, but, on the contrary, the Cuban Government has been recognized as rightfully exercising sovereignty over the Isle of Pines as a de facto government until otherwise provided. It must be treated as foreign, for this Government has never taken, nor aimed to take, that possession in fact and in law which is essential to render it domestic.").

[64] *See, e.g.*, United States v. Huckabee, 83 U.S. 414 (1873).

ternational law,[65] a nontax canon of construction dating back to Chief Justice Marshall in an admiralty case.[66] The Court's practical approach seems to be that it will try to follow international norms in the absence of conflicting federal law,[67] but greater resistance has developed on the Court recently to extending the scope of international law that is binding on federal courts beyond treaties as to which Congress has enacted implementing legislation or the treaty is intended to be self executing.[68]

Most of the Supreme Court's sparse case authority on this subject relates to either the complete subjection of the citizen to taxation on worldwide income or property, or to the taxation of property found in (or income paid from) the United States but owned by nonresidents; as to these subjects no constitutional limits have been found by the Court.

Chief Justice Marshall addressed the subject of taxing jurisdiction indirectly in *Loughborough*, saying that the taxing power extends to all places over which the government extends, which includes the states, the Territories and the District of Columbia.[69] For further discussion of these topics, see the discussions elsewhere in this book of the federal taxing power in the District of Columbia, the Territories, and federal enclaves,[70] as well as Chapter IX on state taxation. The Court several times has made statements indicating that the taxing power of the United States reaches as far as the United States can reach as a matter of legal process or physical control.[71] A very early decision on seizure for taxes stated: "The laws of no nation can justly extend beyond its own territories, except so far as regards its own citizens. They can have no force to control the sovereignty or rights of any other nation, within its own jurisdiction."[72]

Burnet v. Brooks affirmed the power of the United States to collect an estate tax from the estate of a foreign decedent on foreign stocks and bonds physically held in the United States and stocks of domestic corporations, regardless of the location of the certificates. Relying on *DeGanay v. Lederer*, Chief Justice Hughes stated that the issue of jurisdictional power was one of due process and international relations:

---

[65] *See, e.g.*, MacLeod v. United States, 229 U.S. 416 (1913) ("The statute should be construed in the light of the purpose of the Government to act within the limitation of the principles of international law, the observance of which is so essential to the peace and harmony of nations, and it should not be assumed that Congress proposed to violate the obligations of this country to other nations, which it was the manifest purpose of the President to scrupulously observe and which were founded upon the principles of international law." Because the Court construed the statute not to authorize levying duties in the port not under actual military control and occupation, it said the unauthorized tax was an illegal penalty and void.).

[66] Murray v. The Schooner Charming Betsy, 6 U.S. 64 (1804).

[67] *See* Avi-Yonah, at 500-501, *citing* The Paquete Habana, 175 U.S. 677 (1900).

[68] *See* Medellin v. Texas, 552 U.S. 491 (2008).

[69] Loughborough v. Blake, 18 U.S. 317 (1820).

[70] *See* Ch. V.D.3.a(3) and (4) and II.C.6.

[71] *See, e.g.*, Memphis & C. R. Co. v. United States, 108 U.S. 228 (1883) (corporate income earned within the Confederacy, and in Confederate money, was taxable because the corporation was within the control of the United States).

[72] The Apollon, 22 U.S. 362, 370 (1824).

> So far as our relation to other nations is concerned, and apart from any self-imposed constitutional restriction, we cannot fail to regard the property in question as being within the jurisdiction of the United States,—that is, it was property within the reach of the power which the United States by virtue of its sovereignty could exercise as against other nations and their subjects without violating any established principle of international law. This view of the scope of the sovereign power in the matter of the taxation of securities physically within the territorial limits of the sovereign is sustained by high authority and is a postulate of legislative action in other countries. . . . [Taxing] . . . jurisdiction may exist in more than one government, that is, jurisdiction based on distinct grounds—the citizenship of the owner, his domicile, the source of income, the situs of the property . . . .[73]

Sourcing. As to income, sourcing the income in the United States has been assumed to be a ground of taxing jurisdiction, without much analysis. Chief Justice Hughes said so in *Burnet v. Brooks* in passing.[74] At first the Court posited but did not answer the question.[75] Subsequent rulings on the same statute as amended appear to have assumed the answer was yes,[76] at least where the tax was collected from the payor, out of its distributed earnings.[77] Finally, *DeGanay v. Lederer* ruled under the 1913 income tax that a French citizen owed tax on income from stocks and bonds held in trust for her in the United States, reasoning simply that the property was here.[78]

The reference to source in the Sixteenth Amendment—"from whatever source derived"—does not refer to domestic or foreign sourcing of income. Rather, it was intended to overcome the interpretation that had led to striking down the income tax of 1894 in *Pollock*: that the true source of rental income was land and so the income tax was a direct tax on land and was unconstitutional because not apportioned among the states.[79]

Citizens. The 14th Amendment states that "All persons born or naturalized in the United States and subject to the jurisdiction thereof, are citizens of the United States and of the State wherein they reside."[80] Citizens are taxed because citizenship imports a network of rights and responsibilities between the state and the citizen that exist wherever the citizen or the citizen's property may be

---

[73] Burnet v. Brooks, 288 U.S. 378, 396-399 (1938).

[74] 288 U.S. at 399.

[75] Railroad Co. v. Jackson, 74 U.S. 262 (1869) (railroads were not required by the Civil War income tax statute to withhold federal income tax on bond interest paid to nonresident aliens, but would be required to do so under amendment).

[76] Barnes v. R.R., 84 U.S. 294 (1873) (statute was amended to specifically include dividends to nonresident aliens and the Court ordered the corporation to withhold on all dividends).

[77] R.R. Co. v. Collector, 100 U.S. 595 (1880).

[78] DeGanay v. Lederer, 250 U.S. 376 (1919).

[79] *See* Ch. V.D.2.e.

[80] *See* Plyler v. Doe, 457 U.S. 202 (1982), citing United States v. Wong Kim Ark, 169 U.S. 649 (1898). *See generally* Alexander M. Bickel, *Citizenship in the American Constitution*, 15 Ariz. L. Rev. 369 (1973) (asserting that defining citizenship was not important to the original Constitution and became important only in connection with making the freed slaves citizens and reversing the *Dred Scott* decision; that the concept of "the people" and persons was much more important).

found; or perhaps simply because it is an administratively convenient category of persons to tax.[81] The fact of citizenship is a matter of general federal statutory law.[82] In addition Code provisions enacted in 2004 treat certain expatriates as citizens for tax purposes.[83] The loss of citizenship is not easily proven.[84] If a person loses citizenship as the result of an unconstitutional law the person does not cease being subject to the income tax.[85]

The theoretical basis for taxing citizens (and residents) on worldwide income is explained in an unusual place: a decision on state taxation. In a precursor to the breakdown of the intergovernmental immunity doctrine, Justice Stone explained that the source of income, which source might be beyond the state's taxing power, did not govern its ability to tax the income received from that source by residents.[86] This opinion justified breaking the linkage between source and income taxation by distinguishing *Pollock*,[87] which it said did not literally hold that a tax on income was a tax on its source but rather that "there were similarities in the operation of the two kinds of tax which made it appropriate to classify both as direct, ..."[88] Similarly Justice Stone in a later opinion ruled that a state tax on a resident federal employee did not tax the source of the income, the federal government.[89]

Resident aliens. Resident aliens, as defined by the Code, are subject to the power of taxation of the United States because it has the literal power to collect from them in this country. The Court has said that taxation of all of the income of residents, including income from sources outside the country, was an international tax norm.[90]

> . . . [T]he people who pay taxes imposed by laws are entitled to have a voice in the election of those who pass the laws, and that taxes must be assessed and

---

[81] *See* Edward A. Zelinsky, *Citizenship and Worldwide Taxation: Citizenship as an Administrative Proxy for Domicile*, 96 Iowa L. Rev. 1289 (2011); Cook v. Tait, 265 U.S. 47 (1924).

[82] 8 U.S.C. Ch. 12 contains detailed rules for identifying citizens. *See* Rogers v. Bellei, 401 U.S. 815, 830 (1971) ("Thus, at long last, there emerged an express constitutional definition of citizenship. But it was one restricted to the combination of three factors, each and all significant: birth in the United States, naturalization in the United States, and subjection to the jurisdiction of the United States. The definition obviously did not apply to any acquisition of citizenship by being born abroad of an American parent. That type, and any other not covered by the Fourteenth Amendment, was necessarily left to proper congressional action.").

[83] I.R.C. § 877(g). An author has suggested this provision may raise constitutional issues involving the interplay of international norms with federal law; however, as noted above, federal law usually does not bow to international norms. *See* Kirsch, at 408, et seq. (discussing constitutionality of that statute).

[84] *See* Nishikawa v. Dulles, 356 U.S. 129 (1958).

[85] Rev. Rul. 75-357, 1975-2 C.B. 5.

[86] New York ex rel. Cohn v. Graves, 300 U.S. 308 (1937). *See* Ch. II.C.4, 5 and 9.

[87] Pollock v. Farmers' Loan & Trust Co., 157 U.S. 429 (1895), *confirmed and expanded*, 158 U.S. 601 (1895).

[88] 300 U.S. at 315.

[89] Graves v. New York, 306 U.S. 466 (1939).

[90] Okla. Tax Comm'n v. Chickasaw Nation, 515 U.S. 450 (1995) (citing to other authority that emphasized the existence of domicile as well as residence).

> collected for public purposes, and that the duty or obligation to pay taxes by the individual is founded in his participation in the benefits arising from their expenditure . . . do not mean that no person, man, woman or child, resident or non-resident, shall be taxed, unless he was represented by someone for whom he had actually voted, nor do they mean that no man's property can be taxed unless some benefit to him personally can be pointed out. Thus it has been held that personal allegiance has no necessary connection with the right of taxation; an alien may be taxed as well as a citizen. . . . So, likewise, it is settled law that the property, both real and personal, of non-residents may be lawfully subjected to the tax laws of the State in which they are situated.[91]

Territoriality. When the United States conquered and acquired foreign lands, such as California, the territorial military government had the power to collect federal taxes (customs duties).[92] The Court had occasion to define territorial jurisdiction in which foreign persons and their property might be taxed by the United States, relying on the Eighteenth Amendment, which instituted Prohibition. It stated that liquor manufacture, transportation and sale were in "all territory subject to the jurisdiction thereof [*i.e.*, of the United States] for beverage purposes is hereby prohibited." The ocean liners arriving from abroad complained that they were not subject to the jurisdiction of the United States. The Court rejected the argument, stating what might serve as a general principle of taxing jurisdiction geographically:

> Various meanings are sought to be attributed to the term "territory" in the phrase "the United States and all territory subject to the jurisdiction thereof." We are of opinion that it means the regional areas—of land and adjacent waters—over which the United States claims and exercises dominion and control as a sovereign power. The immediate context and the purport of the entire section show that the term is used in a physical and not a metaphorical sense,—that it refers to areas or districts having fixity of location and recognized boundaries. . . . It now is settled in the United States and recognized elsewhere that the territory subject to its jurisdiction includes the land areas under its dominion and control, the ports, harbors, bays and other enclosed

---

91 Thomas v. Gay, 169 U.S. 264, 276-277 (1898).

92 Cross v. Harrison, 57 U.S. 164 (1854). But that did not apply to the port of Tampico, in the Mexican State of Tamaulipas, which was conquered by the United States, but whose port was considered foreign. Fleming v. Page, 50 U.S. 603 (1850).

arms of the sea along its coast and a marginal belt of the sea extending from the coast line outward a marine league, or three geographic miles.[93]

Transactions. Although persons and their property are the sources of tax collections, transactions are commonly the motivating incident of taxation. Payments sourced in the United States are most likely to raise jurisdictional issues. A taxed transaction may itself be criminal.[94] Most of the federal taxes that the Court has ruled unconstitutional have fallen on account of the nature of the transaction taxed, either because it occurred before the enactment of the taxing statute, it was an export, or it was a transaction the United States did not have the power to regulate and the Court found the exaction was not a tax.[95]

Cases. The principal cases illustrating these points are as follows:

- *McCulloch v. Maryland* had to identify the proper subjects of a state's taxing power so as to exclude the Bank of the United States. It did so by starting with the source of the states' taxing power: that power given them by their own people to tax the people and their property.[96] The opinion states: "[The power to tax] is an incident of sovereignty, and is co-extensive with that to which it is an incident. All subjects over which the sovereign power of a State extends, are objects of taxation. . . . The sovereignty of a State extends to everything which exists by its own authority, or is introduced by its permission; . . . ."[97] The latter part of the definition was aimed at entities, but perhaps is reflected in the treatment of resident aliens the same as citizens for income tax purposes; the first part takes a more practical approach, asking what can the state reach.

- In *Providence Bank v. Billings* Chief Justice Marshall refused to find an exclusion from state taxation in a state bank's charter granted by the taxing state, stating that the power to tax operates on all persons and property belonging to the body politic and, somewhat more helpfully, all things brought into the jurisdiction.[98]

---

[93] Cunard S.S. Co. v. Mellon, 262 U.S. 100, 122-125 (1923) (The opinion continues: ". . . When private individuals of one nation spread themselves through another, as business or caprice may direct, mingling indiscriminately with the inhabitants of that other, or when merchant vessels enter for the purposes of trade, it would be obviously inconvenient and dangerous to society, and would subject the laws to continual infraction, and the government of degradation, if such individuals or merchants did not owe temporary and local allegiance, and were not amenable to the jurisdiction of the country. Nor can the foreign sovereign have any motive for wishing such exemption. His subjects thus passing into foreign countries, are not employed by him, nor are they engaged in national pursuits. Consequently, there are powerful motives for not exempting persons of this description from the jurisdiction of the country in which they are found, and no one motive for requiring it. The implied license, therefore, under which they enter, can never be construed to grant such exemption.").

[94] *See, e.g.*, Dep't of Revenue v. Kurth Ranch, 511 U.S. 767, 778 (1994); License Tax Cases, 72 U.S. 462 (1867).

[95] *See* Ch. I.E.2.b.

[96] McCulloch v. Maryland 17 U.S. 316, 428-430 (1819).

[97] *Id. See also* Society for Savings v. Coite, 73 U.S. 594, 606 (1867).

[98] Providence Bank v. Billings, 29 U.S. 514, 563-564 (1830).

- *Nevada Bank v. Sedgwick* ruled that the United States could tax a state bank on the basis of its capital invested in foreign countries, citing *McCulloch* and federal supremacy.[99]
- *Eidman v. Martinez* stated in dictum that the United States could impose an inheritance tax on intangible property sitused here and owned by a nonresident alien decedent, but the statute did not do so.[100]
- In *Metropolitan Street Railway Co. v. New York* the Court reaffirmed, in the context of state taxation, the power of a state to tax all property within its territorial limits.[101]
- *Billings v. United States* ruled that a citizen could be required to pay an excise tax on a foreign built boat used only outside the waters of the United States.[102]
- *United States v. Bennett* involved the same tax and facts as *Billings v. United States* and specifically rejected a due process objection to taxing a citizen's use of property (not just ownership of unused boats) outside the United States.[103] It distinguished cases limiting a state's power to tax property outside its borders on the grounds that the Constitution required such limits under the Due Process Clause and to enforce the states' rights as against each other. In contrast, the taxing power of the United States knows no such limit.[104] The opinion did not discuss the possibility that other nations could have concerns about United States taxation similar to those of the states with respect to other states' taxes; the implicit point is that such an argument is of no concern to a particular taxpayer and not for him to make. Moreover, because the tax is based on citizenship it cannot be said that the thing taxed receives no benefit from the United States; the inherent benefits of citizenship redound to a citizen's property wherever found.
- *United States v. Goelet* dealt with the same boat excise tax as *Billings* and *Bennett*, but the taxpayer was a citizen who was permanently domiciled abroad.[105] The Court stated that the United States had the power to tax such a citizen, but interpreted the statute not to do so.
- *Cook v. Tait* confirmed that the federal taxing power includes citizens domiciled abroad and income from a citizen's property located abroad, citing

---

[99] Nevada Bank v. Sedgwick, 104 U.S. 111 (1881).

[100] Eidman v. Martinez, 184 U.S. 578, 582 (1902).

[101] New York ex rel. Metropolitan Street Ry. Co. v. New York State Bd., 199 U.S. 1 (1905).

[102] Billings v. United States, 232 U.S. 261 (1914).

[103] United States v. Bennett, 232 U.S. 299 (1914).

[104] "[The state tax jurisdiction limit] affords no ground for constructing an imaginary constitutional barrier around the exterior confines of the United States for the purpose of shutting that government off from the exertion of powers which inherently belong to it by virtue of its sovereignty." 232 U.S. at 305-306. *See, e.g.*, Buck v. Beach, 206 U.S. 392 (1907).

[105] United States v. Goelet, 232 U.S. 293 (1914).

Bennett and *Goelet.*[106] The opinion restated, as if obvious, the inherent relationship of benefits (and burdens) that derive from citizenship in a nation, regardless of the location of the citizen or his or her property.

- *Burnet v. Brooks*, quoted above, ruled that securities (*i.e.*, intangible property) owned by a decedent nonresident alien but held in the United States were subject to the estate tax, both as a matter of legislative intent and constitutional power.[107] Chief Justice Hughes grounded the analysis on the power of the sovereign to control international relations by taking control of property within its physical jurisdiction, *i.e.*, at the situs of the property. The opinion refused to apply to the federal government due process limits imposed on states. The opinion identified literal power to levy on property as the proper measure of a nation's taxing jurisdiction.
- *Curry v. McCanless*, although a state tax opinion, contains a general treatment by Justice Stone of sovereign powers in relation to intangibles owned by citizens or domiciliaries. He stated that domicile had long been deemed a sufficient basis to tax and to tax the person's intangibles on the assumption that they were located at his domicile. But because a person may avail himself of the protections of a nondomiciliary state, that state too may tax the intangibles. "If the 'due process' of the Fifth Amendment does not require us to fix a single exclusive place of taxation of intangibles for the benefit of their foreign owner, who is entitled to its protection, *Burnet v. Brooks*, . . . the Fourteenth can hardly be thought to make us do so here, for the Due Process Clause of each amendment is directed at the protection of the individual and he is entitled to its immunity as much against the state as against the national government."[108]

4. *Conceptual Outer Limit on the Sovereign's Power of Taxation*

In theory the illimitable power to tax described above has some outer limit, which usually means the levy escapes the category of a tax, rather than being subject to a limit on a tax. The principal citation to which every proponent of a limitation on the subject of federal taxation inevitably repairs is the statement of Chief Justice Marshall in *McCulloch v. Maryland*, which though made in a tax case, was not specifically addressed to the federal taxing power:

> Should Congress, in the execution of its powers, adopt measures which are prohibited by the Constitution; or should Congress, under the pretext of executing its powers, pass laws for the accomplishment of objects not intrusted to the government; it would become the painful duty of this tribunal, should

[106] Cook v. Tait, 265 U.S. 47 (1924).
[107] Burnet v. Brooks, 288 U.S. 378 (1938).
[108] Curry v. McCanless, 307 U.S. 357, 369-370 (1939).

a case requiring such a decision come before it, to say, that such an act was not the law of the land.[109]

Chief Justice White stated a similarly vague warning in *Baltic Mining*:

> Mark, of course, in saying this we are not here considering a tax not within the provisions of the Sixteenth Amendment, that is, one in which the regulation of apportionment or the rule of uniformity is wholly negligible because the tax is one entirely beyond the scope of the taxing power of Congress, and where consequently no authority to impose a burden, either direct or indirect, exists.[110]

The simplest, if not most illuminating explanation, for when that boundary is reached is when the tax becomes viewed solely as a regulation of a subject the government does not have the power to regulate.[111]

The *Veazie Bank* opinion identified two suspect subjects of taxation:

> There are, indeed, certain virtual limitations, arising from the principles of the Constitution itself. It would undoubtedly be an abuse of the power if so exercised as to impair the separate existence and independent self-government of the States, or if exercised for ends inconsistent with the limited grants of power in the Constitution.[112]

The limited grants refer to the issues discussed in Chapter III.E. The self-government statement was footnoted to the decision that interpreted the Legal Tender Act not to require that state and local tax revenues be collected in paper money (the state required coin).[113]

The opinion in *McCray* upholding the federal tax on colored margarine also closed with one vague caveat, but contained the broadest possible scope for a regulatory tax: that it is proper if any free government can regulate the conduct, whether it be the United States or not.

> Let us concede that if a case was presented where the abuse of the taxing power was so extreme as to be beyond the principles which we have previously stated, and where it was plain to the judicial mind that the power had been called into play not for revenue but solely for the purpose of destroying rights which could not be rightfully destroyed consistently with the principles of freedom and justice upon which the Constitution rests, that it would be the duty of the courts to say that such an arbitrary act was not merely an abuse of a delegated power, but was the exercise of an authority not conferred. This concession, however, like the one previously made, must be without influence upon the decision of this cause for the reasons previously stated; that is, that the manufacture of arti-

---

[109] McCulloch v. Maryland, 17 U.S. 316, 423 (1819); quoted, for example, in J.W. Bailey v. Drexel Furn. Co., 259 U.S. 20, 40 (1922).

[110] Stanton v. Baltic Mining Co., 240 U.S. 103 (1916).

[111] *See* Ch. I.E.2.b and III.E and F.

[112] Veazie Bank v. Fenno, 75 U.S. 533, 541 (1869).

[113] Lane County v. Oregon, 74 U.S. 71 (1868).

> ficially colored oleomargarine may be prohibited by a free government without a violation of fundamental rights.[114]

These caveats are nothing more than the prudent effort of the Court to retain flexibility against the possibility of that set of facts and laws it cannot now anticipate, but which a future Court might want to rule against. The Court does not want to paint itself into a corner, although it usually has little trouble distinguishing or ignoring prior statements. However, the course of decisions as explained in this book reflects a near perfect record of deference to Congress' taxing power, in terms of subject, amount, and confiscatory result, with the sole exception of the period from 1922 to 1936 when the conservative wing of the Court exalted substantive due process, liberty of contract, and states' rights to strike down five federal taxes the bare majorities of the Court thought to be regulatory rather than taxes.[115]

B. The Federal and State Taxing Powers in the Constitution

This chapter addresses both the federal and state taxing powers because of the role of the state taxing power in intergovernmental tax immunity, one of the three most contentious issues in federal taxation as discussed in Chapter I.E.8 and II.C, albeit now largely resolved. See Chapter IX for further discussion of state taxing powers.

1. *The Federal Power to Tax*

Chapter II.A.2 shows that the extent of the sovereign's taxing power in general, and of the federal taxing power in particular, is great. Article I, section 8, clause 1 (the first enumerated power of Congress) of the Constitution states the grant of that power to Congress:

> The Congress shall have Power To lay and collect Taxes, Duties, Imposts and Excises, ...

The most important fact about the power to tax granted in the Constitution is that the grantor is the people, not the states; and the grantee is the Congress, not the executive or the courts.[116] The source of the power is more than symbolic; it forms the foundation for the supremacy of the United States in relation to the states (only the United States received powers from *all* the people), and it differentiates the Constitution from the Articles of Confederation (which made the

---

[114] McCray v. United States, 195 U.S. 27, 64 (1904). *See also* dissent of Justice Harlan in Pollock v. Farmers' Loan & Trust Co., 158 U.S. 601, 674-675 (1895) (referring to the possibility of spoliation if a federal tax on the rich were "repugnant to principles of natural right"); Flint v. Stone Tracy Co., 220 U.S. 107 (1911) (citing *McCray* for identifying the theoretical possibility of a tax that was arbitrary or sought unwarranted ends).

[115] *See* Ch. III.F.

[116] *See* McCulloch v. Maryland, 17 U.S. 316, 412, 428-429 (1819) ("A government is created by the people, having legislative, executive, and judicial powers."). However, when Congress imposes sufficiently clear guidelines, the fixing of the amount of the tax can be delegated to the executive. *See* J. W. Hampton, Jr. & Co. v. United States, 276 U.S. 394 (1928); *see* Ch. VIII.E.2.

Confederation dependent on the states for the collection of revenue; hence the importance of the dual powers to both lay and collect).[117] As a consequence of the supremacy of the federal taxing power in relation to the states' taxing power, for example, Congress can give priority to federal taxes in bankruptcy.[118]

In addition to clause 1, the power of taxation is implied in the Necessary and Proper Clause,[119] the references to modes of taxation in Article I, section 9, clauses 4, 5 and 6, and the regulation of the methods of appropriation in Article I, section 9, clause 7.[120] Congress may both lay and collect taxes, meaning that the requisitions of tax by the United States are not to depend on voluntary compliance, as was the case under the Articles of Confederation.

The Necessary and Proper Clause's role in taxation is often overlooked. Congress can impose a tax as necessary and proper to carry out an enumerated power such as the power to make war.[121] However, in its most extensive analysis of a War Revenue Act it based the tax solely on the taxing power.[122] On the other hand the Prohibition taxes were adopted under the war powers.[123]

The taxing power does not identify the taxpayers, except for import duties, which are usually imposed of necessity on the importer, or at least are imposed at the point of importation. The other major choices were the people, who had created the Constitution and hence the powers of taxation, and the states. Indeed Article I, section 2 says that direct taxes shall be apportioned among the several states, which strongly implies that the states themselves would support the United States government and might determine which of their residents would pay the tax.[124]

However, taxation of the states was not the aim of the authors of the Constitution. On the one hand the Federalists wanted the federal government to have the power to deal directly with the people as a source of taxes due to the bad experience with the Articles of Confederation under which the states had failed to properly supply the general government.[125] And on the other hand the states did not want the responsibility for supplying the federal government; indeed an

---

[117] CHARLES A. BEARD, AN ECONOMIC INTERPRETATION OF THE CONSTITUTION OF THE UNITED STATES 52 (1921).

[118] *See* County of Spokane v. United States, 279 U.S. 80 (1929).

[119] *See* G. Merle Bergman, *The Federal Power to Tax and Spend*, 31 MINN. L. REV. 328 (1946).

[120] *See* Robert B. McKay, *Taxing and Spending for the General Welfare: A Reply to Mr. Nillson*, 48 A.B.A. J. 38, 39 n. 6 (1962).

[121] *See* Ware v. Hylton, 3 U.S. 199 (1796) ("That Congress did not possess all the powers of war is self-evident from this consideration alone, that she never attempted to lay any kind of tax on the people of the United States, ..."). *But see* Nat'l Fed'n of Indep. Bus. v. Sebelius, 567 U.S. 519 (2012) refused to find the Individual Mandate to be necessary and property to carry out some enumerated power of Congress (Roberts' opinion).

[122] Knowlton v. Moore, 178 U.S. 41 (1900).

[123] Ruppert v. Caffey, 251 U.S. 264 (1920). For the Necessary and Proper Clause, see Ch. III.E.4.a. For Common Defense see Ch. III.D.7.

[124] *See* Ch. V.C.

[125] *See* JOSEPH STORY, COMMENTARIES ON THE CONSTITUTION OF THE UNITED STATES, Vol. 1, 228-229 (1833) (explaining defects of the Confederation); Herman M. Knoeller, *The Power to Tax*, 22 MARQ. L. REV. 125, 132 (1937).

important compromise in the immediate aftermath of the Constitution was the assumption by the United States of the war debts of the states (in exchange, inter alia, for locating the capitol in Virginia).[126]

The second most important point about the federal power to tax is that it has long been viewed as one of the most unfettered powers held by the federal government. In addition to the statements referenced in Chapter II.A.1 and 2, the Court has at least twice stated that the Constitution is not self-defeating or self-destructive, meaning that the essential power to tax is not limited by the Due Process Clause.[127] In a 1916 case the Attorney General actually argued to the Supreme Court that Congress had called a levy a tax to "give it a coating of constitutionality."[128] When Frances Perkins inquired of her friends Justices Louis Brandeis and Harlan Fiske Stone for advice on the creation of the social security system, they both recommended reliance on the taxing power.[129] Even the Court's most conservative Justices have upheld the power to tax against Sixteenth Amendment objections, simply on the grounds that the revenue cannot be collected without a strong inclination towards finding the power to tax.[130]

Finally, although the federal taxing power has been limited in practice by the doctrine of intergovernmental immunity,[131] it is not one of those powers that is burdened by the Tenth Amendment: "The Tenth Amendment [which reserves to the states powers not granted to the United States] does not operate as a limitation upon the powers, express or implied, delegated to the national government."[132] And those delegated powers include first and foremost the power to tax.

---

[126] David McCullough, John Adams 425-426 (2001) ("compromise of 1790").

[127] Billings v. United States, 232 U.S. 261, 282 (1914) (Congress could choose to levy an excise tax on foreign built boats chartered by U.S. persons, and not U.S. built boats); Brushaber v. Union Pacific R. Co., 240 U.S. 1, 24 (1916 ("does not conflict with itself" by conferring the taxing power in one clause and taking it away in the Due Process Clause).

[128] United States v. Jin Fuey Moy, 241 U.S. 394, 401 (1916).

[129] Kirstin Downey, The Woman Behind the New Deal 235-236 (2009). *See also* William E. Leuchtenberg, Franklin D. Roosevely and the New Deal 130 (1963) [hereinafter Leuchtenburg] (Justice Brandeis' daughter participated in drafting the unemployment plan and it also was thought to have a better chance of gaining Supreme Court approval because it used a federal-state partnership.). Justice Brandeis' views were generally followed by the Roosevelt administration in fashioning what was called the Second New Deal more carefully than the AAA and NIRA, which were held unconstitutional. Paul L. Murphy, The Constitution in Crisis Times 1918-1969, 146 (1972).

[130] *See, e.g.*, Taft v. Bowers, 278 U.S. 470 (1929) (Justice McReynolds ruled that the donee of an appreciated gift could be taxed on the pre-gift appreciation, when realized, because to rule otherwise would allow that part of the gain to go untaxed upon a well planned gift-sale).

[131] *See* Ch. II.C.7.

[132] Fernandez v. Wiener, 326 U.S. 340, 362 (1945). *See* Ch. III.F.3. But if the tax can be found not to be a taxing power tax, then it might be limited by the Tenth Amendment if it regulates a subject that the federal government lacks power to regulate. *See* Ch. III.E and F.

2. *The States' Power to Tax*

The Tenth Amendment does not create the states' power to tax, though it does provide:

> The powers not delegated to the United States by the Constitution, nor prohibited by it to the States, are reserved to the States respectively, or to the people.

The Tenth Amendment was part of the Bill of Rights, adopted in 1791. It postdated the creation of the states, which started off exercising the power to tax, without benefit of the Tenth Amendment. The Federalist confirmed the "absolute and unqualified" power of the states to tax, well before the adoption of the Tenth Amendment.[133] Article I, sections 9 and 10 of the Constitution assume the states' power to tax, by imposing various limits, particularly on taxing imports and exports.

But just as important as the fundamental power to tax is the fact that Congress can limit the states' taxing power, in pursuit of legitimate powers of the United States. The Supreme Court stated in the important *Van Allen* opinion:

> It is said that Congress possesses no power to confer upon a State authority to be exercised which has been exclusively delegated to that body by the Constitution, and, consequently, that it cannot confer upon a State the sovereign right of taxation; nor is a State competent to receive a grant of any such power from Congress. We agree to this. But as it respects a subject-matter over which Congress and the States may exercise a concurrent power, but from the exercise of which Congress, by reason of its paramount authority, may exclude the States, there is no doubt Congress may withhold the exercise of that authority and leave the States free to act. . . .The power of taxation under the Constitution as a general rule, and as has been repeatedly recognized in adjudged cases in this court, is a concurrent power. The qualifications of the rule are the exclusion of the States from the taxation of the means and instruments employed in the exercise of the functions of the Federal Government.[134]

Thus, when in the 20th Century the Court removed constitutional protection from state taxation of federal contractors, it stated that they still could be extended protection by Congress.[135] Other statutory limits on state taxation exist today.[136]

Although not discussed here, states face the same subject matter jurisdictional issues of taxation as does the United States, discussed in Chapter IV,B.3 and

---

[133] FEDERALIST No. 32, by Alexander Hamilton, p. 194 (Modern Library Ed.).

[134] Van Allen v. Assessors, 70 U.S. 573, 585 (1866).

[135] *See, e.g.*, United States v. New Mexico, 455 U.S. 720, 737 (1982); Carson v. Roane-Anderson Co., 342 U.S. 232 (1952) (Congress made AEC contractors and employees exempt from state tax). *See* Richard A. Paschal, *Congressional Power to Change Constitutional Law*, 77 U. CIN. L. REV. 1053, 1099 (2009) [hereinafter Paschal].

[136] *See, e.g.*, 4 U.S.C. § 114 (states cannot tax pensions received by nonresidents and non domiciliaries); 4 U.S.C. §§ 115-126 (other limitations on state taxation); Dameron v. Brodhead, 345 U.S. 322 (1953) (under the Necessary and Proper Clause and the war powers, the United States could free soldiers from state taxation).

III.D, plus additional complex issues due to the Commerce Clause, the Supremacy Clause, and relations to other states.[137] See generally Ch. IX.

3. *Concurrent Jurisdiction to Tax*

Tax competition and "double taxation," due to dual taxing authorities, were major concerns of the delegates to the Constitutional Convention. The upshot was a system of concurrent taxation, comprised of the direct tax apportionment/uniformity limits on federal taxation, and denial of import and export duties and tonnage fees[138] to the states (neither could the United States tax exports).[139] Justice Jackson eloquently explained the situation in *Allegheny*:

> In arguing the case of *McCulloch v. Maryland*, Luther Martin, Attorney General of Maryland, himself a member of the Constitutional Convention, said, "The whole of this subject of taxation is full of difficulties, which the Convention found it impossible to solve, in a manner entirely satisfactory. The first attempt was to divide the subjects of taxation between the State and the national government. This being found impracticable, or inconvenient, the State governments surrendered altogether their right to tax imports and exports, and tonnage; giving the authority to tax all other subjects to Congress, but reserving to the States a concurrent right to tax the same subjects to an unlimited extent. This was one of the anomalies of the government, the evils of which must be endured, or mitigated by discretion and mutual forbearance." *McCulloch v. Maryland*, 17 U.S. 316, 376. Where discretion and forbearance have failed, it often has fallen to this Court to determine specific cases for which the Convention was unable to agree upon a general rule. Looking backward it is easy to see that the line between the taxable and the immune has been drawn by an unsteady hand.[140]

Contrary to popular conception, the Tenth Amendment, which reserves powers to the states, is not an either-or provision. The Tenth Amendment does not say that some powers are delegated exclusively to the United States, and all the rest of the powers are reserved to the states and so cannot be exercised by the United States. Rather, there are powers exclusively delegated to the United States (regulation of interstate commerce, taxation of imports), and also powers (including reserved powers such as taxation) that are concurrently exercised by both (including the important power held by the United States to tax and spend for

---

[137] *See* Ch. III.E.9. *See generally* HELLERSTEIN & HELLERSTEIN, STATE TAXATION, Part III. A state does not have power to tax within a geographical area within the state but over which the United States has obtained exclusive jurisdiction. James v. Dravo Contracting Co., 302 U.S. 134 (1937). *See also* United States v. Alaska, 521 U.S. 1, 42 (1997).

[138] *See* Ch. VI.

[139] *See* McCulloch v. Maryland, 17 U.S. 316, 425 (1819) ("That the power of taxation is one of vital importance; that it is retained by the States; that it is not abridged by the grant of a similar power to the government of the Union; that it is to be concurrently exercised by the two governments; are truths which have never been denied."); Van Brocklin v. Tennessee, 117 U.S. 151, 155 (1886) ("to be concurrently exercised by the two governments"); Dobbins v. The Commissioners of Erie, 41 U.S. 435, 447 (1842).

[140] United States v. County of Allegheny, 322 U.S. 174, 176 (1944).

the general welfare), and then other powers (such as the general police power) are reserved to the states. A prime example of concurrent powers is the power to tax: the taxing power is not delegated exclusively to the United States by the Constitution as evidenced by the fact that Article I, section 10, clause 2 specifies certain taxes the states cannot impose. Besides those prohibited taxes, the taxing power is reserved to the states, which does not imply any exclusivity whatsoever.

In *Gibbons v. Ogden* Chief Justice Marshall differentiated the concurrent power to tax from the power to regulate commerce:

> The grant of the power to lay and collect taxes is, like the power to regulate commerce, made in general terms, and has never been understood to interfere with the exercise of the same power by the States; and hence has been drawn an argument which has been applied to the question under consideration. But the two grants are not, it is conceived, similar in their terms or their nature. Although many of the powers formerly exercised by the States, are transferred to the government of the Union, yet the State governments remain, and constitute a most important part of our system. The power of taxation is indispensable to their existence, and is a power which, in its own nature, is capable of residing in, and being exercised by, different authorities at the same time. We are accustomed to see it placed, for different purposes, in different hands. Taxation is the simple operation of taking small portions from a perpetually accumulating mass, susceptible of almost infinite division; and a power in one to take what is necessary for certain purposes, is not, in its nature, incompatible with a power in another to take what is necessary for other purposes. Congress is authorized to lay and collect taxes, &c. to pay the debts, and provide for the common defence and general welfare of the United States. This does not interfere with the power of the States to tax for the support of their own governments; nor is the exercise of that power by the States, an exercise of any portion of the power that is granted to the United States. In imposing taxes for State purposes, they are not doing what Congress is empowered to do. Congress is not empowered to tax for those purposes which are within the exclusive province of the States. When, then, each government exercises the power of taxation, neither is exercising the power of the other. But, when a State proceeds to regulate commerce with foreign nations, or among the several States, it is exercising the very power that is granted to Congress, and is doing the very thing which Congress is authorized to do. There is no analogy, then, between the power of taxation and the power of regulating commerce.[141]

Alexander Hamilton in The Federalist stated:

> I mean the power of imposing taxes on all articles other than exports and imports. This, I contend, is manifestly a concurrent and coequal authority in the United States and in the individual states. There is plainly no expression in the granting clause which makes the [taxing] power exclusive in the Union. There is no independent clause or sentence which prohibits the States from exercising it. So far is this from being the case that a plain and conclusive argument to the contrary is to be deduced from the restraint laid upon the States in relation to duties on imports and exports. This restriction implies an admission that,

[141] Gibbons v. Ogden, 22 U.S. 1, 198-199 (1824).

> if it were not inserted, the States would possess the power it excludes; and it implies a further admission, that as to all other taxes, the authority of the States remains undiminished.[142]

In response to the objections that concurrent taxing jurisdiction would lead to "double taxation," Hamilton explained that the sum total of taxation ought to be no more, whether collected by one sovereign or two.[143]

Justice White in *Knowlton v. Moore* stated:

> Under our constitutional system both the National and the state governments, moving in their respective orbits, have a common authority to tax many and diverse objects, but this does not cause the exercise of its lawful attributes by one to be a curtailment of the powers of government of the other, for if it did there would practically be an end of the dual system of government which the Constitution established.[144]

Today the matter of concurrent powers of taxation arises most often in cases involving Native American Tribes, addressed in Ch. IX.J. The Court has restated in these decisions the theory of concurrent taxation by sovereigns that exist in tandem, pointing out that federal taxation does not occupy the field once exercised: both the United States and the states can tax our incomes and our gasoline purchases.[145] Thus true concurrence is in contrast with a power like the federal authority over interstate commerce, which is supreme when exercised.[146] However, when both the federal and state taxing powers seek the same funds, federal supremacy can be invoked.[147]

C. Intergovernmental Tax Immunity

1. *Overview*

"The immunity of the Federal Government from state taxation is bottomed on the Supremacy Clause, but the States' immunity from federal taxes was judicially implied from the States' role in the constitutional scheme."[148]

The concurrent jurisdictions and powers of the states and the United States to levy most types of taxes not only sets up the potential for double taxation of the

---

[142] THE FEDERALIST No. 32, by Alexander Hamilton, p. 195 (Modern Library Ed.); *see also* No. 34, by Hamilton, p. 203.

[143] THE FEDERALIST No. 36, by Alexander Hamilton, p. 222 (Modern Library Ed.).

[144] Knowlton v. Moore, 178 U.S. 41, 60 (1900).

[145] Wagnon v. Prairie Band Potawatomi Nation, 546 U.S. 95 (2005). *See also* Ark. v. Farm Credit Servs., 520 U.S. 821, 826 (1997).

[146] *See* J.A. Grant, *The Scope and Nature of Concurrent Power*, 34 COL. L. REV. 995, 1020 (1934), citing So. Ry. Co. v. Railroad Comm'n, 236 U.S. 439 (1915). A similar area of federal dominance is federal regulation of aliens. *See* Hines v. Davidowitz, 312 U.S. 52 (1941). An early statement of the difference appeared in Prigg v. Pennsylvania, 41 U.S. 539 (1842) (the federal government occupied the area of slave recovery and so Pennsylvania could not prosecute a slave owner who came into the state to catch a runaway slave, which was in contrast to the taxing power, which is exercised by each government independently of the other).

[147] County of Spokane v. United States, 279 U.S. 80 (1929).

[148] Massachusetts v. United States, 435 U.S. 444, 455 (1978).

same persons (which is permitted), but of taxation of one sovereign by the other, *i.e.*, intergovernmental taxation, which generally is not permitted. It is perhaps unthinkable that the states might try to collect taxes from the United States Treasury itself, but the United States might more reasonably expect to collect taxes from the various states' treasuries. After all, the possibility of states bearing the taxes required by the United States is suggested by the Constitution's requirement that "direct taxes" be apportioned to the states based on their relative populations; some of the early direct tax levies allowed the states to pay the tax and then try to collect it from the people, although the states were not required to do so (some did).[149]

Despite the anomaly of states taxing the United States, the intergovernmental immunity issue arose first in connection with an attempted state tax thought to fall on the United States; the state tax bill did not go to the Treasury, but to what at most might be termed today an instrumentality of the United States, the Second Bank of the United States. When the Supreme Court ruled that tax to be unconstitutional, it set in motion two inevitable consequences: (1) a search for more and more remotely burdensome indirect taxes on the United States, violating its supremacy, and (2) a demand for parallel or reciprocal protection of the states from federal taxation, said to be "judicially implied from the States' role in the constitutional scheme."[150] In actuality the second consequence was not promoted by the states any more than was the first promoted by the United States; they were both promoted by private taxpayers who hoped to stand under the umbrella of intergovernmental tax immunity, due to some relationship to a government. Thus intergovernmental tax immunity was the first "tax shelter."

Finding ever more indirect taxation of the United States by the states hinged on the so called substance over form doctrine.[151] The private taxpayers who wanted to share in the United States' tax immunity had to argue that the state or local tax they paid was in substance a tax on the government with which they had some employment or business or investment relationship. Necessarily the taxes were not levied on the other government in form (except in the cases where the governmental character of an entity was the critical issue, as in *McCulloch*), and so the taxpayers had to argue first that form did not control and second that the substance controlled and third that a factual investigation would show an economic impact on the government with which they claimed a relationship.

For a century both this search for substance, and also the process of parallel application of immunity to the states, occurred and expanded in the largest grouping of Supreme Court tax decisions outside the cases on state taxing power under the Commerce Clause and other constitutional constraints. Eventually the tide receded, first as to state immunity (which was never on equal footing with federal immunity) and then as to federal immunity, with the results that (1) the tax must be fairly directly imposed "on" the other government as a govern-

---

[149] *See* Ch. V.C.

[150] Massachusetts v. United States, 435 U.S. 444, 455 (1978).

[151] *See* Ch. I; *see also* Jasper L. Cummings, Jr., The Supreme Court's Federal Tax Jurisprudence (2d ed. 2016), at ch. VI.E.1.

ment for it to be unconstitutional, and (2) the states' protection turned out not to be as robust as that enjoyed by the United States, as discussed in the following Chapters.

It is fairly obvious that by the late 1930s the Supreme Court simply determined that its own substance over form theory, adopted at the urging of numerous private taxpayers, did not work in practice after a century of effort, creating a "confusing maze" of rules that even the federal government did not want to apply to protect its own employees from taxation.[152] It is not possible to understand the constitutional limits on the United States' taxation of the states in isolation from the reciprocal issue; therefore they will both be discussed below, and Chapter IX will further discuss the state cases.[153]

One of the most informative analyses of the issues is found in the amicus brief of the United States in *James v. Dravo*, discussed in Chapter II.C.9. It explains how intergovernmental immunity in the United States derived from different roots than the English "royal prerogative." It also emphasized the overlooked counterpoint to the theory of intergovernmental immunity, which it argued justified allowing nondiscriminatory state taxation of federal contractors: "Taxes are what we pay for civilized society. . . ."[154]

The reader may question the utility of slogging through the history of the rise and fall of intergovernmental immunity in the Supreme Court. First, it comprises a huge proportion of the Court's constitutional tax jurisprudence, which the researcher inevitably stumbles upon in studying a variety of other federal tax subjects. One needs to understand these cases in the context of their peculiar issue so as to separate the wheat from the chaff. Second, hope springs eternal in the breasts of taxpayers wanting to align themselves with a sovereign and claim the immunity; this history can either help or caution them. Finally, the history illustrates three powerful elements of all tax cases: (1) the role of politics in taxation and in the Court's decisions, (2) substance over form, and (3) the relentless quest of taxpayers for tax reduction through litigation if not otherwise.

As shown below, the immunity doctrine started with *McCulloch v. Maryland*, in which Chief Justice Marshall created tax immunity to support the Second Bank of the United States, whose life and work (along with the First Bank and the thwarted Third Bank) were the focus of one of the two most contentious political fights of the first decades of the Constitution (the other being slavery, which was not to be resolved until the Civil War). The weight of the threat of state taxes on the Bank is hard to assess: as many as six states tried to tax its notes in one way or the other. More attenuated in effect on the United States was the tax on the federal bonds at issue in *Weston*, the second important decision in the series. Nevertheless, as discussed below, the Court protected not only the Bank

---

152 *See* ROBERT H. JACKSON, THE STRUGGLE FOR JUDICIAL SUPREMACY 242 (1941).

153 For an entirely different intergovernmental tax issue, *see* Bonaparte v. Tax Court, 104 U.S. 592 (1882) (one state did not have to honor another state's exemption for its bonds).

154 New York ex rel. Cohn v. Graves, 300 U.S. 308, 313 (1937), quoting dissent of Justice Holmes in Compania General De Tabacos De Filipinas v. Collector of Internal Revenue, 275 U.S. 87, 100 (1927).

but the federal bonds from state taxation, most likely also to protect the Bank, which held federal bonds.

So state tax "on" the United States, its instrumentalities and its debt was and still is prohibited. But tax on private persons who do business with the United States or a state has come to be allowed, after a hiatus that lasted from *Dobbins* (1842) to *James v. Dravo* (1937). The explanation for the shift was that the United States government decided that form could control substance and the states were not to be feared at this point in the history of the nation.

2. *Federal Supremacy Established*

Chief Justice Marshall discovered in 1819 in *McCulloch v. Maryland* the freedom of at least the United States from state taxation, though the freedom was not found in the Constitution's words.[155] The Court later said that the limitation on the power of the United States to levy a tax that falls on another sovereign is "not with any express constitutional restriction, but only with an asserted implication."[156] *McCulloch* ruled that the state of Maryland could not require the Second Bank of the United States to pay a stamp tax upon the issuance of its own bank notes (which was, in effect, national currency).

The *McCulloch* opinion did not call the Bank a federal "instrumentality," but did call it an instrument and the opinion was understood to cast the Bank as a federal agency, a view with which many disagreed.[157] Thus the the opinion seemed to treat the tax as one imposed directly on the United States Treasury, and if not then as a tax that impeded the performance of a federal contractor, whether or not it was the government itself.[158] In hindsight, the most appropriate explanation for the tax immunity accorded the Bank is not that it was the sovereign or even a federal instrumentality such as the military, but that it was a semi-independent contractor carrying out a critical governmental function that the Congress had created it to perform: the creation of a national currency.[159] Unfortunately, the independent contractor aspect was followed in later cases, without sufficient attention to the importance of the governmental function.

McCulloch v. Maryland addressed the attempt by Maryland to require the Bank of the United States, chartered by Congress,[160] to either (a) be chartered by

[155] McCulloch v. Maryland, 17 U.S. 316 (1819).

[156] Willcuts v. Bunn, 282 U.S. 216, 231 (1931).

[157] *Daniel Walker Howe*, The Transformation of America 1815-1848 at 145 (Oxford Paperback, 2007) [hereinafter Howe] (plenty of constitutional lawyers of the time disagreed with treating the Bank as the United States, including Luther Martin).

[158] *See* Brief of United States in James v. Dravo, 1937 WL 63782, p. 34 (indicating the latter).

[159] *But cf.* Briscoe v. President & Directors of Bank of Kentucky, 36 U.S. 257 (1837) (ruling that a bank wholly owned by a state did not emit credit in violation of the prohibition on states' creating money, with no mention made of *McCulloch*).

[160] 3 Stat. 266 (April 10, 1816). The United States chartered the bank, but was to buy only 1/5 of its stock. Public investors would buy the rest. The United States could pay with its own debt instruments for the stock. The President would appoint 1/5 of the directors and other shareholders would select the rest. Loans to the United States and the states were limited. The bank was to operate for profit as a commercial bank and pay dividends.

the state (*i.e.*, dual chartering, which would have produced rules and regulations of operation that conflicted with the detailed rules written into its charter by Congress), (b) pay the state $15,000 for the right to operate in the state without being chartered (which the Bank did not pay), or (c) pay a stamp tax for the purchase of stamped paper on which to issue its bank notes. Because Cashier McCulloch of the Baltimore branch issued some bank notes without paying the Maryland tax, and the Bank had not registered with the state, he was sued by the state, evidently for the fine or penalty that was specifically collectible from a cashier who issued bank notes without the stamped paper. Thus the suit was not to recover the tax but to recover a penalty from an individual for failure of the Bank chartered by Congress to pay the $15,000 excise tax, which itself was due because of the Bank's failure to be chartered by Maryland.

The opinion first addressed the power of the United States to incorporate a bank, and that issue took up the bulk of the opinion and is the point for which the opinion is most famous. Chief Justice Marshall also ruled that the state could not tax the Bank because a tax would burden the power of the United States, which was supreme in this instance because Congress had acted in its proper sphere in chartering the Bank.[161] One of those fundamental federal powers was the taxing power. Chief Justice Marshall reasoned that the Bank was a means to transmit federal tax revenues and to conduct federal fiscal operations, presumably meaning holding funds, borrowing and paying federal obligations. In other words, the government of the United States could not be forced to bank with state banks.

Moreover, the opinion explains why the United States may choose to provide for itself a function that could also be provided by "private enterprise" (a topic of recurring interest today):

> The exigencies of the nation may require that the treasure raised in the north should be transported to the south, that raised in the east conveyed to the west, or that this order should be reversed. Is that construction of the constitution to be preferred which would render these operations difficult, hazardous, and expensive? Can we adopt that construction, (unless the words imperiously require it,) which would impute to the framers of that instrument, when granting these powers for the public good, the intention of impeding their exercise by withholding a choice of means? If, indeed, such be the mandate of the constitution, we have only to obey; but that instrument does not profess to enumerate the means by which the powers it confers may be executed; nor does it prohibit the creation of a corporation, if the existence of such a being be essential to the beneficial exercise of those powers. It is, then, the subject of fair inquiry, how far such means may be employed.
>
> It is not denied, that the powers given to the government imply the ordinary means of execution. That, for example, of raising revenue, and applying it to national purposes, is admitted to imply the power of conveying money from place to place, as the exigencies of the nation may require, and of employing

[161] *See also* Providence Bank v. Billings, 29 U.S. 514, 563 (1830), in which Chief Justice Marshall specifically characterizes the holding of *McCulloch* as based on supremacy.

> the usual means of conveyance. But it is denied that the government has its choice of means; or, that it may employ the most convenient means, if, to employ them, it be necessary to erect a corporation.[162]

Once a power such as the power to tax was found to exist in the sovereign under the Constitution, Congress has the power to make all laws "necessary and proper" to carry out these enumerated powers, and the opinion said "necessary" was not restrictive, but meant convenient or useful.[163] The opinion reasoned that once the power is granted the means to carry it out are within the discretion of the government; that the fact that a means (such as incorporation) might be an aspect of sovereignty that the states also claim cannot prevent the United States from selecting that means to carry out its powers. Chief Justice Marshall dealt with the Tenth Amendment and its reservation to the states of powers not delegated to the United States, observing that it did not say "not expressly delegated," thus allowing for implied powers not expressly stated, such as the power to create a bank.

Second, the opinion addressed the state's attempt to tax the proper federal instrumentality and rejected it on grounds of federal supremacy, using several subsidiary grounds. The Supremacy Clause, Article VI, paragraph 2, states that the Constitution and laws enacted by Congress and treaties are the supreme law of the land. This means not only that state judges had to enforce the Constitution, but also that the states could not impede the federal government when acting within its powers, which the first part of the opinion had proved it was in creating the Bank. In explaining this aspect of supremacy Chief Justice Marshall explained that the Constitution came from the people and not from the states; the states did not give to the United States certain powers and thereby make it their tool; rather the people gave those powers to the United States, and because the United States is the only sovereign to which all of the people have spoken, it must be supreme over a sovereign that represents only part of the people (such as Maryland). In contrast, in the Articles of Confederation, the Colonies did create only a league of states. The supremacy of federal law may have the effect of enabling Congress to preempt state laws, but it more fundamentally serves as a constitutional rule to resolve conflicts between state and federal law.[164]

The principal check on supremacy was to ask whether the United States acted within its constitutional powers and sphere of action: "the government of the Union, though limited in its powers, is supreme within its sphere of action."[165] But questioning the scope of federal power in courts is not the sole check on federal overreaching of the states. Chief Justice Marshall also identified the political check:

> The people of all the States, and the States themselves, are represented in Congress, and, by their representatives, exercise this power. When they tax the

---

[162] McCulloch v. Maryland, 17 U.S. 316, 408-409 (1819).
[163] *Id.* at 413.
[164] Viet D. Dihn, *Reassessing the Law of Preemption*, 88 Geo. L. J. 2085, 2090 (2000).
[165] 17 U.S. at 405.

> chartered institutions of the States, they tax their constituents; and these taxes must be uniform.[166]

Subsequently, this political check served as part of the explanation for reversing the expansion of tax intergovernmental immunity.[167]

Maryland did not seek to prevent the federal chartering of the bank; rather it wanted to be paid for letting it operate in Maryland. Actually, the Maryland law may have been less a resistance to federal power than an expression of anger at the fiscal mismanagement of the Maryland branch.[168] The payment was styled a tax and Chief Justice Marshall treated it as a tax, and the actual penalty at issue was a penalty for not paying a tax. The penalty could not be proper if the tax was unconstitutional and because the power to tax involves the power to destroy, Maryland could not have the power to tax the Bank; there was no way to contain the power of the states to tax the United States once allowed, and the subordinate sovereign could not be allowed to destroy the powers of the supreme sovereign. *McCulloch v. Maryland* did not delve into exactly how the effectuation of the enumerated powers of the United States would be affected by state taxation of the Bank notes, aside from the worst case scenario of destruction, but did observe generally that taxation could retard, impede, burden or control the United States.[169]

Chief Justice Marshall also identified what might be viewed as a second ground for federal immunity through supremacy: that the protections that the people have against harsh taxation—the political process—cannot be used by the United States to protect itself from state taxation. In addition he reasoned that the people of a state could not have granted the state as a sovereign the power to tax the United States because the people of one state did not themselves have that power to grant. Moreover, putting within the hands of the people of one state the power to destroy the United States would pit state against state in a way the union was designed to prevent. Thus entered the Supreme Court's lore a political analysis of the interaction of state and federal governments that continues to this day.[170]

---

[166] *Id.* at 435.

[167] Massachusetts v. United States, 435 U.S. 444, 456 (1978) (citing Helvering v. Gerhardt, 304 U.S. 405, 416 (1938)).

[168] *See* Howe, at 144 (the Bank had not only mismanaged the panic of 1819 but also the managers, including McCulloch, had embezzled a great amount of money).

[169] 17 U.S. at 436. Chief Justice Marshall also addressed the argument that Maryland was not trying to tax the United States or even the Bank, but was taxing property (the bank notes that were supposed to be on stamped paper). He dismissed this claim without even bothering to explain how the tax fell on the United States or affected it, relying instead on the extreme example of the potential to destroy a means to carry out an enumerated power.

[170] *See, e.g.*, Garcia v. San Antonio Metro. Transit Authority, 469 U.S. 528 (1985), *discussed in* Ch. III.F.3. Cases on both federal and state immunity in which no immunity is found now remit the respective governments to "political checks" or other political avenues to protect their interests. *See* Ch. II.C.7.a.

McCulloch was reprised in *Osborne*, with the same result.[171] The fact that Ohio did not get the message from *McCulloch* evidences the scope of disagreement with the Chief Justice.[172] Ohio's tax collector had actually collected the taxes it claimed the Bank owed and the bank officers sued for injunctive relief. Ohio levied and collected a tax of $50,000 per office from the bank because it had failed to obtain permission to operate in the state from state authorities. Ohio attacked the governmental status, or the instrumentality status, of the bank, pointing out that it was formed largely by private individuals to carry out a private business. But Chief Justice Marshall stated as a matter of fact that the bank was a "public corporation" established for public and national purposes. He explained again the fiscal operations as involving the creation of the money with which the United States conducted its affairs, and explained that the bank's functioning as a commercial bank facilitated the creation of value in that money. *Osborn* viewed the Bank of the United States as an instrument of the United States to carry out its enumerated powers, albeit not so directly as the post office. However, the opinion stated that the same protection from taxation would be accorded a contractor used by the United States to carry out the same function, a statement that would come back to haunt the issue, because later cases did not limit the tax exemption to taxes burdening the public function, but extended it to almost any tax on the federal contractor or employee as if it were a federal instrumentality.[173]

Chief Justice Marshall refused to bifurcate the Bank into its public and private pursuits, reasoning that the private pursuits were public pursuits in this case. The bank was an agent of the United States, being compensated by the profits it was allowed to make. Admittedly the bank officers were not federal employees, but even as contractors with the government their dealings with or for the government could not be taxed.

Two years after *McCulloch* Chief Justice Marshall wrote another historic opinion in the realm of federal-state interactions, *Cohens v. Virginia*, establishing the principle that the Supreme Court had jurisdiction to hear appeals from state criminal convictions.[174] Commentators generally overlook the fact that the opinion followed a path similar to that in *Marbury v. Madison*, of using a case to establish a procedural point, while letting the substantive point go.[175] Instead of finding the Court did not have jurisdiction, Chief Justice Marshall found it did have jurisdiction, but then affirmed the state conviction of the Cohens for selling lottery tickets issued under an Act of Congress outside the District of Columbia. In line with the approach of *McCulloch* one would have thought *Cohens*

---

171 Osborn v. President, Directors & Co. of Bank, 22 U.S. 738 (1824) (much of the opinion is devoted to jurisdictional and procedural issues).

172 Howe, at 145.

173 22 U.S. at 867.

174 Cohens v. Virginia, 19 U.S. 264 (1821).

175 Marbury v. Madison, 5 U.S. 1 (1803) (first decision to hold a federal statute unconstitutional, the statute purporting to grant the court jurisdiction to hear this appeal). *But see* Hylton v. United States, 3 U.S. 171, 175 (1796) (Justice Chase considered declaring the act of Congress unconstitutional but stated "I will never exercise it, but in a very clear case." This was the first case in which the Court considered the constitutionality of a federal statute.).

would have ruled the state could not impede a lottery authorized by Congress. However, instead it construed the statute not to have contemplated selling the lottery tickets outside the District and thus avoided the clash of sovereignties. *Cohens* actually was the final act of the struggle over Lord Fairfax's devise, which Virginia refused to allow to be settled by the Supreme Court (Chief Justice Marshall not having been able to write for the Court in those cases involving federal supremacy because of personal involvement in the case).[176]

3. *Expansion of Federal Immunity*

McCulloch v. Maryland identified two exceptions to state taxation that might be thought to impinge on the Bank of the United States:

> This opinion does not deprive the States of any resources which they originally possessed. It does not extend to a tax paid by the real property of the bank, in common with the other real property within the State, nor to a tax imposed on the interest which the citizens of Maryland may hold in this institution, in common with other property of the same description throughout the State.[177]

These two exceptions echoed down the decades and were repeatedly cited as the boundaries of taxation of national banks (which were not necessarily in the same posture as the single Bank of the United States).[178] The states relied on these particular subjects of taxation. However, the Chief Justice was overly optimistic of the ability of the federal courts to easily distinguish between the permitted and the impermissible state taxes on federal activities.[179] The issue in *McCulloch* and *Osborn* was not principally the power of the states to tax the federal government or an instrumentality, but the power of the United States to enforce its hard fought and much resisted choice to charter a bank and use it for national purposes as sort of a rough precursor of the Federal Reserve System (which has enjoyed some of the same types of political criticisms as did the Bank of the United States). Some of the states attempted, in effect, to nullify that decision of Congress through taxation. Specifically, at least six states enacted laws

---

[176] Fairfax's Devisee v. Hunter's Lessee, 11 U.S. 603 (1813); Martin v. Hunter's Lessee, 14 U.S. 304 (1816).

[177] 17 U.S. at 436. The City of Charleston cited this statement to the Court in its argument in Weston v. Charleston, 27 U.S. 449, 469 (1829), and Chief Justice Marshall distinguished the cases, apparently on the ground that the city's tax on the United States debt was more closely related to the enumerated power to borrow than would be a tax on the stock of the Bank of the United States. In 1864 Congress allowed the two forms of taxation of national banks sanctioned by Chief Justice Marshall's opinion. ch. 106, 13 Stat. 99 (1864). *See* Van Allen v. Assessors, 70 U.S. 573 (1866) (involving that act). As to restrictions on taxing banks generally, *see* Sandra B. McCray, *Constitutional Issues in State Income Taxes: Financial Institutions*, 51 Alb. L. Rev. 895 (1987); Hellerstein and Hellerstein, State Taxation ¶ 6.29.

[178] *See, e.g.*, Owensboro National Bank v. Owensboro, 173 U.S. 664, 676 (1899).

[179] *See generally* Thomas Reed Powell, *The Waning of Intergovernmental Tax Immunities*, 58 Harv. L. Rev. 633 (1945); Thomas Reed Powell, *The Remnant of Intergovernmental Tax Immunities*, 58 Harv. L. Rev. 757 (1945); Note, *State Taxation of Federal Instrumentalities*, 30 Col. L. Rev. 74 (1930); Carl C. Plehn, *The Taxation of National Banks*, 17 Cal. L. Rev. 357 (1928); Roger J. Traynor, *National Bank Taxation in California*, 17 Cal. L. Rev. 83, 232, 456 (1928).

imposing taxes of various large amounts on the Bank of the United States by name or as a bank not chartered by the state.[180]

Therefore, Chief Justice Marshall evidently felt he had to repel that nullification. However, the Bank was disliked for reasons that went beyond states' rights. At that particular point in its history it was ill managed, had bungled administration of currency and contributed to a recession, and the very Mr. McCulloch for whom the case is named was indicted for malfeasance.[181] Maryland's attorneys argued strongly that the Bank was not a public agency but a private business at best used for certain governmental purposes.[182] Chief Justice Marshall's opinion gave no attention to that argument, and, as shown above, only five years later in *Osborn* undertook to explain further why he thought the Bank was an instrumentality.

Giving the *McCulloch* opinion its maximum respect in this regard, one may say that it viewed the facilitation of federal fiscal matters to have been difficult if not impossible without a bank that would serve the nation's needs, and only one such bank was chosen (with branches allowed), and the fact that the United States allowed it to be mostly privately owned could not diminish its public role, but indeed facilitated it.[183] Of course President Jackson proved that he could get along quite well without the Bank of the United States, and its currency creating function was not sorely needed by the federal government again until the Civil War necessitated the creation of national banks, which could issue currency.[184]

But *McCulloch*'s broad dictum took a crucial turn toward forbidding perceived indirect burdens on the federal government in *Weston*, which prevented the states from taxing United States debt as property in the hands of the creditor.[185] Chief Justice Marshall found federal debt obligations to be instruments of the United States, just as the Bank had been. *Weston v. Charleston* ruled that a local government could not collect a nondiscriminatory property tax (that was actually a form of income tax on net interest) on federal stock (notes) held by

---

[180] Harold J. Plous and Gordon E. Baker, *McCulloch v. Maryland: Right Principle, Wrong Case*, 9 Stan. L. Rev. 710, 717 (1957) [hereinafter Plous and Baker], quoting 1 Warren, The Supreme Court in United States History 505-506 (rev. ed. 1946).

[181] *See* Plous and Baker, at 713-717.

[182] *Id.* at 720-726.

[183] *Id.* at 730.

[184] *See* Carl B. Swisher, Roger B. Taney ch. 12 (1935) (describing how then Attorney General Taney went about removing the federal deposits from the Bank as it was winding down).

[185] Weston v. Charleston, 27 U.S. 449 (1829).

the public, reflecting government borrowing.[186] Chief Justice Marshall did not have to rely on the type of reasoning used in *McCulloch*—that the bank was a means that was necessary and proper to carry out enumerated or implied federal powers—instead, the Constitution specifically authorized the United States to borrow money and Chief Justice Marshall viewed the local tax as falling directly on the federal power.

The *Weston* opinion relied on two facts: (1) that the tax was measured by, and so said to be levied "on," the government instrument (although not collected from the United States), and (2) that the tax indirectly burdened the United States. Like *McCulloch*, the opinion did not find it necessary to explain exactly how the burden occurred, because of (a) the crucial importance of the federal power at issue (borrowing in *Weston*, currency in *McCulloch*), and (b) the "power to destroy," worst case scenario. Although indirect effects on the United States that might result from state taxation are no longer generally grounds for voiding a state tax, federal debt continues to be a special case for exemption from state taxation.[187]

The dissents in *Weston* pointed out that *McCulloch* had said a nondiscriminatory tax on the bank's property and stock would be proper, and so by analogy a nondiscriminatory tax on federal interest should be proper, and asserted that if the tax had been properly understood as an income tax it would have been constitutional.[188] However, the Chief Justice seemed controlled by the fact that the tax was "on" an instrument, which was in the nature of an instrumentality, of the United States. It is possible that Chief Justice Marshall was concerned about the fact that the Second Bank of the United States held United States bonds and that his dictum in *McCulloch* that the Bank's real property could be taxed might be used by states to try to tax the United States bonds held by the Bank.[189]

Over 100 years later Justice Blackmun fingered *Weston* as the case that caused federal tax immunity to be unfortunately expanded beyond its needed scope.[190] Even though *Weston* relied on what appeared to be a formal ground to find a tax on the United States, it was later applied as part of a substance over form approach that allowed the expansion of intergovernmental immunity. Justice

---

[186] The opinion examined the attempt of the city to tax the "stock" issued by the United States in exchange for funds lent to it. It reasoned that the power to borrow was as fundamental as the power to tax because borrowing frequently was necessary when taxation was episodically insufficient; that once the power exists to tax a subject, "it is a right which in its nature acknowledges no limits." Therefore, to allow a state to tax the borrowing of the United States imposed a serious burden on that important power of sovereignty and could not be allowed. The concept of calling debt stock is quite confusing, but evidently it was the practice to call at least long term government debt stock in the 1800s. *See, e.g.*, Ch. 49, 31st Cong., 1st Sess. (Sept. 9, 1850), 9 Stat. 446, 447 (14-year single payment notes bearing five percent interest issued to Texas for the resolution of a boundary issue).

[187] *See* 31 U.S.C. § 3124.

[188] *See* Bryan L. Rakestraw, *The Reciprocal Rule of Governmental Tax Immunity: A Legal Myth*, 3 Okl. L. Rev. 131, 138 (1950) [hereinafter Rakestraw].

[189] 3 Stat. 266 (April 10, 1816) (authorized the United States to pay for its stock with bonds).

[190] United States v. New Mexico, 455 U.S. 720, 731 (1982) (noting that Chief Justice Marshall seemingly disregarded his own dictum).

Johnson in dissent argued that the real problem with the state tax in *McCulloch* was that it wasn't a tax: Maryland was not trying to raise revenue from the Bank, rather it was trying to kill the Bank, or at least prevent its operation in Maryland. In contrast, Charleston's nondiscriminatory tax on debt, governmental and private, was a true tax that was not a "masked attack on the powers of the general government," and should be allowed for that reason.[191]

In 1842 a much greater expansion of federal immunity occurred in *Dobbins*, which invalidated a county tax in the nature of a general property tax on the salary of an officer of a federal revenue cutter (*i.e.*, a tax collector).[192] The opinion expanded the concept of the prior decisions to "emoluments" of the instruments used by the United States, counting individual employees as instruments who received such emoluments.[193] Perhaps the vital tax collecting role performed by the particular federal officer Dobbins influenced the Court's decision, but its reasoning was based on at least a theoretical impact on the United States: either (a) Congress would have to increase the salary to make up for the tax, and do so in varying amounts around the country as local taxes varied, or (b) an act of Congress would simply be thwarted by the officer getting less than Congress intended to pay. Thus *Dobbins* rather than *Weston* may be the more unfortunate extension of federal immunity and was the case in which the indirect burden concept suggested in *McCulloch* and *Weston* (*i.e.*, substance over form) was carried to an extreme; and it laid the foundation for the states' claim to tax immunity, which was confirmed in *Collector v. Day* in 1871.[194]

It took another 99 years for a Justice to even question the dictum of the Great Chief Justice, and only in the late 1930s did the tide of federal immunity actually start to recede. Justice Holmes complained about the over-reading of Chief Justice Marshall's dictum in *McCulloch* in 1928:

> I should say plainly right, but for the effect of certain dicta of Chief Justice Marshall which culminated in or rather were founded upon his often quoted proposition that the power to tax is the power to destroy. In those days it was not recognized as it is today that most of the distinctions of the law are distinctions of degree. If the States had any power it was assumed that they had all power, and that the necessary alternative was to deny it altogether. But this Court which so often has defeated the attempt to tax in certain ways can defeat an attempt to discriminate or otherwise go too far without wholly abolishing the power to tax. *The power to tax is not the power to destroy while this Court sits.* The power to fix rates is the power to destroy if unlimited, but this Court while it endeavors to prevent confiscation does not prevent the fixing of rates. A tax is not an unconstitutional regulation in every case where an absolute

---

[191] 27 U.S. at 472. *See* DONALD G. MORGAN, JUSTICE WILLIAM JOHNSON 249-250 (1954).

[192] Dobbins v. The Commissioners of Erie, 41 U.S. 435, 447 (1842); *implicitly overruled by* Graves v. New York, 306 U.S. 466 (1939). Justice Wayne wrote the unanimous *Dobbins* opinion.

[193] *Osborne* had referred to the alternative of a person performing the duties of the bank and reaping its profits as emoluments. 22 U.S. at 863.

[194] Collector v. Day, 78 U.S. 113 (1871); *overruled by* Graves v. New York, 306 U.S. 466 (1939).

prohibition of sales would be one. Hatch v. Reardon, 204 U.S. 152, 162.[195] (emphasis added)

4. *Destruction to Nondiscrimation*

As Justice Holmes predicted in 1928, the "power to destroy" ground for intergovernmental tax immunity was moderated in the 1930s due to the need of all governments for tax revenues. The Supreme Court came to limit immunity to taxes imposed directly on the federal government itself (and in the case of state and local governments, on their essential government functions), and came to allow nondiscriminatory taxation of private persons who dealt with government, and even of the state and local governments themselves.[196] As explained in *Davis v. Michigan*, the nondiscrimination principle is not only stated in the Public Salary Tax Act of 1939 and other waivers of federal immunity but also is a constitutional principle, so far as the federal immunity is concerned.[197] The following Chapter outlines the core principles, which evolved from *McCulloch*.

5. *Federal Immunity from Chief Justice Marshall to Today*

Chief Justice Marshall's opinions in *McCulloch* and *Weston* discussed in Chapters II.C. 2 and 3 were the foundation stones of the intergovernmental immunity doctrine, as applicable to both federal and state governments. *McCulloch* had an outsized importance because it primarily involved not taxation but the largest political fight of the first half century of the nation: the ability of the federal government to charter and effectively run its own central bank and the supremacy of the federal government vis à vis the states, which that Bank implicated. *Weston* addressed the separate issue of federal debt taxation by the states. If the two opinions had been properly understood, a century of confusion and much litigation over taxation might have been largely avoided. Instead, the "power to destroy" fear provided cover for the expansion of immunity far beyond that likely intended by Chief Justice Marshall, largely at the urging and for the benefit of private taxpayers. The major expansions were to exempt the salaries of

---

[195] Justice Holmes' dissent in Panhandle Oil Co. v. Mississippi, 277 U.S. 218, 223 (1928). A similar statement had appeared in Flint v. Stone Tracy Co., 220 U.S. 107, 169 (1911) (rejected the argument that indirectly taxing state bonds through a corporate excise tax could destroy the states; stated the courts have no authority to forbid a reasonable act because some other act may be impermissible; the remedy is through Congress). *See also* ROBERT H. JACKSON, THE STRUGGLE FOR JUDICIAL SUPREMACY 242 (1941) ("However persuasive the argument for governmental immunity, there was little reason in law and none at all in sound government for holding that officeholders shared the government's immunity from tax.").

[196] Helvering v. Mountain Producers Corp., 303 U.S. 376 (1938) is the principal decision on nondiscrimination. *See* Oklahoma Tax Comm'n v. Texas Co., 336 U.S. 342, 361 (1949).

[197] Davis v. Michigan, 489 U.S. 803, 812-813 (1989). *See* David M. Richardson, *Federal Income Taxation of States*, 19 STETSON L. REV. 411, 433-438 (1990) [hereinafter Richardson] (stating that while in theory even a discriminatory tax might be found not to adversely affect the government involved, in practice discrimination is the fixed dividing line, with the finding of the fact of discrimination being the variable; the discrimination found in *Davis* was entirely facial and not shown to have any actual impact on the state or federal governments).

federal employees and incomes of federal contractors and lessees, and then to turn the doctrine around and apply it to protect states from federal taxation on sovereignty grounds, even though they did not enjoy the supremacy attribute of the federal government.

The largest subset of cases on federal immunity involves the national banks, which were private institutions chartered under Civil War legislation. Like the creation of the Bank of the United States, the chartering of national banks was a huge political issue, because it implicated the federal control over the money supply and the inevitable tug of war between debtors (who enjoyed inflating the money supply) and creditors (who enjoyed "hard money"), and also between federal control of banking and state control of banking. Thus, again the taxing issues were sideshows to a larger political drama.

Core principles. The *McCulloch* opinion identified the core principles of intergovernmental tax immunity that eventually were partly codified and form part of the law today, with one exception (31 U.S.C. § 3124):

- The post office, the mint, the patent office, for examples, are all federal agencies authorized by the Constitution to carry out the powers of the United States and cannot be taxed by the states.
- Somewhat similarly, an instrument (agent, contractor, etc.) used by the United States to carry out its constitutional powers (*e.g.*, the Bank of the United States) cannot be taxed on carrying out those powers (*e.g.*, the issuance of bank notes that Congress intended to form a national currency).
- However, states could collect at least some taxes from even the Bank of the United States if they were not measured by or directly related to its execution of the governmental function, such as a permitted property tax on the Bank's real property.
- This permission to tax some aspects of an instrumentality reflected a nondiscrimination principle, meaning that the agent was taxed in common with similarly situated citizens of the state.
- The separation of shareholder from corporation would be respected and a tax on stock held by shareholders would not be treated as a tax on the corporation that was an instrumentality, such as the Bank of the United States. (However, a state cannot impose a property tax on stock that is computed on the value of federal debt held by the bank under current law.[198])
- Such permitted stock tax also must be nondiscriminatory.

Weston dealt with the distinct issue of a state tax on United States debt instruments, which the Court viewed as an instrument of government just as much as the Bank of the United States. *Weston* approached debt in a different way from *McCulloch*'s approach to stock of the Bank: it was sensitive to any indirect influence that a state tax on federal debt might have on borrowing by the United

---

[198] 31 U.S.C. § 3124; American Bank & Trust Co. v. Dallas County, 463 U.S. 855 (1983).

States. Nevertheless, *Weston* did not indicate any limitation on *McCulloch*'s assertion that corporate stock could be taxed, even though the corporation owned United States debt. Justice Stone later pointed out that *Weston* showed that even nondiscriminatory state taxes could be prohibited.[199]

Current law. The above stated seminal points made by Chief Justice Marshall in *McCulloch* and *Weston* eventually formed the core of the current regime of intergovernmental immunity:

- The United States: A state still cannot send a tax bill to the United States, including governmental agencies that only perform constitutional functions such as the military,[200] and cannot tax instrumentalities on carrying out the federal functions (which was the case with the Bank of the United States issuing bank notes).[201] This rule reflects a distinction between the constitutional prohibition of a state tax whose "legal incidence" falls on the United States, and the permission for nondiscriminatory taxes levied on persons dealing with the United States even though the "economic incidence" of those taxes might fall on the United States.[202]

- The nondiscrimination principle: The Supreme Court eventually reversed the long expansion of federal immunity that had extended to government employees and contractors and other private parties, and their taxability was codified in various general statutes as well as specific statutes creating entities. The first such general waiver was the Public Salary Tax Act of 1939 (4 U.S.C. § 111).[203] The Buck Act of 1940 (4 U.S.C. §§ 105-110) permits nondiscriminatory sales and use and income taxes on transactions and income derived in federal lands.[204] A 1947 act allows nondiscriminatory state motor fuels taxes on federal bases (4 U.S.C. § 104). States can tax those with whom the United States deals, as long as the tax does not discriminate

[199] Helvering v. Gerhardt, 304 U.S. 405, 413 (1938).

[200] 4 U.S.C. § 107 (although the Buck Act allows state sales taxation in federal enclaves, the permission applies only to private parties and not the United States). *See, e.g.*, United States v. Tax Comm'n of Miss., 421 U.S. 599 (1975) (post exchange liquor purchases could not be subject to tax on vendors to be passed on to post).

[201] 4 U.S.C. § 107. *See* South Carolina v. Baker, 485 U.S. 505, 523 (1988). *See, e.g.*, Dep't of Employment v. United States, 385 U.S. 355 (1966) (Red Cross is a federal instrumentality and immune from state taxation).

[202] 485 U.S. at 526.

[203] *See* Davis v. Michigan, 489 U.S. 803 (1989) (interpreting the statute to apply to federal retirees and to impose a fairly strict standard of nondiscrimination vis à vis taxation of state retirees).

[204] The Buck Act applies to franchise and other taxes that are based on income. *See* Humble Oil & Ref. Co. v. Calvert, 478 S.W. 2d 926, 929 (Tex. 1972), *cert. denied*, 409 U.S. 967 (1972) (quoting Senate Finance Committee Report). Although it does not use the word discrimination, it achieves the same effect by authorizing the tax only to the same extent and effect as applied outside the federal area. *See* Polar Ice Cream & Creamery Co. v. Andrews, 375 U.S. 361 (1964) (allowing state tax on distributing milk in federal enclave). As to the broad characterization of income tax, *see* Howard v. Commissioners, 344 U.S. 624 (1947).

against either the United States or those with which it deals.[205] Congress has codified many other waivers of immunity for federal instrumentalities.[206]

- National banks: The nondiscrimination principle is now the only limit left on state taxation of national banks (12 U.S.C. § 548).
- Supremacy: The supremacy of the federal government and the limited nature of its powers aside from taxation, in contrast with the general reserved powers of the states, mean that federal instrumentalities are much more likely (if not certain) to be carrying out an essential function of the United States than are state created entities to be carrying on essential functions of the states. In stating this conclusion the opinion made an overstatement: the United States "performs no 'proprietary' functions."[207] It meant that the Federal Land Bank was not a proprietary lending activity, but the associated footnote did not support ignoring the vast array of federal user fees, such as entry fees for national parks, which are surely proprietary function fees (as discussed in Chapter IV).
- Federal debt obligations: The mechanical refusal of *McCulloch* to look through stock to the holdings of the corporation that issued the stock (in stating that the stock of the Bank of the United States could be taxed nondiscriminatorily by states) has been melded with the substantive emphasis of *Weston* on preventing any sensible influence of state taxation on the federal borrowing power, in 31 U.S.C. § 3124 (first enacted in 1959). This statute prohibits any state tax measured by United States debt, other than nondiscriminatory franchise or other non property taxes imposed in lieu thereof on corporations, and estate and inheritance taxes. Thus even a nondiscriminatory property or income tax on federal debt is unconstitutional; a state property tax on stock is constitutional if the value of the stock is the measure but not if the measure is the value of the corporate assets including federal debt.[208] There is a four part test for identifying a federal obligation: (1) written documents, (2) the bearing of interest, (3) a binding promise by the United States to pay specified sums at specified dates, and (4) specific congressional authorization, which also pledged the faith and credit of the United States in support of the promise to pay.[209] In contrast, the United States can tax interest paid on debt by states and municipalities, although it generally chooses not to do so in section 103.[210]

---

[205] South Carolina v. Baker, 485 U.S. 505, 523 (1988).

[206] *See* Paschal, at 1100-1101.

[207] Federal Land Bank v. Bd., 368 U.S. 146, 150-151 (1961).

[208] American Bank & Trust Co. v. Dallas County, 463 U.S. 855 (1983).

[209] Smith v. Davis, 323 U.S. 111 (1944) (open account obligation not a federal debt). *See also* Rockford Life Ins. Co. v. Ill. DOR, 482 U.S. 182 (1987) (GNMAs not federal debt); Neb. DOR v. Loewenstein, 513 U.S. 123 (1994) (repurchase agreements on federal debt did not burden federal borrowing and were not subject to the statute).

[210] South Carolina v. Baker, 485 U.S. 505 (1988) (overruling *Pollock* as to nondiscriminatory tax on state interest).

- State franchise taxes: The curious treatment of state franchise taxes is the only major feature of the current regime that did not originate with Chief Justice Marshall. In 1868 the Supreme Court allowed a state to tax the franchise of a state institution that held federal debt, on the premise that a franchise tax was an excise tax and not a tax on the property of the corporation, and the federal obligation was merely the measure of the tax.[211] As discussed in Chapter IV, this is based on the formalistic view that the franchise is an act of sovereignty and so supports a tax for the grant, which is not a user fee for a service or property provided by the state; whereas a tax on property is just a tax. This state taxing method was extended to national banks in 1926, resulting in a distinction between a state tax on the capital (*i.e.,* property) of a business that included federal debt (not allowed), and a tax on the shareholders' stock reflecting federal debt held by the corporation (allowed up to 1959, and still allowed if the federal debt held by the corporation is not in the tax base), and a franchise tax measured by the corporation's income from federal debt (allowed). The Supreme Court has remarked on the oddity of the distinctions.[212] As a result of these rules states commonly used franchise taxes to tax national banks up to the 1972 (based on the 1969 amendment), because national banks commonly held substantial federal debt and the income from that debt could be in the franchise tax base but not an income tax base; after the effective date of 1969 amendment national banks could be taxed the same as state banks (*i.e.*, non discriminatorily).[213] Privilege license taxes or excise taxes are similar to franchise taxes, and the same sort of "legerdemain" was applied to uphold the federal corporate income tax of 1909 and to distinguish it from the income tax struck down by *Pollock*, simply by calling it an excise tax (which could tax state obligations).[214]

---

[211] Society for Savings v. Coite, 73 U.S. 594 (1868). *See generally* John B. Sholley, *Corporate Taxpayers and the Equal Protection Clause*, 31 Ill. L. Rev. 567, 580 et seq. (1937) (explaining how the Court treated some nominal franchise taxes as property taxes).

[212] Am. Bank & Trust Co. v. Dallas County, 463 U.S. 855, 866 n. 11 (1983) (quoting a congressional colloquy in 1926: "67 Cong. Rec. 6085-6986 (1926) (colloquy of Reps. Wingo and Cooper) (legalizing franchise tax measured by assets including federal obligations is 'a use of words to conceal an idea'; 'the decision of the Supreme Court which arrived at [that] conclusion gave me a headache, and it took me considerable time to be able to comprehend it'); *id.*, at 6088 (remarks of Rep. Stevenson) ('the Supreme Court of the United States frequently obscures ideas by language as well as statesmen when they are on the stump. . . . When they held that the stock was taxable, although every dollar of it was invested in United States bonds, which were expressly exempt from taxation, they held practically the same thing.'")).

[213] 12 U.S.C. § 548.

[214] *See* Ch. V.D.2.c. *See* Ratner, at 296: "This element [of appearing to indirectly tax property], however, he [Justice Day in *Flint v. Stone Tracy*] felt was lacking in taxes on privilege, because if no business was done in the manner prescribed in the statute, no tax was payable. But astute critics of judicial rationalizations like Thomas Reed Powell pointed out the dialectical legerdemain by which a few words in a statute turned a tax on income into a tax on something else merely measured by income; they believed in it, nevertheless, 'as the gentleman believed in baptism, because he had seen it done.'" [citing Robert M. Haig, Ed., The Federal Income Tax (New York 1954), p. 21.].

- Congress' power. Another element of current federal immunity is the power of Congress to both expand[215] and contract[216] the federal immunity.[217] Perhaps this was implied by *McCulloch* through the power of Congress to invest a bank with federal character and Chief Justice Marshall's easy ability to create a nondiscrimination exception for indirect taxes on its stock. The power to immunize what might not otherwise be immune generally comes from the Necessary and Proper Clause.[218] Scholars debate how Congress can change the Constitution to allow taxation of federal agencies, but the Court says it can.[219]
- Legal incidence on the United States rather than indirect economic effect is the test for immunity violations. After the *Dobbins* opinion in 1842 expanded federal tax immunity to the salary of federal employees, almost a century passed before the Court turned its back on the search for the economic substance of tax falling indirectly on the United States and decided that as to the issue of intergovernmental immunity, form should control (sometimes called "legal incidence" of the tax).[220]
- The federal courts and not the state courts determine whether a state tax is levied on the United States for purposes of immunity analysis, although

---

[215] *See, e.g.*, Pittman v. Home Owners' Loan Corp., 308 U.S. 21 (1939) (federal law made the corporation exempt from state tax).

[216] *See, e.g.*, Owensboro National Bank v. Owensboro, 173 U.S. 664, 668 (1899) (Congress permitted state taxation of national banks); Pacific Coast Dairy, Inc. v. Department of Agriculture, 318 U.S. 285, 296 (1943) (Congress may subject federal activities to state regulation); Maricopa County v. Valley Nat'l Bank, 318 U.S. 357 (1943) (Congress could remove from local taxation the stock of national banks held by the Reconstruction Finance Corporation).

[217] *See* Paschal, at 1098-1099; Rakestraw, at 162-168 (the primary examples of extensions of immunity to state taxation that would not otherwise be required by the Constitution are several statutes exempting soldiers and veterans). *See, e.g.*, Soldiers and Sailors Relief Act, 50 U.S.C. App. 574; enforced in California v. Buzard, 382 U.S. 386 (1966) (car registration fee was tax); but not in Sullivan v. United States, 395 U.S. 169 (1969) (applies only to ad valorem property taxes and not sales taxes). Justice Stone discussed both waivers and extensions of federal immunity in Helvering v. Gerhardt, 304 U.S. 405, 411 n. 1 (1938). *See also* Lawrence v. Shaw, 300 U.S. 245 (1937) (veterans could not be subjected to property tax on bank credits from the United States for their benefit); Oklahoma Tax Comm'n v. Texas Co., 336 U.S. 342 (1949) (stating that Congress could, if it wished, immunize lessee from state taxation).

[218] *See* Federal Land Bank v. Bismark Lumber Co., 314 U.S. 95 (1941) (in furtherance of the lending power).

[219] Paschal, at 1102-1103. *Cf.* Ashton v. Cameron County Water Improvement Dist., 298 U.S. 513, 531 (1936) ("Neither consent nor submission by the States can enlarge the powers of Congress; none can exist except those which are granted." This was not a federal tax case and the statement would bear only on the obverse point: state permission for federal taxation).

[220] *See, e.g.*, Ariz. Dep't of Revenue v. Blaze Constr. Co., 526 U.S. 32, 36 (1999).

the state law does determine the rights and obligation of taxpayers and the states.[221]

Chapter II.C.8 recounts the long chain of decisions from *McCulloch* to the current law of limited federal immunity from state taxation, based principally on the nondiscrimination principle.

6. *Federal Enclaves*

Article I, section 8, clause 17 of the Constitution states:

> The Congress shall have Power . . . To exercise exclusive Legislation in all Cases whatsoever . . . over all Places purchased by the Consent of the Legislature of the State in which the Same shall be, for the Erection of Forts, Magazines, Arsenals, dock-Yards, and other needful Buildings . . . .

Land obtained in this manner is called a "federal enclave." The states have no power to tax within a federal enclave, because it is not part of the state. But when the United States conveys enclave land to a private buyer, it becomes subject to state property taxation, absent other contractual terms.[222]

The Buck Act, 4 U.S.C. § 104-110 (1940), allows states to collect nondiscriminatory sales and use and income taxes from nongovernmental persons operating in federal enclaves.

Issues still can arise about a state's attempt to tax the property of a contractor working in a federal enclave; the question is not federal immunity but the more fundamental power to tax geographically. For example, *Humble Pipe Line* involved a drilling company with drilling equipment and pipelines on the Barksdale Air Force Base, which the United States had acquired from Louisiana under the quoted constitutional provision.[223] The state levied ad valorem taxes on the drill rigs and pipelines and the oil company protested. The Court's opinion said that no issue of federal tax immunity was involved, but only whether the base was a federal enclave in which the federal authority was exclusive; the Court ruled it was a federal enclave. The contract with the driller said it should pay all taxes legally due. The state argued that the United States had thereby waived its exclusivity. The Court disagreed, suggesting that it was not sure such a waiver was possible, but in any event the language did not do so. The terms of a partic-

---

[221] *See, e.g.*, Diamond National Corp. v. State Bd. of Equal., 425 U.S. 268 (1976); Gurley v. Rhoden, 421 U.S. 200 (1975); Society of Savings of Cleveland v. Bowers, 349 U.S. 143 (1955); Kern-Limerick, Inc. v. Scurlock, 347 U.S. 110 (1954); First Agricultural National Bank v. State Tax Comm'n, 392 U.S. 339 (1968). *Cf.* Federal Land Bank v. Bismark Lumber Co., 314 U.S. 95 (1941) (which appears to defer more to state characterization); United States v. Tax Comm'n of Miss., 421 U.S. 599 (1975) (which did not cede control of the characterization to the state but effectively estopped the state from denying it levied the tax on the United States on account of a state letter to vendors so requiring).

[222] S. R. A., Inc. v. Minnesota, 327 U.S. 558 (1946).

[223] Humble Pipe Line Co. v. Waggonner, 376 U.S. 369 (1964). *See also* Shell Oil Co. v. Iowa Dep't of Revenue, 488 U.S. 19 (1988) (outer continental shelf is federal enclave); Polar Ice Cream & Creamery Co. v. Andrews, 375 U.S. 361 (1964) (allowing state tax on distributing milk in federal enclave).

ular federal purchase from a state also may determine the extent of state taxing power within the area.[224]

The Buck Act does not allow taxation of the United States itself within its federal enclave.[225] Cases directly involving that issue are immunity cases and are included in the chronology below in Chapter II.C.8.

7. *States' Implied Immunity from Federal Taxation*

a. *Overview*

The first major role played by the Tenth Amendment was in *Collector v. Day*, the first of the long line of confusing decisions holding that state employees could not be taxed by the United States.[226] Despite the general rule that the Tenth Amendment does not limit the federal taxing power, that opinion cited the Tenth Amendment and indicated that its preservation of state sovereignty and powers meant that the United States could not tax the states indirectly by taxing their employees.

Today the residue of a huge amount of litigation and confusion over state immunity from federal taxation is sections 103 and 115 of the Code, but only section 115 is possibly based on the Constitution. Section 103 excludes interest on state and local debt from gross income, but the Constitution does not mandate the exclusion.[227] Section 115 allows states and their instrumentalities as potential federal taxpayers to exclude from gross income their income from their public utilities and essential governmental functions.[228] These two provisions were in the original 1913 income tax and have consistently appeared in subsequent income tax laws. The case law, however, held unconstitutional the taxation of the compensation of state and local employees and contractors and the incomes of some state and local instrumentality activities beyond those now viewed as essential governmental functions.[229] That expansion has receded into a limitation on taxation that discriminates against states and their instrumentalities, and possibly a limitation on taxing core state functions.[230]

---

[224] Ft. Leavenworth R. Co. v. Lowe, 114 U.S. 525 (1885).

[225] *See, e.g.*, United States v. State Tax Comm'n, 412 U.S. 363 (1973).

[226] Collector v. Day, 78 U.S. 113 (1871); *overruled by* Graves v. New York, 306 U.S. 466 (1939).

[227] South Carolina v. Baker, 485 U.S. 505 (1988) (overruling *Pollock* as to nondiscriminatory tax on state interest). In contrast, 31 U.S.C. § 3124 prohibits most state taxation of federal debt interest and is a constitutional limitation on the states; Superior Oil Co. v. Mississippi, 280 U.S. 390 (1930) (state could not impose property tax on property of contractor in enclave; extensive discussion of rule; changed by Buck Act).

[228] *See* Bittker & Lokken, at ¶ 102.10. *See also* Richardson, at 460 et seq. (arguing that the Service honors a de facto exemption of states and municipalities without regard to section 115 or constitutional immunity).

[229] *See generally* Richardson.

[230] *See* Paschal, at 1091-1092. *Cf.* Massachusetts v. United States, 435 U.S. 444 (1978) (excise tax on police aircraft upheld; Congress intended to tax states, evidently relying in part on the fact that the levy was to be treated as a user fee rather than a tax).

South Carolina v. Baker[231] and *Massachusetts v. United States*[232] indicate that "political checks" can be a principal protector of states from undue federal taxation. Intergovernmental tax immunity began with federal immunity based on the twin supports of sovereignty and supremacy as discussed in Chapter II.C.2, and was expanded in 1871 by *Collector v. Day* to state tax immunity based solely on the limited sovereignty of states and their role in the constitutional system.[233] State immunity from federal tax was an outgrowth of Chief Justice Marshall's statement that the power to tax involves the power to destroy; because the constitutional system requires that states coexist and not be destroyed by the federal government, the federal taxing power cannot be carried to its limit against states; and because it cannot be carried to its limit it cannot be applied at all, because admitting the power to any degree admits the whole power.[234]

The two lines of immunity in effect played off each other to create first a widening of immunity and then a narrowing of immunity (with state tax immunity narrowing first). The current state of the law and its historical origins are summed up in 1988 in *South Carolina v. Baker*, which ruled that the federal income tax exemption for state and municipal bond interest could be conditioned on registration of the bonds, and hence was a matter of the grace of Congress and not a constitutional mandate:

> The sources of the state and federal immunities are, of course, different: the state immunity arises from the constitutional structure and a concern for protecting state sovereignty whereas the federal immunity arises from the Supremacy Clause. The immunities have also differed somewhat in their underlying political theory and in their doctrinal contours. Many of this Court's opinions have suggested that the Constitution should be interpreted to confer a greater tax immunity on the Federal Government than on States because all the people of the States are represented in the Federal Government whereas all the people of the Federal Government are not represented in individual States. . . . In fact, the federal tax immunity has always been greater than the States' immunity. The Federal Government, for example, possesses the power to enact statutes immunizing those with whom it deals from state taxation even if intergovernmental tax immunity doctrine would not otherwise confer an immunity. . . . The States lack any such power. Also, although the Federal Government has always enjoyed blanket immunity from any state tax considered to be "on" the Government under the prevailing methodology, the States have never enjoyed immunity from all federal taxes considered to be "on" a State. . . . *Garcia* . . . may suggest further limitations on state tax immunity. We need not, however, decide here the extent to which the scope of the federal and state immunities differ or the extent, if any, to which States are currently immune from direct

[231] South Carolina v. Baker, 485 U.S. 505, 511 (1988). See discussion in Ch. III.F.3.

[232] Massachusetts v. United States, 435 U.S. 444 (1978) (the last tax opinion referring to political checks; excise tax on police aircraft upheld; Congress intended to tax states, evidently relying in part on the fact that the levy was to be treated as a user fee rather than a tax).

[233] Collector v. Day, 78 U.S. 113 (1871); *overruled by* Graves v. New York, 306 U.S. 466 (1939).

[234] *See* Mass. v. United States, 435 U.S. 444, 455 (1978).

> nondiscriminatory federal taxation. It is enough for our purposes that federal and state tax immunity cases have always shared the identical methodology for determining whether a tax is "on" a government, and that this identity has persisted even though the methodology for both federal and state immunities has changed as intergovernmental tax immunity doctrine shifted into the modern era.[235]

South Carolina v. Baker did not rest the power of the United States to impose an income tax on interest from state debt on the Sixteenth Amendment's authorization of taxation of income "from whatever source derived."[236]

Knowlton v. Moore rejected a powerful challenge to the expansion of state intergovernmental immunity from federal taxation.[237] The taxpayer, an estate, argued that the federal estate tax was levied on the power to transmit property upon death, which was a state created and regulated power of individuals. As such, the tax was a tax on the exclusive power of the state. The Court rejected that argument, saying that if it were so it would be the end of all taxation because most all individual rights were created or allowed by some government, usually the state governments.

The crucial distinction between the Supremacy Clause (protecting the United States' sovereignty from state taxation), and sovereignty alone (protecting the states from federal taxation), has several important consequences (noted in part in the quotation above):

- Although their taxing powers are concurrent due to the characteristic of taxation as a core feature of sovereignty, the taxing power of the United States is supreme relative to the states' (*McCulloch* explained the Bank of the United States as performing a role in collecting taxes and moving federal tax revenues).
- This supremacy most frequently is tested not in cases of federal tax versus state tax, but in cases of federal tax versus some reserved power of the states other than taxation (such as the *License Tax Cases*[238]) or federal instrumentalities being exempt from state tax.
- Most often the plaintiff seeking the exemption from federal taxes was not a state or local government but was a private person seeking to benefit from the state's exemption.[239]
- Federal supremacy is conditioned on the United States acting within the realm of its constitutional powers,[240] which it does whenever it taxes, but

[235] South Carolina v. Baker, 485 U.S. 505, 519 n. 11 (1988).

[236] *Id.* at 523 n. 13 (stating that the Amendment intended solely to remove the apportionment requirement).

[237] Knowlton v. Moore, 178 U.S. 41, 60 (1904).

[238] License Tax Cases, 72 U.S. 462 (1867).

[239] Helvering v. Gerhardt, 304 U.S. 405, 416 (1938).

[240] *Id.* at 411 n. 1.

which it may not do when it claims exemption of a federal instrumentality from state taxation or when a federal levy is not a tax.[241]

- The states are remitted largely to political processes for their protection from federal taxation. That is reasonable because Congress represents all of the people of the states. But no comparable political protection is available to the United States, because the people outside a state who comprise the United States are not represented in that state that may attempt to tax the United States. Consequently those other citizens of the United States are subject to taxation without representation (or more appropriately, are without the requisite political check on state action).[242]
- In contrast with the states' right to exemption, which exists only to the extent recognized by the Supreme Court or Congress, Congress has the power to expand or waive the immunity of federal instrumentalities that are within the power of Congress to create, applying the Necessary and Proper Clause.[243]
- The expanding activities of state and local governments and the increasing revenue needs of the United States made it necessary for the Court to rein in state immunity which is now limited to essential governmental functions of a state or municipality, principally (1) the income received by the governmental entity itself in the exercise of essential governmental functions (I.R.C. § 115), (2) possibly excise taxes that fall on the acts of the entity (such as sales taxes on sales to it),[244] and (3) until *South Carolina v. Baker*, the interest income paid to others by the governmental entity on its debt (still generally exempt under section 103).[245]
- In general states may be directly taxed in a nondiscriminatory fashion.[246]

---

[241] However, the Tenth Amendment is no defense to a federal tax, except a tax on a state. Fernandez v. Wiener, 326 U.S. 340, 361-362 (1945); Flint v. Stone Tracy Co., 220 U.S. 107, 154 (1911); McCray v. United States, 195 U.S. 27, 61 (1904). *See* Ch. III.F.3.

[242] 304 U.S. at 412 and n. 2. *But see* Ch. VIII.8, showing that taxation without representation is not a constitutional fault.

[243] *Id.* at 411 n. 1. *See* for discussion of expansion and waivers Rakestraw, at 162-168 (the primary examples of extensions of immunity to state taxation that would not otherwise be required by the Constitution are several statutes exempting soldiers and veterans). *See, e.g.*, Lawrence v. Shaw, 300 U.S. 245 (1937) (veterans could not be subjected to property tax on bank credits from the United States for their benefit); Oklahoma Tax Comm'n v. Texas Co., 336 U.S. 342 (1949) (stating that Congress could, if it wished, immunize lessee from state taxation); Carson v. Roane-Anderson Co., 342 U.S. 232 (1952) (Necessary and Proper Clause role). *See* Ch. II.C.5.

[244] *See* Indian Motorcycle Co. v. United States, 283 U.S. 570 (1931) (never directly overruled).

[245] 304 U.S. at 417-418 (governmental income including "investments"). But *South Carolina v. Baker* later showed that state bond interest was not constitutionally exempt.

[246] South Carolina v. Baker, 485 U.S. 505, 523 (1988); *see also* quotation in text.

b. Collector v. Day

Just as the intergovernmental immunity of the United States was identified in connection with banking, the immunity of states also first arose in the same context. That reflects the immense historic importance of creating and controlling currency in the United States. The original plan to create a stable currency was based on Alexander Hamilton's Bank of the United States. After its charter ended and a fight over recreating it, the Second Bank of the United States was chartered and was attacked by the states, leading to *McCulloch v. Maryland*, discussed in Chapter II.C.2. They and Andrew Jackson won and the Second Bank was not recreated when its charter ended. As a result, there was no central bank to constrain the creation of money and state banks issued a wide variety of bills of exchange of varying quality. The United States dealt only in gold and silver though it did issue Treasury notes from time to time, which could be used to pay taxes and other debts to the federal government.[247]

That state of affairs was perhaps tolerable until the Civil War, when the financial needs of the United States dramatically increased and dealing in coin in paying and supplying hundreds of thousands of troops became difficult. The Administration looked for a new way to create and stabilize currency, which resulted both in currency issued by the United States itself and not immediately redeemable in coin, and in chartering multiple national banks that would issue bank notes, and which the United States could at least monitor. By 1865 that arrangement had sufficiently succeeded that Congress chose to discourage the inferior currency issued by state chartered banks by levying a ten percent tax on state bank notes when either issued by the state banks or received by national banks. In fact in the 1869 opinion in the case in which the Veazie Bank complained, Chief Justice Chase stated that the tax "very decidedly . . . discriminated" against the state banks and their notes.[248]

The *Veazie* opinion addressed whether the tax was invalid as an unapportioned direct tax, or because it violated intergovernmental immunity by impairing the banking franchise granted by the state, or because it improperly regulated rather than taxed. The opinion first observed the great breadth of the federal taxing power, but said it was subject to a "virtual" (*i.e.*, implied) limitation: "It would undoubtedly be an abuse of the power if so exercised as to impair the separate existence and independent self-government of the States. . . ."[249] This virtual limitation was another way of saying the state's sovereignty itself may preclude its being taxed.

After dispensing with the direct tax argument on the ground that Congress had considerable experience with direct taxes and had never laid an apportioned tax on anything but realty and slaves, the opinion reasoned as to the state immunity as follows:

---

[247] *See* Alonzo Barton Hepburn, A History of Currency in the United States Ch. X (1915).

[248] Veazie Bank v. Fenno, 75 U.S. 533 (1869).

[249] *Id.* at 541.

> We do not say that there may not be such a tax. It may be admitted that the reserved rights of the States, such as the right to pass laws, to give effect to laws through executive action, to administer justice through the courts, and to employ all necessary agencies for legitimate purposes of State government, are not proper subjects of the taxing power of Congress. But it cannot be admitted that franchises granted by a State are necessarily exempt from taxation; for franchises are property, often very valuable and productive property; and when not conferred for the purpose of giving effect to some reserved power of a State, seem to be as properly objects of taxation as any other property. But in the case before us, the object of taxation is not the franchise of the bank, but property created, or contracts made and issued under the franchise, or power to issue bank bills.[250]

It is crystal clear that *Veazie* meant for the Congress to be able to destroy state bank currency through taxation, for purposes of exerting its supremacy. The opinion also stated:

- If the tax is so high as to drive the banks out of the business of issuing notes, that is not an objection for the courts but the legislature (again, the political defense mechanism was early preferred to the legal one).
- In contrast, the United States exercised an implied power when it issues notes and it also had liability to stand behind the credit of national banks if they defaulted on their notes that were in effect part of the national currency.[251]
- In support of that currency Congress could inhibit and control the competing inferior currency.

The majority opinion did not mention *McCulloch v. Maryland*, which had explained why denying Maryland the right to tax the federally chartered bank did not mean that the United States could not tax state chartered banks: the explanation was based on the fact that the supremacy of the United States protected its means of carrying out its enumerated powers, a protection not enjoyed by the states.[252] The dissent mentioned *McCulloch*, but not to ask why the notes of one bank should be exempt from tax and the other not. The Constitution prevented states from making state bank notes legal tender (or from creating currency) and so state bank notes depended for their acceptability solely on the solvency of the bank.[253] Therefore state bank notes were in no sense currency authorized, backed or generated by the states. Even the dissent did not argue to the contrary; rather it argued that the heavy tax was in effect on the power of the state to charter banks (not to create currency), which power was properly reserved to the states and could not be taxed. While this may be true as a matter of economics, it

---

[250] *Id.* at 547.

[251] This was perhaps a new discovery or novel idea because the dissent stated it learned the idea from the majority.

[252] 17 U.S. at 435.

[253] Constitution, Article I, section 10, clause one ("No State shall enter into any Treaty, Alliance, or Confederation; grant Letters of Marque and Reprisal; coin Money; emit Bills of Credit; make any Thing but gold and silver Coin a Tender in Payment of Debts; . . .").

could not be accepted as a reason why the United States could not tax state chartered corporations, banks and otherwise, because it was clear that they would soon be the holders of most of the wealth of the country. Therefore, the indirect burden argument failed in this case.

However, a year later Justice Nelson, who dissented in *Veazie*, wrote the opinion of the court in *Collector v. Day*.[254] That decision brought to an end the era in which only the federal government and persons with whom it dealt were protected from taxation on account of the Supremacy Clause, and began a period of tax immunity expansion extending to 1938 that was marked by a "reciprocal rule and mutual independence."[255] At issue was the federal taxation of the salary of a state judge. *Collector v. Day* established the view that a tax on an instrumentality of a state was a tax on the exercise by the state of a power (the judicial power) reserved by the Tenth Amendment to the states. Just as the Court had ruled in 1842 in *Dobbins*[256] that states could not tax federal officers' salaries, the federal government could not tax state judges' salaries, not because the states were supreme (as the United States is supreme), but because the states are equally sovereign within their realm of sovereignty (the realm protected by the Tenth Amendment) and the federal government cannot impair that sovereignty.

Collector v. Day attempted to distinguish *Veazie* by pointing to language in that opinion that said it would not be extended to state functions more closely related to governmental functions, such as courts. Justices Nelson and Davis had dissented in *Veazie* and Justice Nelson wrote the opinion in *Day*, to which the only new Justice on the Court since *Veazie*, Justice Bradley, dissented alone. Therefore Chief Justice Chase went along with the *Day* decision as did all of the other justices still on the Court, who had been in the majority in *Veazie*. One explanation for this surprising change of heart is that *Veazie* was all about protecting the United States' preeminence in the field of currency creation and regulation, a hot issue dating back to *McCulloch*. Chief Justice Chase should have been particularly interested in that subject as the sponsor of the national banks' bill and Secretary of the Treasury. However, once that federal preeminence was established in *Veazie*, the Court evidently was content to accord the same exemption to state judges that it had accorded to a federal revenue officer in *Dobbins*. It may have helped that the state official involved was from Massachusetts and not a southern state. Also, the Civil War income tax was quickly repealed and a federal income tax did not reappear until it was adopted in 1894, which may have made the income tax immunity issue somewhat academic.[257]

Justice Bradley well forecast the future in his *Collector v. Day* dissent:

---

[254] Collector v. Day, 78 U.S. 113 (1871); *overruled by* Graves v. New York, 306 U.S. 466 (1939).

[255] Rakestraw, at 141.

[256] Dobbins v. The Commissioners of Erie, 41 U.S. 435 (1842) (the plaintiff was a captain in the federal revenue cutter service).

[257] As to Chief Justice Chase's somewhat peculiar jurisprudence, *see* G. Edward White, *Reconstructing the Constitutional Jurisprudence of Salmon P. Chase*, 21 N. Ky. L. Rev. 41 (1993) (explaining the similar change of heart in the *Legal Tender Cases*, but not discussing *Collector v. Day*).

> How can we now tell what the effect of this decision will be? I cannot but regard it as founded on a fallacy, and that it will lead to mischievous consequences. I am as much opposed as any one can be to any interference by the general government with the just powers of the State governments. But no concession of any of the just powers of the general government can easily be recalled. I, therefore, consider it my duty to at least record my dissent when such concession appears to be made. An extended discussion of the subject would answer no useful purpose.[258]

In 1938 Justice Stone commented on the motivations for *Collector v. Day* in *Gerhardt*.[259] He observed that the Court had not yet rendered its decision in the *Slaughter-House Cases*.[260] His implication was that *Slaughter-House* reflected a new found basis for reluctance of the federal government to trench on states' rights (*i.e.*, the Fourteenth Amendment did not preclude the municipal monopolization of slaughter houses in a way that was claimed to violate the then undiscovered substantive due process doctrine).[261] Instead, the most recent and relevant case on the books was *Veazie*, which had used the federal taxing power with "destructive effect" on a state instrumentality. Stone thought that *Collector v. Day* resulted from the fear that the *Veazie* approach would be applied to "the existence of states themselves."[262] In other words, judges were much more closely related to essential state governmental functions than were state chartered banks. Therefore, the Court in *Collector v. Day* was acting to contain *Veazie*.

The ensuing confusion about when a tax on a person was a tax on, or that affected, a state government, should not obscure the fundamental point that state immunity from federal taxation was implied from different sources than federal immunity based on the Supremacy Clause, as explained in *South Carolina v. Baker*, quoted in Chapter II.C.7., above. The states performed essential functions reserved to them under the Tenth Amendment to the Constitution;

---

[258] 78 U.S. at 129.

[259] Helvering v. Gerhardt, 304 U.S. 405, 415 n. 4 (1938).

[260] Slaughter-House Cases, 83 U.S. 36 (1873). Also this decision did not overrule the early holding that the Bill of Rights did not apply to the states, in Barron v. Baltimore, 32 U.S. 243 (1833). This view was restated in Hurtado v. California, 110 U.S. 516 (1884), and the selective incorporation of the Bill of Rights into the Fourteenth Amendment began only in Gitlow v. New York, 268 U.S. 652 (1925) (First Amendment incorporated).

[261] Alexander Bickel explained that *Slaughter-House* turned on "privileges and immunities" of national citizenship, which the independent butchers had argued for and lost. The argument that later succeeded was that due process and equal protection provided substantive rights against state interference. Alexander M. Bickel, *Citizenship in the American Constitution*, 15 ARIZ. L. REV. 369, 379 (1973). For the prime example of substantive due process of that era, *see* Lochner v. New York, 198 U.S. 45 (1905). *See* Ch. V.D.3.b(7).

[262] 304 U.S. at 425 n. 5. It is possible that another influence on *Collector v. Day* (although not cited in the opinion) was the decision two years earlier in Texas v. White, 74 U.S. 700 (1869) and the concerns it reflected. The Court ruled that Texas could recover state assets sold by the Confederate government that had been in control of the state during the Civil War. The opinion contained strong statements about the sovereignty of the states and supported the view known as "dual federalism" protecting the equal sovereignties of the state and federal governments in their spheres.

federal taxation of states might impair those functions; as Chief Justice Marshall had pointed out in *McCulloch v. Maryland* the power to tax involved the power to destroy; and the courts could not well police that line. Consequently, the Court adopted a fairly rigid prohibition of taxes that could economically impact the states. *Willcuts v. Bunn* explained: ". . . the exemption resting upon necessary implication in order effectively to maintain our dual system of government."[263]

However, all of the heat surrounding state immunity from federal taxation over the better part of a century provided little warmth to the states themselves, but instead usually benefitted only private persons. Justice Stone explained how little state immunity from federal taxation had to do with the well-being of the states in a dissent:

> The practical effect of enlargement is commonly to relieve individuals from a tax, at the expense of the government imposing it, without substantial benefit to the government for whose theoretical advantage the immunity is invoked. . . . This is especially the case where, as here, the sole ground of the immunity is that, although the tax is an excise collected by one government from an individual normally subject to it, the incidence of the tax may conceivably be shifted to the other government. In such a case it is not clear how a recovery by the taxpayer would benefit directly the government supposed to be burdened; and the assumption of indirect benefit in the case of a tax of this type necessarily rests upon speculation rather than reality. . . . It is significant that neither the federal nor any state government has appeared by intervention or otherwise to support this claim of immunity in cases in which the taxpayer has urged it upon us.[264]

The immunity tide turned in the late 1930s, as shown in the following chronology.

8. *Chronology of Intergovernmental Immunity Cases*

Because there are so many Supreme Court opinions on both federal and state intergovernmental immunity that came to be reversed in effect, if not explicitly, it is useful to review all of the authorities comprising the rise and fall of immunity to avoid confusion caused by a currently moot precedent.[265] The following chronological list (some entries in which have been discussed above) includes Supreme Court opinions on both state immunity from federal taxation (*date in italics*) and federal immunity from state taxation (in normal typeface). Limits on federal taxation cannot be understood without a contemporaneous review of

---

[263] Willcuts v. Bunn, 282 U.S. 216, 225 (1931).

[264] Dissent of Justice Stone in Indian Motorcycle Co. v. United States, 283 U.S. 570, 582 (1931). *See also* Henry W. Edgerton, *Incidence of Judicial Control over Congress*, 22 CORN. L. Q. 299 (1937) (explaining generally, and specifically with respect to tax cases, how little benefit accrues to states from the invalidation of federal laws on their behalf).

[265] *See also* HELLERSTEIN & HELLERSTEIN, STATE TAXATION ch. 22; Rob Gunning, *Into and Out of the Bog: The Intergovernmental Tax Immunity Doctrine*, 41 WILLAMETTE L. REV. 151 (2005).

the constitutional limits on state taxation of the United States. This list does not include the federal enclave cases.[266]

The following chronological list of major Supreme Court opinions also includes certain related important decisions on federal taxing power that did not involve intergovernmental immunity but did involve private taxpayer objections to the power to tax, usually based on Tenth Amendment reserved regulatory powers of the states.

- 1819: *McCulloch v. Maryland* initiated the intergovernmental immunity line of cases by holding that the state could not collect a tax from the Bank of the United States, deemed a federal instrument, for the "privilege" of operating in the state and of issuing bank notes, activities that the opinion treated as necessary and proper means to carry out the federal taxing and spending powers.[267]
- 1824: *Osborn v. President, Directors & Co. of Bank* reprised *McCulloch*.[268] It stated that the same protection could be enjoyed by other sorts of federal contractors, thus planting the seeds for vast expansion of the intergovernmental immunity doctrine.
- 1829 (federal debt exemption): *Weston v. Charleston* ruled that federal debt could not be taxed.[269]
- 1842 (federal salaries exempt): *Dobbins* ruled that a state could not tax the compensation of a federal revenue officer.[270]
- 1845 (United States mail): *Searight v. Stokes* ruled that state tolls could not be levied on coaches carrying mail.[271] The ruling was based in part on treating a statute ceding the Cumberland Road to Pennsylvania as a contracts with the state.

[266] *See* Ch. II.C.6.

[267] McCulloch v. Maryland, 17 U.S. 316, 425 (1819); *see* Ch. II.C.2_.

[268] Osborn v. President, Directors & Co. of Bank, 22 U.S. 738 (1824); *see* Ch. II.C.2 and 3.

[269] Weston v. Charleston, 27 U.S. 449 (1829); *see* Ch. II.C.3. *See* South Carolina v. Baker (1988), below, containing confusing reference to *Weston*.

[270] Dobbins v. The Commissioners of Erie, 41 U.S. 435, 447 (1842), *implicitly overruled*, Graves v. New York, 306 U.S. 466 (1939); *see* Ch. II.C.4 and 9.

[271] Searight v. Stokes, 44 U.S. 151 (1845).

- 1862 (exemption of federal interest codified): Congress first codified the exemption of United States debt from state taxation (property and income and otherwise).[272]
- 1863 (federal debt exemption extended to indirect tax on corporate capital): *Bank of Commerce* invalidated a New York tax for 1862 on a state bank's capital reflecting the value of investments in United States debt.[273] The Court viewed the levy as clearly a burden on the power of the United States to borrow money because it was not levied on the nominal capitalization but rather on the value of the bank property including the federal debt.
- 1864 (*McCulloch* codified as to national banks): Congress rewrote the act authorizing national banks to provide that states could tax national banks but only nondiscriminatorily on their real property, and could tax shareholders nondiscriminatorily on the value of their stock.[274] *McCulloch* had stated that such methods of state taxation of the Bank of the United States would be permissible.
- 1865 (corporate capital tax exemption for federal debt widened): The *Bank Tax Case* invalidated a New York bank capital tax that had been revised in 1863, which was based on the bank's nominal capital regardless of what it was invested in.[275] This method of taxation appeared to conform to the method implicitly blessed in the 1863 decision, but the Court disagreed. The 1865 decision rested entirely on the facts that the tax was not a tax on the franchise but on the property and that much of the bank's property was federal debt); thus the Court did not concern itself with how the valuation

[272] 12 Stat. 346 (Feb. 25, 1862); this became Revised Statutes 3701. Codification was not thought to be necessary. *See* Home Sav. Bank v. City of Des Moines, 205 U.S. 503, 513-514 (1907) ("It may well be doubted whether Congress has the power to confer upon the States the right to tax obligations of the United States. However this may be, Congress has never yet attempted to confer such a right. Until the time of the Civil War it was not thought to be necessary to express the constitutional prohibition in an act of Congress. But on the occasion of authorizing the issue of Treasury notes it was enacted that 'all stocks, bonds, and other securities of the United States held by individuals, corporations, or associations within the United States shall be exempt from taxation by or under state authority.' Act of February 25, 1862, 12 Stat. at Large, 346. The substance of this enactment is embodied in § 3701 of the Revised Statutes, and has usually, if not invariably, since 1862 been inserted in acts authorizing the issue of bonds.").

[273] New York ex rel. Bank of Commerce v. Commissioners, 67 U.S. 620 (1863) (which ruled that *Weston* could not be distinguished by the fact that there a tax was laid discriminatorily only on the debt of the United States, whereas in the latter case the tax fell on all property reflected by the capital of a corporation, which included the United States debt; the immunity was not based on discrimination but on supremacy). *See* People ex rel. Bank of Commerce v. Commissioners of Taxes, 26 N.Y. 163 (1863) (the decision reversed).

[274] Ch. 106, sec. 41, 13 Stat. 99, 112 (1864).

[275] Bank Tax Case, 69 U.S. 200 (1865). New York changed the statute held unconstitutional in *Bank of Commerce* to tax bank capital on the basis of the fixed paid in capital, rather than valuing the assets annually. Because the bank could invest its capital in United States debt, the Supreme Court again held the state tax unconstitutional.

of the capital was made, which had appeared to be the ground relied on in 1863.[276]

- 1866 (Congress may waive federal immunity): New York next levied a tax on the shareholders on their national bank stock, as permitted by the 1864 federal statute allowing nondiscriminatory taxation of the stock of national banks and their real property (as forecast in *McCulloch v. Maryland*).[277] The national bank at issue in *Van Allen* invested all of its capital in United States bonds, which allowed its shareholders to argue that the tax on the stock was a tax on the bonds. *Van Allen* held the statute that authorized nondiscriminatory state taxation of shares was constitutional, even though the value indirectly reflects the bank's investments in United States bonds; the theory was that the tax was not a tax on the capital of the bank (*i.e.*, a tax on its property), which Congress had not permitted to be taxed.[278] Nevertheless, the taxpayer won because the state tax was not also levied equally on state bank stock: the supposedly parallel tax on state banks was paid by the banks on their capital not including federal debt they held, whereas the shareholders of the national banks paid on the full value (or at least the par value) of their shares, which presumably reflected federal debt.[279] Chief

[276] This extreme application of "burden" may have been caused by the state's admission "for the sake of argument" that an indirect burden on the United States was caused by the tax. 1864 U.S. LEXIS 422, 4. Evidently the result of the decision was only to allow a recovery of the tax to the extent of the value of the United States securities held by the bank.

[277] National banks were first authorized in 1863 as an inextricable part of a new plan to provide currency in the difficult Civil War years. Ch. 58, 12 Stat. 665 (1863). The act created the comptroller of the currency, provided for the creation of national banks to be capitalized by private owners, required at least one third of the capital of the national bank to be invested in United States bonds, and then allowed the banks to pledge the bonds to obtain circulating currency notes from the comptroller, which notes would be secured by the bonds. This scheme had the multiple advantages of raising money for the United States, creating a stable circulating currency, and assuring the public that the currency was sound. Several cases addressed the existence of discrimination in comparison to taxation of state banks' stock. *See, e.g.*, Palmer v. McMahon, 133 U.S. 660 (1890).

[278] Van Allen v. Assessors, 70 U.S. 573 (1866). *See* Owensboro National Bank v. Owensboro, 173 U.S. 664, 677 (1899) (explaining the significance of Van Allen). *See also* People v. Tax Commissioners, 71 U.S. 244 (1866) (shareholder could not deduct value of exempt bonds held by bank from value of stock). The terminology of these cases is confusing because the Court used the term "capital stock" to refer to a tax on the bank measured by its capital, which might be its share par value but was viewed as a tax on property owned by the bank, as contrasted with a tax on the shares levied against the shareholders, which was permitted by the national banking act. The explanation may lie in a statement made in an unrelated opinion, Hecht v. Malley, 265 U.S. 144 (1924) (". . . in statutes relating to taxation . . . the courts will construe 'capital stock' to mean the actual property of the corporation, when necessary to carry out the intent of the statute [citing cases].").

[279] *Cf.* Bradley v. People, 71 U.S. 459 (1867) (said by the Court to be the same as *Van Allen*, and also found to discriminate, and yet the facts of the underlying opinion indicate that the taxes on the state shares paid by the state banks and on the national bank shares paid by the shareholders were computed identically; *see* 39 Ill. 130 (1866)). *See also* San Francisco National Bank v. Dodge, 197 U.S. 70 (1905) (finding discrimination where national banks were taxed on all their property except their franchises and shareholders' stock was taxed on the excess value presumed to reflect the franchises, but state banks were taxed on property value through the franchise tax and shareholders were not necessarily taxed).

Justice Salmon P. Chase, who had been Secretary of the Treasury and responsible for the national banking act creating the federal currency and the taxing rule at issue, wrote a concurrence.[280] He thought the stock could not be taxed at all because it reflected the United States bonds; in other words, he rejected as artificial the distinction between taxing shares to individual shareholders and taxing capital to the corporation. Although normally a states' rights supporter, Chase was a strong nationalist when it came to supporting his bank and bank notes.[281] In 1983 the Supreme Court ruled that Justice Chase had been correct, with the assistance of a 1959 amendment to the statutes, both as discussed below. However, Chase was not saying that Congress could not waive immunity, just that it had not done so to the extent the national banks held United States bonds. This was an odd position to take, given the fact that all national banks were largely invested in federal bonds. In 1938 Justice Stone identified *Van Allen* as the first example of the power of Congress to waive an intergovernmental immunity that the Court would otherwise enforce.[282] Of course *McCulloch v. Maryland* stated that national bank stock was not constitutionally immune from state tax, but Justice Chase's opinion said Chief Justice Marshall did not have federal bonds in mind when he said that.[283]

- 1867: *The Kansas Indians* decision ruled that the federal immunity extended to lands held in trust for Native Americans.[284]
- 1868 (corporate franchise/excise tax could be measured by federal debt, but cannot discriminate): *Coite* distinguished the bank capital tax cases (referring to a tax on the property owned by the bank) from a franchise tax imposed on the amount of deposits of a mutual bank, in part because it was a tax charged for a state granted privilege, and in part because the measure of the tax was actually the bank's debt to the depositors and not the current value of the United States securities in which the bank might have invested its deposits; in other words, because the franchise was property and it was nominally the subject of tax, the tax did not fall on the property that

---

[280] *See* Michael Les Benedict, *Salmon P. Chase and Constitutional Politics*, 22 LAW AND SOCIAL INQUIRY 459 (Spring 1997).

[281] However, Chase's opinions were inconsistent generally. For example, he wrote Hepburn v. Griswold, 75 U.S. 603 (1870), which ruled unconstitutional the Legal Tender Act, also passed under his tenure, which decision was reversed in Knox v. Lee, 79 U.S. 457 (1871) (together, the *Legal Tender Cases*).

[282] Helvering v. Gerhardt, 304 U.S. 405, 411 n. 1 (1938).

[283] 70 U.S. at 596.

[284] The Kansas Indians, 72 U.S. 737 (1867), as stated in Mont. v. Blackfeet Tribe of Indians, 471 U.S. 759 (1985).

was federal debt.[285] It is possible that the fact that the savings institution at issue was a mutual company without stock may have influenced this odd distinction. In contemporaneous decisions on similar taxes in another state the Court stated it felt bound by the decisions of the state courts that the tax was indeed a franchise and not a property tax.[286] However, see *First Agricultural National Bank* (1968), discussed below, asserting federal primacy in characterizing the incidence of a state tax for federal immunity purposes.

- 1868 (Congress can forbid state taxation of a federal instrumentality beyond the scope that the Constitution might require): The Court invalidated a state tax on United States notes (*i.e.*, currency) held by a bank, on the theory that the notes were promises to pay in coin and therefore debt of the United States (which *Weston* had ruled not taxable, though *Weston* was not cited in this opinion).[287] Justice Stone identified this case in 1938 as the earliest to stand for the proposition that Congress can extend federal immunity beyond what the Court otherwise might require.[288]
- 1869 (enforcement action for *Bank Tax Case*): New York refused to refund the taxes as ordered in the *Bank Tax Case* with respect to United States scrip issued for the purchase of goods during the Civil War. The Supreme Court ruled the scrip was protected from state taxation the same as federal bonds.[289]
- 1869 (tax on the shares of national bank could be collected from national bank): *National Bank v. Commonwealth* held that Kentucky could collect tax on shares of a national bank from the bank at a flat rate per $100 of par value, on the theory that the tax was not "on" the bank capital but "on" the

[285] Society for Savings v. Coite, 73 U.S. 594 (1868) (involving Connecticut). This case was the origin of the peculiar rule that a state can impose a franchise tax measured by the income of banks from United States securities but cannot impose an income tax on interest from federal debt. *See* Hellerstein & Hellerstein, State Taxation, ¶ 22.06[1][a]; Flint v. Stone Tracy Co., 220 U.S. 107, 164 (1911) (discussing this line of cases). That rule is not limited to banks. *See* Educational Films Corp. v. Ward, 282 U.S. 379 (1931) (even if income from federally granted copyrights owned by taxpayer was exempt as from a federal instrumentality, it could be taxed indirectly through a franchise tax on the copyright owner measured by net income).

[286] *See, e.g.*, Provident Inst. v. Mass., 73 U.S. 611 (1868) (Massachusetts levied tax on transactions and use of the franchise); Hamilton Co. v. Mass., 73 U.S. 632 (1868) (approved tax on market value of stock, less value of real estate and machinery, of nonbanking corporation because value reflected stock value in the market and not value of United States securities; also tax was franchise and not property tax); Home Ins. Co. v. New York, 119 U.S. 129 (1886) (divided court affirmed state court without opinion); New Jersey Realty Title Ins. Co. v. Division of Tax Appeals, 338 U.S. 665 (1950) (accepting state's characterization; but Justice Black dissented).

[287] Bank v. Supervisor, 74 U.S. 26 (1868). *Cf.* Veazie Bank v. Fenno, 75 U.S. 533 (1869) (The federal government may levy a tax on the notes issued by state-chartered banks.).

[288] Helvering v. Gerhardt, 304 U.S. 405, 411 n. 1 (1938).

[289] Banks v. Mayor, 74 U.S. 16 (1869). *Cf.* Smith v. Davis, 323 U.S. 111 (1944) (open account obligation not a federal debt).

shares, and only collected from the bank as a matter of convenience.[290] The opinion did not discuss whether the bank had a right of recovery against the shareholders for the amount of the tax, but later opinions indicated that was required for the tax method to be constitutional.[291]

- 1869 (railroad with federal franchise could be taxed on its real property): *Thomson v. Pacific Railroad* held the state could tax property of state chartered railroad that had a franchise and grant from the United States to build a railroad. The permission was based on (a) a distinction between impermissibly taxing the agency and permissibly taxing the means, and (b) the increasing value of entities like the railroads that were used for the mails and otherwise by the United States could not be exempted completely from state taxation because that would undermine the ability of the states to support themselves.[292] This case initiated the distinction allowing broader taxation of independent contractors.
- *1869*: *Veazie Bank v. Fenno* ruled that the United States could tax state chartered bank notes at a prohibitive rate.[293]
- 1870 (atypical finding of state nondiscrimination): *Lionberger v. Rouse* ruled that Missouri sufficiently complied with the requirement of the national banking act of 1864 when it taxed the shareholders of national banks at two percent and continued to collect tax on the capital of the two remaining

---

[290] National Bank v. Commonwealth, 76 U.S. 353 (1869). The opinion indicated that only the Bank of the United States was a completely state tax exempt bank, even though Chief Justice Chase stated in his concurrence in *Van Allen* that the national banks served a more important public function than had the Bank of the United States. The opinion made this summary statement of the law at that time: "The principle we are discussing has its limitation, a limitation growing out of the necessity on which the principle itself is founded. That limitation is, that the agencies of the Federal government are only exempted from State legislation, so far as that legislation may interfere with, or impair their efficiency in performing the functions by which they are designed to serve that government. Any other rule would convert a principle founded alone in the necessity of securing to the government of the United States the means of exercising its legitimate powers, into an unauthorized and unjustifiable invasion of the rights of the States. The salary of a Federal officer may not be taxed; he may be exempted from any personal service which interferes with the discharge of his official duties, because those exemptions are essential to enable him to perform those duties. But he is subject to all the laws of the State which affect his family or social relations, or his property, and he is liable to punishment for crime, though that punishment be imprisonment or death." 76 U.S. at 362.

[291] *See* Home Sav. Bank v. City of Des Moines, 205 U.S. 503, 518 (1907) (ruling a similar regime in Iowa applicable to state banks to be unconstitutional because there was no right of recovery).

[292] Thomson v. Pacific Railroad, 76 U.S. 579 (1869); Railroad Co. v. Peniston, 85 U.S. 5 (1873) (same). *Thomson* was the earliest case cited in *Metcalf*, which rejected exemption for an independent contractor's compensation in 1926. *See also* Baltimore Shipbuilding and Dry Dock Co. v. Baltimore, 195 U.S. 375 (1904) (taxpayer subject to tax on real estate even though taxpayer had obtained it from the United States and had to allow United States to use it as a dry dock); Susquehanna Power Co. v. State Tax Comm'n, 283 U.S. 291 (1931) (company with federal license to operate power dam was not entitled to exempt the land under the water from local taxation).

[293] Veazie Bank v. Fenno, 75 U.S. 533, 541 (1869). *See* Ch. III.E.4.

state banks at one percent, because the one percent capital tax was in lieu of all other taxes the state could collect under a contract between the state and the state banks.[294] Thus the opinion allowed the state to rely on its asserted inability to impair an obligation of contract as a limiter on absolute equality of taxing state and national banks.[295]

- *1871*: *Collector v. Day* ruled that the United States could not tax the income of a state judge.[296]
- *1873* (state's immunity extends to municipal corporations and their investment income): The Court ruled that the United States could not require a railroad to withhold an income tax from interest payable to a municipal corporation.[297]
- 1880: *People v. Weaver* ruled that the permission for states to tax national bank shares at same rate did not allow a different method of valuation.[298]
- 1882 (tax on telegraph company's messages was a tax on the federal activity): *Telegraph Co. v. Texas* ruled that because a telegraph company had become in effect an agent of the United States in sending government messages, the state could not impose a tax on messages sent.[299]
- 1883 (Justice Field tries to apply Fourteenth Amendment to protect corporations[300]): In *Santa Clara County v. So. Pac. R. Co.* federally authorized state chartered railroads claimed exemption from Santa Clara County property taxes. Although the Circuit Court, with Supreme Court Justice Field sitting as a circuit court judge, did not find the railroads to be exempt from tax as federal instrumentalities, it found another constitutional fault with the tax. It ruled that the state could not tax the franchise and property of its own corporations because the tax violated the Fourteenth Amendment's equal

---

[294] Lionberger v. Rouse, 76 U.S. 468 (1870). *Cf.* Van Allen v. Assessors, 70 U.S. 573 (1866).

[295] As to state taxes impairing the obligation of contract, *see* Jefferson Branch Bank v. Skelly, 66 U.S. 436 (1862) (state could not change system of bank tax in place when bank was chartered). Compensating tax arguments have a varied treatment in the Supreme Court. It allowed such an argument for purposes of the Privileges and Immunities Clause (Madden v. Kentucky, 309 U.S. 83 (1940)), but denies it in cases of Commerce Clause discrimination (Fulton Corp. v. Faulkner, 516 U.S. 325 (1996), implicitly overruling Darnell v. Indiana, 226 U.S. 390 (1912)).

[296] Collector v. Day, 78 U.S. 113 (1871), *overruled by* Graves v. New York, 306 U.S. 466 (1939). *See* Ch. II.C.4.

[297] United States v. R.R. Co., 84 U.S. 322 (1873).

[298] People v. Weaver, 100 U.S. 539 (1880).

[299] Telegraph Co. v. Texas, 105 U.S. 460 (1882) (the decision was also based on the view that as to messages out of state that were not sent on government business the tax was an improper regulation of commerce).

[300] Justice Field was the chief proponent of what is now called substantive due process as applied to the protection of economic interests. He dissented in the *Slaughter-House Cases* and in *Munn* (discussed in Ch. V.D.3.b(7), not because he sympathized with civil rights but because he opposed economic regulation by states as well as the federal government. He was a particular supporter of the railroads. *See* James MacGregor Burns, Packing the Court 98-99 (2009) [hereinafter Burns]; Ted Nace, Gangs of America ch. 9 "The Judge" (2003).

protection and due process guarantees. Inter alia, the tax was on real property at full value, unreduced by any mortgage, while other taxpayers were allowed to reduce the taxable value to the net amount.[301] See the Supreme Court's 1886 opinion on appeal, below.

- 1886 (corporations become "persons" under the Fourteenth Amendment): On appeal the Supreme Court affirmed Justice Field's decision in *Santa Clara County v. So. Pac. R. Co.*, but on a very different ground: because one element of the valuation of the railroad was fences, which the state statute did not authorize to be taxed, the whole tax was illegal.[302] The opinion specifically did not address the Fourteenth Amendment argument. Nevertheless, the court reporter later added to the official report the following statement: "One of the points made and discussed at length in the brief of counsel for defendants in error was that 'Corporations are persons within the meaning of the Fourteenth Amendment to the Constitution of the United States.' Before argument Mr. Chief Justice Waite said: 'The court does not wish to hear argument on the question whether the provision in the Fourteenth Amendment to the Constitution, which forbids a State to deny to any person within its jurisdiction the equal protection of the laws, applies to these corporations. We are all of opinion that it does.'"[303] This summary conclusion was, however, by no means obvious and was dictum as the Court ruled on the basis of state law.[304]

---

[301] Santa Clara County v. So. Pac. R. Co., 18 Fed. 385 (Cir. Cal. 1883).

[302] Santa Clara County v. So. Pac. R. Co., 118 U.S. 394 (1886). *See also* San Bernardino County v. So. Pac. R. Co., 118 U.S. 417 (1886) (same). However, corporations are not citizens entitled to protection of the Privileges and Immunities Clause, and states can impose license taxes or other requirements on foreign corporations. Pembina Consolidated Silver & Mining Co. v. Pennsylvania, 125 U.S. 181 (1888) (subject to interstate commerce limitations); Henneford v. Silas Mason Co., 300 U.S. 577 (1937) (property tax on property that had come to rest in state was not burden on interstate commerce).

[303] According to the official court Syllabus in the United States Reports, Santa Clara County v. Southern Pacific Railroad Company 118 U.S. 394, 396 (1886).

[304] For an in depth analysis of this amazing turn of events, see Ted Nace, Gangs of America ch. 9 (2003). Also, the winning argument is attributed to Roscoe Conkling, who argued the parallel case San Mateo County v. So. Pac. R. Co., 116 U.S. 138 (1885), as discussed in Benjamin R. Twiss, Lawyers and the Constitution: How Laissez Faire Came to the Supreme Court 61 (1942), and analyzed in ultimate depth by Howard Jay Graham in "Builded Better than They Knew" Part I, The Framers, the Railroads and the Fourteenth Amendment, 17 U. of Pitt. L. Rev. 537 (1956) (concluding the argument of Conkling about the intent of the Amendment was wrong). Justice Douglas, in dissent, later stated that *Santa Clara* was wrongly decided and should be overruled. Wheeling Steel Corp. v. Glander, 337 U.S. 562 (1949). In asking for briefing in the *San Mateo* case Justice Field had suggested to the railroad's counsel the argument it should make: "the artificial entity is composed of natural persons whose rights are protected in those of the corporation," thus ignoring the corporate form. County of San Mateo v. So. Pac. R. Co., 13 Fed. 145 (Cir. Cal. 1882). *See* John B. Sholley, *Corporate Taxpayers and Equal Protection*, 31 Ill. L. Rev. 463, 470-473 (1936) (speculating on why the Supreme Court was so mysterious about this conclusion).

- 1886 (no tax on United States' property): *Van Brocklin v. Tennessee* ruled that a state could not tax real property owned by the United States.[305] Cumulating reasons why the state could not tax the federal lands, the Court said: "But the means employed by the government of the Union are not given by the people of a particular State, but by the people of all the States; and being given by all, for the benefit of all, should be subjected to that government only which belongs to all."[306]
- 1888 (Western Union could be subject to general franchise tax): Distinguishing *Telegraph Co. v. Texas* (1882), *Western Union* ruled that a general apportioned franchise tax on value and not on telegrams sent could be collected from Western Union despite federal privileges conferred on telegraph companies.[307]
- 1888 (no tax on federal franchise granted to railroad): *California v. Central Pacific R. Co.* ruled that the state could not tax as property of a railroad the franchise granted to it by the United States to build the transcontinental railroad or other specific lines.[308]
- 1888 (no tax on telegraph company; Commerce Clause case): *Leloup v. Port of Mobile* ruled that the city could not require a local license tax to be paid by a federally authorized telegraph company because that would regulate interstate commerce.[309] Unlike the 1882 telegraph company case, this one relied entirely on the aspect of regulating interstate commerce and thus is not literally a sovereign tax immunity case.[310]
- 1890 (extension of special rule allowing state franchise taxes on state chartered corporations): In *Home Ins. Co. v. New York* Justice Field cast a protective bubble around any tax on a state chartered corporation that a state characterized as for the privilege granted by its franchise, regardless of whether the means of measurement reflected investments in United States debt.[311] But see 1959 statute below.

---

[305] Van Brocklin v. Tennessee, 117 U.S. 151 (1886). The United States had acquired this realty from delinquent taxpayers of direct taxes under the Civil War direct tax levy.

[306] 117 U.S. at 155.

[307] Western Union Tel. Co. v. Attorney Gen. of Massachusetts, 125 U.S. 530 (1888).

[308] California v. Central Pacific R. Co., 127 U.S. 1 (1888). Later opinions treated this ruling as one protecting interstate commerce and not federal property. *See, e.g.*, Seaboard A. L. R. Co. v. Daniel, 333 U.S. 118 (1948).

[309] Leloup v. Port of Mobile, 127 U.S. 640 (1888). The Court later characterized this decision as one from its early period, when states could not tax interstate commerce at all. Okla. Tax Comm'n v. Jefferson Lines, 514 U.S. 175 (1995).

[310] It cited Brown v. Maryland, 25 U.S. 419 (1827).

[311] Home Ins. Co. v. New York, 134 U.S. 594 (1890) (taxpayer wanted to reduce the value of the stock as the tax base by the percentage that the value of the U.S. debt held by the corporation bore to the entire value of the stock; argument rejected based on the absolute right of states to regulate and tax the franchises they granted to operate corporations; Justices Harlan and Miller dissented). This formalistic approach was superseded by the 1959 statute discussed below, as stated in American Bank & Trust Co. v. Dallas County, 463 U.S. 855, 863 (1983).

- *1893*: *Manhattan Co. v. Blake* upheld a federal tax on deposits in state chartered banks, including deposits by the State of New York.[312]
- *1895* (interest on state debt not taxable): The first *Pollock* opinion ruled that the 1894 income tax was unconstitutional not only because it was a direct tax on real property but also because it tried to tax interest on state bonds. The opinion stated: "As the States cannot tax the powers, the operations, or the property of the United States, nor the means which they employ to carry their powers into execution, so it has been held that the United States have no power under the Constitution to tax either the instrumentalities or the property of a State."[313] The Court has overruled *Pollock* as to this holding in 1988.[314]
- 1896 (franchise tax on state franchise): The Court ruled that a state could tax a state chartered railroad that had a franchise from both the United States and the state to operate a railroad, based on the theory that only the state franchise was taxed.[315]
- 1896 (state could tax bequest to United States): *United States v. Perkins* ruled that the state could impose an inheritance tax on a bequest to the United States because the bequest was not the property of the United States at the moment the tax liability attached.[316]
- 1899 (substance rather than form determined who owned land for tax exemption purposes): *Northern P. R. Co. v. Myers* ruled that the state could impose ad valorem tax on lands of railroads obtained from the United States even though nominal title remained in the United States.[317]
- 1899 (franchise tax on national bank): *Owensboro National Bank v. Owensboro* ruled that the city could not impose an ad valorem tax on the intangible value of a national bank because it was a tax on neither the bank stock nor on property as allowed by the 1864 Act but effectively on its national

---

[312] Manhattan Co. v. Blake, 148 U.S. 412 (1893).

[313] Pollock v. Farmers' Loan & Trust Co., 157 U.S. 429, 584-586 (1895).

[314] South Carolina v. Baker, 485 U.S. 505 (1988).

[315] Cent. Pac. R. Co. v. Cal., 162 U.S. 91 (1896); So. Pac. R. Co. v. Cal., 162 U.S. 167 (1896) (similar).

[316] United States v. Perkins, 163 U.S. 625 (1896).

[317] Northern P. R. Co. v. Myers, 172 U.S. 589 (1899). *See also* Irwin v. Wright, 258 U.S. 219 (1922) (same for taxation by a territory); Wisconsin C. R. Co. v. Price County, 133 U.S. 496 (1890) (distinguishing between lands as to which only ministerial act remained to be done to convey from the United States and lands with respect to which a more substantial decision was to be made; this opinion is also interesting in that it relied on the Constitution, Article IV, section 3, clause 2, for the immunity of the property of the United States from state property taxation).

franchise.[318] The 1926 Act discussed below allowed a state franchise tax on national banks.

- 1900 (formalistic excise tax approach applied to state inheritance tax): *Plummer v. Coler* approved a state inheritance tax measured by value of United States debt securities.[319]
- *1902* (state debt exemption extended): *Ambrosini v. United States* ruled that *Collector v. Day* meant that a federal statute exempting state bonds from a federal stamp tax should be construed to also exempt bonds issued to a state for a liquor license.[320]
- *1903* (federal estate tax approved): *Snyder v. Bettman* ruled that a federal estate tax could be imposed on a bequest to a municipality, under the same theory that allowed taxation of the stock of national banks.[321]
- *1905* (limit on state immunity begins; distinction between governmental and proprietary function applied to states, but not the United States): For the first time in the important *South Carolina v. United States* opinion the Court ruled that a state's immunity from federal taxation ". . . extended only to the 'ordinary' and 'strictly governmental' instrumentalities of state governments and not to instrumentalities 'used by the State in the carrying on of an ordinary private business.'"[322] This distinction seems to have been motivated by the fact that excise taxes on liquor provided a substantial part of the federal revenue and if states took over that business the federal excise taxes would be severely diminished (as they were anyway due to Prohibition).[323]
- 1907 (corporation could pay shareholders' stock tax if it had a right to recover from them): The Court explained the *National Bank v. Commonwealth* (1869) decision and a line of cases following it as allowing a corporation

[318] Owensboro National Bank v. Owensboro, 173 U.S. 664 (1899). *See also* Davis v. Elmira Sav. Bank, 161 U.S. 283 (1896) (Reasoning that national banks are instrumentalities of the United States, the Court ruled that preferences stated in the National Banking Act and not state law determined the distribution of the bank's assets in insolvency).

[319] Plummer v. Coler, 178 U.S. 115 (1900) (estate tax on bonds not a burden). Reversed by 1959 amendment, as stated in American Bank & Trust Co. v. Dallas County, 463 U.S. 855 (1983).

[320] Ambrosini v. United States, 187 U.S. 1 (1902) (The Court went out of its way to make this interpretation).

[321] Snyder v. Bettman, 190 U.S. 249 (1903).

[322] South Carolina v. United States, 199 U.S. 437, 451, 461 (1905) (license tax on state liquor business). *See* Rakestraw, at 146 (identifying this decision as the origin of the "doctrine of functions"). That distinction was rejected by New York v. United States, 326 U.S. 572 (1946), as stated in Garcia v. San Antonio Metro. Transit Authority, 469 U.S. 528, 543 (1985).

[323] *See* Richardson, at 421.

holding federal bonds to be taxed on its stock value when it had the right to recover the tax from the shareholders.[324]

- *1911* (franchises granted by states taxable): *Flint v. Stone Tracy Co.* ruled that the United States could tax a franchise granted by a state, including in the tax base interest received by the corporation on state bonds (because of the long standing exception for franchise taxes on corporations measured by government bond interest).[325]
- 1912: *Williams v. Talladega* ruled that a state could not impose a license tax on a federally authorized telegraph company.[326]
- *1913* (effect of Sixteenth Amendment): The Sixteenth Amendment relieved federal income taxation from apportionment but did not affect exemptions. Therefore, immunities that existed before the Sixteenth Amendment continued.[327]
- *1913* (*Pollock* codified): The first income tax statute exempted interest on state and local government debt, as have all succeeding income tax acts; income of municipalities and public utilities also was exempted.[328]
- 1916 (bonding company not an instrumentality): The Court ruled that an insurance company did not become a federal instrumentality by virtue of being certified under a federal statute as approved for issuing bonds for various governmental purposes, even when an official was bonded; and so the company was subject to a state tax on premiums.[329]

---

[324] Home Sav. Bank v. City of Des Moines, 205 U.S. 503, 518 (1907) (state bank held U.S. bonds for its customers).

[325] Flint v. Stone Tracy Co., 220 U.S. 107 (1911).

[326] Williams v. Talladega, 226 U.S. 404 (1912).

[327] *See, e.g.*, Evans v. Gore, 253 U.S. 245, 259 (1920) (judicial salaries); *overruled in part*, United States v. Hatter, 532 U.S. 557 (2001).

[328] The history of the state exemptions from federal taxation by statute up to that time is as follows. 1861 income tax: no exemption, sec. 49, ch. 45, 12 Stat. 292, 309 (1861). 1862 income tax: no exemption, sec. 90, ch. 119, 12 Stat. 432, 473 (1862). 1894 income tax: no exemption except for states, counties, and municipalities, secs. 27 and 32, ch. 349, 28 Stat. 509, 553 (1894). 1909 corporate excise tax: no exemption for state interest or for municipal corporations (though they were not for profit and thus not covered for that reason), sec. 38, ch. 6, 36 Stat. 11, 112 (1909). 1913 income tax: exemption for state interest and state employee compensation, also federal interest was exempt as were federal salaries for the President and judges to avoid reducing their salaries while in office, sec. II.B.; also state and local governmental function and public utility income was exempt under the precursor of section 115, sec. II.G., ch. 16, 38 Stat. 166, 168 (1913). 1916 income tax (same), sec. 4, ch. 463, 39 Stat. 756, 758-759 (1916).

[329] Fidelity & Deposit Co. v. Pennsylvania, 240 U.S. 319 (1916).

- *1917* (first of two statutory recognitions of *Collector v. Day*): Congress provided that state, local and federal employees' and officers' compensation was temporarily exempt from the 1917 War Excess Profits Tax.[330]
- *1918*: Congress ended the statutory exemption from federal taxation for federal interest.[331]
- 1921: The Court ruled that Congress could make Federal Land Bank bonds exempt from state tax.[332]
- 1922: *Gillespie* ruled that state could not tax lessee of Native American lands.[333]
- *1922* (another estate tax approved): *Greiner v. Lewellyn* ruled that the United States could impose an excise tax (the estate tax) on municipal bonds.[334]
- 1923 (Federal Land Bank instrumentality): The Court ruled that a mortgage given to a Federal Land Bank that was denominated an instrumentality of the United States by federal statute was not subject to a state recordation tax.[335]
- 1923 (war production corporation was a federal instrumentality): *Clallam County v. United States* ruled that a state could not tax a state corporation organized under the direction of a federal statute and whose stock was owned by the United States for the purpose of war production; the corporation clearly was a federal instrumentality.[336]
- *1926* (another important limit on state immunity; state independent contractor taxed): *Metcalf & Eddy v. Mitchell* arose under the 1917 Revenue Act and was a "pivotal decision" allowing the United States to tax the income of an independent contractor of the state.[337] The Court relied on it in 1937

[330] 40 Stat. 300, 303, ch. 63, sec. 201(a) (1917). This exemption continued by official position of the IRS until it was codified retroactively in 1924, through the 1924 year. *See* George T. Altman, *Tax Exemption of Compensation Received from States*, 8 TAX MAG. 18 (1930) [hereinafter Altman] (history of exemption).

[331] 1918 income tax: exempted state and federal interest and specifically taxed the President and federal judges, but limited exemption for federal interest after 1917 to bonds whose issuing authority required exemption; exempted state and local public utility income, sec. 213, ch. 18, 40 Stat. 1057, 1065 (1918); 1921 income tax (same as 1918), sec. 213, ch. 136, 42 Stat. 227, 237; 1924 income tax (same as 1921, with expanded definition of public utilities), ch. 234, sec. 213, 43 Stat. 253 (1924).

[332] Smith v. Kansas City Title & Trust Co., 255 U.S. 180 (1921).

[333] Gillespie v. Oklahoma, 257 U.S. 501 (1922), *overruled by* Oklahoma Tax Comm'n v. Texas Co., 336 U.S. 342 (1949).

[334] Greiner v. Lewellyn, 258 U.S. 384 (1922).

[335] Federal Land Bank v. Crosland, 261 U.S. 374 (1923).

[336] Clallam County v. United States, 263 U.S. 341 (1923).

[337] Metcalf & Eddy v. Mitchell, 269 U.S. 514 (1926) (salaries of consulting engineers employed by city).

in the important *James v. Dravo* opinion.[338] The *Metcalf* decision was pivotal because it broke apart the treatment of "instrumentalities" and United States debt from the taxation of independent contractors. The Court seemed concerned that only private parties were benefiting from the tax immunity. However, its effort to distinguish a judge's salary (*Collector v. Day*) from the contractor's compensation was unconvincing. It was forecast by earlier cases allowing taxation of federally chartered railroads.[339]

- *1926* (second statutory exemption for state salaries): The Court issued the *Metcalf* decision on January 11, 1926 and six weeks later Congress enacted the second and last specific exemption of employees and officers of states and political subdivisions from the normal income tax.[340] This provision was not re-enacted but thereafter the Treasury issued regulations (Treasury Regulation 74, Article 643) under the exemption for income from the exercise of governmental functions exempting the incomes of state and local employees and officers.[341]
- 1926 (federal statute allowed broader state taxation of national banks): Congress allowed states to tax national banks in one of four ways: (1) on their shares, (2) on dividends paid to the shareholders as income, (3) on their own net income, or (4) "measured by" their net income (referring to a franchise tax).[342]
- 1927 (de facto discrimination): In *Miller v. Milwaukee* Justice Holmes ruled unconstitutional a state income tax that generally did not tax dividends except to the extent they reflected untaxed income of the corporations, which

---

[338] James v. Dravo Contracting Co., 302 U.S. 134, 160 (1937) (the fact that a tax on a government contractor "may increase the cost to the Government . . . would not invalidate the tax"); *id.* at 156-157 ("pivotal decision . . . . While the *Metcalf* case was one of a federal tax, the reasoning and the practical criterion it adopts are clearly applicable to the case of a state tax upon earnings under a contract with the Federal Government."). *See* Ch. II.C.9.

[339] *E.g.*, Thomson v. Pacific Railroad, 76 U.S. 579 (1869).

[340] Section 1211, Revenue Act of 1926, ch. 27, 44 Stat. 9 (Feb. 26, 1926) (the section ordered abatement and refund of all such taxes for 1924 and prior years). *See also* 1928 Revenue Act (same as 1926 as to government interest; specific reference to the President and judges eliminated and exemption of public utilities moved to section 116; abatement for state and local salaries eliminated and exemption for income of states, municipalities and political subdivisions added), ch. 852, sec. 22, 45 Stat. 791 (1928); 1932 income tax (same as 1928 except specific reference to the President and federal judges reinstated), ch. 209, sec. 22, 47 Stat. 169; 1934 income tax (same interest exemptions, same state and local income exemptions and same public utility exemptions) secs. 22 and 116, ch. 277, 48 Stat. 680 (1934); 1936 income tax (same) secs. 22 and 116, ch. 690, 49 Stat. 1648 (1936).

[341] *See* Altman, at 19 (quoting Regulations 74, Article 643); John Reid Jr. v. Commissioner, 28 B.T.A. 1217 (1933) (the regulation is based not on the statute but on the Constitution); Sappington v. Commissioner, 25 B.T.A. 1385 (1932) (regulation based on section 116(d) of the 1928 Revenue Act).

[342] Ch. 88, 44 Stat. 223 (1926), codified as 12 U.S.C. § 548. This permission to tax shares of national banks even included such shares held by the federal Reconstruction Finance Corporation. Baltimore National Bank v. State Tax Comm'n, 297 U.S. 209 (1936).

meant that dividends were taxed to the extent the corporation did not pay state tax on its federal bond interest.[343]

- 1928: *Long v. Rockwood* invalidated a state tax on royalties received under a patent granted by the United States Patent Office (Justices Holmes, Brandeis, Sutherland and Stone dissenting).[344] The dissents beginning in this decision were to continue and culminate ten years later in a reversal of the long expansion of intergovernmental immunity.
- 1928 (indirect purchase by United States): *Panhandle Oil Co. v. Mississippi* invalidated a state sales tax on gasoline purchased for United States Coast Guard vessels.[345] This is the case in which Justice Holmes' dissent stated that the taxing power is not a destructive power as long as the Supreme Court sits.
- *1928* (state interest exempt from income tax): *National Life Ins.* held that the United States could not define an insurance company's income (as contrasted with excise) tax base in a way that gave no benefit to the exclusion of interest and state, local and United States bonds (Justices Stone, Holmes and Brandeis dissenting).[346]
- *1930*: The Court ruled that the United States could impose a tax on the transportation of goods purchased by a municipality, where the tax was found to fall on the shipper.[347]
- *1931* (market discount is not protected interest): *Willcuts v. Bunn* ruled that the United States could tax capital gain on sale of municipal bonds.[348]
- *1931* (federal sales tax could not be levied on city): The Court ruled that the United States could not impose a sales tax on sales to a city found to fall on the city.[349]

---

[343] Miller v. Milwaukee, 272 U.S. 713 (1927). *See also* Schuylkill Trust Co. v. Pennsylvania, 296 U.S. 113 (1935) (similar embedded discrimination); Macallen Co. v. Mass., 279 U.S. 620 (1929) (state franchise tax on income measured in part by federal bond interest was unconstitutional). The government's amicus brief in *James v. Dravo* made this statement about such opinions: ". . . if the tax while apparently harmless on its face is de facto discriminatory the courts may still protect against its operation."). 1937 WL 63782. Justice Stone thought later opinions effectively overruled *Macallen*. A.T. Mason, Harlan Fiske Stone 307-310 (1956).

[344] Long v. Rockwood, 277 U.S. 142 (1928), *overruled by* Fox Film Corp. v. Doyal, 286 U.S. 123 (1932).

[345] Panhandle Oil Co. v. Mississippi, 277 U.S. 218 (1928); *overruled by* Alabama v. King & Boozer, 314 U.S. 1 (1941) (overruled to extent it holds that a state tax is unconstitutional if it economically impacts the United States).

[346] National Life Ins. Co. v. United States, 277 U.S. 508 (1928) (the decision presumably relied on the constitutional exemption of state interest ruled in *Pollock*, but *Pollock* was not cited).

[347] Wheeler Lumber Bridge and Supply Co. v. United States, 281 U.S. 572 (1930).

[348] Willcuts v. Bunn, 282 U.S. 216 (1931).

[349] Indian Motorcycle Co. v. United States, 283 U.S. 570 (1931).

- *1931* (oil lessees taxable; turning point): *Group No. 1 Oil Co. v. Bass* ruled that the United States could tax a lessee of the State of Texas on oil profits from leased oil lands; the same rule would apply to a lease granted by the United States.[350] The Court later pointed to the *Bass* decision as a "turning point" in lessee tax liability.[351]Actually it may have been the first lessee case, but that issue had been confused by earlier opinions exempting oil profits from leases on Native American lands, as discussed in the opinion and below in Chapter II.C.10.
- 1931 (property tax on independent mail carrier allowed): *Alward v. Johnson* ruled that the state could tax an independent contractor mail carrier on gross revenues earned from the United States for carrying the mail; the tax was viewed as a property tax, and so the decision did not exactly overlap with the later *James v. Dravo* case, discussed below.[352]
- *1931* (cost of carrying state bonds not deductible): *Denman v. Slayton* upheld the denial of an interest deduction with respect to debt incurred to buy exempt state bonds.[353] This decision refused to extend the 1928 ruling in *National Life Ins.*, above.
- 1932: *Fox Film Corp. v. Doyal* overruled *Long v. Rockwood* (1928) denying a state's right to tax patent royalties.[354]
- *1932*: *Burnet v. Coronado Oil & Gas Co.* ruled the United States could not tax the production of an oil lease obtained from a state.[355] It was overruled by *Helvering v. Mountain Producers Corp.*[356]
- 1932: *Pacific Co. v. Johnson* ruled that a state chartered bank can be taxed by the state through a nondiscriminatory franchise tax based on net income, which reflected federal bond interest.[357] This ruling was not affected by 1959 act discussed below.
- 1933 (indirect property tax allowed): The Court approved a state ad valorem tax on oil extracted from Native American lands, being stored after extraction; any burden on the United States was said to be indirect.[358]

---

[350] Group No. 1 Oil Co. v. Bass, 283 U.S. 279 (1931) (ruling based on fact that all of the oil was sold rather than a fractional interest in oil in place). But lessees continued to claim they were state instrumentalities, and continued to lose. *See* Burnet v. A.T. Jergins Trust, 288 U.S. 508 (1933); Helvering v. Bankline Oil Co., 303 U.S. 362 (1938).

[351] Oklahoma Tax Comm'n v. Texas Co., 336 U.S. 342, 358 (1949).

[352] Alward v. Johnson, 282 U.S. 509 (1931).

[353] Denman v. Slayton, 282 U.S. 514 (1931).

[354] Fox Film Corp. v. Doyal, 286 U.S. 123 (1932).

[355] Burnet v. Coronado Oil & Gas Co., 285 U.S. 393 (1932). *See also* Gillespie v. Oklahoma, 257 U.S. 501 (1922) (federal immunity).

[356] Helvering v. Mountain Producers Corp., 303 U.S. 376 (1938).

[357] Pacific Co. v. Johnson, 285 U.S. 480 (1932).

[358] Indian Territory Illuminating Oil Co. v. Bd., 288 U.S. 326 (1933).

- *1933*: The Court ruled that a state university was not immune from customs duties on imports; importation is not a function of state government immune from federal power.[359]
- 1934 (approved tax on independent contractor that dealt with government): *Trinityfarm Construction Co. v. Grosjean* ruled that the state could impose an excise tax on gasoline used by an independent contractor of the United States because the impact on the United States was only remote.[360]
- 1936 (tax on sales to United States invalid): *Graves v. Texas Co.* invalidated a state tax in the nature of a nondiscriminatory sales tax on the withdrawal of fuel from storage, to the extent it was withdrawn for sale to the United States under a contract that made the seller bear the tax; the tax was viewed as levied on the United States or for dealing with the United States, even though it was not a tax limited to sellers to the United States.[361] The decision was overruled in 1941.[362]
- *1937*: *Liggett & Myers Tobacco Co. v. United States* ruled that the federal excise tax on tobacco manufacturing could be collected in effect from a state that purchased tobacco products.[363]
- 1937 (*Dobbins* applied): *New York ex rel. Rogers v. Graves* ruled that an employee of a federal instrumentality was exempt from state income tax.[364]
- 1937 (beginning of change): In a case not involving intergovernmental immunity but rather a state's power to tax income of residents received from out of state sources, *New York ex rel. Cohn v. Graves*, Justice Stone explained that the source of income, which source might be beyond the state's taxing power (such as a government's income), did not determine the state's ability to tax the income received from that source by residents.[365] This opinion justified breaking the linkage between source and income taxation by distinguishing *Pollock*,[366] which it said did not literally hold that a tax on income was a tax on its source, but rather that "there were similarities in the operation of the two kinds of tax which made it appropriate to classify

[359] Bd. of Trustees v. United States, 289 U.S. 48 (1933).
[360] Trinityfarm Construction Co. v. Grosjean, 291 U.S. 466 (1934).
[361] Graves v. Texas Co., 298 U.S. 393 (1936). Justices Brandeis and Cardozo dissented and Justice Stone did not participate.
[362] Alabama v. King & Boozer, 314 U.S. 1 (1941).
[363] Liggett & Myers Tobacco Co. v. United States, 299 U.S. 383 (1937).
[364] New York ex rel. Rogers v. Graves, 299 U.S. 401 (1937) (opinion by Justice Sutherland; the attempted New York tax was on the salary of the general counsel of the Panama Railroad Co., wholly owned by the United States; the opinion did not even analyze the issue, relying on *Dobbins* and the mirror state tax immunity); *overruled by* Graves v. New York, 306 U.S. 466 (1939). However, the opinion's determination that the Panama Railroad itself was a federal instrumentality was not overruled by the 1939 opinion.
[365] New York ex rel. Cohn v. Graves, 300 U.S. 308 (1937). *See* Ch. II.C.4.
[366] Pollock v. Farmers' Loan & Trust Co., 157 U.S. 429 (1895), *confirmed and expanded*, 158 U.S. 601 (1895).

both as direct, ..."[367] Having thus removed one substance over form technique of looking to the source to classify a tax, Justice Stone moved on in a later opinion that did involve intergovernmental immunity to eliminate the second substance over form argument: that the economic burden of the tax on the individual actually fell on the state and interfered with its sovereign powers.[368]

- *1937* (the last state compensation exemption ruling): *Brush v. Commissioner* invalidated a federal income tax on the salary of an engineer employed in a municipal water plant.[369] Justices Stone and Cardozo concurred, stating that the decision should have been grounded on Treasury Regulation 74, Article 643 rather than the Constitution. The opinion did not question the exemption of the employee's salary but rather investigated whether the water utility was such an instrumentality whose employees' salaries should be exempt from federal taxation. *Garcia* in 1985 identified *Brush* as the decision that turned away from the distinction between governmental and proprietary activities of a state or municipality, although that is not so evident from the *Brush* opinion.[370]
- 1937 (Federal firearms tax upheld): *Sonzinsky v. United States* is not an immunity case, but a Tenth Amendment case.[371] It is a very broad assertion of federal regulatory power that produced "some revenue," and so the Court viewed the tax as a tax and not as a regulation. See Chapter III.F for the 1937 reversal of limits on federal regulation by taxation.
- 1937 (Beginning of major limitation of immunities; *Dobbins* turned back as to federal contractor): In *James v. Dravo* Chief Justice Hughes approved a state tax on the gross receipts of a general contractor for work done for the United States on a dam.[372] The United States weighed in as amicus curiae because the Court ordered reargument and asked for the federal government's view.[373] The United States sided with the state. The opinion characterized the issue as whether the tax laid a "direct burden" on the United States. The distinction rested on characterizing the contractor as an independent contractor and not an instrumentality; it also adopted a sliding scale that ignored indirect and insignificant impact on the United States of

---

[367] 300 U.S. at 315.

[368] Graves v. New York, 306 U.S. 466 (1939).

[369] Brush v. Commissioner, 300 U.S. 352 (1937); *implicitly overruled by* Helvering v. Gerhardt, 304 U.S. 405 (1938).

[370] Garcia v. San Antonio Metro. Transit Authority, 469 U.S. 528, 541 (1985), *discussed in* Ch. III.F.3.

[371] Sonzinsky v. United States, 300 U.S. 506, 513 (1937); United States v. Miller, 307 U.S. 174 (1939) (similar to *Sonzinsky*).

[372] James v. Dravo Contracting Co., 302 U.S. 134, 160 (1937) (the fact that a tax on a Government contractor "may increase the cost to the Government . . . would not invalidate the tax"). *See also* Superior Bath House Co. v. McCarroll, 312 U.S. 176 (1941) (1891 statute had authorized state taxation of contractor on the reservation).

[373] *See* Brief of United States, 1937 WL 63782.

the tax, and distinguished the more rigid line of cases finding burdens on the federal borrowing power of indirect taxes on United States debt. The opinion expanded on the more well established power of states to tax the property of a government contractor (after all, *McCulloch v. Maryland* said the real property of the Bank of the United States could be taxed), to find that a tax on the income paid by the United States was not likely to impose any heavier a burden on the United States. Thus *James v. Dravo* embraced the moderation that Justice Holmes had counseled in 1928. Because of the pivotal role of this decision, it is discussed in more detail at Chapter II.C.9, at the end of this chronology.

- *January 7, 1938*: The Treasury Regulations were changed to limit the exemption of compensation of employees and officers of states and their instrumentalities to the extent the Constitution required immunity.[374]
- *1938*: *Helvering v. Therrell* ruled that fees paid to bankruptcy lawyers from the bankrupt estate were taxable.[375]
- *1938* (income from state government lease taxable): *Mountain Producers Corp.* overruled *Gillespie* (1922) (federal immunity) and its line of cases dating to 1914, and also *Coronado Oil* (state immunity), on the grounds that a tax on income from property leased from the state was not a direct tax on the state; the lessee was not a government instrumentality.[376] In 1939 in *Graves* Justice Stone cited *Mountain* as starting a reexamination of the immunity rules that led to *Gerhardt*, the precursor of the *Graves* decision on federal immunity in a case of state employee immunity.[377]
- *1938* (reversal of state immunity begun): *Helvering v. Gerhardt* upheld federal taxation of employees of the New York Port Authority, based literally on the fact that the Port Authority was a corporation owned by the state and not a state or a state instrumentality.[378] The opinion recognized that the taxation of the judge addressed in *Collector v. Day* might be distinguishable, but that was not this case. Thus *Gerhardt* did not wholly overturn *Collector*

---

[374] *See* Helvering v. Gerhardt, 304 U.S. 405, 423 (1938) ("Compensation received for services rendered to a State is to be included in gross income unless the person receives such compensation from the State as an officer or employee thereof and such compensation is immune from taxation under the Constitution of the United States.").

[375] Helvering v. Therrell, 303 U.S. 218 (1938) (state employee was paid by state and then state was reimbursed by bankrupt estate).

[376] Helvering v. Mountain Producers Corp., 303 U.S. 376 (1938). *See* Burnet v. Coronado Oil & Gas Co., 285 U.S. 393 (1932).

[377] Graves v. New York ex rel. O'Keefe, 306 U.S. 466, 483 (1939), *citing* Helvering v. Gerhardt, 304 U.S. 405 (1938).

[378] Helvering v. Gerhardt, 304 U.S. 405 (1938). As to whether the Supreme Court later changed its mind on the status of the Port Authority, *see* Mineo v. Port Authority of New York and New Jersey, 770 F. 2d 939, 948 n. 16 (3d Cir. 1985). *See also* Sims v. United States, 359 U.S. 108 (1959) (relying on *Gerhardt* for the principle that state salaries could be levied on for federal taxes and that states were "persons" under the code and could be made to cooperate with the federal levy).

v. Day; that occurred in *Graves* (1939). The *Gerhardt* decision was viewed as the impetus for the Public Salary Tax Act of 1939, allowing nondiscriminatory state taxation of federal officers and employees.[379] Justice Stone stated that the 1937 *Brush* opinion had not considered the constitutional issue. *Gerhardt* ended any view of reciprocity in state-federal immunity, by clearly distinguishing the supremacy grounds for federal immunity from the support for state tax immunity.[380] The opinion set out a full rehearsal of the state immunity that *Collector v. Day* had found implied in the Constitution and explained it solely on the "power to destroy" threat against the sovereignty of the states: "The immunity which it implied was sustained only because it was one deemed necessary to protect the states from destruction by the federal taxation of those governmental functions which they were exercising when the Constitution was adopted and which were essential to their continued existence."[381] Finally, it attempted to describe the two guiding principles on which state immunity was warranted: "The one . . . excludes from the immunity activities thought not to be essential to the preservation of state governments even though the tax be collected from the state treasury . . . . The other principle, exemplified by those cases where the tax laid upon individuals affects the state only as the burden is passed on to it by the taxpayer, forbids recognition of the immunity when the burden on the state is so speculative and uncertain that if allowed it would restrict the federal taxing power without affording any corresponding tangible protection to the state government; even though the function be thought important enough to demand immunity from a tax upon the state itself, it is not necessarily protected from a tax which well may be substantially or entirely absorbed by private persons."[382] Therefore nondiscriminatory tax on a state agency employee was upheld.

- *1938* (State liable for excise tax on university football game tickets): *Allen v. Regents* applied a federal excise tax to a state sale, citing both the nondiscriminatory nature of the tax and *South Carolina v. United States*, which allowed federal taxation of non-essential state functions (while public education is essential, the football games were not).[383]

---

[379] *See* Davis v. Michigan, 489 U.S. 803, 811 (1989) (noting that the Act was moving through Congress before *Graves* was finally decided).

[380] *See* Rakestraw, at 151-152.

[381] 304 U.S. at 414.

[382] *Id.* at 419-420. The examples of the non-essential state functions that could be taxed were a liquor business, in South Carolina v. United States, 199 U.S. 437 (1905) and Ohio v. Helvering, 292 U.S. 360 (1934); and a railroad, in Helvering v. Powers, 293 U.S. 214 (1934) (Boston Elevated Railway Co. taken over by the state). The examples of the indirect effect on the state through tax paid by private persons were Metcalf & Eddy v. Mitchell, 269 U.S. 514 (1926) and Willcuts v. Bunn, 282 U.S. 216 (1931).

[383] Allen v. Regents, 304 U.S. 439 (1938). This case was decided the same day as *Gerhardt. Garcia* indicated that this was an example of the superseded approach of trying to separate proprietary from governmental activities. Garcia v. San Antonio Metro. Transit Authority, 469 U.S. 528, 542 n. 7 (1985).

- 1939 (*Dobbins* effectively overruled): *Graves* overruled the federal employee salary immunity from state tax cases.[384] The Court announced: "The theory . . . that a tax on income is legally or economically a tax on its source, is no longer tenable."[385] The opinion went on to say: "So much of the burden of a non-discriminatory general tax upon the incomes of employees of a government, state or national, as may be passed on economically to that government, through the effect of the tax on the price level of labor or materials, is but the normal incident of the organization within the same territory of two governments, each possessing the taxing power. The burden, so far as it can be said to exist or to affect the government in any indirect or incidental way, is one which the Constitution presupposes . . . ."[386] Justice Stone essentially said that the extension of immunity to salaries was a mistake caused by erroneous assumptions. The only economic rationale for the exemption of state salaries, that states might obtain services cheaper without federal taxation, was deemed an inadequate and constitutionally insufficient reason for insulating private persons from taxation. Even though *James v. Dravo* might seem to have resolved the issue, this opinion viewed *James* as deciding only that sourcing of the income to a sovereign could not be used to prove the income tax was on the sovereign; this opinion went on to dismiss searches for economic burden on the sovereign.[387] Justice Jackson identified this case as the one that reflected a decision at the highest levels of the federal government to let the states have these taxes.[388]
- 1939 (*Graves* codified): The Public Salary Tax Act of 1939, 4 U.S.C. § 111, consented to taxation of compensation of federal employees.[389]
- *1941*: In a decision not involving taxation, *Darby* upheld federal regulation of worker wages and hours, effectively limiting *Carter v. Carter Coal* and overruling *Hammer v. Dagenhart*.[390] There may have been a linkage between

---

[384] Graves v. New York ex rel. O'Keefe, 306 U.S. 466 (1939) (taxpayer was employee of Federal Home Owners Loan Corp., thus the tax was two steps removed from being a tax on the United States). *See also* United States v. County of Fresno, 429 U.S. 452, 460 (1977) (stating that *Graves* had overruled *Dobbins*). See 4 U.S.C. § 111 by which the United States consents to nondiscriminatory taxation of officers and employees of the United States, its agencies or instrumentalities, by duly authorized taxing jurisdictions. Violation of this section led to the landmark case Davis v. Michigan, 489 U.S. 803 (1989), which led to refunds of taxes paid by federal retirees on pensions that states taxed though they exempted pensions of their own retirees. *See* Hellerstein & Hellerstein, State Taxation ¶ 22.04[3]; Helvering v. Gerhardt, 304 U.S. 405 (1938) (the parallel state immunity case; although both opinions pointed out the lack of complete parity).

[385] 306 U.S. 480.

[386] *Id.* at 487.

[387] *Id.* at 481.

[388] Robert H. Jackson, The Struggle for Judicial Supremacy 241-244 (1941) (the state viewed the United States intervention and brief as a "gift from the Greeks.").

[389] *See* Jefferson County v. Acker, 527 U.S. 423 (1999) (applied act to county occupational tax on federal judge; this opinion also recognized the linkage between *Graves* and the Act).

[390] United States v. Darby, 312 U.S. 100 (1941). *See* Ch. III.E and F.3.

the Court's attitude toward federal taxation and federal regulation, as suggested also by *Penn Dairies, Inc. v. Milk Control Comm'n*, discussed below.

- 1941 (nondiscriminatory tax on private party never unconstitutional): *Alabama v. King & Boozer* upheld a state sales tax imposed on purchases made by a federal government (independent) contractor even though the financial burden of the tax was entirely passed on, through a cost-plus contract, to the federal government.[391] As usual, the objecting taxpayer was a private party, and in this case the United States sided with Alabama; the opinion noted that Congress could, if it wished, extend federal immunity to the contractor by legislation.[392] "*King & Boozer* thus completely foreclosed any claim that the nondiscriminatory imposition of costs on private entities that pass them on to States or the Federal Government unconstitutionally burdens state or federal functions."[393]
- 1941: *Federal Land Bank v. Bismark Lumber Co.* ruled that Federal Land Banks are exempt from state sales taxation, both by statute and constitutionally.[394] This opinion also made the point that the incidence of a state sales tax was determined by the state law, and here the state law imposed the sales tax on the buyer, which was the Land Bank.[395]
- 1943: In a decision addressing a state regulation of a federal agency, *Penn Dairies, Inc. v. Milk Control Comm'n*, the Court said: "The trend of our decisions is not to extend governmental immunity from state taxation and regulation beyond the national government itself and governmental functions performed by its officers and agents."[396]

---

[391] Alabama v. King & Boozer, 314 U.S. 1, 8-9 (1941) ("The Government, rightly we think, disclaims any contention that the Constitution, unaided by congressional legislation, prohibits a tax exacted from the contractors merely because it is passed on economically, by the terms of the contract or otherwise, as part of the construction cost to the Government. So far as such a nondiscriminatory state tax upon the contractor enters into the cost of the materials to the Government, that is but a normal incident of the organization within the same territory of two independent taxing sovereignties. The asserted right of the one to be free of taxation by the other does not spell immunity from paying the added costs, attributable to the taxation of those who furnish supplies to the Government and who have been granted no tax immunity. So far as a different view has prevailed, we think it no longer tenable." (citations omitted)). *See also* Curry v. United States, 314 U.S. 14 (1941) (similar cost plus contract).

[392] 314 U.S. at 8-9.

[393] South Carolina v. Baker, 485 U.S. 505, 521 (1988).

[394] Federal Land Bank v. Bismark Lumber Co., 314 U.S. 95 (1941).

[395] *But see* First Agricultural National Bank v. State Tax Comm'n, 392 U.S. 339 (1968), discussed below.

[396] Penn Dairies, Inc. v. Milk Control Comm'n, 318 U.S. 261, 270 (1943) (approved a state price control on a U.S. government contractor); *distinguished by* Public Utilities Comm'n of California v. United States, 355 U.S. 534 (1958) (because the price control fell on the United States as buyer, but did not conflict with a federal price policy). *Cf.* Mayo v. United States, 319 U.S. 441 (1943) (state inspection fee could not be imposed directly on United States; *see* Ch. II.C.4.

- 1944 (tax "on" federal property still forbidden): *United States v. County of Allegheny* invalidated a state property tax on machinery the United States "leased" to a munitions manufacturer for $1 a year under a contract that passed any tax through to the United States.[397] The opinion did not depend on the indirect impact of the tax on the United States but rather on the fact that the machinery was owned by the United States, the machinery itself was taxed, and the nominal taxpayer was in the capacity of a bailee of the property of the United States, like any government agency. This case, however, appears to have been an outlier and later cases found many ways to distinguish it.[398]
- *1945* (broad statement of irrelevance of Tenth Amendment to federal taxation): A decision not involving governmental immunity, *Fernandez v. Wiener*, upheld an estate tax on the termination of a marital property interest against a Tenth Amendment objection that evidently was based on the right of the state to control the passage of title. The opinion broadly precludes the Tenth Amendment from controlling federal taxation, but failed to note the obvious exception for a tax on the state itself.[399]
- 1945: *Cleveland v. United States* ruled that a municipality could not require the Federal Housing Authority to pay property tax on low income housing.[400] The decision rested on an exemption in a federal statute.

---

[397] United States v. County of Allegheny, 322 U.S. 174 (1944); *distinguished by* United States v. City of Detroit, 355 U.S. 466 (1958) (on grounds that in *Allegheny* the tax was not on the use of the property by the bailee but on the ownership of the property by the United States).

[398] *See, e.g.*, RFC v. Beaver County, 328 U.S. 204 (1946) (construed federal statute to treat machinery provided to a contractor in similar situation subject to real property taxes); Esso Standard Oil v. Evans, 345 U.S. 495 (1953) (use tax paid by government contractor on value of oil owned by and stored for the United States was not a tax "on" government property and was allowed). *See also* United States v. County of Fresno, 429 U.S. 452, 464 n. 10 (1977) (stating that *Allegheny* has no application where the private persons are taxed only on their interest in the government property).

[399] Fernandez v. Wiener, 326 U.S. 340, 361-362 (1945) (estate tax) ("The Tenth Amendment does not operate as a limitation upon the powers, express or implied, delegated to the national government. United States v. Darby, 312 U.S. 100, 123-4. The amendment has clearly placed no restriction upon the power delegated to the national government to lay an excise tax qua tax. Undoubtedly every tax which lays its burden on some and not others may have an incidental regulatory effect. But since that is an inseparable concomitant of the power to tax, the incidental regulatory effect of the tax is embraced within the power to lay it. It has long been settled that an Act of Congress, which on its face purports to be an exercise of the taxing power, is not any the less so because the tax is burdensome or tends to restrict or suppress the thing taxed. In such a case it is not within the province of courts to inquire into the unexpressed purposes or motives, which may have moved Congress to exercise a power constitutionally conferred upon it. Sonzinsky v. United States, 300 U.S. 506, 513-514, and cases cited."). As to the Tenth Amendment, *see* Ch. III.F.3.

[400] Cleveland v. United States, 323 U.S. 329 (1945).

- 1946 (timber severance tax allowed): *Wilson v. Cook* approved a state severance tax on timber cutting on United States lands even though the tax appeared to be a lien on the United States.[401]
- 1946 (tax not on government property when title held only for security): *S. R. A., Inc. v. Minnesota* approved a state tax on land equitably sold to the taxpayer but for which the United States retained legal title as security.[402]
- *1946* (discards "proprietary" versus "governmental" distinction for purposes of federal taxation of state activity): *New York v. United States* upheld federal taxation of a state water business but purported to discard the categories used in *South Carolina v. United States*.[403] However, the opinion substituted for it a requirement that the tax be "exacted equally from private persons upon the same subject matter."[404] Also the opinion stated that the state and federal immunities were not "correlative."[405] The multiple opinions in concurrence are frequently cited as evidencing lack of any coherent theory other than nondiscrimination and some core governmental functions that cannot be taxed even on a nondiscriminatory basis.[406] The Frankfurter opinion, in which only one other Justice joined, indicated that only things like the State House would escape nondiscriminatory federal taxation; beyond that the states' protection was said to lie in politics and the Court could not resolve the issues, much as it could not enforce the requirement of a republican form of government.[407]
- *1949*: *Wilmette Park Dist. v. Campbell* ruled that a federal admissions tax could apply to tickets sold to a municipal beach; the tax was nondiscriminatory.[408]
- 1954 (sales tax "on" sale to government forbidden): *Kern-Limerick, Inc. v. Scurlock* struck down a state sales tax on machinery purchased by a contractor for use on a federal project because the contract between the contractor and the United States stated that all such machinery would be acquired by and for the United States.[409] The opinion stated that while the state could determine from whom it would collect a tax, the federal courts would de-

---

[401] Wilson v. Cook, 327 U.S. 474 (1946) (actually refused to entertain the lien issue as raised too late).

[402] S. R. A., Inc. v. Minnesota, 327 U.S. 558 (1946).

[403] New York v. United States, 326 U.S. 572 (1946) (sale of mineral water). *See* Garcia v. San Antonio Metro. Transit Authority, 469 U.S. 528 (1985) (confirming that the *New York* opinion shifted from the proprietorship rationale to the nondiscrimination rationale); Massachusetts v. United States, 435 U.S. 444, 457 (1978).

[404] 326 U.S. at 583. South Carolina v. Baker, 485 U.S. 505, 523 n. 14 (1988) observed that the prior test was rejected by all eight justices, but that they could not agree on a new test.

[405] 326 U.S. at 577.

[406] The state tax immunity case history was so cited in Garcia v. San Antonio Metro. Transit Authority, 469 U.S. 528, 540-544 (1985). *See* Richardson, at 450.

[407] 326 U.S. at 581-581. This deferral to political protection is similar to the "political check" theory applied to state taxation of federal entities; *see Fresno* (1977) below.

[408] Wilmette Park Dist. v. Campbell, 338 U.S. 411 (1949).

[409] Kern-Limerick, Inc. v. Scurlock, 347 U.S. 110 (1954).

termine whether the tax was imposed on the United States for immunity purposes.

- 1955: *Society of Savings of Cleveland v. Bowers* refused to accept a state determination that a tax was on depositors in a bank and held it was on the bank and unconstitutionally taxed federal bonds held by the bank.[410] The ruling was superseded by a 1959 statute, as discussed below.
- 1958 (*Allegheny* distinguished): The *City of Detroit* decision was another watershed, limiting the temporary restraint of the *Allegheny* (1944) case, discussed above.[411] The city levied property tax on realty leased by the United States for presumably market rent to a private party for private use, with an offset against the rent for such tax (meaning that the United States economically bore the state tax). The opinion distinguished *Allegheny* as involving a pure tax on property ownership, whereas the tax at issue was on the "use" of the property; however the tax was computed on the full value of the property, not the value of the lease. Another distinction was that the lessee used the property in its own business, not to carry out a government contract. The alleged distinction about the tax being on use rather than property was most important to the Court.[412] Justice Frankfurter said that to share the government's exemption the private taxpayer must actually "stand in the government's shoes."[413] The opinion identified the instrumentalities that would be entitled to the government's exemption as those that are arms of the government performing an essential government function.
- 1959 (exemption of federal debt broadened): Revised Statutes section 3701 concerning United States obligations was amended to say: "This exemption extends to every form of taxation that would require that either the obligations or the interest thereon, or both, be considered, directly or indirectly, in the computation of the tax, except nondiscriminatory franchise or other nonproperty taxes in lieu thereof imposed on corporations and except estate or inheritance taxes." This is now 31 U.S.C. § 3124. Thus the *Coite* exception for franchise taxes that are not capital or property taxes continues. Section 3124 principally restates the constitutional rule.[414]
- 1960 (discrimination against federal lessee): *Phillips Chem. Co. v. Dumas* is a rare example of a state tax on a federal lessee that was held unconstitutional

---

[410] Society of Savings of Cleveland v. Bowers, 349 U.S. 143 (1955).

[411] United States v. City of Detroit, 355 U.S. 466 (1958); United States v. Township of Muskegon, 355 U.S. 484 (1958) (companion case). *See also* United States v. Fresno County, 429 U.S. 452, 462 n. 10 (1977) (stating *Detroit* had overruled *Allegheny*).

[412] *See* City of Detroit v. Murray Corp., 355 U.S. 489 (1958) (applying same distinction to tax on work in process owned by the United States, but in the hands of the taxpayer contractor).

[413] *Id.* at 503.

[414] Memphis Bank & Trust Co. v. Garner, 459 U.S. 392, 397 (1983).

because it discriminated against the federal lessee in comparison to the taxation of lessees of state lands.[415]

- 1961 (Federal Land Bank a federal instrumentality): The Court ruled that because the United States is incapable of performing "proprietary" as opposed to governmental functions, the holding of a lease by its instrumentality, a Federal Land Bank, was a governmental function and could not be taxed by a state.[416]
- 1964: *United States v. Boyd* ruled that federal contractors were subject to a state tax on personal property used in performing the federal contract.[417]
- *1965*: The Court refused to find indirect taxation of municipal bond interest by virtue of denial of a federal income tax deduction for related expenses.[418]
- 1968 (national bank immunity): *First Agricultural National Bank* ruled that national banks continued to enjoy immunities to state taxes other than real property taxes.[419] The opinion stated that the ultimate factual issue of whether the tax impinged on federal sovereignty was controlled by federal law and not the state characterization of the tax.[420]
- 1969 (statutory change for state taxation of national banks): In addition to the four methods by which states could tax national banks allowed in 1926, the 1969 amendment to 12 U.S.C. § 548 allowed nondiscriminatory sales, property and license taxes during a transition period.[421] Then, beginning in 1972 national bank became taxable by states on a nondiscriminatory basis as if it were a state bank organized where its principal office is located.[422]
- 1975 (definition of "legal incidence"): The Court ruled that state sales taxes indirectly falling on military post exchange sales (*i.e.*, federal enclave) were not allowed by 4 U.S.C. § 107 (the Buck Act) because the tax was not a sales tax for sales occurring on the base.[423] Although the tax was nominally levied on the liquor vendors, the state directed the vendors to collect it from

---

[415] Phillips Chem. Co. v. Dumas, 361 U.S. 376 (1960) (the federal lessee was taxed on the value of the fee rather than the value of the leasehold and the terminability of the lease did not relieve the lessee of that burden). *See also* Moses Lake Homes, Inc. v. Grant County, 365 U.S. 744 (1961) (similar facts).

[416] Federal Land Bank v. Bd., 368 U.S. 146 (1961).

[417] United States v. Boyd, 378 U.S. 39 (1964).

[418] United States v. Atlas Life Ins. Co., 381 U.S. 233 (1965).

[419] First Agricultural National Bank v. State Tax Comm'n, 392 U.S. 339 (1968) (could not be taxed on purchase of office supplies).

[420] For a state tax case in which the Court analyzed the bearing of a state determination of the incidence of a tax, see Gurley v. Rhoden, 421 U.S. 200 (1975).

[421] Pub. L. No. 91-156, 83 Stat. 434; 12 U.S.C. 548. *See* HELLERSTEIN & HELLERSTEIN, STATE TAXATION, ¶ 6.30.

[422] "For the purposes of any tax law enacted under authority of the United States or any State, a national bank shall be treated as a bank organized and existing under the laws of the State or other jurisdiction within which its principal office is located." 12 U.S.C. 548.

[423] United States v. Tax Comm'n of Miss., 421 U.S. 599 (1975).

the military. "But the controlling significance of *First Agricultural National Bank* for our purposes is the test formulated by that decision for the determination where the legal incidence of the tax falls, namely, that where a State requires that its sales tax be passed on to the purchaser and be collected by the vendor from him, this establishes as a matter of law that the legal incidence of the tax falls upon the purchaser."[424]

- 1976 (incidence of tax): The Court applied the statutory rule that prior to 1969 a state could not impose sales tax on a national bank.[425] The opinion again stated that the incidence of a state tax as being on the federal instrumentality or not was a question of federal law.
- 1977 (nondiscriminatory tax on federal lessee proper; "political check"): *United States v. County of Fresno* allowed nondiscriminatory use taxes on possessory interests held by federal employees in housing on federal lands, which was supplied as part of their compensation.[426] The opinion created a link between the nondiscrimination principle and the "political check" that provides to the United States the protection against abusive state taxation, which Chief Justice Marshall could not find to exist to protect the Bank of the United States from state taxation. Even though the United States does not vote in the states, its interests can be protected when private persons dealing with the United States can make common cause with a state's other citizens who can oppose through the political process taxes that will fall equally on all of them.[427] However, the opinion is better explained by the fact that the tax was on the interest of the private persons in the federal land rather than the interest of the United States.
- *1978* (intergovernmental immunity not applicable to regulatory charge): *Massachusetts v. United States* ruled that states must pay a nondiscriminatory federal aircraft "tax" referred to as a user fee that Congress intended to support the federal aviation system.[428] The opinion, in effect, declined to extend the concept of intergovernmental immunity to such a charge, but instead tested it as regulatory charges are commonly tested—reasonable approximation of fair share of government cost—plus testing it for possible discrimination against a state as such.[429]
- 1981 (another *Allegheny* type case): The Court ruled that the 1958 *City of Detroit* decision did not entirely overrule the 1944 *Allegheny* decision, holding that a tax on property (a laboratory) owned by the United States but used by Rockwell International to produce nuclear weapons for the gov-

[424] *Id.* at 608, *citing* First Agricultural National Bank v. State Tax Comm'n, 392 U.S. 339, 341 (1968).

[425] Diamond National Corp. v. State Bd. of Equal., 425 U.S. 268 (1976).

[426] United States v. County of Fresno, 429 U.S. 452 (1977).

[427] *Id.* at 463-464 notes 10 and 11.

[428] Massachusetts v. United States, 435 U.S. 444 (1978).

[429] As to fees and charges, *see* Ch. IV.A.

ernment, not as a lessee, was a prohibited tax on the United States' property; the ruling was based on the fact that as between Rockwell and the government, the government was ultimately responsible for the tax.[430]

- 1982 (government contractors not exempt even though tax burden fell directly on the United States): *United States v. New Mexico* ruled federal contractors who paid for purchases by drawing directly on bank accounts created and owned by the United States were not entitled to immunity from state taxation because they made purchases in their own names and vendors did not know that they were dealing with the government.[431] The opinion stated: ". . . tax immunity is appropriate in only one circumstance: when the levy falls on the United States itself, or on an agency or instrumentality so closely connected to the Government that the two cannot realistically be viewed as separate entities, at least insofar as the activity being taxed is concerned. This view, we believe, comports with the principal purpose of the immunity doctrine, that of forestalling 'clashing sovereignty,'. . . . With the abandonment of the notion that the economic—as opposed to the legal—incidence of the tax is relevant, it becomes difficult to maintain that federal tax immunity is designed to insulate federal operations from the effects of state taxation. It remains true, of course, that state taxes on contractors are constitutionally invalid if they discriminate against the Federal Government, or substantially interfere with its activities."[432]
- 1983 (discriminatory corporate excise/franchise tax): *Memphis Bank & Trust Co. v. Garner* ruled that the Tennessee bank tax was an excise or franchise tax that was properly levied on the income from United States debt, but nevertheless was unconstitutional because it allowed exemption of Tennessee debt.[433] This case arose under 31 U.S.C. § 3124.
- 1983 (nondiscriminatory sales tax on federal contractor; "political check"): The Court found a state method for taxing federal contractors not to be discriminatory when viewed in the overall context of state taxes: the contractors (builders) did not pay sales tax on their purchases but charged sales tax on their sales, except to the United States, in which case they paid a use tax on their purchases.[434] Justice Rehnquist's opinion, joined by four other Justices, found that the "legal incidence" of the use tax was on the federal contractor, and because the tax was even less in those cases (labor costs did not inflate the tax base), the federal property was taxed less than others and

---

[430] Jefferson County, Colorado v. United States, 450 U.S. 901 (1981), *affirming* 627 F. 2d 217 (10th Cir. 1980).

[431] United States v. New Mexico, 455 U.S. 720 (1982).

[432] *Id.* at 735-736 and n. 11.

[433] Memphis Bank & Trust Co. v. Garner, 459 U.S. 392 (1983).

[434] Washington v. United States, 460 U.S. 536 (1983). *See also* Montana v. United States, 440 U.S. 147 (1979) (similar facts; contractor had litigated and lost in state court; ruled United States was estopped from relitigating in federal court).

the tax did not discriminate.[435] The opinion relied in part on the fact that a "political check" existed in the form of the general applicability of the sales tax. Justice Blackmun writing for the four dissenters argued that the majority had not adequately considered or proved the equality of the taxation (for example, the contractors must pay the tax earlier than the landowners would and it was unknown whether they could pass it through to the government), and that in any event facially disparate treatment of the United States' contractor should be enough to strike down the tax.[436]

- 1983 (property tax on federal debt): Reversing what had been thought to be the law going back at least to *Van Allen* in 1866, the Court ruled, with the assistance of the 1959 statute, that taxes on the stock of both state and national banks held by shareholders must be adjusted to eliminate the indirect tax on federal debt held by the banks.[437] The key to the ruling was that the statute valued the stock on the basis of the bank's assets and was treated as a property tax. A nondiscriminatory state tax on the value of the stock itself, without reference to the assets of the bank, would have been in compliance with 31 U.S.C. § 3124.
- *1988* (*Pollock* overruled as to state debt): In *South Carolina v. Baker* the state attacked the 1983 amendment to Code section 103 limiting the exemption for state and local bond interest to interest paid on registered bonds. In addition to claim of intergovernmental immunity, South Carolina relied on the Tenth Amendment. The Court disagreed, stating that the Tenth Amendment imposes "structural, not substantive" limits and that normally the only recourse of a state was through the political process, citing as a possible exception Chief Justice Stone's footnote 4 in *Carolene Products*, which it did not find applicable.[438] The opinion then rejected the state's intergovernmental immunity claim, stating that "All federal activities are immune from direct state taxation . . . but at least some state activities have always been subject to direct federal taxation. For a time, only the States' govern-

[435] But the Court retained the ability to evaluate whether an economically heavier tax was imposed on those who dealt with the United States, in which case the tax might be unconstitutional. 460 U.S. 546 n. 11.

[436] 460 U.S. at 551-556. The unusual approach of this opinion has not been repeated by the Supreme Court in a tax case. South Carolina v. Baker, 485 U.S. 505, 521 (1988) characterized it as a typical case holding that the test is not economic effect on the United States.

[437] American Bank & Trust Co. v. Dallas County, 463 U.S. 855 (1983). Later opinions that refined the calculation of the deduction include First National Bank of Atlanta v. Bartow County Bd. of Tax Assessors, 470 U.S. 583 (1985). The rule established is that exemption of income or property does not require that taxable income or taxable property pay less tax than otherwise on account of the ownership of the nontaxable property or income.

[438] South Carolina v. Baker, 485 U.S. 505 (1988), *citing* Garcia v. San Antonio Metro. Transit Authority, 469 U.S. 528 (1985); *citing also* United States v. Carolene Prod. Co., 304 U.S. 144, 152 n. 4 (1938) ("There may be narrower scope for operation of the presumption of constitutionality when legislation appears on its face to be within a specific prohibition of the Constitution, such as those of the first ten amendments, which are deemed equally specific when held to be embraced within the Fourteenth.").

mental, as opposed to proprietary, activities enjoyed tax immunity . . . but this distinction was subsequently abandoned as untenable by all eight Justices participating in *New York v. United States* . . . . We need not concern ourselves here, however, with the extent to which, if any, States are currently immune from direct federal taxation . . . . For our purposes, the important principle *New York* reaffirms is that the issue whether a nondiscriminatory federal tax might nonetheless violate state tax immunity does not even arise unless the Federal Government seeks to collect the tax directly from a State."[439] The opinion also contains confusing dictum concerning the constitutionality of state income tax on federal interest.[440] It states: "Indeed, this Court has in effect acknowledged that a holder of a Government bond could constitutionally be taxed on bond interest in *Memphis Bank & Trust Co. v. Garner*, 459 U.S. 392 (1983), which involved a state tax on federal bond interest. Although that case involved an interpretation of 31 U. S. C. § 742, we premised our statutory interpretation on the observation that 'our decisions have treated § 742 as principally a restatement of the constitutional rule.' 459 U.S., at 397. We then stated: 'Where, as here, the economic but not the legal incidence of the tax falls upon the Federal Government, such a tax generally does not violate the constitutional immunity if it does not discriminate against holders of federal property or those with whom the Federal Government deals.' Ibid. (emphasis added)."[441] But this interpretation by the Court entirely overlooks the fact that *Memphis* involved a corporate franchise tax, or at least a tax that the state claimed was a franchise tax, which has long been allowed to reflect federal bonds.[442] The *Memphis* Court found it unnecessary to resolve the nature of the tax because it was discriminatory. Thus, *Weston v. Charleston* is not overruled by either *South*

---

[439] 485 U.S. at 523 n. 14 (the *South Carolina* opinion also stated in relation to *New York v. United States*: "Two Justices reasoned that any nondiscriminatory tax on a State was constitutional, even if directly collected from the State. . . . (Frankfurter, J., joined by Rutledge, J.). Four other Justices declined to hold that every nondiscriminatory tax levied directly on a State would be constitutional because 'there may be non-discriminatory taxes which, when laid on a State, would nevertheless impair the sovereign status of the State quite as much as a like tax imposed by a State on property or activities of the national government. . . . This is not because the tax can be regarded as discriminatory but because a sovereign government is the taxpayer, and the tax, even though non-discriminatory, may be regarded as infringing its sovereignty" . . . (Stone, C. J., concurring, joined by Reed, Murphy, and Burton, JJ.) (emphasis added) (the cited discussion from *Mayo* stressed the difference between levying a tax on a government and on those with whom the government deals); . . . 'only when and because the subject of taxation is State property or a State activity must we consider whether such a non-discriminatory tax unduly interferes with the performance of the State's functions of government.' The four Justices then concluded that the tax at issue was constitutional even though directly levied on the State because recognizing an immunity would 'accomplish a withdrawal from the taxing power of the nation a subject of taxation of a nature which has been traditionally within that power from the beginning.' Ibid.").

[440] 485 U.S. at 526 (1988), *citing* Memphis Bank & Trust Co. v. Garner, 459 U.S. 392 (1983).

[441] *Id. See also* North Dakota v. United States, 495 U.S. 423, 434 (1990) (a state liquor regulation case that lumped *Weston* with prior overruled cases).

[442] 459 U.S. at 396 n. 6 (unnecessary to decide if it was a franchise tax because it was discriminatory).

Carolina v. Baker or *Memphis*, and no commentators or later cases indicate it was. *South Carolina v. Baker* did not ground its decision on the Sixteenth Amendment authorization of taxation of income "from whatever source derived."[443]

- 1989 (discriminatory state taxation of federal retirees unconstitutional): *Davis v. Michigan* had far reaching impact in upsetting the taxation of state and federal retirees' pensions in many states.[444] The state did not tax its own retirees' pensions and claimed that there were good reasons for taxing the federal retirees, but the Court found no ground justifying the discrimination. It did not matter to the Court that millions of other Michigan residents were taxed the same as the federal retirees.
- 1989: The Court ruled that state taxation of oil and gas upon severance from Native American lands was too indirect a burden on Native Americans, who share federal tax immunity, to prevent state taxation.[445]
- 1989: The Court ruled that a state could impose its sales and use taxes on a federal bankruptcy trustee.[446]
- 1993 (federal contractor case): The Court ruled that the fact that the United States agreed with a contractor to reimburse the state taxes on the contractor does not turn the tax into one imposed by the state on the United States.[447]
- 1994 (repurchase agreement taxable): The Court ruled that a state can tax interest earned from a private party on the sale-repurchase of United States debt.[448]

---

[443] South Carolina v. Baker, 485 U.S. 505, 523 n. 13 (1988).

[444] Davis v. Michigan, 489 U.S. 803 (1989). *See also* Harper v. Va. Dep't of Taxation, 509 U.S. 86 (1993) (addressing remedies). *See* Richardson, at 433 et seq. The states keep trying the same discrimination and the Court had to strike down another one in Dawson v. Steager, 139 S. Ct. 698 (2019).

[445] Cotton Petroleum Corp. v. New Mexico, 490 U.S. 163 (1989) (Native American tribe also taxed severance; applied "interest balancing" analysis). Mont. v. Crow Tribe of Indians, 523 U.S. 696 (1998), called *New Mexico* a "pathmarking" decision. But Ariz. Dep't of Revenue v. Blaze Constr. Co., 526 U.S. 32 (1999) limited the balancing approach, evidently to cases involving multiple taxation by tribe and state of oil severance, and opted for a bright line test allowing taxation of contractors dealing with tribe. Also, result followed though distinguished in Wagnon v. Prairie Band Potawatomi Nation, 546 U.S. 95 (2005) (state tax on oil distributors selling on reservation). *See* Ch. II.C.10.

[446] Cal. State Bd. of Equalization v. Sierra Summit, 490 U.S. 844 (1989).

[447] United States v. California, 507 U.S. 746 (1993).

[448] Neb. DOR v. Loewenstein, 513 U.S. 123 (1994).

- 1997 (Tax Injunction Act): The Court denied jurisdiction for a suit by a Production Credit Association to enjoin a state tax.[449] The case did not decide whether the PCA as a federal instrumentality could be taxed by a state, but it implied that the PCA was not an instrumentality of that status because it did not extend to it the implied exemption from the Tax Injunction Act for suits brought by the United States and its instrumentalities.[450]

9. James v. Dravo: *Back Story*

1937 can fairly be called the pivot point of federal taxation because in that year major shifts occurred in two of the three most important federal tax issues in the history of the United States: taxation versus regulation and intergovernmental tax immunity.[451] On March 29, 1937 the Court issued its decision in West Coast Hotel Co. v. Parrish, 300 U.S. 379 (1937). That decision is generally viewed as marking the so called switch in time that saved the nine by ending the Supreme Court's total rejection of New Deal regulations (although the case itself involved state regulation, and was said to have been decided in conference before the Court packing proposal was aired).[452] On April 26-27 *James v. Dravo* was first argued.[453] On June 1, 1937 the Court ordered reargument and asked that the United States express its views. The United States filed an amicus brief siding with the state tax authority in the fall of 1937.[454] The usual long list of attorneys appeared at the foot of the brief, but the last name, Warner W. Gardner, "Special Attorney," stands out. He was a founder in 1947 of the prominent District of Columbia law firm Shea and Gardner (which merged with Goodwin Procter in 2004). It is likely that the decision to let the states have these taxes was made at

---

[449] Ark. v. Farm Credit Servs., 520 U.S. 821, 831 (1997) ("PCA's are not granted the right to exercise government regulatory authority but rather serve specific commercial and economic purposes long associated with various corporations chartered by the United States."). *See also* Director of Revenue v. CoBank ACB, 531 U.S. 316 (2001) (Bank for Cooperatives was not exempt under the terms of the federal statute, even though it was a federal instrumentality).

[450] *Arkansas v. Farm Credit Servs.* cited as the origin of this judicial exception the decision in Dep't of Employment v. United States, 385 U.S. 355 (1966).

[451] For discussion of the three issues, *see* Ch. I.E.8.

[452] Burns, at 148. However, the subsequent opinion that first approved a New Deal federal law was NLRB v. Jones & Laughlin Steel Corp., 301 U.S. 1 (1937). As to the timing of the decision and the proposal, *see* Bernard Schwartz, A History of the Supreme Court 235 (1993). *See generally* Leuchtenburg, at 236-237 ("The conservative minority, which had dominated the Court for so many years, knew it had been eclipsed . . . Old McReynolds was sore as hell . . ."). The shift embodied in *James v. Dravo* also occurred at the same time that the Court shifted its view on the Commerce Clause and taxation by states of out of state businesses doing business in the state. *See* D.J. Farage, *Whither or Wither Tax Immunities?* 42 Dick. L. Rev. 69 (Oct. 1937) [hereinafter Farage].

[453] James v. Dravo Contracting Co., 302 U.S. 134 (1937).

[454] 1937 WL 63782.

the highest level of the Roosevelt administration.[455] The Court decided the case in favor of the state on December 6, 1937.

The government's brief exhaustively recounts the rise and projected fall of intergovernmental immunity. It specifically asked the Court to reexamine the doctrine insofar as it had protected private persons from nondiscriminatory taxes.[456] It explained that intergovernmental immunity in the United States was not based on the English "royal prerogative," but rather on the special relationship of the United States and the states: reciprocal immunity and dual system of government. Its arguments strongly reflected that the federal government's position was based both on the expanding role of government (*i.e.*, the New Deal) and the Supreme Court's new found understanding that governments could regulate in each other's provinces, and likewise should be able to tax.

The brief is a model of how to argue that a line of Supreme Court authorities should be overruled. The points of the amicus brief included:

- The reciprocity of the immunity doctrine dates only to 1870 (in 1937 that counted as "relatively recent." *Collector v. Day* and not *McCulloch* created the reciprocal approach. *Collector v. Day* was said to introduce a "novel doctrine."

- One of the reasons why the doctrine was objectionable was the subtle and theoretical distinctions it had fostered: while *Pollock* (1895) found income taxation of state interest to be unconstitutional, *Flint v. Stone Tracy* (1911) found excise taxation measured by state interest to be constitutional. Also estate taxes can be imposed on state debt.

- The United States thought contractors should share in the costs of local government, even if it indirectly cost the United States money. Indeed, the brief quoted Justice Holmes' line about taxes being the price of civilized society in the context of the United States indirectly paying the state of West Virginia for providing a local civilized society that benefits the nation.[457] Thus it could have reflected a conscious decision of the federal government to assist the states in the Depression times.

- The brief linked *West Coast Hotel*, the decision marking the shift in favor of governmental regulatory power, to the tax immunity issue, arguing that it stood for the proposition that states could impose regulations that increased costs of the federal government, and so state taxes should not fail when they did the same.

---

[455] However, the subsequent 1939 case of *Graves v. New York* was viewed by Justice Jackson as the one in which the federal government actually established its change of mind. *See* discussion of case in Robert H. Jackson, The Struggle for Judicial Supremacy 241-244 (1941). During this period Jackson was either Assistant Attorney General or Solicitor General.

[456] Amicus brief at p. 12.

[457] *Id.* at p. 25. Dissenting opinion of Justice Holmes, Compania General De Tabacos De Filipinas v. Collector of Internal Revenue, 275 U.S. 87, 100 (1927).

- Although the brief projected that the net benefit would be to the states in any event, it reasoned that there would be an offsetting benefit to the United States from being afforded the reciprocal right to tax state contractors. Also the brief did not see the problem as a zero sum game, stating that more taxes collected by the states likely meant less claims for aid to the United States. However, a tax that affected the performance of the contract rather than its cost would be suspect. Indeed the tax Maryland attempted to collect in *McCulloch* impinged on the performance of the currency generating project of the Bank.
- The brief emphasized the importance of nondiscrimination in taxing governmental contractors. It pointed out that taxes could be discriminatory in effect, though not in terms, by the example of the Bank of the United States, which was the only bank operating in Maryland other than Maryland banks, and thus the only bank subject to the tax at issue in *McCulloch v. Maryland.*
- Another linkage made by the brief with the New Deal was an argument that a reconsideration of the immunity doctrine was made necessary by the increasing importance of governmental activities.
- The same approach should not be applied to the effect of state taxes on interstate commerce because interstate commerce issues always arise solely in connection with private persons.[458]

Needless to say, the Court was primed to agree with the amicus brief, having asked for it.

The 1937 brief appears to have been a rehearsal for a 218 page study written by the same attorney Warner and others for the Justice Department others entitled *Taxation of Government Bondholders and Employees - The Immunity Rule and the Sixteenth Amendment.*[459] The study supported proposed legislation to allow reciprocal taxation of governmental debt and supported the federal taxation of state debt interest on the basis that the Sixteenth Amendment had eliminated the source of state interest as a basis for not taxing it. However, *South Carolina v. Baker* ultimately did not adopt that construction of the Sixteenth Amendment in allowing federal taxation of state bond interest.[460]

10. *Native American Tribes*

Native American Tribes also can enjoy intergovernmental tax immunity. The taxation of Native American Tribes, individual Native Americans, persons dealing with Tribes or Native Americans, and of activities, transactions and property occurring on Native American lands is a substantial subject addressed in Chap-

---

[458] *But see* Farage, explaining that the Court reduced the immunity of interstate commerce from state taxation at the same time.

[459] *A Study Made by the Department of Justice at the Direction of Homer S. Cummings, Attorney General,* transmitted June 24, 1938.

[460] South Carolina v. Baker, 485 U.S. 505, 523 n. 13 (1988).

ter IX as part of state taxation. This Chapter addresses (1) federal taxation of those subjects, and (2) to a lesser extent, state efforts to tax the United States as agent for, or otherwise representing, Native Americans, usually in connection to income from "trust lands."[461] Until fairly recently Native Americans and Native American lands were relatively poor and most tax issues related to oil and minerals removed from Native American lands and to a lesser extent sales to Native Americans. Today many Tribes have developed businesses such as casinos, which have led to an explosion of literature on taxation of such activities.

As to the federal taxing power, several articles have recently summarized the state of the law as follows:[462]

- Federally recognized Tribes and tribal corporations formed under section 17 of the Indian Reorganization Act (25 U.S.C. § 477) or under the Oklahoma Indian Welfare Act (25 U.S.C. §§ 501-509) are exempt from federal income taxation (generally including unrelated business income taxation), at least with respect to activities on the reservation. Although the reasons for Tribes' income tax exemption are obscure, it can be said that Congress intends the exemption, and that the quasi sovereignty of the Tribes allows them to benefit from the intergovernmental immunity doctrine.[463] Of course state tax immunity has waned, but Tribes' immunity remains broader. Code section 7871 provides that Tribes are not automatically treated like states for all purposes, but does not provide the tribal income tax exemption.
- Federal taxes other than income taxes can be levied on Tribes, but there is no consistency in the rules.[464]
- In 2014, Congress attempted to codify the Indian General Welfare Exclusion in section 139E.
- Native Americans are U.S. citizens, and more importantly are individual persons as defined in the Internal Revenue Code, and so subject to federal tax on their worldwide income, except as otherwise provided by treaty or

---

[461] *See generally* STAFF OF THE JOINT COMMITTEE ON TAXATION, OVERVIEW OF FEDERAL TAX PROVISIONS AND ANALYSIS OF SELECTED ISSUES RELATING TO NATIVE AMERICAN TRIBES AND THEIR MEMBERS, JCX-40-12 (May 14, 2012).

[462] Eric M. Jensen, *Taxation and Doing Business in Indian Country*, 60 ME. L. REV. 1, 41 et seq. (2008) [hereinafter Jensen]; John Lentz, *When Canons Go to War in Indian Country, Guess Who Wins?* 35 AM. IND. L. REV. 211, 213 (2011) (explaining that a special canon of construction favors Native Americans in construction of treaties); Mark J. Cowan, *Leaving Money on the Table(s): An Examination of Federal Income Tax Policy Towards Indian Tribes*, 6 FLA. TAX REV. 345, 351 et seq. (2004).

[463] Jensen, at 48; Richard D. Pomp, *The Unfulfilled Promise of the Indian Commerce Clause and State Taxation*, 63 TAX LAW. 897, 1215 (Summer 2010). *See also* Robert N. Clinton, *There Is No Federal Supremacy Clause for Indian Tribes*, 34 ARIZ. ST. L. J. 113 (2002). *See* Merrion v. Jicarilla Apache Tribe, 455 U.S. 130 (1982) (the sovereignty of Tribes is not created or recognized by the Constitution and is not protected by the Tenth Amendment, but the Court has recognized aspects of sovereignty).

[464] *See* I.R.C. § 7871 (treating Tribes like states for purposes of some excise taxes); Chickasaw Nation v. United States, 534 U.S. 84 (2001) (gaming subject to excise taxes).

statute.[465] One statute of particular importance is the 1887 General Allotment Act, which provides for the United States to administer trust lands. This Act has been interpreted to exempt income from such lands from federal taxation.[466]

- Persons dealing with Native American Tribes or Native Americans are subject to tax as they otherwise would be.

Taxation by Native American Tribes and state taxation of Native Americans are addressed by Ch. IX.J.

11. *Native Americans Not Taxed*

The Constitution Article I, section 2, clause 3 states:

> Representatives and direct Taxes shall be apportioned among the several States which may be included within this Union, according to their respective Numbers, which shall be determined by adding to the whole Number of free Persons, including those bound to Service for a Term of Years, and excluding Indians not taxed, three fifths of all other Persons . . . .

Amendment XIV, section 2 states:

> Representatives shall be apportioned among the several States according to their respective numbers, counting the whole number of persons in each State, excluding Indians not taxed . . . .

2 U.S.C. section 2a(a) repeats the phrase in describing the census report. These references to "Indians not taxed" are so startling and confusing that it is worthwhile to explain them here so as to save readers' time in chasing down the explanation, which is: there are no longer any Native Americans not taxed. Rather, the term was an attempt to exclude Native persons from citizenship and to indirectly acknowledge that Native nations were sovereigns. Nevertheless, because the clauses remain in the Constitution, they are part of federal law. Today 2 U.S.C. § 2a(a) continues to exclude "Indians not taxed" from the census for apportionment purposes.

The Supreme Court has never elucidated the phrase. The following, however, explains generally what it means:

- 1831: In a decision having broad national significance, the Court ruled the Cherokee Nation was not a "foreign nation" and so could not bring suit to challenge enforcement of the laws of Georgia within its boundaries.[467] Justice Baldwin's concurrence relied on Article I, section 2, clause 3 by reasoning that "Indians not taxed" (which he referred to as "free Indian popu-

---

[465] *See* Superintendent of Five Civilized Tribes v. Commissioner, 295 U.S. 418 (1935) (citizen and taxpayer); Choteau v. Burnet, 283 U.S. 691 (1931). *See also* Federal Power Comm'n v. Tuscarora Indian Nation, 362 U.S. 99 (1960). Note that early rulings that Native Americans are not citizens are no longer effective. Iowa Mut. Ins. Co. v. LaPlante, 480 U.S. 9 (1987), *distinguishing* Elk v. Wilkins, 112 U.S. 94 (1884).

[466] *See* Squire v. Capoeman, 351 U.S. 1 (1956).

[467] Cherokee Nation v. Georgia, 30 U.S. 1 (1831).

lation") need not have been excluded if they had been a nation or any such body as was not considered part of the population of the state.

- 1866: Congress enacted the Civil Rights Act making all persons born in the United States citizens, except Native Americans not taxed.[468]
- 1868: The second section of the Fourteenth Amendment excluded Native Americans not taxed from the population counted for purposes of apportioning representatives, parroting the original Constitution.
- 1884: A Native American asserted his rights as a citizen to vote under the Fourteenth Amendment. The opinion stated that Native Americans were exempt from taxation "by treaty or statute" and so could not be taxed by a state; that general federal laws did not apply to them unless specified.[469] The Court ruled that a Native American was not a citizen by birth but could only become a citizen by naturalization, citing the fact that the exclusion of Native Americans not taxed had been repeated in the Fourteenth Amendment, as well as the Civil Rights Act. Justice Harlan in dissent explained that the reference to Native Americans not taxed meant that there also were Native Americans that were taxed, being those Natives that had departed from tribal relations; he referred to the Native Americans in tribal relations as "wild Indians" (whom Justice Baldwin had called "free Indian[s]"). Thus he linked taxpaying with citizenship, though the method of shifting from tribal status to taxpaying status was murky.
- 1935: The Court ruled that Native Americans were citizens and subject to general laws like the income tax.[470]
- 1940: Attorney General Robert H. Jackson rendered an opinion to the Department of Interior on the meaning of the phrase.[471] He stated that the question had never been decided, but that there were grounds for concluding that there were no Native Americans not taxed since the Supreme Court had ruled that Native Americans were subject to the federal income tax. He opaquely stated that the Department could continue doing what it had been doing, which presumably was to count all Native Americans in the census for apportionment purposes.

In sum, the clause has no current bearing on the subject whether individual Native Americans are or are not subject to United States taxation.

---

[468] 13 Stat. 774 (1866).

[469] Elk v. Wilkins, 112 U.S. 94 (1884). United States v. Wong Kim Ark, 169 U.S. 649 (1898) limited *Wilkins* to Indians and found a Chinese born in the United States to be a citizen, based on British law principles.

[470] Superintendent of Five Civilized Tribes v. Commissioner, 295 U.S. 418 (1935) (citizen and taxpayer). *See* Indian Citizenship Act (June 2, 1924).

[471] 39 Op. Atty Gen. 518 (Nov. 28, 1940).

12. *Other Federal Supremacy Interactions*

The federal taxing power is so broad that no state law can interfere with it directly or indirectly by burdening federal taxpayers on account of paying federal taxes. *Hanson* ruled that a state cannot require a person who bought a federal liquor license to post it on pain of criminal penalty.[472] The problem with the states trying to piggyback a penalty on a federal taxing regime is that it burdens the federal government by burdening the person paying the federal tax, without any nexus to any subject matter of legitimate state concern.[473] The *Hanson* opinion supported this principle, which it said to be obvious, with citations to *McCulloch* and other federal supremacy decisions.[474]

As to the specifics of state interference with federal taxation, *Hanson* cited *Snyder*, which ruled that a state lien recordation requirement cannot void a federal tax lien.[475] More recently the Court cited *Snyder* in ruling that the United States is not just another creditor when it is collecting taxes, but rather has all the force of the constitutional power to tax behind it.[476]

Another aspect of federal supremacy in taxation is the conflict between federal and state government tax claims on the assets of a debtor taxpayer. The Court ruled that Congress could give federal tax claims priority over state and local tax claims.[477]

Finally, Chief Justice Marshall established in an early and important decision concerning the Court's jurisdiction, *Cohens v. Virginia*, that the Court could properly redetermine federal questions like those concerning federal taxation on appeal from the state courts, because of both federal supremacy and a reasonable suspicion that the state courts would not have the best interests of the nation at heart.[478]

---

[472] North Dakota ex rel. Flaherty v. Hanson, 215 U.S. 515 (1910) (habeas corpus proceeding brought by jailed liquor dealer). In contrast, Printz v. United States, 521 U.S. 898 (1997) ruled unconstitutional a provision of the Brady Act that required state enforcement of a federal scheme for regulating guns. This reflects the statement in *Garcia* that there may be other limits in the structure of government. Garcia v. San Antonio Metro. Transit Authority, 469 U.S. at 556.

[473] 215 U.S. at 524.

[474] *Id.* at 524 n. 1.

[475] United States v. Snyder, 149 U.S. 210 (1893). *See also* United States v. McDermott, 507 U.S. 447 (1993) (citing *Snyder* for not subjecting a federal tax lien to a strong state first to record presumption); United States v. Union Cent. Life Ins. Co., 368 U.S. 291 (1961) (discussing subsequent federal statutes requiring recordation of federal tax lien in certain cases); Michigan v. United States, 317 U.S. 338 (1943) (like *Snyder*).

[476] United States v. Rogers, 461 U.S. 677, 696-697 (1983).

[477] County of Spokane v. United States, 279 U.S. 80 (1929), *citing* United States v. Fisher, 6 U.S. 358 (1805), and discussing confusion in the cases. *See also* New York v. Maclay, 288 U.S. 290 (1933) (which did not rely on the Necessary and Proper Clause but rather federal supremacy).

[478] Cohens v. Virginia, 19 U.S. 264, 386-388 (1821).

Ch. III. Taxes Versus Regulation

A. Overview

The three principal ways that the federal government can affect persons are by direct regulation, taxation and spending. Taxing and spending are the more expansive powers, with direct regulation being limited to matters within the enumerated powers of Congress. As a consequence distinguishing taxing from direct regulation is a recurring issue, along with the linkage of taxing with spending.

Of the three most contentious constitutional issues in the entire history of federal taxation (the other two being intergovernmental immunity and direct taxes),[1] the interaction of the federal taxing power with the limited scope of regulation allowed to the federal government has been the relatively less litigated and is the least resolved today. The other two issues were resolved largely by allowing form to control substance (or abandoning the search for substance), after the Court's experience with trying to discern substance proved too unwieldy to serve as an administrable rule.[2]

The Court can find to be constitutional money exactions that Congress calls a tax or treats as a tax, either under the taxing power or as necessary and proper to another power. Such taxes may incidentally, or primarily, regulate matters that

---

[1] *See* Ch. I.E.8.

[2] With the help of the Public Salary Tax Act and other such statutes the Supreme Court ultimately realized that searching for indirect burdens of state taxes on the United States was more trouble than it was worth (Ch. II.C.4). The Sixteenth Amendment in effect directed form and not substance to determine whether a tax was levied directly on property or heads (Ch. V.D.2.e).

Congress has the power to regulate, whether approved under the taxing power or the Necessary and Proper Clause. Thus if the United States can regulate the matter, it is of only theoretical interest whether a federal exaction is characterized as a tax or not; the United States can exact it either way.[3] However, if the Court holds that Congress does not have the power to regulate a subject that it finds to be regulated by the tax (usually the regulatory power Congress relies on is the Commerce Clause, but has included the power to regulate currency and to enforce Prohibition), then it is not entirely clear whether (1) Congress can constitutionally tax the subject regulated simply by labeling it a tax or treating the exaction as a tax (i.e., a facial test), or (2) the tax potentially should raise at least some federal revenue (the general rule) (i.e., a limited functional test), or (3) some more intrusive inquiry into Congress' motives to regulate as opposed to the motive to tax, or some more expansive analysis of the levy's function, must be applied.

The period 1922-1936 was the heyday of the Court's rulings against federal taxes in form based on finding they were not taxes at all, but were solely regulations of subjects the Court found to be outside the power of Congress to regulate. Before and since that period, the Court has consistently supported the use of federal exactions that were taxes in form to regulate matters beyond the power of direct federal regulation, with the 2012 health insurance tax case being a prime example.[4] Therefore, if the United States lacks the power to regulate the subject that triggers the exaction, and if the exaction can be characterized solely as something other than a tax, then the Court might rule it unconstitutional with a reasoned analysis having case law support.[5] The recurring issues are (1) whether an exaction was treated as a tax by Congress, (2) if so whether any additional proof is needed to evidence an exercise of the taxing power, and (3) whether a supervening regulatory intent or purpose of Congress can nevertheless justify the Court's ignoring the taxing power and finding the exaction wholly regulatory.

The better approach, which the Court has followed throughout most of its history, including the 2012 health insurance tax ruling, is that labeling (or otherwise treating) the exaction as a tax, and it having at least the theoretical possibility of raising even de minimis revenue, provides sufficient support to sustain the tax under the taxing power; to require more proof puts the Court in the inappropriate and impossible position of evaluating Congress' motives, which normally results in political rather than legal decisions against Congress' power.[6]

---

[3] *See, e.g.*, Edye v. Robertson, 112 U.S. 580 (1884) (Head Money Cases); *see* Ch. III.E.4.

[4] Ch. III.E.2.c.

[5] *See* Ch. III.F.

[6] *Cf.* Robert D. Cooter & Neil S. Siegel, *Not the Power to Destroy: A Theory of the Tax Power for a Court that Limits the Commerce Power*, 98 Va. L. Rev. 1195 (2012), SSRN Id. No. 19895371 (2012) [hereinafter Cooter and Siegel] (asserting that legal theory is needed to resolve the confusion of regulatory taxes and that the solution is to treat taxes that raise some revenue and somewhat dampen behavior as taxes and taxes that dampen behavior to the point of raising no taxes as purely regulatory).

Alternately, the Court may assert that it is not evaluating Congress' motives but is only evaluating the levy's function, but that approach should apply only to the levy that is not clearly labeled a tax.[7] Federal exactions not labeled as a tax have been upheld as a tax.[8] However, the Court cannot be precluded from second guessing Congress with respect to a tax that appears to regulate a matter that a taxpayer argues is outside the federal power to regulate and to find an exaction to be an unconstitutional regulation that is not a tax.

The tax versus regulation issue is a misnomer because the Constitution contemplated that taxes can regulate, and the Court has ruled that federal taxes can regulate matters that Congress may not have power to regulate directly.[9] Recognizing this, the Court has been forced to crowd down into the nontax category the federal taxes that it wants to strike on the grounds that Congress has attempted to regulate beyond its powers. The Court has so ruled in five decisions involving four statutes, in two ways (which may be combined): (1) finding a lack of tendency to raise revenue,[10] and (2) finding Congress' sole motive to be to regulate, regardless of substantial revenues raised by the tax.[11] Therefore, the potential for a court to hold a federal tax to be an unconstitutional interference by Congress with matters solely regulated by states exists whenever a federal exaction can be found not to be a tax at all under some version of a substance over form analysis based on Congress' improper motive or an analysis of the functions of a levy not labeled as a tax.

In direct and irreconcilable contrast to the approaches of those five decisions, the Court also has announced in decisions that have never been overruled that if an exaction appears on its face to be a tax, then the tax is constitutional under the taxing power regardless of (1) its tendency to destroy the thing taxed (and thus not raise revenue), (2) its effect on matters the United States does not have the power to regulate, and (3) Congress' intent or motive to regulate such matters.[12] In 1945 the Court broadly indicated that if Congress treats an exaction as a tax, that characterization controls.[13] Congress is almost always prudent enough to do so, though it waffled in the case of the 2010 health insurance tax.[14] Therefore, overturning a federal tax that the government defends as a tax

---

[7] *See* Ch. III.E.2.c.

[8] *See, e.g.*, Inter-Island Steam Navigation Co. v. Hawaii, 305 U.S. 306 (1938) (Hawaiian "fee" upheld as a general tax that did not have to provide benefits to payor).

[9] *See* Ch. III.E.2.

[10] Which was claimed to be the case in *Hill v. Wallace* (tax said by the Court to be "most burdensome" and would never go into effect because compliance enjoined), *Trusler*, *Drexel* and *Constantine*.

[11] Which was the approach taken in United States v. Butler, 297 U.S. 1 (1936).

[12] *See, e.g.*, McCray v. United States, 195 U.S. 27 (1904). The opinion refers to reliance on the face of the statute seven times and does not rely at all on the power of the Congress to regulate the matter said to be affected by the tax, although the taxpayer forcefully argued that Congress lacked that power, and the Solicitor General did not refute that argument.

[13] Fernandez v. Wiener, 326 U.S. 340, 361-362 (1945).

[14] *See* Ch. III.E.2.c.

always requires ruling that the exaction in substance is not a tax, and ruling that substance rather than form controls in this instance.

Justice Stanley Reed, no flaming liberal (although a Roosevelt appointee), aptly summed up the peculiar status of regulatory taxes in one of the most recent opinions on the matter, *Kahriger*, in 1953:

> While the Court has never questioned the above-quoted statement of Mr. Chief Justice Marshall in the *McCulloch* case, the application of the rule has brought varying holdings on constitutionality. Where federal legislation has rested on other congressional powers, such as the Necessary and Proper Clause or the Commerce Clause, this Court has generally sustained the statutes, despite their effect on matters ordinarily considered state concern. When federal power to regulate is found, its exercise is a matter for Congress. *Where Congress has employed the taxing clause a greater variation in the decisions has resulted. The division in this Court has been more acute.* Without any specific differentiation between the power to tax and other federal powers, the indirect results from the exercise of the power to tax have raised more doubts. This is strikingly illustrated by the shifting course of adjudication in taxation of the handling of narcotics. The tax ground in the *Veazie Bank* case, supra, recognized that strictly state governmental activities, such as the right to pass laws, were beyond the federal taxing power. That case allowed a tax, however, that obliterated from circulation all state bank notes. A reason was that "the judicial cannot prescribe to the legislative departments of the government limitations upon the exercise of its acknowledged powers." Id., at 548. The tax cases cited above in the third preceding paragraph followed that theory. *It is hard to understand why the power to tax should raise more doubts because of indirect effects than other federal powers.*[15] (emphasis added)

With due regards to Justice Reed, it is not so hard to understand. What appears to be an insertion by Congress of the taxing power as a cover for regulation or spending outside the powers of Congress strikes many tax avoiders, who are not informed about or sympathetic with the great historic scope of the taxing power, as a ruse that is far more odious than if Congress simply tried to regulate outside of its powers.

Although the Supreme Court's opinions ruling federal taxes to be unconstitutional regulations and not exercises of the taxing power are few in number (five relating to four federal tax acts) and limited to the 15-year period of time from 1922 to 1936, the potential for the Court to find a tax not to be a tax always exists; the Court will never totally defer to Congress' labels or give up the core judicial power to demand that substance control over form. The Court has indicated several times, however, that the ability of a tax to raise revenue, no matter how little, is sufficient to resolve the substance over form question in favor of a

[15] United States v. Kahriger, 345 U.S. 22, 29-31 (1953). A student note examined the authorities facing the Court in *Kahriger* before it was decided, and observed the irreconcilable conflict of what it called the "objective constitutionality" approach of *McCray*, as contrasted with the "penalty" doctrine of the *Child Labor Tax Case*. Note, *The Federal Gambling Tax and the Constitution*, 43 J. of Crim. L., Criminology and Police Science 637 (1953).

tax,[16] except for a tax like the one in *Butler*, which clearly raised revenue but was found not to be a tax anyway.[17] In resolving the issue of the tax's regulatory purpose the Court necessarily engages in speculations about congressional motive, an investigation that the Court generally *says* it will avoid,[18] and try to replace with analysis of the levy's function (when not labeled a tax).[19]

The Court during most of its history has sided firmly with the federal taxing power, based on the form of the exaction as a tax and sometimes on its ability to raise some revenue, and generally has refused to engage in a substantive analysis of whether the tax was intended to, or did, mostly regulate beyond Congress' powers to regulate. However, the Court struck down five federal taxes on the ground that they were not taxes but were unconstitutional regulations of local matters: a federal child labor law enforced by a federal tax in the *Child Labor Tax Case* (1922), two taxes in a federal commodities futures trading law in *Hill v. Wallace* (1922) and *Trusler* (1926), a held over Prohibition penalty after the repeal of Prohibition in *Constantine* (1935), and the New Deal Agricultural Adjustment Act in *Butler* (1936); it also struck down the New Deal Guffy Coal Conservation Act in *Carter Coal* (1936). All of these laws employed federal taxes. All of the opinions (summarized in Chapter I.E.2.b) recognized the almost limitless reach of the federal taxing power (discussed in Chapter II.A.2). For that reason all of the decisions but *Carter Coal* (which was not defended under the taxing power) struck down the taxes by ruling they were not taxes, but were regulations that regulated in areas outside the power of the United States (child labor, commodities futures trading, agricultural price supports, liquor laws after the end of Prohibition).

Although the Court has not directly overruled any of these decisions, their current weight is diminished by subsequent expansions of the Court's views of the Commerce Clause powers of Congress, as well as particular aspects of the opinions that limit their bearing on the tax versus regulation issue:

- *Constantine* was the proverbial hard case that makes bad law in that it involved multiple state and federal prosecutions for a violation of a state liquor law after the United States had repealed Prohibition, where the United States also imposed a tax plus the penalty "tax" at issue, making that much higher penalty look like a usurpation of the state police power rather than a federal tax.[20]

- *Butler* was not defended by the United States under the Commerce Clause and involved a unique scheme by which an administrative agency could

[16] *See* Ch. III.E.5.

[17] United States v. Butler, 297 U.S. 1 (1936).

[18] Fernandez v. Wiener, 326 U.S. 340, 362 (1945) ("It has long been settled that an Act of Congress which on its face purports to be an exercise of the taxing power, is not any the less so because the tax is burdensome or tends to restrict or suppress the thing taxed. In such a case it is not within the province of courts to inquire into the unexpressed purposes or motives which may have moved Congress to exercise a power constitutionally conferred upon it.").

[19] *See* Ch. III.E.2c(3)(c).

[20] United States v. Constantine, 296 U.S. 287 (1935).

impose a variable "tax" by which the government appeared to be taking money from cotton processors and giving it directly to cotton farmers,[21] which made it seem more a regulation than a tax.[22] Indeed, the same type of payments to farmers have been made ever since *Butler*, but not in a way that appears to pay for them through taxes on processors of the same commodity.[23] The tax at issue raised substantial revenue. Nevertheless, *Butler* is the poster child for latter day tax protesters, based on the number of times it is cited in dissenting opinions of the Court. The *Butler* opinion reasoned: (1) the tax was not a "true tax" because it was part of an Act the "sole object" of which was a "prohibited end"; (2) neither was the tax necessary and proper in support of another enumerated power or of spending under the General Welfare Power, because Congress could not spend the tax revenues to support local agriculture (a holding that is no longer viable). *Butler* is in direct and irreconcilable conflict with *McCray*, an earlier decision that the *Butler* opinion of the Court avoided entirely.[24]

- *Carter* was not defended by the United States under the taxing power, but solely under the Commerce Clause, so literally it does not stand for a finding that a regulatory tax is not a tax.[25]
- *Child Labor Tax Case*[26] and *Hill v. Wallace* and *Trusler*[27] as well as *Butler* have come to be viewed as involving matters that certainly could now be, and are, regulated by the United States.[28] Nevertheless, they are probably the purest cases of taxes being invalidated by finding the tax not to be a tax. They did not overrule *McCray* and its approach of looking only to the face of an obviously regulatory statute to rule that it imposes a tax, even if the tax's effect is clearly to penalize or even abolish a practice that the federal government has no power to regulate (in *McCray*, the coloring of margarine).[29]

---

[21] United States v. Butler, 297 U.S. 1 (1936). In response to *Butler*, Congress included in the Revenue Act of 1936 a new Title III-Tax on Unjust Enrichment. It levied a tax of 80% of the unjust enrichment of persons who, instead of paying the excise tax imposed on them, passed the tax on to their customers.

[22] *See* Ch. V.D.3.b(7)(b).

[23] The Supreme Court has never ruled on the constitutionality of the federal agricultural price support programs since the 1933 version at issue in *Butler*. It has entertained a case involving the program without any adverse comment on the support payments. *See* United States v. Guy W. Capps, Inc., 348 U.S. 296 (1955). The broadened Commerce Clause powers of the United States are thought to justify current programs for payments to farmers. *See* Ronald B. Schram, *International Repercussions of National Farm Policies*, 3 Law & Policy Int'l Bus. 239, 250 (1971). However, Horne v. Dep't of Agric., 569 U.S. 513 (2013) ruled that a part of the act might be a taking.

[24] McCray v. United States, 195 U.S. 27 (1904).

[25] Carter v. Carter Coal Co., 298 U.S. 238 (1936).

[26] J.W. Bailey v. Drexel Furn. Co., 259 U.S. 20 (1922).

[27] Hill v. Wallace, 259 U.S. 44 (1922); Trusler v. Crooks, 269 U.S. 475 (1926).

[28] Child labor came to be regulated as approved in United States v. Darby, 312 U.S. 100 (1941). Chicago Bd. of Trade v. Olsen, 262 U.S. 1 (1923) (approved regulation of the board of trade).

[29] McCray v. United States, 195 U.S. 27 (1904).

The 1922-1936 trend in rulings against federal taxes came to an end in 1937, the most clearly identifiable pivotal year in Supreme Court history, and perhaps in the political history of the United States after the Civil War and Reconstruction.[30] In 1937 the Supreme Court did an about face, relative to the decisions of the preceding period, and upheld three federal taxes (social security, unemployment, and firearms taxes) that were clearly intended to regulate, relying principally on an expanded view of the Commerce Clause, although the firearms tax raised minimal revenue and was upheld solely under the taxing power.[31] The 1937 (and later) opinions did not directly overrule the opinions from the preceding 15-year period insofar as they held that the taxes were not taxes but were (then unconstitutional) regulations. Therefore, aspiring tax avoiders can still cite those five earlier opinions and argue (1) the federal tax they wished to avoid did, or was intended to, regulate some subject matter, which (2) the United States does not have the power to regulate, and (3) the exaction falls outside the taxing power of the United States and is therefore unconstitutional. This possibility was most recently illustrated in the attacks on the 2010 health insurance tax.[32]

The decisions upholding New Deal taxes were recognized at the time as pitting the liberal (or literal) approach of the 1904 *McCray* decision, which still stands and has not been overruled, against the 1922 *Child Labor Tax Case*; and it was understood that those two decisions are irreconcilable.[33] *Butler* did not even attempt to reconcile them, not citing *McCray* in the majority opinion.[34] When cases involving this issue arise in the future (as occurred in the attack on the 2010 health insurance tax), no doubt the Court will purport to resolve them on the basis of close legal reasoning and analogies to prior decisions,[35] but the odd clustering of the anti-tax rulings between 1922 and 1936 strongly suggests that the cases' outcomes will largely depend on the politics of the Court at the

---

[30] Paul L. Murphy, The Constitution in Crisis Times 1918-1969, 154 (1972). *See generally* William E. Leuchtenburg, The Supreme Court Reborn (1995). *Cf.* A.T. Mason, The Supreme Court from Taft to Warren 249 et seq. (1968) (identifying and questioning the status of 1937 as a year of judicial revolution; tracing the waxing and waning of the Court's view that it stood between Congress and chaos). Another indication of the pivotal nature of the times for tax is the rise of Republican populist resistance to Democratic taxation, this time the "hidden taxes." *See* Marjorie E. Kornhauser, *Remembering the "Forgotten Man" (and Woman): Hidden Taxes and the 1936 Election*, Studies in the History of Tax Law Vol. 4 (John Tiley, ed, Hart 2010).

[31] Sonzinsky v. United States, 300 U.S. 506, 513-514 (1937) (firearms tax; opinion assumed Congress did not have power to regulate firearms); United States v. Miller, 307 U.S. 174 (1939) (similar to *Sonzinsky*); Helvering v. Davis, 301 U.S. 619, 640 (1937) (social security tax); Steward Machine Co. v. Davis, 301 U.S. 548 (1937) (unemployment tax).

[32] *See* Ch. III.E.2.c.

[33] Kingman Brewster, *Is The Process Tax Constitutional*, 19 A.B.A.J. 419, 422 (1933); Robert E. Cushman, *Social and Economic Control through Federal Taxation*, 18 Minn. L. Rev. 759, 782 (1934).

[34] United States v. Butler, 297 U.S. 1, 53 et seq. (1936).

[35] Distinctions can be perceived based on whether the taxing provision is part of a larger act with a set of regulatory provisions; just how extensive those regulatory provisions are; whether the tax funds the regulation; whether the tax is a mechanism for obtaining "voluntary" compliance with a regulatory scheme, etc.).

moment.[36] This point was illustrated by the 2012 *Sebelius* decision, involving attacks on the health insurance tax brought by almost all states whose legislatures were controlled by Republicans, and other Republican affiliated groups; indeed the most commented upon fact about the lineup of the Justices in the opinions was that Chief Justice Roberts, appointed by President George W. Bush, voted to uphold the tax.[37]

To fully understand the tax versus regulation issue one must understand the anti-tax opinions of those 15 years in the context of (1) the entire chronology of the Court's dealing with tax versus regulation, (2) the development of the Court's view of the Commerce Clause (which will only generally be addressed here), and (3) the Court's Tenth Amendment jurisprudence. The following Chapters attempt to interrelate all three stories.

As stated above, the reason tax avoiders argue so vehemently that an exaction is not a tax is the nearly unstoppable power of the United States to tax, as discussed in Chapter II.A. In capsule form this statement from an important Supreme Court opinion is typical of the Court view of the federal taxing power:

> In approaching this subject we must remember that enactments levying taxes, as other laws of the Federal Government when acting within constitutional authority, are the supreme law of the land. The Constitution contains only two limitations on the right of Congress to levy excise taxes; they must be levied for the public welfare and are required to be uniform throughout the United States. As Mr. Chief Justice Chase said, speaking for the court in License Tax Cases, 5 Wall. 462, 471: "Congress cannot tax exports, and it must impose direct taxes by the rule of apportionment, and indirect taxes by the rule of uniformity. Thus limited and thus only, it reaches every subject and may be exercised at discretion." The limitations to which the Chief Justice refers were the only ones imposed in the Constitution upon the taxing power.[38]

B. Why Characterization Matters

The preceding Chapter explains that the Court has made the unconstitutionality of five federal taxes (in four Acts) turn on the characterization of a tax as

[36] *Cf.* United States v. Butler, 297 U.S. 1, 62-63 (1936) ("There should be no misunderstanding as to the function of this court in such a case. It is sometimes said that the court assumes a power to overrule or control the action of the people's representatives. This is a misconception. The Constitution is the supreme law of the land ordained and established by the people. All legislation must conform to the principles it lays down. When an act of Congress is appropriately challenged in the courts as not conforming to the constitutional mandate the judicial branch of the Government has only one duty,—to lay the article of the Constitution which is invoked beside the statute which is challenged and to decide whether the latter squares with the former. All the court does, or can do, is to announce its considered judgment upon the question. The only power it has, if such it may be called, is the power of judgment. This court neither approves nor condemns any legislative policy. Its delicate and difficult office is to ascertain and declare whether the legislation is in accordance with, or in contravention of, the provisions of the Constitution; and, having done that, its duty ends.").

[37] *See* Ch. III.E.2.c.

[38] Flint v. Stone Tracy Co., 220 U.S. 107, 153-154 (1911).

not a tax but as solely a regulation. However, this is only one of several contexts discussed in this book in which the characterization of taxes as such matters.[39] The reasons classification issues can arise include:

- The United States can tax almost anything to any extent, including subjects it cannot regulate, and can do so subject to very scanty constitutional limits, which have proved hard to enforce;[40] but it cannot regulate or license or penalize everything because the United States does not have a general police power as the states do.
- The amount of a tax (state or federal), once permitted, is limitless. Indeed the issue frequently comes up in disputes over whether a heavy tax is really a penal regulation due to its weight. In these cases the analysis always cites Chief Justice Marshall's injunction that the power to tax involves the power to destroy.[41]
- In contrast, the Court, during its substantive due process heyday, established a different rule about regulations and confiscation that has endured: "the power to regulate is not the power to destroy."[42]
- The practical regulatory result of many federal taxes, and the purpose of Congress to regulate while it taxes, have long been understood and blessed by the Supreme Court, without converting the tax into a regulation for purposes of constitutional analysis.[43]
- If a federal exaction is not a tax, then it must be authorized by some other grant of power in the Constitution.[44]
- If a federal exaction is a tax, the bill enacting it must originate in the House.[45]
- If a federal exaction is a tax on exports, the United States cannot levy it.[46]
- If a state exaction is a tax on imports or exports, the state cannot levy it.[47]

---

[39] *See* Ch. IV, tax versus user fee.

[40] *See* Ch. III.E.

[41] *See* Ch. II.A.2.

[42] *E.g.*, Railroad Com. Cases, 116 U.S. 307, 331 (1886) (regarding railroad rate making by the legislature). *See also* Chicago, M. & St. P. Ry. v. Minnesota, 134 U.S. 418 (1890) (reserving to the courts and not the legislature the ultimate determination of the reasonableness of rates); Permian Basin Area Rate Cases, 390 U.S. 747, 769 (1968) (citing the 1886 opinion).

[43] *See* Ch. III.E.2.

[44] It could be a fee, a penalty for activity the United States has the power to regulate, or a criminal fine; the imposition could be necessary and proper to some other power, such as the power to regulate currency.

[45] *See* Ch. VIII.C.

[46] *See* Ch. VI.D.

[47] *See* Ch. VI.E.

- If a federal exaction is a tax, the use of the revenues raised may (or may not) be limited to pay federal debts or for the common defense or general welfare.[48]
- If a federal exaction is a tax that is a direct tax and is not an income tax, it must be apportioned to the states.[49]
- If a federal exaction is a tax, then by definition it is not in violation of the reserved powers of the states to tax because the power to tax is concurrent; but the same is not necessarily true of a state tax because of the Supremacy Clause.[50] The federal taxing power is not limited by the Tenth Amendment.[51]
- If a federal exaction is a tax that is not a direct tax, it must be uniform throughout the United States; but geographical uniformity is not required for user fees or regulatory charges.[52] Indeed regulatory charges can be confusingly similar to regulatory taxes, with the distinction turning on there actually being some federal regulation that must be paid for in the case of charges.[53]
- Wholly different due process and other Fourth, Fifth and Sixth Amendment, self-incrimination, double jeopardy and other requirements that are specifically related to the imposition of a criminal penalty or punishment do not or may not apply to a tax.[54]
- If the exaction (state or federal) is not a tax, it may be a taking for public use without just compensation in violation of the Fifth or Fourteenth Amendments.[55]

Joseph Story was tempted to describe all contributions imposed by a government on individuals (and other persons) for the use of the state as taxes, regardless of their name.[56] That might have been a good approach, but it has not been adopted by the Court.

C. Definitions of Tax

Despite the important consequences that can depend on the characterization of a governmental exaction as a tax (or not), the Supreme Court has not settled on a clear definition of tax. The reasons include (1) despite the many settings in which classification matters, it is disputed relatively infrequently, so that offhand

---

[48] *See* Ch. III.D.

[49] *See* Ch. V.C.2.

[50] *See* Ch. II.B.

[51] *See* Ch. III.F.3.

[52] *See* Ch. V.D.3.a. *See, e.g.*, Alaska v. Troy, 258 U.S. 101 (1922).

[53] *See* Ch. IV.

[54] *See* Lipke v. Lederer, 259 U.S. 557 (1922) (particularly the dissent of Justice Brandeis). *See also* discussions of *Constantine* and *La Franca*, Ch. III.F.2, and Ch. VII.E, on double jeopardy.

[55] *See* Ch. V.D3.b(8).

[56] *See* JOSEPH STORY, COMMENTARIES ON THE CONSTITUTION OF THE UNITED STATES, Vol. 2, 419 (1833) [hereinafter STORY].

definitions generally suffice for the issues at hand, without having to be complete;[57] (2) as the list in the preceding Chapter shows, the contexts of classification vary widely, a fact that perhaps cautions the Court not to attempt a single definition; (3) the issue inevitably involves the amorphous substance over form approach, which the Court also never defines; because (4) the Court doesn't want to box itself in. It is important to ward off the tendency to seize upon some supposed all-purpose definition of tax that explains all cases: there is none. For example, the Court has rejected the argument that all exactions levied under Title 26 and labeled a tax are necessarily taxes.[58] On the other hand it has stated that the characterization of a tax should be based on the face of the statute,[59] but still has ruled that facial taxes are not taxes at all, as for example in *Butler*.[60] Most recently the Court essayed a so called functional approach, without fully defining the functions of all taxes.[61]

The most that can be said with confidence in defining a tax is that (1) if Congress does not treat an exaction as a tax, it is not likely to be characterized as an Article I, section 8, clause 1 tax; (2) if Congress does treat an exaction as a tax, it must at least also appear on its face to be an attempted exaction of money by Congress from persons whom Congress has the power to tax; (3) the possibility of raising at least some, even de minimis, amount of revenue through the tax is a positive factor, if not required;[62] and in the odd but important case when Congress' treatment of a tax as a tax is ambiguous (*e.g.*, in Title 26 but called a penalty), the Court has said it will apply a functional analysis.[63] The third point may be considered by some to set too low a threshold, but it is supported in the cases, and, as *Butler* shows, has not in practice prevented the Court from ignoring the substantial revenue raising ability of a tax and finding it was not a tax.

General statements that the Court frequently makes tend to be misleading as complete definitions of tax, even though they may describe most taxes. Contrary to common misstatements, taxes are not necessarily levied only for the "general"

---

[57] *See, e.g.*, Bull v. United States, 295 U.S. 247, 259 (1935) ("a tax is an exaction by the sovereign . . . ," but a definition was not relevant to the case because the nature of the levy as a tax was not disputed).

[58] Massachusetts v. United States, 435 U.S. 444 (1978) (no "bright-line test" dependent on enactment in Title 26).

[59] McCray v. United States, 195 U.S. 27 (1904) (refers to the face of the statute seven times).

[60] United States v. Butler, 297 U.S. 1 (1936).

[61] *See* Ch. III.E.2.c, discussing the 2012 health insurance tax ruling in Nat'l Fed'n of Indep. Bus. v. Sebelius, 567 U.S. 519 (2012).

[62] The latter possibility is illustrated best in Trusler v. Crooks, 269 U.S. 475 (1926). Taxpayer's attorney alleged that the amount of the tax was 200 times the value of the contract that was subject to the tax. 70 L. Ed. 365 (1926). Apparently no one ever paid the tax except Mr. Trusler, who bought a single tax stamp for purposes of testing the law. *See* Trusler v. Crooks, 300 F. 996 (W.D. Mo. 1924). In contrast, the 10 cents per pound tax on colored margarine was said to be not prohibitive but high enough to make fraud unprofitable. Herbert F. Margulies, *Federal Police Power by Taxation*, 5 J. S. L. HIST. 1, 7 (1997) (an in depth study of the legislative actions leading to the tax).

[63] *See* Ch. III.E.2.c, discussing the 2012 health insurance tax ruling in Nat'l Fed'n of Indep. Bus. v. Sebelius, 567 U.S. 519 (2012).

support of government, because they may be segregated or identified for some specific use. Taxes are not necessarily levied only from involuntary payors, because payors sometimes elect to pay a license or franchise tax in order to receive a particular benefit. Therefore, taxes are not necessarily levied without regard to benefit received from government by the taxpayer, although generally that is true.

The point about lack of benefits from most tax payments (other than franchise and license taxes) cannot be overemphasized because it is counterintuitive. *Southern Coal & Coke* stated:

> A tax is not an assessment of benefits. It is . . . a means of distributing the burden of the cost of government. The only benefit to which the taxpayer is constitutionally entitled is that derived from his enjoyment of the privilege of living in an organized society, established and safeguarded by the devotion of taxes to public purposes.[64]

The Court rejected a due process objection to state taxes based on the disproportion between the amount of the tax and the benefit they receive.[65] Nevertheless, the Court sometimes slips up and says taxes are a way of apportioning the burdens of benefits, which statement does not literally require that there be any relationship between the two.[66]

Only slightly clearer are the meanings of other types of government exactions, which may be contrasted as aids in identifying a tax by elimination of the other possibilities: a user fee or regulatory charge (both of which are not taxes) imposed for some specific benefit or federal regulation,[67] and a penalty (civil/regulatory or criminal). But a regulatory tax (a tax intended to regulate addressed by Ch. III.E) is different from a regulatory charge (a non-tax charge for the costs of regulation). The matter is confused principally due to the overlapping functions of almost all government exactions, for example:

- The taxes that are most likely to be contested commonly are defined to fall on activities, transactions or property that are relatively undesired by Congress for some reason; hence the taxes likely have a regulatory function or appear to be penal.[68]
- Taxes generally bear no relationship to the receipt of a benefit or to its value. But that is not always true because sometimes the tax may be a precondition to quite specific benefits, as in the case of license, franchise and other priv-

[64] Carmichael v. Southern Coal & Coke Co., 301 U.S. 495, 522-523 (1937). To similar effect are statements in Commonwealth Edison Co. v. Montana, 453 U.S. 609, 623 (1981); Massachusetts v. United States, 435 U.S. 444, 455 (1978); Inter-Island Steam Navigation Co. v. Hawaii, 305 U.S. 306 (1938); Keystone Bituminous Coal Ass'n v. DeBenedictis, 480 U.S. 470 n. 21 (1987).

[65] Commonwealth Edison Co. v. Montana, 453 U.S. 609 (1981) (state tax case).

[66] *See, e.g.*, Welch v. Henry, 305 U.S. 134, 146-147 (1938).

[67] *See* Ch. IV.

[68] *See* Ch. III.E

ilege taxes, which almost always are identified as excise taxes on the pursuit of a business.[69]

- Illegal activity may be the subject of a tax as well as a criminal penalty.[70]
- Even though it is well settled that taxes can be designed to encourage certain responses by taxpayers to avoid the taxes, so are criminal laws designed in part to deter crime.

Analysis of tax characterization also is confusing because there are various ways to approach the subject. One way is to focus on the handful of Supreme Court opinions holding a federal levy that is denominated and defended by the government as a tax, not to be a tax (the five decisions from 1922 to 1936). Another way is to focus on the hints in the Constitution of what is a tax. A third way is to cobble together the disparate comments made by the Supreme Court in finding federal levies to be taxes, and in connection with state taxes. A fourth way is to try to define the other levies: user fees, regulatory charges, and penalties.

As stated above, the use of generalized definitions is most suspect. Many have essayed (usually misleading) definitions. For example:

- "Taxation is the simple operation of taking small portions from a perpetually accumulating mass, susceptible of almost infinite division; and a power in one to take what is necessary for certain purposes, is not, in its nature, incompatible with a power in another to take what is necessary for other purposes."[71]
- Taxes are, as said in *Cooley on Taxation*, p. 1: "The enforced proportional contribution of persons and property, levied by the authority of the State for the support of the government and for all public needs . . . ."[72]
- Taxes are often referred to as being for the general support of the government and unrelated to any specific prospect of benefit, which is clearly incorrect.[73] This definition may have arisen in the context of interpreting contracts, as for example when a government granted land to a railroad and exempted the land from future taxation but later levied a special assessment to pay for improvements, which the Court allowed based on a differentiation between general taxes (to which the contract applied) and taxes that were special assessments.[74]

---

[69] *See* Ch. IV.C.

[70] *See, e.g.*, License Tax Cases, 72 U.S. 462 (1867).

[71] Gibbons v. Ogden, 22 U.S. 1, 198-199 (1824).

[72] Quoted in Patton v. Brady, 184 U.S. 608, 619 (1902).

[73] *See, e.g.*, Puerto Rico v. Russell & Co., 315 U.S. 610 (1942) (levy for a water district found to impair the obligation of contract because it was not a general tax).

[74] *See, e.g.*, Illinois C. R. Co. v. Decatur, 147 U.S. 190 (1893).

- Similarly, generalities are sometimes relied on in defining taxes when the alternative is some unconstitutional limitation, as on the free exercise of religion.[75]
- "A tax, in the general understanding of the term, and as used in the Constitution, signifies an exaction for the support of the Government."[76] This definition is utilized when the Court thinks the tax is an exaction for some other purpose, such as regulating a matter beyond Congress' authority and not for raising revenue.[77]
- Unfortunately, one of the most quoted purported definitions of tax was rendered by Justice Sutherland: "A tax is an enforced contribution to provide for the support of government; a penalty, as the word is here used, is an exaction imposed by statute as punishment for an unlawful act. The two words are not interchangeable, one for the other. No mere exercise of the art of lexicography can alter the essential nature of an act or a thing; and if an exaction be clearly a penalty it cannot be converted into a tax by the simple expedient of calling it such."[78] But a tax need not be an involuntary payment, because taxpayers can voluntarily pay a tax to obtain a license or franchise; and a tax can regulate as opposed to providing for the support of the government, particularly when the subject of regulation is within the federal governments' authority; and taxes can penalize and do so for the purpose of discouraging the taxed conduct, whether or not the conduct is otherwise criminal.

Finally, taxes have different meanings for different purposes. For example:

- The Bankruptcy Code makes distinctions between taxes and penalties and has its own definitions.[79]
- The Origination Clause applies only to revenue raising taxes in certain types of bills.[80]
- A tax that is justified as necessary and proper under another power, such as the power to regulate foreign commerce or immigration, is not subject to the limitations on taxing power taxes, such as the direct tax apportionment requirement.[81]

---

[75] *See, e.g.*, Rosenberger v. Rector and Visitors of the Univ. of Va., 515 U.S. 819 (1995) (student activity fee not a tax).

[76] United States v. Butler, 297 U.S. 1, 61 (1936).

[77] *Id.*

[78] United States v. La Franca, 282 U.S. 568, 572 (1931).

[79] *See* United States v. Reorganized CF&I Fabricators, 518 U.S. 213 (1996); United States v. New York, 315 U.S. 510 (1942); United States v. Sotelo, 436 U.S. 268 (1978). *Cf.* Nat'l Fed'n of Indep. Bus. v. Sebelius, 567 U.S. 519 (2012) (asserting that characterization in *Sotelo* under bankruptcy statutes is generally relevant, as discussed in Ch. III.E.2.c).

[80] *See* Ch. VIII.C; Twin City Bank v. Nebeker, 167 U.S. 196 (1897).

[81] Edye v. Robertson, 112 U.S. 580, 595 (1884) (Head Money Cases).

- The Anti-Injunction Act applies only to taxes assessable under the Internal Revenue Codes of 1954 and 1939 and so did not apply to fees assessed under another federal statute.[82] Similarly Chief Justice Roberts rather surprisingly managed to find in 2012 that Congress did not intend the Anti-Injunction Act to the health insurance tax because it labeled that tax a penalty and not a tax.[83]

D. Clause One's Definition of Taxes: Purposes

1. *The Spending Power*

A primary source of guidance on the differentiation of federal taxes from federal regulation through exactions that are not taxes might be found in Article 1, section 8, clause 1 of the Constitution. It contains both the taxing power and the spending power. The juxtaposition of the two powers might suggest that the identification of federal taxes can be informed in some cases by the purposes for which the revenues raised by taxes are spent. For example, perhaps a tax levied for an improper spending purpose is not a tax at all? By analogy, in the narrow area of taxpayer objections to federal spending for the establishment of religion, a connection between taxes and spending has been recognized for standing purposes.[84]

Supreme Court opinions, both of the Court and in dissent, have implicitly rejected the interpretations that (1) there is no linkage between taxes and spending,[85] and (2) the clause simply lists several unrelated things Congress can do, including legislating for the general welfare, without any connection with spending, much less taxing.[86] However, there generally is no connection in fact between taxing and the spending for which the revenues might be used, simply because most tax revenues cannot be traced to appropriations or spending, and all taxes can find a proper spending home given the huge amount of federal debt. But in the *Butler* decision, discussed in the next Chapter, the Court found that the tax revenues could be traced to a spending program that the Court found to be a regulation of agriculture that was beyond the regulatory power of Congress. The Court further found the related tax to be unconstitutional not as a section 8, clause 1 tax but as an exaction that was not a tax, which was allegedly necessary and proper in aid of an unconstitutional regulation.

Outside of a case like *Butler* involving such a tight connection between taxing and spending in an era when the Court had a very limited view of Congress' regulatory powers under the Commerce Clause, the spending power, like the

---

[82] Federal Energy Administration v. Algonquin SNG, Inc., 426 U.S. 548, 558 n. 9 (1976).

[83] Nat'l Fed'n of Indep. Bus. v. Sebelius, 567 U.S. 519 (2012).

[84] *See* Ch. VIII.D.4.b.

[85] Flemming v. Nestor, 363 U.S. 603 (1960); Western Air Lines v. Board of Equalization, 480 U.S. 123 (1987); Nat'l Fed'n of Indep. Bus. v. Sebelius, 567 U.S. 519 (2012) (Roberts opinion states "Put simply, Congress may tax and spend.").

[86] For example, the Thomas dissent in Nat'l Fed'n of Indep. Bus. v. Sebelius, 567 U.S. 519 (2012) treats the general welfare as part of the "Spending Clause," which is typical.

taxing power, normally is a powerful federal tool over which Congress has wide discretion. For example, because Congress can choose to spend, or not, and because the Court recognizes that tax deductions are like federal spending, Congress can choose not to spend to promote free speech and so can choose not to subsidize free speech through tax deductions for the costs of such speech.[87] Likewise, Congress can condition spending on actions of others that it could not regulate directly.[88] Specifically, Congress may, in the exercise of its spending power, condition its grant of funds to the States upon their taking certain actions that Congress could not require them to take, and that acceptance of the funds entails an agreement to the action,[89] though the Court enforced an uncertain limit to that power in *Sebelius* in 2012.[90] Thus the spending power is like the taxing power in that both can be used to regulate matters that Congress could not regulate directly.

2. Butler *and Spending Purpose*

United States v. Butler uniquely stands for the proposition that when the sole purpose of a tax is to regulate something Congress cannot regulate, then the tax might not be sustained either under the taxing power (despite the fact that substantial revenues are raised) or the Necessary and Proper Clause.[91] Even though *Butler* is thus distinguishable from the rest of the Court's decisions striking down taxes as not taxes, which relied in part on the absence or small amount of revenue raised, it is worth addressing first because of its discussion of spending purposes.

Butler is the last decision striking down a federal tax because the Court would not characterize it as a tax under the taxing power but rather called it a regulation of a subject the United States could not regulate or spend money upon.[92] It relied on Congress' sole purpose to regulate local agriculture despite the substantial tax raised by the levy at issue. *Butler* struck down a federal tax on cotton processors, which tax was not prohibitively high and did produce substantial revenues, because it was neither (1) a "true tax" (meaning it was not an exertion of the taxing power),[93] nor was it (2) necessary and proper to the carrying out of a power possessed by Congress, including spending under the Spending Clause, because it was in aid of a regulation of agriculture, a subject found to be (then) reserved to the states under the Tenth Amendment.[94]

When *Butler* struck down the Agricultural Adjustment Act, which included the tax, it provided a Pyrrhic victory by settling favorably to Congress the question whether it could spend for the general welfare, apart from spending in

---

[87] Regan v. Taxation with Representation, 461 U.S. 540 (1983). *See* Ch. VIII.D.

[88] *See, e.g.*, United States v. Am. Library Ass'n, 539 U.S. 194, 209 n. 4 (2003).

[89] South Dakota v. Dole, 483 U.S. 203 (1987); New York v. United States, 505 U.S. 144 (1992). *See* Ch. III.D.8.b.

[90] *See* Ch. III.E.2.c(5).

[91] United States v. Butler, 297 U.S. 1 (1936).

[92] It was not the last of the anti-New Deal decisions, but the last such decision involved a tax that the government did not defend as a tax. Carter v. Carter Coal Co., 298 U.S. 238 (1936).

[93] 297 U.S. at 61.

[94] 297 U.S. at 68-78.

pursuit of any other enumerated federal power. In doing so *Butler* adopted what is known as the Hamilton/Story expansive view and rejected Madison's view.[95] However, this expansive view, which the Court soon employed to support federal spending on Social Security in 1937,[96] did not save the Agricultural Adjustment Act tax, because the Court found the expanded scope of general welfare to be constrained by the Tenth Amendment. *Steward Machine*, which later upheld the unemployment insurance tax in 1937, tried to limit this constraint by observing that surely relief of the unemployed in a time of national economic crisis was for the general welfare.[97]

The first part of the *Butler* opinion took an all or nothing approach to identifying a "true tax" under the taxing power: once the Court concluded in that part of its analysis that the "sole object" of the Act containing the tax was the regulation of agriculture that it found elsewhere in the Act,[98] including regulation by spending, there was no room for the associated tax to be a "true tax." A casual reader of *Butler* might assume that the Court ruled the tax was not a "true tax" because it was for spending that was beyond the Spending Clause. However, *Butler* did not reason in that fashion. Rather it first ruled the tax was not a "true tax" because it took the character of the regulation to which it was linked, and

---

[95] Robert Eugene Cushman, *The National Police Power under the Taxing Clause of the Constitution*, 4 MINN. L. REV. 247, 257 (1920) [hereinafter Cushman]. *See also* Robert B. McKay, *Taxing and Spending for the General Welfare: A Reply to Mr. Nillson*, 48 A.B.A. J. 38, 39 (1962) [hereinafter McKay] (explaining that Madison was alone in his view). But some academics are still fighting for Madison. *See* John C. Eastman, *Restoring the "General" to the General Welfare Clause*, 4 CHAP. L. REV. 63 (2001); Robert G. Natelson, *Judicial Review of Special Interest Spending: The General Welfare Clause and the Fiduciary Law of the Founders*, 11 TEX. REV. L. AND POL. 239, 243 (2006) (stating that *Butler* departed from the "original meaning"). One writer in 1919 had stated the conclusion that *Butler* reached as "settled," but noted dissenting views. Cushman, at 250 (reciting the various arguments, prior to *Butler*; citing Jefferson and Monroe).

[96] Helvering v. Davis, 301 U.S. 619, 640 (1937) ("There have been great statesmen in our history who have stood for other views. We will not resurrect the contest. It is now settled by decision. *United States v. Butler, supra.*"). *See also* Fullilove v. Klutznick, 448 U.S. 448, 474 (1980) (same); South Dakota v. Dole, 483 U.S. 203, 207 (1987) (explaining this reading of *Butler*; but dissent argued that spending power could not be that expansive). *See* ROBERT H. JACKSON, THE STRUGGLE FOR JUDICIAL SUPREMACY 233 (1941) ("The much criticized opinion in the *Butler* case had helped to lay a foundation for victory in the Social Security cases."); ROBERT H. JACKSON, THE SUPREME COURT IN THE AMERICAN SYSTEM OF GOVERNMENT 60 (1963) ("In the famous Agricultural Adjustments Act case the political branches lost a case and won a cause.").

[97] Steward Machine Co. v. Davis, 301 U.S. 548, 587 (1937) ("It is too late today for the argument to be heard with tolerance that in a crisis so extreme the use of the moneys of the nation to relieve the unemployed and their dependents is a use for any purpose narrower than the promotion of the general welfare. *Cf.* United States v. Butler, 297 U.S. 1, 65, 66, Helvering v. Davis."). *See also* as to the breadth of the General Welfare Power, Buckley v. Valeo, 424 U.S. 1 (1976).

[98] 297 U.S. at 58 ("The tax can only be sustained by ignoring the avowed purpose and operation of the act, and holding it a measure merely laying an excise upon processors to raise revenue for the support of government. Beyond cavil the sole object of the legislation is to restore the purchasing power of agricultural products to a parity with that prevailing in an earlier day; to take money from the processor and bestow it upon farmers who will reduce their acreage for the accomplishment of the proposed end, and, meanwhile to aid these farmers during the period required to bring the prices of their crops to the desired level.").

so should be evaluated solely by asking the question whether it was a necessary and proper adjunct to that regulation; then it decided the regulation, including its spending, was beyond the power of Congress because the subject matter was reserved to the states.[99]

Whether *Butler* stands for the proposition that a taxing power tax must be imposed for a spending purpose authorized in the latter part of section 8, clause 1 is muddled.[100] The opinion stated that the government had conceded that "to provide for the general welfare" qualifies the power to "lay and collect taxes."[101] However, the government brief did not concede a linkage between the two powers, but only argued in the alternative that if the tax were not upheld simply as a tax, then it was levied for a proper spending purpose.[102] In addition, because the Court had already ruled in the first part of its opinion that the tax at issue was not a taxing power tax,[103] its later statements about the linkage of taxes with spending can apply only to taxes that are not "true taxes," but rather are exactions that can only be defended as necessary and property to carry out another power.[104]

The *Butler* opinion in its third part rejected the government's argument that the spending was not regulating matters subject to exclusive state control because the spending occurred only upon the voluntary acceptance by the cotton farmers of the support payments.[105] The Court found the cooperation not to be voluntary because it was due to economic coercion, and even if it were voluntary the spending program (and also the tax) still were unconstitutional because they regulated in an area reserved to the states.[106]

---

[99] *Id.* at 61 (stating that the tax was not unconstitutional simply because it was not a taxing power tax).

[100] *Cf.* United States v. Comstock, 560 U.S. 126, 1967 (2010) (concurrence of Justice Kennedy refusing to agree that the spending power even exists apart from the taxing power).

[101] 297 U.S. at 64.

[102] Brief for the United States, 1935 WL 33033 (U.S.) pages 63-64 (Nov. 18, 1935). As to the controlling status of a government concession in a constitutional tax case, *see* dissent of Justice Kennedy in United States v. IBM, 517 U.S. 843, 870 (1996), pointing out that that the Court had refused to accept such a concession in Massachusetts v. United States, 333 U.S. 611 (1948). But the majority in IBM evidently refused to consider an argument the government had arguably not made, as pointed out in Justice Souter's dissent in Ashcroft v. Iqbal, 556 U.S. 662, 692 (2009). Thus it seems the Court can and will ignore a concession or not when it suits its majority.

[103] "It does not follow that as the act is not an exertion of the taxing power and the exaction not a true tax, the statute is void or the exaction uncollectible. For, to paraphrase what was said in the *Head Money Cases* (supra), p. 596, if this is an expedient regulation by Congress, of a subject within one of its granted powers, 'and the end to be attained is one falling within that power, the act is not void, because, within a loose and more extended sense than was used in the Constitution,' the exaction is called a tax." 297 U.S. at 61.

[104] "The true construction undoubtedly is that the only thing granted is the power to tax for the purpose of providing funds for payment of the nation's debts and making provision for the general welfare." 297 U.S. at 64. While not specifically cited later by the Court, *Helvering v. Davis* implicitly adopted the theory of linkage by stating that once the spending Title of the Social Security Act was found valid, there was no reason to examine the taxing Title. 301 U.S. at 645.

[105] 297 U.S. at 70-71.

[106] *Id.* at 72.

Properly read, the *Butler* opinion has fairly narrow application to federal taxes levied under Article I, section 8, clause 1:

- *Butler* does not require that taxes always be evaluated in relation to associated spending of revenues produced, because, of course, that is seldom possible: the vast majority of tax revenues that are raised by the income tax have no necessary relation to any particular spending; indeed part of the vague definition of a tax is that it usually is not associated with the receipt of any benefit in terms of government spending.[107]

- Even if there is a linkage in a statute between a tax and some spending that the Court finds outside the expansive scope of the Spending Clause, *Butler* does not necessarily exclude the tax from the taxing power, unless by analogy to the facts found in *Butler* the "sole object" of the Act and its tax is not taxation (however that is determined) and so the tax is not a taxing power tax.

- *Butler* is inapposite to cases in which the alleged problem with the tax is not its relation to prohibited spending, but rather to prohibited regulation, as was allegedly the case in *Drexel*, *Hill v. Wallace*, *Trusler*, and *Constantine*, except to the extent the tax produces little or no revenue and so might be said in a *cf.* cite to *Butler* not to be a tax at all.

Therefore, when tax protesters assert the unconstitutionality of a tax on grounds of absence of power in Congress to tax, it is much more likely that they will be making a *Drexel*, *Hill v. Wallace*, *Trusler*, and *Constantine* type of argument (the tax is a regulatory penalty and not a taxing power tax because it will not in fact raise revenue, or for some other reason), than that they are making a *Butler* type of argument that somehow links a tax that clearly raises revenue to unconstitutional spending. If for no other reason than to avoid such attacks, presumably Congress will be wise enough not to link the tax and the appropriation of its proceeds to spending in the same Act (although the wisdom of Congress in drafting tax laws to avoid constitutional problems was brought into serious doubt in the *Sebelius* case, as discussed in Chapter III.E.2.c).

Where does the foregoing analysis then leave the relationship between a tax's purposes and the characterization of taxes (duties, excises, imposts) for purposes of the taxing power? It leaves a confusion of two types of cases:

- If a tax is sufficiently associated in the law with defined spending *purposes*, then a court might find that the spending is not within Congress' powers, that the tax cannot be otherwise justified as a "true tax" because of Congress' *intent or motives* in enacting it, and the tax falls (*e.g.*, *Butler*) because it is not a tax but an improper regulation.

- If a tax is not linked by statute with spending purposes, but rather is found to be motivated by Congress' *intent or motive* to regulate something that Congress cannot regulate, then the tax might fall if it is not a "true tax,"

---

[107] *See* Ch. II.A.2.

which should be based on the face of the statute and perhaps whether it has the potential to raise some revenue (or functions as a tax when not labeled a tax), but also may be based on Congress' *intent or motives* found to be solely to regulate (*e.g.*, *Drexel*, *Hill v. Wallace*, *Trusler*, and *Constantine*).

Observe that in each case the most important factual investigation is not, or is not solely, the spending *purposes* (*e.g.*, the general welfare issue), but rather is an investigation of Congress' *motives*: even though Congress labeled an exaction as a tax, located it in Title 26, or gave it other indicia of a tax, the Court has looked beyond that evidence in five decisions (involving four Acts) to classify the tax solely as a regulation through a conclusion that can only rest on an inference of legislative *motive*. As shown below, it is crystal clear that "true taxes" can regulate as their primary purpose. Any exaction that Congress treated as a tax, and that appears both to collect revenue and to regulate, can be a valid taxing power tax, as the Court has ruled on several occasions both before and after *Butler*. Therefore, to eject a regulatory tax from that permitted category in defiance of Congress' legislation to the contrary, the Court both must infer a sole intent to regulate in disregard of a stated purpose to tax, and be willing to rule on the basis of that inference in defiance of other opinions of the Court that have rejected such an approach, discussed in the following Chapter.[108]

A separate issue about taxing and spending not explored here, is spending through the Internal Revenue Code by tax expenditures, which has attracted substantial academic attention.[109]

3. *Purpose and Motive*

a. *Taxing Purpose*

The evaluation of Congress' purpose in the context of distinguishing a tax from a regulation may involve analysis similar to that applied in statutory interpretation and construction generally, but has a different goal.[110] Whereas statutory interpretation attempts to make the ambiguous clear, investigations of purpose in levying a tax usually aims to unseat Congress' formal treatment of a levy as a tax by resorting to substance said to be informed by Congress' purpose. However, if Congress treats a levy as a tax, then its purpose is thereby expressed and any further investigation actually delves into legislative motives, an area usually off limits even to the Supreme Court, as discussed in the next Chapter. Conversely, if Congress does not clearly treat a levy as a tax, as it arguably did not in the case of the 2010 health insurance tax, then the Court will say it is

---

[108] *See, e.g.*, McCray v. United States, 195 U.S. 27 (1904) (refers to the face of the statute seven times).

[109] *See, e.g.*, Ruth Mason, *Federalism and the Taxing Power*, 99 CAL. L. REV. 975, 984 (2011). *But see* Ch. VIII.D.2.d, discussing tax expenditures and free speech.

[110] *See* JASPER L. CUMMINGS, JR., THE SUPREME COURT'S FEDERAL TAX JURISPRUDENCE 264-271 (2d ed. 2016) [hereinafter CUMMINGS], as discussed further in the following Chapter.

investigating Congress' purpose to tax or regulate by assessing the function of the levy.[111]

In a case like *Butler*, discussed in the preceding Chapter, where the tax actually raised substantial revenue, the Court might evaluate Congress' spending purposes as a way to invalidate the tax. However usually taxes and spending are not so linked. Aside from such a case, the Court is left with inferring a solely regulatory purpose from a tax that does not raise revenue, which it was willing to do during the period 1922-1936.

The text of the Constitution and its history do not require that Congress have a spending purpose, or any other purpose, in enacting a tax. Article I, section 8, clause 1 (the first enumerated power of Congress) states:

> The Congress shall have Power To lay and collect Taxes, Duties, Imposts and Excises, to pay the Debts and provide for the common Defence and general Welfare of the United States; but all Duties, Imposts and Excises shall be uniform throughout the United States; . . . .

In addition the preamble to the Constitution states that it is adopted in order to provide for the common defense and promote the general welfare. The taxes specifically identified in the taxing power are generic taxes that commonly have no linkage with spending: excises are usually taxes on transactions or privileges granted,[112] duties and imposts are types of taxes levied on exports and imports,[113] and taxing power taxes encompass every other type of tax, principally property and head taxes. The latter, being direct taxes, usually were levied to produce a defined sum that Congress thought was needed for a period, usually a period of war. But excises and imposts produce however much revenue the business activities taxed cause them to produce.

Other parts of the Constitutional also refer to taxes without regard to spending. Article I, section 9, clause 4 classifies a capitation tax as a direct tax, and shows that tax and duty are used interchangeably (to refer to levies on exports and imports). Article I, section 9, clause 1 shows that an import duty on slaves was viewed as a tax and actually authorized a a head tax up to $10 without reference to any spending need. Article 1, section 10, clause 2 relates imposts to export duties.

The history of the Confederation shows that taxation and spending can exist independently of each other, but not successfully. In contrast to the Constitution, the Articles of Confederation stated:

---

[111] *See* Ch. III.E.2.c.

[112] Flint v. Stone Tracy Co., 220 U.S. 107, 151 (1911) ("Excises are 'taxes laid upon the manufacture, sale or consumption of commodities within the country, upon licenses to pursue certain occupations, and upon corporate privileges.'").

[113] *Id.* ("Duties and imposts are terms commonly applied to levies made by governments on the importation or exportation of commodities."). *Cf.* James M. Gray, Limitations of the Taxing Power 351 (1906) [hereinafter Gray] (while duties, imposts and excises can refer to all taxes, duty most commonly refers to taxes on imports, exports or consumption; impost is any tax but hardly ever a direct tax; excise duties are inland imposts on manufacture and sale, licenses and special privileges).

> Article VIII. All charges of war, and all other expenses that shall be incurred for the common defense or general welfare, and allowed by the United States in Congress assembled, shall be defrayed out of a common treasury, which shall be supplied by the several States in proportion to the value of all land within each State, granted or surveyed for any person, as such land and the buildings and improvements thereon shall be estimated according to such mode as the United States in Congress assembled, shall from time to time direct and appoint.
>
> The taxes for paying that proportion shall be laid and levied by the authority and direction of the legislatures of the several States within the time agreed upon by the United States in Congress assembled.

Because the Confederation did not have the power of taxation but only of spending, the taxes requisitioned from the states obviously had to be for the authorized spending purposes. In contrast, the Constitution gives the United States both the taxing power and the spending power, and so linking spending and taxing was not inevitable.[114] Moreover, the Court has rejected that linkage in the important area of taxpayer standing to challenge spending generally (outside the Establishment Clause cases): being a taxpayer does not give a person the standing to challenge the purposes for which tax revenues are used.[115]

As discussed in Chapter III.D.2, *Butler*, a decision striking down a federal tax, indicated that purpose mattered in two ways in evaluating the tax: (1) a tax may not be a "true tax" if its purpose is too closely linked to spending, and (2) it ruled that after a tax is determined not to be a "true tax," it can be upheld only if it serves the *purpose* of aiding some other action within Congress' power.[116] As to the suggested linkage, the Court has occasionally stated in passing that the taxing power authorizes taxes for "public purposes," or "in order to" pay for the common defense, etc.[117] But, like Santa Claus, the bad purpose federal tax (as contrasted with the regulation masquerading as a tax) is more discussed than seen. Indeed, the Supreme Court has never held a tax that it agreed was a tax (*Butler* did not agree the tax was a taxing power tax) to be unconstitutional because Congress laid and collected it to raise funds to be used for some purpose other than debts, defense and general welfare.[118] Therefore, the issue of what will tax revenues be used for is largely theoretical.

In practice the tax laws that are in place in the Internal Revenue Code produce a steady stream of revenue without relation to any congressional spending purpose. The federal budget attempts to match revenues with expenditures, which

---

[114] *See* Ware v. Hylton, 3 U.S. 199, 232 (1796).

[115] *See* Ch. VIII.D.4.b.

[116] United States v. Butler, 297 U.S. 1, 65-66 (1936).

[117] *See, e.g.*, South Carolina v. United States, 199 U.S. 437, 450 (1905) ("public purposes"); Cincinnati Soap Co. v. United States, 301 U.S. 308, 313 (1937) (to aid the Philippines); concurrence of Justice Frankfurter in Graves v. New York, 306 U.S. 466, 488 (1939) ("in order to pay . . .".

[118] This is to be distinguished from the handful of decisions that found exactions not to be taxes because they were regulations of intrastate commerce.

comprise the debt payments, defense, and general welfare spending; but the matching follows the imposition of the taxes for the most part, rather than the other way around. In the early days revenue acts contained a preamble stating that revenues were needed to pay debts, support the government and encourage manufactures,[119] and later Congress reenacted biennial revenue acts said to be simply to raise revenue. When Congress codified the revenue laws into the 1939 Code (and then 1954 and 1986), all pretense of stating a spending purpose vanished.[120]

Therefore, no purpose is needed for a revenue bill.[121] The purpose issue cannot arise at all in the case, for example, of the regularly collected income tax, because the statute laying the income tax is not linked with any particular intent to spend or with any appropriation. Moreover, there can be no concern that such general taxes will produce excessive revenues beyond the needs of the country, because the huge federal debt surely can take up any slack in spending. The spending purposes limitation can become a concern only if either (1) the bill enacting a tax states a purpose to use the revenues in a certain way that is found to be unconstitutional (as did not occur in *Butler*), or that bill or a related bill appropriates in advance the revenues of a particular tax to a specific use;[122] or (2) the Court just does not believe the label of a tax as a tax (as occurred in *Butler*).

Even before *Butler*, the Court stated that taxes levied in support of some other power of Congress depended on the constitutional validity of that non tax purpose. *Veazie Bank v. Fenno*, which treated the tax on state bank currency as both a taxing power tax and a necessary and proper tax, stated this very general limit on necessary and proper taxation:

> It would undoubtedly be an abuse of the power if so exercised as to impair the separate existence and independent self-government of the States, or if exercised for ends inconsistent with the limited grants of power in the Constitution.[123]

b. *Congress' Motives*

As proposed in the preceding Chapter, the motives of Congress (more accurately the motives of certain members of Congress) are the real focus of most disputes about the characterization of a tax as a taxing power tax, or not, though sometimes framed in terms of "purposes." The issue here is quite different from the "purposive interpretation" issue that has received broad coverage in the con-

---

[119] *See, e.g.*, ch. II, 1 Stat. 24 (1789) (the first taxing law, an import duty).

[120] This may also reflect the more general principle that federal legislation need not contain recitals of its constitutional underpinnings. *See* Woods v. Cloyd W. Miller Co., 333 U.S. 138, 144 (1948).

[121] *See* G. Merle Bergman, *The Federal Power to Tax and Spend*, 31 MINN. L. REV. 328, 330 (1946) [hereinafter Bergman].

[122] Article I, section 9, clause 7 requires an appropriation as a precondition of all expenditures. *See* Bergman, at 351.

[123] Veazie Bank v. Fenno, 75 U.S. 533, 541 (1869). *Butler* itself cited Edye v. Robertson, 112 U.S. 580 (1884) (Head Money Cases) for this proposition.

text of statutory interpretations and construction.[124] Rather than trying to determine what an ambiguous statute means, the Court sometimes has tried to deny the facial characterization of a tax as a taxing power tax by examining evidence of, or inferring, the motives that led Congress to enact the tax.

And yet, many opinions of the Court state that the Court will neither search for nor be swayed by investigation of the motives of the legislature, which obviously can be applied to motives behind a tax. Many commentators have made the important observation of the difference between a legislature's motive and purpose: motive is usually unexpressed, largely political, and sometimes includes even personal aims of legislators; purpose is the overall objective end of the law.[125]

Most of the opinions discussing Congress' motive in taxation arise in one of three different contexts:

- One group of opinions appears to address the situation where the litigants try to impute a questionable motive or "hidden motives" to Congress in the absence of direct statements by Congress about what it was doing. In such cases the Court almost always eschews assessment of Congress' motive.[126]
- A second group recognizes that Congress was or might have been pursuing some object in addition to revenue collection, but still asserts either disinterest in Congress' motives, or that the motive cannot affect the tax

[124] *See* Cummings, at ch. VI.B.1.d; Ronald Dworkin, Law's Empire (1986) (the entire book addresses the topic, but Chapter 9 particularly addressed it); William D. Popkin, Statutes in Court 131 et seq. (1999) (discussing purposivism). *See, e.g.*, Colgate-Palmolive-Peet Co. v. United States, 320 U.S. 422, 425 (1943) ("Again, if petitioner's argument is sound, the Congressional purpose to create an advantage for domestic oil producers would be frustrated to the extent . . .").

[125] A.M. Bickel, The Unpublished Opinions of Mr. Justice Brandeis 209-210 (1957) [hereinafter Bickel].

[126] *See, e.g.*, Daniel v. Family Sec. Life Ins. Co., 336 U.S. 220 (1949) (not interested in fact that "insurance lobby" urged adoption of act); Fernandez v. Wiener, 326 U.S. 340, 361-362 (1945) ("It has long been settled that an Act of Congress which on its face purports to be an exercise of the taxing power, is not any the less so because the tax is burdensome or tends to restrict or suppress the thing taxed. In such a case it is not within the province of courts to inquire into the unexpressed purposes or motives which may have moved Congress to exercise a power constitutionally conferred upon it."); Sonzinsky v. United States, 300 U.S. 506, 513-514 (1937) ("Inquiry into the hidden motives which may move Congress to exercise a power constitutionally conferred upon it is beyond the competency of courts.").

collection.[127] Indeed, in 1906 on the heels of the *McCray* opinion a careful observer read it to mean that "the motive which animates Congress in enacting tax laws cannot be considered by the courts. . . ."[128]

- The third and smallest group of opinions (total of five) is the focus of this Chapter III of this book: they throw caution to the winds and say the Court cannot turn a blind eye to what Congress obviously is doing, which is a Code term for discerning motive.[129]

Alexander Bickel said of the *Drexel* opinion containing the original blind eye statement:

> In one of the few and not highly reputed cases in which the Court has essayed examination of legislative motives, it declared plaintively that the impermissible motive was one that all others [meaning all others entitled to make the normal rough-and-ready political judgments] can see and understand. And the Court asked, virtually wailing, "How can we properly shut our minds to it?" The answer is that the Court ought to shut its mind to much of what all others think they see. That is precisely what courts are for. They try things out on evidence, by the process of proof and refutation, and shut their minds to the kinds of surmise by which the general public may reach politically sufficient

---

[127] *See, e.g.*, United States v. Doremus, 249 U.S. 86, 93 (1919) ("And from an early day the court has held that the fact that other motives may impel the exercise of federal taxing power does not authorize the courts to inquire into that subject. If the legislation enacted has some reasonable relation to the exercise of the taxing authority conferred by the Constitution, it cannot be invalidated because of the supposed motives which induced it. Veazie Bank v. Fenno, 8 Wall. 533, 541, in which case this court sustained a tax on a state bank issue of circulating notes. McCray . . . where the power was thoroughly considered, and an act levying a special tax upon oleomargarine artificially colored was sustained. *See also* Flint v. Stone Tracy Co. . . ."); McCray v. United States, 195 U.S. 27, 56 (1904) ("The decisions of this court from the beginning lend no support whatever to the assumption that the judiciary may restrain the exercise of lawful power on the assumption that a wrongful purpose or motive has caused the power to be exerted."); Treat v. White, 181 U.S. 264, 269 (1901) ("The power of Congress in this direction is unlimited. It does not come within the province of this court to consider why agreements to sell shall be subject to stamp duty and agreements to buy not. It is enough that Congress in this legislation has imposed a stamp duty upon the one and not upon the other."); A. Magnano Co. v. Hamilton, 292 U.S. 40, 44 (1934) ("Collateral purposes or motives of a legislature in levying a tax of a kind within the reach of its lawful power are matters beyond the scope of judicial inquiry."); *In re* Kollock, 165 U.S. 526, 536 (1897) ("The act before us is on its face an act for levying taxes, and although it may operate in so doing to prevent deception in the sale of oleomargarine as and for butter, its primary object must be assumed to be the raising of revenue.").

[128] Gray, at 348.

[129] J.W. Bailey v. Drexel Furn. Co., 259 U.S. 20, 37 (1922) ("In the light of these features of the act, a court must be blind not to see that the so called tax is imposed to stop the employment of children within the age limits prescribed. Its prohibitory and regulatory effect and purpose are palpable. All others can see and understand this. How can we properly shut our minds to it?"). Justice Taft's statement about blindness was so remarkable, it was called "famous" in United States v. Rumley, 345 U.S. 41, 44 (1953) ("And so, we would have to be that 'blind' Court, against which Mr. Chief Justice Taft admonished in a famous passage, Child Labor Tax Case, 259 U.S. 20, 37, that does not see what 'all others can see and understand' not to know that there is wide concern, both in and out of Congress, over some aspects of the exercise of the congressional power of investigation.").

> conclusions. . . . The holding ultimately was based on an altogether untenable view of the scope of the taxing power. Under the guise of a finding of motive, the case attempted to narrow the power to regulate the economy, which inheres in the power to levy taxes. . . . And so the mysteries of motive must remain largely, like Churchill's Russia, wrapped in their enigma.[130]

Randolph Paul made a similar observation:

> Legislative draftsmen have learned to preserve silence as to ulterior motives beyond tax territory, and the court has learned how to shut its eyes to things it does not care to see. Ostrich playing of this type could be unfavorably compared to the brand of jurisprudence which Bentham condemned as "the art of being methodically ignorant of what everyone knows." But courts must occasionally bow to their own inhibitions, and one must sometimes read between the lines of opinions. The inner lesson may be that the propriety of the motives which produced much current legislation is essentially a "political question" (using "political" in the Aristotelian rather than the invidious sense) into which the judiciary should hesitate to trespass.[131]

The third group is described by *Cincinnati Soap Co.* as follows, again stating that the issue is fundamentally political:

> Primarily, and in a very high degree, whether a tax serves any of these purposes is a practical question addressed to the law-making department. And it will require a very plain case to warrant the courts in setting aside the conclusion of Congress in that regard.[132]

And even when the Court does take the blinders off to envision a tax as not a tax but a regulation, it is not ruling it unconstitutional as a tax for a purpose other than paying debts, general welfare or defense; it is ruling it unconstitutional as a regulation in an area where it finds Congress may not regulate.[133] As to this line of rulings, the practical conclusion about the state of the law is that at least the Supreme Court will not be prevented from ruling that a tax was actually enacted with improper motives, and not for revenue raising, if it wishes to do so.[134] However, to do so today would (1) signal a marked retreat from the uniform course of Supreme Court rulings since 1937, and (2) signal a reversal of over two centuries of judicial solicitude for the federal taxing power. A possible exception to the foregoing analysis is the tax that Congress fails to clearly style as a tax; that situation gives tax opponents grounds to argue the tax is not a tax

---

[130] BICKEL, at 220.

[131] RANDOLPH PAUL, TAXATION FOR PROSPERITY 213 (1947).

[132] Cincinnati Soap Co. v. United States, 301 U.S. 308, 313 (1937).

[133] *See* Ch. III.F.

[134] *See* Nelson Lund, *Congressional Power over Taxation and Commerce: The Supreme Court's Lost Chance to Devise a Consistent Doctrine*, 18 TEX. TECH. L. REV. 729, 747 n. 97 (1987) (citing and agreeing with a 1953 observation that the Court had left open two avenues for ruling on "close" regulatory/tax cases like the *Child Labor Tax Case*).

and when the Court most recently took up such a challenge it purported to rely on objective indicia of tax function in the 2012 health insurance tax decision.[135]

The Court has frequently based its reluctance to delve into Congress' motives in tax cases on the nature of the political role of Congress, and its primacy in the area of political choices. For example, the Court has stated:

- "Within the wide parameters of the common defense and general welfare, arguments as to the expediency of levying such taxes, or of the economic mistake or wrong involved in their imposition, are beyond judicial cognizance"[136]
- ". . . [T]he right to select the measure and objects of taxation devolves upon the Congress and not upon the courts, and such selections are valid unless constitutional limitations are overstepped. 'It is no part of the function of a court to inquire into the reasonableness of the excise, either as respects the amount or the property upon which it is imposed.' Patton v. Brady, 184 U.S. 608; McCray v. United States, 195 U.S. 27, 58 and previous cases in this court there [cited]."[137]
- "This court can know nothing of public policy except from the Constitution and the laws, and the course of administration and decision. It has no legislative powers. It cannot amend or modify any legislative acts. It cannot examine questions as expedient or inexpedient, as politic or impolitic. Considerations of that sort must, in general, be addressed to the legislature. Questions of policy determined there are concluded here. There are cases, it is true, in which arguments drawn from public policy must have large influence; but these are cases in which the course of legislation and administration do not leave any doubt upon the question what the public policy is, and in which what would otherwise be obscure or of doubtful interpretation, may be cleared and resolved by reference to what is already received and established."[138]
- "The first answer to this [the argument by plaintiff that a ten percent tax on bank notes of state chartered banks was so high as to try to destroy them] is that the judicial cannot prescribe to the legislative departments of the government limitations upon the exercise of its acknowledged powers. The power to tax may be exercised oppressively upon persons, but the responsibility of the legislature is not to the courts, but to the people by whom its members are elected. So if a particular tax bears heavily upon a corporation, or a class of corporations, it cannot, for that reason only, be pronounced contrary."[139]

---

[135] *See* Ch. III.E.2.c.
[136] Brushaber v. Union Pacific R. Co., 240 U.S. 1, 25 (1916).
[137] Flint v. Stone Tracy Co., 220 U.S. 107, 167 (1911).
[138] License Tax Cases, 72 U.S. 462 (1867).
[139] Veazie Bank v. Fenno, 75 U.S. 533, 548 (1869).

However, what is political, as contrasted with jurisprudential, is in the eye of the beholder. The former attorney general, Edwin Meese III, stated:

> The Court is what it was understood to be when the Constitution was framed—a political body. The judicial process is, at its most fundamental level, a *political* process. While not a partisan political process, it is political in the truest sense of that word. It is a process wherein public deliberations occur over what constitutes the common good under the words of a written constitution.[140]

The policy based flexibility that Meese's approach seemed to allow to the Supreme Court was suddenly yanked back by his strict constructionism, and "jurisprudence of original intention,"[141] which held, for example, that the Court badly erred when it selectively incorporated the parts of the Bill Of Rights into the Fourteenth Amendment.[142] Meese's argument, of course, ran counter to Justice Hughes' injunction that "the Constitution is what the judges say it is";[143] it hewed close to Chief Justice Taney's ground for the *Dred Scott* decision.[144] However, even a conservative Court can find selective incorporation useful: in 2010 it applied the Second Amendment to the states.[145] Meese's theory, has, of course, taken hold in the Supreme Court. It turns on its head the common understanding of one of Chief Justice Marshall's most famous statements:

> A jurisprudence of original intention would take seriously the admonition of . . . John Marshall in Marbury v. Madison, that the Constitution is a limitation on judicial power, as well as executive and legislative. That is what Chief Justice Marshall meant in McCulloch v. Maryland when he cautioned judges never to forget that it is a constitution they are expounding.[146]

The last sentence normally is read to encourage a flexible interpretation of the Constitution.[147] Indeed later the opinion also stated it was to be "a constitution intended to endure for ages to come, and consequently, to be adapted to the various crises of human affairs."[148] But in a way Meese is right, the Court is a po-

---

[140] Edwin Meese III, *The Supreme Court of the United States: Bulwark of a Limited Constitution*, 27 S. Tex. L. Rev. 455 (1985) [hereinafter Meese].

[141] *Id.* at 464.

[142] *Id.* at 463.

[143] Addresses and Papers of Charles Evans Hughes 185-186 (2d ed. 1916).

[144] Dred Scott v. Sandford, 60 U.S. 393, 426 (1857) (stating that the Constitution "speaks not only in the same words . . . but with the same meaning and intent with which it spoke when it came into the hands of its framers.").

[145] McDonald v. City of Chicago, 561 U.S. 742 (2010).

[146] Meese, at 465.

[147] Barry Friedman, The Will of the People 81 (2009) [hereinafter Friedman] (explaining that Marshall meant to adopt an expansive and flexible reading of the Constitution).

[148] McCulloch v. Maryland, 17 U.S. 316, 415 (1819).

litical institution.[149] Nevertheless, it also is an arbiter rather than a primal force, and so should not enact its own economic views.[150]

The subject of a tax's purpose and Congress' motives cannot be closed without acknowledging the vast academic literature on the subject. Obviously for the Court to hold that a tax is not a tax, it must rely on some inference or factual determination of another congressional motive besides raising revenue. However, studies show that the Court, and commentators, generally have denied the judicial capacity to make that analysis, except during the *Lochner* era.[151] Beginning with the Burger court, scrutiny of congressional motives is said to have expanded.[152] However, there is no evidence yet that it has expanded for the purpose of invalidating federal regulatory taxes. Therefore, statements of the demise of earlier precedents such as *McCray* (federal tax on colored margarine manufacture that Congress presumably could not regulate), due to more liberal views of evidence of motive, are premature;[153] it was not that the Court in *McCray* didn't know what Congress was doing, but rather the Court respected Congress' choice to call the tax a tax.[154]

The ability of the Court to discern Congress' motives is not a new found trait of the Court; Chief Justice Marshall reserved the possibility of its use in *McCulloch*.[155] Rather, it is a matter of the will of the Court, whether or not it will base a ruling on Congress' motives.

c. *Public Purpose Doctrine*

Sometimes taxpayers oppose a tax because it is not levied for a "public purpose." A public purpose doctrine as such has been applied only to states and local governments.[156] Despite the invocation of the doctrine, the Court has a record of broadly approving state taxing powers; striking down a state tax for alleged non public purposes is "rare."[157] For example, in *Olcott* a Wisconsin county had issued bonds to pay for aid to a private railroad.[158] The Wisconsin Supreme Court held the law aiding the railroad illegal under Wisconsin law and a related

---

[149] *See* Robert H. Jackson, The Struggle for Judicial Supremacy 311 (1941) ("The political nature of judicial review generally is either unrecognized or ignored. But it is that which gives significance to constitutional litigation and which makes it transcend mere legal proceedings.").

[150] *Id.* ("The ultimate function of the Supreme Court is nothing less than the arbitration between fundamental and ever present rival forces or trends in our organized society.").

[151] *See generally* Caleb Nelson, *Judicial Review of Legislative Purpose*, 83 N.Y.U.L. Rev. 1784 (2008) (and articles cited therein).

[152] *Id.*

[153] *Id.* at 1794 n. 29.

[154] McCray v. United States, 195 U.S. 27 (1904).

[155] 17 U.S. at 423 (Congress cannot invoke its powers as a "pretext" for interfering with affairs of the states).

[156] Joseph Lesser and Vigdor D. Bernstein, *The Evolution of Public Purpose, General Welfare and American Federalism*, 19 Urb. Law. 603, 640 (1987) [hereinafter Lesser and Bernstein] (arguing that the public purpose doctrine applied to states is the analogue of the General Welfare Power restriction applied to the United States).

[157] Everson v. Bd. of Educ., 330 U.S. 1, 7 (1947).

[158] Olcott v. Supervisors, 83 U.S. 678 (1872).

case held the bonds unenforceable. The Court reversed, stating, inter alia, that it was well accepted that municipalities could condemn land for use by railroads, which necessarily meant that the railroad was a public use even though owned by private persons, because it benefited the public. The Court did twice apply the public purpose doctrine to strike down a general tax levied to pay off what would now be called an industrial development bond, but that approach has been overruled.[159]

The Court's conception of what is a private purpose has shrunk as its willingness to let the legislative department make those decisions has expanded. Thus in a state tax case the Court stated that:

> . . . local conditions are of such varying character that what is or is not a public use in a particular state is manifestly a matter respecting which local authority, legislative and judicial, has peculiar facilities for securing accurate information.[160]

The issue of possible non-public spending purposes and federal taxation can come up only when (1) a tax and spending are sufficiently connected in the statute, and (2) the spending either is for a purpose beyond Congress' power

---

[159] Loan Ass'n v. Topeka, 87 U.S. 655 (1875); Parkersburg v. Brown, 106 U.S. 487 (1883). But similar local bonds are now deemed public purposes. *See, e.g.*, Allbritton v. Winona, 303 U.S. 627 (1938) (dismissing appeal for want of a substantial federal question of a state's affirmance of such a bond issue). Evidently the *Topeka* case was known to Congress and cited by some in 1902 as involving an overreaching tax. *See* Margulies, 5 J. S. Legal Hist. at 15-16 (*Topeka* was cited in congressional debates on the bill that led to the tax at issue in *McCray* as a prior similar bad tax). *Topeka* possibly reiterates the view of Alexander Hamilton that taxation must be for general and not local purposes. United States v. Butler, 297 U.S. 1 n. 15 (1936). *Topeka* has been called a "landmark" case. Lesser and Bernstein, at 610-613 (also pointing out that the opinion cited no constitutional ground and that the opinion was a "constitutional waif"; also showing that in only one other case did the Court apply the public purpose doctrine to strike down a state law); GRAY, at 18 (singling out *Topeka* as reflective of Judge Cooley's view of natural limits on taxation). *Topeka* remains a totem for libertarian opponents of taxation. *See* Gale Ann Norton, *The Limitless Federal Taxing Power*, 8 HARV. J. L. & PUB. POL'Y 591, 618 (1985). *Griswold v. Connecticut* cited it with the handful of prior cases that had relied on the Ninth Amendment, although *Topeka* did not cite the Ninth Amendment specifically. Griswold v. Connecticut, 381 U.S. 479 n. 6 (1965). It was cited by *Everson* as one of the rare cases striking down a tax as not for a public purpose. Everson v. Bd. of Educ., 330 U.S. 1 (1947) (juxtaposing Green v. Frazier, 253 U.S. 233 (1920) (advising extreme caution for such an action). However, the origins and grounding of *Topeka* are highly questionable. *See* Breck P. McCallister, *Public Purpose in Taxation*, 18 CAL. L. REV. 137, 147-148 (1930) (the opinion did not mention the Fourteenth Amendment, was not based on due process, and did not even have to find a federal question existed because the case originated in federal court; so its embrace as an example of a due process public purpose doctrine is weak).

[160] Jones v. Portland, 245 U.S. 217, 221 (1917), casting doubt on an earlier opinion containing a very broad prohibition against taxing one group for the benefit of another: Loan Ass'n v. Topeka, 87 U.S. 655 (1875) (this involved essentially a precursor of the industrial development bond and Justice Miller struck down the bond on the grounds of lack of public purpose, without explaining what federal constitutional provision applied, as pointed out by the dissent). *See also* Green v. Frazier, 253 U.S. 233 (1920) (also stating the widening scope of state and local expenditures). At issue in *Green* were state expenditures for a state bank and other such government owned businesses that the critics labeled "socialistic." The ruling was viewed as important at the time. *See* PAUL MURPHY, THE CONSTITUTION IN CRISIS TIMES 39 (1972).

or appears to benefit a limited group of persons. Both elements were present in *Butler*, as discussed in Chapter III.D.2. In contrast to that decision, the Court sometimes stated in early decisions upholding taxes that tax revenues should be and were spent for public purposes,[161] and has given the concept an expanding meaning in later cases.[162] The Court once shorthanded the general welfare requirement as spending for "general public purposes."[163] When addressing spending alone, general welfare is the standard for federal spending, and Congress has great latitude in making that choice.[164] Because the Court recognized that the scope of general welfare is not static and necessarily increases as needs increase,[165] the Court has come close to stating the its scope is non justiciable.[166]

Another indication that spending should be for public purposes, however, broadly defined, is the fact that tax expenditures also reflect that requirement. The Court has required charities enjoying the benefits of receiving deductible charitable contributions to serve public purposes.[167]

4. *Another Understanding of the Taxing Power*

In 1946 G. Merle Bergman proposed that the taxing power is not the primary source of the federal power to tax; that taxes can be levied under the Necessary and Proper Clause insofar as the taxes support specified powers of the United States; that the taxing power must, therefore, have been introduced for another purpose, and that it is not limited by the following clause referring to paying debts, general welfare and common defense.[168] As to the first point, the argument is surely correct: taxes can be levied in support of enumerated powers. For example the taxes were levied on liquor when Prohibition was in effect. The sec-

---

[161] South Carolina v. United States, 199 U.S. 437, 450 (1905) ("public purposes"); Cincinnati Soap Co. v. United States, 301 U.S. 308, 313 (1937).

[162] Carmichael v. Southern Coal & Coke Co., 301 U.S. 495 (1937) (which upheld the state unemployment compensation tax with citations about public purpose, including Green v. Frazier, 253 U.S. 233 (1920)); *cf.* Steward Machine Co. v. Davis, 301 U.S. 548 (1937) (which upheld the federal unemployment compensation tax, with no discussion of public purpose but with extensive discussion of general welfare).

[163] South Dakota v. Dole, 483 U.S. 203, 207 (1987).

[164] *Id.* ("The first of these limitations is derived from the language of the Constitution itself: the exercise of the spending power must be in pursuit of 'the general welfare.' [citing *Davis* and *Butler*]. In considering whether a particular expenditure is intended to serve general public purposes, courts should defer substantially to the judgment of Congress."). But early opinions mixed the private purpose and general welfare standards. *See* Van Brocklin v. State of Tennessee, 117 U.S. 151, 158 (1886), *cited in* United States v. Insley, 130 U.S. 263, 265 (1889) ("The United States do not and cannot hold property, as a monarch may, for private or personal purposes. All the property and revenues of the United States must be held and applied, as all taxes, duties, imposts and excises must be laid and collected, 'to pay the debts and provide for the common defense and general welfare of the United States.'").

[165] Helvering v. Davis, 301 U.S. 619, 640 (1937).

[166] Buckley v. Valeo, 424 U.S. 1, 90-91 (1976) (per curiam). *See generally*, Lynn A. Baker, *Constitutional Amiguities and Originalism: Lessons From the Spending Power*, 103 Nw. U. L. Rev. 495 (2009).

[167] Bob Jones Univ. v. United States, 461 U.S. 574, 586 (1983).

[168] Bergman.

ond contention hinges almost entirely on the comma separating the two parts of the first clause of Article 1, section 8, which he contended should grammatically and normally indicate two parallel ideas rather than the second part modifying the first. The Court has never directly addressed the import of the comma.[169]

From this argument Bergman concluded that Congress has the power to tax simply to raise revenue, unconstrained by either the following clause or the enumerated powers. Also Congress has power to provide for (appropriate money for) the general welfare. This is slightly different from arguing that Congress has the power to tax to promote the general welfare without raising revenue. He asserted that when the Supreme Court states that Congress can tax for the general welfare, it does not really mean it, because if it did it would allow non-revenue raising taxes to regulate for the general welfare. Therefore, the Court must actually agree with Bergman's argument that taxes can be levied simply for revenue, but if not for revenue, then they are not taxes.

His article then analyzed all of the cases discussed in Chapter III.F holding federal taxes unconstitutional as not taxes and found the Court to be consistent in looking to the face of the statute and distinguishing taxes not for raising revenue (*Child Labor Tax Case* and *Hill v. Wallace*) due to their coercive nature, from taxes that arguably could go either way based on the face of the statute (*Butler*, *Davis*, *Steward*). He concluded that the formalistic test turns on whether the regulatory expenditure or other purpose is in the same statute; if it is not, then the tax probably would be upheld.

This is a quite elegant argument. However, it may be too late in the day for the Court to announce that the taxing power is not limited by raising money to spend for the general welfare. *Butler* stated (incorrectly) that the government conceded that the general welfare power qualified the taxing power. Bergman's argument can backstop the view that the Court should not look behind the face of the statute to determine whether a tax is for revenue, but Bergman did not take account of the scant tax raised by clearly punitive levies like the firearms tax in *Sonzinsky*, which was held to be a tax because it raised a little (very little) cash.

---

[169] *Cf.* Trailmobile Co. v. Whirls, 331 U.S. 40 (1947) (a final clause separated by comma referred to earlier clauses); Singer v. United States, 323 U.S. 338 (1945) (reading a series separated by commas together). Others have made different arguments about the comma, such as contending that it should have been a semicolon, and so the use of the comma suggests a tighter connection between the general welfare and taxation than has generally been admitted

· *See* Paul Moreno, *A Short History of Congress' Power to Tax* A13, WALL STREET JOURNAL (July 7-8, 2012). One version of the disputes claims a semicolon should have separated paying debts from the General Welfare Clause, which would have had an entirely different meaning

· Herman J. Herbert, Jr., *The General Welfare Clauses in the Constitution of the United States*, 7 FORDHAM L. REV. 390, 394 (1938). A careful student of the records concluded that there was no plot afoot in the use of a comma versus a semicolon and showed that the conservative James Madison had no commas at all in the clause except the one between taxes and spending, which would suggest that there was not a link between taxes and spending purposes

· David E. Engdahl, *The Basis of the Spending Power*, 18 SEATTLE U. L. REV. 215, 253 (1995); Robert G. Natelson, *The General Welfare Clause and the Public Trust: An Essay in Original Understanding*, 52 U. KAN. L. REV. 1, 27 (2003) (same).

A somewhat analogous grammatical analysis occurred in the firearms case, *District of Columbia v. Heller*.[170] It hinged on ruling that the "well regulated militia" clause of the Second Amendment did not limit the right to bear arms, even though it appeared as a preamble. This seems inconsistent with the interpretation that the general welfare power modifies the taxing power (as well as being inconsistent with prior holdings of the Court on the Second Amendment).

5. *Actual Use of Funds: Tracing*

The Court's opinions sometimes purport or attempt to trace funds from tax collection to spending uses, but such tracing usually is either impossible or not relevant to identifying a tax.

Article I, section 9, clause 7 of the Constitution provides that no money shall be drawn from the Treasury but in consequence of appropriations made by law. At least since the advent of a national currency provided by the Federal Reserve rather than by national banks (or state banks or the Bank of the United States), it is not possible for the United States to "save" tax revenues in special funds like bank deposits (although it can lend funds to other governmental funds, which does not really produce an asset different from the expectation of future tax revenues). Rather the Treasury has annual revenues and it has annual expenditures and all expenditures must be appropriated by Congress and are paid by the Treasury through the creation of money (with the help of the Federal Reserve), which may or may not match the amount of money collected in taxes. Therefore, tracing of tax revenues now can occur only as a matter of bookkeeping directed by Congress that somehow links the amount of funds appropriated for spending to the amount of revenue collected from a certain tax.

The Court's few opinions and principles on tax revenue tracing are as follows:

- Tax receipts do not have to be segregated for use, even when levied for a particular purpose, although there could be a problem if some department of the government failed to carry out Congress' appropriation directive.[171]
- Conversely, tax receipts can be earmarked for any purpose for which an appropriation would be proper. *Cincinnati Soap* stated: "It is said to be bad because it is earmarked and devoted from its inception to a specific purpose. But if the tax, qua tax, be good, as we hold it is, and the purpose specified be one which would sustain a subsequent and separate appropriation made out of the general funds of the Treasury, neither is made invalid by being bound

[170] District of Columbia v. Heller, 554 U.S. 570 (2008).

[171] Binns v. United States, 194 U.S. 486 (1904) (The excise tax levied for specific support of Alaska was inadequate and so the territorial government costs were paid out of the United States Treasury).

to the other in the same act of legislation."[172] This opinion did assume that a tax law containing its own appropriation could be constitutional only if the associated spending was constitutional.

- The appropriation may be made in the taxing bill itself, and even if spending is improper or appropriation lacking, that does not necessarily void the tax.[173]
- The fact that half of a state tax was paid into a trust fund did not prevent it from being a general revenue tax, which meant it should not be treated as a fee.[174]
- Earmarking for transfer of revenues from tax collections to other persons was a ground for *Butler* holding the Agricultural Adjustment Act unconstitutional in 1936, but the Court later cast doubt on the ground.[175]

6. *Paying Debts*

Because a taxing statute need not have a particular revenue purpose, it need not be for paying debts, but if it is, that is clearly a proper purpose. Paying debts of the United States is usually not a controversial activity, but a peculiar issue came up in *Cincinnati Soap*, which ruled that a tax on domestic manufacture of coconut oil, dedicated to the Philippine treasury, was not only for the general welfare of both the Philippines and the United States, but also was to pay a "debt" of the United States in the general sense. Of course the issue would not have arisen at all if the taxing statute had not undertaken to link the tax and the

---

[172] Cincinnati Soap Co. v. United States, 301 U.S. 308, 312-313 (1937) (An excise tax imposed on domestic soap producers, the entire proceeds of which were to be transferred to the treasury of the Philippines, was upheld as a constitutional tax. Because the levy was a "true tax" it could not be subject to the objection of *Butler* and the *Child Labor Tax Case* that it was the transfer of money from one group to another by tax.). *See also* Carmichael v. Southern Coal & Coke Co., 301 U.S. 495, 522 and n. 14 (1937) (quoting *Cincinnati Soap* and citing examples of tax revenues earmarked for schools, pensions, agriculture and unemployment).

[173] Edye v. Robertson, 112 U.S. 580, 599-600 (1884) (head tax on immigrants paid into immigrants' fund).

[174] Commonwealth Edison Co. v. Montana, 453 U.S. 609 (1981).

[175] United States v. Butler, 297 U.S. 1 (1936), *discussed in* Steward Machine Co. v. Davis, 301 U.S. 548, 592-593 (1937).

expenditure. The opinion defined debt so broadly as to encompass any determination by Congress that a payment should be made.[176]

7. *Common Defense*

As stated above in connection with paying debts, taxing need not be for a purpose, but taxing for the common defense is clearly a proper purpose and is virtually inevitable. Indeed, several taxes have been specifically justified by war, such as the War Excess Profits Tax for World War I. The Civil War produced many experiments in novel federal taxation, including the first income tax and a license tax on intrastate activities that the United States did not have the power to regulate.[177] Most of the limited number of direct taxes were assessed to pay for the War of 1812. There is no Supreme Court authority on taxing for the common defense, likely because defense is a much clearer concept than general welfare, and less disputed.[178] Moreover, so many more surprising powers have been assumed by the federal government under the war powers clause that surely taxes can be levied as necessary and proper to wage war.[179] The Court called a Civil War fee imposed on trading in cotton with the southern states a "bonus" and not a tax; it was levied under the war powers.[180] The Prohibition taxes were adopted under the war powers.[181]

---

[176] Cincinnati Soap Co. v. United States, 301 U.S. 308, 316-317 (1937) ("It is conceded and indeed it cannot be questioned that the debts are not limited to those which are evidenced by some written obligation or to those which are otherwise of a strictly legal character. The term 'debts' includes those debts or claims which rest upon a merely equitable or honorary obligation, and which would not be recoverable in a court of law if existing against an individual. The nation, speaking broadly, owes a 'debt' to an individual when his claim grows out of general principles of right and justice; when, in other words, it is based upon considerations of a moral or merely honorary nature, such as are binding on the conscience or the honor of an individual, although the debt could obtain no recognition in a court of law. The power of Congress extends at least as far as the recognition and payment of claims against the government which are thus founded. To no other branch of the government than Congress could any application be successfully made on the part of the owners of such claims or debts for the payment thereof. Their recognition depends solely upon Congress, and whether it will recognize claims thus founded must be left to the discretion of that body. Payments to individuals, not of right or of a merely legal claim, but payments in the nature of a gratuity, yet having some feature of moral obligation to support them, have been made by the government by virtue of acts of Congress, appropriating the public money, ever since its foundation. Some of the acts were based upon considerations of pure charity. A long list of acts directing payments of the above general character is appended to the brief of one of the counsel for the defendants in error. The acts are referred to not for the purpose of asserting their validity in all cases, but as evidence of what has been the practice of Congress since the adoption of the Constitution [citing cases]."). *See also* United States v. Realty Co., 163 U.S. 427 (1896) (to same effect).

[177] License Tax Cases, 72 U.S. 462 (1867).

[178] *See* La Belle Iron Works v. United States, 256 U.S. 377 (1921) (considering various objections to the 1917 War Excess Profits Tax, which carried rates of up to 60% of invested capital, but there was no objection to the tax itself).

[179] *See, e.g.*, Lichter v. United States, 334 U.S. 742 (1948). *See* Ch. III.E.4.a.

[180] Hamilton v. Dillin, 88 U.S. 73 (1874).

[181] Ruppert v. Caffey, 251 U.S. 264 (1920). For the Necessary and Proper Clause, see Ch. III.E.4.a. For Common Defense see Ch. III.D.7.

8. *General Welfare*

a. *Meaning*

Article I, section 8, clause 1 states:

> The Congress shall have Power To lay and collect Taxes, Duties, Imposts and Excises, to pay the Debts and provide for the common Defence and general Welfare of the United States; but all Duties, Imposts and Excises shall be uniform throughout the United States;

The Supreme Court has attempted to define the meaning of this clause in connection with the general welfare in remarkably few opinions. The principal possible (or at least suggested) meanings of the general welfare power are:

1. Not adopted: Congress can do anything to provide for the general welfare, whatever that takes, and whether it involves taxes or spending or not; in other words the taxing part of the clause and the spending part of the clause are not connected in meaning and are unconnected to legislating for the general welfare.[182]
2. Congress can tax to raise revenue to be used to provide for the general welfare, with two alternative sub meanings
   a. Not adopted: the general welfare purposes of taxation are limited to the enumerated powers of Congress;
   b. Adopted: the general welfare purposes of taxation are not limited to the enumerated powers of Congress (whether or not they include those powers is unclear, as discussed in Chapter III.D.2).[183]
3. Adopted with the exception of the five contrary decisions between 1922 and 1936: Congress can tax with or without any substantial purpose of raising revenue (although some revenue is raised), but with the principal purpose of regulating, as for example by regulating through the imposition of a tax that is designed to inhibit conduct that Congress could not regulate directly.[184]

---

[182] Helvering v. Davis, 301 U.S. 619 (1937) rejected that interpretation: "Congress may spend money in aid of the 'general welfare.'" *See, e.g.*, McKay (listing and rejecting this possible reading; noting it was proposed in a 1926 book on the General Welfare Power and that Story discussed and rejected it in 1891); Cooter and Siegel, *Collective Action Federalism: A General Theory of Article I, Section 8*, 63 STAN. L. REV. 115, 127 (2010) (rejected regulating in addition to taxing and spending for the general welfare). It was purportedly disclaimed by the government in arguing the *Butler* case. United States v. Butler, 297 U.S. 1, 64 (1936) "("The Government concedes that the phrase 'to provide for the general welfare' qualifies the power 'to lay and collect taxes.' The view that the clause grants power to provide for the general welfare, independently of the taxing power, has never been authoritatively accepted."). *But see* Ch. III.d.4.

[183] United States v. Butler, 297 U.S. 1, 64 (1936).

[184] The principal example is McCray v. United States, 195 U.S. 27 (1904) (which did not mention general welfare). *See* Ch. III.E.

4. Adopted: Congress can spend for the general welfare and regulate incident to the spending, apart from taxing.

As discussed in Chapter III.D.2, the anti-New Deal decision *Butler* in 1936 finally announced the Court's view that general welfare as a purpose for federal spending is not a cumulation of the enumerated powers of Congress, but is itself an independent purpose of spending.[185] But *Butler* also rejected what would have been a much greater expansion of the taxing power: that "true taxes" can regulate for the general welfare as opposed to being imposed in some degree for raising revenue to spend for the general welfare; it did so by taking an all or nothing approach to a tax that did raise substantial revenue and calling it purely a regulation and not a "true tax."[186]

On the other hand, *Wickard v. Filburn* made clear that Congress can regulate the activity for which it spends.[187] Thus Congress can regulate campaign finance laws when it provides public financing.[188]

Providing for the general welfare was referred to in the Articles of Confederation and is stated both in the preamble to the Constitution and in the taxing and spending powers as a purpose for which Congress can tax. Analysis of records of the constitutional convention shows that "general welfare" was added at least in part to circumscribe the power of taxation to national rather than local uses.[189] The "general" part of "general welfare" obviously does not mean that spending cannot be targeted. Rather, like many parts of the Constitution, it was written with the state-federal relationship in mind: it means that Congress cannot tax

---

[185] United States v. Butler, 297 U.S. 1 (1936). The reading of *Butler* was confirmed in the case that essentially rejected *Butler* otherwise. Helvering v. Davis, 301 U.S. 619 (1937). *See* Cushman, at 250 and n. 17 (explaining that what was to be *Butler*'s reading was President Monroe's view).

[186] The rejected argument had been made, for example, in support of the tax on butterine in *McCray*. *See* Margulies, 5 J. S. Legal Hist. at 10.

[187] Wickard v. Filburn, 317 U.S. 111, 131 (1942) ("It is hardly lack of due process for the Government to regulate that which it subsidizes."). The Court relied on *Wickard* in upholding federal regulation of marijuana grown for the grower's use; in the earlier case the United States regulated field crops grown for home consumption. Gonzales v. Raich, 545 U.S. 1 (2005).

[188] Buckley v. Valeo, 424 U.S. 1, 90-91 (1976) ("Appellants' 'general welfare' contention erroneously treats the General Welfare Power as a limitation upon congressional power. It is rather a grant of power, the scope of which is quite expansive, particularly in view of the enlargement of power by the Necessary and Proper Clause."). It was not entirely clear whether the spending was necessary and proper to the regulation of federal elections, or regulations of elections were necessary and proper to the spending. *Buckley v. Valeo* might have not included such an expansive statement if it involved a matter as to which states could have claimed a Tenth Amendment right.

[189] *See* Charles J. Bullock, *Direct Taxes Under the Constitution*, 15 Pol. Sci. Q. No. 2 and 3, 217, 224 (1900); John C. Eastman, *Restoring the "General" to the General Welfare Clause*, 4 Chap. L. Rev. 63, 72 et seq. (2001).

for the treasury of a single state.[190] That is consistent with Hamilton's view that the purpose must be general and not local.[191]

The Court has stated that the general welfare power may have limitations, however, in preventing spending for "some mere local purpose."[192] Yet, federal spending on local needs goes back to the founding of the nation when the United States took over the debts of the states, and somewhat later with early grants in aid.[193]

When *United States v. Butler* struck down the cotton processing tax that provided part of the funds used to provide support payments to farmers, it trotted out all of the Court's prior vague injunctions against bad purposes taxes:

- "Should Congress, in the execution of its powers, adopt measures which are prohibited by the constitution; or should Congress, under the pretext of executing its powers, pass laws for the accomplishment of objects not intrusted to the government; it would become the painful duty of this tribunal, should a case requiring such a decision come before it, to say that such an act was not the law of the land."[194]
- "Congress cannot, under the pretext of executing delegated power, pass laws for the accomplishment of objects not entrusted to the Federal Government. And we accept as established doctrine that any provision of an act of Congress ostensibly enacted under power granted by the Constitution, not naturally and reasonably adapted to the effective exercise of such power but solely to the achievement of something plainly within power reserved to the States, is invalid and cannot be enforced."[195]
- "Congress is not empowered to tax for those purposes which are within the exclusive province of the States."[196]

Whether by good fortune or by a shift in the Court's views, it is a fact that the first taxing cases to come before the Court after *Butler* involved matters that

[190] Smith v. Turner, 48 U.S. 283, 446 (1849) (Congress cannot tax to pay the debts of a single state or for its general welfare; but the opinion ignored that fact that Congress did tax to pay the debts of the states in the compromise that located the capital in Washington).

[191] 297 U.S. at 67. *See* Frothingham v. Mellon, 262 U.S. 447 (1923) ("Hamilton in his Report on Manufactures, cited above, although contending for the broad power of appropriation, says: 'The only qualification of the generality of the phrase in question, which seems to be admissible, is this, that the object to which an appropriation of money is to be made must be general and not local,—its operation extending in fact, or by possibility, throughout the Union, and not being confined to a particular spot.' Story, Const., Fifth ed., § 978; Tucker, Const., § 225."). But the case was dismissed for want of standing.

[192] United States v. Gerlach Live Stock Co., 339 U.S. 725, 738 (1950). In practice the spending of federal monies on projects that appear to be purely local is endemic. *See, e.g.*, Fullilove v. Klutznick, 448 U.S. 448 (1980) (which funded local projects and required minority participation); overruled as to racial designations by Adarand Constructors, Inc. v. Pena, 515 U.S. 200 (1995).

[193] *See* McKay, at 40-41.

[194] McCulloch v. Maryland, 17 U.S. 316 (1819).

[195] Linder v. United States, 268 U.S. 5, 17 (1925) (dictum; statutory construction case).

[196] Gibbons v. Ogden, 22 U.S. 1 (1824) (dictum; not a tax case).

the majority then thought (and in hindsight appear clearly) to involve matters of national concern: the unemployment of the Depression and the poverty of the aged. Thus, *Helvering v. Davis*[197] upheld the social security tax and *Steward*[198] upheld the federal unemployment compensation tax. The real evidence that the Court had turned away from *Butler* came in *Sonzinsky*,[199] upholding a tax on firearms, despite an obvious regulatory purpose, but nevertheless some minimal tax revenue was raised. Presumably the Court that ruled in 1922 in *Drexel Furniture* that the United States had no concern with child labor would not have ruled as did the Court in *Davis* and *Steward*.[200]

It is odd that *Butler*, the opinion of a conservative majority that opposed federal regulation of state affairs, should be the vehicle for unleashing the federal spending power from the restraints of the enumerated powers of Congress. This was called a falling of the "legitimacy barrier" to spending.[201] Moreover, in practice the recognition of the general welfare taxing and spending power appears to have aided in eliminating concern with an expenditure being too local.[202] However, as shown above and in Chapter III.D.2, the construction applied to Article I, section 8, clause 1 of the Constitution by *Butler* actually avoided several far more liberal alternatives.

b. *Coercive General Welfare Spending*

Coercing state action through withholding federal spending was one of the questions presented in the *Sebelius* appeals concerning the 2010 Affordable Care Act.

The claimed coercion was not directly related to the tax dispute as to the Affordable Care Act, discussed in Chapter III.E.2.c, but rather was a separate claim of plaintiff states that the Congress was trying to coerce them into expanding certain features of Medicaid on pain of losing all federal Medicaid funding. Medicaid participation is voluntary with the states, but all now participate due to the substantial federal revenues the states receive. The result of the ruling in *Sebelius* is that Congress cannot punish a state's failure to participate in the Medicaid expansion enacted in 2010 by denying federal funding for basic Medicaid, but because there is no opinion of the Court on this issue, there is no holding, just a result.[203]

---

[197] Helvering v. Davis, 301 U.S. 619 (1937).

[198] Steward Machine Co. v. Davis, 301 U.S. 548 (1937). *See also* Pennhurst State Sch. & Hosp. v. Halderman, 451 U.S. 1, 17 (1981) (The Spending Clause permits Congress to "fix the terms on which it shall disburse federal money to the States." "[L]egislation enacted pursuant to the spending power is much in the nature of a contract: in return for federal funds, the States agree to comply with federally imposed conditions.").

[199] Sonzinsky v. United States, 300 U.S. 506, 513 (1937); United States v. Miller, 307 U.S. 174 (1939) (similar to *Sonzinsky*). *See* PAUL L. MURPHY, THE CONSTITUTION IN CRISIS TIMES 1918-1969, 157 (1972) (confirming the parallelism of the decision to *Butler*, with a different result).

[200] J.W. Bailey v. Drexel Furn. Co., 259 U.S. 20, 37 (1922).

[201] Lesser and Bernstein, at 632.

[202] *Id.* at 633.

[203] Nat'l Fed'n of Indep. Bus. v. Sebelius, 567 U.S. 519 (2012).

The complaining states based their claim on *Dole*, but contrary to the suggestion in the issue as framed, *Dole* did not enforce a limitation on Congress; rather it enforced the general rule that Congress can condition its spending, which it need not have spent at all, subject to certain broad limitations not found there to apply.[204] The Court's approvals of conditioned federal grants in aid can be traced at least back to *Massachusetts v. Mellon* and the Maternity Aid Act.[205] *Dole* ruled that loss of certain federal funds if a state lowered its drinking age was not an unconstitutional coercion of the states, because it was not the sort of compulsion to which the *Steward* opinion referred in upholding the unemployment compensation act as not going being beyond the bounds of federal power.[206] *Steward* referred to "destroying or impairing the autonomy of the states" and cited *Cincinnati Soap* for the source of this concern.[207] That opinion did not involve a state but rather a dependency, the Philippines. The United States levied a tax on domestic processing of coconut oil and appropriated the proceeds to the Philippines, where most if not all coconuts came from, but conditioned the appropriation on the Philippines' not paying any subsidies to coconut producers there. The Court reasoned that because Congress "may levy the tax with the collateral purpose of protecting the industries of this country," it can condition the spending on protecting that result. In other words, if Congress can tax with an ancillary purpose to regulate it can spend with the same ancillary purpose to regulate.

Since *Cincinnati Soap* does not appear to be the origin of the coercion concern, perhaps it lies in the phrase "autonomy of the states." The Court first used the term to limit a federal statute in *E. C. Knight*, which emasculated the Antitrust Act of 1890 in finding that manufacturing is not interstate commerce.[208] *Carter v. Carter Coal* cited *E. C. Knight* for the phrase in explaining why the Coal Code was not a proper regulation of interstate commerce.[209] But *Steward* did not depend on the Commerce Clause in upholding the unemployment security system; it relied purely on the taxing power. It identified the federal motivations to raise the funds as including (1) protecting the federal treasury from expenses of mass unemployment, and (2) putting the states on equal footing.

The unemployment security system allowed a credit against a federal tax on employers for 90% of a state tax levied under a program that met federal stan-

---

[204] South Dakota v. Dole, 483 U.S. 203 (1987).

[205] Massachusetts v. Mellon, 262 U.S. 447, 489 (1923) ("Probably, it would be sufficient to point out that the powers of the State are not invaded, since the statute imposes no obligation but simply extends an option which the State is free to accept or reject. But we do not rest here."). But when *Butler* addressed the voluntary cooperation of farmers in the Agricultural Adjustment Act, it found the voluntariness to be illusory and the act to be coercive regulation of a subject Congress could not regulate. United States v. Butler, 297 U.S. 1, 70-71 (1936).

[206] Steward Machine Co. v. Davis, 301 U.S. 548, 591 (1937).

[207] *Id.* at 586 ("There must be a showing in the second place that the tax and the credit in combination are weapons of coercion, destroying or impairing the autonomy of the states."). Cincinnati Soap Co. v. United States, 301 U.S. 308 (1937).

[208] United States v. E. C. Knight Co., 156 U.S. 1 (1895).

[209] Carter v. Carter Coal Co., 298 U.S. 238 (1936).

dards. *Steward* said that the charge that the states were coerced into the system mistook coercion for the motive or temptation of anyone, including a state, that is seeking a rebate.[210] Thus the states had a choice of administering their own system under federal rules or the federal government would administer the system; that is not coercion.

Indeed, the design of the taxes for the unemployment security system was suggested by Justice Louis Brandeis to Frances Perkins, the Secretary of Labor, who was primarily responsible for the plan. Justice Brandeis believed the tax credit method would place the system on solid constitutional ground.[211] Justice Stone also recommended to Perkins that the taxing power be relied on.[212]

The opinion of Chief Justice Roberts in *Sebelius*, in which only two other Justices joined, found that the coercive effect of taking away all Medicaid funding was different in kind and not in degree and so deprived the states of the choice to which federalism entitles them. The joint dissent of Justices Kennedy, Thomas, Scalia and Alito would have more broadly invalidated the Act. Therefore the result was the narrowest result on which a majority of the Justices could agree, eliminating the sanction of total loss of Medicaid funding, even though only three Justices supported that view. There was no holding as to this issue because there was no opinion of the Court. Either the theories in Justice Roberts' opinion or the opinion of the four dissenters may be used by future plaintiffs to mount attacks on federal conditioned spending that has previously been thought proper.

But a new trend in the Court's decisions holds that the United States cannot withhold spending if the recipient fails to conform to some "speech" required as a condition of the spending.[213] This trend promises to allow all manner of individual rights to stymie federal action,[214] but remains a highly malleable doctrine.[215]

E. Taxes Can Regulate

1. *The General Rule*

As shown in the foregoing parts of this Chapter III, taxes Congress enacts under the taxing power in Article 1, section 8, clause 1 of the Constitution (sometimes called a "true tax")[216] can and do regulate. They can regulate as an incidental purpose or effect, a principal purpose or effect, or a sole purpose. The matter regulated can be a matter that is within another enumerated power of Congress, or not. But if the sole effect of the tax is to regulate and no revenue whatsoever is

---

[210] 301 U.S. at 589-590.

[211] Kirsten Downey, The Woman Behind the New Deal 235 (2009).

[212] *Id.* at 235-236.

[213] Agency for Int'l Dev. v. Alliance for Open Soc'y Int'l, Inc., 570 U.S. 205 (2013).

[214] Burwell v. Hobby Lobby Stores, Inc., 573 U.S. 682 (2014).

[215] Agency for Int'l Dev. v. All. for Open Soc'y Int'l, Inc., 140 S. Ct. 2082 (2020) (very similar to the 2013 case but the foreign persons affected had no First Amendment rights).

[216] Dep't of Revenue of Mont. v. Ranch, 511 U.S. 767, 787 (1994); United States v. Butler, 297 U.S. 1, 61 (1936); United States v. Constantine, 296 U.S. 287, 294 (1935).

produced (not even minimal revenue that declines as the regulation takes hold), then the tax will be more subject to attack and may be unconstitutional if Congress lacks the power to regulate the matter taxed.

A true tax that regulates may be dually authorized by both the taxing power and the Necessary and Proper Clause, but need not be based on the Necessary and Proper Clause. Alternately, a federal exaction called a tax may be solely based on the Necessary and Proper Clause if the matter regulated is within the power of Congress. In contrast, a regulatory charge is not a tax.

The following authorities, in addition to the more specific discussion in the following Chapters, prove these points.

- The Constitution Article I, section 9, clause 6, states that no preference shall be given by any regulation of commerce or revenue to the ports of one state, indicating by the reference to revenue that taxes can regulate.[217]
- Alexander Hamilton expounded the benefits of a federal excise or import tax on ardent spirits not only by explaining the large amount of revenue that might be raised, but also stating: "if it should tend to diminish the consumption of it, such an effect would be equally favorable to the agriculture, to the morals, to the economy and to the health of the society. There is, perhaps, nothing so much a subject of national extravagance as these spirits."[218]
- Protective tariffs were thought to be taxes that could be used for accomplishment of purposes that might not be sought directly, such as drawing money from the pockets of one part of the community for the purpose of increasing the business of another part; and such a scheme had been approved by Madison, who believed Jefferson agreed.[219] The second bill enacted by Congress was a protective tariff, which stated its purpose to protect local manufactures.[220] However, in opposition to the Tariff of 1828 John C. Calhoun wrote the Protest and Exposition on which South Carolina relied in attempting to nullify the federal tariff in that state. The Protest grounded its opposition to the tariff in part on the fact that taxes can be levied solely for revenue. President Jackson made South Carolina back down.[221]

---

[217] *See* Ch. VI.C. *See also* Alaska v. Troy, 258 U.S. 101 (1922) (A regulation that shipping to Alaska must be on American registry ships is not a tax and so is not subject to the tax uniformity clause; dissent of Justice Miller in Dooley v. United States, 183 U.S. 151, 168 (1901) (explaining clause 6 as aimed at taxes and commerce regulations having a regulatory effect through discrimination); Knowlton v. Moore, 178 U.S. 41 (1900) (discussing by analogy to the uniformity clause the ports clause and finding the uniformity to require the same geographical uniformity and explaining the course of adoption); Gibbons v. Ogden, 22 U.S. 1 (1824) (described clause 6 as relating to both revenue and commerce regulation).

[218] The Federalist, No. 12, by Alexander Hamilton, p. 75 (Modern Library Ed.).

[219] J. I. Clark Hare, American Constitutional Law 271 (1889).

[220] *See* McKay, at 40. The first tariff act was explained in its section 1: "Whereas it is necessary for the support of the government, for the discharge of the debts of the United States, and the encouragement and protection of manufactures, that duties be laid on goods, wares and merchandises imported: Be it enacted . . . ." The Tariff Act of July 4, 1789.

[221] Friedman, at 96.

- Chief Justice Marshall's famous statement that "the power to tax involves the power to destroy," meant that a sovereign could use its taxing power for regulatory purposes totally unrelated to raising revenue (*i.e.*, aiming to destroy).[222]

- In 1833 Joseph Story examined at length the competing arguments on the question whether the federal government could levy a tax for a purpose other than raising revenue. He stated that "nothing is more clear from the history of commercial nations than the fact that the taxing power is often, very often, applied for other purposes than revenue. It is often applied as a regulation of commerce."[223]

- Chief Justice Taft, no friend of taxes, stated: ". . . [N]o historian, whatever his view of the wisdom of the policy of protection, would contend that Congress, since the first revenue Act, in 1789, has not assumed that it was within its power in making provision for the collection of revenue, to put taxes upon importations and to vary the subjects of such taxes or rates in an effort to encourage the growth of the industries of the Nation by protecting home production against foreign competition. It is enough to point out that the second act adopted by the Congress of the United States, July 4, 1789, ch. 2, 1 Stat. 24, contained the following recital. 'Sec. 1 Whereas it is necessary for the support of government, for the discharge of the debts of the United States, and the encouragement and protection of manufactures, that duties be laid on goods, wares and merchandises imported: Be it enacted, etc.'"[224]

- Justice Kagan stated in a unanimous opinion in 2021: "That is just as true when the tax in question is a so-called regulatory tax—that is, a tax designed mainly to influence private conduct, rather than to raise revenue. This Court has long since "abandoned the view that brightline distinctions exist between regulatory and revenue raising taxes."[225]

Usually paired with the observation that taxes frequently regulate something is the observation that it is undesirable for the courts to be forced to look into the intent or motives of Congress in imposing what it has denominated a tax, as discussed above in Chapter III.D.3. This concern shows that the Court prefers to rely on the form of a tax or Congress' assertion of the taxing power rather than to examine its substance to determine if it is not a tax. Chief Justice Marshall originated this approach when he said duties and imposts on imports and

---

[222] SIDNEY RATNER, AMERICAN TAXATION 19-20 (1942) [hereinafter RATNER] (quoting *McCulloch v. Maryland*, noting that many have asserted the opposite meaning, but that the evidence reveals the framers knew and intended that taxes have the power to destroy commerce, apart from revenue raising).

[223] STORY, at 434. *See also* James M. Beck, *Nullification by Indirection*, 23 HARV. L. REV. 441, 451 (1909) [hereinafter Beck] ("The power to tax imports was always understood as a power to regulate foreign commerce and not a taxing power, . . .").

[224] J. W. Hampton, Jr. & Co. v. United States, 396 U.S. 394, 411-412 (1926).

[225] CIC Servs., LLC v. IRS, 141 S. Ct. 1582 (2021).

exports were taxes and not regulations of commerce, but in the next breath he said that "The idea that the same measure might, according to circumstances, be arranged with different classes of power, was no novelty to the framers of our constitution."[226] Those alternatives allowed Chief Justice Taft to say he knew a regulation when he saw it in the *Child Labor Tax Case*.[227]

The opinions of the Court recognizing the regulatory role of taxes include:

- *Gibbons v. Ogden* explained that taxes can regulate, which is why the Import-Export Clause and Tonnage Clause forbids them to states.[228]
- *Fernandez v. Wiener* upheld a federal estate tax, stating: "Undoubtedly every tax which lays its burden on some and not others may have an incidental regulatory effect. But since that is an inseparable concomitant of the power to tax, the incidental regulatory effect of the tax is embraced within the power to lay it. It has long been settled that an Act of Congress which on its face purports to be an exercise of the taxing power, is not any the less so because the tax is burdensome or tends to restrict or suppress the thing taxed. In such a case it is not within the province of courts to inquire into the unexpressed purposes or motives which may have moved Congress to exercise a power constitutionally conferred upon it."[229]
- *Sonzinsky v. United States* stated in upholding a federal tax: "Every tax is in some measure regulatory. To some extent it interposes an economic impediment to the activity taxed as compared with others not taxed. But a tax is not any the less a tax because it has a regulatory effect . . . ."[230]
- *United States v. Sanchez* ruled that the Marijuana Tax Act was not justified on the basis of the Commerce Clause or other federal regulatory power, but solely on the taxing power.[231]
- *United States v. Doremus* stated in upholding a federal tax that involved a detailed regulatory scheme: "And from an early day the court has held that the fact that other motives may impel the exercise of federal taxing power does not authorize the courts to inquire into that subject. If the legislation enact-

---

[226] Gibbons v. Ogden, 22 U.S. 1, 202 (1824).

[227] J.W. Bailey v. Drexel Furn. Co., 259 U.S. 20, 37 (1922)("In the light of these features of the act, a court must be blind not to see that the so called tax is imposed to stop the employment of children within the age limits prescribed. Its prohibitory and regulatory effect and purpose are palpable. All others can see and understand this. How can we properly shut our minds to it?").

[228] Gibbons v. Ogden, 22 U.S. 1 (1824).

[229] Fernandez v. Wiener, 326 U.S. 340, 361-362 (1945).

[230] Sonzinsky v. United States, 300 U.S. 506, 513 (1937); United States v. Miller, 307 U.S. 174 (1939) (similar to *Sonzinsky*).

[231] United States v. Sanchez, 340 U.S. 42, 44 (1950), citing J. W. Hampton Jr. & Co. v. United States, 276 U.S. 394 (1928) (a tariff case, which indicated an understanding that tariffs sometimes were set for the primary purpose of protecting local industries, although it cited a statement in the *Child Labor Tax Case* indicating that nontax motives might be incidental). *Cf.* Pittsburgh v. Alco Parking Corp., 417 U.S. 369, 375 (1974) (a state tax case upholding a tax that had some ability to raise revenue despite regulatory impact).

ed has some reasonable relation to the exercise of the taxing authority conferred by the Constitution, it cannot be invalidated because of the supposed motives which induced it. *Veazie Bank v. Fenno*, 8 Wall. 533, 541, in which case this court sustained a tax on a state bank issue of circulating notes. *McCray v. United States*, 195 U.S. 27, where the power was thoroughly considered, and an act levying a special tax upon oleomargarine artificially colored was sustained."[232] *Doremus* was one of several cases involving the Harrison Narcotics Act and related drug laws. Congress repealed the Marijuana Tax Act in 1970 and replaced it with criminal penalties that did not involve taxes, which were upheld as proper regulation in *Gonzales v. Raich*.[233]

- The *License Tax Cases* upheld a federal fee for engaging in conduct that was illegal under state law, stating: "There is nothing hostile or contradictory, therefore, in the acts of Congress to the legislation of the States. What the latter prohibits, the former, if the business is found existing notwithstanding the prohibition, discourages by taxation."[234] Unlike the other cases discussed in this section payment of the tax did not authorize the conduct to be pursued, which made it easier for the Court to rule that the tax was a tax (and it was labeled a tax).

- Even the *Child Labor Tax Case* grudgingly admitted to the incidental regulatory purposes and effects of taxation: "Taxes are occasionally imposed in the discretion of the legislature on proper subjects with the primary motive of obtaining revenue from them and with the incidental motive of discouraging them by making their continuance onerous. They do not lose their character as taxes because of the incidental motive."[235]

- *Alaska Fish v. Smith* applied the same principle to state taxes designed to prevent misuse of fish: "If Alaska deems it for its welfare to discourage the destruction of herring for manure and to preserve them for food for man or for salmon, and to that end imposes a greater tax upon that part of the plaintiff's industry than upon similar use of other fish or of the offal of salmon, it hardly can be said to be contravening a Constitution that has known protective tariffs for a hundred years. . . . We know of no objection to exacting a discouraging rate as the alternative to giving up a business, when the legislature has the full power of taxation."[236]

- *In re* Kollock stated in upholding a conviction for failure to pay a tax on colored margarine: "The act before us is on its face an act for levying taxes, and although it may operate in so doing to prevent deception in the sale of oleomargarine as and for butter, its primary object must be assumed to be the raising of revenue. The act may not be declared unconstitutional because

[232] United States v. Doremus, 249 U.S. 86 (1919).
[233] Gonzales v. Raich, 545 U.S. 1 (2005).
[234] License Tax Cases, 72 U.S. 462, 473 (1867).
[235] J.W. Bailey v. Drexel Furn. Co., 259 U.S. 20, 38 (1922).
[236] Alaska Fish Salting & By-Products Co. v. Smith, 255 U.S. 44, 48-49 (1921).

its effect may be to accomplish another purpose as well as the raising of revenue."[237] And a more recent opinion also has used the "must be assumed" formulation.[238]

- *Bob Jones University v. Simon* stated that a tax is intended to raise revenue, but that the Court had in *Sonzinsky* rejected the distinction between regulatory and revenue raising taxes (citing *Hill v. Wallace* and *Lederer*).[239] Evidently this meant that *Bob Jones* and *Sonzinsky* recognized that a tax could also have a regulatory purpose and function, but that understanding did not start with *Sonzinsky*.
- *McCray v. United States* upheld a federal tax intended to discourage the coloring of margarine to look like butter.[240]
- *Veazie Bank v. Fenno* upheld a tax intended to suppress state bank notes so as to favor national bank notes.[241] This case differs from those in which the regulation would not be permitted apart from the power to tax, because it was ruled to be constitutional in part as an adjunct to the power to emit money and to regulate coinage. The opinion makes it crystal clear that the Court understood the tax was not imposed to raise revenue but to eliminate the state banks from the business of creating money, thus proving that the taxing power could be exercised purely to regulate.[242] Nevertheless, the opinion also clearly treats the tax as a taxing power tax.[243] The Court has cited *Veazie Bank* as an example of a power of Congress that stemmed from more than one constitutional source.[244] However, opponents of the taxing power have strained to read *Veazie Bank* as purely a regulatory tax case, presumably

---

[237] *In re* Kollock, 165 U.S. 526, 536 (1897).

[238] *See, e.g.*, Grosso v. United States, 390 U.S. 62 (1968) (wagering tax must be assumed to be for revenue raising and not prosecuting gamblers).

[239] Bob Jones Univ. v. Simon, 416 U.S. 725, 741 n. 12 (1974) (citing Sonzinsky v. United States, 300 U.S. 506, 513 (1937).

[240] McCray v. United States, 195 U.S. 27 (1904). *See* John B. Waite, *May Congress Levy Money Exactions Designed as "Taxes" Solely for the Purpose of Destruction?* 6 Mich. L. Rev. 277, 279, 289-290 (1908) (Disagreeing with the opinion and stating, "Because the tax raised little if any revenue and was clearly for the purpose of destroying the trade in colored oleo, which congress had no right to regulate, how could the power to tax apply? Taxes exclude fees, but should also exclude impositions solely to regulate."); Fred. D. Ragan, *National Police Powers: The Oleomargarine Case*, in John W. Johnson, Historic U.S. Court Cases 456 (2d ed). *See also* Cliff v. United States, 195 U.S. 159 (1904) (also involving the oleo tax).

[241] Veazie Bank v. Fenno, 75 U.S. 533 (1869).

[242] Harry Edward Smith, The United States Federal Internal Revenue Tax History from 1861 to 1871 at 139 (1914).

[243] 75 U.S. at 540, 547 (the opinion considered and rejected a direct tax challenge, which it could have ignored if the tax were not a taxing power tax). *See* Pollock v. Farmers' Loan & Trust Co., 157 U.S. 429, 577 (1895) (explaining *Veazie Bank* as a taxing power tax).

[244] Adickes v. S. H. Kress & Co., 398 U.S. 144, 187 (1970).

enacted under the Necessary and Proper Clause, despite the fact that the Clause was not mentioned in the opinion.[245]

- *Sebelius* stated in 2012: ". . . [T]axes that seek to influence conduct are nothing new . . . indeed, every tax is to some extent regulatory."[246]

Regulation through the taxing power bears an obvious similarity to regulation through the Commerce Clause. Both the taxing power and the Commerce Clause exist for purposes other than general police power regulation: the taxing power exists principally to fund the federal government and the Commerce Clause exists principally to knit the states together into one nation. Nevertheless, the power of the United States to regulate in the nature of a police power through the Commerce Clause was established in *Champion v. Ames*, though not without reversals up to 1937.[247] Thus Congress has used both powers in similar ways.

2. *Federal Taxes Can Regulate Matters Beyond Federal Control*

a. *General*

The hardest cases are those in which federal taxes appear to regulate matters that the federal government could not regulate directly; and yet such taxes clearly are constitutional as a general matter. The most recent example (with a caveat) is the 2012 decision in *Sebelius* upholding the health insurance tax as a tax even though five Justices said that Congress could not regulate individual insurance purchasing under the Commerce Clause (but the Court did not so hold).[248] For and earlier example, in one of several opinions upholding the Harrison Narcotics Act, *Nigro v. United States*, Chief Justice Taft, speaking for the Court, said:

> In interpreting the Act, we must assume that it is a taxing measure, for otherwise it would be no law at all. If it is a mere act for the purpose of regulating

---

[245] In 1910 a Harvard Law Review article by a future Solicitor General in the Harding administration said critics thought *Veazie Bank v. Fenno* had crossed the line in the fundamental dispute as to when a tax ceases to be authorized by the taxing power and is levied for a purpose denied to the federal government. Beck. In contrast, Max Pam stated in 1911 that the power of taxation appeared to be an "even more potent" way to regulate than the commerce clause and control over the mails. Max Pam, *Power of Regulation Vested in Congress*, 24 Harv. L. Rev. 77, 100 (1911). *See* Benjamin R. Twiss, Lawyers and the Constitution 231-241 [hereinafter Twiss] (discussing the important role Beck played in cases attempting to limit federal regulation). *See also* Staff of the Joint Committee on Taxation, The Taxing Power of the Federal and State Governments 6 (1936) (available on Joint Committee website) (stating that *Veazie Bank* upheld the tax under the power to regulate currency).

[246] Nat'l Fed'n of Indep. Bus. v. Sebelius, 567 U.S. 519 (2012). *See* Ch. III.E.2.c.

[247] Champion v. Ames, 188 U.S. 321 (1903). See Margulies, 4 J. S. Legal Hist. 45. The reversals were in Hammer v. Dagenhart, 247 U.S. 251 (1918) (*Child Labor Case*) and Carter v. Carter Coal Co., 298 U.S. 238 (1936) (New Deal Bituminous Coal Act). *Hammer* itself was overruled by United States v. Darby, 312 U.S. 100 (1941), which did not directly overrule *Bailey* (the *Child Labor Tax Case*).

[248] *See* Ch. III.E.2.c.

> and restraining the purchase of the opiate and other drugs, it is beyond the power of Congress and must be regarded as invalid . . . .[249]

Even Justice Sutherland recognized that the taxing power enabled Congress to regulate what it could not regulate directly:

> The statute [Harrison Narcotics Act] is not aimed at sales of the forbidden drugs qua sales, a matter entirely beyond the authority of Congress, but at sales of such drugs in violation of the requirements set forth in §§ 1 and 2, enacted as aids to the enforcement of the stamp tax imposed by the act.[250]

Veazie Bank v. Fenno clearly stands for this proposition, with the only caveat that the opinion relied on both the power of taxation and the power of coinage.[251] The *License Tax Cases* are more on point because they involved federal taxes for licenses required as a precondition to selling liquor when the United States had no power to regulate local liquor sales.[252] As originally enacted the tax was labeled a license tax, but when attacked as unconstitutional, Congress changed the label to "special tax" in hopes that the change would assuage any concern. In the opinion the Court upheld both versions of the tax, stating that the change removed any ambiguity.[253] The heavy pre-Prohibition federal taxes on alcohol were clearly for the purpose of regulation.[254] The Court ruled in 1902 that in taxing the sale of tobacco, which Congress was not thought to have the power to regulate, Congress could choose to impose apparently arbitrary conditions that had regulatory effect or purpose, such as forbidding the seller to package any other item, no matter how insignificant, with the tobacco product.[255]

In 1925 Justice Brandeis for the entire Court identified six different ways in which Congress could constitutionally tax the exercise of the corporate franchise to do business, despite the fact that Congress did not grant the franchise.[256] *Sonzinsky* upheld federal regulation of guns, solely under the taxing power.[257] *Sanchez* and *Kahriger* directly ruled that the United States could tax, and by taxing regulate, a subject that the United States could not regulate directly (much to Justice Frankfurter's distress in *Kahriger*).[258]

---

[249] Nigro v. United States, 276 U.S. 332, 341 (1928).

[250] Blockburger v. United States, 284 U.S. 299, 304 (1932).

[251] Veazie Bank v. Fenno, 75 U.S. 533 (1869).

[252] License Tax Cases, 72 U.S. 462 (1867).

[253] *Id.* at 475. This case was cited in the arguments over the 2010 health care tax as an example of a tax that was not originally labeled a tax; however, Congress added the denomination tax in 1866 not to insure that the levy was viewed as a tax but to combat the misconception that the license authorized the activities taxed. *See* Brief of United States dated January 2012, Dept. of Health and Human Services v. State of Florida, p. 57 (USSC No. 11-398).

[254] *See* Selzman v. United States, 268 U.S. 466 (1925) (explaining why denatured alcohol was relieved of the heavy pre-Prohibition tax on intoxicating liquor).

[255] Felsenheld v. United States, 186 U.S. 126 (1902).

[256] Ray Consol. Copper Co. v. United States, 268 U.S. 373 (1925).

[257] Sonzinsky v. United States, 300 U.S. 506 (1937).

[258] United States v. Sanchez, 340 U.S. 42 (1950); United States v. Kahriger, 345 U.S. 22 (1953).

McCray v. United States upheld federal taxes on colored margarine fairly clearly for the purposes of regulating intrastate activity.[259] The tax did not require interstate shipment as a precondition to its imposition, but rather was imposed upon manufacture and sale. The opinion did not rely on the Commerce Clause to support the tax, because it treated the tax as an exercise of the taxing power. Rather amazingly, it concluded by stating that a regulatory tax is constitutional if any free government can regulate the conduct; that must mean that if the levy is labeled a tax and regulates something that is solely within the power of the states to regulate, it is a valid federal tax:

> Let us concede that if a case was presented where the abuse of the taxing power was so extreme as to be beyond the principles which we have previously stated, and where it was plain to the judicial mind that the power had been called into play not for revenue but solely for the purpose of destroying rights which could not be rightfully destroyed consistently with the principles of freedom and justice upon which the Constitution rests, that it would be the duty of the courts to say that such an arbitrary act was not merely an abuse of a delegated power, but was the exercise of an authority not conferred. This concession, however, like the one previously made, must be without influence upon the decision of this cause for the reasons previously stated; that is, that the manufacture of artificially colored oleomargarine may be prohibited by a free government without a violation of fundamental rights.[260]

In his dissent in *Hammer v. Dagenhart*, Justice Holmes cited *McCray* as an example of the principle that the exercise of a federal power can result in indirect regulation of activities normally subject to only state control:

> The question then is narrowed to whether the exercise of its otherwise constitutional power by Congress can be pronounced unconstitutional because of its possible reaction upon the conduct of the States in a matter upon which I have admitted that they are free from direct control. I should have thought that that matter had been disposed of so fully as to leave no room for doubt. I should have thought that most conspicuous decisions of this Court had made it clear that the power to regulate commerce and other constitutional powers could not be cut down or qualified by the fact that it might interfere with the carrying out of the domestic policy of any State.[261]

George Sutherland, while a Republican senator and before he became one of the most conservative Justices ever to sit on the Supreme Court, characterized *McCray* in a 1910 Senate speech in a way that made clear his understanding that

---

[259] McCray v. United States, 195 U.S. 27 (1904). The government did not argue that it had the power to regulate under the Commerce Clause and the Court did not say it did. This has evidently surprised some commentators. *See, e.g.*, MARIE CAROLYN KLINKHAMER, EDWARD DOUGLAS WHITE CHIEF JUSTICE OF THE UNITED STATES 162 (1943) (indicating that the opinion said the commerce was regulable as commerce).

[260] 195 U.S. at 64.

[261] Hammer v. Dagenhart, 247 U.S. 251, 278 (1918). *See* United States v. Darby, 312 U.S. 100 (1941) (citing the Holmes dissent, Justice Stone stated that *Hammer* had been a departure from the normal principles applied to the Commerce Clause).

so long as a tax raised some revenue it could regulate a matter beyond federal authority to regulate. His statement refutes some later statements of the Court (in the *Child Labor Tax Case* and *Sebelius*) that a federal tax could incidentally but not primarily regulate:

> 4. If the law carries out any constitutional power, it is not rendered invalid because it also, to a greater or less extent accomplishes some other result which is wholly beyond the power of Congress to deal with as a separate and independent matter. And I cite *McCray v. United States* (195 U.S. 27).[262]

In other words, so long as the tax was a true tax (and *McCray* admitted that the federal tax could eliminate the colored margarine business, thus raising no or only declining revenue), the federal government could properly regulate colored margarine, despite the fact that it was not relying on the Commerce Clause but solely on the taxing power.[263] Due to this power of taxes to regulate, and to do so as a primary or even sole object, the threshold identification of a true tax is the only escape valve for an opponent of such a tax, as discussed in Chapter III.F.

b. *Taxes Can Regulate to Strongly Encourage Positive Action*

A common way in which taxes are used to regulate is to encourage taxpayers to avoid the taxed conduct. Indeed, discouragement of certain imports has long been a principal purpose of many import duties. Such regulation might be called compulsion or coercion of the public and even of the states. The Supreme Court upheld against complaints about such compulsion the federal unemployment compensation system and tax in *Southern Coal* and *Steward Machine*.[264]

The Southern Coal Co. sued in federal court to restrain Alabama officials from collecting an unemployment insurance tax imposed by Alabama state law. The Coal Co. argued, inter alia, that the federal government did not have the power to force the states to institute an unemployment compensation system and could not do so by the indirect method of granting a tax credit so that employers in the state could credit against the federal unemployment tax liability the taxes they paid to a qualifying state unemployment plan.[265] In addition the Coal Co. argued that the tax on the hiring of persons was an unconstitutional unapportioned direct tax.

The Coal Co. relied on the three recent Supreme Court decisions striking down New Deal taxes and agencies.[266] Of these three, *Carter Coal* was most analogous to the later unemployment tax cases, except for the fact that the United States did not defend the tax in *Carter Coal* under the taxing power, but rather

---

262 Joel Francis Paschal, Mr. Justice Sutherland A Man Against the State 64 (1951).

263 *See generally* as to taxes and spending and regulation, Ruth Mason, *Federalism and the Taxing Power*, 99 Cal. L. Rev. 975, 1006 (2011) ("the dominant view [among scholars] seems to be that Congress may use taxes to achieve regulatory goals that fall outside its other enumerated powers.").

264 Carmichael v. Southern Coal & Coke Co., 301 U.S. 495 (1937); Steward Machine Co. v. Davis, 301 U.S. 548 (1937).

265 301 U.S. at 525-526.

266 United States v. Butler, 297 U.S. 1 (1936); Carter v. Carter Coal Co., 298 U.S. 238 (1936); Railroad Retirement Bd. v. Alton R. Co., 295 U.S. 330 (1935).

under the Commerce Clause.[267] The Guffy Coal Conservation Act of 1935 and its Coal Code at issue in *Carter* had imposed an "excise tax" on coal producers' sales or production without sales, 90% of which could be "drawnback," meaning credited or not paid, if the producer had accepted the Coal Commission Coal Code. The main goal of the Coal Code was to fix minimum prices for coal, but there were many other requirements affecting the rights of labor. Thus the tax was a means of coercing producer agreement to the Coal Code. With Justices Cardozo, Brandeis and Stone dissenting, Justice Sutherland ruled for Carter Coal on the ground that the tax was not a tax but a penalty (which the government admitted) and that it was a penalty the United States could not impose as a regulation of interstate commerce.

Justice Sutherland's opinion in *Carter Coal* disregarded the long recognized fact explained in the preceding Chapter that all taxes are partly regulatory and found the regulatory nature of the tax to dictate its treatment as a penalty: "One who does a thing in order to avoid a monetary penalty does not agree; he yields to compulsion precisely the same as though he did so to avoid a term in jail."[268] The opinion applied the theory used in *Hammer v. Dagenhart* that regulation of an activity that literally occurs within a state does not affect interstate commerce.[269]

In contrast, Justice Stone, in *Southern Coal*, upheld Alabama's power to levy the tax as a tax, not mentioning the Commerce Clause. It ruled that the United States had not coerced Alabama into levying the tax. In the companion case, *Steward Machine*, Justice Cardozo addressed an attack on the ten percent residual unemployment tax levied by the United States. He also upheld it as a tax because it was paid into the Treasury, and its role as a tax was not defeated by the fact that it might have some other motive or purpose. The *Steward* opinion expressed great reluctance to investigate the motives of Congress, but indicated that a tax would be undermined as a tax only if:

> . . . the conduct to be stimulated or discouraged is unrelated to the fiscal need subserved by the tax in its normal operation, or to any other end legitimately national. The *Child Labor Tax Case*, 259 U.S. 20, and *Hill v. Wallace*, 259 U.S. 44, were decided in the belief that the statutes there condemned were exposed to that reproach. Cf. *United States v. Constantine*, 296 U.S. 287. It is quite another thing to say that a tax will be abated upon the doing of an act that will satisfy the fiscal need, the tax and the alternative being approximate equivalents. In such circumstances, if in no others, inducement or persuasion does not go beyond the bounds of power. We do not fix the outermost line. Enough for present purposes that wherever the line may be, this statute is within it. Definition more precise must abide the wisdom of the future.[270]

[267] 298 U.S. at 289.

[268] *Id.* at 289.

[269] Hammer v. Dagenhart, 247 U.S. 251 (1918). *See also* United States v. Butler, 297 U.S. 1 (1936) (which similarly rejected the government's argument that cotton growers' participation in the cotton price support program was voluntary and thus did not attempt to regulate purely intrastate commerce).

[270] 301 U.S. at 591.

When the 1937 revision of the Bituminous Coal Code came back to the Court, it ruled the tax constitutional, reasoning that despite the fact that the tax was 19 ½ times greater for non-code members than for members, it was properly intended to coerce producers into the Code; it relied primarily on the Commerce Clause, but also on the taxing power used in aid of the Commerce Clause (not as a necessary and proper exaction that was not a tax).[271]

Other cases involving apparently coercive federal tax schemes include:

- An objection to tax coercion was most vehemently argued and rejected in *South Carolina v. Baker*, involving the registration requirement for state tax exempt bonds, which effectively coerced the states to register.[272]
- *Florida v. Mellon* (cited and relied upon by the *Steward* opinion) rejected the argument that an 80% credit for state inheritance taxes in the federal estate tax was intended to coerce the states to adopt an inheritance tax.[273]

However, the argument against federal coercion has enjoyed renewed support in the Court in more recent decisions not involving taxes.[274] For other discussions of coercion, see Ch. III.D.8.b (coercive federal spending); V.D.3.b(9) (due process aspects of coercion).

c. *The 2012 Health Insurance Tax Case*

(1) *Summary of Decision*

On June 28, 2012, *National Federation of Independent Business v. Sebelius* affirmed the constitutionality of 26 U.S.C. section 5000A, imposing a tax beginning in 2014 as part of the 2010 Patient Protection and Affordable Care Act.[275] This important decision is placed under the Chapter on regulating matters that Congress cannot regulate not because the Court held that Congress could not regulate individual purchases of health insurance, but because Chief Justice Roberts so stated in dictum in his sole opinion and four dissenters agreed, without joining his opinion. The general results of the judgment are: (1) the Anti-Injunction Act[276] did not bar the suits to enjoin the tax, (2) the tax that section 5000A would impose on certain individuals who did not buy health insurance would be

---

[271] Sunshine Anthracite Coal Co. v. Adkins, 310 U.S. 381, 393 (1940).

[272] South Carolina v. Baker, 485 U.S. 505 (1988). The potential that a federal requirement imposed on the states through the Spending Clause might be unduly coercive of the states was mentioned in *Steward Machine* and South Dakota v. Dole, 483 U.S. 203 (1987). *See* Ch. III.F.3, discussing the Tenth Amendment.

[273] Florida v. Mellon, 273 U.S. 12 (1927).

[274] *See, e.g.*, New York v. United States, 505 U.S. 144 (1992) (examining the extent to which coercive federal prodding of state action was proper); FMC v. S.C. State Ports Auth., 535 U.S. 743 (2002) (states could not be coerced into a federal adjudicative regime on pain of being subject to the rulings without participating); Agency for Int'l Dev. v. Alliance for Open Soc'y Int'l, Inc., 570 U.S. 205 (2013) (Congress could not condition receipt of funds on speech).

[275] Nat'l Fed'n of Indep. Bus. v. Sebelius, 567 U.S. 519 (2012). *See also* King v. Burwell, 576 U.S. 473 (2015) (ruling that the tax credits also applied to the federal exchange).

[276] 26 U.S.C. § 7421(a).

constitutional, but (3) it is not necessary and proper to the constitutional spending power for Congress to sanction a state by denying all Medicaid funding if the state refuses to participate in the Act's expanded spending on Medicaid.

In sum the opinion of the Court affirmed without praising the vast power of Congress to tax. However, the motives of the five Justices joining in the opinion may have differed. The four "liberal" Justices who joined Part IIIC of the Chief Justice's opinion, which upheld the tax as a tax, likely support the great scope of the taxing power that the Court has previously explained in many opinions beginning with Chief Justice Marshall's opinion in *McCulloch v. Maryland*.[277]

The relative lack of praise for the taxing power in Chief Justice Roberts' opinion can be added to many tea leaves that commentators have read in trying to discern what the Chief Justice, and indeed all the members of the Court, were really thinking when writing this remarkable set of opinions. It is possible that Chief Justice Roberts chose to deftly combine:

1. upholding the tax; with
2. doing so only under the taxing power, which he underplayed; while
3. stating in dictum having no precedential force that the "broccoli theory" prevented him from upholding it under the Commerce Clause;[278] because
4. (a) he did not want to be remembered in the way Chief Justice Taney has been remembered for his opinion in a single decision, the *Dred Scott* case;[279] and (b) he knows that upholding this penalty under the taxing power does not expand that power as a matter of legal precedent; and (c) his opinion on taxing inactivity is unlikely to embolden Congress to tax more, because the taxing power is in extremely bad odor currently;[280] while (d) his dictum adopting the "broccoli theory" of the Commerce Clause can, in the long run, provide added momentum for the Rehnquist Court's reversal of Commerce Clause powers that began in 1995.[281]

---

[277] McCulloch v. Maryland, 17 U.S. 316 (1819). *See* Ch. II.A.2.

[278] This is the argument made in the case by some plaintiffs that Congress might rely on the Commerce Clause to make individuals eat broccoli, if it can regulate inactivity, i.e., failure to eat broccoli.

[279] Dred Scott v. Sandford, 60 U.S. 393 (1857) (which effectively held that Congress had no power to resolve the slavery issue, thus setting the stage for a resolution through different means, which turned out to be the Civil War).

[280] *See* "A Vast New Taxing Power," p. A10, Wall Street Journal (July 2, 2012) (an unusual editorial that ran the full length of the two column editorial space, vehemently attacking the Roberts' opinion but grudgingly noting that the bad press of taxation may reduce the damage of the opinion's reasoning).

[281] In 1937 the Court began abruptly to turn back the anti-New Deal complaints that had met with uniform favor in the Court through 1936. After 1936 the Court held a federal statute unconstitutional as beyond the Commerce Clause powers only in two cases, United States v. Lopez, 514 U.S. 549 (1995) and United States v. Morrison, 529 U.S. 598 (2000).

The immediate attacks on the Roberts' opinion were based mostly on views of political economy, but found handy weapons in two seeming contradictions in his opinion, which will be discussed further below:

- It found the health insurance penalty to be a tax for constitutional purposes, but not a tax for Anti-Injunction Act purposes.
- It stated that Congress cannot regulate individual inactivity under the Commerce Clause, but can tax individual inactivity.

(2) *Future Stare Decisis Effects*

(a) *The Opinions*

With respect to the health insurance tax, Chief Justice Roberts' opinion is the opinion of the Court only as to the Anti-Injunction Act and the taxing power. No other Justice joined his opinion that the Commerce Clause does not authorize the penalty; although the four dissenters presumably agree with that conclusion, they did not concur with that part (or any part) of the Chief Justice's opinion. In addition no Justice joined the Chief Justice's explanation why it was necessary to reach a conclusion on the Commerce Clause, when the taxing power allowed the penalty and thus resolved the issue on appeal.

Justice Ginsburg filed a concurrence, in which three Justices joined, finding the Commerce Clause also to authorize the penalty. Justices Breyer and Kagan joined Chief Justice Roberts' opinion on Medicaid and the four dissenters agreed with the conclusion on Medicaid, although they would have gone farther.[282] Therefore there is no opinion of the Court as to the Medicaid issue, only a result based on the narrowest reasoning of the Justices that disagreed with the Medicaid expansion. Justices Ginsburg and Sotomayor dissented as to the Medicaid judgment.

In sum, the only issues for which the Court provided a definitive statement of its holding and reasoning are the Anti-Injunction Act and taxing power issues, which are the issues in the case that are most relevant to the subjects of this book.

(b) *Stare Decisis*

Tax lawyers and even judges tend not to parse the exact precedential significance of court tax decisions, for reasons that are not clear; perhaps tax experts tend to believe they know what the law is or should be, and assume the court agreed.[283] Repetition does not, however, make the practice correct, and this analysis will focus on the holdings of the Court, which alone have precedential value. It may be that one can count noses by reading all of the opinions and predict

---

[282] Perhaps Justices Breyer and Kagan joined Justice Roberts' opinion on Medicaid in exchange for his opinion on the tax?

[283] This tendency is reflected most unfortunately in the creation of the economic substance doctrine from disparate strands of opinions having no power to create the positive rule of law that the doctrine has become. *See* CUMMINGS, at 198-210.

that five votes might be assembled for some particular legal view, but that does not mean such view exists as a legal precedent for lower courts.

The preclusive effect on the lower federal and state courts of decisions of the Supreme Court of the United States rests on the doctrine of stare decisis, as well as the constitutional supremacy of the Supreme Court relative to other federal courts, and to the state courts as to issues of federal law.[284] The Court itself has more flexibility as to its prior decisions and can ignore, reject, claim to distinguish or change a decision that it finds to be unsound in principle or unworkable in practice.[285] The Court's flexibility is at its greatest in cases of constitutional interpretation, due to the very limited ways in which the Constitution otherwise can be changed.[286]

> The doctrine of stare decisis extends to the holdings of prior decisions, but it does not extend to mere dicta (*e.g.*, statements that were unnecessary to the result in a prior decision).[287]

Therefore other courts must at a minimum reach a result consistent with the result reached by the Supreme Court.[288] When a majority of the Justices constituting the Court agree to one opinion, the holding stated in the opinion is entitled to stare decisis effect.[289] The holding is the determination of an issue of law, not of fact or of mixed law and fact.[290] Holding is in contrast to dictum;[291] although alternative grounds supporting a result are part of the holding, dictum can be identified by asking if it could be deleted without impairing the basis of the court's decision.[292] When there is no opinion of the Court on an issue but concurrence in the result, the narrowest ground of concurrence is the holding of the Court.[293] Sometimes the reasoning of a decision is distinguished from both the holding and the result; generally the reasoning need not be followed.[294] However, the rule of law selected, created or identified by the Court to be ap-

---

[284] Moore's Federal Practice ¶ 134.01[1]. This preclusive effect derives from the fact that the United States has a common law legal system rather than a civil code based system. James Wm. Moore and Robert Stephen Oglebay, *The Supreme Court, Stare Decisis and the Law of the Case*, 21 Tex. L. Rev. 514, 515 (1942) [hereinafter Moore and Oglebay].

[285] Moore's Federal Practice at ¶ 134.02[1][b].

[286] *See* Agostini v. Felton, 521 U.S. 203, 235 (1997) (stare decisis "is at its weakest when we interpret the Constitution because our interpretation can be altered only by constitutional amendment or by overruling our prior decisions").

[287] Moore's Federal Practice at ¶ 134.01[1].

[288] *Op. cit.* at ¶ 134.03[1].

[289] *Op. cit.* at ¶ 134.04[1], ¶ 134.03[2].

[290] *Op. cit.* at ¶ 134.04[2].

[291] *Id.*

[292] *Id.*

[293] *Id.*

[294] *Op. cit.* at ¶ 134.03[3].

plied to the facts to reach the result necessarily is the holding, else stare decisis would have no use in future cases.[295]

Applying these principles of American law to the opinion of Justice Roberts, the preclusive effect of the entire decision can be summarized as follows:

- Anti-Injunction Act: The result is that the Anti-Injunction Act did not remove from the federal courts jurisdiction to hear the complaints against the health insurance penalty. The holding is that the Act does not bar a suit to enjoin a tax that Congress has styled as a penalty rather than a tax, provided Congress has not otherwise indicated the penalty should be treated as a tax for purposes of the Anti-Injunction Act.
- Constitutionality of the health insurance tax: The result is that the tax can be collected because the Constitution authorizes Congress to impose it. The holding is that the penalty is a tax that Congress can impose under the taxing power because it functions (i.e., its "practical operation") as a tax, principally by having the tendency to raise some revenue for the federal government. In response to plaintiffs' arguments, the opinion also holds that (1) a federal taxing power tax can be imposed on account of a so-called failure of the taxpayer to act, and (2) the tax need not be apportioned to the states because it is not like taxes previously held by the Court to be direct taxes.
- Medicaid expansion: The result is that a state can decline to participate in the Medicaid expansion contained in the 2010 Act without losing its pre-existing Medicaid funding. There is no holding because a majority of the Justices did not agree to the Roberts' opinion.

(c) *Holding, Reasoning, and Dicta As to the Tax*

Specifically, Part IIIC of the opinion of the Court holds as follows with respect to the health insurance tax:

- Section 5000A was constitutional because it levied a tax that Analysis 1, section 8, clause 1 of the Constitution empowered Congress to lay and collect.[296]
- The label Congress applies to an exaction does not determine whether the payment may be viewed as an exercise of Congress' taxing power.
- The finding that section 5000A is a taxing power tax must be based on objective facts and not the subjective intent of Congress.

---

[295] *See* Moore and Oglebay, at 516-517 ("Thus, if a court adjudges, in litigation between A and B, that the applicable rule of law is 'X-Y,' this rule is the law of the case for the A-B litigation, but the court also establishes 'X-Y' as the rule of law to be applied by it, and all courts owing obedience to it, in all subsequent litigation between any and all parties where such a rule is relevant and properly applicable.").

[296] Although the section remains in the Code, in 2017 Congress reduced the tax rate to zero for the purpose of setting up another attack on the constitutionality of the entire act based on lack of the tax.

- The objective facts that are relevant to prove that a levy that is not named a tax is a taxing power tax are those that tend to prove whether it functions to an undefined but sufficient extent like taxes as commonly understood. Although the opinion does not define the quantum of tax similarity, it implies that it is fairly low; the Court does not require complete congruity (it is sufficient if it "looks like a tax in many respects.").
- The most important function of a taxing power tax is to produce "at least some revenue for the government."
- Taxes can have the purpose and effect of regulating taxpayers' activities, regardless of whether Congress has a constitutional power to regulate the activities outside the taxing power, and so the tendency of a tax to regulate is not evidence that it is not a tax.[297]
- The Court previously has distinguished a penalty for an unlawful act from a tax that was not conditioned on an unlawful act. Because Congress did not make failure to buy insurance unlawful, this tax cannot be removed from the taxing power under that distinction.
- Failure of a person to perform an act defined by Congress can incur liability for a taxing power tax.
- The health insurance tax is neither a capitation tax nor a tax on property and so is not a direct tax and need not have been apportioned among the states according to their populations.

The opinion's reasoning includes the following:

- It relied on the following characteristics to indicate that the penalty would function as a tax: the payee is the Treasury Department, the criteria for liability for the tax shares at least some common features of the income tax (taxable income, dependents, joint filing), assessment and collection occur in a manner similar to that for the income tax, the requirement for the exaction is located in Title 26 along with other taxes.
- Holding the penalty to be a tax did not require overruling *Bailey v. Drexel Furniture Co.* (also called the *Child Labor Tax Case*) because the Roberts' opinion showed how the insurance penalty could pass a test that was said to have been extracted from, and not satisfied in, the *Child Labor Tax Case*: (1) the size of the penalty was not perceived to be "an exceedingly heavy burden," (2) there is no scienter requirement, and (3) the IRS will collect

[297] Chief Justice Roberts' opinion illustrated this principle by finding no ground for regulation of insurance purchases other than the taxing power. Indeed, the opinion's introductory section, which was not literally joined by any other Justice, stated even more broadly that the taxing power "grant gives the Federal Government considerable influence even in areas where it cannot directly regulate. The Federal Government may enact a tax on an activity that it cannot authorize, forbid, or otherwise control."

the penalty somewhat like a tax, rather than another agency being involved in the enforcement scheme.[298]

- Giving the taxpayer a choice to do something or pay a tax is not the same as making the failure to act unlawful.
- The direct tax category is not going to be expanded by discovery of some new categories of direct taxes.
- Although the *Child Labor Tax Case* and another decision that ruled a tax not to be a tax, *United States v. Butler*, remain on the books, "more recently we have declined to closely examine the regulatory motive or effect of revenue-raising measures."
- Taxes can be imposed on inactivity because the Constitution contains an illustration of such a tax, the capitation tax.

(3) *Discussion of Holdings*

(a) *The Power to Tax*

The most important aspect of Part IIIC is the "dog that didn't bark" (or perhaps barked softly): the Chief Justice did not go out of his way to extol the federal taxing power, in contrast to statements made by even conservative Justices of the past in describing the federal taxing power. However, actions may here speak louder than words: the Court upheld the tax against strong opposition. In addition the opinion of the Court did include statements that imply the great scope of the taxing power: (1) once a tax is found to be a tax, the constitutional analysis is usually over;[299] (2) taxes are as certain as only one other event—death; and (3) the taxing power must run deep because it does not run as broadly as the Commerce Clause.

As an example of point (1) above, the opinion stated "§5000A need not be read to do more than impose a tax. That is sufficient to sustain it." It also quoted Benjamin Franklin that only "death and taxes" are certain, to explain why inactivity could be taxed. Thus, the opinion of the Court holds that once a federal exaction is found to be a taxing power tax, the constitutional analysis is over.

The opinion identified as the "essential feature" of a tax - the culmination of its functional analysis - the production of some revenue for the government, citing *Kahriger*.[300] Although that part of the Roberts' opinion addresses the definition of tax, the citation reveals another reason for protecting the taxing power: taxes are the lifeblood of government. No matter how much some may dislike the federal government, state and local governments must tax to survive. Even if a Justice wanted to bash the federal taxing power, the Justice would be hard pressed

[298] Bailey v. Drexel Furniture Co., 259 U.S. 20 (1922).

[299] Of course if the tax were conditioned on some suspect category such as race, it could be unconstitutional on grounds other than absence of power in Congress. *See* Ch. I.E.4.b.

[300] United States v. Kahriger, 345 U.S. 22 (1953).

to bash taxation in general, lest the states be unable to tax to enforce their police powers, which the conservative Justices are so intent on reserving to the states.[301]

Kahriger ruled unanimously that a person handling wagers could be criminally charged for failing to register to pay the federal tax on wagering. The Court assumed that the United States could not regulate wagering. Nevertheless it rejected the challenge to the criminal charge because regulation of wagering was not the sole purpose of the tax if it produced even negligible revenue, which in *Kahriger* was $4,371,869. The particular *Kahriger* footnote cited by Chief Justice Roberts' opinion stated that federal taxes had been upheld even though they produced $3,501, $914,910, and $28,911. This shows that historically when the Court has said a tax must produce at least some revenue it means even a de minimis amount, due to the centrality of the taxing function.

The Roberts' opinion does discuss some other criteria in its functional analysis, such as the amount of tax that may be owed by a particular taxpayer, but this discussion does not mean that the power to tax is limited (*e.g.*, there is no rule that a tax cannot be "too heavy"). Rather, the opinion discusses such factors in determining whether the exaction is a tax at all. This careful distinction proves that the Court knows that once the tax is a tax, it can be so heavy as to be confiscatory,[302] and it can be levied on some and not others, with an amazing degree of arbitrariness. That is why the Chief Justice was able to say it "need not be read to do more than impose a tax."

Thus the great scope of the power to tax is the linchpin of the opinion of the Court, but the opinion assumed it without explaining, extolling or dwelling on it. This reticence contrasts with the typical approach of earlier Courts.[303] The Roberts opinion not only lacked the extolling language, but in a Part not joined by any other Justice he underplayed the taxing power in another way, by emphasizing the limitation on federal powers rather than the expansiveness of a federal power once enumerated. Roberts did this in a statement in the third paragraph of his opinion: ". . . the National Government possesses only limited powers; the States and the people retain the remainder." At first glance this appears to be an entirely obvious and common statement. However, it turns out that the formulation "only limited powers" dates only to 1991 and appears uniformly

---

[301] There is no Necessary and Proper Clause alternative for states to rely on to support a tax. Thus, for example, if *Sebelius* had ruled that Congress could neither tax inactivity nor regulate inactivity under the Commerce Clause, the states would have been left to rely solely on their police powers if they try to regulate inactivity. The Roberts' opinion shows that it is possible to have different results under different powers, but if the Court had said two out of three powers could not deal with inactivity, that might tip the scales against using the police power at the state and local level.

[302] Chief Justice Marshall said the power to tax involves the power to destroy in recognition of the fact that a tax can be destructively burdensome. McCulloch v. Maryland, 17 U.S. 316, 427 (1818).

[303] *See* Ch. II.A.

in opinions by or joined by the conservative Justices, including only a single opinion of the Court.[304]

The more typical explanation of Congress' powers under the Constitution utilizes and emphasizes the word "enumerated" rather than limited. Chief Justice Roberts' opinion did mention that the Constitution enumerates Congress' powers. But while citing *McCulloch v. Maryland*, which referred to both limitations and enumeration, and quoting the Necessary and Proper Clause, Chief Justice Roberts' opinion lacks the flavor of the emphasis of Chief Justice Marshall. In explaining why Congress could charter a bank, *McCulloch* said that while the powers of Congress are limited to those enumerated, within the enumeration the power is not limited but is quite expansive and supreme over the states. That view is transmuted in the Roberts' opinion introduction into "only limited powers" including taxation and Commerce Clause.

(b) *Substance over Form*

Labels. The rejection of reliance on labels in the opinion of the Court is common practice for the Supreme Court generally, particularly in matters of taxation and in determining federal levies to be taxes and not taxes.[305] While it resulted in finding a penalty to be a tax in this case, the principle historically has served a much more potent role in a handful of decisions finding exactions that Congress intentionally labeled taxes not to be taxes.[306] The result of such an exclusion from the taxing power usually has been a ruling that the tax was unconstitutional, because the Court could not identify any other enumerated power to which the tax could be a necessary and proper adjunct. The *Sebelius* opinion likely had to devote more attention to this subject due to the holding in Part II that for Anti-Injunction Act purposes the penalty was not a tax and the Act did not apply.

In applying the substance over form principle, the opinion of the Court at first seems to make no distinction between levies that Congress labels a tax, and levies that Congress does not label a tax; instead it seems to cite indiscriminately decisions purportedly standing for finding a non tax a tax and vice versa. It is not, however, obvious that these two categories of levies should be viewed the same and the opinions imply agreement.

Part IIIB of the Roberts' opinion not joined by any other Justice treated a levy that Congress did not label as a tax as having to clear a preliminary hurdle (is the tax treatment "fairly possible") before the tax characterization could even be considered. A levy that Congress labels a tax will not have to clear that hurdle, which promotes it at least to that extent. Furthermore, the opinion of the Court strongly implies what it would have done if Congress had labeled the section

---

304 Hilton v. South Carolina Pub. Rys. Comm'n, 502 U.S. 197, 209 (1991) (dissent of O'Connor, J.); United States v. Lopez, 514 U.S. 549, 599 (1995) (Thomas, J., concurring); McDonald v. City of Chicago, 561 U.S. 742, 3037 (2010) (Alito, J., opinion of the Court joined by the conservative Justices).

305 *But see* Ch. I.E.8 discussing the great tax issues that appear to have migrated toward formal resolution.

306 *See* Ch. III.F.

5000A exaction a tax: it would have upheld it without discussion. It states this by analogy to a $50 tax imposed on homeowners for not having energy efficient windows. The opinion states: "No one would doubt that this law imposed a tax and was within Congress' power to tax."[307] Of course Americans for Tax Reform, for example, surely would doubt the $50 energy efficiency tax is constitutional. But the Court does not agree because its example posits that Congress choose to call the $50 levy a tax.

Although the opinion of the Court discussed cases both finding taxes not to be taxes and other levies to be taxes, obviously the latter group of cases are more pertinent to the case at hand. Therefore, it is curious that the opinion faltered in correctly analyzing those precedents. The opinion prominently cited the *License Tax Cases* as an example of the Court's holding a fee to be a tax despite it not being labeled a tax.[308] But the original act under which the cases arose did state that the payment for a federal license was a tax, and the amended statute called it a "special tax" multiple times.[309]

Likewise the *Sebelius* opinion inaccurately described *New York v. United States* as a second example of a federal tax not labeled a tax by Congress.[310] However, the totality of that opinion's discussion of what is a tax is this:

> The second step, the Secretary's collection of a percentage of the surcharge, is no more than a federal tax on interstate commerce, which petitioners do not claim to be an invalid exercise of either Congress' commerce or taxing power.[311]

The *Sebelius* opinion characterized the *New York* decision as upholding a surcharge as a tax, stating that part of the surcharge was paid to the Treasury (the tax part). In fact, the states where waste was stored were to collect a surcharge from other states depositing waste, and a quarter of the surcharge was paid to the Secretary of Energy not Treasury, to be held in escrow for the states, and not as property of the United States.[312] The arrangement was very unusual; the power to tax was not contested; and the opinion stated the surcharge was either an exercise of Commerce Clause or taxing powers. The Court certainly should not

---

[307] The opinion's example assumes that the $50 tax is paid with the income tax return, has an income threshold and shares other indicia of the income tax as currently applied. It is not clear how important these features are to the Court's analysis. The Court must know that the income tax is not the only federal tax. Indeed, it is a relative newcomer to the scene: excises and duties and imposts are identified in the Constitution, none of which involve joint returns and minimum income thresholds.

[308] License Tax Cases, 72 U.S. 462 (1867).

[309] 13 Stat. 223, 248, 249 (sec. 73) (1861-1865) ("besides being liable to the payment of the tax"); 14 Stat. 113 (1863-1867) (the July 13, 1866 act inserted references to "special tax" throughout the prior act, by amendment). What the amendment tried to do was remove the implication that a license to engage in the local businesses was being granted by the United States, rather than to create the impression that a tax and not a fee was being paid, because it was well understood that charges for licenses were taxes in character.

[310] New York v. United States, 505 U.S. 144 (1992).

[311] 505 U.S. at 171.

[312] P.L. 99-240, 99 Stat. 1842, 1849.

want such an arrangement, as properly understood, to be a standard example of a federal tax not labeled as a tax.

Finally, the *Sebelius* opinion also relies on a decision identifying a tax for purposes of references to taxes in the Bankruptcy Code, which is not necessarily the same as the Constitution's usage of taxes.[313]

In sum, the Court's rejection of labels is unremarkable, but its reasoning is questionable and it failed to explain how the analysis might differ when Congress does assert that it is exercising the taxing power by applying the tax label.

Penalties Both Taxes and Not Taxes. The opinion of the Court is not internally inconsistent in respecting a tax label for purposes of the Anti-Injunction Act and not for purposes of the taxing power. Indeed, the first result was entirely forseeable as a practical matter: the Court has a history going back to at least the *Pollock* decision in 1895 of reaching over the Act and other procedural barriers to decide federal tax cases in which there is general public interest.[314] That is, the Court knows how to use various methods of literally interpreting the Anti-Injunction Act to make sure that its scope is narrow when the Court wants to decide a tax case; of course it helped that the United States also wanted the *Sebelius* case decided in 2012 rather than after 2014, which necessitated the appointment of an Amicus to argue for the Anti-Injunction Act.

The legal reasoning the Court employed to reach the merits is entirely standard: the Code deems certain penalties in the Code to be taxes for some or all Code purposes, but none of these deemings includes section 5000A (but for one partial deeming in the section itself that the Court logically distinguished); penalties are not inherently taxes for Code purposes, as arguably shown by the deemings themselves; therefore this penalty is not a tax for Code purposes except to the extent Congress said it was, which it did only as to certain assessment and collection procedures.

Whether the holding as to the Anti-Injunction Act can be applied to any other tax, at least in theory it is a pro-taxpayer precedent. Taxpayers certainly can argue that the Anti-Injunction Act should not bar a suit to enjoin the collection of any other exaction not labeled a tax and not deemed to be a tax for all Code

---

[313] United States v. Sotelo, 436 U.S. 268 (1978). *See also* discussion of *La Franca*, below.

[314] Pollock v. Farmers' Loan & Trust Co., 158 U. S. 601 (1895) (not only had the tax not been paid, the plaintiff was not even the taxpayer, but rather a shareholder suing to enjoin his corporation from paying the corporate income tax in the future). Also, as discussed below, *Atherton Mills v. Johnston*, the first version of the *Child Labor Tax Case*, was organized as a suit to enjoin the mill from refusing to hire a 15-year-old boy, in order to obtain federal court jurisdiction. Similarly, Hill v. Wallace, 259 U.S. 44 (1922) involved a shareholder suit and escaped the Anti-Injunction Act. While these were all decided against the government, Brushaber v. Union Pacific R. Co., 240 U.S. 1 (1916) avoided the Anti-Injunction Act and was decided for the government in an important decision explaining the Sixteenth Amendment. But the Court refused to allow a taxpayer whose time had run out on its claim for abatement of tax to enjoin the tax collector, at least where it was impossible to claim the tax was a penalty. Graham v. Du Pont, 262 U.S. 234 (1923). Even before the Anti-Injunction Act the Court was amenable to early hearings on tax cases, deciding the *Hylton* case after the taxpayer paid the tax and wanted to abandon the suit, so that the government paid for argument of both sides of the case. Hylton v. United States, 3 U.S. 171 (1796), as explained in Carl Brent Swisher, American Constitutional Development 75-76 (1954).

purposes (as most penalties are under section 6665(a)). But such penalties likely would have to share the signal characteristic of the health insurance tax: it is not a penalty for not paying a tax, but rather an independent payment obligation. Such penalties are more likely to be found in levies that are necessary and proper to carrying out some other power of Congress, which usually means they are not taxing power taxes; indeed, that is what the Commerce Clause argument was all about.

(c) *Objective Facts, Congress' Motives*

Congress' Motives and Butler. The Court did not ignore Congress' intent to regulate behavior in enacting the tax; rather it identified it and then ignored it because it is not relevant to resolving the legal issue.[315] The opinion's emphasis on identifying a tax based on objective facts (i.e., the function of the levy) and not Congress' intent or motives is both consistent with statements in prior decisions and tends to distance the Court from what are arguably the two most potent prior holdings that federal exactions are outside the taxing power because they penalize and regulate: the *Child Labor Tax Case* in 1922 (cited above) and *United States v. Butler* in 1936.[316] As to both of these, the *Sebelius* opinion stated:

> A few of our cases policed these limits aggressively, invalidating punitive exactions obviously designed to regulate behavior otherwise regarded at the time as beyond federal authority. . . . More often and more recently we have declined to closely examine the regulatory motive or effect of revenue-raising measures.[317]

This quotation both (1) casts doubt on the current force of the two decisions as to the scope of both the Commerce Clause and the taxing power, and (2) acknowledge that those decisions rested in large part on examination of Congress' motives, which more recently the Court has declined to do. The *Sebelius* opinion does not discuss *Butler* further, which is itself significant. *Butler* was the next to last decision of the Court against New Deal legislation, striking down the Agricultural Adjustment Act and its mechanism that taxed cotton processors, raising substantial revenue that was used to pay farmers to achieve price parity for cotton sold.

Butler has been the anti-New Deal decision most frequently cited in Supreme Court opinions, both by dissenters who would continue to apply it and by others who say it has been passed by (as did the *Sebelius* opinion). Thus *Butler* may now stand for nothing more than a reminder of the fact that so long as the Court sits, a majority can rule a tax not to be a tax. Observe that the tax in *Butler* satisfied what the *Sebelius* opinion says is the "essential feature of any tax": it was designed to and did raise substantial revenue. Indeed, *Butler* conflicts with *Sebelius* in another way: the commodity processors tax was ruled not to be a tax without any reference to the fact that it was (and still is) housed at Title 7 of the

---

[315] *See* Ch. III.D.3.b.

[316] United States v. Butler, 297 U. S. 1 (1936).

[317] Nat'l Fed'n of Indep. Bus. v. Sebelius, 505 U.S. 144 (2012).

United States Code and not in the tax title;[318] also the *Butler* opinion did not indicate that administration by the IRS rather than the Agriculture Department would have made any difference.

The Functional Test. The specific objective facts indicating function that *Sebelius* relied upon in lieu of subjective intent or motives of Congress were functions that the Court chose to fit this case. The opinion did not undertake to provide an all purpose test for the functions of a tax (aside from raising some revenue), or even to provide a laundry list of considerations as it did in *Frank Lyon.*[319] The functions found to exist on the facts of *Sebelius* are not uniformly indicative of tax characterization, and amount to only reasoning in this particular decision. Moreover, the Court's requirement of functional similarity to taxes, aside from revenue raising, was at a fairly low threshold.

For example, the Court's reliance on the housing of tax collection responsibilities solely in the Treasury or the Internal Revenue Service not only is inconsistent with *Butler* (which did not cite that fact) but will turn out to be an imperfect guide to a tax. Customs duties and tariffs are taxing power taxes by definition in the Constitution itself, and yet under the Homeland Security Act of 2002 the collection of customs duties has been delegated to the Secretary of Homeland Security.[320] Similarly, the other features of the penalty that the opinion said are common to taxes are common only to income taxes. Most federal excise taxes, for example, do not vary with or depend on the size of a person's income or marital status as the health insurance was found to do. Likewise, many federal taxes are not collected with the income tax return, as the health insurance penalty happens to be.

Surely the Court was not suggesting that the only sort of tax having features of a taxing power tax is the income tax: after all, it came along after the country had been collecting other types of taxes for over 125 years. Indeed the health insurance tax has so many dissimilarities to income taxes in the area of collection (pointed out by the dissenters) that the Court's efforts to find objective similarities looks more like what it is: an effort to carry out the intent of Congress to levy a tax without having to say so.

And for other reasons the Court's purporting to base its ruling on objective facts as to function, and not on Congress' regulatory motive or effect, is not as judicious as it might seem. The Court had already admitted that Congress can intend to use federal taxation to regulate. Therefore, eschewing analysis of Congress' motive does not really put the grounds of decision on firm footing, as it might in other types of cases; rather it just states the obvious.

What does put the analysis on firm footing is to read the opinion to carry to its logical conclusion the holding that the potential to raise at least some revenue for the government marks a tax.[321] The Court did reach this conclusion in

---

[318] 7 U.S.C. § 609.

[319] Frank Lyon Co. v. United States, 435 U.S. 561, 582-583 (1978) (listing over 20 factors that might inform who owns property).

[320] *See* U.S. Customs and International Trade Guide, Second Edition ¶ 3.02[1].

[321] *See* Ch. III.E.7.

dictum when it said that a nominal $50 tax for failing to have energy efficient windows clearly would be a tax: the Court there broadly indicated that naming a levy a tax plus raising at least some revenue for the Government is nearly the end of the analysis in such cases. The holding, however, relates only to taxes not named as such. Those cases require the functional analysis pursued in the opinion of the Court. The Court required only minimal functional resemblance, because it relied on a fairly vague resemblance to income taxes, and said so ("looks like a tax in many respects").

(d) *Taxes That Regulate*

Primary or Incidental Regulation. The opinion of the Court stated that every tax is in some degree regulatory, some taxes have had as their primary if not sole aim the regulation or prevention of the act that would be taxed (citing the case of import tariffs[322]), and that failing to raise at least some revenue is normally the standard used to show when the regulatory effect totally subsumes a levy and removes it from the taxing power.[323] That could be the end of the analysis, and has been the end of the analysis in other opinions of the Court upholding regulatory taxes, because the production of some revenue is the most objective test of a tax.

In the broad perspective, as discussed elsewhere in this Chapter III the Court has employed three approaches to test the constitutionality of federal taxes that appear to regulate some behavior:

- The *McCray* (1904) opinion upheld a federal tax that clearly regulated an area where Congress then was not thought to have power to regulate, based largely on the fact that Congress said it was acting under the taxing power.[324] This approach later was embodied in a line of decisions cited by the *Sebelius* opinion holding that if Congress called it a tax, and if it raised some revenue for the government, it is a tax (although no opinion in *Sebelius* cited *McCray*).
- The *Child Labor Tax Case* and *Butler* applied the approach that Congress cannot regulate through the taxing power except incidentally, and when Congress' intent to regulate obviously predominates, Congress has strayed from the taxing power.
- *Sebelius* follows the approach that Congress can regulate as a primary purpose under the taxing power only if it makes the regulation look sufficiently like some other taxes, but purports to make the determination through objective facts (here functionality) rather than inferences of Congress' intent.

The *Sebelius* opinion did not adopt the incidental versus principal purpose approach of the *Child Labor Tax Case* and so seems to leave intact the *McCray*

---

322 It is sometimes argued that tariffs are merely necessary and proper to the regulation of foreign commerce and are not authorized by the taxing power, but this belies not only the statement in the Roberts' opinion but the inclusion of "duties" in the taxing power clause.

323 *See* Ch. III.E.1.

324 McCray v. United States, 195 U.S. 27 (1904).

view that a federal tax may primarily regulate and still be a tax. But then *Sebelius* attempts to state a standard that could get to the same result as the *Child Labor Tax Case* by purporting to assess functional similarity to taxes. Whether that standard can ever be objective, at least it does not supplant the view of *McCray* that it is not the business of the Court to deny Congress' power to principally engage in regulation through taxation.

Tax versus Penalty. After completing its functionality analysis, the opinion of the Court addressed a separate argument of the plaintiffs, that the tax was really a non tax penalty.[325] This dichotomy would have been unnecessary if the Chief Justice's opinion had found the tax to be authorized by the Commerce Clause; then it would not have mattered whether the levy was a taxing power tax or a tax (or penalty) levied as necessary and proper to carrying out Commerce Clause powers.

The opinion does not explain how its analysis of the penalty argument differs from the functionality test. Based on both the ordering of the analysis and the length of the discussions, it appears that the Court viewed the functionality standard as primary and the contrast with a penalty secondary, as an aspect of the functionality standard. Presumably the Court believed that a tax that functioned as a penalty as it defined a penalty would flunk the functionality test, even if it otherwise passed it (as by being collected along with the income tax return, etc.). Therefore, the Court held, in effect, that a tax could not function as a tax if it punished conduct that Congress made unlawful. But the Court had great difficulty explaining what unlawful means.

It is significant that the opinion's analysis of the penalty issue did not rely on the *Child Labor Tax Case*. That opinion had already served doubly in Chief Justice Roberts' discussion of (1) how a tax may be treated differently for both Anti-Injunction Act purposes and taxing power purposes, and (2) as one example of the functional approach to identifying taxes. But when a page later the opinion addressed distinguishing taxes from penalties, it did not cite the *Child Labor Tax Case*. Rather, it cited a recent decision involving the meaning of "excise taxes" for purposes of the bankruptcy code, and a double jeopardy decision.[326]

This choice indicates a second demotion of the *Child Labor Tax Case* (the first was the statement that the Court no longer follows its emphasis on congressional intent). Therefore, the Roberts opinion accomplishes a delicate handling of that venerable anti-tax opinion by Chief Justice Taft, which ushered in the anti-tax era that struck down five federal tax provisions during the short period from 1922 through 1936: Roberts relied on it for a procedural distinction and picked its test as one example of a test the health insurance penalty did not flunk, but when it came to the core definition of tax versus penalty, Roberts ignored Taft's opinion.

---

325 *See* Ch. III.F.

326 United States v. Reorganized CF&I Fabricators, 518 U.S. 213 (1996); United States v. La Franca, 282 U.S. 568 (1931).

The two decisions that the Robert's opinion did cite do more or less make the distinction the opinion cited them for, but neither is controlling. The bankruptcy decision interpreted the priority for "excise taxes" in the bankruptcy code, thus interpreting the bankruptcy code not the tax code. Given the distinction the Court already had made between the Anti-Injunction Act and the constitutional taxing power, there is no reason to jump to the conclusion that a bankruptcy code interpretation is controlling for constitutional tax purposes, and the Roberts' opinion did not justify why it should be.

The second opinion relied on, *La Franca*, involved a bootlegger who had been convicted of a violation of a Prohibition law and also had been required to pay $1,000 that the 1924 Revenue Act did not clearly labeled a tax.[327] Because of the prior conviction, the Court relieved him of the "taxes" on double jeopardy grounds, in effect. The opinion ruled that the exaction was not a tax but a punishment for double jeopardy purposes; the facts of the particular levy were highly unusual. Therefore, *La Franca* was based on both the special meaning of punishment applied for double jeopardy purposes, and on an even more narrow interpretation of a particular act. The Court has since disavowed an earlier decision on which *La Franca* relied, at least for tax if not double jeopardy purposes.[328]

Sebelius asserted a distinction between a regulatory penalty and regulatory tax that asks whether Congress made the act or omission taxed unlawful, with the further definition of unlawful being an act or omission that cannot be done or not done as a matter of choice simply by paying a (tax). But an even further refinement was needed, because crooks have a choice not to engage in crime, and the fact of choice does not change the character of the criminal penalty. Therefore the opinion had to proceed even deeper into definition to explain that the act or omission that may be taxed carries with it no other "negative legal consequences" once the person has paid the (tax).

That definition cannot be a holding of the Court because it could convert parking tickets, which are commonly handed out under the police power and constitute punishments for petty crimes, into taxes. If one believes that simply having a criminal record is a "negative legal consequence" then this definition of tax could fit any misdemeanor punishable only by a fine as to which the law provides automatic expungement. If one does not believe having a criminal record is a "negative legal consequence," one could find the monetary penalty to be tax in the case of any crime for which there is no other punishment.[329]

The opinion likely meant that Congress did not attach opprobrium to not buying insurance; Congress only wanted to incentivize individuals to buy insurance. Based on that standard the *Child Labor Tax Case* should have come out the other way, because Congress was not trying to punish manufacturers for

---

[327] United States v. La Franca, 282 U.S. 568 (1931).

[328] Bob Jones Univ. v. Simon, 416 U.S. 725 n. 12 (1974) (cited *Lipke v. Lederer* as no longer representing the Court's views).

[329] The opinion of the Court foresaw this argument in part, because the dissenters made it, and stated in footnote 9 that strict liability crimes could not be converted into acts punished by IRS tax collections, without explaining how that would be prevented.

hiring child labor, it was trying to incentivize them not to hire child labor. That explains why the *Child Labor Tax Case* was not cited at this point. Chief Justice Taft did not believe Congress could regulate child labor, through taxation or otherwise. In contrast, today the Court understands that Congress can regulate child labor and health insurance purchases through taxation, if not otherwise. That understanding has forced the Court to double down on its recognition that taxes can regulate by holding that if the tax does tend to regulate but not punish, then it can be a tax.

If the Court continues down this road it will have to face the fact that criminal penalties also are designed to incentive avoidance of bad conduct (i.e., the deterrent effect). That would bring the Court full circle to have to define bad conduct. Why is speeding bad conduct and not buying health insurance not bad conduct? The tax versus penalty distinction does not hold up, but likely will remain as an escape value to allow a majority of the Court to rule that a tax is not a tax.

(e) *Taxing Inactivity*

Given the large role accorded the regulation of inactivity in Chief Justice Roberts' sole opinion on the Commerce Clause, he must have felt compelled to address the same issue in his taxing power analysis. The opinion rejects the complaint that a tax on inactivity is outside the taxing power for three reasons:

- The Constitution itself shows that inactivity can be taxed because a capitation tax can be viewed as a tax on inactivity.
- Having already determined that the penalty is authorized as a tax under the taxing power after applying all other criteria, there is nothing about taxing inactivity that pushes such a tax beyond the limits of taxation.
- More flexibility can be allowed Congress in taxation than under the Commerce Clause because Congress has less flexibility to regulate under the taxing power. That is, Congress can do all things necessary and proper to carry out its Commerce Clause powers, but it can only tax under the taxing power.

The third point is novel to this opinion. It is a true creation of the Court in this case. It forms the second of the two apparent contradictions in the Roberts' opinion identified above. It highlights the historic juxtaposition of the Commerce Clause and taxing powers, whose story goes something like this (the following summary points are discussed elsewhere in Chapter III.F.2):

- Chief Justice Marshall "created" in a sense the great scopes of both the taxing and Commerce Clause powers in his seminal decisions *McCulloch v. Maryland* and *Gibbons v. Ogden*, among others.[330]
- Direct regulation of business (principally railroads and then trusts and combinations) by states and then by the federal government was a predominant

[330] Gibbons v. Ogden, 22 U.S. 1 (1824).

constitutional issue in the Court after Reconstruction, and the Court eventually succeeded in thwarting such direct regulation through rulings like *Lochner* (1905) (striking down state regulation) and *Hammer v. Dagenhart* (1918) (striking down federal regulation and involving essentially the same law at issue in the *Child Labor Tax Case* (1922), discussed further below).

- A brief exception to the Court's dislike of federal regulation appeared in *Champion v. Ames* (1903) and *Hoke* (1913), upholding federal regulation of businesses that were not of the railroad variety (lotteries and interstate transportation of women for immoral purposes).[331]
- Similar dislike by business had not yet attached to federal taxation generally. Creditors initially liked federal taxation because it enabled the repayment of the substantial debts incurred to wage the Revolutionary War, both state and federal.[332]
- The *Pollock* (1895) decision striking down the second federal income tax is not to the contrary because it reflected not so much opposition to taxation in general as opposition to an income tax, which took business profits, as contrasted with the more typical consumption taxes, which were ultimately borne by the public, including tariffs, which generally benefited domestic business.[333]
- *McCray* (1904) upheld a federal tax designed to eliminate colored margarine for the benefit of the Republican dairy farmers of the Midwest. As explained herein, *McCray* involved pure federal regulation through the taxing power.
- Only when Congress tried to deal with the Court's limitation of its Commerce Clause powers in *Hammer v. Dagenhart*, by turning the child labor regulation into a regulation enforced by a tax, did the Court change its historically expansive view of federal taxation and develop, beginning in the *Child Labor Tax Case* (1922), the ability to "see what all others can see and understand [that a tax is a regulation]" as Chief Justice Taft put it in his opinion.[334]

So the *Sebelius* opinions have provided another interaction of the Commerce Clause and the taxing power to add to this history: the Commerce Clause may not authorize federal regulation of at least individual inactivity (according to Chief Justice Roberts alone), but the taxing power does (according to the Court).

(f) *Direct Taxation*

Just as the absence from the opinion of the Court of a fulsome discussion of the taxing power may reflect a desire not to stir up that subject, the short shrift

---

[331] Champion v. Ames, 188 U.S. 321 (1903) (also known as the *Lottery Case*); Hoke v. United States, 227 U.S. 308 (1913) (White Slave Act).

[332] Carl Brent Swisher, American Constitutional Development 65 (1954).

[333] *E.g.*, Carl Brent Swisher, Stephen J. Field Craftsman of the Law 396-397 (1963).

[334] 259 U.S. at 37.

given to the plaintiffs' direct tax argument may reflect an acknowledgment that this perennial favorite of tax protesters is a dead issue. The opinion of the Court said that heretofore the Court has identified as direct taxes only taxes imposed on individuals as individuals (i.e., capitation taxes), and taxes on property (presumably on property value, with income as a proxy for value), real and personal. The Court was not willing to apply any more analysis than to say the health insurance tax is none of those and so cannot a direct tax.[335]

Thus the Court was unwilling to reopen the box of trying to devise an all purpose definition of direct taxes, instead relying on what the Court has in fact done, which was the view that came to be uniformly followed by the Court up to 1895, when *Pollock* added direct taxes on personal property through the method of an income tax to the list of direct taxes. *Pollock* did not disagree that direct taxes were generally property and capitation taxes, but purported to apply a substance over form analysis to find a tax on property in a tax on income from property.

The *Sebelius* opinion did state in passing the direct tax test applied in the *Hylton* case: the tax cannot be a direct tax if apportionment makes no sense, which in the case of *Hylton* meant that it made no sense for carriages to be taxed at widely varying different rates in different states depending on how many carriages were in the state.[336] If that standard had been applied in *Pollock*, the Court would have had considerably more difficulty ruling the income tax unconstitutional.

In addition to closing the book on the tax avoider's dream of finding an unapportioned direct tax, the other somewhat noteworthy feature of the discussion of direct taxes is the summary conclusion that the health insurance penalty could not be a capitation tax because it did not fall on all individuals without regard to their individual circumstances, quoting *Hylton*.[337] This may not be a definition of direct taxes that can be consistently applied to the precedents. First heads would necessarily be taxed at different rates depending on the state they lived in. Also, slaves might or might not have been included in the head tax count (alternately, they could have been taxed as property). In addition there is a confusing overlap of taxes levied solely as a condition of voting at the polls versus purportedly general poll taxes (*e.g.* $1 per person) that were enforced in practice only when a non-taxpayer presented himself at the polls. Although *Harper v. Virginia* overturned an earlier opinion allowing a poll tax to be a precondition of the right to vote, it did not reject the reasoning of that earlier opinion that poll taxes (evidently referring to capitation taxes) could properly exempt different persons such as women, children and those over age 60.[338] Finally, in 1884 the Attorney General had called the tax levied on immigrants entering ports a capi-

---

335 *See* Ch. V.C.

336 Hylton v. United States, 3 U.S. 171 (1796) (Chase opinion).

337 *Id.* at 175 (Chase opinion).

338 Breedlove v. Suttles, 302 U.S. 277 (1937), *overruled by* Harper v. Virginia State Bd. of Elections, 383 U.S. 663 (1966).

tation tax but the Court upheld it not under the taxing power but as a necessary and proper tax adjunct to the power to control commerce and immigration.[339]

(4) *Discussion of Reasoning*

(a) *The* Child Labor Tax Case

The Roberts' *Sebelius* opinion's handling of the *Child Labor Tax Case* (1922) falls far short of an endorsement of that anti-Congress decision, which occupies the same suspect category of decisions as *Lochner*[340] and *Hammer v. Dagenhart*.[341] As shown above, the *Sebelius* opinion cast doubt on the claim in the 1922 opinion that the Court was not assessing Congress' motives, but the *Sebelius* opinion still chose to apply its interpretation of the purported objective test for a tax found to have been flunked in that case. *Sebelius* did not thereby make such test part of the holding of the Court, as evidenced by the fact that the first paragraph of Part IIIC identifies five functional features of a tax, which includes only the third of the three parts of the test said to have been applied in the 1922 decision: (1) "exceedingly heavy burden" which it said was present in the 1922 case; (2) scienter requirement in the 1922 tax, which was not typical of a tax, and (3) the enforcement authority, which was the IRS in *Sebelius* but also involved other agencies in the 1922 case.[342]

As discussed elsewhere in this book,[343] the desire to regulate child labor grew out of the Progressive Movement, and was emboldened by victories for federal Commerce Clause powers in two decisions, *Champion v. Ames* and *Hoke*, as stated above. The National Child Labor Committee turned to Congress rather than the states because the Court in 1905 had issued its infamous *Lochner* decision, holding that New York could not impose maximum working hours on bakeries.[344] Against the heavy opposition of the National Association of Manufacturers and southern textile manufacturers, Congress enacted a set of child labor regulations for manufacturers whose goods passed into interstate commerce, relying on the Commerce Clause for authority. The textile manufacturers quickly organized a test case and the Court struck down the law on the theory that manufacturing is not interstate commerce for purposes of Commerce Clause regulation.[345] The name of the 1918 decision is as infamous as that of *Lochner*: *Hammer v. Dagenhart*, which the Court overruled in 1941 in *Darby*.[346]

---

[339] Edye v. Robertson, 112 U.S. 580, 595 (1884) (Head Money Cases).

[340] Lochner v. New York, 198 U.S. 45 (1905).

[341] Hammer v. Dagenhart, 247 U.S. 251 (1918).

[342] The Court's staff written Syllabus purports to promote the *Child Labor Tax Case* "test" into part of the holding, but it is not the opinion of the Court.

[343] Ch. III.F. *See also* Stephen B. Wood, Constitutional Politics in the Progressive Era (1968) [hereinafter Wood] (from which most of the background facts in the text are drawn).

[344] Lochner v. New York, 198 U.S. 45 (1905).

[345] Hammer v. Dagenhart, 247 U.S. 251, 272 (1918) ("The making of goods and the mining of coal are not commerce, nor does the fact that these things are to be afterwards shipped or used in interstate commerce, make their production a part thereof.").

[346] United States v. Darby, 312 U.S. 100 (1941).

After World War I Congress turned back to the child labor issue, and decided to try to regulate child labor by reliance on the taxing power as interpreted in *McCray* (1904), which upheld a federal tax on colored margarine that was well understood to be a tax in name only, and to regulate a matter that then was thought to be beyond Congress' power.[347] *McCray* can be viewed as the taxing power analogue to *Champion v. Ames*. No opinion in *Sebelius* cited *McCray*, even though it is stands as the broadest application of the taxing power to a pure regulation.

The revised child labor law imposed a tax of ten percent of net profits from the sale of the product (after deducting other taxes paid) for the entire year in which the manufacturer had knowingly employed child labor even once.[348] The sponsors of the bill had debated whether to have the Labor Department or the Treasury Department administer the act and decided to employ the Treasury Department in order to ward off a claim that the tax was a regulation because it was administered by another agency.[349] The act mentioned the Labor Department twice: it included the Labor Secretary as one of a three member board with the Secretary of the Treasury and the Commissioner of the Bureau of Internal Revenue to devise exemption certificates, and it gave the Labor Secretary secondary authority to inspect plants, if requested by the Commissioner.

The Cotton Manufacturers Association of North Carolina again created a quick test case by inducing a father and his 15-year-old son to sue a Charlotte cotton mill that had been induced to announce that it would cease hiring child labor on account of the new tax, and indeed would discharge child Johnston.[350] The same lawyers that had brought the *Dagenhart* case filed the suit for injunction, *Atherton v. Johnston*, in the same federal district court before the same federal judge that had ruled for them in *Dagenhart*. They won and the case was quickly appealed to the Supreme Court. The government relied primarily on *McCray*, which embodied a near facial test for a tax, written in 1904 by Justice White, who now was Chief Justice. The tax case was argued in 1919 and was not decided for a year and a half, while Chief Justice White lived. After Warren Harding became President, Chief Justice White died, Harding appointed former President Taft as Chief Justice, and the *Atherton* case was consolidated with *Bailey v. Drexel Furniture Co.*, which was decided for the plaintiffs in 1922.[351]

Upon reargument, as in the original case, the United States was represented by Solicitor General James M. Beck, who personally believed the child labor tax

---

[347] McCray v. United States, 195 U.S. 27 (1904). *See* Ch. III.E.2.

[348] 40 Stat. 1138. The tax was computed in much the same way as the income tax was computed, but allowed a deduction for other taxes paid, meaning that the ten percent tax would not be imposed on the regular income tax.

[349] Wood, at 204.

[350] *Id.* at 224-225.

[351] Drexel Furniture Co. actually paid the tax and requested refund, because sufficient time had passed while the Court was holding the *Atherton* case for the law to come into effect.

was unconstitutional.[352] Beck's argument effectively dared the Court to strike down the law by overstating the *McCray* decision and telling the Court it was impotent to stop an "anti-constitutional" (Beck's words) law; the only remedy was with the people.[353]

Chief Justice Taft's opinion that the child labor tax was unconstitutional fundamentally struggled to distinguish *McCray*'s broad implication that if Congress says it is a tax, then it is a tax, even if one may infer that Congress intended principally to regulate that which it lacked power to regulate. He did so by asking whether the tax was "naturally and reasonably adapted to the collection of the tax," which sounded like an objective test, but actually aimed to determine whether Congress' regulatory or taxing "motive" was primary or incidental. Most commentators believe, and the opinion of the Court in *Sebelius* implies, that Taft's opinion was based on finding Congress' primary regulatory motive.[354]

Taft's approach was less a rule of law (i.e., a holding) than a mechanism to give the Court supervisory authority based on subjective considerations.[355] That was not a new approach for the Court. It had invented the doctrine of substantive due process for the same reason. Indeed, the Taft opinion in the *Child Labor Tax Case*, and subsequent decisions that relied on it to strike down taxes through 1936, provided a template for deciding whether a tax was a tax: (1) the facial status of a federal levy as a tax would not control, as it seemed to have in *McCray*, (2) instead an ostensibly objective search would be made to determine Congress' subjective motive as either primarily taxing or regulatory, but (3) the objective criteria were never well identified, leaving the distinct impression that the Court was simply reserving to itself the power to say when Congress had gone too far.

The *Sebelius* opinion attempts to make a more objective holding than the *Child Labor Tax Case*, and does purport to give Congress more leeway than that opinion, but similarly fails to articulate a clear test at least as applied to a levy that Congress does not label a tax, and thereby retains the ultimate flexibility of the Court to call such a levy a regulation.

The *Sebelius* opinion by Chief Justice Roberts deals with the *Child Labor Tax Case* in its merits analysis in three ways: first it adopted the so-called functional analysis, which is the same as Taft's "naturally and reasonably adapted" test; second, it adopted Taft's ultimate conclusion that Congress can go too far in regulating through taxation, while purporting to focus less on Congress' motive than Taft did; and third, it acts as if the *Child Labor Tax Case* is a precedent that

---

352 Wood, at 268-269. *See also* Alpheus T. Mason, William Howard Taft Chief Justice 246 n. (1964) [hereinafter Mason] (quoting letter from Beck to Taft stating that if Beck had won "our form of government would have sustained a serious injury.").

353 Wood, at 271. 66 L. Ed. 817 (1922) (containing the summary of Beck's argument).

354 *See, e.g.*, Mason, at 245 ("Taft's opinion was a striking example of conscious judicial involvement in the policy implications of legislation."). *Sebelius* stated: "More often and more recently we have declined to closely examine the regulatory motive or effect of revenue-raising measures." Nat'l Fed'n of Indep. Bus. v. Sebelius, 567 U.S. 519 (2012).

355 Wood, at 282-283.

at least needs to be distinguished by first restating its test and then showing that the health insurance penalty did not flunk that test.

(b) *The Three Part Test*

The *Sebelius* opinion purports to find in the Taft opinion a three part test to distinguish a penalty for an unlawful act from a tax: (1) did the tax impose an "exceedingly heavy burden," (2) was it imposed only on a person acting with scienter, and (3) was it enforced (in part) by an agency other than the revenue collecting agency? Notably, the *Child Labor Tax Case* opinion does not say that the test required some revenue to be collected, which Roberts had just identified as the "essential feature of any tax." Indeed, Chief Justice Taft's opinion did not discuss the amount of tax raised, thereby implying that fact was not relevant.[356] In fact, the Bureau of Internal Revenue collected $24,233 in child labor tax in 1921 and more monies were outstanding but uncollected.[357]

The *Sebelius* discussion of the *Child Labor Tax Case* test should be viewed as no more than reasoning, for several reasons. First, it was not necessary to the holding. Second, as discussed below, Chief Justice Taft's real test, as even the Roberts' opinion implied, was to find Congress' motive to regulate, effectively rejecting the premise that Chief Justice Roberts started with, that taxes can and do regulate. Third, the *Sebelius* opinion did not accurately discern the holding or test of the *Child Labor Tax Case*, not all of the factors of that test made sense in the context of the *Child Labor Tax Case*, and the test does not make sense as a general test.

The "heavy" part of the test is questionable. Chief Justice Taft did not even say it was "exceedingly heavy," just that it was "heavy." Chief Justice Roberts added "exceedingly." Moreover it is not obvious that a ten percent net profits tax that allowed a deduction for other taxes paid can be accurately characterized as "exceedingly heavy." It would leave the manufacturer employing child labor with over 80% of its net profit from manufacturing and would not tax other nonbusiness income of the manufacturer. The top corporate tax rate for 1921 was ten percent, so the tax did not even double that low rate, much less reach the current corporate income tax rate. Perhaps Taft was peculiarly sensitive to taxes, but subsequently many taxes are or have been indisputably exceedingly heavy, including the income tax that once carried a top rate of 94% and tariffs, which historically have been levied at high rates per item without regard to value.

What the Taft Court may have meant was that it was unduly burdensome to tax a whole year's income on account of the employment of one under age child. In other words, the tax had a trigger and an all or nothing quality based on the commission of a single act. If so, the single act case was as farfetched as the broccoli tax. History shows that child labor was pervasive, particularly in the cotton mills of the south, and it was those plants at which it was aimed. In any

---

356 *Id.* at 282. The *Butler* decision, which Roberts also cited at the same point in the opinion, likewise ignored a substantial amount of taxes collected.

357 Wood, at 262-263, 273.

event, the fear of an inadvertent stumbling into tax liability was substantially lessened by the scienter requirement, discussed below. Moreover, today a variety of tax rules have single act triggers: for example, a charity can lose its entire tax exemption for the year on account of engaging in one prohibited transaction.[358]

Second, the *Sebelius* opinion's statement that the Labor Department "in part" enforced the child labor tax is literally accurate but misrepresents the facts. The Bureau of Internal Revenue spent $130,000 in 1921 inspecting plants,[359] and as shown above the statute was specifically drafted to reduce the involvement of the Labor Department, and made the Treasury primarily responsible for enforcement. In no substantive sense could the child labor tax be said to be a Labor Department regulatory activity.

Third, the scienter test cannot be a reliable indicator of a non-tax punishment. For example, the accumulated earnings tax[360] and the section 1445 withholding tax are based on state of mind or knowledge. Sections 4912, 4941, 4944, 4945, 4951, 4952, 4955, 4958, 4965, 4966, 4967, and 4975, all impose taxes only if an act is "knowing" with respect to some condition of fact, which is a scienter requirement. Several penalties, most prominently the civil fraud penalty, section 6663, are dependent on scienter. Of course the Court indicated that penalties added to taxes may not be taxes unless Congress says so. Does this mean that Title 26 penalties that are based on scienter, and obviously are designed to regulate behavior (i.e., to make people want to pay their taxes), and which can be very heavy (75% of the underpayment due to fraud), cannot be supported by the taxing power directly, but must rely on the Necessary and Proper Clause? If so, that could produce consequences never before examined.

In sum the purported three part test derived from the *Drexel* opinion (1) is not the holding of the Taft Court at all or if it was Taft misconceived the facts of the case, (2) it has been rendered out of date by developments in the tax law, (3) it is in conflict with Roberts' primary test that the hallmark of a tax is raising revenue, and (4) it simply won't work in practice. It is not part of the holding of the Roberts' opinion at all because the Court did not say it would hold the penalty unconstitutional if it were heavier, had a scienter requirement and had been collected by, for example, the Department of Health Education and Welfare.

(5) *Commerce Clause*

This book will not analyze Part IIIA of the Chief Justice's opinion concerning the Commerce Clause because it was not joined by any other Justice and does not directly involve tax. It does, however, have three indirect connections to tax issues. The principal indirect nexus to tax of that part of that opinion is that Part IIIB reasons that the Commerce Clause had to be addressed first because the penalty most naturally appears to be a regulation and not a tax. The Ginsburg dissent disagrees. This procedural theory of the Chief Justice is at odds with the

---

358 I.R.C. § 503.

359 Wood, at 262.

360 I.R.C. § 532(a).

more general statement that his own opinion contains that the Court will search for any reasonable way to avoid holding an act of Congress unconstitutional. Such search obviously does not entail first finding all the ways the act may be held unconstitutional. If it did, the opinion could also have examined the war powers, and the post office powers, etc.

The second indirect nexus is that the Roberts sole opinion adopted the broccoli theory of Commerce Clause regulation largely through a parade of horribles (which presumably includes eating broccoli), in distinct contrast with the quotation in the opinion of the Court of the famous statement of Justice Holmes that the "power to tax is not the the power to destroy while this Court sits."[361] No good explanation was provided why Justice Holmes' injunction is not as applicable to an overreaching of the Commerce Clause as to the taxing power. Indeed, when Justice Stone upheld under the taxing power the unemployment compensation act in 1937 he made exactly that sort of point: that surely Congress had the power to tax to deal with a singular national emergency of unemployment;[362] similarly when Justice Cardozo upheld the social security act tax he described the unique national disaster that Congress had the power to address.[363] Presumably the reason that Roberts and the Scalia dissenters did not see the analogy is that they made the policy decision that in 2010-2012 there is no health care cost crisis akin to the Great Depression.

A third interaction between the Roberts opinion's Commerce Clause analysis and its tax discussion is an analogy to another issue of regulating inactivity: the Court's earlier fights over punishing the inactivity of states and local governments in protecting civil rights. At first the Court thought it had no power to make states cease their inactivity in enforcing civil rights; then it ruled that it could, in decisions like *Wilmington Parking Authority*.[364] But then the Rehnquist Court pushed back, ruling that a local department of social services could not be held liable under the Civil Rights Act even though it knew the petitioner's father was beating him and did not remove the child, after which the father finally beat him so severely that he suffered permanent brain damage and was rendered profoundly retarded.[365] Hence, leaving inactivity be turns out to be a conservative touchstone.

(6) *Conclusion As to* Sebelius

Sebelius will be discussed for generations to come, unless it is quickly reversed due to a change in the makeup of the Court. That has occurred before, for

---

[361] Panhandle Oil Co. v. Mississippi, 277 U.S. 218, 223 (1928) (Holmes, J., dissenting)).

[362] Carmichael v. Southern Coal & Coke Co., 301 U.S. 495, 518 (1937) ("When public evils ensue from individual misfortunes or needs, the legislature may strike at the evil at its source.").

[363] Helvering v. Davis, 301 U.S. 619, 645 (1937).

[364] Burton v. Wilmington Parking Authority, 365 U.S. 715 (1961).

[365] Deshaney v. Winnebago County Dep't of Social Services, 489 U.S. 189 (1989). Justice Blackmun's dissent stated "The Court fails to recognize this duty because it attempts to draw a sharp and rigid line between action and inaction. But such formalistic reasoning has no place in the interpretation of the broad and stirring Clauses of the Amendment. 489 U.S. at 212.

example in the *Legal Tender Cases* (1871), which reversed *Hepburn v. Griswold* (1870), but in that situation the first decision was the one that limited federal power to authorize the creation of a national currency.[366] Thus *Sebelius* may turn out to be either another *Gregory v. Helvering*, or more like *General Utilities* (which took a little longer to reverse). For now, the principal significance of the Court's tax holdings is the fact that they exist and were obtained from the 2012 Court: (1) the Anti-Injunction Act may not apply to an exaction that Congress does not label a tax, and (2) the taxing power stands firm and Congress can use it to regulate.

Because the Court based its holding on the taxing power, congressional opponents repealed the individual mandate, hoping that would undercut the constitutionality of the entire Affordable Care Act. However, when plaintiffs pursued that theory in court, the Supreme Court dismissed their action for lack of standing.[367]

3. *Taxes Can Regulate As Incident to Their Own Collection*

Perhaps the easiest cases in which to uphold federal taxing rules are those in which the regulation at issue is a regulation that is incident to federal tax collection:

- *Nicol v. Ames* ruled that the United States could impose a stamp tax on certain sales or exchanges, without undertaking thereby to regulate the sales or the exchanges; and that the requirement of documentation was not a regulation but incident to the tax collection.[368]
- *Sonzinsky* said that the firearms registration provisions were incident to the tax collection on the firearms sales.[369]
- The registration provisions of the Harrison Narcotics Act were found to be aids in collection of the tax.[370]
- If Congress determines that it is more desirable to collect tax on cigars packed in boxes of a certain size, it can require that all cigars be sold in boxes of that size.[371]
- *South Carolina v. Baker* held constitutional the Code's registration requirement for coupon bonds whose holders claimed an interest exemption under section 103, even when the issuer was a state or local government, because

---

[366] Hepburn v. Griswold, 75 U.S. 603 (1870), *reversed*, Knox v. Lee, 79 U.S. 457 (1871) (the Legal Tender Cases).

[367] California v. Texas, 141 S. Ct. 2104 (2021).

[368] Nicol v. Ames, 173 U.S. 509 (1899).

[369] Sonzinsky v. United States, 300 U.S. 506 (1937); United States v. Miller, 307 U.S. 174 (1939) (similar to *Sonzinsky*).

[370] Nigro v. United States, 276 U.S. 332 (1928).

[371] Felsenheld v. United States, 186 U.S. 126 (1902).

the requirement prevented tax avoidance, even though the requirement indirectly regulated state action.[372]

But there are limits to the degree of connection between a nontax provision and a tax. *Dewitt* ruled unconstitutional the criminalizing of the sale of one type of illuminating oil (in a provision in the federal tax laws), defended as encouraging the sale of the other, taxed, type of illuminating oil.[373] The linkage was "too remote and uncertain" to justify the criminal provision as in aid of the taxing provision; the sale at issue in the crime was not taxed. *Hill v. Wallace* also rejected the government argument that record keeping requirements of the law aided tax collection.[374]

See also the next Chapter discussing the Necessary and Proper Clause, which can justify regulations in aid of taxation.

4. *When Congress Has the Powers to Both Regulate and Tax*

a. *Taxes That Regulate As Necessary and Proper to Another Power*

Article I, section 8, clause 18 authorizes Congress:

> To make all Laws which shall be necessary and proper for carrying into Execution the foregoing Powers, and all other Powers vested by this Constitution in the Government of the United States, or in any Department or Officer thereof.[375]

The Court has ruled that necessary does not mean absolutely necessary, and that it will look to see if Congress had a "rational basis" to select a "choice of means" to carry out an enumerated power, asking only whether the choice is "reasonably adapted" to the end.[376]

The Court's Necessary and Proper Clause case list is sparse in general, relative to subjects like due process and equal protection. It is even sparser in the tax area. Congress can impose a tax as necessary and proper to carry out an enumerated power such as the power to make war.[377] However, in its most extensive

---

[372] South Carolina v. Baker, 485 U.S. 505 (1988). *See* F. Ladson Boyle, *The Rehnquist Court: Nineteen Years of Tax Decisions*, 25 Va. Tax Rev. 451, 459 (2005).

[373] United States v. Dewitt, 76 U.S. 41 (1869).

[374] Hill v. Wallace, 259 U.S. 44 (1922).

[375] *See generally* Randy E. Barrett, *The Original Meaning of the Necessary and Proper Clause*, 6 U. Pa. J. Con. Law 183 (2004) (arguing for a more constricted meaning of the Clause); J. Randy Beck, *The New Jurisprudence of the Necessary and Proper Clause*, 2002 U. Ill. L. Rev. 581 (arguing that the Supreme Court has misused the clause).

[376] United States v. Comstock, 560 U.S. 126 (2010).

[377] *See* Ware v. Hylton, 3 U.S. 199 (1796) ("That Congress did not possess all the powers of war is self-evident from this consideration alone, that she never attempted to lay any kind of tax on the people of the United States, ..."). *But see* Nat'l Fed'n of Indep. Bus. v. Sebelius, 567 U.S. 519 (2012) refused to find the Individual Mandate to be necessary and property to carry out some enumerated power of Congress (Roberts' opinion).

analysis of a War Revenue Act it based the tax solely on the taxing power.[378] On the other hand the Prohibition taxes were adopted under the war powers.[379]

The more common application of the Necessary and Proper Clause to taxation is to enable reporting or other ancillary requirements needed to collect the tax.[380] However, Congress surely can impose a Article I, section 8, clause 1 tax to aid in carrying out another power; indeed that is inevitabe when the regulatory effect of a true tax falls on an activity that Congress has the power to regulate (unless Congress specifically labels the tax as solely a regulation).[381] Such taxes are dually authorized in the Constitution; tariffs are a prime example,[382] although tariffs (customs duties) are clearly understood to be taxing clause taxes,[383] even though Congress levies them for regulation and not just for revenue.[384]

Rarer still are the federal exactions that Congress may call taxes but intends solely as exercises of its Necessary and Proper Clause power in support of another power. Examples include:

- Congress levied an excess profits tax as necessary and proper to its war powers, for the purpose of attempting to insure fair charges for war materials used by the military and to prevent profiteering.[385] Similarly a federal fee was levied on cotton bought from the south during the Civil War, and was explained as a war powers levy, not a federal taxing power tax.[386]
- Congress could both tax and regulate under the Commerce Clause the public utilities in Hawaii.[387]
- When a state university objected on grounds of intergovernmental immunity to an import duty, the Court determined that Congress had not imposed

---

[378] Knowlton v. Moore, 178 U.S. 41 (1900).

[379] Ruppert v. Caffey, 251 U.S. 264 (1920). For the Necessary and Proper Clause, see Ch. III.E.4.a. For Common Defense see Ch. III.D.7.

[380] *See, e.g.*, United States v. Doremus, 249 U.S. 86 (1919); dissent of Chief Justice Warren in Grosso v. United States, 390 U.S. 62 (1968); Heiner v. Donnan, 285 U.S. 312 (1932); County of Spokane v. United States, 279 U.S. 80 (1929) (priority of U.S. tax claim in bankruptcy is rule necessary and proper to tax collection); United States v. Snyder, 149 U.S. 210 (1893); Van Brocklin v. Tennessee, 117 U.S. 151 (1886).

[381] *See, e.g.*, Sunshine Anthracite Coal Co. v. Adkins, 310 U.S. 381, 393 (1940).

[382] *See, e.g.*, McGoldrick v. Gulf Oil Corp., 309 U.S. 414, 427 (1940) (the tariff act recited both raising revenue and encouraging certain imports as reasons for the tariff).

[383] Michelin Tire Corp. v. Wages, 423 U.S. 276 (1976).

[384] J. W. Hampton, Jr. & Co. v. United States, 276 U.S. 394 (1928).

[385] *See* Lichter v. United States, 334 U.S. 742 (1948).

[386] Hamilton v. Dillin, 88 U.S. 73 (1875).

[387] Inter-Island Steam Navigation Co. v. Hawaii, 305 U.S. 306 (1938) (did not identify the Necessary and Proper Clause but appeared to rely on powers other than the taxing power).

the duty under the taxing power, thereby respecting Congress' declaration of the constitutional basis for the tax.[388]

The most commonly cited tax of this type was upheld by the Court in the *Head Money Cases*, which treated a duty imposed on immigrants solely as a regulation.[389] Despite the fact that the opinion also commonly is cited for its interpretation of the meaning of the uniformity requirement in Article I, section 8, clause 1,[390] the opinion wound up concluding that the levy was not a taxing power tax, even though the Attorney General had called it a capitation tax. Therefore, it was not subject to the requirement of apportionment of direct taxes.

Butler in striking down the tax in the Agricultural Adjustment Act, first determined it was not a true tax, but rather was a tax only in "a loose and more extended sense than was used in the Constitution, ..."[391] Then *Butler* considered and rejected the alternative that the tax could be constitutional as necessary and proper for carrying into execution a power possessed by Congress.

Using the taxing power as necessary and proper to carrying out some other enumerated power of Congress through a regulatory effect is analogous to another obvious but seldom discussed power: taxing to produce revenue to carry out some specifically enumerated power rather than for paying debts, the common defense or the general welfare. Surely that is done and is constitutional. Perhaps it could be explained by interpreting the general welfare as encompassing those specific powers and more, but the Court has never said that. The more straightforward explanation is that the linked taxing power and general welfare power is not the sole role of the taxing power and the taxing power may also be used to carry out specifically enumerated powers of Congress.

Another unexplored issue in this area is the freedom of Necessary and Proper Clause taxes from the limitations imposed by Article I, section 8 on taxes levied under the taxing power. Presumably the direct versus other tax dichotomy

---

[388] Bd. of Trustees v. United States, 289 U.S. 48, 57-58 (1933)("But because the taxing power is a distinct power and embraces the power to lay duties, it does not follow that duties may not be imposed in the exercise of the power to regulate commerce. . . . But if the Congress may thus exercise the power, and asserts, as it has asserted here, that it is exercising it, the judicial department may not attempt in its own conception of policy to distribute the duties thus fixed by allocating some of them to the exercise of the admitted power to regulate commerce and others to an independent exercise of the taxing power. The purpose to regulate foreign commerce permeates the entire congressional plan."). *See also* New York v. United States, 505 U.S. 144, 171 (1992) ("which petitioners do not claim to be an invalid exercise of either Congress' commerce or taxing power . . ."). The surcharge on nuclear waste in *New York* was explained as a tax, though this is questionable, in Nat'l Fed'n of Indep. Bus. v. Sebelius, 567 U.S. 519 (2012). *See* Ch. III.E.2.c(e)(b).

[389] Edye v. Robertson, 112 U.S. 580, 595 (1884) (Head Money Cases). Justice Roberts leaned heavily on the *Head Money Cases* as illustrating the right way a "tax" could be used as necessary and proper to carrying out another power that the federal government actually possesses. United States v. Butler, 297 U.S. 1, 61 (1936).

[390] *See* Fernandez v. Wiener, 326 U.S. 340, 359 (1945). *See also* Sunshine Anthracite Coal Co. v. Adkins, 310 U.S. 381, 393 (1940) (viewing the *Head Money Cases* as a true tax in aid of a regulation).

[391] United States v. Butler, 297 U.S. 1, 69 (1936).

would not be relevant and neither would the uniformity clause. A possible example is taxing for a Territory.[392]

b. *When It Doesn't Matter*

As indicated in the preceding Chapters, the fact that a federal tax regulates activities that might be considered potential subjects of state regulation is not a matter of constitutional concern if the United States also has the power to regulate that activity. Therefore, that may be the first question when such a tax is attacked by a taxpayer as a regulation; the regulatory effect of a federal tax certainly is of no concern if Congress possess the exclusive power in the area. This principle was acknowledged by the first Supreme Court opinion to rule that a federal tax was not a tax and was unconstitutional because it regulated in an area where the United States had no power to regulate:

> Where the sovereign enacting the law has power to impose both tax and penalty the difference between revenue production and mere regulation may be immaterial, ...[393]

Other opinions to the same effect include the following:

- *Knowlton v. Moore* stated: "This principle (the power to tax is the power to destroy) is pertinent only when there is no power to tax a particular subject, and has no relation to a case where such right exists."[394]
- But one of the handful of rulings against federal taxes from 1922 to 1936 found a liquor tax to be unconstitutional because the federal power to regulate had been removed by repeal of the Prohibition Amendment.[395]
- In 1884 the Court upheld a federal "duty" on immigrants to be paid by ship owners at ports, principally as a regulation of commerce, but observed that it could have been upheld under the taxing power (although literally that was not the ground of the holding).[396] It could be a tax even though the money was put into an account to assist immigrants, because the funds were clearly for the "general welfare."[397] The opinion explained that the taxes were regulatory in part because "the money thus raised, though paid into the Treasury, is appropriated in advance to the uses of the statute, and does not go to the general support of the government."[398] The opinion analogized *Veazie Bank v. Fenno*,[399] where the power to regulate the national currency was a second ground for the tax along with the power to tax, and *Packet Co.*

---

[392] *See* Ch. V.D.3.a(4).
[393] J.W. Bailey v. Drexel Furn. Co., 259 U.S. 20, 38 (1922) (Child Labor Tax Case).
[394] Knowlton v. Moore, 178 U.S. 41, 60 (1904).
[395] United States v. Constantine, 296 U.S. 287 (1935).
[396] Edye v. Robertson, 112 U.S. 580 (1884) (Head Money Cases).
[397] *Id.* at 595.
[398] *Id.* at 596.
[399] Veazie Bank v. Fenno, 75 U.S. 533, 541 (1869).

v. Keokuk, where the local wharfage charge was a user fee and not an import duty.[400]

- *Cloverleaf Butter* applied the same approach to the tax on colored margarine at issue in *McCray*, which it said was solely a revenue measure, but also justified the regulatory aspects of the taxing regime under the Commerce Clause (reflecting a maturing of the understanding of the Commerce Clause since 1904).[401] *Cloverleaf Butter* is unusual in that the Court was evaluating the extent to which the federal government had exercised its Commerce Clause powers to preempt the field of regulating local butter production, so as to preclude a state from also regulating that production. Because it reasoned the United States had imposed the regulatory aspects of the tax regime in part under the Commerce Clause, it was able to also conclude that the state could not regulate. In contrast, *McCray* in 1904 had justified the tax solely on the taxing power.
- The most obvious example of a regulatory tax whose characterization usually does not matter is the tariff, which is primarily in aid of the power to regulate foreign commerce, but has been a major revenue source as well and should be viewed as doubly authorized since tariffs are surely the "duties" referred to in Article I, section 8.[402]
- *Veazie Bank v. Fenno* is an early example of a tax that the Supreme Court justified in part as in aid of the power of coinage.[403]
- Justice Black explained this category of tax in *Sunshine Anthracite Coal* as a tax whose primary purpose is to serve as a penalty in aid of another enu-

[400] Packet Co. v. Keokuk, 95 U.S. 80 (1877).

[401] Cloverleaf Butter Co. v. Patterson, 315 U.S. 148 (1942).

[402] *See* Bd. of Trustees v. United States, 289 U.S. 48 (1933). *See also* Gibbons v. Ogden, 22 U.S. 1, 191 (1824) (explaining that tariffs could either be purely for revenue raising or in aid of regulation): Constitution, Article I, section 9, clause 6 (regulation of commerce or revenue).

[403] Veazie Bank v. Fenno, 75 U.S. 533, 541 (1869). *See* United States v. Kahriger, 345 U.S. 22 n. 6 (1953) (stating that *Veazie* "depends partly on the alternate ground of the federal power to provide money for circulation"); Hepburn v. Griswold, 75 U.S. 603 (1870) (dissent of Justice Miller states that the tax upheld in *Veazie* was applied under Congress' implied powers, and likewise Congress should have the power to support its bank's currency by making it legal tender). *See also* David P. Currie, *The Constitution in the Supreme Court: Civil War and Reconstruction: 1865-1873*, 51 U. Chi. L. Rev. 131, 173-174 (1984) (alternate argument too glib); John Barker Waite, *May Congress Levy Money Exactions Designated Taxes Solely for the Purpose of Destruction?*, 6 Mich. L. Rev. 277, 288 (1908).

merated power, there the very heavy tax on coal producers who did not join the Coal Code.[404]

The principal, though not only, enumerated power that Congress relies upon to tax what it regulates is the Commerce Clause.[405] The Court broadly construed the Commerce Clause in the early years, only to narrow the concept of interstate commerce from the 1880s through 1936, then to expand it seemingly without limit up to 1995 in *Lopez*.[406] Due to the substantial expansion of Commerce Clause powers into private and seemingly localized economic activity,[407] the application of taxation in support of the Commerce Clause can occur in a variety of settings, as in the case of the health insurance tax case decided in 2012.[408]

c. *Taxes Can Regulate What Is Already Regulated*

Federal taxes can tax activities that the federal government otherwise regulates or forbids, as explained in an early Prohibition tax decision:

> That Congress may under the broad authority of the taxing power tax intoxicating liquors notwithstanding their production is prohibited and punished, we have no question. The fact that the statute in this aspect had a moral end in view as well as the raising of revenue, presents no valid constitutional objection to its enactment. *License Tax Cases* . . . ; *In re Kollock* . . . ; *United States v. Jin Fuey Moy* . . . ; *United States v. Doremus* . . . .[409]

---

[404] Sunshine Anthracite Coal Co. v. Adkins, 310 U.S. 381, 393 (1940) ("Clearly this tax is not designed merely for revenue purposes. In purpose and effect it is primarily a sanction to enforce the regulatory provisions of the Act. But that does not mean that the statute is invalid and the tax unenforceable. Congress may impose penalties in aid of the exercise of any of its enumerated powers. The power of taxation, granted to Congress by the Constitution, may be utilized as a sanction for the exercise of another power which is granted it. Head Money Cases, 112 U.S. 580, 596. *And see* Sonzinsky v. United States, 300 U.S. 506. It is so utilized here.").

[405] *See, e.g.*, New York v. United States, 505 U.S. 144, 171 (1992) (finding it unnecessary to explain whether a "surcharge" was a tax because it was within federal power either as a tax or as a regulation of interstate commerce). The surcharge on nuclear waste in *New York* was explained as a tax in *Nat'l Fed'n of Indep. Bus. v. Sebelius*, 567 U.S. 519 (2012), although that is questionable. *See* Ch. III.E.2.c.

[406] United States v. Lopez, 514 U.S. 549 (1995) (reasoning that because carrying guns around schools was not economic activity, as to which the Commerce Clause has broader reach, it did not have "substantial effect" on interstate commerce; and that deference to Congress' determinations has limits). *See* FRIEDMAN, at 330. *See also* United States v. Morrison, 529 U.S. 598 (2000) (invalidated a section of the Violence Against Women Act of 1994, 42 U.S.C. § 13981, which provided a federal civil remedy for victims of gender motivated violence). *But see* Gonzales v. Raich, 545 U.S. 1, 23 (2005) (indicating that reports of the demise of the Commerce Clause were premature). *See generally* Cooter and Siegel, at 131 et seq.

[407] *See, e.g.*, Katzenbach v. McClung, 379 U.S. 294 (1964) (local restaurant subject to civil rights laws).

[408] *See* Ch. III.E.2.c.

[409] United States v. Yuginovich, 256 U.S. 450, 462 (1921) (liquor tax). *See also*, United States v. Stafoff, 260 U.S. 477 (1923) (prohibition); Lewis v. United States, 348 U.S. 419 (1955) (wagering).

5. *The Self-Defeating Tax*

If the extent of the power to tax be essentially limitless, what of a tax that defeats itself as a tax by being so onerous as to discourage, perhaps completely, the thing taxed? The most common example is a high protective tariff, which Congress has used not only to raise the majority of federal revenue prior to the adoption of the income tax, but also to discourage certain imports and thereby encourage local industry.[410] Such use of taxation is so well established as to be easily overlooked, and so when a high tax appears more clearly to have a regulatory purpose or effect, taxpayers frequently balk.

This Chapter focuses on the contentions that a tax that either confiscates the entire subject matter of a transaction, or effectively takes all profit out of a transaction, is not an exercise of the taxing power but rather is a regulatory penalty or a taking without just compensation in violation of the Fifth Amendment.[411] Because such a tax chokes off the thing to be taxed and so may wind up not producing revenue, it may be called a self-defeating tax.

The Court's uniform response is that taxes are not takings; they are taxes, even if "confiscatory."[412] Indeed the majority opinion in a highly contentious expansion of the Eminent Domain protections in 2013 brushed aside the dissent's concern that the majority's reasoning would put the taxing power in jeopardy by stating "It is beyond dispute that "[t]axes and user fees . . . are not 'takings.'"[413] The Supreme Court has never held a federal tax to be unconstitutional under the Fifth Amendment or otherwise because it was too great in absolute dollar amount or in percentage of the tax base. That should not be surprising in light of (1) Chief Justice Marshall's seminal view that taxes, by their very nature, can be so great as to destroy (Chapter II.A.2), and (2) the Court's repeated reliance on that view, most prominently for the protection of the United States against the states in *Veazie Bank v. Fenno*, ruling that the United States could tax notes issued by state banks so heavily that state banks would stop issuing the notes, which was the purpose of Congress in levying the tax.[414]

Despite these early precedents, taxpayers continued to attack federal taxes on the ground that they were "confiscatory," which usually is paired with an assertion of a taking without compensation, and the Court has always rejected that

---

[410] *See* Margulies, 5 J. S. LEGAL HIST. 1.

[411] As to the Eminent Domain Clause of the Fifth Amendment generally, *see* Ch. V.D.3.b(8).

[412] *Id.*

[413] Koontz v. St. Johns River Water Mgmt. Dist., 570 U.S. 595 (2013) (the dissent was not convinced).

[414] Veazie Bank v. Fenno, 75 U.S. 533, 541 (1869).

claim insofar as the claim was based on the level of taxation.[415] Taxpayers' hopes continue to spring eternal because, as usual, the Court has left itself an out. The opinion in *Knowlton v. Moore* stated, while approving a progressive inheritance tax:

If a case should ever arise, where an arbitrary and confiscatory exaction is imposed bearing the guise of a progressive or any other form of tax, it will be time enough to consider whether the judicial power can afford a remedy by applying inherent and fundamental principles for the protection of the individual, even though there be no express authority in the Constitution to do so.[416]

High taxes that are collected are more discussed than seen, having become a straw man for academic debate. One commentator has proclaimed that "surely" a tax of 100 per cent on Bill Gates' income would violate the Eminent Domain Clause.[417] While there might be constitutional concerns about a federal tax law applicable to Bill Gates by name and directing him alone to pay 100% of all of his income to the Treasury, no one can "surely" opine that a progressive tax on all taxpayers that reached the level of 100% above some income level is a taking to that extent; progressive taxes have been generally upheld in *Knowlton v. Moore* and other decisions of the Court, and the caveat in the quotation from that opinion can be read to refer to an impermissible arbitrariness (*i.e.*, picking on Gates alone) rather than confiscation. After all, the marginal income tax rate reached as high as 94% in 1944, without successful, or apparently any, constitutional challenge.

Others have extended the same concern to an income tax applicable to more persons than Bill Gates, but concentrated at the high end of the income spectrum.[418] They assume, without proof, that a tax that is wholly divorced from benefits to the taxpayer, in part because too much of the burden of taxation is

---

415 *See, e.g.*, Sunshine Anthracite Coal Co. v. Adkins, 310 U.S. 381, 84 L. Ed. 1263 (1940) (argument of taxpayer's counsel); United States v. Butler, 297 U.S. 1, 80 L. Ed. 477 (1936 (argument of taxpayer's counsel); Stewart Dry Goods Co. v. Lewis, 294 U.S. 550 (1935) (even though opinion of Court indicated confiscation occurred); Porter v. Commissioner, 288 U.S. 436 (1933) (rejecting taxpayer argument that including in gross estate property over which decedent reserved a power of appointment was confiscatory); Burnet v. Brooks, 288 U.S. 378 (1933) (rejected confiscatory charge); Alaska Fish Salting & By-Products Co. v. Smith, 255 U.S. 44 (1921) (acknowledging potential of tax to confiscate business and upholding tax); Flint v. Stone Tracy Co., 220 U.S. 107 (1911) (taxpayer argued confiscation and Court upheld tax); McCray v. United States, 195 U.S. 27 (1904) (Court entertained the confiscation argument and said it was permissible for the tax to destroy the business); Helvering v. Davis, 301 U.S. 619 (1937) (argument of counsel).

416 Knowlton v. Moore, 178 U.S. 41, 109-110 (1900). This opinion generally was a remarkable exercise in judicial legerdemain, managing to uphold the progressive inheritance tax five years after the decision in *Pollock*, but interpreting it so that the progressive feature was not measured by the entire estate but each separate inheritance. *See* Ratner, at 244-245.

417 Calvin R. Massey, *Takings and Progressive Rate Taxation*, 20 Harv. J. L. and P. Policy 85, 104 (1996). Senator Grassley cited this argument in questioning Elena Kagan during hearings on her appointment to the Supreme Court. 2010 TNT (TA) 133-21. He also cited Saul Levmore, *Just Compensation and Just Politics*, 22 Conn. L. Rev. 285, 292 (1990).

418 *See* Eric Kades, *Drawing the Line Between Taxes and Takings: The Continuous Burdens Principle, and its Broader Application*, 97 Nw. U. L. Rev. 189 (2002) [hereinafter Kades].

shifted to a small group of taxpayers, is a taking without compensation.[419] That argument is wrong simply because it violates the Marshall view and the *Veazie Bank* holding, and also because it fails to understand that lack of relationship of tax to benefits is the very essence of a tax, at least one that is not a special assessment.[420] However, a 2012 local tax opinion contained the statement in dictum that:

> Petitioners further argue that administrative considerations alone should not justify a tax distinction, lest a city arbitrarily allocate taxes among a few citizens while forgiving many similarly situated citizens on the ground that it is cheaper and easier to collect taxes from a few people than from many. . . . Petitioners are right that administrative considerations could not justify such an unfair system. But that is not because administrative considerations can *never* justify tax differences (any more than they can *always* do so).[421]

One author relies primarily on the works of Thomas M. Cooley as a basis for this view of the Bill Gates problem.[422] But he fails to notice the bias of Cooley. Cooley's major work, *Constitutional Limitations*, became:

> . . . the groundwork of all laissez faire constitutional doctrine, and was so popular among lawyers and judges that the book went through four editions in ten years. . . . Jacksonian democracy and popular sovereignty had given rise between the years of 1837 and 1850 to an extended application of democratic principles and faith in legislative supremacy, . . . Unable to combat such a popular movement the conservatives struck at the seat of power, the legislature, through the courts, the traditional defenders of vested interests. But until Cooley wrote their success had been limited because of the prevalence of state-sovereignty doctrine in the decisions of state courts and the Supreme Court of Chief Justice Taney.[423]

Turning to the allegedly confiscatory taxes that have actually been enacted—the taxes that substantially discourage transactions, either because of their amount or their potential even though relatively modest in amount—the complaining taxpayers tend to improperly conflate with tax law the Eminent Domain Clause law holding that a regulatory statute (not a tax) that effectively destroyed the value of property could be treated as a taking.[424] That is so, but, again, as long as the exaction is a tax, that line of authority cannot apply.

Some opinions of the Court have suggested that whether an exaction is a true tax may depend on the absolute amount of revenue it can raise, implying that if the tax totally discourages the taxed activity and therefore produces no reve-

---

[419] *Id.*

[420] *See* Ch. III.C.

[421] Armour v. City of Indianapolis, 566 U.S. 673 (2012).

[422] Kades, at 198.

[423] Twiss, at 18-19. To the same effect, *see* Arnold M. Paul, Conservative Crisis and the Rule of Law 12-13 (1960, 1976 reprint).

[424] Pennsylvania Coal Co. v. Mahon, 260 U.S. 393 (1922) (statute prohibited owner of coal mining rights to mine in such a way as to upset the house built on the surface; held to be a taking for the private benefit of the homeowner). *See* Ch. V.D.3.b.8 and 9.

nue, it might not be a true tax. This theory has led to searches for, and reliance upon, extremely modest revenues raised in upholding federal taxes in *Sonzinsky* ($5,400 tax collected from 27 taxpayers in 1934 and $4,400 from 22 taxpayers in 1935),[425] *Kahriger* (which involved a tax that collected $4 million, but the opinion canvassed other federal taxes that produced a few thousand),[426] and *Sanchez* ("negligible," but the legislative history said Congress intended to raise revenue).[427] *Alston* stated that a one cent per ounce narcotics tax had produced "substantial revenue," but that is hard to believe.[428] To whatever extent these decisions relied on some tax being raised, those findings may be padding that was not essential to the rulings. *McCulloch* and *Veazie Bank* in effect ruled that taxes that were designed only to regulate were taxes, as did *McCray*. The 2012 *Sebelius* opinion prominently relied on *Kahriger* and stated in its functional analysis that the ability to raise some revenue for the government was the signal feature of a tax.[429]

In any event, the amount of tax revenue actually raised can matter only in cases in which Congress has the power to tax but not to regulate, which was not true in *Veazie* due to the power to regulate coinage but likely was true in *McCray*. Where Congress has both the taxing power and another power, Congress can levy a tax that has a prohibitory effect, without raising a cent, unless the tax violates another constitutional rule, such as freedom of the press, as discussed in connection with *Grosjean*, below. Where the Court decides Congress does not have the power to regulate, the Court has cited a total absence of tax collection to justify ruling that the exaction is not a true tax,[430] and alternately has ignored the substantial revenue produced by a federal tax.[431]

The Court's rulings and statements on taxes tending to eliminate the subject of taxation include:

- *McCulloch v. Maryland* established the fundamental point that the power to tax involves the power to destroy,[432] which *Weston v. Charleston* applied to

---

[425] Sonzinsky v. United States, 300 U.S. 506 (1937); United States v. Miller, 307 U.S. 174 (1939) (similar to *Sonzinsky*). However, it has been suggested that the Firearms Tax was upheld on the basis that it looked like a tax as in *McCray* and not like a penalty as in *Bailey*. Margulies, 5 J. S. Legal Hist. at 4.

[426] United States v. Kahriger, 345 U.S. 22 n. 4 (1953) ($4,371,869 was enough although $400 million had been projected; the opinion also indicated the sufficient amount raised by other regulatory type taxes: "$3,501 collected under the tax on adulterated and processed or renovated butter and filled cheese, the $914,910 collected under the tax on narcotics, including marijuana and special taxes, and the $28,911 collected under the tax on firearms, transfer and occupational taxes.").

[427] United States v. Sanchez, 340 U.S. 42 (1950). *See also* Minor v. United States, 396 U.S. 87 n. 13 (1969) ("negligible" revenue not a problem).

[428] Alston v. United States, 274 U.S. 289 (1927) (affirmed conviction of person who sold narcotics not in original package and not showing payment of 1 cent per ounce tax stamp; "have produced substantial revenue").

[429] Nat'l Fed'n of Indep. Bus. v. Sebelius, 567 U.S. 519 (2012) (health insurance tax projected to raise $4 billion a year by 2017). *See* Ch. III.E.2.c.

[430] *See, e.g.*, Hill v. Wallace, 259 U.S. 44 (1922).

[431] *See, e.g.*, United States v. Butler, 297 U.S. 1 (1936).

[432] *See* Ch. II.A.2.

the attempt of the city to tax the "stock" issued by the United States in exchange for loans. It reasoned that the power of the United States to borrow was as fundamental as the power to tax, because borrowing frequently was necessary when taxation was episodically insufficient; that once the power to tax a subject is found, "it is a right which in its nature acknowledges no limits."[433]

- Another early decision on state tax exemptions, *Billings*, stated: "If the grant of a power to trade in money to a given amount [*i.e.*, a charter for a state bank], implies an exemption of the stock in trade from taxation, because the tax may absorb all the profits; then the grant of any other thing implies the same exemption; for that thing may be taxed to an extent which will render it totally unprofitable to the grantee. Land, for example, has, in many, perhaps in all the states, been granted by government since the adoption of the constitution. This grant is a contract, the object of which is that the profits issuing from it shall enure to the benefit of the grantee. Yet the power of taxation may be carried so far as to absorb these profits. Does this impair the obligation of the contract? The idea is rejected by all; and the proposition appears so extravagant, that it is difficult to admit any resemblance in the cases."[434]
- *Veazie Bank* rejected an argument that the ten percent tax on the bank notes of state chartered banks was "excessive" by explaining that Congress could exercise the taxing power in support of its power to regulate currency and thereby to destroy competing currency if need be.[435] Although Congress had the power to regulate currency, the case was decided on the basis of rejecting a direct tax challenge to the exercise of the taxing power.
- *McCray* upheld a federal tax on colored margarine of ten cents a pound that was intended to make such product economically impossible to sell in competition with butter.[436] The Court said it could not be concerned with the results of taxation, and specifically stated it would not hold a tax invalid because the taxpayer argued it was too high. The opinion did not rely on or decide the power of the United States to regulate margarine; it did not mention the Commerce Clause. It spoke solely of the power of taxation. However, as in the case of the marijuana tax later held constitutional in *Sanchez*, legislative history did indicate an expectation of raising some revenue, evidently from the dramatically lower tax that would be paid on the genuine article, not from the high tax that was attacked.[437] An explanation for the enactment of the margarine tax is that conservative Republicans backed it to aid dairy farmers; and while they might not have been in favor of a broad

---

[433] Weston v. Charleston, 27 U.S. 449 (1829).
[434] Providence Bank v. Billings, 29 U.S. 514, 562 (1830).
[435] Veazie Bank v. Fenno, 75 U.S. 533 (1869).
[436] McCray v. United States, 195 U.S. 27 (1904).
[437] United States v. Sanchez, 340 U.S. 42 (1950). *See* Margulies, 5 J. S. Legal Hist. at 13 n. 49.

Commerce Clause measure, they were in favor of a broad reading of the federal government's taxing power.[438] The "anti-oleomargarine law [has] served as the primary precedent for use of the tax power to expand the federal police power," and Congress was aware of what it was doing.[439]

- *Alaska Fish* approved a heavy territorial tax, which the taxpayer argued would, and the Court assumed could, make the taxpayers stop the activity that was being taxed.[440] Because the Territory of Alaska could exercise the police power, presumably it had both regulatory and taxing power.
- The *Child Labor Tax Case* did not strike down the ten percent tax on net profit from plants using child labor and not complying with the regulatory requirements of the Child Labor Act because the tax was excessively high, or because the plants might be forced to close or otherwise be destroyed, but because the detailed nature of the accompanying regulatory scheme allegedly convinced the Court that the exaction was a regulatory penalty and not a tax.[441]
- *Hill v. Wallace* and *Trusler v. Crooks* involved taxes on certain commodity trading, which taxes were said to halt that activity.[442] One trader paid one of the taxes to set up the test case in *Trusler* and the Solicitor General, William D. Mitchell, wrote a perfunctory brief supporting the tax if the United States had the power to regulate the trades, but surprisingly stated his personal opinion that the United States did not have that power and that the tax was unconstitutional.[443] It is not surprising that the Court agreed with Mitchell's personal opinion.
- *A. Magnano* upheld a state's 15 cents per pound tax on butter substitutes despite the fact that the tax would eliminate the business.[444] The state had both the taxing power and the police power.
- *Grosjean* struck down a Louisiana tax on ad revenues of large newspapers. In explaining how the tax restrained the freedom of the press, the opinion pointed out that because the power to tax was the power to destroy, the

---

[438] 5 J. S. Legal Hist. 1, 18-19 (also there was an argument that the high tax would encourage payment of a low tax on the genuine article).

[439] 5 J. S. Legal Hist. 1, 26-27.

[440] Alaska Fish Salting & By-Products Co. v. Smith, 255 U.S. 44 (1921).

[441] J.W. Bailey v. Drexel Furn. Co., 259 U.S. 20 (1922) (Child Labor Tax Case). *But cf.* reasoning in *Sebelius,* which stated that the amount of the child labor tax was "exceedingly heavy," adding the word "exceedingly," which did not appear in Chief Justic Taft's opinion. Nat'l Fed'n of Indep. Bus. v. Sebelius, 567 U.S. 519 (2012). *See* Ch. III.E.2.c(4)(b).

[442] Hill v. Wallace, 259 U.S. 44 (1922) and Trusler v. Crooks, 269 U.S. 475 (1926).

[443] ". . . we feel under no obligation to conceal our opinion that in this case Congress under the guise of a revenue measure which cannot produce a dollar of revenue (except that paid to make a test case) has attempted to completely prohibit transactions which it has no power under the Constitution to deal with." 70 L. Ed. 365.

[444] A. Magnano Co. v. Hamilton, 292 U.S. 40 (1934).

publications could be destroyed if the tax rate were raised high enough.[445] However, the decision seems to have been prompted by the peculiar facts of the case, as discussed in Chapter VIII.D.3.

- *Pittsburgh v. Alco Parking Corp.* in 1974 reaffirmed *Magnano* and rejected the argument that a tax can be so high as to be a taking without just compensation in violation of the Due Process Clause.[446] The city had both the taxing power and the police power.

When a state attempted to both criminally convict and heavily tax the manufacturer of marijuana, the Court in *Kurth Ranch* struck down the tax not as a too heavy tax but as double jeopardy, treating it like a criminal penalty but not denying its nature as a tax.[447] The opinion acknowledged that the excessiveness of a tax did not necessarily show it was not a tax. *Kurth Ranch*, however, noted the difference in analysis between a tax imposed by a sovereign with the power to regulate and one that does not have that power.

Constantine is the one decision that ruled a federal tax not to be a true tax in part because it was "highly exorbitant.[448] This reflects an alternate usage of the amount of tax to defeat a tax, as opposed to arguing that it is a taking. The $1,000 tax on selling liquor without a special license was in addition to another license tax the person had already paid. The key to the decision was that the tax was a holdover from Prohibition levied at a time when Congress did not have the power to regulate local sales of alcohol. The combination of the absence of regulatory authority and several indicia that the "excise tax" was not a tax convinced the Court to strike it down as an invalid regulation. Thus a tax was not stricken on account of its size; rather the size of the exaction contributed to a factual finding that the exaction was not a tax. The Court similarly suggested that the high amount of a tax can count against a tax finding in the case of a tax not clearly labeled a tax, in *Sebelius*.[449]

In at least one state tax case the Court expressed a view that a tax could be so burdensome as to be "spoliation" and subject to the Eminent Domain Clause.[450]

---

[445] Grosjean v. American Press Co., 297 U.S. 233 (1936). Justice Sutherland originally planned to base the opinion on equal protection, but Justice Cardozo wrote such a persuasive draft based on press freedom that Sutherland adopted it. A.T. Mason, The Supreme Court from Taft to Warren 222 (1968).

[446] Pittsburgh v. Alco Parking Corp., 417 U.S. 369, 375 (1974) (a state tax case in which state tax and federal tax precedents were cited). *See also* Commonwealth Edison Co. v. Montana, 453 U.S. 609 (1981) (relying on *Pittsburgh* for the principle of a state's unlimited power to tax and stating that the Commerce Clause did not impose on that power, thus allowing as high severance tax).

[447] Dep't of Revenue v. Kurth Ranch, 511 U.S. 767, 782 and n. 22 (1994) ("These justifications vanish when the taxed activity is completely forbidden, for the legitimate revenue-raising purpose that might support such a tax could be equally well served by increasing the fine imposed upon conviction.").

[448] United States v. Constantine, 296 U.S. 287 (1935).

[449] *See* Ch. III.E.2.c(4)(b).

[450] Henderson Bridge Co. v. Henderson City, 173 U.S. 592 (1899).

However, that case did not involve a question of the degree of taxation but rather of the jurisdiction to tax.[451]

6. *Poll Taxes*

Making the payment of a poll tax a condition of voting is inherently a regulatory use of taxation. The Twenty-Fourth Amendment was adopted to prevent the states (and the United States) from using "poll tax or other tax" for this purpose as to federal elections. Such usage of the term poll tax can cause confusion because historically the term poll tax was an alternative way of describing a capitation tax,[452] which normally would not refer to a special tax levied as a precondition of voting. The confusion of terminology developed when southern states adopted general poll taxes after the Civil War, which effectively served as preconditions of voting if the state statutes also made them so, even though ostensibly levied as a general tax.[453] Thus even though "poll" can refer to both heads and voting places, the true meaning for the discussion here is a capitation tax that is also made a condition of voting.

Capitation taxes have had at least three common meanings. First they are taxes at so much per person levied under an apportioned federal direct tax.[454] Second they are per person taxes levied to penalize or burden certain activities such as travel.[455] Third, the Court has used the term to refer to poll taxes levied on the right to vote,[456] although sometimes the reference to "polls" is ambiguous and may refer only to persons.[457] Thus a poll tax that is due solely from those who choose to vote may not properly be called a capitation tax.

At first the Court approved a state poll tax, said to have "long been a familiar form of taxation, much used in some countries and to a considerable extent here, at first in the Colonies and later in the States."[458] Even though payment of the tax was a condition of voting for most voters, the Court found that its purpose (in Georgia) was not to burden voting. However, the Court overruled that holding in 1966.[459] The decision was rooted in three concepts: the primacy of the right to vote; the equality required of the right to vote as evidenced by the "one man one vote" rulings of the Court, and the view that wealth was an improper classification at least as to such a core right as the right to vote.

---

[451] *See also* dissent of Justice Harlan in Pollock v. Farmers' Loan & Trust Co., 158 U.S. 601, 674-675 (1895) (referring to the possibility of spoliation if a federal tax on the rich were "repugnant to principles of natural right").

[452] *See, e.g.*, Pollock v. Farmers' Loan & Trust Co., 158 U.S. 601, 625 (1895).

[453] *See* Joseph E. Kallenbach, *Constitutional Aspects of Federal Anti-Poll Tax Legislation*, 45 Mich. L. Rev. 717, 726 (1946-1947). *See, e.g.*, Breedlove v. Suttles, 302 U.S. 277 (1937), *overruled by* Harper v. Virginia State Bd. of Elections, 383 U.S. 663 (1966).

[454] *See, e.g.*, Springer v. United States, 102 U.S. 586 (1881).

[455] *See, e.g.*, Crandall v. Nevada, 73 U.S. 35 (1868); Smith v. Turner, 48 U.S. 283, 412 (1849).

[456] *See, e.g.*, United States v. Reese, 92 U.S. 214 (1876) (dissent of Justice Clifford).

[457] *See, e.g.*, Hylton v. United States, 3 U.S. 171, 175 (1796).

[458] Breedlove v. Suttles, 302 U.S. 277, 281 (1937).

[459] Harper v. Virginia State Bd. of Elections, 383 U.S. 663 (1966).

See also Chapter V.C.3 discussing capitation taxes and the identification of direct taxes.

7. *Taxes That Are Too Light*

Just as a tax may raise little or no revenue because it is too heavy, it may raise little revenue because it is too light, which might indicate it is not levied for revenue but to regulate. Nevertheless, the Court has not stricken down any federal taxes on that basis.

The prime example is the Harrison Narcotics Act (levying a one cent per ounce tax) and the Marijuana Tax Act (levying a one dollar per ounce tax), which taxes obviously neither stamped out the thing taxed nor raised much revenue. Nevertheless the Court affirmed convictions under the Harrison Act multiple times, for failure to pay as little as one cent in tax, against consistent contentions that the crime was not failing to pay a tax but dealing in drugs, which was then thought to be a local matter that the United States could not regulate.[460] The Marijuana Tax Act was hardly more productive, at one dollar per year for registration and one dollar per ounce for sale by registered dealers, nevertheless the Court upheld it as a tax.[461]

8. *Taxation As Punishment*

Taxes are not punishments for wrongdoing because if they were they might be bills of attainder that would violate Article I, section 9, clause 3 of the Constitution.[462] A bill of attainder is a legislative or even an executive punishment

---

[460] *See, e.g.*, United States v. Doremus, 249 U.S. 86 (1919); Alston v. United States, 274 U.S. 289 (1927) (affirmed conviction of person who sold narcotics not in original package and not showing payment of one cent per ounce tax stamp; "have produced substantial revenue"); Nigro v. United States, 276 U.S. 332 (1928); Casey v. United States, 276 U.S. 413 (1928) (affirmed conviction for failure to pay tax of one cent; a dissent stated "It is hard to continue to say that this Act is a taxing measure in order to sustain it. Eagerness to use federal law as a police measure to combat the opium habit—a purpose for which Congress has no power to legislate—should not lead to the enactment or the construction of laws that shock common sense."); Blockburger v. United States, 284 U.S. 299 (1932) (the United States cannot punish the sales as sales but only as an aid to collecting the one cent per ounce tax).

[461] United States v. Sanchez, 340 U.S. 42 (1950); Leary v. United States, 395 U.S. 6 (1969) (while reversing the conviction of Dr. Timothy Leary on self-incrimination grounds, the opinion confirmed the tax was a tax and not a regulation, largely based on Congress calling it a tax). The self-incrimination problem led to a shift away from a tax based anti-drug regime to a Commerce Clause based regime, based on a new found conclusion that national concerns were implicated in the drug trade. *See* Gonzales v. Raich, 545 U.S. 1 (2005).

[462] *See* Annotation: *Supreme Court's Views as to What Constitutes a Bill of Attainder Prohibited by Federal Constitution*, 53 L. Ed. 2d 1273. However, no opinion of the Court analyzes bills of attainder in the context of taxes.

of a designated person or class that is not imposed by a court.[463] Similarly taxes are not subject to the Eight Amendment prohibition against excessive fines or subject to the double jeopardy or due process requirements imposed on criminal penalties.

Nevertheless, the preceding Chapters list many taxes that Congress designed to discourage or encourage certain conduct by imposing penalties, which sometimes could be viewed as not just regulatory but punitive. Therefore, without a way to pigeonhole taxes as such, the courts would never know what limits to impose on such punitive taxes. Applicable here by analogy is Justice White's statement in *Knowlton v. Moore* about the power to tax being the power to destroy: "But this reasoning [that federal taxation might destroy state power to regulate inheritance] has no application to a lawful tax, for if it had there would be an end of all taxation; . . . ."[464] The Court has come to the very practical conclusion that punitive, penalizing, taxes are true taxes and not bills of attainder.

However, there is considerable literature analyzing the intersection of taxes and punishment,[465] because: (1) taxpayers sometimes feel punished by taxation, (2) taxes are enforced by civil penalties denominated as penalties but collected as part of the tax, (3) sometimes different definitions apply to punishment so that what is a civil enforcement mechanism for tax purposes is a punishment for other purposes (for example, double jeopardy and self-incrimination),[466] and (4) in rare cases taxes as such (not enforcement penalties) are so high as to be treated as nontax regulatory penalties (that is, the tax that is not a tax).[467]

As discussed in detail in Chapter III.E.2.c(3)(d), the 2012 *Sebelius* opinion by Chief Justice Roberts set up a functional test for a levy not clearly labeled as a tax, and after finding that the functional test was satisfied, applied an additional test asking whether the tax was instead a penalty for an unlawful act, and determined it was not because Congress did not make failing to buy insurance unlawful.

It is important to acknowledge that taxes well may feel like punishment because of two of their signal features: (1) the amount of tax is not supposed to be related to the amount of benefit to the taxpayer from government services,[468] and (2) substantial discrimination is allowed to vary tax liability from person

---

[463] *Id.* An attainder was the British punishment of forfeiture imposed on felons. *Bouvier's Law Dictionary* 279 (1st Ed.). It could be imposed by the legislature but was unknown in the United States due to the constitutional prohibition. *Id.* An example of a legislative attainder was discussed in Carmell v. Tex., 529 U.S. 513 (2000) (Fenwick's case in England where Parliament eliminated the evidentiary requirement of two witnesses so Fenwick could be convicted). It has been suggested that a punitive and targeted tax could be a bill of attainder. *See* Congressional Research Service, Retroactive Taxation of Executive Bonuses, R40466 (March 25, 2009), *reprinted at* 2009 TNT 57-35 (March 25, 2009).

[464] Knowlton v. Moore, 178 U.S. 41, 60 (1904).

[465] *See, e.g.*, Suellen M. Wolfe, *Recovery from Halper: The Pain from Additions to Tax Is Not the Sting of Punishment*, 25 Hofstra L. Rev. 161 (1996) (and articles cited therein).

[466] *See, e.g.*, Dep't of Revenue v. Kurth Ranch, 511 U.S. 767 (1994). *See* Ch. VIIC and E.

[467] *See, e.g.*, United States v. Constantine, 296 U.S. 287 (1935).

[468] *See* Ch. IV.A.

to person.[469] The role of tax penalties as such is much debated, and is discussed separately in Chapter VI.F and H.

9. *Contrast State Taxation and Regulation*

Care must be taken not to cross fertilize constitutional analysis of state taxes that regulate with analysis of federal taxes that regulate for the simple reasons that states must conform to the additional requirements of the Commerce Clause and do not enjoy the benefit of supremacy that inheres in the United States, but do have a general police power.

A huge issue about state taxation in the late 19th and early 20th Century was whether state taxes improperly regulated interstate commerce and so could not be imposed at all on any business operating across state lines. The Court created a variety of principles to deal with the issue, including the "original package rule" and the "stream of commerce doctrine."[470] An early book was devoted wholly to the issue.[471] Subsequently the restrictions were softened and changed and augmented with equal protection and due process limits.[472] With rare exceptions, none of that extensive case law is pertinent to constitutional limits on federal taxation. The exceptions are the equal protection and due process concerns. The constitutional limits on state taxation are addressed in Chapter IX.

F. Supreme Court Rulings That a Federal Tax Was Not a Tax

1. *Overview*

This Chapter reviews all of the Supreme Court's rulings in this area, the most important of which have been discussed above. The Supreme Court ruled unconstitutional federal taxes in five decisions from 1922 to 1936 on the ground that they were not true taxes but rather were regulations of matters beyond the power of Congress. These five opinions stated various considerations, including principally these [with comments in brackets]:

---

469 *See* Ch. V.D.3.b.

470 *See* Hellerstein & Hellerstein, *State Taxation*, ch. 4.

471 Margaret Spahr, The Supreme Court on the Incedence and Effects of Taxation: An Analysis of Economic Theory Embedded in the Constitutional Law Derived from the Explicit Tax Clauses, Smith College Studies in History (Jan.-July, 1925) (reprinted by Making of the Modern Law, Legal Treatises, 1800-1926).

472 Hellerstein & Hellerstein, *State Taxation*, ch. 3.

- The label "tax" is not necessarily dispositive.[473] [Disregard of labels is standard substance over form jurisprudence.]
- The regulatory or penalizing purpose or effect of the tax so predominated that it was not merely incidental and the Court characterized the tax as wholly regulatory, whether or not it also raised significant revenue.[474] [None of the opinions clearly establish whether the regulatory aim has to be exclusive, but the group of opinions suggests that the Court applied an either/or approach to mixed purpose exactions. In more recent years the Court has admitted that a tax with a primary purpose to regulate is a true tax.[475]]
- The subject of the tax is a disliked circumstance that is being penalized, thus evidencing Congress' intent to coerce avoidance of the taxed circumstance.[476] [This fact should be neutral because it ignores the inherent power of taxes to regulate, including regulation of matters outside the regulatory power of the United States, as discussed above in Chapter III.E.1.]
- The tax is not "naturally and reasonably adapted" to collecting taxes.[477] [This ignores the many taxes upheld despite intent to destroy the taxed object, such as the tax on state bank notes in *Veazie Bank v. Fenno*, and the taxes on various narcotics, as discussed above in Chapter III.E.5.]
- The tax is so exorbitant as to be presumably totally effective in terminating the taxed activity, and thus preclude the possibility of collecting any tax, thus forcing the tax to rely on regulatory authority for justification.[478] [But

---

[473] United States v. Constantine, 296 U.S. 287 (1935) (Invalidated penalty tax on liquor dealing that was illegal under state law only. The tax originally had been adopted to penalize activity that was illegal under the Eighteenth Amendment, but when Prohibition was repealed the federal government had no basis to penalize violation of state law. It could not recharacterize what was initially clearly a penalty into a tax by calling it that). *See* Ch. III.A (explaining how *Constantine* is the hard facts case that made bad law). *Cf.* United States v. Kahriger, 345 U.S. 22 (1952) (that an ambiguous license fee was labeled a tax in its title had some bearing on the Court's determination that it was a tax; a measure bears the indicia of a tax when the statute labels it a tax and locates it in the Revenue Code. Wagering excise tax ruled constitutional); Dep't of Revenue v. Kurth Ranch, 511 U.S. 767 (1994) (discounted labels of a tax in the different context of double jeopardy, as discussed in Ch. VII.E).

[474] J.W. Bailey v. Drexel Furn. Co., 259 U.S. 20 (1922) (child labor); Hill v. Wallace, 259 U.S. 44 (1922) (futures speculation); United States v. Butler, 297 U.S. 1, 60 (1936) (in contrast to the other two cases, the tax at issue here raised substantial revenue and was intended to raise revenue, but the Court found regulation to be the sole purpose of the tax).

[475] United States v. Sanchez, 340 U.S. 42 (1950); Nat'l Fed'n of Indep. Bus. v. Sebelius, 567 U.S. 519 (2012). *Cf.* Pittsburgh v. Alco Parking Corp., 417 U.S. 369, 375 (1974) (state tax).

[476] J.W. Bailey v. Drexel Furn. Co., 259 U.S. 20 (1922) (child labor); Hill v. Wallace, 259 U.S. 44 (1922) (futures speculation).

[477] J.W. Bailey v. Drexel Furn. Co., 259 U.S. 20, 43 (1922).

[478] Trusler v. Crooks, 269 U.S. 475 (1926). *Constantine* suggests this ground on the basis of a comparison of the $1,000 tax at issue with another parallel $20 tax, which was admitted to be a tax. United States v. Constantine, 296 U.S. 287 (1935).

not much tax need be collected to avoid this category, and the Court later seemed willing to accept any amount.[479]]

- The presence of "elaborate specifications" or "detailed specifications" or "detailed regulation of a concern or business" in the tax act describing what was to be taxed indicates a similarity to a regulation.[480] [Several caveats apply to this ground. First the two opinions relying on these grounds purported not to go beyond the face of the statute. Second, the amount of regulation at issue in those two cases was much more limited than in the New Deal cases involving complex industry codes, but which did not rely on that fact.[481] Third, the factor does not apply to procedural requirements (like reporting and record keeping) that are reasonably incident to a tax, even including obtaining a license for criminal conduct and firearms and narcotics dealing regulations and registration.]
- The event that is taxed is the commission of a state crime.[482] [However, other federal taxes have been upheld where the same fact existed; for example the *License Tax Cases* and the narcotics tax cases.[483]]
- The tax is not an exaction for the support of government (the definition of tax applied by the Court in the case), but rather is an expropriation from one group for the benefit of another, as evidenced by its variability depending on market conditions.[484] [This factor is implied by and limited to the *Butler* decision, which dealt with an Act that created a unique system of recapturing what were considered to be excess profits of the commodity

---

[479] *See* Ch. III.E.7 and Sonzinsky v. United States, 300 U.S. 506, 513 n. 1 (1937) ("The $ 200 tax was paid by 27 dealers in 1934, and by 22 dealers in 1935."); United States v. Miller, 307 U.S. 174 (1939) (similar to *Sonzinsky*); United States v. Kahriger, 345 U.S. 22 n. 4 (1953) ($4,371,869 was enough although $400M had been projected; the opinion also indicated the sufficient amount raised by other regulatory type taxes: "$ 3,501 collected under the tax on adulterated and process or renovated butter and filled cheese, the $ 914,910 collected under the tax on narcotics, including marijuana and special taxes, and the $ 28,911 collected under the tax on firearms, transfer and occupational taxes."); United States v. Sanchez, 340 U.S. 42 (1950) ("negligible," but legislative history stated a purpose to raise revenue).

[480] J.W. Bailey v. Drexel Furn. Co., 259 U.S. 20, 41 (1922); relied on by Hill v. Wallace, 259 U.S. 44 (1922).

[481] Neither *Butler* nor *Constantine* involved any objections to allegedly detailed or complex regulations.

[482] United States v. Constantine, 296 U.S. 287 (1935) (while admitting that other taxes had been approved even though the persons taxed were doing illegal acts).

[483] License Tax Cases, 72 U.S. 462 (1867); for narcotics cases, *see* Ch. III.E.1.

[484] United States v. Butler, 297 U.S. 1, 60 (1936).

processors and transferring them to the farmers, which amounts also was indeterminate, in that the amounts varied with the market prices.][485]

None of these five decisions has been explicitly overruled. However, subsequent Supreme Court opinions have cast doubt on them, including principally the following:

- *Bob Jones University* stated that a tax is intended to raise revenue, but that *Sonzinsky* had rejected the distinction between regulatory and revenue raising taxes (citing *Hill v. Wallace* and *Lederer*).[486] Evidently this meant that *Bob Jones* and *Sonzinsky* recognized that a tax could also have a regulatory purpose and function, but that understanding did not start with *Sonzinsky*.[487]
- *Sonzinsky* upheld a firearms tax that imposed a $200 license tax on firearms dealers and a $200 per firearm tax on transfers of guns, which the taxpayer claimed had an average value of $20. Thus the tax could be said to be exorbitant. Nevertheless it was a true tax because (a) it raised some revenue ($5,400 and $4,400 in two years), (b) it "operates as a tax," (c) it is not a subservient part of a larger regulatory scheme (and the registration of dealers and buyers is not such regulation), and (d) the Court cannot inquire into the motives of Congress.[488]
- *Helvering v. Davis* and *Steward Machine* upheld the federal unemployment and social security taxes, basically federalizing the problems of unemployment and old age compensation, which previously had been thought to be local welfare problems.[489]
- *Sanchez* upheld the Marijuana Tax Act without mentioning any of the five decisions finding taxes to be solely regulations in the 1922 to 1936 period, or relying on the Commerce Clause, but reciting the power of a federal tax to regulate what the United States cannot regulate directly.

---

[485] Although *Butler* stated that the purpose and effect of the act was "to take money from the processor and bestow it upon farmers" rather than to raise general revenue, it did not clearly base its reasoning on that fact. 297 U.S. at 58. *Cf.* Calder v. Bull, 3 U.S. 386, 388 (1798) (explaining legislative acts that would fall outside the limits of a republican government's powers to include "a law that takes property from A. and gives it to B: It is against all reason and justice, for a people to entrust a Legislature with SUCH powers; and, therefore, it cannot be presumed that they have done it."). *See* Kermit Roosevelt III, *Forget the Fundamentals: Fixing Substantive Due Process*, 8 *U. Pa. J. Const. Law* 983, 986 (2006) (explaining that defining the outer boundaries of legislative power was the original undertaking that came to be called substantive due process).

[486] Bob Jones Univ. v. Simon, 416 U.S. 725, 741 n. 12 (1974), *citing* Sonzinsky v. United States, 300 U.S. 506, 513 (1937).

[487] *See* Ch. III.E.1.

[488] Sonzinsky v. United States, 300 U.S. 506, 513 n. 1 (1937); United States v. Miller, 307 U.S. 174 (1939) (similar to *Sonzinsky*).

[489] *See* Ch. III.E.2.b.

- *Kahriger* upheld a federal wagering tax under the taxing power, stating "It is hard to understand why the power to tax should raise more doubts because of indirect effects than other federal powers."[490]
- *Minor* upheld a tax on illegal drugs.[491]
- *Sebelius* (2012) did not rely on *Butler*, but cited it and the *Child Labor Tax Case* and described them as one of a few earlier decisions that had aggressively policed the limits of taxation, but that "more often and more recently we have declined to closely examine the regulatory motive or effect of revenue-raising measures."[492]

Some might discern a pattern that the Court takes a more lenient view of regulatory taxes imposed on disfavored activities (drugs, liquor, gambling, firearms) than on more neutral economic activities (using children in manufacturing). No such pattern exists. *Constantine* struck down a tax on liquor dealers. Moreover, there is no way to draw a meaningful line between favored and disfavored activities: today there is quite a resurgence of favor towards gun ownership;[493] and the use of child labor in manufacturing is no longer viewed so benignly as in the 1920s. Therefore, no reasoned explanation for the cases can be based on such a division.

Finally, most of the decisions that struck down taxes by first ruling they were not taxes also relied on a very constricted view of the Commerce Clause, which later decisions have reversed, as reflected in the following Chapter.[494] It is likely that such view colored the tax classification in those cases, supplying another reason that is of substantially diminished current force.

2. *Tax and Regulation Chronology*

Congress' powers to regulate certain subjects and to tax cannot be disentangled, because (1) many if not most taxes, or at least taxing rules, inherently regulate in some degree by influencing the behavior of taxpayers,[495] and (2) the history of each power in the Supreme Court's decisions plays off the other in a fascinating fashion. Moreover, the tax versus regulation dichotomy is at the intersection of four core provisions of the Constitution affecting federal power:

- The taxing power;
- The Commerce Clause;
- The Tenth Amendment;
- The Fifth Amendment's Due Process and Eminent Domain Clauses.

---

490 United States v. Kahriger, 345 U.S. 22, 31 (1953).

491 Minor v. United States, 396 U.S. 87 (1969).

492 Nat'l Fed'n of Indep. Bus. v. Sebelius, 567 U.S. 519 (2012). *See* Ch. III.E.2.c.

493 *See, e.g.*, District of Columbia v. Heller, 554 U.S. 570 (2008).

494 *See* Wickard v. Filburn, 317 U.S. 111, 122 n. 21 (1942).

495 *See, e.g.*, Sonzinsky v. United States, 300 U.S. 506, 513 (1937) ("Every tax is in some measure regulatory."); Steward Machine Co. v. Davis, 301 U.S. 548, 589-590 (1937).

They fit together in this way:

- If the levy is not a tax, is must either be authorized by the Commerce Clause or some other enumerated power (*e.g.*, war power or power over foreign commerce), or it is likely to fail as a regulation of a matter either outside the enumerated powers or deemed reserved to the states under the Tenth Amendment, or possibly as a taking without just compensation.
- If it is a true tax, to date no such tax has been ruled to violate the Tenth Amendment, or the Fifth Amendment except for retroactive taxes, and the applicability of the Commerce Clause is irrelevant.

Governmental regulations, as well as taxation, necessarily restrict rights, usually meaning rights to property or to contract with respect to property. Therefore, the issues of taxation and regulation implicate the broader constitutional subjects of property and contract, liberty and due process, under the Constitution. The latter subjects frequently are not integrated with tax and regulation, but should be. The Court's use of substantive due process to limit state and federal regulation progressed in tandem with its willingness to rule that federal taxes were not true taxes and were regulations beyond the power of Congress.[496] The fight to establish first governmental regulatory power and then federal regulatory power has been well chronicled and is well known to experts in the area but the trends and threads can be invisible to the casual observer.

The chronology presented below attempts to (1) recount the ebb and flow of the major rulings on regulation in a way that shows the general trends, while (2) interrelating the frequently parallel tax rulings that questioned or dealt with the taxes' regulatory aspects. The compressed conclusions one may draw from these cases (and other observations discussed elsewhere in this book) are that (1) the Court brought to the subject of federal taxation a strong willingness to make it work for the country, including refusing to condemn taxes as regulatory, due in large part to an understanding that the inability to tax had been the major shortcoming of the Articles of Confederation; (2) at the height of the Gilded Age when railroads and other business interests were succeeding in opposing federal and state regulation, the Court in *Pollock* (1895) stripped out of the Constitution the ability of the federal government to tax income from capital and made it very difficult to tax wage income alone; (3) nevertheless, the Court generally continued to view the taxing power as so expansive that decisions like *McCray* (1904) continued to hold that the United States could tax that which it could not regulate and could do so for the clear purpose of regulation; but (4) by the 1920s the conservative majority of the Court had solidified its ability and willingness to deny to states and the United States the powers to regulate most business activity and to simply announce that a federal tax was not a tax; (5) which majority waned after 1936, with the Court returning to its respect for a federal tax as a tax, while it also greatly expanded its view of the federal Commerce Clause powers.

---

[496] For discussion of substantive due process, *see* Ch. V.D.3.b(7).

Thus the list includes all of the tax versus regulation decisions of the Court and the major due process and regulation decisions. The latter group necessarily includes certain important state tax cases.

- 1819 (impairment of contract as a limiter of regulation): Chief Justice Marshall interpreted the Contracts Clause in the *Dartmouth College Case* to protect a contract (the college's charter) under which the college could claim a beneficial property right that was enforceable in court.[497] Although Article I, section 10, clause 1 of the Constitution applies only to the states, federal taxpayers later argued for "liberty of contract" under the Due Process Clause of the Fifth Amendment and as an aspect of liberty.[498] Furthermore, many state taxpayers succeeded in avoiding state taxes through an impairment of contract argument.[499]

- 1829 (intergovernmental immunity not dependent on regulation): *Weston v. Charleston* ruled that a nondiscriminatory city tax on notes was an unconstitutional tax on the United States when applied to federal notes.[500] The opinion refused to adopt the approach of the dissent that distinguished the case from *McCulloch v. Maryland*, on the ground that the state was trying to regulate in *McCulloch*, whereas the Charleston levy was not intended to regulate.[501] This case illustrates the difference between the intergovernmental immunity from taxation, which immunity can be absolute as in *Weston*, and regulation of one government by another government, which can be applied without immunity concerns if the regulations is within the first government's power.

- 1837 (contract rights limited to prevent monopoly): The *Charles River Bridge Case* ruled that the state's authorization of a new bridge did not impair an obligation of contract to the company that was chartered to build the pre-existing bridge, based on a narrow construction of the prior contract.[502] Although not a federal case, it reflected the tension between property rights authorities on the one hand (like *Dartmouth College*, which were much more numerous) and cases upholding regulatory power (which continued in the *Slaughter-House Cases* and *Munn v. Illinois*, but started to go

---

[497] Dartmouth College v. Woodward, 17 U.S. 518 (1819). *See also* Sturges v. Crowninshield, 17 U.S. 122 (1819) (holding states could pass debtor relief laws so long as they did not impair the obligation of contract).

[498] *See* Ch. V.D.3.b(7).

[499] *See, e.g.*, New Jersey v. Wilson, 11 U.S. 164 (1812); Dodge v. Woolsey, 59 U.S. 331 (1856); Home of the Friendless v. Rouse, 75 U.S. 430 (1868) (dissenters argued for the reversal of *New Jersey v. Wilson*, which never occurred). The doctrine was limited, however, by requiring great clarity in proving the exemption, as early pointed out in Providence Bank v. Billings, 29 U.S. 514, 545-546 (1830), *see* James L. Kainen, *Nineteenth Century Interpretations of the Federal Contract Clause: The Transformation from Vested to Substantive Rights Against the State*, 31 Buff. L. Rev. 381, 386 (1982) (explaining how the Contract Clause gave way to substantive due process).

[500] Weston v. Charleston, 27 U.S. 449, 466 (1829).

[501] Donald G. Morgan, Justice William Johnson 249-250 (1954).

[502] Proprietors of Charles River Bridge v. Proprietors of Warren Bridge, 36 U.S. 420 (1837).

into decline thereafter, culminating in *Lochner*, *Hammer v. Dagenhart* and the *Child Labor Tax Case*).[503] Astute commentators have viewed the *Charles River Bridge Case* as an activist ruling of the Court that actually favored the interests of property owners who did not want their ability to profit from the expanding economy to be restricted by the monopolies of others, in contrast to the appearance of decreasing the rights of property.[504]

- 1865 (federal excise tax imposed on occupation that United States perhaps could not regulate): *McGuire v. Commonwealth* upheld a state conviction of a person who had illegally operated a bar, but who had paid a federal license tax for running a bar, because the federal law explicitly stated it did not grant authority to run a bar.[505] Although the defendant raised the question of the United States' power to regulate the local liquor business, the Court did not answer it.

- 1867 (federal excise tax imposed on occupation that United States perhaps could not regulate): The same federal tax at issue in *McGuire* was re-examined in the related *License Tax Cases*; the Court addressed federal rather than state prosecution for failure to pay the federal license taxes, even for occupations that were illegal under state law.[506] The Civil War internal revenue tax statute provided that no person shall carry out various occupations unless they obtained licenses from the government for specified dollar amounts to be paid for each license. The amounts were not clearly denominated taxes, although the original legislation did call them taxes in one section.[507] In 1866 the statute was amended to label the fee a "special tax."[508] The Court noted that the amendment clarified the intent of Congress, but it had no trouble treating the 1864 license fee as a tax, principally because it did not serve another function: specifically it did not give authority to carry on the businesses taxed; rather it was a precondition to carrying on the business. This is a rather bold way to circumvent the claim that the federal government was trying to regulate intrastate business by licensing conduct that the

---

503 *See infra* this Chapter.

504 *See* Richard Hofstadter, The American Political Tradition 84 (1974 Vintage Ed.) (citing Charles Warren).

505 McGuire v. Commonwealth, 70 U.S. 387 (1865) (the opinion did not directly evaluate the power to tax, but only ruled that it did not grant a right to run the bar so that the licensee could be convicted by the state).

506 License Tax Cases, 72 U.S. 462 (1867). The federal government can even prosecute a person that violated another federal law against liquor, despite the fact that the person had paid the liquor tax. *See* United States v. Forty-Three Gallons of Whiskey, 108 U.S. 491 (1883).

507 13 Stat. 223, 248-249 et seq. (1864) ("besides being liable to the payment of the tax").

508 Ch. 184, 14 Stat. 113 (1866).

states prohibited: the federal license didn't authorize anything other than avoiding arrest for not paying a tax.[509]

- 1869 (federal tax in aid of another federal power): *Veazie Bank v. Fenno* ruled that the United States could tax state chartered bank notes at a prohibitive rate so as to coerce state banks to stopping issuing notes, leaving the national bank notes unchallenged.[510] As discussed in Chapter II.C.3, the case is an important one in the field of intergovernmental immunity; as discussed in Chapter V.C.3.c, it also raised the issue of direct tax; but it is also important in juxtaposition of regulation and taxation. The opinion is clear that the tax at issue was a true tax; the principal rejected argument against the tax was that it was an unapportioned direct tax. And yet, the Court justified it also as supporting the power to create a national paper currency. Therefore, it also was viewed as a tax levied in aid of another power.[511]
- 1869 (regulatory effect that is too remote from the taxing power to be necessary and proper): As sort of an exception to the *License Tax Cases* that proves the rule that things can be taxed that cannot be regulated, *Dewitt* held that a federal revenue statute making sale of certain oils a crime (but not imposing a tax and not basing the crime on failure to pay a tax) was not ancillary to the taxing power and was an invalid police regulation because the oils specified were not the ones taxed.[512] Rather the government's argument was that by criminalizing the sale of those oils, the sale of the taxed oils would increase, which the Court found too remote a connection to taxation to justify the criminalization. The opinion indicated that regulation of the taxed items would not run afoul of this problem. Even though the criminal penalty was ruled unconstitutional this decision is not categorized as holding a federal tax unconstitutional because it did not do so.
- 1873 (state regulation establishing a monopoly upheld against Fourteenth Amendment challenge): In the important *Slaughter-House Cases* the Court cited the *License Tax Cases* and *Dewitt* as consistent with the view that the

---

[509] 72 U.S. at 471-473 ("It is given in the Constitution, with only one exception and only two qualifications. Congress cannot tax exports, and it must impose direct taxes by the rule of apportionment, and indirect taxes by the rule of uniformity. Thus limited, and thus only, it reaches every subject, and may be exercised at discretion. But it reaches only existing subjects. Congress cannot authorize a trade or business within a State in order to tax it. . . . There is nothing hostile or contradictory, therefore, in the acts of Congress to the legislation of the States. What the latter prohibits, the former, if the business is found existing notwithstanding the prohibition, discourages by taxation. The two lines of legislation proceed in the same direction, and tend to the same result. It would be a judicial anomaly, as singular as indefensible, if we should hold a violation of the laws of the State to be a justification for the violation of the laws of the Union.").

[510] Veazie Bank v. Fenno, 75 U.S. 533, 541 (1869).

[511] *See* United States v. Kahriger, 345 U.S. 22, 31 n. 6 (1953) (*Veazie* depended partly on the alternate ground of the federal power to provide currency); *see* Ch. III.E.4.a.

[512] United States v. Dewitt, 76 U.S. 41 (1869). *See* United States v. Lopez, 514 U.S. 549 (1995) (identifying *Dewitt* as the first case ruling a federal statute unconstitutional due to exceeding the reach of the Commerce Clause).

local government had plenary authority to regulate slaughter houses in New Orleans and did not violate the Constitution by creating a monopoly.[513] Although the Fourteenth Amendment might not seem relevant to a book on constitutional issues in federal taxation, this case is the starting point for substantive due process, which has been argued against federal taxes that regulate. The Fourteenth Amendment does not apply to the United States; it was adopted to protect the newly freed slaves and their progeny in the future from ill treatment at the hands of the southern states. In what is the classic example of lawyers emphasizing the words rather than the intent of laws, the initial history of the Fourteenth Amendment is a story of its use to protect business interests.[514] In the *Slaughter-House Cases* the losing plaintiffs' argument was: ". . . the first interpretation given to the Fourteenth Amendment by a lawyer in a Supreme Court case [and it] was a laissez faire interpretation, based upon a premise of individualism and limited government."[515] Nevertheless, the municipal monopoly on butchering survived the constitutional attack because the Court rejected an expansive reading of the part of the Fourteenth Amendment that the plaintiffs relied on: the Privileges and Immunities Clause. Justice Field's dissent argued for expansion of that Clause (which never occurred), but Justice Bradley's dissent proved most prescient in suggesting that a "liberty of contract" was implied in the Due Process Clause of the Fourteenth Amendment.[516] That argument was to become a foundation of substantive due process.[517] Moreover, Justice Field was to have a big hand in that process.[518] The enduring importance of the *Slaughter-House Cases* in the minds of some is shown by an editorial calling for its reversal on January 5, 2021 by a prominent conservative journalist.[519]

- 1877 (second Fourteenth Amendment loss by business interests): The issue in the *Slaughter-House Cases* was joined again the *Granger Cases*, *Munn v.*

[513] Slaughter-House Cases, 83 U.S. 36 (1873).

[514] *See generally* Twiss.

[515] *Id.* at 55.

[516] *Id.* at 56-57. Justice Bradley played a large role in other important Court decisions, including the *Legal Tender Cases*, Knox v. Lee, 79 U.S. 457 (1871), as discussed in Cortlandt Parker, Mr. Justice Bradley 20 (1893).

[517] It was first used by the majority in Allgeyer v. Louisiana, 165 U.S. 578 (1897), and later in Adkins v. Children's Hospital, 261 U.S. 525 (1923), and most infamously in Lochner v. New York, 198 U.S. 45 (1905). For discussion of *Allgeyer* and *Lochner*, *see* David P. Currie, *The Constitution in the Supreme Court*, 52 U. Chi. L. Rev. 324, 375-382 (1985); Russell Galloway, The Rich and Poor in Supreme Court History 96 (1982). *See* Ch. V.D.3.b(7).

[518] Inter alia, *see In re* Neagle, 135 U.S. 1 (1890) (concerning murder by Justice Field's Marshal).

[519] George F. Will, *It's time for the Supreme Court to curb one of its worst precedents*, Washington Post (Jan. 5, 2021).

Illinois.[520] The *Munn* opinion is viewed as a watershed holding that set in motion substantial business reaction to state and then federal regulatory power, because it involved parties (railroads) that were far more important than the independent butchers in New Orleans.[521] The ultimate result of the business reaction to *Munn* was the invention of the theory of substantive due process, being substantive rights housed in the Due Process Clause, which could place railroads and other large businesses in the posture of the thwarted butchers who lost the *Slaughter-House Cases*. Those substantive due process rights were later applied to strike down various state regulations and taxes and then federal regulations and taxes. Chief Justice Waite's opinion in *Munn* ruled for the state on the basis that the grain business affected the public and the state had the power to change the law to regulate it (harkening back to the *Charles River Bridge* case).[522] *Munn* is most remembered for Justice Field's dissent, which struck these chords that appear frequently in later arguments against federal taxes as well as regulations: "If this be sound law, if there be no protection, either in the principles upon which our republican government is founded, or in the prohibitions of the Constitution against such invasion of private rights, all property and all business in the State are held at the mercy of a majority of its legislature. . . . [T]he doctrine which allows the legislature to interfere with and regulate the charges which the owners of property thus, employed shall make for its use, that is, the rates at which all these different kinds of business shall be carried on, has never before been asserted, so far as I am aware, by any judicial tribunal in the United States."[523] The emphasis is on deprivation of liberty and property and contract without due process of law.

- 1884 (the original regulation through a tax that was not a true tax): The *Head Money Cases* upheld a federal "duty" of 50 cents per person arriving as an immigrant at a port, to be paid by ship owner; the funds were paid into the Treasury to be used to regulate immigration and assist immigrants.[524]

---

[520] Munn v. Illinois, 94 U.S. 113 (1877). At issue in *Munn* was an Illinois constitutional requirement and subsequent statute that regulated grain elevators and railroads in their carriage of grain. The statute required a license and imposed a maximum charge for grain storage. Munn was convicted of operating a grain warehouse without a license. Munn argued that it was being deprived of property without due process of law in violation of the Fourteenth Amendment, in effect depriving Munn of the right to do business without a license.

[521] Friedman, at 115-159.

[522] "From this it is apparent that, down to the time of the adoption of the Fourteenth Amendment, it was not supposed that statutes regulating the use, or even the price of the use, of private property necessarily deprived an owner of his property without due process of law. Under some circumstances they may, but not under all. The amendment does not change the law in this particular: it simply prevents the States from doing that which will operate as such a deprivation." 94 U.S. at 125. But the special treatment of state regulation of business affected with a public interest as determined by the courts was abandoned in Nebbia v. New York, 291 U.S. 502 (1934), which allowed state legislatures to determine which businesses they chose to regulate.

[523] 94 U.S. at 140-141.

[524] Edye v. Robertson, 112 U.S. 580 (1884) (Head Money Cases).

The opinion treated the statute as a regulation of commerce and not a tax, analogizing it to *Veazie Bank v. Fenno*.[525] The Court was firmly of the opinion that the regulatory aspects of the statute were appropriate governmental action and that states had already been excluded from legislating with respect to immigrants; therefore it was inescapable that the federal government could do so. The statute was labeled an immigration act, the "duty" was never called a tax, and the duty was collected by the customs officials.[526] The *Butler* majority thought the tax part of the Agricultural Adjustment Act was like the tax in the *Head Money Cases*, with the signal difference that Congress lacked the power to regulate.[527] Therefore, the *Head Money Cases* is a prime example of a charge as to which it doesn't matter whether it is classed as a tax or not (it is best characterized as a non tax regulatory charge).[528] However, the opinion's alternate discussion of the duty as a tax makes it fairly obvious that if the duty could only have been sustained as a tax, the Court would have called it a tax.

- 1897 (motive of Congress not relevant): *Kollock* upheld a criminal penalty for not paying the federal tax on colored margarine by recognizing its obvious regulatory purpose and effect, but stating that its primary object "must be assumed" to be revenue raising; it was a tax "on its face."[529] The opinion dismissed all consideration of legislative motive as irrelevant under the separation of powers, and stated that the very high rate of tax did not prevent the states from also regulating the product as they would like.
- 1898 (due process limitation on state non tax regulation): *Smyth v. Ames* ruled that while state regulation of railroad rates was constitutional, it must produce a "fair value" return to the railroad, which cannot be finally determined by regulatory agencies, but is subject to judicial review.[530] This important decision put the federal courts squarely in the middle of the state rate making business with a fact based standard supposedly enforcing due process that the Court later came to regret and change.[531] The analogy to regulation by taxation is that relatively contemporaneous tax decisions affirmed taxation despite obvious regulation, without much factual analysis, but the 1922 to 1936 period found the Court in a business similar to that of rate setting: looking for the nontax tax.

---

525 But the Court has recognized that *Veazie* was a dual power tax, not just a tax adopted as necessary and proper to another power. *See* United States v. Kahriger, 345 U.S. 22, 31 (1953).

526 Ch. 376, 22 Stat. 214.

527 United States v. Butler, 297 U.S. 1, 60 (1936).

528 *See* Ch. III.E.4.b.

529 *In re* Kollock, 165 U.S. 526, 536 (1897) ("The act before us is on its face an act for levying taxes, and although it may operate in so doing to prevent deception in the sale of oleomargarine as and for butter, its primary object must be assumed to be the raising of revenue.").

530 Smyth v. Ames, 169 U.S. 466 (1898). *See* Twiss, at 76-77. *See also* Chicago, M. & St. P. Ry. v. Minnesota, 134 U.S. 418, 458 (1890) (similar to *Smyth v. Ames*).

531 *See* Verizon Communs., Inc. v. FCC, 535 U.S. 467 (2002).

- 1900 (federal taxation of a matter purely regulated by states): The important decision *Knowlton v. Moore* ruled that the succession tax did not interfere with the states' ability to regulate transmission of property at death, because it only fell on that universal subject of taxation, the transmission of property.[532] Thus the Court avoided the assertion that because states exclusively regulate estates, the federal taxing power was reduced. This approach rejected the substance over form view of what was being taxed.
- 1903 (regulation under the Commerce Clause): *Champion v. Ames*, a very important constitutional decision, rejected an attack on federal regulation of lotteries under the Commerce Clause.[533] The case is related to tax cases because it reflects the same expansive view of one power that was applied to another power, the taxing power, the next year in *McCray*, and the opinion made clear that taxes could regulate (and when the government levying the tax was a state and the tax impinged on interstate commerce it was an invalid regulation).
- 1904 (federal tax could regulate matter outside of Congress' power to regulate): *McCray* is the earliest case in which a federal tax was *vigorously* contested (*Kollock* was not as vigorously contested; William D. Guthrie[534] appeared for the taxpayer in *McCray*) as improperly regulating local commerce without any constitutional justification other than the taxing power (*i.e.*, distinguished from the tax and regulation of currency in *Veazie Bank v. Fenno* and the regulation of immigration in the *Head Money Cases*), and not involving intergovernmental immunity (such as *Collector v. Day*).[535] It is the first such Supreme Court case in which the taxpayer specifically relied on the Tenth Amendment. The case involved what was clearly a regulatory measure affecting local commerce: the manufacture and sale of butter and margarine. Beginning in 1886 the act aimed to prevent the deceptive packaging and coloring of margarine to look like butter, both by packaging regulations and by taxes on every level of manufacture and sale including a two cents per

---

[532] Knowlton v. Moore, 178 U.S. 41, 59 (1900).

[533] Champion v. Ames, 188 U.S. 321 (1903) (The Lottery Case). *See* United States Dep't of Treasury v. Fabe, 508 U.S. 491 (1993) (identifying *Ames* as the decision exemplifying the Court's recognition of the increased interconnectedness of the national economy); United States v. Kahriger, 345 U.S. 22 n. 6 (1953) (cited by Justice Reed in support of his wondering why taxes sometimes have a harder time than Commerce Clause cases before the Court).

[534] *See* Ch. I.E.3.

[535] McCray v. United States, 195 U.S. 27 (1904). *See also* Cliff v. United States, 195 U.S. 159 (1904) (also involving the oleo tax). The Lawyers' Edition of *McCray* reveals that the taxpayer could not cite any on point authority for his Tenth Amendment arguments. *See* John B. Waite, *May Congress Levy Money Exactions Designed as "Taxes" Solely for the Purpose of Destruction?*, 6 MICH. L. REV. 277, 279, 289-290 (1908) ("Because the tax raised little if any revenue and was clearly for the purpose of destroying the trade in colored oleo, which congress had no right to regulate, how could the power to tax apply? Taxes exclude fees, but should also exclude impositions solely to regulate."); Fred. D. Ragan, *National Police Powers: The Oleomargarine Case*, in JOHN W. JOHNSON, HISTORIC U.S. COURT CASES 456 (2d Ed); Margulies, 5 J. S. LEGAL HIST. at 3.

pound tax on manufacture.[536] If the taxes were not paid and the rules not followed, a penalty of $1,000 to $5,000 could be applied. Effective July 2, 1902 Congress amended the Act to tax margarine at 10 cents a pound unless it had not been colored to look like butter, in which case the tax dropped to ¼ cent per pound.[537] The taxpayer attacked the 1902 amendment in what appears to have been a test case.[538] *McCray* ruled that (1) the motive of Congress in levying a tax would not be looked into (although the regulatory motive was clear); and (2) whether or not the Tenth Amendment reserved to the states the exclusive power to regulate butter and butter substitutes, the Congress could choose to tax in a way that also had the effect of regulating butter substitutes. Therefore, the *McCray* opinion means that Congress can raise taxes for reasons that might tend to regulate something it does not have the power to regulate, so long as it does not violate some fundamental right of persons, as opposed to the rights of states under the Tenth Amendment. *Flint v. Stone Tracy Co.* cited *McCray* in upholding the 1909 corporate excise tax.[539] *McCray* may be paired with *Champion v. Ames* decided one year earlier as two decisions establishing federal power to regulate, either under the Commerce Clause or the Taxing Power.[540]

- 1905 (tax plus criminal punishment): Frequently a state has made an act, such as selling cigarettes, a crime punishable in a certain way, and then has imposed a tax on a failure to obtain a license to sell cigarettes, even though the license would not permit the act to occur legally. The Court treated the state tax as a tax even though designed to prevent the thing that would be taxed.[541]
- 1905 (substantive due process applied to state regulation): *Lochner* struck down a state law imposing maximum hours for labor on the basis of Fourteenth Amendment "freedom of contract," also known as "substantive due

---

[536] Ch. 840, 24 Stat. 209 (Aug. 2, 1886).

[537] Ch. 784, 32 Stat. 193 (May 9, 1902).

[538] Within seven months after the 1902 Act was passed, the Court heard argument on the constitutionality of the amendment. In that time the government had to sue McCray for not paying the tax and McCray had to lose in the trial court, and the case went up to the Supreme Court, was briefed and argued. The taxpayer's attorney was William D. Guthrie; *see* Ch. I.E.3. The butterine tax had been adopted in 1886 during the administration of Grover Cleveland, the first Democrat elected President after the Civil War, and viewed as a reformer. The income tax that was ruled unconstitutional in *Pollock* was enacted during Cleveland's second administration through the efforts of William Jennings Bryan to add an income tax onto the tariff act. Justice White, who wrote the *McCray* opinion, with Justice Harlan dissented in *Pollock*.

[539] Flint v. Stone Tracy Co., 220 U.S. 107 (1911).

[540] Champion v. Ames, 188 U.S. 321 (1903) (also known as the *Lottery Case*).

[541] Hodge v. Muscatine County, 196 U.S. 276 (1905).

process."[542] Justice Holmes said in dissent that "This case is decided upon an economic theory which a large part of the country does not entertain. . . . [and the Fourteenth Amendment does not] enact Mr. Herbert Spencer's Social Statics." But other rights such as free speech that merit strict scrutiny of limitations, have begun to replace the substantive due process grounds of *Lochner*.[543] When a similar type of regulation of child labor was tried at the federal level it was struck down as a regulation,[544] and then when Congress relied on the taxing power, the the *Child Labor Tax Case* ruled it unconstitutional as not a tax but a regulation.[545]

- 1908: *Muller* surprisingly approved a maximum hour law for women, distinguishing *Lochner* on the basis of the gender of the persons protected.[546] This was not an indication of a turning by the Court but rather of the power of the Brandeis Brief.
- 1913 (regulatory tax): The Court viewed the McKinley Tariff Act tax of $10 a pound on manufacturing opium to be a tax, regardless of the indication that it was designed to discourage opium manufacture.[547] However, it construed the tax not to apply to secondary recovery of opium because a tax would not have been so intended; this uses the tax classification to limit the application of the tax when to expand it would be to make the tax more prohibitive and thus decrease revenue (a novel interpretive approach).
- 1916 (federal narcotics regulation through taxation): *United States v. Jin Fuey Moy* is the first decision of the Court to deal with the Harrison Narcotics Act. Justice Holmes affirmed quashing the indictment under the Harrison Act of a physician who prescribed opium, and who was charged with conspiring with the patient, who was the individual that had not paid the

[542] Lochner v. New York, 198 U.S. 45 (1905). The Court began to draw back from the broad freedom of contract statements in *Lochner* almost immediately. *See* Chicago, B. & Q. R. Co. v. McGuire, 219 U.S. 549, 567 (1911) ("There is no absolute freedom to do as one wills or to contract as one chooses. The guaranty of liberty does not withdraw from legislative supervision that wide department of activity which consists of the making of contracts, or deny to government the power to provide restrictive safeguards. Liberty implies the absence of arbitrary restraint, not immunity from reasonable regulations and prohibitions imposed in the interests of the community."). *Lochner* was overturned by *West Coast Hotel*. For substantive due process, *see* Ch. V.D.3.b(7).

[543] Sorrell v. IMS Health Inc., 564 U.S. 552 (2011) ("The Constitution 'does not enact Mr. Herbert Spencer's Social Statics.' [citing *Lochner*] (Holmes, J., dissenting). It does enact the First Amendment." The opinion struck down state limits on pharmaceutical drug salesmen.).

[544] Hammer v. Dagenhart, 247 U.S. 251 (1918).

[545] J.W. Bailey v. Drexel Furn. Co., 259 U.S. 20 (1922).

[546] Muller v. Oregon, 208 U.S. 412 (1908).

[547] United States v. Shelley, 229 U.S. 239 (1913).

required license tax.[548] Evidently the doctor was exempt on his own. The government attempted to show that "any person" in violation could include the entire population, and not just those who manufactured or dispensed opium. The opinion agreed that the unpaid levy was a true tax, noted that if it were a regulation it would be in serious doubt as invading a local matter, but construed the words not to apply to the opium buyer. The opinion clearly recognized that the tax also had a "moral end."

- 1918 (*Lochner* approach applied to federal regulation): *Hammer v. Dagenhart* struck down a child labor law enacted in 1916, which was not enforced by a tax.[549] Justice Holmes' dissent saw no difference between the regulation of margarine in *McCray* and of cotton manufacturing in *Dagenhart.* But others saw a difference and the stage was set for a showdown on whether a regulatory tax could avoid the *Dagenhart* result by being treated as a tax. In the interregnum between *Dagenhart* and the *Child Labor Tax Case*, Charles Warren observed that *Hammer v. Dagenhart* had "finally settled" the rule that the "National police powers may be restricted under the commerce clause," [but] . . ."there seem to be very little restrictions on the extent to which the National Government may regulate, under the taxing power, the production, manufacture, sale and transportation of articles within the states."[550] He was wrong both about *Hammer v. Dagenhart* and the taxing power. *Dagenhart* was overruled by *United States v. Darby.*[551]
- 1919 (light regulatory tax): *Doremus*, a second Harrison Narcotics Act case, followed *McCray* and *Jin Fuey Moy*, upholding the Harrison Narcotics Act tax as a tax.[552] The tax at issue again was a low one ($1 per year) on distributors, but it was accompanied by a detailed regulatory scheme that was upheld as a necessary incident of the tax. The small amount of the tax called its function as a tax, rather than a prohibitive amount, into question.[553] Again the Court expressed disinterest in investigating Congress' motives, understood that the act had regulatory purposes, and thought those pur-

---

[548] United States v. Jin Fuey Moy, 241 U.S. 394 (1916). *See also* Casey v. United States, 276 U.S. 413 (1928) (stating that the statute was even more tax-like after certain amendments and that it was too late in the day to apply the *Child Labor Tax Case* approach to the Harrison Narcotics Act); Linder v. United States, 268 U.S. 5 (1925) (finding that as a revenue statute it should be interpreted so as to avoid unconstitutionality, which apparently meant if it applied too harshly on physicians it would be subject to the *Child Labor Tax Case* approach; the doctor was released); United States v. Balint, 258 U.S. 250 (1922) (a taxing act with the incidental purpose to prevent the spread of addiction).

[549] Hammer v. Dagenhart, 247 U.S. 251 (1918).

[550] CHARLES WARREN, THE SUPREME COURT IN UNITED STATES HISTORY, Vol. II, pp. 738-739 (1922).

[551] United States v. Darby, 312 U.S. 100 (1941).

[552] United States v. Doremus, 249 U.S. 86 (1919). There were several cases upholding the Harrison Act, including Alston v. United States, 274 U.S. 289 (1927). The Act involved a detailed regulatory and record keeping scheme.

[553] *See* Nelson Lund, *Congressional Power over Taxation and Commerce: The Supreme Court's Lost Chance to Devise a Consistent Doctrine*, 18 TEX. TECH. L. REV. 729, 744 (1987).

poses not to be "arbitrary and unreasonable," but suited to the purpose of identifying the opium trade, and approved the levy as a tax. The purported tax need have only "some reasonable relation to the exercise of the taxing authority . . . ," and the Court will not inquire into Congress' other purposes; if it is within the taxing power it may regulate a matter within the exclusive jurisdiction of the states.[554] *Doremus* was decided a week before Congress began considering the bill that resulted in the *Child Labor Tax Case*.[555]

- 1921 (destructive federal tax): *Alaska Fish* upheld a tax intended to prevent wastage of herring, even though it was so heavy as to destroy the business taxed.[556]
- 1922 (Court examines Congress' motives): The *Child Labor Tax Case* tends to prove that the Court should not have abandoned its oft-stated injunction not to succumb to the temptation to evaluate Congress' motives in passing tax laws. Chief Justice Taft revealed almost too much when he said: "In the light of these features of the act, a court must be blind not to see that the so called tax is imposed to stop the employment of children within the age limits prescribed. Its prohibitory and regulatory effect and purpose are palpable. All others can see and understand this. How can we properly shut our minds to it?"[557] After *Hammer v. Dagenhart* Congress had set about immediately to replicate the child labor law through a brief taxing provision that was not a complicated regulatory system but simply a tax on mines and mills that employed child labor.[558] Nevertheless, in hindsight some opinions have characterized the child labor law as having a "detailed scheme of administration beyond the obvious fiscal needs . . . ."[559] The same mill operators involved in *Dagenhart* set about just as quickly to oppose the new statute, using the same federal district judge who had ruled against the

---

[554] 249 U.S. at 93.

[555] Margulies, 5 J. S. Legal Hist. at 3.

[556] Alaska Fish Salting & By-Products Co. v. Smith, 255 U.S. 44 (1921). *See also* Pacific American Fisheries v. Alaska, 269 U.S. 269 (1925) (same law imposed by territory).

[557] J.W. Bailey v. Drexel Furn. Co., 259 U.S. 20, 37 (1922). *See, e.g.*, Watts v. Indiana, 338 U.S. 49, 52 (1949) (applying the injunction to looking through to the facts in a civil rights setting). Chief Justice Taft's statement about blindness was so remarkable, it was called "famous": "And so, we would have to be that 'blind' Court, against which Mr. Chief Justice Taft admonished in a famous passage, Child Labor Tax Case, 259 U.S. 20, 37, that does not see what 'all others can see and understand' not to know that there is wide concern, both in and out of Congress, over some aspects of the exercise of the congressional power of investigation." United States v. Rumley, 345 U.S. 41, 44 (1953).

[558] The Revenue Act of 1918, 40 Stat. 1057, 1138 (1919). The act described the taxable mines and mills in one short paragraph, dependent solely on employing children under a certain age. The tax was an excise tax specially computed on the net income of the mill, at the non-confiscatory rate of ten percent. IRS officers were authorized to inspect work sites to determine taxability.

[559] Dissent of Justice Frankfurter in United States v. Kahriger, 345 U.S. 22, 39 (1953); Hill v. Wallace, 259 U.S. 44, 67 (1922) ("detailed regulations").

original child labor law.[560] The answer, and a reprise of the entire question of the alleged distinction between a valid tax and a valid or invalid regulation, was fully articulated in this excerpt from Chief Justice Taft's opinion in the *Child Labor Tax Case*, officially known as *J. W. Bailey v. Drexel Furn. Co.*: "Where the sovereign enacting the law has power to impose both tax and penalty the difference between revenue production and mere regulation may be immaterial, but not so when one sovereign can impose a tax only, and the power of regulation rests in another. Taxes are occasionally imposed in the discretion of the legislature on proper subjects with the primary motive of obtaining revenue from them and with the incidental motive of discouraging them by making their continuance onerous. They do not lose their character as taxes because of the incidental motive. But there comes a time in the extension of the penalizing features of the so called tax when it loses its character as such and becomes a mere penalty with the characteristics of regulation and punishment. Such is the case in the law before us. Although Congress does not invalidate the contract of employment or expressly declare that the employment within the mentioned ages is illegal, it does exhibit its intent practically to achieve the latter result by adopting the criteria of wrongdoing and imposing its principal consequence on those who transgress its standard. . . . The case before us cannot be distinguished from that of Hammer v. Dagenhart, 247 U.S. 251."[561] [Note: *Hammer* was overruled by *United States v. Darby*, 312 U.S. 100 (1941).] The opinion then said this was one of those laws Chief Justice Marshall had described as going too far.[562] The Court explained how a tax that was incidentally a regulation and a regulation that employed a tax as enforcement could be distinguished, largely based on (1) the extensive regulatory regime that accompanied the tax, and (2) the obvious purpose (which the Court normally says is

---

[560] *See* Cushman, at 247-249. As James MacGregor Burns put it: "Reformers had been fighting for a congressional ban on child labor for at least 20 years when in 1922 Taft voided Congress' levy of a child labor tax in *Bailey v. Drexel Furniture*." JAMES MACGREGOR BURNS, PACKING THE COURT 133 (2009) [hereinafter BURNS]. Chief Justice White died on May 19, 1921. An earlier attack on the tax had been argued before him in 1919 in the case of Atherton Mills v. Johnston, 259 U.S. 13 (1922). Presumably he delayed ruling because it was argued December 10, 1919, and it was restored to docket for reargument on June 6, 1921, after his death and shortly before President Harding nominated William H. Taft to be Chief Justice. The case was reargued March 7, 8, 1922 with the *Bailey* case and was dismissed as moot because the child who obtained the injunction preventing his firing under the labor law had moved from the state. Presumably Chief Justice White, who wrote the *McCray* opinion in 1904, was not sympathetic with the opponents of the tax.

[561] 259 U.S. at 36-40. Justice Sutherland cited this as the test in A. Magnano Co. v. Hamilton, 292 U.S. 40 (1934), which upheld the same margarine tax at issue in *McCray*.

[562] 259 U.S. at 39 (". . . This case requires as did the *Dagenhart* Case the application of the principle announced by Chief Justice Marshall in McCulloch v. Maryland, 4 Wheat. 316, 423, in a much quoted passage: 'Should Congress, in the execution of its powers, adopt measures which are prohibited by the Constitution; or should Congress, under the pretext of executing its powers, pass laws for the accomplishment of objects not intrusted to the government; it would become the painful duty of this tribunal, should a case requiring such a decision come before it, to say, that such an act was not the law of the land.'").

not relevant).[563] However, the regulatory scheme at issue in the *Child Labor Tax Case* was by no means extensive; it was simply intensive in the one act it taxed. The *Child Labor Tax Case* did not overrule *McCray*. Although the Court never overruled The *Child Labor Tax Case*, it severely distinguished it in *Steward*,[564] and diminished it in *Sebelius* (2012) while purporting to apply its three part test.[565]

- 1922 (monopoly wins against regulatory tax): *Hill v. Wallace* struck down one Futures Trading Act tax designed to force the exchange to adopt certain rules because it was so closely tied to regulation of the commodity exchange that it was not a tax but a regulation of a matter Congress could not regulate.[566] It was decided on the same day the Court decided the *Child Labor Tax Case* and indeed the opinion referred to the *Child Labor Tax* opinion for its reasoning.[567] It found the act not to be a revenue act but to be a regulatory measure and to be outside the power of the United States to regulate interstate commerce, because the operation of the Chicago Board of Trade was not in interstate commerce (or at least Congress did not have interstate commerce "in mind" when it enacted the tax[568]). Although never overruled, the Supreme Court subsequently lumped *Hill v. Wallace* with a group of decisions such as *Hammer v. Dagenhart* from a prior era of limited view of

[563] 259 U.S. at 36-37 ("It provides a heavy exaction for a departure from a detailed and specified course of conduct in business. That course of business is that employers shall employ in mines and quarries, children of an age greater than sixteen years; in mills and factories, children of an age greater than fourteen years, and shall prevent children of less than sixteen years in mills and factories from working more than eight hours a day or six days in the week. If an employer departs from this prescribed course of business, he is to pay to the Government one-tenth of his entire net income in the business for a full year. The amount is not to be proportioned in any degree to the extent or frequency of the departures, but is to be paid by the employer in full measure whether he employs five hundred children for a year, or employs only one for a day. Moreover, if he does not know the child is within the named age limit, he is not to pay; that is to say, it is only where he knowingly departs from the prescribed course that payment is to be exacted. Scienter is associated with penalties not with taxes. The employer's factory is to be subject to inspection at any time not only by the taxing officers of the Treasury, the Department normally charged with the collection of taxes, but also by the Secretary of Labor and his subordinates whose normal function is the advancement and protection of the welfare of the workers.").

[564] Steward Machine Co. v. Davis, 301 U.S. 548, 591 (1937) (the earlier case was decided "in the belief" that the United States had no interest in the activities regulated, and did not address a federal fiscal need); Sonzinsky v. United States, 300 U.S. 506, 513 (1937) (*Child Labor Tax Case* found a tax to be a penalty enforcing a regulation).

[565] *See* Ch. III.E.2.c(4).

[566] Hill v. Wallace, 259 U.S. 44 (1922).

[567] *Id.* at 67.

[568] Board of Trade v. Olsen, 262 U.S. 1, 32 (1923).

the Commerce Clause,[569] and also stated that it abandoned the distinction between regulatory and revenue raising taxes.[570]

- 1922 (due process federal tax case): *Lipke v. Lederer* was a difficult case producing a problematic decision that the Court has disavowed.[571] It involved the original Volsted Act section 35 that attempted to retain the federal liquor excise taxes that had been in place when liquor was legal at the federal level, but also doubled the taxes, and added a $500 or $1,000 amount that was clearly denominated as a penalty. The section did not attempt to label the penalty a tax; and it was not a penalty for nonpayment of the doubled tax because the tax could become due only after the illegal act was committed and evidently only upon assessment by the government after it had identified the crime, as opposed to a self-assessed tax. Therefore, the penalty of $500 was fairly clearly a regulatory penalty and not a tax. The ruling did not decide that the doubled tax was not a tax because it ruled that whichever it was, Lipke was entitled to pre-deprivation due process: "Section 35 prescribes no definite mode for enforcing the imposition which it directs, and, if it be interpreted as above stated [immediately above it was discussed as a tax], *we do not understand counsel for the United States claim that relief should be denied to the appellant.* [emphasis added] Before collection of taxes levied by statutes enacted in plain pursuance of the taxing power can be enforced, the taxpayer must be given fair opportunity for hearing—this is essential to due process of law. . . . And certainly we cannot conclude, in the absence of language admitting of no other construction, that Congress intended that penalties for crime should be enforced through the secret findings and summary action of executive officers. The guarantees of due process of law and trial by jury are not to be forgotten or disregarded. . . . A preliminary injunction should have been granted."[572] Therefore, it seems that the United States Attorney agreed with the Court that the relief should be granted, and that relief was simply a preliminary injunction. Justice Brandeis dissented, similarly addressing the exactions as possibly either tax or penalty, and not indicating that the Court had firmly fixed them as one or the other.
- 1923 (famous non tax substantive due process decision): *Adkins v. Children's Hospital* ruled a federal minimum wage law for women unconstitutional under the Fifth Amendment Due Process Clause as infringing the liberty

[569] Wickard v. Filburn, 317 U.S. 111, 122 n. 21 (1942).

[570] Bob Jones Univ. v. Simon, 416 U.S. 725, 741 n. 12 (1974) (citing Sonzinsky v. United States, 300 U.S. 506, 513 (1937), which did not so clearly abandon the distinction, although it did uphold a firearms tax that was fairly clearly regulatory). *See also* Steward Machine Co. v. Davis, 301 U.S. 548, 591 (1937) (indicating disagreement with the prior "belief" of the Court as to the lack of relationship of the tax to the fiscal need).

[571] Lipke v. Lederer, 259 U.S. 557 (1922). Bob Jones Univ. v. Simon, 416 U.S. 725 n. 12 (1974), cited *Lipke* along with *Hill v. Wallace* as no longer representing the Court's views.

[572] 259 U.S. at 562.

of contract.[573] Thus the victory in *Muller* based on protecting women was only temporary. Note that what the impairment of contract argument could do to state taxes, the liberty of contract argument could do to federal taxes, although the concepts were quite different.

- 1925 (federal regulation through taxation allowed): The Court again ruled the Harrison Narcotics Act to be a taxing act, but strictly construed it, because if it were a regulatory provision it would exceed the power of Congress by attempting to regulate medical practice, which was within the control of the states.[574]
- 1926 (if the potential taxpayers are smart enough to universally avoid the tax, then it may not be a tax): *Trusler v. Crooks* is a companion case with *Hill v. Wallace*, striking down a high tax on commodity futures trading that effectively would prohibit the sort of trading taxed if paid.[575] It was paid only once for purposes of this test case. The *Trusler* opinion relied on the reasoning of *Hill v. Wallace* and said the tax was not a tax. In contrast, if the potential taxpayer group were drug addicts, gamblers or other illegal actors, who are not able to completely avoid being caught, then the tax is almost certainly constitutional. *Trusler* was not likely to have been won by the government in light of the fact that the Attorney General stated in oral argument that he personally thought the tax unconstitutional.[576] Between 1922 and 1926 the regulatory portions of the Act were reenacted without the tax and upheld.[577]
- 1927 (federal regulation through taxation allowed): *Alston v. United States* again upheld the Harrison Narcotics Act.[578] The United States argued that the opium trade was a serious problem that had to be dealt with, but still did not rely on the Commerce Clause. Justice McReynolds stated that the act ". . . contain[s] nothing to indicate that by colorable use of taxation Congress is attempting to invade the reserved powers of the States."[579] This shows the willingness of even a conservative judge to accept a facial designation of a tax that clearly regulated as a tax.
- 1928 (regulation through a tariff tax): In *J. W. Hampton* an importer attacked the "flexible tariff," whereby President Coolidge had been authorized by Congress to adjust a tariff to more exactly remove the competitive

---

573 Adkins v. Children's Hospital, 261 U.S. 525 (1923), *overruled by* West Coast Hotel Co. v. Parrish, 300 U.S. 379 (1937).

574 Linder v. United States, 268 U.S. 5 (1925).

575 Trusler v. Crooks, 269 U.S. 475 (1926).

576 70 L. Ed. 365.

577 Bd. of Trade v. Olsen, 262 U.S. 1 (1923).

578 Alston v. United States, 274 U.S. 289 (1927). *See also* Blockburger v. United States, 284 U.S. 299 (1932) (rejected argument that multiple sales without paying stamp tax should not be separate crimes).

579 274 U.S. at 294.

advantage of lower foreign production costs.[580] The taxpayer argued that this system proved too clearly that the tariff was not a revenue raising tool but a local industry protection tool. Chief Justice Taft firmly rejected the argument on the grounds of the long history of tariffs as protective tools and the rubric that the primary purpose was revenue raising and the incidental purpose was protection.[581] In 1950 and 1974 the Court characterized *Hampton* as being a case in which it had recognized the revenue purpose as "only secondary."[582]

- 1928 (federal regulation through taxation): *Nigro v. United States* again upheld the Harrison Act.[583] Chief Justice Taft, speaking for the Court, said: "In interpreting the Act, we must assume that it is a taxing measure, for otherwise it would be no law at all. If it is a mere act for the purpose of regulating and restraining the purchase of the opiate and other drugs, it is beyond the power of Congress and must be regarded as invalid . . . ."[584]
- 1931 (civil penalty): *La Franca* involved a bootlegger in a position similar to that of *Lipke v. Lederer* (1922) except that La Franca also had been convicted of the Prohibition criminal violation rather than just charged, and had been required to pay $1,000 imposed by section 701 of the 1924 Revenue Act, which was not clearly labeled a tax.[585] Because of the prior conviction he was relieved of the "taxes" because another statute precluded a double "prosecution." The opinion ruled that the tax was not a tax but a punishment for purposes of applying the other statute, although it did not clearly call it a criminal punishment. The Court has since disavowed the distinction made in *Lipke*, at least for tax if not double jeopardy purposes.[586] For all these reasons, neither *La Franca* nor *Lipke* stands for any general principles about nominal or regulatory taxes not being taxes, although they may reflect how multiple punishments for double jeopardy purposes reflect a sui generis

---

[580] J. W. Hampton, Jr. & Co. v. United States, 276 U.S. 394 (1928).

[581] 276 U.S. at 412-413 ("So long as the motive of Congress and the effect of its legislative action are to secure revenue for the benefit of the general government, the existence of other motives in the selection of the subjects of taxes cannot invalidate Congressional action. As we said in the Child Labor Tax Case, 259 U.S. 20, 38: 'Taxes are occasionally imposed in the discretion of the legislature on proper subjects with the primary motive of obtaining revenue from them, and with the incidental motive of discouraging them by making their continuance onerous. They do not lose their character as taxes because of the incidental motive.' And so here, the fact that Congress declares that one of its motives in fixing the rates of duty is so to fix them that they shall encourage the industries of this country in the competition with producers in other countries in the sale of goods in this country, cannot invalidate a revenue act so framed. Section 315 and its provisions are within the power of Congress. The judgment of the Court of Customs Appeals is affirmed.").

[582] United States v. Sanchez, 340 U.S. 42 (1950); Pittsburgh v. Alco Parking Corp., 417 U.S. 369, 375 (1974).

[583] Nigro v. United States, 276 U.S. 332 (1928).

[584] 276 U.S. at 341.

[585] United States v. La Franca, 282 U.S. 568 (1931).

[586] Bob Jones Univ. v. Simon, 416 U.S. 725 n. 12 (1974) (cited *Lipke* along with *Hill v. Wallace* as no longer representing the Court's views).

definition of punishment.[587] That did not, however, stop opinions like *Carter Coal* from citing them for such a proposition.[588]

- 1934 (state tax designed to destroy): *A. Magnano Co. v. Hamilton* upheld a state tax on butter substitutes that was admittedly so high as to destroy the business taxed.[589] The Court stated that such a result, and even purpose of the government, was permissible so long as the power being employed was the power to tax and not some other invalid power, such as "the confiscation of property."[590] The opinion observed that if the amount of the tax had been lower, likely no one would have protested; and that the fact that a tax was heavy, indeed so heavy as to diminish or prevent the thing taxed, could not be a ground for ruling it unconstitutional, so long as it was a tax.
- 1935 (unique case inconsistent with later *Sonzinsky* and *Sanchez* rulings based on commission of state law crime): *Constantine* is both a unique case involving the peculiar circumstances of the repeal of the Eighteenth Amendment, and also a decision based on specific fact finding.[591] The defendant Constantine had been convicted of a federal crime specified in the taxing statute for nonpayment. The issue was not the punishment of federal tax nonpayment through a criminal enforcement but rather the constitutionality of a federal tax upon a state crime: it could be upheld as a tax but not as a punishment. The Court found the $1,000 amount must be a penalty for an act Congress no longer had the power to penalize, and therefore not a tax, also because it was imposed upon the commission of a state crime. The Internal Revenue Act of 1864 had created a series of federal license taxes, of which Section 79, ¶ Five, imposed a $25 tax on retail liquor dealers.[592] The Revenue Act of 1918 was approved in 1919 about a month after the Prohibition Amendment was ratified and about a year before it went into effect

---

[587] *See* dissent of Justice Stevens in Hudson v. United States, 522 U.S. 93 (1997) (explaining *La Franca*); Dep't of Revenue v. Kurth Ranch, 511 U.S. 767 n. 15 (1994) ("Notably, in reaching that conclusion we relied in part on an earlier case recognizing that a tax statute might be considered punitive in character for double jeopardy purposes. . . . That case, *United States v. La Franca* . . ."). *See also* Kennedy v. Mendoza-Martinez, 372 U.S. 144 (1963) (citing all of *Lipke*, *La Franca*, and *Constantine* in the context of whether deportation is a punishment that requires certain due process protections).

[588] Carter v. Carter Coal Co., 298 U.S. 238 (1936). *La Franca* also was cited for a suspect point in *Sebelius*, discussed in Ch. III.E.2.c(3)(d). Nat'l Fed'n of Indep. Bus. v. Sebelius, 567 U.S. 519 (2012).

[589] A. Magnano Co. v. Hamilton, 292 U.S. 40 (1934).

[590] *Id.* at 44.

[591] United States v. Constantine, 296 U.S. 287 (1935). Justices Cardozo, Brandeis and Stone dissented.

[592] Ch. 173, 1st Sess. 38th Cong., 13 Stat. 223, 252 (June 30, 1864). These were the taxes at issue in the *License Tax Cases* and clearly did not authorize the licensee to conduct the business, and the business might even be illegal under state law. License Tax Cases, 72 U.S. 462 (1867). The punishment for engaging in the business without the license was two years in jail and a $500 fine. Section 73. The fine was increased to $1,000 in 1868. 15 Stat. 143 (1868). The tax appeared in the Second Revised Statutes at page 622.

in 1920.[593] Section 1001(12) referenced the license taxes in the Revised Statutes and imposed a "special tax" of $1,000 on retail liquor dealers who were operating in 1919 in violation of state law (liquor dealing then being legal under federal law). This was the twelfth of a series of special taxes; the other 11 "special taxes" in section 1001 were in the range of $10 to $100. The Revenue Act of 1926 added the phrase "special excise tax" to directly refer to the $1,000 amount.[594] Nonpayment of this amount was the crime Constantine was convicted for violating as to the 1933-1934 year. The Twenty First Amendment was adopted December 5, 1933. For the July 1934-July 1935 year Constantine registered with the Treasury and paid the $25 tax for a retail liquor dealer; no earlier than September 13, 1934 the Treasury developed a tax stamp for an additional $1,000 tax, which it demanded of Constantine on October 1, 1934 and criminally charged him with selling liquor without paying on November 21, 1934.[595] From 1926 (immediately after the addition of the phrase "special excise tax" to the statute) to September 13, 1934 the Treasury treated the $1,000 as a penalty and not a tax in published guidance.[596] The factors cited by the opinion were (1) the liability was conditioned on the commission of a state crime (not just that the thing taxed might also be a crime, but the taxpayer must have violated a state law in order to owe the tax), (2) it was imposed in addition to an excise tax, and (3) it was exorbitant in relation to the amount of the excise tax.[597] However, the reasoning is inconsistent with the Court's unanimous 1950 opinion in *Sanchez*.[598] The Marijuana Tax Act also had a two level tax structure, with a $1 per ounce tax for registrants and a $100 per ounce tax for nonregistrants. *Sanchez* upheld the $100 tax as a true tax and explained it was intended to enforce registration. *Constantine* relied on both *Lipke* and *La Franca*. The Court has since disavowed the distinction between tax and penalty made in *Lipke*, and relied on in *La Franca*, at least for tax if not double jeopardy purposes.[599]

- 1936 (most prominent ruling that federal regulatory tax was not a tax): *Butler* stands for the proposition that a tax linked to a specific appropriation of the tax proceeds as part of a regulatory scheme is not a tax at all, based on an all or nothing approach to the act; and because the appropriation and regulation were for a purpose wholly reserved to the states by the Tenth

---

[593] 40 Stat. 1057.
[594] Revenue Act of 1926 § 701, 44 Stat. 9.
[595] Brief of United States, 1935 WL 32911 (Oct. 1935).
[596] *Id.* and Brief of Constantine, 1935 WL 32912 (Oct. 19, 1935).
[597] 296 U.S. 287, 292 n. 7 (1935).
[598] United States v. Sanchez, 340 U.S. 42 (1950).
[599] Bob Jones Univ. v. Simon, 416 U.S. 725 n. 12 (1974) (cited *Lipke* along with *Hill v. Wallace* as no longer representing the Court's views).

Amendment, the tax and the entire act were unconstitutional.[600] The tax differed from that in the *Child Labor Tax Case* and *Hill v. Wallace* in that the government wanted to and did collect substantial tax, as contrasted with taxing to discourage certain activities. As in the *Child Labor Tax Case*, the government did not defend *Butler* on the basis of the Commerce Clause; therefore, the entire defense rested on the taxing and spending powers.[601] The majority opinion interpreted the Constitution to authorize taxing and spending to provide for the general welfare, without being limited to taxing and spending only for the other enumerated powers.[602] But this did not reflect any liberality on the part of the otherwise conservative majority; it is fairly clear from the opinion itself that the Court was trying to avoid the other alternative and even more expansive interpretation that a tax could be for the purpose of regulating for the general welfare and not just to raise revenues to spend for the general welfare.[603] The opinion relied on the same sharpened vision used in the *Child Labor Tax Case*.[604] See Chapter III.F.

- 1936 (tax defended only under Commerce Clause): *Carter Coal* struck down the bituminous coal mining tax and code.[605] *Carter Coal* cannot be viewed as a ruling of tax unconstitutionality because the government did not even try to defend the tax as a tax but defended it wholly under the Commerce Clause.[606] The tax allowed a 90% credit to encourage the producers to join the code that imposed various operating and marketing requirements on the industry. The Court ruled the regulatory effort to be outside the bounds authorized by the Commerce Clause and so the tax was a penalty to enforce an unconstitutional regulation.
- 1937: The so called switch in time that saved the nine, *West Coast Hotel Co. v. Parrish*, upheld a state economic regulation.[607]

---

[600] United States v. Butler, 297 U.S. 1 (1936). *Butler* struck down the Agricultural Adjustment Act and its processing tax. The Act was a comprehensive effort to pump up the cotton market, which required processors to pay a tax designed to be the difference between the price they paid the farmer for the cotton and the "fair value." The Act appropriated the taxes to pay benefit and other support payments to farmers.

[601] 297 U.S. at 63.

[602] The ruling has stuck. *See, e.g.*, opinion of Chief Justice Rehnquist in South Dakota v. Dole, 483 U.S. 203, 207 (1987); United States v. Gerlach Live Stock Co., 339 U.S. 725, 738 (1950). *See generally* Cooter and Siegel, *Collective Action Federalism: A General Theory of Article I, Section 8*, 63 Stan. L. Rev. 115, 127 (2010). *See* Ch. III.D.2.

[603] 297 U.S. at 64. *See* Bergman, at 341.

[604] 297 U.S. at 61 ("To do this would be to shut our eyes to what all others than we can see and understand.").

[605] Carter v. Carter Coal Co., 298 U.S. 238 (1936).

[606] "There is general agreement that the statute rests upon the commerce power. The tax provision stands or falls with the validity of the scheme of regulation under the commerce power." Summary of argument of United States in 80 L. Ed. 1160 (1936).

[607] West Coast Hotel Co. v. Parrish, 300 U.S. 379 (1937) (upholding state regulation). *See also* NLRB v. Jones & Laughlin Steel Corp., 301 U.S. 1 (1937) (upholding federal regulation). *See* Burns, at 148.

- 1937 (insubstantial tax raised): *Sonzinsky* stands for the proposition that even insubstantial revenue raised normally will justify finding a true tax, though the regulatory purpose is obvious.[608] A unanimous Court decided *Sonzinsky* on the same day as *West Coast Hotel*, which suggests that it might have been part of an implicit understanding among the Justices about the switch in *West Coast Hotel*. It rejected a Tenth Amendment challenge and reached over the *Child Labor Tax Case* (1922), back to *McCray* (1904), for support. Justice Stone affirmed the conviction of a firearms dealer for not paying the $200 license tax (roughly ten times the value of the gun), against a states' rights challenge. The United States did not argue that it had the power to regulate firearms sales. The opinion distinguished *Carter Coal* and *Butler* and relied on the face of the statute.[609] In 1950 and 1974 the Court characterized *Sonzinsky* as a case in which it had recognized the revenue as "obviously negligible" and the revenue purpose as "insubstantial."[610]

- 1937: *Southern Coal* upheld a state unemployment compensation system and tax.[611] Because the federal tax was not at issue, Justice Stone had only to refute the Fourteenth Amendment argument.

- 1937 (excise tax upon employment justified unemployment security tax): *Steward Machine* upheld the federal unemployment security tax solely on

---

[608] Sonzinsky v. United States, 300 U.S. 506 (1937).

[609] "The case is not one where the statute contains regulatory provisions related to a purported tax in such a way as has enabled this Court to say in other cases that the latter is a penalty resorted to as a means of enforcing the regulations. *See* Child Labor Tax Case . . . Hill v. Wallace . . . Carter v. Carter Coal Co. . . . Nor is the subject of the tax described or treated as criminal by the taxing statute. *Compare* United States v. Constantine. . . . Here § 2 contains no regulation other than the mere registration provisions, which are obviously supportable as in aid of a revenue purpose. On its face it is only a taxing measure, and we are asked to say that the tax, by virtue of its deterrent effect on the activities taxed, operates as a regulation, which is beyond the congressional power. Every tax is in some measure regulatory. To some extent it interposes an economic impediment to the activity taxed as compared with others not taxed. But a tax is not any the less a tax because it has a regulatory effect, United States v. Doremus, . . . Nigro v. United States, License Tax Cases, . . . ; *see* Child Labor Tax Case, . . . ; and it has long been established that an Act of Congress which on its face purports to be an exercise of the taxing power is not any the less so because the tax is burdensome or tends to restrict or suppress the thing taxed. Veazie Bank v. Fenno, . . . ; McCray v. United States, . . . ; *cf.* Alaska Fish Co. v. Smith. . . . Inquiry into the hidden motives which may move Congress to exercise a power constitutionally conferred upon it is beyond the competency of courts. Veazie Bank v. Fenno, . . . ; McCray v. United States, . . . ; United States v. Doremus, . . . ; *see* Magnano Co. v. Hamilton. . . . They will not undertake, by collateral inquiry as to the measure of the regulatory effect of a tax, to ascribe to Congress an attempt, under the guise of taxation, to exercise another power denied by the Federal Constitution. McCray v. United States, . . . ; *cf.* Magnano Co. v. Hamilton. . . . Here the annual tax of $200 is productive of some revenue [$4,400 in one year]. We are not free to speculate as to the motives, which moved Congress to impose it, or as to the extent to which it may operate to restrict the activities taxed. As it is not attended by an offensive regulation, and since it operates as a tax, it is within the national taxing power. [citing Harrison Narcotics Act cases]." 300 U.S. at 512-514.

[610] United States v. Sanchez, 340 U.S. 42, 44 (1950); Pittsburgh v. Alco Parking Corp., 417 U.S. 369, 375 (1974).

[611] Carmichael v. Southern Coal & Coke Co., 301 U.S. 495 (1937).

the traditional grounds that an excise tax on employment was a permissible excise under the Constitution.[612] In discussing the purportedly coercive aspect of the credit of 90% of the state tax against the federal tax it stated that any national problem that impinges on the United States government economically can support such a program under the General Welfare Power. Thus, it rejected a Tenth Amendment challenge to the unemployment compensation portion of the Social Security Act. The opinion's reasoning included (1) the inevitable regulatory aspect of taxes,[613] (2) the "robust common sense" that must be applied to charges that taxes are coercive,[614] (3) distinguishing cases in which it was determined that the United States had no legitimate interest,[615] and (4) the *Butler* decision is distinguishable on the grounds of the earmarking and the lack of cooperation of the state. The opinion distinguished *Butler* as follows: it was decided by a divided court; in contrast the proceeds of the tax in controversy here are not earmarked for a special group; and the conditions in the law are not directed to the attainment of an unlawful end, but to an end, the relief of unemployment, for which nation and state may lawfully cooperate.[616] Perhaps the most important ground of *Steward Machine* was that the national unemployment was the federal government's fiscal problem and for that reason alone it was entitled to try to remedy it. Nevertheless, *Steward* upheld the tax as a tax separate and apart from its analysis of the spending and credit offset aspects of the law.

- 1937 (excise tax upon employment justified social security tax): *Helvering v. Davis* is almost identical to *Steward* in upholding the social security tax solely because it was an excise tax on the transaction of employment; it

[612] Steward Machine Co. v. Davis, 301 U.S. 548, 579-583 (1937).

[613] 301 U.S. at 589-590 ("Every tax is in some measure regulatory. . . . In like manner every rebate from a tax when conditioned upon conduct is in some measure a temptation. But to hold that motive or temptation is equivalent to coercion is to plunge the law in endless difficulties. The outcome of such a doctrine is the acceptance of a philosophical determinism by which choice becomes impossible.").

[614] 301 U.S. at 589-591 ("Till now the law has been guided by a robust common sense which assumes the freedom of the will as a working hypothesis in the solution of its problems. The wisdom of the hypothesis has illustration in this case. Nothing in the case suggests the exertion of a power akin to undue influence, if we assume that such a concept can ever be applied with fitness to the relations between state and nation. Even on that assumption the location of the point at which pressure turns into compulsion, and ceases to be inducement, would be a question of degree,—at times, perhaps, of fact. The point had not been reached when Alabama made her choice. We cannot say that she was acting, not of her unfettered will, but under the strain of a persuasion equivalent to undue influence, when she chose to have relief administered under laws of her own making, by agents of her own selection, instead of under federal laws, administered by federal officers, with all the ensuing evils, at least to many minds, of federal patronage and power. There would be a strange irony, indeed, if her choice were now to be annulled on the basis of an assumed duress in the enactment of a statute which her courts have accepted as a true expression of her will. *Beeland Wholesale Co. v. Kaufman, supra.* We think the choice must stand.").

[615] 301 U.S. at 590-592.

[616] *Id.* at 592-593.

also upheld the spending under the General Welfare Power against a Tenth Amendment attack, but the spending and the taxing were treated separately.[617] Justice Cardozo grounded the opinion on spending on the power of the federal government to spend for the general welfare and found that the old age pensions protected the general welfare due to the national disaster. The opinion stated: "Counsel for respondent has recalled to us the virtues of self-reliance and frugality. There is a possibility, he says, that aid from a paternal government may sap those sturdy virtues and breed a race of weaklings. If Massachusetts so believes and shapes her laws in that conviction, must her breed of sons be changed, he asks, because some other philosophy of government finds favor in the halls of Congress? But the answer is not doubtful. One might ask with equal reason whether the system of protective tariffs is to be set aside at will in one state or another whenever local policy prefers the rule of laissez faire. The issue is a closed one. It was fought out long ago. When money is spent to promote the general welfare, the concept of welfare or the opposite is shaped by Congress, not the states. So the concept be not arbitrary, the locality must yield. Constitution, Art. VI, Par. 2."[618] Despite the invitation of the parties the Court did not discuss whether the tax regulated, was too high, was a penalty, or had any other shortcoming that had previously justified striking down a tax. The opinion simply stated that it was an excise tax on employment. In 1954, just before his death, Justice Jackson characterized *Helvering v. Davis* as follows: "It was early perceived that to allow the federal government to spend for internal improvements would aggrandize its powers as against those of the states. It was not until the famous decision holding the Social Security Act constitutional that this controversy over the federal power to tax and spend for the general welfare was settled, and settled in favor of the existence of that power in the Federal Government."[619]

- 1938 (penalty in aid of federal tax): Justice Brandeis said the penal nature of a tax is irrelevant if the power to tax exists, as in taxing the income of corporations to their shareholders through the undistributed earnings tax.[620]
- 1940 (tax enforcing Commerce Clause): *Sunshine Anthracite Coal* ruled constitutional the 1937 revision of the Bituminous Coal Act, whose labor provisions had been ruled unconstitutional in *Carter Coal*.[621] The Act imposed a one cent tax per ton for code members and a 19½ % tax on others. The Court avoided the issue of tax versus regulation by concluding that the principal power being exerted was regulation of interstate commerce

[617] Helvering v. Davis, 301 U.S. 619, 645 (1937). *See also* Bowen v. Public Agencies Opposed to Soc. Sec. Entrapment, 477 U.S. 41 (1986) (ruling that states cannot opt out of social security).

[618] 301 U.S. at 644-645.

[619] Robert H. Jackson, The Supreme Court in the American System of Government 67 (1963).

[620] Helvering v. National Grocery Co., 304 U.S. 282, 288-289 (1938).

[621] Sunshine Anthracite Coal Co. v. Adkins, 310 U.S. 381 (1940).

and that the taxing power was applied in aid of that, which meant that the main purpose of the exorbitant tax did not need to be revenue raising but was properly in aid of the regulation. The opinion did not reference the Necessary and Proper Clause and appears to treat the tax as a tax under the taxing power.

- 1941 (substantive due process reversed): *Darby* upheld federal regulation of worker wages and hours, effectively limiting *Carter v. Carter Coal* and overruling *Hammer v. Dagenhart.*[622]
- 1950 (regulation of subject Congress cannot regulate, through the taxing power): *Sanchez* upheld the Marijuana Tax Act despite the fact that it imposed a $100 per ounce tax on non registrants and a $1 per ounce tax on registrants, a regime somewhat similar to that in *Constantine* (1935).[623] The Court acknowledged that the two level tax structure was intended to penalize transfers of marijuana (by the $100 tax) if they were not within the narrow range of legal transfers by registered dealers. The tax was upheld solely under the taxing power and not under the Commerce Clause or any other enumerated power of Congress, even though the revenue raising purpose might be secondary to the regulatory purpose. The opinion cited the facts that the tax was not levied upon "the commission of a crime," legislative history indicated Congress had a purpose to raise revenue, though only negligible revenue was raised, civil procedure is provided for collection (thus distinguishing *Lipke* (1922)), and the $100 tax was intended to enforce the basic regime. Thus *Sanchez* is a ringing endorsement of federal regulatory taxes in an area where the United States could not regulate directly.[624]
- 1953 (regulation of subject United States cannot regulate, through the taxing power): *Kahriger* rejected a Tenth Amendment challenge and ruled that a license tax on wagering did not infringe state police power, because it was a tax.[625] It distinguished *Constantine* (on which the district court had relied), by noting that in the next term *Sonzinsky* had ruled contrary to *Constantine* in effect, and because the bootlegging tax in *Constantine* was dependent on a state crime having been committed, whereas the tax on accepting wagers applied without regard to a crime (although the activity was criminal in most states). It noted that the $4 million raised by the wagering tax was substantially more than was raised by other taxes that had been upheld. Both the majority opinion, Justice Jackson's concurrence, and the dissent

---

[622] United States v. Darby, 312 U.S. 100 (1941).

[623] United States v. Sanchez, 340 U.S. 42 (1950) (unanimous opinion denied taxpayer's motion to dismiss suit for collection of taxes). *See also* Leary v. United States, 395 U.S. 6 (1969) (reversing the conviction of Dr. Timothy Leary of failing to pay the $100 tax as a nonregistrant, because to register would have required self-incrimination).

[624] *See* Reina v. United States, 364 U.S. 507, 511 (1960) (confirming that *Sanchez* involved a narcotics regulation based on the taxing power).

[625] United States v. Kahriger, 345 U.S. 22 (1953). *See also* Lewis v. United States, 348 U.S. 419 (1955) (similar case arising in District of Columbia).

acknowledged the difficulties peculiarly attending cases questioning the taxing power. Justice Reed's majority opinion noted that the issue gave rise to "diverse decisions" and had baffled judges and legislators. He quoted Chief Justice's Marshall's vague and general warning against laws that went beyond the federal powers, and noted that courts generally sustained statutes adopted under the Necessary and Proper Clause or the Commerce Clause, despite their effect on matters ordinarily considered state concern; but that when the taxing power was relied on, a greater variation in the decisions has resulted when indirect results of the tax were involved. "It is hard to understand why the power to tax should raise more doubts because of indirect effects than other federal powers."[626] The opinion pointed out how *Butler* struck down a tax, but later in *Mulford v. Smith* and *Wickard v. Filburn* the same regulation was obtained under the Commerce Clause without taxation. It pointed out that *Hill v. Wallace* and *Trusler v. Crooks* struck down taxes that were said to regulate markets, whereas *Chicago Bd. of Trade v. Olsen*, 262 U.S. 1, had upheld regulations based on the Commerce Clause to the same effect. It observed that the departure in *Hammer v. Dagenhart* from this line of decisions was overruled by *United States v. Darby*. Justice Jackson reluctantly concurred, on the grounds that it was better to uphold the taxing power than to invalidate a tax and create a precedent with unknowable ramifications.[627] Justice Frankfurter dissented. He wanted to say the emperor had no clothes and the Court should not keep ignoring the obvious fact that regulations were being passed off as taxes. He was more jaded about the subject than we are today, saying: "To review in detail the decisions of this Court, beginning with *Veazie Bank v. Fenno* . . . dealing with this ambivalent type of revenue enactment, would be to rehash the familiar." Then Justice Frankfurter neatly capsulized the entire issue: "Two generalizations may, however, safely be drawn from this series of cases. Congress may make an oblique use of the taxing power in relation to activities with which Congress may deal directly, as for instance, commerce between the States. Thus, if the dissenting views of Mr. Justice Holmes in *Hammer v. Dagenhart* . . . had been the decision of the Court, as they became in *United States v. Darby* . . ., the effort to deal with the problem of child labor through an assertion of the taxing power in the statute considered in *Child Labor Tax Case* . . . would by the latter

---

[626] 345 U.S. at 31.

[627] "The United States has a system of taxation by confession. That a people so numerous, scattered and individualistic annually assesses itself with a tax liability, often in highly burdensome amounts, is a reassuring sign of the stability and vitality of our system of self-government. What surprised me in once trying to help administer these laws was not to discover examples of recalcitrance, fraud or self-serving mistakes in reporting, but to discover that such derelictions were so few. It will be a sad day for the revenues if the good will of the people toward their taxing system is frittered away in efforts to accomplish by taxation moral reforms that cannot be accomplished by direct legislation. But the evil that can come from this statute will probably soon make itself manifest to Congress. The evil of a judicial decision impairing the legitimate taxing power by extreme constitutional interpretations might not be transient. Even though this statute approaches the fair limits of constitutionality, I join the decision of the Court." 345 U.S. at 36.

case have been sustained. However, when oblique use is made of the taxing power as to matters which substantively are not within the powers delegated to Congress, the Court cannot shut its eyes to what is obviously, because designedly, an attempt to control conduct which the Constitution left to the responsibility of the States, merely because Congress wrapped the legislation in the verbal cellophane of a revenue measure."[628] Justice Frankfurter's sentiment about shutting eyes, is, of course, essentially the same as Chief Justice Taft's statement in the *Child Labor Tax Case*. This dissenting view of Justice Frankfurter reflects an inflexibility in his views of regulation (and taxation), which also got him in trouble in the area of civil rights.[629]

- 1969: *Leary* ruled unconstitutional the statutory presumption of knowledge of importation in the Marijuana Tax Act but otherwise did not question the constitutionality of the Act.[630]
- 1969: *Minor* again upheld the Harrison Narcotics Act and the Marijuana Tax Act.[631] It stated a summary of the law of taxation that did not differ from that stated in the 1930s New Deal laws opinions: "A statute does not cease to be a valid tax measure because it deters the activity taxed, because the revenue obtained is negligible, or because the activity is otherwise illegal."[632] It is interesting to note that the opinion states the validity of the taxes has long been established, but cites cases involving statutes on opium importation and heroin sales; opium is not produced in the United States and so always involves importation, which is always a federal issue.
- 1988: *South Carolina v. Baker* viewed the federal requirement that state bonds be issued in registered form (and if not, the state and local bond interest would lose its federal tax exemption) as purely regulatory and not designed to raise revenue and yet upheld the requirement as within the proper scope of federal regulation.[633] Even though the registration requirement itself did not raise revenue directly, its purpose was in large part to protect the federal tax base both as to taxable and municipal and state bonds (as to which capital gains and estate taxes could be levied).[634] Therefore, it can be viewed as a regulation in aid of federal tax collection.[635]

---

[628] 324 U.S. at 37-38.

[629] Justice Frankfurter so absorbed the New Deal/Holmes view that states should be allowed to regulate, that when it came to regulations like requiring school children to say the pledge of allegiance, he deferred to the school board, as in Minersville School District v. Gobitis, 310 U.S. 586 (1940), only to find himself in dissent in a case overruling *Gobitis* three years later. West Virginia State Bd. of Education v. Barnette, 319 U.S. 624 (1943). *See* Friedman, at 238-240.

[630] Leary v. United States, 395 U.S. 6 (1969).

[631] Minor v. United States, 396 U.S. 87 (1969).

[632] *Id.* at 98 n. 13.

[633] South Carolina v. Baker, 485 U.S. 505, 527 n. 16 (1988) ("That § 310(b) is purely regulatory in purpose and effect and was never intended to raise any federal revenue does not alone render it unconstitutional.").

[634] 485 U.S. at 510.

[635] *See* Ch. I.

- 1994 (state tax): *Kurth Ranch* ruled that a state tax on marijuana imposed on a person only if arrested for the crime of possessing the marijuana constituted double jeopardy.[636] The opinion contains some broad statements about taxes and regulation and penalties, but no holding that is relevant here because it is limited to the unique definition of punishment ("jeopardy") applied for double jeopardy purposes: "Taken as a whole, this drug tax is a concoction of anomalies, too far removed in crucial respects from a standard tax assessment to escape characterization as punishment for the purpose of double jeopardy analysis."[637]
- 1995 and 2000: The Court for the first time since 1936 held that Congress lacked the power to regulate under the Commerce Clause.[638]
- 2005: *Gonzales v. Raich* upheld the Controlled Substances Act of 1970 regulation of marijuana on the basis of the Supremacy Clause and the Commerce Clause.[639] The opinion explained how prior to 1970 the federal war on drugs had been conducted through taxes under the Harrison Narcotics Act of 1914, repealed in 1970, and the Marijuana Tax Act. The regulation of marijuana under the Commerce Clause was justified as a "quintessentially economic" activity.[640]
- 2012: As discussed in detail in Ch. III.E.2.c, *Sebelius* held that the health insurance tax was a taxing power tax and thus constitutional, even though five of the Justices thought that it could not be sustained under the Commerce Clause.

3. *Tenth Amendment*

The Tenth Amendment to the Constitution states that:

> The powers not delegated to the United States by the Constitution, nor prohibited by it to the States, are reserved to the States respectively, or to the people.

The Tenth Amendment is paired with Article I, section 10, which contains a series of "no state shall" injunctions.

The Tenth Amendment does not limit the powers the Constitution grants to the federal government, including not only the taxing power but powers exercised under the Necessary and Proper Clause.[641] Chief Justice Stone stated in the opinion of the Court in *Fernandez v. Wiener* (1945) that the federal taxing power is not burdened by the Tenth Amendment:

---

[636] Dep't of Revenue v. Kurth Ranch, 511 U.S. 767 (1994).

[637] *Id.* at 783.

[638] United States v. Lopez, 514 U.S. 549 (1995); United States v. Morrison, 529 U.S. 598 (2000).

[639] Gonzales v. Raich, 545 U.S. 1 (2005).

[640] *Id.* at 25.

[641] United States v. Comstock, 560 U.S. 126 (2010).

> The Tenth Amendment does not operate as a limitation upon the powers, express or implied, delegated to the national government.[642]

The case involved the federal estate tax, which treated a marital estate differently from the state's treatment. To whatever extent this difference might be though to regulate state property law, it did not involve the Tenth Amendment because Congress was exercising an express or implied power, the power to tax. Justice Stone stated more generally in the unanimous opinion in *Darby* (1941), cited by *Fernandez v. Wiener*:

> The amendment states but a truism that all is retained which has not been surrendered. There is nothing in the history of its adoption to suggest that it was more than declaratory of the relationship between the national and state governments as it had been established by the Constitution before the amendment or that its purpose was other than to allay fears that the new national government might seek to exercise powers not granted, and that the states might not be able to exercise fully their reserved powers.[643]

The Stone formulation reversed the implied insertion of the word "[expressly] delegated to the national government" that had occurred in *Hammer v. Dagenhart* and *Butler*.[644]

Nevertheless, the Tenth Amendment has served as the defense of last resort for opponents of federal taxation. It long predated, of course, the Civil War, and was temporarily eclipsed by the subjugation of states' rights that was the essence of the Civil War's outcome and of Reconstruction. The Tenth Amendment and states' rights contentions said to be based on the Tenth Amendment, were pillars of the southern justification for secession.[645] The Court used the Tenth Amendment to strike down the Civil Rights Act of 1875, marking a resurgence of the Amendment.[646] Although this important ruling is generally viewed as severely undermining the Reconstruction era amendments intended to protect the freed slaves, a somewhat more positive observation is that it effectively turned over the "race problem" to the southern states to resolve, which they did by creating a caste system acquiesced in by the northern states, which in practice allowed the southern states to reenter the Union in fact as well as in law.[647]

---

642 Fernandez v. Wiener, 326 U.S. 340, 362 (1945).

643 United States v. Darby, 312 U.S. 100, 124 (1941).

644 Alpheus T. Mason, Harlan Fiske Stone 407-412 (1956) (Stone explained that "the tail goes with the hide" in terms of spending or taxing power and regulation; that the slippery slope argument "hardly rises to the dignity of argument"; that the historical record shows that the Constitutional Convention specifically considered putting the word "specifically" into the Tenth Amendment and chose not to do so on Madison's recommendation; the same sort of judicial reaction to perceived unwisdom of laws lessens the power not only of Congress to make bad laws but also to make good laws).

645 *See* Jefferson Davis, The Rise and Fall of the Confederate Government Vol. 1, ch. 9 (1881).

646 Civil Rights Cases, 109 U.S. 3 (1883).

647 Ralph H. Gabriel, The Course of American Democratic Thought 135-137 (1940).

The Court usually refers to the Tenth Amendment to encompass any "implied constitutional limitation on Congress' authority to regulate state activities, whether grounded in the Tenth Amendment itself or in principles of federalism derived generally from the Constitution."[648]

The Tenth Amendment has played a huge role in creating two of the three major long running issues of constitutional confusion in federal taxation: intergovernmental immunity and allegedly improper federal regulation through federal taxation. The third major area of confusion, apportioned direct taxes, did not directly involve the Tenth Amendment, though it did involve similar concerns that the states not to be "overtaxed"; also the plaintiffs argued it protected the bonds of states from direct taxation and the *Pollock* opinion cited it in that light.[649]

The first major role played by the Tenth Amendment in federal taxation was as a basis for *Collector v. Day*, the first of the long line of confusing decisions holding that state employees could not be taxed by the United States.[650] Of the cases involving federal tax versus regulation disputes, *McCray* is the earliest in which a federal tax was vigorously contested as improperly regulating local commerce without any justification other than taxation, and thus violating the Tenth Amendment, to which Justice White responded:

> Whilst undoubtedly both the Fifth and Tenth Amendments qualify, in so far as they are applicable, all the provisions of the Constitution, nothing in those amendments operates to take away the grant of power to tax conferred by the Constitution upon Congress. The contention on this subject rests upon the theory that the purpose and motive of Congress in exercising its undoubted powers may be inquired into by the courts, and the proposition is therefore disposed of by what has been said on that subject.[651]

In 1954 Justice Jackson stated:

> I know that it is now regarded as more or less provincial and reactionary to cite the Tenth Amendment, which reserves to the states and the people the powers not delegated to the Federal Government. That Amendment is rarely mentioned in judicial opinions, rarely cited in argument. But our forefathers made it a part of the Bill of Rights in order to retain in the localities certain powers and not to allow them to drift into centralized hands. Perhaps the Tenth Amendment is drifting into oblivion as constitutional provisions may sometimes do. [Explaining how the Ninth Amendment has so drifted.][652]

Justice Jackson, no doubt, was speaking from the vantage point of the effective reversal of the anti-tax opinions of the era from 1922 to 1936 (*Child Labor Tax*

---

648 South Carolina v. Baker, 485 U.S. 505, 511 n. 5 (1988).

649 Pollock v. Farmers' Loan & Trust Co., 157 U.S. 429, 584 (1895).

650 Collector v. Day, 78 U.S. 113 (1871); *overruled by* Graves v. New York, 306 U.S. 466 (1939). *See* Ch. II.

651 McCray v. United States, 195 U.S. 27, 61 (1904).

652 Robert H. Jackson, The Supreme Court in the American System of Government 73-74 (1963).

Case, Hill v. Wallace, Trusler v. Crooks, Butler, Constantine), by *Southern Coal, Davis, Steward Machine, Sonzinsky*, etc.[653] And yet, seven decades later the Tenth Amendment does not look so quaint, as a conservative majority on the Court has gradually replaced the New Deal majority and its moderate followers on the Warren Court. The Tenth Amendment will always stand as an uncertain dividing line between state and federal power.[654] It inevitably will be asserted against any federal law impacting a state in a way that the state political powers do not like. More importantly and more typically it inevitably will be asserted against any federal tax that taxpayers can claim circumvents state power. Therefore, the Tenth Amendment is best viewed as a tool of private litigants rather than a rule of law.

The political nature of the Tenth Amendment is reflected in the fact that in the 20th Century the basic view of the Supreme Court on the Tenth Amendment switched positions at least five times:[655]

- The Court early upheld federal regulatory schemes and taxes that appeared to invade areas of historical and exclusive state control.[656]
- But in 1918 *Hammer v. Dagenhart* denied federal power to regulate child labor.[657]
- When the supposed regulation of activities reserved to the states was in the form of a grant-in-aid with conditions attached, the Court found no Tenth Amendment violation.[658]
- But *Darby* reversed *Hammer* in 1941.[659] *Darby* was part of New Deal Court rulings, several of which involved taxes.
- In 1976 *National League of Cities v. Usery* "sent shockwaves through the constitutional world" when it reversed the federal effort to subject cities and states to the Fair Labor Standards Act.[660] In contrast to most disputes over

---

[653] *See* Ch. III.F.2.

[654] *See* Gary Lawson, *A Truism with Attitude, The Tenth Amendment in Constitutional Context*, 83 Notre Dame L. Rev. 469, 504 (2008) [hereinafter Lawson] ("indeed, a string of 5-4 decisions going in different directions may well be the most appropriate answer [to what the Tenth Amendment means]"). *See, e.g.*, Murphy v. NCAA, 138 S. Ct. 1461 (2018) (applying the Tenth Amendment to strike down a sports betting statute but not disputing Congress' general Commerce Clause powers over the subject matter).

[655] *See generally* Thomas H. Odom and Marc R. Baluda, *The Development of Process-Oriented Federalism: Harmonizing the Supreme Court's Tenth Amendment Jurisprudence from Garcia through Prinz*, 31 Urban Law. 993 (1999) [hereinafter Odom and Baluda].

[656] *See, e.g.*, Champion v. Ames, 188 U.S. 321 (1903) (lotteries); McCray v. United States, 195 U.S. 27, 58 (1904) (margarine).

[657] Hammer v. Dagenhart, 247 U.S. 251 (1918). And a second attempt to regulate child labor through taxation also was denied. J.W. Bailey v. Drexel Furn. Co., 259 U.S. 20 (1922).

[658] *See, e.g.*, Massachusetts v. Mellon, 262 U.S. 447 (1923) (the first test of a conditioned grant in aid).

[659] United States v. Darby, 312 U.S. 100 (1941).

[660] National League of Cities v. Usery, 426 U.S. 833 (1976). *See* Lawson, at 501. *Usery* effectively overruled Maryland v. Wirtz, 392 U.S. 183 (1968), decided eight years earlier.

the Tenth Amendment, this one actually involved state and local governments as plaintiffs, rather than taxpayers or other private parties resisting federal regulation.

- But in 1985 *Garcia* reversed course and appeared to remit Tenth Amendment issues to the political process, except in cases of "process failure."[661] It stated that the Tenth Amendment did not define substantive areas reserved to state control. *South Carolina v. Baker* relied on this distinction as to a federal tax issue.[662] It has been suggested that the talisman of those cases not likely to receive judicial review is the generally applicable law that incidentally impacts states.[663]
- In 1991 *Ashcroft* imposed a "plain statement" requirement to test whether Congress had properly warned of a rule overriding states' Tenth Amendment rights, so that the political process might work.[664] The *Ashcroft* test is heartily asserted by the Court's conservative wing in dissents and is grudgingly followed by the rest of the Court.[665]
- In 1992 the Court did not reject *Garcia* as to generally applicable regulations, but imposed a stricter view of the federal power when the United States tries to use the states to regulate, as contrasted with direct federal regulation of individuals; it struck down a regulation on radioactive waste.[666] Later it struck down a requirement that states participate in enforcing the Brady Act (in 1997).[667]
- In 2005 *Gonzales v. Raich* held that the Supremacy Clause requires that Congress' Commerce Clause powers override a state's regulatory authori-

[661] Garcia v. San Antonio Metro. Transit Authority, 469 U.S. 528 (1985) (overruling *Usery*).

[662] South Carolina v. Baker, 485 U.S. 505 (1988) (rejecting a Tenth Amendment argument by South Carolina against a Code requirement that state issued bonds had to be registered in the name of the holders in order for the holders to exclude interest received under section 103).

[663] Odom and Baluda, at 999-1000. The Court keeps avoiding whether this is the sole test, as in Reno v. Condon, 528 U.S. 141 (2000) where a unanimous Court upheld the Driver's Privacy Protection Act of 1994 with the explanation that it applied to all persons, including states, despite the fact that the basic information that is being protected by the Act necessarily originates with states.

[664] Gregory v. Ashcroft, 501 U.S. 452 (1991).

[665] As to the last case following it, *see* Nixon v. Mo. Mun. League, 541 U.S. 125 (2004).

[666] New York v. United States, 505 U.S. 144, 166 (1992) ("In providing for a stronger central government, therefore, the Framers explicitly chose a Constitution that confers upon Congress the power to regulate individuals, not States."). *See* Robert G. Natelson, *Judicial Review of Special Interest Spending: The General Welfare Clause and the Fiduciary Law of the Founders*, 11 TEX. REV. L. AND POL. 239, 271 (2006) (*New York* abandoned the political process approach of *Garcia*, although the opinion itself says that *Garcia* is distinguished and not affected).

[667] Printz v. United States, 521 U.S. 898 (1997).

ty.[668] The case involved the Controlled Substances Act and its application to marijuana used for medical purposes. The opinion stated that the Commerce Clause powers override the state's power to legislate for the general welfare of its citizens.

In 2008 one scholar wrote:

> There are two camps within the Court today, each with a wildly different view of the Tenth Amendment's importance. The conservative federalist camp has shown a propensity to enforce the Amendment and respect the ideal of federalism. The liberal nationalist camp adheres to the *Darby* Court's attitude that the Tenth Amendment is a mere 'truism' with no substantive power of its own and values the accomplishments of the Federal Government more than state sovereignty.[669]

Although several of the more recent Tenth Amendment decisions of the Supreme Court involve federal laws trying to make states do something (such as comply with the Fair Labor Standards Act,[670] or register their bonds[671]), or prevent amateur sports betting,[672] the tax cases in which the Tenth Amendment has been asserted are almost all brought by taxpayers who don't want to pay tax, and almost all of those taxpayers have been businesses.[673] Nevertheless, the overriding point about the Tenth Amendment and federal taxation is that so long as the

---

[668] Gonzales v. Raich, 545 U.S. 1 (2005). *See also* Reno v. Condon, 528 US 141 (2000) (Congress could regulate drivers' license information because driving was in interstate commerce). *See* Scott A. Keller, *How Courts Can Protect State Autonomy from Federal Administrative Encroachment*, 82 S. Cal. L. Rev. 45, 53 (2008) ("After *Gonzales v. Raich*, the Supreme Court appears unwilling or unable to interpret the Constitution to impose meaningful, substantive limits on Congress' enumerated powers. Although the Rehnquist Court flirted with substantive limits on congressional power, the specter of such meaningful limits is now water over the dam. *Raich* therefore signals that 'the political safeguards of federalism' will largely drive the Court's Commerce Clause jurisprudence.").

[669] Keith Stover, *Restoring the Tenth Amendment: A Call to Overrule United States v. Darby and Reinstate National League of Cities v. Usery*, 25 T.M. Cooley L. Rev. 555, 585 (2008). Note that this author has converted the term "federalist" from its revolutionary roots in strong central government, to a new meaning reflecting the power of states under concepts of federalism. Whether the political process should be the sole remedy for a nondiscriminatory tax falling on an essential government function (if there is such a tax) is uncertain. *See generally* David M. Richardson, *Federal Income Taxation of States*, 19 Stetson L. Rev. 411, 451-510 (1990).

[670] National League of Cities v. Usery, 426 U.S. 833 (1976) and Garcia v. San Antonio Metro. Transit Authority, 469 U.S. 528 (1985).

[671] South Carolina v. Baker, 485 U.S. 505 (1988) (the most recent Supreme Court decision involving a Tenth Amendment challenge to a federal tax, and deciding it in favor of the United States).

[672] Murphy v. NCAA, 138 S. Ct. 1461 (2018).

[673] *See* Robert H. Jackson, The Struggle for Judicial Supremacy 20-21 (1941) ("Few decisions of the Supreme Court can be cited in which any state of the Union has been able to obtain protection from the Court of its own constitutional rights, *upon its own demand*.") (emphasis in original). Justice Jackson cited *Massachusetts v. Mellon* and *Florida v. Mellon* as examples of cases brought by states and dismissed by the Court; but then private litigants purported to represent the state in *Carter v. Carter Coal*, which struck down the Coal Act.

federal exaction is a tax, the Amendment has no application: it cannot place any limit on the federal taxing power.

> In McCray v. United States, 195 U.S. 27, this court sustained a Federal tax on oleomargarine, artificially colored, and held that while the Fifth and Tenth Amendments qualify, so far as applicable, all the provisions of the Constitution, nothing in those Amendments operates to take away the power to tax conferred by the Constitution on the Congress. In that case it was contended that the subject taxed was within the exclusive domain of the States, and that the real purpose of Congress was not to raise revenue, but to tax out of existence a substance not harmful of itself and one which might be lawfully manufactured and sold; but, the only constitutional limitation which this court conceded, in addition to the requirement of uniformity, and that for the sake of argument only so far as concerned the case then under consideration, was that Congress is restrained from arbitrary impositions or from exceeding its powers in seeking to effect unwarranted ends. The limitation of uniformity was deemed sufficient by those who framed and adopted the Constitution. The courts may not add others. . . . We must remember, too, that the revenues of the United States must be obtained in the same territory, from the same people, and excise taxes must be collected from the same activities, as are also reached by the States in order to support their local government.[674]

As stated above, the Court last ruled a federal tax that was defended under the taxing power to violate the Tenth Amendment in 1936. Since then, it has rejected several Tenth Amendment attacks on federal taxes as listed in Chapter III.F.2, most recently in *South Carolina v. Baker*, *Minor*, and *Sebelius* (2012) (where the opinion of the Court and the Roberts' opinion did not mention the Tenth Amendment, but the Scalia dissent relied upon it). In another case not listed it ruled that the accumulated earnings tax did not violate the Tenth Amendment by interfering with the state's power to authorize corporations to distribute dividends or not.[675]

Efforts to periodically revive the Tenth Amendment are inherently suspect because they seek to deny the reality of the movement of history. Charles Evans Hughes, no liberal, stated:

> . . . [F]ar more important to the development of the country, than the decisions holding acts of Congress to be invalid, have been those in which the authority of Congress has been sustained and adequate national power to meet the necessities of a growing country has been found to exist within constitutional limitations.[676]

---

[674] Flint v. Stone Tracy Co., 220 U.S. 107, 154 (1911).
[675] Helvering v. National Grocery Co., 304 U.S. 282, 286-287 (1938).
[676] Charles Evans Hughes, The Supreme Court of the United States 96 (1928).

Justice Holmes made a similar statement:

> I do not think that the United States would come to an end if we lost our power to declare an act of Congress void. I do think the Union would be imperiled if we could not make that declaration as to the laws of the several states.[677]

[677] Oliver Wendell Holmes, Collected Legal Papers 295-296 (1920).

Ch. IV. User Fees, Regulatory Charges, Special Assessments, and Privilege License Taxes

A. User Fees and Regulatory Charges

1. *Overview*

Each of taxes (including regulatory taxes, privilege license taxes, and most special assessments) and fuser fees and regulatory charges (both of which are not taxes) generally aims to raise revenue for the government as a greater or lesser part of its purposes, which is the root cause of confusion about distinguishing one from the other.[1] Although the possible recharacterization of a tax as a regulation of a subject the government lacks power to regulate is the more highly charged political issue (see Chapter III), a more straightforward definitional at-

[1] Taxes need not necessarily raise revenues (a regulatory tax can aim to eliminate the taxed item or transaction, as discussed in Ch. III.E.2 and 5), but user fees and regulatory charges must raise revenues because they must be evaluated in comparison to the value of the benefit or the government cost to be funded. For a review of the fee versus tax issue from an economists' perspective, *see* Congressional Budget Office, The Growth of Federal User Charges, 93 TNT 205-41 (August 1, 1993). Loose terminology causes part of the confusion. *See, e.g.*, Berkman v. United States, 250 U.S. 114 (1919) (referring to a one percent fee paid to the clerk of court on a $25,000 cash bail deposit as a tax, as in "taxing costs"). *See generally* Jasper L. Cummings, Jr., *Meandering from Income to Consumption Taxes via User Fees*, 152 Tax Notes (TA) 1241 (Aug. 29, 2016).

tack that may fit some taxes is that it is really a user fee or regulatory charge (even though the opinions do not well distinguish between those two categories), and as such is too high relative to the value provided or cost incurred, or unconstitutional for some reason that hinges on the non-tax characterization. A user fee is charged in the government's proprietary and not sovereign capacity, either for property or a service provided. Alternately, the disgruntled payor could claim the tax was a regulatory charge that was too high relative to the government's cost of regulation, even if it had the power to regulate the matter. A regulatory charge is not charged for provision of a property or service, but is imposed in the government's sovereign capacity (regulatory or police powers but not the taxing power). But because the other sovereign power of taxation can be imposed in any amount, identification of a levy as a tax or not is generally the threshold issue.

This chapter differentiates user fees from regulatory charges even though the Supreme Court has never used the latter term and its opinions have not clearly made the distinction. While this book generally reports what the Court says rather than what it should have said, in this area the opinions are so confused that a mere recitation of what the Court has said is not very illuminating.

In general a user fee is a voluntarily incurred charge imposed by a government in its proprietary capacity, paid in exchange for property or a service received, which fee should somehow reasonably approximate the value of the benefit, which benefit (and hence the fee) may vary with usage of the benefit.[2] Thus a user fee shares some common features of license and franchise taxes (voluntarily incurred and benefit received); but the government need not (and usually does not) incur a cost in providing a license or franchise, and the license or franchise tax amount need not (and usually cannot) be related in amount to a cost to the government; most importantly, the government grants licenses and franchises in its sovereign and not proprietary capacity.[3] Also a user fee shares some features with a regulatory charge in that the payor may seem to be receiving a service, but it is not a proprietary service; rather a regulatory charge is for a sovereign exercise of regulatory power for which the payor is bearing the cost. Also user fees share some common features with special assessment taxes (benefits usually received and governmental costs incurred), but the special assessment tax is usually imposed for a sovereign act within a special taxing district.[4] A tax is not usually voluntarily incurred (except for franchise and license taxes), and need not produce any identifiable benefit to the payor or reflect governmental costs. Federal user fees are not the product of a revenue law enacted under Article I, section 8, clause 1.[5]

---

[2] Voluntariness need not be complete. For example in United States v. Sperry Corp., 493 U.S. 52 (1989), the Court acknowledged that the plaintiff might have preferred not to use the adjudication process it was required to use and pay for; nevertheless, the payment was a valid user fee.

[3] *See* Ch. IV.C, as to license and franchise taxes.

[4] *See* Ch. IV.B.

[5] United States v. Hill, 123 U.S. 681 (1887) (fees and emoluments charged by federal clerk of court were not federal taxes).

The distinctions described above are based on the sources of power of the government imposing the charge: sovereignty versus proprietary actions. Within the sovereign power is the taxing power and the power to regulate. The taxing power also may be used to regulate (the prime example being tariffs). There is no limit on the amount of a tax. There are limits on the amounts of regulatory charges that are not taxes. There are limits on user fees imposed in the proprietary capacity. The seeds of many confusions are obvious from these principles and the Supreme Court has not explicitly adopted the framework imposed on the cases by this Chapter, but the composite of its opinions strongly leads to the framework.

The alternative characterizations (including state fee cases) that can be applied to governmental levies labeled in these various ways include:

- Federal regulatory charge versus possibly unconstitutional tax on a state.[6]
- Federal regulatory charge set by an agency versus a tax that is not authorized by Congress.[7]
- User fees, and regulatory charges, which both are subject to limits on amount, as contrasted with taxes, which are not subject to the Eminent Domain Clause.[8]
- Federal user fee for use of harbor versus unconstitutional tax on exports.[9]
- Regulation versus fee for service versus tax.[10]

---

[6] Massachusetts v. United States, 435 U.S. 444 (1978). This opinion is cited for multiple points within this analysis and yet it is not a typical case because it involved the additional issue of intergovernmental immunity. The Court analogized the question to that arising in a Commerce Clause attack on local fees. 435 U.S. at 466 (three prong test: no discrimination, fair approximation of cost of benefit, and fee not designed to collect more than cost). However, the focus on discrimination and benefits should not apply to test regulatory charges purely on their amounts. *See* Ch. IV.A.2 for discussion of tests.

[7] National Cable Television Ass'n v. United States, 415 U.S. 336, 340-341 (1974) (statute authorized administrator to set a fee, which could not be a tax because only Congress can tax).

[8] Even Justice Field agreed that taxes are not subject to the just compensation requirement. *See* dissent in regulatory case but not involving a regulatory charge, Munn v. Illinois, 94 U.S. 113 (1877) ("The power of the State over the property of the citizen under the constitutional guaranty is well defined. The State may take his property for public uses, upon just compensation being made therefor. It may take a portion of his property by way of taxation for the support of the government."). *See* Ch. V.D.3.b(8) on Eminent Domain Clause.

[9] United States v. United States Shoe Corp., 523 U.S. 360 (1998) (Harbor Maintenance Tax was a tax and not a user fee because not properly correlated to benefit; there may be a stricter standard where the potential for an unconstitutional export tax exists).

[10] The *Head Money Cases* is a good illustration of a situation in which the government had the power to impose a regulatory charge that need not be a fee for services and perhaps could have imposed a fee for services, but could not impose a capitation tax. Edye v. Robertson, 112 U.S. 580 (1884).

- State user fee versus unconstitutional state import duty.[11]
- State user fee for property actually owned and provided by the state versus unconstitutional impediment to interstate commerce.[12]
- State user fee versus unconstitutional tonnage duty.[13]
- State fee versus deprivation of property without due process in violation of Fourteenth Amendment.[14]
- State regulatory charge versus 14th Amendment violations.[15]
- And sometimes the distinction really makes no difference, despite being bruted in the opinion.[16]

The distinction between a user fee and a tax has received the most scrutiny in the federal tax laws in the context of the foreign tax credit allowed by section 901. The law is concerned with limiting the credit to compulsory taxes as opposed to a levy that the person voluntarily incurred on account of receiving a "specific economic benefit."[17] The definition of tax for this purpose is largely consistent with the view that a tax promises no specific benefit to the payor, with two exceptions: customs duties are not taxes for foreign tax credit purposes and neither are privilege license taxes.[18]

---

[11] *See, e.g.*, Cooley v. Bd. of Wardens, 53 U.S. 299 (1852) (State harbor half pilot fee that applied if ship did not take on a pilot and pay a full fee was not a tax, and so did not violate the constitutional prohibition of state imposts and duties on imports and exports. The fees collected were paid into a society for relief of distressed and decayed pilots. "It cannot be denied that a tonnage-duty, or an impost on imports or exports, may be levied under the name of pilot-dues or penalties; and certainly it is the thing, and not the name, which is to be considered." The decision was based on the typicality of such a penalty in encouraging use of harbor pilots for purposes of safety and as part of such regulations.).

[12] *See, e.g.*, Packet Co. v. Keokuk, 95 U.S. 80 (1877) (wharfage fee not a regulation of commerce); Cannon v. New Orleans, 87 U.S. 577 (1874) (docking fee); Evansville-Vanderburgh v. Delta Airlines, Inc., 405 U.S. 707 (1972) (per passenger fee); Case of State Freight Tax, 82 U.S. 232 (1873).

[13] *See, e.g.*, Packet Co. v. Keokuk, 95 U.S. 80 (1877) (wharfage fee not a tonnage duty); Packet Co. v. St. Louis, 100 U.S. 423 (1880).

[14] *See, e.g.*, Sands v. Manistee River Improvement Co., 123 U.S. 288 (1887) (tolls); Carson v. Brockton Sewerage Com., 182 U.S. 398 (1901) (sewer charge based on usage).

[15] Charlotte, C. & A. R. Co. v. Gibbes, 142 U.S. 386 (1892) (fee/tax charged to regulated industry).

[16] Rosenberger v. Rector and Visitors of the Univ. of Va., 515 U.S. 819 (1995) (The issue was whether a student activity fee of $14 violated the Establishment Clause because the proceeds could be used, nondiscriminatorily by religious organizations. The Court seemed to draw some comfort from the fact that the fee was not a general tax, but it hardly could have been, since levied by a University); Mayo v. United States, 319 U.S. 441 (1943) (inspection fees that state tried to exact directly from the United States; unconstitutional whether they be fees or taxes, unless the United States consents).

[17] Reg. § 1.901-2(a)(2)(ii)(B). *See* PPL Corp. v. Commissioner, 569 U.S. 329 (2013) (the most recent discussion of the difference between income and ad valorem taxes).

[18] *Id.* and Reg. § 1.901-2(a)(i).

2. *Constitutional Standards and Amounts*

a. *Range of Constitutional Provisions*

Evaluating the constitutionality of, and sometimes identifying, user fees and regulatory charges is made more difficult because the Supreme Court has implied different standards for fees under different parts of the Constitution, and the question arises under even more parts of the Constitution:

- Eminent Domain Clause: For purposes of just compensation a user fee need only be a fair approximation of the benefits received.[19] However, twhen the Court decides a fee is a taking, it has required it approximate the cost to the government.[20] Justice Alito waved aside the objection that the new rule announced in *Koontz* could apply to taxes and user fees by asserting that taxes and user fees are not takings. Earlier rulings had so held where the state provided a benefit.[21]

- Commerce Clause: State tax discrimination against interstate commerce is discussed in Chapter IX, but the same standards apply to regulatory charges and user fees. The Court has observed that it has applied a more stringent standard in user fee cases involving a discrimination against commerce than otherwise.[22] More generally, the standard requires the fee to bear some fair approximation to the amount of use, not discriminate against interstate commerce and not be excessive in comparison to the benefits received.[23] The Commerce Clause standard has been applied in an intergovernmental immunity case, because of the analogous concern with discrimination.[24]

- Export Clause: An unconstitutional export tax can be saved as a user fee (or regulatory charge; the opinion was unclear) only if it does not vary in amount based on the size or value or other variable measuring the export and its amount is no more than necessary to recompense the government cost (or the payor's benefit).[25]

---

[19] United States v. Sperry Corp., 493 U.S. 52 (1989) (assumed rather than decided applicability of Eminent Domain Clause). *See* Ch. V.D.3.b(8).

[20] Koontz v. St. Johns River Water Mgmt. Dist., 570 U.S. 595 (2013).

[21] Sands v. Manistee River Improvement Co., 123 U.S. 288 (1887) (tolls are not takings); United States v. Sperry Corp., 493 U.S. 52 (1989) (user fees are not takings; a 1.5 percent recovery fee is not a taking; contrasting FCC v. Florida Power Corp., 480 U.S. 245 (1987), which involved how much a telephone company could charge a cable company for pole use); and Webb's Fabulous Pharms. v. Beckwith, 449 U.S. 155 (1980).

[22] 493 U.S. 52 at 61 n. 7.

[23] American Trucking Ass'ns v. Scheiner, 483 U.S. 266, 289-290 (1987); Northwest Airlines v. County of Kent, 510 U.S. 355 (1994), citing Evansville-Vanderburgh v. Delta Airlines, Inc., 405 U.S. 707 (1972).

[24] Massachusetts v. United States, 435 U.S. 444, 454, 466 (1978).

[25] United States v. United States Shoe Corp., 523 U.S. 360 (1998). The Export Clause is in Article I, section 9, clause 5 of the Constitution.

- Supremacy Clause: States cannot impose either fees or taxes on the United States.[26]
- Intergovernmental Immunity: The Supreme Court created this constitutional doctrine and then substantially downsized it in the 1930s.[27] A federal regulatory charge may be collected from a state whereas a federal tax might violate the doctrine of intergovernmental immunity.[28]
- Separation of Powers: Federal taxes must be enacted by Congress, so agency created charges need to be user fees or regulatory charges.[29] In some cases an agency can set the amount of or rules defining taxes; the nondelegation doctrine applies the same to taxes as to fees.[30]
- Taxing Power: A regulatory penalty imposed on an activity that the United States does not have the power to regulate must be a tax to be constitutional.[31]
- Tonnage Clause: States cannot impose tonnage duties,[32] but can charge user fees.[33]
- Excessive Fines Clause: Limits excessive fines for crimes, which the Court has extended to forfeitures of criminal's property, and punitive civil fines and forfeitures, but not remedial fines that do not serve to punish.[34] It does not apply to excessive regulatory taxes.[35]
- Poll Taxes Amendment: Bans only poll taxes as an impediment to voting. But any effort to impose a voting fee to cover costs would be subject to strict scrutiny.[36]

---

[26] Mayo v. United States, 319 U.S. 441 (1943) (not even a "reasonable inspection fee").

[27] *See* Ch. II.C.

[28] *See* Massachusetts v. United States, 435 U.S. 444 (1978) (state must pay nondiscriminatory federal aircraft "tax" that functioned as a regulatory charge and was called a user fee). *But see* Pittman v. Home Owners' Loan Corp., 308 U.S. 21, 30 (1939) (Court approved "a reasonable fee to meet the expenses of the registry" of mortgages given to a federal lender); Mayo v. United States, 319 U.S. 441 (1943) (when the fee was imposed directly on the United States, and not an agent, like a loan corporation, and on an action that was a function of government (soil protection), it was forbidden without discussion of the reasonableness of the cost).

[29] *See* Nat. Cable TV Ass'n v. United States, 415 U.S. 336 (1974).

[30] Skinner v. Mid-America Pipeline Co., 490 U.S. 212 (1989).

[31] *See* Edye v. Robertson, 112 U.S. 580 (1884); National Federation of Independent Business v. Sebelius, 567 U.S. 519 (2012) (penalty versus tax).

[32] Polar Tankers, Inc. v. City of Valdez, 557 U.S. 1 (2009) (struck down Alaska city tax).

[33] Packet Co. v. Keokuk, 95 U.S. 80 (1877) (wharf fee).

[34] Hudson v. United States, 522 U.S. 93 (1997); Browning-Ferris Indus. v. Kelco Disposal, 492 U.S. 257 (1989); Alexander v. United States, 509 U.S. 544 (1993) (criminal court costs are not user fees but part of the regulation); Austin v. United States, 509 U.S. 602 (1993); United States v. Halper, 490 U.S. 435 (1989).

[35] *See* United States v. Kahriger, 345 U.S. 22 (1952).

[36] *See* Bullock v. Carter, 405 U.S. 134 (1972) (ballot access fee charged candidates to be placed on ballot was too high and prevented fair access to candidacy); Lubin v. Panish, 415 U.S. 709 (1974); Morse v. Republican Party, 517 U.S. 186 (1996) (Republican Party $5 fee to attend state nominating convention to cover costs violated the Voting Rights Act).

- Free Exercise of Religion Clause: *Hobby Lobby* in effect applied the Religious Freedom Restoration Act to make federal specialty taxes and fees targets for religious and other objections; only a "national systems of taxation," of which the income tax and social security taxes are the only identified examples, are safe.[37]
- Free Exercise Clause—State Regulation: A state fee may be found to burden exercise of a constitutional right, religion.[38]
- Origination Clause: Revenue laws must originate in the House.[39] But a properly enacted bill can delegate aspects of the taxing power to an agency under proper limitations.[40]
- Equal Protection Cause: It is a rational choice for a state to charge user fees to cover the cost of public services and is not an invidious discrimination between rich and poor; heightened scrutiny is not warranted.[41]

b. *Amount of User Fee*

A user fee generally should not exceed the value of the benefit received or made available to the taxpayer, although it may be less, including recovery of cost or less than cost; the general principle is subject to modification as part of application of specific constitutional requirements (e.g., Commerce Clause), as discussed above.

The signature difference between the amount measurements for user fees and regulatory charges is that user fees can approximate benefit value whereas regulatory charges generally must approximate and not exceed governmental cost, as discussed below. If the charge is a tax, neither limit applies.

Proving these amount standards for fees and charges is somewhat difficult due to the tendency of the Court's opinions not to distinguish between user fees and regulatory charges, and the tendency to refer to cost and benefits in combination, without noting a distinction. In addition, since 1952, 31 U.S.C. section 9701 (and its predecessor) has directed federal agencies to charge for each service or thing of value, with the amount to reflect a variety of considerations including

---

[37] Burwell v. Hobby Lobby Stores, Inc., 573 U.S. 682 (2014). *See* Cummings, Hobby Lobby *and Federal Taxes*, 145 TAX NOTES 519 (Nov. 3, 2014).

[38] *See* Murdock v. Pennsylvania, 319 U.S. 105 (1943) (license fee for right to go door to door was an unconstitutional tax on religious because it was not used to defray costs of regulation).

[39] *E.g.*, United States v. Sperry Corp., 493 U.S. 52 (1989) (a fee was contested as a tax that did not originate in the House; ruled a user fee). See excerpt from Congressional Record, titled Rosty Loses Bid to Strike Fees from Clean Air Bill, 90 TNT 115-45 ("For 200 years, that constitutional prerogative has been jealously guarded by the House and reluctantly respected by the Senate. If, however, the clean air bill is passed in its current form, the House of Representatives and its officers will present the other body an open invitation to originate revenue legislation in the future under the guise of 'fees.'").

[40] Skinner v. Mid-America Pipeline Co., 490 U.S. 212 (1989).

[41] Kadrmas v. Dickinson Pub. Sch., 487 U.S. 450 (1988).

cost and value. In practice the agencies and courts have applied the act to both user fees and regulatory charges, compounding confusion.

OMB Circular No. A-25 interprets the requirement and fortunately recognizes the distinction discussed in this chapter between charges imposed in the government's capacity as a sovereign (called here regulatory charges) and otherwise (as a proprietor, called here user fees). Because the act and the Circular are primarily focused on recovering cost, they refer to cost as a baseline requirement for all types of charges, without well distinguishing between user fees and regulatory charges; but the Circular does refer to benefits in authorizing the use of "market prices" when the government does not act as a sovereign. The Circular recognizes the obvious fact that the federal government acts in many settings as a proprietor (charge to enter a park) although some early opinions deny that the federal government could be a proprietor.

Linking benefits to user fees is doubly hard because of a variety of competing and confusing factors: (1) charges for governmental licenses and franchises, which are sovereign acts that generally afford benefits, are taxes and not user fees;[42] (2) similarly, regulated industries pay regulatory fees and often benefit from the regulation (e.g., monopolization); (3) the Court has upheld user fees despite the failure of the charging government to solely devote the collections to providing the benefit charged for; (4) the fee payor need not actually take advantage of the service offered;[43] (5) even though the payor benefits, the government cannot charge for a service or property it does not provide.[44]

Where a city is only charging for a service like a wharf, which it provides in a proprietary and not necessarily governmental capacity, the Court has refused to investigate whether the fees produced excess revenues and how they were used by the city, so long as not "exorbitant."[45]

c. *Amount of Regulatory Charge*

The principle that a regulatory charge must be designed to recover government costs can be traced to the one constitutional provision that discusses such a charge: a particular type of fee that the Constitution treats as a tax is the state inspection fee that can be imposed on imports and exports.[46] Article I, section 10, clause 2, sometimes called the Import/Export Clause, forbids state duties,

---

[42] Jefferson County v. Acker, 527 U.S. 423 (1999).

[43] Cooley v. Board of Wardens, 53 U.S. 299 (1852); Massachusetts v. United States, 435 U.S. 444 (1978), citing Clyde Mallory Lines v. Alabama ex rel. State Docks Comm'n, 296 U.S. 261 (1935), "in which the Court held that a vessel that has not been the recipient of any police services could be required to pay a charge designed to defray their costs since the services redounded to the benefit of all vessels in the port." *Cf.* Federal Power Comm'n v. New England Power Co., 415 U.S. 345 (1974) (regulatory fee could not charge for service not used).

[44] *See* Cannon v. New Orleans, 87 U.S. 577 (1874) (wharf fee charged but there was no wharf provided); Packet Co. v. Keokuk, 95 U.S. 80 (1877) (explained the river bank versus wharf distinction); Case of State Freight Tax, 82 U.S. 232 (1873) (not a toll because state did not own the road).

[45] Ouachita Packet Co. v. Aiken, 121 U.S. 444 (1887).

[46] *See* Ch. VI.E.

except to the extent they are reasonable charges to pay for the "absolutely necessary" inspections of property imported and exported.[47] The clause requires the "net Produce" of such inspection fees to be paid to the United States.[48] Presumably this refers to the gross fee less the government cost, with the excess being an import/export tax that only the United States can enjoy.

Inspection fees should be regulatory charges, although in some cases they could also perform a service for the payor, who benefits from having its goods receive an inspection approval. The Court has basically eyeballed the challenged inspection fees for indications that a state meant it for other than cost recovery,[49] which appears also to be the Court's approach to testing the amount of regulatory charges.[50] When the regulatory charge was so new that its ability to cover the cost was unknown, the Court did not reject it as a burden on interstate commerce.[51] And the Court assumed that if the regulatory charge (inspection fee) produced much more than cost the state would reduce the fee.[52] And when part of the fee proceeds were used for other purposes in addition to the cost of regulation the burden fell on the state to explain why that was reasonable.[53]

One opinion suggests that in apportioning cost to payors of regulatory charges, the cost of providing an incidental benefit to the public must be subtracted.[54] However, this concept is suspect because it would be exceedingly hard

---

[47] *See* Youngstown Sheet & Tube Co. v. Bowers, 358 U.S. 534, 552 (1959) (dissent of Justice Frankfurter: "the only constitutional permission in terms so drastically limited").

[48] *Cf.* D. E. Foote & Co. v. Stanley, 232 U.S. 494 (1914) (not addressing payment of such net produce, but placing on the state the burden of proving its costs as to this type of fee).

[49] *See, e.g.*, Patapsco Guano Co. v. North Carolina Bd. of Agriculture, 171 U.S. 345, 353-354 (1898) ("Entertaining these views of the legislative intention, it does not appear to us that evidence tending to show that money collected from this source was applied to other than the purposes for which it was received should be entered into on this inquiry into the validity of the act. If the receipts are found to average largely more than enough to pay the expenses, the presumption would be that the legislature would moderate the charge. But treating the question whether the charge of twenty five cents per ton was shown to be so excessive as to demonstrate a purpose other than that which the law declared, as a judicial question we are satisfied that comparing the receipts from this charge with the necessary expenses, such as the cost of analyses, the salaries of inspectors, the cost of tags, express charges, miscellaneous expenses of the department in this connection, and so on, we cannot conclude that the charge is so seriously in excess of what is necessary for the objects designed to be effected, as to justify the imputation of bad faith and change the character of the act.").

[50] *See* Pace v. Burgess, 92 U.S. 372 (1875) (charge never more than cost); United States v. Sperry Corp., 493 U.S. 52 (1989) (government need not prove its costs with bills and records); Postal Telegraph-Cable Co. v. Taylor, 192 U.S. 64 (1904) (calling the "license fee" a tax even though it was a regulatory charge that was far in excess of cost; Mass. v. United States, 435 U.S. 444 (1978) (The amount of a fee must approximate the cost of the benefit received); Evansville-Vanderburgh v. Delta Airlines, Inc., 405 U.S. 707 (1972) (per passenger fee; fee is valid if it is based on some fair approximation of the usage, is not discriminatory and is not excessive in comparison with the benefit conferred); Northwest Airlines v. County of Kent, 510 U.S. 355 (1994) (states that Evansville's test has been adopted in a variety of settings).

[51] Bourjois, Inc. v. Chapman, 301 U.S. 183 (1937).

[52] Red "C" Oil Mfg. Co. v. Board of Agriculture, 222 U.S. 380 (1912).

[53] Great Northern Ry. Co. v. Washington, 300 U.S. 154 (1937).

[54] National Cable Television Ass'n v. United States, 415 U.S. 336, 340-341 (1974).

to enforce; OMB Circular A-25 says the fact of incidental benefit to the public will not prevent cost from being allocated to an identifiable recipient of special benefits.

3. *Summary Principles*

In addition to the principles governing amounts of user fees and regulatory charges, others that can be drawn from the often confusing opinions of the Court include the following (some already mentioned):

- Taxes are not required to have any relationship to the taxpayer's receipt of a benefit or not (although taxes may be paid to obtain a benefit, in the cases (a) of special assessments, and (b) of excise tax licenses and franchises for governmental privileges).[55]
- But user fees are always supposed to be imposed only on those receiving some benefit from a specific government service or provision of property.
- Although there is a "not excessive" theoretical limit,[56] the amount of the benefit usually need not be measured because the payor is presumed to be satisfied with the benefit, having elected to pay the fee in most cases; but the Court will be exacting of a state charge affecting interstate commerce,[57] and a charge affecting exports.[58]
- Regulatory charges may vary with usage of the government provided regulatory regime (*i.e.*, the "fair share" aspect of the definition), although flat fees are permissible.[59]
- The power to impose a regulatory charge does not depend on the government having a property right in some property used, but rather on its incurring a cost that may produce a private benefit.[60]
- User fees generally do not regulate as their primary purpose, although regulatory taxes can.[61]
- There is no "bright line" test for whether a levy imposed in Title 26 is necessarily a tax because it is in Title 26; rather the Court seeks to learn how Congress conceived the levy and if it has the indicia of a fee rather than a

[55] *See* Ch. IV.B and C.
[56] Northwest Airlines, Inc. v. Cty. of Kent, 510 U.S. 355 (1994).
[57] Ingels v. Morf, 300 U.S. 290 (1937).
[58] United States v. United States Shoe Corp., 523 U.S. 360 (1998).
[59] 435 U.S. at 463-464 (rough approximation is sufficient).
[60] *Id.* at 464 n. 19.
[61] *Id.* at 461. An example of a regulatory tax is the tax on oleomargarine in McCray v. United States, 195 U.S. 27 (1904).

tax,[62] which was a highly contentious issue decided in favor of a tax in the Obamacare ruling.[63]

4. *Case Chronology*

Most of these cases involve state and local fees or taxes, and involve the Constitution's prohibition on state taxation of imports and exports and tonnage duties, as well as taxation of or interference with interstate commerce. States and localities are much more likely to charge user fees for benefits or services and to impose regulatory charges, because two of their major functions as governments are to provide local services and improvements as proprietors of such improvements, and to regulate through the police power; Congress does not have a plenary police power, only enumerated powers.[64] They are also much more likely to charge license and privilege taxes (which may be called fees but are treated as taxes because the rights are granted in the state's sovereign and not proprietorship capacity), because they traditionally license and authorize so many local occupations and undertakings.

The Court's decisions in the area are as follows. After the chronology appears a summary of the factors distinguishing both user fees and regulatory charges from taxes drawn from the cases.

- 1824 (state regulatory inspection fees discussed): The seminal Commerce Clause opinion, *Gibbons v. Ogden*, did not involve a state tax or fee but discussed inspection fees as an aspect of a state's police power applied to interstate commerce.[65] The Court struck down a monopoly license New York had granted on navigation that the Court found to be part of interstate commerce. The owner of the license argued that the Constitution's prohibition of state taxes on exports and imports showed that the states retained the power to regulate interstate commerce so long as they did not tax it. The opinion rejected that argument, saying that the Import-Export and Tonnage Clauses address the taxing power,[66] not the police power, and so proved

[62] *Id.* at 453-454 (fact that federal aircraft tax was in Title 26 did not prevent the Court from treating it as a user fee).

[63] National Federation of Independent Business v. Sebelius, 567 U.S. 519 (2012) (penalty versus tax).

[64] United States v. Lopez, 514 U.S. 549 (1995).

[65] Gibbons v. Ogden, 22 U.S. 1 (1824).

[66] The opinion stated that the writers of the Constitution fully understood that a duty or impost could be motivated by intent to regulate, and it was for that reason that the Constitution prohibits them. That would seem to contradict the initial statement that the prohibition was on the taxing power, but Chief Justice Marshall reasserted that it was on the taxing power because of the fresh example of taxation by a foreign sovereign that had started the Revolutionary War. "The right to regulate commerce, even by the imposition of duties, was not controverted." 22 U.S. at 202.

nothing about the states' power to regulate commerce.[67] The opinion then turns to inspection laws, admitting that the Constitution permits states to have inspection laws, but ascribes them to the general police power ("system of police"), which Congress does not possess, and not as evidence of a power to regulate commerce among the states.[68] Thus the opinion differentiated the taxing power, the power over interstate commerce and the police power to regulate matters internal to a state, and made an observation that explains the continuing confusion in the area: "All experience shows, that the same measures, or measures scarcely distinguishable from each other, may flow from distinct powers; but this does not prove that the powers themselves are identical. Although the means used in their execution may sometimes approach each other so nearly as to be confounded, there are other situations in which they are sufficiently distinct to establish their individuality."[69] The Court ruled that New York could not restrict by license that subject (interstate commerce) over which it had no power.

- 1827 (state "license" tax is a tax and not a user fee or regulatory tax): *Brown v. Maryland* ruled unconstitutional as a burden on foreign commerce a $50 state license for selling "imported" items in the "original package" (this case coined the original package doctrine), in violation of Article I, section 10, clause 2: "No State shall, without the Consent of the Congress, lay any Imposts or Duties on Imports or Exports, except what may be absolutely necessary for executing it's inspection Laws. . . ."[70] As a charge for a government license the $50 surely was a tax and also had nothing to do with inspection, but Chief Justice Marshall went far afield to state that an inspection charge on exports would be a tax, because it had to be part of the category of taxes from which it was excepted. It is likely that he was using the term "duty" in the broader sense of any levy incident to an export.[71] He said inspection fees would be for a service, and perhaps they might be and so be user fees, but more commonly would seem to be regulatory charges. In conjunction with *Cooley* (1852), discussed below, and several other opinions, this decision illustrates the rule applied in practice that a license that grants a right to do something is not for a governmental service or benefit and so the cost is not a fee but a tax.

---

[67] *See also* State Tonnage Tax Cases, 79 U.S. 12 (1870) (confirming that *Gibbons* determined the duties at issue in the Constitution are taxes, with the consequence that the states had the power to lay them under the Confederation, except as limited by the Constitution, unlike interstate commerce, which the states did not have the power to regulate). The police power broadly refers to the general powers of government, which frequently can regulate private property and so recognition of states' police power can be undesirable to property rights. *See* BERNARD SCHWARTZ, A HISTORY OF THE SUPREME COURT 80 (1993) [hereinafter SCHWARTZ] (citing the *Passenger Cases*, Smith v. Turner, 48 U.S. 283, 403 (1849) and Norris v. Boston, 48 U.S. 283 (1849)).

[68] 22 U.S. at 203.

[69] 22 U.S. at 204.

[70] Brown v. Maryland, 25 U.S. 419 (1827).

[71] *Id.* at 438. This appears to be at odds with the reasoning in *Gibbons* that the inspection laws were allowed under the states' police power. *Brown* did not discuss this aspect of *Gibbons*.

- 1847: The *License Cases* distinguished *Brown v. Maryland* and upheld state laws requiring licenses to sell products, most importantly alcoholic beverages, some of which had come from interstate commerce.[72] The opinion did not discuss whether the $1 Maryland license tax was a tax or fee, but treated it as a tax.
- 1849 (possible use of tax to provide possible benefit to taxpayer does not make state tax a fee): The *Passenger Cases, Smith v. Turner*, considered flat per head taxes charged by two ports on immigrants ostensibly for the operation of a marine hospital for their future benefit or some other vague protections.[73] In part because the use of the funds was not limited to any such purpose, the opinions of Justices McLean and Wayne (who tried to list the salient points of the multiple opinions) did not even consider the tax might be a fee for services, but struck it down as a tax on commerce.[74] The unconstitutional state tax was quite similar to the constitutional federal duty in the *Head Money Cases* (1884).
- 1852 (state user fees for services not taxes): *Cooley*, also known as the *Pilot Case*, interpreted the Import-Export Clause not to prohibit state fees for pilots, wharfage, pilotage and other services rendered to ships or cargo.[75] Thus a distinction was drawn between charges for inspection that a state could not impose (at least inspection of imports, under *Brown v. Maryland*) and charges for services, which might be allowed. Presumably the Court thought inspection could not occur without an import or export, whereas the services are not so limited. *Cooley* is the first opinion to state clearly that fees for services are not taxes. It even allowed a half fee for ships that were offered and declined the pilotage. It has been cited many times for its definition of governmental services. However, the *Cooley* decision primarily

---

[72] Thurlow v. Mass., 46 U.S. 504 (1847).

[73] Smith v. Turner, 48 U.S. 283, 403 (1849) (also stated in dictum that even the United States could be made to pay a toll for use of state roads because the toll was not a tax but a compensation for the advantage of using the improvement); Norris v. Boston, 48 U.S. 283 (1849). These cases reflect an exclusivity view of Congress' interstate commerce regulatory powers, which has been repudiated. *See* Southern Pac. Co. v. Arizona, 325 U.S. 761, 766-767 (1945). See Louis B. Boudin, Government by Judiciary 418-429 (1932, 1968 reprint) [hereinafter Boudin] (explaining the intense slavery issue dispute reflected in this case); Carl B. Swisher, Roger B. Taney 402-406 (1935) (Chief Justice Taney dissented, relying on a previous statement of the Court that people were not imports and so a state could regulate the migration of people, which would include slaves, but not citizens, who have the right to travel from state to state without being taxed).

[74] *See* Boudin, at 415-418. *Smith v. Turner* attempted to distinguish an earlier opinion allowing a state fee on immigrants as an early application of the states' police power, New York v. Miln, 36 U.S. 102 (1837). These two cases reflected concerns about importation of slaves as well as state versus federal authority, and so their tax implications are suspect. The *Cooley* decision discussed next somewhat resolved the confusion of these cases.

[75] Cooley v. Bd. of Wardens, 53 U.S. 299 (1852). *But see* Smith v. Turner, 48 U.S. 283, 401-402 (1849) (explaining that the states' pilot laws were incorporated by Congress into federal regulation of commerce). *Cooley* is viewed as establishing the doctrine that Congress' power over interstate commerce is selectively exclusive. *See* Schwartz, at 83.

turned on the issue of national Commerce Clause power versus the state's regulatory powers, with the Court creating a ground for distinction based on the pilotage services and fees being inherently local, regardless of their impact on imports.[76]

- 1867 (federal regulatory "license" tax that does not authorize anything is a tax): The *License Tax Cases* upheld the federal tax required for licenses to engage in intrastate activities, not interstate commerce, which the United States could not regulate (such as selling alcohol).[77] The tax could even fall on activities illegal under state law. The licenses did not purport to authorize the activities; rather the person could be prosecuted by the United States if he performed the wholly intrastate activities without the federal license. Therefore, because the license granted no benefit (except protection from prosecution) it could not have been a true license tax or a user fee and was a regulatory tax that did not invade the state's rights.[78] This opinion presents a startling, if now commonplace, usage of the term license: a paper that does not grant a right (because the sovereign may not have the power to grant the right), but without which the licensee may be criminally charged.[79]
- 1867 (a state user fee must at least purportedly be for some benefit): A $5 tax on all ships entering the port was an unconstitutional tonnage duty (tax) and not a user fee.[80] It was not analogous to the half pilot fee allowed in *Cooley* even though no service was provided there, because there a service was offered. Here no service was offered and the tax was said to be for the general support of the port warden; it evidently did not depend on wharfing, but solely on entering the port. This case was appealed from Louisiana and bridged the Civil War from start to finish, which likely had something to do with the outcome.[81] In contrast, *Packet Co. v. St. Louis* (1880) where the city did provide a wharf.

---

[76] Carl Brent Fisher, American Constitutional Development 205 (1954) (explaining that the rule established was that while Congress was supreme in regulating commerce, it could leave to the states matters as to which diversity rather than uniformity was required).

[77] License Tax Cases, 72 U.S. 462 (1867). The opinion does not indicate that the tax would not be a tax if the United States had the power to grant a license. It explains that license taxes are just taxes.

[78] *See* Nat'l Fed'n of Indep. Bus. v. Sebelius, 567 U.S. 519 (2012), (citing the *License Tax Cases* as a primary example of a federal exaction that was not labeled a tax but that function as a tax).

[79] *See, e.g.*, N.C. Admin. Rules 17 NCAC 04B.0604 (imposing a privilege license tax on CPAs and specifically stating that it is not a regulatory measure and CPAs must obtain separate approval to practice).

[80] S.S. Co. v. Portwardens, 73 U.S. 31 (1867) (treated as an unconstitutional tonnage duty even though not based on tonnage); *implicitly overruled by* Clyde Mallory Lines v. Alabama, 296 U.S. 261 (1935) (which found a similar charge for general port supervision to be a fee).

[81] This case languished on appeal for eight years. 14 La. App. 595 (1859).

- 1870: The *State Tonnage Tax Cases* did not juxtapose a tax and a fee (while observing that a fee for inspection was proper) but ruled that a tonnage duty could not be disguised as a property tax based on tonnage.[82]
- 1873 (sovereignty versus proprietorship): The *Case of State Freight Tax* found a state tax on freight shipped on railroads to be an unconstitutional burden on interstate commerce because it could not be a toll (user fee) because the state did not provide the road.[83] Thus it could only be a tax, and as a tax it had the ability to be increased to any amount, which is why states could not tax interstate commerce.[84] This opinion applied the phrase and concept that taxation is a right of sovereignty (as discussed in Chapter II.A), whereas a toll or charge for use of property requires acting as a proprietor of property.
- 1874 (state proprietorship charge for use of property was not aspect of sovereignty): *Cannon* identified a category of government fees that were not taxes: fees charged by a proprietor, which happened to be a city, for use of improved city property, in this case a wharf.[85] The fact that the charge varied with the ship's tonnage did not make it an unconstitutional duty on tonnage because the charge was for a service that could reasonably relate to tonnage. But because the charge applied both to ships that used the dock and ships that docked on the riverbank, the charge was a duty on interstate commerce and void.[86]
- 1874 (state inspection fee based on tonnage not an inspection fee): In contrast with the earlier 1874 case and the 1886 case below, *Peete* struck down as a tax an inspection fee to enforce a necessary quarantine, because it was measured by the ship's tonnage and evidently did not depend on an inspection.[87]
- 1875 (federal regulatory charge may be arbitrary in amount so long as not grossly excessive): *Pace* found to be a regulatory charge and not an unconstitutional tax on exports a 25 cent stamp that an exporter could affix to a package of any size to prove that it was for export and was not to be taxed

---

[82] State Tonnage Tax Cases, 79 U.S. 204 (1870).

[83] Case of State Freight Tax, 82 U.S. 232 (1873).

[84] The jurisprudence of state taxation of interstate commerce underwent several transformations and cases such as this are not representative of current law, at least as to whether the state can tax. *See* Oklahoma Tax Comm'n v. Jefferson Lines, 514 U.S. 175 (1995).

[85] Cannon v. New Orleans, 87 U.S. 577 (1874). *See also* Packet Co. v. Keokuk, 95 U.S. 80 (1877).

[86] *Cf.* Clyde Mallory Lines v. Alabama, 296 U.S. 261 (1935) (allowing port charge where port policing accrued to benefit of all, even though no specific service used, as stated in Massachusetts v. United States, 435 U.S. 444 n. 23 (1978), which analogized the federal fee for airspace use to *Mallory*).

[87] Peete v. Morgan, 86 U.S. 581 (1874).

under another provision.[88] The Court waived aside discussion of the actual cost of the stamp and said that the amount might be arbitrarily fixed so long as not obviously excessive (although the cost exceeded the charge). The opinion acknowledged that stamps usually were for taxes but not in this case. The Court later indicated that the rule of *Pace* for Export Clause purposes is stricter than outside that context.[89] Although the fee might also be viewed as a fee for service, it seems most congruent with a regulatory charge.

- 1877 (state tonnage prohibition is particularly strict): A fee based on tonnage on all ships entering the port is an unconstitutional tonnage duty.[90] The fee may pay for important port regulation, but because it is measured by nothing but tonnage and charged for entering the port without docking, it cannot be said to be compensation for anything.

- 1880: The Court upheld a wharfage duty of 7 and ½ cents per ton as a user fee because it was reasonably related to the value of the benefit to the ship, the benefit being the generalized availability of a well regulated harbor and not the specific use of the wharf.[91] The opinion also implied that the fee approximated the cost because it stated the city was not trying to raise excess revenue. It did not mention the 1867 opinion that seems contrary, except that the charge there was not dependent on using the wharf and was a flat amount.

- 1881 (state user fees for improvements are not limited to one time collections): The Court rejected the argument that the city could not continue to collect fees for docking after it had recovered the cost of the improvements; the fee could be paying for the ongoing costs of the wharf.[92]

---

[88] Pace v. Burgess, 92 U.S. 372 (1875). *See also* Carson v. Brockton Sewerage Com., 182 U.S. 398 (1901) (the legislature can set the rate and so long as it is not grossly excessive or out of all proportion to the benefit received, it is allowed).

[89] United States v. United States Shoe Corp., 523 U.S. 360, 369-370 (1998).

[90] Inman S.S. Co. v. Tinker, 94 U.S. 238 (1877).

[91] Packet Co. v. St. Louis, 100 U.S. 423 (1880). *See also* Vicksburg v. Tobin, 100 U.S. 430 (1880) (upholding a wharfage fee against an assertion that the city was charging for docking at the unimproved river bank; found city had improved the wharf and was charging for docking there).

[92] Packet Co. v. Catlettsburg, 105 U.S. 559 (1881). The plaintiff did not actually claim the fee was excessive in terms of the value provided. The opinion also implied that an excessive wharfage fee is not a tax but is an unconstitutionally excessive fee.

- 1883 (state inspection of exports): Outage charge levied for inspection of tobacco exports was a permitted inspection duty.[93] The inspection regime appears to have been a method of market regulation designed to require all tobacco grown in the state to pass through the local warehouses where inspection would occur, which supports the treatment as a regulatory charge.
- 1883 (state inspection of imports): A New York law and fee were not for inspection of imports because that term applies only to inspection of property and the law purported to inspect immigrants; moreover the inspection involved taking testimony as to character and mental capacity.[94]
- 1883 (state wharfage fee): In another case attacking a wharfage fee the Court essentially refused to evaluate whether the user fee was excessive, stating that was for the state to decide.[95]
- 1884 (federal duty in aid of regulating immigration; likely regulatory charge): The famous *Head Money Cases* opinion ruled that a federal duty on immigrants per head was constitutional under the power to regulate commerce and so whether the duty qualified under the taxing power was not controlling, although uniformity was discussed (but the amount of the duty was not discussed).[96] It has been suggested that the *Head Money Cases* opinion provides a standard for governmental fees; that is not necessarily true.[97] The opinion did analogize the duty to the charge in a wharfage fee case, but it also analogized it to the levy that clearly was not a fee for service in *Veazie Bank*.[98] Just because an amount charged with respect to a subject the United States has the power to regulate (immigration) is not a tax (which it might have been in this case, although the opinion has been viewed as not calling it a tax) does not mean it must be a fee for service, which would require that the benefit or cost be approximated in the fee. Rather, there is an ample third category of regulatory charges that are designed to make the subjects of regulation pay for the regulation, and which may incidentally be related to some benefit to the payor.
- 1886 (regulatory charge for quarantine): A ship could be made to pay a fee for its own inspection under quarantine laws.[99] *Peete* was distinguished as

---

[93] Turner v. Md., 107 U.S. 38 (1883) (containing an extensive recitation of the Colonies' inspection laws at the time of the Constitutional Convention).

[94] People v. Compagnie Generale Transatlantique, 107 U.S. 59 (1883).

[95] Transp. Co. v. Parkersburg, 107 U.S. 691 (1883). It is not clear that the Court actually believed this. *See, e.g.*, Minnesota Rate Cases, 230 U.S. 352 (1913) (citing *Parkersburg* for that principle); Hopkins v. United States, 171 U.S. 578, 596 (1898) (stating that a remedy "would probably be forthcoming" if the rate was excessive).

[96] Edye v. Robertson, 112 U.S. 580 (1884) (Head Money Cases).

[97] Jason Burge, *Rethinking Fees and Taxes in Light of the New York City Health Care Security Act*, 61 N.Y.U. Ann. Sur. Am. L. 679 (2006).

[98] 112 U.S. at 595.

[99] Morgan's S.S. Co. v. Louisiana Bd. of Health, 118 U.S. 455 (1886) (and any excess could be used for general revenue purposes).

involving a fee charged whether any inspection was done or not. Also the fee was a flat dollar amount per type of ship, not per ton as in *Peete*.

- 1887 (administrative power to fix tolls but not taxes): Tolls are neither taxes nor are they a taking of property to which a due process claim could apply; they are a user fee for a supposed benefit from using property.[100] Not being taxes, tolls need not be set by the legislature.
- 1887 (excess funds from user fees): Where neither interstate commerce nor the Import-Export Clause was involved, the Court refused to declare a local wharfage fee to be excessive simply because excess funds were produced over and above the costs of maintaining the wharf and were paid into the state treasury. The opinion indicated that so long as the fee was not exorbitant under an undefined standard, a state could earn a profit on the fees that was used for general revenue purposes, and the fee would not be converted into a tax.[101]
- 1888 (state privilege license fee is a tax): Ruled that a state license tax (fee) for the right to have an office in the state based on the amount of capital of a foreign corporation was a tax that did not violate the equal protection clause.[102]
- 1892 (in case of regulated industry, state regulatory charge could reflect benefit to public and not business): Railroads were made to pay the costs of the state railroad commissioners even though their activities were largely for the benefit of the public.[103]
- 1893 (sovereignty versus property): The Court ruled that a city's charge per pole erected along streets by a telegraph company was not a privilege or license tax but was a fee for use of property, the streets.[104] It stated that taxes are demands of sovereignty, whereas tolls (like this charge was found to be) are demands of proprietorship.
- 1898 (state inspection fee): State could charge for quality inspection of imports, including imports from other states; we would categorize the fee as a regulatory charge.[105]

---

[100] Sands v. Manistee River Improvement Co., 123 U.S. 288 (1887).

[101] Ouachita Packet Co. v. Aiken, 121 U.S. 444 (1887) ("Clearly it must be by the local municipal law, at least until some superior or paramount law has been prescribed. . . . The courts of the United States do not enforce the common law in municipal matters in the States because it is Federal law, but because it is the law of the State."). *See also* Huse v. Glover, 119 U.S. 543 (1886) (same statement about using surplus funds for general purposes).

[102] Pembina Consol. Silver Mining & Milling Co. v. Pennsylvania, 125 U.S. 181 (1888).

[103] Charlotte, C. & A. R. Co. v. Gibbes, 142 U.S. 386 (1892).

[104] St. Louis v. Western Union Tel. Co., 148 U.S. 92 (1893). *See also* Mackay Tel. & Cable Co. v. Little Rock, 250 U.S. 94 (1919) (pole rental).

[105] Patapsco Guano Co. v. North Carolina Bd. of Agriculture, 171 U.S. 345 (1898)(quoted Chief Justice Marshall's opinions stating that the Import/Export Clause inspection fees could apply to imports).

- 1903 (state telephone pole charge): In a confused opinion the Court insisted a license tax on a telegraph company was not a tax but a police power regulatory charge, although it was priced like a use fee for polls.[106]
- 1906 (territorial inspection fee): The Court upheld a territorial inspection fee for exports and likened it to an inspection fee permitted under the Import/Export Clause (which did not apply).[107]
- 1906 (inspection fee): police power inspection fee regulatory charge.
- 1911 (grazing fees): Federal agency could set charges for grazing cattle on federal lands, a user fee.[108]
- 1915 (auto licenses): Licensing vehicles for road use was a fee for use of the improvements made by state to the roads and not a tax on interstate commerce.[109]
- 1923 (recording fee/tax): County could charge a user fee for recording a federal mortgage but could not charge the United States an additional 15 cents per hundred dollars, which was a tax.[110]
- 1928 (state excise tax that is for use of roads called a tax but likely was a user fee): State charged one cent per mile excise "mileage tax" for use of roads by interstate carriers, but carriers in intrastate travel paid a percentage of gross receipts.[111] The opinion ruled the tax constitutional; it viewed the taxes as for support of the roads but did not indicate it was other than a tax. Later opinions referred to it as a toll.[112]
- 1928 (state occupation or privilege license tax was a tax): Justice Brandeis examined a flat charge for the privilege of driving a bus in a city.[113] He found that it could not be a fee because it was not used to maintain the roads and was not said to do so and was not proportioned to use. It could be an occupation tax (otherwise called a license tax or privilege license), if it did not discriminate against interstate travel, which it did because it was applicable to solely interstate transportation.
- 1929 (state franchise tax labeled a license fee): The Court treated as a franchise tax without discussion a license fee imposed on the capital of corporations by a state for the privilege of operating in the state.[114]

---

[106] Atlantic & Pacific Tel. Co. v. Philadelphia, 190 U.S. 160 (1903). *See also* Western Union Tel. Co. v. New Hope, 187 U.S. 419 (1903).

[107] New Mexico ex rel. E. J. McLean & Co. v. Denver & R. G. R. Co., 203 U.S. 38 (1906).

[108] United States v. Grimaud, 220 U.S. 506 (1911).

[109] Hendrick v. Maryland, 235 U.S. 610 (1915).

[110] Federal Land Bank v. Crosland, 261 U.S. 374 (1923).

[111] Interstate Busses Corp. v. Blodgett, 276 U.S. 245 (1928).

[112] Evansville-Vanderburgh v. Delta Airlines, Inc., 405 U.S. 707 (1972); United Air Lines v. Mahin, 410 U.S. 623 (1973).

[113] Sprout v. South Bend, 277 U.S. 163 (1928).

[114] New York v. Latrobe, 279 U.S. 421 (1929).

- 1935 (state user fee can be for general and not specific benefit): The *Clyde Mallory* opinion found a $7.50 charge for large ships to defray the city's costs of policing the harbor to be a fee and not a duty of tonnage even though the benefit to the ship was only general.[115] It analogized the fee to the half fee for declined pilot services in *Cooley*, as a "cost of regulation."
- 1937 (state user fee excessive as burden on interstate commerce): Because the state chose to label and defend as a fee a per car charge for "caravaning" cars by dealers, and could not trace the funds into a use for highway improvement, the Court held it failed the stated purpose and found that the cost of that purpose was about one tenth of the sum raised, hence the fee was excessive and unconstitutional as a burden on interstate commerce.[116]
- 1938 (federal/Hawaii "fee" for general regulation is not a fee but a tax): Despite being denominated a fee, Justice Black without hesitation upheld as a tax a levy on gross income of shipping companies allowed by federal statute, which placed such shipping under the territorial control of Hawaii (thus removing Commerce Clause questions). The taxpayer protested that the tax was out of proportion to the amount of regulation (*i.e.*, "benefit") it received, but the Court said that was irrelevant because it found the tax to be a "general tax" for protection of the public and subject to the general rule that "a tax is not an assessment of benefits."[117] This reflects an extreme willingness to treat a federally approved exaction as a tax, despite (1) the failure to call it a tax, (2) the targeting of the fee at a limited number of payors, and (3) the intended use of the revenues in relation to the industry of the taxpayers.
- 1943 (state license fee charged to exercise civil rights is a tax if it is not a regulatory charge): Justice Douglas ruled that a city could not require payment of a license tax to go door to door because the requirement infringed the freedom of religion; if the charge had been for a right the city could grant it could have been a valid license tax.[118] It was not a nominal fee to defray the costs of policing. Justice Frankfurter dissented.[119] As usual, Justice Jackson's dissent in a companion case was more cogent.[120] Among other things, he

[115] Clyde Mallory Lines v. Alabama, 296 U.S. 261 (1935).

[116] Ingels v. Morf, 300 U.S. 290 (1937) (probably regulatory charge).

[117] Inter-Island Steam Navigation Co. v. Hawaii, 305 U.S. 306 (1938).

[118] Murdock v. Pennsylvania, 319 U.S. 105 (1943). *See also* Forsyth County v. Nationalist Movement, 505 U.S. 123 (1992) (parade fee unconstitutional because it could vary in amount based on content of speech).

[119] He stated that exercise of a constitutional right (such as publishing) could be conditioned on payment of a license tax. Presumably only for purposes of the freedom of religion analysis, Frankfurter said it made no difference whether the levy was a license tax or a regulatory fee designed to cover the cost of regulation; he said governments can choose to earmark revenues and that did not change their character. He turned the usual distinction between tax and fee on its head by stating that the ultimate question about a tax was whether the state has given something for which it may charge; his point was that religious groups benefit from an ordered society and should pay for it.

[120] Douglas v. City of Jeannette, 319 U.S. 157 (1943).

thought Justice Douglas' distinction between a nominal fee and the license tax failed. He stated: "This Court is forever adding new stories to the temples of constitutional law, and the temples have a way of collapsing when one story too many is added. So it was with liberty of contract, which was discredited by being overdone."[121]

- 1948 (fishing license taxes): The first of a series of cases on fishing license discrimination, which generally treat the license fees as taxes.[122]
- 1951 (charge for privilege granted by state is a tax): *Spector Motor Service* treated a charge for the privilege of conducting interstate carriage in the state to be a tax for a privilege the state could not grant.[123] *Complete Auto Transit* overruled *Spector* on other grounds (see below).
- 1952: Congress enacted the predecessor of 31 U.S.C. section 9701, which directs federal agencies to charge for each service or thing of value, with the amount to reflect a variety of considerations including cost and value. This statute has been applied to authorize both user fees and regulatory charges.[124]
- 1953: A city called a tax on income of individuals an occupational license fee and the Court deemed it an income tax under the Buck Act.[125]
- 1972 (local airport user fee): A $1 per passenger airport fee was a reasonable approximation of costs where it did not exceed the costs; it was not relevant that the funds were not earmarked for use in the terminals.[126]
- 1974 (federal regulatory charge limited by fee statute): The Court remanded for determination whether a 30 cents per customer fee for services charged by FCC to cable TV operators was reasonable.[127] The FCC levied the annual fees, which were not for licenses, under 31 U.S.C. section 9701, enacted in 1052. Primarily because the statute let the agency set the fee, the opinion concludes it was a fee and not a tax. Arguably based on an interpretation of the specific statute authorizing the fee, the Court determined that the fee improperly attempted to recover the entire costs of regulation even though part of the benefit of regulation went to the public. The Court later explained

---

[121] 319 U.S. at 181. *Cf.* Barry Friedman, The Will of the People 189 (2009) (Learned Hand said to construe liberty of contract into liberty "is entirely to disregard the whole juristic history of the word") and Thomas Reed Powell said "no such doctrine is stated in the Constitution.").

[122] Toomer v. Witsell, 334 U.S. 385 (1948). *See also* Mullaney v. Anderson, 342 U.S. 415 (1952); Baldwin v. Fish & Game Comm'n, 436 U.S. 371 (1978).

[123] Spector Motor Serv. v. O'Connor, 340 U.S. 602 (1951).

[124] National Cable Television Ass'n v. United States, 415 U.S. 336 (1974) (regulatory charge).

[125] Howard v. Commissioners of Sinking Fund, 344 U.S. 624 (1953).

[126] Evansville-Vanderburgh v. Delta Airlines, Inc., 405 U.S. 707 (1972).

[127] National Cable Television Ass'n v. United States, 415 U.S. 336 (1974). *See also* FPC v. New England Power Co., 415 U.S. 345 (1974) (companion case). *See* Cummings, *Meandering From Income to Consumption Taxes via User Fees*, 152 Tax Notes 1241 (Aug. 29, 2016).

this case as saying that if the payor did not benefit then the levy might be a tax and to avoid that possibility it interpreted the statute strictly.[128]

- 1976: A federal "license fee" system for restricting oil imports was reasonable.[129] The Court said the fee was not a tax for purposes of the Anti-Injunction Act because it was not enacted under Title 26, but rather it was in aid of the regulation of imports (therefore, it need not be a tax under the taxing power and the characterization as a tax or fee was not controlling). It must have been a regulatory charge.
- 1977 (new proportional use standard for Commerce Clause tax compliance by states): *Complete Auto Transit* overruled *Spector Motor Service.*[130] The tax was levied on the gross receipts of an interstate bus company for the "privilege" of operating in the state. The Court indicated that the privilege label was not relevant and treated it as a tax. The opinion established a four part test for Commerce Clause compliance, one of which is "reasonably related to benefits provided."[131] This "benefits" test is not, however, the same as the user fee benefits standard and does not mean that state charges subject to the test are user fees (which most are clearly not). It also does not mean that these taxes must produce benefits to the taxpayer in any context other than the interstate commerce analysis.
- 1978 (expansive view of federal regulatory charge): The United States could impose a flat "registration tax" on civil aircraft because it functioned as a "user fee."[132] The opinion substantially confuses the issues of this chapter because it persistently called the federal aviation regulatory charge a user fee despite the fact that the federal government was not giving the aircraft use of any property or service, but rather of the right to fly under federal regulation, a sovereign act. The United States did not have to own the property of the airports in order to be able to impose the charge and the fact that the tax was flat did not prevent it so long as it was a rough approximation of the cost. Because it was not a tax it was not subject to Chief Justice Marshall's fears about destructive taxes, and the amount could be set by the agency. The opinion unfortunately flips back and forth between tax and fee terminology, but it is clear that the Court treated the tax as a regulatory charge.
- 1987: The Court found flat taxes on trucks in interstate commerce to be discriminatory and violate the Commerce Clause.[133] The opinion consistently referred to the fees as taxes. Evidently the state made no effort to prove that the amount was a reasonable charge for use of the roads, and so waived the potential of calling the levy a fee; the focus of the opinion was

---

[128] Skinner v. Mid-America Pipeline Co., 490 U.S. 212 (1989).
[129] Federal Energy Administration v. Algonquin SNG, Inc., 426 U.S. 548 (1976).
[130] Complete Auto Transit, Inc. v. Brady, 430 U.S. 274 (1977).
[131] *See also* American Trucking Ass'ns v. Scheiner, 483 U.S. 266 (1987).
[132] Massachusetts v. United States, 435 U.S. 444 (1978).
[133] American Trucking Ass'ns v. Scheiner, 483 U.S. 266 (1987).

on the discrimination, which resulted in the effective overruling of several earlier opinions.

- 1989 (no stricter standards for delegation of federal power to fix fees or taxes): Plaintiff argued that federal fee for safety measures related to pipelines were actually taxes, and so subject to more strict nondelegation standards (as had been ruled in earlier cases).[134] The Court disagreed that there was a stricter nondelegation standard for taxes, ruling that it did not matter whether or not the fee was a tax because the standards for delegation of authority to the agency to fix the amount was the same, and was met in this case (and did not decide whether the fee was a tax, although it probably was a regulatory charge).
- 1989: Reasonable user fees (court costs) are not subject to just compensation as for a taking if imposed to recompense federal government cost.[135] The government does not need to record invoices and billable hours to justify its fee. All that is required is a fair approximation of the cost of benefits (citing *Massachusetts v. United States*). One and one half percent of a recovery was not an excessive fee. Deduction of fee from funds to which plaintiff was entitled did not make it more of a "taking." The user did not have to be willing. Retroactive application of the fee was permissible.
- 1992: The federal surcharge on out of state nuclear waste shipments levied on states was confirmed as a regulatory tax, based on either Congress's Commerce Clause powers or taxing power.[136]
- 1994: The local airport authority could recover all of the costs of operating the airport from user fees charged to the airlines and not to concessionaires that also used the facility.[137]
- 1996: (federal tax violated Import-Export Clause) *IBM* relied in part on the view that "imposts and duties" on imports and exports is a narrower concept than taxes.[138]
- 1998 (purported federal user fee amount not correlated to benefits was a tax): The Court ruled the federal Harbor Maintenance Fee to be an unconstitutional export duty and not a fee.[139] The fee was a fixed percentage of the cargo's value. It was deposited in the Harbor Maintenance Trust Fund from which Congress could appropriate moneys for harbor maintenance. The

---

[134] Skinner v. Mid-America Pipeline Co., 490 U.S. 212 (1989). *See also* Federal Energy Administration v. Algonquin SNG, Inc., 426 U.S. 548 (1976) (Congress can delegate to administration power to vary taxes based on a standard).

[135] United States v. Sperry Corp., 493 U.S. 52 (1989).

[136] New York v. United States, 505 U.S. 144 (1992) ("is no more than a federal tax on interstate commerce, which petitioners do not claim to be an invalid exercise of either Congress' commerce or taxing power.").

[137] Northwest Airlines, Inc. v. Cty. of Kent, 510 U.S. 355 (1994).

[138] United States v. IBM, 517 U.S. 843 (1996) (involved the Export Clause).

[139] United States v. United States Shoe Corp., 523 U.S. 360 (1998).

opinion distinguished *Pace v. Burgess* and said that the ad valorem fee did not correlate sufficiently with harbor maintenance costs or benefits to be a fee for purposes of the Export Clause, indicating that an unusually strict test should be applied in such cases.

- 1999 (license fee is a tax): A county could levy a license tax on a federal judge based on income because the tax applied to all judges in the county.[140] The Public Salary Tax Act was satisfied. The opinion implied that if the license had granted a right to be a judge or had involved a regulatory scheme, then it would not be a tax, which is in contrast to other cases treating license taxes as taxes, but perhaps this statement is limited to the Public Salary Tax Act interpretation. The opinion disregarded the fact that the statute made it a crime to be a judge without paying the tax, by stating that in practice the government only tried to collect the tax. The holding is essentially similar to that in the *License Tax Cases.*[141]
- 2009 (services generally available to all taxpayers cannot be charged for by a fee). In an important tonnage tax case the Court rejected a claim that a tax on ships taking on oil in a harbor was a fee for services rendered because it was for the general benefit of police, fire, environmental, etc., services that are available to all taxpayers.[142] Therefore it was an unconstitutional tonnage duty. Presumably the case would have come out differently if the fee had been for specific harbor maintenance.
- 2012: In the highly contested attack on the Obamacare "individual mandate" the Court barely ruled that it was a tax and hence not invalidated because it was an attempt to regulate conduct the Court could not agree that Congress could regulate.[143]

5. *User Fee/Regulatory Charges/Tax: Distinguishing Factors*

The criteria for distinguishing user fees and regulatory charges (both state and federal) from taxes relied on by the Court in the preceding cases include the following:

- As discussed in Chapter IV.C, below, taxes are in general charged under the powers of a sovereign, while user fees generally are charged in a proprietary status, like other private proprietors, which explains why privilege license taxes generally are taxes and not fees even though they grant a benefit to the

---

[140] Jefferson County v. Acker, 527 U.S. 423 (1999).

[141] License Tax Cases, 72 U.S. 462 (1867).

[142] Polar Tankers, Inc. v. City of Valdez, 557 U.S. 1 (2009). The dissent explained an often overlooked distinction between property taxes based on value and levied only when the ship had taxing situs in the jurisdiction, versus impermissible tonnage duties where the ship could not be subject to a property tax based on situs and the charge bore no relation to the services. But the majority said situs was too easy to establish to make that principle controlling; it asked instead whether the alleged property tax was uniformly imposed on others.

[143] National Federation of Independent Business v. Sebelius, 567 U.S. 519 (2012) (penalty versus tax). *See* Cummings, 136 Tax Notes 599 (July 30, 2012).

payor.[144] However, a government sometimes can choose to impose the same fee as an excise tax or a regulatory tax.[145]

- Terminology and labels don't control: it is the thing, not the name, which is to be considered.[146] The Court frequently says that, but it is not clear that it has firmly in mind the substantive alternatives.
- The Court will give credence to a commercial understanding of the difference between a fee and a tax (particularly in the context of the constitutional drafting).[147]
- The Court will consider that the nature of an alleged fee is such that it obviously could not conform to the asserted constitutional tax rule.[148]
- Relation of user fee to permitted and denied measures: The fact that a state fee is based on a ship's tonnage does not necessarily make it a tonnage duty if it is charged for a service that varies with tonnage.[149]
- To be a user fee a charge must be in exchange for some actual benefit conferred by service or property or use of property, usually by the expenditure of state money, rather than for a right as in the nature of a toll where there is no road.[150]
- The relatively few opinions that say a user fee must not be substantially out of proportion to the benefits provided are either very early cases or involved

---

[144] The distinction between a state acting its sovereign capacity and its proprietary capacity is stated here as a conceptual distinction and is not analogous to the rejected similar distinction in the intergovernmental immunity area. *See* Garcia v. San Antonio Metro. Transit Authority, 469 U.S. 528, 542 n. 7 (1985).

[145] *See* Staff of the Joint Committee on Taxation, Background and Present Law Relating to Funding Mechanisms of the "E-Rate" Telecommunications Program, Background and Present Law, sec. C, n. 13, JCX-59-98 (July 31, 1998), *available on* JCT Website (indicating that Congress could choose to charge a regulatory fee as an excise tax).

[146] Cooley v. Bd. of Wardens, 53 U.S. 299, 314 (1852). *See also* Packet Co. v. Keokuk, 95 U.S. 80 (1877) (wharfage fee); Massachusetts v. United States, 435 U.S. 444, 453-454 (1978) (even though called a tax and located in the Internal Revenue Code, determined to be a fee that was a regulatory charge); United States v. United States Shoe Corp., 523 U.S. 360 (1998) (harbor maintenance tax was a tax and hence an impermissible export duty and was not a user fee simply because it was said to be levied for the benefit of using the harbor); Pace v. Burgess, 92 U.S. 372, 375-376 (1875) (a fee was not tax and the fee was not excessive, taking into account the cost of arrangements needed both "to give to the exporter the benefit of exemption from taxation, and . . . to secure . . . against the perpetration of fraud."); Inter-Island Steam Navigation Co. v. Hawaii, 305 U.S. 306 (1938) (fee was a constitutional tax). *Cf.* United States v. IBM, 517 U.S. 843 (1996) (tax on insurance policies on exports; government did not even assert that excise tax in the Internal Revenue Code was a fee).

[147] Cooley v. Bd. of Wardens, 53 U.S. 299, 314 (1852).

[148] *Id.* (pilot fees necessarily vary with local conditions).

[149] Packet Co. v. Keokuk, 95 U.S. 80 (1877) (wharfage fee).

[150] Cannon v. New Orleans, 87 U.S. 577 (1874) (docking fee where the ships had to dock on the river bank); Packet Co. v. St. Louis, 100 U.S. 423 (1880) (improved wharf).

an issue of discrimination against interstate commerce or actually mean the fee can vary with usage, and may actually involve a regulatory charge.[151]

- The regulatory charges paid by a regulated industry normally can reflect benefits to the public from the regulation, but not exclusively.[152]
- The Court will consider the purposes behind the constitutional limits, such as hindering commerce, to determine whether the user fee hinders or helps commerce.[153]
- Tolls are for the use of property or improvements thereon and the amount is determined by factors including cost and the need for return as well as the value of benefits and is best left to administrators.[154]
- The amount of a user fee may be determined by a federal agency,[155] and the general statute directing agencies to charge fees is Congress' general delegation of authority to agencies.[156]
- An exaction that is linked to cost for providing a benefit has the indicia of a regulatory charge and not a tax although the opinion called it a user fee.[157]
- A regulatory charge need not be related to the amount of usage of a benefit.[158]
- But when the measure of the fee is unrelated to the benefit it is more likely to be a tax in some cases.[159]

---

[151] *See, e.g.*, Packet Co. v. St. Louis, 100 U.S. 423 (1880); Massachusetts v. United States, 435 U.S. 444 (1978) (repeatedly referring to relation to cost, which supports its treatment as a regulatory charge).

[152] *See* Charlotte, C. & A. R. Co. v. Gibbes, 142 U.S. 386 (1892). *Cf.* National Cable Television Ass'n v. United States, 415 U.S. 336 (1974) (where the words of the statute authorizing the fee were interpreted to preclude their paying for public benefit).

[153] Packet Co. v. Keokuk, 95 U.S. 80 (1877) (wharfage fee).

[154] Sands v. Manistee River Improvement Co., 123 U.S. 288 (1887) (did not involve interstate commerce).

[155] United States v. Grimaud, 220 U.S. 506 (1911).

[156] National Cable Television Ass'n v. United States, 415 U.S. 336 (1974) ("The lawmaker may, in light of the 'public policy or interest served,' make the assessment heavy if the lawmaker wants to discourage the activity; or it may make the levy slight if a bounty is to be bestowed; or the lawmaker may make a substantial levy to keep entrepreneurs from exploiting a semipublic cause for their own personal aggrandizement. Such assessments are in the nature of 'taxes' which under our constitutional regime are traditionally levied by Congress."); Sands v. Manistee River Improvement Co., 123 U.S. 288 (1887). *But see* contrary view in Skinner v. Mid-America Pipeline Co., 490 U.S. 212 (1989) and Federal Energy Administration v. Algonquin SNG, Inc., 426 U.S. 548 (1976) (Congress also can delegate to administration power to vary taxes based on a standard, so fees and taxes are not distinguishable on that basis); J. W. Hampton, Jr. & Co. v. United States, 276 U.S. 394 (1928) (power to set tariff rates delegated).

[157] Massachusetts v. United States, 435 U.S. 444 (1978).

[158] *Id.* (flat annual fee).

[159] United States v. United States Shoe Corp., 523 U.S. 360 (1998) (Export Clause case where the definition of tax may be more strict than in other cases).

- A state cannot charge a user fee for something that it does not own,[160] but can impose a regulatory charge for use of private property (a garbage dump).[161]
- In a state tax case, the fact that half of the tax was paid into a trust fund did not prevent it from being a general revenue tax.[162]
- The fact that fee produced revenues in excess of cost does not make it a tax.[163]
- An inspection fee per item may be commuted into a flat annual fee.[164]
- When the question about a state inspection fee is interference with imports and exports, a more strict limit to actual costs may be applied.[165]

B. Special Assessments

1. *Assessments for Benefits*

The United States does not normally impose special assessments but can, as in the case of the District of Columbia and Territories.[166] Therefore most of the case law involves state and local taxation, but will be discussed here rather than Chapter IX. They round out the discussion of user fees for purchased benefits (which the special assessment is not).

The identifying feature of the special assessment is that it is a tax that is not subject to the normal rule that a taxpayer has no right to expect a correlation between the tax paid and the enjoyment of any particular benefit on account of the taxes paid.[167] However, precisely how a government signals that it is limiting its discretion in taxation that way is unclear and may simply be the choice to call the levy an assessment, which indistinctly invokes a benefits concept.[168]

---

[160] Case of State Freight Tax, 82 U.S. 232 (1873) (A state freight tax was not a toll and so was an unconstitutional tax).

[161] Or. Waste Sys. v. Dep't of Envtl. Quality, 511 U.S. 93 (1994).

[162] Commonwealth Edison Co. v. Montana, 453 U.S. 609, 622 n. 11 (1981).

[163] Ouachita Packet Co. v. Aiken, 121 U.S. 444 (1887). *See also* Huse v. Glover, 119 U.S. 543 (1886) (same statement about using surplus funds for general purposes).

[164] Standard Stock Food Co. v. Wright, 225 U.S. 540 (1912) (although plaintiff was large dealer paying the flat fee and opinion stated it did not have the right to complain).

[165] D. E. Foote & Co. v. Stanley, 232 U.S. 494 (1914).

[166] Wight v. Davidson, 181 U.S. 371 (1901).

[167] *See* Ch. III.C. Illinois C. R. Co. v. Decatur, 147 U.S. 190 (1893). The special assessment tends to be viewed as sui generis, which contributes to the confusion of its role. *See* John B. Sholley, *Equal Protection in Tax Legislation*, 24 Va. L. Rev. 229 and 388, 396 (1938) (extensively discussing equal protection in taxation but excluding special assessments from the discussion because the case law has been "entirely independent and unrelated" to the rest of the tax discrimination case law). Also for the particular purposes of review of municipal levies under state constitutions, special assessments frequently were not subject to the same rules as "taxes." Robert Desty, American Law of Taxation 5-6 (1883) [hereinafter Desty].

[168] *See* Harry Hubbard, *Fourteenth Amendment and Special Assessments on Real Estate: Norwood v. Baker, 172 U.S. 269*, 14 Harv. L. Rev. 1 (1900-1901).

Professor Seligman captured the confusion around the subject by stating both that special assessments are taxes and that they are not taxes (of the normal sort), and also said correctly: "The primary test of a [general] tax is that it imposes a common burden; the primary test of a special assessment is that it implies a special benefit."[169] Unquestionably the Court has consistently treated special assessments as taxes, and that is the basis of the categorization adopted here.[170]

One reason a special assessment should be treated as a tax is that it is payment for a sovereign act that is not usually regulatory, which leaves the category of sovereign taxes. For example, when the city makes a special assessment for running a sewer line through a neighborhood, it is a sovereign charge because only governments can force a landowner to pay for something it did not ask for.

Perhaps the practical reason why special assessments are taxes is that the states have treated them as simply the taxes imposed within a special taxing district, which is a subdivision within which any local tax might be imposed.[171] This is more than merely practical because it reflects the flexibility needed by state governments to decide whether public projects should be paid for generally or by taxpayers in the vicinity, and exactly how closely they need to be related to the project.[172]

The Court has held that a general tax exemption granted by a state to a railroad did not as a matter of interpretation exempt it from a special assessment because "ordinary taxes" are imposed to pay for public burdens whereas the assessment to pave a road by the taxpayer's house is for a special benefit to that person; the Court also listed a variety of other possible factual distinctions between the two types of taxes that might explain why the exemption was not intended.[173] For better or worse, the intense scrutiny of special assessments by the Supreme Court around 1900 has waned substantially and they are a mostly forgotten tax whose status has not been re-examined lately (as in 75-100 years, unless attacked as takings).

The special assessment appears to be freed from the normal rule that the payor need not benefit at all for the somewhat unusual reason that the taxing authority is held to its own self-limitation: if the taxing authority (or the state statute, or the state court that first considered the issue) denominates or defends a tax as for a particular benefit to a particular taxpayer group, then the authority may be required to show some rational relationship of the tax to the benefit. It appears that no commentator has identified this signal feature of the special assessment, and some have confusingly argued that its requirement of approximate benefits

---

[169] *See* E.R.A. Seligman, Essays in Taxation 282 *et seq.* (1895) (special assessments found to be somewhat peculiar to the United States, and definitely to be taxes, citing People v. Brooklyn, 4 N. Y. 419 (1851), but then stating they were not taxes, at 288).

[170] For a most recent example in which a city sewer assessment was treated as a tax without recognition of any issue about tax characterization, *see* Armour v. City of Indianapolis, 566 U.S. 673 (2012).

[171] Chadwick v. Kelley, 187 U.S. 540 (1903).

[172] French v. Barber Asphalt Paving Co., 181 U.S. 324 (1901).

[173] Illinois C. R. Co. v. Decatur, 147 U.S. 190 (1893).

should apply to all taxes,[174] or is analogous to tolls for bridges (which they are not because bridge tolls are fees that need to approximate cost not benefits).[175] However, this self-declarative feature of special assessments is not unique. The Court has observed that fees can be justified on the basis of the government's declaration that the fee is imposed to recover the costs of service.[176]

The principal characteristic of a user fee for a benefit, as reflected by the cases discussed above in Chapter IV.A, is the payment for a specific service enjoyed by the particular payor, although others also may enjoy the same benefit electively by choosing to use the same service. The classic example of the fee is a toll for driving on a toll road. In contrast, special assessments are taxes that otherwise would be unremarkable as taxes except for the facts that (a) the government usually earmarks the proceeds for some improvement, and (b) defines a subset of taxpayers who will pay the tax due to some determination of particularized benefit to the group of taxpayers from the improvement.

The fixing of amounts of special assessments is limited to costs incurred by the government and to some rough approximation of benefits received. As explained by Justice Holmes in one of the few decision of the Court holding a special assessment to be unconstitutionally large, normally "The chance of the cost being greater than the benefit is slight, and the excess, if any, would be small."[177] But in that case the lots adjoining an alley being widened were assessed portions of the cost that appeared to assume the widening had trebled the value of the lots, which Justice Holmes found to be most improbable. The real reason for the rejection of the tax was likely that it was set by a jury that was told it should simply allocate the cost without reference to the benefit.

2. *Specific Rulings*

Other aspects of the special assessment cases include:

- When the exaction was not justified as a safety measure and only benefitted one other person, then it was a taking for private benefit without due process of law.[178]

---

[174] *See* Gale Ann Norton, *The Limitless Federal Taxing Power*, 8 HARV. J. L. & PUB. POL'Y 591, 618 n. 164 (1985); Eduardo Moises Penalver, *Regulatory Taxings*, 104 COLUM. L. REV. 2182, 2202 (2004) (discussing special assessments as narrowly targeted taxes, but failing to explain why).

[175] W.H. BURROUGHS, TREATISE ON THE LAW OF TAXATION AS IMPOSED BY THE STATES AND THEIR MUNICIPALITIES § 145 and ch. 22 (1877) (also limited special assessments to levies on real property, which is mostly true).

[176] United States v. Sperry Corp., 493 U.S. 52, 60 (1989), citing Pittsburgh v. Alco Parking Corp., 417 U.S. 369 (1974).

[177] Martin v. District of Columbia, 205 U.S. 135, 139 (1907).

[178] Chicago, S.P.M. & O.R. Co. v. Holmberg, 282 U.S. 162 (1930). Property may not be taken for private purposes even if just compensation is paid. Hawaii Housing Authority v. Midkiff, 467 U.S. 229 (1984).

- A special assessment district could not include as a taxpayer a person wholly without benefit from the public improvement, because taxing that person amounted to taxing for the private benefit of the group benefited.[179]
- In earlier times the same principle (called the "public purpose doctrine") was applied to strike down a general tax to pay off what would now be called an industrial development bond, but that approach has been overruled.[180] The public purpose doctrine is the analogue of the General Welfare Power.[181]
- *Norwood* ruled that a city that condemned a street, and evidently paid the landowners for the land condemned, could not assess the same landowners still abutting the new street for 100% of its costs because they were not the only persons benefited and the city did not even attempt to determine the value of the benefit.[182] The levy was in "substantial excess" of the benefits accruing to that taxpayer. For special tax assessments the standard is whether the tax is palpably arbitrary and a plain abuse of power.[183] *Norwood* involved the hotly contested and recurring question whether a road assessment based solely on front footage abutting the road was per se arbitrary. Because an arbitrary payment can be viewed as a taking, particularly when the roadway also was taken from the taxpayer, *Norwood* has recently been cited in takings cases.[184]
- But the Court later ruled that 100% of the cost of paving an existing street could be assessed against the abutting landowners,[185] except when the allocation formula was totally illogical because of a glitch in the drafting of the statute.[186] These conflicting cases show that the Court has tried to stay out of measuring a disproportion between tax and benefit but leaves open the

---

[179] Myles Salt Co. v. Bd. of Comm'rs, 239 U.S. 478 (1916). *Cf.* Thompson v. Consolidated Gas Utilities Corp., 300 U.S. 55 (1937) (striking down a state order limiting gas production so that efficient producers could not produce all of the gas they needed to fulfill their contracts and so had to buy it from inefficient producers).

[180] Loan Ass'n v. Topeka, 87 U.S. 655 (1875). See Ch. III.D.3.c.

[181] Joseph Lesser and Vigdor D. Bernstein, *The Evolution of Public Purpose, General Welfare and American Federalism*, 19 URB. LAW. 603, 640 (1987).

[182] Norwood v. Baker, 172 U.S. 269 (1898).

[183] Kansas City S. R. Co. v. Road Improv. Dist., 266 U.S. 379 (1924).

[184] *See* Martin v. District of Columbia, 205 U.S. 135 (1907); Horne v. Dep't of Agric., 576 U.S. 351 (2015).

[185] French v. Barber Asphalt Paving Co., 181 U.S. 324 (1901) (also ruling that no notice is required to taxpayers of a tax's adoption).

[186] Gast Realty & Inv. Co. v. Schneider Granite Co., 240 U.S. 55 (1916) (approving a frontage foot apportionment). *See also* Kansas City S. R. Co. v. Road Improv. Dist., 256 U.S. 658 (1921).

possibility that at the margin the taxpayer can prove complete arbitrariness or no benefit.[187]

- A public improvement could be charged for twice: when built and for operations.[188]
- A special assessment for a street may in fact exceed the benefit but generally will not and so an episodic overage will not invalidate such assessments.[189]
- The Court treated as a tax a special assessment for a tunnel on the basis that it benefited the surrounding taxed lands.[190]
- A special assessment could exceed in total the cost of the improvement where it was intended to pay for maintenance and future costs.[191]
- A special assessment could be charged for an improvement already paid for.[192]
- An unusual special or targeted assessment was upheld under a so-called "government speech doctrine."[193] The Agriculture Act, outside of Title 26, authorizes "checkoff" assessments of $1 per head on cattle sold to be collected by private associations and used for meat promotion under the direction of the USDA. Because the Court found the speech funded to be government and not private speech, it ruled that the payors of what it treated as a tax could be required to subsidize speech with which they disagreed.

3. *Contrast Police Power*

Because almost all of the Court's special assessment decisions involve state and local taxes, it is important to understand that just as special assessments can be confused with fees for services, they can be confused with regulatory charges

---

[187] Georgia R. & Electric Co. v. Decatur, 295 U.S. 165 (1935) (state refused to allow taxpayer to prove no benefit and tax was more than value of the property taxed); Myles Salt Co. v. Board of Comm'rs, 239 U.S. 478 (1916) (no benefit to taxpayer at all); French v. Barber Asphalt Paving Co., 181 U.S. 324 (1901) (entire cost of street could be collected from abutting property owners, but that continued to be a contentious issue, with taxpayers arguing others were benefited by the street).

[188] Carson v. Brockton Sewerage Com., 182 U.S. 398 (1901).

[189] Martin v. District of Columbia, 205 U.S. 135 (1907); Louisville & N. R. Co. v. Barber Asphalt Paving Co., 197 U.S. 430 (1905).

[190] Milheim v. Moffat Tunnel Improv. Dist., 262 U.S. 710 (1923).

[191] Parsons v. District of Columbia, 170 U.S. 45 (1898).

[192] Phillip Wagner, Inc. v. Leser, 239 U.S. 207 (1915).

[193] Johanns v. Livestock Mktg. Ass'n, 544 U.S. 550 (2005).

required by a state or local government under its police power.[194] For example, if a business creates a nuisance the state may require the business to pay to remove the nuisance as a regulation under its police power. This is not a tax and does not relate to any benefit intended for the payor (in contrast with a fee).

The police power is one of what may be viewed as the four fundamental powers of government: the military power, the taxing power, the police power and the power of eminent domain.[195] A fair definition of the most diffuse of these, the police power, is that power that aims to promote the public welfare by constraint and compulsion.[196] Thus the same exaction from a person may be justified by a government as a police power regulation, as a tax and as a tax that is a special assessment for a benefit. Generally the tax classification will be accepted with hardly any real likelihood of rejection.[197] The police power classification can be attacked by arguing the charge is really a special assessment or is otherwise a violation of due process as a police regulation. But when the charge is labeled a special assessment the taxing authority must deal with the equation of benefits and cost.

A 1935 opinion by Justice Brandeis explains the relationship of police power regulation and special assessments. The Court ruled in favor of a railroad that did not want to pay one half of the cost of building an overpass over an inter-

---

[194] The police power is the states' analogue to the United States' Commerce Clause and General Welfare powers, except that the Commerce Clause powers are constrained by a required connection to interstate commerce, whereas the local police powers are said to be broad and plenary, except to the extent they intersect with supreme federal authority. *See, e.g.*, Am. Trucking Ass'ns v. Mich. PSC, 545 U.S. 429 (2005) (ruling that a state fee that is imposed under the police power is proper where it does not conflict with the federal government's Commerce Clause regulation of the same subject); United States v. Morrison, 529 U.S. 598 (2000) (the Commerce Clause is not a general police power); Hodel v. Va. Surface Mining & Reclamation Ass'n, 452 U.S. 264 (1981) (Congress' exercise of Commerce Clause power can displace state's police power action). That intersection generally allowed the states to regulate for safety and health, including matters such as protection from fraud, except when Congress had preempted the field, but generally did not allow the states to regulate for economic protectionism. H. P. Hood & Sons, Inc. v. Du Mond, 336 U.S. 525 (1949). When a state exercises its police power to regulate by requiring a business to buy a safety appliance, the United States may pre-empt the field by exercising its Commerce Clause powers to require the same business to buy similar or different safety appliances. Southern Ry. Co. v. Railroad Comm'n, 236 U.S. 439 (1915). Moreover, the police power concept encompasses "general welfare" regulation, which at the federal level depends on the power to tax and spend for the general welfare. *See, e.g.*, Mountain Timber Co. v. Washington, 243 U.S. 219, 238 (1917) ("The authority of the States to enact such laws as reasonably are deemed to be necessary to promote the health, safety, and general welfare of their people, . . .").

[195] Ernst Freund, The Police Power: Public Policy and Constitutional Rights 1-2 (1904). *But see* Carl Brent Swisher, American Constitutional Development 200-201 (1954) (explaining that state police powers were originally identified not by "states' rights" advocates but by nationalists who sought an explanation for otherwise unexplainable deviations from federal control; ultimately the states' police power came to be viewed less as a residuum than as an enumerated power, as stated in the text).

[196] Freund at 3. Sections 36-39 explain how licenses may be accompanied by taxes that may be for regulatory or revenue purposes, and that it is generally unnecessary and impossible to separate the two.

[197] *See* Ch. IV.B.

state highway, basically because the railroad did not cause the problem (i.e., not a nuisance) and the state did not argue it was benefited by the assessment.[198] The opinion explained that the trial court may have been correct in finding that the original state law on railroad liability for bridges was passed in a day when the police power was properly exercised to protect the public from dangerous railroads.[199] However, the bridge at issue was to carry the existing railroad over an interstate highway to be constructed, not under the police power but as a public convenience designed to promote highway transportation in competition with railroads. This was a change in circumstances. Rather than the railroad being a cause of danger to be remedied under the police power, the railroad needed protection from the automobile, both physically and economically (or at least the state court should have considered that argument). The opinion usefully, if elliptically, explained the distinction between the varieties of taxes discussed here.

- First are the usual sort of taxes that do not have to be tied to any particular benefit to a taxpayer.
- Second, police power regulations can require private spending in the form of taxes to promote public health, safety and morals, which presumably must bear some relationship to the payor's culpability or nexus to the problem. (This chapter calls these regulatory taxes.)
- Third, slightly different police power regulations require private spending to promote public convenience and welfare, which must bear some reasonable relationship to "the evils to be eradicated". (This chapter calls these regulatory charges.)
- Fourth, special assessments may be imposed ("assessments for public improvements," citing *Gast*, *Myles Salt*, and *Kansas City*, discussed in Chapter IV.B), which are not police power regulations but taxes that must bear some relationship to the benefic received.[200]

The opinion did not call the special assessment a tax but cited cases in which it was called a tax. The point seems to be that a payment required to produce a public benefit and levied on a subset of persons said to have some connection to the benefit but who did not cause a nuisance might be treated as a special assessment tax if the financed improvement benefits the taxpayer not unreasonably out of proportion to the tax, and might be treated as a police power exaction for public convenience, which is subject to different standards. The railroad could not be made to bear half the cost of grade separation improvements for public

[198] Nashville, C. & S. L. Railway v. Walters, 294 U.S. 405 (1935).

[199] *See* James M. Gray, Limitations of the Taxing Power 1010-1013 (1906) (discussing assessments under the police power to remove nuisances and the like).

[200] *See* Norwood v. Baker, 172 U.S. 269 (1898) (treating a special assessment as a tax; quoted Cooley on Taxation for the principle that special assessments on land were a "peculiar species of taxation" that taxed particular persons for public improvements on the theory that they received a particular benefit, and so the tax should not exceed the benefit, else there would be a taking without just compensation).

safety and convenience under the Commerce Clause and the exaction evidently was not defended as a special assessment, so the railroad won, without the Court exactly concluding what requirement would have been proper.[201]

In early cases the Court treated as exercises of the police power state or local license taxes on taxpayers who argued they were protected by the Commerce Clause; in the process a few opinions made confusing references to police power exactions imposed to raise revenue.[202] The view that police power regulation and state taxation may be looked at differently for Commerce Clause purposes persists, whether the outcomes are actually different.[203] Like the case in which Justice Brandeis laid out the alternatives, discussed above, there are many cases in which the exaction might be constitutional either as a special tax assessment, a regulatory tax or a regulatory charge. For example, requiring certain landowners to clean up a nuisance was called an exercise of the police power and may appear not to have general public benefit but likely does benefit the group of payors physically adjacent to the nuisance.[204] *Decatur* is a case illustrating that the way a state chooses to characterize an exaction determines how it will be tested. A railroad protested being charged with the cost of road paving and the state court decided the case on the basis of benefits to the railroad, which would have been consistent with a special assessment. On appeal the state argued the exaction was levied under the police power, but the Court would not consider that argument and found the railroad was not benefited at all.[205] Similarly in *Pace* the state court said the tax levied on the railroad's property for general road improvements was not levied under the special assessments law but as a general tax; therefore the benefit to the taxpayer need not be measured and the tax could be invalid only if "palpably arbitrary or unreasonably discriminatory."[206]

The police power is an additional basis for conflating taxation and regulation at the state level in contrast with the federal level. In *Great Atlantic & Pacific* the Court justified ruling in favor of heavier state taxation on chain stores by stating that taxation could be used to carry out police power aims.[207] However, the one federal tax case it cited in support was not a case in which the taxing power was

---

[201] *Cf.* Atchison, T. & S. F. R. Co. v. Public Utilities Com., 346 U.S. 346 (1953) (*citing* Chesebro v. Los Angeles County Flood Control Dist., 306 U.S. 459 (1939), and distinguishing *Nashville, C. & S. L. Railway v. Walters*, 294 U.S. 405 (1935), on the basis that the 50% allocation of cost there was specified in the statute and not determined to be appropriately related to the railroad, whereas here the state court had determined its propriety and the amount was not arbitrary; the opinion appeared to uphold the levy as a police power charge rather than a special assessment).

[202] *See, e.g.*, Caldwell v. North Carolina, 187 U.S. 622 (1903) (ruling a license tax imposed on out of state photographers was a tax and not a police power exercise and violated the Commerce Clause); Postal Telegraph Cable Co. v. Charleston, 153 U.S. 692 (1894); Postal Telegraph-Cable Co. v. Richmond, 249 U.S. 252 (1919).

[203] *See, e.g.*, Freeman v. Hewit, 329 U.S. 249 (1946), *overruled on other grounds*, Complete Auto Transit, Inc. v. Brady, 430 U.S. 274 (1977).

[204] Wurts v. Hoagland, 114 U.S. 606 (1885) (confusingly stating that the drainage project did not have general benefit, but calling it an exercise of police power and not tax).

[205] Georgia R. & Electric Co. v. Decatur, 295 U.S. 165 (1935).

[206] Memphis & C. R. Co. v. Pace, 282 U.S. 241 (1931).

[207] Great Atlantic & Pacific Tea Co. v. Grosjean, 301 U.S. 412 (1937).

exercised in support of the Commerce Clause; rather it was *Sonzinsky*, which depended solely on the power to tax, with incidental regulation of firearms (a regulatory tax).[208] A better cite is a typically epigrammatic opinion by Justice Holmes upholding a state's differential tax on oleomargarine by saying: "It may express and carry out its policy [of regulating or destroying that product] as well in a revenue as in a police law."[209]

And confusion continues about the police power. In 2008 Justice Kennedy stated that the police power is simply all local powers not denied by the Constitution.[210] Justice O'Connor stated that a state could use its taxing power to favor local business and cited in support of that statement an opinion supporting the use of the police power for that purpose.[211] Instead, the correct categorization is that states exercise police powers and also taxing and spending powers,[212] and by analogy the Congress exercises Commerce Clause and other specifically enumerated powers and the taxing and spending (for the general welfare) powers.

C. The Tax-Sovereignty Connection: Privilege License Taxes

1. *For a Sovereign Grant*

In concluding this Chapter IV by discussing privilege license taxes it is useful to focus again on the relationship of taxation and sovereignty.[213] A core principle of taxation, that taxes are an attribute of sovereignty, provides a solid starting point for distinguishing taxes from fees and also for identifying license and privilege taxes as taxes. If the levy can be found to be for or explained by the fact of sovereignty, as opposed to a charge for a service or benefit, then it is a tax, assuming it is not a criminal penalty (which is a third levy solely exercisable by sovereigns). If not a tax, then it must be collected by the sovereign in a dual capacity as a proprietor, and it is a fee for service or other benefit (and may be an excessive fee that is an unconstitutional taking).

Under this guiding principle, license taxes and franchise taxes are taxes and not fees; even though they are paid for a benefit, it is a benefit that only a sovereign can grant.[214] There appears to be no clear authoritative statement of this

---

208 Sonzinsky v. United States, 300 U.S. 506 (1937).

209 Hammond Packing Co. v. Montana, 233 U.S. 331 (1914).

210 Dep't of Revenue v. Davis, 553 U.S. 328 (2008) (dissent).

211 Metro. Life Ins. Co. v. Ward, 470 U.S. 869 (1985) (dissent of Justice O'Connor).

212 *See, e.g.*, Moorman Mfg. Co. v. Bair, 437 U.S. 267, 287-288 (1978) ("It is a basic principle of Commerce Clause jurisprudence that '[neither] the power to tax nor the police power may be used by the state of destination with the aim and effect of establishing an economic barrier against competition with the products of another state or the labor of the residents.'"); Kidd v. Pearson, 128 U.S. 1 (1888) (the police power is as plenary as the taxing power); Emert v. Missouri, 156 U.S. 296 (1895) (identifying only the taxing power and the police power as the two powers that a state might exercise concerning a local business).

213 *See* Ch. II.A.

214 *See* Ch. IV.A.4 for listing of opinions distinguishing fees from license taxes.

view,[215] but it is implicit in Chief Justice Marshall's explanation why New York did not have the power to license interstate shipping in *Gibbons v. Ogden*:

> The word "license," means permission, or authority; and a license to do any particular thing, is a permission or authority to do that thing; and if granted by a person having power to grant it, transfers to the grantee the right to do whatever it purports to authorize. It certainly transfers to him all the right which the grantor can transfer, to do what is within the terms of the license. Would the validity or effect of such an instrument be questioned by the respondent, if executed by persons claiming regularly under the laws of New-York? The license must be understood to be what it purports to be, a legislative authority to the steamboat Bellona, "to be employed in carrying on the coasting trade, for one year from this date."216

In the 19th Century governmental license charges generally were considered taxes, although not clearly.[217] However, the decisions identified in Chapter IV.A.4 as privilege license taxes cases or referring to such taxes—*Brown v. Maryland, Blodgett, Sprout v. South Bend, Murdock*, the fishing license cases, *Spector*, and *Jefferson County v. Acker*—are good evidence that the Court views payments for benefits that only government can grant to be taxes and not fees for services.

Similarly, taxes charged by a sovereign for using natural resources of the state can be viewed as similar to license taxes.[218]

Sometimes the sovereignty/proprietor cases overlap, as in the early cases on automobile licenses. Although the state presumably had the power to grant the driving privilege or not, because of amounts spent on roads and the stated purposes to collect for them, the Court treated an early driving license as a user fee and not a tax.[219] In at least one decision the Court has allowed a taxing jurisdiction to vary the cost of a license geographically within the jurisdiction because it was worth more in more populous areas than in rural areas.[220]

Sometimes license fees are explained as police power regulations, although imposed in part to raise revenue.[221] Many of such early cases involved local efforts to regulate interstate businesses and it did not matter to the Court under

---

[215] The Court came close in New Jersey v. Anderson, 203 U.S. 483 (1906) (explaining why a corporate franchise tax is a tax and not a debt for bankruptcy purposes, based on the power of the state to charter or authorize the corporation; the dissent thought that the fact that the taxes were paid voluntarily and in exchange for corporate privileges prevented them from being taxes in the sense used in the bankruptcy act).

[216] Gibbons v. Ogden, 22 U.S. 1, 213-214 (1824)

[217] *See City Licenses*, 14 Central L. J. 422, 424 (1882) (stating that license fees were not necessarily taxes but that in general they were evaluated as taxes, citing Cooley on Constitutional Limitations 201-202 (1868), which went both ways as to municipal license taxes); Desty, at 3 ("a license is not a tax").

[218] *See, e.g.*, Lacoste v. Dep't of Conservation, 263 U.S. 545 (1924) (wildlife).

[219] *See* Hendrick v. Maryland, 235 U.S. 610 (1915); *so explained in* Evansville-Vanderburgh v. Delta Airlines, Inc., 405 U.S. 707 (1972).

[220] Toyota v. Hawaii, 226 U.S. 184 (1912).

[221] *See* Postal Telegraph Cable Co. v. Charleston, 153 U.S. 692 (1894), *citing*, Wiggins Ferry Co. v. East St. Louis, 107 U.S. 365, 376 (1882) (it was a matter of indifference to the Court which category applied; police power licensing may be exercised for purpose of raising revenue).

its then view of local taxation whether the regulation was a regulation or a tax. A governmental charge for a license that is made a precondition of doing a certain business in the jurisdiction can be either a tax or an exercise of the police power, but particularly if there is no accompanying regulation of the business activities, it is likely a tax.[222] "Undoubtedly every tax which lays its burden on some and not others may have an incidental regulatory effect."[223]

A practical explanation why license or franchise taxes must be viewed as taxes and not user fees is that the government usually has not incurred any cost in providing the right licensed, and so there would be no way to test the reasonableness of the charge. For example in the 1900s cities were not allowed to charge for docking at unimproved river banks because the city had done nothing, but the federal government is allowed to impose a charge for maintenance of the air traffic control.[224]

2. *Another Sovereign's Grant*

Finally, another source of confusion as to franchise taxes is that a sovereign can impose a tax on the use of the franchise granted by another sovereign, at least if the tax collector is federal. This occurred in the case of the corporate excise tax of 1909. The Court upheld the tax as an excise tax on the use of state granted corporate franchises to do business.[225] In 1925 Justice Brandeis for the unanimous Court identified six different ways in which Congress could constitutionally tax the exercise of the corporate franchise to do business, despite the fact that Congress did not grant the franchise.[226]

Alternately, the United States has levied a true tax styled as a license tax on the pursuit of an occupation that it could not license the taxpayer to perform.[227] These were not true licenses or franchises at all and so are not the subject of this chapter. Rather they are excise taxes that the United States called a license tax, presumably meaning that if the taxpayer did not pay it could be criminally liable and thus effectively prevented from carrying on its business. Indeed the Supreme Court has stated that such license taxes could be so great as to tax the business out of business. The Court stated "Looking, therefore, at the Constitution in the light of the conditions surrounding at the time of its adoption, it is obvious that the framers in granting full power over license taxes to the National Government meant that that power should be complete, . . ." and also stated that there was

---

[222] Brennan v. Titusville, 153 U.S. 289 (1894).
[223] Fernandez v. Wiener, 326 U.S. 340, 362 (1945).
[224] *See* Ch. IV.A.
[225] Flint v. Stone Tracy Co., 220 U.S. 107 (1911).
[226] Ray Consol. Copper Co. v. United States, 268 U.S. 373 (1925).
[227] McGuire v. Commonwealth, 70 U.S. 387 (1865); License Tax Cases, 72 U.S. 462 (1867).

no constitutional limit on the amount of the federal license tax on local liquor dealers.[228]

Similarly, a state may tax a franchise issued by it or another sovereign as property.[229] And a state may tax the income of a federally licensed business.[230]

[228] South Carolina v. United States, 199 U.S. 437 (1905).

[229] *See* Veazie Bank v. Fenno, 75 U.S. 533 (1869) (discussing the taxation of a bank franchise as a tax on valuable property).

[230] Broad River Power Co. v. Query, 288 U.S. 178 (1933).

Ch. V. Direct Taxes and Other Taxes

A. Summary

Contrary to common usage, the Constitution does not refer to indirect taxes; rather it authorizes Congress to lay and collect "taxes, duties, imposts and excises." There has never been a doubt that duties, imposts and excises are taxes. Therefore, the clause can be read to authorize taxes, including duties, imposts and excises. Duties and imposts normally refer to taxes on imports and exports (but Congress cannot tax exports), and excises normally refers to taxes on transactions in goods, but can apply to other transactions such as earning income.[1] The Constitution does refer to direct taxes in identifying a category of tax that must be apportioned among the states according to census populations, and in that context uses only the term taxes. Ad valorem taxes levied on the ownership of property were generally understood to be direct taxes for constitutional purposes, as were capitation (poll) taxes, which the Constitution specifically identifies as direct taxes.[2]

When Congress episodically chose during the 1800s to collect taxes from persons based on the value of property they owned, it apportioned the total tax revenue desired among the states, according to the census. When Congress did not so apportion a tax that was a regular ongoing tax levy, and such tax was chal-

---

[1] For example, the Court upheld the 1909 federal income tax on corporations because it was an excise tax. Flint v. Stone Tracy Co., 220 U.S. 107 (1911).

[2] Constitution, Article I, Section 9. As to poll taxes, see Ch. IIIE.6.

lenged, the Court uniformly concluded all such taxes were not direct taxes, up to the *Pollock* decisions in 1895.[3] *Pollock* took that power of identification away from Congress and created a lookthrough definition for direct tax that presumably could turn any tax into a direct tax if one could find that a tax on something else somehow indirectly burdened land or other property.

Despite focusing on the indirect economic relationship of an income tax on rent to the land producing the rent, the *Pollock* opinions mostly employed the term indirect as a simplistic label for imposts, duties and excises. The Court assumed these could not be direct taxes due principally to the fact that the Constitution imposed a uniformity requirement solely on taxes that are imposts, duties and excises; as a practical matter, a tax could not be both uniform throughout the United States and also apportioned according to the census. In addition the Constitution clearly contemplated federal import duties, which could not be apportioned because importation did not occur in inland states; also no one doubted Congress' ability to levy consumption taxes of the usual sort (such as excise taxes on alcohol) without apportionment.

Thus when the Court extracted imposts, duties and excises from the larger category of taxes, what was left stood a very good chance of being a direct tax in the Court's eyes.[4] The Court inferred this method of identifying direct taxes by elimination from the constitutional language despite the facts that an income tax could be described as an excise, and that the lookthrough theory was not logically bound by the form of the tax (indeed, that was the theory's whole purpose, to ignore the form of the tax). The Sixteenth Amendment directed that such lookthrough efforts cease, at least as to an income tax.

Hence the primary role of the concept of indirection in the direct tax controversies has been the Supreme Court's short-lived effort to find taxes levied directly on earning rent, for example, to be levied indirectly on the land that produced the rent and thus be "direct." Nevertheless, the primary terminology came to be a direct versus indirect dichotomy that exists in the cases, but not in the Constitution. Chapter V.C.4 discusses the Constitution's reasons for differentiating direct taxes, the identification of direct taxes and the limits on direct taxation. However, that history is just that: largely of historical interest.

In contrast the Constitution's limits on other taxes that escape the direct classification are now much more important, as discussed in Chapter V.D. The limit stated in the Constitution is uniformity, which came to be understood as geographical uniformity. However, various potential limits on federal taxation have been urged under the Fifth Amendment, which are discussed in Chapter V.D.3.b; the Court has not found any federal tax rule to be unconstitutional under the Fifth Amendment other than three retroactive estate tax provisions. By far the more popular means of holding a federal tax to be unconstitutional has been to find it is not a tax at all, usually accompanies by a Tenth Amend-

---

[3] Pollock v. Farmers' Loan & Trust Co., 157 U.S. 429 (1895), *confirmed and expanded*, 158 U.S. 601 (1895). *See* Ch. V.D.2.c.

[4] *See, e.g.*, 157 U.S. at 566.

ment ground, which is discussed in Chapter III.F. Other grounds on which the Court has ruled unconstitutional federal taxes that were not direct taxes are intergovernmental immunity discussed in Chapter II.C, export taxes discussed in Chapter VI.D, and taxes on federal judges' salaries discussed in Chapter VIII.F.

B. Two Types of Federal Taxes

Article I, section 8, clause 1 of the Constitution states:

> The Congress shall have Power To lay and collect Taxes, Duties, Imposts and Excises, to pay the Debts and provide for the common Defence and general Welfare of the United States; but all Duties, Imposts and Excises shall be uniform throughout the United States; . . . .

Article I, section 9, clause 4 states:

> No capitation, or other direct, Tax shall be laid, unless in Proportion to the Census or Enumeration herein before directed to be taken.

Article I, section 2, clause 3 stated prior to amendment:

> Representatives and direct Taxes shall be apportioned among the several States which may be included within this Union, according to their respective Numbers, which shall be determined by adding to the whole Number of free Persons, including those bound to Service for a Term of Years, and excluding Indians not taxed, three fifths of all other Persons

The Constitution thus refers to four types of taxes—taxes, duties (including duties of tonnage), imposts and excises—but for purposes of constitutional evaluation there are only two: direct taxes and taxes that are not direct (though issues can arise about federal imposts on exports, which Congress cannot lay).[5] As to the identification of any particular tax as direct or not the only thing that can be known for sure from the face of the Constitution is that poll taxes are direct taxes; in addition there is a textual implication that taxes that were then commonly known as imposts, excises and duties were not direct taxes, which the *Pollock* opinions adopted.[6]

The Constitution established this grand division for a variety of political reasons that were of profound importance to the states forming the union and to their varying interests. The unifying political theme of the two categories was uniformity of some type: (1) to the extent the federal government undertook to tax people (polls) and whatever else was directly taxed (and all agreed this included realty value), the drafters wanted the aggregate levy apportioned among the states based on their populations, with the uniformity being upset purposefully by counting slaves as three fifths of a person; and (2) as for taxes that were not direct, the drafters wanted the taxes to be uniformly applied across the

[5] *See* Joseph Story, Commentaries on the Constitution of the United States, Vol. 2, 419 (1833) [hereinafter Story] (stating this view, which will be further defended in the text). Observe that there was never any doubt that duties, imposts and excises are taxes as a generic matter.

[6] Pollock v. Farmers' Loan & Trust Co., 157 U.S. 429 (1895), *confirmed and expanded*, 158 U.S. 601 (1895). *See* Ch. V.D.2.c.

United States, so that one region would not be picked upon for heavier taxation (at least in terms of tax rates and imposition or not of a tax).[7] Because imposts, duties and excises had to be uniform, the text provides a strong implication that they are not normally direct.

Of course land acreage and value and polls (including particularly slaves) started off being unequally distributed across the country. This fact was one of the many considerations that had a profound influence on the creation of the division. This and other motivating factors are discussed further in Chapter V.C.4.

Section 8 notably does not extend the uniformity requirement to taxes that are not imposts, duties and excises. The intuitive explanation why taxes, other than duties, imposts and excises, are not so limited is that taxes must refer to direct taxes, the same category of impositions that is subject to another and different limit in section 9. That is, assuming taxes in section 8 means the same as direct Tax in section 9, taxes do not need to be, indeed could not be, uniform (at least geographically) throughout the United States because they must be apportioned among the states on the basis of the population as determined by census (as modified for slaves). In fact direct taxes by this definition had to be nonuniform geographically, with landowners, for example, paying different amounts of tax per valuation or acreage of property in one state versus another state, because the tax was only partially based on value and acreage; it also was based on the census apportionment.

The Supreme Court has adopted this reading. *Pollock* affirmed this interpretation and identified as the two great classes of tax the direct and the "indirect," and the two great limitations on federal taxes: the one of apportionment on direct taxes and the other of uniformity on indirect taxes (in addition to the denial of export taxes).[8] *Pollock* was able to find the tax on income to be a direct tax on property that produced the income by looking to the substance rather than the form of the tax and finding that it burdened the ownership of the property that produced the income, in substance.[9] Thus, the tax on the income from land did not fall directly on the land (as an ad valorem tax) but it fell directly on the landowner and indirectly on the land. The basic theory of *Pollock* was that since an ad valorem tax on land was admitted to be a direct tax, a different sort of tax that indirectly burdened the land must also be a direct tax.

The Supreme Court had previously recognized the linkage of the apportionment requirement and the uniformity requirement to achieve one larger goal,

---

[7] *Cf.* Dodge v. Woolsey, 59 U.S. 331, 351-351 (1856) (explaining the type of uniformity of direct taxation in all states that was required of direct taxes).

[8] Pollock v. Farmers' Loan & Trust Co., 157 U.S. 429, 557 (1895). *See also* Flint v. Stone Tracy Co., 220 U.S. 107, 151 (1911) (confirmed this reading that "duties, imposts and excises" meant indirect taxes); Hylton v. United States, 3 U.S. 171, 173 (1796) (only two rules limit imposing taxes). *See* Francis W. Bird, *Constitutional Aspect of the Federal Tax on the Income of Corporations*, 24 Harv. L. Rev. 31, 32 (1911) [hereinafter Bird].

[9] 157 U.S. at 581; *as explained in* Brushaber v. Union Pacific R. Co., 240 U.S. 1, 16 (1916).

quoting Alexander Hamilton.[10] And five years after *Pollock*, *Knowlton v. Moore* linked the two limitations on the two classes of taxes as both designed to protect the states from discrimination:

> Now, that the requirement that direct taxes should be apportioned among the several States, contemplated the protection of the States, to prevent their being called upon to contribute more than was deemed their due share of the burden, is clear. Giving to the term uniformity as applied to duties, imposts and excises a geographical significance, likewise causes that provision to look to the forbidding of discrimination as between the States, by the levying of duties, imposts or excises upon a particular subject in one State and a different duty, impost or excise on the same subject in another; and therefore, as far as may be, is a restriction in the same direction and in harmony with the requirement of apportionment of direct taxes. And the conclusion that the possible discrimination against one or more States was the only thing intended to be provided for by the rule which uniformity imposed upon the power to levy duties, imposts and excises, is greatly strengthened by considering the state of the law in the mother country and in the colonies, and the practice of taxation which obtained at or about the time of the adoption of the Constitution.[11]

Justice Cardozo confirmed this view of the meaning of direct taxes in the pivotal decision *Steward Machine Co. v. Davis*.[12] In rejecting various objections to the social security tax, Justice Cardozo evaluated the uniformity objection and stated that it was not critically important to classify a tax as an excise or otherwise because so long as the tax was not direct (which the social security tax certainly was not), it had to be an excise, duty or impost subject to the uniformity requirement; in the long history of the Constitution and taxation no one had ever been able to identify a third category of taxes that was neither direct nor subject to the uniformity requirement;[13] therefore, the social security tax being

---

[10] Scholey v. Rew, 90 U.S. 331, 348 n. 26 (1875). It is likely that the desire to promote different forms of uniformity among the states was motivated in part by concerns about regional rebellions such as Shay's Rebellion. *See* THE FEDERALIST, No. 21, by Alexander Hamilton, pp. 126-127 (Modern Library Ed.).

[11] Knowlton v. Moore, 178 U.S. 41, 89 (1900).

[12] Steward Machine Co. v. Davis, 301 U.S. 548 (1937). *See also* Brushaber v. Union Pacific R. Co., 240 U.S. 1, 17 (1916) (stating that an income tax was an excise that might or might not impose a direct tax, based on whether substance over form principles applied, as to which the Sixteenth Amendment dictated that such principles should not be applied, but rather income could be taxed "from whatever source derived"); Flint v. Stone Tracy Co., 220 U.S. 107 (1911) (the 1909 corporate income tax was denominated an excise tax and was not a direct tax).

[13] *See also* Pollock v. Farmers' Loan & Trust Co., 157 U.S. 429, 557 (1895) (also not finding a third type of tax).

an excise (because not a direct tax), it must conform only to the requirement of uniformity, which is geographical and not intrinsic, and it did so conform.[14]

As Justice Cardozo stated, the meaning of direct tax is best informed by distinguishing it from a duty, impost or excise, and it is fairly certain that a duty, impost or excise was understood in colonial times, as now, as contingent on the happening of an event, *i.e.*, levied on continuing or repeatable events (such as purchases, manufacturing, imports, or uses) as they occur, in contrast to a tax levied on a thing or state of ownership as a static set of facts. Therefore, the opposite of an excise is a tax that is not contingent on anything but being or existence: the existence of a head to tax (capitation) or the existence of property, whose ownership is taxed by value (ad valorem tax).

Chief Justice Chase said that the restrictions on direct and indirect taxes were not limits on power but directions as to the mode of taxation:

> These are not strictly limitations of power. They are rules prescribing the mode in which it shall be exercised. It still extends to every object of taxation, except exports, and may be applied to every object of taxation, to which it extends, in such measure as Congress may determine.[15]

The foregoing generalities forecast the difficult questions: what about taxes that appeared to be imposed on the ownership of property other than land, and what about taxes that fell indirectly on land; are excises on the use of property in a certain way direct or indirect? The very first Supreme Court case to evaluate the constitutionality of any federal statute addressed a federal tax and answered the question as to a personal property tax in favor of limiting the direct tax category to a tax on land (and polls), finding a "duty" on carriages that were used for certain purposes to be indirect.[16] The Supreme Court was consistent in so limiting the meaning of direct taxes to land and poll taxes up to *Pollock*, which involved the tax on income enacted in 1894 (not the first federal income tax), and ruled it to be a direct tax on land when paid upon rents, and also ruled a tax on the income from at least "invested personal property" to be direct.[17] See Chapter V.D.2.c. In 2012 the Court in the health insurance tax case reaffirmed the traditional view that only taxes on property and heads can be direct.[18]

---

[14] *See* Ch. V.D.3.a. *See also* Thomas v. United States, 192 U.S. 363 (1904) (as to the existence of only two classes of taxes; the stamp tax fell on the sale of stock and was not direct; "There is no occasion to attempt to confine the words duties, imposts and excises to the limits of precise definition. We think that they were used comprehensively to cover customs and excise duties imposed on importation, consumption, manufacture and sale of certain commodities, privileges, particular business transactions, vocations, occupations and the like."). The possibility of another category had been left open in *Hylton*, and recognized in 1833 by Story. *See* STORY, at 419.

[15] Veazie Bank v. Fenno, 75 U.S. 533, 541 (1869).

[16] Hylton v. United States, 3 U.S. 171 (1796).

[17] Pollock v. Farmers' Loan & Trust Co., 157 U.S. 429 (1895), *confirmed and expanded*, 158 U.S. 601 (1895).

[18] *See* Ch. III.E.2.c(3)(f).

C. Direct Taxes

1. *The Direct Tax Issue*

Direct taxes and other taxes (including at least duties, imposts and excises) are the categories of federal taxation that were of the greatest constitutional significance up to the adoption of the Sixteenth Amendment, which promoted the importance of an income tax, a term not used in the original Constitution, and effectively freed a federal income tax from possible treatment as a direct tax and hence from apportionment. This change in 1913 was critically important to the nation, because direct taxes (principally ad valorem taxes apportioned to the states) were difficult for the nation to collect, at least in the amounts needed on a regular basis. Although Congress levied a handful of direct taxes to raise specified sums to pay for the War of 1812 and the Civil War, thereafter it became apparent that such an episodic federal property tax could not be converted into a regular baseline tax. Furthermore, the other types of federal taxes, duties and imposts on imports, and excises on transactions in goods, had the unfortunate ability to decrease the subject taxed when rates were increased to provide emergency revenue, thus making the revenue stream somewhat uncertain. One thing was for sure, however, at the dawn of the 20th Century, at least some Americans were earning a lot of income and a tax on incomes looked like a much more reliable revenue source.

But the recipients of that income knew just as well as Congress how attractive the income source appeared and deployed against the income tax the charge that it was a direct tax that Congress could impose only if it identified a dollar amount of tax it wanted to raise and then apportioned that amount among the states for collection from incomes. That, of course, was not going to happen for a variety of reasons. Therefore the income tax brought to a head the uncertainty about just what was a direct tax.

Implicitly recognizing the impracticality of direct taxes as a source of regular tax revenues, from the 1790s to 1895, Congress and the Court effectively treated as not direct all federal taxes other than a few episodic ad valorem taxes on land and poll taxes that Congress clearly labeled as direct taxes and apportioned among the states. For example, simply by choosing in 1794 not to apportion a tax on personal property (carriages), Congress showed that it did not consider that tax to be a direct tax. And it did so despite the fact that a tax on carriages looked like a direct tax on property ownership (although the tax did not depend directly on the property value but rather taxed by categories, which approach also had been applied to realty, *i.e.*, by number of windows). The Court went along with Congress' tax classification decisions, at least up to 1895, when a new federal tax—the second federal income tax, adopted in 1894—struck too directly at capital. In 1895 the Court rendered its only decisions striking down a federal tax because it was an unapportioned direct tax, leading to the adoption of the Sixteenth Amendment in 1913.

In those few instances when Congress did levy clearly labeled direct taxes, it did so only under financial duress when extraordinary additional tax revenue was needed. Moreover the states did not like federal direct taxes because they trenched on state methods of ad valorem taxation. Therefore, Congress found it much more commodious throughout the 19th Century for the United States to finance itself mainly through import duties, which came to serve the additional purpose of protecting local manufactures, while being somewhat invisible to domestic consumers (like many of the other excise taxes). If a federal tax were thought to be direct, and thus subject to apportionment, it probably would not be imposed by Congress at all, as contrasted with being refashioned as a direct tax. For that reason, Congress apportioned only the taxes that all agreed were direct: taxes on real property value and poll taxes; otherwise, it avoided those taxes (or called them excises or at least duties, as in the *Hylton* 1794 carriage tax[19]).

But whenever a taxpayer did not want to pay some new form of federal tax that was not clearly indirect (and few were clearly indirect aside from import duties), the taxpayer most likely would claim that it was an unconstitutional unapportioned direct tax. That assertion held the promise of the particular protesting taxpayer escaping the new tax burden altogether. It still does. Foes of the health insurance tax imposed under the 2010 health care act on individuals failing to obtain health insurance coverage filed multiple suits attacking the tax as an unapportioned direct tax, and the Court rejected the direct tax argument rather summarily in 2012 in *Sebelius*, indicating that the issue is a dead one, so long as the tax is not fairly clearly imposed on property or heads.[20]

The 1895 ruling that Congress violated the Constitution by failing to apportion a direct tax was not only the first but also the last time it has so ruled.[21] That decision in *Pollock*[22] ranks just below the *Dred Scott*[23] decision as among the worst in Supreme Court history.[24] Fortunately, the adoption of the Sixteenth Amendment and other factors discussed below have caused this issue of direct

---

[19] 1 Stat. 373 *et. seq.* (June 5, 1794).

[20] *See* Ch. III.E.2.c(3)(f).

[21] *Cf.* Eisner v. Macomber, 252 U.S. 189 (1920) (ruling that the Sixteenth Amendment did not authorize taxation of certain stock dividends, under a prior understanding of income).

[22] Pollock v. Farmers' Loan & Trust Co., 157 U.S. 429 (1895), *confirmed and expanded*, 158 U.S. 601 (1895).

[23] Dred Scott v. Sandford, 60 U.S. 393 (1857) (effectively ruling the Missouri Compromise unconstitutional and setting the stage for resolution of the issue of the expansion of slavery into new states by the Civil War).

[24] *See* Charles Evans Hughes, The Supreme Court of the United States 50 (1928) (listing as worst *Dred Scott*, *Pollock* and *Hepburn v. Griswold*, the quickly reversed ruling against the government in the *Legal Tender Cases*; Hughes' standards appear largely to have related to stability and public perception thereof). Illinois Governor John Peter Altgeld likened the *Pollock* decision to *Dred Scott*. Randolph Paul, Taxation for Prosperity 13 (1947). *See also* Charles Warren, The Supreme Court in United States History, Vol. II, 316-317 (1926) (concluding that most historians had rejected the earlier view that the *Dred Scott* decision was the most potent force in bringing on the Civil War, but agreeing with Edward Corwin's view that the decision was a "gross abuse of trust" that had the effect of removing the Supreme Court from its usual role of supervision during the Civil War and causing broad loss of confidence in the Court); Bernard Schwarz, Super Chief 502 (1983) (quoting retired Justice Frankfurter as criticizing a recent one man-one vote ruling by the Warren Court by saying that not since *Pollock* had the Court "rendered a decision so disruptive of the time-honored operations of our Government. . . .").

taxes to be largely one of historical significance. However, the related but separate uniformity requirement, which is applied to all federal taxes other than direct taxes, is quite alive, as discussed in Chapter V.D.3.a.

2. *Limit on Direct Taxes*

The Constitution requires Congress to apportion direct federal taxes among the states on the basis of their populations determined by the federal census. Understanding the nature of the apportionment requirement is informed by understanding its origin. It sprang from dissatisfaction with the inability of the Confederation to levy taxes directly on persons or property; instead the Continental Congress had to depend on amounts paid to it by the states.[25] The founders wanted the United States to be able to levy taxes directly on the people and their property, but because of the unequal distribution of people and property the apportionment requirement was applied.

Knowlton v. Moore explained a direct tax as one in which the Congress identified a gross amount desired to be raised, apportioned it among the states, then directed how it should be raised within each state, without being subject to the uniformity clause.[26] The method of application within each state was limited to a per capita amount or, more commonly, a tax on property value. This means if Congress required $20 million from the states by direct taxation, the adjusted census population of each state would be the numerator, over a denominator of the total adjusted census populations of all states, and that fraction times $20 million would be that state's share, to be collected from the direct subjects of taxation directed by Congress, either by federal tax collectors or by the states as agents for the United States.

But even this view was not obvious. Justice Story in 1833 used the $10 per carriage tax (if *Hylton* had come out the other way, as a direct tax) to try to devise a scheme to first determine the total number of taxable carriages, multiply that by $10, and then apportion the total tax derived among the states. He explained how that could be done mathematically, but would produce absurd results, thus evidencing why the carriage tax could not be a direct tax.[27]

The Fourteenth Amendment, section 2, modified Article I, section 2, clause 3 of the Constitution to remove the Three Fifths Clause. However, the Amend-

---

[25] 157 U.S. at 559-560. *See also* Lane County v. Oregon, 74 U.S. 71 (1869); Cross v. Harrison, 57 U.S. 164 (1854) (explaining the procedure under the Articles of Confederation: "The means to defray the expenses of government, under the Confederation, for common defense or general welfare were obtained by requisitions on the several States, for such sums of money as should be in proportion to the value of the lands and improvements in possession, or in grant to the citizens of the State, (Journals of Congress of Confederation, October Fourteenth, 1777, vol. 2, 288,) to be estimated in such way as Congress should appoint. See Confederation, article 8, vol. 2, Journal of Congress, 330, November 15, 1777. These quota were fixed by Congress, from time to time, according to the number of the white inhabitants in each State. Art. 9, Confederation; see vol. 2 of Journals of Confederation, 336, 337; also *id.* 346, November 23d, 1777, and the Report of the Committee of the Board of Treasury, *id.* 332.").

[26] 178 U.S. at 88.

[27] *See* STORY, at 426-427.

ment required apportionment according to all persons but "Indians not taxed," counting all persons as whole persons, only as to apportionment of representatives. Technically this left intact the requirement that direct taxes be apportioned on the basis of counting slaves as three fifths of a person.[28] Justice White's dissent in *Pollock* adverted to this fact and suggested that if anyone had thought that income taxes would be subject to such a rule of apportionment then taxes would have been included in the amendment.[29] Presumably, if anyone thought of it, they reasoned that after the Emancipation there were no slaves and the point was moot.

3. *Identifying Direct Taxes*

a. *Overview*

Today almost the only things that matter about identifying direct taxes are (1) that identification rarely if ever must be attempted due to the Sixteenth Amendment, and (2) the Supreme Court's cumulative pronouncements have left the subject in a state of relative clarity.[30] The Court's controlling opinions reflect a resounding affirmation of all congressional decisions, explicit or implicit, to levy taxes without apportionment, with *Pollock* being the exception that proves the rule.[31]

Under those controlling decisions, including *Pollock* (which was never overruled on this point, except to the extent overruled by the Sixteenth Amendment as to income), a direct tax is either (1) a poll tax levied on persons as persons,[32] or (2) a tax on the value of real property or "invested personal property,"[33] which is not levied on account of or with respect to the property's use, creation, transfer, or any other transaction, right or business activity related to it. As to personalty (and probably also as to realty), any reasonable designation by Congress of the

---

[28] *See* ROGER FOSTER, COMMENTARIES ON THE CONSTITUTION OF THE UNITED STATES, Vol. I, 413-415, 421 (1895) [hereinafter FOSTER].

[29] 158 U.S. 601, 715 (1895).

[30] Although it was not consulted in writing this book, the reader may wish to compare the views of another author with time on his hands who has recently written an article covering much of the same ground; *see* Joseph M. Dodge, *What Federal Taxes Are Subject to the Rule of Apportionment under the Constitution?* 11 U. PA. J. CON. L. 839 (2009). *See also*, Bruce Ackerman, *Taxation and the Constitution*, 99 COL. L. REV. 1 (1999) (arguing that the direct tax clause is of very little current importance); Robert G. Natelson, *What the Constitution Means by 'Duties, Imposts, and Excises' - and 'Taxes' (Direct or Otherwise)*, 66 CASE W. RES. L. REV. 297 (2015). Also, a substantial literature has arisen debating the constitutionality under the direct tax clause of recent proposals for flat taxes and the like. *See, e.g.*, Lawrence M. Zelenak, *Radical Tax Reform, the Constitution, and the Conscientious Legislator*, 99 COL. L. REV. 833 (1999) (concluding that a flat tax would not be unconstitutional).

[31] Pollock v. Farmers' Loan & Trust Co., 158 U.S. 601, 637 (1895).

[32] *See* Ch. III.E.6.

[33] This is the term used in *Pollock*, where it referred to stocks and bonds, and in Brushaber v. Union Pacific R. Co., 240 U.S. 1 (1916); McCoach v. Minehill & S. H. R. Co., 228 U.S. 295 (1913); Flint v. Stone Tracy Co., 220 U.S. 107 (1911); and Spreckels Sugar Refining Co. v. McClain, 192 U.S. 397 (1904).

tax as an excise tax upon some aspect of the property's use or consumption will be respected.[34]

The relevance of the Sixteenth Amendment to the determination is that it bans the application of the substance over form approach to the characterization of an income tax, thus making it an excise tax on receipt of income and not a tax on the property from which the income was derived.[35] However, even before 1913 when the Amendment was adopted the Court had backed away from such economic analysis of direct taxation in *Knowlton v. Moore*.[36]

When the Supreme Court began to try to make sense of the direct or not distinction, it early announced that direct taxes included taxes on heads and property,[37] which was entirely consistent with the British view. Property clearly included real property and this category was understood to include slaves in those several states that treated slaves as realty; if slaves were not realty, then tax was levied with respect to them on the basis of capitation.[38] *Hylton*, which ruled a federal tax on certain types of carriages to be indirect, stood either for the proposition that personal property was not subject to direct tax or that a tax on at least consumable personal property could be styled as an excise and that necessarily removed it from the direct tax class.[39] *Pollock* extended direct taxation to at least investment personal property (stocks and bonds), effectively limiting *Hylton* to the excise justification.[40]

Although the cases contrast direct with indirect taxes, the Constitution actually contrasted direct taxes with excises, duties and imposts; the direct-indirect dichotomy is a shorthand. A chart of other dichotomies that influenced the direct-indirect dichotomy can serve to summarize and illustrate the state of affairs and competing considerations when the Constitution was drafted. The categories and analogies are not perfect but close enough to suggest patterns in the process. The specific categories are discussed in Chapters V.C and C.

---

[34] Hylton v. United States, 3 U.S. 171 (1796) (ruled that a "duty," which later opinions characterized as an excise tax, on carriages was not a direct tax); Flint v. Stone Tracy Co., 220 U.S. 107 (1911) (ruled that an income tax on corporations in the form of an excise tax was constitutional, just 16 years after *Pollock*, and before the Sixteenth Amendment).

[35] *See* Ch. V.D.2.e.

[36] Knowlton v. Moore, 178 U.S. 41 (1900).

[37] *See, e.g.*, Justice Chase's opinion in Hylton v. United States, 3 U.S. 171 (1796).

[38] Pollock v. Farmers' Loan & Trust Co., 158 U.S. 601, 649-650 (1895).

[39] Hylton v. United States, 3 U.S. 171 (1796). *See* Brushaber v. Union Pacific R. Co., 240 U.S. 1, 14-15 (1916) (stating the alternate meanings). Note also that the carriage tax in *Hylton* was not exactly based on value but was a flat type that varied based on type of carriage, like a license.

[40] Pollock v. Farmers' Loan & Trust Co., 158 U.S. 601, 628-629 (1895) (but it left the excise definition applicable to a tax on business, which the Court relied on in Flint v. Stone Tracy Co., 220 U.S. 107 (1911) to uphold a corporate income (excise tax)).

Direct Tax	**Not Direct (Indirect) Tax**
Tax incurred by ownership (and poll tax)	Tax incurred by transaction
Tax that cannot be avoided; subject to "absolute and unavoidable demand"[41]	Tax that can be avoided by avoiding the transaction or the "privilege" taxed
Tax that is more likely to fall on the wealthy who own property	Tax that can fall on all classes
Tax on wealth or capital	Not viewed as a tax on wealth or capital so much as on wages
Tax on individuals	Tax on trade or business transactions
More difficult to shift economic incidence of the tax away from the immediate payor	Less difficult to shift the economic incidence of the tax away from the immediate payor
Therefore more likely to be noticed by ultimate payor[42]	Therefore less likely to be noticed by ultimate payor
Lends itself to episodic (as needed) levy	Lends itself to continuous levy
Tax base more likely to be known in advance	Tax base less likely to be known in advance, i.e., variable
Internal tax	Internal and external taxes
Not a tax on consumption	Tax on consumption
Historically called a tax in England (the "land tax"), which was apportioned to the counties and towns	Normally called something else: Duties and imposts (generally on imports) and excises (on internal transactions), generally uniform throughout a geographical territory
More likely to reflect the intent of the legislature to tax the immediate payor rather than to regulate	More likely to serve purposes both of raising revenue and regulating transactions
Tax on land	Tax on anything other than land
Difficult to administer and collect; not likely to be levied	Easier to administer and collect; more likely to be levied

Many have studied the records of the Constitutional Convention, the Federalist Papers, the debates on the Constitution's ratification and other sources to try to ascertain what the Constitution means by direct taxes, to little avail. We know that the research has been complete because of the money at stake: the

[41] *See* Thomas v. United States, 192 U.S. 363 (1904) (which first used this phrase to explain why a stamp tax on a particular business was not a direct tax).

[42] This usage was current in 1861. *See A Benefit of Direct Taxation*, New York Times (Aug. 9, 1861) (favoring the imposition of the Civil War income tax because it would be directly felt by the payors and might cause them to be more advertent to the fraud and waste of government).

most assiduous students have been lawyers who were trying hard to prove that their clients' taxes were direct and not apportioned and thus unconstitutional. Perhaps the most famous statement about the lack of definition of direct taxes is that in Madison's notes on the Constitutional Convention. Mr. King asked what was the precise meaning of direct taxes and "No one answered."[43] Hamilton's briefs contained this statement:

> What is the distinction between direct and indirect taxes? It is a matter of regret that terms so uncertain and vague in so important a point are to be found in the Constitution. We shall seek in vain for any antecedent settled legal meaning to the respective terms. There is none.[44]

In light of this history it is curious that discussions about the Civil War income tax commonly called it a direct tax.[45]

Capitation taxes. The meaning of capitation or poll taxes, which all agree would be direct taxes, is relatively clear. Article I, section 9 of the Constitution states that capitation taxes are direct. Capitation taxes generically can encompass not only a flat tax per person living at a certain time and place but also per person doing a certain thing, such as crossing a state line[46] or voting.[47] They also can vary by class or rank or some other method aimed at approximating the payor's wealth.[48] The records of the Constitutional Convention show that direct taxes were considered as taxes on heads and property.[49] The concept of poll taxes is not obsolete, as illustrated by the Twenty Fourth Amendment, ratified in 1964, which prohibits conditioning voting on the payment of a poll tax, state or federal.

Interest in capitation taxes enjoyed a small revival in 2012 when the Court considered the argument that the health insurance tax will be a capitation tax

---

[43] Pollock v. Farmers' Loan & Trust Co., 157 U.S. 429, 562 (1895) (citing MADISON'S JOURNAL OF THE CONSTITUTIONAL CONVENTION (Aug. 20, 1787)). For other statements made during the debates, *see* FOSTER, at 417-418 (Chancellor Livingston said direct taxes were taxes on land and specific duties; John Jay said they were general and specific but were items that were uniformly found throughout the states; John Marshall said the term was "well understood" to mean land, slaves, stock and a few other articles of domestic property).

[44] *Quoted in* Springer v. United States, 102 U.S. 586, 597 (1880).

[45] *A Benefit of Direct Taxation*, NEW YORK TIMES (Aug. 9, 1861); *Direct Taxation: A Sketch of the Rise, History and Development of the British Income Tax*, NEW YORK TIMES (Jan. 6, 1862); *Some Suggestions in Regard to Direct Taxation: An Income Tax*, NEW YORK TIMES (July 26, 1861); *Direct Taxation: Views of Mr. C.A. Bristed*, NEW YORK TIMES (Jan. 13, 1862).

[46] *See* Colgate v. Harvey, 296 U.S. 404, 430 (1935); Crandall v. Nevada, 73 U.S. 35 (1868) (the Court did not question that a flat tax on persons leaving the state was a tax and a capitation tax, but declined to rule that it was a tax on imports or exports, and held it unconstitutional as a burden on interstate commerce; it contrasted earlier cases involving tax on importation of slaves, which were both persons and property and so could be imports).

[47] *See* United States v. Reese, 92 U.S. 214 (1875).

[48] ADAM SMITH, AN INQUIRY INTO THE NATURE AND CAUSE OF THE WEALTH OF NATIONS 514-515 (1776, Harvard Classics ed. 1909) [hereinafter ADAM SMITH]

[49] *See* Michelin Tire Corp. v. Wages, 423 U.S. 276, 293 n. 12 (1976) (quoting Luther Martin); Pollock v. Farmers' Loan & Trust Co., 157 U.S. 429, 565 (1895) (quoting Luther Martin, letter to Maryland legislature).

because a person must pay it by virtue of being an individual.[50] The opinion of the Court quickly dismissed this argument, discerning that more was required than the fact that an individual exists: the individual must also fail to buy health insurance when that is a condition of the tax.[51]

b. *Identification: The British Background*

Edward B. Whitney, the Assistant Attorney General who argued *Pollock* as well as other important cases of that era in the Supreme Court,[52] wrote in 1907 as part of a detailed analysis of *Pollock* and the income tax, his conclusions about the drafters' meaning of direct taxes.[53] He reasoned that because they were mostly lawyers and not economists, and because the Colonies' taxing laws were so inconsistent, they would have relied on their understanding of the English taxes.[54] For a century the English statutes had levied a "tax" on property by valuation and by apportionment, and the only such general tax was on land. Everything else was a duty. Duties were not laid by apportionment but by uniformity. "This unvarying distinction in terms in the statute books cannot have been accidental, and must have been familiar to lawyers."[55]

On the other hand some have pointed to Mr. King's inability to obtain an answer to his quest for a definition of direct tax at the Constitutional Convention, and suggested that the reason was there was none and the term was simply ambiguous.[56] Hamilton's brief quoted above said we may seek in vain for an antecedent meaning and find none and it must be arbitrarily determined. Justice Patterson in *Hylton* said the words direct tax "present no clear and precise idea to the mind."[57]

The earliest taxes in England were the feudal levies, which drew funds up through the ranks of the feudal system to support the King.[58] Those levied on land, which was the fundamental thing of value in the feudal system, were called direct taxes. As the nature of wealth shifted in England the King shifted to trying to tax personal property and revenues. The demise of feudalism was followed by the rise of the British Empire, which provided to the Crown a variety of revenue sources, only some of which were called taxes, but the most obvious of which

---

[50] Nat'l Fed'n of Indep. Bus. v. Sebelius, 567 U.S. 519 (2012).

[51] *See also* Ch. III.E.6.

[52] *Edward B. Whitney Retires*, New York Times (June 15, 1897).

[53] Edward B. Whitney, *The Income Tax and the Constitution*, 20 Harv. L. Rev. 272 (1907) [hereinafter Whitney].

[54] *Id.* at 292-293.

[55] *Id.* at 293. Whitney points out that due to the imposition of British taxes on the Colonies the colonial lawyers were intimately familiar with the British tax statutes and would have known that they clearly differentiated taxes on land, which were apportioned by counties and towns, from unapportioned taxes on personalty, which were called duties. *Id.* at 294.

[56] *See, e.g.*, Dwight Morrow, *The Income Tax Amendment*, 10 Col. L. Rev. 379, 397-398, and 401 (1910) [hereinafter Morrow] (stating that Richard Lee said different men understand the words differently).

[57] 3 U.S. at 176.

[58] William Stubbs, Constitutional History of England in its Origins and Development, Vol. 1, 576-587 (1880).

were customs duties. Nevertheless, the English land tax continued to exist and to be apportioned among the counties, thus bearing strong resemblance to the Constitution's direct taxes if applied to land.[59]

Maitland explained in 1888 that when even earlier the King turned from indirect taxation (customs duties on imports, which initially were thought to be a type of regulation of trade) to direct taxation (requiring "loans" from knights), the Parliament rebelled and in the Petition of Right in 1628 forbade the King to require any forced loan or tax without common consent by act of Parliament.[60] This prohibition did not clearly encompass customs duties, which presumably were not viewed as "direct taxes." Eventually Parliament concluded that such duties were taxes, no matter how closely they might be related to the King's near absolute power to control commerce. In 1689 the Declaration of Rights and the Bill of Rights established that the King could lay no taxes without the consent of Parliament. Maitland said this was the last word on the matter, which was closed (in 1888).

In the mid-1700s Blackstone categorized the then extant British taxes in two different groups that did not employ the term direct tax: annual and perpetual.[61] The annual taxes were annual land tax and malt tax; these were in the nature of direct taxes. The perpetual taxes were customs on imports from and exports to other countries, excise duties or "inland impositions," and duties on salt, stamps, houses and windows, carriages and offices and pensions. Income taxes did eventually arise in England in 1799, obviously after the writing of the Constitution, which tends to disprove the view that the drafters could have had British income taxes in mind.[62]

Thus it is entirely logical that the American lawyers writing the Constitution would have acted consistently with the British statutes' view of "tax" as the land tax, with the confusion arising mainly from the absence of the term "direct tax" in the British law.[63]

c. *Identification: The Economic Explanation*

Was the Constitution's dichotomy of direct versus other taxes derived from the relatively new (in 1787) theory that the direct payors of a tax were not necessarily those who ultimately bore its burden due to an ability of that payor to shift the economic burden of the tax to others through increasing rents, prices and other charges? Perhaps.

More likely the economic explanation is no more complicated than the common sense understanding that a tax on the value of property owned by an indi-

---

[59] FOSTER, at 417.

[60] F.W. MAITLAND, A CONSTITUTIONAL HISTORY OF ENGLAND 306-311 (1908).

[61] WILLIAM BLACKSTONE, AN ANALYSIS OF THE LAWS OF ENGLAND 17-18 (1858, 3d Ed.); 1 WILLIAM BLACKSTONE, COMMENTARIES ON THE LAWS OF ENGLAND 298 *et seq.* (1765).

[62] *See* Meade Emory, *The Early English Income Tax: A Heritage for the Contemporary*, 9 AM. J. LEGAL HIST. 286 (1965); dissent of Justice Jackson in Pollock v. Farmers' Loan & Trust Co., 158 U.S. 601, 701 (1895).

[63] Bird, at 32-33.

vidual, or on heads and due from the individuals (or their owners in the case of slaves), will necessarily be paid by the property owners or the individuals, both as a matter of initial liability and as an economic matter, if one does not search too deeply for tax shifting. Conversely, it was commonly understood that a tax collected at the port on imported goods raised prices on goods used by the general population, and hence was likely not a burden ultimately borne by the importer but was indirectly borne by the general population. In other words tax shifting had been experienced in the Colonies as to import duties and perhaps excises on manufactures; but beyond that the common sense understanding was not sufficiently advanced to see that even a tax on property value could be shifted (for example to property tenants in the form of rent). Therefore, it is not likely that a full-fledged economic explanation underlies the Constitutional rule for direct taxes. Nevertheless, the Court in *Pollock* discerned such advanced shifting in the form of an income tax bearing on land that produced taxed rental income, but failed to discern that land was no more an ultimate bearer of the tax burden than was the income.[64]

Shifting was first analyzed in a major way by French economists called the physiocrats, who argued that all wealth could be traced back to land.[65] This has been a recurring theme in popular tax discussions, showing up in the single tax theory of Henry George, in his book *Progress and Poverty*.[66] Close on the heels of the physiocrats was Adam Smith, whose enormously important book, *The Wealth of Nations*, was published in 1776.

If one could find that the physiocrats or Adam Smith used direct and indirect taxes as common terms of art, that might go a long way toward explaining what the drafters of the Constitution meant. The majority in *Pollock* thought so, but Justice White in dissent stated that it served no purposes at that late date to resort to the theoretical opinions of economists, because the Constitution had been uniformly interpreted for over 100 years to employ a more narrow definition of direct tax, and what was at issue was "American law."[67] Most commentators have doubted that Smith's ideas could have so quickly influenced the

---

[64] Pollock v. Farmers' Loan & Trust Co., 157 U.S. 429 (1895), *confirmed and expanded*, 158 U.S. 601 (1895). *See* Ch. V.D.2.c.

[65] E.R.A. Seligman, The Shifting and Incidence of Taxation 95 *et seq.* (2d Ed. 1899) [hereinafter Seligman] (But the story of economic analyses of tax incidence shifting is vastly more complicated than that, as explained by Seligman, who is the father of the U.S. income tax).

[66] *See* Cummings, *The Great American Tax Reformer*, 144 Tax Notes 79 (July 7, 2014); Edwin S. Todd, *The Single Tax on Land Rent*, 12 Taxes 346 (1934). *See generally*, Ralph H. Gabriel, The Course of American Democratic Thought 198-215 (1940) (describing the vast influence in its day of George's idea of a single tax on land on the theory that land was a limited resource on which all ultimately depended).

[67] 157 U.S. at 614.

drafters of the Constitution, but they might have.[68] At least Franklin did meet Adam Smith twice before the drafting of the Constitution and perhaps read early drafts of parts of the *Wealth of Nations*,[69] and certainly was exposed to the physiocrats (as was Hamilton).[70] However, ultimately the economic explanation has not prevailed in practice.

Veazie Bank v. Fenno stated:

> The great work of Adam Smith, the first comprehensive treatise on political economy in the English language, had then been recently published; but in this work, though there are passages which refer to the characteristic difference between direct and indirect taxation, there is nothing which affords any valuable light on the use of the words "direct taxes" in the Constitution.[71]

The physiocrats thought that all taxes ultimately fall on the land and the income of land, regardless of who is the payor; their ideas can be traced back to John Locke.[72] Perhaps one evidence of the lack of advertence of the drafters to physiocrats is that section 9 of Article I of the Constitution specifically labeled capitation taxes as direct, without providing any other definition; the physiocrats were in disagreement on the point.[73]

Evidently Francois Quesnay, a leading physiocrat, used the distinction of direct versus indirect tax to refer to taxes on what he considered to be the ultimate source of all tax revenues, land, versus taxes on anything else; he viewed a tax on land rent as a direct tax on the land.[74] Therefore, so long as a tax was levied on land or its rent, it was applied directly to the ultimate source of all tax revenues, but if not it would be indirectly derived from land because that was the ultimate source of value.[75]

Adam Smith agreed with the need to examine whether a tax directly paid by one person could be shifted to another person through pricing, but Smith's disagreement with the physiocrats was more fundamental than a disagreement about which shifts occurred. His entire theory of taxation was based on the view that all taxes must ultimately fall on either rents, profits or wages, a very different

---

68 Bird, at 33-34; Foster, at 416. *But see* Margaret Spahr, The Supreme Court on the Incidence and Effects of Taxation: An Analysis of Economic Theory Embedded in the Constitutional Law Derived from the Explicit Tax Clauses, Smith College Studies in History 97, 117-121 (Jan.-July, 1925) (reprinted by Making of the Modern Law, Legal Treatises, 1800-1926) [hereinafter Spahr] (noting that the separate opinion of Justice Paterson in *Hylton*, 3 U.S. at 181, quoted The Wealth of Nations).

69 Walter Isaacson, Benjamin Franklin: An American Life 196, 260-261.

70 *See* Seligman, at 109-110, stating that Turgot wrote a special memo on tax shifting to Franklin.

71 Veazie Bank v. Fenno, 75 U.S. 533, 542 (1869).

72 Bird, at 33. *See also* Spahr, at 97, 121; Adam Smith, at 481 (discussing what he called the oeconomists); Foster, at 416.

73 Foster, at 416-417.

74 *See* Gianni Vaggi, The Economics of Francoise Quesnay 27, and 220 n. 12 (1987) (citing the Second Probleme Economique as espousing a single tax on land rent in lieu of all indirect taxes).

75 Seligman, at 99.

approach than that of the physiocrats.[76] Thus he did not even admit of a tax on the holding of land because he was focused on the practical necessity for taxes to be paid out of something other than capital. His view of shifting was based largely on whether the taxed person was a monopolist (if it was a monopolist then presumably it was already charging the maximum amount for the item taxed and could not raise its prices and shift the tax further) or otherwise able to raise its prices to recoup the tax.[77]

A major problem with relying on Smith for the direct versus indirect tax dichotomy is that Smith did not consistently categorize taxes as direct or indirect or external or internal, but rather as falling on either rents, profits or wages, which are ultimate sources of cash flows that he thought most appropriate for taxation.[78] At some points he indicated that a tax whose incidence could not be shifted was direct.[79] At other points he called a tax a direct tax even when it could be shifted, evidently using the word direct tax simply to refer to the person who directly pays the tax; in that sense all taxes are direct taxes.[80]

Seligman's 1899 review of the thinking on tax shifting over the centuries included the following: (1) in the 1600s a distinction appeared between a direct tax on wages and an indirect excise tax on necessities, which would be shifted to the workingman and hence paid from his wages;[81] (2) also in the 1600s there were discussions of indirect consumption taxes (imposed on the manufacturer of consumables) and direct consumption taxes (imposed on expenditures and collected from the consumer);[82] (3) in the 1700s there were discussions of direct tax on luxuries;[83] (4) the physiocrats' discussed direct taxes on land or land rent and referred to all other taxes as indirect;[84] (5) later the so called socialistic theory viewed as better those direct taxes that were imposed on the individual's income and property and as worse all other indirect taxes because they indirectly fell on the poor when levied on consumption;[85] and (6) another old theory viewed a direct tax on wages as being shifted to profits.[86] Seligman concluded:

---

[76] Harry Edward Smith, The United States Federal Internal Tax History from 1861 to 1871 476 (1914).

[77] *Id.* at 489, 491-492 (landlord usually can raise rent but not pure land rent, which presumably is set at highest monopoly price).

[78] *Id.* at pp. 476-548.

[79] *Id.* at pp. 496-497. Smith explains that the normal return of business (which he calls interest) generally can be taxed directly because the tax cannot affect the interest return required, whereas the extra profit above the return of interest cannot be taxed directly because the tax would either drive the person out of business or be shifted; but the earner of interest is not such a monopolist as the owner of land.

[80] *Id.* at 512 (taxes on wages are direct taxes even though they tend to raise wages and be shifted to the employer); at 516 (capitation taxes are indirectly wage taxes).

[81] Seligman, at 16.

[82] *Id.* at 55.

[83] *Id.* at 36.

[84] *Id.* at 95 *et seq.*

[85] *Id.* at 163.

[86] *Id.* at 297.

> In common parlance the distinction between direct and indirect taxes is practically relegated to the mind of the legislator: what he wishes to have borne by the original taxpayer is called a direct tax, what he intends to have borne by someone else than the original taxpayer is called indirect. Unfortunately the intention of the legislator is not identical with the actual result. We must, then, either revise our nomenclature or declare the present distinction of little value.[87]

Just five years after *Pollock*, *Knowlton v. Moore* ruled that an estate tax was not direct. More importantly, it rejected the view that direct taxes should be defined in terms of whether the tax could be shifted.[88] *Scholey v. Rew* had already presaged this position by saying that citations to "foreign political economists" were trumped by Hamilton's brief in *Hylton*.[89] In *Brushaber*, upholding the 1913 income tax, Justice White summarized the analysis of the direct versus indirect classification in *Pollock*, and brought it up to date with a statement of the "practical construction" and "legislative practice" that prevailed: direct taxes were only taxes imposed on property because of its ownership (with the two examples being land and slaves).[90] As a consequence, taxes that were not direct came to be characterized by their relationship to a transaction. This gave the distinction a legal rather than an economic tone, like the rest of the interpretation of the tax laws.

d. *Identification: The Colonies, the Confederation, and the New Congress*

To identify a direct tax *Knowlton v. Moore* advised considering the "state of the law . . . in the colonies, and the practice of taxation which obtained at or about the time of the adoption of the Constitution."[91] That consideration shows that most of the Colonies had derived revenues principally from poll taxes and real property taxes;[92] that the Confederation had attempted to use the same revenue sources; and that the early Congress apportioned property taxes in episodic levies for the War of 1812, but regularly relied on import duties and excises. These facts suggest that real property taxes and poll taxes were viewed as the principal revenue source for the Colonies, and thus for the states; that while this revenue source would not be denied to the United States, it was not to be the principal revenue source and when used was tightly constrained by the apportionment requirement.

Professor Rabushka's extensive analysis of colonial taxation shows that during the period leading up to the revolutionary era the Colonies depended predomi-

---

[87] *Id.* at 311.

[88] Knowlton v. Moore, 178 U.S. 41, 88 (1900). *See also* Murdock v. Ward, 178 U.S. 139 (1900) (similar).

[89] Springer v. United States, 102 U.S. 586, 602-603 (1880).

[90] Brushaber v. Union Pacific R. Co., 240 U.S. 1, 14-15 (1916). *See also* Tyee Realty Co. v. Anderson, 240 U.S. 115 (1916).

[91] Knowlton v. Moore, 178 U.S. 41, 89 (1900).

[92] *See* Chapter V.C.4.c, for further discussion of this history.

nantly on poll and property taxes for revenues.[93] For example in 1762 and 1763, Massachusetts derived approximately 79% of its tax revenue from poll taxes and real property taxes;[94] the "overwhelming bulk" of Connecticut's tax revenues were from poll and property taxes;[95] New York was able to collect significant revenue from import duties and tonnage duties due to its port, but did in some years levy direct taxes on real and personal property, which when levied produced vastly greater sums than the excises;[96] Pennsylvania depended principally on excises, but when war needs arose substantial direct taxes on property were required, and the counties regularly taxed property for local revenue;[97] Virginia depended primarily on export duties (tobacco) and poll taxes (including a poll tax on slaves) until the war, when it turned to property taxes, which appeared to raise more than the prior taxes;[98] North Carolina depended primarily on the poll tax, at both the state and county levels;[99] South Carolina derived substantially more revenue from a variety of direct taxes (poll, property) than from duties on imports and exports, where also were significant.[100]

The Confederation had attempted to appropriate from the states taxes based either on land or people, including the technique of counting slaves as three fifths of a person.[101] At the time of the Constitution no general income tax had been levied in the states or in England, although certain receipts and occupation taxes had been levied; so the drafters could not have had a specific intent about a general net income tax.[102]

The taxes that Congress adopted in the years immediately after ratification of the Constitution, when its meaning presumably was better understood, indicate that any tax other than taxes on lands, houses and slaves was not considered to be direct. As explained in *Veazie Bank v. Fenno*, Congress levied direct taxes only 5 times: 1798, 1813, 1815, 1816, 1861.[103] In the first levy slaves were taxed

---

[93] Alvin Rabushka, Taxation in Colonial America (2008) [hereinafter Rabushka].

[94] *Id.* at 582-599 (Rabushka states that it is difficult to determine what was actually collected relative to what was levied, but the taxes on polls and property levied were the percentage of the total stated, with the indirect taxes being mainly excises and import duties).

[95] *Id.* at 601.

[96] *Id.* at 631-636 (although it was difficult to determine what was actually collected, for example in 1763 about 46,000 pounds was collected from direct taxes in comparison with duties of about 8,000 pounds).

[97] *Id.* at 641-647.

[98] *Id.* at 668-678

[99] *Id.* at 690-695.

[100] *Id.* at 708-709.

[101] *See* David Waldstreicher, Slavery's Constitution: From Revolution to Ratification 55 (2010) [hereinafter Waldstreicher] (in addition to an unsuccessful tax on imports). *See also* Charles J. Bullock, *Direct Taxes Under the Constitution*, 15 Pol. Sci. Q. No. 2 and 3, 217-219 (1900) [hereinafter Bullock].

[102] Many have made this observation, including Whitney, at 292.

[103] Veazie Bank v. Fenno, 75 U.S. 533, 542 (1869) (the citations for the five taxes in the Statutes at Large appear in the opinion). *See also* Harry Smith, at ch. II (recounting the direct taxes and extensively discussing the Civil War direct taxes). Foster, at 413-415, 420 (explaining that the final direct tax was refunded).

per capita and the last 4 acts as realty. The *Springer* opinion found three more statutes in 1815, 1861 and 1862, which related to the basic levies.[104] The direct tax was never laid on anything other than lands, houses and slaves and never as a poll tax.[105] However, because the uniformity requirement was not applicable to direct taxes, Congress could choose to levy taxes within the states on different subjects state by state, so long as the apportionment was satisfied.[106]

The most important evidence of congressional understanding of direct taxes is the first such tax on carriages, examined in *Hylton v. United States.*[107] The tax was effectively a luxury tax.[108] The Supreme Court gave short shrift to the taxpayers and proclaimed the tax was not direct because it would be difficult to apportion. An alternate explanation was that the Court viewed the tax as one on expense rather than capital (or revenue from capital), which view was assisted by the fact that the tax fell on what was perceived as a luxury.[109] Madison complained to Jefferson that the tax had been upheld despite the Constitution, was aimed at luxuries, and threatened all persons of wealth.[110] *Hylton* further explained that the apportionment requirement was the result of a compromise and so should be strictly construed against taxation, implying that the whole idea of apportioned direct taxes was a bad one and the practicalities difficult and producing unfairness.

4. *Direct Taxes: Reasons for the Distinction*

This Chapter surveys the various factors that may have produced the direct versus indirect categories in the Constitution. These factors obviously can inform the identification issue discussed above.

a. *Reasons: Political Motivations Overview*

The political motivations that affected the taxing provisions of the Constitution were many and, like all political compromises, resulted in rules that are sometimes obscure (what is a direct tax?) and sometimes conflicting (are direct taxes not to be uniform?). The most important political motivations are discussed below. This ground has been plowed heavily by far more expert historians than this author. The purpose here is not to find any undiscovered insight, but to assemble the interpretations, including general scholarship on the Constitution, and apply the latter to tax, which has not necessarily been the focus of such studies.

---

[104] Springer v. United States, 102 U.S. 586 (1880).

[105] Foster.

[106] Knowlton v. Moore, 178 U.S. at 88.

[107] Hylton v. United States, 3 U.S. 171 (1796).

[108] Carl Brent Swisher, American Constitutional Development 75-76 (1954) (also the suit was contrived to be brought before the Supreme Court, because the taxpayer did not want to bear the expense of litigation and actually paid the tax before judgment).

[109] *See* Foster, at 420 (quoting statement of Albert Gallatin in 1796 to that effect).

[110] Letter dated May 7, 1794, quoted at Foster, at 418.

Scholars have identified many competing interests at work in the writing of the Constitution. They included protectors of mercantile interests versus populist interests,[111] and protectors of landed interests (primarily slave holders) versus others.[112] Sidney Ratner succinctly summarized the political dynamics in his 1942 book:

> . . . [T]he direct tax provisions were designed to prevent the manufacturing states from shifting the burdens of taxation to the sparsely settled farming regions and that these direct taxes were viewed only as a last resort when indirect taxes, especially the customs duties, failed to produce sufficient revenue. It is rather ironic that the direct tax provisions should have become the means of preventing the farmers in 1895 from forcing the industrial Northeast to assume its due share of the tax burden.[113]

And the political explanations evolved. As concern about Socialism appeared in the latter 1800s (Karl Marx published *Das Kapital* in 1867), the term "direct taxation" came to be a shorthand for a socialistic tax that the government must collect directly from the people, as contrasted with collection through some withholding (as in excises and duties and imposts) or tolls that appeared to be fees for services, which perhaps were not perceived by the people as taxes at all.[114] Presumably the threat of imposing a direct tax was thought to be the ultimate political weapon against such a tax: direct taxation would not be pursued in practice because the taxpayers would be too cognizant of the tax. As a result of these concerns and the fact that the Constitution made direct taxes difficult to impose, the people got a taxing system "placing practically all of the national burden on the consumer," prior to the adoption of the income tax in 1913.[115]

b. *Reasons: Regions and Large States Versus Small States*

The conflicting interest of large and small states permeated the Constitutional Convention. Small states tended to be northern and mid-Atlantic, not to have substantial numbers of slaves, to be more densely populated in terms of whites, to have less valuable land in the aggregate but more valuable commerce in terms

---

[111] *See generally* CHARLES A. BEARD, AN ECONOMIC INTERPRETATION OF THE CONSTITUTION OF THE UNITED STATES (1921) [hereinafter BEARD].

[112] LOUIS H. POLLAK, THE CONSTITUTION AND THE SUPREME COURT: A DOCUMENTARY HISTORY, Vol. 1, pp. 114-115 (1966) [hereinafter POLLAK].

[113] SIDNEY RATNER, AMERICAN TAXATION 19 (1942) [hereinafter RATTNER]. By this statement Ratner refers to the fact that the income tax of 1894 that *Pollock* ruled unconstitutional was part of the populist program, which included loosening the money supply to encourage inflation and help debtors, and was generally supported by southern Democrats, who were the heirs of the former slave owners, in some sense.

[114] *See, e.g.*, Editorial, *Democratic Doctrine Destroys the Populist Income Tax*, NEW YORK TIMES (May 21, 1895) (stating that the west and the south combined to tax the east and the north and the wealthy only; labeled as "socialists and populists" those responsible for the income tax of 1864); *Republicanism in Kentucky*, NEW YORK TIMES (July 13, 1860) (Henry Clay contrasted direct taxation "on the people" with customs duties); *Governor King's Message*, NEW YORK TIMES (Jan. 6, 1858) ("if tolls don't produce enough income we will have to resort to direct taxation").

[115] BEARD, at 170.

of interests such as shipping and manufacturing, and to be less concerned about exportation and perhaps more concerned about preventing importation of some items (cloth, for example) or encouraging importation of other items (sugar, for example, which was used to make rum). The major shipping interests were in the smaller northern states and would have been more concerned about customs duties.[116] The larger states tended to be in the south, to have large numbers of slaves, to have large and valuable lands, to export agricultural goods, and to want cheap imports of goods they did not manufacture. The southern colonies thought that direct taxation of heads and land would hurt them the most and wanted to prevent the taxing power from being used against them.[117]

Charles Beard said it was the consensus of knowledgeable persons that the direct tax limitation was intended to prevent the smaller states from shifting the burden of taxation to the sparsely populated (by whites) southern states.[118] This might have been done by imposing a direct tax on property found in larger amounts or values in certain states, such as land and slaves and possible even farm products in the south.[119] Bullock strongly contests that view, attributing the limitation entirely to the slavery compromise.[120] Beard quoted an explanation by the North Carolina delegates to the Constitutional Convention pointing out the combination of benefits to the south, which made the following points: 50 citizens of North Carolina will pay no more tax on their land than 50 citizens of one of the "Eastern States"; the problem of counting slaves has been ameliorated by counting them only as three fifths of a person; our land is much more valuable than the lands of the eastern states; if there are poll taxes, slaves will be charged as three fifths of a person; in addition, the south will receive better security for the return of its escaped slaves under the union; and the federal government would take over the debts of the states, which would be paid through the taxing power.[121]

Of course, the most basic compromise of the Constitution, the creation of a bicameral legislature elected on differing bases, reflected the competing needs of each group of states.[122] Clearly the competing Randolph Plan (Virginia) and Patterson Plan (New Jersey) paved the way for that compromise by which the states were not to have equal voices (except in the Senate) but rather proportional representation would apply, with many modifications (for example, slaves were counted as three fifths of a person).[123]

---

[116] WALDSTREICHER, at 92.

[117] This explanation appears in Hylton v. United States, 3 U.S. 171, 177 (1796). It is obviously closely linked to the concerns about slavery.

[118] BEARD, at 169.

[119] CARL BRENT SWISHER, AMERICAN CONSTITUTIONAL DEVELOPMENT 35 n. 6 (1954). While slaves were valuable property concentrated in the south, it is not clear that southern land was as valuable as northern land, but there was more of it. *See* HINTON ROWAN HELPER, THE IMPENDING CRISIS OF THE SOUTH (1857).

[120] Bullock, at 217 *et seq.*

[121] BEARD, at 169-170.

[122] WALDSTREICHER, at 80-83.

[123] POLLAK, at Vol. 1, pp. 60-63.

c. *Reasons: Primary Source of Tax*

As pointed out in Chapter V.C.3.d, a very practical explanation for the direct versus indirect distinction was that the direct taxes were of the sort that states (and their local governments, counties) might be most likely to depend on. Ad valorem taxes on land, which were generally acknowledged to be direct taxes, were typical local taxes of the colonial period, as were poll taxes to a lesser extent.[124] By making federal taxation of land and poll taxes hard to impose (the troublesome apportionment was required), the states preserved for themselves primary access to their historic primary source of funds.[125]

Even though the federal and state taxing powers were to be concurrent,[126] in practice the states were more likely to rely on certain types of taxes that preferably differed from those the federal government might rely upon.

> Nothing can be clearer than that what the Constitution intended to guard against was the exercise by the general government of the power of directly taxing persons and property within any State through a majority made up from the other States.[127]

Presumably this statement from the *Pollock* opinion assumed that direct taxes on persons and property somehow were the province of each state for itself.

While the states fought for the right to tax imports, which they had historically taxed, along with exports,[128] it was almost inevitable that the power to levy tariffs on imports would be granted exclusively to the United States, given the success of Hamilton's conception of various national powers encouraging commerce and hence economic growth. But the states were rightly protective of their primary revenue source: land taxes and poll taxes. Whatever direct taxes meant, it surely meant taxes levied on the ownership of land and polls. Hamilton thought that a "small land tax" would be the natural and sufficient tax for the states to levy after their war debts were paid, and that the federal government would choose to avoid that tax to which the states "first had recourse," just as the states would choose to avoid the internal imposts and excises to which the federal government would first have recourse.[129] Hamilton referred to this as mutual abstention.

Poll or capitation taxes are always recognized as direct taxes; Hamilton stated that they were a favorite source of revenue of some of the states, though he viewed them with disapprobation and not suitable for the federal government.[130]

---

[124] *See* Ch. III.E.6 and V.C.3.a.

[125] *See* Herman Vandenburg Ames, The Proposed Amendments to the Constitution of the United States 241-242, Vol. II (1897) [hereinafter Ames] (no poll tax was ever imposed by the United States; and the feeling was general throughout the states that the federal government should not lay direct taxes if it could be avoided).

[126] *See* Ch. II.B.3.

[127] Pollock v. Farmers' Loan & Trust Co., 157 U.S. 429, 582 (1895).

[128] *See* Ch. VI.D.

[129] The Federalist, No. 36, by Alexander Hamilton, pp. 219-221 (Modern Library Ed.).

[130] *Id.* at 223.

They were never levied at the federal level; because most southern states treated slaves as realty, slaves were more likely to be taxed as property than by poll tax.[131]

Conversely, Hamilton thought that the federal government would be dependent primarily on excises, duties and imposts, as was Britain.[132] He viewed commercial imposts as the "most convenient branch of revenue" for the federal government.[133] But as among duties, excises and imposts he strongly favored import duties, noting that excises would have to be limited to a narrow compass due to their annoying "inquisitive and peremptory spirit," the only exception to which might be consumption taxes that were not apparent to the taxpayer.[134] Indeed, Hamilton foresaw correctly, because in 1811 Jefferson explained that virtually all federal taxation was borne by those paying import duties on luxuries.[135]

Indirect taxes were "most convenient" because it was generally understood that the machinery for apportioning, identifying, and collecting direct taxes was so cumbersome as to be a last resort.[136] To the extent the federal government levied apportioned taxes on land they would be administered, valued and collected by the local collectors, thus preserving to the states the control of this method of taxation.[137]

Finally, it was clear that only the national government had the ability to regulate trade with foreign countries and duties and imposts on imports were viewed as regulations by the federal government in addition to raising revenue.[138] Hamilton urged that the promotion of trade that would be fostered by federal regulation of trade would result in a concomitant expansion of that mercantile activity that would lend itself to the excises and imposts, not to speak of import duties that could be more easily collected nationally, on which the federal government would primarily depend.[139]

---

[131] *See* Veazie Bank v. Fenno, 75 U.S. 533, 542-543 (1869) (after the first of the five direct tax levies, slaves were treated as realty, with the result that the land did not have to be more heavily taxed).

[132] THE FEDERALIST, No. 12, by Alexander Hamilton, p. 72 (Modern Library Ed.).

[133] THE FEDERALIST, No. 36, by Alexander Hamilton, p. 222 (Modern Library Ed.). But Hamilton foresaw that import duties alone might not be sufficient, which is why the Constitution appropriately granted all sources of taxation to the federal government. THE FEDERALIST, No. 30, by Alexander Hamilton, pp. 184-185 (Modern Library Ed.).

[134] THE FEDERALIST, No. 12, by Alexander Hamilton, pp. 72, 75 (Modern Library Ed.).

[135] *See* 1811 letter of Thomas Jefferson to Pierre S. Dupont de Nemours explaining that all taxation is borne by the wealthy by way of tariffs on imported goods that the poor cannot buy, except for sale. SAUL K. PADOVER, EDITOR, THOMAS JEFFERSON ON DEMOCRACY (1939).

[136] *See* BEARD, at 170-171; THE FEDERALIST, No. 12, by Alexander Hamilton, p. 72 (Modern Library Ed.).

[137] THE FEDERALIST, No. 36, by Alexander Hamilton, pp. 219-220 (Modern Library Ed.); Printz v. United States, 521 U.S. 898, 946-947 (1997) (dissent explaining how federal use of local officials to carry out federal programs can be traced back to use of local tax collectors to collect direct taxes). However, the Civil War caused the United States to have to collect its own taxes in the rebel states where it could, as in Virginia. *See* Bennett v. Hunter, 76 U.S. 326 (1869).

[138] THE FEDERALIST, No. 44, by Alexander Hamilton, p. 292 (Modern Library Ed.).

[139] THE FEDERALIST, No. 12, by Alexander Hamilton, pp. 72-74 (Modern Library Ed.).

Obviously this division of preferred taxes between the states and the United States was the roughest of approximations, as explained by Luther Martin, a delegate to the Constitutional Convention:

> The whole of this subject of taxation is full of difficulties, which the Convention found it impossible to solve, in a manner entirely satisfactory. The first attempt was to divide the subjects of taxation between the State and the national government. This being found impracticable, or inconvenient, the State governments surrendered altogether their right to tax imports and exports, and tonnage; giving the authority to tax all other subjects to Congress, but reserving to the States a concurrent right to tax the same subjects to an unlimited extent. This was one of the anomalies of the government, the evils of which must be endured, or mitigated by discretion and mutual forbearance.[140]

d. *Reasons: Favored Versus Disfavored Taxes*

Taxes on land (*i.e.*, direct taxes) were generally disfavored relative to taxes on imports and excises, for a variety of reasons. The drafters were, of course, well aware of British taxation methods. Historically the King of England taxed land in various ways beginning with the feudal system. If the land did not produce the rents or profits to pay the taxes, they were a dead "oppressive" weight upon the owner.[141] In contrast, taxes on imports might appear to be paid by the importer or the vendor, or a foreign person, or at least might not be recognized as having been paid at all.[142] Taxes on commercial transactions, such as excises and import duties were thought to reflect the growing economic wealth of the country, a good thing.[143] Hamilton called them "fluid," finding their own level as the payors had the means to pay them.[144] He also viewed them as self-regulating: if the tax was too high the consumption would diminish, as would the tax revenue.[145] However, taxes on internal transactions such as local liquor production had been disliked in the Colonial period.[146]

Moreover, taxes that had to be provided to the central government through contributions from the states based on quotas (as might direct apportioned taxes), as occurred under the Articles of Confederation, were disliked for many reasons, not the least of which was the imprecision of allocating the total funds

---

[140] Argument in McCulloch v. Maryland, as quoted in United States v. County of Allegheny, 322 U.S. 174, 176 (1944).

[141] The Federalist, No. 12 at 75-76 (decrying the possibility that without other sources all taxes might burden the landowner).

[142] The Federalist, No. 12 at 72 (suggesting that farmers would pay taxes on personal property only by the "imperceptible agency of taxes on consumption").

[143] The Federalist, No. 12 at 70 *et seq.*

[144] The Federalist, No. 21, by Alexander Hamilton, p. 129 (Modern Library Ed.) ("the rich may be extravagant, the poor may be frugal").

[145] *Id.* at 130.

[146] Waldstreicher, at 69, 92. Excises had a bad odor in the Colonies due to the British stamp tax experience. New York tried to have the power to lay excises eliminated from the Constitution by amendment, but Hamilton defeated the attempt and went further to encourage Congress to impose excises. Ames, at 240-241.

needed; Hamilton pointed out that neither amount nor value of land or population was an accurate measure of the wealth of a state.[147] Of course, the apportionment of direct taxes in the Constitution was by census population, which counted the slaves as three fifths of a person. That was intended to ameliorate the apportionment of taxes to the slave holding states somewhat, but Hamilton said that too heavy reliance on unfair quotas would lead to disunion. He thought that the population of a county was a barometer of the state of its agriculture and hence of its land value and because the population was much easier to count than the land value he preferred its use, which, of course, was used in the Constitution.[148]

The view of direct taxes as disfavored also is supported by the fact that the interests that opposed the Constitution's taxing restrictions complained that states would be limited to direct taxes and internal excises, which was viewed as a poor trade-off.[149]

e. *Reasons: Internal Versus External Taxes*

One of the many causes of confusion is the juxtaposition of the direct versus other taxes dichotomy in the Constitution with the internal versus external dichotomy that was regularly employed in the debates on the Constitution. The internal versus external dichotomy was well known to the colonists due to its centrality to their disputes with England. Some opponents of the Constitution tried to carry that dispute over to claim for the states the exclusive power of internal taxation, leaving to the federal government only the power of external taxation, meaning duties on imports from abroad.[150]

Hamilton helpfully explained that internal taxes could be both direct and indirect.[151] That is one reason for his disagreement with those who would reserve the internal taxes to the states and leave the federal government with only external taxes. Another reason is that Hamilton claimed that the potential of internal taxation was two thirds of the taxing power of the nation, whereas the states had to carry but one tenth of the expense.[152] Hamilton evidently counted the potential direct internal taxes on the value of lands and houses at one third of the potential total revenue, internal excise taxes as a second third of the total potential available tax revenues, and external duties on imports as one third.[153] He thought the United States would bear nine tenths of the governmental costs and the states one tenth.[154]

---

[147] THE FEDERALIST, No. 21, by Alexander Hamilton, pp. 128-129 (Modern Library Ed.).

[148] *Id.* at 130.

[149] *See* Camps Newfound/Owatonna v. Town of Harrison, 520 U.S. 564, 631-632 (1997) (citing authorities).

[150] THE FEDERALIST, No. 36, by Alexander Hamilton, pp. 217-218 (Modern Library Ed.).

[151] *Id.* at p. 218.

[152] THE FEDERALIST, No. 34, by Alexander Hamilton, p. 208 (Modern Library Ed.).

[153] *Id.* at 208-209.

[154] *Id.*

The British had imposed taxes on the Colonies that were external as to Britain, but could appear internal as to the Colonies, not only to raise revenue from the Colonies but also to tightly control their trade. Of the regulatory variety was the Sugar Act of 1764 (an import duty as to sugar and other goods).[155] However, the French and Indian War caused the British to need revenue to pay for its American activities. The Stamp Tax of 1765 (an internal excise imposed on the use of paper and other items requiring purchase of a stamp as a tax) produced more colonial dislike than revenue because it was imposed purely for revenue and not for trade regulation.[156] It was replaced by the similarly disliked Townshend Act of 1767 (in which customs duties were laid on many items including tea), which was amended to apply only to tea.[157]

The colonists as well as the British debated the power of Parliament to levy these taxes in terms of internal and external taxes, not direct and indirect taxes.[158] At first some in the Colonies were willing to allow external taxes in the form of customs duties on the understanding that they were a byproduct of regulation of trade throughout the British Empire, presumably for some general benefit to the Empire, including the American Colonies.[159] But the Stamp Act taxes were not customs duties and were clearly taxes and the Townshend duties were clearly external but also were clearly taxes (at least to the colonists). Consequently the distinction broke down insofar as it served to differentiate what the Parliament could and could not do without the consent of the Colonies, at least in the eyes of the colonists.[160]

This progression of opinion or understanding about taxes, depending on nomenclature, passed through the phase of tolerating a regulation (customs duty) that incidentally raised revenue if that were not its purpose;[161] but when the Townshend Act relied on the distinction to cloak a tax in a customs duty the colonists abandoned the name game.[162] The most practical politician of them

---

[155] RANDOLPH G. ADAMS, POLITICAL IDEAS OF THE AMERICAN REVOLUTION 8-9 (3d Ed. 1958) [hereinafter ADAMS]. *See also* John Phillip Read, *In an Inherited Way: English Constitutional Rights, the Stamp Act Debates, and the Coming of the American Revolution*, 49 S. CAL. L. REV. 1109, 1111-1112 (1986); RABUSHKA, at 737 (explaining how the Sugar Act limited where American exports could go).

[156] RABUSHKA, at 754-755.

[157] *Adams*, at 97; RABUSHKA, at 755, *et seq.* Indeed, there was a reason for the colonists' dislike of the tea tax that differed substantially from the general dislike of taxes imposed by Parliament: the special tea tax applied only to tea sold by the East India Company, was lower than the tax otherwise applied to tea, and gave the East India Company what was perceived as an unfair advantage in selling cheaper tea as compared with the American merchants. HERBERT AGAR, THE PRICE OF UNION, 8 (1966).

[158] ADAMS, at 15.

[159] *Id.* at 15-19, 91, 94-95, 100, 120-121.

[160] *See* RABUSHKA, at 756-757 (discussing the huge amount of scholarly debate on the impact of resistance to British taxes on the colonists' attitude toward the King).

[161] ADAMS, at 95.

[162] *Id.* at 96-97, 104-105. *See also* WALDSTREICHER, at 35 (explaining the initial objection to internal taxes and then to external taxes for revenue).

all, John Adams, summed it up by saying "the distinction between taxation and legislation has been found to be a distinction without a difference."[163]

What is most curious about this period's discussion of taxes is that the internal-external dichotomy was abandoned in the Constitution in favor of the direct and not direct dichotomy. Perhaps the best explanation is that the colonists viewed the internal-external labels from the viewpoint of a colony on which the external taxes were imposed, which would not occur in the future as to the United States. Hence the external taxes became duties and imposts and the internal taxes became excises, and taxes that the King never attempted to levy in the Colonies at all (polls and property) mostly were reserved in practice to the states and localities.

f. *Reasons: Episodic Versus Ongoing Taxes*

Several of the Colonies were accustomed to running their own revenue systems on the basis of recurring taxes providing baseline needs and episodic taxes to pay for wars and other such occasional revenue needs; indeed the episodic financing frequently was in the form of what we would call revenue anticipation bonds, to be paid off by poll and property taxes levied specifically for that purpose.[164] Also, the Colonies were accustomed to a relationship with the Confederation in which the latter called on the Colonies to produce stated amounts of tax revenue per colony from time to time, as needed, and they did so as they saw fit.[165] The uncertainty of this method of raising revenues was one of the main reasons for adopting the Constitution of the United States. The type of revenue on which the United States was expected to depend under the Constitution primarily was the regular, recurring type produced by duties, excises and imposts, not the episodic variety.[166]

However, it makes sense that the two classes of taxation were viewed together in terms of differing needs. The revenues from continuous taxes might decline in times of war, and therefore direct taxes might be needed.[167] These different roles for the types of federal taxes were not much discussed in the debates but likely were generally understood. The different roles suggests what seems like an obvious point about the meaning of direct taxes: the term must refer to taxes that can be called for in a fixed total amount, levied and collected episodically, without having to wait for uncertain events to occur such as the earning of

[163] ADAMS, at 122.

[164] *See* RABUSHKA, at chapters 21, 22 and 23 surveying taxation in each colony in the period before the Revolutionary War.

[165] *See* THE FEDERALIST, No. 30, by Alexander Hamilton, pp. 83-184 (Modern Library Ed.).

[166] THE FEDERALIST, No. 36, by Alexander Hamilton, p. 221 (Modern Library Ed.).

[167] *See* STORY, at 503-504. *See also* Bullock, at 470-471, 474 (explaining, based on the failure of the first apportioned direct taxes to yield the desired collections, that the method was not tried again until the second war with Great Britain caused import duties to fall and necessitated resort to another taxing source; he calculated the total net direct taxes collected in the then 109-year history of the country as one tenth of one percent of the total ordinary revenues of the United States since 1789); Bennett v. Hunter, 76 U.S. 326 (1869) (explaining that a $20 million direct tax had been levied on account of the Civil War).

rents, payment of wages, transfer of property, sale of goods, or importation and exportation.

This view of direct taxes might make the 1794 tax on carriages seem direct, contrary to the ruling in *Hylton.*[168] The tax at issue was a fixed amount per carriage and did not apply to carriages used in business but only for transportation of persons, whether for hire or owned by the user. The tax was per year for two years and was labeled a duty. It did not vary with the value of the carriage, although there were $10, $8, $6 and $2 taxes for different types of carriages. The carriage tax was not levied to produce a fixed dollar amount of revenue. Moreover, the *Hylton* opinions were written by Justices who were intimately familiar with the adoption of the Constitution, was argued by Hamilton, whose knowledge of the Constitution and persuasiveness were unparalleled, and the Court effectively adopted a sui generis definition of the opaque term direct tax, which walled off taxes on consumables, particularly luxuries, of which carriages were one example. Hamilton had argued that the line must be drawn arbitrarily because there was no logical differentiation.[169] Also, the carriage tax at issue was adopted as an annual tax, not a one-time tax. At least in hindsight *Pollock* viewed the tax in *Hylton* as an excise tax, which prevented it (however arbitrarily) from being a direct tax;[170] but the Court later viewed *Hylton* as based on either the view that the tax was an excise or the view (rejected by *Pollock*) that only land and slaves were property for purposes of direct taxation.[171]

g. *Reasons: Consumption or Not*

Another way to look at the distinction between direct and other taxes is that the latter are imposed on consumption and the former are not. Excise taxes, which generally did fall on consumption (such as production or purchase of liquor) seemed to fit the indirect category well, except when they appeared also to fall on property itself (*e.g.* carriages). Hamilton viewed indirect taxes as taxes on consumption, whose increase might cause a decrease in the revenue raised, due to decrease in consumption, whereas the quantity of land could not diminish.[172] Hamilton argued the *Hylton* case for the government. The Supreme Court in *Hylton* (Justice Chase) thought that a tax on carriages was a tax on "expence . . . a consumeable commodity" and thus not direct.[173]

---

[168] Hylton v. United States, 3 U.S. 171 (1796). However, *Hylton* may be explained in the same way an excise tax on certain goods was explained not to be a tax on property in Patton v. Brady, 184 U.S. 608, 619 (1902) (". . . it is not a tax upon property as such but upon certain kinds of property, having reference to their origin and their intended use.").

[169] *See* Morrow, at 402-403 (quoting Hamilton's brief in *Hylton*).

[170] Pollock v. Farmers' Loan & Trust Co., 157 U.S. 429, 576 (1895).

[171] Brushaber v. Union Pacific R. Co., 240 U.S. 1, 14 (1916).

[172] The Federalist, No. 21, by Alexander Hamilton, p. 130 (Modern Library Ed.).

[173] 3 U.S. at 175.

Similarly, in somewhat more modern times but before the demise of *Pollock*, an excise tax on foreign built boats was ruled constitutional so long as the tax was on the use of the boat, but mere availability for use was not taxed.[174]

Adam Smith's views on the subject may have influenced the founders' thinking, but are fairly convoluted relative to the legal dichotomy between a tax on a transaction and a tax on property. He labeled taxes on consumable commodities as indirect taxes on expense, in lieu of "directly" taxing the buyer's income.[175] Smith's main concern was with the shifting incidence of taxation. He thought that indirect taxes on consumption of laborers must come out of their wages, and so their wages would have to rise to enable the payment of the tax, thus shifting the incidence of the tax to others (the employer will have to charge more for the goods made, etc.). Then Smith explains that taxes on luxuries bought by the wealthy do not raise the price of any goods but the luxuries.[176] Smith said all taxes should fall on luxuries rather than necessities because taxes on necessities would ultimately be paid by the wealthy through higher wages or otherwise.[177]

Thus Adam Smith, and also the physiocrats, discussed at Chapter V.C.3.c, focused on the shifting incidence of taxes, using the terms direct and indirect to indicate the likelihood of shifting. Whether or not the drafters thought about it, the theories of tax shifting must have seeped into the usage in the Constitution. It certainly influenced the *Pollock* opinion (which thought that a tax on income was shifted to land), and is commonly discussed today in the theory that the corporate income tax may be paid by everyone else in the society but the corporation, through tax shifting.

h. *Reasons: Administrability*

The difficulties of administering apportioned direct taxes were identified from the start, thus suggesting their limitation to the most administrable cases (land and heads). Indeed the insertion of direct taxes into the Constitution may have been a red herring. In *Hylton* the concurring opinion of Justice Patterson pointed out that land taxes had not been levied in some states for several years and so for that reason and others the collection of an apportioned land tax would be quite difficult.[178] He said much the same for apportioning a tax on carriages, which supported treating the tax as indirect. The principal opinion by Justice Chase is based in part on the need for a direct tax to be easily collectible by

[174] *See* Pierce v. United States, 232 U.S. 290 (1914) (taxpayer did not use boat and was not subject to tax as a matter of statutory construction, not constitutionality); Billings v. United States, 232 U.S. 261 (1914) (upholding tax in part because it was imposed on use as an excise tax).

[175] Adam Smith, at 517-518.

[176] *Id.* at 520.

[177] *Id.* at 532.

[178] Hylton v. United States, 3 U.S. 171, 178-180 (1796).

apportionment and not produce inequality and injustice. In practice the direct taxes sometimes were paid by the states.[179]

Gouverneur Morris prophetically warned that the three fifths compromise that supposedly linked representation to taxation would not have the effect of reducing taxation because federal direct taxation would be so hard to administer that it would be little used.[180] He also pointed out a different aspect of administrability: collectibility. Reflecting the view that direct taxes are property or head taxes on land and persons that do not require or depend on any flows of income or payments, he foresaw that direct taxes would be hard to collect from a poor populace and could mean the federal tax collector would "Seize and sell their effects and you push them into Revolts."[181]

Finally, an interesting issue in the collection of direct taxes was raised by *Dodge v. Woolsey* in an illustration.[182] The case concerned the jurisdiction of the Supreme Court to give a remedy as to a state tax, but in deciding it the Court posited a direct federal tax that might be levied in the future to which taxpayers in a particular state successfully objected in state court on the ground that it was not direct (just the opposite of the usual complaint). The opinion stated that the uniformity and certainty of collection across the country that was the aim of federal taxation in general and direct taxation in particular would be thwarted if such cases could not be reviewed by the Supreme Court.

i. *Reasons: Slaves*

A significant likely explanation of use of the term "direct tax" in the Constitution is that it was a ruse to avoid having to spell out the rule that slaves could be taxed only by apportionment, and because apportioned taxes were less likely to occur than indirect taxes, slaves were less likely to be taxed. This is just

---

[179] *See* Turner v. Smith, 81 U.S. 553, 562-563 (1871) ("In the act of August Fifth, 1861, apportioning the tax of $20,000,000 among the States, according to population, provision is made for its collection out of the lands within those States, if not paid by the States. Under the provisions of that act it might admit of some doubt whether the tax was in its essence a tax on the land, and on all the various estates into which the fee may have been divided, or was a tax on the owner of the land, and levied on the interest of the owner in it, and on no other subordinate or incorporeal interest. But no tax was ever collected, or any land sold under that act. The States which, in the war for the support of which this tax was levied, supported the General Government, assumed and paid the portion allotted to each. With regard to the States which were in insurrection, Congress passed a new law for the assessment and collection of their portion, under which the sale in this case was made.").

[180] WALDSTREICHER, at 92.

[181] *Quoted in* United States v. IBM, 517 U.S. 843, 873 (1996).

[182] Dodge v. Woolsey, 59 U.S. 331 (1856).

one of many such ruses concerning slaves that the Constitution employed.[183] The slavery concern is an aspect of the regionality concern discussed in Chapter V.C.4.b.[184]

The Constitution clearly defines capitation taxes as direct taxes, no matter what other taxes might occupy that category. Capitation taxes clearly would fall on people, of which the slaves were a large, perhaps the largest, group in the south. The three fifths compromise and the direct tax apportionment requirement both would serve to ameliorate the tax threat to the south.[185] Slavery and the concerns of the states in which slave holding predominated permeated the political considerations that went into the compromise that is the Constitution, and nowhere is this more true, and less apparent, than in the taxing provisions.[186] As explained in David Waldstreicher's important treatment of the subject, the connections between slaves and taxes included:

- In trying to answer the question of how much a slave should be counted for purposes of taxation, the Confederation found itself contemplating the very nature of slavery and what it meant to be a slave, certainly far afield from the usual issues of taxation.[187]
- Concerns of the slave states about taxation during the period of Confederation stymied attempts to raise taxes and ultimately contributed to the Constitutional Convention.[188]
- The New Englanders, who might be tainted as slave traders, nevertheless found a way to base an argument against taxation without representation by saying such a method of taxation would treat them as slaves.[189]

---

[183] Article I, section 2 states that representatives and taxation shall be determined by the number of free persons and three fifths of all other persons, without ever mentioning slavery. Article I, section 9 addresses the importation of persons, without mentioning slavery. Article I, section 9 limits capitation taxes to the census (which counted slaves as three fifths of a person); the purpose of this express limitation was to prevent Congress from estimating the population and heavily taxing slaves so as to effectively prohibit them. Bullock, at 238. Article IV, section 2 provides for extradition both for crimes and for escape, without mentioning slavery, but mentioning persons held in service or labor. The prohibition of taxes on exports was intended to protect the sale of the products of the labor of slaves, tobacco, rice and indigo. Bullock, at 225-226; SPAHR, at 193. Article I, section 7 states that revenue bills must originate in the House, which stood a better chance of being controlled by the southern states as a result of counting slaves as three fifths of a person. Of course the stated reason for the Origination Clause was more democratic: it was closer to the people. *See* J. Michael Medina, *The Origination Clause in the American Constitution: A Comparative Survey*, 23 TULSA L. J. 165 (1987) (quoting James Madison's explanation in The Federalist).

[184] *See* Hylton v. United States, 3 U.S. 171, 177 (1796).

[185] ARNOLD M. PAUL, CONSERVATIVE CRISIS AND THE RULE OF LAW 187 N. 6 (1960, 1976 Reprint) [hereinafter PAUL].

[186] *See generally* WALDSTREICHER.

[187] *Id.* at 52-53.

[188] *Id.* at 62, 66.

[189] *Id.* at 32-33.

- The massive agricultural production that slavery facilitated made the southern states exporters and most interested in preventing taxation of exports.[190]
- Taxation was linked to the crucial issue of representation in the national government through the common question of how to count slaves.[191]
- By applying the Three Fifths Clause to taxation and representation, the northern states, whose representatives might therefore have more power to vote for taxes (than if slaves were counted equally with other persons), might also be more subject to those taxes (because slaves were counted as three fifths of a person for apportionment of direct taxes), thus hopefully moderating their taxing tendency (as to direct taxes); also due to the relative numbers of slaves in the various southern states, the three fifths compromise drove a wedge between Virginia's interests and those of South Carolina and Georgia.[192]
- As parts of the price paid to southern interests in exchange for national supremacy, the Constitution, clause 1, section 9, of Article I, insured that importation of slaves could continue until 1808 and no more than $10 per person duty (also labeled a tax) could be levied; no capitation tax (slaves counting three fifths) could be levied before a census was taken; no export duty could be levied.[193]
- The pro slave state elements of the Constitution were needed to win its acceptance by the south.[194]

Justice Story also thought that the category of direct taxes and the limitation thereon was rooted in the desire of the southern states to protect their slaves

---

[190] *Id.* at 89.

[191] *Id.* at 73, 77. Indeed, the linkage of direct taxation to the number of representatives and the counting of slaves was the reason for the tax apportionment rule being inserted into the discussion Bullock, at 234-235, 452-453 ("Historically the provision must be viewed as a relic of the great compromise upon the subject of slavery."). But the article admits others disagreed, citing other reasons, most importantly a check on the power of Congress and a check on sectional attacks; the article successfully repels both arguments. *Id.* at 455, *et seq.* At 462 the article considers the arguments in North Carolina that the apportionment clause was intended to prevent over taxation of slaves and finds it confused as specifically referring to the method of apportioning a direct tax, as opposed to a capitation tax. "The proceedings of the constitutional convention, interpreted fairly and explained by Morris, Madison and King, give countenance to only one theory—that the apportionment rule was merely a bait for extremists, in the north and in the south, thrown out in order to secure the adoption of the compromise over representation for the slaves." *Id.* at 464.

[192] Waldstreicher, at 79, 84-85.

[193] *Id.* at 90-91. However, the tax on slave importation may have been viewed as a welcome potential use of such a tax to regulate and reduce slave importation, because prior to the invention of the cotton gin in 1794 many slave owners both did not need any more slaves and did not want continued importation to reduce the value of the slaves they had. Wilfred E. Binkley, American Political Parties 24 (3d. ed. 1958); Herbert Agar, The Price of Union 186-87 (Sentry edition 1966).

[194] Waldstreicher, at 114.

from heavy taxation.[195] He cited Justice Patterson's statement in *Hylton* that the rule of apportionment was adopted to guard the southern states from undue taxation of slaves.

Direct taxes certainly encompassed at least capitation taxes and taxes on real property. Slaves could be treated as real property. Therefore, there is strong reason to suspect that the limitation on direct taxes was in large part intended as a limitation on the ability of the federal government to tax slaves and the land they worked on (and incidentally non slave lands). That the taxing power was imbued with slavery concerns is entirely consistent with the fact that the Commerce Clause also was imbued with slavery concerns.[196]

Finally, *Pollock* confirms these views:

> Thus was accomplished one of the great compromises of the Constitution, resting on the doctrine that the right of representation ought to be conceded to every community on which a [direct] tax is to be imposed, but crystallizing it in such form as to allay jealousies in respect of the future balance of power [*i.e.*, to link taxation with representation as it changes from time to time]; to reconcile conflicting views in respect of the enumeration of slaves [the 3/5 compromise]; and to remove the objection that, in adjusting a system of representation between the States, regard should be had to their relative wealth, since those who were to be most heavily taxed ought to have a proportionate influence in the government [slaves might be fully taxed on their value as realty, so at least 3/5 should count toward representation].
>
> The compromise, in embracing the power of direct taxation, consisted not simply in including part of the slaves in the enumeration of population, but in providing that as between State and State such taxation should be proportioned to representation. The establishment of the same rule for the apportionment of taxes as for regulating the proportion of representatives, observed Mr. Madison in No. 54 of the Federalist, was by no means founded on the same principle, for as to the former it had reference to the proportion of wealth, and although in respect of that it was in ordinary cases a very unfit measure [meaning that it was odd to reduce the taxation of wealthy states on account of relatively smaller population], it "had too recently obtained the general sanction of America, not to have found a ready preference with the convention," while the opposite interests of the States, balancing each other, would produce impartiality in enumeration. By prescribing this rule, Hamilton wrote (Federalist, No. 36) that the door was shut "to partiality or oppression," and "the abuse of this power of taxation to have been provided against with guarded circumspection;" and obviously the operation of direct taxation on every State tended to prevent resort to that mode of supply except under pressure of necessity and to promote prudence and economy in expenditure.[197]

---

195 STORY, at 425.

196 *See* CHARLES WARREN, THE SUPREME COURT IN UNITED STATES HISTORY, Vol. I, p. 627 (1926) (". . . throughout the long years when the question of the extent of the Federal power over commerce was being tested in numerous cases in the Court, that question was, in the minds of Southerners, simply coincident with the question of the extent of the Federal power over slavery.").

197 Pollock v. Farmers' Loan & Trust Co., 157 U.S. 429, 563-564 (1895).

j. *Reasons: The Advantage of Ambiguity*

A final explanation for the direct versus other taxes categories in the Constitution, for the lack of definition of direct tax, and for the brevity of the coverage of federal taxes generally, is planned confusion and obfuscation, not limited to slavery. The preceding chapter illustrates the obfuscation that attended the important issue of slavery, which was intimately linked to taxation. While at least one region liked slavery, no one liked taxes at the time of the Constitution, although the federalists well understood the need for them to be collectible by the federal government. But for tax opponents the ambiguity of the term direct tax served a purpose of providing a potential means of thwarting a disliked federal tax. Indeed, an early proposed amendment in 1793 would have specifically defined all taxes other than duties, imposts and excises as direct taxes, apparently for this very purpose of making it hard to levy taxes.[198]

Furthermore, specific evidence exists that the Constitution intentionally obscured the drafters' intent and understandings about taxation in the absence of any reference to a stamp tax in the document:

> Thus it was intended to give Congress the power to levy stamp duties, but members were desired to say as little as possible on this unpopular subject, and if fully reported, Ellsworth observed this precaution in his explanation to the Connecticut convention.[199]

D. Other Taxes

1. *Overview*

The Constitution does not use the term indirect taxes, but rather clause 4 of section 9 of Article I, when read together with clause 1 of section 8, walls off duties, imposts and excises in a way that has led to their treatment as synonymous with taxes that are not direct, and so are called indirect taxes. Duties and imposts are terms that historically applied generally to taxes, or more specifically to customs levies on imports.[200] Excises more often referred to an inland imposition on the consumption of articles.[201]

So long as the tax did not lay on the ownership of land or slaves, or the head of each person, the constitutional compromise allowed the tax to be levied by the United States, if it were uniform "throughout the United States." Both the apportionment requirement for direct taxes and the uniformity requirement for imposts, duties and excises, reflected a desire that one state not be pitted against another, or a group of states not be able to dictate disproportionate taxation within another state.

The principal forms of indirect tax in the early days of the United States were tariffs or customs duties and excise taxes on liquor. They have the admirable

198 Ames, at 243.

199 Whitney, at 291.

200 *See* Story, at 422.

201 *Id.* at 423; Adam Smith, at 523; Patton v. Brady, 184 U.S. 608, 617 (1902).

qualities of usually not informing the ultimate indirect payors that they were being taxed, and of falling mainly on the more well off who could afford the relatively luxurious items that were imported.[202] A major exception was the Whiskey Rebellion of 1794 of farmers who did not like the tax on whiskey, which was the major product of their corn production and effectively served as a currency.[203]

However, the means of protection against state by state discrimination through indirect taxes, the uniformity requirement, was obviously imprecise because the various items and transactions that might be taxed occurred in varying degrees in various states—for example, ports existed only on the seacoast—and duties and excises might be selected in a way that would fall more heavily on one state or group of states than on another. This type of inequality had been "the pith of the controversy during the Confederation."[204] It also was a central controversy in the Constitutional Convention: ". . . those who opposed the ratification of the Constitution clearly understood that the uniformity clause as to taxation imported but a geographical uniformity, and made that fact a distinct ground of complaint."[205] But the low geographical uniformity threshold for imposts, duties and excises also is why taxpayers brought so many cases claiming that a federal tax was a direct tax.

Dissatisfaction with the constitutional compromise on taxation is reflected in the statements of Mr. Singletary in the Massachusetts debates on ratification of the Constitution:

> They tell us Congress don't lay dry taxes upon us, but collect all the money they want by impost. I say, there has always been a difficulty about impost. Whenever the general court was going to lay an impost they would tell us it was more than trade could bear, that it hurt the fair trader, and encouraged smuggling; and there will always be the same objection: they won't be able to raise money enough by impost, and then they will lay it on the land, and take all we have got.[206]

---

[202] *See* 1811 letter of Thomas Jefferson to Pierre S. Dupont de Nemours explaining that all taxation is borne by the wealthy by way of tariffs on imported goods that the poor cannot buy, except for sale. Saul K. Padover, editor, Thomas Jefferson on Democracy (1939).

[203] Leland D. Baldwin, The Whiskey Rebels (1939).

[204] 178 U.S. at 104. *See also* United States v. Ptasynski, 462 U.S. 74, 80-82 (1983) (stating that the issue was analyzed in the greatest depth in *Knowlton*; and that nondiscrimination among the states was the primary goal of the uniformity requirement).

[205] 178 U.S. at 106 ("Thus in the report made to the legislature of Maryland by Luther Martin, attorney general of the State, detailing and commenting upon the proceedings of the convention of 1787, of which convention Mr. Martin was a delegate, in the course of comments upon the tax clause of the Constitution Mr. Martin said (1 Ib. p. 369): 'Though there is a provision that all duties, imposts and excises shall be uniform—that is, to be laid to the same amount on the same articles in each State—yet this will not prevent Congress from having it in their power to cause them to fall very unequally and much heavier on some States than on others, because these duties may be laid on articles but little or not at all used in some other States, and of absolute necessity for the use and consumption in others; in which case, the first would pay little or no part of the revenue arising therefrom, while the whole or nearly the whole of it would be paid by the last, to wit, the States which use and consume the articles on which imposts and excises are laid.'").

[206] Quoted in Pollak, Vol. 1, p. 113.

2. *Identifying Taxes That Are Not Direct*

a. *Imposts, Duties, and Excises, and What Else?*

Federal taxes that are not direct usually are identified just that way: by defining direct taxes and finding that the tax at hand does not fit the description. But as discussed in Chapter V.B, that approach is less than clear. One indicator that is clear, starting with the definition of taxes that are not direct, is that Article I, section 8, clause 1 of the Constitution shows that federal imposts, duties and excises are not direct taxes because they must be uniform geographically;[207] a federal tax cannot be uniform geographically and also be apportioned based on the states' census population. Of course identifying an impost, duty and excise is not always easy, but it helps if Congress labels the tax an excise, which it did not do as to the income tax of 1894, thus aiding *Pollock* to find the income tax to be direct.[208]

The Supreme Court never had as much trouble or spent as many pages identifying taxes that are not direct as it did in 1895 in the two *Pollock* opinions, and never again has it found an unapportioned tax to be direct, except for *Eisner v. Macomber*, which focused almost entirely on whether a stock dividend was income, and finding that it was not, assumed it was a tax on property, citing *Pollock*.[209] Income taxes are not direct taxes because (a) they can be properly viewed as excises upon the receipt of income, and (b) the Sixteenth Amendment removed the possibility of looking through the form of the tax to the substance, for example by categorizing a tax on rent as a tax on the property from which the rent derived. Indeed, categorizing a tax as an excise tax upon an event or transaction is the best way to insure it is not a direct tax.

A practical test for a tax that is not direct, which the Supreme Court effectively applied in the decisions that preceded *Pollock*, is to ask whether the tax could be collected in practice if it had to be apportioned; if it could not in practice be administered, then Congress must have understood that the tax was indirect. Put another way:

> . . . [S]ince Congress had been granted a plenary power over taxation, direct taxes were only those taxes that could as a matter of practicality be apportioned according to population. . . . [I]f by presuming a tax to be direct, the constitutional requirement of apportionment would result in such manifest injustice as to preclude the tax in question from ever being levied at all, then the tax in question was not a direct tax within the meaning of the Constitution.[210]

---

[207] *See* Thomas Reed Powell, *The Judiciality of Minimum Wage Legislation*, 37 HARV. L. REV. 56-58 (1924) [hereinafter Powell] (explaining the treatment of excises and the impact of the Sixteenth Amendment).

[208] Pollock v. Farmers' Loan & Trust Co., 157 U.S. 429 (1895), *confirmed and expanded*, 158 U.S. 601 (1895).

[209] Eisner v. Macomber, 252 U.S. 189 (1920).

[210] PAUL, at 166, 169.

The first case involving and upholding as not direct a federal tax was *Hylton v. United States*, which also was the first reported decision in which the Supreme Court decided a constitutional challenge to a federal statute.[211] The tax at issue was a "duty" on carriages for personal and not business use (although it included carriages for hire) and the tax was a fixed amount dependent on the type of carriage, not on its cost or value. Justice Samuel Chase suggested that the types of taxes enumerated in the Constitution were not exclusive and that a tax could be both direct and indirect (which suggestions were not later adopted by the Court), but found the carriage tax not to be direct because (a) it would be hard to apportion, producing gross inequality of taxation of carriages in different states, and (b) it was a tax on expense which was not a direct tax, and (c) he did not think any tax was direct except on land or polls.[212]

Justice Chase had not been a delegate to the Constitutional Convention but was a signer of the Declaration of Independence and undoubtedly was familiar with the Convention's proceedings. His suggestion that an apportioned tax of a fixed dollar amount on carriages would produce inequalities was applicable to any tax in which the federal government specified a dollar amount per article, as opposed to a rate of tax based on value, intended to produce a total sum nationwide.[213]

The Court did not again decide a direct versus indirect federal tax case until after the Civil War, and the decisions include most prominently:

- *Pac. Ins. Co. v. Soule* ruled that a tax on insurance company premiums was not direct, in part because it would produce discrimination if an effort were made to apportion it (the same ground cited by Justice Chase in *Hylton*).[214] The tax was an income tax, albeit not on net income.

- *Collector v. Hubbard* ruled that the Civil War income tax on undistributed corporate earnings imposed on shareholders was not a direct tax.[215] *Eisner v. Macomber* stated *Pollock* overruled *Hubbard*.[216]

- *United States v. Singer* ruled that a tax on spirits to be distilled is an excise tax.[217]

- *Scholey v. Rew* ruled that a succession tax was not a direct tax.[218]

---

[211] Hylton v. United States, 3 U.S. 171 (1796).

[212] As to taxes on consumption being indirect taxes, *see* Pollock v. Farmers' Loan & Trust Co., 157 U.S. 429, 562 (1895) (quoting Gouverneur Morris as stating that a tax on consumption was an indirect tax). In addition, withdrawal of items for consumption was viewed as parallel to importation, which was taxable on an indirect basis. *See* Tariff Act of 1894 (which contained the income tax at issue in *Pollock*), 28 Stat. 509 (1894).

[213] *See* Story, at 426-427 (trying to make sense of treating a carriage tax as a direct tax, as Justice Chase had, and failing, calling it an absurdity).

[214] Pacific Ins. Co. v. Soule, 74 U.S. 433 (1869).

[215] Collector v. Hubbard, 79 U.S. 1 (1871).

[216] Eisner v. Macomber, 252 U.S. 189 (1920).

[217] United States v. Singer, 82 U.S. 111 (1872).

[218] Scholey v. Rew, 90 U.S. 331 (1875).

- *Knowlton v. Moore* ruled that a estate tax was not direct, relying on *Scholey v. Rew*.[219] The opinion explained a direct tax as one in which the Congress identified a gross amount it desired to raise, and then apportioned the amount among the states, which decided how it should be raised within each state; such direct taxes obviously could not be subject to the uniformity requirement. *Knowlton* rejected the view that direct taxes should be defined in terms of whether the tax could be shifted. *Knowlton* was followed as to the 1916 estate tax by *New York Trust*.[220] Even when the property taxed did not literally transfer upon death because it was entireties property, the Court ruled in a later decision that the tax arose upon the event of death and that was enough to prevent it from being a tax on property.[221] The Court later summarized the test applied by *Knowlton* as based "on the practical and historical ground that this kind of tax always has been regarded as the antithesis of a direct tax; 'has ever been treated as a duty or excise, because of the particular occasion which gives rise to its levy.' 178 U.S. 81-83. Upon this point a page of history is worth a volume of logic."[222]
- *Billings* ruled that a tax on the use of foreign built boats was an excise tax.[223]
- *Eisner v. Macomber* held a tax on a stock dividend unconstitutional by ruling that because a stock dividend was not income under the Sixteenth Amendment it could not be taxed without apportionment.[224] The focus of the opinion was on the definition of income, utilizing the now outmoded definition of "gain derived from capital, from labor, or from both combined."[225] The opinion gave no thought to the fact that it had rendered stock dividends totally free from tax (or perhaps the Court gave much thought to that but said nothing), because the only course it left to Congress was to define a dollar amount of total direct tax to be derived from taxing stock dividends and apportion that amount among the states to be derived from a special tax on stock dividends. Of course the amount of stock dividends could not be known until the year was over. *Eisner* basically enshrined *Pollock*'s look through approach as continuing outside the Sixteenth Amendment.
- *Bromley v. McCaughn* ruled that a gift tax was not a direct tax.[226] The opinion stated: "... [T]his Court has consistently held, almost from the founda-

---

219 Knowlton v. Moore, 178 U.S. 41, 88 (1900). *See also* United States v. Mfrs. National Bank, 363 U.S. 194 (1960) (estate tax on insurance proceeds where decedent paid premiums is not a direct tax).

220 New York Trust Co. v. Eisner, 256 U.S. 345, 349 (1921) (this is the opinion in which Justice Holmes said "a page of history is worth a volume of logic.") *See generally* Louis Eisenstein, *Estate Taxes and the Higher Learning of the Supreme Court*, 3 Tax L. Rev. 395, 397–408 (1948).

221 Tyler v. United States, 281 U.S. 497 (1930).

222 New York Trust Co. v. Eisner, 256 U.S. 345, 349 (1921).

223 Billings v. United States, 232 U.S. 261 (1914); United States v. Bennett, 232 U.S. 299 (1914).

224 Eisner v. Macomber, 252 U.S. 189 (1920).

225 *Id.* at 207.

226 Bromley v. McCaughn, 280 U.S. 124 (1929).

tion of the government, that a tax imposed upon a particular use of property or the exercise of a single power over property incidental to ownership, is an excise which need not be apportioned, and it is enough for present purposes that this tax is of the latter class."[227]

- *Helvering v. Independent Life* ruled that requiring the insurance company to include an imputed rental value for occupying its own building as a condition of deducting expenses was not an unconstitutional direct tax on the building.[228] The language in this opinion is far reaching. It states that an income tax on the value of property or the rental value of that property to the user or owner would be an unconstitutional unapportioned direct tax. However, that statement was not necessary to the holding because the opinion stated that in any event Congress could condition the deductions on the inclusion of the rental value. This opinion presents a hurdle for any effort to impute income from property under a Haig-Simons approach.[229]
- *Fernandez v. Wiener* upheld an estate tax, stating: "An excise tax, which the Constitution requires to be uniform, laid upon the shifting at death of some of the incidents of property, could hardly be thought to be a direct tax which must be apportioned. . . . The contention that such a tax is direct because measured by the property whose incidents are shifted at death, was rejected in *Bromley v. McCaughn*, and in *Tyler v. United States*, 501-4, and *Phillips v. Dime Trust & Safe Deposit Co.*, 284 U.S. 160, 165. A tax imposed upon the exercise of some of the numerous rights of property is clearly distinguishable from a direct tax, which falls upon the owner merely because he is owner, regardless of his use or disposition of the property. 'The persistence of this distinction and the justification for it rest upon the historic fact that [excise] taxes of this type were not understood to be direct taxes when the Constitution was adopted and, as well, upon the reluctance of this Court to enlarge, by construction, limitations upon the sovereign power of taxation by Article I, § 8, so vital to the maintenance of the national government.' *Bromley v. McCaughn*, 137."[230]
- *Mfrs. National Bank* ruled that a tax on a transfer in contemplation of death was not a direct tax but was a tax on the transfer of property, *i.e.*, an excise, despite the fact that the transfer only matured at death, the decedent having given a life insurance policy years before, and having continued to pay the premiums.[231]

---

[227] *Id.* at 136.

[228] Helvering v. Independent Life Ins. Co., 292 U.S. 371 (1934).

[229] *See* Jasper L. Cummings, Jr., The Supreme Court's Federal Tax Jurisprudence ch. VI.A (2d ed. 2016) [hereinafter Cummings] (discussing the fact that the Court has never relied on the Haig-Simons definition of income for purposes of economics in deciding a federal income tax case).

[230] Fernandez v. Wiener, 327 U.S. 340, 352 (1946).

[231] United States v. Mfrs. National Bank, 363 U.S. 194 (1960).

- *Sebelius* (2012) ruled that the health insurance tax would not be a direct tax because it was neither a tax on property nor a capitation tax.[232]

b. *Income Taxation and the Sixteenth Amendment: The Politics*

The pivotal event in United States taxation was the adoption of the Sixteenth Amendment and the ensuing creation of the federal income tax. However, contrary to popular belief the Amendment neither permitted federal income taxation for the first time, nor did it explicitly recognize that an income tax was a direct tax and relieved it from the requirement of apportionment.[233] Rather, the Supreme Court has interpreted it to forbid the look through approach that the Court applied in *Pollock* to rule that the substance rather than the form of the tax required that a tax on rental income must be treated as a tax on land and hence an unapportioned direct tax.[234] In other words, because the income tax purports to be levied upon transactions producing income, it shall be categorized as falling on its immediate subject, the earning of income (presumably as an excise).

Not only is the income tax a pivotal event in the history of federal taxation, it is a pivotal event in the history of the United States after the Civil War. As Justice Jackson pointed out, the rich and poor of the north had combined to break the hold of slavery on the south, but when the war was over, the rich and poor (including the southern poor, which was most of the southern population) faced each other with uncertainty, an uncertainty that reached its high point in the Populist Era of the late 1890s and the campaigns of William Jennings Bryan. Justice Jackson believed that the legislatures of that day, including Congress, saw the disparate pulls of rich and poor and addressed the problem first by adopting an income tax, second by regulating "the power of wealth where the premise of competition failed," and third, fostering the right of the poor worker to organize.[235] The income tax was clearly an effort to make taxation more progressive, whether the rates were progressive or flat, because in most of the prior history of the country taxation had meant consumption taxes, which fell disproportionately on the poorer classes.[236]

In the latter part of the 20th and the beginning of the 21st centuries that congressional solution came under heavy attack, with the power of unions being in eclipse, regulation of business being generally attacked with success by the right, and the income tax being questioned, with suggestions that it be replaced by

---

[232] *See* Ch. III.E.2.c(3)(f).

[233] *Cf.* statement of Elihu Root that the Sixteenth Amendment merely relieved the income tax from apportionment, *quoted in* Morrow, at 380 (containing another extensive history of the Constitutional Convention).

[234] *See* Ch. V.D.2.e.

[235] Robert H. Jackson, The Struggle for Judicial Supremacy 39-40 (1941) [hereinafter Jackson].

[236] James C. Carter, who defended the tax in the *Pollock* case, directly defended it on that basis. Paul, at 190-191. Of course some of the consumption taxes were on luxuries, but the basic taxes were on necessities (including liquor).

various versions of consumption taxes. These changes could return the United States largely to the status quo ante the 20th Century, at least as to these political choices.

c. *The* Pollock *Case*

In 1869 the Supreme Court ruled that an insurance company gross income receipts tax was an indirect tax.[237] In 1881 the *Springer* opinion ruled that a general income tax was not a direct tax, saying that the only direct taxes were on the value of realty and by capitation.[238] The tax in *Springer*, the 1865 income tax, explicitly fell on rents from real property.[239] And in a little noticed ruling the Court had approved what it called a Civil War excise tax on the income of corporations in 1880, without any concern about taxing income.[240]

However, in 1895 the Supreme Court in *Pollock*,[241] addressing a new income tax that was not motivated by the exigencies of war, distinguished the 1881 decision because the taxpayer at issue had not reported rent income.[242] But neither had the taxpayer in *Pollock* reported rent income; indeed it had reported no income at all, because the suit was a shareholder suit to enjoin the corporation from paying any tax, and it never did.

The income tax at issue in *Pollock* had been added to a major tariff reduction bill. The tariff reform sought by President Cleveland was largely undercut when enacted by many amendments to the bill, but the income tax remained.[243] When the income tax was stricken down, the tariff portion remained, which Justice Harlan called a "disaster to the country."[244]

What distinguished *Pollock* from the earlier decisions upholding unapportioned taxes on income was (1) that the income on which the plaintiffs focused their legal attack was income from property, particularly real property and stocks, (2) the tax at issue fell on the capital of well financed corporations and the wealthy, which were quite exercised about the imposition of an income tax, because (3) the income tax case was inextricably linked with a more pervasive reaction of conservative forces to the Populist Movement, the William Jennings Bryan campaign, calls for free silver, and most importantly the proliferation of

---

[237] Pacific Ins. Co. v. Soule, 74 U.S. 433 (1869). Citing *Soule*, the Court later stated that a tax on banks was in the nature of an income tax and so was not a direct tax. Veazie Bank v. Fenno, 75 U.S. 533, 547 (1869).

[238] Springer v. United States, 102 U.S. 586 (1881). For a complete explanation of the Civil War income tax, *see* HENRY SMITH, at Ch. III.

[239] Ch. 173, Sec. 116, 13 Stat. 281 (1864). It is notable that corporations were taxable under that act only by being required to deduct and withhold a tax from dividends and interest paid. Sec. 122, 13 Stat. 284.

[240] Railroad Co. v. Collector, 100 U.S. 595 (1880).

[241] Pollock v. Farmers' Loan & Trust Co., 157 U.S. 429 (1895), confirmed and expanded, 158 U.S. 601 (1895).

[242] *See generally*, for discussion of *Pollock*, Charlotte Crane, *Pollock, Macomber and the Role of the Federal Courts in the Development of the Income Tax in the United States*, 73 LAW & CONTEMP. PROB. 1 (2010) [hereinafter Crane]; RATNER, at ch. 10.

[243] PAUL, at 161-162.

[244] 158 U.S. at 685.

labor strikes in the 1890s.[245] It was one thing to impose an income tax in time of war; it was quite another to give every indication of a shift in general taxation methods away from excises and imposts (*i.e.*, consumption taxes like tariffs) to an income tax falling on capital. Therefore, it is explainable mainly on a political basis that the income tax enacted in 1894 produced the opposite constitutional conclusion from that of the earlier cases, indeed it reversed them as to their tenor if not their narrow holdings.[246]

The New York Times report of the oral argument stated that the Attorney General admitted the income tax was "class legislation," not an auspicious defense for a tax that the plaintiffs attacked as "socialistic" and even "communistic":[247]

> Congress has adopted as the minimum income for purposes of taxation the limit of $4,000. The limit may be said now to divide the upper from the lower middle class, financially speaking, in the larger cities, or to divide the middle class from the wealthy in the country districts.[248]

The political foundations of *Pollock* are further evidenced by the fact that is is generally viewed as part of a trilogy of reactionary opinions, the other two being *E. C. Knight* (holding that manufacturing was local and so not part of commerce and not subject to the monopoly laws),[249] and *In re* Debs (upholding labor injunctions in the Pullman strike of 1894).[250] Section 32 of the 1894 Act imposed a tax of two percent on the net incomes of corporations.[251] Section 27 imposed a tax of two percent of net income on individuals, with a $4,000 per family exemption, which tax was authorized only for five years.[252] Unfortunately, the statute did not label the tax either as an excise tax or a duty.[253] Very few individuals had incomes of $4,000, and so for that reason, plus the limited life of the individual income tax, the individual tax must have been far less important than the corporate tax. Indeed the cases before the court involved shareholder suits to restrain their corporations from paying the tax for the first year it was due.

The 1894 income tax was political also from a regional viewpoint. The two original dissenters (Justices White and Harlan) and the dissenter who returned

---

[245] *See* Paul, generally, and at 163 (The press claimed the income tax was "class legislation on a tremendous scale.").

[246] For a detailed history of the enactment of the 1894 income tax as well as of the prior history of taxation in the United States, plus analyses of the constitutional objections to the income tax prior to the *Pollock* decision, *see* Foster and Abbott, A Treatise on the Federal Income Tax Under the Act of 1894 (1895); another history is provided in Morrow; another history is provided in Bullock; a briefer statement appears in David P. Currie, *The Constitution in the Supreme Court*, 52 U. Chi. L. Rev. 324, 350-352 (1985) (the result was surprising in light of precedents, was produced in protection of business and property and the opinion was poorly reasoned).

[247] Argument of Joseph Choate in *Pollock*, quoted in Jackson, at 46.

[248] *Income Tax Battle Is On*, New York Times (March 9, 1895); *see also Its Inequalities Shown*, New York Times (March 8, 1895) (reporting original oral argument).

[249] United States v. E. C. Knight Co., 156 U.S. 1 (1895).

[250] *In re* Debs, 158 U.S. 564 (1895). *See* Jackson, at 39-40; Paul, at ch. 7 and 178-183.

[251] Tariff Act of 1894, 28 Stat. 509, 556 (Aug. 27, 1894).

[252] 28 Stat. 509, 553 (1894).

[253] *Id.* at 553-560 (referred to only as tax).

to the bench from sickness to participate in the second decision (Jackson), were from the south.[254] The warning of Gouverneur Morris at the Constitutional Convention seemed to have come true: the populous states of the south and west could be said to have ganged up on the smaller commercial states of the northeast to impose an income tax that might fall most heavily on their commercial incomes and the wealthy, or at least the plaintiffs so argued.[255] Joseph Choate argued for the plaintiffs that at least four fifths of the unapportioned income tax would fall on taxpayers in New York, New Jersey, Pennsylvania and Massachusetts.[256] That *Pollock* was viewed as a case of class or regional rivalry is reflected not only by the United States' own attorney's statement quoted above, but also in the view of even an acute legal observer that it dealt with "odious class legislation" that trampled "state's rights" and the decision would check waste of the national treasury.[257] Another way to look at it was that Congress found itself needing funds, which it felt the usual excises and duties could not produce without undue burden on the poor, and so decided to tax the wealthier classes.[258]

The able advocates for the shareholders in *Pollock* brought to the Supreme Court's attention the inevitability that their corporations' incomes would include income from property, including real property, which provided the nexus to direct taxes that the Supreme Court relied upon to find the tax direct and hence unconstitutional because not apportioned. Property is, of course, another word for capital, and so *Pollock* was a case of capital taxes versus consumption taxes.

The Supreme Court's treatment of the *Pollock* litigation was procedurally unusual, befitting the great public interest, or the desire to resolve the case before (or as it turned out shortly after) the initial tax returns were due. With the acquiescence of the government, the Court swept aside the seemingly insurmountable procedural hurdles and decided the case within nine months of the enactment of the tax. It was argued over five days, and initially decided on April 8, 1895, less than a month after the end of the argument and just seven days before the due date for the first returns: the Court ruled the income tax on rents and municipal bond interest unconstitutional, and reversed the lower court's refusal to enjoin the corporation from paying the tax and remanded; the Justices were equally divided as to the unconstitutionality of the entire act (Justice Jackson being absent).[259]

When the Chief Justice announced a rehearing it was thought the Court meant to reverse itself; the Attorney General said a week of argument for each

---

254 *See* Irving Schiffman, *Escaping the Shroud of Anonymity: Justice Howell Edmunds Jackson and the Income Tax Case*, 37 TENN. L. REV. 334, 337 (1970) ("Fuller's opinion was as welcome to the South as a plague of boll weevils").

255 Foster, at 421.

256 *Id.*

257 Foster, at 423.

258 *See* Whitney, at 284 (containing a detailed account of the course of the *Pollock* litigation).

259 Pollock v. Farmers' Loan & Trust Co., 157 U.S. 429 (1895).

side would be required,[260] but that is not the way it turned out. It was reargued and redecided after 3 days of argument on May 20, 1895.[261] Because the original decision invalidated the tax only as to income from bonds and land, the taxpayers asked for rehearing, hoping to extend the reach of the decision to all income; their petition was filed April 15, the last day for payment of the initial tax: the Court ruled that no income from personalty could be taxed, and because the two income tax sections of the 1894 act were "one entire scheme of taxation," those income taxing sections were entirely invalid.[262]

The *Pollock* decision was met with approval in some quarters, mostly on socio-political grounds rather than for its legal reasoning. The New York Times stated that in enacting the income tax the west and the south had combined to tax the east and the north and the wealthy only; it labeled as "socialists and populists" those responsible for the income tax of 1894.[263] However, the majority of contemporaneous legal writers viewed the court's analysis, if not its social jurisprudence, with skepticism. For example:

> Direct taxes are taxes on land, poll taxes, and as long as a majority of the Supreme Court are of the same mind, taxes on rents and general taxes on personal property and incomes which are not confined to a special class, although with large classes of exemptions.[264]

Other contemporary comments, which evinced the singularity both of the tax as one on "wealth" and of the denial of the constitutionality of the tax, included:

> . . . Never before [has the Court] interposed an interference in regard to the laying of taxes for the support of the government. For the first time in our national history Congress is thwarted in the exercise of its constitutional right. . . . While all the states of the Union as well as all the civilized countries of the world, have taxed wealth for their support, the government of the United States has alone, except for a short period during the Civil War, exempted it from taxation. All of its revenues were directed from imposts and taxes on business.[265]

> It is to be noted that in both the elaborate opinions delivered by the Chief Justice no case is cited by him in support of the conclusion of the Court. . . . [I]f there ever was a direct tax it was the carriage tax, the constitutionality of which

---

260 *To Be a Decisive Hearing*, New York Times (April 26, 1895).

261 Pollock v. Farmers' Loan & Trust Co., 158 U.S. 601 (1895).

262 *A Fuller Decision Asked*, New York Times (April 16, 1895).

263 Editorial, *Democratic Doctrine Destroys the Populist Income Tax*, New York Times (May 21, 1895).

264 Foster, at 422.

265 Sylvester Pennoyer, *The Income Tax Decision and the Power of the Supreme Court to Nullify Acts of Congress*, 29 Am. L. Rev. 550, 554 (1895) (Note that this is an admittedly biased article, virtually rejecting the right of judicial review of acts of Congress, but the statement about the facts is correct).

> was supported in *Hylton v. United States*, and the succession tax . . . supported in *Scholey v. Rew*. . . . It is begging the question utterly to call them excises.[266]
>
> . . . [T]he term "direct taxes" was used in as loose and indefinite way by our ancestors as it is by our modern political economists. Since the words themselves will bear almost any construction which the court chooses to put upon them, and since to declare a tax a direct tax is practically to say that Congress has no power to pass such a tax, every consideration of public policy would seem to urge the court to . . . [confine the term to] a capitation tax and a tax on land.[267]

Professor Ratner convincingly showed that throughout the history of the nation the Congress, including many of the Founders, had never considered an income tax to be a direct tax.[268] Current commentators are equally dismissive of the reasoning of the *Pollock* opinion, in part based on the fact that it was one of a set of three highly conservative opinions from the Court in 1895.[269] For example:

> . . . [T]he highly technical ruling could not cloak the fact that the majority saw the tax as an attempt to alter what [Justice] Brewer called "the unvarying law" of civilization, "that the wealth of a community will be in the hands of a few."[270]

However, the historic confusion about the meaning of direct taxes created a situation ready made for resolution favoring the taxpayers at the hands of a willing Court. As it turned out a 5 to 4 majority had to be cobbled together to reach the ultimate result in the second opinion, possibly including a vote switch.[271]

Although not entirely novel, a tax on net income was somewhat of an oddity at the time of the Constitution,[272] probably not specifically considered by Hamilton and the other founders. In addition, while it looked like a tax that was contingent on something occurring (earning income), which was typical of excises and imposts, it could be viewed as indirectly a tax on property to the extent it taxed income from property (rents, dividends, interest). That the ability to perceive such an indirect burden did not necessarily make the tax "direct" was a nuance overlooked by the *Pollock* Court, because it was not interested in reaching that result.[273] Given the zone of ambiguity, the Supreme Court had all of the room it needed to invalidate the 1894 income tax.

---

[266] Francis R. Jones, *Pollock v. Farmers' Loan & Trust Co.*, 9 Harv. L. Rev. 198, 203, 208 (1895) [hereinafter Jones]. *See also* Whitney, at 288 ("The distinction is verbal. But a legal rule which can be avoided by a mere form of words is not really based upon public policy.").

[267] William Lewis Draper, *Constitutionality of the Income Tax*, 49 Am. Law Rev. 189, 191 (1895).

[268] Ratner, at 34 (1815 proposal of income tax), and 67 (civil war income tax).

[269] The other two were United States v. E. C. Knight Co., 156 U.S. 1 (1895) (limiting the reach of the Sherman Act), and *In re* Debs, 158 U.S. 564 (1895) (enjoining the Pullman strike).

[270] James MacGregor Burns, Packing the Court 109 (2009) [hereinafter Burns]

[271] *See* Bernard Schwartz, Super Chief 185 (1983) [hereinafter Schwartz].

[272] *See* Crane, at 6.

[273] *See* Ch. I.E.8, as to substance over form generally.

On the one hand the Court was probably right that a tax on rents was of a kind with the English land taxes and the taxes the physiocrats would have viewed as levied directly on the landowners; nevertheless, the opinion rejected 100 years of the Court's own precedent, starting with *Hylton* and running through *Springer*, which actually had considered and upheld an income tax.[274] The political nature of the Court's dislike for the income tax is reflected in its failure to consider the greatest practical argument against its holding: that it had effectively removed the taxation of income from property (but not from labor) from the federal tax base because it would be practically impossible to administer an apportioned tax on capital income.[275]

Pollock conflated the factual ability to deduce an indirect burden on land with the legal issue of whether the tax was direct.[276] Such conflation was not new. *McCulloch v. Maryland* had ruled that the states could not indirectly burden the United States by requiring the Bank of the United States to pay a stamp tax on the notes it issued.[277] While that opinion did not explicitly discuss direct and indirect burdens, it set in motion a chain of cases on intergovernmental immunity that struggled with how indirect a taxing burden had to be before it did not have the tendency to "destroy" the central government. Eventually, the Court came to see that it had to abandon that factual analysis due to the difficulties it caused.[278] But at the time of *Pollock* the law stood that federal contractors could not be taxed, as in the case of a license tax on a telegraph company performing work for the postal service.[279]

The Court began backing away from *Pollock* even before it was over. Upon rehearing Chief Justice Fuller stated that the original decision concerned only income from invested real and personal property and did not concern income from business and employments, which had been previously treated as excises.[280] Five years later in *Knowlton v. Moore* the Court rejected as a talisman of a direct tax a close analysis as to whether the incidence of the tax could be shifted, and instead relied on the more straightforward distinction based on an estate tax

---

[274] Foster, at 423.

[275] *See* Edward A. Harriman, *Original Power to Levy Income Tax*, 7 A.B.A.J. 303-304 (1921) (explaining that Congress could have imposed an excise tax on business income and wages and an apportioned tax on capital income, in theory, but not in practice).

[276] *See* Jones, at 204-205.

[277] McCulloch v. Maryland, 17 U.S. 316 (1819).

[278] *See* Ch. I.E.8 and II.C.4.

[279] Leloup v. Port of Mobile, 127 U.S. 640 (1888); *see generally* HELLERSTEIN & HELLERSTEIN, STATE TAXATION ¶ 22.01 (3d Ed.) [hereinafter HELLERSTEIN & HELLERSTEIN].

[280] 158 U.S. at 635.

being a tax on an event, transmission of property.[281] Likewise, in 1902 an excise tax on inventory held for sale was ruled not a tax on property because it was on a particular type of property as defined by the transactions involved.[282]

In conclusion, the *Pollock* case was highly political, as one leg of a massive conservative resistance to the populism of the 1890s: the other two legs being the defeat of labor in *In re* Debs, and the weakening of the antitrust laws in *E. C. Knight*.[283] The opponents of the income tax correctly predicted that it was the nose under the tent of a huge shift in federal taxation. In 1913, before the implementation of the 1913 income tax, taxes on commodities yielded 94.6% of federal revenues; in 1930 income taxes yielded 66.5% of federal revenues and taxes on commodities produced only 29.5%.[284]

d. *1909 Corporate Tax*

In 1909 Congress enacted an excise tax payable by corporations, foreign and domestic, doing business in the United States and possessions.[285] The brief statute contained several features that have endured in the corporate income tax, even though the tax was labeled an excise tax measured by net income: (1) the tax base was net, not gross, income; (2) the income taxed was "from all sources"; (3) there was a dividends received deduction limited to dividends from corporations also subject to the tax; (4) foreign corporations, as determined by place of organization, were taxed only on income sourced in the United States; and (5) the tax did not apply to non-profit corporations.

---

[281] Knowlton v. Moore, 178 U.S. 41, 80-82 (1900) (denying that *Pollock* had adopted this "disputable theory"). *See also* Spreckels Sugar Refining Co. v. McClain, 192 U.S. 397 (1904) (gross receipts tax on a business); Nicol v. Ames, 173 U.S. 509 (1899) (rejecting argument that tax on market sales was direct tax because it could not be shifted, because tax was on a transaction; Justice Peckham stated: "In deciding upon the validity of a tax with reference to these requirements, no microscopic examination as to the purely economic or theoretical nature of the tax should be indulged in for the purpose of placing it in a category which would invalidate the tax. As a mere abstract, scientific or economical problem, a particular tax might possibly be regarded as a direct tax, when as a practical matter pertaining to the actual operation of the tax it might quite plainly appear to be indirect. Under such circumstances, and while varying and disputable theories might be indulged as to the real nature of the tax, a court would not be justified, for the purpose of invalidating the tax, in placing it in a class different from that to which its practical results would consign it. Taxation is eminently practical, and is in fact brought to every man's door, and for the purpose of deciding upon its validity a tax should be regarded in its actual, practical results, rather than with reference to those theoretical or abstract ideas whose correctness is the subject of dispute and contradiction among those who are experts in the science of political economy." *Id.* at 515-516.).

[282] Patton v. Brady, 184 U.S. 608 (1902). *See also* Thomas v. United States, 192 U.S. 363 (1904) (stamp tax was clearly the second class of tax, not requiring apportionment).

[283] *In re* Debs, 158 U.S. 564 (1895); United States v. E. C. Knight Co., 156 U.S. 1 (1895). *See generally* PAUL.

[284] Henry W. Edgerton, *The Incidence of Judicial Control over Congress*, 22 CORN. L. QUAR. 299, 339 (1937) [hereinafter Egerton]. Prohibition and the drastic reduction in liquor excise tax revenues had something to do with this shift as well.

[285] 36 Stat. 11, 112, ch. 6, sec. 38 (1909). *See generally* RATNER, at 287-297.

The reason the corporate income tax was possible in the face of *Pollock* was that *Pollock* left open the possibility that income derived from industry and business and not from property still could be subject to an excise tax rather than an income tax.[286] *Flint v. Stone Tracy Co.* adopted that approach and found that the 1909 tax was an excise on doing business by corporations and not on the holding of the property.[287] Other features of the opinion include:

- It implied that if the income that measured the tax had been limited to income from property then the Court might have viewed the tax as an indirect method of taxing property, but because the statute used the phrase "from all sources" several times, the Court did not find it to be targeted at property income.[288] That, of course, was quite different from the approach of *Pollock*, which invalidated the entire income tax because some of the taxed income would be rents and dividends from stock. If the corporation held property that did not produce business income, that was its problem and did not invalidate the tax so long as the corporation was in business.
- "The difference between the [1894 and 1909] acts is not merely nominal, but rests upon substantial differences between the mere ownership of property and the actual doing of business in a certain way."[289] The Court resolutely insisted that an excise tax "measured by" income was different from a tax "on" income, which might be a tax on the property from which the income flowed. That reflects a substantial willingness to rely on form over substance, despite the Court's protestation that it was not controlled by the tax's label as an excise. It was justified due to the generic view of excises as including a charge for a privilege. However, the federal government did not license corporations as such, and failure to pay the new tax did not preclude the state-chartered corporations from doing business; the only penalty for failure to pay the tax was a fine of $1,000 to $10,000. The ruling was better justified on the basis that the Court had already ruled that a franchise tax on corporations measured by income on federal government bonds did not

---

[286] *See* Morrow, at 407. The Supreme Court had so observed in Spreckels Sugar Refining Co. v. McClain, 192 U.S. 397 (1904). A corporate tax was promoted by Simeon E. Baldwin, *Federal Taxation of Interstate Commerce*, 22 Harv. L. Rev. 27 (1908), in which he reasoned that a tax on large corporations that enjoyed interstate commerce could be imposed under the taxing power with the indirect effect on interstate commerce, but not being an export duty. Another justification for the 1909 corporate tax law was that it would allow the federal government to investigate domestic corporations. James M. Beck, *Nullification by Indirection*, 23 Harv. L. Rev. 441, 450 (1909). Aside from the legal reasoning, the Court's about face was simply an about face, as stated by Thomas Reed Powell, who said that what mattered was that the Court believed in its new found distinction between taxing income and measuring an excise tax by income, just "as the gentleman believed in baptism, because he had seen it done." Robert M. Haig, ed., The Federal Income Tax 54 (1921).

[287] Flint v. Stone Tracy Co., 220 U.S. 107 (1911). *See also*, United States v. Whitridge, 231 U.S. 144 (1913) (relying on *Flint* as to the same tax); Eliot v. Freeman, 220 U.S. 178 (1911) (but since a trust did not derive special powers from the state it was not subject to the corporate tax).

[288] 220 U.S. at 146-147.

[289] *Id.* at 150.

violate principles of intergovernmental immunity by taxing federal bond interest because the tax was on the franchise and not the bond interest.[290]

- The Court got around the objection that it was taxing a state created right by insisting that the excise tax only taxed the business that was pursued with the assistance of the corporate charter, but did not tax the corporate charter. Moreover, even if it were taxing a state created right, it was not taxing a state instrumentality because the private businesses involved were distinguishable from, for example, the Bank of the United States (a federal instrumentality that Justice Marshall ruled the state could not tax). But when the opinion turned to the equal protection argument, it justified the tax on corporations and not partnerships on the basis of the special privileges accorded by the franchise, which seems inconsistent with the former justification.
- The Court also relied on the distinction between a tax that could be avoided and one that could not: the corporation could avoid the tax by avoiding the privilege of conducting the business.

Whether a corporation was conducting a business became a line of defense to the 1909 corporate excise tax, as a matter of statutory construction.[291] *McCoach* ruled that a company that had leased its railroad to another railroad company was not in business and was not subject to the 1909 tax, even upon its investment income, distinguishing a case in which the investment income was in the nature of working capital and so related to its business income.[292] This opinion also made the interesting point that the fact that the rent was deductible to the tenant railroad but not taxable income to the lessor railroad did not affect the result; the tax was not on income but on business measured by income and if there was no business there was no tax.

The Court rejected a second attack on the 1909 excise tax in *Stratton's*.[293] It ruled that a mine was a business and so the excise tax applied and the absence of any stated deduction for the wasting asset that was the mine did not invalidate the excise tax, noting that human brains also wasted and it was not thought that individuals should be allowed brain depreciation. *Stratton's* is also important as perhaps the first interpretation of what is now section 165, as not allowing a deduction for losses on the basis of estimation.[294] *Stratton's* also affirmed that an

---

[290] *Id.* at 164, citing Home Ins. Co. v. New York, 134 U.S. 594 (1890).

[291] *See* Zonne v. Minneapolis Syndicate, 220 U.S. 187 (1911) (not operating business because operated solely to collect passive rent and distribute it to shareholders); Eliot v. Freeman, 220 U.S. 178 (1911) (a common law trust did not enjoy state corporation powers); United States v. Whitridge, 231 U.S. 144 (1913) (receivers of a corporation did not owe the corporate tax); United States v. Emery, Bird, Thayer Realty Co., 237 U.S. 28 (1915) (realty holding company not engaged in business).

[292] McCoach v. Minehill & S. H. R. Co., 228 U.S. 295 (1913).

[293] Stratton's Independence v. Howbert, 231 U.S. 399 (1913).

[294] 231 U.S. at 421-422 (the taxpayer assumed the entire profit of the mine should be the depletion allowance, evidently arguing that if a trespasser had stolen the ore that would be the measure of the loss). *See also* Von Baumbach v. Sargent Land Co., 242 U.S. 503 (1917) (rejecting another argument for mine depletion).

excise tax measured by gross income was not an income tax. However, because the Treasury by regulation allowed taxpayers to compute gain by treating as basis the fair market value on the date of enactment (1913) of property sold, the Court allowed a company cutting and using trees in products to deduct such "stumpage" basis, which could be accurately determined.[295]

The 1909 tax not only did not allow a mineral depletion deduction, it also limited the interest deduction. The Court ruled that the general concept of net income did not trump the statute's specific limitation on the interest deduction.[296]

Justice Holmes noted the inconsistency between the Court's support for the 1909 tax and its rejection of the federal child labor law in his dissent in *Hammer v. Dagenhart*.[297] He pointed out that the Court had already decided that the United States could tax oleomargarine, and tax it almost out of existence, despite the general authority of states to regulate local manufactures of that sort.[298] The Court also had approved a tax on state banks, the purpose of which was clearly to drive them, or at least their currency, out of business.[299]

Flint v. Stone Tracy Co. and the 1909 corporate excise tax were a way station to the adoption of the Sixteenth Amendment, which by this time even the Republicans agreed was needed,[300] but possibly as a ruse to prevent the 1909 act from being viewed as a constitutional general corporate income tax that was not an excise tax.[301]

e. *The Sixteenth Amendment*

The Sixteenth Amendment states:

> The Congress shall have power to lay and collect taxes on incomes, from whatever source derived, without apportionment among the several states, and without regard to any census or enumeration.

The Amendment can only refer to Article I, section 9, clause 4, and section 2, clause 3, which link direct taxes with a proportionality to the state by state census or enumeration. The Amendment assumes that an income tax might be subject to that limitation, and rightly so because the Supreme Court had so ruled in *Pollock*, the motive cause of the Amendment.[302] Presumably the drafters

---

295 Doyle v. Mitchell Bros. Co., 247 U.S. 179 (1918).

296 Anderson v. Forty-Two Broadway Co., 239 U.S. 69 (1915).

297 Hammer v. Dagenhart, 247 U.S. 251, 279 (1918), *overruled by* United States v. Darby, 312 U.S. 100 (1941).

298 McCray v. United States, 195 U.S. 27 (1904).

299 Veazie Bank v. Fenno, 75 U.S. 533 (1869).

300 President Taft had proposed the 1909 corporate excise tax and the constitutional amendment. *See* William E. Dorman, *The Federal Corporation Tax Constitutional?* 22 Green Bag 168 (1910) (containing an analysis of the 1909 tax that accurately predicted its outcome in *Flint v. Stone Tracy*).

301 Kelly, Harbison and Belz, The American Constitution: Its Origin and Development, Vol. II 431-432 (7th ed.) (Taft supported a corporate excise tax but not a pure corporate income tax).

302 Pollock v. Farmers' Loan & Trust Co., 157 U.S. 429 (1895), *confirmed and expanded*, 158 U.S. 601 (1895).

of the Amendment thought it most logical to avoid saying the Supreme Court got the definition of direct tax wrong, and to avoid implying that without the Amendment Congress had no power to tax incomes at all without apportionment. It is odd that the Amendment did not just eliminate reference to direct taxes from the Constitution and require that all taxes be uniform.[303]

But the Amendment left open the possibility of the previously discussed but unseen third category of tax; a tax subject to neither the apportionment nor uniformity requirement.[304] However, we now know that is not the meaning of the Amendment.[305] The purpose and function of the Sixteenth Amendment is to say that in the classification of an income tax, form shall control: Congress doesn't care about the indirect sourcing of the income ("from whatever source derived"), which view had been presaged by *Knowlton* and by *Springer*'s rejection of income shifting analysis.[306] Therefore the effect of the Sixteenth Amendment is to categorize an income tax according to its form, which is naturally an indirect excise tax levied on a transaction, the receipt of income.[307] Moreover, there is no third category of taxes and so an income tax is treated as an indirect tax, one of "duties, imposes and excises."[308] The part of *Pollock* that the Sixteenth Amendment rejects is the look through approach.

The described interpretation of the Sixteenth Amendment is not necessarily clear on the face of it. In *Brushaber* Justice White accomplished this feat of construction by stating that the 1913 income tax was a direct tax under *Pollock*'s view;[309] that unless the Sixteenth Amendment created some third category of taxes, all taxes either were direct and subject to the apportionment requirement or indirect and subject to the uniformity requirement;[310] that the exhaustive nature of the taxing power surely encompassed an income tax and the Sixteenth Amendment did not for the first time authorize an income tax; moreover, it did not exempt the income tax as a direct tax from the apportionment rule; rather it directed that the source of the income not be the basis of categorizing the

---

[303] Recommended by Morrow, at 413.

[304] *See* Morrow, at 412, making this argument in 1910, citing Justice Chase's views in *Hylton*, and noting that Charles Evans Hughes agreed with Chase; Elihu Root disagreed.

[305] Steward Machine Co. v. Davis, 301 U.S. 548, 581-582 (1937) (also stating that it was not important whether a tax could be labeled an excise; if not that it would be an impost or a duty if it was not a direct tax).

[306] *See* Ch. V.D.2.c. *Cf.* Hubbard, *From Whatever Source Derived*, 6 A.B.A.J. 202, 204-206 (1920) (suggesting that the taxation of municipal bond interest and state employee salaries was intended).

[307] However, even the Justices miss or gloss over its accurate interpretation. *See* Utah v. Evans, 536 U.S. 452, 492 n. 2 (2002) (concurrence of Justice Thomas: "Adoption of the Sixteenth Amendment, however, removed the requirement of apportionment for direct taxes. U.S. Const., Amdt. 16 . . ."); Baldrige v. Shapiro, 455 U.S. 345 n. 8 (1882) (Chief Justice Burger: "The ratification of the Sixteenth Amendment in 1913 amended Art. I, § 2, to provide for direct taxation without apportionment.").

[308] 301 U.S. at 581-582.

[309] Brushaber v. Union Pacific R. Co., 240 U.S. 1 (1916).

[310] *Id.* at 12.

income tax as direct or indirect, and thus it would be an indirect tax based on the event of income and not the ownership of property that produced income.[311]

In so construing the Amendment, the opinion also managed to leave the income tax subject to any pre-existing limits on the power to tax income, other than the apportionment limitation, which meant that to the extent state and local bond interest could not be taxed due to intergovernmental immunity, that had not been changed by the Sixteenth Amendment.[312] Thus the abandonment of look-through was limited, not only leaving intergovernmental immunity untouched but also presumably leaving any other federal tax that was not an income tax subject to being found to be a tax on property ownership. This failure to interpret the Sixteenth Amendment to expansively define income contributed to its only significant subsequent limitation in *Eisner v. Macomber*, discussed below, which ruled a stock dividend not to be income and thus not subject to tax without apportionment.[313]

f. *What Is Income?*

By far the most important constitutional issue of the early days of the 1913 income tax was identifying income: for if the taxed item were not income it was not protected by the Sixteenth Amendment, and if found to be a direct tax and governed by *Pollock*, the tax could be invalidated as an unconstitutional unapportioned direct tax.[314] Indeed attacking a part of the income tax as not falling on income turned out not to be a two part undertaking but a one part argument as to income from property: if the taxed item could be excluded from the constitutional meaning of income, its taxation would be an unapportioned direct tax. That result has occurred only once when the taxpayer actually received valuable property, in a decision that can be viewed as the exception that proves

[311] 240 U.S. at 18-19. Stanton v. Baltic Mining Co., 240 U.S. 103 (1916) decided a month later and also written by Justice White states somewhat more forcefully that income taxes inherently belonged in the not direct category, but then reasserted the function of the Sixteenth Amendment as explained above: "... [W]e are here dealing solely with the restriction imposed by the Sixteenth Amendment on the right to resort to the source whence an income is derived in a case where there is power to tax for the purpose of taking the income tax out of the class of indirect, to which it generically belongs, and putting it in the class of direct, to which it would not otherwise belong, in order to subject it to the regulation of apportionment."

[312] South Carolina v. Baker, 485 U.S. 505, 523 n. 13 (1988).

[313] *See* Ratner, at 337-338 (citing Justice Holmes' dissent in Eisner v. Macomber, 252 U.S. 189, 219-220 (1920).

[314] *See generally* Crane; Bernhaard Knollenberg, *Taxable Income under the Sixteenth Amendment*, 9 Taxes 87 (1931).

the rule: *Eisner v. Macomber*.[315] That decision and several confusing opinions of the Court following it (either upholding the constitutionality of the tax or invalidating a tax as a matter of statutory construction) were all made difficult by *Eisner v. Macomber*'s mechanistic definition of income as gain that must be derived from capital, labor or both.[316] Eventually, the Court broadened the definition of income, which effectively resolved the constitutional question of what is income.[317]

A second major issue in the early years was whether the recognition of income predated the Sixteenth Amendment and the income tax statute; the Court ruled that income that was inchoate in 1913 could be taxed when received thereafter.[318]

Some of the major issues that have arisen as to the definition of income after *Macomber* include:

- Gross income can be taxed under the Sixteenth Amendment. The Court had approved a gross receipts tax on sugar refiners in 1904, after *Pollock* and before the Sixteenth Amendment.[319] Even if a tax on gross product or receipts of a business somehow fell outside the Sixteenth Amendment, it would not be subject to apportionment because it is an excise tax not a direct tax on the property.[320] *Sanford & Brooks* assumed without deciding that only net income could be taxed.[321] But the Court later stated that "Unquestionably Congress has power to condition, limit or deny deductions from gross income in order to arrive at the net that it chooses to tax [citing *Burnet*

---

[315] Eisner v. Macomber, 252 U.S. 189 (1920). For a general analysis of Macomber, see Cummings, at 47-54. *Cf.* Helvering v. Indep. Life Ins. Co., 292 U.S. 371 (1934) (stated that a tax on the value or rental value of property occupied by the owner would be a direct tax because it would not be a income tax and so would have to be apportioned, but did not find such a direct tax on the facts of the case and upheld the tax at issue); Helvering v. Northwest Steel Rolling Mills, Inc., 311 U.S. 46 (1940) (ruled that the undistributed income of a single year of a corporation could be taxed even though the corporation had no undistributed income in the aggregate because it had a deficit). Other early decisions found taxed items not to be income as a matter of statutory construction, prior to the expansion of the understanding of income as stated in Commissioner v. Glenshaw Glass Co., 348 U.S. 426 (1955). *See, e.g.*, Bowers v. Kerbaugh-Empire Co., 271 U.S. 170 (1926) (diminution in amount debtor must repay due to deflation of the German mark did not produce taxable income); Edwards v. Cuba R. Co., 268 U.S. 628 (1925) (contribution by government to corporate capital not income); *distinguished by* Texas & P. R. Co. v. United States, 286 U.S. 285 (1932).

[316] 252 U.S. at 207.

[317] Later opinions looked only for "undeniable accessions to wealth, clearly realized, and over which the taxpayers have complete dominion." Commissioner v. Glenshaw Glass Co., 348 U.S. 426, 431 (1955). *See generally* Bittker & Lokken, Federal Taxation of Income, Estates and Gifts ¶ 5.1.

[318] United States v. Safety Car Heating & Lighting Co., 297 U.S. 88 (1936) (disputed claim).

[319] Spreckels Sugar Refining Co. v. McClain, 192 U.S. 397 (1904). *See also* Nicol v. Ames, 173 U.S. 509 (1899) (upholding federal gross receipts tax). *See* Cummings, *Cost of Goods Sold and the Constitution*, 156 Tax Notes 77 (July 3, 2017).

[320] Stanton v. Baltic Mining Co., 240 U.S. 103 (1916), citing Stratton's Independence v. Howbert, 231 U.S. 399 (1913) (the 1909 corporate income tax on net incomes as applied to a mine, which did not allow depreciation of the mine as a wasting asset).

[321] Burnet v. Sanford & Brooks Co., 282 U.S. 359 (1931).

v. Thompson Oil & Gas, Stanton v. Baltic Mining and *Brushaber v. Union Pacific R. Co.*]"[322] *Stewart* invalidated a state gross receipts tax on retailers that had progressive rates and contained language suggesting that ability to pay had to be considered, but a later opinion indicated that the flaw was in the combination of progressivity and gross taxation and not gross sales tax alone.[323]

- The selection of post 1913 gains as income to be taxed is a matter of governmental policy and not of constitutional power.[324]
- There is no constitutional reason why the income of corporations cannot be taxed directly to their shareholders, although *Macomber* implies the contrary.[325]
- *Brushaber* made clear that the Sixteenth Amendment did not introduce any new limitations on the power to tax.[326] That power is granted in Article I, section 8 of the Constitution and was not negatively affected by the Amendment. This affirmation also related to a concern that the Amendment had overturned the ruling in *Pollock* that the interest on state and local bonds could not be taxed.[327]

---

[322] Helvering v. Indep. Life Ins. Co., 292 U.S. 371, 380 (1934). This is, perhaps, a version of the statements that deductions are a matter of grace not of right. *See* Commissioner v. Sullivan, 356 U.S. 27 (1958).

[323] Stewart Dry Goods Co. v. Lewis, 294 U.S. 550 (1935); distinguished by New York Rapid Transit Corp. v. New York, 303 U.S. 573 (1938). *See also* Louis K. Liggett Co. v. Lee, 288 U.S. 517 (1933) (graduated license tax with each additional store opened by chain store violated equal protection clause); *distinguished by* Fox v. Standard Oil Co., 294 U.S. 87 (1935)(state tax on chain stores); *preceded to the contrary by* State Bd. of Tax Comm'rs v. Jackson, 283 U.S. 527 (1931); *overruled by* North Dakota Pharmacy Bd. v. Snyder's Drug Stores, Inc., 414 U.S. 156 (1973).

[324] Willcuts v. Bunn, 282 U.S. 216 (1931), citing Merchants' Loan and Trust Co. v. Smietanka, 255 U.S. 509, 519, 520 (1921); Goodrich v. Edwards, 255 U.S. 527 (1921); Walsh v. Brewster, 255 U.S. 536 (1921); Eldorado Coal & Mining Co. v. Mager, 255 U.S. 522 (1921).

[325] Helvering v. National Grocery Co., 304 U.S. 282, 286-287 (1938) (accumulated earnings tax was collected from corporation, but alternately could have been paid by shareholders on undistributed corporate income). *See also* Dougherty v. Commissioner, 60 T.C. 917 (1973) (income of controlled foreign corporation taxed to shareholders; distinguished from *Macomber* on basis of control; the foreign corporation did recognize the income). *See generally* Jasper L. Cummings, Jr., *Consolidating Foreign Affiliates*, 11 Fla. Tax Rev. 143, 198-206 (2011) (explaining why it is constitutional to tax the undistributed income of foreign affiliates currently to domestic shareholders).

[326] Brushaber v. Union Pacific R. Co., 240 U.S. 1 (1916).

[327] *See* Morrow, at 380.

- Unrealized appreciation can be taxed as income.[328] Of course this occurs by consent of the taxpayer when "mark to market" is applied by election (as under section 1256), and can be forced on a taxpayer (as under section 475). It is to be distinguished from taxing a shareholder on income actually recognized by the corporation, because that is not so much a matter of taxing unrealized appreciation as of identifying the shareholder's portion. Other opinions of the Court thought to have undercut *Macomber* as to unrealized appreciation are *Midland Mutual, Bruun* and *Horst.*[329]
- The Court stated in dictum that the rental value of property owned could not be taxed without apportionment.[330] This may or may not raise issues different from taxing unrealized income.
- Illegal income can be taxed.[331]

---

[328] Cottage Sav. Ass'n v. Commissioner, 499 U.S. 554, 559 (1991) ("Rather than assessing tax liability on the basis of annual fluctuations in the value of a taxpayer's property, the Internal Revenue Code defers the tax consequences of a gain or loss in property value until the taxpayer 'realizes' the gain or loss. The realization requirement is implicit in § 1001(a) of the Code, 26 U.S.C. § 1001(a), which defines 'the gain [or loss] from the sale or other disposition of property' as the difference between 'the amount realized' from the sale or disposition of the property and its 'adjusted basis.' As this Court has recognized, the concept of realization is 'founded on administrative convenience.' Helvering v. Horst, 311 U.S. 112, 116 (1940)."). *See* Noel B. Cunningham and Deborah H. Schenk, *Taxing without Realization: A "Revolutionary" Approach to Ownership*, 47 Tax L. Rev. 725, 741 (1992) ("The realization requirement is not constitutionally mandated.").

[329] Helvering v. Midland Mut. Life Ins. Co., 300 U.S. 216 (1937) (mortgagee that bid in principal and interest of mortgage for property that was not worth the principal had to include the interest bid into income; Justice Brandeis thought the taxpayer received a "credit" even though it did not receive any asset it could put on its books, based on the broad definition of income); Helvering v. Bruun, 309 U.S. 461 (1940) (landlord realized income when tenancy lapsed and improvements left on property; this is more clearly a case of realization because the landlord got the improvements); Helvering v. Horst, 311 U.S. 112 (1940) (father realized income when son collected interest due on interest coupons the father clipped from his bond and gave to son before maturity of the coupon). *See also* Helvering v. Griffiths, 318 U.S. 371, 393-394 (1943) (which declined to interpret what is now section 305 to overturn *Macomber*, but stated: ". . . Helvering v. Bruun, . . . rejected the concept that taxable gain could arise only when the taxpayer was able to sever increment from his original capital. It preceded by ten days the decision in Helvering v. Zich held that there was no exemption from taxation where economic gain is enjoyed 'by some event other than the taxpayer's personal receipt of money or property.' . . . Each of these decisions undermined further the original theoretical bases of the decision in Eisner v. Macomber."). The demise of *Macomber* was not immediately obvious. *Cf.* Roswell Magill, Taxable Income 42 (1945) (who thought that *Macomber* was still good law purely as to unrealized appreciation, but did not distinguish between unrealized appreciation reflecting market rise and appreciation reflecting earned income); Irving Fisher and Herbert W. Fisher, Constructive Income Taxation 184-188 (1942) (who doubted a tax on the rise in value of land could be taxed as income). And some commentators don't agree. *See* Henry Ordower, *Revisiting Realization: Accretion Taxation, the Constitution, Macomber and Mark to Market*, 13 Va. Tax Rev. 1 (1993).

[330] Helvering v. Independent Life Ins. Co., 292 U.S. 371 (1934). This dictum conflicts with the implication of the decisions cited immediately above.

[331] *See, e.g.*, Rutkin v. United States, 343 U.S. 130 (1952) (taxing moneys derived from extortion).

- However, Treasury regulations retain the possibility that income is not taxable under the Constitution.[332]
- In trying to help a corporation claim a foreign tax credit for a British tax on the value of a British subsidiary the Court treated a tax based on a multiple of corporate earnings as an income tax, which might be a template for other property taxes computed based on the property's income.[333]

3. *Limits on Duties, Imposts, and Excises*

After the Sixteenth Amendment resolved the direct versus indirect issue concerning an income tax, the constitutional limits on indirect taxes took center stage. These range from the uniformity requirement specifically stated in the Constitution to a variety of implied rules under the Fifth Amendment, as addressed in the following Chapters.

a. *The Uniformity Requirement*

(1) *General Rule*

Article I, section 8, clause 1 of the Constitution states:

> The Congress shall have Power To lay and collect Taxes, Duties, Imposts and Excises, to pay the Debts and provide for the common Defence and general Welfare of the United States; but all Duties, Imposts and Excises shall be uniform throughout the United States; . . . .

Even though grammatically the sentence appears not to require uniformity of "Taxes," it does apply to taxes that are not direct taxes, which must be apportioned to the states and obviously could not be geographically uniform.

The Court has never directly invalided a federal tax for lack of uniformity. It did uphold an injunction against enforcement of a tax where the IRS had acquiesced in injunctions issued in favor of other similarly situated taxpayers in other states, stating that collecting the tax from this taxpayer would violate the requirement for uniformity of taxation, which justified ignoring the Anti-Injunction Act.[334] However, the Court had already determined that the tax was not due and so the ground of the substantive ruling was not lack of uniformity.

The uniformity requirement, like the apportionment requirement for direct taxes, does not limit the federal power to tax but rather prescribes the mode of exercising that power.[335] The uniformity to which section 8 of Article I refers is uniformity of application "throughout the United States," meaning geographical

---

[332] *See* Reg. § 1.312-6(b) (inclusion in earnings and profits).

[333] PPL Corp. v. Commissioner, 569 U.S. 329 (2013).

[334] Miller v. Standard Nut Margarine Co., 284 U.S. 498, 510 (1932).

[335] Veazie Bank v. Fenno, 75 U.S. 533, 541 (1869). *See generally* Ruth Mason, *Federalism and the Taxing Power*, 99 Cal. L. Rev. 975, 995 (2011) (discussing the tax uniformity requirement, and the ports and bankruptcy uniformity requirements, and arguing uniformity also should apply to the Commerce Clause); Thomas B. Colby, *Revitalizing the Forgotten Uniformity Constraint on the Commerce Power*, 91 Va. L. Rev. 249, 275 (2005) (linking the taxing and commerce powers).

uniformity.[336] The United States does not include Territories for this purpose.[337] The fact that the subjects of federal taxation are not uniformly distributed across the United States does not make a tax nonuniform.

The Supreme Court most recently explained uniformity in *United States v. Ptasynski*, which now stands for the unfortunate principle that a geographical variation in the description of the tax base does not necessarily violate the Uniformity Clause, but will require additional scrutiny.[338] That relaxed what was firmly understood to be the one role of the Clause. The plaintiffs were crude oil producers in one area who complained about the more favorable taxation of crude oil produced in another area (oil from certain areas in Alaska was exempt), under the crude oil windfall profits tax; they claimed the windfall profits tax they had paid violated the Uniformity Clause due to the discrimination. The windfall profit tax was an imputed income tax labeled as an excise and collectible upon the removal of the oil from the ground.[339] Therefore, oil removed in certain area of Alaska did not incur a tax, whereas other oil did (and rates differed).

Justice Powell for a unanimous Court ruled that the tax did not violate the uniformity requirement, stating:

> Subsequent cases have confirmed that the Framers did not intend to restrict Congress' ability to define the class of objects to be taxed. They intended only that the tax apply wherever the classification is found.[340]

That statement is certainly true but does not explain the holding. If the tax had been imposed on all producers' sales of oil, with exemptions for sales of certain oil that happened to be produced in certain states, that would be a typical and proper tax classification, applicable to all taxpayers alike, though bearing

---

[336] Brushaber v. Union Pacific R. Co., 240 U.S. 1, 24 (1916); Flint v. Stone Tracy Co., 220 U.S. 107, 158 (1911); Knowlton v. Moore, 178 U.S. 41, 84-106 (1900) (extensively examining the possibility that taxes must be intrinsically uniform, charging each taxpayer the same amount, and rejecting that; showed linkage of clause prohibiting preference for ports with uniformity of taxation); Patton v. Brady, 184 U.S. 608, 622 (1902); Edye v. Robertson (Head Money Cases), 112 U.S. 580, 594 (1884) (this cases is primarily known for establishing the rule that treaties are not supreme over later acts of Congress; although it found the duty on immigrants to be a regulation of commerce rather than a tax, it stated that if it were a tax it was uniform because it applied to all ports, no matter that immigrants might not arrive other than through ports, and that they arrived more frequently as some ports than at others); United States v. Doremus, 249 U.S. 86 (1919) (the Court upheld the criminal conviction of a doctor who had failed to register and pay the $1 annual excise tax to dispense narcotics, stating that the Uniformity Clause required only geographical uniformity and nothing else, and the court cannot add other limits); Fernandez v. Wiener, 326 U.S. 340 (1945).

[337] Downes v. Bidwell, 182 U.S. 244 (1901). For discussion of federal taxation in federal Territories, *see* Ch. V.D.3.a(4).

[338] United States v. Ptasynski, 462 U.S. 74 (1983). The *Ptasynski* opinion stated that the Court had not had occasion to reconsider the uniformity requirement since Knowlton v. Moore. 462 U.S. at 83.

[339] Former I.R.C. § 4986(a) called the tax they paid an excise; § 4988(a) defined windfall profit as the excess of the removal price of oil over its adjusted basis plus a severance tax adjustment; § 4988(c) defined removal price as the sales price, with certain variations.

[340] 462 U.S. at 82.

differently on differently situated taxpayers. If the tax had been on the extraction of oil of a type that happened to exist only in Alaska, that would have been a proper classification (just as taxes on ports are uniformly applied, even though ports are not uniformly distributed among the states). However, taxing an act (extracting oil) one way in identified parts of Alaska and another way in other places appears to violate geographical uniformity as commonly understood; the commentators agreed.[341]

Perhaps the Court was unwilling to tangle with the issues that would arise from the refund ordered by the lower court, which ruled the exemption unconstitutional, meaning that every payor of the tax would get its money back.[342] The Court was able to camouflage its reasoning by adopting a similar rejection of geographical limitation in a bankruptcy case involving a supposedly analogous rule.[343]

Ptasynski relied primarily on the *Head Money Cases*, which most clearly illustrated the lack of geographical discrimination when a taxed subject happened to be distributed in a nonuniform manner around the country (ports).[344] That opinion linked the uniformity requirement to the clause preventing Congress from giving preference to any ports, as part of a general theme to prevent discriminatory regulation of trade within the United States.[345]

The Court first extensively analyzed the uniformity requirement in *Knowlton v. Moore*, concerning the federal estate tax with progressive rates adopted in 1898, which decision had to deal with some loose statements appearing in earlier opinions that had not extensively addressed the requirement.[346] The taxpayers' arguments went to the heart of the republican form of government and the separation of powers in the Constitution. *Knowlton v. Moore* recognized this and stated:

> The grave consequences which it is asserted must arise in the future if the right to levy a progressive tax be recognized involves in its ultimate aspect the mere assertion that free and representative government is a failure, and that the grossest abuses of power are foreshadowed unless the courts usurp a purely legislative function. If a case should ever arise, where an arbitrary and confiscatory exaction is imposed bearing the guise of a progressive or any other form of tax, it will be time enough to consider whether the judicial power can afford a rem-

---

[341] Peter R. Mounsey, *Comment: The Constitutionality of the Alaska Exemption*, 18 LAND AND WATER L. REV. 575 (1983); Ellen Eggleston, *Comment: United States v. Ptasynski, A Windfall for Congress*, 61 DENV. L. J. 395 (1984); *Comment, The Uniformity Clause*, 51 U. CHI. L. REV. 1193 (1984).

[342] Ptasynski v. United States, 550 F. Supp. 549 (D. Wyo. 1982).

[343] Regional Rail Reorganization Act Cases, 419 U.S. 102 (1974). *See also* Ry. Labor Executives' Ass'n v. Gibbons, 455 U.S. 457, 468-469 (1982) (the bankruptcy laws must be uniform but laws based on the Commerce Clause need not be uniform).

[344] Edye v. Robertson (Head Money Cases), 112 U.S. 580 (1884). However, the uniformity discussion in this opinion was mostly dictum because the Court found the duty not to be a taxing power tax but a regulation of foreign commerce. 112 U.S. at 595.

[345] 112 U.S. at 594. *See* Bullock, at 227-228.

[346] Knowlton v. Moore, 178 U.S. 41 (1900).

edy by applying inherent and fundamental principles for the protection of the individual, even though there be no express authority in the Constitution to do so. That the law which we have construed affords no ground for the contention that the tax imposed is arbitrary and confiscatory, is obvious.[347]

The Court's subsequent opinions reflect a variety of issues and reject a variety of specific attacks on federal taxes based on the uniformity requirement:

- A tax only on foreign leased vessels did not violate the uniformity requirement because the boats might be used anywhere in the U.S. by taxpayers.[348]
- The consent by the federal government for a state to levy an impost under the Import-Export Clause (referring to an inspection duty that exceeded the state's costs) conflicts with the requirement that imposts be uniform throughout the United States; the Court did not resolve which would prevail.[349]
- *Hanson* invalidated a state law that required persons who bought a federal liquor license to post it on pain of criminal penalty, because this sort of piggybacking on federal tax could result in non-uniform application of federal tax.[350]
- *Snyder* ruled that a state law requiring recordation of liens could not apply to prevent a federal court from enforcing a federal tax lien, both because it would limit the sovereignty of the United States, and because it would render application of the federal tax laws non-uniform; the system of assessment and collection must be uniform, which precludes state preconditions and state statutes of limitations.[351]
- The *Regional Rail Reorganization Act Cases* analogized the bankruptcy uniformity provision as applied to differential treatment of railroads in a certain part of the country to the tax uniformity requirement and stated that both required uniform application throughout the country wherever the event at issue occurs; but the fact that it does not occur in all areas does not make the rule non-uniform.[352] *Ptasynski* relied on this reasoning, as discussed above.
- The uniformity requirement does not apply to taxes imposed by states, such as a tax on a foreign insurance company for the privilege of doing business in the state, on a theory that the federal government has adopted the

---

[347] 178 U.S. at 109-110.

[348] Billings v. United States, 232 U.S. 261 (1914).

[349] Michelin Tire Corp. v. Wages, 423 U.S. 276, 301 n. 13 (1976). *See* Ch. VI.E.

[350] North Dakota ex rel. Flaherty v. Hanson, 215 U.S. 515 (1910).

[351] United States v. Snyder, 149 U.S. 210, 214 (1893). Subsequently Congress required filing of federal tax liens in accordance with state laws. *See* United States v. Union Cent. Life Ins. Co., 368 U.S. 291 (1961); United States v. Estate of Romani, 523 U.S. 517 (1998).

[352] Regional Rail Reorganization Act Cases, 419 U.S. 102 (1974). In addition to the bankruptcy uniformity requirement there is an immigration uniformity requirement in Article I, section 8, clause 4. Neither influences the meaning of the tax uniformity requirement. *See* Ry. Labor Executives' Ass'n v. Gibbons, 4555 U.S. 457, 473 (1982).

non-uniform tax by allowing it; it applies only to the federal taxing power when it is exerted without reference to any state action.[353]

- An estate tax on the termination of the marital community in states applying community property law did not violate the uniformity clause.[354]
- Tax rate progressivity does not violate uniformity.[355]
- Differing state laws causing different federal taxation of otherwise similarly situated taxpayers do not violate uniformity.[356]
- However, even geographically uniform federal taxes are subject to the principle applied to federal statutes generally, that "Statutes are subjected to a higher level of scrutiny if they interfere with the exercise of a fundamental right, such as freedom of speech, or employ a suspect classification, such as race."[357]
- A "grandfather clause" will not be invalidated if there is any state of facts rationally justifying it.[358]
- But what would normally be viewed as Fifth Amendment lack of equal protection has been referred to as lack of uniformity at least once by the Court.[359]
- Rifle-shot provisions in federal tax statutes are no more likely to succumb to the uniformity requirement than are any other apparently arbitrary distinctions.[360]

---

[353] Prudential Ins. Co. v. Benjamin, 328 U.S. 408 (1946).

[354] United States v. Rompel, 326 U.S. 367 (1945); *followed* Fernandez v. Wiener, 326 U.S. 340, 359 (1945) (which stated: "The amendment taxing community property interests is applicable throughout the territory of the United States wherever such interests may be found. There is no lack of geographical uniformity because in some states they are not found. For a taxing statute does not fall short of the prescribed uniformity because its operation and incidence may be affected by differences in state laws."). *See also* Poe v. Seaborn, 282 U.S. 101 (1930).

[355] Bromley v. McCaughn, 280 U.S. 124, 183 (1929) (federal gift tax). *See also* Magoun v. Illinois Trust & Savings Bank, 170 U.S. 283 (1898) (progressive state inheritance tax).

[356] Knowlton v. Moore, 178 U.S. 41 (1900); Poe v. Seaborn, 282 U.S. 101 (1930); Phillips v. Commissioner, 283 U.S. 589 (1931); Riggs v. Del Drago, 317 U.S. 95 (1942); Florida v. Mellon, 273 U.S. 12, 17 (1927) ("Congress cannot accommodate its legislation to the conflicting or dissimilar laws of the several states nor control the diverse conditions to be found in the various states which necessarily work unlike results from the enforcement of the same tax.").

[357] Regan v. Taxation with Representation, 461 U.S. 540, 547 (1983) (not specifically addressing the uniformity requirement; also a distinction between veterans and other groups did not merit strict scrutiny). *See* Ch. I.E.4.b.

[358] United States v. Maryland Savings-Share Ins. Corp., 400 U.S. 4, 6 (1970) (listing other cases; not specifically addressing the uniformity requirement). *See* Ch. V.D.3.b(3).

[359] Miller v. Standard Nut Margarine Co., 284 U.S. 498, 510 (1932) (in discussion of Anti-Injunction Act).

[360] *See* Lawrence Zelenak, Are Rifle Shot Transition Rules and Other Ad Hoc Tax Legislation Constitutional?, 44 Tax L. Rev. 563, 599-594 (1989) (exhaustively analyzing the rifle-shot provisions and their possible treatment if attacked).

See Chapter V.D.3.b for further discussion of uniformity in connection with discrimination.

(2) *Uniformity: The* Golsen *Rule and Circuit Disuniformity*

Disuniformity of interpretation or application of the federal tax laws can occur as a result of differing lower court rulings not resolved by the Supreme Court. For several decades the surest way for a federal tax issue to receive review by the Supreme Court has been for the petitioner to show a conflict in rulings on the issue in two or more courts of appeal.[361] When the Court decides such cases it obviously eliminates the conflict and creates uniform federal tax law. However, obviously not all circuit conflicts are resolved by the Court, either because it chooses not to issue the writ of certiorari or because the parties do not seek review. Furthermore, conflicts in legal interpretation and hence outcomes in court can exist as a result of differing rulings of lower federal courts: the Tax Court may conflict with the Claims Court, and lacking appellate precedent each federal district court tends to follow the rulings of other judges in the district and will not feel bound by the Tax Court or the Claims Court.

Is court created disuniformity a violation of the uniformity requirement for federal indirect taxes? The Court has not spoken on the issue directly, but has implied the answer is no.[362] In theory such disuniformity might be thought to violate the Constitution's tax uniformity requirement,[363] but in practice that makes no sense, either because the uniformity requirement speaks to what Congress does and not what the courts do,[364] or because court created disuniformity is inevitable and accepted and the Court will not allow an event that is inevitable and accepted to stymie the operation of a power so important as the federal taxing power.[365] If the Court thought such disuniformity were a problem, it would review all federal tax cases with such conflicts.

The natural disuniformity that can be created by the existence of the various federal courts is recognized and exacerbated by the Tax Court's *Golsen* Rule, which the Supreme Court declined to review and has not disapproved.[366] In *Golsen* (1971) the Tax Court imposed on itself as a principle of procedure the rule

[361] *See, e.g.*, Pasquantino v. United States, 544 U.S. 349, 354 (2005).

[362] It refused to review the *Golsen* case, which exacerbated the disconformity as discussed further in the text. Golsen v. Commissioner, 54 T.C. 742, *affirmed*, 445 F. 2d 985 (10th Cir. 1971), *cert. denied*, 404 U.S. 940 (1971).

[363] *See* Jeffrey S. Kinsler, *Circuit-Specific Application of the Internal Revenue Code: An Unconstitutional Tax*, 81 Denver U. L. Rev. 113 (2003) (which does not cite the *Golsen* rule).

[364] However, as the following discussion of the *Golsen* Rule shows, much of the court based disuniformity stems from the decision of the Tax Court to follow the rule adopted by the circuit to which the case normally would be appealed; the Tax Court is part of Congress, being formed in the legislative branch. *See* Ch. VIII.E.3.b.

[365] *Cf.* Knowlton v. Moore, 178 U.S. 41, 60 (1904) (refused to view a federal estate tax as a tax on the state's power to regulate transmission of property at death because that would be "the end of all taxation.").

[366] Golsen v. Commissioner, 54 T.C. 742, *affirmed*, 445 F. 2d 985 (10th Cir. 1971), *cert. denied*, 404 U.S. 940 (1971). *See also* Commissioner v. Portland Cement Co., 450 U.S. 156, 164 n. 14 (1981).

that it would follow the legal decision in a case on all fours with the instant case of the court of appeals to which the case could be appealed. However, in doing so the Tax Court recognized the broader duty to promote uniform application of the internal revenue laws.[367] When it had first addressed the issue in *Lawrence* (1957) the Tax Court thought that uniformity concerns meant it should not follow the circuit (noting that the parties could agree to appeal to any circuit), but *Golsen* reversed that decision without abandoning the goal of nationwide uniformity. *Golsen* asserted that the question was one of efficient judicial administration only (i.e., not beating the Tax Court's head against the brick wall of the circuit's contrary view), and was not as important as critics had asserted, because in 13 years *Golsen* was the first case to have to reevaluate the earlier decision. *Golsen* asserted that its decision to follow the circuits:

> . . . does not jeopardize the Federal interest in uniform application of the internal revenue laws which we emphasized in Lawrence. We shall remain able to foster uniformity by giving effect to our own views in cases appealable to courts whose views have not yet been expressed, and, even where the relevant Court of Appeals has already made its views known, by explaining why we agree or disagree with the precedent that we feel constrained to follow.[368]

Assuming that natural federal court-based disuniformity cannot violate the tax uniformity requirement, how about administrative disuniformity? The IRS Chief Counsel can recommend in an Action on Decision that the IRS not follow any federal tax court ruling by issuing a nonacquiescence.[369] The IRS has issued such nonacquiescences for almost a century. While this may appear to promote administrative uniformity it does not when the court with which the IRS disagrees is a court of appeal: in those cases the nonacquiescence means the IRS will follow that circuit's ruling with respect to taxpayers in that circuit, and otherwise will follow its own view. As a result, the IRS creates disuniformity.

Again, there is no indication that the Supreme Court views this type of disuniformity as a constitutional problem. To do so would implicate deep structural issues in the separation of powers.[370]

---

[367] Estate of Munter v. Commissioner, 63 T.C. 663, 670 n. 3 (1975), citing Lawrence v. Commissioner, 27 T.C. 713 (1957) (which was overruled by *Golsen*).

[368] 54 T.C. at 757.

[369] I.R.M. section 36.3.1 ("Nonacquiescence signifies that, although the decision was not appealed or was not reviewed by the Supreme Court, the Service does not agree with the holding of the court and will not follow it nationwide in disposing of other cases. With respect to opinions of an appellate court, the Service will generally follow the holding of the circuit court in cases appealable to that circuit due to the binding nature of that opinion in lower courts, even when the office concludes that the opinion is erroneous.").

[370] In practice the IRS is much more likely to allow a single appellate ruling to dictate the nationwide course of the law. *See, e.g.*, Rite Aid Corp. v. United States, 255 F.3d 1357 (Fed. Cir. 2001), which led to the abandonment of the consolidated return loss disallowance rule. *See* JASPER L. CUMMINGS, JR. & ROBERT P. HANSON, SELECTIVE ANALYSIS OF THE AMERICAN JOBS CREATION ACT OF 2004 ¶3.05 (2005).

(3) *Uniformity: Taxing Power in the District of Columbia*

The United States, throughout which duties, excises and imposts must be uniform, includes the District of Columbia, even though the District is not considered a state for this purpose.[371] This means that a *lower* tax cannot be imposed in the District of Columbia, nor can the District be exempted from a generally applicable tax (such as the income tax); but a *higher* tax rate presumably can be charged in the District, under the separate power of Congress to tax within the District.[372]

Several provisions of the Constitution relate to the federal taxing power in the District of Columbia, beginning with Article I, section 8, clause 1:

> The Congress shall have Power To lay and collect Taxes, Duties, Imposts and Excises, to pay the Debts and provide for the common Defence and general Welfare of the United States; but all Duties, Imposts and Excises shall be uniform throughout the United States; . . . .

Article I, section 8, clause 17 also grants to Congress power:

> To exercise exclusive Legislation in all Cases whatsoever, over such District (not exceeding ten Miles square) as may, by Cession of particular States, and the Acceptance of Congress, become the Seat of the Government of the United States, and to exercise like Authority over all Places purchased by the Consent of the Legislature of the State in which the Same shall be, for the Erection of Forts, Magazines, Arsenals, dock-Yards, and other needful Buildings;[373]

Article I, section 2, clause 3 is not directly applicable to the federal power to impose indirect taxes, but does preclude voting in the District for Representatives:

> Representatives and direct Taxes shall be apportioned among the several States which may be included within this Union, according to their respective Numbers, which shall be determined by adding to the whole Number of free Persons, including those bound to Service for a Term of Years, and excluding Indians not taxed, three fifths of all other Persons [Modified by Amendment XIV] as to representatives only; Amendment XIII abolished slavery]. The actual Enumeration shall be made within three Years after the first Meeting of the

---

[371] Loughborough v. Blake, 18 U.S. 317 (1820); Downes v. Bidwell, 182 U.S. 244 (1901). *See generally* Forrest Revere Black, *Tax Uniformity and the Incorporated Territories*, 26 GEO. L. J. 343 (1937) [hereinafter Black] (which cites a 1936 Joint Committee on Taxation Report entitled *The Taxing Power of the Federal and State Governments*, which explained the inclusion of the District of Columbia in the United States for this purpose, and cited the *Blake* decision, but Black disputes the dictum in *Blake*, which was a direct tax case).

[372] Ross O'Donoghue, *The Power To Tax In Respect To The District of Columbia*, 31 GEO. L. J. 146, 161 (1943) [hereinafter O'Donoghue] (this article appears to be the only one addressing the general subject).

[373] For discussion of taxation in federal enclaves, to which this clause also refers, see Ch. II.C.6.

> Congress of the United States, and within every subsequent Term of ten Years, in such Manner as they shall by Law direct.[374]

Also Article I, section 9, clause 4 states:

> No capitation, or other direct, Tax shall be laid, unless in Proportion to the Census or Enumeration herein before directed to be taken.

The District of Columbia is subject to federal taxation under both clause 1, for the support of the national government, and clause 17 for its own benefit. Congress, directly or by delegation, exercises both powers of taxation. In addition, the Necessary and Proper Clause augments the taxing power.

If Congress were to levy a direct tax (a property tax) nationally it could choose to include the District in the levy or not; if it did, the District would bear its apportioned part based on the census. Indirect taxes that Congress does regularly levy, such as the income tax and excise taxes, are levied uniformly in the District along with the rest of the United States, as a matter of practice. However, Congress also can and does levy property taxes (which otherwise would be limited as direct taxes if imposed nationally) and other forms of taxes within the District for the use of the District without reference to either any apportionment among the states or uniformity of application in other parts of the United States.

Chief Justice Marshall had occasion to address all of these provisions directly, or by dictum, in *Loughborough v. Blake*,[375] which upheld an apportionment of one of the early direct taxes in part to the District. Due to the unusual direct feature of the tax involved, the opinion is somewhat confusing as applied to more typical taxes. The opinion held or stated in dictum:

- The District had been carved out of Maryland and Virginia and could not, therefore, be less treated as part of the United States than those states.
- Congress' power to tax in the District derives both from clause 17 and from the general taxing power, because as to the latter the United States includes the Territories and the District.[376]
- The uniformity requirement for indirect taxes applies to the whole United States as defined (including the District).[377]
- Therefore, direct taxes must be applicable as broadly as uniform imposts, meaning they can be levied in the Territories and the District.

---

[374] Also Article IV, section 3, clause 2 grants powers as to property belonging to the United States, but the Court has not ruled that it applies to the District of Columbia (most of which now is privately owned): "The Congress shall have Power to dispose of and make all needful Rules and Regulations respecting the Territory or other Property belonging to the United States; and nothing in this Constitution shall be so construed as to Prejudice any Claims of the United States, or of any particular State."

[375] Loughborough v. Blake, 18 U.S. 317 (1820).

[376] However, *Downes v. Bidwell* held that certain Territories were not part of the United States for certain purposes of the revenue clauses of the Constitution. *See* Ch. V.D.3.a(4).

[377] But this does not prevent a direct tax being levied in the District alone. *See* Gibbons v. District of Columbia, 116 U.S. 404 (1886).

- Article I, section 2, clause 3 (quoted above) does not restrict direct taxes to the states. Rather, Article I, section 9, clause 4 shows that direct taxes can be levied anywhere, but only in proportion to the census that is also taken to establish the apportionment of taxes among the states.
- The foregoing analysis illustrates that section 2, clause 3 and section 9, clause 4 are not duplicative. Also Chief Justice Marshall observed that apportionment for taxation does not track apportionment of representatives even as to the states, and so it is not a constitutional concern that direct taxation may occur without representation because it already occurs without proportional representation.[378]
- But a census need not be taken and direct taxes need not be apportioned to the Territories or the District if Congress chooses not to take a census there.
- The "no taxation without representation" theme does not prevent levying direct taxes in the District by apportionment because (1) that theme related to the peculiar situation with Great Britain, whereby (2) there was no principle of apportionment as here, and (3) there was neither a progression toward statehood (as in the case of the western Territories) nor a voluntary relinquishment of sovereignty to Congress (as in the case of the District).
- Moreover, the Constitution directs that indirect uniform taxes be levied in the United States, which includes the District and the Territories, and so directs that there be indirect taxation without representation. Thus the District is protected by the principles of uniformity and apportionment without having any representation.
- Therefore, the holding of the opinion is that Congress can levy direct taxes in the District in proportion to the census.

The *Loughborough* opinion would seem to severely constrain taxation in the District to indirect taxes uniformly applied across the entire United States and to apportioned direct taxes if the census were extended to the District (which it, of course, was). That would leave no room for a system of taxation within the District analogous to that applied by states within their borders. The taxpayer in the case contended that Congress could act in either of two capacities with respect to the District, as the national government and as a local legislature. Chief Justice Marshall declined to accept or decide the "soundness of this distinction," but chose to ground the power to tax on the general powers of Congress rather than that of a "mere local legislature."

When the Court came to examine the Act of 1875 that authorized property taxation within the District, it stated that *Loughborough* recognized the power

[378] His illustration concerns a state that is entitled to 2 representatives if it has 60,000 persons counted in the census but 1 representative if the census counted 59,000; in contrast the apportionment of direct taxes would be based on the actual census numbers, not the representatives.

of Congress to tax in the District as if it were a local legislature.[379] Although this was an over-reading of the earlier opinion, it was a necessary one, recognizing that Congress can levy in the District a direct tax on property without apportionment to the census, as a state could do. Subsequent opinions have recognized that clause 17 giving Congress power of exclusive legislation over the District empowers it to tax there (which it has delegated to the D.C. local government).[380] The District tax revenues must be used for the District but need not be segregated, at least as a constitutional matter.[381]

(4) *Uniformity: Taxing Power in the Territories*

The United States, throughout which duties, excises and imposts must be uniform, includes the so called incorporated Territories, but not the so called unincorporated Territories.[382] Therefore, when Congress enacts duties, imposts and excises under the general taxing power, they apply within the incorporated Territories and are subject to the uniformity requirement. The uniformity requirement does not apply in the unincorporated Territories, within which Congress may levy taxes as necessary and proper to its control of those Territories. Generally, Territories themselves can tax for their own benefit, as permitted by Congress.[383]

As to the federal power to tax in the Territories, Article IV, section 3, clause 2 states:

> The Congress shall have Power to dispose of and make all needful Rules and Regulations respecting the Territory or other Property belonging to the United States; and nothing in this Constitution shall be so construed as to Prejudice any Claims of the United States, or of any particular State.

The Constitution also authorizes taxation in the Territories in the general taxing power and other rules quoted above in Chapter V.D.3.a(3) on the District

---

[379] Gibbons v. District of Columbia, 116 U.S. 404 (1886) (a direct tax could be levied in the District alone, which of course occurs when property is taxed). However, one of the few commentators on the subject protests that it is not appropriate to view the Congress as exercising anything but a single unified power. *See* O'Donoghue, at 159.

[380] *See, e.g.*, Palmore v. United States, 411 U.S. 389 (1973); Heald v. District of Columbia, 259 U.S. 114 (1922); Wight v. Davidson, 181 U.S. 371 (1901) (ruling the Fourteenth Amendment did not apply to local assessments in the District).

[381] *See* Binns v. United States, 194 U.S. 486 (1904) (concerning the incorporated territory of Alaska and stating that "In order to avoid any misapprehension we may add that this opinion must not be extended to any case, if one should arise, in which it is apparent that Congress is, by some special system of license taxes, seeking to obtain from a Territory of the United States revenue for the benefit of the nation as distinguished from that necessary for the support of the territorial government.").

[382] Downes v. Bidwell, 182 U.S. 244 (1901). *See generally* Black (citing a 1936 Joint Committee on Taxation Report entitled *The Taxing Power of the Federal and State Governments*, which explained the inclusion of the "incorporated" Territories for uniformity purposes; but Black disputes the reliability of *Bidwell*'s multiple opinions for this conclusion).

[383] For a full discussion of taxation in the Territories, see Staff of the Joint Committee on Taxation, Federal Tax Law and Issues Related to the United States Territories, JCX-41-12 (May 14, 2012).

of Columbia. In addition Chief Justice Marshall said a power to govern accompanies the power to acquire,[384] and clause 2 quoted above makes it clear that the Constitution views a Territory as property acquired and owned by the United States. Moreover, the President as Commander in Chief can direct collection of tariffs in a conquered Territory.[385]

This overlap of sources of power led to a constitutional crisis around the turn of the 19th Century that was said to be "now scarce remembered" in 1926.[386] To understand the crisis it is important to distinguish those parcels of real property "belonging" to the United States that are not states, and how they differ: (1) the Northwest Territory, which had turned into states and had theretofore been treated as part of the United States for various purposes, and (2) Puerto Rico and other Territories acquired in the latter part of the 19th Century and not necessarily expected to become states.

The first clause in section 3 of Article IV authorizes admitting new states to the Union. The juxtaposition of the two clauses suggests that by "Territory" the Constitution contemplated primarily those contiguous parcels of land that were expected to become states. Indeed, since 1785 the Confederation had a compact with the Northwest Territory that was to become Ohio, Indiana, Illinois and Michigan.[387] The early compact shows that the Territories were to be set up like states, with their own legislatures and courts, presumably in preparation for statehood. It precludes taxation of federal property by the Territory, and so contemplated taxation by the Territories of themselves, but also contemplated taxation in the Territories by the Confederation (or at least on behalf of the Confederation).

We are concerned here with taxation by the United States of the Territories and not taxation by the Territories,[388] or with state taxation of the Territories.[389]

---

[384] Sere v. Pitot, 10 U.S. 332 (1810) (the Territory of New Orleans). *See also* De Lima v. Bidwell, 182 U.S. 1 (1901) (suggesting other sources of governing power).

[385] Cross v. Harrison, 57 U.S. 164 (1854).

[386] Frederic R. Coudert, *The Evolution of the Doctrine of Territorial Incorporation*, 26 COL. L. REV. 823 (1926) [hereinafter Coudert]. The author litigated *Downes v. Bidwell.*

[387] First Cong., Sess. I, ch. 8, 1 Stat. 50 (1789).

[388] As to taxation by the Territories, see Anthony Ciolli, *The Power of United States Territories to Tax Interstate and Foreign Commerce: Why the Commerce and Import-Export Clauses Do Not Apply*, 63 TAX LAW. 1223 (Summer 2010). *See also* Gromer v. Standard Dredging Co., 224 U.S. 362 (1912) (*Gromer* likened a Territory to a state and allowed Puerto Rico to tax property of a contractor used in work for the United States); Pacific American Fisheries v. Alaska, 269 U.S. 269 (1925) (Alaska could impose graduated canning tax falling more heavily on larger canners); Haavik v. Alaska Packers Ass'n, 263 U.S. 510 (1924) (Territory of Alaska could impose a poll tax and a tax on non-resident fishermen, who were not mere tourists, because it exercised the same taxing powers Congress could have exercised in the Territories); Bonet v. Yabucoa Sugar Co., 306 U.S. 505 (1939) (The Court refused to overturn an interpretation of the taxing statute by the Puerto Rican Supreme Court, which ruled that there was no right to sue for refund of taxes voluntarily paid, believing that the local courts are due substantial deference).

[389] *See* Farmers & Mechanics Sav. Bank v. Minnesota, 232 U.S. 516 (1914) (held that a State cannot tax bonds issued by a Territory of the United States; that a tax upon the bonds is a tax on the government issuing them; that such a tax, if allowed at all, may be carried to an extent that will entirely arrest governmental operations).

In fact all Territories now are governed by federal statutes setting up taxing regimes.[390]

Downes v. Bidwell (one of the *Insular Cases*) clarified that Territories simply by virtue of being Territories are not part of the United States under the Constitution and therefore the federal taxing power in the Territories depends on the clause quoted above rather than the general taxing power, nothing else appearing.[391] The multiple opinions in that case are confusing because the opinion of the Court by Justice Brown was based on a theory that ultimately has not been followed by the Court. Rather the opinion by Justice White created the "incorporation theory."[392] According to Justice White, the Constitution's general taxing power applied to the Territory as if it were a state only if Congress had incorporated the Territory into the United States by some affirmative act.

The issue in *Downes* was not taxation within a Territory but rather the taxability of an import into New York from Puerto Rico under a special reduced rate established in the Foraker Act. The taxpayer did not want to pay any import duty because it claimed the Constitution does not allow tax on "imports" from one part of the United States to another. The tax issue was probably not the core concern to the Justices, who remembered, and felt constrained by, the unfortunate opinion of Chief Justice Taney in the *Dred Scott* decision.[393] It ruled that slavery existed in the Territories as a matter of constitutional law, and so Dred Scott had no right to escape from his owner and be free by virtue of moving into a Territory. However, the positive feature of *Dred Scott* that the *Insular Cases* reaffirmed was that the Constitution governed the question of the law in the Territories.[394]

That view of *Dred Scott* appeared to mean that all of the provisions of the Constitution apply in the Territories. However, the Justices in *Downes* perceived many problems with such a doctrine, generally that the residents of the Territories could be automatically invested with all the rights of citizens, from which they could not be divested if the United States decided to dispose of the Territory.[395] Conversely, the dissenters in *Downes*, including particularly Justice Harlan, were appalled at the thought that the United States might go around the world conquering Territories and treating their inhabitants as subjects not entitled to rights.[396]

---

[390] *See* Karla Hoff, *U.S. Federal Tax Policy Towards the Territories: Past, Present and Future*, 37 Tax L. Rev. 51 (1981).

[391] Downes v. Bidwell, 182 U.S. 244 (1901) (see particularly opinion of Justice White). This with two other decisions, De Lima v. Bidwell, 182 U.S. 1 (1901), and Dooley v. United States, 182 U.S. 222 (1901), were sometimes called the *Insular Cases*. Opinions about the *Insular Cases* continue to run hot. *See, e.g.*, Gabriel A. Terrasa, *The United States, Puerto Rico, and the Territorial Incorporation Doctrine: Reaching a Century of Constitutional Authoritarianism*, 31 John Marshall Law Review 55 (Fall 1997). *Downes* relied on the earlier opinion in Fleming v. Page, 50 U.S. 603 (1850) (the *Tampico Duties Case*).

[392] Coudert, at 830.

[393] Dred Scott v. Sandford, 60 U.S. 393 (1857).

[394] *See* Schwartz, at 117.

[395] Coudert, at 832.

[396] *Id.* at 836-837.

Ultimately the doctrine created by Justice White in *Downes* was accepted as the law: Congress must incorporate a Territory into the United States in order for the general taxing (and most other) constitutional rules to apply.[397] It is not that the Constitution does not apply in the Territories, but rather what parts of the Constitution apply.[398] However, the *Insular Cases* have been much criticized and might be revisited by the Court.[399]

Of course the constitutional rule with which we are most concerned here is the rule requiring uniformity of taxation. The last time the Court spoke to the issue it allowed a nonuniform regulation of commerce in the incorporated Territory of Alaska because it was not a tax, which presumably had to be uniform throughout the United States.[400] However, the effect of nonuniformity can be had in the incorporated Territories by imposing the general federal taxes, and then imposing territorial taxes in addition.

The Constitution does not require that funds raised by taxation in Territories be segregated.[401] As in the case of the District of Columbia, discussed in the preceding Chapter, if Congress chose to take a census in the Territories it could levy a direct tax in the Territories also, based on apportionment by census.[402]

b. *Fifth Amendment*

Amendment V to the Constitution states:

> . . . [N]or shall any person be subject for the same offence to be twice put in jeopardy of life or limb; nor shall be compelled in any criminal case to be a witness against himself, nor be deprived of life, liberty, or property, without due process of law; nor shall private property be taken for public use, without just compensation.

It is not literally addressed to the federal government, but the Preamble to the Bill of Rights so indicates. It does not contain an equal protection requirement, in contrast to the Fourteenth Amendment, which states:

> . . . [N]or shall any State deprive any person of life, liberty, or property, without due process of law; nor deny to any person within its jurisdiction the equal protection of the laws.

Amendment V applies the requirement of due process of law not only to deprivation of property but also of "liberty." In addition to protecting property and liberty, it has several other potential impacts on federal taxation: double jeopardy, self-incrimination, and taking without just compensation. The

---

[397] *Id.* at 847. *See* Dorr v. United States, 195 U.S. 138 (1904); Balzac v. Porto Rico, 258 U.S. 298 (1922). Later opinions differ on the extent of the particular protections to be provided to inhabitants of the Territories. *See* Boumediene v. Bush, 553 U.S. 723 (2008).

[398] United States v. Verdugo-Urquidez, 494 U.S. 259, 268 (1990).

[399] Fin. Oversight & Mgmt. Bd. for P.R. v. Aurelius Inv., LLC, 140 S. Ct. 1649 (2020).

[400] Alaska v. Troy, 258 U.S. 101 (1922).

[401] Binns v. United States, 194 U.S. 486 (1904); Gibbons v. District of Columbia, 116 U.S. 404 (1886).

[402] *See also* James M. Gray, Limitations of the Taxing Power 371 (1906) [hereinafter Gray].

Equal Protection Clause of the Fourteenth Amendment was read into the Fifth Amendment at least by 1954,[403] and before that time similar requirements (*i.e.*, not arbitrary and capricious) were applied. This relatively recent event of constitutional construction makes some earlier opinions on tax discrimination confusing, but did not change the law in any practical way.

Additional confusion is caused by the different terminologies and theories used by taxpayers and the Court in discussing due process as applied to the taxing power, including:

- Equal protection/discrimination;[404]
- Substantive due process;[405]
- Confiscation and taking;[406]
- Lack of procedural due process, which can implicate equal protection;[407]
- Arbitrary and capricious taxation (*e.g.*, conclusive presumptions);
- Lack of jurisdiction to tax.[408]

Although there is a substantial body of Supreme Court authority on the subject of the Fifth Amendment and federal taxes, the Court has held only three federal tax provisions unconstitutional under the Fifth Amendment. All three involved retroactivity and/or conclusive presumptions, which have features of equal protection, arbitrariness and procedural due process, and the three decisions involving the two federal statues came in the short period from 1927 to 1932 and all involved estate taxes. For these reasons the retroactivity cases appear to be sui generis and will discussed separately.

Therefore one can state with confidence that the Court has applied the Fifth Amendment to federal taxes with a very light hand; it has never ruled a federal tax unconstitutional simply because it made distinctions in taxation. The Court is aware of this fact and has explained itself this way: the Constitution is not self-destructive.[409] The Constitution would not take away with one hand (the Fifth Amendment) the power it gave with the other. *McCray v. United States* stated:

> . . . [N]othing in those amendments [Fifth and Tenth] operates to take away the grant of power to tax conferred by the Constitution upon Congress. The

[403] Bolling v. Sharpe, 347 U.S. 497 (1954).

[404] *See* Ch. V.D.3.b(2).

[405] *See* Ch. V.D.3.b(7).

[406] *See, e.g.*, Steward Machine Co. v. Davis, 301 U.S. 548, 585 (1937).

[407] *Id.* at 585. Ch. V.D.3.b(1).

[408] *See, e.g.*, Burnet v. Brooks, 288 U.S. 378, 400 (1933). This subject is discussed in Ch. II.A.3.

[409] Billings v. United States, 232 U.S. 261, 282 (1914) (Congress could choose to levy an excise tax on foreign built boats chartered by U.S. persons, and not on U.S. built boats); Brushaber v. Union Pacific R. Co., 240 U.S. 1, 24 (1916 ("does not conflict with itself" by conferring the taxing power in one clause and taking it away in the Due Process Clause). *Cf.* Powell, at 58 (questioning the logic of the "not self-destructive" view and pointing out that the Court always holds open the possibility that a tax is not really a tax).

> contention on this subject rests upon the theory that the purpose and motive of Congress in exercising its undoubted powers may be inquired into by the courts, and the proposition is therefore disposed of by what has been said on that subject. . . . The judicial power may not usurp the functions of the legislative in order to control that branch of the government in the performance of its lawful duties. This was aptly pointed out in the extract heretofore made from the opinion in Treat v. White, 181 U.S. 264.[410]

Sometimes the Court has referred to a vague constitutional standard of fairness in taxation, which even it cannot define. In a handful of opinions it attempted to encapsulate the outer limit placed on the otherwise limitless taxing power as that line beyond which "free governments" cannot go in taxation or other regulation.[411] One of those opinions also referenced the similarly fundamental but vague principle that one person may not be taxed on the income of another:[412]

> It may be doubted by some, aside from express constitutional restrictions, whether the taxation by Congress of the property of one person, accompanied with an arbitrary provision that the rate of tax shall be fixed with reference to the sum of the property of another, thus bringing about the profound inequality which we have noticed, would not transcend the limitations arising from those fundamental conceptions of free government which underlie all constitutional systems.[413]

But in one of its most recent comments on the subject of the taxing power and the Due Process Clause generally the Court stated:

> It should be emphasized that the Court finds it unnecessary to examine the history of the Due Process Clause to determine whether it was intended as a "specific limitation" upon Congress' spending and taxing powers.[414] [It was not.]

(1) *Procedural Limits*

Historically due process of law meant only "the right of trial according to the process and proceedings of the common law."[415] The meaning gradually expanded into a variety of notions of procedural fairness, mostly involving notice and the right to be heard. The most important procedural defect (with substantive overtones) that the Court has discovered in federal taxes, retroactivity, has caused three federal tax provisions to be ruled unconstitutional, as discussed in Chapter V.D.3.b(4).

---

[410] McCray v. United States, 195 U.S. 27, 61 (1904).

[411] Billings v. United States, 232 U.S. 261, 283 (1914); United States v. Bennett, 232 U.S. 299, 305 (1914); McCray, 195 U.S. 27, 63 (1904) (unless "no free government" could pass such a law to destroy); Knowlton v. Moore, 178 U.S. 41, 77 (1900).

[412] *See* Ch. V.D.3.b(7)(c). *See also* Cummings, at ch. VI.F.2.a.

[413] Knowlton v. Moore, 178 U.S. 41, 77 (1900).

[414] Flast v. Cohen, 392 U.S. 83 n. 11 (1968).

[415] Story, at 661 (and this was related only to criminal trials). *See also* Davidson v. New Orleans, 96 U.S. 97 (1878) (state tax case).

Taxpayers (mostly in state tax cases discussed in Chapter IX) have objected on due process grounds to methods of (1) enacting taxes, (2) computing taxes, (3) assessing taxes, (4) collecting taxes, and (5) refunding taxes paid. Generally there are no due process rights as to enactment or assessment, minimal rights as to collection, and rights to notice and hearing only as to refund or before an individual is "finally" deprived of property.[416]

Specific principles of procedural due process in federal taxation that have been discussed by the Court include the following (including some state tax citations):

- Generally no notice is required of the adoption of a tax,[417] or of the specific taxpayer's liability under a general tax.[418] The theory is that the legislature has such a broad power to determine the subjects and rate of tax that there is nothing the taxpayer could say to avoid the tax by right, and so the taxpayer must rely on political rights and whatever "sunshine" laws generally apply to legislation. However, the principle does not extend to the part of tax determinations that require, for example, case by case determinations such as property valuations, if viewed as part of the tax adoption process.[419]
- The United States can assess tax first, and require the taxpayer to dispute the tax liability later, even though it has chosen not to do so in most cases.[420]
- The United States can collect first and require the taxpayer to dispute later.[421] The due process need not be a pre-deprivation remedy.[422] This is an application of the general rule that where property rights are concerned, prior review is not required as long as ultimate judicial review of the liability is available.[423] However, a non tax ruling indicated that a person need not

[416] *See, e.g.*, Central of Georgia R. Co. v. Wright, 207 U.S. 127 (1907) (state tax case; notice and an opportunity to be heard); McKesson Corp. v. Div. of Alcoholic Bevs., 496 U.S. 18, 37 n. 17 (1990) (state tax case). *See generally* Nina E. Olson, *Taking the Bull by Its Horns: Some Thoughts on Constitutional Due Process in Tax Collection*, 63 TAX LAW. 227 (2010).

[417] Parsons v. District of Columbia, 170 U.S. 45 (1898) (deemed to know the potential for taxation); Carson v. Brockton Sewerage Com., 182 U.S. 398, 401-403 (1901) (state tax case); Hagar v. Reclamation Dist. No. 108, 111 U.S. 701 (1884) (state tax case).

[418] Bell's Gap R. Co. v. Pennsylvania, 134 U.S. 232, 239 (1890) (state tax case).

[419] Hagar, 111 U.S. at 710. *See also* Chesebro v. Los Angeles County Flood Control Dist., 306 U.S. 459 (1939) (state tax case).

[420] Murray's Lessee v. Hoboken Land & Improv. Co., 59 U.S. 272 (1856) (an early analysis of the "law of the land"); G. M. Leasing Corp. v. United States, 429 U.S. 338 n. 18 (1977); Phillips v. Commissioner, 283 U.S. 589 (1931). *See also* Bell's Gap R. Co. v. Pennsylvania, 134 U.S. 232, 239 (1890) (state could tax on nominal value where taxpayer refused to file return).

[421] Murray's Lessee v. Hoboken Land & Improv. Co., 59 U.S. 272 (1856) (an early analysis of the "law of the land"); G. M. Leasing Corp. v. United States, 429 U.S. 338 n. 18 (1977); Phillips v. Commissioner, 283 U.S. 589 (1931). *See also* George Moore Ice Cream Co. v. Rose, 289 U.S. 373 (1933) (state tax case; due process demands that a taxpayer be allowed to present his defenses, but not necessarily before "entry of judgment").

[422] *See* McKesson Corp. v. Div. of Alcoholic Bevs., 496 U.S. 18 (1990) (state tax case); United States v. Clintwood Elkhorn Mining Co., 553 U.S. 1 (2008).

[423] Phillips v. Commissioner, 283 U.S. 589, 596 (1931); Carson v. Brockton Sewerage Com., 182 U.S. 398 (1901) (state tax case).

pay and sue for refund when it has a constitutional objection to an agency's claim for payment;[424] if that principle were extended to federal taxes it would entirely upset the federal tax assessment system (at least as to constitutional objections, which might proliferate).

- The power to distrain personal property (as well as real property) for the payment of taxes is not a deprivation of property without due process of law.[425] This reflects the need for taxes to be promptly collected, which is always important to the public welfare.[426] Therefore, when the IRS levies on a bank account the bank must pay and may not await a determination of the taxpayer's disagreement.[427]
- However, seizure of a taxpayer's property under a jeopardy assessment without any opportunity for the taxpayer to contest the seizure can provide due process grounds to avoid the Anti-Injunction Act where there are extraordinary circumstances causing irreparable harm for which the taxpayer had no adequate remedy at law, and it was apparent that, under the most liberal view of the law and the facts, the government could not establish its claim.[428]
- Due process of law for tax determination purposes does not necessarily mean a judicial proceeding; taxation is by nature administrative and not judicial; it is sufficient that the law provides for administrative appeal (with ultimate judicial review).[429]

---

[424] Horne v. Dep't of Agric., 569 U.S. 513 (2013); Horne v. Dep't of Agric., 576 U.S. 351 (2015).

[425] Springer v. United States, 102 U.S. 586 (1881). *See also* G. M. Leasing Corp. v. United States, 429 U.S. 338, 351-352 (1977); Bull v. United States, 295 U.S. 247, 260 (1935) (assessment "is given the force of a judgment, and if the amount assessed is not paid when due, administrative officials may seize the debtor's property to satisfy the debt."); Cheatham v. United States, 92 U.S. 85, 87-90 (1876); State Railroad Tax Cases, 92 U.S. 575, 612-615 (1876); Graham v. Du Pont, 262 U.S. 234, 255 (1923).

[426] The rationale underlying these decisions is that the very existence of government depends upon the prompt collection of the revenues. *See* Phillips v. Commissioner, 283 U.S. 589, 596-597 (1931) (The Court rejected a constitutional challenge to the statutory system under which taxes may be collected summarily without a pre-seizure judicial hearing. It was held that as long as there was an adequate opportunity for a post-seizure determination of the taxpayer's rights, the statute met the requirements of due process.); Commissioner v. Shapiro, 424 U.S. 614, 630-633 (1976); Fuentes v. Shevin, 407 U.S. 67, 91-92 (1972).

[427] United States v. National Bank of Commerce, 472 U.S. 713 (1985).

[428] Commissioner v. Shapiro, 424 U.S. 614 (1976). *Cf.* South Carolina v. Regan, 465 U.S. 367 (1984) (allowing the state's suit to proceed without a claim for refund by a taxpayer).

[429] Palmer v. McMahon, 133 U.S. 660 (1890); French v. Barber Asphalt Paving Co., 181 U.S. 324 (1901) (state tax case); Anniston Mfg. Co. v. Davis, 301 U.S. 337 (1937) (tax refunds may be required to be pursued first through an exclusive administrative remedy before Treasury employees, as long as it allows a full and fair consideration and retains the possibility of judicial review); United States v. Clintwood Elkhorn Mining Co., 553 U.S. 1, 9 (2008) (administrative exhaustion can be required of constitutional claims, including tax claims); United States v. Felt & Tarrant Mfg. Co., 283 U.S. 269, 272 (1931).

- The same procedures of appeal need not be provided to all taxpayers so long as due process is provided.[430] But some procedure of protest must be provided.[431] In a jeopardy assessment situation, the taxpayer is entitled to a deficiency notice so that it may petition the Tax Court.[432]
- Should the Supreme Court declare a statutory provision unconstitutional after liability based thereon has been determined by a closing agreement, the agreement stands.[433]
- The statute giving the United States priority to collect a tax debt in bankruptcy is constitutional. Chief Justice Marshall said that the Necessary and Proper Clause did not require that the act be "indispensably necessary" to give effect to a specified power.[434] Congress must possess the choice of means and cannot be denied a means because a court believes the end could be achieved in another way.[435] Tax debts have priority for other purposes as well.[436]
- The taxpayer may be required to bear the burden of proof or show why proof is impossible.[437] This includes proving that it did not pass a sales tax it paid to the government on to its customer, as a precondition of refund.[438]
- The tax Anti-Injunction Act does not deny constitutional rights to address the courts.[439]

---

[430] Kentucky Railroad Tax Cases, 115 U.S. 321, 337 (1885) (state tax case; railroad property could be assessed separately from other realty, and by a different method of procedure). However, this case relied on Missouri v. Lewis, 101 U.S. 22 (1880), which was based on different procedures in different parts of a thinly populated western state.

[431] Davidson v. New Orleans, 96 U.S. 97 (1878) (state tax case; a property tax levied for an improvement that is supposed to benefit the property can be made a personal liability of the owner and is not limited by the Constitution to a levy on the land.).

[432] *See* Laing v. United States, 423 U.S. 161 (1976) (but Justice Blackmun dissented, arguing that other remedies were available).

[433] *See* Rev. Rul. 56-322, 1956-2 C.B. 963, for authority and cases on point.

[434] United States v. Fisher, 6 U.S. 358, 396 (1805); County of Spokane v. United States, 279 U.S. 80 (1929).

[435] 6 U.S. 358.

[436] *See, e.g.*, Massachusetts v. United States, 333 U.S. 611 (1948) (insolvency).

[437] Anniston Mfg. Co. v. Davis, 301 U.S. 337 (1937) (this opinion also approved the shift in refund procedure from suing the local tax collector to suing the United States); United States v. Jefferson Elec. Mfg. Co., 291 U.S. 386 (1934) (taxpayer could be required to show that it had borne the tax for which it sued). One exception was found in Speiser v. Randall, 357 U.S. 513 (1958), holding that a state violated due process by requiring a taxpayer to take an oath as a condition of a tax exemption.

[438] United States v. Jefferson Elec. Mfg. Co., 291 U.S. 386, 401 (1934) (sales tax collector had to prove it had not passed on the tax to its customer; requirement was adopted after the refund accrued).

[439] Alexander v. "americans united," 416 U.S. 752, 759 (1974). *See* 26 U.S.C. § 7421.

- There is a possible category of exactions in the guise of a tax that are facially unconstitutional and therefore not subject to the tax Anti-Injunction Act.[440]
- Constitutional claims (for tax refunds) can be time barred just as other claims may be time barred.[441]
- The United States can require taxpayers to create paperwork to memorialize the transactions the United States desires to tax.[442]
- The taxpayer has no right to any particular form of assessment, because "The exact truth always lies in the knowledge of the manufacturer. His books show, or ought to show, everything that he has produced, and in an investigation of this kind, if he shows that his returns or stamps fully equal the amount of his production and sale, the burden will then be on the government to show a deficiency."[443]
- Taxpayer can be given a choice between paying tax one time on receipt of property or annually.[444]
- The federal "common law" of tax allowed the United States to collect interest on tax deficiencies even in the absence of a statute fixing an obligation to pay interest.[445] The rule was otherwise in many state courts. The taxpayer did not make a constitutional challenge to the interest, which the Court characterized as a penalty.
- As to secrecy of matters relating to taxation, the Court did not have to reach due process to reject the secrecy of a Special Tax Court Trial Judge opinion.[446] The Court did not even seriously entertain the possibility that

---

[440] United States v. Clintwood Elkhorn Mining Co., 553 U.S. 1, 12 (2008), *citing* Enochs v. Williams Packing & Nav. Co., 370 U.S. 1 (1962). *See also* South Carolina v. Regan, 465 U.S. 367 (1984); Commissioner v. Shapiro, 424 U.S. 614 (1976) (irreparable injury from jeopardy assessment, without any proof of liability by IRS); Bob Jones University v. Simon, 416 U.S. 725, 743 (1974) ("In 1922, the Court seized upon these dicta and permitted pre-enforcement injunctive suits against tax statutes that were viewed as penalties or as adjuncts to the criminal law. Hill v. Wallace, 259 U.S. 44 (1922); Lipke v. Lederer, 259 U.S. 557 (1922) (ruled that whether or not the exaction was a tax, the defendant did not receive due process); Regal Drug Corp. v. Wardell, 260 U.S. 386 (1922). Shortly thereafter, however, the Court made clear that *Hill*, *Lipke*, and *Regal Drug* were of narrow scope and had no application to pre-enforcement challenges to truly revenue-raising tax statutes. Graham v. Du Pont, 262 U.S. 234 (1923). Thus, the Court's first departure from a literal reading of the Act produced a prompt correction in course."

[441] United States v. Clintwood Elkhorn Mining Co., 553 U.S. 1, 9 (2008).

[442] Nicol v. Ames, 173 U.S. 509, 515-516 (1899).

[443] Dandelet v. Smith, 85 U.S. 642, 647 (1873); Bergdoll v. Pollock, 95 U.S. 337 (1877) (the taxpayer has only to refer to his books, which speak for themselves).

[444] Billings v. United States, 232 U.S. 261 (1914) (pay import duty on foreign built leased boats or annual excise tax).

[445] *Id.*

[446] Ballard v. Commissioner, 544 U.S. 40 (2005).

there might be a constitutional right to secrecy of one's tax returns.[447] The President is thought to have a constitutional right to see tax returns.[448]

- See Chapter VII.G for discussion of void for vagueness claims under the Due Process Clause in criminal cases.

Though important, the Anti-Injunction Act, 26 U. S. C. § 7421, referenced above, is not addressed further here beyond its constitutional support. It is of concern not only to taxpayers, who are generally remitted to the exclusive Tax Court and refund remedies, but also to non-taxpayers who cannot enjoy those remedies and must seek to avoid the Act if they are to contest taxes at all.[449]

(2) *Discrimination and Equal Protection*

(a) *General Principles*

Federal taxes today are subject to what has come to be called the equal protection component of the Due Process Clause of the Fifth Amendment. The Court read that component of the Fourteenth Amendment into the Fifth Amendment most clearly in an important 1954 civil rights opinion.[450] That component in effect subsumed or replaced an earlier argument by taxpayers that arbitrariness in federal taxation violated due process and could be rectified by judicially removing the "tax" from the category of tax and treating it as a taking of property, which was necessarily without just compensation (because there generally is no correlation between tax and benefits received),[451] and thus unconstitutional under the Fifth Amendment Due Process Clause (without regard to equal protection).

Although taxation might seem to be an area in which it is relatively easy to apply principles of equality due to the mathematical exactness with which differential taxation can be measured,[452] that exactitude disappears when one allows for differential taxation based on relatively minor differences in characteristics of the taxpayers, which always has been the rule in the United States.

---

[447] Flint v. Stone Tracy Co., 220 U.S. 107 (1911); United States v. Dickey, 268 U.S. 378 (1925).

[448] *See* Staff of the Joint Committee on Taxation, Confidentiality of Tax Returns (1975), JCS-38-75 (stating that a Chief Counsel so advised the President and citing constitutional provisions).

[449] *See, e.g.*, Alexander v. "americans united," 416 U.S. 752, 759 (1974); Bob Jones Univ. v. Simon, 416 U.S. 725 (1974); Enochs v. Williams Packing & Nav. Co., 370 U.S. 1 (1962); United States v. American Friends Service Committee, 419 U.S. 7 (1974). *See generally*, Cummings, *Standing to Sue About Taxes, Part 2*, Tax Notes Federal, July 15, 2019, p. 323; Cummings, *Standing to Sue About Taxes*, Tax Notes Federal, July 1, 2019, p. 45.

[450] Bolling v. Sharpe, 347 U.S. 497 (1954). This was the District of Columbia analogue to *Brown v. Board of Education*. There has been considerable scholarly debate about the wisdom of this reading, and wondering why the Due Process Clause could not have served as well, or better. *See* Kermit Roosevelt III, *Forget the Fundamentals: Fixing Substantive Due Process*, 8 U. Pa. J. Const. Law 983, 997 (2006) [hereinafter Roosevelt].

[451] *See* Ch. III.C.

[452] *See* Gray, at 4-5.

In practice, the Court has found discrimination in state and federal taxation to violate the Fifth Amendment's Due Process Clause (or the Fourteenth Amendment's Equal Protection Clause), in cases where nothing else was going on (such as a discrimination against interstate commerce or a perceived violation of "states' rights"), only due to (1) inequality based on a "fundamental right" or a "suspect classification,"[453] (2) retroactivity,[454] or (3) a truly arbitrary and totally inexplicable distinction rather than an odious one. The Supreme Court so far has not found any such defects in federal taxes, aside from three federal estate tax provisions ruled unconstitutional on account of their retroactivity within a narrow band of years.[455] The Court has recognized that tax laws are allowed even more leeway to be arbitrary than nontax commercial regulations not involving strict scrutiny, stating in a state tax decision " . . . in taxation, even more than in other fields, legislatures possess the greatest freedom in classification."[456]

True arbitrariness that the Court has found in state taxes is best exemplified by a taxing formula that simply had a mistake in its design, based on an incorrect factual assumption, rather than a rule that is explainable logically but for a reason that is disliked, or an approximation for administrative convenience.[457]

The historical progression of the federal tax equal protection rulings of the Court, like the Court's intergovernmental tax immunity rulings,[458] benefits from being studied in conjunction with the parallel state tax rulings (addressed in Ch. IX), particularly because state taxes were explicitly subject to equal protection under the Fourteenth Amendment, before equal protection was read into the Fifth Amendment in 1954. However, it must be kept in mind that the grounds of state and federal tax authority differ not only (1) because the recognition of a nondiscrimination element occurred earlier for state taxes than for federal taxes, but more importantly (2) because the majority of discrimination complaints against state taxes have involved at least in part claims of discrimination against

---

[453] *See* Ch. I.E.4.b, as to suspect classifications.

[454] *See* Ch. V.D.3.b(4).

[455] *Id.* But when DOMA was ruled unconstitutional on equal protection grounds the plaintiff got a tax refund. United States v. Windsor, 570 U.S. 744 (2013).

[456] Levin v. Commerce Energy, Inc., 560 U.S. 413 (2010), quoting Madden v. Kentucky, 309 U.S. 83, 88 (1940). *See also* Armour v. City of Indianapolis, 566 U.S. 673 (2012) ("And we have repeatedly pointed out that '[l]egislatures have especially broad latitude in creating classifications and distinctions in tax statutes.'").

[457] *See, e.g.*, Gast Realty & Inv. Co. v. Schneider Granite Co., 240 U.S. 55, 59 (1916) (The statutory criteria for defining the district to be taxed for a street improvement was based on lines drawn half way the distance to the next street. On one side of the new street the next street was 300 feet back; but on the taxpayer's side it was 1,000 feet back and taxpayer's lot ran all the way to that far off street. Taxpayer's lot was within the taxing district back 400-500 feet, half the way to the next street, which the opinion crucially found to be "much farther than the distance within which paving could be supposed to be a benefit." Based on that finding of fact, the opinion found the formula to be facially arbitrary, presumably because it resulted in treating opposite sides of the street differently, with no limit on the presumption of equal benefit. The opinion made clear in an addendum that it did not void the entire assessment district but only the tax on this taxpayer and those similarly situated.) *See* Ch. V.D.3.b(4), as to arbitrary and capricious taxes.

[458] *See* Ch. II.C.

interstate commerce or travel or newcomers, which has its own peculiarities based on the supremacy of the federal government in regulation of interstate commerce,[459] and (3) because indirect federal taxes were subject only to the uniformity requirement of Article I, section 8, clause 1, which was interpreted to require only geographical uniformity,[460] thus seeming to leave federal taxes unsusceptible to discrimination claims.

Likewise the course of the Court's federal and state tax equal protection rulings is analogous to the course of the tax versus regulation rulings:[461] a quite large percentage of the rulings striking down taxes is clustered in the 1920s and 1930s, up to the so called switch in time that saved the nine, the cessation of the Court's rulings against New Deal regulations and tax provisions.[462]

By eschewing wide ranging efforts to equalize federal taxation the Court has, in effect, rejected a form over substance approach to equal protection in taxation: if the subjects of taxation differ in form (as they almost always will) then they can be taxed differently, as discussed in the next chapter.

Beyond that, any effort to impose a structure on the Court's opinions in the area is frustrating. Sholley in 1938 proposed a classification of equal protection tax cases that imposes some needed order on the cases: tax classifications or distinctions based on (1) factual differences in the persons taxed and their transactions, (2) differences in their relationship to the fiscal interests of the state (for example, they paid other taxes), and (3) differences in the public interests (*i.e.*, a public interest in discouraging use of alcohol).[463]

Here we are concerned mostly with the category (1) cases, which prove the observation stated above that things that are different in fact can be taxed differently, even if the difference in the things taxed is insubstantial. In a sense these cases make the issue as simple as asking the question: are the things taxed differently of the same class or different classes, which difference alone justifies a difference in taxation. However, the cases are not so simple, because as Justice Stone pointed out, what appear to be the taxing distinctions made between

---

[459] *See* HELLERSTEIN & HELLERSTEIN, at ch. 3. *See* Armour v. City of Indianapolis, 566 U.S. 673 (2012) ("With but one exception, however, the cases to which they refer involve discrimination based on residence or length of residence. *E.g.*, Hooper v. Bernalillo County Assessor, 472 U. S. 612 (1985) (state tax preference distinguishing between long-term and short-term resident veterans); Williams v. Vermont, 472 U. S. 14 (1985) (state use tax that burdened out-of-state car buyers who moved in-state); Metro. Life Ins. Co. v. Ward, 470 U. S. 869 (1985) (state law that taxed out-of-state insurance companies at a higher rate than in-state companies); Zobel v. Williams, 457 U. S. 55(1982) (Alaska oil revenue "dividend" distribution system that favored long-term residents was unconstitutional, as would be a state tax that varied with length of residence).

[460] *See* Ch. V.D.3.a.

[461] *See* Ch. III.F.2.

[462] *See* BURNS, at 148.

[463] *See* John B. Sholley, *Equal Protection in Tax Legislation*, 24 VA. L. REV. 229, 234 (1938). Factual differences (*i.e.*, one type of coal versus another) have almost always been allowed to justify tax differences. *Id.* at 234-267. Distinctions based on compensating taxes, special benefits to the taxpayer, special burdens cast on the state, and administrative convenience, have faced greater resistance by the Court. *Id.* 388-404. The distinctions based on government intent to regulate face the most variation in decision. *Id.* at 404-414.

members within one class "must be presumed to rest on [a rational] basis if there is any conceivable state of facts which would support [a distinction]."[464] As to Sholley's category (2), generally the Court has not concerned itself with compensating federal taxes,[465] or the overall tax burden of one taxpayer relative to another or to some absolute amount.[466] The use of taxes to regulate, category (3), is discussed in Chapter III.E.

But as in other areas of the law, in theory even federal tax discriminations would have to survive stricter scrutiny if taxing distinctions were based on certain suspect categories (such as race or alienage, and limitations on free speech), a requirement commonly attributed to footnote 4 in *Carolene Products* (not a tax case and involving due process and not equal protection).[467] So far such strict scrutiny has not been applied to a federal tax rule.[468] However, as early as 1900 the Court identified in a state tax case the types of taxing distinction that could have no possible justification:

> . . . [I]f such discrimination were purely arbitrary, oppressive or capricious, and made to depend upon differences of color, race, nativity, religious opinions, political affiliations or other considerations having no possible connection with the duties of citizens as taxpayers, such exemption would be pure favoritism, and a denial of the equal protection of the laws to the less favored classes."[469]

See Chapter I.E.4.b, for discussion of heightened constitutional scrutiny for certain types of discrimination. See Chapter V.D.3.b(6), for discussion of discrimination through a general tax that does not encompass substantially similar cases due to use of a common definition established for administrative convenience. See Chapter IX for discussion of the state tax constitutional decisions of the Court generally.

---

[464] Carmichael v. Southern Coal & Coke Co., 301 U.S. 495, 509 (1937).

[465] *Cf.* Minneapolis Star & Tribune Co. v. Minn. Comm'r of Revenue, 460 U.S. 575 (1983) (discussing how sales and use taxes compensate for the inability to levy one or the other, but not finding the use tax on the press to fit into that mold); National Paper & Type Co. v. Bowers, 266 U.S. 373, 375-376 (1924) (Congress may have decided not to tax foreign corporations because they are taxed in their own countries); Kidd v. Alabama, 188 U.S. 730 (1903) (analyzing solely the Equal Protection Clause, Justice Holmes ruled that states could tax stock of foreign corporations because it could not tax their foreign, property, whereas it did tax the local property of local corporations whose stock was not taxed).

[466] *See, e.g.*, Swiss Oil Corp. v. Shanks, 273 U.S. 407 (1927) (crude oil tax plus state, county and local property taxes on oil company). *See also* Davidson v. New Orleans, 96 U.S. 97 (1878) (property had already been assessed for the same improvement project, swamp drainage); Patton v. Brady, 184 U.S. 608 (1902) (an excise tax on inventory could be increased and reapplied to the same inventory); United States v. Hudson, 299 U.S. 498 (1937) (in addition to the regular income tax a special tax equal to 50% of profit earned was imposed on transactions in silver bullion).

[467] United States v. Carolene Prod. Co., 304 U.S. 144, 152 n. 4 (1938); see Ch. I.E.4.b. The Court most recently harkened back to *Carolene* in Armour v. City of Indianapolis, 566 U.S. 673 (2012) for this principle.

[468] *See* Ch. I.E.4.b.

[469] American Sugar Refining Co. v. Louisiana, 179 U.S. 89, 92 (1900).

(b) *Tax Discrimination and Equal Protection*

Separate and quite distinct from the geographical uniformity required for indirect taxes under Article I, section 8, clause 1, the equal protection component of the Due Process Clause is an aspect of liberty guaranteed in the Fifth Amendment that also is applicable to federal taxes.[470] The Supreme Court has never ruled a federal tax law unconstitutional for lack of equal protection, outside the three rulings based on retroactivity of various rules of the federal estate tax.[471]

However, the Court has held out the possibility that discrimination in federal taxation could be so palpably arbitrary as to remove the exaction from the category of tax and place it in the category of a taking without compensation. The opinions generally dismiss that possibility by observing that the subject taxed is different, without feeling compelled to explain why the difference should make a difference in taxation, with two identified possible exceptions: (1) the discrimination arguably interferes with the exercise of a fundamental right, such as freedom of speech, or employs a suspect classification, such as race (in which case strict scrutiny will be applied);[472] or (2) interstate commerce is potentially discriminated against, in the case of state taxes (where Privileges and Immunities Clause issues also can arise).

Nevertheless, the Court will venture speculation about why a tax differentiation made sense to Congress or the state.[473] No doubt one reason the Court may choose not to examine too carefully the congressional thought processes is that Congress' favoring of various groups and special interests through taxation, and using taxes to regulate,[474] is so pervasive that it could hardly be unconstitutional, and is at the core of the political process.

The current state of equal protection law in the tax field was stated in a 2012 state tax equal protection decision, *Armour*:[475]

- The taxing distinction must have a rational relationship to a legitimate governmental purpose.

---

[470] Bolling v. Sharpe, 347 U.S. 497 (1954) (not a tax case but incorporating the equal protection analysis into due process as an aspect of liberty guaranteed by the Fifth Amendment); Regan v. Taxation with Representation, 461 U.S. 540, 547 (1983) (the opinion assumed the application of equal protection to a federal tax provision). *Cf.* Prudential Ins. Co. v. Benjamin, 328 U.S. 408, 431 n. 39 (1946) ("a different thing entirely" is the equal protection requirement applied to states from anything like the geographical uniformity requirement imposed on the federal government as to taxation).

[471] *See* Ch. V.D.3.b(4).

[472] Regan v. Taxation with Representation, 461 U.S. 540, 547 (1983) (but speech subsidy by taxation does not requires strict scrutiny). *See, e.g.*, Nancy E. Shurtz, *Gender Equity and Tax Policy: The Theory of Taxing Men*, 6 So. Cal. Rev. of Law and Women's Studies 485 (1997); Karen B. Brown, *Not Color- or Gender-Neutral: New Tax Treatment of Employment Discrimination Damages*, 7 So. Cal. Rev. of Law and Women's Studies 223 (1998).

[473] Regan v. Taxation with Representation, 461 U.S. 540, 550 (1983).

[474] *See* Ch. III.E.

[475] Armour v. City of Indianapolis, 566 U.S. 673 (2012).

- The government need not articulate the purpose (which makes the first principle dubious).
- Rationality means the legitimate government purpose is plausibly served by the distinction.
- When the distinction affects a fundamental right or is based on a suspect classification, stricter scrutiny will be applied, which means less deference is accorded the legislature.
- Subject matters that are local (in the case of state and local legislation), economic, social, and commercial matters and taxation generally do not require such strict scrutiny.
- When strict scrutiny is not applied, deference is accorded to the legislature, and even more deference is accorded in tax cases (which may mean that the court need not discover the purpose served by the distinction in taxation).
- Therefore, absent strict scrutiny a distinction will be presumed to rationally advance some legitimate purpose unless the complaining party carries the burden of proving otherwise, which requires disproving every conceivable basis for the distinction. Since the government need not have articulated its purpose, this process of proof entails hypothesizing purposes and disproving them. If the taxpayer wins it means the two legislative classifications will be taxed as one (although that does not necessarily dictate the remedy).

Federal equal protection—Bolling v. Sharpe. The Fifth Amendment does not contain an Equal Protection Clause, in contrast to that stated in the Fourteenth Amendment. However, the Court read the Equal Protection Clause of the Fourteenth Amendment into the Due Process Clause of the Fifth Amendment beginning in 1954 with a finding that a type of discrimination can be so unjustifiable as to violate the rights to liberty and due process.[476] Soon equal protection was promoted to a full-fledged, if implied, component of due process.[477] The component forbids an extremely unjustifiable form of discrimination.[478] The 1954 decision in *Bolling v. Sharpe* was a companion case to *Brown v. Board of Edu-*

---

[476] Bolling v. Sharpe, 347 U.S. 497 (1954).

[477] *See* United States Dep't of Ag. v. Moreno, 413 U.S. 528, 533 (1973) (the first Supreme Court opinion to use the term "equal protection component"). Later the Court said the the Due Process Clause imposes on the federal government requirements comparable to those that the Equal Protection Clause of the Fourteenth Amendment imposes on the states, citing Schweiker v. Wilson, 450 U.S. 221, 226 n. 6 (1981). When the *Bolling v. Sharpe* opinion was drafted, Justice Black evidently objected to a strict reliance on due process and citation of opinions such as Pierce v. Society of Sisters, 268 U.S. 510 (1925), written by Justice McReynolds and applying a sort of substantive due process to social issues. As a consequence, those cites were dropped and equal protection added as an aspect of due process. The shift was not viewed at the time as a major change. *See* SCHWARTZ, at 98-100.

[478] *See, e.g.*, Schneider v. Rusk, 377 U.S. 163, 168 (1964) (the statute made an impermissible distinction by assuming that naturalized citizens were less reliable than native born citizens).

cation,[479] but because *Sharpe* concerned the District of Columbia's segregated schools, it required Fifth and not Fourteenth Amendment analysis. It reached the same conclusion as *Brown*, based on finding freedom from such discrimination to be an aspect of liberty protected by the Fifth Amendment and stating:

> . . . "[E]qual protection of the laws" is a more explicit safeguard of prohibited unfairness than "due process of law," and, therefore, we do not imply that the two are always interchangeable phrases. But, as this Court has recognized, discrimination may be so unjustifiable as to be violative of due process.[480]

The earliest Supreme Court opinion that *Bolling v. Sharpe* cited for this principle of equal protection due process was an important federal tax opinion, *Steward Machine*.[481] The Court issued *Steward* on May 24, 1937, just weeks after the March 29, 1937 and April 12 decisions in *West Coast Hotel Co. v. Parrish* and *NLRB v. Jones & Laughlin Steel*, which upheld the Washington state minimum wage law and the National Labor Relations Act and marked the end of the Supreme Court's conservative resistance to progressive legislation, not only of the New Deal but in the states, sometimes called the switch in time that saved nine.[482] *Steward* upheld the federal unemployment compensation act and accompanying tax against various constitutional attacks, including one of discrimination based on the exemption of small employers. Justice Cardozo recognized the possibility of a discrimination challenge (which *Bolling* characterized as an equal protection challenge) to a tax, stating:

> The act of Congress is therefore valid, so far at least as its system of exemptions is concerned, and this though we assume that discrimination, if gross enough, is equivalent to confiscation and subject under the Fifth Amendment to challenge and annulment.[483]

Thus, this seminal statement of nondiscrimination under the Fifth Amendment is indirectly based on the high hurdle required to reclassify a tax from the category of tax to the category of a taking without just compensation, before equal protection was understood to apply to the Fifth Amendment. Because the Court had long recognized such a reclassification to be theoretically possible (it so ruled five times from 1922 to 1936 in federal tax cases), the standards for equal protection as to federal taxes should not really have changed when the component was discovered in 1954 to reside under due process.

Indeed there is no evidence that discovery of the component has made any decisional difference in Supreme Court federal tax cases, though the rhetoric changed (compare *Regan v. Taxation with Representation*, which is the first opinion to address equal protection in federal taxation since 1954, and the only one besides *Carlton*, a retroactivity case, and *Windsor*, which invalidated a non tax

---

[479] Brown v. Board of Education, 347 U.S. 483 (1954).

[480] 347 U.S. at 499.

[481] Steward Machine Co. v. Davis, 301 U.S. 548, 585 (1937).

[482] West Coast Hotel Co. v. Parrish, 300 U.S. 379 (1937); NLRB v. Jones & Laughlin Steel Corp., 301 U.S. 1 (1937). *See* BURNS, at 148.

[483] 301 U.S. at 585.

statute that affected the federal tax).[484] It is possible that the more liberal equal protection standards recited in civil rights cases could influence a greater skepticism of tax inequality, but it should not, except as to the "suspect categories" of race, and protected interests such as voting and perhaps free speech and the press that are specially protected.[485]

Discrimination before equal protection. Before the equal protection component of due process was recognized, the Court refused to entertain equal protection claims as such against federal taxes, refused to find that the Fifth Amendment contained an equal protection requirement, and remitted the taxpayers to the remote possibility of proving that the tax was "so wholly arbitrary as to amount to confiscation."[486] Such proof would remove the tax from its natural exclusion from the just compensation clause and treat it as any other taking without just compensation and so unconstitutional under the Fifth Amendment's Taking Clause, not the Due Process Clause, or perhaps in violation of the Tenth Amendment (if the United States could not regulate the thing taxed and the tax was not a tax). Thus before 1954 the classification of a levy as a tax determined the standard under which it was measured for discrimination purposes, which was (and is) a very low standard indeed.

As discussed in Chapter II.A.2, once the power to tax is found to exist with respect to a subject of taxation, taxes can be imposed to the maximum in terms of rate and scope; this explains why the power to tax involves the power to destroy. The "power to destroy" statement was first made with respect to a state tax targeted at the bank notes issued by the Bank of the United States branch in Maryland, a highly discriminatory tax. Nevertheless, *McCulloch v. Maryland* ruled it unconstitutional on supremacy grounds, not discrimination grounds.[487] And when the shoe was on the other foot and the United States imposed a tax only on the bank notes of state chartered banks, *Veazie Bank v. Fenno* upheld the tax despite (or perhaps because of) its purpose and effect to discriminatorily destroy the state bank currency.[488] Therefore, the touted ability of taxes to destroy could hardly work if federal taxes could not discriminate, because no tax has ever been designed to uniformly destroy the entire possible tax base, but rather only parts of it.

As a consequence, a huge body of case law built up allowing all manner of distinctions in federal taxation, justified in part by (1) the extremely broad grant of the taxing power (see Chapter II.A.2), (2) the Court's general view that the Constitution is not self-destructive, meaning that the Fifth Amendment was not

---

[484] Regan v. Taxation with Representation, 461 U.S. 540 (1983). *See* Ch. V.D.3.b(4), on retroactivity. The Court struck down DOMA on equal protection grounds, resulting in a tax refund. United States v. Windsor, 570 U.S. 744 (2013).

[485] *See* Ch. I.E.4.b.

[486] *See, e.g.*, La Belle Iron Works v. United States, 256 U.S. 377, 393 (1921) (not arbitrary); Steward Machine Co. v. Davis, 301 U.S. 548, 584 (1937); Sunshine Anthracite Coal Co. v. Adkins, 310 U.S. 381, 401 (1940) (neither does the Commerce Clause require equal treatment).

[487] *See* Ch. II.B.

[488] Veazie Bank v. Fenno, 75 U.S. 533 (1869).

meant to be a specific limitation on the taxing power,[489] and (3) the absence of an Equal Protection Clause from the Fifth Amendment. In addition the Court distinguished taxation from antitrust and similar regulatory schemes in which certain uniformity standards were applicable that did not apply to taxes; in contrast in taxation discrimination was allowed "between different trades and callings when not obviously exercised in a spirit of prejudice or favoritism [citing cases]."[490] In fact, taxing discrimination could be, can be, and is exercised in the spirit of favoritism all the time (federal taxation commonly benefits particular industries, such as the oil industry, ethanol producers and other farmers). Therefore, even the loose prohibition of prejudice is an empty gun.

Uniformity as the federal tax standard. The early discussions of equality of federal taxation arose in connection with the Constitution's uniformity requirement for indirect taxes in Article I, section 8, clause 1, and were resolved by the ruling that the only uniformity required was geographical.[491] Therefore, the analysis of discrimination in federal taxes is inextricably linked to the uniformity requirement and that is the fundamental explanation for the extremely loose standard. Once the Court found an indirect tax to be uniform throughout the United States, little if any more analysis was necessary: the Court dismissed seemingly unexplainable distinctions in federal taxation, indicating that there was no limit on the taxing distinctions that could be made by Congress.[492] Because territorial and not intrinsic uniformity was required, exemptions were unassailable.[493]

Most discussions of inequality or discrimination in taxation arose in cases involving state taxes that arguably discriminated against interstate commerce or involved intergovernmental immunity (as in *McCulloch v. Maryland*). See generally Chapter IX. In the 1870s cases started to arise questioning equality of treatment under state laws or constitutions, which themselves required some sort of equality in state taxation.[494] A remarkable number of the complaining taxpayers were railroads, whose litigation against taxes and regulations, both state and federal, effectively created large parts of the case law of those subjects.

---

[489] Billings v. United States, 232 U.S. 261, 282 (1914) (Congress could choose to levy an excise tax on foreign built boats chartered by U.S. persons, and not U.S. built boats); Brushaber v. Union Pacific R. Co., 240 U.S. 1, 24 (1916).

[490] *See, e.g.*, Cook v. Marshall County, 196 U.S. 261 (1905), *citing* Kentucky Railroad Tax Cases, 115 U.S. 321 (1885); Magoun v. Illinois Trust & Savings Bank, 170 U.S. 283 (1898); American Sugar Refining Co. v. Louisiana, 179 U.S. 89 (1900); Bell's Gap R. Co. v. Pennsylvania, 134 U.S. 232 (1890); Connolly v. Union Sewer Pipe Co., 184 U.S. 540 (1902).

[491] *See* Ch. II.C.2.

[492] *See* Treat v. White, 181 U.S. 264 (1901) (Congress can choose to require a stamp tax for a call but not a put on stock, with no reason discussed or needed; Fifth Amendment not mentioned, possibly because taxpayer was *pro se*); Flint v. Stone Tracy Co., 220 U.S. 107, 158-159 (1911) (listing cases).

[493] *See, e.g.*, Edye v. Robertson, 112 U.S. 580 (1884) (Court rejected arguments that head taxes on persons arriving by ship could not be uniform because no tax was levied on train travel and ports were not evenly distributed in the nation); Knowlton v. Moore, 178 U.S. 41 (1900). *See also* La Belle Iron Works v. United States, 256 U.S. 377 (1921) (stating that the Fifth Amendment has no equal protection clause).

[494] *See, e.g.*, La. v. Pilsbury, 105 U.S. 278 (1882).

In those cases and analogous federal tax cases the Court began to entertain the possibility of a distinction so arbitrary as to be wholly unexplainable, without finding such to exist on the facts.[495] Then federal taxpayers began to assert the Equal Protection Clause of the Fourteenth Amendment by implication to federal taxes and the Court began to assume that the due process requirement of the Fifth Amendment and Equal Protection Clause of the Fourteenth Amendment were similar (but Congress should not be subject to any stricter standard than that applied to the states),[496] or at least asserted that a discrimination would stand under the Fourteenth Amendment and so necessarily will stand under the Fifth.[497]

The very high threshold that the Court previously had established for equal protection of the law claims against state taxes obviously informs the Court's later evaluation of equal protection claims against federal taxes (taking care to disentangle the Commerce Clause discrimination component of many of those cases). The state tax cases required only some basis that appeared to the Court adequate or reasonable for a classification.[498] The Court's opinions frequently cite *Bell's Gap* as the origin of the expansive reading of state taxing powers in the face of an equality claim:

---

[495] *See* McCray v. United States, 195 U.S. 27, 62 (1904) ("for the sake of argument" but finding an explanation for taxing colored margarine and not colored butter).

[496] *See* Flint v. Stone Tracy Co., 220 U.S. 107, 161 (1911) ("even if the principles of the Fourteenth Amendment were applicable to this case . . ."); a note at p. 159 contains a list of federal taxes that obviously picked and chose seemingly random objects of taxation); Fernandez v. Wiener, 326 U.S. 340 (1945) (held that the fact that estate tax falls on community property and not similar private contractual arrangements does not violate the Uniformity Clause and there is no other more restrictive uniformity requirement under the Equal Protection Clause; if there were, Congress would be subject to an equality requirement more restrictive than that imposed on the states).

[497] Steward Machine Co. v. Davis, 301 U.S. 548, 584 (1937) ("The Fifth Amendment unlike the Fourteenth has no equal protection clause. . . . But even the states, though subject to such a clause, are not confined to a formula of rigid uniformity in framing measures of taxation. Swiss Oil Corp. v. Shanks . . . They [states] may tax some kinds of property at one rate, and others at another, and exempt others altogether. Bell's Gap R. Co. v. Pennsylvania . . .; Stebbins v. Riley . . .; Ohio Oil Co. v. Conway . . . . They may lay an excise on the operations of a particular kind of business, and exempt some other kind of business closely akin thereto. Quong Wing v. Kirkendall . . .; American Sugar Refining Co. v. Louisiana . . .; Armour Packing Co. v. Lacy . . .; Brown-Forman Co. v. Kentucky . . .; Heisler v. Thomas Colliery Co. . . .; State Bd. of Tax Comm'rs v. Jackson . . . . If this latitude of judgment is lawful for the states, it is lawful, a fortiori, in legislation by the Congress, which is subject to restraints less narrow and confining. Quong Wing v. Kirkendall."). In the latter case, Quong Wing v. Kirkendall, 223 U.S. 59 (1912), Justice Holmes stated: "Like the United States, although with more restriction and in less degree, a state may carry out a policy, even a policy with which we might disagree."

[498] *See, e.g.*, Swiss Oil Corp. v. Shanks, 273 U.S. 407, 413 (1927) ("Unlike the state constitution . . . the Fourteenth Amendment does not require equality of taxation."); Gulf, C. & S. F. R. Co. v. Ellis, 165 U.S. 150, 165 (1897), *cited in* Magoun v. Illinois Trust & Savings Bank, 170 U.S. 283 (1898); Kentucky Railroad Tax Cases, 115 U.S. 321, 337 (1885) (railroad property could be assessed separately from other realty, and by a different method of procedure).

> It may, if it chooses, exempt certain classes of property from any taxation at all, such as churches, libraries and the property of charitable institutions. It may impose different specific taxes upon different trades and professions, and may vary the rates of excise upon various products; it may tax real estate and personal property in a different manner; it may tax visible property only, and not tax securities for payment of money; it may allow deductions for indebtedness, or not allow them. All such regulations, and those of like character, so long as they proceed within reasonable limits and general usage, are within the discretion of the state legislature, or the people of the State in framing their Constitution. But clear and hostile discriminations against particular persons and classes, especially such as are of an unusual character, unknown to the practice of our governments, might be obnoxious to the constitutional prohibition. It would, however, be impracticable and unwise to attempt to lay down any general rule or definition on the subject, that would include all cases. They must be decided as they arise. We think that we are safe in saying, that the Fourteenth Amendment was not intended to compel the State to adopt an iron rule of equal taxation. If that were its proper construction, it would not only supersede all those constitutional provisions and laws of some of the States, whose object is to secure equality of taxation, and which are usually accompanied with qualifications deemed material; but it would render nugatory those discriminations which the best interests of society require; which are necessary for the encouragement of needed and useful industries, and the discouragement of intemperance and vice; and which every State, in one form or another, deems it expedient to adopt.[499]

As to the degree of grossness of a distinction that will invalidate a tax, the terminology ranges from gross in *Bell's Gap* to "arbitrary and capricious" in a more recent federal tax opinion of the Court.[500]

Current federal tax equal protection law. Most recently the Court has purported to state its views on Fifth Amendment equal protection in federal taxation generally in *Regan v. Taxation with Representation.*[501] The taxpayer complained that it was discriminated against in comparison with veterans groups, which could both receive tax deductible contributions and lobby. The Court's holding rejected the claim by refusing to apply strict scrutiny, since the alleged discrimination was not based on the content of the speech. In describing equal protection's application to taxation generally the opinion at first recited the broad civil rights cases mantra requiring a search for a "rational relation to a legitimate governmental purpose." But it short-circuited such search by then referring back to the historically broad pass given to tax discrimination; that is, taxes are different and

---

[499] Bell's Gap R. Co. v. Pennsylvania, 134 U.S. 232, 238 (1890). *See also* Carmichael v. Southern Coal & Coke Co., 301 U.S. 495, 514 (1937): ("Neither due process nor equal protection imposes upon a state any rigid rule of equality of taxation. . . . This Court has repeatedly held that inequalities which result from a singling out of one particular class for taxation or exemption, infringe no constitutional limitation. . . . [numerous citations omitted].").

[500] Fernandez v. Wiener, 326 U.S. 340, 358 (1945).

[501] Regan v. Taxation with Representation, 461 U.S. 540 (1983).

are not subject to even the reasonableness standard, unless it be read as referring to no more than the hypothetical wholly arbitrary tax that is a taking.

(c) *Tax Discrimination: The Equal Protection Cases*

Although it is important to include many state tax cases in this review, most of the decisions based on multiple state taxation of interstate commerce are excluded as peculiar to state taxation. Inclusion of some state tax decisions of the Court makes it necessary to have a firm grip on the somewhat counterintuitive rules for state taxation of foreign corporations (as most of these cases involved corporations): (1) corporations are not citizens of the United States for purpose of the protection of privileges and immunities of citizenship;[502] (2) corporations are entitled as "persons" to equal protection of the laws of states;[503] (3) as a result, once admitted to operate in a state, they must be treated as domestic corporations, meaning that taxing distinctions generally cannot be based on their foreign origin (almost like a suspect category);[504] (4) admission to engage in business in the state can be conditioned on payment of fees and other requirements and licenses not imposed on domestic corporations, but such additional requirements must not impinge on constitutional rights; although this statement of principle retains the theoretical possibility of a differential entry tax, it probably means in practice that states cannot impose a domestication tax or fee that is greater than the incorporation tax or fee;[505] and (5) under the Commerce Clause a state's tax regime cannot discriminate against interstate commerce.[506]

The Supreme Court's federal tax equal protection and discrimination decisions, and selected state tax decisions, plus certain important nontax decisions and other pertinent events, are listed below.[507] They support the general principles stated in Chapter V.D.3.a. All of the federal tax decisions invalidating a tax

---

[502] *See* Pembina Consolidated Silver & Mining Co. v. Pennsylvania, 125 U.S. 181 (1888).

[503] *See* Wheeling Steel Corp. v. Glander, 337 U.S. 562 (1949) (in which Justice Jackson wrote a separate opinion to his own majority opinion to explain how this principle had become established, be it right or wrong).

[504] *Id.*

[505] Western & Southern Life Ins. Co. v. State Bd. of Equalization, 451 U.S. 648 (1981) (this case involved an insurance company, which is a good laboratory for equal protection claims because the Commerce Clause did not apply to state regulation of insurance; the opinion stated: "whatever the extent of a State's authority to exclude foreign corporations from doing business within its boundaries, that authority does not justify imposition of more onerous taxes or other burdens on foreign corporations than those imposed on domestic corporations, unless the discrimination between foreign and domestic corporations bears a rational relation to a legitimate state purpose."). Many states charge a lower fee for incorporating a new corporation than for a certificate of authority for a foreign corporation to do business in the state, but the amounts are usually small. However, Mississippi charges $50 for incorporation and $500 for a certificate of authority. *See* Chapter IX.

[506] *See, e.g.*, Complete Auto Transit, Inc. v. Brady, 430 U.S. 274 (1977). *See generally* HELLERSTEIN & HELLERSTEIN, at ¶ 4.12[1].

[507] *See generally*, John B. Sholley, *Corporate Taxpayers and the Equal Protection Clause*, 31 ILL. L. REV. 567 (1937) [hereinafter Sholley]. That article, a Ph.D. dissertation, chronicles all equal protection tax cases up to 1938, citing many not contained in this Chapter.

on equal protection or discrimination grounds involved retroactivity of an estate tax provision.

- 1796 (federal): The Court's first federal tax decision declined to treat a tax on carriages as a direct tax, in part, because trying to apportion such a tax as a direct tax among the states would cause the "grossest inequality."[508] This observation reflects the understanding that one aim of the direct-indirect tax rules was equality of the sorts that concerned the Founders: the Uniformity Clause should produce identical treatment wherever the taxed subjects were found; direct taxes would be spread about roughly on the basis of relative populations of the states, but that sort of equality (or proportionality) could not also produce equal taxation of the same objects of taxation wherever found.[509]

- 1804 (federal): Chief Justice Marshall said of the difference between a tax on home distilling and commercial sugar production: "it is not for the courts to beat down these distinctions on the allegation that they are capriciously made, and therefore to be disregarded. It is the duty of the court to discover the intention of the legislature, and to respect that intention."[510]

- 1852 (federal): A statute allowed a reduction in tariffs for leakage of liquor taxed by the gallon; the taxpayer wanted to apply that reduction to liquor taxed by value; the Court said that despite any discrimination, Congress created the difference by the plain meaning of the section and it would be so limited.[511]

- 1868 (state): On July 9, 1868 the Fourteenth Amendment to the Constitution was ratified.

- 1870 (state): Congress enacted a voting rights act, ch. 114, section 16 of which stated that all persons shall be subject to the same state taxes as "white citizens" of states.[512] This was perhaps the only aspect of the equal protection of the laws that the Negro citizens quickly enjoyed.

- 1873 (state): In an argument not to be repeated again by a taxing authority, a state was the first party to raise the Fourteenth Amendment in the *Case of State Freight Tax*.[513] The taxpayer was a railroad that did not want to pay a local tax and the state argued that if the interstate freight could not be taxed then the local persons would be discriminated against because they would be taxed unequally on their local shipping. The Court ruled that the tax was invalid because it was not a fee and was on interstate commerce, which at that time was thought to be beyond the state's power to tax.

---

[508] Hylton v. United States, 3 U.S. 171 (1796).
[509] *See* Ch. V.B.
[510] Pennington v. Coxe, 6 U.S. 33 (1804).
[511] Lawrence v. Caswell, 54 U.S. 488 (1852).
[512] This became section 1977 of the Revised Statutes of 1873, p. 348.
[513] Case of State Freight Tax, 82 U.S. 232 (1873).

- 1878 (state): The Court announced generally that the Fourteenth Amendment did not prohibit unequal taxation by the states.[514] Even though the opinion recited the Equal Protection Clause, it only addressed due process, which it treated as wholly directed to procedural rights of notice and hearing.[515]
- 1884 (federal): The *Head Money Cases* considered briefly and rejected the claim that the tax on immigrants was not uniform, linking the Ports Clause with the Uniformity Clause.[516]
- 1885 (state): The *Kentucky Railroad Tax Cases* was the first decision specifically considering (and rejecting) an equal protection argument by the taxpayer. It ruled that the state could classify railroad companies differently from other companies for purposes of the method of valuing their property for ad valorem tax, and so long as all within the class were treated alike the valuation provided equal protection.[517] The right to classify arose out of the "inherent nature of the property" and the power of the state to tax.
- 1886 (state nontax): The important decision in *Yick Wo v. Hopkins* ruled that Chinese persons could not be discriminated against explicitly in the operation of laundries, under the Fourteenth Amendment, based on the accompanying statute giving all persons rights equal to those of white citizens.[518]
- 1886 (state): As in several other decisions involving railroads, the Court sought for statutory grounds to rule taxes on railroads invalid (here that the tax improperly included fences that the railroads did not own), evidently in part to avoid ruling on the constitutional assertions that Mr. Justice Field wanted to address (his concurrence asserted an equal protection ground).[519]
- 1886 (state): A state did not deny equal protection when it required a license tax to be paid by a foreign insurance corporation (not in interstate commerce) even though no such tax was imposed on local corporations.[520]

---

514 Davidson v. New Orleans, 96 U.S. 97 (1878). *See generally* Sholley. The article observes that this view was in line with the minimal scope the Court initially accorded the Fourteenth Amendment in the *Slaughter-House Cases*; *see* Ch. V.D.3.b(7). However, Justices Field and Bradley attacked this position as they did the similar position on economic regulation. Sholley, at 230.

515 The opinion also made a curious distinction of the frequently cited opinion in Loan Ass'n v. Topeka, 87 U.S. 655 (1874), which purported to say that a tax had to be levied for a "public purpose" but was decided that way because it arose from a circuit court; the same approach would not be applied in an appeal from a state supreme court.

516 Edye v. Robertson, 112 U.S. 580 (1884). Similarly, Knowlton v. Moore, 178 U.S. 41, 104-106 (1900) stated that the meaning of the ports clause and the taxing power was identical insofar as the required uniformity was concerned.

517 Kentucky Railroad Tax Cases, 115 U.S. 321 (1885). Railroads continued to make and lose the same argument. *See* Nashville, C. & S. L. Railway v. Browning, 310 U.S. 362 (1940).

518 Yick Wo v. Hopkins, 118 U.S. 356 (1886).

519 San Bernardino County v. So. Pac. R. Co., 118 U.S. 417 (1886).

520 Philadelphia Fire Ass'n v. New York, 119 U.S. 110 (1886); *see also* Pembina Consol. Silver Mining & Milling Co. v. Pennsylvania, 125 U.S. 181 (1888).

The ruling relied on the prior ruling that corporations are not entitled to "privileges and immunities" protections under Article IV, section 2.[521] But this line of cases allowing discrimination against out of state corporations in state taxation is at odds with the Commerce Clause and also was eventually overturned if not overruled under the Equal Protection Clause.[522]

- 1890 (state): *Bell's Gap* (quoted above) is the most widely cited early opinion holding that states can make almost any sort of distinctions in taxation.[523] It ruled against the railroad plaintiff and approved differentiation "within reasonable limits and general usage."[524] However unremarkable the statements in this opinion now may appear to be, it imposed by dictum an outer limitation that did not previously exist.[525]
- 1892 (state): The Court recognized that true equality of taxation actually requires differentiation among differently situated taxpayers.[526] This is an insightful, but seldom discussed, concept.[527]

---

[521] *See* Paul v. Virginia, 75 U.S. 168 (1869) (ruling that out of state corporations are not citizens of the United States and so are not entitled to privileges and immunities of citizenship; also that insurance was not an interstate commerce transaction), *overturned*, United States v. South-Eastern Underwriters Association, 322 U.S. 533 (1944) (insurance is a transaction in interstate commerce).

[522] Western & Southern Life Ins. Co. v. State Bd. of Equalization, 451 U.S. 648 n. 15 (1981) (overruling *Paul v. Virginia* as to discrimination in allowing foreign corporations to operate in the state). The beginning of this line of cases was Bank of Augusta v. Earle, 38 U.S. 519 (1839), which ruled that a corporation chartered by another state could do business in other states, subject to regulation, which set up the issue of what regulation was reasonable, as discussed in *W. & S. Life Ins. Co.* The ability of corporations to operate outside their states of incorporation was, of course, crucial to the economic development of the country and the *Earle* decision was very important.

[523] Bell's Gap R. Co. v. Pennsylvania, 134 U.S. 232 (1890).

[524] 134 U.S. at 237.

[525] Sholley identifies this decision as the starting point of the development of the Equal Protection Clause as a limitation on state taxing power, citing dictum in Justice Bradley's opinion, even though the tax at issue was upheld. *See* Sholley, at 231. *Cf.* Davidson v. New Orleans.

[526] Pacific Express Co. v. Seibert, 142 U.S. 339, 351 (1892) (". . . that a system which imposes the same tax upon every species of property, irrespective of its nature or condition or class, will be destructive of the principle of uniformity and equality in taxation and of a just adaptation of property to its burdens.").

[527] *See* Tappan v. Merchants' National Bank, 86 U.S. 490, 504 (1874) ("Absolute equality in taxation can never be attained. That system is the best which comes the nearest to it. The same rules cannot be applied to the listing and valuation of all kinds of property. Railroads, banks, partnerships, manufacturing associations, telegraph companies, and each one of the numerous other agencies of business which the inventions of the age are constantly bringing into existence, require different machinery for the purposes of their taxation. The object should be to place the burden so that it will bear as nearly as possible equally upon all. For this purpose different systems, adjusted with reference to the valuation of different kinds of property, are adopted. The courts permit this. Thus, in a case in Illinois, involving the system adopted for the taxation of bank shares, it was said by the Supreme Court, 'in view of this legislation it must be apparent that a system of taxation for bank shares was designed peculiar to itself and independent of the general revenue laws of the State;' and the authority of the law was sustained and enforced."); State Railroad Tax Cases, 92 U.S. 575 (1876).

- 1897 (state nontax): Railroad prevailed against a state statute that required only railroads to pay a plaintiff's attorney's fee up to $10.[528] The discrimination was said to be arbitrary, with this general statement: "It is apparent that the mere fact of classification is not sufficient to relieve a statute from the reach of the equality clause of the Fourteenth Amendment, and that in all cases it must appear not only that a classification has been made, but also that it is one based upon some reasonable ground—some difference which bears a just and proper relation to the attempted classification—and is not a mere arbitrary selection."[529] However, the application of such a formula to taxes seems meaningless, because, for example, different taxes from butchers and bakers have always been assumed to be constitutional, despite a total absence of any distinction in protection received from the government.[530]

- 1898 (state): *Magoun* upheld a state inheritance tax that applied different rates and exemptions depending on degree of relationship.[531] It referred back to *Bell's Gap* for an explanation of the outer limits of distinctions in state taxation allowable under the Fourteenth Amendment. The distinction in the law at issue was based on a difference in the taxpayer's ability to pay.

- 1899 (federal): *Nicol v. Ames* is the first ruling on a federal tax that considered a uniformity argument not involving interstate commerce or governmental instrumentalities and that spoke in some terms other than geographical uniformity.[532] It upheld a gross receipts tax on sales, without deductions for costs. The opinion ruled that sales on commodity exchanges may be taxed although identical sales not made on exchanges are not taxed, stating the guiding principle as follows, citing state tax cases: "The question always is, when a classification is made, whether there is any reasonable ground for it, or whether it is only and simply arbitrary, based upon no real distinction and entirely unnatural."[533] The opinion, perhaps simply speaking in the same terms in which the taxpayer had argued the case, implied that the uniformity requirement for indirect federal taxes had an alternate "meaning [of] uniformity as to all the taxpayers similarly situated with regard to the subject-matter of the tax, ..."[534]

- 1900 (federal): *Knowlton v. Moore* is an extensive and important opinion upholding the federal estate tax.[535] It rejected arguments of non-uniformity based on every distinction made by the taxing statute, deciding that unifor-

---

[528] Gulf, C. & S. F. R. Co. v. Ellis, 165 U.S. 150 (1897).
[529] 165 U.S. at 165-166.
[530] *See* Sholley, at 233.
[531] Magoun v. Illinois Trust & Savings Bank, 170 U.S. 283 (1898).
[532] Nicol v. Ames, 173 U.S. 509 (1899). This case involved sales on the Chicago Board of Trade, a frequent source of federal tax litigation. *See* Hill v. Wallace, 259 U.S. 44 (1922).
[533] 173 U.S. at 521.
[534] *Id.* This theory evidently was not later repeated by the Court, which defined uniformity solely on the basis of geography in *Knowlton v. Moore*.
[535] Knowlton v. Moore, 178 U.S. 41 (1900).

mity of indirect taxes required not intrinsic equality of a tax as applied to each individual but geographical uniformity wherever the subject of taxation was found within the United States. The rejected arguments included: the tax could not apply with intrinsic equality because of its progressive rates; and the estate of one individual would pay more per amount of value than that of another individual because of the overall larger size of the estate or other factors on which the statute varied the tax. Although the 1884 *Head Money Cases* said that uniformity meant the federal tax operates the same throughout the United States, *Knowlton* treated the question as one of "original impression."[536] It pointed out a major problem that likely encouraged many challenges to federal taxes for lack of uniformity: state constitutions frequently contained requirements that taxes be "equal and uniform," which "with practical unanimity" had been interpreted to require intrinsic uniformity.[537] The opinion employed a variety of reasons to distinguish the federal uniformity requirement from the state requirements: (1) ruling for the taxpayer would establish a much stricter equality rule for duties, excises and imposts while direct taxes obviously would be non-uniform because of the need to apportion the taxes based on states' populations; (2) England never applied such a rule of equality; (3) the Colonies did not either; (4) in practice Congress made many distinctions for tax purposes from the earliest days, particularly as to imports to be subject to tariffs (indeed statutes levying import duties are hugely detailed, making all sorts of distinctions with no apparent reason, or with purely regulatory or political reasons); (5) to rule otherwise would produce a paralysis akin to that which the Confederation imposed on the general government (the records of the Constitutional Convention show that the Founders intended only general operation of taxes throughout the country); and (6) the Ports Clause and the Uniformity Clause had the same uniformity requirement, and ports obviously are not equally distributed among the states. *Knowlton* finally considered and rejected the all-purpose Fifth Amendment objection that the tax was just excessive and unfair, referring back to the statement in *Magoun*, which had quoted *Bell's Gap*.

- 1900 (state): The Court ruled that a state could choose to exempt farmers who refined their own sugar from tax while taxing refiners.[538] The United States had made a similar exemption in 1815. The opinion included this early statement that can be viewed as a precursor of Justice Stone's footnote 4 in *Carolene Products*: "Of course, if such discrimination were purely arbitrary, oppressive or capricious, and made to depend upon differences of

---

536 178 U.S. at 87.

537 *Id.*

538 American Sugar Refining Co. v. Louisiana, 179 U.S. 89 (1900). *Distinguished*, because it involved taxes, by Connolly v. Union Sewer Pipe Co., 184 U.S. 540 (1902) (an antitrust regulation case). Note that the Sugar Refining Company was part of the Sugar Trust that escaped regulation as a monopoly in United States v. E. C. Knight Co., 156 U.S. 1 (1895).

color, race, nativity, religious opinions, political affiliations or other considerations having no possible connection with the duties of citizens as taxpayers, such exemption would be pure favoritism, and a denial of the equal protection of the laws to the less favored classes."[539]

- 1901 (federal): *Treat v. White* ruled that Congress can choose to require a stamp tax for a call but not a put on stock, with no reason discussed or needed; the Fifth Amendment was not mentioned.[540] The pro se plaintiff was a lawyer, member of the stock exchange and Republican member of Congress. *Treat* is the support cited by *Hill v. Wallace* for its dictum that a second commodities exchange tax not there at issue would be constitutional, but which it was ruled not to be in *Trusler v. Crooks*.[541]
- 1902 (state nontax): The Court in an antitrust case contrasted a state's greater ability to make taxing distinctions under the Fourteenth Amendment with stricter standards applied to limit the state's exercise of the police power.[542] This contrast was already seen in the 1900 loss of the Sugar Trust member in *American Sugar Refining*, cited above, and the Trust's 1895 victory in the *E. C. Knight* ruling against the Sherman Act application.
- 1902 (federal): *Patton v. Brady* ruled that the rate of an excise tax on tobacco could be increased between the date the taxpayer bought the tobacco and paid the original rate and when it sold the tobacco.[543] Although the plaintiff did not raise the Fifth Amendment, it raised uniformity, as to which the Court said: ". . . [C]ourts may not add new conditions, and the statute in question fully complies with that requirement. It is not the province of the judiciary to inquire whether the excise is reasonable in amount, or in respect to the property to which it is applied. Those are matters in respect to which the legislative determination is final."[544] The decision also is viewed as approving double taxation.[545]

---

[539] 179 U.S. at 92. United States v. Carolene Prod. Co., 304 U.S. 144, 152 n. 4 (1938). *See* Ch. V.D.3.b(3), for discussion of discrimination standards.

[540] Treat v. White, 181 U.S. 264 (1901).

[541] For discussion of these two decisions see Ch. III.F.

[542] Connolly v. Union Sewer Pipe Co., 184 U.S. 540, 563 (1902) ("It is one thing to exert the power of taxation so as to meet the expenses of government, and at the same time, indirectly, to build up or protect particular interests or industries. It is quite a different thing for the State, under its general police power, to enter the domain of trade or commerce, and discriminate against some by declaring that particular classes within its jurisdiction shall be exempt from the operation of a general statute making it criminal to do certain things connected with domestic trade or commerce. Such a statute is not a legitimate exertion of the power of classification, rests upon no reasonable basis, is purely arbitrary, and plainly denies the equal protection of the laws to those against whom it discriminates.").

[543] Patton v. Brady, 184 U.S. 608 (1902).

[544] *Id.* at 623.

[545] Staff of the Joint Committee on Taxation, The Taxing Power of the Federal and State Governments 70-71 (1936) (available on Joint Committee website).

- 1903 (state): Analyzing solely the Equal Protection Clause, Justice Holmes ruled that states could tax stock of foreign corporations because it could not tax their foreign, property, whereas it did tax the local property of local corporations whose stock was not taxed.[546] This and other decisions stand for the proposition that purely under equal protection analysis the place of incorporation is a permissible distinguishing factor; but this view has been bypassed by later Commerce Clause decisions that require strict scrutiny of discriminations against out of state corporations.[547]
- 1904 (federal): The very important *McCray* decision considered "for the sake of argument" the inequality of taxation of colored margarine and natural butter, but found an explanation (one was butter and the other not).[548] The Court had already ruled that general regulation by a state forbidding coloring of margarine was constitutional and so the tax ruling was hardly an extension as to discrimination.[549] The *McCray* opinion restated the theoretical possibility that a tax that destroyed something beyond the power of the United States to destroy might cause it to find the tax unconstitutional, but not this tax. *McCray* is important for the fact that the Court made this statement in the context of a power to regulate that was solely derivative of the power to tax, and not separately justified under the Commerce Clause, which the opinion did not mention.
- 1905 (state): *Cook v. Marshall County* approved a distinction in taxation between selling at retail and wholesale.[550]
- 1905 (state): *Metropolitan Street Railway* rejected W. D. Guthrie's attack (see Chapter I.E.3) on a tax on street railroads that differed in amount from the tax imposed on underground railroads.[551]
- 1906 (state): The Court ruled that the state could choose to levy different taxes on packing houses according to what they packed, here meat.[552]
- 1910 (state tax invalidated): An important group of decisions overturned the rule of the 1886 decision that entry of foreign corporations into a state to do business could be conditioned on payment of an unapportioned capital tax.[553] Moreover, once admitted to the state as the taxpayer was, its foreign incorporation could not be a basis for differential taxation.

---

[546] Kidd v. Alabama, 188 U.S. 730 (1903).

[547] *See* Fulton Corp. v. Faulkner, 516 U.S. 325 (1996).

[548] McCray v. United States, 195 U.S. 27, 62 (1904). *See* Ch. III.E.5.

[549] Capital City Dairy Co. v. Ohio, 183 U.S. 238 (1902).

[550] Cook v. Marshall County, 196 U.S. 261 (1905).

[551] New York ex rel. Metropolitan Street Ry. Co. v. New York State Bd., 199 U.S. 1 (1905) (also rejected objection to unequal allowance of deductions for debts).

[552] Armour Packing Co. v. Lacy, 200 U.S. 226 (1906).

[553] Southern R. Co. v. Greene, 216 U.S. 400 (1910), *explained in* Western & Southern Life Ins. Co. v. State Bd. of Equalization, 451 U.S. 648 (1981). *See also* Looney v. Crane, 245 U.S. 178 (1917).

- 1910 (state): The Court ruled that Kentucky could impose a higher license tax on distillers of blended spirits than non blended spirits, even though it appeared to reflect favoritism toward the classic Kentucky spirits.[554]

- 1911 (federal): *Flint v. Stone Tracy*, the important decision approving the federal excise tax on corporate incomes, issued just 16 years after *Pollock* had ruled the general income tax unconstitutional,[555] also ruled it was not discriminatory to tax corporations and not unincorporated businesses, and rejected a host of other claims of discrimination, stating: "In levying excise taxes the most ample authority has been recognized from the beginning to select some and omit other possible subjects of taxation, to select one calling and omit another, to tax one class of property and to forbear to tax another."[556] The plaintiff argued that the equal protection requirement of the Fourteenth Amendment implicitly applied as part of due process in the Fifth Amendment. The opinion neither agreed nor disagreed but simply pointed out that even under the Fourteenth Amendment states had wide leeway to select subjects for taxation, with citations starting at *Bell's Gap*.

- 1912 (state): In a surprising contrast to *Yick Wo* (1886), Justice Holmes ruled hand laundries could be taxed more heavily than steam laundries, despite the common knowledge that Chinese laundries tended to be hand laundries.[557] Justice Holmes stated: "Like the United States, although with more restriction and in less degree, a state may carry out a policy, even a policy with which we might disagree."

- 1912 (Territory): *Toyota v. Hawaii* ruled that Hawaii could impose a much heavier license tax on auctioneers in Honolulu as compared with other areas.[558] The brief opinion suggested that the legislature could have found that a license was worth much more in Honolulu than elsewhere. This implies that governmental licenses, which are in the nature of franchises, are evaluated somewhat like special assessments, although that view has never been applied generally.[559]

- 1913 (state): The Court ruled that grading the license taxes of theaters according to the price asked for the highest price seat did not violate equal protection.[560]

- 1913 (state): The Court ruled that taxing only telephone companies with more than $500 gross receipts was not discriminatory.[561]

---

[554] Brown-Forman Co. v. Kentucky, 217 U.S. 563 (1910) (the plaintiff was not an importer and so the Commerce Clause was not at issue).

[555] *See* Ch. V.D.2.d.

[556] Flint v. Stone Tracy Co., 220 U.S. 107, 158 (1911).

[557] Quong Wing v. Kirkendall, 223 U.S. 59, 62 (1912).

[558] Toyota v. Hawaii, 226 U.S. 184 (1912).

[559] *See* Ch. IV.C.

[560] Metropolis Theatre Co. v. Chicago, 228 U.S. 61 (1913) (not "palpably arbitrary").

[561] Citizens' Tel. Co. v. Fuller, 229 U.S. 322 (1913).

- 1914 (federal): The important *Billings* decision ruled that use of foreign built boats could be taxed while use of domestic built boats was not taxed.[562] *Billings* contained the frequently repeated statement that the Constitution is not self-destructive; it does not give the taxing power in one clause and take it away in the Fifth Amendment. It also contained a version of the general statement about the outer reaches of tolerance of discrimination: "[the tax is not] so beyond the power of classification, so abhorrent to the sense of justice, and so repugnant to the conceptions of free government as to be void even in the absence of express constitutional limitation."[563]
- 1916 (state tax invalidated): *Gast* is a rare Fourteenth Amendment victory for a taxpayer on account of a wholly arbitrary taxing statute, with the arbitrariness amounting to a formula that simply did not work under any explanation of its purposes, whether good or bad. Justice Holmes found the statutory formula for a special assessment apportioning the costs of a street to the property on either side to produce a grossly unequal apportionment that had no basis in an attempt to charge for benefits, could not be defended as the occasional bad result of a generally reasonable scheme, but was an "ordinance that is a farrago of irrational irregularities throughout."[564] The typically brief Holmes opinion was based on the fact that the mechanical rules of the statute produced grossly unequal results simply by virtue of the operation of a formula that neither responded to some special considerations of benefit nor operated reasonably most of the time.
- 1916 (federal): Although *Knowlton v. Moore* and *Magoun* had already approved progressivity in federal estate and state inheritance taxes, *Brushaber* approved it in the much more contentious setting of the income tax.[565] It distinguished the theoretical case of a distinction so arbitrary as not to be a tax at all but a taking without just compensation. *Brushaber* also rejected a variety of other discrimination charges against the income tax in two ways: first, the uniformity requirement did not apply because it requires only geographical uniformity, and second the Due Process Clause does not limit the taxing power. The opinion left open the theoretical possibility that a tax could be so arbitrary as to not be a tax at all but a confiscation.[566] But none of the usual distinctions in taxation that might make taxpayers think they had been discriminated against were even close to that extreme.[567]
- 1921 (federal): *La Belle Iron Works* points out again that the Fifth Amendment has no Equal Protection Clause and only the tax uniformity require-

[562] Billings v. United States, 232 U.S. 261 (1914); Rainey v. United States, 232 U.S. 310 (1914).

[563] *Id.* at 283.

[564] Gast Realty & Inv. Co. v. Schneider Granite Co., 240 U.S. 55, 59 (1916).

[565] Brushaber v. Union Pacific R. Co., 240 U.S. 1 (1916) (1913 income tax).

[566] *See* Ch. V.D.3.b(8)(b).

[567] *See also* Stanton v. Baltic Mining Co., 240 U.S. 103 (1916) (rejecting similar discrimination claims based on *Brushaber*).

ment limits federal taxes.[568] The taxpayer complained that basing the War Excess Profits tax on "invested capital" rather than current fair market value resulted in baseless and arbitrary variation in tax liability between taxpayers. The Court did entertain the arbitrariness claim under the Due Process Clause but dismissed it due to the breadth of the power of Congress to make taxing distinctions and the fact that the the rule applied equally to all, whether or not it had unequal effects as applied.

- 1922 (state): The Court ruled that the state could tax bituminous and anthracite coal differently.[569] The difference need not be based on competition between the types of coals but could be based on the simple fact that they have different names and different qualities. If some goal is intended by the state it is not for the court to investigate the facts of the likelihood of success.
- 1924 (federal): *Barclay & Co. v. Edwards* ruled that domestic corporations could be taxed on income from exports even though foreign corporations were not taxed on income from exports of goods made in the United States.[570] The opinion stated that even if the Court were to concede, which it could not, that the Fifth Amendment demanded equality of taxation, it would not prevent differently taxing foreigners who were subject to taxation in other countries. It noted that the exemption might be designed to lure foreign business.
- 1925 (Territory): The Court upheld a graduated tax on salmon canneries according to the number of fish packed under Fifth Amendment as to the Territory of Alaska.[571]
- 1925 (state): The Court ruled that a state inheritance tax could deny a deduction from value for the amount of federal estate tax paid, which denial would tend to burden larger estates more than smaller estates.[572]
- 1926 (state tax invalidated): *Schlesinger v. Wisconsin* struck down a six year contemplation of death presumption under the Fourteenth Amendment.[573]

---

[568] La Belle Iron Works v. United States, 256 U.S. 377 (1921).

[569] Heisler v. Thomas Colliery Co., 260 U.S. 245 (1922), *overruled on other grounds*, Commonwealth Edison Co. v. Montana, 453 U.S. 609 (1981).

[570] Barclay & Co. v. Edwards, 267 U.S. 442 (1924); National Paper & Type Co. v. Bowers, 266 U.S. 373 (1924).

[571] Pacific American Fisheries v. Alaska, 269 U.S. 269 (1925).

[572] Stebbins v. Riley, 268 U.S. 137 (1925) ("It is not necessary that the basis of classification should be deductible from the nature of the thing classified. It is enough that the classification is reasonably founded in the 'purposes and policies of taxation.' . . . It is not open to objection unless it precludes the assumption that the classification was made in the exercise of legislative judgment and discretion.").

[573] Schlesinger v. Wisconsin, 270 U.S. 230 (1926). The Court last cited *Schlesinger* in support of its dislike of irrebuttable presumptions in Vlandis v. Kline, 412 U.S. 441 (1973) (concerning in state tuition status). In dissent in *Vlandis* Justice Rehnquist grouped these cases with *Lochner* and *Adkins*. 412 U.S. at 467-468.

The case was analyzed as involving an irrebuttable presumption.[574] It also was said to be the then leading case for the proposition that a class could not be expanded merely to promote administrative efficiency.[575]

- 1926 (Territorial rule invalidated): The Court held unconstitutional under the Constitution of the Philippines the Chinese Bookkeeping Act by which the Philippines forbade Chinese merchants from keeping a set of books in Chinese.[576] The opinion stated that it was permissible to require tax records or business records to be maintained in a certain language, but also maintaining them in another language could not be a crime. The case is not directly a tax case because the defendant was convicted of a crime as to the bookkeeping. Chief Justice Taft, who wrote the opinion, indicated special knowledge of the prevalence of Chinese businessmen in the Philippines, which knowledge he no doubt acquired as Governor General to the Philippines from 1900 to 1904.
- 1926 (state): The Court formally rejected the prior view that a state could impose heavier requirements on foreign corporations, as forecast in the 1910 opinions.[577]
- 1927 (federal tax invalidated): The application of an estate tax rule requiring the inclusion of a gift made before the enactment, which was to take effect at death (which was after the enactment), was held to be so arbitrary and capricious as to amount to a confiscation of property in violation of the

---

[574] Justice McReynolds explained the discrimination as follows: "Gifts inter vivos within six years of death, but in fact made without contemplation thereof, are first conclusively presumed to have been so made without regard to actualities, while like gifts at other times are not thus treated. There is no adequate basis for this distinction. Secondly, they are subjected to graduated taxes which could not properly be laid on all gifts or, indeed, upon any gift without testamentary character." The real objection appears to have been to the progressivity. Justice Holmes' dissent (in which Justices Brandeis and Stone concurred) stated that no one would have disagreed that a six month presumption was permissible and therefore there was no reason a state legislature could not select a period of six years, so long as it was in the penumbra of reasonable possibility, which it was. The majority opinion was the origin of this objection to a presumption on equality grounds: [It is not right that] "'A' may be required to submit to an exactment forbidden by the Constitution if this seems necessary in order to enable the State readily to collect lawful charges against 'B'." 270 U.S. at 240. *Cited in* Heiner v. Donnan, 285 U.S. 312 (1932).

[575] *See* Sholley, at 401, 404 (in this and related cases the Court divided 6 to 3 along conservative and liberal lines, and so it was unlikely that the Court would change its view on administrative convenience until the personnel changed).

[576] Yu Cong Eng v. Trinidad, 271 U.S. 500 (1926).

[577] "It is not necessary to challenge the proposition that, as a general rule, the state, having power to deny a privilege altogether, may grant it upon such conditions as it sees fit to impose. But the power of the state in that respect is not unlimited; and one of the limitations is that it may not impose conditions which require the relinquishment of constitutional rights. If the state may compel the surrender of one constitutional right as a condition of its favor, it may, in like manner, compel a surrender of all. It is inconceivable that guaranties embedded in the Constitution of the United States may thus be manipulated out of existence." Frost & Frost Trucking Co. v. Railroad Com. of California, 271 U.S. 583, 593-594 (1926).

Due Process Clause of the Fifth Amendment.[578] *Nichols v. Coolidge* and the related decisions did not literally involve an equal protection argument under the Fifth Amendment but they did involve the Fifth Amendment and represented the first finding by the Court of the rare completely arbitrary federal tax that so many earlier opinions stated could exist: the tax that amounted to a confiscation. Therefore, since this category was often said to be the repository of the theoretical arbitrary discrimination, it is relevant to the equal protection cases. Justices Holmes, Brandeis, Sanford and Stone concurred but did not join the opinion. The majority seems to have been exercised by the fact that the decedent had no notice of the possibility that her conveyance to take effect at death could be taxed at her death. Also, the majority was appalled by the possibility that a small gift could have grown into a much more valuable property when taxed (exactly the purpose of the contemplation of death statute). It found as a fact that death was not contemplated when the gift was made, even though the gift was to take effect on death. The Court has since cast serious doubt on the viability of these decisions.[579]

- 1927 (state): *Swiss Oil Corp. v. Shanks* ruled that the Fourteenth Amendment does not prevent double taxation.[580] Assuming the tax on oil produced to be a property tax and not a license tax, the fact that the property of the oil producer was otherwise taxed in the state does not render the tax unconstitutional.
- 1928 (state tax invalidated): *Louisville Gas & Electric Co. v. Coleman* ruled that a statute excepting from a tax upon recording mortgages instruments in which the indebtedness matures within five years unconstitutionally deprives mortgagees not within the exception clause of the equal protection of the laws.[581] This ruling is clearly out of line with preceding opinions.[582] It admitted that the recordation, which protected the lien's priority, was worth more the longer the debt was outstanding; but it reasoned that a difference in value could not be reflected in a complete exemption for short term notes and a full fee for longer term notes. Thus the opinion seemed to treat the

[578] Nichols v. Coolidge, 274 U.S. 531 (1927). Blodgett v. Holden, 275 U.S. 142 (1927) and Untermeyer v. Anderson, 276 U.S. 440 (1928) relied on *Nichols* in striking down a gift tax applied to gifts that preceded the enactment in the same year.

[579] United States v. Carlton, 512 U.S. 26 (1994) ("long since been discarded" and limited to a new tax); Commissioner v. Estate of Church, 335 U.S. 632 n. 10 (1949).

[580] Swiss Oil Corp. v. Shanks, 273 U.S. 407 (1927) (crude oil tax plus state, county and local property taxes on oil company). *See also* Davidson v. New Orleans, 96 U.S. 97 (1878) (property had already been assessed for the same improvement project, swamp drainage); Patton v. Brady, 184 U.S. 608 (1902) (an excise tax on inventory could be increased and reapplied to the same inventory); United States v. Hudson, 299 U.S. 498 (1937) (in addition to the regular income tax a special tax equal to 50% of profit earned was imposed on transactions in silver bullion).

[581] Louisville Gas & Electric Co. v. Coleman, 277 U.S. 32 (1928). This decision was last followed by *Quaker City Cab*, which has been overruled.

[582] *See* Sholley, at 242 ("Rarely is a judicial opinion so vulnerable as this one.").

tax as a fee for services that should be proportion to the benefits received, but purported to reject that basis. In effect, Justice Sutherland's opinion branded any differentiation in taxation discriminatory, without regard to the reasons or their reasonableness.[583] Justices Holmes, Brandeis, Stone and Sanford dissented.[584]

- 1928 (state tax invalidated): The Court struck down a gross receipts tax only on corporate taxi cabs. Justices Holmes, Brandeis and Stone dissented; the decision was later overruled.[585]
- 1929 (federal): *Bromley v. McCaughn* ruled that progressive gift tax rates were proper under the Fifth Amendment.[586]
- 1930 (state): The Court ruled that the use of a measure of the gravity content of oil was not a palpably arbitrary method of taxing it because the standard had some relationship to the quality of the oil.[587]
- 1930 (federal): *Tyler v. United States* ruled that including in the gross estate of a decedent, for the purpose of computing the tax "upon the transfer of the net estate," the value of property held by him and another as tenants by the entirety, where such property originally belonged in no part to the survivor but came to the tenancy as a pure gift from the decedent, is neither arbitrary nor capricious and does not violate the Due Process Clause of the Fifth Amendment.[588]

---

[583] *See* JOEL FRANCIS PASCHAL, MR. JUSTICE SUTHERLAND A MAN AGAINST THE STATE 132 (1951).

[584] The brief Holmes dissent contains one of his classic statements of legal realism on drawing lines: "When a legal distinction is determined, as no one doubts that it may be, between night and day, childhood and maturity, or any other extremes, a point has to be fixed or a line has to be drawn, or gradually picked out by successive decisions, to mark where the change takes place. Looked at by itself without regard to the necessity behind it the line or point seems arbitrary. It might as well or nearly as well be a little more to one side or the other. But when it is seen that a line or point there must be, and that there is no mathematical or logical way of fixing it precisely, the decision of the legislature must be accepted unless we can say that it is very wide of any reasonable mark." 277 U.S. at 41. This was quoted by Yale Kamisar in *The Right to Die: On Drawing and Erasing Lines*, 35 DUQ. L. REV. 481, 521 (1996). The dissenting opinion, written by Justice Brandeis, contains an extensive set of citations of Supreme Court opinions approving discrimination in state tax (many of which are not in the list in this book). It states that "in taxation there is a broader power of classification than in some other exercises of legislation," citing Citizens' Tel. Co. v. Fuller, 229 U.S. 322, 329 (1913). 77 U.S. at 43. Justice Brandeis may have taken a particular interest in the Kentucky law because his family lived in Louisville; the law school at the University of Louisville is now named for Justice Brandeis.

[585] Quaker City Cab Co. v. Pennsylvania, 277 U.S. 389 (1928), *overruled by* Lehnhausen v. Lake Shore Auto Parts Co., 410 U.S. 356 (1973).

[586] Bromley v. McCaughn, 280 U.S. 124 (1929).

[587] Ohio Oil Co. v. Conway, 281 U.S. 146 (1930).

[588] Tyler v. United States, 281 U.S. 497 (1930).

- 1931 (state). The Court ruled that a state could charge more tax on chain stores selling the same goods than it charged local stores.[589] Besides stating the obvious that chain stores were different in terms of management and operation, the only indication the opinion gave of why the difference mattered was that chain store operation proved advantageous.
- 1931 (federal): *Milliken v. United States* upheld against retroactivity charges an increase in the estate tax rate on gifts in contemplation of death, where the gift was made after the statute including gifts in contemplation of death was enacted, but before the rate increase.[590]
- 1931 (state tax invalidated): *Hoeper* struck down on due process and equal protection grounds a state income tax that combined the incomes of husband and wife.[591] The 1945 decision in *Fernandez v. Wiener* reaches an inconsistent result for the estate tax. The state tax at issue in *Hoeper* taxed the husband on the income of the wife and minors in the home. It was not elective as is the current federal joint return, and the tax was not merely computed on a joint basis but was primarily levied upon the husband. Therefore, the Court could rely on the principle that one person cannot be taxed on, or his liability determined with respect to, the income of another.[592]
- 1932 (federal): *Standard Nut Margarine* is an unusual case that is like *McCray*,[593] except that the Court found that the margarine was not of the type covered by the colored margarine tax.[594] The taxpayer sought an injunction against the imposition of the tax and the IRS pleaded in defense the Anti-Injunction Act. The Court rejected that defense because the IRS had discriminated against the taxpayer in attempting to enforce the tax against it, while not enforcing it against other taxpayers.[595] Thus, lack of uniformity was not a reason to hold a tax unconstitutional, but it was a reason to waive the Anti-Injunction Act.
- 1932 (federal): While not admitting the possibility of an equality claim under the Fifth Amendment, the Court stated that taxpayer partners could

---

[589] State Bd. of Tax Comm'rs v. Jackson, 283 U.S. 527 (1931).

[590] Milliken v. United States, 283 U.S. 15 (1931).

[591] Hoeper v. Tax Comm'n of Wisconsin, 284 U.S. 206 (1931). Justices Holmes, Brandeis and Stone dissented.

[592] *Citing*, Knowlton v. Moore, 178 U.S. 41 (1900) (which concluded that the total amount of the estate did not govern the tax rate as a matter of statutory construction, and so the indication about the use of another's amount to govern one's tax rate was dictum). *See* Ch. V.D.3.b(7)(c).

[593] McCray v. United States, 195 U.S. 27 (1904).

[594] Miller v. Standard Nut Margarine Co., 284 U.S. 498 (1932). *But see* Bob Jones Univ. v. Simon, 416 U.S. 725, 744 (1974) (casting doubt on the reasoning).

[595] "Petitioner [the IRS] acquiesced in the injunctions granted in Rhode Island and the District of Columbia and did not assess any tax upon identical products contemporaneously being made by complainants in such suits, and directed enforcement against respondent's entire product. Such discrimination conflicts with the principle underlying the constitutional provision directing that excises laid by Congress shall be uniform throughout the United States." 284 U.S. at 510.

not complain about being subjected to a different refund regime because the 1923 partnership income was reported in their 1924 returns.[596]

- 1932 (federal tax invalidated): *Heiner v. Donnan* ruled that an irrebuttable presumption that a gift within two years before death was in contemplation of death and thus taxable in the gross estate violated the Due Process Clause on two grounds: (1) "there was no adequate basis" to distinguish between such transfers just within and just without the two-year period, and (2) to the extent that the presumption was over inclusive its justification—that improperly taxing A was a reasonable price to pay for properly taxing B—violated due process.[597] The Court had previously ruled the same way in state tax cases and stated the principle involved as follows: a statute that imposes a tax upon an assumption of fact that the taxpayer is forbidden to controvert, is so arbitrary and unreasonable that it cannot stand under the Fourteenth Amendment.[598] Although never overruled, the Court has not relied on the retroactivity aspect of the decision in a tax case and implicitly rejected it in *Whitney* (1940).[599]
- 1933 (state tax invalidated): The Court ruled that a graduated chain store tax could not differentiate between chain stores operating in only one county versus those operating in multiple counties.[600]
- 1934 (state): *Magnano Co. v. Hamilton* ruled that a tax can be based on the distinction between butter and margarine (essentially same as *McCray*).[601]

---

[596] Shearer v. Burnet, 285 U.S. 228 (1932).

[597] Heiner v. Donnan, 285 U.S. 312 (1932). The Court last cited *Heiner* in support of its dislike of irrebuttable presumptions in Vlandis v. Kline, 412 U.S. 441 (1973) (concerning in state tuition status). In dissent Justice Rehnquist stated: "The majority's reliance on cases such as Heiner v. Donnan . . . harks back to a day when the principles of substantive due process had reached their zenith in this Court. Later and sounder cases thoroughly repudiated these principles in large part. Ten years ago, the Court reviewed these doctrines in Ferguson v. Skrupa, 372 U.S. 726, 730 (1963), and made the following observation: 'The doctrine that prevailed in *Lochner*, *Coppage*, *Adkins*, *Burns*, and like cases—that due process authorizes courts to hold laws unconstitutional when they believe the legislature has acted unwisely—has long since been discarded. We have returned to the original constitutional proposition that courts do not substitute their social and economic beliefs for the judgment of legislative bodies, who are elected to pass laws. As this Court stated in a unanimous opinion in 1941, 'We are not concerned . . . with the wisdom, need, or appropriateness of the legislation." " 412 U.S. at 467-468.

[598] *Citing* Coolidge v. Long, 282 U.S. 582, 596 (1931) (a state tax decision stating that a confiscatory tax was invalid under the Fourteenth Amendment, as it would be under the Fifth Amendment).

[599] Whitney v. State Tax Com., 309 U.S. 530 (1940) (Justice Frankfurter's opinion vaguely dismisses *Heiner* as involving "differences of opinion"). *Whitney* involved the estate of Cornelius Vanderbilt and the inclusion of powers of appointment in the estate of his wife who died 35 years later under New York law. *Whitney* rejected a uniformity claim based on the alleged arbitrary fixing of the effective date of a statute.

[600] Louis K. Liggett Co. v. Lee, 288 U.S. 517 (1933). Justices Brandeis, Stone and Cardozo dissented on the ground that the taxes applied were different types of taxes.

[601] Magnano Co. v. Hamilton, 292 U.S. 40 (1934).

- 1934 (state tax invalidated): The Court ruled that a state could not tax the casualty insurance premiums received by a multiline foreign insurer and not tax the casualty insurance premiums received by a foreign insurer that sold only casualty insurance.[602]

- 1935 (federal): *Helvering v. City Bank Farmers Trust Co.* upheld as an anti-abuse mechanism the inclusion of property in the taxable estate because it was subject to a revocable trust.[603]

- 1935 (state tax invalidated): *Stewart Dry Goods* is a rather remarkable ruling that runs contrary to the long string of opinions upholding progressive rates and also comes perilously close to stating that only net income can be taxed because the progressivity that is acceptable in an income tax is not acceptable in a gross receipts tax.[604] It ruled a gross receipts sales tax to violate equal protection because it was graduated.[605] The majority's reasoning seemed to be that a state cannot levy a gross receipts tax at any but a minimal amount unless it can be passed on to the customers because the tax might unduly impinge on the vendor's profits in an unequal way; in other words the opinion favors income taxes over gross receipt taxes because the former are payable only if the taxpayer earns profits. The dissent of Justice Cardozo, Brandeis and Stone thought that the state could have reasonably presumed that vendors with more sales were more efficient. Justice Cardozo's dissent contained the memorable phrase: "Socially, the theory is that just as in taxes upon income or upon transfers at death, so also in imposts upon business, the little man, by reason of inferior capacity to pay, should bear a lighter load of taxes, relatively as well as absolutely, than is borne by the big one."[606] The Court has not relied on the decision since the companion cases. In effect *Stewart* applied the constraint that the Court had placed on regulatory rate making to taxation.[607]

- 1936 (state tax invalidated): *Binney v. Long* struck down an unusual state inheritance tax discrimination because it taxed the exercise of a power of appointment created before a date two years before the legislation but not a similar power created after that date.[608] And before that earlier date there had been no inheritance tax at all. So the current policy of the state was not

[602] Concordia Fire Ins. Co. v. Illinois, 292 U.S. 535 (1934). Justices Cardozo, Brandeis and Stone dissented.

[603] Helvering v. City Bank Farmers Trust Co., 296 U.S. 85 (1935) (not "unreasonably harsh or oppressive").

[604] *See* Sholley, at 263.

[605] Stewart Dry Goods Co. v. Lewis, 294 U.S. 550 (1935); *followed by* Valentine v. Great Atlantic & Pacific Tea Co., 299 U.S. 32 (1936); *distinguished by* New York Rapid Transit Corp. v. New York, 303 U.S. 573 (1938).

[606] 294 U.S. at 567. This is the only time a Supreme Court opinion ever used the term "little man" to reflect the Justice's own thinking.

[607] *See* Chicago, M. & St. P. Ry. v. Minnesota, 134 U.S. 418 (1890).

[608] Binney v. Long, 299 U.S. 280 (1936) (Justices Cardozo and Brandeis dissented in part; Justice Stone did not participate); *distinguished by* Whitney v. State Tax Com., 309 U.S. 530 (1940).

to tax such exercises and it adopted a law taxing exercise of a power created when there was not inheritance tax.

- 1936 (state tax invalidated): The Court struck down under the First and Fourteenth Amendments a discriminatory tax on large newspapers.[609]
- 1937 (state): The Court upheld a heavier tax on chain stores, which effectively discriminated against national chain stores relative to local stores.[610]
- 1937 (federal): *Steward Machine Co. v. Davis* upheld the unemployment compensation tax imposed under the Social Security Act against a variety of constitutional objections, including Fifth Amendment due process and equality of application (the tax exempted employers of fewer than eight).[611] The opinion noted the absence of an Equal Protection Clause from the Fifth Amendment and then said even the states would be allowed to permit exemptions as used in the tax.
- 1938 (state): The Court ruled that utilities could be taxed on their gross incomes, stating "[t]he power to make distinctions exists with full vigor in the field of taxation, where no 'iron rule' of equality has ever been enforced upon the states."[612]
- 1938 (state): *Welch v. Henry* ruled that the state could eliminate a dividend received deduction for dividends received from corporations that had paid tax in the state on at least half of their income, and the repeal could operate retroactively for two years.[613]
- 1940 (state): *Whitney* rejected an equal protection objection to a change in a New York inheritance tax statute that brought under the tax a power of appointment made before the change.[614] The taxpayer (the estate of Mrs. Cornelius Vanderbilt) relied on *Heiner v. Donnan*, *Schlesinger* and *Hoeper*, which Justice Frankfurter dismissed with this statement: ". . . differences of opinion to which these cases gave rise are not here relevant."[615] He dealt with *Binney v. Long* by contrasting with an allegedly arbitrarily selected date the logical explanation for the effective dates of the statute at hand, citing *Madden v. Kentucky* for the freedom of the legislature to make distinctions.[616]

---

609 Grosjean v. American Press Co., 297 U.S. 233 (1936).

610 Great Atlantic & Pacific Tea Co. v. Grosjean, 301 U.S. 412 (1937).

611 Steward Machine Co. v. Davis, 301 U.S. 548 (1937).

612 New York Rapid Transit Corp. v. New York, 303 U.S. 573, 578 (1938).

613 Welch v. Henry, 305 U.S. 134 (1938) (the law was enacted in 1935 and made applicable for the 1933 and 1934 years; taxation is not a penalty or a contract with the taxpayer).

614 Whitney v. State Tax Com., 309 U.S. 530 (1940). However, *Whitney* was not the end of the dispute over legislative powers. In 1945 Justices Black and Douglas in a nontax case were complaining in dissent about Justice Stone pursuing the "super legislature" approach. S. Pac. Co. v. Arizona, 325 U.S. 761 (1945).

615 309 U.S. at 541.

616 Madden v. Kentucky, 309 U.S. 83, 88 (1940) ("The burden is on the one attacking the legislative arrangement to negative every conceivable basis which might support it.").

- 1941 (federal): *Lerner Stores* ruled that despite the absence of an Equal Protection Clause in the Fifth Amendment the taxpayer had not been harmed by being held to its low reported capital stock value, which caused it to have a high excess profits tax; the taxpayer could have originally reported the stock capital value higher.[617]
- 1945 (federal): *Fernandez v. Wiener* ruled a federal estate tax on community property constitutional despite the fact that Congress did not tax similar property created by private agreements. "There can be no doubt that the selection of such a class for taxation would not offend against the Fifth Amendment, or even the Fourteenth, merely because it did not attempt to reach casual arrangements resulting from individual agreements. Taxes must be laid by general rules. Considerations of practical administrative convenience and cost in the administration of tax laws afford adequate grounds for imposing a tax on a well-recognized and defined class, without attempting to extend it so as to embrace a penumbra of special and more or less casual interests which in each case may or may not resemble the taxed class. Such interests would be but isolated specimens of the attorney's art, and likely to resist efforts to identify them with the taxable subject."[618] The opinion did not cite *Hoeper*, the earlier decision that had ruled a state income tax scheme unconstitutional because of differential treatment of community property, despite the fact that the taxpayer's brief cited it six times.[619]
- 1959 (state): The Court ruled that equal protection was not violated by a state granting a property tax exemption to inventory stored temporarily in the state by nonresidents.[620] The statute was not palpably arbitrary because of its valid justification based on attracting business to the state.
- 1966 (state tax invalidated): *Harper v. Virginia State Bd. of Elections* ruled that a poll tax levied as a prerequisite for voting discriminates on the basis of affluence in violation of the Equal Protection Clause.[621] The ruling is based on the fundamental nature of the right to vote.[622] Justice Harlan and Stewart in dissent discerned that the decision was based on the high value accorded the right to vote, which had led the Court away from its traditional equal protection approach. They cited Justice Holmes' injunction that the Constitution does not embody a particular economic theory, be it laissez faire or otherwise. The decision is much more a voting rights case than a tax case.

---

[617] Helvering v. Lerner Stores Corp., 314 U.S. 463 (1941).

[618] Fernandez v. Wiener, 326 U.S. 340, 360-361 (1945); United States v. Rompel, 326 U.S. 367 (1945) (companion case).

[619] 1945 WL 48225. And the Supreme Court has never cited both *Fernandez* and *Hoeper* in the same opinion.

[620] Allied Stores of Ohio, Inc. v. Bowers, 358 U.S. 522, 527 (1959).

[621] Harper v. Virginia State Bd. of Elections, 383 U.S. 663 (1966).

[622] "We have long been mindful that where fundamental rights and liberties are asserted under the Equal Protection Clause, classifications which might invade or restrain them must be closely scrutinized and carefully confined." 383 U.S. at 670.

- 1973 (state): *Lehnhausen v. Lake Shore Auto Parts Co.* ruled that corporations and individuals can be taxed differently; the decision rejected *Quaker City* as a "relic of a bygone era."[623]
- 1974 (state): *Kahn v. Shevin* ruled that widowers could be denied a property tax exemption allowed to widows.[624] This opinion stated what generally has gone unstated: that the permitted variations under the Equal Protection Clause do not include distinctions based on specific federal rights (presumably including to this point racial discrimination, interstate commerce discrimination, voting discrimination). The opinion stated that gender had never been rejected as a basis for discrimination in all cases, citing *Muller.*[625] This was one of Ruth Bader Ginsburg's few losses.
- 1983 (federal): *Regan v. Taxation with Representation* is the first federal tax equal protection case to employ the newly discovered equal protection component of the Fifth Amendment.[626] It purported to require a rational relation to a legitimate government purpose,[627] which is a somewhat more restrictive test than applied when the Court only thought that confiscatory taxes could violate due process, which the opinion recognized by then referring to a 1940 opinion that explained the extreme degree of discrimination allowable in taxation.[628] "The presumption of constitutionality can be overcome only by the most explicit demonstration that a classification is a hostile and oppressive discrimination against particular persons and classes. The burden is on the one attacking the legislative arrangement to negate every conceivable basis which might support it."[629] However, even tax statutes are subject to a higher degree of scrutiny if they interfere with the exercise of a fundamental right, such as freedom of speech, or employ a suspect classification, such as race.[630] The Court refused to apply heightened strict scrutiny where one exempt organization could lobby and also receive tax deductible contributions and another could not, because (1) this was no more than a choice to subsidize some activities and not others (*i.e.*, the Court equated the tax benefit to spending programs), (2) there was no evidence that Congress had created the distinction with the intent of favoring or disfavoring any particular form of speech or legislative influence, and (3) tax classifi-

[623] Lehnhausen v. Lake Shore Auto Parts Co., 410 U.S. 356 (1973) (stating that Quaker City Cab Co. v. Pennsylvania, 277 U.S. 389 (1928) was a relic of a bygone era).

[624] Kahn v. Shevin, 416 U.S. 351 (1974).

[625] Muller v. Oregon, 208 U.S. 412 (1908) (the case in which Louis Brandeis convinced the Court to uphold a labor law designed to protect women).

[626] Regan v. Taxation with Representation, 461 U.S. 540 (1983).

[627] The Court has not since applied that formulation to a federal tax case.

[628] Madden v. Kentucky, 309 U.S. 83, 87-88 (1940).

[629] 461 U.S. at 547-548.

[630] *Id. See* United States v. Carolene Prod. Co., 304 U.S. 144, 152 n. 4 (1938) ("There may be narrower scope for operation of the presumption of constitutionality when legislation appears on its face to be within a specific prohibition of the Constitution, such as those of the first ten amendments, which are deemed equally specific when held to be embraced within the Fourteenth.").

cations in general are accorded great leniency.[631] Thus, the subsidy analogy helps avoid a constitutional equal protection problem, whereas in the case of Establishment Clause issues it creates a problem.[632]

- 1983 (state tax invalidated): The Court struck down under the First and Fourteenth Amendments a use tax on paper and ink, which without any reasonable explanation singled out newspapers, and a particular group of newspapers.[633]
- 1987 (state tax invalidated): The Court struck down under the First Amendment a state sales tax that varied on the basis of the content of magazines.[634]
- 1989 (state tax invalidated): *Allegheny Pittsburgh Coal Co.* struck down a "welcome stranger" method of taxing new property owners more heavily than long time property owners by using the purchase price as the value, while not revaluing other property so long as it was not sold.[635] The opinion found the state law to create a right to have property taxed at fair value, and allowed approximations and delays in adjusting values only when such procedures did not result in intentional undervaluation that produced exceedingly high disproportions in value. The opinion reasoned that the differential taxation was unfair because similarly situated taxpayers ("the same class") were taxed differently, evidently refusing to view the recent sale of property as a sufficient reason for differentiation. However, footnote 4 of the opinion forecast a different result in *Nordlinger* by saying that the holding was limited to an episodic decision of the tax collector in one county to tax this way, in apparent disregard of the statutory requirement. In a 2012 opinion the Court emphasized that *Allegheny* was a "rare" case that turned on the state law requiring equality, which precluded finding any other legitimate government purpose to be served by the distinction.[636]
- 1992 (state): *Nordlinger* purported to distinguish *Allegheny* (calling the "rare" exception), by now finding that the difference of recent sales of property justified not treating the owners of similar property as similarly situated. It relied on the fact that the State of California, through Proposition 13, had decided as a political decision to make that distinction, stating: "The Equal Protection Clause is satisfied so long as there is a plausible policy reason for the classification, the legislative facts on which the classification is apparently based rationally may have been considered to be true by the

[631] 461 U.S. at 548.

[632] *See* Ch. VIII.D.4.

[633] Minneapolis Star & Tribune Co. v. Minn. Comm'r of Revenue, 460 U.S. 575 (1983). *See* Ch. VIII.D.3.

[634] Arkansas Writers' Project, Inc. v. Ragland, 481 U.S. 221 (1987). But the Court rejected a First Amendment claim by cable TV operators. Leathers v. Medlock, 499 U.S. 439 (1991).

[635] Allegheny Pittsburgh Coal Co. v. Commission of Webster Cty., 488 U.S. 336 (1989). John G. Roberts, Jr., before he was appointed Chief Justice, wrote the brief for the taxpayer.

[636] Armour v. City of Indianapolis, 566 U.S. 673 (2012).

governmental decision maker, and the relationship of the classification to its goal is not so attenuated as to render the distinction arbitrary or irrational."[637] The Court also said that while a state need not identify its purpose in making a taxing distinction, a court must be able to discern one (which the Court refused to attempt to do in *Allegheny*). The discerned purpose was to help existing homeowners avoid having to sell their houses because they had trouble paying increased taxes that reflected increased property values. The Court accepted the theory that the "welcome stranger" system was designed to get to a current value approach (despite the fact that only strangers got the current valuation). In one sense *Nordlinger* was a return to a more traditional tax discrimination approach, but is very close to the line, and probably would not have withstood Mr. Justice Holmes analysis in *Gast* (1916) (mechanical formula, mindlessly followed).

- 1994 (federal): *Carlton* refused to find an estate tax change to be improperly retroactive.[638] The opinion contains an extensive review of retroactivity cases, and states that the general rules applied to all economic legislation also applies in tax cases. It ruled that tax laws are not a promise to the taxpayer and approved the retroactive change to plug a loophole. The amendment was adopted at the end of 1987 to be effective in 1986.
- 2003 (state): *Fitzgerald v. Racing Association* ruled that a tax benefit helps one industry or group of taxpayers and can be viewed as hurting another group that feels itself similarly situated is no grounds to label it unconstitutional; in other words, if a legislature wants to help river boats by having them pay less tax on slot machines than other slot operators, it may do so.[639] Indeed the opinion actually states: "Here, 'the facts' do not 'preclude' an inference that the reason for the different tax rates was to help the riverboat industry or the river communities."[640] The opinion lists the discrimination bases that are not subject to the normal tests: race, gender (*cf. Muller*), interstate commerce and recent arrivals in the state (*cf. Allegheny*).[641]
- 2010 (state): *Levin v. Commerce Energy* stated "in taxation, even more than in other fields, legislatures possess the greatest freedom in classification."[642]

---

[637] Nordlinger v. Hahn, 505 U.S. 1, 11-12 (1992). The Howard Jarvis Taxpayers Association filed a brief on the side of the tax collector because the tax collector in *Nordlinger* defended California Proposition 13, which instituted the "welcome stranger" method of taxing recently purchased homes more heavily than long held homes. Proposition 13 is viewed as starting the "taxpayer revolt" later pursued by Americans for Tax Reform and its anti-tax pledge.

[638] United States v. Carlton, 512 U.S. 26 (1994).

[639] Fitzgerald v. Racing Ass'n, 539 U.S. 103 (2003).

[640] *Id.* at 110.

[641] *Id.* at 107. It is perhaps significant that the opinion cited a different case for the recent arrival point: Hooper v. Bernalillo County Assessor, 472 U.S. 612 (1985).

[642] Levin v. Commerce Energy, Inc., 560 U.S. 413 (2010), quoting Madden v. Kentucky, 309 U.S. 83, 88 (1940).

- 2012 (state): *Armour* ruled that a city could terminate a sewer special assessment regime by forgiving all unpaid installments but not refunding taxes to those who had paid in full without installments.[643] The opinion effectively ruled that the city had a legitimate purpose to save money, which was rationally served by not paying refunds that would result in equal treatment of all taxpayers.

As stated in *Fitzgerald v. Racing Association*, stricter scrutiny applies to taxation in equal protection cases when the claimed discrimination is with respect to a suspect classification such as race or religion, or certain constitutionally protected rights, such as the press and free speech.[644] However, the Court's general approach to equal protection objections to government actions is that intent to discriminate must be shown and facially neutral statutes generally pass muster, despite discriminatory impact.[645] The ultimate discrimination may be falling outside of a "rifle-shot" targeted tax benefit enacted to assist a particular taxpayer or small group. So far the Supreme Court has not ruled in such a case.[646]

The next Chapter discusses the equal protection and discrimination decisions that specifically utilized the "arbitrary or capricious" terminology.

(3) *Arbitrary or Capricious*

The Court first used the term arbitrary or capricious to describe proper, if unexplainable, tax distinctions that illustrated the great scope of the taxing power.[647] Then it shifted to use the term to describe the outer limits on tax discrimination. In a sense both uses can be correct. To say that the state can with apparent arbitrariness choose to charge plumbers a $100 license tax and carpenters a $200 license tax, is to say that the legislature has discretion and the Court is not to look behind the exercise of that discretion. As long as in some sense carpenters and plumbers are not of the same class, they can be taxed differently (at least for license purposes). Such seemingly arbitrary and unexplainable distinctions have been common in the tariff schedules. Refusing to go behind a facial distinction to look for some similarity in substance is a way to defer to the politically superior branch of government and to avoid entangling the Court in speculation about congressional motives.[648] Of course, if the facial distinction is

---

[643] Armour v. City of Indianapolis, 566 U.S. 673 (2012).

[644] *See* Ch. VIII.D.

[645] *See* Washington v. Davis, 426 U.S. 229 (1976); *see generally* Linda Sugin, *Tax Expenditure Analysis and Constitutional Decisions*, 50 HAST. L. J. 407, 422 (1998).

[646] Tracy A. Kaye and Stephen W. Mazza, *United States—National Report: Constitutional Limitations on the Legislative Power to Tax in the United States*, 15 MICH. ST. J. INT'L LAW 481, 519 (2007).

[647] Sometimes it appears as "arbitrary and capricious," or in a series "arbitrary, capricious, or . . . ," or "arbitrary or capricious." The latter formulation was used most recently in a federal tax opinion in Mayo Found. for Med. Educ. & Research v. United States, 562 U.S. 44 (2011). That decision addressed the *Chevron* Doctrine; the next preceding major decision of the Court addressing the *Chevron* Doctrine used the term "arbitrary and capricious." Nat'l Cable & Telecomms. Ass'n v. Brand X Internet Servs., 545 U.S. 967, 981 (2005).

[648] *See* Ch. III.D.3.

facially discriminatory in a way requiring strict scrutiny, as in the case of race, then a different approach is applied.[649]

On the other hand, assessing reasonableness of a law was a fundamental goal of the theory of substantive due process of law.[650] It put the courts in the business of second guessing the wisdom of legislation under the guise of the Constitution. That role is entirely proper and necessary when suspect categories are involved, but not otherwise in economic legislation. Therefore, it is not surprising that the bulk of the Court's rulings that have cited arbitrary or capricious as a ground for striking down a federal tax have come in the conservative era when substantive due process developed, from *Pollock* in 1895, through the 1920s when the Court used such terminology to find three retroactive estate tax provisions violated due process. Beyond those decisions, the references to the specter of the arbitrary or capricious taxes are principally dicta, setting up a standard that is easily met, usually by finding that there is a difference in fact, sometimes with added speculation about the particular reasoning of Congress.

To the extent it is a standard, arbitrary or capricious is not separate from due process, but rather states one of the most commonly used labels for discrimination that goes too far. The Court used the term before it read the equal protection component into the Due Process Clause of the Fifth Amendment in 1954 (see Chapter V.D.3.b(2)), and perhaps understandably so due to lack of the equal protection terminology. The term still serves as a ground for Fifth Amendment tax rulings under the equal protection component.

None other than Justice Field first applied the term "arbitrary or capricious" in support of states' rights to tax arbitrarily despite the Commerce Clause. *The Delaware Railroad Tax* opinion first applied the arbitrary or capricious term to a tax; indeed it seems to be the first use by the Court of the term in any case. Justice Field was intent on preventing the interstate commerce power of the United States from limiting the states' power to tax. Therefore, he was willing to rule against the railroad to find that the tax was constitutional. In that context he said:

> The State may impose taxes upon the corporation as an entity existing under its laws, as well as upon the capital stock of the corporation or its separate corporate property. And the manner in which its value shall be assessed and the rate of taxation, however arbitrary or capricious, are mere matters of legislative discretion. It is not for us to suggest in any case that a more equitable mode of assessment or rate of taxation might be adopted than the one prescribed by the legislature of the State; our only concern is with the validity of the tax; all else lies beyond the domain of our jurisdiction.[651]

The tax at issue in *The Delaware Railroad Tax* case was a capital stock tax imposed on the railroad, in the proportion of its total track mileage in the state of Delaware. Justice Field admitted that if the tax had been imposed on the

---

[649] *See* Ch. I.E.4.b.
[650] *See* Ch. V.D.3.b(7).
[651] Del. R.R. Tax, 85 U.S. 206, 231 (1874).

value of corporate property, using an approximation based on that proportion would be unconstitutional, because it was admitted that the property value in the state was not proportional to the track mileage.[652] However, because the tax was on the corporate capital, though arbitrary it was "approximately just."[653] Therefore *The Delaware Railroad Tax* opinion is a prototype of several themes in constitutional taxation: the apportionment of the tax base of corporate value or income among the states based on some reasonable measure of relative activity in the state,[654] the practice of holding the taxing authority to the theory of the tax applied (if it is a tax on value of property then due process standards relative to measuring value are applied, but if not, then they are not applied), and use of approximations for administrative ease.

The railroad in *The Delaware Railroad Tax* had raised the arbitrariness issue and also asserted that the state was infringing on the federal power over interstate commerce by taxing an interstate railroad at all. It relied on the recent *Case of State Freight Tax* ruling, which had entirely prohibited a state tax on freight carried out of state because it was imposed "on" the interstate carriage and not "on" the franchise or local property, etc.[655] The *Delaware* opinion rejected both arguments, but did view the mileage proportionality rule as a rough approximation and so not capricious, although it might be arbitrary.

Although the opinion's language appears to place no limit on taxation (it can be arbitrary and capricious), it did find that the proportionality rule was based on some reason, however, tenuous. In contrast, if the tax had reflected a choice based on no reason, and in fact in disregard of all relevant reasons, it could be arbitrary or capricious.[656] The term derived from equity jurisprudence and was used to contrast a sound exercise of discretion, with the unsound discretion being one exercised for the whims or predilections of the judge.[657] In that context the question raised by the term arbitrary or capricious is not just that there be a reason for a distinction, but that the reason be relevant to the subject matter and within some realm of propriety.

The scope of the realm of propriety is what really causes confusion, compounded by the difference between the expectations that might be applied to equity judges as contrasted with democratically elected legislative bodies. For example, James Madison referred to the conduct of the King with regard to the Colonies as "arbitrary and capricious."[658] Perhaps he meant the King was crazy, but it is likely that the King's actions had logical explanations that were appro-

---

652 *Cf.* Nordlinger v. Hahn, 505 U.S. 1 (1992) (allowing a variation from fair value that Mr. Justice Field might not have allowed under his test).

653 *Id.*

654 *See* HELLERSTEIN & HELLERSTEIN, at ch. 8C.

655 Case of State Freight Tax, 82 U.S. 232 (1872).

656 *See, e.g.*, Buttz v. Northern P. Railroad, 119 U.S. 55 (1886) (the second opinion to use the term, again by Justice Field; a path selected for a rail line would be arbitrary and capricious if not selected with some regard to the topography, as for example if a straight line were drawn on a map without regard to mountains).

657 Nickerson v. Nickerson, 127 U.S. 668, 676 (1888) (quoting STORY ON EQUITY).

658 JAMES MADISON, THE DEBATES IN THE FEDERAL CONVENTION OF 1787 at 586 (1920).

priate from the viewpoint of the King, though not of the Colonies. So applying the term to evaluate legislation raises unique problems: legislators are expected to transfer their predilections, if not whims, into legislation, although perhaps not their personal leanings but rather the sometimes arbitrary leanings of their constituents.[659] In contrast, administrative agencies normally do not have that political prerogative; but most of the law on arbitrary and capricious action relates to administrative action.[660] Therefore, applying the historical dislike of arbitrariness in judges to statutes can lead to error, as occurred in *Pollock* and other rulings that are effectively substantive due process rulings.

Both of the Court's most recent applications of the test to a tax statute involve state statutes that impose taxes, the first being *Nordlinger v. Hahn*, discussed above.[661] The opinion states that to avoid the arbitrary and capricious category there must be a "plausible policy reason" for the classification.[662] It found two such reasons: (1) discouraging housing turnover, and (2) protecting the old owners' expectation interest in their low tax valuations. Justice Stevens' dissent argued that it should not be enough to identify a reason; there must be a rational relationship between the reason and the law. He said the classification swept too broadly to be rational. In the second decision the Court approved different business taxes on two types of businesses by reverting to the more traditional view that almost any sort of differentiation between businesses is not arbitrary.[663] Thus the meaning of arbitrary and capricious in taxation remains undefined.

After Justice Field, who wrote *The Delaware Railroad Tax* opinion, departed the Court in 1897, the term came to be used to denote the outer limit of the taxing power. Opinions of the Court using "arbitrary and capricious," other than the retroactivity cases discussed in Chapter V.D.3.b(4), and including some but not all of the equal protection cases already mentioned in the preceding chapter, include the following:

- 1890 (state): Justice Field quoted himself as to the right of a state to tax arbitrarily in upholding a state tax on dividends against a charge that it indirectly taxed United States bond interest.[664] Again he sided with state taxing power against the United States.

---

[659] *See* Kathryn A. Watts, *Proposing a Place for Politics in Arbitrary and Capricious Review*, 119 YALE L. J. 2 (2009) (this article address the issue in the context of rule-making).

[660] Attributable primarily to 42 U.S.C. § 7607(d)(9)(A) imposing the arbitrary, capricious, or abuse of discretion standard on rule-making; and 5 U.S.C. § 706(2)(A). *See, e.g.*, Judulang v. Holder, 565 U.S. 42 n. 7 (2011) (explaining that the APA standard and not the similar second prong of the *Chevron* test applies when the agency is not interpreting the statute); *cf.* Mayo Found. for Med. Educ. & Research v. United States, 562 U.S. 44 (2011) (applying *Chevron* because the agency was interpreting the statute and the regulation was not arbitrary or capricious).

[661] Nordlinger v. Hahn, 505 U.S. 1 (1992).

[662] *Id.* at 11.

[663] Fitzgerald v. Racing Ass'n, 539 U.S. 103 (2003).

[664] Home Ins. Co. v. New York, 134 U.S. 594 (1890).

- 1892 (state): Justice Field quoted himself a second time to sustain a state tax against a charge of interfering with interstate commerce.[665]
- 1895 (federal): In *Pollock* Justice Field wrote a concurring opinion that turned on its head his former views about arbitrary and capricious taxes, finding distinctions in the federal income tax of 1894 to be "arbitrary and capricious and sometimes merely fanciful," and thus reasons to rule it unconstitutional.[666]
- 1900 (state): The shift was complete when the Court upheld a state tax stating: "Of course, if such discrimination were purely arbitrary, oppressive or capricious, and made to depend upon differences of color, race, nativity, religious opinions, political affiliations or other considerations having no possible connection with the duties of citizens as taxpayers, such exemption would be pure favoritism, and a denial of the equal protection of the laws to the less favored classes."[667]
- 1902 (state): The Court lapsed back into approving arbitrary and capricious state tax distinctions.[668]
- 1910 (state): The Court returned to the arbitrary and capricious standard as a limit, ruling that distinction between taxation of blended and non blended spirits was not arbitrary and capricious, even though obviously intended to favor local manufactures.[669]
- 1916 (state): Justice Holmes used his own term "a farrago of irrational irregularities throughout" to strike down a special assessment.[670]
- 1920 (federal): *Simpson* ruled that the use of mortality tables and assumed rates of return for valuation purposes is not arbitrary.[671]
- 1921 (Territory): *Alaska Fish Salting* ruled that a tax is not arbitrary and capricious simply because it is confiscatory.[672]
- 1924 (federal): *Barclay & Co. v. Edwards* ruled that so long as a tax is not arbitrary and capricious the Fifth Amendment cannot apply.[673]

---

[665] Horn Silver Mining Co. v. New York State, 143 U.S. 305 (1892).

[666] Pollock v. Farmers' Loan & Trust Co., 157 U.S. 429, 600 (1895).

[667] American Sugar Refining Co. v. Louisiana, 179 U.S. 89, 92 (1900). Note that this statement predated footnote 4 in *Carolene Products* by 38 years. United States v. Carolene Prod. Co., 304 U.S. 144 (1938), *discussed at* Ch. I.E.4.b.

[668] Florida C. & P. R. Co. v. Reynolds, 183 U.S. 471 (1902).

[669] Brown-Forman Co. v. Kentucky, 217 U.S. 563 (1910).

[670] Gast Realty & Inv. Co. v. Schneider Granite Co., 240 U.S. 55 (1916).

[671] *See* Simpson v. United States, 252 U.S. 547 (1920) (justified on the basis of being generally applied).

[672] *See* Alaska Fish Salting & By-Products Co. v. Smith, 255 U.S. 44 (1921) (demurrer of United States sustained even though taxpayer alleged destruction of its business by the tax).

[673] Barclay & Co. v. Edwards, 267 U.S. 442 (1924).

- 1929 (federal): *Taft v. Bowers* upheld the use of carryover basis for purpose of computing the income of donees of gifts upon disposition of the property, against an arbitrary and capricious argument based largely on the unreality of according a loss to a donee who took a high basis in depreciated property (which is no longer the law).[674]
- 1931 (state): In a questionable decision the Court stated, inter alia, that one person cannot be taxed on the income or property of another.[675] There are, however, many departures from this idea, as for example in the case of carryover basis of gift property.[676]
- 1933 (federal): *Burnet v. Wells* and *Reinecke Trust* ruled that the trust grantor could be taxed on the trust income used for his benefit because his relationship with the income was sufficiently close to treat him as a taxpayer liable to support the government's providing of benefits.[677]
- 1938 (federal): The Court ruled that the "formed or availed of" approach of the accumulated earnings tax was not arbitrary and capricious.[678]
- 1941(federal): The Court rejected an arbitrary and capricious challenge to a taxing scheme that allowed the taxpayer to put any value on stock, whether or not correct, for purposes of an excise tax, because the taxpayer would be bound by that value as its basis for purposes of an income tax.[679]
- 1943 (federal): The Court rejected a Fifth Amendment challenge to the effectiveness of an unrecorded federal tax lien against purchasers for value.[680]
- 1945 (federal): The Court ruled it was not arbitrary or capricious to apply the estate tax to tax both transfers of property and the shifting of interests in property.[681]
- 1953 (federal): *Kahriger* ruled that it is not arbitrary to tax some wagering and not others.[682]
- 1960 (federal): The Court ruled that Congress did not act arbitrarily when it placed the donor of an insurance policy in the position of having to decide

[674] Taft v. Bowers, 278 U.S. 470 (1929).

[675] Hoeper v. Tax Comm'n of Wisconsin, 284 U.S. 206 (1931) (due process and equal protection violated by forcing husband to report with wife and include her income in computation) (Justices Holmes, Brandeis and Stone dissented). *See* Ch. V.D.3.b(7)(c).

[676] *See* Taft v. Bowers, 278 U.S. 470 (1929).

[677] Burnet v. Wells, 289 U.S. 670 (1933); Reinecke Trust v. Smith, 289 U.S. 172 (1933). The Court intimated that the income of a trust could be taxed to the grantor solely on the basis of a short duration. *See* Du Pont v. Commissioner, 289 U.S. 685 (1933).

[678] Helvering v. National Grocery Co., 304 U.S. 282 (1938).

[679] Helvering v. Lerner Stores Corp., 314 U.S. 463 (1941).

[680] Detroit Bank v. United States, 317 U.S. 329 (1943) (not so arbitrary as to violate due process).

[681] Fernandez v. Wiener, 326 U.S. 340 (1945) (estate tax).

[682] United States v. Kahriger, 345 U.S. 22 (1953).

whether to stop paying the premiums and have the policy lapse, or pay the premiums and have it taxed in his estate.[683]

- 1970 (federal): The Court ruled that a grandfather clause was not arbitrary.[684] Congress had a reason for imposing a cut-off date that exempted insurers organized before a certain date to reduce the number of state deposit insurers and strengthen the hand of federal deposit insurance. This reasoning was akin to that in *Veazie Bank*, approving federal taxation of state bank notes in order to encourage the use of national bank notes.[685]
- 1976 (federal): *Shapiro* ruled that an arbitrary and capricious assessment can relieve a taxpayer from the Anti-Injunction Act.[686]
- 1989 (state): *Allegheny Pittsburgh Coal Co.* ruled that the "welcome stranger" property valuation method was arbitrary and capricious because the recent purchaser and the long time owner were found to be of the same class.[687] But the Court effectively reversed itself in *Nordlinger*.[688]

The arbitrary or capricious term appears to have been particularly associated with the cases involving retroactivity issues, as discussed next. But when the Court last considered a claim of retroactivity, it shifted to "consider the nature of the tax and the circumstances in which it is laid before it can be said that its retroactive application is so harsh and oppressive as to transgress the constitutional limitation."[689]

Under the heading of arbitrary or capricious, academics have pondered philosophical limits on taxation, which ponderings never play a role in the Court's rulings, at least on paper. For example, one author stated the obvious: that another way of looking at the extreme power of Congress to discriminate in taxation is that fairness is not a standard by which tax laws are judged, at least for constitutional purposes.[690] Similarly, notions of horizontal and vertical equity, while prominent in tax policy discussions, do not rise to the level of a constitutional standard. The Supreme Court does not enforce fairness on the tax laws.[691]

---

[683] United States v. Mfrs. National Bank, 363 U.S. 194 (1960).

[684] United States v. Maryland Savings-Share Ins. Corp., 400 U.S. 4 (1970) (relying on legislative history to show that Congress had some reason to exempt certain entities formed before a stated date).

[685] Veazie Bank v. Fenno, 75 U.S. 533 (1869).

[686] Commissioner v. Shapiro, 424 U.S. 614 (1976). *See also* Miller v. Standard Nut Margarine Co., 284 U.S. 498 (1932).

[687] Allegheny Pittsburgh Coal Co. v. Commission of Webster Cty., 488 U.S. 336 (1989).

[688] Nordlinger v. Hahn, 505 U.S. 1 (1992). See discussion above.

[689] United States v. Hemme, 476 U.S. 558, 568-569 (1986) (quoting Welch v. Henry, 305 U.S. 134, 147 (1938)).

[690] *See* Leo P. Martinez, *The Trouble with Taxes: Fairness, Tax Policy and the Constitution*, 31 HAST. CONST. L. Q. 413 (2003) [hereinafter Martinez]; Henry Ordower, *Horizontal and Vertical Equity in Taxation as Constitutional Principles: Germany and the United States Contrasted*, 7 FLA. TAX REV. 259 (2006).

[691] Martinez, at 415.

Finally, Alexander Bickel provided an excellent explanation of the arbitrary versus the illogical and why legislatures are allowed to be illogical if not arbitrary:

> [Our legislatures] are political institutions and we should not require them also to be disinterested; . . . There are some conceivable groupings of victors and losers which we do not recognize as legitimate because they do not correspond to groups that actually operate as such, or that may be expected to operate as such, in society and that may therefore rationally be thought to need regulation or deserve protection. . . . To want to foster farming . . . is not a rational choice in the sense that reason compels it. [But it is not illogical as contrasted with]the fostering of red-heads [which] would be counter-rational, the product of sheer unreasoned will or emotion.[692]

(4) *Retroactive Tax*

(a) *General*

As an exception that proves the rule that inequality is rarely a ground for invalidating a federal tax, the Court's dislike of retroactivity in taxation led it during a five year period to reject two retroactive federal estate and a gift tax provisions in three decision on due process grounds.[693] In the same period it similarly struck down a state provision on related grounds.[694] Although these decisions may purport to be based on equal protection, they more likely are attributable to a visceral objection to catching a taxpayer unawares, or to imposing a tax that the taxpayer cannot avoid by some counter maneuver. Three of the four retroactivity rulings also involved conclusive presumptions for gifts in contemplation of death, to some extent, and the Court's dislike of denying an opportunity to prove out of the tax may have been the root of the rulings.[695] Perhaps most importantly, the three federal tax provisions found to be unconstitutional all involved newly imposed estate and gift taxes, not just increases in rates.[696] Outside the case of a newly imposed tax regime, retroactivity of tax changes for the current calendar year and even to the beginning of the preceding calendar year are common and accepted by the Court.[697]

The due process and equal protection arguments taxpayers make in these cases are based on the fact that Congress has drawn a line based on timing: either the event that triggers the tax liability occurred before an enactment that either created or increased the tax liability, or some related event (such as the pre-death

---

[692] Alexander M. Bickel, The Supreme Court and the Idea of Progress 226 (1970).

[693] *See generally* Robert R. Gunning, *Back from the Dead: The Resurgence of Due Process Challenges to Retroactive Tax Legislation*, 47 Duq. L. Rev. 291 (2009) [hereinafter Gunning].

[694] Schlesinger v. Wisconsin, 270 U.S. 230 (1926) (ruling based on an irrebuttable presumption in the taxing statute).

[695] *See* Ch. V.D.3.b(5). *Schlesinger* was last cited for this point in Vlandis v. Kline, 412 U.S. 441 (1973).

[696] Gunning, at 299-300.

[697] *See* as to likely constitutionality if Congress had chosen to reenact an estate tax retroactively for 2010, Peter J. Kosydar, III, *Death and Taxes or Death Without Taxes?* 37 J. Leg. 224 (2012).

gift) occurred before such dates. Drawing lines can hardly be avoided in taxation (as Justice Holmes said in a famous dissent),[698] and indeed is what every discrimination case is about. But the income tax, in particular, may have gotten the discussion off to a bad start by drawing a line in the sand at 1913 for basis and other purposes, thus encouraging the idea that things that happen before the tax is adopted should not count.[699]

The three unconstitutionality rulings involving retroactive federal provisions are no longer in good odor. In all of them some combination of Justices Holmes, Brandeis and Stone dissented, or concurred on statutory grounds without joining the majority opinion that depended on the Fifth Amendment. While the decisions have never been overruled, they have been limited and are seldom relied on by the Court. The three decisions are:

- *Nichols v. Coolidge* (1927) held the application of an estate tax rule requiring the inclusion of a gift made before the enactment, and which was to take effect at death (which was after the enactment), to be so arbitrary and capricious as to amount to a confiscation of property in violation of the Due Process Clause of the Fifth Amendment.[700] The Court later cast serious doubt on the viability of the decision.[701]

- *Blodgett v. Holden* (1927)[702] and *Untermeyer v. Anderson* (1928)[703] struck down the application of a gift tax to gifts made earlier in the year of enactment. *Untermeyer* differed from *Blodgett* in that the statutory change had already been introduced in Congress when the gift was made. The Court later cast serious doubt on the viability of the decisions.[704]

The great bulk of the Court's decisions on the subject approve retroactivity of tax law changes to at least the second tax year prior to the year of enactment. All of the decisions listed below involve federal taxes except as indicated.

---

[698] *See* Schlesinger v. Wisconsin, 270 U.S. 230, 241 (1926) ("and while I should not dream of asking where the line can be drawn, since the great body of the law consists in drawing such lines, yet when you realize that you are dealing with a matter of degree you must realize that reasonable men may differ widely as to the place where the line should fall." Dissent of Justice Holmes).

[699] 26 U.S.C. § 1053.

[700] Nichols v. Coolidge, 274 U.S. 531 (1927). Justices Holmes, Brandeis, Sanford and Stone concurred without joining the opinion. *See also* Helvering v. Helmholz, 296 U.S. 93 (1935) (interpreted trust not to retain power of appointment, and so not includable under the statute; but if it were includable it would be improperly retroactive); White v. Poor, 296 U.S. 98 (1935) (same); Bingham v. United States, 296 U.S. 211 (1935).

[701] United States v. Carlton, 512 U.S. 26 (1994) ("long since been discarded" and limited to wholly new tax).

[702] Blodgett v. Holden, 275 U.S. 142 (1927). Justices Holmes, Brandeis, Sanford and Stone concurred without joining the opinion.

[703] Untermeyer v. Anderson, 276 U.S. 440 (1928). Justices Holmes, Brandeis and Stone dissented.

[704] United States v. Carlton, 512 U.S. 26 (1994) ("long since been discarded" and limited to wholly new tax).

- 1874: *Stockdale* approved an extension of the Civil War income tax for part of a year after it had expired.[705] It is the first Supreme Court opinion to address and approve a short retroactive period for taxation in the context of an extension of an expired tax, although it contained a confusing discussion of Congress' confused effort at "construction" of the prior law in a later law.[706]
- 1907: It is not retroactive taxation or a violation of the Fifth Amendment for Congress to ratify the doing of an act in the past (collection of a tariff) that it could have authorized to begin with.[707] Of course, this principle could entirely eliminate the possibility of unconstitutional retroactivity. The case involved a delegated power to impose a tariff, later determined to be illegal, but ratified by Congress. The taxpayer also complained that the later legislation occurred after the suit was filed, but the Court rejected that argument.
- 1914: On August 5, 1909 Congress required a tax to be paid on September 1, 1909 for foreign vessels used in the prior year. *Billings* stated that normally a tax would be interpreted not to be retroactive if possible, but found the partial retroactivity to be permissible.[708]
- 1916: *Brushaber* approved the retroactive application of the income tax from the October 3, 1913 statutory enactment to March 1, 1913, the date the Sixteenth Amendment was effective, citing *Stockdale*.[709]
- 1924: *Hecht v. Malley* approved the retroactive effect of a statute making Massachusetts Business Trusts liable for a corporate excise tax that was due

---

[705] Stockdale v. Ins. Cos., 87 U.S. 323 (1874).

[706] The confusing opinion has several potentially important features. The Civil War corporate tax fell on distributed as well as undistributed corporate income, with taxes on both paid by the corporation. The tax on the undistributed income was subject to an expiration before 1870 but the tax on the dividends was not. However, reenactment of the sections evidently confused the cut-off date and Congress acted in 1870 to make clear that all of the taxes expired in August 1870, the statute stating that Congress so "construed" the former statutes. The majority in *Stockdale* either ruled or assumed that the tax expired in 1869 and treated the "construction" as if it were a new adoption of the tax, which the Court said could be retroactive for two years, presumably meaning 1869 corporate earnings distributed in the second year, 1870. However, the opinion also stated that Congress could "construe" a statute without invading the province of the Court. The dissent violently disagreed, viewing the original tax as expired and not subject to revival by construction or retroactive enactment. The concurrence of Justice Bradley and the Chief Justice evidently got it right, as later stated by Justice Swayne: Congress had been right all along, the 1869 cut off was never intended to apply to the tax on dividends, as a matter of construction. *See* R.R. Co. v. Rose, 95 U.S. 78 (1877) (adopting that view).

[707] United States v. Heinszen & Co., 206 U.S. 370 (1907). *See* concurrence of Justice Brandeis in Untermeyer v. Anderson, 276 U.S. 440 (1928) (citing this case as one of many examples of retroactive taxation). *Cf.* Lincoln v. United States, 202 U.S. 484 (1906) (analogous ratification case, but ratifying act did not cover the tariff at issue).

[708] Billings v. United States, 232 U.S. 261 (1914).

[709] Brushaber v. Union Pacific R. Co., 240 U.S. 1 (1916). *See also* Lynch v. Hornsby, 247 U.S. 339 (1918) (income derived from a surplus of corporate assets existing before the 16th Amendment could be taxed).

before the statute was enacted, at a time when the trust was not required to pay the tax under the Court's interpretation of prior law.[710]

- 1926 (state): *Schlesinger v. Wisconsin,* struck down a six-year contemplation of death presumption under the Fourteenth Amendment.[711] The case was analyzed as involving an irrebuttable presumption.[712]
- 1930: *Cooper v. United States* ruled that an income tax can be retroactive to tax income earned in the year.[713]
- 1931: The Court allowed a defense of the government against refund of a tax to be revived by statute after the government had failed to assess the tax within the time allowed by the statute of limitations.[714] The opinion described the statute as "curative" and not creating a liability where none had ever existed.
- 1931: *Milliken* approved the application of rates increased in 1918 to a gift in contemplation of death in 1916 by a decedent who died in 1920, reasoning that the decedent was on notice that gifts in contemplation of death could be taxed at death.[715]
- 1931: (state tax) *Coolidge v. Long* in effect ruled that a state could not retroactively tax a completed gift.[716]
- 1932: The Court ruled that gain may be taxed even though the gain accrued before the taxing act was adopted, so long as it accrued after 1913.[717]

---

[710] Hecht v. Malley, 265 U.S. 144 (1924).

[711] Schlesinger v. Wisconsin, 270 U.S. 230 (1926). The Court last cited *Schlesinger* in support of its dislike of irrebuttable presumptions in Vlandis v. Kline, 412 U.S. 441 (1973) (concerning in state tuition status). In dissent in *Vlandis* Justice Rehnquist grouped these cases with *Lochner* and *Adkins.* 412 U.S. at 467-468.

[712] Justice McReynolds explained the discrimination as follows: "Gifts inter vivos within six years of death, but in fact made without contemplation thereof, are first conclusively presumed to have been so made without regard to actualities, while like gifts at other times are not thus treated. There is no adequate basis for this distinction. Secondly, they are subjected to graduated taxes which could not properly be laid on all gifts or, indeed, upon any gift without testamentary character." The real objection appears to have been to the progressivity. Justice Holmes' dissent (in which Justices Brandeis and Stone concurred) stated that no one would have disagreed that a six month presumption was permissible and therefore there was no reason a state legislature could not select a period of six years, so long as it was in the penumbra of reasonable possibility, which the dissent thought to be the case. The majority opinion was the origin of this objection to a presumption on equality grounds: [it is not right that] "'A' may be required to submit to an exactment forbidden by the Constitution if this seems necessary in order to enable the State readily to collect lawful charges against 'B'."

[713] Cooper v. United States, 280 U.S. 409 (1930).

[714] Graham & Foster v. Goodcell, 282 U.S. 409 (1931).

[715] Milliken v. United States, 283 U.S. 15 (1931) (also not a direct tax). *See also* Phillips v. Dime Trust & Safe Deposit Co., 284 U.S. 160 (1931) (not arbitrarily retroactive).

[716] Coolidge v. Long, 282 U.S. 582 (1931).

[717] MacLaughlin v. Alliance Ins. Co., 286 U.S. 244 (1932). *See also* United States v. Safety Car Heating & Lighting Co., 297 U.S. 88 (1936).

- 1937: *Hudson* ruled that the Silver Purchase Act could constitutionally impose a 50% tax on profits from dealing in silver bullion or futures, including transactions within 35 days before enactment.[718] The Court relied not only on the general pattern of income tax changes retroactive within the year but also the notoriety of the legislation.
- 1938: Penalties are a form of retroactive taxation that the Court has approved.[719]
- 1938 (state): *Welch v. Henry* approved a two-year retroactive state tax (enacted in 1935 for 1933) and noted that Congress frequently legislates with respect to the whole year or the prior year.[720] It is frequently cited for the general rule: "Taxation is neither a penalty imposed on the taxpayer nor a liability which he assumed by contract. It is but a way of apportioning the cost of government among those who in some measure are privileged to enjoy its benefits and must bear its burdens. Since no citizen enjoys immunity from that burden, its retroactive imposition does not necessarily infringe due process . . . [unless the changes are] so harsh and oppressive as to transgress the constitutional limitation."[721] The practical distinction between *Welch* and the four earlier decisions holding taxes unconstitutional may have been the difference between an ongoing income tax and a relatively new estate or gift tax (in addition to the conclusive presumptions).
- 1939: *Jacobs* ruled that the mere fact that the events on which the tax was based came into existence before the statute was enacted does not make a tax unconstitutionally retroactive.[722]
- 1945: *Wheeler* ruled that a tax statute was not unconstitutionally retroactive despite a stated retroactive effect date, where the same rule was contained in a valid pre-existing regulation.[723]
- 1960: *Manufacturer's National* approved an estate tax on the transfer of insurance during life where the decedent retained a life interest, even though the transfer occurred (in 1936) before the statute was enacted (in 1942), because the death occurred later (in 1954), despite the fact that the decedent's payments of premiums were almost all before the enactment.[724]

---

[718] United States v. Hudson, 299 U.S. 498 (1937).

[719] Helvering v. National Grocery Co., 304 U.S. 282, 290 (1938).

[720] Welch v. Henry, 305 U.S. 134 (1938).

[721] *Id.* at 146-147.

[722] United States v. Jacobs, 306 U.S. 363 (1939) (estate tax could tax the full value of tenancy by entirety created before adoption of statute).

[723] Commissioner v. Wheeler, 324 U.S. 542 (1945).

[724] United States v. Mfrs. National Bank, 363 U.S. 194 (1960) (and to the extent they preceded the enactment, regulations had been proposed in 1941).

- 1981: *Darusmont* rejected an objection to the application of the alternate minimum tax to a transaction occurring before the enactment.[725] It cited *Stockdale* for the general rule that a statute could surely reach back to the first part of the year of enactment and the prior year. The taxpayer argued the AMT was a "new tax" and that was subject to a different rule, but the Court dodged that argument by tracing the minimum tax back to 1969.
- 1984: A nontax opinion equated the "harsh and oppressive" standard cited in some tax retroactivity decisions with the "arbitrary and irrational" standard.[726]
- 1986: *United States v. Hemme* distinguished *Untermeyer* and *Blodgett* because they were related to the first gift tax, not an amendment.[727] It rejected an objection to a change in the exemption as applied to a contemplation of death transfer, which occurred in the transition from the prior annual $60,000 exemption and the post 1976 unified credit. The opinion noted that while the particular change cost the taxpayer more tax, the overall change reduced the net tax.
- 1994: *United States v. Irvine* ruled that the exercise of a disclaimer can be a taxable gift even though the interest disclaimed was created by the creation of a trust in 1917 before the gift tax law was enacted.[728]
- 1994: *Carlton* is the most recent general statement by the Court on tax retroactivity.[729] It upholds what the opinion called a "curative" measure that was retroactive a little over 12 months. It states: "The due process standard to be applied to tax statutes with retroactive effect, therefore, is the same as that generally applicable to retroactive economic legislation: 'Provided that

---

725 United States v. Darusmont, 449 U.S. 292 (1981). *See* O'Connor v. United States, 479 U.S. 27 (1986) (avoiding a retroactivity issue).

726 Pension Ben. Guaranty Corp. v. R. A. Gray & Co., 467 U.S. 717 (1984). This case also has been explained as adopting a "legislative purpose" test. *See* Gunning, at 304.

727 United States v. Hemme, 476 U.S. 558 (1986).

728 United States v. Irvine, 511 U.S. 224 (1994).

729 United States v. Carlton, 512 U.S. 26 (1994) (holding the amendment was neither illegitimate nor arbitrary because made to correct what Congress viewed as a mistake in the original legislation, which would have caused a large revenue loss). The case involved a glitch in drafting of an estate tax deduction in the Tax Reform Act of 1986 for half the sale proceeds of sales by estates to an ESOP. Congress had not contemplated that estates would go out and buy stock (in this case the stock of MCI) specifically for the purpose of selling it to the ESOP. It changed the law in December 1987, effective back to the enactment of the 1986 Act; the taxpayer estate had done its deal in December 1986 (buying and selling MCI stock). The Court had no trouble finding such a correction to be proper. Justices Scalia and Thomas concurred but found major fault with the majority's reasoning, which they thought fell into the category of "substantive due process." They cited *Nichols*, *Blodgett* and *Untermeyer* and wondered why they were not controlling. For a recent confused authority in the retroactivity area, see E. Enters. v. Apfel, 524 U.S. 498 (1998) (retroactive imposition of duty to pay more money into retirement fund was unconstitutional, with Justice Kennedy relying on the Due Process Clause to provide the needed fifth vote in favor of the company).

the retroactive application of a statute is supported by a legitimate legislative purpose furthered by rational means, judgments about the wisdom of such legislation remain within the exclusive province of the legislative and executive branches . . . .' To be sure, . . . retroactive legislation does have to meet a burden not faced by legislation that has only future effects. . . . 'The retroactive aspects of legislation, as well as the prospective aspects, must meet the test of due process, and the justifications for the latter may not suffice for the former' . . . . But that burden is met simply by showing that the retroactive application of the legislation is itself justified by a rational legislative purpose."[730]

- 2012: *Home Concrete* did not directly deal with retroactivity but bears mentioning as the most recent tax decision with any mention of the issue.[731] The Court ruled that the overstatement of the basis of property sold, resulting in a substantial understatement of gain, is not an omission from gross income, and so the three-year and not the six-year statute of limitations applied to the taxpayer's assessment, meaning the assessment came too late. Therefore, the Court did not have to address the retroactivity of the regulation that the Treasury adopted in 2010 and asserted applied to the taxpayer's 1999 year. However, the dissent stated that the regulation was not unconstitutionally retroactive because it "worked no change in the law, and instead . . . interpreted a statutory provision without an established meaning . . . ."[732] A somewhat analogous decision previously rejected a challenge to an additional procedural hurdle placed before a taxpayer seeking refund, after the refund accrued.[733]

(b) *Ex Post Facto Clause*

The Ex Post Facto Clause has no direct application to the tax retroactivity issue.[734] It applies only to crimes and to the creation of a crime or an amendment making it easier to convict of a crime, after the act was committed.[735] The Clause can be applied to: "Every law that alters the legal rules of evidence, and receives less, or different, testimony, than the law required at the time of the commission of the offence, in order to convict the offender."[736] However, an ex post facto issue can arise when a court changes the interpretation of a tax statute and a tax

[730] 512 U.S. at 31.

[731] United States v. Home Concrete & Supply, LLC, 566 U.S. 478 (2012), *affirming*, 634 F.3d 249 (4th Cir. 2011).

[732] *Citing* Smiley v. Citibank (South Dakota), N.A., 517 U.S. 735, 741, 744, n. 3 (1996); Manhattan Gen. Equipment Co. v. Commissioner, 297 U.S. 129, 135 (1936).

[733] United States v. Jefferson Elec. Mfg. Co., 291 U.S. 386, 401 (1934) (sales tax collector had to prove it had not passed on the tax to its customer).

[734] UNITED STATES CONSTITUTION, ARTICLE I, SECTION 9, CLAUSE 3. The ex post facto clause does not encompass taxes, but only a penalty or a forfeiture. Locke v. New Orleans, 71 U.S. 172 (1867).

[735] *See* Calder v. Bull, 3 U.S. 386 (1798).

[736] *Id.* at 390.

crime is involved. For example in *Wilcox* the Court ruled that embezzled money was not includible in gross income.[737] *James* reversed that interpretation, but declined to apply it to the taxpayer who had been convicted of willfully failing to report embezzled income, thus giving the new interpretation prospective only application because the defendant did not act willfully.[738]

Burgess v. Salmon is a confusing ex post facto federal tax precedent.[739] It appears to treat a tax increase as an ex post facto violation, but does not. A tobacco tax was raised from 20 cents to 24 cents per pound and the act made the increase applicable only after the act became effective. The taxed removal of the tobacco from the warehouse occurred in the morning of the day on which the President signed the law in the afternoon; and the Court ruled that it could not be effective earlier than it was signed. Rather than leaving the opinion to rest on this statutory construction of the effective date, the opinion went on to imply that the extra four cents tax was a criminal punishment because failure to pay the tax could alternately have been punished as a crime. In fact it seems to have been making a garbled statement of the unfounded reasoning in the court below that because the new statute had criminal and civil aspects, and the criminal aspects could not be retroactive under the Ex Post Facto Clause, neither could the civil elements.[740] Later the Court cited *Burgess* as simply explaining other earlier decisions applying the Clause to "novel disabilities" that were in effect criminal punishments.[741]

(c) *Contracts Clause*

The state analogue to the Ex Post Facto Clause is in Article I, section 10, clause 1, which also contains the Contracts Clause: a state shall make no law "impairing the obligation of contracts." As to state taxation, the Contracts Clause can appear to play a role similar to that of the the Ex Post Facto Clause, but applicable to civil matters, as discussed in Chapter IX.D.7. The Contracts Clause was interpreted by Chief Justice Marshall in the *Dartmouth College Case* to apply to contracts respecting property under which an individual could claim a beneficial property right that was enforceable in court.[742]

There is no "Contracts Clause" in the Constitution applicable to the United States, but the concept has been suggested as an aspect of due process although

---

[737] Commissioner v. Wilcox, 327 U.S. 404 (1946).

[738] James v. United States, 366 U.S. 213 (1961).

[739] Burgess v. Salmon, 97 U.S. 381 (1878).

[740] Salmon v. Burgess, 21 F. Cas. 254 (1875).

[741] Harisiades v. Shaughnessy, 342 U.S. 580, 595 (1952). The last citation to the opinion by the Court treats it as turning on timing of effective date of an act. United States v. Will, 449 U.S. 200 (1980).

[742] Dartmouth College v. Woodward, 17 U.S. 518 (1819).

its boundaries are somewhat obscure,[743] and indeed substantive due process in practice took the place of Contract Clause rights, which receded in the late 1800s.[744] *Murdock v. Ward* declined to consider an objection that a tax violated a contract between the taxpayer and the United States, which it labeled an estoppel issue.[745] The United States does not impair its obligation of contract with persons to whom it owes money by taxing the receipts.[746]

The Contracts Clause must be distinguished from the "freedom of contract" theory developed under the Due Process Clause and used to justify injunctions against labor strikes,[747] and to strike down a minimum wage for women and children in *Adkins*.[748] It was recognized even at that time that no such doctrine existed in the Constitution; it came from Justice Sutherland.[749] The Supreme Court ultimately abandoned "freedom of contract" due process.[750]

(5) *Presumption*

(a) *Conclusive*

Heiner v. Donnan (1932) ruled that the United States could not conclusively presume that a gift within two years of death was in contemplation of death for estate tax purposes.[751] *Schlesinger* ruled the same way in a state tax cases on a six-year presumption.[752] Generally the substantive due process objection to certain "permanent irrebuttable presumptions" is still part of constitutional jurispru-

---

[743] *See* United States v. Winstar Corp., 518 U.S. 839, 876 (1996) (unmistakability doctrine requires high standard for contractual abrogation of legislative power to reverse itself; it arises under the Contracts Clause as to state contracts and under the Due Process Clause as to federal contracts). *See also* dissent of Justice Douglas in Reg'l Rail Reorganization Act Cases, 419 U.S. 102 (1974).

[744] *See* James L. Kainen, *Nineteenth Century Interpretations of the Federal Contract Clause: The Transformation from Vested to Substantive Rights Against the State*, 31 Buff. L. Rev. 381 (1982), citing as an illustration of the shift from preventing regulation of business by finding a contract right against regulation to finding a substantive due process right not to be regulated, Chicago, M. & St. P. Ry. v. Minnesota, 134 U.S. 418 (1890).

[745] Murdock v. Ward, 178 U.S. 139 (1900).

[746] United States Trust Co. v. Helvering, 307 U.S. 57 (1939).

[747] *E.g., In re* Debs, 158 U.S. 564 (1895).

[748] Adkins v. Children's Hospital, 261 U.S. 525 (1923); *overruled by* West Coast Hotel Co. v. Parrish, 300 U.S. 379 (1937).

[749] Powell, at 545, 555.

[750] *See, e.g.*, Ferguson v. Skrupa, 372 U.S. 726, 729 (1963); Lincoln Federal Labor Union v. Northwestern Iron & Metal Co., 335 U.S. 525 (1949) (repudiating *Lochner*). *See* Ch. V.D.3.b(7).

[751] Heiner v. Donnan, 285 U.S. 312 (1932) (Justices Stone and Brandeis dissented). Handy v. Delaware Trust Co., 285 U.S. 352 (1932) is to the same effect. *Cf.* United States v. Gainey, 380 U.S. 63 (1965) (allowing rebuttable presumption that presence at an illegal still meant defendant was operating it for liquor tax crime purposes); United States v. Provident Trust Co., 291 U.S. 272 (1934) (permitting rebuttal of a presumption that a woman could have children). Justice Stone's dissent in *Heiner* illustrated how the IRS had tried in 102 cases to prove contemplation of death, showing the practical need for a presumption, but to no avail against the majority. *See* Alpheus T. Mason, Harlan Fiske Stone 342 (1956).

[752] Schlesinger v. Wisconsin, 270 U.S. 230 (1926).

dence and the Court applies it with unusual inflexibility.[753] However, in *Vlandis v. Kline* Justice Rehnquist stated in dissent:

> The majority's reliance on cases such as *Heiner v. Donnan* . . . harks back to a day when the principles of substantive due process had reached their zenith in this Court. Later and sounder cases thoroughly repudiated these principles in large part. Ten years ago, the Court reviewed these doctrines in *Ferguson v. Skrupa*, 372 U.S. 726, 730 (1963), and made the following observation: "The doctrine that prevailed in *Lochner*, *Coppage*, *Adkins*, *Burns*, and like cases—that due process authorizes courts to hold laws unconstitutional when they believe the legislature has acted unwisely—has long since been discarded. We have returned to the original constitutional proposition that courts do not substitute their social and economic beliefs for the judgment of legislative bodies, who are elected to pass laws. As this Court stated in a unanimous opinion in 1941, 'We are not concerned . . . with the wisdom, need, or appropriateness of the legislation.'"[754]

And Justice Rehnquist pretty much reversed *Kline* in *Salfi*.[755] The test for conclusive presumptions continues to be whether the presumption has a rational relationship to a legitimate governmental interest.[756]

As discussed in the next Chapter, approximations in taxation can be justified on the basis of administrative convenience. Therefore, the key for taxing authorities seems to be to avoid calling something a presumption of a fact, and simply to state a rule, such as "all gifts within two years of death will be included in the gross estate." That can be viewed as line drawing, for which Congress has great discretion in taxation as illustrated by the Equal Protection Clause decisions.

(b) *Rebuttable Presumptions*

Rebuttable presumptions can violate the Due Process Clause if the court finds there is no rational relationship between the fact to be proved and the fact rebuttably presumed.[757] The constitutional problem is not fixed solely by letting the party try to prove out of the presumption. The Court has applied this rule to strike down several federal tax laws.[758]

---

[753] *See* Vlandis v. Kline, 412 U.S. 441 (1973) (conclusive presumption about college student's residence for purposes of in state tuition violated due process).

[754] 412 U.S. at 467-468.

[755] Weinberger v. Salfi, 422 U.S. 749 (1975). *See also* Usery v. Turner Elkhorn Mining Co., 428 U.S. 1 (1976) (*Salfi* applied to economic matters).

[756] Mobile, J. & K. C. R. Co. v. Turnipseed, 219 U.S. 35 (1910).

[757] Mobile, J. & K. C. R. Co. v. Turnipseed, 219 U.S. 35 (1910).

[758] United States v. Romano, 382 U.S. 136 (1965) (can't presume operating a still by being found near it); Leary v. United States, 395 U.S. 6 (1969) (possessor of marijuana cannot be presumed to know it was imported); Helvering v. Taylor, 293 U.S. 507 (1935) (naked assessment unconstitutional). *See also* Webre Steib Co. v. Commissioner, 324 U.S. 164 (1945) (in this case the presumption favored the taxpayer). *See* Cummings, *Presumptions, Tax Law, and the Constitution*, __ TAX NOTES __.

(6) *Administrative Convenience*

Approximations and generalizations in classification for tax purposes frequently are justified on the basis of administrative convenience, in response to due process objections. Generally, the Court accepts these explanations, with some exceptions (in addition to the exceptions for the three federal estate tax retroactivity rules held unconstitutional):

- One of the earliest appearances of approval of approximations in state taxation was in *The Delaware Railroad Tax* opinion in which Justice Field approved approximating the portion of the capital stock to be taxed based on the portion of trackage in the state.[759] Of course this became a template for multistate corporation taxation by apportionment. But Justice Field's lenience in favor of the state and against a railroad was likely designed to thwart application of the Commerce Clause to limit state powers.

- Administrative convenience justified federal taxation of community property created by statute differently from similar community property rights created by contract.[760]

- *Allegheny* effectively rejected administrative convenience as an excuse for using current sale price values for ad valorem tax purposes for recently purchased houses and not revaluing houses that had not been sold, but *Nordlinger* approved essentially the same regime, without discussing administrative convenience.[761] Then in *Armour* the Court relied entirely on administrative convenience, stating that "ordinarily, administrative considerations can justify a tax-related distinction."[762] *Armour* found any convenience purpose in *Allegheny* to have been precluded by a state statute requiring equal tax valuations. *Armour* ruled that a city could decide to end a tax system under which some persons had paid the tax in full and some were paying in installments, by forgiving future installments but not refunding paid taxes. Not only would continuing to collect the installments be an administrative burden that the city could choose to avoid, but paying refunds would also be an administrative burden that could be reasonably avoided. Even though the state law required equal taxation, as in *Allegheny*, the Court somehow distinguished the two cases on the theory that the tax was initially equally apportioned, and that subsequent refund decisions were not covered by the state equality requirement.

---

[759] Del. R.R. Tax, 85 U.S. 206, 231 (1874).

[760] Fernandez v. Wiener, 326 U.S. 340, 360-361 (1945); United States v. Rompel, 326 U.S. 367 (1945) (companion case).

[761] Allegheny Pittsburgh Coal Co. v. Commission of Webster Cty., 488 U.S. 336 (1989); Nordlinger v. Hahn, 505 U.S. 1, 11-12 (1992). *See* Ch. V.D.3.b(3).

[762] Armour v. City of Indianapolis, 566 U.S. 673 (2012). The considerations applied in *Armour* could be implicated in decisions of taxing authorities to forgive unpaid taxes in other settings, and in deciding how to remedy unconstitutional inequality in taxation (refunds versus taxing all equally).

- The issues of administrative convenience, conclusive presumptions and retroactivity have sometimes overlapped.[763]
- The use of mortality tables and assumed rates of return for valuation purposes is not arbitrary.[764]
- However, *Gast* (state tax) shows that a formula used for purposes of approximation can produce results so grossly illogical as to violate due process.[765]
- A surprising reliance on administrative convenience was allowed in *Madden* where a state taxed interest on local bank deposits at five times the rate for interest on out of state bank deposits, based on the convenience that the local banks collected the tax and the account owner had to report and pay the tax on interest paid by out of state banks.[766]
- In the closely clustered decisions (three federal tax, one state tax) ruling unconstitutional estate tax provisions found to be retroactive, in effect the Court rejected the defense of administrative convenience.[767]

(7) *Substantive Due Process*

(a) *General*

Even Justice Sutherland said that in general the Due Process Clause is not a limitation on the taxing power.[768] And yet, on rare occasions in the 1920s the Court applied what is called substantive due process to strike down three federal tax provisions as unreasonable in substance, not in procedure. Therefore it is useful to examine the origins, history and meaning of this amorphous legal tool even though the Court has not used it, directly or indirectly, to strike down a federal tax in nearly a century.

Substantive due process is any positive rule of federal common law applied by courts to measure the reasonableness of governmental action, which rule does not find direct support in the Constitution but rather is inferred from the Fifth or Fourteenth Amendments' Due Process Clauses, sometimes in combination

---

[763] Schlesinger v. Wisconsin, 270 U.S. 230 (1926) (administrative convenience did not justify conclusive presumption as to retroactive contemplation of death statute).

[764] *See* Simpson v. United States, 252 U.S. 547 (1920).

[765] Gast Realty & Inv. Co. v. Schneider Granite Co., 240 U.S. 55, 59 (1916).

[766] Madden v. Kentucky, 309 U.S. 83 (1940), cited favorably in Armour v. City of Indianapolis, 566 U.S. 673 (2012).

[767] *See* Ch. V.D.3.b(4). *E.g.* Schlesinger v. Wisconsin, 270 U.S. 230, 240 (1926) (The majority opinion was the origin of this objection to a presumption on equality grounds: [it is not right that] "'A' may be required to submit to an exactment forbidden by the Constitution if this seems necessary in order to enable the State readily to collect lawful charges against 'B'."); Heiner v. Donnan, 285 U.S. 312 (1932) (citing *Schlesinger*).

[768] A. Magnano Co. v. Hamilton, 292 U.S. 40, 44 (1934). In 1906 a careful observer stated: "So far as unequal, unjust, or oppressive taxation is concerned, the due process of law clause in the Fifth Amendment, if it be a limitation on congressional power at all, is a limitation of so vague and elastic character as to be hardly worth mentioning." GRAY, at 378.

with other parts such as the Eminent Domain Clause or the Equal Protection Clause, and does not enforce only rights to fair governmental procedure.[769] The Court applied substantive due process, whether or not it used the term, within a five-year period to strike down three federal estate tax rules due to retroactivity and a conclusive presumption.[770]

The reasons for the Court's relative lack of reliance on substantive due process in federal tax cases include the facts that (1) the Court successfully relied (during the same period as the three cases) instead on the Tenth Amendment in cases of federal taxes that the Court found not to be taxes but to regulate local matters, (2) it retained the "out" of striking down a tax under the even more undefined category of taxes that were so arbitrary as to be confiscations without just compensation,[771] and (3) the Court was somewhat hemmed in by the expansiveness of the federal taxing power, which had been installed by Chief Justice Marshall himself (see Chapter II.A.2). Thus, Justice Sutherland stated in 1934, the heyday of substantive due process, in a case refusing to strike down a state regulatory tax scheme:

> Except in rare and special instances, the due process of law clause contained in the Fifth Amendment is not a limitation upon the taxing power conferred upon Congress by the Constitution. . . . That clause is applicable to a taxing statute such as the one here assailed only if the act be so arbitrary as to compel the conclusion that it does not involve an exertion of the taxing power, but constitutes, in substance and effect, the direct exertion of a different and forbidden power, as, for example, the confiscation of property. . . . Collateral purposes or motives of a legislature in levying a tax of a kind within the reach of its lawful power are matters beyond the scope of judicial inquiry. . . . Nor may a tax within the lawful power of a state be judicially stricken down under the Due Process Clause simply because its enforcement may or will result in restricting or even destroying particular occupations or businesses . . . unless, indeed, as already indicated, its necessary interpretation and effect be such as plainly to demonstrate that the form of taxation was adopted as a mere disguise, under which there was exercised, in reality, another and different power denied by the Federal Constitution to the state.[772]

---

[769] *See Due Process - Substantive*, THE OXFORD GUIDE TO THE SUPREME COURT 274-276 (2005).

[770] Nichols v. Coolidge, 274 U.S. 531 (1927); Blodgett v. Holden, 275 U.S. 142 (1927) and Untermeyer v. Anderson, 276 U.S. 440 (1928) (same statute); Heiner v. Donnan, 285 U.S. 312 (1932). *See* Ch. V.D.3.b(4) and (5).

[771] *See* Ch. V.D.3.b(8)(b).

[772] A. Magnano Co. v. Hamilton, 292 U.S. 40, 45 (1934). Note also that McCray v. United States, 195 U.S. 27 (1904) had already approved essentially the same tax. The taxpayer in *McCray* made Fifth Amendment challenges both to the destructive nature of the tax and its arbitrary discrimination, as well as objecting to Congress' lack of power to regulate the subject taxed; Justice White gave the surprising response that Congress can regulate that which it does not have the power to regulate through the taxing power, so long as a state could tax the same way without violating the Fifth (or Fourteenth) Amendment. 195 U.S. at 63 (unless "no free government" could pass such a law to destroy).

Despite a long term decline in reliance on substantive due process as such, the Court maintains a love-hate relationship with it, the degree of affection depending somewhat on whose ox is being gored. When first used to strike down regulation of economic activity (*e.g.*, *Lochner*[773]), substantive due process was championed by conservative Justices. The same conservatives also used substantive due process to protect certain individual rights in the same era (*e.g.*, *Pierce v. Society of Sisters*,[774] ruling that Catholics could not be forced to attend public schools). Later, more liberal Justices cited the *Pierce* line of cases for the exceptions that would prove the rule that substantive due process should not be used to strike down economic legislation (*i.e.*, footnote 4 in *Carolene Products*[775]). But some of those liberal Justices could not stomach relying on a Justice McReynolds opinion such as *Pierce* to strike down school segregation in the District of Columbia, and so the Court imported equal protection into the Due Process Clause of the Fifth Amendment to explain its 1954 decision in *Bolling v. Sharpe*.[776] The most recent turn of the wheel finds conservative Justices bemoaning the inconsistency of the liberal Justices and the lack of substantial guarantees in the procedural protection of the Due Process Clause.[777]

However, Justices of both persuasions may say things like it is "too late in the day" [to say substantive due process does not exist], while also saying they "should be reluctant" to expand it.[778] In other cases the term substantive due process is accompanied by modifiers like "generalized notion,"[779] "'scarce and open ended' guideposts, . . . infinitely plastic, . . . incoherence,"[780] "wonderfully malleable concept,"[781] and "now discredited"[782] to quote a few. Substantive due process is like the cat with nine lives, except that in the early years it was not even identified as a cat, but once seen (and adopted as a category by the legal publishers), it has often been discussed by the Court in the last half century. The current approach of the would-be users of substantive due process is to find substantive rights in the words of the Constitution (*e.g.*, "free exercise").[783]

Justice Jackson best explained the shortcoming of substantive due process as applied to government regulation:

> Invalidation of a statute or ordinance on due process grounds leaves ungoverned or ungovernable conduct which many people find objectionable. Invo-

---

[773] Lochner v. New York, 198 U.S. 45 (1905).

[774] Pierce v. Society of Sisters, 268 U.S. 510 (1925).

[775] United States v. Carolene Prod. Co., 304 U.S. 144, 153 n. 4 (1938).

[776] Bolling v. Sharpe, 347 U.S. 497 (1954). *See* SCHWARTZ, at 98-100 (explaining Justice Black's objection to reliance on *Pierce*).

[777] *See, e.g.*, Vlandis v. Kline, 412 U.S. 441 (1973) (dissent of Justice Rehnquist); McDonald v. City of Chicago, 561 U.S. 742 (2010) (dissent of Justice Scalia); Perry v. New Hampshire, 565 U.S. 228 (2012) (concurrence of Justice Thomas).

[778] Dissent of Justice Stevens in Philip Morris USA v. Williams, 549 U.S. 346 (2007).

[779] Turner v. Rogers, 564 U.S. 431 (2011).

[780] NASA v. Nelson, 562 U.S. 134 (2011).

[781] Stop the Beach Renourishment, Inc. v. Fla. Dep't of Envtl. Prot., 560 U.S. 702 (2010).

[782] Gundy v. United States, 139 S. Ct. 2116 (2019) (Gorsuch dissent).

[783] Roman Catholic Diocese v. Cuomo, 208 L. Ed. 2d 206 (2020) (Gorsuch concurrence).

> cation of the equal protection clause, on the other hand, does not disable any governmental body from dealing with the subject at hand. It merely means that the prohibition or regulation must have a broader impact.[784]

Justice Jackson also noted the inevitable desire of the "well-to-do minority" to grasp for any tool, such as judicial review of the reasonableness of Congress' action, to free itself from that otherwise uncontrollable threat (like taxation or regulation) to their financial well-being.[785] He counted 228 times from 1890 to 1941 when the Court invalidated state laws under the Due Process Clause of the Fourteenth Amendment.[786]

Many opinions have been identified as the first instances of substantive due process,[787] but the most prominent precursor was *Dred Scott*, ruling that the property rights of the slave owners were protected by due process notions against the act of Congress known as the Missouri Compromise, which might have resulted in the freedom and hence citizenship of the former slave, Dred Scott.[788] However, the doctrine did not really take hold until (1) the Fourteenth Amendment transplanted the Due Process Clause into the evaluation of state statutes, at a time when state economic regulatory efforts were much more robust than federal economic regulatory efforts, and (2) the post-Civil War changes in American society shifted national concerns from states versus the nation, to business and corporations versus the states and the nation. Justice Miller remarked upon the strange juvenation of the Due Process Clause when it appeared in the Fourteenth Amendment.[789]

The Court was called on by business, particularly the railroads, which were the first big business corporations in the United States, for protection from economic regulations and taxation, in what is called the Gilded Age, the period from the

---

[784] Railway Express Co. v. New York, 336 U.S. 106, 110 (1949).

[785] JACKSON, at 23 n. 27, quoting Edgerton.

[786] JACKSON, at 50.

[787] *See, e.g.*, Chicago, B. & Q. R. Co. v. Chicago, 166 U.S. 226 (1897) (applying the Eminent Domain Clause to the states through the Due Process Clause); Murray's Lessee v. Hoboken Land & Improv. Co., 59 U.S. 272, 276 (1856) (containing a precursor of substantive due process); Chicago, M. & St. P. Ry. v. Minnesota, 134 U.S. 418 (1890) (ruled that courts not state commissions must determine whether railroad rates are reasonable and not just fairly determined as a matter of procedure); Allgeyer v. Louisiana, 165 U.S. 578 (1897) (the subcategory of substantive due process based on liberty of contract).

[788] *See* SCHWARTZ, at 117-118; JACKSON, at 36 ("It [*Dred Scott*] first suggested the due process clause as a basis for reviewing federal legislation and so foreshadowed the enormous scope of the judicial power which was to be later exercised . . . It had never been used as the basis of judicial review of the content of legislation . . ."). *Cf.* Louise Weinberg, *An Almost Archeological Dig: Finding a Surprisingly Rich Early Understanding of Substantive Due Process*, 27 CONST. COMM. 163 (2010) (analyzing an 1840 argument in the Supreme Court).

[789] "It is not a little remarkable that while this provision has been in the Constitution of the United States as a restraint upon the authority of the federal government, for nearly a century, . . . [it] has rarely been invoked . . . [but now] the docket of this court is crowded with cases in which we are asked to hold that state courts and state legislatures have deprived their own citizens of life, liberty or property without due process of law." Davidson v. New Orleans, 96 U.S. 97, 103 (1878).

end of the Civil War to 1900.[790] The 1937 so called switch in time that saved the nine seemed to mark the demise of substantive due process at the hands of the growing liberal majority on the Court. But what Justice Stone described as a residual possibly substantive due process inquiry about the mere rationality of a law of economic regulation, surged back in the direction of a more free floating investigation of reasonableness of law rather than its bare rationality.[791]

As a phrase substantive due process first appeared in at least the Lawyer's Edition of the Supreme Court Reports in the arguments made by the A.L.A. Schechter Poultry Company against the New Deal Agricultural Adjustment Act

---

[790] *See, e.g.*, Railroad Com. Cases, 116 U.S. 307 (1886) (regulation cannot confiscate or destroy), *cited by* Atlantic C. L. R. Co. v. North Carolina Corp., 206 U.S. 1 (1907) (which the abstractors have identified as a substantive due process case). A brief history of the beginnings of substantive due process: In the *Slaughter-House Cases* the Court at first appeared to support regulation of commerce, this time by a municipality. Slaughter-House Cases, 83 U.S. 36 (1873), rejected a challenge by butchers to what was effectively a local monopoly on butchering. The opinion is most remembered for eviscerating the Fourteenth Amendment by finding that there were no special "privileges and immunities" of United States citizenship. *See* BARRY FRIEDMAN, THE WILL OF THE PEOPLE 143 (2009) [hereinafter FRIEDMAN]. However, it also declined to find any protection from regulation in the Due Process and Equal Protection Clauses. The Court applied the same approach in support of a more sympathetic regulation when it upheld state regulation of grain elevator rates in Munn v. Illinois, 94 U.S. 113 (1877) (the *Granger Cases*), which is viewed as a watershed decision that set in motion substantial business reaction to growing regulation of business. FRIEDMAN, at 115-159. This backlash produced the fleshed out theory of substantive due process, which placed railroads and the like in the posture of the thwarted butchers who lost the *Slaughter-House Cases*. Former Justice Campbell's losing argument in that case likely influenced Justice Field, a primary architect of substantive due process, who dissented in both *Slaughter-House* and *Munn*. The latter dissent asserted the idea that substantive due process could protect property rights, chiefly of business, from government interference. This contention converted what had theretofore been a vague set of procedural safeguards (notice and hearing, etc.) into substantive, positive rights found to inhere in the expanded concept of due process. Due process was selected for this task when "privileges and immunities" and "impairment of the obligation of contract" and "taking without just compensation" failed to carry the day for propertied interests. Justice Field grounded his dissent on the Fourteenth Amendment and free markets economics, and stated, inter alia: "The question presented, therefore, is one of the greatest importance,—whether it is within the competency of a State to fix the compensation which an individual may receive for the use of his own property in his private business, and for his services in connection with it. . . . [If the majority be right] all property and all business in the State are held at the mercy of a majority of its legislature. . . . If the legislature of a State, under pretence of providing for the public good, or for any other reason, can determine, against the consent of the owner, the uses to which private property shall be devoted, or the prices which the owner shall receive for its uses, it can deprive him of the property as completely as by a special act for its confiscation or destruction." 94 U.S. at 136-154. Substantive due process finally took hold in a majority opinion in Allgeyer v. Louisiana, 165 U.S. 578 (1897), and was applied to federal law in Adair v. United States, 208 U.S. 161 (1908). The story of substantive due process is well told by Felix Frankfurter in *Mr. Justice Holmes and the Constitution: A Review of His Twenty five Years on the Supreme Court*, 41 HARV. L. REV. 121, 141-142 (1927); and SCHWARTZ, at 151-170.

[791] *See* Louise Weinberg, *Back to the Future: The New General Common Law*, 35 J. MAR. L. & COM. 523, 546-547 (2004) (commenting on Justice Stone's opinion in United States v. Carolene Prod. Co., 304 U.S. 144 (1938) and listing the substantive due process rationality questions as (1) rationality, (2) relevance, and (3) legitimacy of the governmental interest).

(which arguments the Court adopted, without using the phrase).[792] The term first appeared in an opinion in the dissent of Justice Rutledge to the dismissal of a complaint of a gas company about regulation.[793] Then Justices Black and Douglas used the term in dissent, without defining it but contrasting it to the "more elemental and less flexible" procedural due process.[794] Finally Justice Frankfurter in a majority opinion referred to substantive due process as a broad limiter on the powers of Congress in 1954, but again without definition.[795]

In 1955 Justice Jackson said of the 1936 *Tipaldo*[796] opinion (similar to *Schechter*):

> For more than half a century the Supreme Court found in the Fourteenth Amendment authority for striking down various social experiments by the states. The history of judicial nullification of state social and economic legislation is too well known to justify repetition here. It came to its culmination when the Court wound up the October 1935 Term by declaring that there was no power in either state or nation to enact a minimum wage law, a position repudiated within a few months by the conventions of both political parties and retracted by the Court itself with some haste. That retraction probably brought an end to the use of the Fourteenth Amendment to prevent experiments by the states with economic and social and labor legislation.[797]

In 1962 Justice White, in dissent, stated that the present Court had an allergy to substantive due process and would not apply it to an economic regulation (although it applied it to a narcotics regulation). In 1963 Justice Black linked substantive due process to the pre-1937 anti-regulation cases and rejected it in ruling that a state could regulate debt collectors.[798] In 1968 Justice Douglas concurring in *Flast v. Cohen* identified 1923 as the heyday of substantive due process "when courts were sitting in judgment on the wisdom or reasonableness of legislation."[799]

When the Court shifted the use of substantive due process to create substantive rights for individuals, in what are called civil rights cases in three areas—(1) the criminal area (*e.g.*, *Miranda* warnings),[800] (2) the recognition of personal lib-

---

[792] A. L. A. Schechter Poultry Corp. v. United States, 295 U.S. 495 (1935).

[793] Republic Natural Gas Co. v. Oklahoma, 334 U.S. 62 (1948).

[794] Shaughnessy v. United States, 345 U.S. 206 (1953).

[795] Galvan v. Press, 347 U.S. 522 (1954).

[796] Morehead v. New York ex rel. Tipaldo, 298 U.S. 587 (1936).

[797] JACKSON, at 68.

[798] Ferguson v. Skrupa, 372 U.S. 726 (1963) ("The doctrine that prevailed in *Lochner*, *Coppage*, *Adkins*, *Burns*, and like cases—that due process authorizes courts to hold laws unconstitutional when they believe the legislature has acted unwisely—has long since been discarded").

[799] Flast v. Cohen, 392 U.S. 83 (1968). The statement evidently referred to Adkins v. Children's Hospital, 261 U.S. 525 (1923), *overruled by* West Coast Hotel Co. v. Parrish, 300 U.S. 379 (1937).

[800] *See* Susan R. Klein, *Miranda Deconstitutionalized: When the Self Incrimination Clause and the Civil Rights Act Collide*, 143 U. PA. L. REV. 417, 420 (1995).

erties (*e.g.*, *Roe v. Wade*),[801] (3) the strict scrutiny/suspect classification area (*e.g.*, *Bakke*)[802]—generally the shift was not welcomed by the conservative Justices. Substantive due process seems to have been under greatest attack since the dawn of the Rehnquist Court,[803] even by the Court's centrists. In 1970 in *Williams v. Illinois* Justice Harlan disassociated himself from the equal protection grounds for ruling that an indigent who had served his time and could not pay the fine to get out of jail should be released by reasoning that there was no governmental purpose whatsoever that could be served by keeping him in jail, which also seems to reject the more amorphous substantive due process:

> The "equal protection" analysis of the Court is, I submit, a "wolf in sheep's clothing," for that rationale is no more than a masquerade of a supposedly objective standard for subjective judicial judgment as to what state legislation offends notions of "fundamental fairness." Under the rubric of "equal protection" this Court has in recent times effectively substituted its own "enlightened" social philosophy for that of the legislature no less than did in the older days the judicial adherents of the now discredited doctrine of "substantive" due process. I, for one, would prefer to judge the legislation before us in this case in terms of due process, that is to determine whether it arbitrarily infringes a constitutionally protected interest of this appellant.[804]

So there seem to be three major reasons why at least some of the conservative members of the Court currently seem less ready to create new rights under substantive due process: (1) they have found other somewhat more targeted, albeit novel, constitutional grounds for the positions they want to support, (2) they can interpret new rights into words of the Constitution such as "free exercise," and (3) they want to limit the potential for use of the much more diffuse substantive due process to create rights they are not interested in creating. As to the more targeted provisions, for example, Justice Thomas did not have to interpolate the right to bear arms through substantive due process; rather he relied on privileges and immunities in his concurrence.[805] Majority opinions have empowered

---

[801] Roe v. Wade, 410 U.S. 113 (1973). *See* Linda Greenhouse and Reva B. Siegel, *Before (and after) Roe v. Wade: New Questions about Backlash*, 120 YALE L. J. 2028 (2011) (arguing that the decision has not become notorious due to a backlash to the court's action alone, but due to the Republican political interests deciding (1) to make abortion an issue to attract Catholic and conservative voters before the decision, and (2) to further promote the decision as a talisman for political purposes substantially after the decision).

[802] Regents of Univ. of Cal. v. Bakke, 438 U.S. 265 (1983).

[803] *See, e.g.*, Vlandis v. Kline, 412 U.S. 441 (1973) (dissent of Justice Rehnquist); McDonald v. City of Chicago, 561 U.S. 742 (2010) (dissent of Justice Scalia); Perry v. New Hampshire, 565 U.S. 228 (2012) (concurrence of Justice Thomas).

[804] Williams v. Ill., 399 U.S. 235 (1970). *See also* Mackey v. United States, 401 U.S. 667 (1971) (Justice Harlan concurrence objecting to new substantive due process in a criminal tax case).

[805] McDonald v. City of Chicago, 561 U.S. 742 (2010).

money in elections by relying on the First Amendment.[806] Also, the Eminent Domain Clause has trumped substantive due process.[807] And freedom of speech increasingly is turned to the protection of business' commercial speech.[808] The Court struck down an exception from a robocall ban for government debt collection under the First Amendment, requiring strict scrutiny.[809] Justice Breyer's dissent wondered whether the same approach could bring tax reporting forms under strict scrutiny.

In contrast, the curtailment of the diffuse substantive due process as a catch-all support for individual freedoms is seen in the Court's refusal to create a due process right of criminals to DNA testing,[810] and to find a protected property interest in a restraining order.[811] One reason for these shifts is that substantive due process was tainted politically by its role in such conservative-hated rulings as *Roe v. Wade* and *Planned Parenthood v. Casey*.[812] Trying to make the best of a bad situation, Justice Scalia and Thomas have emphasized that substantive due process applies only to "fundamental rights" that are historically rooted (which to them did not cover Texas' sodomy laws).[813] They also have spelled out the interesting history by which Justice Stone's famous footnote 4 in *Carolene Products* cited and relied upon such conservative favorites as *Pierce v. Society of Sisters*, which actually broke the ground for converting substantive due process from solely a protection of property rights to protection of other more personal rights.[814]

Professor Kermit Roosevelt wrote has written a very helpful synthesis of Supreme Court opinions on substantive due process and academic thinking about them.[815] He shows that what came to be called substantive due process began in opinions of the Court that attempted to identify limits to legislative power as a matter of constitutional doctrine, the prototype of such cases being *Lochner*.[816] But in the problematic cases, the limits imposed could not be attributed to any particular statement in the Constitution, and instead were remitted to the broad concept of "due process." Those decisions depended on categorization: either a law was within the reach of legislative power, which effectively meant the law

---

[806] *See, e.g.*, Citizens United v. FEC, 558 U.S. 310 (2010). Justice Stevens stated in dissent: "The majority's rejection of this principle "elevate[s] corporations to a level of deference which has not been seen at least since the days when substantive due process was regularly used to invalidate regulatory legislation thought to unfairly impinge upon established economic interests." *See also* Ariz. Free Enter. Club's Freedom Club PAC v. Bennett, 131 U.S. 2806 (2011).

[807] *See* Lingle v. Chevron U.S.A. Inc., 544 U.S. 528 (2005).

[808] *See, e.g.*, Sorrell v. IMS Health Inc., 564 U.S. 552 (2011) (drug vendors have right to get patient information about drug prescriptions).

[809] Barr v. Am. Ass'n of Political Consultants, 140 S. Ct. 2335 (2020).

[810] DA's Office v. Osborne, 557 U.S. 52 (2009).

[811] Town of Castle Rock v. Gonzales, 545 U.S. 748 (2005).

[812] Roe v. Wade, 410 U.S. 113 (1973); Planned Parenthood v. Casey, 505 U.S. 833 (1992).

[813] Lawrence v. Texas, 539 U.S. 558 (2003).

[814] United States v. Carlton, 512 U.S. 26, 38-42 (1994).

[815] Roosevelt.

[816] Lochner v. New York, 198 U.S. 45 (1905).

was in the public interest or had a net benefit to society, or not.[817] When the law in question appeared to benefit or harm a relatively limited group of persons in their private capacities, the Court sometimes purported to find it difficult to discern benefit to the public interest (as in *Lochner*, involving working hour limits, where the employer won). Thus the public interest was often found lacking in legislation adversely affecting some (though obviously not all) private interests.

In the 1930s the realization grew, both outside and within the Court, that the Court's application of the doctrinal principle of due process, based on defining Congress' power in terms of categories, resulted in decisions that were not in the public interest. In other words the proof was not in the pudding: results of applying the doctrine of limited power/due process didn't work in practice (although this epiphany was by no means universal, and did not necessarily reflect only objective analysis, but also a combination of power politics and institutional self-preservation).[818]

As a consequence, the Court shifted in 1937 and thereafter to a more fact-dependent balancing approach when evaluating the constitutional limits of Congress' power under the Due Process Clause.[819] And because fact-dependent balancing is primarily within the competence of Congress and state legislatures, the Court began to broadly defer to Congress' choices.[820] But the balancing/deference approach still needed some boundaries.[821] The only discernible requirement of due process was that the law be in the public interest; however, the public interest could no longer be viewed as including only broad scale "general welfare," but also must somehow encompass benefits targeted to particular groups, given practical political realities.[822]

The substantive due process boundary that the Court eventually found to limit Congress' power to legislate in the public interest was one that protected persons who merited or needed special protection, introduced in Justice Stone's footnote 4 in *Carolene Products*.[823] That footnote summarized types of laws that

---

[817] Roosevelt, at 989. Roosevelt states that the origin of the "public interest" category is obscure, but links it to Munn v. Illinois, 94 U.S. 113 (1877). He also traces it back to Justice Chase's opinion in Calder v. Bull, 3 U.S. 386 (1798).

[818] *See* BURNS, at 148.

[819] Roosevelt, at 989. The process began earlier. The "Brandeis brief" that Louis D Brandeis used to win an early victory in Muller v. Oregon, 208 U.S. 412 (1908), influenced this recognition of the importance of fact finding in assessing the public interest. But another way of looking at it is that the Brandeis Brief either pandered to or adopted the view of the Court of the day that it had the authority to assess the general reasonableness of the legislative decision.

[820] Roosevelt, at 989.

[821] *Id.* at 991.

[822] *Id.* at 992.

[823] United States v. Carolene Prod. Co., 304 U.S. 144, 153 n. 4 (1938). But note, Justice Stone did not discover the special suspicion to be applied to a tax discrimination based on race. *See* American Sugar Refining Co. v. Louisiana, 179 U.S. 89, 92 (1900) ("Of course, if such discrimination were purely arbitrary, oppressive or capricious, and made to depend upon differences of color, race, nativity, religious opinions, political affiliations or other considerations having no possible connection with the duties of citizens as taxpayers, such exemption would be pure favoritism, and a denial of the equal protection of the laws to the less favored classes.").

might not be entitled to as broad a presumption that the choices reflected were exclusively within Congress' competence: (1) those choices specifically prohibited by the Constitution, particularly the first ten amendments; (2) laws restricting the political processes, including voting, the press, political organizations and assembly; and (3) laws aimed a religion or "discrete and insular minorities." The Burger and Rehnquist Courts substantially slowed the identification of such minorities.[824]

Roosevelt calls the Court's movement to use the Due Process Clause to protect "fundamental rights" (and hence to function again as substantive due process) the crafting of a "decision rule," *i.e.*, a way to practically apply the due process limitation on legislating in the public interest.[825] The decision rules can be defended as avoiding the high cost of errors by Congress in certain areas of law.

Roosevelt assesses the *Carolene Products* footnote 4, in the context of its strange migration into equal protection analysis.[826] He observes that when the Court came to decide the *Brown v. Board of Education* issue in the District of Columbia in 1954 it did not apply due process and treat the minority as one to be protected thereunder, but rather imported the Equal Protection Clause into the Fifth Amendment Due Process Clause.[827] His point is not so much the illogic of the reverse-incorporation (which has been widely criticized), but the error of overlooking the due process tool.[828] Then the Court began to apply due process as the protector of "fundamental rights," beginning in 1963 in *Griswold v. Connecticut* (reversing a conviction for dispensing birth control),[829] where it shifted ground away from the doctrinal principle of power boundaries to discover a new set of decision rules for due process analysis based on discovered "fundamental rights." While the fundamental rights approach could be sourced to *Carolene*, it was set adrift from the anchoring substantive due process doctrine of assessing limits on Congress' power, and set the Court on an unmoored search to identify fundamental rights.[830]

Whether or not this application of the Due Process Clause has produced correct results, it is very different from applying substantive due process to limit Congress' power as a matter of impacting positively the public interest (the basic doctrinal principle to be enforced). As Roosevelt puts it:

---

[824] *See* San Antonio Independent School District v. Rodriguez, 411 U.S. 1 (1973) (ruling that there was no duty to equalize school spending in poor districts; that is wealth is not a suspect category); Bowen v. Gilliard, 483 U.S. 587 (1987) (rejected due process objection to reduction of welfare payments).

[825] Roosevelt, at 993.

[826] *Id.* at 996.

[827] Bolling v. Sharpe, 347 U.S. 497 (1954).

[828] As to whether this was an error, *see* SCHWARTZ, at 98-100 (explaining that the choice was a conscious one because some of the Justices did not want to cite such substantive due process rulings as Pierce v. Society of Sisters, and so the alternate approach was required).

[829] Griswold v. Connecticut, 381 U.S. 479 (1965) (the opinion did not cite *Carolene*).

[830] Roosevelt, at 1000 ("remarkably free-wheeling and anti-democratic").

> The focus on fundamentality is not a plausible due process approach because the operative proposition behind the Due Process Clause, as I have described it, is not about fundamental rights at all.[831]

Thus Roosevelt recommends returning substantive due process to its proper role of asking first whether the law serves the public interest, and then applying decision rules that assess whether too high a cost has been placed on groups that need special protection.

As applied to tax, this should mean that the three anti-retroactivity tax rulings of the Court (the only decisions based directly or indirectly on due process, discussed in Chapter V.D.3.b(4)) should come out differently, because the Court has turned away from applying substantive due process to economic and tax regulations, no suspect classification or protected class is involved, and there is a plausible explanation for the exercise of the government's power (as long as it does not box the reasoning in by calling it a preclusive presumption of a required fact).

As a final evidence of the danger of due process grounding for civil liberties rulings, Ruth Bader Ginsburg grounded her arguments for gender equality in the Equal Protection Clause.[832]

(b) *Taking from One to Give to Another*

A recurring theme in substantive due process cases is the specter of unconstitutionally taking property from one person in order to give that property to another. The assertion contains within it an inherent weakness when applied to taxation because taxation by definition is not an apportionment of the costs of governmental to the benefits received,[833] and so inevitably the taxes raised from one person can and very likely will be spent in ways that benefit others.

Taking from one to give to another was one basis of the reasoning in *Butler*, striking down a statutory scheme that forced cotton processors to pay, in the form of taxes, the difference between the market value of the cotton and what they paid for it.[834] The same act that imposed the tax also appropriated funds to pay a like amount to the cotton farmers, in price supports. The key to the Court's ruling in *Butler* was that it found the tax not to be a taxing power tax, but rather to be an exaction imposed under the Necessary and Proper Clause in support of an attempt to carry out another activity that the Court found to be outside the powers of the federal government.[835] The attacks on the AAA con-

---

[831] *Id.*

[832] *See* Reva B. Siegel, *Equality and Choice: Sex Equality Perspectives on Reproductive Rights in the Work of Ruth Bader Ginsburg*, 25 Colum. J. Gender & L. 63 (2013).

[833] *See* Carmichael v. Southern Coal & Coke Co., 301 U.S. 495, 522-523 (1937); Commonwealth Edison Co. v. Montana, 453 U.S. 609, 623 (1981); Massachusetts v. United States, 435 U.S. 444, 455 (1978); Inter-Island Steam Navigation Co. v. Hawaii, 305 U.S. 306 (1938); Keystone Bituminous Coal Ass'n v. DeBenedictis, 480 U.S. 470 n. 21 (1987).

[834] United States v. Butler, 297 U.S. 1 (1936).

[835] *See* Ch. III.F.

tinue to this day, with a recent success by treating the law's enforcement rules as takings, which is a version of taking from one to give to another.[836]

In contrast, when the same argument was raised against a tax on domestic soap producers, the proceeds of which were paid over to the treasury of the Philippines, Justice Sutherland rejected the argument by characterizing the soap tax a "true tax," and distinguishing *Butler* as a case in which the "sole aim" of the statute was regulation that was beyond the power of the United States, and in which there was a "naked taking" of property from one group and giving it to another.[837]

Justice Roberts used an approach similar to that in *Butler* in a highly reactionary nontax case striking down railroad retirement funds: "Thus the Act denies due process of law by taking the property of one and bestowing it upon another."[838] The opinion admitted that the problem could not affect a tax (presumably meaning that taxes do not require a linkage between the amount paid and benefit received by the payor, so necessarily the benefit must be expected to be received by others).[839] The source of this observation actually contained a different nuance: taxes obviously are one case, but not the only case, where cash is taken from one for the benefit of another (an opinion by Justice Holmes.)[840] Justice Roberts also admitted the "principle that an ulterior public advantage may justify the taking of a comparatively insignificant amount of private property for what in its immediate purpose is a private use."[841] Again, the source of his quotation, the same opinion of Justice Holmes, upheld a state requirement that seemed to go considerably beyond insignificance: banks had to deposit five percent of their average daily deposits in a state run account guarantee fund, and the Court rejected attacks on the requirement.

Similarly Justice Alito waived aside an objection that his reasoning in a takings decision could be applied against a tax by blandly asserting that taxes were not takings.[842]

The negative view of taking from one to give to another seems to have arisen automatically to the mind of the Justices who espoused substantive due process. For example, Justice Van Devanter cited it in ruling unconstitutional a state statute requiring a railroad to pay for killed cattle within 30 days, or face double damages if a jury ruled against it (which now seems hardly unreasonable, much less unconsti-

---

836 Horne v. Dep't of Agric., 569 U.S. 513 (2013); Horne v. Dep't of Agric., 576 U.S. 351 (2015).

837 Cincinnati Soap Co. v. United States, 301 U.S. 308, 312-313 (1937).

838 Railroad Retirement Bd. v. Alton R. Co., 295 U.S. 330, 360 (1935). *See* William E. Leuchtenburg, The Supreme Court Reborn ch. 2, "Mr. Justice Roberts and the Railroaders" (1994).

839 295 U.S. at 360 ("It was further said that there may be cases other than those of taxation in which the share of each party . . .").

840 Noble State Bank v. Haskell, 219 U.S. 104, 111 (1911).

841 295 U.S. at 360 (referring to *Noble State Bank*).

842 Koontz v. St. Johns River Water Management District, 570 U.S. 595 (2013).

tutional).[843] However, it is likely that the theory was not an immaculate conception. A speech by future Justice George Sutherland to the New York State Bar Association in 1921 reveals that the theory is rooted in a fear or socialism or communism:

> . . . [F]or if the hand of power shall ever be permitted to take from A and give to B merely because A has much and B has little, we shall have taken the first step upon that unhappy path which leads from a republic where every man may rise in proportion to his energy and ability, to a commune where energy and sloth, ability and ignorance, occupy in common the same dead level of individual despair. Any attempt to fix a limit to personal acquisition is filled with danger . . . .[844]

In sum, the cause of discomfort with taking from one and giving to another arises when (1) a sufficiently tight linkage can be discerned as a matter of fact, (2) the receipt by the other person is thought not to be a "public use" under the Eminent Domain Clause, and (3) neither compensation nor proper purpose is found, and the taking arguably is not a tax.

(c) *Taxing One on the Income or Property of Another*

In a questionable decision the Court stated, inter alia, that one person cannot be taxed on the income or property of another.[845] An analogous statement was made with respect to property.[846]

(d) *Double Taxation*

Double taxation of the same subject by the United States (or in conjunction with some other taxing power) does not violate the Due Process Clause (or other constitutional rule).[847]

---

[843] St. Louis v. Wynne, 224 U.S. 354 (1912) (a surprisingly unanimous opinion not involving tax). *See* Richard S. Kay, *The Equal Protection Clause: 1873-1903*, 29 BUFF. L. REV. 667, 709-712 (1980) (speculating how the Court managed to reach different conclusions in similar cases involving railroads). *Cf.*, for an analogous statement in the area of presumptions, Schlesinger v. Wisconsin, 270 U.S. 230, 240 (1926) ("That is to say, 'A' may be required to submit to an exactment forbidden by the Constitution if this seems necessary in order to enable the State readily to collect lawful charges against 'B.'").

[844] *Quoted in* JOEL FRANCIS PASCHAL, MR. JUSTICE SUTHERLAND A MAN AGAINST THE STATE 109 (1951).

[845] Hoeper v. Tax Comm'n of Wisconsin, 284 U.S. 206 (1931) (due process and equal protection violated by forcing husband to report with wife and include her income in computation) (Justices Holmes, Brandeis and Stone dissented). *See also* CUMMINGS, at ch. VI.F.2.a.

[846] Knowlton v. Moore, 178 U.S. 41, 77 (1900) ("It may be doubted by some, aside from express constitutional restrictions, whether the taxation by Congress of the property of one person, accompanied with an arbitrary provision that the rate of tax shall be fixed with reference to the sum of the property of another, thus bringing about the profound inequality which we have noticed, would not transcend the limitations arising from those fundamental conceptions of free government which underlie all constitutional systems. On this question, however, in any of its aspects, we do not even intimate an opinion, as no occasion for doing so exists, since, as we understand the law, we are clearly of opinion that it does not sustain the construction which was placed on it by the court below.").

[847] Patton v. Brady, 184 U.S. 608 (1902); United States v. Hemme, 476 U.S. 558 (1986); Hellmich v. Hellman, 276 U.S. 233 (1926) (shareholder and corporate income taxes). *See* Ch. IX.

(8) *The Eminent Domain Clause*

(a) *General Rule*

The Court has repeatedly and clearly ruled that taxes are not subject to the Eminent Domain Clause of the Fifth and Fourteenth Amendments.[848] The reasons are both that the Eminent Domain Clause does not apply to the taxing power, and that cash exactions are not subject to the Eminent Domain Clause.[849] However, the Court identified an exception to that principle, when the cash exaction could be found to burden a piece of property.[850] Moreover, the Constitution is not self-defeating,[851] which precludes the Eminent Domain Clause taking away what the taxing power grants. Finally, the fact that there is no necessary connection between taxation and benefits, whether the benefits are direct arm's length payments or otherwise, makes it impossible to apply the Eminent Domain Clause to taxes.[852] The possibility that a confiscatory regulatory tax could be a taking is addressed above in Chapter III.E.5.

Other statements about the Clause and federal taxes include:

- Justice Scalia indicated that the Eminent Domain Clause does not apply to disproportionate taxation.[853]
- The Court explained that general regulations that produce some benefits and some burdens are not subject to the Eminent Domain Clause, just as

[848] *See, e.g.*, Brushaber v. Union Pacific R. Co., 240 U.S. 1 (1916) (1913 income tax not subject to Takings Clause analysis; the Constitution does not conflict with itself); County of Mobile v. Kimball, 102 U.S. 691 (1881) (this case is a popular citation for the point, but is a local bond case); Pittsburgh v. Alco Parking Corp., 417 U.S. 369 (1974) (stating that the taxing power is not subject to the Eminent Domain Clause); dissent of Justice Field in Munn v. Illinois, 94 U.S. 113 (1877) ("The power of the State over the property of the citizen under the constitutional guaranty is well defined. The State may take his property for public uses, upon just compensation being made therefor. It may take a portion of his property by way of taxation for the support of the government."). The requirement of just compensation is not stated in the Fourteenth Amendment and was read into the concept of due process in several cases culminating in Chicago, B. & Q. R. Co. v. Chicago, 166 U.S. 226 (1897).

[849] *See* E. Enters. v. Apfel, 524 U.S. 498 (1998). Moises Penalver, *Regulatory Taxings*, 104 Colum. L. Rev. 2182, 2202 (2004) [hereinafter Penalver], states that five Justices can be cobbled together for a majority against counting cash as a taking, citing the concurrence of Justice Kennedy. *See* Ch. III.E.5.

[850] Koontz v. St. Johns River Water Mgmt. Dist., 570 U.S. 595 (2013).

[851] Billings v. United States, 232 U.S. 261, 282 (1914) "not self destructive"); Brushaber v. Union Pacific R. Co., 240 U.S. 1, 24 (1916 ("does not conflict with itself" by conferring the taxing power in one clause and taking it away in the Due Process Clause).

[852] *See* Ch. III.C., IV.A.

[853] Harmelin v. Mich., 501 U.S. 957 n. 11 (1991) (Scalia delivered the opinion of the Court but only the Chief Justice joined in this part) ("It seems to us no more reasonable to hold that the Eighth Amendment forbids 'disproportionate punishment' because otherwise the State could impose life imprisonment for a parking offense than it would be to hold that the Eminent Domain Clause forbids 'disproportionate taxation' because otherwise the State could tax away all income above the subsistence level.").

a taxpayer may not claim recompense for a shortfall between the taxes paid and value of general government benefits received.[854]

- Justices Breyer, Stevens, Souter and Ginsburg, dissenting to a ruling that invalidated a provision of the Coal Act that is lodged in Title 26, but is not a taxing provision, stated that applying the Eminent Domain Clause in that context (to which they objected) was as incorrect as applying it to a tax.[855]

- The Seventh Circuit listed Eminent Domain Clause objections of tax protesters as one the seven grounds it never considered reasonable for not paying taxes, but the Supreme Court reversed on other grounds in *Cheek*.[856]

- *Koontz* found a taking through regulation requiring payment of an impact fee, but Justice Alito waved aside the objection that the new rule could apply to taxes and user fees by asserting that taxes and user fees are not takings. The Breyer dissent agreed that taxes were not subject to the Court's holding but then stated that the Court's holding could apply to user fees (without explanation other than the difficulty of identification) and license taxes (liquor licenses), without noticing that license taxes are taxes.[857]

But the Eminent Domain Clause is an exceedingly hot topic in academic writings some of which pose the possibility that taxes should be subject to the Eminent Domain Clause. The most vocal has been Richard Epstein.[858] Given the current Court's increased appetite for applying the Takings Clause, they may be prescient.

Other aspects of the Eminent Domain Clause and tax include:

- Reasonable fees are not taxes and are not subject to just compensation as for a taking if imposed to reimburse government cost.[859]

- Third parties cannot complain under the Eminent Domain Clause if their interest came into effect after the enactment of a federal tax lien rule, and are otherwise protected by the statutes as to pre-existing rights.[860]

- At one time the Court ruled that it might be possible to hold a tax to violate the Fifth Amendment if the tax is used for private and not public purposes.

---

[854] Keystone Bituminous Coal Ass'n v. DeBenedictis, 480 U.S. 470, 492 n. 21 (1987) ("The Eminent Domain Clause has never been read to require the States or the courts to calculate whether a specific individual has suffered burdens under this generic rule in excess of the benefits received. Not every individual gets a full dollar return in benefits for the taxes he or she pays; yet, no one suggests that an individual has a right to compensation for the difference between taxes paid and the dollar value of benefits received.").

[855] E. Enters. v. Apfel, 524 U.S. 498 (1998). Penalver, at n. 107.

[856] Cheek v. United States, 498 U.S. 192 (1991). *See* Ch. VII.B. The IRS has a different list of frivolous tax protester arguments. IRS Notice 2006-31, 2006-1 C.B. 751.

[857] Koontz v. St. Johns River Water Management District, 570 U.S. 595 (2013).

[858] Richard A. Epstein, Takings: Private Property and the Power of Eminent Domain (1985); Amnon Lehavi, *The Taking/Taxing Taxonomy*, 88 Tex. L. Rev. 1235, 1255-1257 (2010).

[859] *See, e.g.*, United States v. Sperry Corp., 493 U.S. 52 (1989). *See* Ch. IV.A.

[860] United States v. Rogers, 461 U.S. 677 (1983). *See also* United States v. National Bank of Commerce, 472 U.S. 713 (1985).

This principle was stated in a state tax case that analyzed the lack of a taking restriction on states but imputed it through the Due Process Clause in the Fourteenth Amendment and stated it could be violated by either a tax or a direct taking for nonpublic purposes.[861]

(b) *Confiscation*

The Fifth Amendment states, independent of the Due Process Clause: "nor shall private property be taken for public use, without just compensation." As discussed in the preceding Chapter, neither taxes nor reasonable governmental fees are subject to the just compensation requirement. But as discussed in the preceding Chapter, the Eminent Domain Clause is relevant to due process because it has been referenced when a tax or fee is ruled not to be a tax or fee. Because there is virtually no way an exaction that is a tax can be accompanied by just compensation, taxpayers frequently argue that the exaction is not a tax (or a reasonable fee) but a taking that is confiscation.

The term generally applied to taxes that turn out to be nontax takings without just compensation is "confiscatory," a category of tax more often discussed (usually by taxpayers' attorneys) than seen. In this sense, confiscatory may be an alternate epithet to arbitrary and capricious. *Brushaber* stated in dictum that the Fifth Amendment would prevent taxation based on the most gross forms of discrimination, when it appears that the tax is:

> . . . not the exertion of taxation but a confiscation of property, that is, a taking of the same in violation of the Fifth Amendment, or, what is equivalent thereto, was so wanting in basis for classification as to produce such a gross and patent inequality as to inevitably lead to the same conclusion.[862]

But the term also has been applied to suggestions of unconstitutionality of taxes so heavy as to be confiscatory, meaning taking all of the subject taxed. This complaint is amiss because taxes can be confiscatory in the sense of being excessively large, and still be constitutional.[863]

Nichols v. Coolidge ruled a retroactive federal tax provision unconstitutional, citing *Brushaber* and indicating that the government had effected a "taking" because the provision was arbitrary and capricious and thus a confiscation.[864] In a

---

[861] Fallbrook Irrigation Dist. v. Bradley, 164 U.S. 112, 158 (1896). *Cf.* Carmichael v. Southern Coal & Coke Co., 301 U.S. 495, 514 (1937) (a state tax case, but one involving the federal unemployment act; paying unemployment benefits found to be a public purpose).

[862] Brushaber v. Union Pacific R. Co., 240 U.S. 1, 24 (1916). *See also* La Belle Iron Works v. United States, 256 U.S. 377 (1921) ("so wholly arbitrary as to amount to confiscation"). *Cf.* Patton v. Brady, 184 U.S. 608, 621 (1902) (suggesting that spoliation and confiscation were not possible in the context of a government realizing it had to tax and re-tax to meet its needs).

[863] *See, e.g.*, Veazie Bank v. Fenno, 75 U.S. 533 (1869); Alaska Fish Salting & By-Products Co. v. Smith, 255 U.S. 44, 48-49 (1921); Pittsburgh v. Alco Parking Corp., 417 U.S. 369 (1974) (citing Veazie Bank v. Fenno, which similarly ruled that the state bank notes could be taxed out of existence so as to promote the national bank notes; also a taxpayer can be taxed in order to promote the competing business of the government).

[864] Nichols v. Coolidge, 274 U.S. 531 (1927).

state tax case Justice Stevens indicated as part of a double jeopardy analysis that a tax on marijuana was confiscatory when the tax was eight times the value of the property, among other reasons, and therefore "for purposes of double jeopardy" analysis was treated as a punishment (without holding it was not also a tax).[865] Justices Black and Douglas suggested in a dissent that double taxation of embezzled property would be confiscation in violation of the Fifth Amendment.[866] But the Court has rejected a double taxation challenge to the estate and gift taxes in *United States v. Hemme* and also in decisions involving other federal taxes.[867]

(9) *Coercion Through Taxation*

Coercive features of taxation frequently cause taxpayer kickback, and are discussed in Chapter III.E.2.b, in connection with taxes that regulate so as to coerce action, and in Chapter III.D.8.b, in connection with spending that coerces, usually by states. Although coercion has a negative aura, it has not itself been considered as a violation of due process in tax cases decided by the Court. This Chapter collects the types of coercion cases.

The fundamental reason why taxes as such can coerce is explained in Chapter III.E: taxes can regulate and regulation is necessarily coercive to some degree. Indeed virtually all deductions, differentiation in deductions, and differentiation in taxation of income are if not coercive, at least potentially stimulating taxpayer action to reduce taxation in a variety of ways that requires different conduct in everyday life (*e.g.*, buying houses, holding investments for a long term gain holding period, charities not pursuing political activities or lobbying). In addition to the general category of decisions holding that federal taxes can regulate, the Court has addressed particular types of tax (and spending) coercion as follows:

- Conditioning a deduction on an act that possibly could not be forced under the Constitution: *Helvering v. Independent Life* stated in dictum that an insurance company could not be made to include the imputed value of use of its own property as rental income, because it would run afoul of the direct tax prohibition, but the taxpayer could be required to include that amount as a condition of deducting expenses related to the property.[868]

- Under the First not the Fifth Amendment, *Speiser v. Randall* ruled that a person could not be coerced to say something (that he did not intend to commit a crime) as a condition of a tax exemption.[869]

---

[865] Dep't of Revenue v. Kurth Ranch, 511 U.S. 767, 783 (1994) ("If a statute that amounts to a confiscation of property is unconstitutional, . . . a tax on previously confiscated goods is at least questionable.").

[866] James v. United States, 366 U.S. 213, 229 (1961).

[867] United States v. Hemme, 476 U.S. 558 (1986). *See also* Patton v. Brady, 184 U.S. 608 (1902) (excise tax); Hellmich v. Hellman, 276 U.S. 233 (1926) (shareholder and corporate income taxes).

[868] Helvering v. Independent Life Ins. Co., 292 U.S. 371 (1934).

[869] Speiser v. Randall, 357 U.S. 513 (1958).

- Coercing state action other than by spending: *South Carolina v. Baker* ruled that Congress could effectively require states to change the way they issued bonds if they wished to retain the federal tax exclusion for interest earned by bondholders, which states believe they must retain as a practical matter.[870] It reasoned that imposing requirements on states was a common and inevitable result of the federal government's exercise of its specific powers under the Commerce Clause, the taxing power and otherwise. The fact that the South Carolina legislature would feel coerced to change the state's laws and actions did not make the federal requirement for the interest exclusion unconstitutional.[871] When the federal estate tax allowed a credit for state estate tax, the Court rejected an argument that somehow the credit improperly coerced the states to enact estate taxes.[872]
- Coercing private action beyond the power of the federal government to regulate (citing the Tenth Amendment): As discussed in Chapter III.F, the *Child Labor Tax Case* was based in part on the view that the federal government lacked the authority to coerce local manufacturers to limit child labor.[873] *Hill v. Wallace* was based on the absence of the power of the United States to coerce the Chicago Board of Trade to comply with certain regulations in order that its members' trades might avoid a tax.[874]
- Coercive spending: As discussed in Chapter III.D.2, *Butler* addressed coercion in the context of federal spending, not taxing. It reasoned that the tax on cotton processors was not a tax because it was linked with a regulatory system that required the farmers who got support payments to agree to reduce their acreage, a result that the Court thought the United States could not have required by direct regulation; in other words Congress could not condition proper spending on an improper (according to *Butler*) requirement to act.[875] Later the Court ruled the state components of both unemployment security and social security taxes properly could have been coercive on the states, but in fact were not.[876]
- Coercive tax payment to support spending the taxpayer dislikes: *Flast v. Cohen* is based on the premise that a taxpayer should not be forced to pay tax to support the establishment of religion.[877]

---

[870] South Carolina v. Baker, 485 U.S. 505 (1988).

[871] The opinion distinguished cases ruling that Congress could not force states to enforce federal regulations. 485 U.S. at 513-515.

[872] Florida v. Mellon, 273 U.S. 12 (1927).

[873] J.W. Bailey v. Drexel Furn. Co., 259 U.S. 20 (1922).

[874] Hill v. Wallace, 259 U.S. 44 (1922).

[875] United States v. Butler, 297 U.S. 1 (1936).

[876] Carmichael v. Southern Coal & Coke Co., 301 U.S. 495, 525 (1937); Steward Machine Co. v. Davis, 301 U.S. 548 (1937).

[877] Flast v. Cohen, 392 U.S. 83 (1968). *See* Ch. VIII.D.4.b.

Ch. VI. The Taxation of Imports and Exports

A. Overview

The Constitution states more, and more particularized, rules for the taxation of imports and exports than for any other form of taxation, save the seldom seen direct tax. Generally speaking, (1) the United States can tax imports but not exports, and (2) the states can tax neither. The latter limitation is an aspect of the supremacy of the United States in conducting foreign relations and foreign commerce, it prevents diversion of revenues from the United States to the states and it protects the inland states.[1] The former is a legacy of frustration over British taxation of the Colonies, reflects fear that the agricultural exports of the slave-owning states might be hindered at the hands of the northern states, and perhaps intends to place exclusively in the coffers of the United States the lucrative import duty taxes (to offset effectively reserving direct taxation to the states).[2] That revenue considerations motivated these rules is also supported by the fact that Chief Justice Marshall stated in *Gibbons v. Ogden* (a Commerce Clause case) that the subject matter of taxing imports and exports is one of taxation and not regulation.[3]

---

[1] Michelin Tire Corp. v. Wages, 423 U.S. 276 (1976).

[2] Brown v. Maryland, 25 U.S. 419, 436 (1827) (speculating on these reasons, in other words).

[3] Gibbons v. Ogden, 22 U.S. 1, 201 (1824) (he made this statement in the context of the Import-Export Clause as applied to states). *See* Cummings, *Tariffs Are Taxes and Politics*, 166 Tax Notes Federal 1613 (Mar. 9, 2020).

The subject is important because the Supreme Court has relied on the Export Clause in six of the twenty five rulings that federal tax provisions were unconstitutional,[4] two since 1995.[5] The following chapters focus on the subject of this book: the federal tax cases. Chapter IX addresses the Import-Export Clause and the Tonnage Clause, applicable to states.

The role of import duties is a huge one in the history of the United States. They were considered the lesser of evils in federal taxation for various reasons by various groups for many years. Jefferson stated that "we are all the more reconciled to the tax on importations, because it falls exclusively on the rich, and with the equal partition of intestate's estates, constitutes the best agrarian law."[6] If not then, certainly later, tariffs' effects were not limited to the rich.

B. Import Duties

The taxation of imports is the subject of four provisions in the Constitution, most importantly the Taxing Clause, Article I, section 8, clause 1, which states:

> The Congress shall have Power To lay and collect Taxes, Duties, Imposts and Excises, to pay the Debts and provide for the common Defence and general Welfare of the United States; but all Duties, Imposts and Excises shall be uniform throughout the United States; . . . .

The uniformity requirement does not speak in terms of duties on imports or customs, but only of duties, imposts and excises. However, the Court has always understood all of these terms to refer to taxes, that duties and imposts are synonymous for practical purposes and refer to customs taxes on imports, while excises refer to inland taxes.[7] In reliance on this part of the taxing power Congress supported the nation through customs duties, as supplemented by excises and the occasional direct tax, up to the Civil War income tax and thereafter until the need for a greater source of tax revenue in the form of a permanent income tax, became obvious.

In addition, Article I, section 9, clause 6, the Regulation of Revenue Clause, discussed in the next Chapter, also requires uniformity of import duties and insures that import duties do not extend to imports from one state to another. Article I, section 10, clause 2, as discussed in Chapter VI.E, allows Congress to authorize the states to levy duties or imposts on imports (and exports) and turn over the net taxes to the Treasury. The United States has never attempted to enlist the states to collect import duties. Finally, Article I, section 9, clause 1 authorized a tax of up to ten dollars per persons for slaves imported, until Congress acted to stop importation after 1807.

---

[4] "No Tax or Duty shall be laid on Articles exported from any State." U. S. Constitution, Art. I, sec. 9, cl. 5 (the "Export Clause").

[5] *See* Ch. VI.D.

[6] Sidney Ratner, American Taxation 32 (1942). *See also* Sidney Ratner, The Tariff in American History (1972).

[7] *See, e.g.*, Pacific Ins. Co. v. Soule, 74 U.S. 433, 445 (1869).

Import duties clearly can have and have had the purpose and effect of preferring certain imports over others and protecting domestic industries, and that does not affect their legality.[8] An import must enter the territorial jurisdiction of the United States and if discarded on the voyage is not an import.[9] The uniformity requirement, discussed extensively in Chapter V.D.3.a, applies to import duties and means only they must be uniform geographically, and it matters not that ports are unequally distributed among the states.[10] In practice tariffs have been the most unequal of all federal taxes, differentiating thousands of products with different rates, usually for political purposes (every congressman could protect his own local industry).

Dooley dealt with the unusual issue of whether a tax could be imposed upon the import of goods into Puerto Rico upon their exportation from the United States; the case actually arose under the Export Clause.[11] The Court reasoned that by analogy to *Parham*, exports must mean exports only to foreign countries.[12] Because Puerto Rico was by statute not a foreign country, the shipment from New York to Puerto Rico could not be an export. Moreover, it characterized the levy as an import levy because the proceeds were to be used for Puerto Rico (even though originally paid into the federal Treasury). Nevertheless, the levy could not be an import duty for purposes of the Constitution because that term refers only to imports into the United States, and evidently the Court viewed Puerto Rico as not the United States, although the majority opinion did not say that specifically; therefore the uniformity requirement did not apply, and the tax was not on an import.[13] Thus *Dooley* identified possibly the only situation in which a federal tax is subject to neither the apportionment requirement for direct taxes nor the uniformity requirement for indirect taxes: the tax is not a tax for the United States at all, but for a territory.[14]

One of the key features of tariffs has been the ability of the President to vary them under delegations of authority from Congress, which the Court has upheld.[15]

When Congress reduced tariffs on sugar in the 1890s it felt obliged to otherwise protect domestic sugar manufacturers and did so by providing "sugar bounties," which were effectively payments to the protected industry in lieu of protecting them with tariffs. The constitutionality of the sugar bounties was upheld and the Court also upheld Congress' decision to pay them to taxpayers

---

[8] J. W. Hampton, Jr. & Co. v. United States, 276 U.S. 394 (1928).

[9] Lawder v. Stone, 187 U.S. 281 (1902).

[10] *See* Hadden v. Collector, 72 U.S. 107 (1867) (statute interpreted so as to apply uniformly to all ports that exist).

[11] Dooley v. United States, 183 U.S. 151 (1901). See Ch. V.D.3.a(4), for further discussion of the *Insular Cases*.

[12] *See* Woodruff v. Parham, 75 U.S. 123, 131 (1869) (imports in the Import-Export Clause referred only to imports from other countries); Brown v. Maryland, 25 U.S. 419, 437 (1827) (same, although dictum in the opinion had to be explained in *Woodruff*).

[13] *See* concurrence of Justice White, 183 U.S. 157 *et seq.*, explaining that Downes v. Bidwell, 182 U.S. 244 (1901) had established that Puerto Rico was not part of the United States.

[14] *See* Ch. V.D.3.a(4).

[15] Marshall Field & Co. v. Clark, 143 U.S. 649 (1892). *Cf.* Clinton v. City of New York, 524 U.S. 417 (1998) (distinguishing the tariff delegation in finding another delegation unconstitutional).

who had qualified for them before their repeal, as an exercise of the power of Congress to determine what the just debts of the United States were.[16]

C. Imports: Regulation of Revenue

Article I, section 9, clause 6 states:

> No Preference shall be given by any Regulation of Commerce or Revenue to the Ports of one State over those of another; nor shall Vessels bound to, or from, one State, be obliged to enter, clear, or pay Duties in another.

The Court explained that that clause plus the clause forbidding taxing exports:

> . . . were intended to prevent the application of the power to lay taxes or duties, or the power to regulate commerce, so as to discriminate between one part of the country and another. The regulation of commerce by a majority vote and the exemption of exports from duties or taxes were parts of one of the great compromises of the Constitution.[17]

This no-preference rule does not differ in substance from the requirement of uniformity of import duties except that it is addressed specifically to a state's ports, which were the primary, but not only, venues for imports (imports could come across land).[18] The clause restricts only the national government.[19] The

---

[16] United States v. Realty Co., 163 U.S. 427 (1896).

[17] Dooley v. United States, 183 U.S. 151 (1901).

[18] "The substantial effect of the first clause of the paragraph was to require that all regulations of commerce or of revenue affecting commerce through the ports of the States should be the same in all ports. It follows from the collocation of the two clauses that the prohibition as to preferences in regulations of commerce between ports and the uniformity as to duties, imposts and excises, though couched in different language, had absolutely the same significance. The sense in which the word 'uniform' was used is shown by the fact that the committee, whilst adopting in a large measure the proposition of Mr. McHenry and General Pinckney, 'that all duties, imposts, excises, prohibitions or restraints . . . shall be uniform and equal throughout the United States,' struck out the words 'and equal.' Undoubtedly this was done to prevent the implication that taxes should have an equal effect in each State. As we have seen, the pith of the controversy during the Confederation was that even, although the same duty or the same impost or the same excise was laid all over the United States, it might operate unequally by reason of the unequal distribution or existence of the article taxed among the respective States." Knowlton v. Moore, 178 U.S. 41, 104 (1900).

[19] Morgan's S.S. Co. v. Louisiana Bd. of Health, 118 U.S. 455 (1886); Munn v. Illinois, 94 U.S. 113 (1877). *But cf.* Cooley v. Bd. of Wardens, 53 U.S. 299 (1852), which ruled that a local half pilotage fee was not a regulation of commerce, without stopping to consider whether the clause applies to the states. *See also* Smith v. Turner, 48 U.S. 283 (1849). When states tried to levy taxes in the "importation" of passengers or immigrants, Smith v. Turner (*Passenger Cases*), ruled the taxes unconstitutional. The tax was said to provide "hospital money" to run the hospital on Staten Island. The Court concluded Congress has exclusive power to regulate foreign commerce and the issue was whether the tax was a regulation. It was a tax on imports because men are imports. The Court rejected the state's contentions about the revenue needs fulfilled by the tax by firmly asserting that taxes on imports were generally and perhaps normally regulatory as much as they were revenue raising; in other words regulation was unavoidable. Moreover, different taxes imposed by different states necessarily would produce a lack of uniformity of both regulation and taxation. The path to decision was not easy, however, as each of the five Justices in the majority wrote an opinion and four Justices dissented, including the Chief Justice. The decision was more properly decided under the Import-Export Clause.

clause had to extend to nontax regulations because the uniformity clause applies only to taxes.[20] The clause does not preclude reasonable fees for services.[21] The clause forbids preferences between states, not preferences between ports.[22] The word state does not include Territories.[23] The Court's most extensive analysis of the clause indicated that the revenue part was relatively unimportant.[24] But the most interesting feature of the clause is the juxtaposition of the concepts of regulating commerce and revenue. It clearly illustrates that the Constitution contemplates that revenue laws, which are not regulations of commerce in form, may in practice regulate commerce.[25] The *Head Money Cases* called the federal duty a regulation of commerce without even referring to the clause.[26]

The last time an opinion in the Court referred to the clause was in a 1995 concurrence by Justice Thomas in the opinion striking down the Gun-Free School Zone Act of 1990.[27] He reasoned by analogy that the word commerce was limited to sale and/or transport rather than business generally.

D. No Tax on Exports

The Constitution flatly precludes both federal and state taxation of exports. This absoluteness reflects a clear understanding by the Founders of the economic future that lay ahead of the United States as an exporter to the world. In the early days the principal exports were from the south of agricultural products.[28] Article I, section 9, clause 5 of the Constitution, the Export Clause, states that no tax or duty shall be laid by the Congress on articles exported from any state.

---

[20] A regulation that shipping to Alaska must be on American registry ships is not a tax and so is not subject to the tax uniformity clause. Alaska v. Troy, 258 U.S. 101 (1922).

[21] Cooley v. Bd. of Wardens, 53 U.S. 299 (1852) (half pilotage fee, albeit of a locality).

[22] Alabama G. S. R. Co. v. United States, 340 U.S. 216 (1951); Louisiana Public Service Com. v. Texas & N. O. R. Co., 284 U.S. 125 (1931).

[23] Alaska v. Troy, 258 U.S. 101 (1922); Downes v. Bidwell, 182 U.S. 244 (1901).

[24] "So far as the regulation of revenue is concerned, the prohibition in the clause does not seem to have been very important, as, in a previous section, (8) it was declared, that 'all duties, imposts, and excises shall be uniform throughout the United States'; and, as to a preference by a regulation of commerce, the history of the provision, as well as its language, looks to a prohibition against granting privileges or immunities to vessels entering or clearing from the ports of one State over those of another. That these privileges and immunities, whatever they may be in the judgment of congress, shall be common and equal in all the ports of the several States. This much is undoubtedly embraced in the prohibition; and it may, certainly, also embrace any other description of legislation looking to a direct privilege or preference of the ports of any particular State over those of another. Indeed, the clause, in terms, seems to import a prohibition against some positive legislation by congress to this effect, and not against any incidental advantages that might possibly result from the legislation of congress upon other subjects connected with commerce, and confessedly within its power." Pa. v. Wheeling & Belmont Bridge Co., 59 U.S. 421, 435 (1856).

[25] *See, e.g.*, Ward v. Md., 79 U.S. 418 (1871); Gibbons v. Ogden, 22 U.S. 1, 191 (1824) (not limited to revenue raising laws).

[26] Edye v. Robertson, 112 U.S. 580 (1884) (Head Money Cases).

[27] United States v. Lopez, 514 U.S. 549 (1995).

[28] Staff of the Joint Committee on Taxation, The Taxing Power of the Federal and State Governments 20 (1936) (available on Joint Committee website).

Article I, section 10, clause 2, the Import-Export Clause discussed in Chapter IX, states:

> No State shall, without the Consent of the Congress, lay any Imposts or Duties on Imports or Exports, except what may be absolutely necessary for executing it's inspection Laws: and the net Produce of all Duties and Imposts, laid by any State on Imports or Exports, shall be for the Use of the Treasury of the United States; and all such Laws shall be subject to the Revision and Controul of the Congress.

Article I, section 10, clause 3, the Tonnage Clause discussed in Chapter IX, contains a similar prohibition on state taxation of tonnage "without the consent of Congress."

The Court has speculated that the permission in clause 2 for states to tax exports or tonnage that they could not otherwise tax could not be used as a way around the uniformity requirements otherwise imposed on the United States taxes, without resolving the issue.[29] But the Court has stated in dictum that under clause 2 the states and the United States could agree to do what neither can do alone: tax exports.[30] This makes sense if all of the states agreed, because all interested parties would be represented (but the people). However, clauses 2 and 3 are addressed to actions of individual states ("no state shall").[31]

Because the Constitution forbids both state and federal taxation of exports, the state tax cases as well as the federal tax cases can inform the meaning of a tax on exports, although the terminology of the two clauses does differ,[32] and many of the state export cases involve interstate commerce rather than foreign commerce.[33] The current rule seems to be that the tax can run afoul of the Export Clause only if it is levied "on" the transit of goods in export, with a fairly limited appetite to search for indirect burdens on exports, except when the nominal subject of the tax is not the export but some related transaction like insurance on the export, or the tax is a facially nondiscriminatory tax that falls principally on exporting carriers. Thus a tax can be unconstitutional as applied. The major decisions of the Court follow.

- 1876: *Pace v. Burgess* ruled that a federal stamp tax levied on tobacco that was being exported was not a tax on exports because the charge was nominal

---

[29] Michelin Tire Corp. v. Wages, 423 U.S. 276, 301 n. 13 (1976).

[30] Prudential Ins. Co. v. Benjamin, 328 U.S. 408, 436 n. 47 (1946).

[31] *Cf.* Dooley v. United States, 183 U.S. 151, 156 (1901) (stating that Congress could not levy a tax on exports from one state to another because it would not be uniform).

[32] *Cf.* United States v. IBM, 517 U.S. 843 (1996); Michelin Tire Corp. v. Wages, 423 U.S. 276 (1976).

[33] *See generally* Abramson, *State Taxation of Exports: The Stream of Constitutionality*, 54 N.C.L.Rev. 59 (1975).

and the purpose of the stamp was solely to prove a tax had already been paid on manufacturing.[34]

- 1901: The United States cannot impose a stamp tax on a foreign bill of lading under the clause forbidding taxation of exports.[35] The opinion distinguished *Pace v. Burgess*, unconvincingly. Justices Harlan, Gray, White and McKenna dissented.
- 1901: *Dooley* ruled that shipment from New York to Puerto Rico was not exportation.[36]
- 1904: *Cornell v. Coyne* upheld a federal tax on filled cheese that was slated for exportation because it was not levied on account of the export but applied generally; the opinion stated that a bounty need not be conferred on exports.[37] *IBM* later explained this decision as applying to pre-exportation taxes.[38]
- 1915: *Hvoslef* held a Federal stamp tax on charter parties to foreign ports to be a disguised tax on the goods to be exported on the charter.[39] The Court read the intent of the export clause to broadly prevent any direct or indirect burden on exports. *IBM* explained this as a nondiscriminatory tax that was not facially applied to exports but functioned as a tax on exports.[40]
- 1915: *Thames & Meresy Ins. Co.* held that the United States cannot impose a tax on insurance for marine risks issued to insure export transportation, because insurance is a necessity of exportation.[41]
- 1918: The important *Peck & Co. v. Lowe* decision ruled that the federal income tax could fall on export income of taxpayers.[42]
- 1923: *Spalding & Bros. v. Edwards* ruled that a three percent federal sales tax on the sale of baseball bats (and other sporting goods) was unconstitutional as applied to sales to a commission agent buying for export to the ultimate

---

[34] Pace v. Burgess, 92 U.S. 372 (1876). *See also* Almy v. Cal., 65 U.S. 169 (1861) (state tax on a bill of lading is a tax on the exports by a state); Turpin v. Burgess, 117 U.S. 504 (1886) (similar to *Pace*); United States v. P. Lorillard Co., 267 U.S. 471, 473 (1925) (Congress chose to allow an exporter to drawback a stamp tax on goods that turned out to be exported, which the Court characterized as "beyond its [the Export Clause's] strict requirement and [designed] to let the event decide about the tax").

[35] Fairbank v. United States, 181 U.S. 283 (1901).

[36] Dooley v. United States, 183 U.S. 151 (1901). *See* Ch. V.D.3.a(4), for further discussion of this case. *See also* Swan & Finch Co. v. United States, 190 U.S. 143 (1903) (shipment to a possession is not exportation).

[37] Cornell v. Coyne, 192 U.S. 418 (1904). *See also* Thompson v. United States, 142 U.S. 471 (1892) (discussing when exportation begins).

[38] United States v. IBM, 517 U.S. 843 (1996).

[39] United States v. Hvoslef, 237 U.S. 1 (1915).

[40] United States v. IBM, 517 U.S. 843, 847-848 (1996).

[41] Thames & Mersey Ins. Co. v. United States, 237 U.S. 19 (1915).

[42] William E. Peck & Co. v. Lowe, 247 U.S. 165 (1918).

purchaser.[43] Because the Court was able to find that the tax was levied "on the article exported" rather than income from the sale, it mattered not that the tax was general. Justice Holmes stated that the issue was one of timing and a sales tax necessarily fell on the goods in the process of exportation.

- 1924: *National Paper* and *Barclay* ruled again that a federal net income tax on export income is not a prohibited tax on exports and went further to find that the nontaxation of foreign corporations exporting from the United States did not render the taxation of domestic exporters unconstitutional.[44]
- 1996: *IBM* ruled that the Export Clause prohibits tax on insurance on exports. It contains an extended discussion, distinguishing the Import-Export Clause as somewhat more lenient.[45] Its general rule is that no matter how broadly applicable or nondiscriminatory may be the tax in appearance, if it is viewed as being imposed on goods in (or because of) export transit it is prohibited. See Ch. IX for the Import-Export Clause.
- 1998: *United States Shoe Corp.* ruled the federal Harbor Maintenance Tax was a tax on exports and not a fee.[46] The tax was a percentage of value, imposed on the loading of the goods for export.
- 2008: *Clintwood Elkhorn Mining Co.* ruled that no special constitutional rules applied to refunds claimed under the Export Clause (the tax was not ruled unconstitutional in the opinion).[47]

[43] Spalding & Bros. v. Edwards, 262 U.S. 66 (1923).
[44] National Paper & Type Co. v. Bowers, 266 U.S. 373 (1924); Barclay & Co. v. Edwards, 267 U.S. 442 (1924).
[45] United States v. IBM, 517 U.S. 843 (1996).
[46] United States v. United States Shoe Corp., 523 U.S. 360 (1998).
[47] United States v. Clintwood Elkhorn Mining Co., 553 U.S. 1 (2008).

Ch. VII. Criminal Tax Constitutional Issues

A. Tax Crimes

Today the criminal law is a relatively rarely used backstop to civil tax collection efforts of the IRS that mostly serves an in terrorem purpose; indeed, it is so selectively used that it might be subject to the charge of improper selective enforcement.[1] However, in the early days criminal enforcement of the tax laws appears to have been more nearly the norm. For example, when a person carried on a business without paying a federal license tax he was indicted.[2]

Criminal tax defendants are likely to raise any constitutional argument they can think of in defense, but only the principal ones are discussed here: the standard of willfulness required for the crime, self-incrimination, search and seizure, double jeopardy, excessive fines, and the vagueness of the criminal standard.[3] Chapter VII.H, also discusses forfeitures in tax cases, both civil and criminal,

---

[1] *See generally* as to tax crimes, Bittker & Lokken, Federal Taxation of Income, Estates and Gifts ¶ 117.10. But the standard for proving selective prosecution is very high. *See* United States v. Armstrong, 517 U.S. 456 (1996). *Cf.* Miller v. Standard Nut Margarine Co., 284 U.S. 498 (1932) (selective enforcement prevented the IRS from defending under the Anti-Injunction Act).

[2] *See, e.g.*, License Tax Cases, 72 U.S. 462 (1867) (although these taxes were somewhat unusual, being imposed on selling liquor, which was illegal as a matter of state law).

[3] *See generally* Comisky, Feld and Harris, Tax Fraud and Evasion (6th ed.); Townsend, Campagna, Johnson and Schumacher, Tax Crimes (2015) [hereinafter Townsend]; Matthew Angelo, Edward Welles Hasen, Uriel Hindberg, Ryan Kesselring, & Howard Perlman, *Tax Violations*, 57 Am. Crim. L. Rev. 1349 (2020) (annually updated review).

because the same set of constitutional defenses has been implicated in forfeiture cases.

Most of the Supreme Court's criminal tax opinions deal with statutory interpretation and not the Constitution. The Court may be even more likely to apply its maxim of avoiding constitutional rulings if possible in criminal cases. Generally, the constitutional principles applied in criminal tax cases are not peculiar to tax, in contrast to most other constitutional tax issues discussed in this book. In addition, many civil tax rulings necessarily have criminal implications due to the tendency of criminal prosecutions to follow civil audits.[4]

Tax crimes are clustered in Chapter 75 of the Code but can be prosecuted under other general criminal provisions.[5]

Grand jury proceedings. Lawn v. United States contained several miscellaneous rulings: a taxpayer cannot go behind the grand jury indictment; the taxpayer was not denied due process by use of a copy of a check at the trial; and the taxpayer's counsel was not improperly limited in cross examination at trial.[6] *Neder v. United States* ruled that the failure to charge the jury on materiality of a $5 million omission from income was harmless error.[7]

B. Willfulness

The application of the willfulness requirement found in most criminal tax statutes is mainly a matter of statutory construction and raises constitutional issues only tangentially. Generally, ignorance of the law is no defense to a criminal prosecution.[8] But due to the "complexity" of the tax laws and the possibility of bona fide misunderstandings of what the tax law requires, certain criminal tax laws—including most importantly tax evasion under Code section 7201, filing materially false returns under Code section 7206(1), making materially false statements under Code section 7207, and willful failure to file or pay under Code section 7203—include the word "willfully," which the Court has interpreted to make specific intent to violate the statute an element of the crime.[9] In addition, to convict under the "omnibus clause" of section 7212(a) the Government must prove the defendant was aware of a pending tax-related proceeding, such as a particular investigation or audit, or could reasonably foresee that such a proceeding would commence.[10] The current state of the law on willfulness in tax crimes rests on the 1991 decision in *Cheek*.

---

[4] United States v. Clarke, 573 U.S. 248 (2014) is the Court's most recent ruling on civil summons enforcement; the opinion did not mention a crime.

[5] *See, e.g.*, Pasquantino v. United States, 544 U.S. 349 (2005) (wire fraud statute violated by Canadians seeking to avoid Canadian tax).

[6] Lawn v. United States, 355 U.S. 339 (1958).

[7] Neder v. United States, 527 U.S. 1 (1999).

[8] Cheek v. United States, 498 U.S. 192, 200 (1991).

[9] *Id.* at 199-200; Bryan v. United States, 524 U.S. 184, 193-194 (1998). *See generally* Sharon L. Davies, *The Jurisprudence of Willfulness: An Evolving Theory of Excusable Ignorance*, 48 DUKE L. J. 341 (1998); Daniel Anker, *Cheek v. United States: Beliefs that Tax Credulity Still Get to the Jury*, 41 CASE W. RES. L. REV. 1311 (1991) [hereinafter Anker].

[10] Marinello v. United States, 138 S. Ct. 1101 (2018).

Cheek was a "tax protester" case in which the nontaxpayer criminal defendant thought wages were not income, both as a matter of statutory interpretation and of constitutionality. The Court interpreted the word willfully to require an intentional violation of a known legal duty; it concluded that a taxpayer could not know it had a duty if the taxpayer held a "good faith" belief that the tax was not owed (on grounds other than constitutionality of the tax); and it stated that the unreasonableness of the belief might go to the weight of the evidence of what the taxpayer knew or did not know about his duty, but that an unreasonable belief did not preclude proof of good faith.[11] The Court differentiated belief in unconstitutionality on the grounds that Congress intended other ways of contesting constitutionality besides not paying the tax;[12] however, this differentiation does not explain how it makes the defendant's act any the more willful.[13]

Even though the Court ruled only that the trial judge should not have taken from the jury the consideration of the taxpayer's belief because it was objectively unreasonable as a matter of law, the opinion went on to say that a good faith belief did not depend on the belief being objectively reasonable, whether or not the objective reasonableness was left to the jury. The trial court had effectively taken from the jury the question of whether the belief could be reasonably held and the court of appeals went so far as to list seven beliefs about the tax system that were unreasonable as a matter of law.[14] The Supreme Court's opinion worried about the application of irrebuttable presumptions in criminal cases, supposedly raising Sixth Amendment or due process concerns.[15] Presumably the Court concluded that if the word willful, and the gloss put on that word requir-

---

[11] 498 U.S. at 204-208.

[12] *Id.* at 206.

[13] Justice Scalia's concurrence points out the inconsistency. *Id.* at 207-209.

[14] The Seventh Circuit was alone in its views on tax protester irrationality. *See* Anker, at 1315-1316.

[15] *Citing* Francis v. Franklin, 471 U.S. 307 (1985), and Morissette v. United States, 342 U.S. 246 (1952). The latter opinion of Justice Jackson is a strong endorsement of the importance of intent (as in intent to steal) in criminal cases. The Court reversed the conviction of the junk dealer who picked up used shell casings from government property because the trial judge had refused to allow the jury to consider that the defendant did not actually intend to do anything wrong. But the Court clearly believed it possible that the defendant could have reasonably believed he was not stealing: "They might have concluded that the heaps of spent casings left in the hinterland to rust away presented an appearance of unwanted and abandoned junk, and that lack of any conscious deprivation of property or intentional injury was indicated by Morissette's good character, the openness of the taking, crushing and transporting of the casings, and the candor with which it was all admitted." 342 U.S. at 276. *See* Mark D. Yochum, *Cheek is Chic: Ignorance of the Law Is an Excuse for Tax Crimes—A Fashion that Does Not Wear Well*, 31 Duq. L. Rev. 249, 253 (1993) (rebutting Sixth Amendment argument). *See* Ch. V.D.3.b(5), on conclusive presumptions. For an example of a nontax criminal case in which an irrebuttable presumption required reversal of conviction, *see* Carella v. California, 491 U.S. 263 (1989) (failure to return rental car allowed a conclusive presumption of fraud).

ing disregard of a known duty, is to mean anything, it has to refer to subjective knowledge of the duty, not objective knowledge.[16]

Cheek turned on the assumption that if the belief were required to be unreasonable in order to convict, then that "transforms the inquiry into a legal one and would prevent the jury from considering it."[17] But this is not a necessary result. If willfulness were defined as unreasonable disregard of law then the question what a reasonable person would conclude based on all of the facts about the state of the law would be a question of fact that could be submitted to the jury; that occurs in negligence cases all the time.

The tax crime decisions leading up to *Cheek* did not forecast its conclusions:

- *Murdock*: This opinion is the beginning of the line of Supreme Court tax rulings on willfulness. The Court reversed the conviction for criminally withholding information from the IRS because the trial judge in effect had told the jury the defendant could not reasonably hold the view he did about the law (that the Fifth Amendment privilege against self-incrimination extended to state crimes), and so the defendant must have acted willfully.[18] The reason the Court found that instruction to be error was not that it had inserted a reasonableness requirement into the law, but that the defendant's view of the law was not unreasonable at that time because the law in fact was unsettled (it was settled only in the first appeal of the same defendant to the Supreme Court).[19] But to repeat: the Court said that in the context of a belief that the taxpayer could reasonably hold as a matter of law because the law was unsettled.

- *Bishop*: Affirmed a conviction of tax fraud in which the trial judge had charged the jury to convict if it found "the defendant intended with evil motive or bad purpose either to disobey or to disregard the law."[20] The Court's opinion in *Bishop* introduced what turned out to the talismanic phrase that allowed the distinction made in *Cheek*: willfulness connotes "a voluntary, intentional violation of a known legal duty."[21]

---

[16] *Cf.* Ratzlaf v. United States, 510 U.S. 135, 142 (1994) (involving another supposedly complex area of the law and citing *Cheek* in ruling that a person might not specifically know that it was illegal to break up deposits so as to avoid reporting a cash deposit larger than $10,000, and so could be acquitted based on subjective lack of willfulness).

[17] 498 U.S. at 203.

[18] United States v. Murdock, 290 U.S. 389 (1933) (at time defendant refused to answer revenue agents on grounds of self-incrimination; the Supreme Court had not yet determined that incrimination under state law did not count).

[19] The Court said: "The trial court could not, therefore, properly tell the jury the defendant's assertion of the privilege was so unreasonable and ill-founded as to exhibit bad faith and establish willful wrongdoing. This was the effect of the instructions given. We think the Circuit Court of Appeals correctly upheld the respondent's right to have the question of absence of evil motive submitted to the jury, and we are of opinion that the requested instruction was apt for the purpose." 290 U.S. at 396.

[20] United States v. Bishop, 412 U.S. 346, 350 (1973).

[21] This was based on Spies v. United States, 317 U.S. 492, 501 (1943).

- *Pomponio*: Affirmed a conviction of tax fraud in which the trial judge charged the jury that motive did not matter and the court of appeals reversed and said the jury should have been told that the defendants had to act in bad faith, which they may not have because they may legitimately have thought that disputed distributions were loans.[22] The Supreme Court wanted to extract any reference to bad motive from the jury charge and leave the issue to be whether the defendant intentionally violated a known duty.[23] The Supreme Court in *Cheek* had agreed with the trial court's charge that "good motive alone is never a defense . . ."[24]

Cheek somehow read the per curiam opinion in *Pomponio* to preclude not consideration of subjective state of mind of the defendant, but consideration of the objective reasonableness of the belief. It is not clear how that reading occurred, except that by limiting itself to the "known duty" talisman, the Court only had the word "known" to work with. Therefore, it felt it had to define such knowledge subjectively, regardless of how unreasonable it might be.

In sum, the tax crime cases leading up to *Cheek* did not support its rejection of a standard of reasonableness of belief, which Justices Blackmun and Marshall pointed out in dissent in *Cheek*:

> That being so, it is incomprehensible to me how, in this day, more than 70 years after the institution of our present federal income tax system with the passage of the Income Tax Act of 1913, 38 Stat. 166, any taxpayer of competent mentality can assert as his defense to charges of statutory willfulness the proposition that the wage he receives for his labor is not income, irrespective of a cult that says otherwise and advises the gullible to resist income tax collections. One might note in passing that this particular taxpayer, after all, was a licensed pilot for one of our major commercial airlines; he presumably was a person of at least minimum intellectual competence.
>
> The District Court's instruction that an objectively reasonable and good-faith misunderstanding of the law negates willfulness lends further, rather than less, protection to this defendant, for it adds an additional hurdle for the prosecution to overcome. Petitioner should be grateful for this further protection, rather than be opposed to it.
>
> This Court's opinion today, I fear, will encourage taxpayers to cling to frivolous views of the law in the hope of convincing a jury of their sincerity. If that ensues, I suspect we have gone beyond the limits of common sense.[25]

---

[22] United States v. Pomponio, 528 F.2d 247 (4th Cir. 1975).

[23] United States v. Pomponio, 429 U.S. 10 (1976). *But see* Bryan v. United States, 524 U.S. 184, 195 n. 17 (1998), which describes the jury instruction approved in *Pomponio* as not typical of the high mens rea bar set in tax cases.

[24] Cheek v. United States, 498 U.S. 192, 200 (1991).

[25] 498 U.S. at 209-210.

Subsequently the Court has limited the *Cheek* rule to situations involving what it could call highly complex laws, like the tax laws.[26] However, it has not clarified what was "highly complex" about wages being taxable income. *Cheek* did not mention *James*, in which the Court ruled that an embezzler could not be criminally convicted for not reporting the embezzlement income because at the time the law was not clear enough to support the willful intent.[27]

An explanation for the shift in the Court's view of willfulness and tax crimes subsequent to *Murdock* (1933) may lie in the Court's ruling in *Screws* (1945) that such an interpretation of the word willfulness in criminal statutes can be used to save it from unconstitutional vagueness.[28] The Court has upheld prosecutions under what might seem to be vague statutes (void for vagueness is discussed further in Chapter VII.G), in reliance on the statutes' additional requirement of willfulness or bad faith, which appears to mean that the defendant's understanding that he was violating the statute was enough to give the statute constitutional definiteness as applied to him.[29]

But this approach cannot mean that a subjective belief that one is breaking the law results in a felony, when the belief is unreasonable. The correct meaning of this line of authority is illustrated by the 1918 opinion to which it is traced: a brief opinion by Justice Brandeis holding that a rancher could be convicted of allowing sheep to graze where cattle had previously grazed.[30] The sole explanation in the opinion was: "Men familiar with range conditions and desirous of observing the law will have little difficulty in determining what is prohibited by it." Justice Brandeis was not announcing a subjective interpretation of the statue but rather found that there was no ambiguity in its application as an objective fact: whether cattle had grazed the land was generally knowable and known.

Similarly the Court upheld prosecution of a trucking company for knowingly failing to follow the shortest route: liability require both proof of the fact of a shorter route and proof that the defendant knew it and failed to follow it.[31] However, the mens rea concept took an odd turn that seemed to be toward subjective self-indictment in the 1941 decision in *Gorin*.[32] It affirmed the conviction of a Russian spy who had both obtained information related to national defense (which might be a vague concept) and also intended to use it to the advantage of a foreign nation. The Court thought the term national defense was sufficiently well understood, but implied that whether or not the definition of information

---

[26] Bryan v. United States, 524 U.S. 184 (1998); Ratzlaf v. United States, 510 U.S. 135, 149 (1994) (citing *Cheek* for exceptions to the general rule that ignorance of the law is no defense to a criminal charge).

[27] James v. United States, 366 U.S. 213 (1961).

[28] Screws v. United States, 325 U.S. 91 (1945).

[29] *Id.* at 102. *See also* Skilling v. United States, 561 U.S. 358 (2010) (citing *Screws* for the statutory mens rea requirement, which insures constitutionality). *See* Andrew E. Goldsmith, *The Void for Vagueness Doctrine in the Supreme Court, Revisited*, 30 AM. J. CRIM. LAW 279, 301-302 (2003) [hereinafter Goldsmith].

[30] Omaechevarria v. Idaho, 246 U.S. 343 (1918).

[31] Boyce Motor Lines, Inc. v. United States, 342 U.S. 337 (1952).

[32] Gorin v. United States, 312 U.S. 19 (1941).

related to national defense is by itself too vague, the requirement of intent to use it against the United States was an independent and objective grounds for prosecution. Similarly, while conspiring to interfere with interstate travel might be vague (for example, does it include robbing a person who happens to be traveling interstate?), if a defendant is proven to have intended to interfere with interstate travel as such, then as to that defendant the statute is not vague.[33]

The subjective reading of willfulness is most closely associated with the decision in *Screws*.[34] Justice Douglas reversed the federal conviction under the Civil Rights Act of 1866 of a Georgia sheriff (whom the state would not prosecute) who had killed a black man in the course of arresting him for stealing a tire. The trial judge had simply charged that the sheriff should be found guilty if he applied more force than was necessary to make the arrest, rather than if he intended to deprive the victim of his civil rights. The Court was faced with a very difficult set of choices that included eviscerating the Civil Rights Act as well as expanding it to potentially supplant state criminal law.[35] The Court reached a contentious compromise by remanding for a new trial in which the jury must be instructed to consider whether the sheriff intended to deprive the person of his civil rights, which was understood to be an unlikely finding.[36]

In other words, the willfulness requirement could save the Civil Rights Act from vagueness, but then willfulness must be proven to convict. The suspect nature of the emphasis on willfulness to save a vague statute was pointed out by the minority opinion in *Screws*:

> It is as novel as it is an inadmissible principle that a criminal statute of indefinite scope can be rendered definite by requiring that a person "willfully" commit what Congress has not defined but which, if Congress had defined, could constitutionally be outlawed.[37]

Nevertheless, the approach has been justified under the theory that it is better to have some light than to curse the darkness; or that the existence of some grey does not destroy the black and white.[38] In summary, the leniency allowed to tax protesters by *Cheek* may be traced to *Screws*, which reflected a strained interpretation designed to save the Civil Rights Act of 1866.[39]

---

[33] United States v. Guest, 383 U.S. 745 (1966).

[34] Screws v. United States, 325 U.S. 91 (1945). For an analysis of the lengths to which Justice Douglas went to uphold the statute through reliance on the willfulness requirement, *see* Dean Alfange, Jr., *"Under Color of Law," Classic and Screws Revisited*, 47 Corn. L. Q. 395, 407 (1961).

[35] *See* J. Woodford Howard, Mr. Justice Murphy A Political Biography, 355-356 (1968).

[36] *Id.* The *Screws* opinion was not an opinion of the Court because only four Justices joined, reflecting the fracturing of the Court.

[37] 325 U.S. at 153.

[38] Julius Cohen, *The Screws Case: Federal Protection of Negro Rights*, 46 Col. L. Rev. 94 (1946).

[39] But note that the petitioner in *Cheek* did not argue *Screws*; instead a cite to Screws appeared in the government's brief. *Brief for the United States*, Cheek v. United States, 1989 U.S. Briefs (Lexis) 658; *Brief for the Petitioner*, Cheek v. United States, 1989 U.S. Briefs (Lexis) 658.

C. Self-Incrimination

The Fifth Amendment states that "no person . . . shall be compelled in any criminal case to be a witness against himself." Corporations and other organizations that exist by virtue of the laws of the state have no Fifth Amendment right against self-incrimination.[40] Therefore the self-incrimination privilege is confined to individuals. The privilege applies to tax crimes, but there are many exceptions to the privilege as to taxes due to overriding obligations to properly report tax liabilities.

Scope of privilege. The privilege protects only that individual taxpayer's testimony, not the testimony of a third party, even an agent, unless it is an attorney holding information, which if obtained from the individual, would be subject to the privilege.[41] An individual's business records are not in themselves protected because they were voluntarily created.[42] Turning over documents in response to a subpoena or other order is not normally testimonial and subject to protection by the privilege, but can be if the turnover evidences the documents' existence, authenticity and custody and would be a link in the chain of the evidence needed to prosecute (including turnover by an attorney).[43] Documents in the hands of an accountant are not privileged because the privilege attaches to possession not ownership.[44] Individuals may sometimes object to turning over records of organizations on the ground that the records will incriminate them, but the privilege will be effective only if the testimonial act of production incriminates the individual.[45] Although the privilege is designed to protect against criminal prosecutions it can be applied to civil forfeitures that are punishments in nature.[46]

Special rules have grown up around taxes and required filings with respect to activities that are themselves illegal; generally the individual can successfully assert the privilege against such filings or punishment for failure to make such filings when the returns are particularized and necessarily identify the illegality of the income,[47] but not for failure to report illegal income on generally applica-

---

[40] *See* California Bankers Ass'n v. Schulz, 416 U.S. 21, 71 (1974). The theory is that because the organizations depend on the state for their existence, unlike individuals, they can be required to reveal their business affairs and documents; otherwise there would be no way for the state to police its creations. Hale v. Henkel, 201 U.S. 43 (1906).

[41] *See, e.g.*, Couch v. United States, 409 U.S. 322 (1973) (distinguishing between documents given to an accountant and to the taxpayer's lawyer; the attorney-client privilege is a major protector of self-incrimination); Fisher v. United States, 425 U.S. 391 (1976).

[42] United States v. Doe, 465 U.S. 605 (1984).

[43] *Id. See also* United States v. Hubbell, 530 U.S. 27 (2000). *See generally* Townsend, at 235-239 ("First, voluntarily prepared documents are generally not privileged. In addition, documents that are business records, and not personal, are also not subject to a claim of privilege. The privilege applies only to compelled testimony. . . . Corporations and other collective entities have no Fifth Amendment privilege.").

[44] Couch v. United States, 409 U.S. 322 (1973).

[45] *See, e.g.*, Braswell v. United States, 487 U.S. 99 (1988).

[46] United States v. United States Coin & Currency, 401 U.S. 715 (1971).

[47] *See, e.g.*, Marchetti v. United States, 390 U.S. 39 (1968); Grosso v. United States, 390 U.S. 62 (1968).

ble income tax returns.[48] But an individual cannot file false information to avoid incriminating himself.[49]

Cases. The Supreme Court rulings on self-incrimination in federal tax cases, reflected in the summary above, are as follows:

- 1886: *Boyd* must be noted, not because it states the current law but because "subsequent history is largely one of escaping the *Boyd* dictum."[50] *Boyd* reversed the forfeiture of imported goods, which had been forfeited on the basis of evidence supplied by the defendant under court order: the invoice that proved the goods were imported. The opinion tied the Fourth and Fifth Amendment protections together and extended the Fourth Amendment protection beyond entry into premises and seizing of property. Subsequently, as shown below, the Court has ruled that the taxpayer can be required to produce documentation so long as the act of production itself is not so testimonial as to violate the privilege.[51] However, *Boyd* still stands as the case that made exclusion of the evidence the remedy for violation of the Fifth Amendment.[52] The Court later explained that *Boyd* did not involve the government seeking documents that the tax law required to be maintained, but rather purely private records.[53]

- 1911: *Stone Tracy* rejected a Fourth Amendment objection to requiring returns to be filed under oath and to the publication of tax returns filed under

---

[48] *See, e.g.*, Mackey v. United States, 401 U.S. 667 (1971). The Court summarized this law in a non tax opinion, United States v. Ward, 448 U.S. 242, 258-259 (1980) (" . . . statutes that are plainly designed to obtain information from a limited class of persons engaged in criminal activity in order to facilitate their prosecution and conviction are invalid under the Fifth Amendment. On the other hand, when the general income tax laws require a full reporting of each taxpayer's income in order to fulfill the Government's regulatory objectives, the fact that a particular answer may incriminate a particular taxpayer is not a sufficient excuse for refusing to supply the relevant information required from every taxpayer.").

[49] United States v. Knox, 396 U.S. 77 (1969).

[50] Boyd v. United States, 116 U.S. 616 (1886). *See* Kenneth Culp Davis, *The Administrative Power of Investigation*, 56 YALE L. J. 1111, 1128 (1947) [hereinafter Davis].

[51] Fisher v. United States, 425 U.S. 391 (1976) stated as to *Boyd* and its progeny: the application of the Fourth Amendment to subpoenas has been substantially limited; nontestimonial material can be searched for and seized; testimonial material sometimes can be seized; the compulsion prohibited by the Fifth Amendment is limited to a testimonial communication that is incriminating; partnership documents can be compelled; *Boyd* based the Fifth Amendment protection of production of private papers on the Fourth Amendment violation of requiring them to be produced, but there is no longer a Fourth Amendment protection, and so now any Fifth Amendment protection against producing papers pursuant to a documentary summons must rest on some other ground; if the papers are another's, such as accountant's work papers, the possessor has no privilege against producing them because of the absence of any significant testimonial effect through only admitting the existence and possession of documents; *Boyd* did not decide whether implicit authentication occurs when the person produces his own documents.

[52] That result was extended to Fourth Amendment violations by Weeks v. United States, 232 U.S. 383 (1914).

[53] Shapiro v. United States, 335 U.S. 1, 33 n. 42 (1948). *Cf.* I.R.C. § 6001 (general record keeping requirement).

the corporate income excise tax of 1909, and said that no Fifth Amendment self-incrimination issue was presented on the facts.[54]

- 1927: *United States v. Sullivan* ruled that an income taxpayer, a bootlegger during Prohibition, must report and pay tax on illegal income and if the taxpayer has concerns about self-incrimination it should "test it in the return so that it could be passed on."[55] The Court continues to cite *Sullivan* for the rule that incriminating evidence may properly be the "byproduct" of complying with regulatory requirements such as filing income tax returns.[56] Nevertheless, *Marchetti* distinguished *Sullivan*, because the general income tax return at issue in *Sullivan* did not have the "direct and unmistakable consequence of incriminating" the defendant, whereas a wagering tax return at issue in *Marchetti* would.[57]
- 1953: *Kahriger* ruled that a registration requirement for illegal wagering did not require the taxpayer to confess to illegal acts already committed and so did not violate the protection against self-incrimination.[58] *Marchetti* rejected this view that the privilege did not apply to prospective acts and the filing could not implicate past criminality and overruled *Kahriger* in effect in 1968.[59] *Kahriger* played a role in a very important Fourth Amendment case, *Irvine v. California*.[60] The local police illegally entered Irvine's home and planted a listening device, which they used to gather evidence of Irvine's gambling activities that were illegal under state law. In the prosecution the state also introduced into evidence Irvine's federal gambling license, of the type held constitutional in *Kahriger*. The issue in *Irvine* was whether to extend to the states the federal exclusionary rule that would have precluded using illegally obtained evidence. The Court declined to extend the rule to the states, later doing so in *Mapp v. Ohio*.[61] Justice Jackson's opinion in *Irvine* in which Chief Justice Warren joined on this point somewhat relied on the ability and right of Irvine to obtain redress against the police for their illegal conduct. Researchers have learned that Chief Justice Warren was upset by the failure of the authorities to punish the police and his dismay led to his later willingness to reverse even state convictions due to blunders of the police.[62]

---

[54] Flint v. Stone Tracy Co., 220 U.S. 107, 176-177 (1911). Although the Court had ruled in 1906 that corporations were not protected by the privilege against self-incrimination. Hale v. Henkel, 201 U.S. 43 (1906).

[55] United States v. Sullivan, 274 U.S. 259 (1927).

[56] *See* United States v. Hubbell, 530 U.S. 27 n. 14 (2000).

[57] Marchetti v. United States, 390 U.S. 39, 48 (1968).

[58] United States v. Kahriger, 345 U.S. 22 (1953).

[59] Also overruled was Lewis v. United States, 348 U.S. 419 (1955).

[60] Irvine v. California, 347 U.S. 128 (1954).

[61] Mapp v. Ohio, 367 U.S. 643 (1961).

[62] Gerald T. Dunne, Hugo Black and the Judicial Revolution 311 (1978); Bernard Schwartz, Super Chief 137 (1983) (Warren tried to get the United States Justice Department to do something about the California police illegality and the Justice Department would not).

- 1963: The privilege against self-incrimination would prevent the IRS from using information obtained under a voluntary disclosure policy addressed to taxpayers generally, but either the offer should be deemed withdrawn or its condition not satisfied when the taxpayer made a fraudulent disclosure.[63]
- 1964: A law firm that turned over client tax information to an accounting firm could not maintain an independent action to restrain the enforcement of a summons by the IRS against the accountants but should appear in the enforcement proceeding for the summons.[64]
- 1966: The fact that the IRS possesses evidence obtained in violation of the privilege against self-incrimination does not bar prosecution altogether.[65]
- 1968: *Marchetti* and *Grosso* ruled that gamblers could not be convicted for failure to pay wagering excise tax where to do so required filing a form that revealed at least the intent to illegally wager, which would violate various state and federal laws in the future and likely encourage the authorities to suspect prior wagering; however the power to tax unlawful activities is unquestioned.[66] *Kahriger* was overruled on the self-incrimination point. The distinction the Court made is between a filing that presents an "imaginary and insubstantial" hazard of self-incrimination (as in *Sullivan* where the bootlegger refused to file a general income tax return on which he presumably could have entered the illegal income without pointing out its source) as contrasted to one that presents a "real and appreciable" hazard of self-incrimination (because the return was not for general income but for the specifically illegal income). The Court did not invalidate the statutes but ruled that one asserting his privilege against self-incrimination could not be convicted for violating them.
- 1968: *Haynes* ruled a criminal defendant's failure to file a firearms registration (and pay the accompanying tax) was subject to a valid self-incrimination defense because of the high likelihood that making the filing would have led to his criminal prosecution.[67] The opinion purported not to limit the broad power to tax, but effectively made impossible the collection of tax by voluntary filings reflecting the possession of illegal firearms; it did not invalidate the statute.
- 1968: *Mathis* ruled that statements obtained by revenue agents in a routine civil tax investigation of a state prisoner without *Miranda* warning were inadmissible because the taxpayer was in the custody of a state for

---

[63] Shotwell Mfg. Co. v. United States, 371 U.S. 341 (1963) (claimed cost of goods sold, which were not incurred).

[64] Reisman v. Caplin, 375 U.S. 440 (1964) (substantive defenses not discussed).

[65] United States v. Blue, 384 U.S. 251 (1966).

[66] Marchetti v. United States, 390 U.S. 39 (1968); Grosso v. United States, 390 U.S. 62 (1968).

[67] Haynes v. United States, 390 U.S. 85 (1968). *See also* United States v. Freed, 401 U.S. 601 (1971) (ruling that an amendment the Firearms Act did not require self-incrimination of the purchaser).

nontax crimes.[68] Later opinions limited this rule fairly strictly to custodial interrogation.[69]

- 1969: The case of Dr. Timothy Leary extended the reasoning of the gambling and firearms tax and registration cases to the Marijuana Tax Act because, like those taxes, filing the required form would have been highly likely to lead to criminal charges.[70] The decision also ruled unconstitutional a presumption outside the tax statute that possession of the marijuana supported a presumption that the possessor knew it was unlawfully imported. The enforcement problems raised by the *Leary* decision caused the government to shift from a taxing regime to a Commerce Clause based regime to penalize drug transactions.[71]
- 1969: *Knox* ruled that a gambler could be convicted for supplying false information on a form as to which he claimed the truth would have incriminated him.[72] Although he could have filed the form and asserted his privilege against self-incrimination, he could not lie and avoid conviction.
- 1969: In *Minor* the defendant appealed a criminal conviction of violating the Harrison Narcotics Act and Marijuana Tax Act by selling narcotics to buyers who had failed to provide the completed forms required by law.[73] Defendant argued that providing the forms would have incriminated the buyers. The Court agreed this was true and noted also that if the buyers had complied they would have subjected themselves to the $100 per ounce tax. But that was not the seller's problem. The seller was not compelled to sell to unregistered buyers. *Minor* stated: "The dissent suggests that the courts should refuse to enforce § 4705 (a) as part of a revenue measure. But these very order form provisions were upheld long ago as valid revenue laws even though they operated to prevent large classes of people from obtaining order forms—and hence from acquiring drugs—at all. United States v. Doremus, 249 U.S. 86 (1919); Webb v. United States, 249 U.S. 96 (1919); *see* Nigro v. United States, 276 U.S. 332 (1928). A statute does not cease to be a valid tax measure because it deters the activity taxed, because the revenue obtained is negligible, or because the activity is otherwise illegal. *See, e. g.*, Marchetti v. United States, 390 U.S. 39, 44 (1968); United States v. Kahriger, 345 U.S. 22, 28 (1953); License Tax Cases, 5 Wall. 462 (1867)."[74]

---

[68] Mathis v. United States, 391 U.S. 1 (1968).

[69] Beckwith v. United States, 425 U.S. 341 (1976) (even though agents might be looking for evidence of criminality, and it was produced in the responses of the defendant, the defendant was not in custody and the privilege did not apply).

[70] Leary v. United States, 395 U.S. 6 (1969. *See also* United States v. Covington, 395 U.S. 57 (1969) (companion case).

[71] *See* Gonzales v. Raich, 545 U.S. 1 (2005).

[72] United States v. Knox, 396 U.S. 77 (1969).

[73] Minor v. United States, 396 U.S. 87 (1969).

[74] 396 U.S. at 98 n. 13.

- 1971: Defendant Mackey, unlike Marchetti and Grosso, filed the wagering tax return but failed to include the wagering income in his income tax and was convicted for tax evasion.[75] There was no majority opinion but the plurality opinion said the *Marchetti* and *Grosso* decisions should not be applied retroactively to the facts of this case; the conviction stood.
- 1971: *Donaldson* stated that a taxpayer has no Fourth or Fifth Amendment right to prevent the IRS obtaining information about him from his employer and its accountant and the taxpayer so conceded.[76] The taxpayer's principal objection was misuse of the civil summons power, which the Court rejected because the taxpayer's case had not been referred for criminal prosecution.
- 1971: In a case like *Marchetti* and *Grosso* the Court extended the privilege to protection from the penalty of a forfeiture of the gambler's winnings.[77] Even though the forfeiture was a civil proceeding, the Court relied on *Boyd* to rule that it was criminal in nature because it effectively punished the gambler for committing a crime.[78]
- 1971: *Freed* ruled contrary to *Haynes* that the possessor of an illegal firearm could be convicted for having an unregistered illegal weapon because only possessors of legal firearms were required to register the firearm under the statute as revised in response to *Haynes*; therefore, the taxpayer was not forced to choose between not registering and giving up the privilege.[79]
- 1973: *Couch* ruled that the privilege relates to possession not ownership and therefore the IRS could obtain the taxpayer's records from the taxpayer's accountant.[80] The taxpayer could not "enlarge" his constitutional rights by causing the accountant to deliver the records to his lawyer; the accountant's obligation was fixed when the summons was served.
- 1974: *Bellis* ruled that partners can be required to produce partnership records because for this purpose partnerships are viewed as entities.[81]
- 1975: *Bisceglia* approved enforcement of a John Doe summons against a bank; the dissent argued that the Fifth Amendment issues were unresolved,

---

[75] Mackey v. United States, 401 U.S. 667 (1971).

[76] Donaldson v. United States, 400 U.S. 517 (1971). *See also* United States v. La Salle National Bank, 437 U.S. 298 (1978) (dissent of Justices Stewart, Burger, Rehnquist and Stevens points out that no one claims there is any constitutional basis for limiting the summons authority to before the referral of a case for criminal prosecution; *see* I.R.C. § 7602).

[77] United States v. United States Coin & Currency, 401 U.S. 715 (1971).

[78] Boyd v. United States, 116 U.S. 616, 634 (1886). *See* discussion of *Boyd* in double jeopardy context in Ch. VII.E.

[79] United States v. Freed, 401 U.S. 601(1971) (hand grenades).

[80] Couch v. United States, 409 U.S. 322 (1973). *See also* Andresen v. Maryland, 427 U.S. 463 (1976) (a person's business records are not protected, only his testimonial verification is protected).

[81] Bellis v. United States, 417 U.S. 85 (1974).

but ignored the fact that a third party cannot enforce another person's self-incrimination rights.[82]

- 1976: *Garner* rejected a self-incrimination defense asserted in a nontax criminal gambling case in which the government had used the gambler's income tax return that identified the taxpayer as a "professional gambler" and listed gambling income.[83] The Court said he had to file the return but could assert the privilege, as *Sullivan* had directed ("test" the claim). It rejected his argument that he was compelled to file the return. It distinguished between testimonial compulsion, by which the government has the right to make the witness appear and either speak or claim the privilege, from (a) custodial interrogation to which the *Miranda* warnings apply, (b) *Marchetti*, *Grosso* and *Mackey*, which involved a return targeted at illegal gamblers the filing of which was much more likely to lead to a prosecution,[84] and (c) a case in which a bad consequence necessarily would flow from claiming the privilege. Defendant could have filed the return and claimed the privilege and would not have been indictable for willfully failing to supply information or file a return ("A § 7203 conviction cannot be based on a valid exercise of the privilege."). The fact that the defendant had to face a possible criminal prosecution in which he would have to successfully defend his self-incrimination argument was not the type of compulsion that could render his self incrimination coerced.
- 1976: As noted above, *Fisher* explained the substantial reversal of *Boyd*. *Fisher* ordered a taxpayer's attorney to turn over documents created by the taxpayer's accountant in preparing his tax returns and obtained by the taxpayer from the accountants and delivered to the lawyer.[85] The documents were the accountant's work papers, the returns themselves and correspondence and so the person who might be incriminated was not called on to do anything, certainly not to incriminate himself. The attorney-client privilege did not justify extending the privilege because the client could not have avoided turning over the documents in his hands because (1) they were not documents he had created, and (2) his turnover would not constitute testimonial self-incrimination although it would have had a testimonial element. In *Hubbell* the Court later characterized *Fisher* as relating to voluntarily created

[82] United States v. Bisceglia, 420 U.S. 141 (1975).

[83] Garner v. United States, 424 U.S. 648 (1976).

[84] *Cf.* Roberts v. United States, 445 U.S. 552 (1980) (explained *Garner* by indicating that the general requirement to file Form 1040 did not give the IRS substantial reason to believe that the taxpayer would incriminate himself).

[85] Fisher v. United States, 425 U.S. 391 (1976). *See* Andresen v. Maryland, 427 U.S. 463 (1976) (production of the person's own documents may compel authentication or other testimonial evidence that is protected).

documents, which would include the taxpayer's own business records, and limited its reach.[86] *Fisher* originated the act-of-production doctrine.[87]

- 1980: A taxpayer can be required to provide a handwriting exemplar without violating the privilege.[88]
- 1983: *Rylander* ruled that a corporate officer could not hide behind a self-incrimination defense to avoid explaining why he could not produce corporate records to avoid civil contempt.[89] Defendant was held in civil contempt for failing to produce the corporate books. He claimed he did not have them and to say more would be self-incrimination; in effect he wanted to place on the IRS the burden of proving he had the books.
- 1984: An individual's business records are not themselves protected by the Fifth Amendment because they are considered to have been created voluntarily.[90] However, the act of producing the records in response to an IRS request or summons may verify their accuracy and that they are the documents sought and thus the act of production may be protected as self-incriminating.[91] This opinion decides the issue about the taxpayer's own papers left undecided in *Fisher*. The Court was bound by the facts found by the trial court as to self-incrimination: "With few exceptions, enforcement of the subpoenas would compel [respondent] to admit that the records exist, that they are in his possession, and that they are authentic. These communications, if made under compulsion of a court decree, would violate [respondent's] Fifth Amendment rights. . . . The government argues that the existence, possession and authenticity of the documents can be proved without [respondent's] testimonial communication, but it cannot satisfy this court as to how that representation can be implemented to protect the witness in subsequent proceedings."[92]
- 1984: *Arthur Young & Co.* did not involve any consideration of constitutional rights but did conclude that accountant's work papers can be obtained by the IRS.[93]
- 1988: A corporate officer could not resist the grand jury subpoena of corporate records on the grounds that the records might incriminate him personally.[94]

---

[86] United States v. Hubbell, 530 U.S. 27, 36 (2000).

[87] *See* Note, *The Act of Production Privilege Post Hubbell*, 17 GEO. MASON L. REV. 863, 867 (2010).

[88] United States v. Euge, 444 U.S. 707 (1980).

[89] United States v. Rylander, 460 U.S. 752 (1983).

[90] United States v. Doe, 465 U.S. 605 (1984).

[91] *Id.*

[92] 465 U.S. at 614 n. 11.

[93] United States v. Arthur Young & Co., 465 U.S. 805 (1984). *See also* Tiffany Fine Arts, Inc. v. United States, 469 U.S. 310 (1985).

[94] Braswell v. United States, 487 U.S. 99 (1988).

- 1988: Defendant could not assert the privilege against self-incrimination against a grand jury demand that he execute forms authorizing access to foreign (Cayman) bank account records because that act in itself was not testimonial.[95] The records were not privileged in the hands of the bank; the defendant had no right to assert the privilege against disclosure by the bank. Even though the form would be a link in possible inculpating evidence, because its signing was not testimonial it was not prevented.
- 2000: Webster Hubbell, former Assistant Attorney General and friend of President Clinton, obtained a dismissal of his indictment on tax fraud because the indictment was based on documents under subpoena from Hubbell and his production involved a compelled testimonial aspect, although the documents themselves were not protected, citing *Doe* and *Fisher*.[96] The opinion relied on the principles that (1) the incriminating evidence need not be used at the trial itself but may be privileged if it would be a link in the chain of evidence needed to prosecute, (2) the "existence, authenticity and custody" of the subpoenaed documents that were established by the defendant's answer and production need not be themselves introduced into evidence but the privilege would be violated if the prosecution used the "existence, authenticity and custody" to locate evidence needed to prosecute, which it did. This expansion appears to significantly restrict the *Fisher* limitation of the privilege, at least when the defendant has to exercise substantial knowledge to identify and gather the documents requested in what might be described as a "fishing expedition" by the government.[97]

The Court subsequently has been silent on self-incrimination issues, outside of custodial interrogation cases.

D. Fourth Amendment

The Fourth Amendment states:

> The right of the people to be secure in their persons, houses, papers, and effects, against unreasonable searches and seizures, shall not be violated, ...

The right against government entry to search has roots in the British tax law. In a 1763 Parliamentary debate, about searches made to enforce a tax, William Pitt the Elder orated as follows: "The poorest man may in his cottage bid defiance to all the forces of the Crown. It may be frail; its roof may shake; the wind may blow through it; the storm may enter; the rain may enter; but the King of England cannot enter—all his force dares not cross the threshold of the ruined tenement!"[98]

Although corporations and other organizations are not literally excluded from Fourth Amendment protections, they do not have the same expectation of pri-

---

[95] Doe v. United States, 487 U.S. 201 (1988).

[96] United States v. Hubbell, 530 U.S. 27 (2000).

[97] 17 Geo. Mason L. Rev. at 873.

[98] Cited in Lange v. California, 141 S. Ct. 2011 (2021).

vacy under the Fourth Amendment with respect to their documents and affairs as individuals because corporations exist only by permission of the state, and are endowed with public attributes.[99]

As discussed in the preceding Chapter in relation to the Fifth Amendment, an early but now misleading authority as to the Fourth Amendment and tax collections is *Boyd v. United States*, of which it has been said that "subsequent history is largely one of escaping the *Boyd* dictum."[100] That dictum tied together the Fourth and Fifth Amendments and ruled that when a taxpayer turned over incriminating evidence under a court order authorized by statute, the taxpayer's Fourth Amendment rights were violated and therefore it was compelled to incriminate itself in violation of the Fifth Amendment.

Subsequently the Court has established that the taxpayer's books and records can be obtained under a valid search warrant without a violation of the Fourth Amendment, and also can be obtained under compulsion from the taxpayer unless the taxpayer's act of turning over documents is testimonial in nature, which is a separate issue under the Fifth Amendment, as discussed in the preceding Chapter. In other words, it is not "unreasonable" to seek the documents on which the tax return is based. Although the requirements for obtaining a search warrant are rather strict, once that hurdle is cleared, the documents obtained can be used to prosecute the taxpayer and such use does not raise issues of self-incrimination.[101] Generally third parties like banks have no Fourth Amendment grounds to prevent turnover of records reflecting taxpayer's transactions, and neither does the taxpayer.

Because of the apparent expansion of the privilege against self-incrimination in the Supreme Court's last Fifth Amendment tax decision, *Hubbell*, the IRS may be forced to rely more heavily on the search warrant in criminal cases.[102]

The federal tax Fourth Amendment decisions of the Supreme Court reflecting the foregoing summary are the following:

- 1911: *Flint v. Stone Tracy Co.* rejected Fourth Amendment objections to the publicity of returns filed under the 1909 corporate excise tax on the grounds that the power to tax justified the means selected by Congress; the Court could see that disclosure of returns could have the benefit of making them more complete and accurate.[103]
- 1955: *Lewis* raised the issue whether having to buy and display a license to engage in illegal activity would unfairly attract a search; the Court ruled the

[99] California Bankers Ass'n v. Shultz, 416 U.S. 21, 65 (1974) ("law-enforcing agencies have a legitimate right to satisfy themselves that corporate behavior is consistent with the law and the public interest," *citing* United States v. Morton Salt Co., 338 U.S. 632, 652 (1950)).

[100] Boyd v. United States, 116 U.S. 616 (1886). Davis, at 1128.

[101] Andresen v. Maryland, 427 U.S. 463 (1976).

[102] Mark A. Cowen, Note, *The Act-of-Production Privilege Post Hubbell*, 17 GEO. MASON L. REV. 863, 883.

[103] Flint v. Stone Tracy Co., 220 U.S. 107 U.S. 176-177 (1911).

defendant did not have standing to raise the issue because the defendant had not bought the license.[104]

- 1963: *Lopez v. United States* rejected an entrapment defense asserted by a taxpayer convicted of attempting to bribe a revenue agent.[105] The dissent of Justice Brennan asserted that the defendant's Fourth Amendment rights had been violated. The Court later cited *Lopez* for the ruled that the Fourth Amendment provides "no protection to an individual against the recording of his statements by the IRS agent to whom he was speaking."[106]
- 1966: *Black* remanded for a new trial a criminal tax prosecution in which another branch of the government had intercepted telephone calls between the defendant and his attorney discussing the case.[107]
- 1970: Treasury officials were authorized to inspect premises of liquor dealer and when it refused to allow inspection it would be subject to fine; but officials could not enter forcibly without a warrant.[108]
- 1974: Discussing but not resolving all Fourth and Fifth Amendment objections of banks to reporting various transactions, *California Bankers Ass'n v. Shultz* explained that Treasury regulations have long required records to be maintained and such requirements do not violate the Fourth or Fifth Amendments.[109] The full protections of the Fourth Amendment are not available to corporations.[110] The Court rejected Fourth Amendment objections to laws requiring banks to report domestic and foreign money transactions exceeding $10,000. Among other reasons, any wrongdoings involved were not the banks'.
- 1975: *Bisceglia* ruled that the IRS could issue a John Doe summons to a bank officer requiring turnover of records of all large deposits without identifying any particular person.[111] The opinion did not discuss constitutional issues but the dissent argued that the Fourth Amendment issues had been left unresolved by *California Bankers Ass'n v. Shultz.*
- 1976: *Miller* ruled that taxpayer had no expectation of privacy in a bank's records of defendant's transactions.[112] Taxpayer had neither ownership nor

[104] Lewis v. United States, 348 U.S. 419 (1955).

[105] Lopez v. United States, 373 U.S. 427 (1963).

[106] United States v. Caceres, 440 U.S. 741, 750 (1979).

[107] Black v. United States, 385 U.S. 26 (1966).

[108] Colonnade Catering Corp. v. United States, 397 U.S. 72 (1970).

[109] California Bankers Ass'n v. Shultz, 416 U.S. 21 (1974).

[110] *Id.* at 65-66.

[111] United States v. Bisceglia, 420 U.S. 141 (1975). *Cf.* United States v. Stuart, 489 U.S. 353 (1989) (enforced a summons from the Canadian tax authorities against a domestic bank, which was provided for under a treaty; constitutional issues were not discussed).

[112] United States v. Miller, 425 U.S. 435 (1976). This opinion also stated that *Boyd* had been deeply undercut as explained in *Fisher*.

possession of the records. Even though some of the documents were taxpayer's checks, he had no expectation of privacy as to them.

- 1976: *Janis* ruled that the IRS could use in a civil proceeding material obtained in a state criminal proceeding in violation of the Fourth Amendment.[113]
- 1977: *G.M. Leasing Corp.* upheld seizure of property that occurred without entry into private property, but found a violation of the Fourth Amendment in the revenue agent's entry into taxpayer's premises without a warrant for the purpose of searching, finding and taking property to satisfy a tax lien.[114]
- 1980: A taxpayer can be required to furnish a handwriting exemplar without violating the Fourth Amendment.[115]
- 1980: A taxpayer had no Fourth Amendment rights in the search of a bank officer's brief case by the revenue agents, but the Court suppressed the fruit of the illegal search under its inherent supervisory power.[116]
- 1992: *Church of Scientology* ruled that a taxpayer can obtain appellate review of a summons compliance order in a criminal tax investigation.[117]

It is thought that the President has constitutional rights to tax return information, a potential Fourth Amendment issue.[118]

E. Double Jeopardy

1. *Overview*

The Fifth Amendment to the Constitution states: "nor shall any person be subject for the same offence to be twice put in jeopardy of life or limb. . . ." It is not limited to "life or limb" punishments, but extends to monetary penalties, so long as they are punishments for a criminal offense.[119] The words of the Amendment do not refer to either a prosecution or punishment or crime, so the required criminal nexus of the Double Jeopardy Clause derives from the reference to either "offence" or "jeopardy of life or limb." In practice it derives from both: there must be at least one clearly defined offense that Congress labels criminal, which is once pursued by the government to the point that jeopardy attaches (conviction or acquittal, not a hung jury); if so the United States cannot put the

---

[113] United States v. Janis, 428 U.S. 433 (1976).

[114] G. M. Leasing Corp. v. United States, 429 U.S. 338, 352 (1977). Note that "G.M." is not an abbreviation for General Motors.

[115] United States v. Euge, 444 U.S. 707 (1980).

[116] United States v. Payner, 447 U.S. 727 (1980).

[117] Church of Scientology v. United States, 506 U.S. 9 (1992). *See also* United States v. Jose, 519 U.S. 54 (1996) (allowing immediate appeal of a final summons compliance order).

[118] *See* Staff of the Joint Committee on Taxation, Confidentiality of Tax Returns, p. 8, JCS-38-75 (Sept. 25, 1975) (citing Article II, sections 1, 2 and 3; also discussing Congress' rights).

[119] Dep't of Revenue of Mont. v. Ranch, 511 U.S. 767, 769 n. 1 (1994).

defendant in jeopardy of life or limb (*i.e.*, a criminal punishment) a second time with respect to the same criminal offense.

Contrary to some statements in opinions, the Double Jeopardy Clause does not forbid multiple criminal punishments for the same criminal offense; indeed, many crimes can be punished by both fines and imprisonment.[120] Rather it forbids first pursuing one punishment to acquittal or conviction, and then pursuing a second criminal punishment in a separate prosecution for the same criminal offense. Because the Double Jeopardy Clause is limited to criminal punishments, it obviously does not forbid multiple punishments in the generic sense of multiple sanctions; that is why it does not forbid one punishment that is in nature criminal, and another that is in nature civil, for the same offense that is treated as a criminal offense for purposes of the criminal sanction and as a civil offense for purposes of the civil sanction.

Therefore, applying the Double Jeopardy Clauses to taxes and tax penalties usually involves deciding whether the tax or tax penalty is intended by Congress to be a criminal punishment for a criminal offense. After some uncertainty, in *Hudson* (discussed in Chapter V) the Court came down on the side of form rather than substance and decided the nature of an ambiguous sanction through more traditional statutory interpretation.[121] This approach has made even rarer the possibility that a sanction or tax imposed on a taxpayer must be treated as a criminal punishment, even though it is not labeled as a punishment for crime and is not imposed in a criminal proceeding.

In addition to giving great deference to Congress' indicia of civil and criminal punishments in the statute, and treating the issue as one of statutory construction, the Court recognizes that sanctions can be treated as civil even though they punish in the sense that they can be imposed for some of the same purposes

---

[120] *See, e.g.*, 18 U.S.C. § 81 (arson punishable by prison, fine equal to cost of fire damage, or both). *See generally* Anne Bowen Poulin, *Double Jeopardy and Multiple Punishment: Cutting the Gordian Knot*, 77 U. Colo. L. Rev. 595 (2006). However, if one of the punishments is not authorized by statute, then it is viewed as a double jeopardy. *See* Ex Parte Lange, 85 U.S. 163 (1874).

[121] Hudson v. United States, 522 U.S. 93 (1997). *See* dissent of Chief Justice Roberts in Caperton v. A. T. Massey Coal Co., 556 U.S. 868 (2009) ("Consider the cautionary tale of our decisions in United States v. Halper, . . . and Hudson v. United States. . . . Historically, we have held that the Double Jeopardy Clause only applies to criminal penalties, not civil ones. *See, e.g.*, Helvering v. Mitchell, . . . But in *Halper*, the Court held that a civil penalty could violate the Clause if it were 'overwhelmingly disproportionate to the damages [the defendant] has caused' and resulted in a 'clear injustice.' . . . We acknowledged that this inquiry would not be an 'exact pursuit,' but the Court assured litigants that it was only announcing 'a rule for the rare case, the case such as the one before us.' . . . Just eight years later, we granted certiorari in *Hudson* 'because of concerns about the wide variety of novel double jeopardy claims spawned in the wake of *Halper*.' . . . The novel claim that we had recognized in *Halper* turned out not to be so 'rare' after all, and the test we adopted in that case—'overwhelmingly disproportionate'—had 'proved unworkable.' . . . We thus abandoned the *Halper* rule, ruing our 'ill considered' 'deviation from longstanding double jeopardy principles.'").

that criminal punishments are imposed (retribution and deterrence[122]), and they need not be imposed solely for remedial purposes (*i.e.*, to make the government whole). This recognition makes the Court's heavily reliance on the formal indicia of a civil penalty given by Congress in the statute exceedingly important, because without that reliance the identification of a punitive sanction as civil would be difficult (as illustrated by the *Halper* opinion, discussed in Chapter VII.E.3). The individual mandate upheld by *Sebelius* is a good example of a civil penalty that was a punitive tax but not a criminal punishment.[123]

As applied to taxpayers, the double jeopardy questions that arise almost always ask whether the tax itself, or a civil tax penalty, is a criminal punishment for the same offense for which the taxpayer has already been (or will later be) prosecuted as a criminal offense, either to conviction or acquittal. The other unambiguous criminal offense causing the double jeopardy concern will be either a criminal tax offense or a nontax criminal offense. Generally a tax offense in the generic sense (*i.e.*, failure to pay tax) can be punished as both a civil offense and a criminal offense by both civil and criminal penalties (only one criminal jeopardy); and a nontax offense can be punished criminally and also taxed, unless the tax is interpreted to be a criminal punishment for a criminal offense (now a very rare possibility).

Determining whether a sanction imposed on a taxpayer is a criminal punishment for a criminal offense is an issue that can arise in multiple settings in addition to double jeopardy cases: (1) cases involving the legislative power of Congress to punish or regulate in the area if the sanction is found to be regulatory (*i.e.*, a criminal punishment) and not a tax;[124] (2) cases involving procedural rights;[125] (3) cases involving self-incrimination;[126] and possibly (4) cases involving Eighth Amendment excessive fines and cruel and unusual punishment issues.[127] Although the Court tends to intermingle cites to its own opinions from this variety of settings involving criminal proceedings, the standards for finding a criminal punishment are not necessarily the same. For example, the Court has specifically stated that the Eighth Amendment applies to both civil and criminal

---

[122] As to the propriety of deterrence in a civil proceeding, *see also* United States v. Ursery, 518 U.S. 267, 292 (1996) ("Third, though both statutes may fairly be said to serve the purpose of deterrence, we long have held that this purpose may serve civil as well as criminal goals."); Hudson v. United States, 522 U.S. 93, 99 (1997); Bennis v. Michigan, 516 U.S. 442, 452, (1996) ("Forfeiture . . . serves a deterrent purpose distinct from any punitive purpose").

[123] National Federation of Independent Business v. Sebelius, 567 U.S. 519 (2012).

[124] *Cf.* United States v. Sanchez, 340 U.S. 42 (1950) (Congress could impose a tax on marijuana even though it could not regulate it).

[125] When a taxpayer's property was to be seized for payment additional due process must be provided, whether the amount to be collected was a tax or criminal penalty. Lipke v. Lederer, 259 U.S. 557 (1922); *cf.* Helwig v. United States, 188 U.S. 605 (1903) (a penalty for excessive understatement of value for customs purposes was a penalty and not revenue for purposes of a jurisdictional statute).

[126] *See* United States v. United States Coin & Currency, 401 U.S. 715 (1971).

[127] *Cf.* Murphy v. United States, 272 U.S. 630 (1926) (the nuisance that was a liquor establishment could be abated to the financial detriment of the bootlegger, in addition to his criminal conviction).

forfeitures and is not to be considered parallel to the double (criminal) jeopardy rule.[128] The same opinion stated that a civil in rem forfeiture by its very nature usually cannot be a "punishment" for double jeopardy purposes (although the opposite might be shown in the clearest cases).[129] In its most recent opinion holding a state drug tax to be a punishment the Court took care to state:

> Taken as a whole, this drug tax is a concoction of anomalies, too far removed in crucial respects from a standard tax assessment to escape characterization as punishment *for the purpose of double jeopardy analysis.* (emphasis added).[130]

Little of the Supreme Court's law in this area is in federal tax cases, with two major exceptions. First, the *Mitchell* decision, discussed below, holds that the same failure to pay tax can be punished by a criminal punishment and a civil tax fine that the Court viewed as "remedial."[131] *Mitchell* is a seminal opinion in the area, placing the emphasis on statutory construction and the legislature's intent to punish or not.[132]

Second, the *License Tax Cases* ruled that Congress could impose a tax on conduct that was illegal at the state level, which could result in criminal punishment by the state and criminal punishment by the United States for failing to pay the tax.[133] The Court has explained the possibility of constitutional dual criminal punishment by a state and the United States, without referring to double jeopardy, because the punishments and laws "occupy different planes," meaning that the state exercised its police power and the United States exercised its taxing power, despite the obvious fact that the conduct was illegal and the tax was intended to provide an additional discouragement.[134]

2. *Where the Crime Is the Nonpayment of the Tax*

Multiple detriments to a taxpayer can result from failing to pay a federal tax on time, including: accuracy related and fraud penalties, including a 75% civil fraud penalty, in sections 6662 through 6664; the general criminal penalties in

---

[128] *See* United States v. Ursery, 518 U.S. 267, 281, 286 (1996), *discussing* Austin v. United States, 509 U.S. 602 (1993).

[129] United States v. Ursery, 518 U.S. 267, 289 n. 3 (1996).

[130] Dep't of Revenue of Mont. v. Ranch, 511 U.S. 767, 783 (1994).

[131] Helvering v. Mitchell, 303 U.S. 391 (1938). *Mitchell* also stated that collection of criminal tax penalties by distraint would be unconstitutional. As to civil fraud penalty and double jeopardy generally, *see* SALTZMAN & BOOK, IRS PRACTICE AND PROCEDURE ¶ 12.06[5][b].

[132] *See* Robin W. Sardegna, *No Longer in Jeopardy: The Impact of Hudson v. United States*, 33 VAL. U. L. REV. 115, 120-121 (1998).

[133] License Tax Cases, 72 U.S. 462 (1867). The state and federal government can each make the same conduct illegal and prosecute without violating double jeopardy. Fox v. Ohio, 46 U.S. 410 (1847); Heath v. Alabama, 474 U.S. 82, 88-89 (1985). *See generally* Anthony J. Colangelo, *Double Jeopardy and Multiple Sovereigns: A Jurisdictional Theory*, 86 WASH. U. L. REV. 769 (2009).

[134] *In re* Heff, 197 U.S. 488 (1905), *overruled on other grounds* by United States v. Nice, 241 U.S. 591 (1916). The Court explicitly embraced the dual sovereignty theory allowing multiple criminal punishments for the same act in United States v. Lanza, 260 U.S. 377 (1922) (liquor law violations). Gamble v. United States, 139 S. Ct. 1960 (2019) reaffirmed the dual sovereignty doctrine for separate state and federal prosecutions but was not a tax case.

section 7201 through 7217; and forfeitures, under section 7301 through 7304. The federal civil tax penalties denominated as such are not criminal punishments, as ruled in the *Mitchell* decision.[135] Charles E. (called "Sunshine Charlie," presumably because he never saw a down market) Mitchell, the former Chairman of National City Bank, was acquitted of criminal tax fraud (*i.e.*, the first jeopardy attached), but was found to owe substantial tax due to underreporting and to a sale of stock at a loss to his wife in 1929, and also to owe a 50% fraud penalty.[136] Mitchell argued that the 50% fraud penalty imposed on his underreporting of almost $3 million of income for 1929 was a criminal penalty and thus placed him in double jeopardy for the crime of tax evasion for which he had already been tried and acquitted.

He appealed the fraud penalty and Justice Brandeis wrote the opinion rejecting his claims, finding: (1) although the facts required for the civil fraud penalty may have been the same as the facts required to convict in the criminal case, res judicata did not bar the fraud penalty because the issues were different (the degree of the burden of proof differed); (2) the Double Jeopardy Clause was not violated because as a matter of statutory construction Congress did not intend the civil fraud penalty to be a "punishment" for crime, but intended it to be a "remedial sanction" (remedying the government's loss of the tax and cost of collection) that is part of the tax; and (3) *Coffey*, a case that indicated a forfeiture of property was criminal, was inapplicable.[137]

Mitchell is the cornerstone of federal tax double jeopardy law, although the *Hudson* opinion discussed in the next Chapter updates the legal standards. *Mitchell* contains these principles:

- Congress may impose both civil and criminal sanctions for the same conduct. Therefore, the fundamental regime of civil and criminal sanctions for failure to pay taxes is constitutional. Earlier the Court had upheld the Harrison Narcotics Act as a revenue measure, despite the fact that it also had criminal penalties designed to make it more effective as a revenue measure.[138]

- The identification of a sanction as criminal punishment or civil penalty is a matter of statutory interpretation and so the tools usually used by courts in statutory construction will be applied, beginning with the indicia in the statute of how Congress classified the penalty.

---

[135] Helvering v. Mitchell, 303 U.S. 391 (1938). *See* Kenneth Mann, *Punitive Civil Sanctions: The Middle Ground Between Criminal and Civil Law*, 101 Yale L. J. 1795, 1825 *et seq.* (1992) [hereinafter Mann] (asserting that *Mitchell* reflected a so called remedial approach to penalties, citing Stockwell v. United States, 80 U.S. 531 (1871) and also limited Boyd v. United States, 116 U.S. 616 (1886) by declining to apply special procedural requirements to quasi-criminal punishments).

[136] Helvering v. Mitchell, 303 U.S. 391 (1938). *See* Michael Perino, The Hellhound of Wall Street (2010) (primarily devoted to description of Ferdinand Pecora's interrogation of Mitchell in relation to Wall Street Crash of 1929 and related bank activities).

[137] Coffey v. United States, 116 U.S. 436 (1886).

[138] United States v. Wong Sing, 260 U.S. 18 (1922).

- A remedial sanction is a polar opposite of a punishment sanction. A sanction is viewed as remedial when it is in aid of the fundamental power being exercised by Congress, here the taxing power. The remedial function of civil tax penalties is to protect the revenue (by coercing compliance) and to reimburse the government for the heavy expense of investigation (where self-reporting is the keystone of the system) and the losses from the fraudulent conduct of the taxpayer.
- Congress indicates that a penalty is remedial when it gives administrative agencies the power to enforce it without resort to the judicial power (an element of statutory interpretation). An example of a remedial penalty is revocation of a license or other privilege previously granted.
- Civil forfeitures in support of the revenue laws have existed since the first revenue law of 1789 and the Court has consistently upheld them without requiring the criminal enforcement mechanisms, although they may raise self-incrimination concerns.[139]
- However, the Court's opinions have not well distinguished between civil tax penalties and criminal tax punishments.
- The Court has ruled that even a penalty of double the value of imports on which duties were not paid is a proper civil penalty due to the costs to the government of noncompliance.
- The 50% fraud penalty at issue in *Mitchell* was a civil penalty in part because Congress allowed it to be collected by distraint (a non-judicial remedy), which would be unconstitutional for a criminal penalty; thus Congress intended that it be treated as civil because Congress provided a civil procedure for its collection.
- However, a civil penalty may be enforceable by criminal procedure and still be a civil penalty.
- The government may recover costs in a suit and such costs are not criminal penalties.
- The existence within the Revenue Act of separately stated civil and criminal penalties supports the characterization of the civil penalties as civil.
- The label "additions to tax" denotes a civil penalty.
- The interpretive criterion is not the severity of the sanction but rather the procedure by which Congress directed the application of the penalty, which was a civil procedure.
- Mitchell distinguished the earlier *Coffey* decision on the basis of the burden of proof: where the burden of proof was identical in the civil and criminal

[139] *See* United States v. Ursery, 518 U.S. 267 (1996); United States v. United States Coin & Currency, 401 U.S. 715 (1971). *See* Ch. VII.C.

charges and the same facts underlay both charges, double jeopardy could occur, as may have happened in *Coffey*; but where the facts to be proved or the burden of proof differ, *Coffey* is distinguishable.[140] Mr. Coffey distilled liquor without paying the federal tax. He was acquitted in a criminal trial. Then the United States required the forfeiture of what evidently were two separate stills and appurtenant product. In response to each forfeiture Coffey pleaded his acquittal in the separate criminal case. As to one forfeiture, the Court denied his claims based on a pleading error.[141] That error did not infect the second forfeiture, which the Court reversed on the basis of the prior acquittal.[142] The opinion did not mention double jeopardy and could have been based on collateral estoppel, but primarily viewed the forfeiture as part and parcel of the criminal punishment; one later opinion said it was based on double jeopardy[143] and another labeled it collateral estoppel.[144] In 1984 the Court stated: "The time has come to clarify that neither collateral estoppel nor double jeopardy bars a civil, remedial forfeiture proceeding initiated following an acquittal on related criminal charges. To the extent that *Coffey v. United States* suggests otherwise, it is hereby disapproved."[145]

Chouteau is an early example of a civil penalty that was imposed in aid of collection of a tax.[146] The federal tax on liquor distributors required certain bookkeeping and maintenance of the liquor inventory in identified warehouses, with penalties enforcing these requirements, which were themselves in aid of tax collection. The taxpayer previously had been indicted for evading the tax and had obtained dismissal of that indictment by entering into a compromise agreement with the government, which purported to settle the prosecution for the events that included the acts on which the civil penalty could be based. Subsequently the government initiated a civil proceeding to collect on a bond for a penalty that also could have been collected in the prior criminal proceeding. The Court denied the second remedy, ruling that it was covered by the prior settlement, but the opinion also contained some statements that sound like a reference to

[140] For this explanation of *Coffey*, *see* One Lot Emerald Cut Stones & One Ring v. United States, 409 U.S. 232 (1972) (a customs duty, and hence a tax, case; forfeiture allowed of the jewels on which the duty was not paid after smuggler was acquitted of criminal charge). The explanation was confirmed in discussion of *Mitchell* by United States v. One Assortment of 89 Firearms, 465 U.S. 354 (1984).

[141] Coffey v. United States, 116 U.S. 427 (1886).

[142] *Id.* at 436, *as explained in* Coffey v. United States, 117 U.S. 233 (1886).

[143] Stone v. United States, 167 U.S. 178 (1897).

[144] Ashe v. Swenson, 397 U.S. 436 (1970). This opinion has been credited with inventing a collateral estoppel ingredient of double jeopardy; it applies when an essential element of the current prosecution was necessarily decided in the prior prosecution. *See* Note, Jessica Greenwood, *Double Jeopardy—Supreme Court Denies Relevance of Hung Counts to Collateral Estoppel*, 63 S.M.U.L. Rev. 243, 245 (2010).

[145] United States v. One Assortment of 89 Firearms, 465 U.S. 354 (1984). *See also* Payne v. Tenn., 501 U.S. 808 n. 1 (1991) (states that *89 Firearms* overruled *Coffey*). *Mitchell* also distinguished United States v. La Franca, 282 U.S. 568 (1931) in which Justice Sutherland treated a tax as a punishment as a matter of statutory construction.

[146] United States v. Chouteau, 102 U.S. 603 (1880).

double jeopardy. The *Chouteau* opinion has been characterized as finding that a civil tax penalty was in fact a criminal punishment;[147] the Court erroneously suggested this view in *La Franca*, which nevertheless ruled for the taxpayer on a ground other than double jeopardy.[148] But *Chouteau* is properly viewed as a case deciding the scope of a contractual compromise settlement.[149]

Forfeitures. Civil forfeitures have received relatively recent treatment in *Ursery* (not a tax case), which reaffirmed the generally non-criminal nature of most forfeitures.[150] Specifically, the opinion divided the question into two parts for double jeopardy purposes: (1) is the forfeiture a punishment? (never); and is the proceeding criminal? (evidently this is possible, but not found on the facts). As *Ursery* showed, in rem forfeiture proceedings in tax cases traditionally were not subject to the Double Jeopardy Clause at all. *One Ford Coupe* involved the seizure and forfeiture of a car used to transport nontax paid liquor.[151] The car owner protested that the unpaid tax was not a tax but a penalty and so he did not attempt to defraud the United States out of a tax, which was the precondition for the forfeiture. The Court ruled that the illegality of the act required to be taxed and the unlikelihood of the payment did not render the tax a penalty, but even if it did, a forfeiture still could be triggered. In another case, an importer was criminally convicted for evading the import duties (taxes) and also made to forfeit the merchandise.[152] However, a civil forfeiture may violate the Eighth Amendment's proscription against excessive fines.[153] See further discussion of forfeitures in Ch. VII.H.

Therefore, based on *Mitchell* and the forfeiture cases, not only civil tax penalties denominated as such, but also forfeitures, are permissible civil remedies for failure to pay tax, which failure also has been criminally prosecuted. In theory there remains a potential for a double jeopardy claim as to civil tax penalties and forfeitures: a taxpayer (and even the IRS) can argue that they are a criminal punishment or are imposed in a criminal proceeding, under the current *Hudson* standard, discussed below. For example, the Court ruled that a forfeiture related to a federal liquor law violation was a criminal penalty despite the fact that the United States Code labeled it a forfeiture.[154] That case reversed the usual dynam-

---

[147] *See* Mann, at 1817.

[148] United States v. La Franca, 282 U.S. 568 (1931) (the opinion never mentioned double jeopardy and interpreted a statute precluding another "punishment" to encompass a federal tax that was a penalty, presumably civil). *See* United States ex rel. Marcus v. Hess, 317 U.S. 537 (1943) (concurrence of Justice Frankfurter, indicating that "dialectical subtleties may serve well enough for purposes of explaining away uncritical language in earlier cases" in connection with *Chouteau* and *La Franca*).

[149] *See also* Huntington v. Attrill, 146 U.S. 657, 667 (1892) (citing *Chouteau* for the point that penalty has both a civil and a criminal usage).

[150] United States v. Ursery, 518 U.S. 267 (1996).

[151] United States v. One Ford Coupe Auto, 272 U.S. 321 (1926).

[152] One Lot Emerald Cut Stones & One Ring v. United States, 409 U.S. 232 (1990) (the distinction was the difference in burden of proof).

[153] Austin v. United States, 509 U.S. 602 (1993). *See also* Bennis v. Mich., 516 U.S. 442, 452 (1996).

[154] United States v. Dixon, 347 U.S. 381 (1954).

ics because the government needed the forfeiture to be a criminal penalty in order to explain the indictment it had used to seek the forfeiture. As discussed below in connection with *Kurth Ranch*, a court may in a rare case find a penalty to be so tightly connected to the crime that it is not a civil remedy. Forfeitures are discussed further in Chapter VII.H.

Alternately, and even more hypothetically, a court might find the tax itself not to be a tax, which leaves the government in the unhappy posture of seeking a federal justification for the tax, such as exercise of the Commerce Clause power rather than the federal police power that is said not to exist.[155] If the court finds that other power to be an exercise of criminal punishment, then any additional punishment that is found to be criminal will constitute double jeopardy.

Finally, distinguishing a civil penalty from a criminal punishment is not the same as distinguishing a civil penalty from a remedial payment to the government, a differentiation made relevant by section 162(f).

3. *Where the Crime Is Not Directly Related to Tax Collection*

Taxpayers may tend to raise double jeopardy defenses more often against taxes that Congress has imposed on conduct that is a crime, usually under state law, such as bootlegging, gambling and buying, selling or possessing marijuana or narcotics.[156] The *License Tax Cases* held that Congress could impose a tax on conduct that was illegal at the state level, which could result in criminal punishment by the state and criminal punishment by the United States for failing to pay the tax.[157] Of course double jeopardy cannot arise directly from one crime punished by two sovereigns.[158] However, if a heavy federal tax is imposed on the same facts that constitute a federal crime, as occurred in *Kurth Ranch*, an analogous state law case discussed below, a double jeopardy defense might be asserted.

Hudson defines the current state of the law of double jeopardy that applies to both the tax or tax penalty imposed on account of a nontax crime, as well as to the *Mitchell* type of tax case discussed in the preceding chapter.[159] *Hudson* ruled that if Congress labels a sanction as a criminal punishment, then it is; if Congress does not do so, it is up to the Court to interpret the statute to determine if it imposes a criminal punishment. That much is unsurprising; Justice Brandeis said the same in *Mitchell*. The added features of *Hudson* are (a) the illustrative

---

155 As to a tax ruled not to be a tax, but not for double jeopardy purposes, *see* United States v. Constantine, 296 U.S. 287 (1935).

156 Justices Black and Douglas warned in dissent against criminalizing embezzlement as a tax crime, as leading to double jeopardy or double punishment that presumably would escape the constitutional limit. James v. United States, 366 U.S. 213, 230 (1961).

157 License Tax Cases, 72 U.S. 462 (1867).

158 *See, e.g.*, United States v. Lanza, 260 U.S. 377 (1922); Gamble v. United States, 139 S. Ct. 1960 (2019).

159 Hudson v. United States, 522 U.S. 93 (1997). *See generally* Robin W. Sardegna, *No Longer in Jeopardy: The Impact of Hudson v. United States*, 33 Val. U. L. Rev. 115 (1998). If the courts have to analyze the statute to determine its nature they apply factors under Kennedy v. Mendoza-Martinez, 372 U.S. 144 (1963) (not a double jeopardy case). *See* Aaron Xavier Fellmeth, *Civil and Criminal Sanctions in the Constitution and Courts*, 94 Geo. L. J. 1, 34 (2005).

contrast it creates with the *Halper* opinion, which it basically overruled, and (b) the explanation that interpretation is informed by these factors as "useful guideposts" (among others):

> (1) "whether the sanction involves an affirmative disability or restraint"; (2) "whether it has historically been regarded as a punishment"; (3) "whether it comes into play only on a finding of scienter"; (4) "whether its operation will promote the traditional aims of punishment—retribution and deterrence"; (5) "whether the behavior to which it applies is already a crime"; (6) "whether an alternative purpose to which it may rationally be connected is assignable for it"; and (7) "whether it appears excessive in relation to the alternative purpose assigned." It is important to note, however, that "these factors must be considered in relation to the statute on its face," . . . , and "only the clearest proof" will suffice to override legislative intent and transform what has been denominated a civil remedy into a criminal penalty. . . .[160]

This test appears to leave little room for double jeopardy in federal tax cases where the second punishment is not labeled criminal and is financial (as a tax will always be). The factors usually will be applied to a penalty that Congress has labeled "civil," and that was true of the money fine in *Hudson*; despite protestations to the contrary, the Court gave considerable weight to that label (which tends to undercut the seven factors). In finding the criminal's fine and debarment to be civil, the Court was influenced by (1) the similarity of the proceeding that imposed the punishment to an administrative and not criminal proceeding, (2) a general view that fines and denial of a privilege previously granted is not punitive in the criminal sense, (3) a view that if the punishment is not like imprisonment, then it isn't criminal punishment (which would effectively take care of all penalties but imprisonment), (4) the fact that bad intent is not required for the penalties at issue, (5) the facts that the penalties are imposed for an act that is also criminal and has a deterrent effect are insufficient to make the punishment criminal, and (6) the fact that the "clearest proof" that the fines and debarment were criminal punishment was not made. *Hudson* effectively overruled or abandoned the more permissive approach in *Halper*, which was based on a vaguer test giving great weight to the severity of the penalty relative to the Court's weighting of the offense.[161]

The most recent Supreme Court double jeopardy tax decision (in a state case) is *Kurth Ranch*, which predated *Hudson* and postdated *Halper* and has not been disavowed by the Court.[162] It ruled that what a state called a tax and imposed upon the taxpayer's drug law violation was in substance a second criminal punishment for the same conduct as the criminal prosecution. The opinion stated that it was the first time a tax had been held to violate double jeopardy, but recalled that *Mitchell* (discussed in Chapter VII.E) thought that possible.

[160] 522 U.S. 99-100.

[161] United States v. Halper, 490 U.S. 435 (1989). For the progression of the law to Halper, see Mann. See also for comments on the *Hudson* replacement of the *Halper* test, Robertson v. United States, 560 U.S. 272 (2010); Caperton v. A. T. Massey Coal Co., 556 U.S. 868 (2009).

[162] Dep't of Revenue v. Kurth Ranch, 511 U.S. 767 (1994).

Kurth Ranch appears to be sui generis. It relied heavily on the discredited *Halper* decision, and that opinion's emphasis on the excessive amount of the tax. The Court called the purported taxing statute "a concoction of anomalies," which together removed it too far from the realm of tax.[163] Specifically, *Kurth Ranch* relied on the highly unusual facts that (1) the tax was not merely imposed on conduct that also constituted a state criminal offense, but could be imposed only if a crime had been committed and the taxpayer had been arrested, and (2) the tax purported to be a tax on property, but at the time (after arrest) when the tax was imposed the taxpayer did not possess the property. Also, the opinion considered and rejected the possibility that the labeled tax might be a civil sanction for the criminal act. In doing so it emphasized its non-remedial character.[164]

It is not clear where *Hudson* leaves *Kurth Ranch*. *Hudson* left room for civil sanctions that are not purely remedial, and that may also have elements of retribution and deterrence (*i.e.*, section 162(f) penalties).[165] Indeed, this has to be the law because it is commonly understood that the heavy federal tax penalties are intended to have a general deterrence effect (see, for example, the penalties imposed on taxes found to have been underpaid due to violation of the economic substance doctrine.)[166] The majority in *Hudson* did not mention *Kurth*, but concurring opinions did and asserted it stood for the proposition that the label did not control and that a variety of factors could cause rejection of the civil label.

Kurth Ranch is inconsistent with *Sanchez*, in which the Court ruled that a high tax on marijuana ($100 per ounce) was a tax and not a penalty.[167] *Sanchez* illustrates one reason why federal civil penalties may particularly be subject to question as criminal punishment: the United States does not have a general or "plenary" police power (although the question has been quite contentious in the Supreme Court since 1995).[168] Therefore, exactions, penalties, punishments and other levies made on persons usually must find their source in some specific

---

[163] 511 U.S. at 783.

[164] *Id.* at 777.

[165] *Cf.* Bennis v. Mich., 516 U.S. 442, 452 (1996) (deterrence is not punitive). As to the propriety of deterrence in a civil proceeding, *see also* United States v. Ursery, 518 U.S. 267, 292 (1996) ("Third, though both statutes may fairly be said to serve the purpose of deterrence, we long have held that this purpose may serve civil as well as criminal goals."); Hudson v. United States, 522 U.S. 93, 99 (1997).

[166] I.R.C. §§ 7701(o), 6662.

[167] United States v. Sanchez, 340 U.S. 42 (1950). *See also* Leary v. United States, 395 U.S. 6 (1969) (reversing the conviction of Dr. Timothy Leary of failing to pay the $100 tax as a nonregistrant, because to register would have required self-incrimination).

[168] *See* United States v. Comstock, 560 U.S. 126 (2010), *citing* United States v. Morrison, 529 U.S. 528 (2000), which relied on United States v. Lopez, 514 U.S. 549 (1995). *See, e.g.*, Alderman v. United States, 562 U.S. 1163 (2011) (Thomas and Scalia dissent to denial of certiorari, explaining view that the Commerce Clause should not be expanded into a police power; this dissent shows very clearly that at least these Justices are determined to return to the days when the Court ruled manufacturing to be a local activity that was not in interstate commerce).

power of Congress such as the taxing power, as augmented by the Necessary and Proper Clause.[169]

The most important ruling on a federal nontax crime that did not find that a federal "tax" was double jeopardy was *La Franca*, which has not been overruled.[170] The taxpayer was convicted of selling liquor in violation of the Prohibition laws, and taxed $1,000 under the Willis-Campbell Act. But the Court thought the tax looked like a punishment, and in order to avoid an unspecified constitutional issue construed the Act's prohibition of multiple "punishment" not to require its payment.[171]

F. Eighth Amendment

The Eighth Amendment states: ". . . nor excessive fines imposed, nor cruel and unusual punishments inflicted."[172] The prohibition is not limited to criminal punishments, unlike the Double Jeopardy Clause. A civil forfeiture may violate the Eighth Amendment's proscription against excessive fines.[173] This means that the forfeiture may be viewed as punishment for Eighth Amendment purposes, but that analysis is entirely separate from the definition of criminal punishment for Double Jeopardy Clause purposes.[174] The test is to ask whether the forfeiture is purely remedial, in which case it cannot be an excessive punishment, but if it is not purely remedial then it may be evaluated as an excessive punishment, whether or not it is a punishment for double jeopardy purposes.[175]

Pervear v. Commonwealth addressed a state fine and imprisonment for a liquor law violation that also was subject to the federal license tax and pointed out that the Eighth Amendment did not apply (at that time) to the states but in any event the punishment was not excessive.[176]

G. Vagueness

A criminal indictment violates the Due Process Clause of the Fifth Amendment and the Sixth Amendment's guarantee of the right to be informed of the nature and cause of the accusation when the statute on which the criminal charge is based is so vague as to fail to warn the defendant of the crime. The Court has never ruled a criminal tax conviction unconstitutional because the statute was void for vagueness.

---

[169] *See* United States v. Dewitt, 76 U.S. 41 (1869) (a statute criminalizing but not taxing the sale of certain oils was clearly a police statute that was not in aid of taxation and so was unconstitutional).

[170] United States v. La Franca, 282 U.S. 568 (1931).

[171] *See* Ryan H. Stuart, *Penalties and Taxes May Break My Bones, but Forfeitures Will Never Punish Me*, 41 St. L. L. Rev. 1367, 1375-1376 (1997) (*La Franca* profoundly influenced double jeopardy law).

[172] Timbs v. Indiana, 139 S. Ct. 682 (2019) extended the Clause to the states.

[173] Austin v. United States, 509 U.S. 602 (1993).

[174] United States v. Ursery, 518 U.S. 267 (1996).

[175] *Id.* at 286-287. *See also* Helvering v. Mitchell, 303 U.S. 391 (1938) (civil fraud penalty was remedial and could be imposed even though taxpayer had been acquired of criminal fraud).

[176] Pervear v. Commonwealth, 72 U.S. 475 (1867).

The defendant raised the void for vagueness defense in the criminal tax case *Kahriger*, which ruled that usually being engaged in the business of wagering was not too vague to enforce criminally.[177] Similarly "so-called slot machines" is not too vague a description of the gambling devices to be taxed to avoid criminal conviction.[178] Tax fraud is sufficiently clearly a "crime involving moral turpitude" to justify deportation.[179]

The most commonly cited opinion explaining when a statute is void for vagueness is *Cohen Grocery* concerning price controls:

> [The question is whether the words] "That it is hereby made unlawful for any person willfully . . . to make any unjust or unreasonable rate or charge in handling or dealing in or with any necessaries," constituted a fixing by Congress of an ascertainable standard of guilt and are adequate to inform persons accused of violation thereof of the nature and cause of the accusation against them. That they are not, we are of opinion, so clearly results from their mere statement as to render elaboration on the subject wholly unnecessary. Observe that the section forbids no specific or definite act. It confines the subject-matter of the investigation which it authorizes to no element essentially inhering in the transaction as to which it provides. It leaves open, therefore, the widest conceivable inquiry, the scope of which no one can foresee and the result of which no one can foreshadow or adequately guard against . . . to attempt to enforce the section would be the exact equivalent of an effort to carry out a statute which in terms merely penalized and punished all acts detrimental to the public interest when unjust and unreasonable in the estimation of the court and jury [as reflected by numerous conflicting decisions without an ascertainable standard].[180]

The Supreme Court addressed the vagueness issue in deciding the appeal of Jeffrey Skilling, former Enron executive (not a tax case). The opinion stated:

> To satisfy due process, "a penal statute [must] define the criminal offense [1] with sufficient definiteness that ordinary people can understand what conduct is prohibited and [2] in a manner that does not encourage arbitrary and discriminatory enforcement." Kolender v. Lawson, 461 U.S. 352, 357 . . . (1983).[181]

---

[177] United States v. Kahriger, 345 U.S. 22 (1953); *overruled on other grounds* by Marchetti v. United States, 390 U.S. 39 (1968).

[178] United States v. Korpan, 354 U.S. 271 (1957).

[179] Kawashima v. Holder, 565 U.S. 478 (2012); Jordan v. De George, 341 U.S. 223 (1951).

[180] United States v. L. Cohen Grocery Co., 255 U.S. 81, 89-91 (1921). *See also* United States v. Brewer, 139 U.S. 278 (1891) (statute was not sufficiently definite to support the criminal charge); Connally v. General Constr. Co., 269 U.S. 385 (1926). *Cohen* was cited in dissent in a tax case, James v. United States, 366 U.S. 213 (1961) (if ruling on meaning of statute in criminal case is so surprising that it should be made prospective only that may indicate the statute is too vague to be enforced). *See generally* Goldsmith. *Cohen Grocery* also involved a substantial issue of also delegation of congressional authority, which was not addressed.

[181] Skilling v. United States, 561 U.S. 358 (2010). But void for vagueness rulings seem to be on the rise. *See also* Johnson v. United States, 576 U.S. 591 (2015) (enhanced punishment rule void for vagueness); United States v. Davis, 139 S. Ct. 2319 (2019).

The Court in *Skilling* stressed its obligation to avoid a void for vagueness finding if possible by construing the statute.[182] It did so by construing a 1988 amendment of the mail fraud statute to include "a scheme or artifice to deprive another of the intangible right of honest services" to refer only to bribery, based on the inferred intent of Congress to reverse a 1987 opinion of the Court limiting the crime to property crimes.[183]

The Court found a criminal statute using the word "kosher" to be no more vague than the commercial law requirement of fair dealing that would apply in contract disputes as to whether the goods supplied as kosher were in fact kosher.[184] In contrast to an impermissibly vague statute is a clear statute to be applied in a case involving disputed facts. It is not unconstitutional, for example, to leave to the jury the determination of whether a payment from a corporation to shareholders is a dividend or a commission for tax purposes (*i.e.*, the factual question of reasonableness of the commission amount), and to allow the jury to find criminal tax evasion if the taxpayer willfully mischaracterized the payments.[185]

Finally, several criminal tax statutes have been saved from a void for vagueness defense through the willfulness requirement, as discussed in Chapter VII.B.

Vagueness of a statute also can be a ground for a due process defense to a tax in a civil proceeding, although the standard applied to the statute is not as strict.[186] *Helvering v. National Grocery Co.* ruled that the accumulated earnings tax standard was not too vague to pass due process muster even though the taxpayer characterized it as a tax on a state of mind.[187] Such an objection might be asserted against the application of the economic substance doctrine, partially codified in section 7701(o).[188] The statute has left the "relevance" of the doctrine entirely undefined, except as prior case law may illuminate situations to which it has been applied and future case law may apply it to other situations.

H. Forfeitures

The Internal Revenue Code contains four principal groups of civil forfeiture provisions, all of which are in rem rather than in personam remedies:

- The general forfeiture sections in Subchapter C of Chapter 75 entitled "Crimes, Other Offenses, Forfeitures" (sections 7301-7328);
- Forfeitures in connection with alcohol taxes, Chapter 51 (sections 5601-5691);

---

182 *Id.*

183 *Id. referring to* McNally v. United States, 483 U.S. 350 (1987).

184 Hygrade Provision Co. v. Sherman, 266 U.S. 497 (1925).

185 United States v. Ragen, 314 U.S. 513 (1942).

186 Kolender v. Lawson, 461 U.S. 352, 358-9 n. 8 (1983).

187 Helvering v. National Grocery Co., 304 U.S. 282, 289 (1938) (basing tax on taxpayer's state of mind was not unreasonably vague). *See also* FCC v. Fox TV Stations, Inc., 567 U.S. 239 (2012) (rejecting FCC penalty due in part to vagueness of the rule).

188 *See* Jasper L. Cummings, Jr., The Supreme Court's Federal Tax Jurisprudence 193 *et seq.* (2d ed. 2016).

- Forfeitures in connection with tobacco taxes, Chapter 52 (section 5763);
- Forfeitures in connection with firearms taxes, Chapter 53 (section 5872).[189]

These provisions are dependent on a finding of a connection between the property to be forfeited and a "violation" of the tax laws or some fraudulent conduct, or an attempt to avoid the tax laws. Section 7321 appears to authorize the IRS to effect a forfeiture without court action and section 7323(a) provides that a judicial action to enforce a forfeiture shall be in the nature of an action in rem. One can easily infer from the words of the statute that Congress intends these forfeitures to be independent of criminal punishment of the taxpayer, and the Internal Revenue Manual agrees: it states that Title 26 forfeitures, which it calls Code Forfeitures, are not criminal forfeitures.[190] A criminal forfeiture would be a forfeiture as punishment for a crime, which is possible.[191] The IRS also has forfeiture authority under title 18 and title 31.[192]

However, the Court in 1971 in *United States Coin & Currency* construed section 7302 and related sections to condition the forfeiture on the owner also being a criminal, and as a result at least the Fifth Amendment privilege against self-incrimination applied.[193] The opinion bridges a gap between the very old decision in *Boyd* and current law.[194] That 1886 opinion involved a revenue statute that stated forfeiture in a series with prison and fines as punishments for a crime. On those facts it was not hard for the Court to rule that the privilege against self-incrimination, as well as the Fourth Amendment protection against unreasonable search and seizure, applied. Because section 7302 is not identical to the statute at issue in *Boyd* (it does not state the forfeiture as a punishment for a crime), the 1971 opinion recognized that a plausible argument could be made that section 7302 is one of those unusual in rem civil proceedings against the thing and not the person. However, it rejected that interpretation, at least for self-incrimination purposes, because the statutes read together showed that forfeiture could occur in practice only to take the property of one "significantly involved in a criminal enterprise," because the statute provided protections for

---

[189] *See generally* COMISKY, FELD & HARRIS, TAX FRAUD & EVASION VOL. 2: MONEY LAUNDERING, ASSET FORFEITURE, SENTENCING ch. 12 (WG&L) [hereinafter COMISKY].

[190] I.R.M. 9.7.13.1.

[191] *See* COMISKY, at ¶ 12.01[1][b].

[192] I.R.M. 38.1.3.1. Originally when forfeitures of property were required by revenue statutes the seizure could be made without notice, and subsequent "judicial condemnation" confirmed the United States' ownership of the property, which related back to the seizure. *See, e.g.*, United States v. Stowell, 133 U.S. 1 (1890). Later the Court ruled that lack of prior notice and hearing applied only to moveables and not to land. United States v. James Daniel Good Real Prop., 510 U.S. 43 (1993).

[193] United States v. United States Coin & Currency, 401 U.S. 715 (1971).

[194] Boyd v. United States, 116 U.S. 616, 617 (1886). *See* United States v. Ward, 448 U.S. 242, 253 (1980) (indicating that *Boyd* had been limited).

the innocent owner of property that has somehow gotten mixed up with a taxpayer's tax avoidance scheme.[195]

The process by which *United States Coin & Currency* found the nominally civil Internal Revenue Code forfeitures to be criminal punishment at least for self-incrimination purposes is not inevitably applicable to forfeiture statutes generally. For example, the next year the Court found a forfeiture in a nontax case to be a civil proceeding when the only trigger needed was an importation.[196] Moreover, in a more recent nontax case on the subject the Court did not cite *United States Coin & Currency* at all but rather relied on a more generic analysis of the form and purposes of the forfeiture statute, noting that *Mitchell* had ruled that the very same conduct could give rise to civil and criminal penalties.[197]

Other constitutional protections with regard to forfeitures generally have been addressed in decisions including principally the 1993 *Austin* opinion, which did not involve a federal tax forfeiture.[198] It undertook to explain the applicability of constitutional protections to in rem forfeitures, based on a fairly literal reading of the Constitution, and a somewhat more substantive evaluation of the nature of forfeiture proceedings:

- Self-incrimination: *Austin* ruled that this Fifth Amendment right is limited to criminal prosecutions, but that *United States Coin & Currency* treated the Internal Revenue Code forfeitures as in effect criminal because the Code made the (presumably criminal) "culpability" of the owner of the forfeited property "relevant" to the forfeiture (presumably meaning it was the cause of the forfeiture), or at least the owner could be criminally charged.[199]
- Sixth Amendment: The Confrontation Clause does not logically apply to in rem forfeiture, because the forfeiture does not involve the person being placed on trial for a crime.[200]
- Beyond a reasonable doubt: This Fifth Amendment standard for proof of criminal conviction does not apply to in rem forfeiture.[201]

---

[195] 401 U.S. at 722 (n. 8 states: "Although this statute appears in Title 19, regulating forfeitures under the customs laws, 26 U. S. C. § 7327, provides that: 'The provisions of law applicable to the remission or mitigation by the Secretary or his delegate of forfeitures under the customs laws shall apply to forfeitures incurred or alleged to have been incurred under the internal revenue laws.'"). But the protections provided to the innocent owner may have been reduced by the subsequent ruling in Bennis v. Michigan, 516 U.S. 442 (1996).

[196] One Lot Emerald Cut Stones & One Ring v. United States, 409 U.S. 232 (1972). *See also* Calero v. Pearson Yacht Leasing Co., 416 U.S. 663 (1974) (similar but stating that nevertheless certain constitutional protections might be applied).

[197] United States v. One Assortment of 89 Firearms, 465 U.S. 354 (1984).

[198] Austin v. United States, 509 U.S. 602 (1993).

[199] *Id.* at 608 n. 4 (1993).

[200] *Id.* citing United States v. Zucker, 161 U.S. 475 (1896).

[201] 509 U.S. at 608 n. 4, citing Lilienthal's Tobacco v. United States, 97 U.S. 237 (1878). *See also* United States v. Regan, 232 U.S. 37 (1914).

- Fourth Amendment: Search and seizure protections can apply to civil in rem forfeiture because the protection is not dependent on a criminal prosecution.[202]
- Double Jeopardy: This rule is limited to criminal prosecutions and so might be applied to civil in rem forfeiture only if it could be characterized as a criminal punishment for double jeopardy purposes.[203] However, *Ursery* (not a federal tax case) in 1996 substantially limited the possibility of such a finding.[204] *Ursery* opined that if Congress expresses on the face of the statute an intent that the forfeiture be a civil proceeding and a civil penalty, even though the forfeiture is triggered by a crime, and even though it serves some deterrent function, the forfeiture will not be treated as a criminal proceeding, and hence the Double Jeopardy clause will not apply, unless there is the clearest proof that the form and effect of forfeiture is criminal punishment.[205] *Ursery* explained the peculiar origin of forfeiture statutes whereby the common law viewed the thing itself as the wrongdoer. Although the Court has rejected the wooden approach that an in rem forfeiture is a proceeding against the property and does not affect persons for self-incrimination purposes,[206] it has relied on that distinction for double jeopardy purposes because a forfeiture has no fixed value, making it impossible to determine whether a forfeiture is in more punitive than remedial.[207] See Chapter VII.E, for further discussion of forfeitures and double jeopardy.
- Eighth Amendment: Excessive fines and penalties can be found in both civil and criminal cases, and so the Amendment can apply to a civil forfeiture if it is not purely remedial.[208] The Eighth Amendment was the protection at issue in *Austin*. In another case not involving taxes the Court ruled a civil forfeiture to be excessive in violation of the Eighth Amendment, but purported to distinguish tax forfeitures, and later Congress changed the character of the forfeitures at issue in the case to criminal punishments.[209]
- Takings: *Bennis v. Michigan* indicated that an otherwise permissible forfeiture is not a taking because it is not an exercise of the power of eminent domain.[210] Forfeitures are to be distinguished from confiscation, as in confiscation of the property of the enemy in times of war.[211]

---

[202] 509 U.S. at 608 n. 4, citing criminal prosecution cases.

[203] *Id.* The opinion cited *Halper*, which has since been rejected by the Court. *See* Ch. VII.E.3.

[204] United States v. Ursery, 518 U.S. 267 (1996).

[205] *Id.* at 290.

[206] Austin v. United States, 509 U.S. 602, 615 n. 9 (1993).

[207] 518 U.S. at 283.

[208] *Id. But see* Bennis v. Mich., 516 U.S. 442 (1996) (criticizing *Austin* for misreading an earlier opinion and ruling that an innocent owner's car could be forfeited on account of crime of owner's husband).

[209] United States v. Bajakajian, 524 U.S. 321 (1998).

[210] Bennis v. Mich., 516 U.S. 442, 452-453 (1996).

[211] *See* Ware v. Hylton, 3 U.S. 199 (1796).

Ch. VIII. Other Constitutional Issues

A. Taxing Corporate Income

Preceding chapters have addressed the major constitutional issues of taxing corporate income; indeed, corporations have been at the center of almost all of the major constitutional tax fights: *McCulloch v. Maryland* addressed a state's attempt to tax the corporation that was the Bank of the United States;[1] *Veazie Bank v. Fenno* addressed the destructive federal taxation of the local corporate banks' currencies;[2] the *Pollock* case struck down an income tax on a corporation and *Stone Tracy* upheld an income/excise tax on corporations;[3] the anti-New Deal and pro-New Deal decisions all involved corporations;[4] and last but not least, the numerous railroad tax cases of the late 1800s, both state and federal, powerfully defined the constitutional issues in taxation.[5]

But after the income tax became established as constitutional only one ruling of the Court found a provision of the income tax related to (but not imposed on) corporations to be unconstitutional: *Eisner v. Macomber*, which can be viewed as the exception that proved the rule that corporate income can be

---

[1] *See* Ch. II.C.2.

[2] *See* Ch. II.C.7.b.

[3] *See* Ch. V.D.2.c and d.

[4] *See* Ch. III.F.

[5] *See, e.g.*, Thomson v. Pacific Railroad, 76 U.S. 579 (1869); Railroad Co. v. Peniston, 85 U.S. 5 (1873).

taxed any way Congress chooses.[6] Subsequently Justice Brandeis stated that a corporation's income can be taxed to its shareholders, if Congress chooses.[7] The same opinion also stated that the corporate retained earnings tax was not upon a "state of mind" and thus was not unconstitutional as not an income tax, when it was levied on income and a condition of liability was a state of mind.[8]

However, the Court attributed religious interests to a corporation in *Hobby Lobby*, which was indirectly related to the tax in the Affordable Care Act.[9] And in a free speech ruling the Court accorded substantial effect to the separate incorporation of a foreign subsidiary.[10]

B. No Taxation Without Representation

The slogan "no taxation without representation" is probably the best known statement about taxation in the United States (followed by the power to tax being the power to destroy).[11] Nevertheless, the law is otherwise. Moreover, the statement is disingenuous. As Prof. Swisher pointed out, the Colonists did not want representation in Parliament, they just didn't want to pay taxes to the King.[12] And there was a general resistance to taxes as illustrated by the signal inability of the Congress of the Confederation to levy taxes despite the fact of representation of the states.

As Justice Brandeis stated in 1922: "There is no constitutional provision which so limits the power of Congress that taxes can be imposed only upon those who have political representation."[13] *Loughborough v. Blake* ruled that Congress could lay taxes in the District of Columbia despite the absence of representation in Congress.[14] The decision of the Constitution not to require representation as

---

[6] Eisner v. Macomber, 252 U.S. 189 (1920). *See* Ch. V.D.2.f.

[7] Helvering v. National Grocery Co., 304 U.S. 282 (1938).

[8] *Id.*

[9] Burwell v. Hobby Lobby Stores, Inc., 573 U.S. 682 (2014). *See* Cummings, *Hobby Lobby and Federal Taxes*, 145 Tax Notes (TA) 519 (Nov. 3, 2014).

[10] Agency for Int'l Dev. v. All. for Open Soc'y Int'l, Inc., 140 S. Ct. 2082 (2020) (Breyer dissent contrasted *Regan*).

[11] More accurately, the original phrase may have been "taxation without representation is tyranny." *See* Staff of the Joint Committee on Taxation, The Taxing Power of the Federal and State Governments 1-2 (1936) (available on Joint Committee website) (citing this quotation as a motivation for the requirement that tax bills originate in the House of Representatives).

[12] Carl Brent Swisher, American Constitutional Development 13 (1954).

[13] Heald v. District of Columbia, 259 U.S. 114, 124 (1922).

[14] Loughborough v. Blake, 18 U.S. 317 (1820).

a prerequisite of federal taxation was noted in the *Dred Scott* decision.[15] *Binns* ruled the same for the Territories (Alaska).[16]

Loughborough v. Blake confronted the question whether direct taxes could be levied in the District of Columbia and if so on what basis.[17] The taxpayer objected that because the District had no representation in Congress, it could not be apportioned any part of the tax. The Court disagreed because the District and Territories are within the United States and the taxing power extends to the whole United States.[18] The opinion pointed out that the direct taxation at issue was on a fairer basis than representation in Congress, because a state with 59,000 people might have 1 congressman and a state with 60,000 might have 2, but census proportionality was applied to apportion direct taxes.[19] The opinion advanced two explanations for taxation without representation (but they are not exclusive): (1) the Territories were in a state of infancy advancing toward manhood in the form of statehood, or (2) in the case of the District, the people had voluntarily relinquished their right to representation and adopted the whole Congress as their legitimate government.[20]

The early origins of the slogan are two: (1) the Colonies' dislike of the British taxes imposed on the Colonies, and (2) the apportionment of representation and taxation together through the Direct Tax Clause. As to the Revolutionary origin, Justice Bradley's dissent in the *Slaughter-House Cases* (see Ch. V.D.3.b(7)) likened the fundamental privileges and immunities that he thought the plaintiff butchers possessed to practice their trades without the regulation of the city to the right he found in the unwritten British constitution to no taxation without representation, over which the Revolutionary War was fought.[21] As to the second, the important *Pollock* decision striking down the income tax was based on a version of the slogan: taxation and representation must be apportioned

---

[15] "In the case of Loughborough v. Blake, (5 Whea., 324,) the question arose, whether Congress has power to impose direct taxes on persons and property in this District. It was insisted, that though the grant of power was in its terms broad enough to include direct taxation, it must be limited by the principle, that taxation and representation are inseparable. It would not be easy to fix on any political truth, better established or more fully admitted in our country, than that taxation and representation must exist together. We went into the war of the Revolution to assert it, and it is incorporated as fundamental into all American Governments. But however true and important this maxim may be, it is not necessarily of universal application. It was for the people of the United States, who ordained the Constitution, to decide whether it should or should not be permitted to operate within this District. Their decision was embodied in the words of the Constitution; and as that contained no such exception as would permit the maxim to operate in this District, this court, interpreting that language, held that the exception did not exist." Dred Scott v. Sandford, 60 U.S. 393, 621 (1857).

[16] Binns v. United States, 194 U.S. 486 (1904).

[17] Loughborough v. Blake, 18 U.S. 317 (1820). As to direct taxes, *see* Ch. V.C.

[18] 18 U.S. at 319.

[19] This was apparently drawn from Jefferson's *Opinion on the Apportionment of 1792*, reprinted in Roger Foster, Commentaries on the Constitution of the United States 424 *et seq.* (1895).

[20] *See* Francis Hilliard, The Law of Taxation 44-46 (1875).

[21] Slaughter-House Cases, 83 U.S. 36, 115 (1873).

together.[22] However, the apportionment of direct taxes by the Constitution was rooted in the efforts to deal with and protect slavery, not to protect some notion of democracy.[23]

In addition to those two references, the slogan has been employed in a variety of other ways in the Court's opinions.

- The Court acknowledged as a "general principle" the desirability of representation in taxation but stated that there is no right to avoid taxation unless one is represented, likening the disconnect to the lack of need for a benefit from a tax in order to be subject to it; and stating that one need not owe allegiance to a taxing authority to owe it tax.[24]
- An early use of the slogan occurred in the intergovernmental immunity cases.[25] The fact that all of the people of the country are represented in Congress supports certain taxation of state instrumentalities by the United States, but the reverse is not true.[26]
- Justices Rehnquist and Stevens dissented from the reversal of the conviction of a flag burner. They applied the no taxation without representation slogan in a novel way: those who pay taxes should be able to pass laws that criminalize "conduct that is regarded as evil and profoundly offensive to the majority of people—whether it be murder, embezzlement, pollution, or flag burning."[27]
- Justice Jackson dissented from the conviction of a warehouse company for failing to obtain a city license and pay a license tax for temporary holding of coal being shipped through the state. He asserted the slogan in the context of the tax being indirectly borne by residents of other states who bought the coal and indirectly paid the tax and had no representation in the taxing jurisdiction, explaining that this sort of tax was exactly what the Founders intended to head off in the Commerce Clause.[28]
- Justice Thomas in concurrence asserted that "no taxation without representation" bolstered his view that only voters should count in the "one person one vote" apportionment of state legislatures.[29]

C. Origination Clause

Article I, section 7, clause 1 states:

---

[22] Pollock v. Farmers' Loan & Trust Co., 157 U.S. 429 (1895).
[23] *See* Ch. V.C.4.i.
[24] Thomas v. Gay, 169 U.S. 264 (1898).
[25] Helvering v. Gerhardt, 304 U.S. 405 (1938).
[26] *See, e.g.*, Helvering v. Gerhardt, 304 U.S. 405 (1938).
[27] Tex. v. Johnson, 491 U.S. 397 (1989).
[28] Independent Warehouses, Inc. v. Scheele, 331 U.S. 70 (1947).
[29] Evenwel v. Abbott, 136 S. Ct. 1120 (2016).

> All Bills for raising Revenue shall originate in the House of Representatives; but the Senate may propose or concur with Amendments as on other Bills.

According to a Supreme Court opinion, the purpose of the Origination Clause was to place one control over the taxing power in the House of Congress closest to the people, who originally directly elected only the House of Representatives.[30] A more informed reporter states that it was to protect the more populous states.[31]

As generally understood, this clause carries two kinds of prohibitions. First, the Senate may not originate any measure that includes a provision for raising revenue, and second, the Senate may not propose any amendment that would raise revenue to a non-revenue measure. However, the Senate may generally amend a House-originated revenue measure as it sees fit.[32] When the House of Representatives disapproves of a tax added by the Senate it "blue slips" the bill and sends it back to the Senate.[33] The clause has no bearing on Congress' ability to delegate rule-making authority as to taxes.[34]

A revenue bill is a tax bill in what the Supreme Court called the strict sense of the word, referring to the overall categorization of the bill, not of the specific levy. Therefore identification of taxes for purposes of the Origination Clause does not inform identification of taxes generally:

> Both parties agree that "revenue bills are those that levy taxes in the strict sense of the word, and are not bills for other purposes which may incidentally create revenue." . . . The Court has interpreted this general rule to mean that a statute that creates a particular governmental program and that raises revenue to support that program, as opposed to a statute that raises revenue to support Government generally, is not a "Bil[l] for raising Revenue" within the meaning of the Origination Clause."[35]

---

[30] Skinner v. Mid-America Pipeline Co., 490 U.S. 212 (1989). For a very extensive history and analysis of the Origination Clause, *see* James V. Saturno, The Origination Clause of the U.S. Constitution: Interpretation and Enforcement, Congressional Research Service Report No. R46558 (Oct. 1, 2020).

[31] Carl Brent Swisher, American Constitutional Development 35 (1954).

[32] *See, e.g.*, Rainey v. United States, 232 U.S. 310 (1914).

[33] James V. Saturno, Blue-Slipping: Enforcing the Origination Clause in the House of Representatives, Congressional Research Service Report No. R46556 (Oct. 1, 2020).

[34] Skinner v. Mid-America Pipeline Co., 490 U.S. 212 (1989).

[35] United States v. Munoz-Flores, 495 U.S. 385, 397-398 (1990) (the levy was an unusual one, imposing a "special assessment" on criminals to be paid into a fund for crime victims; the opinion never directly labeled it a tax). *Cf.* United States v. Norton, 91 U.S. 566 (1876) (creation of postal money order system was not a revenue law even though revenue might be raised; issue was longer statute of limitations for crime under revenue laws); Twin City Bank v. Nebeker, 167 U.S. 196 (1897) (a tax levied on national banks as part of the act authorizing them to issue bank notes did not make the bill a revenue bill that had to originate in the House). *See also* Staff of the Joint Committee on Taxation, Background and Present Law Relating to Funding Mechanisms of the "E-Rate" Telecommunications Program, JCX-59-98 (July 31, 1998) (quoting an interpretation of a House Rule that the Ways and Means Committee had jurisdiction over "broad based fees," which it could also treat as excise taxes, as well as pure taxes).

The Supreme Court has evidenced firm and consistent disinterest in objections raised to tax acts under the Origination Clause:

- *Flint v. Stone Tracy Co.* entertained but rejected a challenge to a revenue bill that had originated in the House and been modified by a germane amendment in the Senate to substitute a corporation tax for an inheritance tax.[36]
- Revenue measures do not include laws for another purpose as to which revenue raising is incidental.[37] This is consistent with the fact that there are taxing power taxes and taxes not enacted under the taxing power but rather as necessary and proper to another power, usually regulation of interstate commerce.[38]
- The Court ruled that a taxpayer cannot go behind the congressional determination that a tariff was properly enacted.[39] This came to be called the *Marshall Field* Doctrine,[40] and it arguably extends to Origination Clause questions.[41]
- The fact that a user fee was not enacted in the same act that created the program for which the fee was charged does not necessarily make the fee a revenue raising tax measure.[42]
- The fact that a user fee is collected into the United States Treasury and not earmarked to a particular fund does not make the bill enacting it a revenue raising bill if the fee is in fact a user fee.[43]
- The Origination Clause does not alter the normal rules governing the power of Congress to delegate rule making under a taxing statute.[44]

---

[36] Flint v. Stone Tracy Co., 220 U.S. 107, 143 (1911) ("In thus deciding we do not wish to be regarded as holding that the journals of the House and Senate may be examined to invalidate an act which has been passed and signed by the presiding officers of the House and Senate and approved by the President and duly deposited with the State Department.").

[37] Millard v. Roberts, 202 U.S. 429, 436 (1906) (case involved a tax in the District of Columbia and the Court stated it assumed without deciding that a citizen of the District could raise the issue, which presumably means that it assumed without deciding that the Origination Clause applied to taxes in the District, although that would seem to be a separate issue).

[38] *See* Ch. III.E.4.a.

[39] Marshall Field & Co. v. Clark, 143 U.S. 649 (1892) (The opinion also discussed other parts of Article I, section 7, and Article I, section 5, requiring each House to keep a journal of its proceedings.). *See* United States Nat'l Bank v. Independent Ins. Agents of Am., 508 U.S. 439, 455 n. 7 (1993) ("The *Marshall Field* doctrine concerns 'the nature of the evidence' the Court [may] consider in determining whether a bill had actually passed Congress . . .'").

[40] United States Nat'l Bank v. Independent Ins. Agents of Am., 508 U.S. 439 n. 7 (1993).

[41] *See* concurrence of Justice Scalia in United States v. Munoz-Flores, 495 U.S. 385, 408-409 (1990).

[42] Sperry Corp. v. United States, 925 F.2d 399 (Fed. Cir. 1991), *cert. denied*, 505 U.S. 809 (1991), on remand from United States v. Sperry Corp., 493 U.S. 52 (1989).

[43] *Id.*

[44] Skinner v. Mid-America Pipeline Co., 490 U.S. 212, 220 (1989).

- However, in the most recent decision the Supreme Court rejected the government's challenge to the justiciability of an Origination Clause issue as a political question.[45]

A related provision is the Presentment Clause, Article I, section 7, clause 2, which was applied to strike down a line item veto for tax and spending legislation.[46]

In 2011 and in each Congress thereafter the House of Representatives adopted House Rule XII.7(c)(1) requiring that all bills, which would include all tax bills, have a constitutional authority statement.[47]

D. First Amendment

1. *The First Amendment in Constitutional History*

The First Amendment states:

> Congress shall make no law respecting an establishment of religion, or prohibiting the free exercise thereof; or abridging the freedom of speech, or of the press; or the right of the people peaceably to assemble, and to petition the Government for a redress of grievances.

The First Amendment contains at least six separate prohibitions on Congress. So far the Establishment Clause, the Free Exercise Clause, the Free Speech Clause and the Freedom of the Press Clause have all been implicated in decisions of the Court striking down state taxes, but the Court has never held a federal tax to violate one of these prohibitions. Indeed the Court had never ruled any act of Congress unconstitutional under the First Amendment until 1965.[48] However, the 2014 *Hobby Lobby Stores, Inc.* ruling in effect freed the taxpayer from the possibility of having to pay a penalty tax for exercising the corporation's religious freedom, as protected by the Religious Freedom Restoration Act, which Congress adopted to implement the First Amendment.[49]

Currently, the First Amendment is emerging as a protector of property rights, perhaps joining if turning a constitutional rule meant for one purpose in another not replacing substantive due process as a primary weapon in the evolving struggle by owners of property to protect their property rights through appeals

---

[45] United States v. Munoz-Flores, 495 U.S. 385 (1990). *Cf.* Texas Ass'n of Concerned Taxpayers, Inc. v. United States, 476 U.S. 1151 (1986) (one of the earlier cases raising the justiciability issue).

[46] Clinton v. City of N.Y., 524 U.S. 417 (1998) (ruling unconstitutional a line item veto applicable to spending and taxing; applying). *See also*, as to veto, Raines v. Byrd, 521 U.S. 811 (1997) (ruling that Senator Byrd and other congresspersons did not have a personal stake in the constitutionality of the line item veto law and dismissed their suit against the OMB to have the law declared unconstitutional).

[47] Andres Nolan, Constitutional Authority Statements and the Powers of Congress: An Overview, Congressional Research Service Report No. R44729 (updated March 11, 2019).

[48] Lamont v. Basic Pamphlets, 381 U.S. 70 (1965) (involving Post Office).

[49] Burwell v. Hobby Lobby Stores, Inc., 573 U.S. 682 (2014). *See* Cummings, *Hobby Lobby and Federal Taxes*, 145 Tax Notes (TA) 519 (Nov. 3, 2014).

to the Supreme Court. As shown throughout this book, that struggle has employed against taxation, a major threat to property, several constitutional tools that were more or less intended for other purposes: (1) the prohibition against unapportioned direct taxes (discussed in Chapter V.D.2, and which produced the *Pollock* decision); (2) intergovernmental immunity (which was extended to those who dealt with the government, as discussed in Chapter II.C); and (3) most importantly the Due Process Clause of the Fifth and Fourteenth Amendments, the Tenth Amendment and limitations of the Commerce Clause powers, which the Court combined to prevent not procedural unfairness or denial of rights to freed slaves or invasion of state powers but to reduce tax bills (examples being *Butler*, *Hill v. Wallace*, *Trusler*, and *Drexel Furniture*).

Justice Stone in *Carolene Products* picked out certain rights, including primarily First Amendment rights, the protection of which might justify the application of strict scrutiny of governmental actions, but if they only affected economic interests would not receive strict scrutiny.[50] This procedural shift came to supplant substantive due process, because strict scrutiny usually amounts to substituting the Court's assessment of reasonableness for that of Congress (or a state legislature). However, what one Court sees as an invasion of fundamental rights, a later Court can see as only affecting economic interests. In another example of turning a constitutional rule meant for one purpose in another direction, the Warren Court ruled that a state's one-year residency requirement for public assistance impinged on the protected right to travel under a strict scrutiny approach.[51] But shortly thereafter the Burger Court treated a similar restriction as a matter of economic regulation and thus not subject to strict scrutiny.[52] In effect the Court had taken the earlier approach that had indirectly made wealth a suspect category and given property rights status to welfare and similar government benefits, and turned it into a reason to treat distinctions made on the basis of wealth as economic regulations that get a pass from the Supreme Court.[53]

So far, the principal impact of applying strict scrutiny to economic matters on the basis of a free speech or other protected rights has been a wavering line of decisions under the Establishment Clause involving state taxation and spending,[54] and another group of nontax decisions striking down limits on political speech and economic speech that can be viewed as invasions of First Amendment rights.[55] So far this approach has not led to ruling any federal tax provision unconstitutional under the First Amendment, aside from *Hobby Lobby*. The Court struck down an exception from a robocall ban for government debt col-

---

[50] *See* Ch. I.E.4.b, discussing strict scrutiny in the context of presumptions of constitutionality.

[51] Shapiro v. Thompson, 394 U.S. 618 (1969).

[52] Dandridge v. Williams, 397 U.S. 471 (1970).

[53] *See* Kelly, Harbison and Belz, The American Constitution: Its Origin and Development, Vol. II 680-681 (7th ed.). This was made most apparent in San Antonio Independent School District v. Rodriguez, 411 U.S. 1 (1973), ruling that there was no duty to equalize school spending in poor districts; that is wealth is not a suspect category.

[54] *See* Ch. VIII.D.4.c.

[55] *See* Ch. II.B.

lection under the First Amendment, requiring strict scrutiny.[56] Justice Breyer's dissent wondered whether the same approach could bring tax reporting forms under strict scrutiny.

However, the First Amendment has played a large role in state tax cases, as discussed in Chapter IX.

2. *Federal Taxation and Freedom of Speech Issues Not Involving Churches*

a. *Deductions and Exemptions for Lobbying*

Lobbying is an exercise of free speech and of the right to petition the government (also guaranteed by the First Amendment); nevertheless, the Court has ruled that the United States is not required by the Constitution to subsidize speech in the form of lobbying by providing a deduction or exemption, even if the expense appears to be helpful or essential to a business. As a result, the Code can and does discriminate against speech in the form of lobbying, but not based on its content.

The no deduction rule reflects the general principles that taxpayers can claim only those deductions that are allowed by a specific Code section,[57] and that deductions are a matter of legislative grace.[58] There is no specific deduction for the expenses of speech as such, and they may appear to be personal expenses for which section 262 denies any deduction, without a business nexus. Consequently, taxpayers have searched for grounds for deductions of the costs of speech: ordinary and necessary business expenses, losses, interest expense, etc. Such search is largely cut off by a deduction disallowance rule, section 162(e), which denies a business expense deduction for most lobbying expenditures with respect to legislation, federal, state and local.

The Court recognized the no deduction rule originally in approving a Treasury regulation interpreting the allowance of deduction for "ordinary and necessary business expenses."[59] The opinion did not discuss free speech issues, perhaps because the claimant in 1941 was in such an unfavorable posture (a corporation trying to recovery property lost under the Trading with the Enemy Act during World War I).

The Court addressed the free speech question and ruled in *Cammarano* that the taxpayer failed to carry the burden of proving discrimination against speech based on its content, approving the denial of a federal deduction for lobbying costs as an ordinary and necessary business expense.[60] That opinion also created a crucial concept to rebut the First Amendment claim (later used by the Court in *Regan v. Taxation with Representation*) that the taxpayer was not being denied

---

[56] Barr v. Am. Ass'n of Political Consultants, 140 S. Ct. 2335 (2020).

[57] I.R.C. § 161.

[58] Commissioner v. Sullivan, 356 U.S. 27 (1958).

[59] Textile Mills Sec. Corp. v. Commissioner, 314 U.S. 326 (1941).

[60] Cammarano v. United States, 358 U.S. 498 (1959). *See* Cummings, *Lobbying and Political Expenditures*, BNA Tax Management Portfolio No. 453-1st (2020) (containing extensive discussion of constitutional issues).

a benefit on account of exercising free speech, but rather was being required to pay for its own free speech; the government is not required to subsidize it.[61] The *Cammarano* opinion states:

> . . . [E]veryone in the community should stand on the same footing as regards its purchase [referring to the purchase of lobbying] so far as the Treasury of the United States is concerned.[62]

In effect the Court declined to apply strict scrutiny,[63] at least insofar as the Court finds that the denial does not vary based on who is spending the money (other than that it is a business taxpayer) or the content of the speech.[64] The Court has continued to view tax deductions as cash subsidies, which the government cannot be required to make, as contrasted with denying a benefit on account of exercising First Amendment rights.[65] However, the Court has made encroachments on this view in state taxation, as discussed in Chapter IX.

The Court next approved the denial of the exempt status that permits an organization to receive deductible contributions to an organization that used the contributions received to lobby. Section 501(c)(3) in conjunction with section 170(c)(2)(D) limits the ability of charities to attempt to influence legislation (or to campaign) and also retain their exemption and the ability to receive contributions that donors can deduct. Although these limitations might seem to relate primarily to the organization's exemption, in fact they relate more importantly to the donor's deductions, because the organizations probably can qualify under another exemption category than section 501(c)(3) and also lobby (if not campaign), but those other exemption categories generally do not allow the organization to receive deductible contributions. In contrast to the limitations on lobbying and campaigning by section 501(c)(3) charities that can receive income tax deductible contributions, only one of the other more than 30 types of organizations granted exemptions in section 501(c) faces any limitation on lobbying.[66]

The Supreme Court upheld the restriction effected through the income tax on the charitable donee's lobbying in *Regan v. Taxation with Representation* against a claim of abridgement of free speech.[67] The charity aspired to lobby Congress on

---

[61] Regan v. Taxation with Representation, 461 U.S. 540 (1983).

[62] 358 U.S. at 513.

[63] *See* Miriam Galston, *When Statutory Regimes Collide: Will Citizens United and Wisconsin Right To Life Make Federal Tax Regulation of Campaign Activity Unconstitutional?* 13 U. of Pa. J. of Const. L. 867, 892 (2011) (this article discusses the extent to which application of deduction denials and exemption denials with respect to campaigning may be challenged as limitations on free speech).

[64] *See* Leathers v. Medlock, 499 U.S. 439, 450 (1991).

[65] Matal v. Tam, 137 S. Ct. 1744 (2017).

[66] I.R.C. § 501(c)(29) (co-op health insurers, authorized by the 2010 health care law). In addition, section 501(h) defines lobbying for purposes of charities, section 501(p) denies exemption for terrorist organizations, and prior to 2014 section 501(s) referenced the non-exemption of Communist controlled organizations.

[67] Regan v. Taxation with Representation, 461 U.S. 540 (1983).

tax issues and contended that the IRS' refusal to recognize its exemption under section 501(c)(3), based on its plan to lobby as a substantial part of its activities, violated both the freedom of speech guarantee of the First Amendment and the equal protection aspect of due process under the Fifth Amendment (because veterans organizations could both receive deductible contributions and lobby).[68] The *Regan* opinion surprisingly recommended to the organization how to minimize the effect of its ruling: organizations like Taxation with Representation should split themselves into a section 501(c)(4) lobbying arm and a charity to which deductible contributions could be paid, which has become the norm.

Regan v. Taxation with Representation did not even apply strict scrutiny, which is normally the standard for a government restriction claimed to impinge on a fundamental right like free speech and petitioning the government, both because the Court did not see any discrimination based on the content of the speech, and because it did not see the limitation on the deduction as a restriction at all (*i.e.*, no level playing field for lobbying speech is required by the Constitution).[69] By turning the case into a spending case (through a tax expenditure) rather than a benefit restriction case the Court was able to circumvent the organization's claim of injury.

The opinion purported to make a distinction between placing an obstacle in the path of exercising a right and paying to enable the person to exercise the right, by labeling the former an "independent benefit" that was denied;[70] more likely, the path the Court has indicated through the cases depends on whether the act of Congress appears to single out "dangerous ideas" or other specific speech based on content. Thus the *Regan* decision stands for the proposition that tax breaks are subsidies whose denial may be unconstitutional on free speech grounds only in the more blatant cases of content discrimination,[71] or discrimination based on other protected categories such as race or national origin.[72] The Court also has relied on *Regan v. Taxation with Representation* to support a state's refusal to subsidize union activities by maintaining a right to work law.[73]

It is not clear whether the flexibility of the charity to use a section 501(c)(4) organization to lobby was just an observation of fact or an element of denying

---

[68] The opinion stated that strict scrutiny is not required just because Congress subsidizes some lobbying speech and not others, where the discrimination was not based on the content of the speech. 461 U.S. at 548.

[69] The opinion distinguished Speiser v. Randall, 357 U.S. 513, 518 (1958), which had stated "a discriminatory denial of a tax exemption for engaging in speech is a limitation on free speech," by asserting that the "Code does not deny TWR the right to receive deductible contributions to support its nonlobbying activity, nor does it deny TWR any independent benefit on account of its intention to lobby. Congress has merely refused to pay for the lobbying out of public moneys. This Court has never held that Congress must grant a benefit such as TWR claims here to a person who wishes to exercise a constitutional right." 461 U.S. at 545.

[70] 461 U.S. at 545.

[71] *See, e.g.*, Tex. Monthly, Inc. v. Bullock, 489 U.S. 1, 14 (1989) (religious magazines only exempt from sales tax).

[72] 461 U.S. at 548.

[73] Ysursa v. Pocatello Educ. Ass'n, 555 U.S. 353 (2009).

the exemption/lobbying combination to the charity. A more recent opinion suggests it was just a fact.[74]

The Court has ruled that an objection of a lobbying organization to loss of exempt status is not such an irreparable harm as to justify avoidance of the Anti-Injunction Act.[75]

First National Bank v. Bellotti, a decision not involving tax deductions, ruled unconstitutional a state statute criminalizing a corporation's spending for the purpose of opposing the adoption of a graduated individual income tax.[76] The opinion refused to distinguish between tax proposals that might more directly affect the corporation and this proposal that appeared not to directly affect it. Rather the opinion rested on the support of the First Amendment for free discussion of ideas, no matter what the source.

Deductions for contributions to religious organizations are discussed in Chapter VIII.D.4.

b. *Political Speech*

The Code attempts to neither aid nor hinder political speech:

- Section 162(e) denies a deduction for political expenditures.
- Section 84 requires a donor of appreciated property to a political organization to recognize the gain. The requirement is typical of gain recognition without exchange requirements when the two persons are not closely related, as in section 311(b).
- Political organizations are generally tax exempt under section 527 with respect to "exempt function income" and the gift tax does not apply under section 2501(a)(4) to a transfer to a political organization as defined in section 527(e).
- Section 271 denies a bad debt deduction for certain debts owed by political parties to the creditor (such as an advertising agency).

The Court has not ruled on these Code provisions, but outside the tax area restrictions on campaign finance for political speech now receive strict scrutiny from the Court.[77] However, the Court's approach did not start out that way. The seminal decision in *Buckley v. Valeo* upheld against a variety of constitutional challenges (First Amendment, Ninth Amendment, Fifth Amendment and taxing power) the federal tax return check off system for directing small amounts of tax to presidential election campaign funds, under section 6096, which entailed both public funding and the imposition of limits on spending for a candidate

[74] Agency for Int'l Dev. v. All. for Open Soc'y Int'l, Inc., 140 S. Ct. 2082 (2020) (but see Justice Breyer dissent); Agency for Int'l Dev. v. Alliance for Open Soc'y Int'l, Inc., 570 U.S. 205 (2013) (not essential to ruling, according to Justice Scalia dissent, but Chief Justice Robert's majority opinion gave more weight to dual structure option).

[75] Alexander v. "Americans United" Inc., 416 U.S. 752 (1974).

[76] First National Bank v. Bellotti, 435 U.S. 765 (1978).

[77] *See* Citizens United v. FEC, 558 U.S. 310 (2010).

that accepted public funding.[78] The checkoff system was intended to provide a more level playing field for candidates. *Buckley v. Valeo* also made important rulings that Congress can limit campaign contributions to candidates, but cannot limit campaign spending by candidates using their own funds, and Congress cannot limit independent spending on campaigns. Thus *Valeo* both recognized the propriety of a level playing purpose for federal campaign legislation, and limited its extent. Although it struck down the limit on a candidate spending her own money, it severed that part of the statute. The crucial distinction between (1) the candidate's own unlimited "spending" (presumably from the candidate's own resources) plus independent unlimited spending for the candidate (which came to be facilitated by unaffiliated political action committees), as opposed to (2) limited "contributions" to the candidate, has driven the development of campaign finance in the 21st Century.[79] These two categories of spending and contributions often puzzle persons trying to fathom the federal election laws limits on dollars and reporting thereof.

But in 2011 the Court struck down on First Amendment grounds a somewhat similar campaign funding scheme in Arizona that was paid for out of general tax revenue funds.[80] The majority opinion did not mention *Buckley*, but Justice Kagan's dissent did, arguing that the facts were not distinguishable from *Buckley* and that the scheme imposed no limitation on speech. The dissent emphasized the playing field leveling mechanism in *Buckley* rather than the spending limitation.

c. *Content of Speech*

When denial of an exemption or deduction or some other tax benefit can be characterized as based on the content of speech or on requiring speech, the denial is not likely to survive. The Court has stated: "A tax based on the content of speech does not become more constitutional because it is a small tax."[81]

Speiser v. Randall ruled unconstitutional California's precondition to a property tax exemption for veterans, which required the owner to swear he did not advocate the forcible overthrow of the government.[82] The Court explained that the condition was an indirect way of forcing the taxpayer to say something the

---

[78] Buckley v. Valeo, 424 U.S. 1 (1976).

[79] *See* Cummings, *Citizens United Spurs Social Welfare*, 146 Tax Notes 1141 (Mar. 2, 2015).

[80] Ariz. Free Enter. Club's Freedom Club PAC v. Bennett, 564 U.S. 721 (2011). Also McCutcheon v. FEC, 572 U.S. 185 (2014) struck down a federal election law limit on contributions.

[81] Forsyth County v. Nationalist Movement, 505 U.S. 123, 136 (1992) (parade fee unconstitutional because it could vary in amount based on content of speech), discussing Murdock v. Pennsylvania, 319 U.S. 105 (1943). See also Ch. VIII.D.3, on freedom of the press.

[82] Speiser v. Randall, 357 U.S. 513 (1958) (the case was decided under the Due Process Clause of the Fourteenth Amendment; the facts were particularly egregious; the plaintiff was an honorably discharged World War II veteran who was denied a veteran's exemption); Prince v. City and County of San Francisco, 357 U.S. 513 (1958) (companion case). *See also* First Unitarian Church of Los Angeles v. County of Los Angeles, 357 U.S. 545 (1958) (involving a church's exemption under the same statute, but not decided on Free Exercise Clause grounds).

government could not otherwise force him to say.[83] Because the taxpayer was required to say that he would not make criminal statements, he in effect was being forced to carry the burden of proof that he had not committed (or would not commit) a crime, which the Court found to be unconstitutional on due process grounds for exemption purposes, just as it is in an actual criminal trial.[84]

The majority placed heavy weight on the possible chilling effect of what it called the process of proving entitlement to the exemption. Indeed, the opinion emphasized that the usual tax rule that a taxpayer has the burden to prove an exemption or deduction must be abated when the result is to penalize speech.[85] *Cammarano* characterized *Speiser v. Randall* as a case of procedural due process.[86]

Speiser v. Randall was relied on by the taxpayer in *Regan v. Taxation with Representation*, discussed in Chapter VIII.D.2.a, which wanted to be able to lobby using deductible contributions.[87] Although the Court agreed that *Speiser* stood for the principle that the government may not deny a benefit to a person because he exercises a constitutional right, it relied on the theory applied in *Cammarano* that distinguished between a benefit denial and refusing to subsidize speech.[88]

Spending by an exempt organization was at issue in *Rosenberger*.[89] It distinguished a student activity fee paid to a public university from a tax. The University refused to allow funds from the fees to be used by a religious group, the plaintiff in the case. The Court found that limitation to violate the plaintiff's free speech rights by creating "viewpoint discrimination," and rejected the University's defense that it acted to avoid violating the Establishment of Religion Clause.

Cornelius v. NAACP involved an unusual free speech tax issue that is related to charitable deductions.[90] Several charities complained about being excluded from the combined federal campaign for charitable donations on the basis that they

---

[83] 357 U.S. at 526. *See also* Fed. Election Com. v. Mass. Citizens for Life, Inc., 479 U.S. 238, 256 (1986).

[84] 357 U.S. at 542. The history of loyalty oaths in the Supreme Court dates back at least to the Reconstruction era, as discussed in Note, *Loyalty Oaths*, 77 YALE L. J. 739 (1968). After several decisions against Communists in the Cold War era, the Court substantially limited the use of such oaths. *See* Communist Party of Indiana v. Whitcomb, 414 U.S. 441 (1974).

[85] 357 U.S. at 525.

[86] Cammarano v. United States, 358 U.S. 498, 513 (1959).

[87] Regan v. Taxation with Representation, 461 U.S. 540 (1983).

[88] 358 U.S. at 513. The Court relied on *Cammarano* and Regan v. Taxation with Representation as to the failure to subsidize speech activity not being a constitutional violation outside the tax area in Rust v. Sullivan, 500 U.S. 173 (1991).

[89] Rosenberger v. Rector and Visitors of the Univ. of Va., 515 U.S. 819 (1995). Justice Thomas in concurrence urged recognition of the equivalence of tax expenditures and governmental spending, the point being that the dissent admitted governments make tax expenditures favoring religion in the form of tax exemptions and deductions and so too should the government be able to spend in support of religion. Out of little more than this have entire regimes of theories about tax expenditure and constitutionality been spun. *See* Linda Sugin, *Tax Expenditure Analysis and Constitutional Decisions*, 50 HAST. L. J. 407 (1999) [hereinafter Sugin]; Edward A. Zelinsky, *Are Tax Benefits Constitutionally Equivalent to Direct Expenditures?* 112 HARV. L. REV. 379 (1998). *See also* Regan v. Taxation with Representation, 461 U.S. 540, 548 (1983) ("For the purposes of these cases appropriations are comparable to tax exemptions and deductions . . .").

[90] Cornelius v. NAACP Legal Def. & Educ. Fund, 473 U.S. 788 (1985).

either did not provide direct services to individuals or provided legal defense or political advocacy. The Court entertained the objections but remanded for determination whether the discrimination against the plaintiffs was based on their viewpoints.[91]

d. *Tax Expenditures and the Level Playing Field for Free Speech*

Because the Court finds no constitutional right to a level playing field for free speech, it finds no right to tax expenditures (deductions, exemptions and credits) benefiting organizations that attempt to assert their free speech rights in certain ways (political and lobbying activities). In other words, engaging in certain free speech activities can constitutionally result in loss of tax benefits to which an organization otherwise would be entitled, despite the fact that freedom of speech is generally viewed as the most important (or one of the two most important, with freedom of religion) rights of Americans. The peculiarity of this view is heightened when contrasted with the willingness of the Court to allow tax expenditures in support of organizations for which Congress (or the states) cannot spend directly.[92]

The Court understands that governments spend through allowing tax deductions and exemptions.[93] In *Regan v. Taxation with Representation* the Court both recognized this equation and ruled that a level playing field for speech is not constitutionally required. Because the opinion in that case explained that the organization could lobby as (or through) a section 501(c)(4) exempt organization, the real issue was the charitable deduction allowed by section 170, which was limited to section 501(c)(3) charities that do not carry on substantial lobbying. The opinion rejected the taxpayer's argument that denial of the charitable deduction to its donors was unconstitutional because (1) it explicitly found that both a tax exemption and a tax deduction were like (but not identical to) direct cash subsidies to the charity (*i.e.*, the Court understands the concept of "tax expenditures"); and (2) it implicitly ruled that the Constitution does not impose any duty on Congress to provide a level playing field for lobbying. Therefore,

---

[91] On remand the district court granted the injunction, but it was reversed as moot. NAACP Legal Def. & Educ. Fund v. Horner, 636 F. Supp. 762 (D.D.C. 1986), *reversed*, 795 F. 2d 215 (D.C. Cir. 1986).

[92] *See, e.g.*, Hernandez v. Commissioner, 490 U.S. 680, 696 (1989) (churches); Ariz. Christian Sch. Tuition Org. v. Winn, 563 U.S. 125 (2011).

[93] *See, e.g.*, Regan v. Taxation with Representation, 461 U.S. 540 (1983); Bob Jones Univ. v. United States, 461 U.S. 574, 591 (1983) (relying on the similarity between exemption and direct support). *See also* Comm. for Pub. Educ. and Relig. Liberty v. Nyquist, 413 U.S. 756, 774 (1973) (struck down a state tax deduction for parents who paid tuition at religious and other private schools); *reasoning rejected in* Mueller v. Allen, 463 U.S. 388, 390–391 (1983) (purported to rely on independent choice of persons to direct government spending by making deductible contributions).

Congress could not be forced either to appropriate money to assist in lobbying or provide a tax expenditure to the same end.[94]

The reasoning of *Regan v. Taxation with Representation* cannot rest on the premise that there is no constitutional right to force Congress to spend on anything, because there clearly are instances in which the courts can force Congress to spend, as for example to provide legal representation to criminal indigents.[95] If Congress can be made to spend on something, presumably it can be made to provide a tax expenditure for the same object. Therefore, the Court must have reasoned, in effect, that there is no right to a somewhat level playing field for the expression of ideas, where leveling the playing field requires some equalization of the finances required to make speech effective.

Regan's no-level-playing-field reasoning in the area of federal taxation and free speech is a profound concept that has received little notice outside the tax area. Even the Court did not notice it in *Citizens United*, which did not cite *Regan*, although the premises of the two decisions seem related.[96] Because Congress has no duty to level the playing field for free speech (as stated in *Regan v. Taxation with Representation*), *Citizens United* struck down federal restrictions on campaign expenditures by groups not officially affiliated with the candidate. It did cite the portion of the per curiam opinion in *Buckley v. Valeo* that ruled against a limit on certain campaign spending, which stated:

> It is argued, however, that the ancillary governmental interest in equalizing the relative ability of individuals and groups to influence the outcome of elections serves to justify the limitation on express advocacy of the election or defeat of candidates imposed by § 608 (e)(1)'s expenditure ceiling. But the concept that government may restrict the speech of some elements of our society in order to enhance the relative voice of others is wholly foreign to the First Amendment, which was designed "to secure 'the widest possible dissemination of information from diverse and antagonistic sources,'" and "'to assure unfettered interchange of ideas for the bringing about of political and social changes desired by the people.'" . . . The First Amendment's protection against governmental abridgment of free expression cannot properly be made to depend on a person's financial ability to engage in public discussion.[97]

Perhaps *Citizens United* did not cite *Regan* because *Regan* was a lobbying case and not a campaigning case; but the First Amendment level playing field implications are the same. The notion that playing field leveling is not part of the First Amendment, however, seems contrary to the Court's acceptance of the

---

[94] 461 U.S. at 544-545. *See also* Harris v. McRae, 448 U.S. 297 (1980) and Maher v. Roe, 432 U.S. 464 (1977) (Congress could choose not to subsidize abortions and strict scrutiny was not applied).

[95] *See* Gideon v. Wainwright, 372 U.S. 335 (1963).

[96] Citizens United v. FEC, 558 U.S. 310 (2010) ("The rule that political speech cannot be limited based on a speaker's wealth is a necessary consequence of the premise that the First Amendment generally prohibits the suppression of political speech based on the speaker's identity."). The Court extended the rule of *Citizens United* to state law. Am. Tradition P'ship v. Bullock, 567 U.S. 516 (2012).

[97] Buckley v. Valeo, 424 U.S. 1, 48-49 (1976).

"equal time rule" and other FCC requirements once placed on licensed media companies.[98]

The *Cammarano* and *Regan v. Taxation with Representation* theory that the First Amendment has no business trying to level the playing field to exercise First Amendment rights was carried to new heights in 2011 when the Court struck down an Arizona public financing system that subsidized publicly financed candidates and did not restrict anyone's speech.[99] Justice Kagan pointed out in dissent that:

> . . . what petitioners demand is essentially a right to quash others' speech through the prohibition of a (universally available) subsidy program. Petitioners are able to convey their ideas without public financing—and they would prefer the field to themselves, so that they can speak free from response. To attain that goal, they ask this Court to prevent Arizona from funding electoral speech—even though that assistance is offered to every state candidate, on the same (entirely unobjectionable) basis. And this Court gladly obliges.[100]

The dissent explained that even though *Buckley v. Valeo* struck down a campaign spending limitation, it also and primarily upheld the checkoff system for public financing of presidential campaigns ("That is exactly what we approved in *Buckley v. Valeo*.").[101] It is likely that the Court will be asked to reconsider the theory of *Regan* that there is no duty to subsidize access to Congress, or the same theory as applied to political campaigns, or to other free speech issues. The ability of spending to amplify speech and to make speech unequal is too obvious to ignore.[102] However, the Court did ignore it in 2020. The Court in effect required a state to subsidize private (including specifically church) schools by preventing a state from ending a program for tax credits for giving to fund private school vouchers; only the dissent cited *Regan*.[103]

The Court addressed tax expenditures in general in 2011 in *Arizona Christian School Tuition Organization v. Winn*, rejecting on standing grounds an objection to a state tax expenditure, a state tax credit that was allowed solely for contributions to funds providing tuition scholarships to private schools.[104] The issue was, in effect, expansion of the allowance of tax expenditures for donations to church organizations (most of the private schools were church affiliated). Justice Kagan in dissent pointed out the total lack of economic distinction between tax expenditures through credits and deductions for religious purposes and state spending. The key to the distinction made by the majority of the Court appears to be

---

[98] *See, e.g.*, CBS v. FCC, 453 U.S. 367 (1981) (rejecting First Amendment objections to FCC rules).

[99] Ariz. Free Enter. Club's Freedom Club PAC v. Bennett, 564 U.S. 721 (2011).

[100] 564 U.S. at 766.

[101] *Id.* dissent at n. 3.

[102] *Cf.* dissent of Justice Douglas in United States v. International Union United, 352 U.S. 567, 594 (1957) ("it costs money to make a speech").

[103] Espinoza v. Mont. Dep't of Revenue, 140 S. Ct. 2246 (2020).

[104] Arizona Christian Sch. Tuition Org. v. Winn, 563 U.S. 125 (2011). *See* Congressional Research Service, Public Aid to Sectarian Schools, 2011 STT 67-1 (4/5/2011).

that the state does not select the religious recipient of payments when it spends through a tax expenditure. The dissent discussed *Walz* and other decisions, in which the Court effectively ruled that Congress could support religion through tax expenditures in ways it could not through direct spending.[105]

The expanding application of the First Amendment to taxation may eventually run into the boundary applied when a university refused to reveal peer review information in response to an EEOC complaint: at some point the connection of the impingement on academic freedom is too attenuated to deny normal processes, including taxation as a cited example.[106] Also, the Court's willingness to overlook a limitation on a charity in *Regan* because it could speak through a noncharitable tax exempt organization was brought into question by a holding that for free speech purposes a parent corporation and its foreign subsidiary have no connection.[107]

e. *Taxes As Compelled Speech*

"[C]compelled funding of government speech does not alone raise First Amendment concerns."[108] Therefore taxpayers suffer no constitutional wrong when their tax dollars are spent for government sponsored messages with which they disagree. This is true whether the taxpayer's contribution is through general taxes or a targeted assessment.[109] The so-called "government speech doctrine" does not apply, however, to non government speech funded by compelled payments.[110] Therefore, there is tension in the cases involving fees as to whether they are taxes or not. The student activity fee at issue in *Rosenberger* was unconstitutional because the program spending the funds discriminated on the basis of content; Justice Souter argued in dissent that the fee was a tax.[111] *Southworth* upheld a similar fee's collection and did not treat it as a tax.[112] The Court has become extremely strict in preventing compelled funding of speech through contractually required funding of certain private organizations, i.e., labor unions.[113]

In a discussion of the relationship of conduct to speech in a decision not involving taxes, the Court stated:

---

[105] Walz v. Tax Com. of New York, 397 U.S. 664, 666–667 (1970). *See* Ch. VIII.D.4.c.

[106] Univ. of Pa. v. EEOC, 493 U.S. 182 (1990).

[107] Agency for Int'l Dev. v. All. for Open Soc'y Int'l, Inc., 140 S. Ct. 2082 (2020) (Breyer dissent contrasted *Regan*).

[108] Johanns v. Livestock Mktg. Ass'n, 544 U.S. 550, 559 (2005).

[109] *Id.* at 262, citing United States v. Lee, 455 U.S. 252, 260 (1982) ("There is no principled way . . . to distinguish between general taxes and those imposed under the Social Security Act" in evaluating the burden on the right to free exercise of religion).

[110] United States v. United Foods, Inc., 533 U.S. 405 (2001).

[111] Rosenberger v. Rector and Visitors of the Univ. of Va., 515 U.S. 819, 873-874 (1995). As to fees generally, see Ch. IV.

[112] Bd. of Regents v. Southworth, 529 U.S. 217 (2005).

[113] *See* Knox v. SEIU, Local 1000, 567 U.S. 298 (2012) (non union members could not be required to pay increased dues to fund political speech, without prior request); Janus v. AFSCME, Council 31, 138 S. Ct. 2448 (2018).

> . . . [I]f an individual announces that he intends to express his disapproval of the Internal Revenue Service by refusing to pay his income taxes, we would have to apply *O'Brien* to determine whether the Tax Code violates the First Amendment. Neither *O'Brien* nor its progeny supports such a result.[114]

Alternately, taxes as compelled speech or participation in some activity that violate religious freedoms could be the subject of complaints under the Religious Freedom Restoration Act.[115]

f. *Taxes and Commercial Speech*

Although the decision substantially predated the Court's modern sympathy to commercial speech, in 1902 the Court ruled that Congress could wholly forbid tobacco sellers from packaging any advertising material with the tobacco product that was subject to the federal excise tax.[116] The opinion pointed out that the seller was free to advertise the product in any other way it desired. However, a recent ruling prohibiting stores from discriminating against credit card charges by price could be applied against any advertising of the amount of tax that would be due or not due on a sale.[117]

3. *Freedom of the Press*

The First Amendment provides: "Congress shall make no law . . . abridging the freedom of speech, or of the press; . . . ."[118] The current state of the tax law concerning press freedom is that (1) a generally applicable tax (such as a general sales or income tax) can be imposed on the press despite the exemption of limited smaller segments of the press, and that (2) a special tax that is generally applicable to the entirety of the press, or even most of it in terms of number of taxed entities, could pass muster if it were levied on some feature peculiar to the press, such as circulation, and did not appear to have the purpose or effect of limiting free speech.[119] Beyond those types of taxes, the appearance of press discrimination can arise and a constitutional violation may be found.

A tax can have the purpose or effect of abridging the freedom of speech and of the press, and so taxes payable by the press are subject to First Amendment analysis.[120] Nevertheless, generally applicable economic regulations and taxes can be applied to the press without violating the Constitution.[121] The distinguishing features of an unconstitutional tax on the press (absent direct proof of legislative intent to penalize certain speech by content) are of two distinct kinds: the tax and its exemptions appear on their face either (1) to single out the press as a whole for a differential tax burden (most problematic is a different form of

---

[114] Rumsfeld v. Forum for Academic & Institutional Rights, Inc., 547 U.S. 47, 66 (2006).
[115] *See* Cummings, *Hobby Lobby and Federal Taxes*, 145 Tax Notes (TA) 519 (Nov. 3, 2014).
[116] Felsenheld v. United States, 186 U.S. 126 (1902).
[117] Expressions Hair Design v. Schneiderman, 137 S. Ct. 1144 (2017).
[118] *See generally* David A. Anderson, *Freedom of the Press*, 80 Tex. L. Rev. 429, 495-505 (2002).
[119] *See* Arkansas Writers' Project, Inc. v. Ragland, 481 U.S. 221, 229 (1987).
[120] Speiser v. Randall, 357 U.S. 513, 518 (1938).
[121] Minneapolis Star & Tribune Co. v. Minn. Comm'r of Revenue, 460 U.S. 575, 581 (1983).

taxation imposed on the press, but the differential could be in rate of tax) that appears to be aimed at suppressing or rewarding the press generally (a relatively rare case); or (2) to impose a differential and usually heavier tax on one segment of the press compared with another, actually or presumably based on the content of that segment's speech, in a way that cannot be categorized as a general tax with exemptions not designed to reward or penalize certain speech by content.

In neither case of differential taxation can Congress rely on its normal broad powers to discriminate in taxation,[122] because the subject of the differential taxation is the press. The major difficulty (in addition to identifying the press in the first place) is to distinguish the constitutional generally applicable tax that exempts some segments of the press in a way that avoids being viewed as discriminatory taxation, from the unconstitutional generally applicable tax that singles out some segment of the press for relatively heavier taxation, actually or presumably based on the content of its speech. The cases below show that the intent of the tax differential can be determined based on evidence of actual legislative intent, but lacking that, the Court has trended away from inferring such intent from the structure of the tax; rather it is more willing to infer it from a wholly different form of tax applied to the press than from simply exempting some of the press from a general tax.

Heavier taxation of the press generally might have the purpose or effect of diminishing public discussion generally. Alternately, the press might initially receive differential and more lenient taxation, and so be subject to self-censorship, also rendering the differential tax suspect. The Court views discriminatory taxation of the press as potentially a double discrimination, first against the press or information dissemination generally, and then against some content of speech.[123]

Once differential taxation and a facial tax discrimination against or within segments of the press is identified, a relatively heavy burden falls on the government to justify it by compelling proof of an overriding governmental interest, which cannot just be revenue raising, but rather might be some inherent characteristic of the press appropriately related to its differential taxation.[124] If the discrimination appears to be based on the content of the speech (which is always a possibility if it applies to some segment of the press), a compelling justification is required.[125] But if the Court does not view differential taxation as carrying a facial discrimination, evidently the burden rests on the taxpayer to prove the violation.[126]

Legislative intent to muzzle the press need not be proved by the taxpayer or disproved by the government,[127] but rather facial differential taxation without a

---

[122] *See* Ch. V.D.3.b(2)(b).

[123] Grosjean v. American Press Co., 297 U.S. 233, 245 (1936).

[124] Minneapolis Star & Tribune Co. v. Minn. Comm'r of Revenue, 460 U.S. 575, 582 (1983).

[125] Leathers v. Medlock, 499 U.S. 439, 447 (1991).

[126] *Id.* at 453 (1991).

[127] Arkansas Writers' Project, Inc. v. Ragland, 481 U.S. 221, 228 (1987) ("Both types of discrimination can be established even where, as here, there is no evidence of an improper censorial motive.").

compelling explanation can doom a tax; a government may have entirely legitimate aims and still be unable to defend a differential tax.[128] However, *Leathers v. Medlock* stated that "differential taxation of speakers, even members of the press, does not implicate the First Amendment unless the tax is directed at, or presents the danger of suppressing, particular ideas."[129] Therefore, some such inference from the face of the statute must be plausible.

In practice, the principal cases of differential press taxation that have come to the Court have involved differential state taxation of a segment of the news media, usually targeting larger newspapers or magazines. Such larger entities frequently make up a small minority of the total members of the press, thus isolating them politically, and making the Court more sympathetic to their inability to protect themselves from taxation by lobbying. Perhaps more so than in other constitutional tax issues, free press tax issues cannot be treated in isolation from the general First Amendment jurisprudence of the Court, which is not addressed here.[130] The Court's principal free press tax opinions all involve state taxation:

- *Grosjean* (1936). This decision was based on inferred actual intent to punish one segment of the press. The Court ruled that a Louisiana tax violated the freedom of the press: the tax was two percent of ad revenues of newspapers and other periodicals with weekly circulation in Louisiana of more than 20,000 copies.[131] The opinion listed these factors: (1) although freedom of the press principally prohibits prior restraint, that is not its sole function, and so post publication taxation can violate the First Amendment; (2) the tax had the effect of a restraint on the freedom of the press because it reduced ad revenues and discouraged circulation (and if the tax rate were sufficiently increased could destroy circulation); (3) the First Amendment was drafted specifically to prevent regulation of the press of just this sort, which had occurred in Britain through stamp taxes on newspapers and taxes on ad revenues that Parliament imposed not for revenue but to limit press freedom; (4) newspapers are properly subject to "ordinary forms of taxation"; and (5) the Court inferred from (a) the odious British history of taxes that were similar to the Louisiana tax and (b) the "present circumstances," including the facts that no other state has ever imposed such a tax and it appears to be aimed at a select group of the largest newspapers, that "it is seen to be a deliberate and calculated device in the guise of a tax to limit the circulation of information to which the public is entitled in virtue of the constitutional guaranties."[132] In other words, the Court imputed a bad motive to the Louisiana legislature, without identifying any direct evidence thereof, showing that freedom of the press defenses to a tax need not bear a

---

[128] 460 U.S. at 592-593.

[129] 499 U.S. at 453.

[130] *See* Sonja R. West, *Awakening the Press Clause*, 58 U.C.L.A. L. Rev. 1025 (2011) (discussing the submergence of the press clause in freedom of speech generally and arguing for a limited definition of the press).

[131] Grosjean v. American Press Co., 297 U.S. 233 (1936).

[132] 297 U.S. at 250.

heavy burden to succeed; indeed, Justice Stone listed *Grosjean* in the famous footnote 4 in *Carolene Products* as involving one of the rights to which strict scrutiny might be appropriate.[133] The Court later characterized *Grosjean* as involving a discrimination against newspapers,[134] and also as likely motivated by the fact that Louisiana Governor Huey Long and the legislature intended to penalize the part of the press that was critical of Long.[135]

- *Minneapolis Star* (1983). This decision involved such an unusual special tax on one segment of the press that the Court in effect inferred bad intent to the legislature because it refused to try to figure out how the special tax might be explained as reasonable. The Court ruled unconstitutional a use tax limited to the largest newspapers on paper and ink they used; no sales tax was imposed on the sale of any newspapers.[136] The opinion explained the reason why differential (in form) taxes on the press such as this scheme can be bad and general taxes acceptable: when the press is part of a sufficiently larger group of taxpayers, the larger group can effectively lobby against a tax, whereas the press when taxed alone perhaps cannot protect itself;[137] also the differential taxation of the press places the press in position to be influenced by the legislative taxing decisions, whether the differential be more heavy taxation than that imposed on other taxpayers or less.[138] The instant case was not controlled by *Grosjean* because evidence of specific legislative intent to discriminate was lacking, whether by inference or otherwise; but also, such proof was not necessary because the tax facially discriminated against the press.[139] The opinion identified the threshold issue as whether the tax imposed a differential (presumably but not necessarily heavier[140]) tax on the press as such; and if does, the state must carry a heavy burden to justify the discrimination by proving some compelling and overriding governmental interest. Like *Grosjean*, it stated that the misuse of taxes on the press by the

---

[133] United States v. Carolene Prod. Co., 304 U.S. 144, 152 n. 4 (1938).

[134] Lehnhausen v. Lake Shore Auto Parts Co., 410 U.S. 356, 360 n. 3 (1973).

[135] Minneapolis Star & Tribune Co. v. Minn. Comm'r of Revenue, 460 U.S. 575 (1983). *See also* Fair Assessment in Real Estate Ass'n v. McNary, 454 U.S. 100, 109 (1981) (stating that *Grosjean* was a case where no adequate remedy was available in the state courts).

[136] Minneapolis Star & Tribune Co. v. Minn. Comm'r of Revenue, 460 U.S. 575 (1983). *See also* Village Pub. Corp. v. North Carolina Dep't of Revenue, 472 U.S. 1001 (1985) (dissent to denial of certiorari); Texas Monthly, Inc. v. Bullock, 489 U.S. 1 (1989) (one member of the Court relied on the freedom of the press).

[137] 460 U.S. at 585. Alternately, the press will not have to involve itself in the political process if it can stand under the protection of the masses of taxpayers, thus effecting editorial freedom. RANDALL P. BEZANSON, TAXES ON KNOWLEDGE IN AMERICA 262-264 (1994) [hereinafter BEZANSON] (it mattered not how logical were the state's explanations for the differential form of taxation of large newspapers; it tended to force the large newspapers to concern themselves with the legislation of their own taxation, which was the evil to be avoided).

[138] BEZANSON, at 257.

[139] Leathers v. Medlock, 499 U.S. 439, 445 (1991) (explaining *Minneapolis Star*).

[140] The Court rejected the state's argument that such an economic examination would show that the press was taxed more favorably, because that sort of favorable discrimination could put the press in the position of muzzling itself for fear of losing its favorable taxation. 460 U.S. at 588.

British in revolutionary times justifies a strict scrutiny of such taxes under the First Amendment. The face of the statute showed differential taxation of the press because newspapers had been removed from the general sales tax and instead the tax on paper and ink imposed on the press alone.[141] The opinion rejected the state's argument that special characteristics of the press justified this treatment, saying there was no good reason a sales tax could not have been levied on the papers sold to consumers. But more fundamentally, the Court refused to undertake the task of weighing the equivalence of the paper and ink tax versus a general sales tax levied on the papers, at least in the area of freedom of the press.[142] This refusal highlights the high threshold the Court applies to facially discriminatory taxation of the press; it thought that the possibility of error in attempting to determine the economic equivalence of taxing the press in alternatives ways was too great for press freedom to bear. Despite swearing off analysis of purpose, the majority found evidence of an improper purpose in the limitation of the ink and paper tax to the largest newspapers, which sort of limitation also had been present in *Grosjean*.

- *Arkansas Writers' Project* (1987). Unlike the taxes in the two preceding cases, the tax at issue here was the general Arkansas sales tax. The Court ruled unconstitutional application of the sales tax to general interest magazines, because all other more specialized magazines (church, sports, etc.) were exempted.[143] Although the category of general interest is a broad one, the Court viewed it as a discrimination based on content apparently because it applied to newspapers that were more likely to carry general interest news. The Court thought such discrimination was substantially more damning than differential taxation of the press in general, justifying (a) imposing a "heavy burden" on the state to prove a "compelling state interest," and (b) requiring that the discrimination be "narrowly drawn" to serve that interest (later called "heightened scrutiny").[144] Just as the Court was unwilling to

---

[141] The state's argument was based on the fact that use and sales taxes are appropriately viewed as potentially equivalent, as where a purchaser from an out of state vendor must pay a local use tax because it has not paid a sales tax. However, here the state attempted to impose a tax on certain inputs of newspapers, which did not exactly match up with the value of the output (the newspapers). The state tried to prove that less tax was incurred than if a sales tax had been levied on the papers sold, but the Court refused to consider the factual question.

[142] 460 U.S. at 589-590. But the Court was careful not to swear off its ability to evaluate economic equivalencies in matters of taxation, limiting its statement to the critical issue of free press. In the state tax area, compensating taxes are frequently examined. *See* HELLERSTEIN & HELLERSTEIN, STATE TAXATION ¶ 4.14.[3][c] (3d Ed.) (the complementary tax doctrine).

[143] Arkansas Writers' Project, Inc. v. Ragland, 481 U.S. 221 (1987) (the opinion did not need to reach the "additional basis" of discrimination between newspapers and the general interest magazines). The ruling relieved the general interest magazine of the discriminatory tax, which presumably would lead to a refund and effective extension of the exemption enjoyed by other publications. The Court explained that the taxpayer had standing to complain about the discriminatory exemption of other publications.

[144] 481 U.S. at 231.

evaluate compensating taxes in *Minneapolis Star*, because the exemptions were both overinclusive and underinclusive relative to the claimed purpose of aiding fledgling publications, the Court was not willing to accept that broad brush argument by the state.[145]

- *Leathers v. Medlock* (1991). This case involved the same generally applicable Arkansas sales tax at issue in *Arkansas Writers' Project*, but which now exempted all print publications (evidently in response to *Arkansas Writers' Project*), and had been extended to tax the sales receipts of the new lucrative cable TV industry, other than satellite TV (allegedly to encourage dish TV in rural areas).[146] This regime appeared to create a discrimination against TV medium "news," and against cable TV vis à vis dish TV. However, the Court distinguished *Arkansas Writers' Project* from the facial discrimination in *Leathers v. Medlock* and rejected challenges to both differentials in taxation. Some view *Leathers v. Medlock* as an effective overruling of *Arkansas Writers' Project* and *Minneapolis Star*.[147] The *Leathers v. Medlock* opinion describes as "heightened scrutiny" the test for a content-based discrimination within the press,[148] but did not find it applicable because the Court found no evidence of (or could not infer) intent to discriminate based on content (as perhaps existed in *Grosjean*) and could not infer such intent from the structure of the tax and exemptions (as it had been willing to do in *Arkansas Writers' Project* and *Minneapolis Star*).[149] Evidently this meant that cable TV news was not likely to reflect any particular content that was different from the news carried by print medium or satellite TV, both of which were exempt from the sales tax. Also cable TV was a numerous enough medium (over 100 cable TV providers) that the tax did not look like a discrimination against a narrow segment. Put another way, cable TV was big enough to protect itself politically. The opinion referred back to the fact that the Court had deemed moot the "additional basis" argued by the taxpayer in *Arkansas*

---

[145] Indeed, the Court's unwillingness to engage in close economic comparisons to discern tax discrimination has been repeated over and over. *See* Dep't of Revenue v. Davis, 553 U.S. 328, 355-356 (2008) ("Fulton Corp., 516 U.S., at 342, . . . [stated] '[C]ourts as institutions are poorly equipped to evaluate with precision the relative burdens of various methods of taxation. The complexities of factual economic proof always present a certain potential for error, and courts have little familiarity with the process of evaluating the relative economic burden of taxes' (quoting Minneapolis Star & Tribune Co. . . .").

[146] Leathers v. Medlock, 499 U.S. 439 (1991). *See* Note, *First Amendment Limits on the Use of Taxes to Subsidize Selectively the Media*, 78 Corn. L. Rev. 106 (1993). The pattern of a discriminatory tax first being refunded to the complaining taxpayers, and then the exemption being extended to that class of taxpayers by statutory amendment, is a common and almost inevitable one in state taxation. *See* Fulton Corp. v. Faulkner, 516 U.S. 325 (1996) (refund allowed to first taxpayer); Smith v. State, 349 N.C. 332 (1998) (allowing refunds to class of similar taxpayers); subsequently the intangibles tax at issue was repealed entirely.

[147] *See* Bezanson, at 271-272.

[148] 499 U.S. at 447.

[149] 499 U.S. at 453 ("differential taxation of speakers, even members of the press, does not implicate the First Amendment unless the tax is directed at, or presents the danger of suppressing particular ideas.").

Writers' Project that discrimination between newspapers and magazines was inherently content based. Taking up a similar "additional basis" argument, the Court ruled that differentiation between print and TV medium was not inherently discriminatory but rather fell on the side of those inevitably arbitrary distinctions in taxation that governments are allowed to make; perhaps the rather formal distinction between a tax that is different in form and one that is different in rate explains the different outcomes of the cases.[150] Just as *Regan v. Taxation with Representation* refused to find discrimination in the fact that one type of exempt organization is allowed to lobby (veterans' organizations) and others are not, *Leathers v. Medlock* stated that facial discrimination is not unconstitutional in the absence of actual or reasonably inferable legislative intent to encourage or discourage speech based on content.[151] The case was remanded for consideration of equal protection claims, but because strict scrutiny should not apply for equal protection purposes since no discrimination against the press was found for free press purposes, the taxpayer was unlikely to succeed, and did not.[152]

4. *Establishment Clause*

a. *General*

The First Amendment states:

> Congress shall make no law respecting an establishment of religion, or prohibiting the free exercise thereof . . . .

The First Amendment is treated as containing two distinct rules: the Establishment Clause and the Free Exercise Clause.[153] The Supreme Court ruled in 1940 and 1947 respectively that the Fourteenth Amendment to the Constitution incorporates the Free Exercise Clause and the Establishment Clause as binding on the states.[154] The two clauses have generated two quite distinct lines of Supreme Court authorities. The tax issues similarly are quite distinct, with standing issues predominating in the Establishment Clause cases and discrimination issues predominating in the Free Exercise Clause cases. As is true of the free speech tax cases, many of the Court's tax decisions in this area concern state and local taxes, which also will be discussed here. See also Chapter IX.

---

[150] *See* BEZANSON, at 272.

[151] Regan v. Taxation with Representation, 461 U.S. 540 (1983) (the Court approved an apparent discrimination between veterans' organizations and other charities with respect to lobbying; the discriminated against charities were a large enough group to protect themselves politically, meaning that Congress does not create a discrimination when it differentially *benefits* a small group in taxation).

[152] The Arkansas Supreme Court rejected the equal protection claim, which by the time of the remand had morphed into an objection to the taxation of cable TV but exemption of satellite TV. Medlock v. Leathers, 311 Ark. 175 (1992), *cert. denied*, 508 U.S. 960 (1993) (rational basis to assist provision of TV services to remote areas not serviced by cable).

[153] *See, e.g.*, Cantwell v. Connecticut, 310 U.S. 296, 303 (1940).

[154] Cantwell v. Connecticut, 310 U.S. 296 (1940); Everson v. Bd. of Educ., 330 U.S. 1 (1947).

b. *Taxpayer Suits and Standing*

(1) *Overview*

Because many citizens become exercised about some government action or expenditure that seems to violate the Establishment Clause, many plaintiffs have sought ways to present themselves as appropriate plaintiffs in suits challenging such spending. The most obvious hook on which most plaintiffs have relied is their status as taxpayers, to establish the required "standing," which is a relatively recent gloss on the ancient concept of actually having a case or controversy that is worthy of judicial determination.[155] As a consequence there is a close relationship between the issues of taxpayer standing and the Establishment Clause.

The Supreme Court most recently quoted an earlier opinion in restating its general test for standing to pursue a case or controversy in the federal courts as follows:

> First, the plaintiff must have suffered an "injury in fact"—an invasion of a legally protected interest which is (a) concrete and particularized, and (b) "actual or imminent, not "conjectural" or "hypothetical." Second, there must be a causal connection between the injury and the conduct complained of—the injury has to be "fairly . . . trace[able] to the challenged action of the defendant, and not . . . th[e] result [of] the independent action of some third party not before the court." Third, it must be "likely," as opposed to merely "speculative," that the injury will be "redressed by a favorable decision."[156]

The current law is that taxpayers have standing, purely as taxpayers, to complain about some federal government activity other than their own tax liability, only if that action violates a specific constitutional limitation on the taxing and spending power, and the only such specific limitation recognized for this purpose is the Establishment Clause.[157] The Court's current test for taxpayer standing, as taxpayer, to challenge the constitutionality of some action of the federal government, is to ask whether the action challenged is controlled by a specific constitutional limitation on the taxing and spending powers of Article I, section 8.[158] The Court has identified only the Establishment Clause as having such a specific limitation, and has excluded the Tenth Amendment and the Due

[155] *See generally* Daniel E. Ho and Erica L. Ross, *Did Liberal Justices Invent Standing Doctrine? An Empirical Study of the Evolution of Standing 1921-2006*, 62 Stan. L. Rev. 591 (2010) (arguing that the doctrine of standing was invented without significant political tilt, but then was applied to prevent attacks on New Deal legislation; by the 1950s it came to be applied by liberals to promote suits, whereas conservatives used it to deny suits).

[156] Ariz. Christian Sch. Tuition Org. v. Winn, 563 U.S. 125 (2011), *quoting* Lujan v. Defenders of Wildlife, 504 U.S. 555, 560-561 (1992).

[157] *See, e.g.*, United States v. Richardson, 418 U.S. 166, 173-174 (1974) (no standing to complain about CIA; contrasts Establishment Clause cases). *See generally* Micah Schwartzman, *Conscience, Speech and Money*, 97 Va. L. Rev. 317, 322 (2011).

[158] 418 U.S. at 173-174.

Process Clause.[159] And as the following Chapter will show, even Establishment Clause challenges are allowed only to congressionally directed spending. This standing requirement of nexus between the spending power and a constitutional spending limitation is unique to standing based on taxpayer status and does not apply to citizens' suits where injury and causal connection can be otherwise proven.[160]

And yet taxpayer standing to contest Establishment Clause taxing and spending is under assault from the Republican-appointed Justices, who complain that it is anti-religion.[161] They succeeded in limiting it in the *Winn* decision, discussed below.

A variety of other considerations apply if the plaintiff claiming unconstitutional governmental action involving tax stands in another posture than merely a taxpayer complaining about his own taxes or about spending of tax revenues.[162]

(2) *Taxpayer Refund Standing Generally*

Of course taxpayers can sue to recover their own tax payments on account of a wide variety of constitutional violations discussed in this book that directly affect that liability. Indeed, almost all of the 25 federal tax provisions that the Supreme Court has ruled unconstitutional, as listed in Chapter I.E.2.b, were attacked by payors (or potential payors) of the contested taxes, with the exception of *Pollock*, in which shareholders sued to prevent the corporation from paying the income tax, and *Hill v. Wallace* in which members of the Chicago Board of Trade sued to enjoin a tax before it could be applied.[163]

Some constitutional violations can clearly be direct causes of the particular tax liability attacked by a taxpayer: for example, illegally retroactive taxes and taxes on exports. Other violations are less directly related to the taxpayer's particular tax liability, but the taxpayer still may obtain a tax refund in the normal way, for example if either (1) the taxpayer can claim exemption under an intergovernmental immunity, or (2) the taxpayer can prove that Congress did not exercise

---

[159] *Id.* at 180-185 (concurrence of Justice Powell, explaining Flast v. Cohen). *See also* Valley Forge Christian College v. Americans United for Separation of Church and State, 454 U.S. 464, 508 n. 18 (1982) (Dissent of Justice Brennan, who was a member of the Court that issued Flast v. Cohen, stating that he knew of no other specific limitation beside the Establishment Clause).

[160] *See* Duke Power Co. v. Carolina Envtl. Study Group, 438 U.S. 59, 78-79 (1978) (Note also that footnote 25 observed that "there have been questions as to whether the nexus requirement, even in the context of taxpayers' suits, is constitutionally mandated or is instead simply a prudential limitation.").

[161] Espinoza v. Mont. Dep't of Revenue, 140 S. Ct. 2246 (2020) (concurrence of Justices Thomas, Alito and Gorsuch).

[162] *See, e.g.*, Allen v. Wright, 468 U.S. 737 (1984) (parents did not have standing to challenge grant of tax exemption to racially discriminatory schools); Simon v. East Ky. Welfare Rights Org., 426 U.S. 26 (1976) (indigents lacked standing to challenge tax exemption for hospitals that did not provide them services). *Cf.* Baker v. Carr, 369 U.S. 186 (1962) (citizen-voter could assert equal protection violation in voting).

[163] Pollock v. Farmers' Loan & Trust Co., 157 U.S. 429 (1895), *confirmed and expanded*, 158 U.S. 601 (1895); Hill v. Wallace, 259 U.S. 44 (1922).

the power to tax but rather tried to regulate an activity under exclusive state control (Tenth Amendment violations).

Very few of the intergovernmental immunity and Tenth Amendment claims have been brought by the states themselves, and when they have been, the state appears to have been a stalking horse for private interests. In 1941 Justice Jackson wrote:

> Few decisions of the Supreme Court can be cited in which any state of the Union has been able to obtain protection from the Court of its own constitutional rights, *upon its own demand.* (emphasis in original).[164]

As a consequence the important immunity and Tenth Amendment cases have been mostly brought by taxpayers, with the major examples being the last anti-New Deal decisions, *Carter Coal* and *Butler.*[165]

But when the taxpayer's constitutional objection bears a less direct relationship to his tax payment than occurs in immunity and Tenth Amendment claims (which, if successful, can eliminate the tax liability), the standing issue can begin to arise. Nevertheless, the Supreme Court has allowed taxpayers to assert equal protection or discrimination claims without questioning their standing, most recently in *Windsor,* which did discuss and find standing.[166] However, it has stated that a taxpayer cannot complain that the tax he paid discriminates against some other taxpayer.[167] Also a taxpayer who benefited from an illegality is not in a position to contest the illegality (not involving a constitutional illegality).[168]

The inability to complain about discrimination against another taxpayer is one application of the general principle governing standing stated above: a person does not have standing to complain about the unconstitutionality of a federal tax unless the person has been harmed by the unconstitutional feature of the tax.[169] Such complaints presumably fit within the Supreme Court's general re-

---

[164] Robert H. Jackson, The Struggle for Judicial Supremacy 20 (1941). Jackson cited as examples, Massachusetts v. Mellon, 262 U.S. 447 (1923) and Florida v. Mellon, 273 U.S. 12 (1927). An example to the contrary that proves the rule was South Carolina v. United States, 199 U.S. 437 (1905) in which the state had paid the disputed tax and had to sue to recover it. *Cf.* Hopkins Savings Assn. v. Cleary, 296 U.S. 315 (1935) (state savings and loan commission sued to prevent conversion from state to federal institutions).

[165] Carter v. Carter Coal Co., 298 U.S. 238 (1936); United States v. Butler, 297 U.S. 1 (1936).

[166] United States v. Windsor, 570 U.S. 744 (2013). *But see* Ariz. Christian Sch. Tuition Org. v. Winn, 563 U.S. 125 (2011) (explaining that Establishment Clause standing can be proven in various ways: direct intangible harm, as by being made to pray; the incurrence of a tax imposed cost or benefit to another, as by a required religious affiliation for a tax benefit; or the mere status as taxpayer); Espinoza v. Mont. Dep't of Revenue, 140 S. Ct. 2246 (2020) (a Free Exercise Clause case allowed a parent to sue because its child attended a school whose students could not benefit from a tax credit funded tuition program that the plaintiff did not use; no discussion of standing).

[167] Shearer v. Burnet, 285 U.S. 228 (1932).

[168] Magee v. United States, 282 U.S. 432 (1931).

[169] Heald v. District of Columbia, 259 U.S. 114 (1922) (residents of the District of Columbia complained that nonresidents also had to pay the tax). *Cf.* Raines v. Byrd, 521 U.S. 811 (1997) (ruling that Senator Byrd and other congresspersons did not have a personal stake in the constitutionality of the law and dismissed their suit against the OMB to have the law declared unconstitutional).

quirements for standing: that the plaintiff has suffered a concrete injury in fact; there must be a causal link between the injury and the allegedly unconstitutional act; and the injury can be redressed by the court's ruling.[170]

(3) *Taxpayer Lack of Standing Without Refund: The Establishment Clause Exception*

The interrelationship of the Establishment Clause and taxation has been quite confused, but this much is relatively clear:

> No tax in any amount, large or small, can be levied to support any religious activities or institutions, whatever they may be called, or whatever form they may adopt to teach or practice religion.[171]

The Court based this view on the peculiar or special relationship between government sponsored religion and a government's power to tax and spend.[172] Partly because of that special connection between taxing, spending and the establishment of religion, the Court has recognized that federal taxpayers can have standing to contest federal spending that supports religion.

The current posture of the Court is to limit that standing to the clearest cases of congressionally directed spending that promotes religion, as discussed below. First, *Frothingham v. Mellon* denied standing to a federal taxpayer, suing in that capacity alone, to contest federal spending of tax dollars. But later, *Flast v. Cohen* generally lifted this preclusion when the issue is spending that violates the Establishment Clause. However, the Court has been carving back *Flast v. Cohen* in recent years in various ways, without completely overruling it.[173]

Background. Usually tax discrimination can be redressed by a refund or perhaps by eliminating the preferential treatment of others; but when the remedy sought is refund, that is likely to be the remedy allowed.[174] In contrast, when the injury cannot be redressed by a tax refund, but rather the taxpayer seeks to have the government cease some activity funded by taxes or cease applying taxes in

---

[170] *See* Nancy C. Staudt, *Taxpayers in Court: A Systematic Study of a (Misunderstood) Standing Doctrine*, 52 Emory L. J. 771, 783 (2003) [hereinafter Staudt]; Mark C. Rahdert, *Forks Taken and Roads Not Taken: Standing to Challenge Faith Based Spending*, 32 Cardozo L. Rev. 1009, 1014-1019 (2011) [hereinafter Rahdert]; Cummings, *Standing to Sue About Taxes*, 164 Tax Notes Federal (TA) 45 (July 1, 2019); Cummings, *Standing to Sue About Taxes, Part 2*, 164 Tax Notes Federal (TA) 323 (July 15, 2019).

[171] McGowan v. Maryland, 366 U.S. 420, 443 (1961).

[172] Flast v. Cohen, 392 U.S. 83, 103 (1968) ("Our history vividly illustrates that one of the specific evils feared by those who drafted the Establishment Clause and fought for its adoption was that the taxing and spending power would be used to favor one religion over another or to support religion in general.").

[173] Perhaps one reason for carving back Flast v. Cohen is the arbitrariness of identifying the Establishment Clause as the one constitutional rule that can be enforced by taxpayers, as pointed out by Alexander M. Bickel, The Supreme Court and the Idea of Progress 64 (1970).

[174] *See, e.g.*, Fulton Corp. v. Faulkner, 516 U.S. 325 (1996) (invalidating a state tax on Commerce Clause discrimination grounds and leaving to the state the choice of refunding the complaining shareholder, and perhaps others similarly situated, or eliminating the preference afforded to others, which is very difficult for a taxing authority to accomplish retrospectively).

a way that unconstitutionally benefits some persons (for example, religious tax exemptions), then a broader conception of standing for taxpayers as taxpayers generally had to be developed if they were to be allowed to sue at all, and it has been developed in fits and starts and retreats over the last 90 years.

A 1960 survey of historical taxpayer standing cases made findings that are still applicable:[175]

- Taxpayer suits started with suits against municipalities and then states, and were widely allowed by the state courts.[176]
- Although the opinions (mostly in state courts) speak in terms of the degree of a taxpayer's financial interest in the governmental expenditures as justifying, or not, their standing, more realistically "[t]axpayers' litigation seems designed to enable a large body of the citizenry to challenge governmental action, which would otherwise go unchallenged in the courts because of the standing requirement. Such litigation allows the courts, within the framework of traditional notions of 'standing,' to add to the controls over public officials inherent in the elective process the judicial scrutiny of the statutory and constitutional validity of their acts. Taxpayers' suits also extend the uniquely American concept of judicial review of legislative action by allowing minorities without political power to invalidate statutes or ordinances on constitutional grounds. Because the motive of a plaintiff-taxpayer is viewed as irrelevant, taxpayers' suits afford a means of mobilizing the self-interest of individuals within the body politic to challenge legislative programs, prevent illegality, and avoid corruption. Taxpayers' suits thus create an army of potential private attorneys general acting on whatever private incentives may induce them to spend the time and money to bring a taxpayer's suit: personal economic gain, partisan political objectives, desire to attract personal publicity, or to delay unwanted public projects, or to prevent expenditures believed to be socially or economically unwise."[177]
- Taxpayers' suits are effectively class actions, and despite being suits against the sovereign are not subject to the sovereign immunity defense at the state level.[178]

---

[175] Note, *Taxpayers' Suits: A Survey and Summary*, 69 YALE L. J. 895 (1960).

[176] *Id.* at 898-902.

[177] *Id.* at 904. The explanations for taxpayer standing have not advanced much since 1960. *See* Rahdert, at 1033-1034 ("Absent taxpayer standing, a spending measure like the one in *Flast* would probably never receive judicial review, meaning that its constitutionality might never be determined."). The *Journal* also conducted a study of municipal and state attorneys and found the following motives for taxpayers' suits, in declining order: (1) benefit to one's particular industry or business, (2) general displeasure over any new community action or public expenditure, (3) partisan political reasons, as for example to embarrass elected officials, (4) publicity, (5) suits by losing contractors, (6) idealistic or solely for community welfare, (7) hoping to collect attorneys' fees, and (8) other.

[178] *Id.* at 906.

The 1960 Note's bullishness on taxpayer actions was mostly limited to state court actions, and rightly so, because since 1960 there has been considerable tension on the Court about how many private attorneys general it wants to tolerate in the federal arena. Subsequently, academic writing on taxpayer standing has exploded, both because of the high tension issues involved and the vacillations of the Court as to taxpayer standing, as outlined below.[179]

Frothingham v. Mellon. Federal taxpayers generally cannot bring declaratory judgment actions to dispute federal taxes.[180] State taxpayers have only limited rights to initiate such suits in federal courts.[181] The denial of standing to federal taxpayers to contest the constitutionality of federal expenditures began in the 1923 decision in *Frothingham v. Mellon.*[182] Justice Sutherland for a unanimous Court ruled that Mrs. Harriet A. Frothingham of Boston, claiming damages solely as a federal taxpayer, did not have standing to contest on due process grounds her taxation for the allegedly unconstitutional purposes of a federal appropriation intended to improve the health of mothers and children. The taxpayer did not seek return of any particular amount of tax paid but rather complained vaguely that her taxes would somehow be increased by the illegal government spending. The State of Massachusetts also attacked the use of tax funds under the Sheppard-Towner Maternity Act, the first major federal social welfare program in the United States.[183] The cases were consolidated in the Supreme Court.[184]

The Court rejected the right of a taxpayer such as Mrs. Frothingham to sue on these grounds due to (1) the vague and uncertain relationship of the alleged illegality to any damage to the taxpayer (*i.e.*, not rising to the level of a legally cognizable damage), (2) the practical reason that the pool of potential plaintiffs would be virtually limitless (all taxpayers), thus providing an unlimited supply

---

[179] *See* articles cited in Rahdert and in Staudt.

[180] 28 U.S.C. § 2201 (except as provided in 26 U.S.C. § 7428).

[181] It is almost impossible for state taxpayers to sue states and municipalities for tax refunds in federal court due to the federal Tax Injunction Act ("TIA") (to be distinguished from the 1867 Anti-Injunction Act, which normally prevents prepayment litigation about federal taxes outside the Tax Court), which Congress adopted in 1937, now codified at 28 U.S.C. § 1341. It is arguably the most important federal statute applicable to state taxes. The TIA reads: "The district courts shall not enjoin, suspend or restrain the assessment, levy or collection of any tax under State law where a plain, speedy and efficient remedy may be had in the courts of such State." *See* Jefferson County v. Acker, 527 U.S. 423 (1999) (recounting the history and interrelationship of the two acts).

[182] Frothingham v. Mellon, 262 U.S. 447 (1923). And in the context of the companion consolidated case, Massachusetts v. Mellon, the Court ruled that a state could not sue on behalf of its citizens to contest the tax.

[183] Massachusetts v. Mellon, 262 U.S. 447 (1923).

[184] The Act at issue was signed by President Warren G. Harding in 1921. It created a Board of Maternity and Infant Hygiene. Note that this case reflects one of the two typical patterns of such cases: attack on a "liberal" scheme by "conservative" plaintiffs; the other pattern is attack on a "conservative" scheme, usually some sort of federal support for religious education, by "liberal" plaintiffs. The startling fact about the *Frothingham* case is that the plaintiffs were even more conservative than the Harding administration, which (with a Republican controlled House and Senate) had enacted the federal health care program.

of litigation, and (3) the belief that entertaining suits on such a basis would effectively put the courts in the business of reviewing every act of Congress spending money, which would upset the constitutional balance that precludes the courts from acting as a general court of review for the acts of other branches, outside of a valid case or controversy.

The *Frothingham* opinion differentiated taxpayer attacks on municipal spending, on the grounds that the relationship of a municipal taxpayer and municipality was akin to that of a shareholder and the corporation.[185] But in 2006 the Court made clear that the *Frothingham* exception for municipal matters did not extend to state taxpayers complaints about state taxing and spending.[186] In any event the federal courts have been much more receptive to state and local taxpayer litigation.[187]

The next major development occurred in 1936 when the taxpayer in *Butler* claimed it should not have to pay the federal tax because of the unconstitutional

---

[185] 262 U.S. at 487 ("The reasons which support the extension of the equitable remedy to a single taxpayer in such cases are based upon the peculiar relation of the corporate taxpayer to the corporation, which is not without some resemblance to that subsisting between stockholder and private corporation. . . . But the relation of a taxpayer of the United States to the Federal Government is very different. His interest in the moneys of the Treasury—partly realized from taxation and partly from other sources—is shared with millions of others; is comparatively minute and indeterminable; and the effect upon future taxation, of any payment out of the funds, so remote, fluctuating and uncertain, that no basis is afforded for an appeal to the preventive powers of a court of equity.").

[186] DaimlerChrysler Corp. v. Cuno, 547 U.S. 332 (2006). The Tax Injunction Act was not a problem because the state removed the suit from state court; the taxpayer was trying to increase not decrease state tax collections. The Court, however, dismissed the action for lack of standing. *See* 15-101 MOORE'S FEDERAL PRACTICE § 101.60. *See also* Miller v. Standard Nut Margarine Co., 284 U.S. 498 (1932) (enjoined tax collection because taxpayer's product was definitionally not subject to the tax; dissent by Justices Stone and Brandeis).

[187] *See* Staudt, showing that in fact the federal courts have continued to be much more receptive to state and local taxpayer actions on these grounds than to federal taxpayer actions.

use to be made of the tax revenue and the regulatory scheme associated with it.[188] The Court distinguished *Frothingham* on the ground that the taxpayer could establish a more direct linkage between the particular tax paid and a particular use of the tax funds claimed to be unconstitutional; in fact, the linkage was thought to be so tight that the tax ceased to be a tax and was an unconstitutional regulation of commerce within states. *Butler* was one of the principal anti-New Deal decisions of the Supreme Court, striking down the Agricultural Adjustment Act, which involved, inter alia, the collection of a tax from crop processors and the payment of price supports to farmers. Because the decision as to standing hinged on the Court ruling that the tax was not a tax but a regulation and the regulation was unconstitutional, the plaintiff could not be denied standing because he sued merely as a taxpayer.

Although the two opinions just discussed both involved federal taxes, *Frothingham* had already distinguished municipal taxes, which had a long history of taxpayer complaints. Indeed in 1947 *Everson*, without any reference to standing, rejected on the merits a taxpayer's objections to the spending of local tax monies to provide transportation to church school students.[189] In 1952 *Doremus* rejected on standing grounds a taxpayer's challenge to reading the Bible in public schools.[190] It distinguished *Everson* because there a specific expenditure was involved, which would not otherwise have been made. *Doremus* also illustrates that federal courts can redetermine standing even for purposes of their appellate jurisdiction.

---

188 United States v. Butler, 297 U.S. 1 (1936), *discussed in* Maurice S. Culp, *Methods of Attacking Unconstitutional Legislation*, 22 VA. L. REV. 723, 730 (1935). *See* Ch. III.D.2. The contrast with *Frothingham* made by the *Butler* opinion claims to depend on the tightness of the linkage between the tax and the payments to farmers, but the linkage in the statute was not all that tight: the Secretary of Agriculture could cause a processing tax to be collected from crop processors, in an amount intended to recapture the difference between the market price and the price paid to farmers, less reasonable processing costs; the Secretary was authorized to enter into rental or benefit contracts with farmers by which they would agree to reduce production in return for payments; the Act appropriated a fixed amount of money, $100 million, plus the proceeds of the tax, to pay all of the expenses of the agriculture program described in the Act (which authorized a variety of loans, plus purchases of surplus crops), including the rental and benefits payments to farmers; although the case involved the cotton processors' tax, the Act pooled all processing taxes in the appropriation to pay all crop benefit payments, which could include wheat, cotton, corn, tobacco, rice, as well as hogs and milk products. 48 Stat. 31 et seq. (1933). Thus the worst that could be said of the Act was that the same act that appropriated the spending also levied the tax. Therefore, the Act was a far cry from collecting a tax from the processors of a particular commodity and paying its proceeds to the growers of that commodity. No doubt other factors were at work, including the fact that the AAA was a lightning rod of New Deal legislation not only due to the processing taxes but also due to the portion of the Act authorizing the President to devalue the dollar in terms of gold exchangeability. Title III of the Act, 48 Stat. at 51.

189 Everson v. Bd. of Educ., 330 U.S. 1 (1947).

190 Doremus v. Bd., 342 U.S. 429 (1952). *Cf.* Sch. Dist. of Abington Twp. v. Schempp, 374 U.S. 203 (1963) (which ruled against Bible reading in public schools and distinguished *Doremus* on the ground that the plaintiffs had the more direct standing of being parents of children in the school).

In 1968 *Flast v. Cohen* created a major exception allowing standing for federal taxpayer complaints under the Establishment Clause.[191] Normally federal tax disputes must be pursued in refund litigation, or in the Tax Court. The United States is protected by the constitutional doctrine of sovereign immunity from suit, and waivers of immunity are strictly construed.[192] Nevertheless, without discussing sovereign immunity, *Flast v. Cohen* allowed plaintiffs to complain of the use of federal funds under the Elementary and Secondary Education Act of 1965 to pay expenses of church schools. The opinion observed that there was controversy about the grounds of *Frothingham*: was it based on a constitutional preclusion of the power of courts or on judicial discretion? The opinion effectively ruled it was the latter, stating:

> A taxpayer may or may not have the requisite personal stake in the outcome, depending upon the circumstances of the particular case. Therefore, we find no absolute bar in Article III to suits by federal taxpayers challenging allegedly unconstitutional federal taxing and spending programs. There remains, however, the problem of determining the circumstances under which a federal taxpayer will be deemed to have the personal stake and interest that impart the necessary concrete adverseness to such litigation so that standing can be conferred on the taxpayer qua taxpayer consistent with the constitutional limitations of Article III.[193]

The method discerned by Chief Justice Warren was to ask whether the taxpayer's complaint was based on a limitation on the taxing and spending power itself, as contrasted with a general claim that the government had exceeded its powers. The latter was the claim in *Frothingham*, that the federal government was infringing on state territory by meddling in womens' and childrens' health; whereas the Constitution explicitly directs that religion is not to be established by taxing and spending. The opinion left open the possibility that other parts of the Constitution also limited the taxing and spending powers.[194] The Court effectively has applied *Flast v. Cohen* to taxpayer suits attacking state spending.[195]

In 1982 the Court ruled *Flast v. Cohen* inapplicable to an executive decision to spend money (or rather to transfer property), in contrast to congressional action

---

[191] Flast v. Cohen, 392 U.S. 83 (1968).

[192] Flora v. United States, 357 U.S. 63 (1957), *reaffirmed in* 362 U.S. 145 (1960).

[193] 392 U.S. at 101.

[194] *See* Schlesinger v. Reservists Com. to Stop the War, 418 U.S. 208 (1974) (assumed that if a challenge to the Incompatibility Clause, Art. I, sec. 6, cl. 2, violation had been based on congressional spending, *Flast* would have permitted the suit). Justice Scalia has pointed out that the Establishment Clause has no claim to a special nexus to taxing and spending and that *Frothingham* could have similarly involved Article I, section 8. Hein v. Freedom from Religion Foundation, Inc., 551 U.S. 587, 625 (2007).

[195] *See* School Dist. v. Ball, 473 U.S. 373 (1985), *citing*, inter alia, Lemon v. Kurtzman, in which the trial court found Flast applicable and the Supreme Court evidently affirmed as to standing, though it reversed on the merits. Lemon v. Kurtzman, 310 F. Supp. 35, 41-42 (E.D. Pa. 1969), *reversed*, 403 U.S. 602 (1971).

under the spending power.[196] In 2007 *Hein* again denied federal taxpayer standing when the action complained of was not direct congressional spending.[197]

In 2011 the Court limited taxpayer standing even more in *Arizona Christian School Tuition Organization v. Winn*, involving a state tax.[198] The decision substantially limited the reach of *Flast v. Cohen* by refusing to apply it to a state tax credit that was allowed solely for contributions to funds providing tuition scholarships to private schools. The majority opinion distinguished *Flast v. Cohen* on the basis that a tax credit did not literally involve the state's spending of dollars actually paid into the treasury by the plaintiff taxpayers (somewhat like *Valley Forge* and *Hein*).[199] Therefore, by analogy to the federal system, the taxing and spending power was not implicated and the plaintiffs did not have standing by virtue of being taxpayers.

Justice Kagan in dissent in *Arizona Christian School Tuition Organization v. Winn*, also identified the five cases (including *Winn*) in which the Court had considered taxpayer suits alleging that tax expenditures unlawfully subsidized religion and had not denied standing in the first four.[200] The outcomes of the other four were as follows:

---

[196] Valley Forge Christian College v. Americans United for Separation of Church and State, Inc., 454 U.S. 464 (1982) (executive agency decision to transfer property to church school).

[197] Hein v. Freedom from Religion Foundation, Inc., 551 U.S. 587 (2007) (Office of the President spent generally appropriated funds for allegedly religious purpose; Justice Scalia's concurrence viewed this decision as effectively overruling *Flast v. Cohen*). The line between a congressional appropriation and executive action is hard to discern. *See* Bowen v. Kendrick, 487 U.S. 589 (1988) (finding standing although linkage of spending to Congress' act less direct). But when spending occurred under an act of Congress standing was not questioned. Mitchell v. Helms, 530 U.S. 793 (2000) (spending federal education funds on church schools, attacked by taxpayers).

[198] Arizona Christian Sch. Tuition Org. v. Winn, 563 U.S. 125 (2011). *See* Congressional Research Service, Public Aid to Sectarian Schools, 2011 STT 67-1 (4/5/2011).

[199] The opinion did not take account of the widely accepted concept of tax expenditures. Since 1974 Congress has required that tax expenditures be identified and quantified in the budget. 31 U.S.C. § 1105. "The term 'tax expenditures' means those revenue losses attributable to provisions of the Federal tax laws which allow a special exclusion, exemption, or deduction from gross income or which provide a special credit, a preferential rate of tax, or a deferral of tax liability; and the term 'tax expenditures budget' means an enumeration of such tax expenditures." 2 U.S.C. § 622(3). The Estimate of Tax Expenditures prepared by the Joint Committee on Taxation reflects the charitable deduction in three places: deduction for charitable contributions to educational institutions, to health organizations and to other than education and health. Staff of the Joint Committee on Taxation, Estimates of Federal Tax Expenditures for Fiscal Years 2010-2014, JCS-3-10 (Dec. 15, 2010). The Treasury's analysis of tax expenditures is the same. Analytical Perspectives, Federal Receipts, Budget of the United States Government 2012, Office of Budget and Management. In contrast tax exemptions for charitable organizations are not treated as tax expenditures, presumably on the theory that the organizations do not have income. Sugin, at 422. Sugin also opines that the Court's facial neutrality standard for Equal Protection and Establishment Clause cases make tax expenditures safe from attack. *Id.* at 662. *See also* Edward A. Zelinsky, *Winn and the Inadvisability of Constitutionalizing Tax Expenditure Analysis*, 121 Yale L.J. Online 25 (2011).

[200] Arizona Christian Sch. Tuition Org. v. Winn, 563 U.S. 125 (2011).

- *Walz* rejected a taxpayer attack on property tax exemptions for churches on grounds of historical precedent and as a means of avoiding entanglements.[201] See Chapter VIII.D.4.c.
- *Hunt v. McNair* approved a tax exempt bond program of a state that was used by church related colleges but passed the *Lemon* test (discussed in the next Chapter) because the purpose was secular, and the effect was not to promote religion, in part because the college was not sectarian.[202]
- *Nyquist* struck down a state tax deduction for parents who paid tuition at religious and other private schools.[203]
- *Mueller* upheld a state income tax deduction for expenses of tuition, textbooks and transportation needed to attend schools, including church schools.[204]

In none of the four earlier decisions did the Court question taxpayer standing. The refusal of the Court in *Winn* to equate direct appropriations with deductions and exemptions is opposed to its view in *Regan v. Taxation with Representation* that exemptions and deductions are a form of subsidy administered through the tax system.[205]

c. *Establishment of Religion: The Substantive Law*

(1) *General*

Section 501(c)(3), which describes almost all religious organiations, provides:

> Corporations, and any community chest, fund, or foundation, organized and operated exclusively for religious, charitable, scientific, testing for public safety, literary, or educational purposes, . . . no part of the net earnings of which inures to the benefit of any private shareholder or individual, no substantial part of the activities of which is carrying on propaganda, or otherwise attempting, to influence legislation (except as otherwise provided in subsection (h), and which does not participate in, or intervene in (including the publishing or distributing of statements), any political campaign on behalf of (or in opposition to) any candidate for public office; . . . .

The identified organizations are the principal authorized recipients under section 170(c) of contributions that the donor can deduct. This combination of tax benefits is so rich that one wonders how it arose. The best of the scanty evidence

---

[201] Walz v. Tax Com. of New York, 397 U.S. 664, 666–667 (1970). As to validity of the historical precedents, *see* John Witte, Jr., *Tax Exemption of Church Property: Historical Anomaly or Valid Constitutional Practice?* 64 S. Cal. L. Rev. 363 (1991). *See also* Boris I. Bittker, *Churches, Taxes and the Constitution*, 78 Yale L. J. 1285 (1969). For the later *Lemon v. Kurtzman* test and subsequent developments under the Establishment Clause, see Ch. VIII.D.4.

[202] *Hunt v. McNair*, 413 U.S. 734, 735–736, 738–739 (1973).

[203] Comm. for Pub. Educ. and Relig. Liberty v. Nyquist, 413 U.S. 756, 774 (1973).

[204] Mueller v. Allen, 463 U.S. 388, 390–391 (1983).

[205] Regan v. Taxation with Representation, 461 U.S. 540, 544 (1983). *See* Ch. VIII.D.2.a.

of the congressional purpose behind the charitable deduction suggests it aimed to relieve government of burdens by encouraging donation to organizations that perform functions that otherwise might fall on the government.[206] However, the Court has recognized that the application of this purpose as a standard to be applied to religious organizations is constitutionally problematic because it could place the government in the position of evaluating how much good works churches do.[207] Also, if true, this would permit justifying the charitable deduction under the doctrine that a regulation (to encourage socially beneficial activities) does not violate the Establishment Clause merely because it coincides with the beliefs of some religions (to encourage socially beneficial activities).[208] Alternately, the deduction would be justifiable because the benefits to the religious organizations were "indirect . . . remote . . . or incidental" in relation to the general purpose of relieving the government of burdens or pursuing other non religious objectives, such as education.[209]

Whatever the justification, two types of objections can arise concerning the exemption or deduction: does allowance of a tax benefit tend to establish religion, and in those cases where the tax benefits are denied, has the free exercise of religion been limited? As to the latter, the Court has rejected claims that lack of a deduction for religious donations inhibited free exercise.[210] Sometimes the issues arise together in the same case.

The Court does not believe that a deduction for gifts to churches has the primary effect of encouraging and thereby establishing religion.[211] The explanations for this counterintuitive conclusion are that the deduction cannot be viewed as a

---

[206] McGowan v. Maryland, 366 U.S. 420, 442 (1961). *See also* Walz v. Tax Com. of New York, 397 U.S. 664, 680 *et seq.* (1970) (concurrence of Justice Brennan tracing the history of state and local tax exemptions for religious organizations). *See generally* Bittker & Lokken, Federal Taxation of Income, Estates and Gifts ¶ 35.1.1 (one early congressional report evidenced intent to encourage charitable contributions and another stated that the charities' conduct relieves the United States of financial burdens and promotes the general welfare; referring to H.R. Rep. No. 1860, Fifth Cong., 3d Sess. (1938)). *See also* E.C. Lashbrooke, Jr., *An Economic and Constitutional Case for Repeal of the I.R.C. Section 170 Deduction for Charitable Contributions to Religious Organizations*, 27 Duq. L. Rev. 695 (1988) [hereinafter Lashbrooke].

[207] Walz v. Tax Com. of New York, 397 U.S. 664, 674 (1970) ("To give emphasis to so variable an aspect of the work of religious bodies would introduce an element of governmental evaluation and standards as to the worth of particular social welfare programs, thus producing a kind of continuing day-to-day relationship which the policy of neutrality seeks to minimize. Hence, the use of a social welfare yardstick as a significant element to qualify for tax exemption could conceivably give rise to confrontations that could escalate to constitutional dimensions." *See also* Nina J. Crimm and Lawrence H. Winer, Politics, Taxes and the Pulpit: Provocative First Amendment Conflicts 145 (2011) [hereinafter Crimm and Winer].

[208] Bob Jones Univ. v. United States, 461 U.S. 574 (1983).

[209] *See* Comm. for Pub. Educ. and Relig. Liberty v. Nyquist, 413 U.S. 756, 770 (1973).

[210] *See* Bob Jones Univ. v. United States, 461 U.S. 574 (1983) (denial of exempt status due to racial segregation); Jimmy Swaggart Ministries v. Bd. of Equalization, 493 U.S. 378 (1990) (denial of sales tax exemption for religious material did not violate the free exercise clause, where tax was generally applicable); Tex. Monthly, Inc. v. Bullock, 489 U.S. 1, 24-25 (1989) (plurality held that free exercise clause not violated by taxing religious sales).

[211] *See* Hernandez v. Commissioner, 490 U.S. 680, 696 (1989).

direct endorsement of religion.[212] *Hernandez* is the Supreme Court opinion that gives the most attention to the federal charitable deduction for contributions to churches.[213] This decision denied a deduction for payments to the Church of Scientology and involved only the statutory construction of what was a charitable gift versus a payment for services. The opinion recognized but left unanswered the constitutional issue whether Congress could grant a deduction for payment in exchange for religious benefits; the opinion specifically noted that tuition payments to church schools could be viewed as payments for religious benefits.

Thus churches are swept into the charitable deduction tax expenditure based on a hope that they provide some general welfare benefits and some services that government would otherwise have to provide, purposefully avoiding careful examination of the realities. That the deduction supports or subsidizes religion is beyond question.[214] However, some believe the imprecision of the subsidy justifies treating it as different from direct government payments, at least insofar as legal analysis in court is concerned.[215] Indeed, it is said that support for religion is incidental to broader general welfare goals that support exemptions and deductions for charities generally, which happen to include religious organizations.[216]

A more theoretical issue is whether the United States could tax churches. Scholars dispute the issue but the better answer seems to be in the affirmative in theory,[217] though the excessive entanglements from actually enforcing such a tax would cause the effort to be unconstitutional in effect.[218] The *Bob Jones University* decision resulted in either taxing a church related institution or forcing it to abandon certain practices deemed to be contrary to a public policy limitation against racial discrimination construed into the statute.[219]

Code section 107 provides:"[220]

> In the case of a minister of the gospel, gross income does not include—(1) the rental value of a home furnished to him as part of his compensation; or (2) the rental allowance paid to him as part of his compensation, to the extent used by him to rent or provide a home and to the extent such allowance does not ex-

---

[212] *Id.*; Wallace v. Jafree, 472 U.S. 38, 69 (1985).

[213] Hernandez v. Commissioner, 490 U.S. 680 (1989).

[214] *See* Lashbrooke, at 703.

[215] *See* Sugin.

[216] Donna D. Adler, *The Internal Revenue Code, the Constitution and the Courts: The Use of Tax Expenditure Analysis in Judicial Decision Making*, 28 Wake Forest L. Rev. 855, 889 (1993) [hereinafter Adler].

[217] Crimm and Winer, at 145.

[218] See Kenneth C. Halcom, Taxing God, 38 McGeorge L. Rev. 729 (2007) (citing contrary views).

[219] Bob Jones Univ. v. United States, 461 U.S. 574 (1983). *See* David A. Brennen, *Charities and the Constitution*, 5 Fal. Tax Rev. 781 (2002).

[220] *See* John R. Dorocak, *Income Tax Exclusion of the Housing Allowance for Ministers of the Gospel Per I.R.C. Section 107: First Amendment Establishment of Religion or Free Exercise Thereof—Where Should the Warren Court Have Gone?* 54 S.D. L. Rev. 233 (2009).

ceed the fair rental value of the home, including furnishings and appurtenances such as a garage, plus the cost of utilities.

(2) *The Establishment Cases*

In 1970 *Walz* rejected a taxpayer attack on property tax exemptions for churches on the grounds of historical precedent and as a means of avoiding entanglements.[221] Justice Brennan's concurring opinion is one of the few times the Court has entertained the issue of how religious organizations support the general welfare, and stated without explanation that they do provide services that government otherwise would have to provide.[222] His analysis indicated a two prong purpose for the tax exemption for churches, which is based in the scant congressional record on the charitable deduction: (1) general welfare spending powers, and (2) relief of the government from such general welfare spending. However, Chief Justice's Burger's opinion for the Court refused to engage in a social welfare analysis of exactly how churches provided public goods and how such goods might be quantified, so as to avoid difficult entanglements.[223] Burger's opinion did, however, embrace the notion that a tax exemption for a religious organization (which the Court approved) was clearly distinguishable from a direct money subsidy, which would likely be unconstitutional.[224] This has been viewed as rejecting the tax expenditure basis for finding government sponsorship of religion.[225] However, the only real difference is that the former would require significant entanglement while the latter can operate on automatic pilot,[226] except to the extent questions are raised about the nature of the entity and its qualification for the exemption or deduction.

The next year, *Lemon v. Kurtzman* established a test for evaluating government action under the Establishment Clause (apparently in response to the confusion generated by *Everson*, which allowed public spending on transportation to

---

[221] Walz v. Tax Com. of New York, 397 U.S. 664, 666–667 (1970). As to validity of the historical precedents, *see* John Witte, Jr., *Tax Exemption of Church Property: Historical Anomaly or Valid Constitutional Practice?* 64 S. Cal. L. Rev. 363 (1991). *See also* Boris I. Bittker, *Churches, Taxes and the Constitution*, 78 Yale L. J. 1285 (1969).

[222] 397 U.S. at 687. *See also* Bob Jones Univ. v. United States, 461 U.S. 574, 587-588 (1983) (section 170 encourages organizations that serve useful public purposes; note the exemption for Bob Jones was denied on statutory not constitutional grounds, the meaning of "charitable"); *discussed by* Paul B. Stephan III, *Bob Jones University v. United States: Public Policy in Search of Tax Policy*, 1983 Sup. Ct. Rev. 33 (1983) [hereinafter Stephan] (discussing how the opinion revived the public policy grounds for rejecting the plain meaning of a tax law).

[223] 397 U.S. at 674.

[224] *Id.* at 675 (citing a difference in the degree of possible entanglement).

[225] *See, e.g.*, Tracy A. Kaye and Stephen W. Mazza, *United States—National Report: Constitutional Limitations on the Legislative Power to Tax in the United States*, 15 Mich. St. J. Int'l Law 481, 490-491 (2007).

[226] *See* Lashbrooke, at 717-718.

church schools).[227] The test provided that the United States may indirectly support religious organizations so long as (1) a purpose of the government action is secular, (2) the principal or primary effects are not advancing or inhibiting religion, and (3) the action does not produce excessive entanglements between the religious institutions and the state. Subsequently support for the *Lemon v. Kurtzman* test has frayed and at least two Justices have stated alternate tests: the endorsement test (like the *Lemon* test but substituting a hypothetical reasonable observer to measure effects, rather than actual effects), and the coercion test.[228]

Lemon v. Kurtzman's secular purpose requirement is easy to satisfy. The effects test has risen in nominal importance but shifted to be a facial test of nondiscrimination.[229] The effects test does not concern itself so much with the actual effect of aiding religion as with whether religious subjects or organizations were treated on a nondiscriminatory basis with similarly situated nonreligious subjects or organizations.[230] *Mueller v. Allen* applied the nondiscrimination approach; it rejected a challenge to deductions claimed for state income tax purposes for the cost of attending church schools because the taxpayer not the state made the choice to benefit a church school.[231] Where a tax benefit that aids religion is allowed because a taxpayer chooses to claim it, such "private choice" apparently now acts like a circuit breaker between the state and the religion.[232]

The identification of the religious donee as fitting within the charitable category is key to any such deduction. The Supreme Court has long since eschewed

---

[227] Lemon v. Kurtzman, 403 U.S. 602, 612-613 (1971); Everson v. Bd. of Educ., 330 U.S. 1, 7 (1947). In evaluating whether a denominational preference exists a facial discrimination test is applied first, before the *Lemon v. Kurtzman* test. Hernandez v. Commissioner, 490 U.S. 680, 695 (1989).

[228] Lynch v. Donnelly, 465 U.S. 668, 687-688 (1984) (endorsement test, O'Connor concurrence); Lee v. Weisman, 505 U.S. 577, 587 (1992) (coercion test, Kennedy opinion).

[229] *Id.* at 506.

[230] *Id.* at 506-508 (pointing out that this is not neutrality but equality). *Cf.* Comm. for Pub. Educ. and Relig. Liberty v. Nyquist, 413 U.S. 756, 774 (1973).

[231] Mueller v. Allen, 466 U.S. 388 (1983) (approving state tax deduction for costs of attending both church and non church schools).

[232] This concept plays an important role in the voucher cases; the Court found the ability of the parent to choose to use the educational voucher to pay for church related education sanitized the use of government funds to aid churches. Zelman v. Simmons-Harris, 536 U.S. 639 (2002). *Contrast* Comm. for Pub. Educ. and Relig. Liberty v. Nyquist, 413 U.S. 756, 783, 794 (1973) (which struck down tuition reimbursement to parents, not schools, which parents happened to predominantly choose Roman Catholic schools, stating "Indeed, it is precisely the function of New York's law to provide assistance to private schools, the great majority of which are sectarian . . ." and "As the parties here must concede, tax reductions authorized by this law flow primarily to the parents of children attending sectarian, nonpublic schools. Without intimating whether this factor alone might have controlling significance in another context in some future case, it should be apparent that in terms of the potential divisiveness of any legislative measure the narrowness of the benefited class would be an important factor."). *Cf.* Burton v. Wilmington Parking Authority, 365 U.S. 715 (1961) (discrimination by lessee restaurant in government owned facility constituted state action).

an examination into the truth of religious claims although sincerity of beliefs can be examined, a distinction that Justice Jackson found impossible to make.[233]

The Court's reliance in applying the neutrality test on facial neutrality and "private choice" totally ignores any actual disproportionate benefit for churches or related religious institutions. Thus, if the government is seeking some appropriate nonreligious purpose (under a low threshold), it can do so in a way that indirectly or directly benefits religion so long as the opportunity for benefit is stated with neutrality and nondiscrimination on its face.[234] Nevertheless the Court struck down a tax benefit limited to religious activity in *Texas Monthly*,[235] even though *Walz* had generally approved a tax exemption for churches.[236] The distinction between *Walz* and *Texas Monthly* seems to be the breadth of the class of taxpayers allowed the exemption.[237]

The final test under *Lemon v. Kurtzman*, the entanglement test, has been demoted to function as an adjunct of the formalistic effects test. However, it plays the surprising role of justifying exemptions for church organizations (to avoid entanglements).[238] Unfortunately it can play that role because it is not well enforced.

The current formalistic state of the law reflects a 180 degree reversal of Justice Powell's statements in *Nyquist* in 1973, based on *Lemon v. Kurtzman*, despite the Court's protestations to the contrary.[239] *Nyquist* struck down a New York "maintenance and repair" grant to non public schools attended by low income

---

[233] United States v. Ballard, 322 U.S. 78 (1944) (Jackson in dissent said: ". . . as a matter of either practice or philosophy I do not see how we can separate an issue as to what is believed from considerations as to what is believable.").

[234] *Id.* at 516. *See also* Rosenberger v. Rector and Visitors of the Univ. of Va., 515 U.S. 819 (1995), analyzed by Sugin, at 462 ("The *Rosenberger* opinion appears to set up two conditions that must be present for a tax to violate the establishment clause: (1) it must be collected as a general public assessment, and (2) it must be directly paid to an organization engaged in religious activity. These conditions are formal, rather than functional, and they limit the exactions that can violate the establishment clause. The majority's reliance on these formal distinctions suggests that the Court would consider the similarly formal distinctions between direct expenditures and tax expenditures to be legally significant. Tax expenditures would fail to constitute taxes under the *Rosenberger* majority's definition of a tax: the spending inherent in tax expenditures is indirect by definition because the subsidy never actually moves through the government's hands to the organization's coffers.").

[235] Tex. Monthly, Inc. v. Bullock, 489 U.S. 1, 14 (1989) (which adopted the view of *Bob Jones* that an exemption is a subsidy).

[236] Walz v. Tax Com. of New York, 397 U.S. 664 (1970).

[237] Adler, at 902.

[238] *See* Comm. for Pub. Educ. and Relig. Liberty v. Nyquist, 413 U.S. 756, 793 (1973), *citing* Walz v. Tax Com. of New York, 397 U.S. 664, 676 (1970).

[239] *See, e.g.*, Jonathan D. Boyer, *Education Tax Credits: School Choice Initiatives Capable of Surmountnig Blaine Amendments*, 43 COLUMB. J. L. AND SOC. PROBLEMS 117, 126 (2009) (*Mueller* "implicitly broke step" with *Nyquist*); Kevin Pybas, *Religious Groups in a Free Society*, 86 UNIV. OF D. MERCY L. REV. 685, 717 (2009) ("The shift from strong to weak establishment enforcement began in Mueller v. Allen."); Mark Strasser, *Repudiating Everson: On Buses, Books and Teaching Articles of Faith*, 78 MISS. L. J. 567, 605-606 (2009) (*Mueller* misrepresented *Nyquist*); Adler, at 906 (*Mueller* undercut the analytical underpinnings of *Nyquist*).

children because the Court found it clearly benefited religion, apparently because "virtually all" of the schools that received the grants were Roman Catholic schools; the Court did not even consider that the availability of the grants to secular schools could save the support for religion. It also struck down a state income tax "deduction" allowed to parents of private school students who did not receive one of the tuition grants (also ruled unconstitutional), and which had the effect of a credit because the deduction was allowed in a fixed amount, without regard to actual expenditure.

The effective rejection of *Nyquist* came in *Mueller*, a 5 to 4 opinion written by Chief Justice Rehnquist.[240] Chief Justice Rehnquist distinguished *Nyquist* on the grounds that the deductions were available to all parents of public as well as private school students (despite the fact that public school students do not pay tuition, and normally do not pay for books or transportation to the extent they ride the school bus). He introduced the circuit breaker—private choice—distinction that cleanses deductions relative to direct grants. He refused to concern himself with details of how much the deductions tended to apply only to private, and then to church school students, because that would veer away from the certainty of which the field was in need, which was supplied by the facial nondiscrimination standard used in the case. He went further to implicitly embrace the benefit of the deduction to church schools because they provide "wholesome competition with our public schools." Justice Marshall wrote a dissent in this 5 to 4 decision, explaining the majority's disingenuous attempt to distinguish *Nyquist*: "*Nyquist* also established that financial aid to parents of students attending parochial schools is no more permissible if it is provided in the form of a tax credit than if provided in the form of cash payments."

The tension between the two decisions was partly resolved against *Nyquist* in *Zelman* in 2002, stating:

> To the extent the scope of *Nyquist* has remained an open question in light of [*Mueller* and] later decisions, we now hold that *Nyquist* does not govern neutral educational assistance programs that, like the program here, offer aid directly to a broad class of individual recipients defined without regard to religion.[241]

In 2020 the Court extended *Zelman* by holding that Free Exercise concerns trump Establishment Clause concerns, and a state could not protect its public schools by ending a scholarship program that could be used at church schools; the opinion did not concern itself with standing, even though the standing of the plaintiff was doubtful.[242] Thus the Court currently (1) applies substantially relaxed scrutiny to tax expenditures favoring religion as compared with direct spending, (2) but even as to direct spending embraces the view that government

---

[240] Mueller v. Allen, 466 U.S. 388 (1983) (approving state tax deduction for costs of attending both church and non church schools).

[241] Zelman v. Simmons-Harris, 536 U.S. 639, 662 (2002) (held that public funds can flow to church schools as long as the funds symbolically flow through the hands of private individuals in school vouchers).

[242] Espinoza v. Mont. Dep't of Revenue, 140 S. Ct. 2246 (2020).

intent to support religion must be the paramount determinant in order to prove an establishment claim,[243] (3) precludes the inference of government intent from the necessary consequences of the deduction allowance, through reliance on facial neutrality and private choice, and (4) promotes private choice for religious as a reason to tolerate what otherwise might appear to be an Establishment Clause violation. This approach is somewhat similar to the Court's approach to equal protection claims: facial neutrality and lack of purpose to discrimination can outweigh discrimination in effect.[244]

The ability of government to directly or indirectly support private schools, much of which happens to be church related, is a major cause pursued by conservative political groups. It is related both to the libertarian interest in keeping the government out of the business (*i.e.*, the education) of people, and to the Chicago School style economic viewpoint of education as appropriately subject to market forces.[245] It can trace its history back to an early victory of William D. Guthrie (see Chapter I.E.3) in *Pierce v. Society of Sisters*, ruling that children could not be required to attend public school.[246]

5. *Free Exercise Clause*

a. *In General*

In 1990 the Court ruled in a nontax case, *Employment Division v. Smith*, that strict scrutiny was not required for state laws of general application that denied certain benefits and thereby impinged on the free exercise of religion.[247] In re-

---

[243] *See, e.g.*, Mitchell v. Helms, 530 U.S. 793 (2000) (rejected taxpayer suit challenging spending of 30% of federal education funds on sectarian schools in a Louisiana parish).

[244] *See* Washington v. Davis, 426 U.S. 229, 248 (1976) ("A rule that a statute designed to serve neutral ends is nevertheless invalid, absent compelling justification, if in practice it benefits or burdens one race more than another would be far reaching and would raise serious questions about, and perhaps invalidate, a whole range of tax, welfare, public service, regulatory, and licensing statutes that may be more burdensome to the poor and to the average black than to the more affluent white.").

[245] *See, e.g.*, Steven Menashi, *Toward a More Enlightened and Tolerant View: Educational Choice and the Regulation of Religious Institutions*, 66 N.Y.U. Annual Surv. of Am. Law 31, 32 (2010) (citing Milton Friedman, The Role of Government in Education, in Educational Vouchers: Concepts and Controversies (1972)).

[246] Pierce v. Society of Sisters, 268 U.S. 510 (1925) (affirming the right of persons to pursue private education without the interference of government).

[247] Employment Division v. Smith, 494 U.S. 872 (1990). Prior to *Smith* the cases generally required a compelling governmental interest and a narrow tailoring of a rule if it burdened religion. The Court upheld three federal tax statutes against attack under this earlier approach: United States v. Lee, 455 U.S. 252 (1982) (Amish could be compelled to pay social security tax because it was essential to accomplishing an overriding governmental interest); Bob Jones University v. United States, 461 U.S. 571 (1983) (section 501(c)(3) status conditioned on racial nondiscrimination); Hernandez v. Commissioner, 490 U.S. 680 (1989) (rejecting free exercise challenge to payment of income taxes alleged to make religious activities more difficult).

action Congress enacted the Religious Freedom Restoration Act of 1993.[248] In general it requires that strict scrutiny be applied in determining whether the Free Exercise Clause has been violated. The Court has upheld a challenge to federal law under the Act, but has indicated that its prior rejections of attacks on federal taxes, such as the social security tax, would not change under the standard of the Act.[249] Then the Court struck down a threatened tax penalty, applying the RFRA in favor of a for profit corporation.[250] In addition, Congress indicated that certain pre-Act decisions of the Court in fact had applied strict scrutiny (*Lee*, *Bob Jones University*, and *Hernandez*).[251]

Churches have both been prominent participants in political campaigns and also have been under weak scrutiny by the IRS for such activities. Therefore, restrictions on church political activities, which restrictions apply to all section 501(c)(3) charities, might be said to restrict freedom of religion. As of yet, no denial of a church exemption on account of political activity has reached the Court.[252] Additional developments in this area seem likely, if for no other reason than the plethora of potential and interested plaintiffs and the receptiveness of the Supreme Court. The only thing lacking is active IRS enforcement.

The Court ruled that a free exercise claim did not justify failing to apply the Anti-Injunction Act.[253]

b. *Direct Tax Burdens*

In the rare case where the taxpayer can object to a tax that it paid on account of a religious activity, the standing to complain is clear.[254] In *Murdock*, *Opelika* and *Follett v. Town of McCormick* when the Court discerned that the effect of license taxes on door to door salespersons was to impose a tax on preaching by Jehovah's Witnesses, who sell tracts door to door, it differentiated the taxes from nondiscriminatory and permissible general taxes on the incomes and property

---

[248] Pub. L. No. 103-141, 107 Stat. 1488 (Nov. 16, 1993), codified at 42 U.S.C. § 2000bb through 42 U.S.C. § 2000bb-4. It was held partly unconstitutional as applied to state and local governments. City of Boerne v. Flores, 521 U.S. 507 (1997). *See generally* Lloyd Hitoshi Mayer, *Politics at the Pulpit: Tax Benefits, Substantial Burdens, and Institutional Free Exercise*, 8 Int'l J. Civ. Soc'y L. 117, 134 *et seq.* (2010).

[249] Gonzales v. O Centro Espirita Beneficente Uniao do Vegetal, 546 U.S. 418, 435 (2006).

[250] Burwell v. Hobby Lobby Stores, Inc., 573 U.S. 682 (2014). *See* Cummings, *Hobby Lobby and Federal Taxes*, 145 Tax Notes (TA) 519 (Nov. 3, 2014).

[251] H.R. Rep. No. 103-88, at 5 n.13; S. Rep. No. 103-111, at 5 n. 5 (citing identical cases).

[252] *See generally* Johnny Rex Buckles, *Does the Constitutional Norm of Separation of Church and State Justify the Denial of Tax Exemption to Churches that Engage in Partisan Political Speech*, 84 Ind. L.J. 447 (2009).

[253] Cal. v. Grace Brethren Church, 457 U.S. 393 (1982) (challenge to federal unemployment tax). However, the unemployment compensation tax exempts churches and church organizations and so objections are usually addressed first by statutory construction. *See, e.g.*, St. Martin Evangelical Lutheran Church v. S.D., 451 U.S. 772 (1981).

[254] *See, e.g.*, Follett v. Town of McCormick, 321 U.S. 573 (1944) (tax on preaching).

of preachers.[255] The theory of the decisions was that the door to door selling is analogous to preaching from the pulpit, for which more mainstream preachers make a living through donations in the collection plate; because the latter would not be taxed, neither should the former.[256] However, the Court later limited the publication sales tax cases by stating:

> To the extent that our opinions in *Murdock* and *Follett* might be read, however, to suggest that the States and the Federal Government may never tax the sale of religious or other publications, we reject those dicta.[257]

c. *Religious Objections to Government Actions and Spending*

Religious groups tend to have many concerns about government spending, which concerns do not directly relate to the operation of their own activities (for example, opposition to war). Although a person can have standing to object to government spending, based on the person's religious beliefs, substantively religious objections to government spending are rejected.[258] Such objections would seriously inhibit the ability of the tax system to function.

> The obligation to pay the social security tax initially is not fundamentally different from the obligation to pay income taxes; the difference—in theory at least—is that the social security tax revenues are segregated for use only in furtherance of the statutory program. There is no principled way, however, for purposes of this case, to distinguish between general taxes and those imposed under the Social Security Act. If, for example, a religious adherent believes war is a sin, and if a certain percentage of the federal budget can be identified as devoted to war-related activities, such individuals would have a similarly valid claim to be exempt from paying that percentage of the income tax. The tax system could not function if denominations were allowed to challenge the tax system because tax payments were spent in a manner that violates their religious belief. See . . . Because the broad public interest in maintaining a sound tax system is of such a high order, religious belief in conflict with the payment of taxes affords no basis for resisting the tax.[259]

---

[255] Murdock v. Pennsylvania, 319 U.S. 105, 112 (1943) (Justices Reed and Frankfurter stated in dissent that churches could be taxed); Follett v. Town of McCormick, 321 U.S. 573 (1944); Jones v. Opelika, 319 U.S. 103 (1943). *See also* Jimmy Swaggart Ministries v. Bd. of Equalization, 493 U.S. 378 (1990) (observed that these two cases involved prior restraint and were so limited). In an earlier Jehovah's Witnesses case not involving a tax the Court in effect adopted Justice Stone's footnote 4 in *Carolene Products*, without citing it, stating that "Mere legislative preferences or beliefs respecting matters of public convenience may well support regulation directed at other personal activities, but be insufficient to justify such as diminishes the exercise of rights so vital to the maintenance of democratic institutions." Schneider v. Irvington, 308 U.S. 147, 161 (1939).

[256] 321 U.S. at 577.

[257] Texas Monthly, Inc. v. Bullock, 489 U.S. 1, 24 (1989).

[258] *E.g.*, United States v. American Friends Service Committee, 419 U.S. 7 (1974) (per curiam rejection under Anti-Injunction Act of employee's objection to 51% of their withheld tax, which employees deemed to be attributable to the war to which they objected on religious grounds).

[259] United States v. Lee, 455 U.S. 252, 260 (1982). *See generally* Marjorie E. Kornhauser, *For God and Country: Taxing Conscience*, 1999 Wisc. L. Rev. 939. *See also* Ch. III.D.1.

However, the Religious Freedom Restoration Act, discussed above, could be claimed to exempt taxpayers on account of disliked government spending.

d. *Exemptions, Charitable Deductions, and Free Speech of Religious Organizations*

After *Taxation with Representation* pointed out that non-religious charities could set up parallel organizations to lobby,[260] and *Citizens United* ruled that corporations can effectively spend in unlimited amounts on political campaigns,[261] religious organizations may feel that they are left almost alone in being excluded from the political arena through exercise of free speech rights, at least insofar as their tax treatment is concerned.[262] If a church engages in political campaigning, it runs the serious risk of losing not only its federal income tax exemption (which might not be a mortal blow in light of the potential to zero out net taxable income), but more importantly its ability to receive deductible charitable contributions.[263]

So far the Court has not addressed this issue in the context of churches. The Court's basic approach to denial of tax benefits for exercising free speech is stated in *Cammarano*, ruling that the government is not required to subsidize speech, in the business context.[264] *Regan v. Taxation with Representation* applied the same concept to section 501(c)(3) organizations, but can be distinguished because that organization could form a lobbying arm that was exempt under section 501(c)(4).[265] Indeed, the Court has tended to limit the *Regan* approach to conditioned federal spending to situations in which the spending recipient had an alternative way to engage in speech.[266] The restrictions on church speech might be defended on the ground that churches are not constitutionally entitled to any exemption and so a conditioned exemption is permissible under the "greater

---

[260] Regan v. Taxation with Representation, 461 U.S. 540 (1983).

[261] Citizens United v. FEC, 558 U.S. 310 (2010) ("The rule that political speech cannot be limited based on a speaker's wealth is a necessary consequence of the premise that the First Amendment generally prohibits the suppression of political speech based on the speaker's identity.").

[262] Crimm and Winer, at 9. Numerous articles have raised similar possibilities. *See, e.g.*, Miriam Galston, *When Statutory Regimes Collide: Will Citizens United and Wisconsin Right to Life Make Federal Tax Regulation of Campaign Activity Unconstitutional?*, 13 U. Pa. J. Const. L. 867 (2010-2011).

[263] IRS publication "Election Year Activities and the Prohibition on Political Campaign Intervention for Section 501(c)(3) Organizations" (FS-2006-17, February 2006) reminds tax-exempt entities not to engage in any issue advocacy that "functions as political campaign intervention." The document states in part, "Even if a statement does not expressly tell an audience to vote for or against a specific candidate, an organization delivering the statement is at risk of violating the political campaign intervention prohibition if there is any message favoring or opposing a candidate."

[264] Cammarano v. United States, 358 U.S. 498 (1959). *See* Ch. VIII.d.2.a and b.

[265] Regan v. Taxation with Representation, 461 U.S. 540 (1983), *discussed in* Ch. VIII.d.2.a.

[266] *See, e.g.*, FCC v. League of Women Voters, 468 U.S. 364, 407 (1984).

powers doctrine," but that doctrine may have been abandoned by the Court, at least in the free speech area.[267]

Speiser v. Randall ruled unconstitutional California's precondition to a property tax exemption for veterans, which required the owner to swear he did not advocate the forcible overthrow of the government.[268] *Rust v. Sullivan* ruled that refusing to fund clinics that counseled abortion was a permitted spending choice, akin to the greater powers doctrine reasoning.[269] But a more recent decision ruled that Congress could not condition funding of legal services programs on a limitation of the way the clinics represented their clients, drawing a distinction between government speech that may be restricted and private speech.[270]

While the exact path through these and other authorities that the Court might follow is unknown, it is known that free speech and free exercise rights are at the forefront of the liberties the Court currently is interested in protecting, and that political activities of churches have been at the forefront of national politics since at least the 1980s. The combination of these factors with the increasingly unique tax limitations on churches and campaigning likely will produce some movement in the law.

e. *Melding Establishment and Free Exercise*

The 5:4 opinion of the Court in *Espinoza* in 2020 ruled that the Free Exercise Clause trumps Establishment Clause concerns of the state; that the Montana Supreme Court's enforcement of the Montana Constitution's Establishment Clause amounted to a facial discrimination against persons on account of someone's religious status; that a person cannot be denied public benefits (the tax credits) on account of someone's religious status; and that the applicable strict scrutiny was not satisfied by a state desire to protect public schools.[271] So the Montana Supreme Court's application of the Montana Constitution's version of the Establishment Clause violated the federal Free Exercise Clause, although the Court did not entirely strike down the Montana Constitutional provision.

The reasoning of the opinion will make it difficult to apply the federal Establishment Clause or pursue state law Establishment Clause concerns, because a state's attempts to avoid funding religion (i.e., establishing religion) frequently will also appear to negatively impact some person who is pursuing what the person views as the free exercise of religion.[272]

---

[267] 44 Liquormart, Inc. v. Rhode Island, 517 U.S. 484 (1996). *See* Brooks R. Fudenberg, *Unconstitutional Conditions and Greater Powers: A Separability Approach*, 43 UCLA L. Rev. 371 (1995-1996).

[268] Speiser v. Randall, 357 U.S. 513 (1958) (the case was decided under the Due Process Clause of the Fourteenth Amendment; the facts were particularly egregious; the plaintiff was an honorably discharged World War II veteran who was denied a veteran's exemption).

[269] Rust v. Sullivan, 500 U.S. 173 (1991).

[270] Legal Servs. Corp. v. Velazquez, 531 U.S. 533 (2001).

[271] Espinoza v. Mont. Dep't of Revenue, 140 S. Ct. 2246 (2020).

[272] *See* Cummings, *Churches, Obamacare, Indians and Taxes*, __ Tax Notes __ (2021).

E. Administrative Authority and Enforcement

1. *General*

A variety of miscellaneous constitutional issues (in addition to those discussed above in Chapter V.D.3.b in connection with due process) have arisen with respect to the authority and enforcement activities of the IRS:

- The Necessary and Proper Clause justifies ancillary administrative powers needed to collect the revenue: "In accord with this settled judicial construction the legislation of Congress from the beginning, not only as to tariff but as to internal revenue, taxation and other subjects, has proceeded on the conception that it was within the competency of Congress, when legislating as to matters exclusively within its control, to impose appropriate obligations and sanction their enforcement by reasonable money penalties, giving to executive officers the power to enforce such penalties without the necessity of invoking the judicial power."[273]
- A debtor could be required to withhold tax owed by the creditor on interest paid.[274]
- The Seventh Amendment, which requires that in suits at common law the right to a jury trial shall be preserved, and the Sixth Amendment, which affirms various procedural rights in the criminal process, are not violated when Congress delegates to the IRS the power to assess tax and impose penalties.[275] See Chapter VIII.E.2 below for discussion of *Chevron* and delegation.
- The federal government (and its earlier Legal Tender Act requiring federal currency to be accepted in payment of debt) cannot require a state to collect its taxes in other than gold, because a tax is not a debt.[276] On the federal tax side, many tax resisters have tried to argue that Federal Reserve Notes are

---

[273] Oceanic Steam Navigation Co. v. Stranahan, 214 U.S. 320, 339 (1909).

[274] United States v. R.R. Co., 84 U.S. 322, 326-327 (1873) (however, this opinion contained a strident objection to one person paying the taxes of another: "A tax is understood to be a charge, a pecuniary burden, for the support of government. Of all burdens imposed upon mankind that of grinding taxation is the most cruel. It is not taxation that government should take from one the profits and gains of another. That is taxation which compels one to pay for the support of the government from his own gains and of his own property.").

[275] Atlas Roofing Co. v. Occupational Safety & Health Review Comm'n, 430 U.S. 442, 450-451 (1977), *citing*, Phillips v. Commissioner, 283 U.S. 589, 599-600 (1931); Murray's Lessee v. Hoboken Land & Improv. Co., 59 U.S. 272, 284 (1856); Helvering v. Mitchell, 303 U.S. 391 (1938). *See also* Brushaber v. Union Pacific R. Co., 240 U.S. 1, 26 (1916) (dismissing the delegation argument out of hand).

[276] Lane County v. Oregon, 74 U.S. 71 (1869).

not taxable, or are not taxable at face value; the Court has never addressed these claims, but lower courts have rejected them.[277]

- The Fifth Amendment is not violated either as to the husband or the wife when the IRS sells a home in which both have an ownership interest but only the husband has a tax liability, so long as the financial interest of the wife is protected from the tax lien.[278]
- A state quiet title action brought by the federal taxpayer against the buyer of his property from the IRS after a collection proceeding could be removed to federal court by the buyer to pursue a constitutional or federal statutory issue.[279]
- The Court ruled unconstitutional under the Constitution of the Philippines the Chinese Bookkeeping Act by which the Philippines forbade Chinese merchants from keeping a set of books in Chinese.[280]
- The government can require extensive information from the taxpayer to prevent taxpayers from committing fraud in understating their tax liability.[281]
- Congress can delegate the setting of tariffs to the President and so long as some hearing is allowed the rate setting is final.[282]

2. Chevron *and Delegation of Authority*

The Constitution grants the taxing power to Congress and not to the IRS or Treasury.[283] Although the power of Congress to authorize various collection and administrative actions by the IRS under the Necessary and Proper Clause has always been recognized,[284] taxpayers have asserted the so called "nondelegation doctrine" to question delegation by Congress to an agency of interpretive powers

---

[277] *But see* Cheek v. United States, 498 U.S. 192 n. 7 (1991) (the 7th Circuit had listed as one of its automatically rejected taxpayer complaints the belief that Federal Reserve Notes do not constitute cash or income). *See also* Pearson v. McGraw, 308 U.S. 313 (1939) (an unusual opinion upholding the power of a state to impose an inheritance tax on a gift in contemplation of death, which the decedent accomplished by having an out of state trustee hold Federal Reserve Notes and then buy stock with the notes; the state supreme court had thought the out of state holding of the chattels (*i.e.*, the currency) precluded the state's taxation under the Fourteenth Amendment, but the Court ruled that the multiple steps were one integrated transaction engaged in by a state resident and could be taxed).

[278] United States v. Rogers, 461 U.S. 677 (1983).

[279] Grable & Sons Metal Prods. v. Darue Eng'g & Mfg., 545 U.S. 308 (2005).

[280] Yu Cong Eng v. Trinidad, 271 U.S. 500 (1926).

[281] United States v. Singer, 82 U.S. 111 (1872) (required information about still capacity; no limit on excise tax but geographical uniformity).

[282] Norwegian Nitrogen Products Co. v. United States, 288 U.S. 294 (1933). *See also* Auffmordt v. Hedden, 137 U.S. 310 (1890) (determination of dutiable value final).

[283] *See generally* JASPER L. CUMMINGS, JR., THE SUPREME COURT'S FEDERAL TAX JURISPRUDENCE Ch. VI.D (2d ed. 2016) [hereinafter CUMMINGS].

[284] *See* Ch. III.E.4.a.

that border on law making.[285] When applied to attack a delegation of the legislative power to the executive, the nondelegation doctrine has been found by the Court to apply only twice, and in neither case to a tax.[286] The delegation issue not only involves the separation of powers between Congress and the Treasury but also between the Treasury and the courts. Most recently the Supreme Court has reasserted the historic role of the courts dating back to *Marbury v. Madison* to interpret federal statutes to achieve Congress' intent.[287] That is a way around ruling that a delegation is improper.[288]

Although the Court has invalidated numerous Treasury tax regulations,[289] it has done so because it found the regulations not to measure up to the statute passed by Congress, not because Treasury was exercising a power to make law granted by Congress in violation of the Constitution.[290] Congress does have considerable flexibility to authorize administrative rule-making. This flexibility is not lessened by the fact that taxes are involved: for example, the Court has ruled that the Origination Clause does not bear on Congress' ability to delegate certain decision making concerning taxes,[291] and the Court recently referred to the nondelegation doctrine in stating that the standard for testing Treasury reg-

---

[285] *Cf.* concurrence of Justice Rehnquist in Indus. Union Dep't, AFL-CIO v. API, 448 U.S. 607, 686 (1980) (arguing that the nondelegation doctrine should not fall into disuse as had substantive due process and restrictive interpretation of the Commerce Clause).

[286] *See* Whitman v. Am. Trucking Ass'ns, 531 U.S. 457, 474 (2001) ("In the history of the Court we have found the requisite 'intelligible principle' lacking in only two statutes, one of which provided literally no guidance for the exercise of discretion, and the other of which conferred authority to regulate the entire economy on the basis of no more precise a standard than stimulating the economy by assuring 'fair competition.' *See* Panama Refining Co. v. Ryan, 293 U.S. 388 (1935); A. L. A. Schechter Poultry Corp. v. United States, 295 U.S. 495 (1935)."). The "intelligible principle" that Congress must specify to guide administrative action was found to exist and the principle was articulated in a tax case, J. W. Hampton, Jr. & Co. v. United States, 276 U.S. 394, 409 (1928). *See also* Federal Energy Administration v. Algonquin SNG, Inc., 426 U.S. 548 (1976) (federal import fee set by the President was within scope of congressional authorization).

[287] *See* United States v. Home Concrete & Supply, LLC, 566 U.S. 478 (2012) (the agency is authorized to trump a court interpretation only if there is a gap in the statute as opposed to a facial ambiguity that can be resolved by standard statutory interpretation, according to plurality opinion).

[288] *See* Gundy v. United States, 139 S. Ct. 2116 (2019) (narrowly upholding delegation in non tax case, but dissent forecast heavy push back against delegation suggesting that agencies can only "fill up details." *See* Cummings, *What Is Anti-Deference Really About?* 164 Tax Notes 2075 (Sept. 23, 2019).

[289] *See generally* Cummings, at 343.

[290] *See generally* Thomas W. Merrill, *Rethinking Article I, Section I: From Nondelegation to Exclusive Delegation*, 104 Col. L. Rev. 2097, 2103 (2004) [hereinafter Merrill] (confirming that essentially no federal actions have been stricken in recent decades based on improper delegation; "The only arguable imprint of the nondelegation doctrine in recent years has been as a canon of interpretation supporting narrow constructions of statutes so as to 'avoid' the constitutional question of excessive delegation.").

[291] Skinner v. Mid-America Pipeline Co., 490 U.S. 212 (1989) (this decision refused to apply a stricter nondelegation doctrine to tax, although it declined to decide whether the user fee at issue was a tax).

ulations was not different from that applied to other agencies' regulations.[292] Congress exercised this flexibility generally in section 7805(a), which authorizes the Secretary to prescribe all needful rules and regulations for the enforcement of Title 26, including all rules and regulations as may be necessary by reason of any alteration of law in relation to internal revenue.

Now Treasury Regulations and other regulations appear to be even less likely to be rejected by the Court due to the rise of the *Chevron* Doctrine, giving substantial deference to regulations so long as (a) Congress has granted the agency discretion, and (b) the agency's exercise of that discretion is not arbitrary or capricious in substance, or manifestly contrary to the statute.[293] However, the Court has begun to carve back *Chevron* by enforcement of a variety of procedural limits on agency rule making.[294]

The Court's decisions uphold administrative rule-making for tax in a variety of settings:

- The Court ruled that while Congress could not delegate its legislative authority it could declare the rule (sometimes called an intelligible principle) by which an administrative agency could fix a customs duty.[295]
- The Court ruled that Congress could delegate to the administration the definition of what acts violated a stamp tax.[296]
- *Helvering v. National Grocery Co.* ruled that the accumulated earnings tax standard was not too vague to pass due process muster; it is not improper delegation to authorize the Commissioner to find facts.[297]

---

[292] Mayo Found. for Med. Educ. & Research v. United States, 562 U.S. 44 (2011).

[293] Chevron, U.S.A., Inc. v. NRDC, Inc., 467 U.S. 837 (1984); Mayo Found. for Med. Educ. & Research v. United States, 562 U.S. 44 (2011). *See generally* Cummings, at ch. VI.D. *See also* Judulang v. Holder, 565 U.S. 42 n. 7 (2011) (explaining that the Administrative Procedure Act standard, which is virtually identical to the second prong of the *Chevron* test, is more appropriate in cases where the agency was not attempting to interpret a statute).

[294] *See* Kisor v. Wilkie, 139 S. Ct. 2400 (2019).

[295] J. W. Hampton, Jr. & Co. v. United States, 276 U.S. 394 (1928) (rejected challenge to a provision of the tariff laws directing the President to determine which imports should be subjected to a stated amount of tariff, and giving reasonably specific guidelines to control his determinations). *But see* Clinton v. City of N.Y., 524 U.S. 417 n. 39 (1998) (which suggests that *Hampton* might be limited to issues related to foreign affairs). *See also* Touby v. United States, 500 U.S. 160, 165 (1991) (". . . the nondelegation doctrine does not prevent Congress from seeking assistance, within proper limits, from its coordinate Branches. Thus, Congress does not violate the Constitution merely because it legislates in broad terms, leaving a certain degree of discretion to executive or judicial actors. So long as Congress 'lay[s] down by legislative act an intelligible principle to which the person or body authorized to [act] is directed to conform, such legislative action is not a forbidden delegation of legislative power.'" [citing *Hampton*]); Whitman v. Am. Trucking Ass'ns, 531 U.S. 457 (2001) (affirming that *Hampton* controls).

[296] *In re* Kollock, 165 U.S. 526 (1897). However, in dissent Justices point to this case to prove that delegation is only for "filling up the details." Gundy v. United States, 139 S. Ct. 2116 (2019).

[297] Helvering v. National Grocery Co., 304 U.S. 282 (1938).

- The delegation to the President to determine when a tariff could be eliminated based on a foreign bounty was not unconstitutional.[298]
- The standard for delegation of setting fees and setting taxes is the same.[299] Authorizing the legislature of Philippines to enact tax laws did not violate the nondelegation doctrine.[300]

The intersection of the nondelegation doctrine and deference to Treasury regulations can be a confusing one. As Thomas Merrill has pointed out:

> Thus, *Chevron* and the nondelegation doctrine, if not inconsistent, are at the very least pointed in opposite directions when it comes to determining the judicial response to discretionary agency power.[301]

The practical effect of the *Chevron* Doctrine is to shift power away from the courts to the federal agencies to which Congress has given discretion. The *Chevron* decision was a victory for a Reagan administration regulation, but when presidents of a different party took office, some of the same Justices displayed less enthusiasm for deference.[302]

The *Mayo* opinion in 2011 cleared up a lingering hope that somehow tax regulations were "special" and not subject to the general *Chevron* jurisprudence, although the outcome is largely the same as keeping them "special." *Mayo* rejected a challenge to Treasury's 2004 regulation having the effect of treating a medical resident as an employee and not an exempt student for purposes of FICA taxation.[303] In doing so the Court made clear that the standard of deference to regulations announced in *Chevron* applied to this and most Treasury regulations, rather than a standard peculiar to tax regulations (known as the *National Muffler*

---

[298] Marshall Field & Co. v. Clark, 143 U.S. 649 (1892).

[299] Skinner v. Mid-America Pipeline Co., 490 U.S. 212 (1989). *See also* Federal Energy Administration v. Algonquin SNG, Inc., 426 U.S. 548 (1976) (Congress can delegate to administration power to vary taxes based on a standard).

[300] Cincinnati Soap Co. v. United States, 301 U.S. 308 (1937).

[301] Merrill, at 2172.

[302] *Chevron* itself was a pro-Reagan decision, although it appeared to come from the liberal wing of the Court. It was a unanimous decision of six justices: Stevens, Brennan, White, Powell, Blackmun and Burger. Rehnquist, Marshall and O'Connor did not participate. It rejected the complaint of an environmental interest group against the Reagan administration's narrowing of the scope of a pollution regulation between the time it was proposed by the Carter administration and its ultimate adoption. This explains why *Chevron* was originally satisfactory to the conservative wing of the Court (at that time mostly Justices Rehnquist, Powell and Burger). Since then the increasingly conservative Supreme Court has affirmed and expanded the reach of *Chevron* deference. Either this is attributable to a new found respect for Hamiltonian federalist power or (more likely) to an understanding that the two step *Chevron* test accords the Court sufficient leeway to do what it wants in most cases. *But see* United States v. Home Concrete & Supply, LLC, 566 U.S. 478 (2012) (Justices Roberts, Alito and Thomas would expand the ability of courts to say what the statute means, while Justices Ginsburg, Sotomayor and Kagan would expand the power of the agencies to say what the statute means).

[303] Mayo Found. for Med. Educ. & Research v. United States, 562 U.S. 44 (2011).

test[304]) or the lesser *Skidmore* deference accorded to what used to be called interpretive regulations (which was not even cited in the *Mayo* opinion).[305]

Mayo Clinic argued that its medical residents were not employees for FICA tax purpose, but rather were exempted students. Mayo's residents fit the definition of students, however Treasury regulations long had limited the exemption to an employment that was "incident to and for the purposes of pursuing a course of study." After the Eighth Circuit ruled in 1998 that medical students could not be eliminated automatically from the student category, Treasury revised the regulations to preclude a student working a normal work week of 40 hours from ever being treated as a student. The Court upheld the new regulation, reasoning that the statute was inherently ambiguous as applied to a full time employee who also was a full time student; due to that ambiguity the arbitrary or capricious standard applied, and choosing to treat full time work as work and not study is a reasonable choice for administrability that is supported by the fact that work and study are distinct in the vast majority of the cases.

In its most recent application of *Chevron* to a tax regulation the Court in *Home Concrete* rejected a Treasury regulation without discussing notice and hearing because the Court had 54 years earlier decided the meaning of the statute and had foreclosed the possibility that it was ambiguous.[306]

---

[304] National Muffler Dealers Ass'n, Inc. v. United States, 440 U.S. 472 (1979).

[305] Skidmore v. Swift & Co., 323 U.S. 134 (1944). The *Mayo* opinion does not contain the terms "legislative regulation" or "interpretive regulation" and does not refer to *Skidmore*, which it previously has cited as establishing a lower level of deference for interpretive regulations. Up until *Chevron*, and reinterpretations of *Chevron* in hindsight, it had been thought that "legislative regulations" (like the consolidated return regulations) are entitled to extra deference, whereas mere "interpretive regulations," (in the case of Treasury, thought to be regulations issued under section 7805(a)) are not entitled to any special deference, on the theory that courts are as able to discern the proper interpretation of a statute as the agency. This theory was out of date even before *Chevron*, because *National Muffler* accorded substantial deference to Treasury's regulation issued under section 7805. We know that the *Mayo* Court did not concern itself with such distinctions because it began the opinion by applying *Chevron* and assessing the statute's ambiguity under the first step of the *Chevron* analysis, without investigating or defending its applicability. If the Court had found the statute not to be ambiguous, it would have announced its clear meaning and either affirmed or rejected the regulation. Therefore, the interpretive versus legislative distinction in effect has been subsumed in the unambiguous versus ambiguous distinction. For tax regulations this means that a regulation can be afforded *Chevron* deference whether it is issued under a specific grant of authority like section 1502 or under the more general grant of authority in section 7805. The finding of ambiguity depends on discerning the difference between so called "gap filling" as contrasted with interpretation of words of the statute. This choice is rarely as clear as *Mayo* suggests. It reflects one of the two giant loopholes the Supreme Court has left for itself in applying the *Chevron* Doctrine: the flexibility to announce that the statute is clear enough to the Court, and the flexibility to announce that the regulatory choice is reasonable enough to the Court.

[306] United States v. Home Concrete & Supply, LLC, 566 U.S. 478 (2012). Justices Breyer, Roberts, Alito and Thomas asserted a two stage determination of ambiguity: facial ambiguity versus ultimate ambiguity. This approach allows a court to say what a statute unambiguously means even though it might appear ambiguous on its face, which the statute at issue clearly did. In contrast the liberal dissenting Justices plus Justice Kennedy desired a greater zone of power for the agencies, and thus were unwilling to admit that an ambiguous statute could have one court determined meaning.

3. *Other Separation of Powers Issues*

a. *Joint Committee*

Section 6405 forbids any refund of tax in excess of $2,000,000 until 30 days after the Treasury Department has reported to the Joint Committee on Taxation the name of the taxpayer, the amount of the refund, and provided a summary of the facts and the decision on the refund. The Committee does not have power to prevent the refund, but the practice of the IRS is to treat the Joint Committee's agreement as essential to issuing the refund.[307] This procedure places the legislative branch of government in the business of executing the tax laws and raises separation of powers issues that appear to have been ignored.

Congress created the Joint Committee in 1926 and gave it the power to review large refunds in 1928.[308] The threshold for review has been raised over the years. In 1933 Congress attached to an act appropriating funds for tax refunds a requirement that large refunds not be made without Joint Committee approval. President Hoover vetoed the act. The Attorney General wrote an explanation to Congress asserting that the approval procedure interfered with the executive powers and conflicted with the constitutional separation of powers.[309] Congress failed to override the veto.[310] Thus the Joint Committee review is a constitutional "report and wait" provision, at least nominally.[311] Presumably Congress has never pressed the issue again because the IRS conforms to its wishes in practice; and presumably JCT staff attorneys use prudence in exercising their de facto power. Moreover, the IRS is sufficiently beholding to Congress that it would make no sense for the IRS to pick a fight with the Joint Committee over a refund issue.

The continuing validity of the Attorney General's opinion is reflected in *INS v. Chadha*.[312] The Court found unconstitutional a statute that allowed one house of Congress to veto a decision of the Attorney General on deportation. The limitation of the Joint Committee's review power also reflects the anti-aggrandizement principle that Congress may inform itself about the execution of the laws it makes but it may not itself execute them.[313]

---

307 I.R.M. 8.7.9.5.6 (closing agreement may not be executed until the review clears the Joint Committee).

308 *See* Donald L. Korb, Jeffrey J. Erney and Gregory J. Gawlik, *Rethinking Refund Review: Understanding the Joint Committee on Taxation*, 4 Corp. Bus. Tax'n Monthly 3, 3-4 (2002).

309 76 Cong. Rec. 2445-2449 (Jan. 24, 1933) (the veto message, the Attorney General's opinion and the override vote); 37 Ops. of the Attorney General 56 (1933). *See, e.g.*, Myers v. United States, 272 U.S. 52, 116 (1926) ("From this division on principle, the reasonable construction of the Constitution must be that the branches should be kept separate in all cases in which they were not expressly blended, and the Constitution should be expounded to blend them no more than it affirmatively requires.").

310 76 Cong. Rec. 2445-2449 (Jan. 24, 1933); 37 Ops. of the Attorney General 56 (1933).

311 *See* Buckley v. Valeo, 424 U.S. 1, 137-38 (1976).

312 INS v. Chadha, 462 U.S. 919 (1983). *But see* Note, *Chadha and the Nondelegation Doctrine: Defining the Restricted Legislative Veto*, 94 Yale L. J. 1493 (1985) (arguing that the proliferation of standardless delegations of power to the executive could be offset by legislative vetoes).

313 *See* Bowsher v. Synar, 478 U.S. 714, 733-34 (1986).

b. *Tax Court*

Why can Congress authorize a legislative court, here the United States Tax Court, which is not created under the judicial power of Article III, to supervise assessments proposed by the IRS? The best answers are that the taxpayer voluntarily chooses review by the Tax Court, and that no pre-assessment review need be provided.[314] The practical answer is that the Court has implicitly approved the status of the Tax Court as a legislative court in multiple decisions.[315]

Congress created the United States Tax Court (the Board of Tax Appeals) initially as an executive agency,[316] and later denominated it an Article I court, meaning it was in the legislative branch under Article I rather than Article III, which generally governs federal courts of law.[317] This odd change reflects a combination of difficulties facing Congress: (1) the unseemliness of the executive branch judging its own tax assessment process, (2) reluctance to expand the pool of Article III judges, and (3) concern about the possible exclusion of non-attorney tax professionals from representing taxpayers in the Tax Court.[318] The possibility for federal courts outside of Article III to exercise judicial powers is explained in part by the fact that the judicial power is not exclusively lodged in Article III of the Constitution,[319] and in part by the doctrine that "public rights" can be determined by executive (and also legislative) agencies.[320]

However, the exercise of judicial functions outside of an Article III court can cause confusion about the application to the Tax Court of various constitutional principles and statutes that govern "courts of law." There is little consistency in the decisions evaluating these issues. For example, Article II, section 2, clause 2 of the Constitution authorizes Congress to invest the appointment of inferior

---

[314] *See* John C. Calhoun, *The New Tax Court: The Status and the Rules*, 44 U. Cin. L. Rev. 207, 211 (1975) (stating that the constitutionality of the Article 1 court was settled, citing Williams v. United States, 289 U.S. 553, 565 (1933) (Claims Court upheld as a legislative court, analogous to a territorial court, but was not identified as an Article 1 court). *See also* Freytag v. Commissioner, 501 U.S. 868 (1991) (assuming without deciding that the Tax Court properly exercises judicial power in the legislative branch).

[315] *See, e.g.*, Weiss v. United States, 510 U.S. 163 (1994) (analogizing Court of Military Appeals judges); Hinck v. United States, 550 U.S. 501 (2007) (Tax Court jurisdiction to abate interest); Ballard v. Commissioner, 544 U.S. 40 (2005) (special trial judges considered). *Cf.* Springer v. Government of the Philippine Islands, 277 U.S. 189, 211 (1928) (Holmes, J., dissenting) ("Congress long ago established the Smithsonian Institution, to question which would be to lay hands on the Ark of the Covenant.").

[316] As part of an executive agency, the Board of Tax Appeals also was not a court. Old Colony Trust Co. v. Commissioner, 279 U.S. 716, 725 (1929).

[317] The concurrence of Justice Scalia in Freytag v. Commissioner, 501 U.S. 868 (1991) recounts the history of the Tax Court. *See also* Cummings, at 116-118.

[318] *See generally*, Harold Dubroff, *The United States Tax Court: An Historical Analysis*, 41 Alb. L. Rev. 1 (1977).

[319] *See* Williams v. United States, 289 U.S. 553, 565 (1933); Freytag v. Commissioner, 501 U.S. 868, 889 (1991).

[320] 501 U.S. at 910. As to the public rights doctrine generally, *see* Stern v. Marshall, 564 U.S. 462 (2011). *See generally*, Harold Dubroff, *Federal Taxation*, 1973 Annual Survey of American Law 265, 272-285.

officers in the President, the courts or heads of departments. The Court ruled that special trial judges in the Tax Court are such inferior officers, and the Tax Court is a court (of law) for this purpose, and not a department, even though it is established under Article I rather than Article III. Therefore Congress could properly authorize the Chief Judge of the Tax Court to appoint the special trial judges.[321]

There has been some confusion about whether the Tax Court has jurisdiction to rule on constitutional issues; of course it does. *Dobson* stated that the finding of facts by the Tax Court, which in those days the statute granted the Tax Court almost absolute authority to determine, did not preclude the Supreme Court from deciding on appeal constitutional tax issues involving facts, implying that the Tax Court had initially decided the issue.[322] However, the Court later stated that

> On the other hand, constitutional adjudication, . . . are outside the special province of the Tax Court. See Paul, Dobson v. Commissioner: the Strange Ways of Law and Fact (1944) 57 Harv. L. Rev. 753, 847-48.[323]

But all Paul said was that the ultimate resolution of constitutional issues is reserved to the Supreme Court. Many important Supreme Court constitutional tax decisions came up from the Tax Court, which ruled on the constitutional issues.[324]

A separate constitutional issue concerning the Tax Court is the absence of a jury trial, which could raise Seventh Amendment issues. The Court has not directly ruled on this issue but has explained in a case involving an analogous tribunal that Congress can create new rights and condition them on use of a tribunal that does not employ a jury.[325]

---

[321] Freytag v. Commissioner, 501 U.S. 868 (1991). *See also* Ballard v. Commissioner, 544 U.S. 40 (2005) (involving special trial judges but no colorable constitutional issue; due process was argued but not decided). For an extended analysis of the Appointments Clause as it related to a proposal to have an IRS Oversight Board appoint the IRS Commissioner, *see* Staff of the Joint Committee on Taxation, Description and Analysis of Proposals Relating to the Recommendations of the National Commission on Restructuring the Internal Revenue Service 35-46 (1998), JCS-1-98.

[322] Dobson v. Commissioner, 320 U.S. 489 (1943). *Dobson* peripherally implicates another issue not discussed in the decision: to what extent can the finding of a fact by an administrative agency preclude the determination of a constitutional issue. *See* St. Joseph Stock Yards Co. v. United States, 298 U.S. 38 (1936) (indicating that it cannot).

[323] Trust of Bingham v. Commissioner, 325 U.S. 365, 381 (1945).

[324] *See, e.g.*, Hernandez v. Commissioner, 490 U.S. 680 (1989).

[325] Atlas Roofing Co. v. Occupational Safety & Health Review Comm'n, 430 U.S. 442 (1977). *Cf.* Phillips v. Commissioner, 283 U.S. 589 (1931) (appeal from a Board of Tax Appeals ruling, rejecting a Seventh Amendment claim to lack of jury trial because the Seventh Amendment does not guarantee a right to jury trial); Wickwire v. Reinecke, 275 U.S. 101 (1927) (involving a suit for refund in district court and stating that the Seventh Amendment was not the source of the right to protest a tax).

c. *Public Policy Doctrine*

The IRS and the courts have taken it upon themselves to apply an uncodified public policy doctrine to deny the application of the code according to its terms, usually in cases of deductions or exemptions.[326] The most prominent and recent example is the denial of a tax exemption to Bob Jones University.[327] In these cases the Court may be said to infer a congressional intent on the basis of very slight to nonexistent textual support. Where the support is nonexistent the rulings might be questioned on separation of powers grounds. Although that does not seem to have been seriously considered by the Court, the intermittent nature of these rulings suggests the uncertainty of the Court.[328]

It should be obvious that whatever the scope of public policy, it does not encompass relieving individuals from hardship. The Court has stated that when Congress has made its intention clear in the statute "the courts are not at liberty to modify the act by construction in order to avoid special hardship."[329]

d. *Executive, Legislative, and Judicial Responsibility*

The Court can avoid requiring the IRS to enforce a tax law by citing separation of powers considerations. For example in *Allen v. Wright* the plaintiffs attempted to force the IRS to enforce its requirements that tax exempt schools not discriminate on the basis of race. The Court refused, stating that the Executive and not the Judicial Branch is charged by the Constitution with the duty to see that the laws are faithfully executed.[330]

The unwillingness of the Court to make "federal common law" is a feature of the separation of powers. The Court carried it to an extreme in *Rodriguez*, where the "doctrine" rejected was not actually federal common law.[331] Similarly, the current Court relies heavily on plain meaning to avoid unconstitutionally rewriting the tax laws, even when the meaning is not so plain.[332]

Although the Court has mostly trended to the plain meaning approach to tax statutes, it performed a major exception in interpreting the Affordable Care Act in *King v. Burwell* according to overall congressional intent, sort of the exception that proves the rule.[333]

---

[326] *See* Stephan (discussing prior Supreme Court decisions based on public policy doctrine, although the Court did not call it a "doctrine").

[327] Bob Jones Univ. v. United States, 461 U.S. 574 (1983).

[328] *See generally* Stephan.

[329] Lang v. Commissioner, 289 U.S. 109, 112 (1933). Of course, that statement leaves plenty of room for the courts to maneuver when the statute can be found to be ambiguous.

[330] Allen v. Wright, 468 U.S. 737 (1984).

[331] Rodriguez v. FDIC, 140 S. Ct. 713 (2020). *See* Cummings, *The Supreme Court's 2019 Term in Tax*, 168 TAX NOTES FEDERAL 2175 (Sept. 21, 2020).

[332] Wis. Cent. Ltd. v. United States, 138 S. Ct. 2067 (2018).

[333] King v. Burwell, 576 U.S. 473 (2015).

e. *Sovereign Immunity*

A plaintiff suing the United States or its agencies must find a waiver of the defense of sovereign immunity.[334] Sovereign immunity applies to both suits for money and for other remedies that would require the sovereign to do something.

The grants of jurisdictions to courts to hear certain types of disputes do not waive sovereign immunity, because they do not directly address suits against the government. Thus section 1340 grants jurisdiction for actions arising under the tax laws, but section 1346(a)(1) grants jurisdiction for the recovery of taxes erroneously collected, and is the relevant waiver of sovereign immunity;[335] also section 1491 grants a right of recovery in the Court of Federal Claims. Of course suits for refund are subject to procedural limits in section 7422. No waiver is needed to petition the Tax Court, but section 6512(b)(1) functions as a waiver of sovereign immunity in allowing the Tax Court to redetermine an overpayment.[336]

Waiver has more importance in the district court actions concerning taxation that do not seek refunds. Suits for declaratory or injunctive relief must rely for waiver of sovereign immunity on 5 U.S.C. section 702 of the APA,[337] when plaintiff claims that an agency or one of its officers or employees acted or failed to act in an official capacity or under color of legal authority with regard to an "agency action": an agency rule, order, license, sanction, relief, or the equivalent or denial thereof, or failure to act.[338] Most such suits seek declaratory judgments, but the DJA does not waive sovereign immunity; it only authorizes a type of remedy.[339] Other waivers of sovereign immunity exist for specialized tax issues.[340]

There are important limits on the APA waiver. First, it should not apply to a complaint about something Congress wrote into the code, without the intervention of agency action.[341] Second, it is limited to complaints about "agency action," which related to "rules" and "orders." Rules include all published IRS guidance such as Notices,[342] but should not include the audit and assessment process (which also is not an order or sanction as defined in the APA).[343] However, some opinions have ignored the definition of "agency action" in 5 U.S.C.

---

334 15A Moore's Federal Practice - Civil § 105.21 (2019).

335 *See* United States v. Williams, 514 U.S. 527 (1995) (third party holding property subject to lien for another person's taxes had "standing" to sue under section 1346).

336 *E.g.*, Borenstein v. Commissioner, 149 T.C. 263 (2017).

337 *See* Cohen v. United States, 650 F.3d 717 (D.C. Cir. 2011).

338 5 U.S.C. section 702, 551. *See* 15A Moore's Federal Practice - Civil § 105.45 (2019) (if Congress' action is solely at issue, there is no waiver; but there is authority for waiver for any non monetary claim against an agency, regardless of agency action).

339 *See* A.E. Finley & Assoc., Inc. v. United States, 898 F.2d 1165 (6th Cir. 1990).

340 *E.g.*, sections 7432 and 7433.

341 *See, e.g.*, Freedom from Religion Found., Inc. v. United States, 2012 U.S. Dist. LEXIS 89905 (W.D. Wisc. 2012) (Congress not IRS agency action denied housing exemption to non ministers, and so 5 U.S.C. section 702 did not waive sovereign immunity).

342 Cohen v. United States, 650 F.3d 717 (D.C. Cir. 2011).

343 *See* Mallas v. United States, 993 F.2d 1111 (4th Cir. 1993).

section 551 and applied the term in a generic sense. Agency action probably should not include a letter rulings, although there is little direct authority.[344]

F. Other Explicit Limits on the Subjects of Federal Taxation

Article III, section 1 of the Constitution states that the compensation of federal judges shall not be diminished during their time in office. The Supreme Court ruled in *Evans v. Gore* that the 1913 income tax could not be applied to a federal judge appointed in 1899.[345] The principle was limited to judges appointed prior to the adoption of the income tax.[346] It also was applied to federal judges appointed prior to the extension of social security to federal employees in 1983.[347] However, the social security ruling depended on the exemption for other federal employees; there being no exemption for the new medicare tax, it was applicable to all federal judges.[348] Thus currently all federal taxes that do not target federal judges can be applied to them during their tenure.

Article II, section 1 similarly states that the compensation of the President cannot be decreased, but that clause has not been litigated in the Supreme Court.

Periodically there is interest in the adoption of a balanced budget amendment to the Constitution, which could raise constitutional issues.[349]

G. Novelty

The novelty of a tax (or other law) should not itself be a ground of objection to its constitutionality.[350] Chief Justice Burger made this statement in a manner indicating it was a foregone conclusion in *Buckley v. Valeo*, in reference to the "novel" public financing of campaigns: "The uniqueness of the plan is not relevant, of course, to whether Congress has power to enact it."[351] He evidently thought no citation was needed. Similarly, the unique status of the District of Columbia neither prevented taxation of its domiciliaries nor required abnormal rules for determination of domicile in the District.[352] More recently Chief Justice Roberts agreed with this sentiment, stating that "there is a first time for

---

[344] *Cf.* Pierson v. United States, 428 F. Supp. 384 (D. Del. 1977) (ordered discovery against IRS in refund action of administrative files on revocation of taxpayer's letter ruling, and rejected IRS argument that APA did not allow review of that matter; not obvious why APA was relevant); Investment Annuity v. Blumenthal, 609 F.2d 1 (D.C. Cir. 1979), cert. denied, 446 U.S. 981 (1980) (plaintiff had standing but AIA prevented complaint about letter ruling plaintiff received).

[345] Evans v. Gore, 253 U.S. 245 (1920).

[346] O'Malley v. Woodrough, 307 U.S. 277 (1939). *See* Robert H. Jackson, The Struggle for Judicial Supremacy 244-247 (1941).

[347] United States v. Hatter, 532 U.S. 557 (2001).

[348] *Id.*

[349] *See* Congressional Research Service, A Balanced Budget Amendment: Background and Congressional Options, R41907, 2011 TNT 133-21 (July 8, 2011).

[350] Dissent of Chief Justice Burger in Buckley v. Valeo, 424 U.S. 1 (1976).

[351] *Id.* at 247.

[352] District of Columbia v. Murphy, 314 U.S. 441 (1941).

everything," while opining in dictum that there was not a first time for applying the Commerce Clause to control individual inactivity.[353]

Of course the singular nature of a government action that an injured citizen sees as abusive will inevitably be pointed out.[354]

---

[353] Nat'l Fed'n of Indep. Bus. v. Sebelius, 567 U.S. 519 (2012). ("At the very least, we should 'pause to consider the implications of the Government's arguments' when confronted with such new conceptions of federal power.").

[354] *See* dissent of Justice Field in Henderson's Distilled Spirits, 81 U.S. 28, 65 (1872) (". . . this singular and, I venture to say, unprecedented fact, in the history of judicial decisions in this country . . ." referring to forfeiture of good sold on account of improper act of seller).

Ch. IX. Constitutional Issues in State Tax

A. Rethink the Subject

1. *Needless Confusion*

Litigious state taxpayers routinely claim violations of the Constitution of the United States. State tax practitioners often say that any state tax dispute worth its salt has a federal constitutional issue. Therefore state tax controversies are on an entirely different footing than federal tax controversies, which seldom involve the Constitution (despite the eight chapters above).

And yet few provisions of the Constitution directly address the subject of state taxation; those that do are extremely vague or address subjects rarely of interest (*e.g.*, tonnage and exports). Nevertheless, railroads and other early multistate business litigants against state and local taxes routinely claimed protection under the Equal Protection, Due Process and Commerce Clauses, at a minimum, plus several other even less likely provisions. As a result, the Supreme Court has effectively made up the constitutional limits on state taxes in hundreds of opinions over two centuries. Anyone concerned about the Supreme Court being too activist might be troubled by its state tax opinions.

That over-abundance of Supreme Court opinions is dwarfed by the much larger set of state court opinions. But there are not many lower federal court opinions because state tax litigants usually could not get into lower federal courts and so most of the cases came up to the Supreme Court of the United States directly from state supreme courts.

It seems that every railroad, ship line, bus line, telegraph company and oil company disputed every state and local tax touching them in the post-Civil War period, through the middle of the 20th Century. They frequently lost, sometimes because state courts tended to be very protective of local revenues when attacked by nonresident nontaxpayers. And the state courts also may have been insensitive to federal constitutional limits on state taxation, particularly when the U.S. Supreme Court was making them up and changing them as it went along.

This combination of factors produced an amazing volume of Supreme Court opinions on state taxation, because up to 1988 the Supreme Court was obliged to hear appeals as of right from state supreme courts that upheld their state and local taxes against federal constitutional objections.[1] In addition state taxpayers were not precluded by statute from pursuing state tax claims in federal trial courts until 1937.[2] As a result of the appeal right and exercise of equity jurisdiction, many constitutional disputes over state tax laws were eligible for review by the Supreme Court and it decided hundreds of such cases. Not only are the rulings numerous, but the Court's opinions often spend a lot of words batting down spurious constitutional claims. The resulting welter of Supreme Court writings still did not make clear what the law was (or is).

This chapter continues the general approach of this book that the opinions that matter most on state tax constitutional issues are those of the Supreme Court, both for the usual reasons—they are authoritative and ubiquitous, and all lower courts must work from them—and because the Supreme Court has mostly made the law up in this field. That limitation makes it easier to attempt to restate the constitutional law of state taxation in hornbook fashion, because the numerous state court opinions can be ignored (a luxury not enjoyed by general state tax law treatises).

Also the hornbook approach does not try to wrestle a synthesis out of every set of opinions addressing a subject. Sometimes there is no synthesis. Sometimes a synthesis would be a guess or an argument. Instead, the aim is to report what the Supreme Court has held; a grouping of decisions does not always fit together as neatly as a law review article would hope to show. Sometimes this Chapter

---

[1] *See* Eugene Stern and Robert L. Gressman, Supreme Court Practice: Jurisdiction, Procedure, Arguing and Briefing Techniques, Forms, Statutes, Rules for Practice in the Supreme Court of the United States, sec. 3-4 (3d ed.) (for prior jurisdictional rule); 28 U.S.C. § 1257 now provides only certiorari jurisdiction to review state court rulings. In contrast, the United States had a right of appeal to the Supreme Court from a lower federal court ruling that a federal statute, including a tax provision was unconstitutional. Stern and Gressman, at sec. 2.5. The first case attacking a state tax on constitutional grounds proved the value of giving the losing taxpayer an absolute right to appeal to the Supreme Court, because the Maryland courts saw nothing wrong with taxing the Bank of the United States. McCulloch v. Maryland, 17 U.S. 316 (1819). The early jurisdictional statute provided for a writ of error when the state statute was upheld and a writ of certiorari when it was voided under the constitution. *See* Dahnke-Walker Milling Co. v. Bondurant, 257 U.S. 282 (1921).

[2] The Tax Injunction Act was adopted at 50 Stat. 738 (1937).

does attempt a synthesis, but not in all cases, else it would be the length of 200 law review articles.

The principal stumbling block, even with this constricted approach to constitutional state tax issues, is that the Court's views have shifted over time on several key issues, to a far greater degree than the Court's usual pace of departing from stare decisis. These shifts include (1) away from a formalistic refusal to allow any tax on "interstate commerce," which also meant deciding when interstate commerce "ended"; (2) away from the view that states could charge foreign corporations any amount for admission to doing business in the state; (3) away from finding indirect taxation of the federal and state governments through taxing private parties claiming intergovernmental immunity; (4) away from approving flat taxes on persons engaged in interstate commerce, such as flat vehicle taxes; and (5) the Court has adjusted its views on when imports and exports are deemed to be taxed.

As a result many of the Court's earlier opinions on state taxation are obsolete, making research in the area treacherous.[3] Many writers attempt to deal with the layers of precedent by recounting the history of every current holding, back through all of its predecessors. Although fascinating, that method can be an impediment to knowing what the law is.

Writers have mostly addressed state tax constitutional issues as issues of interstate commerce because the majority of the Supreme Court's state tax opinions have been sought by interstate businesses not wanting to pay taxes.[4] Also writers have tended to categorize the issues in terms of the common state taxes and the particular attacks on them.[5] Thomas M. Cooley popularized the notion in the 19th Century that constitutions exist to limit and not grant state powers, in taxation and otherwise.[6] His *Constitutional Limitations* treatise identified the two subjects to be protected by constitutions: persons and property. Cooley observed that the assumed territorial limits on taxation could be satisfied if either the person or the property were in the state, and identified the vexing ambiguity of locating personal property with its owner or where it was found.[7] However, increasingly state taxes were triggered by transactions rather than persons or property.

These differing approaches of commentators illustrate the difficulty of organizing the subject. State taxation is not mostly about the Commerce Clause. It should not be viewed as a scramble of states to escape many limitations. It may

---

[3] An interesting source for annotations explaining the history of the constitutional tax provisions is Constitution Annotated in the Library of Congress' online Constitution section. *See* also Walter Nagel and Timothy B. Dyk, Leading U.S. Supreme Court State Tax Cases (BNA 1995).

[4] *E.g.*, Paul J. Hartman, State Taxation of Interstate Commerce (1953).

[5] *E.g.*, Jerome R. Hellerstein, State and Local Taxation: Cases and Materials (1952) (see table of contents and introduction).

[6] Thomas M. Cooley, Treatise on the Constitutional Limitations Which Rest upon the Legislative Power of the States of the American Union (5th ed.).

[7] Thomas M. Cooley, Treatise on the Law of Taxation, including the Law of Local Assessments 56 (2d ed.).

be triggered by transactions, but the transactions do not pay tax, people and property do. Focusing on categories of tax types like gross receipts taxes and franchise taxes is the wrong focus, as those categories do not relate to persons, property and transactions or the underlying constitutional limitations.

The constitutional limits on state taxation should not be so hard to understand. And yet state tax experts tend to want to lead you through recitations of Supreme Court opinions from decades and sometimes centuries ago, and explain where the Court went wrong, and how this nuance means that, and what the law should be, as stated in some mid-level state appellate court. They also routinely criticize outmoded Supreme Court decisions that the Court has not overruled. And such information and views can be valuable.

However, this book is based on the premise that we should be able to know what the Supreme Court has said the constitutional rules are today for state taxation. Therefore this chapter only mentions Supreme Court opinions that the Court has not overruled and that are not clearly within the several swaths of decisions that are no longer viable; for example it ignores most of the cases addressing taxation of national banks and many of the early Commerce Clause rulings. Chapter II.C addresses the intergovernmental immunity decisions.

This book mentions many of the Court's older state tax rulings that are still viable, but which may not appear in the major treatises due to the way those books accreted their citations over relatively recent times. It leaves to the reader the fascinating project of reading the tea leaves and figuring out which way the Court might go based on concurrences and dissents. It eschews detailed analysis of the "reasoning" in newer opinions of the Court, which often obscures the holdings. In other words, this is a practitioner's hornbook chapter on state tax constitutional issues.

So the "subjects" of state taxation must be identified for purposes of organizing this chapter. The approach chosen here uses the inevitable basic moving parts of any such analysis but rearranges them as explained below. It does not attempt to do several tasks undertaken by treatises on state taxation. It does not explore the inner workings of various types of state taxes. It does not address procedural issues, except as they have constitutional relevance. It is not concerned with state constitutional or interpretational issues. It only addresses currently relevant federal constitutional issues in state taxation. Of course it treats local taxation as part of state taxation.

Finally, the proliferation of state tax constitutional rulings of the Supreme Court reflects more on the desire of mostly large corporations not to pay state tax than on the lawlessness of state legislators. Justice Frankfurter expressed this caution in an opinion reversing a state supreme court's ruling that its own state tax violated the federal constitution:

> Ambiguous intimations of general phrases in opinions torn from the significance of concrete circumstances, or even occasional deviations over a long course of years, not unnatural in view of the confusing complexities of tax problems, do not alter the limited nature of the function of this Court when state taxes come before it. At best, the responsibility for devising just and pro-

> ductive sources of revenue challenges the wit of legislators. Nothing can be less helpful than for courts to go beyond the extremely limited restrictions that the Constitution places upon the states and to inject themselves in a merely negative way into the delicate processes of fiscal policy-making. We must be on guard against imprisoning the taxing power of the states within formulas that are not compelled by the Constitution but merely represent judicial generalizations exceeding the concrete circumstances which they profess to summarize.[8]

Other Chapters of this book also address subjects addressed here that affect federal taxation, and will be cross referenced.

2. *Jurisdiction Versus Other Issues*

The Due Process Clause controls jurisdiction of both state courts and state tax collectors over persons and property. The Commerce Clause in effect controls state jurisdiction to tax some persons and property because it enforces a constitutional preclusion of state discrimination against interstate commerce. Discrimination against interstate commerce can look like a type of violation of the Equal Protection Clause and many opinions have addressed both claims as one. Therefore the Commerce Clause sits in both the discrimination zone (with the Equal Protection Clause and sometimes the Privileges and Immunities Clause) and the jurisdiction zone (with the Due Process Clause). That duality substantially contributes to confusion in writings on state taxation and even in the Court's opinions.

A solution to the confusion is to treat the Due Process Clause and the Commerce Clause as the only jurisdictional limits on state taxation, and to separately treat the Equal Protection Clause as one of a large group of what this Chapter calls "recurring issues," involving constitutional limitations that also may preclude state taxation of a particular subject that the state has jurisdiction to tax. The recurring issues are addressed separately below. They include some components of Due Process Clause and Commerce Clause issues, *e.g.*, what is commerce, to keep those peripheral issues out of the jurisdictional analysis towards the end of this Chapter. There the Chapter addresses jurisdiction to tax in various fact patterns, with emphasis on Due Process and then Commerce Clause limits on state taxing jurisdiction.

The Due Process Clause did not become applicable to the states until the adoption of the 14th Amendment in 1868. Earlier opinions addressing state jurisdiction to tax were based on the common law conception of taxing power, or upon the Commerce Clause, but commonly are cited as in the line of Due Process authorities.[9]

Most opinions discussing taxing jurisdiction use the term nexus. Nexus generally means no more than connection of some sort. It is the "sort" that is important, rather than the connection. The Supreme Court rarely used the term before using it in 1940 in a state tax opinion. The state imposed a special tax on foreign

---

[8] Wisconsin v. J. C. Penney Co., 311 U.S. 435 (1940).

[9] See concurrence of Justice Black in Central R. Co. v. Pennsylvania, 370 U.S. 607 (1962).

corporations when they paid dividends. The state supreme court thought that the out of state decision to, and actual payment of, dividends was a transaction that did not have a nexus to the taxing state. The Court reversed, finding that the foreign corporation was licensed to do business in the state, and already was subject to its general corporate income tax; the special income tax had as much nexus as the general tax because the state court had focused on the wrong subject of nexus.[10] The point here is that nexus is not a constitutional term but a shorthand sometimes used to describe taxing jurisdiction.

B. The Constitution's State Tax Rules

The provisions of the Constitution that address state taxation, or that the Supreme Court has applied in considering state taxes, include primarily the following (but always open to expansion).

Article I, Section 8, clause 3 (Commerce Clause, Foreign Commerce Clause, Indian Commerce Clause):

> The Congress shall have Power To regulate Commerce with foreign Nations, and among the several States, and with the Indian Tribes; . . .

Article I, Section 8, clause 17:

> To exercise exclusive Legislation in all Cases whatsoever, over such District (not exceeding ten Miles square) as may, by Cession of particular States, and the Acceptance of Congress, become the Seat of the Government of the United States, and to exercise like Authority over all Places purchased by the Consent of the Legislature of the State in which the Same shall be, for the Erection of Forts, Magazines, Arsenals, dock-Yards, and other needful Buildings;

Article I, Section 8, clause 18 (Necessary and Proper Clause):

> To make all Laws which shall be necessary and proper for carrying into Execution the foregoing Powers, and all other Powers vested by this Constitution in the Government of the United States, or in any Department or Officer thereof.

Article I, Section 9, clause 5, the Export Clause, is considered to apply only to the federal government. Similarly, Article I, Section 9, clause 6, the Port Preference Clause, is considered to apply only to the federal government.[11]

Article I, Section 10, clause 1 (The Contracts Clause):

> No State shall enter into any Treaty, Alliance, or Confederation; grant Letters of Marque and Reprisal; coin Money; emit Bills of Credit; make any Thing but gold and silver Coin a Tender in Payment of Debts; pass any Bill of Attainder, ex post facto Law, or Law impairing the Obligation of Contracts, or grant any Title of Nobility.

Article I, Section 10, clause 2 (The Import-Export Clause):

---

[10] Wisconsin v. J. C. Penney Co., 311 U.S. 435 (1940).

[11] Alabama G. S. R. Co. v. United States, 340 U.S. 216 (1951); Morgan's S.S. Co. v. Louisiana Bd. of Health, 118 U.S. 455 (1886).

> No State shall, without the Consent of the Congress, lay any Imposts or Duties on Imports or Exports, except what may be absolutely necessary for executing it's inspection Laws: and the net Produce of all Duties and Imposts, laid by any State on Imports or Exports, shall be for the Use of the Treasury of the United States; and all such Laws shall be subject to the Revision and Controul of the Congress.

Article I, Section 10, clause 3 (The Tonnage Clause; the Compact Clause):

> No State shall, without the Consent of Congress, lay any Duty of Tonnage, keep Troops, or Ships of War in time of Peace, enter into any Agreement or Compact with another State, or with a foreign Power, or engage in War, unless actually invaded, or in such imminent Danger as will not admit of delay.

Article IV, Section 1 (The Full Faith and Credit Clause):

> Full Faith and Credit shall be given in each State to the public Acts, Records, and judicial Proceedings of every other State. And the Congress may by general Laws prescribe the Manner in which such Acts, Records and Proceedings shall be proved, and the Effect thereof.

Article IV, Section 2, clause 1 (The Privileges and Immunities Clause):

> The Citizens of each State shall be entitled to all Privileges and Immunities of Citizens in the several States.

Article IV, Section 3, clause 2 (The Property Clause):

> The Congress shall have Power to dispose of and make all needful Rules and Regulations respecting the Territory or other Property belonging to the United States; and nothing in this Constitution shall be so construed as to Prejudice any Claims of the United States, or of any particular State.

Article IV, Section 4 (the Guarantee Clause or Republican Form of Government Clause):

> The United States shall guarantee to every State in this Union a Republican Form of Government, and shall protect each of them against Invasion; and on Application of the Legislature, or of the Executive (when the Legislature cannot be convened) against domestic Violence.[12]

Article VI, Section 2 (the Supremacy Clause):

> This Constitution, and the Laws of the United States which shall be made in Pursuance thereof; and all Treaties made, or which shall be made, under the Authority of the United States, shall be the supreme Law of the Land; and the Judges in every State shall be bound thereby, any Thing in the Constitution or Laws of any State to the Contrary notwithstanding.

Amendment 1 (Free Speech, Freedom of Religion, Establishment of Religion):

> Congress shall make no law respecting an establishment of religion, or prohibiting the free exercise thereof; or abridging the freedom of speech, or of

[12] Pacific States Tel. & Tel. Co. v. Oregon, 223 U.S. 118 (1912).

> the press; or the right of the people peaceably to assemble, and to petition the Government for a redress of grievances.

Amendment 5 (Double Jeopardy Clause, Due Process Clause, Takings Clause):

> . . .; nor shall any person be subject for the same offence to be twice put in jeopardy of life or limb; nor shall be compelled in any criminal case to be a witness against himself, nor be deprived of life, liberty, or property, without due process of law; nor shall private property be taken for public use, without just compensation.

The 7th Amendment has no application to special assessments proceedings in court.[13]

Amendment 8 (Excessive Fines):

> Excessive bail shall not be required, nor excessive fines imposed, nor cruel and unusual punishments inflicted.[14]

Amendment 10 (Reserved Powers):

> The powers not delegated to the United States by the Constitution, nor prohibited by it to the States, are reserved to the States respectively, or to the people.

Amendment 11 (Suits against States):

> The Judicial power of the United States shall not be construed to extend to any suit in law or equity, commenced or prosecuted against one of the United States by Citizens of another State, or by Citizens or Subjects of any Foreign State.

Amendment 14, Section 1 (Citizenship Clause, Privileges and Immunities Clause, Due Process Clause, Equal Protection Clause):

> All persons born or naturalized in the United States, and subject to the jurisdiction thereof, are citizens of the United States and of the state wherein they reside. No State shall make or enforce any law which shall abridge the privileges or immunities of citizens of the United States; nor shall any State deprive any person of life, liberty, or property, without Due Process of law; nor deny to any person within its jurisdiction the equal protection of the laws.

Amendment 21, Section 2: (Interstate Liquor Sales):

> The transportation or importation into any State, Territory, or possession of the United States for delivery or use therein of intoxicating liquors, in violation of the laws thereof, is hereby prohibited.[15]

Amendment 24, Section 1: (Poll Taxes):

---

[13] St. Louis & Kansas City Land Co. v. Kansas City, 241 U.S. 419 (1916).

[14] Timbs v. Indiana, 139 S. Ct. 682 (2019) extended the Clause to the states. *See also* Pervear v. Commonwealth, 72 U.S. 475 (1867) (excessive fines limit applies only to federal government).

[15] United States v. State Tax Comm'n, 412 U.S. 363 (1973) (state could not tax liquor sales on federal property); State Bd. of Equalization v. Young's Market Co., 299 U.S. 59 (1936).

The right of citizens of the United States to vote in any primary or other election for President or Vice President, for electors for President or Vice President, or for Senator or Representative in Congress, shall not be denied or abridged by the United States or any state by reason of failure to pay any poll tax or other tax.

C. The States' Power to Tax and Its Limits

1. *The Power to Tax: Sovereignty*

The Constitution does not grant to the states the power to tax those subjects within their jurisdiction; that power is inherent in the states' powers as sovereigns; but because it is in effect granted by the people of the state it is subject to the specific limits of the Constitution because the power of the United States derives from all the people.[16] The taxing power of the states over subjects within their jurisdiction is as great as the taxing power of the federal government, subject to the particular limits on state taxation in the Constitution and on the preferred rights of the United States to tax when the two tax the same subjects.[17] The Tenth Amendment reserves to the states their taxing power.[18] The Court has looked to the tax attributes of the sovereign power of the states at the time of the adoption of the Constitution as the measure of the reserved power of states to tax.[19] The Constitution only restricts that power in certain ways, as addressed by this chapter.

The Constitution does not require the states to spend or tax. The United States offered to participate in funding unemployment compensation to encourage states to adopt unemployment compensation taxes. When the scheme was attacked, the Supreme Court rejected the argument that the United States had coerced the states to tax, violating their sovereignty.[20] In enforcing desegregation orders the Court has been hesitant to set local property tax rates and instead has fashioned indirect means of trying to insure that local tax collections will be sufficient to carry out its mandate.[21] When local bond issuing districts failed to levy taxes to pay their bonds, the Court refused to order the collection of taxes, saying it was a purely legislative function.[22] Taxes can be levied by the constitution of a state adopted by the people and not a legislative body.[23]

---

[16] McCulloch v. Maryland, 17 U.S. 316 (1819); State Tax Comm'n v. Aldrich, 316 U.S. 174 (1942). *See* Merrion v. Jicarilla Apache Tribe, 455 U.S. 130 (1982) (one of numerous Supreme Court opinions stating the inherent power of Indian tribe to tax).

[17] Lane County v. Or., 74 U.S. 71 (1869); R.R. Co. v. Peniston, 85 U.S. 5 (1873).

[18] Collector v. Day, 78 U.S. 113 (1870).

[19] Carmichael v. Southern Coal & Coke Co., 301 U.S. 495 (1937).

[20] Carmichael v. Southern Coal & Coke Co., 301 U.S. 495 (1937).

[21] Missouri v. Jenkins, 495 U.S. 33 (1990).

[22] Heine v. Levee Comm'rs, 86 U.S. 655 (1873). But sometimes the Court did order specific local officials to levy a tax that state law required them to levy. Graham v. Folsom, 200 U.S. 248 (1906).

[23] N. M. R. Co. v. Maguire, 87 U.S. 46 (1874).

The sovereign territory of a state includes its territorial waters.[24] Article I, Section 8, clause 17, of the Constitution states that the states may cede jurisdiction to the United States over lands for certain purposes. However, such cessation does not eliminate the state's taxing power on the lands.[25]

A state tax that violates the Constitution is not outside of its sovereign powers but is a taking without due process in violation of the 14th Amendment.[26]

See also Ch. II.B.2. for the states' power to tax.

2. *The Subjects and Sources of State Taxation*

a. *For Jurisdictional Purposes*

There is confusion about the subjects of taxes imposed by states. The Supreme Court often describes the subjects in business terms like sales, incomes, gross receipts, or the transactions that produced them (the transactional focus).[27] But there are only two sources of tax dollars, which can also be subjects of taxation: property taxed in rem and persons that can be compelled to pay a tax with respect to their property or their transactions. The state can collect a tax from property if it can levy on the property and take or sell it. The state can collect a tax from a person if it can find the person or its property and enforce in personam tax liability.

But the state cannot collect tax from a transaction by itself. That means that one of the three most common subjects of taxation is not a source of tax collections; however, transactions can give the state jurisdiction to extract tax from persons and property. The Court has struggled with the confusion of subjects, sources and jurisdiction, even saying that a tax on income of a nonresident was an in rem tax, but in that case the nonresident owed the tax on income and the sheriff tried to collect it from his property in the state, not from the income itself.[28] Nevertheless, the Court sometimes states that the taxing power applies to three subjects: property in the state, persons in the state, and activities or transactions in the state including the receipt of income.[29]

The tripartite reference to taxing jurisdiction can be traced back to Justice Jackson's opinion in *Miller Bros.* After identifying state taxation of property and persons, it said: "Certain activities or transactions carried on within a state, such as the use of property, may give jurisdiction to tax whomsoever engages therein, . . ."[30] Justice Jackson recognized that there are only two sources of tax—property and persons—and persons may be taxed on account of their property

[24] Alaska v. Arctic Maid, 366 U.S. 199 (1961).

[25] Silas Mason Co. v. Tax Com. of Washington, 302 U.S. 186 (1937).

[26] Frick v. Pennsylvania, 268 U.S. 473 (1925). The opinion referred to "power," but the principle probably is not limited to jurisdiction.

[27] South Dakota v. Wayfair, Inc., 138 S. Ct. 2080 (2018).

[28] Shaffer v. Carter, 252 U.S. 37 (1920).

[29] N.C. Dep't of Revenue v. Kimberley Rice Kaestner 1992 Family Trust, 139 S. Ct. 2213 (2019).

[30] Miller Bros. Co. v. Maryland, 347 U.S. 340 (1954).

and their transactions. The *Miller Bros.* opinion contains a remarkable compendium of nearly all of the Court's state tax ruling to that date.

In rem taxes imposed on property without regard to its owner are relatively rare today; usually the state looks for a person to tax with respect to its property, although it will seize the property and sell it as a second best collection method. The state may or may not have jurisdiction over the person but surely has jurisdiction over property in the state. Indeed much of the Court's confusing case law can be explained by its single minded search for property in the state, either actually or constructively in case of intangibles (usually deemed to travel with the owner).

So analyzing state taxes in terms of property, persons and transactions can seem like an iterative process that turns in on itself. Attempting to reduce the confusion, Chapter IX.E., F. and G. prioritize the person that is the taxpayer in all but in rem cases (when property is the subject of the tax). Then Chapter IX.F. and G. divide those persons into residents and non-residents of the taxing state because different rules of taxing jurisdiction can apply to each group. Then each of Chapters IX.F. and G. divides each group's taxes among the property or generic activities that are described in the state taxing statutes. And they address jurisdiction as to each in terms of Due Process Clause and Commerce Clause jurisdiction, where appropriate.

Therefore, for example, if the reader is concerned with a nonresident's duty to pay tax on an investment activity in the state, the reader can go to the discussion of investment activities of nonresidents and find the relevant Supreme Court rulings on taxing jurisdiction, both Due Process Clause and Commerce Clause. As noted, the recurring issues aside from taxing jurisdiction are addressed first, separately.

Finally, the discussion above assumes that the subject of taxation can be easily identified in all cases: it cannot. Normally the Court will accept the state's highest court's construction of the tax, but not its application of the Constitution.[31] Therefore, when constitutional questions are involved the Court reserves the power to determine what the state taxed and is not controlled by the state's characterization.[32] This issue was most fraught in the era when the Court thought states could not tax interstate commerce, and so it often found a tax claimed to be levied on property to be levied on a transaction in interstate commerce.[33] Alternately it found the interstate business item to have come to rest in the form of property that the state could tax. The Court came to reject many of its earlier distinctions based on the subject of the state tax.[34]

---

[31] Crew Levick Co. v. Pennsylvania, 245 U.S. 292 (1917).

[32] Wisconsin v. J. C. Penney Co., 311 U.S. 435 (1940); Senior v. Braden, 295 U.S. 422 (1935) (unfortunately the Court probably picked the wrong subject in this opinion, which treated an income tax on a trust interest as a property tax on the trust res).

[33] Railway Express Agency, Inc. v. Virginia, 347 U.S. 359 (1954).

[34] Okla. Tax Comm'n v. Jefferson Lines, 514 U.S. 175 (1995).

However, when high tension constitutional distinctions are not at issue the Court has usually respected the state court's characterization of a tax.[35] For example, even when the issue was potentially high tension the Court accepted a state court's determination that a franchise tax measured by a savings institution's U.S. bonds was not a tax on the property of the bonds but on the franchise.[36] That occurred in a sensitive area in which the Court for its own reasons was willing to decline to look through a franchise tax to the value taxed that includes federal bond interest.[37] Those rulings may have become obsolete when Congress tightened the rule in 31 U.S.C. § 3124, which excludes only nondiscriminatory franchise taxes from the prohibition on taxing federal debt.

Indeed, because license and franchise taxes often must be based on some underlying measurement, the Court seems to routinely defer to the state's characterization of the tax as a license tax.[38] The general approach is that a state can tax a corporate franchise it grants and the tax is on the corporation (or charged for the right) and not on property owned by the corporation, which may measure the tax.[39] For example it ruled that a franchise tax was not imposed indirectly on the nonresident shareholder's shares but on personal property in the state.[40] But the Court has been inconsistent in its view of corporate franchise taxes; it found a franchise excise tax that functioned like an income tax to fall on the interest from federal obligations, not the franchise.[41]

Similar confusion arose with respect to taxes on the value of capital stock, even when the trading price of the stock limited the value. Because the Pennsylvania Supreme Court ruled that the capital stock tax was levied on the value of the property owned, the U.S. Supreme Court tested the capital stock tax on that basis.[42] In another context it held that a tax on a national bank's capital stock was not a tax on the shareholders.[43]

In addition, the character of property may be uncertain: is it tangible or intangible property; is it real or personal? The Court once assumed without deciding that federal reserve notes were tangible property.[44] And many decisions finding taxing jurisdiction are based on notes and stock certificates or receivables being located in the state, treating them as tangible property.

The Court often applies what looks like linear, geometric deductive logic, to prove that a state can tax a subject. For example because a state can tax a person's

---

[35] United Air Lines v. Mahin, 410 U.S. 623 (1973).

[36] Provident Inst. v. Mass., 73 U.S. 611 (1868).

[37] Werner Machine Co. v. Director of Div. of Taxation, 350 U.S. 492 (1956).

[38] Brown-Forman Co. v. Kentucky, 217 U.S. 563 (1910).

[39] Soc'y for Sav. v. Coite, 73 U.S. 594 (1868); Educational Films Corp. v. Ward, 282 U.S. 379 (1931).

[40] Susquehanna Power Co. v. State Tax Comm'n, 283 U.S. 297 (1931).

[41] Macallen Co. v. Massachusetts, 279 U.S. 620 (1929).

[42] Delaware, L. & W. R. Co. v. Pennsylvania, 198 U.S. 341 (1905) (and decisions cited therein).

[43] First Nat'l Bank v. Adams, 258 U.S. 362 (1922).

[44] Pearson v. McGraw, 308 U.S. 313 (1939).

property, it can tax the person's exercise of various rights with respect to the property such as storage and withdrawal from storage.[45]

Sales taxes and gross receipts taxes seem analogous and often are analyzed together. However, the Court allows a state to tax all of the receipts from sales of goods in the state, while requiring apportionment of gross receipts taxes on similar sales of services because the former is on the buyer and the latter is on the seller that operated in several states.[46]

In sum, while the Court's reasoning sometimes seems inconsistent, it usually has a clear logic: states' have jurisdiction to tax persons and property with respect to taxing subjects—property and persons and transactions—that are somehow "in" the state, which is a limitation based on the reach of a sovereign that is older than the Due Process Clause. The Court repurposed that Clause and then wove in and substantially altered the additional made-up limits of the Commerce Clause to foster a national trading union that would not be unduly impeded by state taxation. These two jurisdictional limits are the primary subject of Chapter IX.F. and G., below.

b. *Tax Shifting*

In an unusual early decision the Court observed that the nominal taxpayer usually can shift the economic incidence of a business tax to another person with whom it deals. It ruled that tax laws generally are not interpreted to forbid that as a matter of some unwritten public policy, much less constitutional rule.[47]

However, when the tax may indirectly fall on a protected category, or directly falls on that category, the Court has at times considered the effect of passing on the tax to another person (the protected category or a person with whom the protected category dealt). For example, it required Native Americans to collect a tobacco tax that would be effectively passed on to non-Natives because the tax did not effectively fall on the Natives even though they bore the legal incidence; and several other cases took a look through approach involving Native American taxation.[48] In other cases the Court required a focus on "legal incidence" of tax levied on Native Americans, against state arguments that the nominal taxpayers passed on the tax to others.[49]

Generally the Court has rejected an argument that a tax on persons handling exports was a tax on the export.[50] Generally legal incidence controls the Court's

[45] Nashville, C. & S. L. Ry. v. Wallace, 288 U.S. 249 (1933).

[46] Okla. Tax Comm'n v. Jefferson Lines, 514 U.S. 175 (1995).

[47] American Express Co. v. Michigan, 177 U.S. 404 (1900) (a federal tax was at issue but a state argued it was being improperly shifted to customers of the Express Co.).

[48] California State Bd. of Equalization v. Chemehuevi Indian Tribe, 474 U.S. 9 (1985). *See also* Ramah Navajo Sch. Bd. v. Bureau of Revenue, 458 U.S. 832 (1982); Atkinson Trading Co. v. Shirley, 532 U.S. 645 (201).

[49] Okla. Tax Comm'n v. Chickasaw Nation, 515 U.S. 450 (1995); Wagnon v. Prairie Band Potawatomi Nation, 546 U.S. 95 (2005).

[50] Canton R. Co. v. Rogan, 340 U.S. 511 (1951).

constitutional analysis of state taxes.[51] However, the primary exception can be for burdens on interstate commerce, which the Court is keen to find by indirection.

As discussed in Ch. I.E.8, the Court's focus mostly on legal incidence of tax reflects an across the board shift by the Court from substance to form in applying the Constitution to taxation.

3. *Constitutional Limits on the Jurisdiction of States to Tax*

a. *Due Process and Commerce Clauses*

The Due Process Clause of the 14th Amendment is the principal constraint on the jurisdiction of states to tax. Because the power to tax is an inherent feature of sovereignty, and because states can only collect tax from "local" subjects, the Due Process Clause necessarily requires some minimum connection between the state and the subject of taxation.[52] That minimum connection is generally the same as the Due Process Clause requires for judicial jurisdiction over persons.[53]

The Due Process Clause as applied to state tax has a second component applied to income and gross receipts taxes and sometimes to property that moves among states: the state's taxing jurisdiction is limited to income rationally related to values connected with the taxing State.[54] This second limit is analogous to the judicial jurisdictional distinction between general jurisdiction over the person and special jurisdiction over the person limited to the subject of litigation, known as quasi in rem jurisdiction or specific jurisdiction.[55] In the context of judicial jurisdiction, the Supreme Court has made personal jurisdiction the primary focus, while retaining the possibility that in some cases the presence of property alone in the state can support judicial jurisdiction over the owner.[56] By analogy, the presence of property or activities of a nonresident in the state can support taxing jurisdiction of the nonresident that may be limited in scope.

The second constitutional limit on the jurisdiction to tax is the Commerce Clause, often referred to as the dormant Commerce Clause or the negative Commerce Clause. It requires "substantial nexus" of the nonresident's "activity" with the state.[57] The Supreme Court continues to treat substantial nexus as independent from Due Process Clause minimum contacts, although there often is

---

[51] Gurley v. Rhoden, 421 U.S. 200 (1975).

[52] N.C. Dep't of Revenue v. Kimberley Rice Kaestner 1992 Family Trust, 139 S. Ct. 2213 (2019).

[53] Quill Corp. v. N.D., 504 U.S. 298 (1992); N.C. Dep't of Revenue v. Kimberley Rice Kaestner 1992 Family Trust, 139 S. Ct. 2213 (2019).

[54] Quill Corp. v. N.D., 504 U.S. 298 (1992), citing Moorman Mfg. Co. v. Bair, 437 U.S. 267 (1978).

[55] Walden v. Fiore, 571 U.S. 277 (2014); Ford Motor Co. v. Montana, 141 S. Ct. 1017 (2021).

[56] 16 Moore's Federal Practice - Civil § 108.80 (2020). *See* Burnham v. Superior Court of Cal., 495 U.S. 604 (1990); Shaffer v. Heitner, 433 U.S. 186 (1977).

[57] South Dakota v. Wayfair, Inc., 138 S. Ct. 2080 (2018).

no distinction.[58] Again, the "activity" is akin to the "transactions" that are really proxies for taxing persons, as in the case of the retailer in *Wayfair*.

Sometimes the wording of the Constitution does not make it clear whether a prohibition applies to the states or the federal government. The Import-Export Clause limits state impost and duties on imports and exports. Article 1, Section 9, clause 5 (the Export Clause) states a similar prohibition (No Tax or Duty shall be laid on Articles exported from any State), but has only been applied to the United States.[59]

The other limits on state taxation are discussed in the recurring issues Chapter.

b. *Federal Enclaves*

Article I, Section 8, clause 17, gives the United States exclusive jurisdiction over the District of Columbia and other places purchased from the states, as for various military installations. Although not referred to as an enclave, Yosemite National Park was granted by California to the United States under an agreement that reserved to California the power to tax private persons within the Park.[60] But the state could not levy a license tax on a military base when it had ceded full authority over the base to the United States.[61] See Ch. II.C.6 for discussion of state taxation within federal enclaves.

c. *Territories*

Territories are treated as states for purpose of their own taxing powers,[62] subject to the powers of Congress over the territories, as discussed in Ch. V.D.3.a(4). By authorizing the Territory of Hawaii to tax, Congress permitted it to tax inter-island shipping without regard to interstate commerce.[63]

4. *Taxes Versus Fees Versus Regulations*

a. *Principles*

This Chapter will examine the distinction between state taxes and fees. All of the decisions on both federal and state fee/taxes are listed in Ch. IV.A.4, which Chapter contains the main treatment of this subject. The basic principles are: (1) state user fees for services or property supplied by the state are not taxes,[64] but should correlate with the benefit charged for (or the cost of providing the

---

[58] *See* Cummings, *Judicial Activism and the Commerce Clause*, 89 State Tax Notes 889 (Aug. 27, 2018).

[59] *See* Congressional Research Service Report Export Clause: Limitation on Congress's Taxing Power, No. R42780 (October 18, 2012).

[60] Collins v. Yosemite Park & Curry Co., 304 U.S. 518 (1938).

[61] Standard Oil Co. v. California, 291 U.S. 242 (1934).

[62] Talbott v. Silver Bow County, 139 U.S. 438 (1891) ("Under the general territorial system, as expressed in the various organic acts, the power of taxation is absolute, save as restricted by the Constitution or congressional enactments.").

[63] Inter-Island Steam Navigation Co. v. Hawaii, 305 U.S. 306 (1938).

[64] Cooley v. Bd. of Wardens, 53 U.S. 299 (1852).

services or property);[65] (2) taxes need not correlate with any benefit received by the taxpayer; (3) both user fees and taxes can also or only regulate a subject taxed; (4) purely regulatory charges are not taxes and should correlate with the cost of regulation; (5) state charges for privileges that only a sovereign can grant such as corporate franchises and licenses are taxes and are not charges for services or property; and (6) because states have general police powers but the United States does not, federal regulatory taxes largely developed as taxes, whereas the Supreme Court might call state regulatory taxes police power taxes, causing substantial confusion between the state and federal fee opinions.

b. *When Distinction Matters*

State user fees can violate the Commerce Clause,[66] the Due Process Clause (as a taking), and intergovernmental immunity,[67] whether or not they are taxes; but user fees can violate the Import-Export Clause and the Tonnage Clause only if they are actually duties or taxes. If a state charge is a user fee, then reasonableness in amount can justify it,[68] while there is no such requirement for reasonableness in amount for taxes (except to the extent the Commerce Clause cases ask whether income is properly apportioned to a state). The Court has applied different standards to user fees for violations of different constitutional limits.[69]

The Commerce Clause opinions are particularly likely to muddy the distinction between taxes and user fees because a state might try to justify either on the basis of reasonable allocation of costs or benefits to the taxpayer, but the Court will apply the same standard to interference with interstate commerce, although the state's arguments based on reasonableness may lead the Court to discuss a tax as if it were a user fee.[70] The distinction can matter when the amount of the fee is in issue: a tax can be in any amount, but a user fee or regulatory charge will be a taking unless it bears some relationship to the service or property provided.[71]

The state tax versus regulation versus fee distinctions are basically the same as for federal levies except that states have general powers to regulate whereas the federal regulatory powers are mostly limited to interstate commerce,[72] and states more frequently supply goods and services for which they charge user fees.[73] Therefore, unlike Congress, states less often have to shoehorn levies into the

---

[65] *See* Ch. IV.A.3.

[66] Atlantic Refining Co. v. Virginia, 302 U.S. 22 (1937) (accepted the state's characterization of the charge as a fee and not a tax but applied the same standard, which is not the current standard).

[67] Mayo v. United States, 319 U.S. 441 (1943). *But see* Federal Land Bank v. Crosland, 261 U.S. 374 (1923) (government instrumentality had to pay fee to record a mortgage but could not be charged a tax on the mortgage amount).

[68] Evansville-Vanderburgh v. Delta Airlines, Inc., 405 U.S. 707 (1972).

[69] Ch. IV.A.2.

[70] *E.g.*, American Trucking Ass'ns v. Scheiner, 483 U.S. 266 (1987) (taxes defended as user fees; opinions on both fees and taxes cited indiscriminately).

[71] Ouachita Packet Co. v. Aiken, 121 U.S. 444 (1887); Ingels v. Morf, 300 U.S. 290 (1937).

[72] *See* Ch. III.E.9; Ch. IV as to fees, special assessments and licenses.

[73] *See* Ch. IV.A.4.

regulatory tax category to avoid regulating a subject they cannot regulate,[74] unless it is a subject denied by the Constitution such as state taxes on imports and exports.[75] But a levy that is not a tax may be a taking without just compensation in violation of the 14th Amendment.[76]

c. *Fewer Constraints on Tax*

"General revenue" taxes (which logically should mean all taxes that are not special assessments) can be in any amount, and can regulate without needing to be correlated to the benefit received or cost incurred by the government, and do not violate the Due Process Clause regardless of the amount.[77] Although opinions sometimes refer to taxes as for general revenue or not, there is no such constitutional classification. Even dedicating a substantial part of the tax to a particular purpose does not change its character into a user fee.[78] And saying that a tax is for a particular purpose but not using the revenues for that purpose does not change the tax to a user fee.[79]

d. *Self-Imposed Limits*

However, if a state imposes a levy called either a tax or a fee and imposes on itself a use for a particular purpose, either by putting the collections into a fund for that purpose or by stating or otherwise showing a limited purpose for the levy, then the Court may find that the levy must be reasonable in amount for that purpose under the Due Process Clause.[80] For example a tax levied to improve a road and for which the landowners were to be taxed according to the benefit received violated the Due Process Clause because the tax was far in excess of the benefit.[81] However, that was likely an example of a special assessment, which is the major exception to the rule that there is no limit on the amount of taxation.[82]

A ship inspection fee can implicate the Commerce Clause, the Import-Export Clause and the Tonnage Clause. However, because the Import-Export Clause references inspections, the Court generally respects state inspection fees as such

---

[74] Ch. III.B.

[75] *See* Ch. VI.E.

[76] Ch. V.D.3.b(8).

[77] Pittsburgh v. Alco Parking Corp., 417 U.S. 369 (1974); Commonwealth Edison Co. v. Mont., 453 U.S. 609 (1981); Rast v. Van Deman & Lewis Co., 240 U.S. 342 (1916) ("prohibitory" $1000 per county license tax was upheld).

[78] Commonwealth Edison Co. v. Mont., 453 U.S. 609 (1981).

[79] Smith v. Turner, 48 U.S. 283 (1849) (tax charged on immigrants to support hospital).

[80] Morf v. Bingaman, 298 U.S. 407 (1936) (tax); Ingels v. Morf, 300 U.S. 290 (1937) (similar fee).

[81] Road Improv. Dist. v. Missouri P. R. Co., 274 U.S. 188 (1927). *Cf.* Roberts v. Richland Irrigation Dist., 289 U.S. 71 (1933) (tax apportioned based on estimated benefits; upheld even though benefits not achieved).

[82] *See* Ch. IV.B.

so long as an inspection actually occurs,[83] and the fee is reasonably related to the cost of inspection.[84]

But if the state fee or tax affects interstate commerce, and is for a particular purpose either as shown by use of the funds or by other evidence of legislative purpose, then for Commerce Clause purposes it had to be commensurate with the benefit provided, even before *Complete Auto*.[85]

e. *Regulatory Taxes*

Levies that a state denominates as taxes can have a purely regulatory purpose. Alaska as a territory could discriminate in license taxation for the purpose of preventing the use of certain fish for fertilizer.[86] The Court accepted the characterization as a tax without question even though the tax might destroy an industry and that might be its purpose, rejecting a Due Process Clause claim.

As discussed in Ch. IV, states have a general police power and the United States does not. Therefore a federal regulatory tax needs to be a tax where Commerce Clause or other regulatory power does not exist, as was at issue in the attacks on the individual mandate in Obamacare. But states can label a regulatory charge as a tax and still rely on broader police power authority. Consequently, many earlier opinions state that state regulatory taxes were exercises of the police power. This tendency waned,[87] but unfortunately a 2005 truck/fee/tax opinion confusingly mixed the fee/tax terms and cited the police power.[88]

f. *Labels*

The Court does not normally question the state's label of a levy as a tax.[89] However, when the classification is constitutionally relevant the Court can look past the form to the substance of the levy.[90] A tax on passengers arriving at a port from outside the United States was not a tax but a regulation of foreign commerce in violation of the Foreign Commerce Clause.[91] A charge for wharfage was not a user fee but a privilege tax when the city did not provide substantial wharfs.[92] A purported inspection fee on imported oil was a privilege tax because

---

[83] *E.g.*, Morgan's S.S. Co. v. Louisiana Bd. of Health, 118 U.S. 455 (1886); Askren v. Continental Oil Co., 252 U.S. 444 (1920).

[84] D. E. Foote & Co. v. Stanley, 232 U.S. 494 (1914).

[85] Ingels v. Morf, 300 U.S. 290 (1937) (regulatory charge).

[86] Alaska Fish Salting & By-Products Co. v. Smith, 255 U.S. 44 (1921).

[87] Toomer v. Witsell, 334 U.S. 385 (1948) seems to be one of the last, and the references to police power were incidental.

[88] Am. Trucking Ass'ns v. Mich. PSC, 545 U.S. 429 (2005).

[89] Commonwealth Edison Co. v. Mont., 453 U.S. 609 (1981).

[90] Cooley v. Bd. of Wardens, 53 U.S. 299 (1852). Many other opinions state this principle, including Galveston, H. & S. A. R. Co. v. Texas, 210 U.S. 217 (1908) (one of many early rulings that almost any tax on an interstate railroad was a tax on interstate commerce, even if called an occupation tax).

[91] Smith v. Turner, 48 U.S. 283 (1849).

[92] Cannon v. New Orleans, 87 U.S. 577 (1874).

the state did no inspection except to collect the "fee."[93] A state could not convert a tax on gross receipts into a property tax by a label.[94]

The amount of a user fee must be reasonable in relation to the benefit conferred.[95] But a government can charge a user fee even when the payer receives no benefit, as when a harbor charged half fee when the ship did not take on a pilot and the full fee when it did, to encourage the use of pilots.[96] A user fee or purported charge for services was found to be a tax when its purpose was general revenue raising.[97]

g. *Licenses and Franchises*

A charge imposed for a privilege or license granted by a state, as contrasted with a service or property, is a tax and not a user fee or even a regulatory charge.[98] However a charge for a "license" that authorizes use of state property, such as an auto license to drive on roads, has been held to be a fee for use of the roads and not a tax.[99] The Court has not been consistent in this area and has upheld as a tax a state charge for the privilege of using the roads, which the Court found to be compensation for that use; the opinion cited the fee cases without noticing that they were not tax cases; the most charitable explanation is that the Court weighted the "privilege" aspect of the facts more than the compensatory function of the tax.[100] A city cannot charge a privilege license fee for a privilege it cannot grant (door to door soliciting; charge violated free exercise of religion).[101]

A state taxing authority may receive both fees such as oil royalties and taxes with respect to the same activity of the taxpayer.[102]

Tolls charged for use of highway and waterways are user fees and not taxes and are not unconstitutional takings when reasonable in amount,[103] but only if there is some causal link between the usage of the property and the toll; simply calling

---

[93] Askren v. Continental Oil Co., 252 U.S. 444 (1920).

[94] Aloha Airlines v. Dir. of Taxation, 464 U.S. 7 (1983).

[95] *See* Ch. IV.A.

[96] Cooley v. Bd. of Wardens, 53 U.S. 299 (1852). Or the benefit may be to the public. *See* Charlotte, C. & A. R. Co. v. Gibbes, 142 U.S. 386 (1892).

[97] Polar Tankers, Inc. v. City of Valdez, 557 U.S. 1 (2009).

[98] Ch. IV.C. *See* Packet Co. v. St. Louis, 100 U.S. 423 (1879); Brown v. Maryland, 25 U.S. 419 (1827); Pembina Consol. Silver Mining & Milling Co. v. Pennsylvania, 125 U.S. 181 (1888) (foreign corporation having office in the state); Sprout v. South Bend, 277 U.S. 163 (1928) (occupation tax for driving a bus in city); New York v. Latrobe, 279 U.S. 421 (1929) (corporate franchise tax); Toomer v. Witsell, 334 U.S. 385 (1948) (commercial fishing boat license); Spector Motor Serv. v. O'Connor, 340 U.S. 602 (1951), overruled on other grounds by Complete Auto Transit, Inc. v. Brady, 430 U.S. 274 (1977). *But see* Atlantic Refining Co. v. Virginia, 302 U.S. 22 (1937) stating that a tax imposed as a condition to entry into the state as a franchise fee was a fee and not a tax because not measured by post entry events.

[99] Hendrick v. Maryland, 235 U.S. 610 (1915).

[100] Interstate Busses Corp. v. Blodgett, 276 U.S. 245 (1928) (also the proceeds were general revenue).

[101] Murdock v. Pennsylvania, 319 U.S. 105 (1943).

[102] Merrion v. Jicarilla Apache Tribe, 455 U.S. 130 (1982) (oil production royalties and severance taxes).

[103] Sands v. Manistee River Improv. Co., 123 U.S. 288 (1887).

a charge for general right to drive on highways a toll does not turn the tax into a toll.[104] Similar to tolls are user fees charged for passengers using airports.[105] A charge imposed on a telephone company for the right to install poles by streets was a user fee.[106] But in another case the state supreme court found that it was a franchise fee and not a property tax and so could substantially exceed the value of the lines, and the Court agreed.[107]

The Court has not been consistent as to whether the amount of a user fee must relate to the cost or the benefit or be justified by devoting all receipts to the cost, whether or not they cover the cost. Chapter IV.A. shows that the correct standard for a user fee is no more than the value of the benefit, which may be measured by cost. The charge need not cover the costs but may only help to defray the costs.[108] However, what is important is that the state actually supplies some property or service that the fee payor used or was able to use, and that the charge, relative to others, bears some logical relation to the use. The latter condition is not explored further here, but is somewhat arbitrary, as indicated by the different road use toll criteria discussed as treated differently in the *Delta* opinion.

Finally, a government may charge a license tax for licenses it did not grant. That occurs in cases of local license taxes on federally chartered corporations, or corporations operating under federal licenses to conduct such activities as telegraph. Generally, the state can impose a license tax in such situations for authorization to operate locally, but not to the extent it burdens the federal license.[109]

h. *Commerce Clause*

A fee that the Court may view as benign in other contexts can become a lightning rod for discrimination if the fee payor claims Commerce Clause discrimination. Rather than trying to integrate these decisions into the body of constitutional fee cases they should be viewed as sui generis to Commerce Clause jurisprudence.[110]

i. *Bonus Charges*

An odd decision held that states could require railroads to pay to them a "bonus" for the right to run the railroad, which looked like a tax but was not.[111] However, later opinions lumped it with rulings approving franchise taxes as being on the franchise and not the underlying property of the taxpayer.[112] The theory was that the state might have built the railroad and charged tolls for its

[104] Carley & Hamilton, Inc. v. Snook, 281 U.S. 66 (1930).
[105] Evansville-Vanderburgh v. Delta Airlines, Inc., 405 U.S. 707 (1972).
[106] St. Louis v. Western Union Tel. Co., 148 U.S. 92 (1893).
[107] New York, Philadelphia & Norfolk Tel. Co. v. Dolan, 265 U.S. 96 (1924).
[108] Evansville-Vanderburgh v. Delta Airlines, Inc., 405 U.S. 707 (1972).
[109] Williams v. Talladega, 226 U.S. 404 (1912).
[110] For example, American Trucking Ass'ns v. Scheiner, 483 U.S. 266 (1987) (fee might be a reasonable charge in the abstract, but not by comparison).
[111] Railroad Co. v. Maryland, 88 U.S. 456 (1875).
[112] Covington & Cincinnati Bridge Co. v. Kentucky, 154 U.S. 204 (1894).

use; and if it authorized a company to build the railroad and pay it 1/5 of the passenger fee revenue, that was not a tax but like a toll in the nature of return on property owned or controlled by the state, called a bonus charge.

A similar decision involved oysters. Maryland required the harvesters of oysters to remit one tenth of the oysters or their value to the state. The Court upheld the requirement not as a tax but as a sharing in the oysters, which the state owned.[113]

j. *Eminent Domain*

Many state taxpayers, particularly subject to special assessments, claimed that the entire effect of the "improvement" and the tax got the identity of the project exactly backward: that it was a taking of their property without just compensation, as opposed to a tax. The Court uniformly rejected those arguments, with explanations like this:

> But neither is taxation for a public purpose, however great, the taking of private property for public use, in the sense of the Constitution. Taxation only exacts a contribution from individuals of the State or of a particular district, for the support of the government, or to meet some public expenditure authorized by it, for which they receive compensation in the protection which government affords, or in the benefits of the special expenditure.[114]

Of course states also can take property by eminent domain, so long as just compensation is paid. The confiscatory power of state taxation is based on the Court not viewing a tax as a taking (as indicated in the quote above: "however great"). At times opinions of the Court have hinted that tax can be unconstitutional because confiscatory, but Justice Jackson rightly stated the rule in *Miller Bros.* that a tax can be confiscatory and violate Due Process only when the state does not have jurisdiction to tax.[115] A state could maintain the tax value of railroad property in a period of declining values and the result was not confiscatory because it was the same as raising the rates.[116]

However, the dissent of Justice Stephen G. Breyer in *Apfel* (1998) explained the possibility that the majority's new willingness to find unconstitutional takings could lead to finding a tax to be a taking.[117] Then in *Koontz* (2013) the Court found a taking when a government refused to grant a permit because the landowner refused to pay charges intended to offset the detriment the development would have caused if it had occurred.[118] Thus, impact fees must be

---

[113] Leonard & Leonard v. Earle, 279 U.S. 392 (1929).

[114] County of Mobile v. Kimball, 102 U.S. 691 (1880); Norwood v. Baker, 172 U.S. 269 (1898) (this opinion shows the close connection between takings and special assessment districts).

[115] Miller Bros. Co. v. Maryland, 347 U.S. 340 (1954). *See also* Fox v. Standard Oil Co., 294 U.S. 87 (1935). *Cf.* Ft. Smith Lumber Co. v. Arkansas, 251 U.S. 532 (1920) (Justice Holmes made a passing reference to a confiscatory tax).

[116] Nashville, C. & S. L. Railway v. Browning, 310 U.S. 362 (1940).

[117] Eastern Enterprises v. Apfel, 524 U.S. 498 (1998). *See* Cummings, *No Vested Right in the Internal Revenue Code*, 167 Tax Notes 759 (May 4, 2020).

[118] Koontz v. St. Johns River Water Management District, 570 U.S. 595 (2013).

"roughly proportional" to the damage to be caused by the development because the Court viewed those fees as a taking. Justice Samuel A. Alito Jr. waved aside the objection that the new rule could apply to taxes and user fees by asserting that taxes and user fees are not takings.

The Breyer dissent in *Koontz* agreed that taxes were not subject to the Court's holding but then stated that the Court's holding could apply to user fees (without explanation other than the difficulty of identification) and license taxes (liquor licenses), without noticing that license taxes are taxes.

D. Recurring Issues

1. *Persons*

Except for the true in rem taxes, all state taxes seek to impose tax obligations on persons. 1 U.S.C. § 1 states with respect to acts of Congress "the words "person" and "whoever" include corporations, companies, associations, firms, partnerships, societies, and joint stock companies, as well as individuals . . ." But that section does not apply to the constitution or state statutes. Similarly the Internal Revenue Code defines persons because the Code commonly uses that term.[119] Lacking any such definition applicable to the states, it is reasonable to assume that persons that may be subject to state taxes must be either individuals (humans) or entities recognized as separate from their owners by local law; but trustees are usually viewed as responsible for their trusts in some cases.

There are four principal issues that turn on the type of person being taxed by a state: (1) as to entities, (a) whether the taxpayer will be the entity or its owners or beneficiaries, and (b) whether a state's jurisdiction over either one gives it jurisdiction over the other; (2) whether Constitutional rights protect that person from state taxation; and (3) what is the residence (domicile, citizenship) of that person?

Issue (1)(a) is not a constitutional issue but a state choice. However, that choice can affect issues (1)(b), (2) and (3). The discussion of jurisdiction to tax below is organized on the assumption that the residence of the taxpayer matters to issue (2).

As to entities that are trusts, the Due Process Clause is concerned with jurisdiction over the trustee (the relevant person) of a trust and not the trust itself, and that jurisdiction may be based on the trustee's domicile.[120] The state of residence of the beneficiary of a trust generally does not have power to tax a foreign trustee, unless the beneficiary is the grantor, and absent other contacts of the trustee.[121]

States can have taxing jurisdiction over corporations without regard to the location of their shareholders because corporations long have been regarded

[119] I.R.C. § 7701(a)(1).

[120] Curry v. McCanless, 307 U.S. 357 (1939).

[121] N.C. Dep't of Revenue v. Kimberley Rice Kaestner 1992 Family Trust, 139 S. Ct. 2213 (2019).

as taxable entities with respect to their own activities.[122] States can have taxing jurisdiction over shareholders of S corporations without regard to their jurisdiction to tax the corporation if the states choose to tax income on a pass through basis.[123] C corporations are separate from and not conduits for their shareholders.[124]

States can have taxing jurisdiction over partnerships without regard to the location of their partners. States can have taxing jurisdiction over partners without regard to their jurisdiction to tax the partnership. The more difficult issue is whether states have taxing jurisdiction over nonresident partners of partnerships resident or doing business in the state. The Supreme Court has not decided that issue.

The Constitution refers only to persons and citizens. It clearly contemplated that persons and citizens would be human beings but the question of extending constitutional rights to entities eventually arose. Justice Stephen Field engineered a treatment of corporations as persons under the 14th Amendment. In the *Santa Clara County* case the court reporter added to the opinion after it was issued the oral statement of the Chief Justice from the bench that corporations were persons entitled to 14th Amendment protection of their civil rights.[125] The Court has operated on that assumption ever since, despite its dubious origin and logic.

At least certain corporations (closely held?) were invested with certain First Amendment rights to the free exercise of religion by the *Hobby Lobby* opinion.[126] Also corporations have certain First Amendment free speech rights under *Citizens United*.[127] The Court has applied other parts of the Constitution to corporations in relation to state taxes without question: Tonnage Clause;[128] Full Faith and Credit Clause;[129] Equal Protection Clause and Due Process Clause;[130] but not the Privileges and Immunities Clause because corporations are not citizens.[131] Neither the Privileges and Immunities Clause nor the Equal Protection Clause protects states as a collective of their citizens, but only protects "citizens" and "people."[132]

---

[122] *See* Jasper L. Cummings, Jr., The Supreme Court's Federal Tax Jurisprudence Ch. VI.F.3 (2d ed. 2016).

[123] Comptroller of the Treasury v. Wynne, 575 U.S. 542 (2015).

[124] Klein v. Board of Tax Supervisors, 282 U.S. 19 (1930).

[125] Santa Clara County v. Southern Pacific Railroad Company, 118 U.S. 394 (1886).

[126] Burwell v. Hobby Lobby Stores, Inc., 573 U.S. 682 (2014). *See* Cummings, Hobby Lobby *and Federal Taxes*, 145 Tax Notes 519 (Nov. 3, 2014).

[127] Citizens United v. FEC, 558 U.S. 310 (2010). *See* Cummings, *Citizens United Spurs Social Welfare*, 146 Tax Notes 1141 (Mar. 2, 2015).

[128] *See* Ch. IX.D.8.a.

[129] Milwaukee County v. M. E. White Co., 296 U.S. 268 (1935) (county relied on full faith and credit against corporate taxpayer).

[130] Grosjean v. American Press Co., 297 U.S. 233 (1936).

[131] Paul v. Virginia., 75 U.S. 168 (1868) (overruled on other grounds).

[132] Pennsylvania v. New Jersey, 426 U.S. 660 (1976) (dismissed state's dispute over commuter tax).

2. *Residency and Nonresidency of Persons*

a. *Citizens*

The 14th Amendment makes each individual a citizens of the state where the individual resides.[133] The Supreme Court has equated the state of citizenship through residence with the concept of domicile, which creates the most fundamental ground for a state's taxing jurisdiction.[134] Most of the Constitution's limits on state taxes refer to citizens and if a state discriminates against "nonresidents," that term necessarily includes within it citizens of other states.[135] A corporation chartered by a state has a residence in the state, which the Supreme Court has called its domicile and it also has called the corporation a "citizen" of that state.[136]

b. *Residents, Domiciliaries (Multiple)*

Sometimes the Court refers to domiciliaries as permanent residents.[137] Residence in fact, coupled with the purpose to make the place of residence one's home, are the essential elements of domicile.[138] But a U.S. citizen may be domiciled abroad and not in any state.[139]

The Court also recognizes that an individual's contacts with a state may be either domicile, residence that does not arise to domicile, mere presence in the state (as for example a commuter), and ownership of property located in the state. All four can support taxing jurisdiction of some kinds.[140] However, a state's determination of a person's domicile for purposes of taxing that person as a domiciliary is not a constitutional question and may be decided inconsistently by two states with respect to the same person.[141] But the Court has exercised its discretion to hear a dispute between two states both claiming the decedent to be a domiciliary, not because the issue presented a constitutional question but because the combined estate taxes could exceed the total estate.[142]

If identifying the state of domicile is not a constitutional issue then surely identifying the state of residence is not. Rather the duration or character of a

---

133 Recited in many Supreme Court opinions, including Miller Bros. Co. v. Maryland, 347 U.S. 340 (1954).

134 Curry v. McCanless, 307 U.S. 357 (1939) ("domiciled resident"); Graves v. Schmidlapp, 315 U.S. 657 (1942).

135 Travis v. Yale & Towne Mfg. Co., 252 U.S. 60 (1920).

136 Newark Fire Ins. Co. v. State Bd. of Tax Appeals, 307 U.S. 313 (1939).

137 Austin v. New Hampshire, 420 U.S. 656 (1975); Toomer v. Witsell, 334 U.S. 385 (1948); Blodgett v. Silberman, 277 U.S. 1 (1928).

138 Texas v. Florida, 306 U.S. 398 (1939).

139 Billings v. United States, 232 U.S. 261 (1914).

140 Miller Bros. Co. v. Maryland, 347 U.S. 340 (1954); Travis v. Yale & Towne Mfg. Co., 252 U.S. 60 (1920).

141 Worcester County Trust Co. v. Riley, 302 U.S. 292 (1937). *Cf.* Tilt v. Kelsey, 207 U.S. 43 (1907) (after New Jersey had probated will and taxed the estate, New York, which also claimed domicile, could not tax the entire estate without reference to location of property in the state).

142 California v. Texas, 457 U.S. 164 (1982).

non-domiciliary's residence in a state may bear on the level of contacts needed for Due Process and Commerce Clause jurisdiction to tax.[143]

A state could not use the federal interpleader statute to have the federal courts determine the domicile of a decedent.[144]

c. *Commercial Domicile*

As to corporations, states often use the concept of "commercial domicile"[145] in addition to "doing business" as proxies for what would be residence or other presence of an individual, but these terms have constitutional relevance only by way of the level of contacts they require, which contacts are the constitutional determinants of jurisdiction to tax.[146] The Court seems to assume that a commercial domicile gives the state the same taxing rights as a legal domicile (chartering state), and seems to have assumed that the states of commercial domicile and legal domicile can both tax nonbusiness income, producing multiple taxation.[147]

The commercial domicile concept is odd because it is based on the location of business assets and management in the state but it can then be applied to justify taxation of the corporation's intangibles by that state, even though intangibles normally are taxed solely at the place of legal domicile. In practice, however, the intangibles that the Court has allowed to be taxed also by the state of commercial domicile usually have been business intangibles generated in that state and not true "investment assets."[148] The threat of multiple taxation is less as to income taxes because the Court requires apportionment by all states with tax jurisdiction for Commerce Clause purposes.[149]

Even when the Court was not allowing other states to tax what was presumed to be interstate commerce, it allowed the state of commercial domicile to tax the

---

[143] States attempt to differentiate residents for purposes of various benefits in many contexts, which produce constitutional disputes. Vlandis v. Kline, 412 U.S. 441 (1973).

[144] Cory v. White, 457 U.S. 85 (1982).

[145] First Bank Stock Corp. v. Minnesota, 301 U.S. 234 (1937); Wheeling Steel Corp. v. Fox, 298 U.S. 193 (1936). These two opinions seem to have been the first to use the term; a commentator at the time said it was of uncertain origin and meaning; he called it "business situs" mostly related to taxing intangibles. Wisconsin v. J. C. Penney Co., 311 U.S. 435 (1940) cited *Wheeling* as the origin of the concept. *See also* Charles Sapp, Taxation - Commercial Domicile and Multi-State Property Taxation of Intangibles, 16 Tex. L. Rev. 227 (1938). But it was not recognized in Ozark Pipe Line Corp. v. Monier, 266 U.S. 555 (1925) (even though principal office of nonresident was in the state, franchise could not be taxed due to interstate commerce; did not refer to commercial domicile; ruling no longer valid).

[146] Allied-Signal, Inc. v. Dir., Div. of Taxation, 504 U.S. 768 (1992) (one of several opinions referencing the commercial domicile but not attaching particular significance to it).

[147] Moorman Mfg. Co. v. Bair, 437 U.S. 267 (1978) (footnote 15). *See also* Container Corp. of Am. v. Franchise Tax Bd., 463 U.S. 159 (1983).

[148] Wheeling Steel Corp. v. Fox, 298 U.S. 193 (1936); Newark Fire Ins. Co. v. State Bd. of Tax Appeals, 307 U.S. 313 (1939); First Bank Stock Corp. v. Minnesota, 301 U.S. 234 (1937).

[149] Mobil Oil Corp. v. Comm'r of Taxes, 445 U.S. 425 (1980) (the chartering state was also the commercial domicile and the case involved another state's income tax).

business profits.[150] In fact, an early reason to identify the commercial domicile may have been to allow that state to tax an interstate business when the Court otherwise was forbidding taxation of interstate business.[151]

The concept of commercial "domicil" is an old one, which evidently first denominated an individual's place of business as contrasted with his personal residence; it also may have had a special meaning for Chinese merchants but not laborers.[152] The commercial domicile concept also may have derived from the law of judicial jurisdiction. Under the Due Process Clause general jurisdiction is found at the principal place of business or headquarters and also the place of formal chartering of the corporation.[153]

3. *Equal Protection*

a. *Scope and Persons*

The 14th Amendment states that "No state shall . . . deny to any person within its jurisdiction the equal protection of the laws." Chapter V.D.3.b(2) lists and reviews the most important Supreme Court decisions applying the Equal Protection Clause to taxes, both state and federal, because the issues are the same. The state tax cases can be harder to classify because plaintiffs routinely also attack state tax discriminations with claims under the Commerce Clause, the Due Process Clause aside from equal protection, the First Amendment, the Privileges and Immunities Clause, and other grounds.

This section addresses only the Court's Equal Protection Clause rulings on state taxes. It will not rehearse the opinions explained in Chapter V but will integrate them, along with others, into a synthesis of the Court's current process for applying the Equal Protection Clause to state taxes.

State action that might deny equal protection includes local taxes authorized by the state,[154] because all local governmental powers flow from authorization by their states.[155] "The laws" that a state must provide equal protection under are that state's laws. A state is not required to take account of other state's taxes in setting its own,[156] which can lead to double taxation, which is not an Equal Protection violation, although it can run afoul of the Commerce Clause.[157]

Actions of nongovernmental persons might be tested as state action, but the Court has not considered such a case. A tax on private action that encourages ra-

---

[150] Memphis Natural Gas Co. v. Beeler, 315 U.S. 649 (1942).

[151] Southern Natural Gas Corp. v. Alabama, 301 U.S. 148 (1937).

[152] Lau Ow Bew v. United States, 144 U.S. 47 (1892); Lem Moon Sing v. United States, 158 U.S. 538 (1895); Juragua Iron Co. v. United States, 212 U.S. 297 (1909).

[153] Daimler AG v. Bauman, 571 U.S. 117 (2014). However, an entity may have consented to jurisdiction in another forum by seeking a charter, etc.

[154] Armour v. City of Indianapolis, 566 U.S. 673 (2012).

[155] Hunter v. Pittsburgh, 207 U.S. 161 (1907).

[156] Gurley v. Rhoden, 421 U.S. 200 (1975); Colgate v. Harvey, 296 U.S. 404 (1935), overruled on other grounds by Madden v. Kentucky, 309 U.S. 83 (1940).

[157] Container Corp. of Am. v. Franchise Tax Bd., 463 U.S. 159 (1983).

cial discrimination could be state action based on private action.[158] A restaurant in a public tax-exempt facility could not discriminate because of the significant state participation in the facility.[159]

The lack of a general definition of persons for purposes of state taxation is discussed above. A tangled history somehow established that private corporations were to be treated as persons for purposes of the 14th Amendment.[160] Persons protected by the Equal Protection Clause include corporations,[161] whether or not properly admitted to do business in the state.[162] Persons is a broader category than citizens to which the Privileges and Immunities Clause applies.

The Court has not ruled that partnerships and limited liability companies are persons for purposes of equal protection in state taxation. However, it ruled in favor of a corporation that was taxed differently than "natural persons and partnerships," implying that partnerships would be similarly protected.[163] And a trust may enforce the Equal Protection Clause rights of beneficiaries.[164] However, the Court has stated that the trust itself generally is not an entity, but the trustee is and can be taxed by states and claim constitutional protections as a person even though the trustee only controls and does not beneficially enjoy the trust property.[165]

The terms of the Equal Protection Clause apply only to persons within the state's taxing jurisdiction. Therefore, the jurisdiction to tax the plaintiff (or defendant) taxpayer should be resolved first. Moreover, that tax treatment should only be compared with others similarly within the state's taxing jurisdiction.[166]

Finally, the Court stated a surprisingly thoughtful view of equal protection when it said "a system which imposes the same tax upon every species of property, irrespective of its nature or condition or class, will be destructive of the principle of uniformity and equality in taxation and of a just adaptation of property to its burdens."[167]

---

[158] Adickes v. S. H. Kress & Co., 398 U.S. 144 (1970) (concurrence and dissent of Justice Brennan).

[159] Burton v. Wilmington Parking Authority, 365 U.S. 715 (1961).

[160] Smith v. Indiana, 191 U.S. 138 (1892) and opinions cited therein.

[161] Wheeling Steel Corp. v. Glander, 337 U.S. 562 (1949); Home Ins. Co. v. New York State, 134 U.S. 594 (1890).

[162] Bethlehem Motors Corp. v. Flynt, 256 U.S. 421 (1921). This decision found a non-admitted corporation to be doing business in the state through agents and to be discriminated against by the state taxing statute; it bypassed the then standard rule that a state could impose any sort of condition on entry.

[163] Quaker City Cab Co. v. Pennsylvania, 277 U.S. 389 (1928), overruled as to violation of equal protection by Lehnhausen v. Lake Shore Auto Parts Co., 410 U.S. 356 (1973).

[164] Binney v. Long, 299 U.S. 280 (1936); Orr v. Gilman, 183 U.S. 278 (1902).

[165] N.C. Dep't of Revenue v. Kimberley Rice Kaestner 1992 Family Trust, 139 S. Ct. 2213 (2019); Greenough v. Tax Assessors of Newport, 331 U.S. 486 (1947).

[166] Applied in Wheeling Steel Corp. v. Fox, 298 U.S. 193 (1936).

[167] W. Union Tel. Co. v. Indiana, 165 U.S. 304 (1897), quoting Pacific Express Co. v. Seibert, 142 U.S. 339 (1892).

b. *Discrimination*

(1) *Fact of Different Taxation*

To prove that the taxing state has unequally taxed the complaining person within its taxing jurisdiction, that person usually must prove (1) that some other person within the state's taxing jurisdiction was or could have been taxed less, (2) that the words of the state laws required such different treatment on their face or the difference arose in practice under the state laws as properly administered,[168] and (3) that the persons taxed differently did not differ from the plaintiff in a constitutionally significant way.

The actual existence of some other more lightly taxed person need not be proved if the discrimination will naturally result from the operation of the state laws, usually reflecting facial discrimination; but the chance incidence of the tax in particular instances or with respect to particular taxpayers normally has not violated the Equal Protection Clause.[169] One plaintiff made the unusual argument that it had paid less than other similar taxpayers in the state; the Court refused to consider the claim because the lower court had not considered it and there were no such other potential taxpayers paying the tax in the year.[170]

The proof of discrimination that violates the Equal Protection Clause is not the same as proof of discrimination against interstate commerce, as discussed below. Unlike Commerce Clause cases, which may or may not be based on facial discrimination (because states learned to obscure discriminations against interstate commerce), Equal Protection Clause cases normally are based on facial discriminations because all taxing statutes draw lines and taxpayers commonly object to those lines drawn. Therefore the focus of most Equal Protection Clause opinions is the constitutional relevance of the admitted taxing distinction.

The state did not violate the Equal Protection Clause when assessors adopted a practice of valuing certain property held by one type of taxpayer different from similar property held by another type of taxpayer, because the taxpayer failed to prove that the differing methods produced unfair valuations.[171]

A railroad was not taxed more heavily on its property than other taxpayers because it paid property tax and also paid a privilege license tax measured by property values; the privilege tax was not a property tax.[172] And a railroad was not denied equal protection by apportioning its moveable property in the state among the counties in which its cars moved, rather than entirely to its principal

[168] For example in Stebbins v. Riley, 268 U.S. 137 (1925) the Court observed that denial of a deduction for the federal estate tax caused larger estates to be taxed more heavily than smaller estates, but did not violate the Equal Protection Clause.

[169] Colgate v. Harvey, 296 U.S. 404 (1935), overruled on other grounds by Madden v. Kentucky, 309 U.S. 83 (1940).

[170] Oliver Iron Mining Co. v. Lord, 262 U.S. 172 (1923).

[171] Charleston Federal Sav. & Loan Asso. v. Alderson, 324 U.S. 182 (1945).

[172] Southern R. Co. v. Watts, 260 U.S. 519 (1923).

office county, even though the different counties had different percentage tax rates, which applied equally to all taxpayers.[173]

Once imported gasoline had come to rest in a state it was not different from other gasoline whose storage in state was taxed.[174] When a statute aimed at discouraging futures exchanges in commodities imposed a stamp tax on every form of business organization imaginable that might engage in such an exchange, it embraced every possible subject in the class and so could not violate the 14th Amendment.[175] A state tax on an oil company selling oil to the United States did not discriminate because the state exempted a local government from tax on property it leased from the oil company.[176]

(2) *Compensating Tax*

Equality of treatment may be proved by the application of other taxes by the taxing state on other taxpayers, which result in some equivalence of taxation in the aggregate.[177] However, such rulings, which may still be correct under the Equal Protection Clause, are irrelevant to the extent the discrimination affects interstate commerce and the Commerce Clause may be applied to require a different result.[178]

A state could charge a property tax on railroad cars of nonresident corporations, which they could avoid by obtaining a local residence and paying roughly similar local property taxes, without violating the Equal Protection Clause;[179] but the Court later said that approach did not reflect current Commerce Clause jurisprudence.[180] The Court approved taxing independent express companies but not express companies attached to railroads because the railroads paid taxes on their tracks.[181] The Court explained an income tax that taxed resident individuals on out of state business income while not taxing resident corporations on similar income by pointing out that the dividends on the untaxed income would be taxed to the corporations' shareholders (but probably did not view that

---

[173] Columbus S. R. Co. v. Wright, 151 U.S. 470 (1894).

[174] Gregg Dyeing Co. v. Query, 286 U.S. 472 (1932).

[175] Brodnax v. Missouri, 219 U.S. 285 (1911).

[176] Esso Standard Oil Co. v. Evans, 345 U.S. 495 (1953).

[177] Travellers' Ins. Co. v. Connecticut, 185 U.S. 364 (1902) (Commerce Clause not considered); Colgate v. Harvey, 296 U.S. 404 (1935) (as to dividends there was a compensating tax on local corporations, but not as to interest on loans from different borrowers), but overruled on other grounds by Madden v. Kentucky, 309 U.S. 83 (1940). *See also* Baldwin v. Fish & Game Comm'n, 436 U.S. 371 (1978), discussed below; Lionberger v. Rouse, 76 U.S. 468 (1870) (allowing a compensating tax to prevent discrimination between state and national banks).

[178] Fulton Corp. v. Faulkner, 516 U.S. 325 (1996) (stating that earlier decisions under the Equal Protection Clause had been bypassed by Commerce Clause decisions: Darnell v. Indiana, 226 U.S. 390 (1912); Kidd v. Alabama, 188 U.S. 730 (1903)). *See also* Klein v. Board of Tax Supervisors, 282 U.S. 19 (1930) (stock not taxed if 75 percent of corporate property taxed in state; Commerce Clause not considered; possibly not implicitly overruled as was *Kidd* because involved only property taxes).

[179] General American Tank Car Corp. v. Day, 270 U.S. 367 (1926).

[180] Associated Indus. v. Lohman, 511 U.S. 641 (1994).

[181] Pacific Express Co. v. Seibert, 142 U.S. 339 (1892).

as a compensating tax).[182] A 6 percent tax on freezer ship canning was the same as a 6 percent tax on fish canning in factories in the state.[183]

The important ruling on retroactive tax changes in *Welch v. Henry* involved an individual dividends received deduction that was allowed if the corporation did a sufficient amount of business in the state and thus paid tax in the state; the state revoked it retroactively and taxed the dividends more than other income was taxed for the same year, without violation of equal protection; the prior escape of taxation was a satisfactory distinction.[184]

The most common compensating tax is the use tax, which compensates for the state's inability to impose a sales tax on a resident's purchases of goods out of state brought into the state (because the sales tax is imposed, by convention, on the seller). Although the use tax so obviously produces equality, it raises Commerce Clause questions and so was primarily attacked under the Commerce Clause and upheld where near equality was achieved.[185]

(3) *Approximation*

The Court usually has not invalidated under the Equal Protection Clause a state's discrimination between identifiable classes of taxpayers resulting from inexact or approximate methods used to identify the classes.[186] A general formula for adjusting the value of non recently purchased property can be sufficient for Equal Protection purposes.[187] It was not discriminatory to tax a railroad's property at about 45 percent of its value and tax others' property at about 50 percent of value.[188] In another case Justice Holmes said that because the state might exempt various businesses entirely, the complaining taxpayer had no equal protection claim on account of the property of various interstate businesses being valued at substantially less than fair market value (presumably relative to his own).[189] But a rural county could not just estimate the "benefit" of county wide road building to a railroad passing through the county without any explanation for how the estimate was made, particularly when the railroad was assessed $67,000 for 9 miles of track and town lots were assessed $10.[190]

---

182 Lawrence v. State Tax Com., 286 U.S. 276 (1932).

183 Alaska v. Arctic Maid, 366 U.S. 199 (1961).

184 Welch v. Henry, 305 U.S. 134 (1938).

185 Henneford v. Silas Mason Co., 300 U.S. 577 (1937); Associated Indus. v. Lohman, 511 U.S. 641 (1994).

186 Great Atlantic & Pacific Tea Co. v. Grosjean, 301 U.S. 412 (1937); Ohio Oil Co. v. Conway, 281 U.S. 146 (1930); General American Tank Car Corp. v. Day, 270 U.S. 367 (1926) (ignore "minute differences between its application in practice"). *Cf.* Associated Indus. v. Lohman, 511 U.S. 641 (1994) (emphasizing that the approximation approach did not necessarily extend to the Commerce Clause).

187 Allegheny Pittsburgh Coal Co. v. County Com., 488 U.S. 336 (1989).

188 Baker v. Druesedow, 263 U.S. 137 (1923).

189 Missouri v. Dockery, 191 U.S. 165 (1903).

190 Kansas City S. R. Co. v. Road Improv. Dist., 256 U.S. 658 (1921). But the Court ruled otherwise where the state statute directed the railroad to pay for the road (numbers not appearing). Branson v. Bush, 251 U.S. 182 (1919).

(4) *Intent or Inadvertence; Nonenforcement*

The Court ruled that if tax discrimination exists in the state's tax statute, it violates the Equal Protection Clause whether by design or inadvertence of the statutory design.[191] And when the discrimination was facial, the Court rejected the state's argument that it did not enforce a discriminatory provision.[192]

But the Court has refused to correct a local property tax valuation error, or mistake of judgment,[193] not due to statutory discrimination against the nonresident owner,[194] and not due to fraud or error so gross as to violate Due Process Clause,[195] or not due to intentional discrimination by the assessor,[196] and not intentional and systematic.[197] The Court early recognized broad state discretion to value property of domestic railroads.[198]

The Court ruled that unauthorized intentional discrimination by taxing officials causing unequal treatment is per se proof of violation of the Equal Protection Clause: the Equal Protection Clause discrimination will be assumed without further investigation when it results from an unlawful preferring of one taxpayer over another by administrative action.[199] This is the best explanation of the *Allegheny* decision.[200]

The state may retroactively tax property that was not previously taxed by inadvertence, if it could have taxed that property differently from other property in the first place.[201]

---

[191] F. S. Royster Guano Co. v. Virginia, 253 U.S. 412 (1920) (although in this case the design was not inadvertent).

[192] Bethlehem Motors Corp. v. Flynt, 256 U.S. 421 (1921).

[193] Baker v. Druesedow, 263 U.S. 137 (1923); Western Union Tel. Co. v. Missouri, 190 U.S. 412 (1903); Sunday Lake Iron Co. v. Wakefield, 247 U.S. 350 (1918).

[194] Beeson v. Johns, 124 U.S. 56 (1888) (decided under the Ordinance of 1787, to the effect that in no case shall non-resident proprietors be taxed higher than residents, and also to a similar provision contained in the act of Congress of March 3, 1845, providing for the admission of the States of Iowa and Florida into the Union); Rowley v. Chicago & N. R. Co., 293 U.S. 102 (1934); Coulter v. Louisville & N. R. Co., 196 U.S. 599 (1905); Maish v. Arizona, 164 U.S. 599 (1896).

[195] Pittsburgh, C., C. & S. L. R. Co. v. Backus, 154 U.S. 421 (1894); Chicago, B. & Q. R. Co. v. Babcock, 204 U.S. 585 (1907) ("it is improper to cross-examine the members in an attempt to exhibit confusion in their minds").

[196] Sioux City Bridge Co. v. Dakota County, 260 U.S. 441 (1923).

[197] Cumberland Coal Co. v. Board of Revision of Tax Assessments, 284 U.S. 23 (1931); Southern R. Co. v. Watts, 260 U.S. 519 (1923); Mackay Tel. & Cable Co. v. Little Rock, 250 U.S. 94 (1919); Chicago G. W. R. Co. v. Kendall, 266 U.S. 94 (1924).

[198] State Railroad Tax Cases, 92 U.S. 575 (1875).

[199] Iowa-Des Moines National Bank v. Bennett, 284 U.S. 239 (1931) (and the plaintiff need not wait for the state to tax the benefitted class properly). But an earlier decision held that a writ of error would not permit review where the statute was not questioned. Jett Bros. Distilling Co. v. Carrollton, 252 U.S. 1 (1920).

[200] Allegheny Pittsburgh Coal Co. v. County Com., 488 U.S. 336 (1989). *Cf.* Nordlinger v. Hahn, 505 U.S. 1 (1992).

[201] Florida C. & P. R. Co. v. Reynolds, 183 U.S. 471 (1902). *See also* Welch v. Henry, 305 U.S. 134 (1938).

(5) *Double Taxation*

Multiple state and local taxes on the same subject of taxation obviously could be viewed as double taxation within that state, and could be viewed as unequal taxation relative to a single taxed subject. However, double taxation within the state does not violate the Equal Protection Clause, whether the multiple taxes be labeled by the state as the same or different types or be imposed by different subdivisions of the state.[202] The state can tax both the property and its income.[203]

See discussion of double taxation below in relation to the Due Process Clause; and also in relation to double taxation considerations, which are at the heart of Commerce Clause apportionment of income, discussed below.[204]

(6) *Retroactivity or Prospectivity*

The Court struck down a six year contemplation of death presumption under the Fourteenth Amendment.[205] The case was analyzed as involving an irrebuttable presumption, but under the Equal Protection Clause; the inequality lay in other presumably similarly situated taxpayers being allowed to avoid the presumption. The Equal Protection Clause also was violated by a statute that included in the taxable estate property in a trust created for which a power of appointment was not exercised; the inclusion did not apply to property of later created trusts.[206] The decision appears to have been based on Due Process Clause decisions of the Court striking down retroactive federal tax legislation involving contemplation of death gifts. But when a state changed the statute that had included trusts made after a certain date to include also trusts made before that date, the Court found no discrimination, but rather an attempt to achieve equal treatment.[207]

Cases involved national banks that could not be taxed directly, so the state attempted to require the banks to pay retroactive taxes on shares held by their shareholders. The Court found that the law discriminated against national banks to the extent applied to nonresident shareholders who had not been required to list the shares for taxation in prior years,[208] but not as to resident shareholders as to whom the law presumably was not retroactive.[209]

---

[202] Swiss Oil Corp. v. Shanks, 273 U.S. 407 (1927).

[203] Ohio Tax Cases, 232 U.S. 576 (1914).

[204] *See* for example, Japan Line, Ltd. v. County of Los Angeles, 441 U.S. 434 (1979) (double taxation of foreign commerce).

[205] Schlesinger v. Wisconsin, 270 U.S. 230 (1926). The Court last cited *Schlesinger* in support of its dislike of irrebuttable presumptions in Vlandis v. Kline, 412 U.S. 441 (1973) (concerning in state tuition status). In dissent in *Vlandis* Justice Rehnquist grouped these cases with *Lochner* and *Adkins*. 412 U.S. at 467-468.

[206] Binney v. Long, 299 U.S. 280 (1936). The law was an odd one in that the statute went out of its way to tax a power exercised after the act with respect to a trust created before the act, but did not tax the exercise of powers created after the act; and at the time the trust was created there was not inheritance tax.

[207] Whitney v. State Tax Com., 309 U.S. 530 (1940).

[208] Covington v. First Nat'l Bank, 198 U.S. 100 (1905).

[209] Citizens Nat'l Bank v. Kentucky, 217 U.S. 443 (1910).

Taxpayers also attacked retroactive state taxes under the Ex Post Facto Clause, which the Court early ruled did not apply.[210]

(7) *Hypotheticals*

The Court refused to find a violation of the Equal Protection Clause when the other presumed favored class did not exist in the state.[211] The Court ruled that Equal Protection was not violated as to the plaintiff, one of two categories of disadvantaged taxpayers; it refused to consider the treatment of the other category.[212]

(8) *Systematic and Intentional Unequal Treatment*

In an unusual ruling the Court found Georgia to have systematically and intentionally overtaxed railroad property.[213] Illinois was found to have similarly singled out on of its own railroads for discriminatory high taxation that would have bankrupted the road if paid, and so the Court enjoined the tax.[214]

(9) *Market Participant: Equal Protection*

A city did not violate the Equal Protection Clause by imposing a tax on a private electric company with which it competed.[215]

c. *Rational Basis*

(1) *General*

The Equal Protection Clause requires a state to have a "rational basis" for applying different tax treatment to different persons subject to its taxing jurisdiction.[216] The Court further defines rational basis as a rational relationship between the disparity of treatment and some legitimate governmental purpose; the Court requires more than a mere rational relationship if a classification involves fundamental rights or is based on certain suspect categorizations.[217]

The Equal Protection Clause applies to state tax discriminations in generally the same way that it applies to non-tax discriminations (usually called economic

---

210 Locke v. New Orleans, 71 U.S. 172 (1867); Bankers Trust Co. v. Blodgett, 260 U.S. 647 (1923).

211 Pullman Co. v. Knott, 235 U.S. 23 (1914).

212 Farmers & Mechanics Sav. Bank v. Minnesota, 232 U.S. 516 (1914).

213 Bohler v. Callaway, 267 U.S. 479 (1925).

214 Raymond v. Chicago Union Traction Co., 207 U.S. 20 (1907).

215 Puget Sound Power & Light Co. v. Seattle, 291 U.S. 619 (1934); Seattle Gas Co. v. Seattle, 291 U.S. 638 (1934).

216 Armour v. City of Indianapolis, 566 U.S. 673 (2012); Fitzgerald v. Racing Ass'n, 539 U.S. 103 (2003); Nordlinger v. Hahn, 505 U.S. 1 (1992); Amerada Hess Corp. v. Dir., 490 U.S. 66 (1989); Metro. Life Ins. Co. v. Ward, 470 U.S. 869 (1985); Williams v. Vermont, 472 U.S. 14 (1985); Exxon Corp. v. Eagerton, 462 U.S. 176 (1983); Board of Education v. Illinois, 203 U.S. 553 (1906) (upheld a state law providing an inheritance tax exemption to in-state charities but denying a similar exemption to out-of-state charities).

217 Armour v. City of Indianapolis, 566 U.S. 673 (2012); Fitzgerald v. Racing Ass'n, 539 U.S. 103 (2003).

and commercial regulations), except that state taxation has received even more leeway because taxation is an inherently legitimate purpose of state governments.[218] It requires less scrutiny than even "ordinary commercial transactions," which require the baseline rational basis, dating back to the Supreme Court's opinion in *Carolene Products*.[219] The very low bar for tax distinction rationality is so easy to jump that plaintiffs frequently try to avoid treating an exaction as a tax if possible. The Court also attributes the low bar ("greatest freedom") to the multiplicity of considerations and to the legislature's special knowledge of the tax subjects in the localities.[220] Other government exactions such as fees also are viewed as economic legislation.[221]

So to survive an equal protection challenge a tax distinction should have a rational basis that pursues a legitimate state interest, and the two subjects taxed differently should be objectively different in some way that has some connection to that purpose. Taxpayers have attacked all of those elements. Another line of attack is that despite the tax classifications being permissible in theory, they just don't work on the facts of the case and produce an entirely illogical differential tax, which the Court has applied on at least one rare occasion.[222]

A legitimate interest includes a choice to impose a higher estate tax on property that was less taxed when owned by the decedent than other property also transferred at death.[223]

(2) *Examples*

There are exceptions that prove the rule, but the rule seems to be, despite statements of the Court to the contrary, that any difference in fact (a plumber is not an electrician) will justify different taxation. The states learned the trick from Congress, which has long imposed tariffs in different amounts on the importation of goods based on minute differences in the measurable characteristics of the goods. The following examples prove the general rule.

The first ruling on state tax discrimination may have been the *Kentucky Railroad Tax Cases* in 1885, which allowed railroad property to be classified differently for taxation.[224] That ruling no doubt fueled more disparate taxation of railroads and a huge amount of complaints by railroads in cases winding up in the Supreme Court. The most commonly cited opinion giving states wide latitude to make tax distinctions is *Bell's Gap*.[225]

---

[218] Nordlinger v. Hahn, 505 U.S. 1 (1992); Exxon Corp. v. Eagerton, 462 U.S. 176 (1983).

[219] United States v. Carolene Products Co., 304 U.S. 144 (1938), cited in Armour v. City of Indianapolis, 566 U.S. 673 (2012).

[220] Madden v. Kentucky, 309 U.S. 83 (1940), citing Bell's Gap R. Co. v. Pennsylvania, 134 U.S. 232 (1890).

[221] Kadrmas v. Dickinson Pub. Sch., 487 U.S. 450 (1988).

[222] Gast Realty & Inv. Co. v. Schneider Granite Co., 240 U.S. 55 (1916).

[223] Watson v. State Comptroller, 254 U.S. 122 (1920).

[224] Kentucky Railroad Tax Cases, 115 U.S. 321 (1885).

[225] Bell's Gap R. Co. v. Pennsylvania, 134 U.S. 232 (1890).

Railroads with tracks solely within the state were held to be different from railroads with tracks in and out of the state.[226] Railroads with less than 25 miles of track within the jurisdiction could be taxed at a lower rate than other roads.[227] Street railroads and subsurface railroads and steam railroads could be taxed differently.[228] Railroads could be taxed more heavily than other common carriers,[229] and other utilities,[230] and other taxpayers.[231] A city could tax the street railway that used the street substantially more heavily than abutting landowners.[232] A state could deny deductions from income from railroad property that were allowed to other corporate businesses because the railroad applied federal commission accounting.[233] A railroad could be taxed under a special act that would subject it to a special taxing regime if it paid its back taxes, which it disputed.[234] A state could authorize special assessments on property including the railroad's right of way, the same as other adjoining property, despite the fact that the railroad made only limited use of the property.[235]

A state could tax common carriers for use of the roads at different rates from private carriers and other business users.[236]

A state could tax ore lands subject to depletion differently from other lands.[237] A state could exempt electricity sales for irrigation because irrigation benefitted the state generally.[238] A state could tax property located in some counties and not others.[239] Graduated oil severance taxes could apply different rates to different gravity oils, and some oils might be taxed the same if they had similarities but were sold for different prices.[240] When land has been undervalued in the past and the state undertakes to create equality of taxation by backtaxing the undervalued property, the Equal Protection Clause was not violated by limiting this process to corporate owners.[241] A state could include one cemetery in a special assessment district and exclude others.[242]

---

[226] Central R. Co. v. Pennsylvania, 370 U.S. 607 (1962).

[227] Columbus & G. R. Co. v. Miller, 283 U.S. 96 (1931).

[228] New York ex rel. Metropolitan Street Ry. Co. v. New York State Bd., 199 U.S. 1 (1905); Puget Sound Power & Light Co. v. County of King, 264 U.S. 22 (1924); Savannah, T. & I. O. H. Railway v. Savannah, 198 U.S. 392 (1905).

[229] Nashville, C. & S. L. Ry. v. Wallace, 288 U.S. 249 (1933).

[230] New York Rapid Transit Corp. v. New York, 303 U.S. 573, 579, 58 S. Ct. 721, 82 L. Ed. 1024 (1938).

[231] Nashville, C. & S. L. Railway v. Browning, 310 U.S. 362 (1940).

[232] Durham Public Service Co. v. Durham, 261 U.S. 149 (1923).

[233] Atlantic C. L. R. Co. v. Doughton, 262 U.S. 413 (1923).

[234] McHenry v. Alford, 168 U.S. 651 (1898).

[235] Louisville & N. R. Co. v. Barber Asphalt Paving Co., 197 U.S. 430 (1905).

[236] Bekins Van Lines, Inc. v. Riley, 280 U.S. 80 (1929); Hicklin v. Coney, 290 U.S. 169 (1933).

[237] Lake Superior Consol. Iron Mines v. Lord, 271 U.S. 577 (1926).

[238] Utah Power & Light Co. v. Pfost, 286 U.S. 165 (1932).

[239] Kentucky Union Co. v. Kentucky, 219 U.S. 140 (1911).

[240] Ohio Oil Co. v. Conway, 281 U.S. 146 (1930).

[241] White River Lumber Co. v. Arkansas, 279 U.S. 692 (1929) (the opinion cited many other examples of back taxation, which seemed to be a common process; the retroactivity was not attacked).

[242] Mount St. Mary's Cemetery Ass'n v. Mullins, 248 U.S. 501 (1919).

A state could tax a domestic insurance company more than a foreign insurance company because more of its reserves and property were in the state.[243] Banks could be taxed more heavily than other moneyed capital lending businesses.[244] The fact that banks holding federal debt enjoy a certain exemption does not mean that the state must tax other corporations the same way.[245] A legislature could provide for collecting back taxes on real property without making a like provision respecting back taxes on personal property.[246] A state could tax emigrant agents who hired laborers for work out of state, but not for work in state.[247]

A state could apply an inheritance tax to personalty in the state of a decedent who held realty in the state but exempt the personalty of a decedent who did not own realty in the state.[248] A state could impose a graduated inheritance tax and the rate may vary according to the degree of relationship to the decedent.[249] Trusts that must distribute their incomes were different from trusts that could make discretionary distributions.[250] A state could charge different inheritance taxes by distinguishing between the lineal and collateral relatives of a testator.[251]

A state could apply a transfer tax to stock and not other property, and levy it on par value and not actual value.[252] Measurement of the tax at a flat rate per share on non-par value stock and at a fixed percentage of par value on par-value stock was based on a reasonable classification because of the different characteristics of the two kinds of shares.[253] The different treatment of stock with no par value did not violate Equal Protection Clause.[254]

A state could require the same flat license tax to drive on the state's roads from a nonresident, whether he drives one times or many times.[255] Alternately, the state could exempt various classes of carriers, such as local and small carriers.[256] A state could tax "caravanning" of cars to be sold into the state, but exempt "in-trazone" caravanning and caravanning not for sale.[257]

A manufacturer selling at its plant could be tax differently from an out of state manufacturer shipping its products into the state for sale.[258] The Court

[243] Northwestern Mut. Life Ins. Co. v. Wisconsin, 247 U.S. 132 (1918).

[244] First Nat'l Bank v. Louisiana Tax Com., 289 U.S. 60 (1933); Union Bank & Trust Co. v. Phelps, 288 U.S. 181 (1933) (and further discrimination against state banks by not taxing national banks does not violate Equal Protection Clause).

[245] Schuylkill Trust Co. v. Pennsylvania, 302 U.S. 506 (1938).

[246] Winona & St. Peter Land Co. v. Minnesota, 159 U.S. 526 (1895).

[247] Williams v. Fears, 179 U.S. 270 (1900) (taxpayer also made Privileges and Immunities argument).

[248] Beers v. Glynn, 211 U.S. 477 (1909).

[249] Keeney v. Comptroller of New York, 222 U.S. 525 (1912).

[250] Guaranty Trust Co. v. Virginia, 305 U.S. 19 (1938).

[251] Billings v. Illinois, 188 U.S. 97 (1903); Campbell v. California, 200 U.S. 87 (1906).

[252] New York ex rel. Hatch v. Reardon, 204 U.S. 152 (1907).

[253] New York v. Latrobe, 279 U.S. 421 (1929).

[254] St. Louis-San Francisco R. Co. v. Middlekamp, 256 U.S. 226 (1921).

[255] Kane v. New Jersey, 242 U.S. 160 (1916).

[256] Continental Baking Co. v. Woodring, 286 U.S. 352 (1932).

[257] Clark v. Paul Gray, Inc., 306 U.S. 583 (1939).

[258] Armour & Co. v. Virginia, 246 U.S. 1 (1918).

has approved of distinctions between utilities—including a railroad—and other corporations;[259] between wholesalers and retailers;[260] between meat packers and packers of other farm products;[261] between chain retail stores and independent retail stores;[262] between anthracite coal mines and bituminous coal mines;[263] between sellers of coal oil and sellers of coal;[264] and between distillers of straight and blended liquor.[265] A beer manufacturer can be charged a different license tax than a beer importer (21st Amendment).[266]

The distinction for property tax purposes between normal vehicles and vehicles used in a transportation service on the roads is plain enough.[267] A state could impose a personal property tax only on corporations and entities and not individuals,[268] and could tax an individual in business out of state on that income while not taxing the same out of state income of domestic corporations.[269] And the tax on different types of retail stores could be at progressive rates as the number rises (but Equal Protection was violated when the rate changed on account of stores being located in more than one county).[270] Electric power generators powered by different sources could be taxed differently.[271] A state could tax wages different from business income, allowing expenses to be deducted in the latter but not the former.[272] Theaters could be taxed differently according to their top ticket price.[273]

(3) *No Rational Basis if the Same*

One way to show lack of a rational basis for different taxation of the plaintiff relative to some other group of taxpayers is to prove that they are the same; but the method is hardly ever that simple and similarity is in the eye of the beholder. Usually some concern important to the Court is involved (*e.g.*, interstate commerce).

(a) *No Actual Difference Cases*

Virginia could not exempt the income of domestic corporations earned out of state when the corporation earned no income in the state, while taxing all of the

---

259 New York Rapid Transit Corp. v. New York, 303 U.S. 573 (1938).

260 Caskey Baking Co. v. Virginia, 313 U.S. 117 (1941); Cook v. Marshall County, 196 U.S. 261 (1905).

261 Armour Packing Co. v. Lacy, 200 U.S. 226 (1906).

262 State Board of Tax Comm'rs v. Jackson, 283 U.S. 527 (1931); Fox v. Standard Oil Co., 294 U.S. 87 (1935).

263 Heisler v. Thomas Colliery Co., 260 U.S. 245 (1922).

264 Southwestern Oil Co. v. Texas, 217 U.S. 114 (1910).

265 Brown-Forman Co. v. Kentucky, 217 U.S. 563 (1910).

266 State Bd. of Equalization v. Young's Market Co., 299 U.S. 59 (1936).

267 Alward v. Johnson, 282 U.S. 509 (1931).

268 Lehnhausen v. Lake Shore Auto Parts Co., 410 U.S. 356 (1973).

269 Lawrence v. State Tax Com., 286 U.S. 276 (1932).

270 Louis K. Liggett Co. v. Lee, 288 U.S. 517 (1933) (chain stores).

271 Broad River Power Co. v. Query, 288 U.S. 178 (1933).

272 Walters v. St. Louis, 347 U.S. 231 (1954).

273 Metropolis Theatre Co. v. Chicago, 228 U.S. 61 (1913).

income of domestic corporation earned in and out of the state.[274] The state argued that the reason for the distinction was that earning income out of the state did not require use of local government services, which the Court said was true also of the out of state income of local corporations doing business in the state. This decision proves that a difference in fact is not alone sufficient to justify a difference in taxation, if the Court cares about the discrimination.

In rare cases the Court has refuses to agree with a state's logical purpose for a distinction, which effectively treats the classes as the same. For example in *Louisville Gas* the five man majority refused to allow Kentucky to exempt short term mortgages mostly given by small borrowers and homeowners from the recording tax, while charging the tax for recording what were generally longer term loans.[275] The Court assumed that the term might bear on the value and might permissibly justify a differential rate but not a complete exemption. Justices Holmes, Brandeis, Stone and Sanford dissented, stating that the state had a purpose to help small borrowers and identified them by the term of their notes, which was a reasonable approach. Unfortunately, later opinions of the Court have recited Justice Sutherland's view that the discrimination was of "an unusual character" requiring special analysis, as in *Windsor*.[276] Aside from that citation, the most recent citation of *Louisville* in a state tax case, cited the Brandeis dissent.[277]

(b) *Deemed No Difference Cases*

Residents must be treated the same as nonresidents for some taxing purposes, without treating nonresidence as a suspect category. Once admitted to the state, a foreign corporation must be taxed the same as domestic corporations on property value.[278] The Court has applied the same deemed equality to individuals paying sales and use taxes.[279] But some of these decisions are based on the Commerce Clause.[280]

---

[274] F. S. Royster Guano Co. v. Virginia, 253 U.S. 412 (1920). This opinion has been cited as an origin of the rational basis standard, which has come under attack when applied to particular discriminations. *See* United States v. Windsor, 570 U.S. 744 (2013) (Roberts dissent).

[275] Louisville Gas & Electric Co. v. Coleman, 277 U.S. 32 (1928).

[276] United States v. Windsor, 570 U.S. 744 (2013).

[277] Madden v. Kentucky, 309 U.S. 83 (1940).

[278] Wheeling Steel Corp. v. Glander, 337 U.S. 562 (1949) (ruled discriminatory taxation of receivables of foreign corporation and not of residents); Hanover Fire Ins. Co. v. Harding, 272 U.S. 494 (1926) (property tax); WHYY, Inc. v. Borough of Glassboro, 393 U.S. 117 (1968) (out of state nonprofit corporation admitted to state entitled to same property tax exemption as domestic non profit corporations; cited additional authorities). There are some contrary early cases but one from that period that should still be good law is Southern R. Co. v. Greene, 216 U.S. 400 (1910) (after being admitted to state a railroad acquired permanent improvements and then state imposed heavier annual license tax than imposed on domestic corporations denied equal protection). *See* W. & S. Life Ins. Co. v. State Bd. of Equalization, 451 U.S. 648 (1981) fn. 16.

[279] Williams v. Vermont, 472 U.S. 14 (1985) (use tax credit for sales tax paid to another state could not be limited to sales taxes paid by persons who were residents of the use tax state at the time of purchase).

[280] Halliburton Oil Well Cementing Co. v. Reily, 373 U.S. 64 (1963) (relied on by *Williams v. Vermont*).

The Equal Protection Clause prevents unequal treatment of recently arrived residents or resident aliens in receiving public benefits based on not contributing to state taxes in the past when nonresident.[281] And yet *Nordlinger v. Hahn* approved a "welcome stranger" policy of valuing newly purchased property at its price and long held properties at their original purchase prices.[282]

However, the principle that nonresidents must be treated the same as residents will not prevent a taxing distinction based on characteristics that might be more likely shared by nonresidents, but for which the state proves another purpose exists, such as to benefit small producers.[283]

d. *Legitimate Purpose*

(1) *General*

The requirement of a "legitimate governmental purpose" for the unequal treatment traces back to at least the earliest Chinese laundry case (not a tax case) in 1885 when Justice Field said prohibiting work in (largely wooden) laundries overnight furthered a "public purpose" of preventing fires.[284] But when the city adopted an ordinance that banned wooden laundries unless specifically allowed by the city, the Court found that the purpose of the ban was to preclude Chinese laundries, which overwhelmingly were operated in wooden buildings and were the predominant laundries in the city; the city evidently being unwilling to defend on the basis that it was discriminating against Chinese, and unable to give any other reason, the Court concluded that there was no public purpose for the discrimination and applied the Equal Protection Clause.[285]

Thus, without calling the Chinese heritage of the class a suspect or protected category, the Court in effect applied that limitation on the states' power to draw lines in applying its police powers. The potential for such an improper purpose (although the category was ill defined) to have motivated the distinction likely led the Court to begin to actually examine the legislative purposes as contrasted with simply presuming that the state had its reasons for drawing lines in taxation and otherwise.

The Court has also referred to the "legitimate governmental purposes" as "a legitimate state interest."[286] Raising tax revenue is always a legitimate governmental purpose. Does the purpose to raise revenue always provide a rational basis

---

[281] Shapiro v. Thompson, 394 U.S. 618 (1969) (public benefits); Graham v. Richardson, 403 U.S. 365 (1971) (welfare benefits could not be denied to aliens).

[282] Nordlinger v. Hahn, 505 U.S. 1 (1992). *Cf.* Zobel v. Williams, 457 U. S. 55 (1982) (Alaska oil revenue "dividend" distribution system that favored long-term residents was unconstitutional, as would be a state tax that varied with length of residence).

[283] American Sugar Refining Co. v. Louisiana, 179 U.S. 89 (1900); Great Atlantic & Pacific Tea Co. v. Grosjean, 301 U.S. 412 (1937).

[284] Barbier v. Connolly, 113 U.S. 27 (1885).

[285] Yick Wo v. Hopkins, 118 U.S. 356 (1886). *Cf.* Quong Wing v. Kirkendall, 223 U.S. 59 (1912) (Court recognized the possibility that the hand laundry tax was improperly aimed at the Chinese, but plaintiff did not argue that ground).

[286] Nordlinger v. Hahn, 505 U.S. 1 (1992).

for a tax on the plaintiff that happens to be greater than the tax on some other person? The answer must be no. The distinction or classification that caused the plaintiff to pay a tax that some other persons did not pay must be tested for furthering the governmental purposes.

And yet, finding the purposes is an uncertain process. The Court does not hold state legislatures to the standards of the federal Administrative Procedure Act, requiring them to explain their reasons at the time of enactment;[287] rather the Court usually will infer logical reasons, usually meaning accepting the after the fact explanations provided by the state's attorneys in litigation.[288] In fact the Court may not even need to infer good reasons, but will "presume" a rational basis for a taxing difference from the rational ability to differentiate two groups of persons based on non tax facts, unless the taxpayer proves otherwise.[289]

Although opinions say that the state's taxing distinction must have a legitimate purpose, in practice that means something less than a wide-ranging analysis of legislative thought processes. It means that (1) it may not have a purpose to discriminate against a protected category unless it passes stricter scrutiny (beginning with the Chinese laundry cases and discussed below), and (2) if it does not violate (1), the purpose will be deemed legitimate (approximating the "pass" that such choices originally were given) so long as there is actually a difference between the two categories that are taxed differently, with this caveat: a difference in fact between the categories may be disregarded if (a) it is not rationally related to a purpose for the taxing distinction asserted by the state or inferred by the Court,[290] or (b) it is a difference that the Supreme Court has ruled must be disregarded for Equal Protection Clause purposes (separate and apart from suspect categories). Thus at least at one time the Court believed that a state's interest in helping widows justified giving them a state tax preference not available to widowers.[291]

Therefore, there are no illegitimate purposes that do not involve protected categories or deemed equal categories. For example a tax on lessees of land of the United States violated Equal Protection when lessees of state lands were not taxed; dealing with the United States is a protected category even though this

---

[287] Carmichael v. Southern Coal & Coke Co., 301 U.S. 495 (1937) ("In the nature of the case it cannot record a complete catalogue of the considerations which move its members to enact laws.").

[288] Allied Stores of Ohio v. Bowers, 358 U.S. 522 (1959); Carmichael v. Southern Coal & Coke Co., 301 U.S. 495 (1937).

[289] Carmichael v. Southern Coal & Coke Co., 301 U.S. 495 (1937); Stebbins v. Riley, 268 U.S. 137 (1925) "I(t is not necessary that the basis of classification should be deductible from the nature of the thing classified. It is enough that the classification is reasonably founded in the 'purposes and policies of taxation.' . . . It is not open to objection unless it precludes the assumption that the classification was made in the exercise of legislative judgment and discretion.").

[290] And in most cases where, for example, the license tax on electricians is different from that for plumbers the state will be wise enough not to state a purpose and the Court will cite *Bell's Gap* and say the distinction is in the discretion of the legislature, which is aware of a multitude of facts.

[291] Kahn v. Shevin, 416 U.S. 351 (1974).

was not literally an intergovernmental immunity ruling.[292] The classic example of deemed equal categories is "redhaired men and black-haired men and the classification would immediately be seen to be wrong; it would have only arbitrary relation to the purpose and province of legislation."[293] But it is not arbitrary to define a taxed class in a way that happens to apply to only one taxpayer.[294]

States often create tax distinctions in pursuance of a desire to regulate through taxation. Because regulation can also be an exercise of the police power, occasionally older opinions referred to taxes as exercise of the police power.[295] But they usually are not; they are the use of the taxing power to effect the police power: regulatory taxes.[296] The incorrect linkage seems to be limited to vehicle license taxes for driving in a state,[297] and taxes on industries to which police regulation is important like alcohol.[298] Because of a state's police power to regulate and control wild animals in the state it could impose a tax on dealers in hides while not taxing other merchants.[299]

If a reason exists for the taxing distinction, the fact that the state made it retroactive does not change the Equal Protection Clause analysis.[300]

A distinction required to satisfy the Commerce Clause cannot cause a violation of the Equal Protection Clause.[301]

(2) *No Rational Relationship to Purpose*

Even though a purpose might be legitimate, the actual discrimination at issue may not logically relate to that purpose. The Court invalidated a property tax exemption for Vietnam veterans who had a defined long residency in the state because it neither served the purpose of encouraging veterans to move to the state nor the purpose of honoring those who served; the purpose were not illegitimate but the discrimination failed.[302]

---

[292] Phillips Chemical Co. v. Dumas Independent School Dist., 361 U.S. 376 (1960).

[293] Tanner v. Little, 240 U.S. 369 (1916).

[294] Independent Warehouses, Inc. v. Scheele, 331 U.S. 70 (1947) (commercial warehouses but not private warehouses taxed; plaintiff owned only commercial warehouse in the city).

[295] Reymann Brewing Co. v. Brister, 179 U.S. 445 (1900) (liquor tax); Rast v. Van Deman & Lewis Co., 240 U.S. 342 (1916) (tax on merchants using trading stamps; opinion theorized that the state viewed the stamps as akin to a lottery, which was a suspect activity that was subject to the policy power); Tanner v. Little, 240 U.S. 369 (1916) (companion case); Pitney v. Washington, 240 U.S. 387 (1916) (companion case).

[296] Hammond Packing Co. v. Montana, 233 U.S. 331 (1914). *See* Ch. IX.C.4.e.

[297] Bode v. Barrett, 344 U.S. 583 (1953); Hendrick v. Maryland, 235 U.S. 610 (1915).

[298] Phillips v. Mobile, 208 U.S. 472 (1908); De Bary & Co. v. Louisiana, 227 U.S. 108 (1913) (the federal Wilson Act intended to allow state taxation of "all" imported liquor, whether from other states or foreign countries); Nashville, C. & S. L. Railway v. Walters, 294 U.S. 405 (1935) (an unusual opinion finding that a state had failed to rationally explain why a railroad should bear the cost of a bridge required by the national highway system).

[299] Lacoste v. Department of Conservation, 263 U.S. 545 (1924).

[300] Welch v. Henry, 305 U.S. 134 (1938).

[301] Matson Navigation Co. v. State Bd. of Equalization, 297 U.S. 441 (1936); Hart Refineries v. Harmon, 278 U.S. 499 (1929) (during era when imported gas could not be taxed under Commerce Clause, sales tax could be limited to domestic gas).

[302] Hooper v. Bernalillo County Assessor, 472 U.S. 612 (1985).

A use tax imposed on nonresidents' cars to support the roads could not logically exempt from the use tax residents who also use the roads.[303] A state tax regime designed to encourage nonresident insurance companies to invest in the state failed of its stated purpose, which might have been a proper purpose, because the nonresidents could never bring their taxes into parity with local insurers no matter how much they invested.[304] The Court rejected on Equal Protection grounds an early effort to apportion a tax base of authorized no par shares because it did not rationally relate the amount of tax to the amount of business done in the state (also Commerce Clause).[305]

A rural county could not just estimate the "benefit" of road building in the county to a railroad passing through the county without any explanation for how the estimate was made, particularly when the railroad was assessed $67,000 for 9 miles of track and town lots were assessed $10.[306] The Court ruled that a state could not tax the casualty insurance premiums received by a multiline foreign insurer and exempt the casualty insurance premiums received by a foreign insurer that sold only casualty insurance; there was no purpose served by the distinction.[307]

Particularly the Vietnam veterans' case cited above shows that if the Court wants to find a distinction, or find absence of a distinction, or find illogic in a state's logic, it can usually do so; the determinant is usually whether the Justices get interested in the discrimination.

(3) *Administrative Considerations Creating Actual Difference*

Administrative concerns can be legitimate purposes and create a difference in otherwise similar taxpayers and defeat an Equal Protection Clause claim. For example railroads owning tracks located in other states obviously are subject to tax in other states but a railroad with solely in-state tracks had to prove that its cars could be subject to taxation in another state.[308] A state could exempt from tax employers with less than eight employees, which might be explained by administrative convenience.[309] A state ad valorem tax on residents did not violate the Equal Protection Clause by applying a lower rate of tax to local bank deposits (collected by the local bank), and a higher rate to deposits in out of state banks, because the difference might be explained by difficulties of collection.[310] In a

---

303 Williams v. Vermont, 472 U.S. 14 (1985).

304 Metro. Life Ins. Co. v. Ward, 470 U.S. 869 (1985).

305 Air-Way Electric Appliance Corp. v. Day, 266 U.S. 71 (1924).

306 Kansas City S. R. Co. v. Road Improv. Dist., 256 U.S. 658 (1921). But the Court ruled otherwise where the state statute directed the railroad to pay for the road (numbers not appearing). Branson v. Bush, 251 U.S. 182 (1919).

307 Concordia Fire Ins. Co. v. Illinois, 292 U.S. 535 (1934). Justices Cardozo, Brandeis and Stone dissented.

308 Central R. Co. v. Pennsylvania, 370 U.S. 607 (1962).

309 Carmichael v. Southern Coal & Coke Co., 301 U.S. 495 (1937).

310 Madden v. Kentucky, 309 U.S. 83 (1940).

relatively recent ruling, administrative convenience justified the unusual choice to forgive unpaid installments of a tax but not refund those who paid early.[311]

Although not specifically explained as for administrative convenience, the Court upheld a state stock tax that valued non par stock at $100 (or imposed a flat rate on non par stock) rather than either valuing it or basing the tax on paid in capital, as was done for other types of stock.[312]

The state could impose on a temporary resident a tax for the privilege of driving, which it chose not to impose on out of state persons enjoying shorter stays, presumably as a matter of administrative convenience.[313] The difference between vested and contingent remainders and the uncertainty of valuation explained the unequal taxation for inheritance tax purposes.[314]

See discussion of administrative convenience in Chapter V.D.3.b(6).

(4) *Progressivity*

Generally, differences in the amount of the tax base justify increasing rates, called progressivity.[315] Progressive rate inheritance tax did not violate the Equal Protection Clause.[316] The city license tax could be different fixed amounts for sellers whose sales fell within bands, meaning that sellers at the top and bottom of one band paid the same tax, but less than sellers with more sales (a cliff effect).[317] The tax on salmon canneries could increase with the amount of production because the profit was likely to increase as the volume increased.[318]

However, in a questionable ruling the Court found there was no rational basis to levy a progressive gross receipts tax as contrasted with a progressive income tax; in the case of incomes the taxpayer with more income is different from the taxpayer with less income; but the seller's more numerous sales are all like its first sale and should not be subject to a higher rate.[319] This decision may be the exception that proves the rule that progressivity is permissible. Evidently the state defended on the ground that its purpose was to tax higher net income's more heavily. The plaintiff evidently proved that the gross receipts were not in

---

[311] Armour v. City of Indianapolis, 566 U.S. 673 (2012).

[312] International Shoe Co. v. Shartel, 279 U.S. 429 (1929); New York v. Latrobe, 279 U.S. 421 (1929).

[313] Storaasli v. Minnesota, 283 U.S. 57 (1931).

[314] Salomon v. State Tax Com., 278 U.S. 484 (1929).

[315] Louis K. Liggett Co. v. Lee, 288 U.S. 517 (1933) (chain store tax; but Equal Protection was violated when the rate changed on account of stores being located in more than one county).

[316] Magoun v. Illinois Trust & Savings Bank, 170 U.S. 283 (1898); Stebbins v. Riley, 268 U.S. 137 (1925).

[317] Clark v. Titusville, 184 U.S. 329 (1902) ("All license laws and all specific taxes have in them an element of inequality; nevertheless they are universally imposed, and their illegality has never been questioned.").

[318] Pacific American Fisheries v. Alaska, 269 U.S. 269 (1925).

[319] Stewart Dry Goods Co. v. Lewis, 294 U.S. 550 (1935) (Cardozo, Brandeis and Stone dissented).

fact related to net income and so the progressivity could not be justified as based on increased ability to pay.[320]

A tax pro rata to gross receipts obviously collects unequal taxes from taxpayers but the disproportion is rational.[321] Progressivity may be called a graduated tax and the state may apply higher taxes to larger vehicles because they may do more damage to the roads.[322]

(5) *Promoting Local Interests*

(a) *Overview*

The most confusing state tax discriminations are based on the in state versus out of state characteristics of persons, activities or property taxed. In addition to the potential for Commerce Clause, Privileges & Immunities Clause and even Supremacy Clause overlays, these cases are confusing because state legislators generally want to prefer their own residents or local activities and either don't think or care about discrimination. Sometimes they believe equality is achieved by compensating taxes on locals, discussed above in Chapter IX.D.3.b(2).

States necessarily first tax local persons, property and activities because the distinction is real and taxing local activities is the most natural course of state taxation and persons with no connection to the state cannot be taxed; indeed Equal Protection is not violated by not taxing the out of state activities on which the in state taxpayers are taxed when the foreigners or the transactions are beyond the state's taxing jurisdiction.[323] Moreover, states understand that the jurisdictional limits on state taxation necessarily leads to taxing local persons, property and activities more. Evidently that necessity leads to efforts to offset the natural local burden by promoting local interests in designing other features of the state's tax system.

(b) *Non-Admitted Foreigners*

A charitable bequest to a foreign charity was different in kind and could be taxed differently because the state did not regulate the charity and could not benefit from it.[324] But when the foreign charity is admitted to the state it must be treated equally as to tax benefits.[325]

---

[320] Great Atlantic & Pacific Tea Co. v. Grosjean, 301 U.S. 412 (1937) (dissent of Justice Sutherland, who wrote the *Stewart* opinion); New York Rapid Transit Corp. v. New York, 303 U.S. 573 (1938).

[321] Charlotte, C. & A. R. Co. v. Gibbes, 142 U.S. 386 (1892).

[322] Carley & Hamilton, Inc. v. Snook, 281 U.S. 66 (1930).

[323] Brown-Forman Co. v. Kentucky, 217 U.S. 563 (1910).

[324] Board of Education v. Illinois, 203 U.S. 553 (1906) (out of state charity denied exemption from inheritance tax enjoyed by local charities).

[325] WHYY, Inc. v. Glassboro, 393 U.S. 117 (1968) ("This is not a case in which the exemption was withheld by reason of the foreign corporation's failure or inability to benefit the State in the same measure as do domestic nonprofit corporations. Compare Board of Education v. Illinois. . ."); and Camps Newfound/Owatonna v. Town of Harrison, 520 U.S. 564 (1997) (applying Commerce Clause to prevent discrimination against local charity that served out of state persons).

(c) *Admission of Foreigners*

Once admitted to the state a foreign corporation is entitled to assert the Equal Protection Clause against discrimination in taxation.[326] However, for a long time the corollary of that rule was that the price of admission could be arbitrarily set. Eventually the Court ruled that the state cannot charge foreign entities a higher tax to qualify to do business in the state,[327] even if the higher charge is for the purpose of encouraging relocation.[328] The 1981 opinion establishing this principle recites the long path to reversal of the *Paul v. Virginia* rule;[329] earlier opinions on the issue will not be reviewed here.[330] And so, the state could not deny an otherwise qualified nonprofit corporation an exemption because it was a nonresident that qualified to operate in the state.[331]

But there is a different rule for admitting nonresidents to recreational activities and possibly other non-tax benefits. The Equal Protection Clause did not prevent charging nonresidents substantially higher hunting license fees (taxes) because the local residents supported wildlife through their own taxes.[332] Evidently that is a sort of compensating tax analysis showing no actual discrimination.

---

[326] Hanover Fire Ins. Co. v. Harding, 272 U.S. 494 (1926); Concordia Fire Ins. Co. v. Illinois, 292 U.S. 535 (1934) (state could not tax other property at 60 percent of value but tax net receipts of foreign insurance company at 100 percent of value).

[327] Western & Southern Life Ins. Co. v. State Bd. of Equalization, 451 U.S. 648 (1981) (primarily addressing retaliatory insurance taxes but first stating that nonresident could not be more heavily taxed without a proper purpose, which the equalization of foreign taxes on local insurers was found to be); Southern R. Co. v. Greene, 216 U.S. 400 (1910). *See also* Bethlehem Motors Corp. v. Flynt, 256 U.S. 421 (1921) (this early finding of unequal treatment in effect ruled that the state could not charge the foreign corporation more to operate in the state; the formula charged the same as for local corporations if the foreign corporation fulfilled a condition that was impossible for most foreign corporations but easy for local corporations; lacking that the foreign corporation paid $500 rather than $100; the $500 tax was not prohibitive but the condition for obtaining equal treatment was).

[328] Metro. Life Ins. Co. v. Ward, 470 U.S. 869 (1985) (higher privilege tax applied to foreign insurance company premiums not justified by encouraging insurance companies to organize in the state; Justice Powell's opinion is not the opinion of the Court because the decision appealed was affirmed by a divided Court). The dissent asserted that Prudential Insurance Co. v. Benjamin, 328 U.S. 408 (1946) had interpreted the McCarran-Ferguson Act to also free states from the Equal Protection Clause, but that opinion mentioned equal protection only in passing, and even if it so interpreted that Act, it does not stand for a rule allowing nonresidents to be taxed more heavily in general.

[329] Paul v. Virginia, 75 U.S. 168 (1868).

[330] *Western & Southern* named only *Lincoln National* in the category of the former line that had already been implicitly rejected. Lincoln National Life Ins. Co. v. Read, 325 U.S. 673 (1945), which had been based on the important early rulings in *Paul v. Virginia*; also Philadelphia Fire Ass'n v. New York, 119 U.S. 110 (1886); Atlantic Refining Co. v. Virginia, 302 U.S. 22 (1937) (accepted the state's characterization of the charge as a fee and not a tax but applied the same standard). New York State v. Roberts, 171 U.S. 658 (1898) is likely no longer correct. The Court early moved away from *Paul* where the nonresident corporation was engaged in interstate commerce, which was often the case. Western Union Tel. Co. v. Kansas, 216 U.S. 1 (1910) (although these decisions also precluded any tax on interstate commerce, which is no longer the law).

[331] WHYY, Inc. v. Glassboro, 393 U.S. 117 (1968).

[332] Baldwin v. Fish & Game Comm'n, 436 U.S. 371 (1978).

(d) *Favoring Nonresidents*

A state's purpose to encourage investment in or business in the state can be a legitimate purpose for lower taxation of nonresidents on account of investment in the state.[333] The Court upheld under the Equal Protection Clause a fixed amount franchise tax on domestic corporations while nonresident corporations were charged an amount based on their capital employed in the state.[334]

(e) *Retaliatory Taxes*

A state could impose higher premium tax on out of state insurance companies resident in states that imposed higher taxes on their own insurance companies to encourage other states to lower their taxes on the taxing state's own insurance companies.[335] That opinion described the retaliatory tax this way:

> [California] imposes a retaliatory tax on out-of-state insurers doing business in California, when the insurer's State of incorporation imposes higher taxes on California insurers doing business in that State than California would otherwise impose on that State's insurers doing business in California.

Retaliatory insurance premium taxes illustrate the principle stated above that when a state asserts a purpose for differential taxation it creates a burden for itself to show that the tax regime carries out that purpose. The Court found the purpose to favor local insurance companies was proper and that it was reasonable for California to believe that the retaliatory tax furthered that purpose.

But when the Court did not believe the reason for the distinction was to encourage change of other states laws but was to discriminate against commerce in other states, it found an Equal Protection Clause violation.[336]

And the Commerce Clause takes a more restrictive view of one state's use of its tax system to force other states to tax differently. The Court struck down under the Commerce Clause an Ohio statute that gave a credit against the sales tax per gallon of gasoline produced in the state (which violated the Commerce Clause), and did not allow the discrimination to be rehabilitated by offering the same credit to gasoline produced in another state that provided the same benefit for gasoline produced in Ohio.[337]

(f) *Favoring Investment in State*

As long as the rule does not discriminate against nonresidents, a state exemption or tax benefit possibly encouraging the development of oil and gas wells that

---

333 Allied Stores of Ohio v. Bowers, 358 U.S. 522 (1959) (allowed discrimination in favor of nonresident retailer that stored goods in state); Youngstown Sheet & Tube Co. v. Bowers, 358 U.S. 534 (1959).

334 Kansas City, M. & B. R. Co. v. Stiles, 242 U.S. 111 (1916).

335 Western & Southern Life Ins. Co. v. State Bd. of Equalization, 451 U.S. 648 (1981).

336 Williams v. Vermont, 472 U.S. 14 (1985) (only buyer who was Vermont resident at time he paid other state's sales tax can claim the credit).

337 New Energy Co. v. Limbach, 486 U.S. 269 (1988).

necessarily would be in the state did not violate the Equal Protection Clause.[338] But a condition on obtaining a lower tax rate that is necessarily easy for local businesses to meet but effectively impossible for nonresident businesses to meet denied equal protection because it was effectively a higher tax due solely to the fact of nonresidence.[339] A state could impose a tax on domestic and foreign corporations that operated within and without the state while exempting those that operated solely within the state (at least for equal protection purposes).[340]

(g) *Promoting Some Local Interests*

Apart from interstate commerce concerns, favoring a particular local class of business does not violate the Equal Protection Clause; indeed, it is the root of all state tax differentiation. It is shocking to many taxpayers to learn that a state can choose to regulate business by preferring some types and treating others less beneficially. Also the state may wholly exempt from a tax certain classes of business that it perceives would more benefit the public interest (such as agriculture).[341] It is rational to tax public companies differently from private companies (subsidiary corporations).[342] A state can levy a tax only on taxpayers for the purpose of paying for certain state benefits, including the benefit of regulation.[343] A state could exempt from sales and use taxes gas sold by public utilities but not independent sellers because the utilities perform a public service of serving large numbers of small customers.[344]

Nordlinger v. Hahn approved the purposes of neighborhood preservation and the reliance interest in paying low property taxes as sufficient to justify a "welcome stranger" policy of valuing newly purchased property at its price and long held properties at their original purchase prices.[345]

e. *Stricter Scrutiny*

The Court has invented several degrees of scrutiny for equal protection cases generally, including strictest (race or ethnic origin),[346] strict (religion,[347] content

---

338 Exxon Corp. v. Eagerton, 462 U.S. 176 (1983).

339 Metro. Life Ins. Co. v. Ward, 470 U.S. 869 (1985); Bethlehem Motors Corp. v. Flynt, 256 U.S. 421 (1921).

340 New York State v. Roberts, 171 U.S. 658 (1898).

341 Carmichael v. Southern Coal & Coke Co., 301 U.S. 495 (1937).

342 Citizens' Tel. Co. v. Fuller, 229 U.S. 322 (1913).

343 Charlotte, C. & A. R. Co. v. Gibbes, 142 U.S. 386 (1892). Dictum stated that it would not be rational to tax one class of taxpayer for the purpose of paying for a benefit to another class of taxpayers. But that cannot be right because many taxes do not benefit the payor.

344 GMC v. Tracy, 519 U.S. 278 (1997).

345 Nordlinger v. Hahn, 505 U.S. 1 (1992). *Cf.* Zobel v. Williams, 457 U. S. 55 (1982) (Alaska oil revenue "dividend" distribution system that favored long-term residents was unconstitutional, as would be a state tax that varied with length of residence).

346 Rucho v. Common Cause, 139 S. Ct. 2484 (2019); Fisher v. Univ. of Tex., 570 U.S. 297 (2013). *See* Regan v. Taxation with Representation, 461 U.S. 540 (1983).

347 Espinoza v. Mont. Dep't of Revenue, 140 S. Ct. 2246 (2020).

or viewpoint based speech,[348] fundamental right of gays and lesbians to vote,[349] and to marry,[350] and other "fundamental rights"), heightened or exacting (sex, commercial speech),[351] and rational basis scrutiny for regulation of economic and commercial matters, which the Court views as "lenient."[352]

But a state tax that might pass a rational basis test might not pass the "strictest scrutiny" applied to discrimination against interstate commerce.[353]

4. *Interstate Commerce*

A substantial number of Commerce Clause decisions are omitted from this Chapter. They all precede the *Complete Auto Transit* decision and either automatically struck down state taxes deemed to fall on interstate commerce or automatically approved taxes deemed to fall on local transactions because the interstate commerce had come to rest; or use outmoded principles such as the home port doctrine. However, the Chapter does cite those earlier decisions that seem to have continued relevance.

a. *Definition*

A person and the person's property or activities may be within a state's taxing jurisdiction under the Due Process Clause but effectively outside of its taxing jurisdiction under the Commerce Clause. In addition the subject of state taxation may be taxable under the Due Process and Commerce Clauses, but the amount of tax may be excessive under the Commerce Clause (and possibly also under the Due Process Clause). So the Commerce Clause functions as an on-off switch if Commerce Clause nexus to the taxing state does not exist, as well as a "how much" switch since the Supreme Court determined (as reflected in *Complete Auto Transit*, but predating it) that the perils of multiple taxation can be overcome by proper apportionment of the tax base; and so it became less necessary to determine when interstate commerce begins and ends and inappropriate to hinge the Commerce Clause result on that fact. Both uses of the Commerce Clause require showing that the state tax affects interstate commerce.

The bar is low to finding interstate commerce and usually any differential taxation can affect the interstate commerce: the taxpayer is a nonresident doing business (or not) in the state; the foreign business is taxed more heavily than the local business; the local person is taxed more lightly due to some connection to

---

348 Reed v. Town of Gilbert, 576 U.S. 155 (2015); Regan v. Taxation with Representation, 461 U.S. 540 (1983).

349 Romer v. Evans, 517 U.S. 620 (1996); Dunn v. Blumstein, 405 U.S. 330 (1972) (residency durational requirements for voting).

350 Obergefell v. Hodges, 576 U.S. 644 (2015).

351 Sorrell v. IMS Health Inc., 564 U.S. 552 (2011). Craig v. Boren, 429 U.S. 190 (1976) (found gender based discrimination but did not identify a scrutiny level). However, the Kahn v. Shevin, 416 U.S. 351 (1974) dissent referred to strict scrutiny of gender discrimination while majority found the discrimination reasonable.

352 Exxon Corp. v. Eagerton, 462 U.S. 176 (1983).

353 *See* Camps Newfound/Owatonna v. Town of Harrison, 520 U.S. 564 (1997); Fulton Corp. v. Faulkner, 516 U.S. 325 (1996); Associated Indus. v. Lohman, 511 U.S. 641 (1994).

local activities as contrasted with out of state activities. The Court routinely has viewed all of these types of differences as affecting interstate commerce.

But sometimes the tax falls on an activity that appears to be entirely local. That does not preclude an effect on interstate commerce, as for example when the tax is on a step in the movement of a product into the "stream of interstate commerce," where the tax "substantially affects" interstate commerce.[354] Transmission of radio waves by a radio station was interstate commerce, even though the station is local.[355] The Court treated the state taxation of receipt of dividends by a nonresident corporation from its foreign subsidiaries as affecting commerce because it necessarily involved "interstate business."[356] Similarly dividends received from a foreign subsidiary were characterized as part of the "flow of value" between the parent corporation and the subsidiary that created the unitary relationship for Foreign Commerce Clause purposes.[357] Interstate commerce was affected by an exemption from a state tax on stock held by residents to reflect state income tax paid by the corporation, which indirectly might discourage holding stock of corporations that did business out of state.[358]

Although any tax or fee charged to a nonresident in the state may affect that person's interstate commerce, when the Court finds the tax not to discriminate against interstate commerce, in effect the Court finds the tax not to affect interstate commerce in a constitutional sense, which can mean the Court did not find a real effect although an effect was hypothetically possible.[359] That means the bare dislike of paying a tax is not itself an effect on interstate commerce or a nonresident or a resident engaging in commerce.

The Commerce Clause is not limited to commerce as normally understood in connection with business, and also can apply to discrimination against non profit organizations.[360] However, the formation of a contract, apart from its performance, was not subject to the Commerce Clause.[361] At one time gross receipts taxes were thought to fall on interstate commerce while net income taxes did not, but the Court discarded that distinction.[362] The Court rejected a ruse by an oil purchaser to take advantage of the early exclusion of interstate commerce from any tax by creating documents that made the oil purchases appear to be for use out of state.[363]

---

[354] Commonwealth Edison Co. v. Mont., 453 U.S. 609 (1981) (severance of coal; any contrary statements in Heisler v. Thomas Colliery Co., 260 U.S. 245 (1922) were disapproved).

[355] Fisher's Blend Station, Inc. v. State Tax Com., 297 U.S. 650 (1936).

[356] Mobil Oil Corp. v. Comm'r of Taxes, 445 U.S. 425 (1980).

[357] Kraft Gen. Foods v. Iowa Dep't of Revenue & Fin., 505 U.S. 71 (1992).

[358] Fulton Corp. v. Faulkner, 516 U.S. 325 (1996).

[359] Am. Trucking Ass'ns v. Mich. PSC, 545 U.S. 429 (2005) (plaintiff did not prove that it had changed routes to avoid the tax, which presumably might have proved effect). *Cf.* Fulton Corp. v. Faulkner, 516 U.S. 325 (1996) (no proof required that tax scheme discouraged investments).

[360] Camps Newfound/Owatonna v. Town of Harrison, 520 U.S. 564 (1997) (see footnote 27).

[361] Western Live Stock v. Bureau of Revenue, 303 U.S. 250 (1938) (better known as a decision freeing the Commerce Clause from formalism).

[362] Comptroller of the Treasury v. Wynne, 575 U.S. 542 (2015).

[363] Superior Oil Co. v. Mississippi, 280 U.S. 390 (1930).

The other major area in which the definition of interstate commerce is relevant is in Congress' enumerated powers. Congress can legislate in controlling interstate commerce but does not otherwise have general police powers. In the 2012 Obamacare ruling the Roberts opinion agreed that health insurance was an interstate activity but not buying it was not.[364] But the Court upheld the tax under the taxing power not the Commerce Clause. The rulings on the reach of federal regulatory powers will not be reviewed here, but include such principles as the inclusion of learned professions (lawyers) in commerce.[365]

b. *Market Participant Exception*

A state may tax differently those who deal with it as a market participant, without Commerce Clause limitation, as for example by exempting from its income tax the interest it pays on its bonds.[366] However, the *Davis* opinion indicated that there could be a limit to the market participant exception by applying *Pike* to balance the competing interests.[367] Also a state tax exemption for a favored business or taxpayer does not make the state a market participant via the taxpayer's activities.[368] Most of the opinions on this exception are outside the state tax area and are not cited here.

c. *General Standard*

(1) *Domestic Commerce*

When the state tax facially discriminates against interstate commerce (meaning taxes differently due to in and out of state characteristics) is it almost "per se" invalid.[369] If a state nevertheless attempts to justify the discrimination based on a legitimate local purpose that cannot be adequately served by reasonable nondiscriminatory alternatives, the Court applies the "strictest scrutiny," which the Court has said is an extremely difficult burden, "so heavy that 'facial discrimination by itself may be a fatal defect.'"[370] The compensating tax discussed below is about the only exception and the compensation must be exact.

Denial of reduced property tax to nonprofit camps catering primarily to out of state campers did not meet that burden.[371] Likewise, a reduction of the tax on dividends from local corporations that presumably paid more income tax to the state did not justify the facial discrimination against multistate corporations through heavier taxation of the value of their stocks to residents of the state.[372] Ohio could not limit the tax credit for sales of ethanol to ethanol produced

---

[364] Nat'l Fed'n of Indep. Bus. v. Sebelius, 567 U.S. 519 (2012).

[365] Goldfarb v. Virginia State Bar, 421 U.S. 773 (1975).

[366] Dep't of Revenue v. Davis, 553 U.S. 328 (2008) (the Court also doubted an actual effect on interstate commerce), citing Bonaparte v. Tax Court, 104 U.S. 592 (1882).

[367] Pike v. Bruce Church, 397 U.S. 137 (1970).

[368] Camps Newfound/Owatonna v. Town of Harrison, 520 U.S. 564 (1997).

[369] Fulton Corp. v. Faulkner, 516 U.S. 325 (1996).

[370] Camps Newfound/Owatonna v. Town of Harrison, 520 U.S. 564 (1997).

[371] Camps Newfound/Owatonna v. Town of Harrison, 520 U.S. 564 (1997).

[372] Fulton Corp. v. Faulkner, 516 U.S. 325 (1996).

in the state or in other states that adopted a reciprocal rule (meaning that the retaliatory tax regime allowed for insurance premium taxes would not work under the Commerce Clause).[373] Hawaii could not exempt only locally produced liquor and wine from its alcohol sales tax.[374]

The test for facial tax discrimination implies that there can be state tax discriminations that are not facial and that a different standard may be applied. However, all purported state tax discriminations depend on some statutory provision that can differentially impact nonresidents or interstate commerce (except for intentional but unauthorized discrimination by tax officials); the real issue is how far is the Court willing to look for the rules producing the discriminatory effect. In a decision perhaps nearing the outer limits, the Court ruled that a facially nondiscriminatory tax on milk producers that was in effect rebated only to in state producers violated the Commerce Clause.[375] In contrast, a tax on severance of coal for use that in practice fell mostly on out of state users was not discriminatory because the imposition of the tax was facially neutral, and varied by use, which was determined by the customers.[376] Also the Court refused to find Commerce Clause discrimination based on some hypothetical amount of tax that the domiciliary state law might impose on the complaining nonresident corporation taxpayer.[377]

The "close enough for government work" standard does not apply for Commerce Clause discrimination purposes.[378]

See discussion of *Complete Auto Transit*, below.

(2) *Foreign Commerce*

Taxation of foreign commerce by states is subject to the same tests as the domestic Commerce Clause application, plus it presents two additional concerns: (1) additional ways the taxpayer can be subject to multiple taxation by taking account of foreign country taxes (sometimes), and (2) the supremacy of the federal government in international relations.[379] The taxpayer in *Japan Line* won because Japan in fact had taxed the property taxed in the state. Also in *Japan Line* the state charge actually violated a Customs Convention, which would seem to have invalidated it without more, under the Supremacy Clause. In contrast, *Barclays Bank* rejected a challenge to California's worldwide corporate income apportionment method because it was designed to prevent international multiple taxation and Congress had not spoken against it.

Japan Line assumed that the state would attempt to apportion the value of the foreign property to be taxed and asked "notwithstanding apportionment,

[373] New Energy Co. v. Limbach, 486 U.S. 269 (1988).

[374] Bacchus Imps. v. Dias, 468 U.S. 263 (1984).

[375] West Lynn Creamery, Inc. v. Healy, 512 U.S. 186 (1994).

[376] Commonwealth Edison Co. v. Mont., 453 U.S. 609 (1981).

[377] Mobil Oil Corp. v. Comm'r of Taxes, 445 U.S. 425 (1980).

[378] Associated Indus. v. Lohman, 511 U.S. 641 (1994).

[379] Japan Line, Ltd. v. County of Los Angeles, 441 U.S. 434 (1979); Barclays Bank Plc v. Franchise Tax Bd., 512 U.S. 298 (1994).

[whether the state's tax] creates a substantial risk of international multiple taxation." Once the taxpayer showed that the property in fact was taxed in Japan it had won because the Court thought multiple taxation was inevitable. However, the opinion did not say that Japan taxed 100 percent of the ships' value. Perhaps what that means is a "substantial risk" will be shown by any home country taxation of property. In contrast, moveable property can be taxed by more than one state, but on an apportioned basis.[380]

Florida's tax on the sale of aviation fuel to a Canadian carrier did not threaten multiple taxation because there could be only one place of sale, and Congress had not spoken to prohibit the tax.[381] Similarly a state sales tax on the purchase of containers for international shipping did not violate the Foreign Commerce Clause because it fell on a transaction that could occur only in the state and was not prohibited by federal law.[382]

A state income tax violated the Foreign Commerce Clause by allowing a deduction for dividends received from domestic subsidiaries but not from foreign subsidiaries, because the fact that the foreign subsidiary was unitary established a flow of commerce and the state statute facially discriminated against it.[383] The *Kraft* opinion also stated that foreign commerce could be harmed even if intra state commerce was not preferred: the relevant question is discrimination against foreign commerce. A state sales tax on fuel used on ships interfered with foreign commerce in violation of federal tariff laws.[384] The operator of a bridge to Canada was not engaging in foreign commerce.[385]

A much more serious attempt at state regulation of foreign commerce by a purported tax was stricken down in the *Passenger Cases*.[386]

(3) *Dormant Commerce Clause*

It is well established that the Commerce Clause creates a zone of exclusive jurisdiction of Congress over interstate commerce and its application by the courts need not await a federal statute denying some right to the states. The parameters of that zone and the means used to identify it and offending state statutes have varied in the Court's opinions over time. This chapter ignores most of the bypassed or overruled opinions in this area. But the exclusivity of the unexercised power of Congress must be firmly understood.

Chief Justice Marshall in the important *Gibbons v. Ogden* opinion decided that a federal ship license preempted the claimed exclusivity of a state shipping license.[387] Even though that did not clearly involve a case Congress had not

---

[380] Ch. IX.F.2 and G.2.

[381] Wardair Canada, Inc. v. Florida Dep't of Revenue, 477 U.S. 1 (1986).

[382] Itel Containers Int'l Corp. v. Huddleston, 507 U.S. 60 (1993).

[383] Kraft Gen. Foods v. Iowa Dep't of Revenue & Fin., 505 U.S. 71 (1992).

[384] McGoldrick v. Gulf Oil Corp., 309 U.S. 414 (1940).

[385] Detroit International Bridge Co. v. Corporation Tax Appeal Board, 294 U.S. 83 (1935).

[386] Smith v. Turner, 48 U.S. 283 (1849) (tax per passenger on arriving ships); Henderson v. Mayor of N.Y., 92 U.S. 259 (1875) (commutation tax on immigrants).

[387] Gibbons v. Ogden, 22 U.S. 1 (1824).

addressed, the opinion indicated that Congress' power was exclusive even if unexercised. However, Chief Justice Taney went out of his way in *Thurlow v. Massachusetts* to undercut Marshall's view.[388] It is not hard to see the tension between the Federalist views of Marshall and the states' rights views of Taney.

And yet, Taney left a loophole to find a state law repugnant to the Constitution even in the absence of a federal statute: the state law had to be "in the execution of its police and health laws." That loophole allowed the Court to strike down a tax on immigrants coming off ships, but Chief Justice Taney dissented, sticking to his argument that the federal power was not exclusive unless exercised.[389] Taney went along with the important *Cooley v. Board of Wardens* ruling because it upheld state regulation of pilots, but he must not have liked this statement in the opinion of the Court:

> Either absolutely to affirm, or deny that the nature of this power requires exclusive legislation by Congress, is to lose sight of the nature of the subjects of this power, and to assert concerning all of them, what is really applicable but to a part. Whatever subjects of this power are in their nature national, or admit only of one uniform system, or plan of regulation, may justly be said to be of such a nature as to require exclusive legislation by Congress. That this cannot be affirmed of laws for the regulation of pilots and pilotage is plain.[390]

The term "dormant Commerce Clause" did not appear in a Supreme Court opinion until 1982.[391] Then in 2015 Justice Alito, no fan of the dormant Commerce Clause, grudgingly recited much of the history stated above and doubled down by applying it to protect an individual resident from possible double taxation of multistate income.[392]

d. *Compensatory Tax*

As discussed above, states collect a use tax on the value of goods bought out of state for use in the state and to which the state's sales tax could not have applied. Therefore, it appears to discriminate against interstate commerce but is the sole example of a so called compensatory tax that can be justified under the Commerce Clause because it is not difficult to measure the relationship of the credited out of state sales tax and the state's use tax.[393] The Court generally

---

[388] Thurlow v. Massachusetts, 46 U.S. 504 (1847).

[389] Smith v. Turner, 48 U.S. 283 (1849).

[390] Cooley v. Bd. of Wardens, 53 U.S. 299 (1852). Also based on the exclusive power of Congress are Nathan v. Louisiana, 49 U.S. 73 (1850), and Case of State Freight Tax, 82 U.S. 232 (1873).

[391] Merrion v. Jicarilla Apache Tribe, 455 U.S. 130 (1982).

[392] Comptroller of the Treasury v. Wynne, 575 U.S. 542 (2015).

[393] Fulton Corp. v. Faulkner, 516 U.S. 325 (1996) fn. 8 (ordinarily will be limited to sales use taxes due to difficulty of measurement, citing Henneford v. Silas Mason Co., 300 U.S. 577 (1937)).

rejects other state efforts to claim that facial discrimination can be overcome by a compensating tax.[394]

e. *Discrimination Without Effect*

There is no differential taxation of interstate commerce when the domestic sellers serve a different market than the interstate sellers; the domestic sellers were locally regulated public utilities.[395] This appears to be a narrow exception. In an analogous area, discrimination against interstate commerce does not occur simply because the items taxed come solely from out of state (oil).[396]

f. *Direct and Indirect Taxpayers*

The customer of the taxed person can have standing to complain under the Commerce Clause.[397]

g. Complete Auto Transit *Test*

(1) *Four Prongs*

When the tax base of a taxpayer doing business in more than one state is apportionable, each such state, including the domiciliary state,[398] must limit the portion of the tax base subject to its tax according to the four requirements briefly referred to in *Complete Auto Transit*.[399] Presumably the Court did not invent tests, but undertook to synthesize prior opinions, while finally abandoning the sometimes applied policy that interstate commerce could never be taxed by states.

In an extremely short opinion not containing much reasoning, the Court ruled that on the facts of that case, the Commerce Clause allowed the state to impose a privilege license tax on a nonresident corporation's gross income earned solely from transporting cars within the state, because (1) the taxpayer had a substantial nexus with the taxing state (because it performs services in the state), (2) the tax was fairly apportioned (because only gross income earned from purely in state services counted), (3) the tax did not discriminate against interstate commerce (because the transports were wholly in state), and (4) the tax fairly related to the services provided by the state (because only income earned wholly in the state was taxed).[400] It is unfortunate that hundreds of later cases have had to attempt to discern the meaning of these words, which the Court may not initially have intended to become an iconic formula, which were largely

394 Tyler Pipe Indus. v. Washington State Dep't of Revenue, 483 U.S. 232 (1987); Armco Inc. v. Hardesty, 467 U.S. 638 (1984).

395 GMC v. Tracy, 519 U.S. 278 (1997).

396 Texas Co. v. Brown, 258 U.S. 466 (1922).

397 GMC v. Tracy, 519 U.S. 278 (1997).

398 Comptroller of the Treasury v. Wynne, 575 U.S. 542 (2013).

399 Complete Auto Transit, Inc. v. Brady, 430 U.S. 274 (1977).

400 Complete Auto Transit, Inc. v. Brady, 430 U.S. 274 (1977). The taxpayer had receipts from intrastate deliveries, but they were not taxed.

irrelevant to the facts of the case, and which may or may not have been an accurate distillation of prior rulings.

Discrimination can often be identified without resort to apportionment. When heavier taxation or loss of a tax benefit hinges on an out of state element, the rest of the prongs are irrelevant.

(2) *Fair Apportionment*

Fair apportionment has two features: internal consistency ("the formula must be such that, if applied by every jurisdiction, it would result in no more than all of the unitary business' income being taxed"), and external consistency ("the factor or factors used in the apportionment formula must actually reflect a reasonable sense of how income is generated.").[401] Actually the external consistency test is more of a know it when I see it test, for which the 1991 opinion cited opinions substantially predating *Complete Auto*.[402]

(3) *Internal Consistency*

The Supreme Court's internal consistency test is a shortcut to identifying discrimination against interstate commerce.[403] It asks a hypothetical question: Would interstate commerce suffer discrimination if all jurisdictions adopted the challenged state regime? The *Wynne* majority used the internal consistency test to show hypothetical double taxation of the taxpayer's S corporation income earned in interstate commerce, but only as a makeweight.[404]

Justice William J. Brennan Jr. invented the internal consistency test in 1983 in his *Container Corp.* opinion, which did not even cite *Complete Auto Transit*.[405] He used it to test whether the California apportionment formula was fair, the second prong of *Complete Auto Transit*. The excuse for the hypothetical test is that the Court did not want the analysis to turn on messy facts of actual discrimination.[406] However, the Court has not been consistent in its use of internal consistency, which befits its status as an adjunct to a made up gloss on a notoriously vague constitutional provision on interstate commerce.[407]

Actually internal consistency is just a repackaging of a mode of analysis that protected many state taxes from Commerce Clause attacks during the era when the Court believed states could not tax interstate commerce at all. The Court would uphold a tax by finding that the tax fell on an aspect of the interstate

[401] Trinova Corp. v. Mich. Dep't of Treasury, 498 U.S. 358 (1991).

[402] Hans Rees' Sons, Inc. v. North Carolina, 283 U.S. 123 (1931) ("out of all appropriate proportions to the business transacted . . . in that State"); Norfolk & W. R. Co. v. Missouri State Tax Comm'n, 390 U.S. 317 (1968) ("led to a grossly distorted result").

[403] *See* Cummings, *Internal Consistency and the Federal Income Tax*, 77 State Tax Notes 185 (July 13, 2015).

[404] Comptroller of the Treasury v. Wynne, 575 U.S. 542 (2013).

[405] Container Corp. of Am. v. Franchise Tax Bd., 463 U.S. 159 (1983).

[406] Armco Inc. v. Hardesty, 467 U.S. 638 (1984).

[407] Am. Trucking Ass'ns v. Mich. PSC, 545 U.S. 429 (2005).

business that could not be replicated by a tax imposed by another state, such as a tax on local property.[408]

(4) *Direct Apportionment: Gross Receipts*

A major source of confusion is when *Complete Auto Transit* style apportionment of an item reflecting multistate activity is not required because only one state can tax the item; therefore, it cannot run the risk of double taxation, and it can, in effect, be directly apportioned to that one state, which can tax it all.

Justice Alito increased rather than reduced the confusion in his *Wynne* opinion, which required apportionment of a resident's multistate business income., which happened to be nationwide gross receipts, not localized to Maryland.[409] He asserted that prior rulings were wrong if they indicated that gross receipts taxes were not subject to apportionment the same as net income taxes. However, he neglected to notice that many of those opinions involved tax items that could only be taxed by one state.

Indeed, in 1995 the Court had upheld such a directly apportioned gross receipts tax in *Jefferson Lines*, cited by *Wynne*.[410] Moreover, *Complete Auto* itself upheld a state tax that was not apportioned under a formula, but rather the state only taxed gross income that could be traced to the state ("cover only transportation 'between points within this state.'")[411] Similarly, the Court found the test satisfied by a use tax on those catalogs a merchandiser causes to be mailed into the state, for which a credit was allowed for out of state sales tax.[412]

The point is, that while net income of a multistate business necessarily reflects out of state activities, items linkable solely to the taxing state, such as certain gross receipts (*e.g.*, only gross receipts from sales in the state are taxed), do not. As a result the former tendency of the Court—to see gross receipts taxes as falling directly on interstate commerce and net income taxes as only indirectly affecting interstate commerce and perhaps constitutional for that reason—should be exactly reversed, with net income taxes necessarily requiring apportionment to satisfy *Complete Auto*, and gross receipts taxes all being subject to tax when the tax base is limited to the receipts with a solely local connection. But if the gross receipts are from interstate travel, then the domiciliary state could not tax all of them.[413]

See also Ch. IX.G.3.b, below.

---

[408] Memphis Natural Gas Co. v. Stone, 335 U.S. 80 (1948).

[409] Comptroller of the Treasury v. Wynne, 575 U.S. 542 (2015).

[410] Okla. Tax Comm'n v. Jefferson Lines, 514 U.S. 175 (1995).

[411] Complete Auto Transit, Inc. v. Brady, 430 U.S. 274 (1977); Itel Containers Int'l Corp. v. Huddleston, 507 U.S. 60 (1993) (sales tax imposed solely on leases into the state necessarily satisfied the four tests); Ewing v. Leavenworth, 226 U.S. 464 (1913).

[412] D. H. Holmes Co. v. McNamara, 486 U.S. 24 (1988).

[413] Philadelphia & Southern Mail S. S. Co. v. Pennsylvania, 122 U.S. 326 (1887).

h. *Other than Dormant Rules*

(1) *Public Law 86-272*

Section 101(a) of Public Law 86-272, 73 Stat. 555, 15 U. S. C. § 381, prohibits a State from taxing the net income of a corporation whose only business activities within the State consist of "solicitation of orders" for tangible goods, provided that the orders are sent outside the State for approval and the goods are delivered from out of state.[414] Congress enacted it in pursuance of its Commerce Clause powers. A wholesaler did more than that in the state when it sent its products to its local representative who transferred them to a local wholesaler, even though it was required to do so by state liquor regulation.[415] 15 U. S. C. § 383 defines net income as any tax measured by net income, to catch franchise and license taxes so measured. The rule is confusing because the solicitation of orders that can go along with not taxing the income supports the imposition of other taxes such as the sales tax.[416]

(2) *Insurance*

The McCarran-Ferguson Act precludes application of the Commerce Clause to state taxation of insurance companies.[417] But the Court struck down a state tax on insurance that had no relation to the state other than the location of the insured property in the state owned by a nondomiciliary corporation that was doing business in the state, because the Act does not give states power over insurance that they would not otherwise have; in that case the Due Process Clause prevented taxation of the premium payments.[418] In addition the Court has applied the Equal Protection Clause to invalidate a state tax on insurance.[419]

(3) *States' Rights*

The Court allowed Wyoming to sue Oklahoma in the Supreme Court and struck down an Oklahoma law requiring local power plants to use at least 10 percent locally produced coal, which caused a reduction of coal sales out of Wyoming and a reduction of the state's severance tax revenues.[420]

---

[414] Wisconsin Dep't of Revenue v. William Wrigley, Jr., Co., 505 U.S. 214 (1992) (performance in the state of independent business functions quite separate from the requesting of orders caused loss of the exemption).

[415] Heublein, Inc. v. South Carolina Tax Comm'n, 409 U.S. 275 (1972).

[416] South Dakota v. Wayfair, Inc., 138 S. Ct. 2080 (2018).

[417] 59 Stat. 33 (Mar. 9, 1945), codified at 15 U.S.C. § 1011 ("The Congress hereby declares that the continued regulation and taxation by the several States of the business of insurance is in the public interest, and that silence on the part of the Congress shall not be construed to impose any barrier to the regulation or taxation of such business by the several States."). *See* Prudential Ins. Co. v. Benjamin, 328 U.S. 408 (1946). Congress was motivated by a reversal of the Court's prior view that life insurance was not commerce in United States v. South-Eastern Underwriters Ass'n, 322 U.S. 533 (1944).

[418] State Bd. of Ins. v. Todd Shipyards Corp., 370 U.S. 451 (1962).

[419] Metro. Life Ins. Co. v. Ward, 470 U.S. 869 (1985).

[420] Wyoming v. Oklahoma, 502 U.S. 437 (1992).

(4) *Other*

Title 15 of the U.S. Code imposes several other specific limits on state regulation of interstate commerce involving specific industries. It applies a specific nondiscrimination rule to state taxation of generation of electricity.[421] The Court enforced it against a New Mexico tax.[422]

By authorizing the Territory of Hawaii to tax, Congress permitted it to tax inter-island shipping without regard to interstate commerce.[423]

5. *Intergovernmental Immunity*

a. *General*

Chapter II.C examines intergovernmental tax immunity, both of the federal government from state taxation and of the states from federal taxation, plus the Supremacy Clause. It lists most of the Supreme Court decisions in the area, many of which have been obsoleted by the major shift that occurred in the law in the 1930s away from finding taxes to indirectly fall on the other sovereign. Therefore, this Chapter will not restate the general subject but will briefly review the principal currently relevant decisions on state taxation of the federal government, its employees and instrumentalities.[424]

In 2019 the Court rehearsed the issues in striking down another attempt by a state to tax state employees' retirement benefits more lightly than federal retirees.[425] The Court unanimously held that West Virginia's exemption for the pensions of some state government retirees unlawfully discriminated against federal retirees whose pensions are taxed, in violation of 4 U.S.C. section 111, which consents to state taxation of federal pay only if the state tax does not discriminate on the basis of the federal source of the pay.[426]

The 2019 opinion emphasized these aspects of the federal statute's permission for state taxation of federal compensation: (1) if a "similarly situated" federal payee does not get the same tax treatment as a state payee, the state tax violates the principle of intergovernmental tax immunity; (2) characterizing the size of the preferred state employee group as de minimis is not likely to work; (3) the Court was unwilling to look into whether the state tax break compensated for low pay for the state employees relative to federal employees; (4) pretty much any state tax break for a state employee is likely to violate the statute because

---

421 15 U.S.C. § 391.

422 Ariz. Public Serv. Co. v. Snead, 441 U.S. 141 (1979).

423 Inter-Island Steam Navigation Co. v. Hawaii, 305 U.S. 306 (1938).

424 As to instrumentalities, see Ark. v. Farm Credit Servs., 520 U.S. 821 (1997) (plaintiffs could not sue as federal instrumentalities without the United States' joinder; barred by Tax Injunction Act).

425 Dawson v. Steager, 139 S. Ct. 698 (2019), based on Davis v. Michigan Department of Treasury, 489 U.S. 803 (1989). *See* Harper v. Va. Dep't of Taxation, 509 U.S. 86 (1993) (remedies in this type of case); Barker v. Kan., 503 U.S. 594 (1992).

426 *See* Cummings, *The Supreme Court's 2018 Term in Tax*, 164 Tax Notes (TA) 1001 (Aug. 12, 2019).

almost necessarily there will be a similarly situated federal payee (although plaintiffs usually try to look like the preferred group, such as law enforcement officers);[427] and (5) the standard is different from that applied in Equal Protection Clause cases and having a rational basis for the distinction is not enough to protect the state tax exemption.

Federal employees almost always win these cases, with the sole exception being the 1999 *Acker* ruling.[428] A county privilege license tax imposed on all judges and based on compensation income did not violate the Public Salary Tax Act of 1939, 4 U.S.C. § 111, because it did not discriminate against federal judges. Evidently the ruling was based on the factual finding that "similarly situated" state judges and other state employees also paid the tax.

Another relatively recent decision ruled that Arizona could collect a gross receipts tax on a private business that earned compensation from the federal government.[429] The Court applied law that had been well established for many years since the drawback of intergovernmental tax immunity began in the 1930s.

The dissent of Justice Holmes in *Panhandle Oil* has been frequently cited, both for its disagreement with intergovernmental immunity and its clear-sightedness about tax:

> It seems to me that the State Court was right. I should say plainly right, but for the effect of certain dicta of Chief Justice Marshall which culminated in or rather were founded upon his often quoted proposition that the power to tax is the power to destroy. In those days it was not recognized as it is today that most of the distinctions of the law are distinctions of degree. If the States had any power it was assumed that they had all power, and that the necessary alternative was to deny it altogether. But this Court which so often has defeated the attempt to tax in certain ways can defeat an attempt to discriminate or otherwise go too far without wholly abolishing the power to tax. The power to tax is not the power to destroy while this Court sits. The power to fix rates is the power to destroy if unlimited, but this Court while it endeavors to prevent confiscation does not prevent the fixing of rates. A tax is not an unconstitutional regulation in every case where an absolute prohibition of sales would be one.[430]

But the reversal of the preclusion of intergovernmental taxation was also forecast by a variety of moderating opinions, as for example, the value of property taxed by a state may reflect the increase in value attributable to a federal permit.[431]

---

[427] Barker v. Kan., 503 U.S. 594 (1992) (federal military retirees are substantially similar to all state government retirees, although the opinion did not use that term).

[428] Jefferson County v. Acker, 527 U.S. 423 (1999).

[429] Ariz. Dep't of Revenue v. Blaze Constr. Co., 526 U.S. 32 (1999).

[430] Panhandle Oil Co. v. Mississippi ex rel. Knox, 277 U.S. 218 (1928).

[431] Susquehanna Power Co. v. State Tax Comm'n, 283 U.S. 291 (1931).

b. *Federal Statutes Precluding State Tax; the Supremacy Clause*

(1) *General*

In addition to the Commerce Clause, the Supremacy Clause allows Congress to forbid state taxation in the exercise of a federal power. Certain federal statutes clearly do so, but more often plaintiffs have unsuccessfully claimed that other federal statutes indirectly precluded state taxation. When Congress creates an agency to engage in commerce it can sue and be sued and presumably a state DOR can sue it to enforce state tax law.[432] In addition various federal statutes specifically allow state taxation of federal instrumentalities and on federal lands.[433] Not all of these will be discussed here.

A federal statute that supersedes state laws insofar as they "relate to" any employee benefit plan covered by ERISA did not preclude a state gross receipts tax on medical centers' gross receipts for patient services.[434]

A state tax on copyright royalties does not impede the federal right to copyright; the decision found a copyright to be property, and the Court cited it in a 2020 decision on copyright for that point.[435] The Supremacy Clause did not prevent states from criminally prosecuting falsifying federal tax forms used as identification.[436]

31 U.S.C. § 3124(a) exempts from state taxation U.S. debt when the form of taxation would require the obligation or interest to be considered in computing the tax.[437] It excepts nondiscriminatory corporate franchise or other non property taxes and estate and inheritance taxes.[438] The Court ruled that it did not apply to "repos" because the U.S. debt was collateral for loans to the repo counterparty; in addition repos involving state debt were not treated differently.[439] But it did apply to a property tax on bank shares to the extent the value reflected

---

[432] Franchise Tax Bd. v. United States Postal Service, 467 U.S. 512 (1984).

[433] 4 U.S.C. section 105 allows state sales and use taxation in federal jurisdictions; 4 U.S.C. section 104 (motor fuels sold for private use);12 U.S.C. section 3019 (cooperative bank).

[434] De Buono v. Nysa-Ila Med. & Clinical Servs. Fund, 520 U.S. 806 (1997).

[435] Fox Film Corp. v. Doyal, 286 U.S. 123 (1932); Allen v. Cooper, 140 S. Ct. 994 (2020).

[436] Kansas v. Garcia, 140 S. Ct. 791 (2020).

[437] Smith v. Davis, 323 U.S. 111 (1944) (not applicable to open account obligation); American Bank & Trust Co. v. Dallas County, 463 U.S. 855 (1983) ("except as otherwise provided" was not in Statutes at Large and so should be ignored); New Jersey Realty Title Ins. Co. v. Division of Tax Appeals, 338 U.S. 665 (1950) (applying statute to property tax on insurance company); Rockford Life Ins. Co. v. Illinois Dep't of Revenue, 482 U.S. 182 (1987) (not applicable to Ginnie Maes); Shotwell v. Moore, 129 U.S. 590 (1889) (ignored effort to convert holdings to exempt debt on one day); Banks v. Mayor, 74 U.S. 16 (1869) (includes federal scrip); New Jersey Realty Title Ins. Co. v. Division of Tax Appeals, 338 U.S. 665 (1950) (found state tax to be a property tax even though state court said it was not); Northwestern Mut. Life Ins. Co. v. Wisconsin, 275 U.S. 136 (1927) (license tax based on gross receipts including bond interest, invalid).

[438] Werner Machine Co. v. Director of Div. of Taxation, 350 U.S. 492 (1956) (franchise tax allowed, before statute enacted); Memphis Bank & Trust Co. v. Garner, 459 U.S. 392 (1983) (tax discriminated against federal obligations held by bank).

[439] Neb. Dep't of Revenue v. Loewenstein, 513 U.S. 123 (1994).

the U.S. debt.[440] Another decision, however, approved a limited deduction for the federal debt.[441] An unusual decision that appeared to be based on equal protection struck down a state franchise tax that purported to exclude from the tax base stock of subsidiaries already taxed in the state while not excluding the stock of national banks that had also been taxed in the state and U.S. bonds.[442] The Court struck down a state statute that appeared not to tax the federal bonds' interest to corporations but to their shareholders as part of dividends.[443]

A federal statute requires nondiscriminatory state taxation of national banks the same as the state would tax a state banks organized in the state where the national bank has its principal office.[444] The 1969 change to that provision substantially simplified the earlier statute and intergovernmental immunity disputes involving national banks, which had been heavily litigated, and many earlier rulings are now obsolete.[445] An analogous provision applies to federal thrift institutions.[446] An early decision surprisingly allowed a state to require national banks to withhold a tax on depositors' interest similar to the franchise tax it imposed on state banks.[447] Not all of the national bank decisions are cited here.

49 U.S.C. § 11501, the Railroad Revitalization and Regulatory Reform Act (4-R Act), deems certain defined forms of state taxation of railroads to unreasonably burden interstate commerce. The railroads have been very successful in enforcing it against state taxation.[448]

49 U.S.C. § 40116 limits state taxation of airlines and air travel, but allows an in lieu tax completely used for airport and aeronautical purposes, which the Court found exempted a South Dakota property tax that took the place of all

---

[440] Am. Bank & Trust Co. v. Dallas County, 463 U.S. 855 (1983).

[441] First Nat'l Bank v. Bartow County Bd. of Tax Assessors, 470 U.S. 583 (1985); United States v. Atlas Life Ins. Co., 381 U.S. 233 (1965).

[442] Schuylkill Trust Co. v. Pennsylvania, 296 U.S. 113 (1935); Schuylkill Trust Co. v. Pennsylvania, 302 U.S. 506 (1938) (statute reinterpreted not to discriminate).

[443] Miller v. Milwaukee, 272 U.S. 713 (1927).

[444] 12 U.S.C. § 548. Diamond Nat'l Corp. v. State Bd. of Equalization, 425 U.S. 268 (1976) (sales tax fell on bank and not on vendor and so statute exempted bank); Tradesmens Nat'l Bank v. Oklahoma Tax Comm'n, 309 U.S. 560 (1940) (not violated by lesser taxation of a few random banks).

[445] *See* Michigan Nat'l Bank v. Michigan, 365 U.S. 467 (1961); First Nat'l Bank v. Hartford, 273 U.S. 548 (1927); Georgetown Nat'l Bank v. McFarland, 273 U.S. 568 (1927). There are numerous national bank tax cases not discussed here.

[446] 12 U.S.C. § 1464(h). *See* First Fed. Sav. & Loan Ass'n v. Tax Comm'n of Mass., 437 U.S. 255 (1978) (not finding discrimination).

[447] Clement Nat'l Bank v. Vermont, 231 U.S. 120 (1913).

[448] Ala. Dep't of Revenue v. CSX Transp., Inc., 575 U.S. 21 (2015); CSX Transp., Inc. v. Ala. Dep't of Revenue, 562 U.S. 277 (2011); CSX Transp., Inc. v. Ga. State Bd. of Equalization, 552 U.S. 9 (2007); Burlington N. R.R. v. Oklahoma Tax Comm'n, 481 U.S. 454 (1987). But the railroad lost in Dep't of Revenue of Or. v. ACF Indus., 510 U.S. 332 (1994) (the fact that other property is exempt from a generally applicable tax but not railroad property does not violate the Act).

other taxes.[449] When Congress allows or prohibits certain types of state taxes the characterization of the state tax is a matter of federal law.[450]

Congress barred taxation of the personal property of a serviceman domiciled in one state who is assigned to military duty in another state.[451] The Atomic Energy Act of 1946 prevented a state from collecting sales tax on sales to government contractors.[452] The Natural Gas Policy Act of 1978 prevented a state from forbidding an oil producer to pass through a state severance tax to customers in interstate commerce.[453]

The Supremacy Clause precluded state taxation of the first use of gas in a state by pipeline companies because it was inconsistent with the federal regulatory scheme for the interstate sale of natural gas.[454] The Supremacy Clause did not preclude local ad valorem taxation of goods in custom bonded warehouses long term for domestic use.[455] But Congress' comprehensive regulation of customs duties preempted local property tax on goods in custom bonded warehouses, between transit into and out of the United States; the Court did not apply the Import-Export Clause.[456] The Container Convention did not preclude a state sales tax on containers in foreign commerce into the state.[457] The Military Leasing Act did not preclude state tax of a lessee.[458] A state could tax Forestry Service employees on use of federally owned houses.[459]

The Outer Continental Shelf Lands Act did not prevent Iowa from including income earned from the sale of OCS oil and gas in its apportionment formula even though it stated state tax laws should not apply to the income.[460] The fact that Congress chartered the Central Pacific Railroad did not exempt it from state tax.[461]

---

[449] Western Air Lines v. Board of Equalization, 480 U.S. 123 (1987).

[450] Aloha Airlines v. Dir. of Taxation, 464 U.S. 7 (1983) (involving a prohibition on airline taxes and a state effort to mislabel its tax); Chase Manhattan Bank, N. A. v. Finance Administration of New York, 440 U.S. 447 (1979).

[451] Dameron v. Brodhead, 345 U.S. 322 (1953). And the property tax could not be made a condition of an auto license. California v. Buzard, 382 U.S. 386 (1966). But the statute did not prevent sales taxation. Sullivan v. United States, 395 U.S. 169 (1969). Veterans' wages deposited in bank account could not be taxed. Lawrence v. Shaw, 300 U.S. 245 (1937).

[452] Carson v. Roane-Anderson Co., 342 U.S. 232 (1952).

[453] Exxon Corp. v. Eagerton, 462 U.S. 176 (1983).

[454] Maryland v. Louisiana, 451 U.S. 725 (1981).

[455] R. J. Reynolds Tobacco Co. v. Durham County, 479 U.S. 130 (1986).

[456] Xerox Corp. v. County of Harris, 459 U.S. 145 (1982); McGoldrick v. Gulf Oil Corp., 309 U.S. 414 (1940).

[457] Itel Containers Int'l Corp. v. Huddleston, 507 U.S. 60 (1993).

[458] Offutt Housing Co. v. County of Sarpy, 351 U.S. 253 (1956). *See also* Rohr Aircraft Corp. v. County of San Diego, 362 U.S. 628 (1960) (Surplus Property Act).

[459] United States v. County of Fresno, 429 U.S. 452 (1977).

[460] Shell Oil Co. v. Iowa Dep't of Revenue, 488 U.S. 19 (1988).

[461] Cent. P. R. Co. v. Cal., 162 U.S. 91 (1896).

(2) *Federal Licenses*

Generally a state cannot impose a license tax on a business that has a federal license to do what the state wants to license; Chicago could not impose a license tax to navigate the Chicago River on tugs licensed by the United States to work on those waters.[462] This principle dates back to *Gibbons v. Ogden*.[463] But a general business license tax that Charleston imposed on the Postal Telegraph Company licensed by Congress to set up a telegraph system did not violate the federal license.[464]

(3) *Foreign Sovereign Immunity*

The Foreign Sovereign Immunities Act of 1976 (FSIA) did not immunize a foreign government from a lawsuit to declare the validity of tax liens on property held by the sovereign for the purpose of housing its employees.[465]

6. *First Amendment*

Freedom of Speech decisions predominantly involve state taxes and are discussed in Ch. VIII.D.2. Freedom of the Press decisions predominantly involve state taxes and are discussed in Ch. VIII.D.3. Establishment Clause decisions predominantly involve state taxes and are discussed chapter VIII.D.4. Free Exercise Clause decisions predominantly involve state taxes and are discussed in chapter VIII.D.5.

7. *Contracts Clause*

Many taxpayers have claimed that a state law impaired the obligation of contracts in violation of the Contracts Clause in connection with taxes. The contracts at issue in these cases mostly involve contracts with the state or taxing authority granting some sort of exemption. A minority of the cases involve contracts with third parties.

Particularly in the exemption cases, often contract interpretation and the Contracts Clause analysis go together. The Court decided many cases against taxpayers claiming their tax exemption state contracts had been breached without even mentioning the Contracts Clause, as a matter of contract interpretation.[466] And occasionally it decided a case for the taxpayer without mentioning the need to strictly construe the exemption.[467] Often the Court avoided the issue by interpreting the contract not to apply to the particular type of tax or the current

---

[462] Harman v. Chicago, 147 U.S. 396 (1893).

[463] Gibbons v. Ogden, 22 U.S. 1 (1824), as discussed in Huron Portland Cement Co. v. Detroit, 362 U.S. 440 (1960).

[464] Postal Tel. Cable Co. v. Charleston, 153 U.S. 692 (1894).

[465] Permanent Mission of India to the UN v. City of New York, 551 U.S. 193 (2007).

[466] Illinois C. R. Co. v. Decatur, 147 U.S. 190 (1893); Wilmington R.R. v. Reid, 80 U.S. 264 (1871). Although the Court is bound by a state's courts interpretation of its own laws, it can interpret the state's contracts. Mobile & O. R. Co. v. Tennessee, 153 U.S. 486 (1894).

[467] Gordon v. Appeal Tax Court, 44 U.S. 133 (1845).

owner of previously exempt property.[468] Even when a state contracted against taxation of some property (bonds), the Court found that the tax was not on the property but on a license or franchise measured by the value of the property.[469] The Court will be slow to overturn a finding of the state court that a statute did not create a contract against taxation of mortgages.[470] Maryland passed a blanket ban on all contracts limiting its right to tax except as barred by the Contracts Clause and the Court approved it.[471]

In applying the Contracts Clause to exemptions, the Court generally will not imply any limitation on the power to tax into a contract between the taxing authority and the taxpayer, such as a license or franchise or transfer of land.[472] The Court requires that any contract with a state to limit its sovereign taxing power must be clear and unambiguous.[473] The Court will construe the contract against exemption.[474] That extends to construing the powers of a territory to grant exemptions.[475] Silence will not be interpreted as exemption.[476] If the state court did not find a contractual tax exemption, the Supreme Court will be very hesitant to disagree.[477] The fact that Congress aided western railroads did not mean that they were supposed to be exempt from state taxation (although Congress might have made them exempt).[478]

For example of the strict construction of exemptions the Court ruled that a charter requiring a tax on each share of capital stock in lieu of all other taxes

---

[468] Tucker v. Ferguson, 89 U.S. 527 (1874); Smith v. Hunter, 48 U.S. 738 (1849) (state tax did not include local tax); Chi. Theol. Seminary v. Ill., 188 U.S. 662 (1903); Jetton v. University of South, 208 U.S. 489 (1908) (tenant of exempt university could be taxed); Bank of Kentucky v. Kentucky, 207 U.S. 258 (1907) (changing assessment date did not violate the contract not to impose any other tax); Atlantic C. L. R. Co. v. Phillips, 332 U.S. 168 (1947) (1833 charter limiting tax on stock did not apply to income tax state adopted in 1937); Boston v. Jackson, 260 U.S. 309 (1922) (city's lease of railroad to private operators not impaired by state tax on operations).

[469] Pacific Co. v. Johnson, 285 U.S. 480 (1932).

[470] New York ex rel. Clyde v. Gilchrist, 262 U.S. 94 (1923).

[471] Commissioners of Wicomico County v. Bancroft, 203 U.S. 112 (1906).

[472] Providence Bank v. Billings, 29 U.S. 514 (1830) (very important early statement of this principle); New York Rapid Transit Corp. v. New York, 303 U.S. 573 (1938) (holding that no such contract existed on the facts and explaining that the taxing power is of such vital importance that a very clear contractual exemption will be required to upset it); New York ex rel. Metropolitan Street Ry. Co. v. New York State Bd., 199 U.S. 1 (1905); Memphis Gas Light Co. v. Taxing Dist. of Shelby County, 109 U.S. 398 (1883); Phila. & W. R. Co. v. Md., 51 U.S. 376 (1851); J. W. Perry Co. v. Norfolk, 220 U.S. 472 (1911).

[473] Erie R. Co. v. Pa., 88 U.S. 492 (1874); N. M. R. Co. v. Maguire, 87 U.S. 46 (1874); Ohio Life Ins. & Trust Co. v. Debolt, 57 U.S. 416 (1854).

[474] Central R. & Banking Co. v. Wright, 164 U.S. 327 (1896); New York ex rel. Troy Union R. Co. v. Mealy, 254 U.S. 47 (1920).

[475] Berryman v. Board of Trustees, 222 U.S. 334 (1912).

[476] Bailey v. Magwire, 89 U.S. 215 (1875); Phoenix Fire & Marine Ins. Co. v. Tennessee, 161 U.S. 174 (1896).

[477] New York ex rel. Clyde v. Gilchrist, 262 U.S. 94 (1923); New York ex rel. Interborough Rapid Transit Co. v. Sohmer, 237 U.S. 276 (1915).

[478] Thomson v. Pacific Railroad, 76 U.S. 579 (1869).

did not preclude a tax imposed on the corporation measured by its stock.[479] The Court ruled that a charter exemption did not apply because the incorporators did not organize the corporation until after the state constitution was changed to deny such exemptions.[480] A charter authorizing one insurance company to have all the "terms, powers, rights, reservations, . . ." of another tax exempt insurance company did not authorize the same tax exemption.[481]

A state granting a license upon the payment of a license tax did not breach its contract by imposing a separate tax on the corporate property.[482] Corporations seem to have been surprised when they leased property from a city to build a railroad or other utility and then found themselves taxed; but the tax was due.[483] The Court rejected a double taxation claim under the Contracts Clause, saying a corporation could be taxed on its capital and the shareholders on their shares.[484] The state did not violate the obligation of contracts when it adopted a tax on the interest paid on state and local bonds; the bonds' stated tax exemption applied only to property tax.[485] The bondholders of a taxing district did not have a constitutional objection to a later change in state law allowing exemption of some land in the district from its taxes.[486] A retroactive tax change was not an ex post facto law.[487]

However, some early rulings struck down state taxes under contracts that were interpreted to grant a permanent tax exemption, in unusual circumstances.[488]

Pennsylvania did contract away its power to require a New York railroad to collect tax from interest paid to Pennsylvania residents.[489] The Court ruled Ohio had contracted not to impose additional taxes on banks,[490] and even a new state constitution could not undo a charter exemption.[491] A 1872 decision referenced the Contracts Clause to prevent a 5 percent withholding tax on bond interest paid to out of state bond holders, but actually was a Due Process ruling that the

---

[479] Shelby County v. Union & Planters' Bank, 161 U.S. 149 (1896). *See also* Wells v. Savannah, 181 U.S. 531 (1901) (exemption limited to one year).

[480] Planters' Ins. Co. v. Tennessee, 161 U.S. 193 (1869).

[481] Home Ins. & Trust Co. v. Tennessee, 161 U.S. 198 (1896).

[482] New York ex rel. Brooklyn C. R. Co. v. New York State Bd., 199 U.S. 48 (1905).

[483] St. Louis v. United R. Co., 210 U.S. 266 (1908); Honolulu Rapid Transit & Land Co. v. Wilder, 211 U.S. 137 (1908); Trimble v. Seattle, 231 U.S. 683 (1914) (not a railroad).

[484] Bank of Commerce v. Tennessee, 161 U.S. 134 (1896).

[485] Hale v. State Board of Assessment & Review, 302 U.S. 95 (1937).

[486] Gilman v. Sheboygan, 67 U.S. 510 (1863); Ingraham v. Hanson, 297 U.S. 378 (1936) (later change in method of collecting district taxes).

[487] Kentucky Union Co. v. Kentucky, 219 U.S. 140 (1911).

[488] New Jersey v. Wilson, 11 U.S. 164 (1812) (land sold to Native Americans would be forever exempt, even in hands of others; this may have been the first state tax case decided by the Court); Home of the Friendless v. Rouse, 75 U.S. 430 (1869) (contract exempted property so long as held by the charity); Wash. Univ. v. Rouse, 75 U.S. 439 (1869). But Armstrong v. Treasurer of Athens County, 41 U.S. 281 (1842) found the state's exemption policy had changed and declined to imply an exemption; Pac. R. Co. v. Maguire, 87 U.S. 36 (1874).

[489] New York, L. E. & W. R. Co. v. Pennsylvania, 153 U.S. 628 (1894).

[490] Piqua State Bank v. Knoop, 57 U.S. 369 (1854); Jefferson Branch Bank v. Skelly, 66 U.S. 436 (1862).

[491] Dodge v. Woolsey, 59 U.S. 331 (1856).

bonds were being taxed as property outside of the state's jurisdiction.[492] A tax on the shares of a railroad was found to violate a contract that had extended the franchise upon payment of a defined amount by the railroad, which contract had been approved by, and was held to be made for the benefit of, the shareholders.[493] A state could not get around a contract not to tax a corporation by requiring it to pay a tax on its shares, when the tax had no relation to earnings; it was a tax on the corporation.[494] A foreign corporation that qualified to do business in a state under a statute stating that thereafter it would be taxed the same as domestic corporations could use the Contracts Clause to avoid a later divergence in tax treatment.[495] The state could not change a corporate charter to repeal an exemption originally granted in the charter.[496] Failure to impose a license tax for 58 years supported the interpretation of the exemption to preclude a license tax.[497] Where a State had sold land under a tax title which was valid with the help of a statute curing irregularities in the tax proceeding, but invalid without it, a repeal of the curative statute impaired the obligation of the contract between the State and its vendee, in violation of the Contracts Clause.[498] If the exemption had been in a general tax law it could have been revoked, but it was in the special law granting the title to the land exempted and could not be revoked and had broad application.[499] A state created a contract with taxpayers by agreeing to take coupons on state bonds in payment for license taxes in the license tax statute applicable to the taxpayer, and later changed the statute to require payment in cash, which the Court found to be unconstitutional.[500]

But charter based exemptions usually were found not to be transferrable. A railroad that was originally tax exempt but was acquired by the state in foreclosure after the state constitution forbade tax exemptions could not be made exempt again, even by a new act of the legislature.[501] The purchaser of railroad property from a state tax exempt railroad did not acquire the exemption.[502] The exemption usually did not carry over upon a corporate merger or consolida-

---

[492] Case of State Tax on Foreign-Held Bonds, 82 U.S. 300 (1872).
[493] Gordon v. Appeal Tax Court, 44 U.S. 133 (1845).
[494] New Orleans v. Houston, 119 U.S. 265 (1886).
[495] American Smelting & Refining Co. v. Colorado, 204 U.S. 103 (1907).
[496] N.J. v. Yard, 95 U.S. 104 (1877); Humphrey v. Pegues, 83 U.S. 244 (1873).
[497] Citizens' Bank v. Parker, 192 U.S. 73 (1904).
[498] Wood v. Lovett, 313 U.S. 362 (1941).
[499] McGee v. Mathis, 71 U.S. 143 (1866).
[500] Royall v. Virginia, 116 U.S. 572 (1886).
[501] Trask v. Maguire, 85 U.S. 391 (1874); Chesapeake & O. R. Co. v. Miller, 114 U.S. 176 (1885); Great Northern Ry. Co. v. Minnesota, 216 U.S. 206 (1910).
[502] Morgan v. Louisiana, 93 U.S. 217 (1876).

tion.[503] But it did carry over to a long term lessee of the railroad (99 years),[504] but not to the lessee of a canal.[505]

A state did not impair the obligation of a municipal contract by taxing an untaxed street railway and relieving it of its contractual duty to maintain the streets.[506] A state could change the charter of a special taxing district.[507] A state could limit the power of a local government to apply a special tax to a railroad.[508] But a state could not eliminate taxing districts that were obligated to levy taxes to pay bonds as a means of avoiding the payment of the bonds.[509] A charter granting exemption was subject to an earlier general statute stating that such exemptions could be revoked.[510] A college lost an exemption granted by statute because the exemption was not in its original charter.[511]

To make such a contract of exemption immutable it must be part of the origination of the exempt entity or exempt property; otherwise it may be revoked as a mere gratuity or bounty (*i.e.*, received without consideration).[512] The default rule has been that even a clear exemption in a statute (as contrasted with a charter) is at the pleasure of the state and can be revoked.[513] A taxing statute that recognized an exemption could be changed to eliminate the exemption without impairing any contract.[514] A tax statute that exempted certain types of railroads was not a contract with the railroads exempted not to change the statute.[515]

However, the allowance of general taxation despite a contract or charter from the state does not prevent the contract from forbidding other government exactions. *Puerto Rico v. Russell & Co.* held that a territorial levy to pay for water was

---

[503] Tomlinson v. Branch, 82 U.S. 460 (1872) (exemption carried over in railroad merger); St. Louis, I. M. & S. R. Co. v. Berry, 113 U.S. 465 (1885) (consolidation produced a new corporation that was subject to then current state law and would not have exemption of prior corporation); Northern C. R. Co. v. Maryland, 187 U.S. 258 (1902) (exemption did not survive merger and new state constitution; this may have involved the very first railroad charter granted in 1827); People's Gas Light & Coke Co. v. Chicago, 194 U.S. 1 (1904) (exemption did not carry over in consolidation); Del. R.R. Tax, 85 U.S. 206 (1873) (three roads merged; did not carry over); Rochester R. Co. v. Rochester, 205 U.S. 236 (1907) (exemption ceased due to corporate acquisition); Yazoo & M. v. R. Co. v. Vicksburg, 209 U.S. 358 (1908) (not exempt after consolidation).

[504] Wright v. Louisville & N. R. Co., 236 U.S. 687 (1915); Wright v. Central of Georgia Ry. Co., 236 U.S. 674 (1915).

[505] Morris Canal & Banking Co. v. Baird, 239 U.S. 126 (1915).

[506] Worcester v. Worcester C. S. R. Co., 196 U.S. 539 (1905).

[507] Houck v. Little River Drainage Dist., 239 U.S. 254 (1915).

[508] Arkansas S. R. Co. v. Louisiana & A. R. Co., 218 U.S. 431 (1910).

[509] Graham v. Folsom, 200 U.S. 248 (1906).

[510] Louisville Water Co. v. Clark, 143 U.S. 1 (1892); Citizens' Sav. Bank v. Owensboro, 173 U.S. 636 (1899).

[511] Seton Hall College v. South Orange, 242 U.S. 100 (1916).

[512] Grand Lodge F. & A. Masons v. New Orleans, 166 U.S. 143 (1897); Powers v. Detroit, 201 U.S. 543 (1906). In contrast, an exemption granted as part of an extension of a grant to a street railroad was a binding contract. City Ry. Co. v. Citizens' Street R. Co., 166 U.S. 557 (1897) (not a tax case).

[513] Rector v. County of Phila., 65 U.S. 300 (1861).

[514] Commissioners of Wicomico County v. Bancroft, 203 U.S. 112 (1906).

[515] Wisconsin & M. R. Co. v. Powers, 191 U.S. 379 (1903).

not a tax and thus the levy impaired the obligation of contract not to charge for water and was void, under the Organic Act of Puerto Rico.[516]

Claims of impairing a contract between a taxpayer and third parties have failed. The adoption of an estate tax on the transfer of securities under a pre-existing power of appointment did not impair the obligation of the power of appointment.[517] The adoption of an estate tax on the exercise of a power of appointment over a trust created before the tax was enacted did not violate the Contracts Clause or the Due Process Clause.[518] A state's sealing of safe deposit boxes after death neither violated the Contracts Clause nor was a taking.[519] The state did not violate the Contracts Clause by adopting a property tax upon ore lands after the owners entered leases;[520] even if the lessee was obligated to pay one eight of the oil proceeds to the landowner free of costs.[521]

The Contracts Clause did not prevent a state from forbidding a taxpayer to pass through the tax to its customers even though the taxpayer would have to amend its contracts to follow that rule.[522] The state did not impair the obligation to provide free water for sewerage by charging for drinking water.[523]

The Court's view of the Contracts Clause in relation to taxation likely was informed by its view of the Clause in the early important *Charles River Bridge* case, which was a Contracts Clause decision containing an important statement about tax. The Court ruled that the Charles River Bridge Co. did not have an exclusive contract to bridge the Charles River next to Harvard because such contracts were to be strictly construed in protection of the public interest.[524] Taney recalled the *Providence Bank* case and said:

> Speaking of the taxing power, he says, "as the whole community is interested in retaining it undiminished, that community has a right to insist that its abandonment ought not to be presumed, in a case in which the deliberate purpose of the state to abandon it does not appear." The case now before the Court, is, in principle, precisely the same.

See also Chapter V.D.3.b(4)(c) for additional discussion of Contracts Clause.

8. *Imports, Exports, Tonnage*

a. *Tonnage*

Article I, Section 10, clause 3, the Tonnage Clause, states:

---

516 Puerto Rico v. Russell & Co., 315 U.S. 610 (1942).
517 Orr v. Gilman, 183 U.S. 278 (1902).
518 Binney v. Long, 299 U.S. 280 (1936).
519 National Safe Deposit Co. v. Stead, 232 U.S. 58 (1914).
520 Lake Superior Consol. Iron Mines v. Lord, 271 U.S. 577 (1926).
521 Barwise v. Sheppard, 299 U.S. 33 (1936) (oil).
522 Exxon Corp. v. Eagerton, 462 U.S. 176 (1983).
523 New Orleans Tax Payers' Protective Ass'n v. Sewerage & Water Bd., 237 U.S. 33 (1915).
524 Proprietors of Charles River Bridge v. Proprietors of Warren Bridge, 36 U.S. 420 (1837).

> No State shall, without the Consent of Congress, lay any Duty of Tonnage . . . [or do a number of other acts implicating interstate commerce and foreign commerce and relations].

The Constitution separately forbids states to tax ships according to size or carrying capacity, out of an abundance of concern that duties on the goods would be converted into duties on the ships carrying the goods.[525] The Court first prominently considered the issue in the *State Tonnage Tax Cases*.[526] Early on many disputes concerned the distinction between state fees versus unconstitutional tonnage duties.[527]

In 2009 the Court applied the Tonnage Clause to strike down an Alaskan city tax graduated with size on ships entering the port to load oil.[528] The *Polar Tankers* opinion reviewed most of the earlier cases. The city tried to apply its general real property tax rate to the value of a large ship owned by a nonresident (its only personal property taxed by the city), which had acquired a taxable situs in the city (by docking and loading $1 million worth of oil), after applying an apportionment formula designed to avoid multiple property taxation by all ports in which the ship had taxable situs.[529] The tax was in effect a tonnage duty because it was imposed on a proxy for the capacity of the ship, as contrasted with its cargo, duties on which would have been subject to the Import-Export Clause; thus reference to tonnage in the taxing formula, or even to a variation of rate based on size is not the key identifier of a tonnage duty. Rather it is any "charge for the privilege of entering, trading in, or lying in a port,"[530] which it was found to be because almost every large ship that entered the port paid the fee proportional to value.

Any charge on ships that varies with size is highly likely to be found to be a duty of tonnage. A fee for inspecting ships quarantined to prevent disease was a duty of tonnage because it varied with tonnage and did not depend on an

---

525 Clyde Mallory Lines v. Alabama, 296 U.S. 261 (1935) (tonnage duties are not limited to charges based on weight).

526 State Tonnage Tax Cases, 79 U.S. 204 (1871). The earliest opinion mentioning the Tonnage Clause was in Cooley v. Bd. of Wardens, 53 U.S. 299 (1852) (contrasting a tonnage tax to a fee for services).

527 *See, e.g.*, Packet Co. v. Keokuk, 95 U.S. 80 (1877); (Packet Co. v. St. Louis, 100 U.S. 423 (1880). *See also* Cannon v. New Orleans, 87 U.S. 577 (1874).

528 Polar Tankers, Inc. v. City of Valdez, 557 U.S. 1 (2009) (It agreed that a state could levy a property tax that was not an invalid tonnage fee, but it must be levied in the same manner as on local property, which this tax was not. It also noted that the home port doctrine had waned and moveables could establish property tax nexus based on situs.).

529 Polar Tankers, Inc. v. City of Valdez, 557 U.S. 1 (2009). The corporation was previously Arco Marine, which at least at one time was headquartered in California. *See* Campbell v. Arco Marine, Inc., 42 Cal. App. 4th 1850 (Cal. App. 1996). Also the Supreme Court called it a nondomiciliary.

530 *See also* Cannon v. New Orleans, 87 U.S. 577 (1874) stating that a fixed and not proportionate tax could be a duty of tonnage; S.S. Co. v. Portwardens, 73 U.S. 31 (1867) (flat $5 fee unrelated to any service).

inspection being made.[531] A tonnage charge for simply entering a harbor was an unconstitutional tonnage duty even though the harbor generally provided some benefits to the ship.[532]

However, the Court ruled that a wharfage fee proportional to tonnage was a constitutional user fee and not an unconstitutional duty after finding the character of the charge to be a fee for wharfage.[533] A flat fee per ship for inspection was not a tonnage duty.[534] A flat fee imposed on large ships was a fee for policing the harbor and not a duty of tonnage.[535]

The prohibition against state tonnage duties is not limited to imports from abroad or imports from another state but applies whenever the duty functions as a regulation of commerce that is not wholly intrastate.[536]

Although not a Tonnage Clause case, the Court ruled that the exclusive federal jurisdiction over navigable waters did not prevent a state from applying its unemployment insurance tax to seamen.[537]

b. *Import-Export Clause*

Article I, Section 10, clause 2, the Import-Export Clause, sometimes called the Export-Import Clause,[538] provides:

> No State shall, without the Consent of the Congress, lay any Imposts or Duties on Imports or Exports, except what may be absolutely necessary for executing it's inspection Laws: and the net Produce of all Duties and Imposts, laid by any State on Imports or Exports, shall be for the Use of the Treasury of the United States; and all such Laws shall be subject to the Revision and Controul of the Congress.

It primarily addresses state taxation but implicates federal taxation (federal import/export taxation is addressed in Ch. VI) in at least three ways. First, in the first important decision applying the clause Chief Justice Marshall reasoned that inspection duties must be taxes because they had to be excepted from taxes in

---

531 Peete v. Morgan, 86 U.S. 581 (1873) (the result was helped by a federal statute authorizing the quarantine but stating that the legislation did not consent to duties of tonnage).

532 Inman S.S. Co. v. Tinker, 94 U.S. 238 (1877).

533 Packet Co. v. Keokuk, 95 U.S. 80 (1877); Packet Co. v. St. Louis, 100 U.S. 423 (1879); Transp. Co. v. Parkersburg, 107 U.S. 691 (1882) (gave considerable credence to city's label as wharfage fee).

534 Morgan's S.S. Co. v. Louisiana Bd. of Health, 118 U.S. 455 (1886).

535 Clyde Mallory Lines v. Alabama, 296 U.S. 261 (1935).

536 Packet Co. v. Keokuk, 95 U.S. 80 (1877) (ships on navigable waters).

537 Standard Dredging Corp. v. Murphy, 319 U.S. 306 (1943).

538 Joy Oil Co. v. State Tax Comm'n, 337 U.S. 286 (1949); Bacchus Imps. v. Dias, 468 U.S. 263 (1984).

this clause.[539] As discussed in Chapter IV.A, this conclusion cannot be universally applied and reflects an early substance over form sensitivity in constitutional interpretation.[540] Second, the clause indicates an alternate way the United States could tax imports (and exports): authorize states to do so and take the funds. The Court has speculated that this could not be used as a way around the tax uniformity requirements (*i.e.*, by allowing different states to impose different taxes), without resolving the issue.[541] Third, it implies a test for this particular charge that is typical of a regulatory charge: it approximates the government's cost of the regulation.[542]

The very important *Parham* decision ruled that the Import-Export Clause does not apply to commerce between states and so prohibits only taxes on goods imported from other countries.[543] Therefore, only the Commerce Clause and the Privileges and Immunities Clause may limit state taxes on imports from other states as such.[544] However, the Justices at times implied that the Import-Export Clause might apply to imports from other states.[545] The practical reason why the Import-Export Clause could not apply between states is that it might prevent the application of use taxes.

A few principles are certain:

- The Court interprets the clause strictly, because the Constitution lists only one exception, implying there are no others (although the Court interprets the Export Clause more strictly).[546]
- Inspection relates only to property, not persons.[547]

---

[539] Brown v. Maryland, 25 U.S. 419 (1827). Inspection of exports, rather than imports, may have been more common in the early days of the nation. *See* MARGARET SPAHR, THE SUPREME COURT ON THE INCIDENCE AND EFFECTS OF TAXATION: AN ANALYSIS OF ECONOMIC THEORY EMBEDDED IN THE CONSTITUTIONAL LAW DERIVED FROM THE EXPLICIT TAX CLAUSES, SMITH COLLEGE STUDIES IN HISTORY 228-229 (Jan.-July, 1925) (reprinted by Making of the Modern Law, Legal Treatises, 1800-1926).

[540] For example, compare treatment of the same fees as police power regulation in Gibbons v. Ogden, 22 U.S. 1, 231 (1824).

[541] Michelin Tire Corp. v. Wages, 423 U.S. 276, 301 n. 13 (1976).

[542] *See* Ch. IV.

[543] Woodruff v. Parham, 75 U.S. 123 (1869) (holding that the original package doctrine was not necessarily the talisman for taxing imports, but rather the issue was one of discrimination or not against imports). *See also* Dooley v. United States, 183 U.S. 151 (1901) (concurrence of Justice White); Coe v. Errol, 116 U.S. 517 (1886); Brown v. Houston, 114 U.S. 622 (1885).

[544] *See* discussion in Tenn. Wine & Spirits Retailers Ass'n v. Thomas, 139 S. Ct. 2449 (2019) (extensive discussion of early cases on interstate alcohol sales).

[545] Comptroller of the Treasury v. Wynne, 575 U.S. 542 (2015) (opinions of Justices Alito and Scalia); Franchise Tax Bd. v. Hyatt, 139 S. Ct. 1485 (2019) (Breyer dissent incorrectly implied that Import-Export Clause addressed commerce among the states).

[546] *See* Richfield Oil Corp. v. State Bd. of Equalization, 329 U.S. 69 (1946) ("The fact of a single exception suggests that no other qualification of the absolute prohibition was intended."); Youngstown Sheet & Tube Co. v. Bowers, 358 U.S. 534, 552 (1959) (dissent of Justice Frankfurter: "the only constitutional permission in terms so drastically limited").

[547] People v. Compagnie Generale Transatlantique, 107 U.S. 59 (1883).

- In this area the Court has basically eyeballed state inspection fees for indications that the legislature meant it for other than cost recovery.[548]
- Eventually, the Court moved away from a search for indirect impacts on imports and exports of general state taxes to a more formal approach, in keeping with its rejection of substance over form in its intergovernmental immunity jurisprudence.[549]
- The clause is alive and well: *United States v. IBM* dealt with the Export Clause as applied to the United States and distinguished the Import-Export Clause as applied to the states, which uses the term duties, defined in a way that differs from the more general term taxes appearing in the Export Clause.[550]

The Court found the Import-Export Clause was not violated by the Tennessee sales tax on leases of international shipping containers to shippers in the state, because it did not violate the Foreign Commerce Clause or the Commerce Clause and did not function as a tax on imports or exports.[551] That opinion applied the test established in *Michelin Tire*, which upheld a property tax on imported tires in a wholesaler's warehouse because it was not imposed on an import as such, did not affect the federal government's power to tax imports, and did not interfere with the free flow of imported goods among the states.[552] As a result of *Michelin*, imported goods in the original package could be subject to property tax.[553] Imported goods in a custom bonded warehouse for long term storage (2 years) were not "in transit" and so an annual county property tax did not violate the Import-Export Clause.[554] But when a local tax on similarly imported goods for resale was imposed on account of the importation and not under a regular property tax, the tax violated the Clause.[555]

A tax on seafood taken in coastal waters was not a tax on imports.[556] A state's business tax on stevedoring did not violate the Import-Export Clause even though the stevedores handled imports and exports because the tax was not

---

[548] *See, e.g.*, Patapsco Guano Co. v. North Carolina Bd. of Agriculture, 171 U.S. 345, 353-354 (1898); New Mexico ex rel. E. J. McLean & Co. v. Denver & R. G. R. Co., 203 U.S. 38 (1906) (inspection between states only).

[549] *See* Michelin Tire Corp. v. Wages, 423 U.S. 276 (1976); Canton R. Co. v. Rogan, 340 U.S. 511 (1951); Western Maryland R. Co. v. Rogan, 340 U.S. 520 (1951). *See* Ch II.C.

[550] United States v. IBM, 517 U.S. 843 (1996).

[551] Itel Containers Int'l Corp. v. Huddleston, 507 U.S. 60 (1993).

[552] Michelin Tire Corp. v. Wages, 423 U.S. 276 (1976), overruling, Low v. Austin, 80 U.S. 29 (1871). Earlier decisions had ruled the same way because the imports were not taxed as such but as goods held for sale. Gulf Fisheries Co. v. MacInerney, 276 U.S. 124 (1928).

[553] Limbach v. Hooven & Allison Co., 466 U.S. 353 (1984). The original package doctrine related solely to imports from outside the United States, although sometimes it is loosely referred to in connection with interstate commerce.

[554] R. J. Reynolds Tobacco Co. v. Durham County, 479 U.S. 130 (1986).

[555] Department of Revenue v. James B. Beam Distilling Co., 377 U.S. 341 (1964) (it is curious that *Reynolds* did not cite this opinion).

[556] Toomer v. Witsell, 334 U.S. 385 (1948).

imposed on the goods, did not affect the federal tariff power and did not impede commerce among the states.[557] The holding of the important early *Brown* decision is probably still the law: a state license tax on the occupation of being an importer was an unconstitutional state duty on imports.[558]

Although much of the Court's Import-Export Clause authorities preceding its 1976 *Michelin* opinion have been superseded if not overruled, its 1946 ruling that a sales tax levied upon the delivery of oil into tankers for direct export out of U.S. ports violates the Clause likely endures and is referred to as "in transit" taxation.[559] An early stamp tax on bills of lading was a tax on exports.[560] A local property tax levied on the part of a property being sold out of the country but not yet shipped was not a tax on exports.[561] A local property tax could be levied on oil marked for shipment out of state but stored for an extended period of time in the jurisdiction prior to shipment.[562] The local property tax could be imposed on goods for sale after the import duties had been levied.[563]

A fee for use of harbor pilots charged ships by the harbor government (called "pilotage") was not a tax on imports.[564] A reasonable "charge for outage" for inspection of exported tobacco came within the exception for inspection laws and did not violate the Import-Export Clause;[565] and inspection fees may apply to imports.[566]

A state could impose an inheritance tax solely on property inherited by aliens and the Court found no constitutional impediment; it was not an indirect tax on exports even though the property would have to be shipped to the heir.[567]

See also Chapter VI for discussion of the Constitution's limitations on federal taxation of exports.

c. *Treaties*

Federal tax treaties with other countries can preclude state taxation.[568] However, the Court has stated that federal tax treaties "do not generally cover the

---

[557] Department of Revenue of Wash. v. Association of Wash. Stevedoring Cos., 435 U.S. 734 (1978), citing Canton R. Co. v. Rogan, 340 U.S. 511 (1935). In addition, "Imposts or Duties" are a particular sort of taxes that fall on the property, which means the prohibition does not apply to tax on earnings from services to the business of exporting the property (stevedoring).

[558] Brown v. Maryland, 25 U.S. 419 (1827).

[559] Richfield Oil Corp. v. State Bd. of Equalization, 329 U.S. 69 (1946), discussed in Itel Containers Int'l Corp. v. Huddleston, 507 U.S. 60 (1993). *See also* Carson Petroleum Co. v. Vial, 279 U.S. 95 (1929).

[560] Almy v. Cal., 65 U.S. 169 (1861).

[561] Empresa Siderurgica, S. A. v. County of Merced, 337 U.S. 154 (1949); Coe v. Errol, 116 U.S. 517 (1886); Kosydar v. National Cash Register Co., 417 U.S. 62 (1974).

[562] Joy Oil Co. v. State Tax Comm'n, 337 U.S. 286 (1949); Independent Warehouses, Inc. v. Scheele, 331 U.S. 70 (1947) (commercial storage facility).

[563] May v. New Orleans, 178 U.S. 496 (1900).

[564] *See* Cooley v. Bd. of Wardens, 53 U.S. 299 (1852).

[565] Turner v. Md., 107 U.S. 38 (1882) (extensive discussion of meaning of inspection laws).

[566] Patapsco Guano Co. v. North Carolina Bd. of Agriculture, 171 U.S. 345 (1898).

[567] Mager v. Grima, 49 U.S. 490 (1850).

[568] Nielsen v. Johnson, 279 U.S. 47 (1929); Petersen v. Iowa, 245 U.S. 170 (1917).

taxing activities of subnational governmental units such as States."[569] The Court relied on the fact that Congress had not banned states from using worldwide combined reporting in its tax treaties.[570]

9. *Privileges and Immunities Clause*

Unhappy nonresident taxpayers commonly assert the Privileges and Immunities Clause and learn that the "fundamental" rights it protects are few. Indeed, the things nonresidents can't do in a state can be quite surprising: for example, in Virginia they can't get access to government records through the state FOIA.[571] The clause requires only "rough parity" and so is much less precise than the Commerce Clause; and also requires some justification for the lack of parity, at a low threshold. Corporations are not protected by the Privileges and Immunities Clause because corporations are not citizens.[572] Also a resident was denied protection under the Clause for dealing with an out of state debtor.[573]

For examples of the losers, the Clause did not protect "an incident" of business (evidently as contrasted with the doing of the business), such as investment in bank accounts, for which the state applied a higher tax rate on interest paid by out of state banks relative to interest paid by in state banks.[574] The Clause did not preclude limiting an inheritance tax charitable deduction to in state charitable corporations.[575]

Likewise, a state could allow residents to deduct their losses wherever incurred, but limited the nonresident to deductions for expenses and losses incurred in the state because the nonresident was only taxed on income earned in the state.[576] The Court found a state to have a substantial justification for charging substantially higher hunting license fees or taxes to nonresidents on the ground that the right to hunt was not within the national interests that the Privilege and Immunities Clause protects.[577] It distinguished the *Toomer* holding that nonresidents could not be charged a higher commercial fishing license, evidently on the ground that the fundamental right to earn money was not the same as the nonfundamental right to enjoy wildlife as recreation in another state. A state could tax nonresidents on the full value of stock of domestic corporations while taxing residents on the net of the value of the stock and the value of real property owned by the corporations.[578] A taxpayer could not assert the privileges

---

[569] Container Corp. of Am. v. Franchise Tax Bd., 463 U.S. 159 (1983).

[570] Barclays Bank Plc v. Franchise Tax Bd., 512 U.S. 298 (1994).

[571] McBurney v. Young, 569 U.S. 221 (2013) (real estate tax records sought by out of state business that wanted to sell access to the tax information).

[572] Paul v. Virginia, 75 U.S. 168 (1868).

[573] Kirtland v. Hotchkiss, 100 U.S. 491 (1879); Jennings v. Coal Ridge Improv. & Coal Co., 147 U.S. 147 (1893).

[574] Madden v. Kentucky, 309 U.S. 83 (1940), overruling Colgate v. Harvey, 296 U.S. 404 (1935) (which applied a national privilege from unequal taxation).

[575] Board of Education v. Illinois, 203 U.S. 553 (1906).

[576] Shaffer v. Carter, 252 U.S. 37 (1920); Travis v. Yale & Towne Mfg. Co., 252 U.S. 60 (1920).

[577] Baldwin v. Fish & Game Comm'n, 436 U.S. 371 (1978).

[578] Travellers' Ins. Co. v. Connecticut, 185 U.S. 364 (1902) (Commerce Clause not considered).

and immunities of nonresident workers who would be barred from working on the street for which he was being assessed, even if the workers had such a right, which they did not.[579] A municipality could not rely on the Clause to claim its own state could not exempt a railroad from city taxes.[580]

However, a tax discrimination on a local business activity by a nonresident is likely to fall under the Privileges and Immunities Clause. The important *Toomer* opinion ruled that one of the privileges that the Clause guarantees to citizens of State A is that of doing business in State B on terms of substantial equality with the citizens of that State: a disproportionately heavy tax on nonresidents doing a type of business in the state violates the Clause when the fact of nonresidency is not logically related to the evil the tax purports to remedy (over-fishing).[581] Likewise, a higher commercial fishing license fee was not logically related to increased enforcement costs.[582] A state could not charge a four times higher license tax for a person in the construction business with an out of state headquarters compared with an in state headquarters.[583]

A state violated the Privileges & Immunities Clause by taxing nonresident commuters on their compensation earned by working in the state while not taxing the income of residents earned within or without the state.[584] The opinion indicated the Court would have considered a compensating tax on residents' compensation income earned in the state, but there was none. A state could not provide a personal exemption to resident workers and not to nonresidents who earned compensation in the state.[585]

But tax discrimination against nonresidents that violates the Privileges and Immunities Clause is not necessarily limited to business or employment income. It included a denial of a personal deduction for payment of alimony, denied only to nonresidents without any substantial justification for the difference.[586] Because that was the most recent ruling of the Court on the subject it suggests that the Court might expand the focus of the clause and not limit it to protecting the conduct of business in a state by nonresidents.

The Supreme Court applied a principle akin to the Privileges and Immunities Clause before the adoption of the Fourteenth Amendment to strike down a $1

---

579 Chadwick v. Kelley, 187 U.S. 540 (1903).

580 Williams v. Baltimore, 289 U.S. 36 (1933).

581 Toomer v. Witsell, 334 U.S. 385 (1948); Ward v. Md., 79 U.S. 418 (1871) (an early peddler case decided under the Privileges and Immunities Clause).

582 Mullaney v. Anderson, 342 U.S. 415 (1952). *Cf.* Haavik v. Alaska Packers Ass'n, 263 U.S. 510 (1924) (different result based on territorial status of Alaska).

583 Chalker v. Birmingham & N. R. Co., 249 U.S. 522 (1919). The facts were unusual. The contractor was suing the railroad for work he did and the railroad defended that he had not obtained the required state license. He proved that the license he would have had to acquire was unconstitutional.

584 Austin v. New Hampshire, 420 U.S. 656 (1975).

585 Travis v. Yale & Towne Mfg. Co., 252 U.S. 60 (1920).

586 Lunding v. New York Tax Appeals Tribunal, 522 U.S. 287 (1998).

per head state tax on persons leaving the state by stagecoach.[587] The Clause does not protect persons from other parts of the taxing state.[588]

Opponents of the narrow scope of the Privileges and Immunities Clause trace its problems to the original rejection by the Court of a claim under the Clause by butchers objecting to a city regulation of butchering, which they thought was a monopoly (and which was a monopoly). The *Slaughter-House Cases* rejected a national citizenship right to be a butcher, thus kick starting a trend to regulation, which blossomed briefly in *Munn*, only to be quenched for a while in *E. C. Knight* and other decisions of the 1890s through 1936.[589] Of course that case did not involve the treatment of nonresidents by the home state, but rather the plaintiffs sought a right that later blossomed into substantive due process.[590]

At one time the denial of rights, privileges or immunities under federal law was a ground for federal question jurisdiction in the federal courts. The Court decided a case on that ground when a state obtained an order requiring the American Express Company not to shift the burden of a stamp tax on its services receipts to the customers.[591] It held there is no public policy that precludes shifting any tax.

10. *Double Jeopardy*

The *Kurth Ranch* opinion is the principal authority on state tax double jeopardy and is discussed in detail in Ch. VII.E.[592]

11. *Due Process other than Jurisdiction*

The tax jurisdictional requirements of the 14th Amendment Due Process Clause are discussed in Ch. IX.F. and G. This Chapter addresses all other issues that have been raised under the Due Process Clause, mostly to be batted down by the Supreme Court. The Due Process Clause is a ready vessel for disparate arguments because it is inherently vague, and can mean equal protection, substantive due process, procedural due process, or a complaint about irrationality, arbitrariness, and confiscation. The Court applies the Due Process Clause of the 14th Amendment to state taxes the same way it applies the Due Process Clause of the 5th Amendment to federal taxes.[593]

---

587 Crandall v. Nevada, 73 U.S. 35 (1868) (a "right to travel").

588 Downham v. Alexandria, 77 U.S. 173 (1869).

589 Slaughter-House Cases, 83 U.S. 36 (1873); Munn v. Illinois, 94 U.S. 113 (1877); United States v. E. C. Knight Co., 156 U.S. 1 (1895). *See generally*, Michael Kent Curtis, *Historical Linguistics, Inkblots, and Life after Death: The Privileges and Immunities of Citizens of the United States*, 78 U.N.C. L. Rev. 1071 (April 2000).

590 Ch. V.D.3.b(7).

591 American Express Co. v. Michigan, 177 U.S. 404 (1900).

592 Dep't of Revenue v. Kurth Ranch, 511 U.S. 767 (1994).

593 French v. Barber Asphalt Paving Co., 181 U.S. 324 (1901). *But see* Wight v. Davidson, 181 U.S. 371 (1901) (stating just the opposite, but perhaps in the context of the power of Congress over the District of Columbia).

As a general matter, the due process of law requirement takes the place of regular judicial proceedings to impose or collect tax, and implies administrative processes to permit routinized tax collections.[594]

a. *Public Use*

The Due Process Clause requires a state tax to be imposed for a public purpose and not a private purpose, based on the jurisprudence of governmental takings.[595] Therefore, even though a taxpayer need not benefit from the tax it pays,[596] the tax collections must be for some public use, encompassed within the "general welfare."[597] That includes a regulatory tax whose purpose is not for revenue, but which produces revenues paid into the government's treasury. A general income tax did not violate due process when its proceeds were paid to reimburse cities and towns for increase of educational salaries.[598] Spending tax dollars on books for children in church schools is a public use.[599]

The origins of the theory that taxes must be levied for a public use are obscure and the Court has more often stated it than applied it. It seems to have originated in an 1872 opinion that relied on state court opinions and stated: "It was asserted (what nobody doubts), that the taxing power of a state extends no farther than to raise money for a public use, as distinguished from private, or to accomplish some end public in its nature, ..."[600] The only decision that applied it against a government action was not actually a tax case but decided that a city could not issue what today would be called industrial development bonds because they would have to be repaid with tax revenues and so the tax would be spent for private purposes.[601] The 1937 *Southern Coal & Coke* opinion reviewed the cases and concluded that the states have broad authority to determine what is in the public interest and that it "would require a plain case of departure from every public purpose which could reasonably be conceived to justify the intervention of a court."

A major and confusing exception to the public benefit principle is special assessments, which are taxes imposed for the benefit of the adjacent property owners, in most cases. See Ch. IV.B.

---

[594] Kelly v. Pittsburgh, 104 U.S. 78 (1881).

[595] Carmichael v. Southern Coal & Coke Co., 301 U.S. 495 (1937); Green v. Frazier, 253 U.S. 233 (1920) (upheld taxes to spend on New Deal type program in the post War depression); Jones v. Portland, 245 U.S. 217 (1917); Fallbrook Irrigation Dist. v. Bradley, 164 U.S. 112 (1896) ("It is not essential that the entire community or even any considerable portion thereof should directly enjoy or participate in an improvement in order to constitute a public use."); Everson v. Bd. of Educ., 330 U.S. 1 (1947) (transportation to school was for public purpose, including to Catholic schools).

[596] Carley & Hamilton, Inc. v. Snook, 281 U.S. 66 (1930).

[597] Carmichael v. Southern Coal & Coke Co., 301 U.S. 495 (1937).

[598] Knights v. Jackson, 260 U.S. 12 (1922).

[599] Cochran v. Louisiana State Bd. of Education, 281 U.S. 370 (1930).

[600] Olcott v. Supervisors, 83 U.S. 678 (1872).

[601] Loan Ass'n v. Topeka, 87 U.S. 655 (1874); Parkersburg v. Brown, 106 U.S. 487 (1882).

b. *Double Taxation*

Double taxation of the same subject matter by different taxing units of the same state does not violate the Due Process Clause,[602] nor does double taxation by the state itself.[603] Although not always explained, the principle seems to be based on the idea that if the state could impose the total as one tax, it can impose it as two taxes.[604] And a state can tax the same value to two different taxpayers,[605] as when it taxes the property of the corporation and its shareholders' stock values.[606] The United States and a state can tax the same subject.[607]

Likewise taxation of the same subject by different states producing double taxation does not violate the Due Process Clause.[608] These holdings are particularly confusing because double taxation is at the heart of Commerce Clause analysis, and most cases, outside of insurance company cases, are also reviewed under the Commerce Clause when the taxes of two or more states are potentially involved. As to domiciliary state taxation, see discussion of *Central R. Co.* in Ch. IX.F.2.a(1). As to taxation of nonresidents, see Ch. IX.G.3.a(2). Whereas the Commerce Clause is concerned with multiple taxation of interstate commerce by two states, the Due Process Clause is concerned with different issues: jurisdiction to tax and irrational taxation. The two different concerns can produce the same or similar conclusions as to taxation of multistate values, but it is not because the Due Process Clause precludes double taxation in the same sense or for the same reason as the Commerce Clause. The issue is of mostly theoretical interest because the Commerce Clause will address double taxation in most cases not involving insurance companies.

Double taxation as it might involve foreign country taxes is confused. *Mobil Oil* upheld a nondomiciliary state's inclusion of dividends from unitary foreign subsidiaries in the apportionable tax base and did not even consider double taxation to be a Due Process Clause issue; the Court refused to consider foreign country taxation in considering multiple taxation for Commerce Clause purposes.[609] It distinguished *Japan Line*, which found a Foreign Commerce Clause

---

602 Carley & Hamilton, Inc. v. Snook, 281 U.S. 66 (1930).

603 Shaffer v. Carter, 252 U.S. 37 (1920).

604 Ft. Smith Lumber Co. v. Arkansas, 251 U.S. 532 (1920) (capital stock tax on parent took account of value of subsidiaries; and subsidiaries also paid the capital stock tax).

605 Ft. Smith Lumber Co. v. Arkansas, 251 U.S. 532 (1920) (stock of subsidiaries can be taxed to subsidiaries and the value of that property taxed to the parent corporation); Cudahy Packing Co. v. Minnesota, 246 U.S. 450 (1918) (rail cars earnings counted in taxing owners of cars and railroad).

606 Tennessee v. Whitworth, 117 U.S. 129 (1886).

607 Gibbons v. Ogden, 22 U.S. 1 (1824).

608 Cream of Wheat Co. v. County of Grand Forks, 253 U.S. 325 (1920) (state of domicile might tax all of corporation's intangible property and other states might tax apportioned value); Fidelity & Columbia Trust Co. v. Louisville, 245 U.S. 54 (1917) (bank account held out of state of residence could be property taxed by both states).

609 Mobil Oil Corp. v. Comm'r of Taxes, 445 U.S. 425 (1980).

violation in double property taxation, including the foreign country property tax.[610]

However, sometime the Court complained of double taxation when it invalidated a state tax on other grounds, usually that the taxing state did not have jurisdiction to tax (usually intangible property).[611]

c. *Taxpayer Benefit*

The Due Process Clause does not require that taxes be used for the benefit of the taxpayer or that the tax be downsized to be proportional to the public uses (such as highways) that the taxpayer actually uses.[612] Moreover, the Court will not police the state's choices of recipients of tax revenues as long as the spending is for a public purpose.[613] The Due Process Clause does not require that the amount of taxation approximate the value of government services rendered and the fact that the subject of tax has some relation to commerce does not change that conclusion.[614]

A state taxing scheme did not violate either the Due Process Clause or the Equal Protection Clause by taxing within localities in greater amounts than the spending in the localities.[615]

Taxpayer benefit may be relevant to determine if special assessments are arbitrary, which seems to be a special case.[616] In one special assessment case the Court ruled for the taxpayer railroad because the state had refused to allow it to present any evidence of lack of benefit, which the Court found to be a denial of due process.[617] In another case the Court affirmed enjoining a special assessment because the law precluded considering benefit to the taxpayer from the improvement to be financed.[618] But the Court cautioned against overreading

---

610 Japan Line, Ltd. v. County of Los Angeles, 441 U.S. 434 (1979). Evidently the impracticality of allocating income with foreign countries dissuaded the Court from being concerned with double international income taxation.

611 Safe Deposit & Trust Co. v. Virginia, 280 U.S. 83 (1929) (state of residence of trust beneficiaries could not impose property tax on securities in the trust held by Maryland trustee); Farmers Loan & Trust Co. v. Minnesota, 280 U.S. 204 (1930) (state of residence of bond issuer could not tax transfer of bonds at death of nonresident owner); Guaranty Trust Co. v. Virginia, 305 U.S. 19 (1938) ("Those cases go upon the theory that the taxing power of a state is restricted to her confines and may not be exercised in respect of subjects beyond them."). To the extent these cases stood for proposition that two states could not tax property transmitted at death they were overruled by State Tax Comm'n v. Aldrich, 316 U.S. 174 (1942).

612 Carley & Hamilton, Inc. v. Snook, 281 U.S. 66 (1930); Nashville, C. & S. L. Ry. v. Wallace, 288 U.S. 249 (1933) (a railroad can be taxed to raise funds to spend on roads); Memphis & C. R. Co. v. Pace, 282 U.S. 241 (1931); Kelly v. Pittsburgh, 104 U.S. 78 (1881) (farm land could be assessed, even above its value, for city taxes).

613 Carmichael v. Southern Coal & Coke Co., 301 U.S. 495 (1937).

614 Cotton Petroleum Corp. v. New Mexico, 490 U.S. 163 (1989).

615 Dane v. Jackson, 256 U.S. 589 (1921).

616 *See* Ch. IV.B.

617 Georgia R. & Electric Co. v. Decatur, 295 U.S. 165 (1935).

618 Norwood v. Baker, 172 U.S. 269 (1898) (this opinion shows the close connection between takings and special assessment districts). Taxpayers began to cite the opinion to object to all special assessments and the Court declined to extend it. Webster v. Fargo, 181 U.S. 394 (1901).

Norwood to upset the long tradition of taxing abutting landowners for road improvements without regard to benefit.[619] The Court also ruled that an assessment could exceed the estimated benefits.[620] So long as the state provides a procedure for contesting the amount of a special assessment relative to benefits, due process is satisfied and the state process can be conclusive.[621]

d. *Market Participant: Due Process*

A government does not violate the Due Process Clause by taxing a competitor.[622]

e. *Absolute Limits*

There is no Due Process Clause cap on state taxation because by analogy states have the police powers to regulate property use to nothing and the police (or regulatory) power may be exercised through the taxing power.[623] A government does not violate the Due Process Clause by taxing an activity so heavily as to destroy it,[624] although the element of the government being in competition with the taxpayer might make taking without due compensation a more relevant consideration.[625]

The amount of state tax on a particular business activity may be so great as to effectively prohibit the conduct of that business, as that is within the state's police powers.[626] Neither the Due Process Clause nor the Commerce Clause limits the absolute amount of state tax (the rate) so long as the tax is fairly apportioned under the Commerce Clause; rather the tax need only be measured by the activity taxed and not some unrelated measure.[627] The Due Process Clause did not limit the time or amount of a transfer tax imposed on account of death and so the state could tax the transfer of the remainder after a life estate at the death date value of the entire property and at the time the life estate ends.[628] The state could charge a 50 percent tax penalty for nonpayment.[629] However, in the case of special assessments the tax may so far outweigh the benefits of the special project funded that a due process limit might be reached, if the taxpayer so proves.[630]

See Ch. IX.B.4.j for discussion of eminent domain.

---

619 Tonawanda v. Lyon, 181 U.S. 389 (1901).

620 Missouri P. R. Co. v. Western Crawford Road Improv. Dist., 266 U.S. 187 (1924).

621 Hibben v. Smith, 191 U.S. 310 (1903).

622 Pittsburgh v. Alco Parking Corp., 417 U.S. 369 (1974).

623 Pittsburgh v. Alco Parking Corp., 417 U.S. 369 (1974); Hammond Packing Co. v. Montana, 233 U.S. 331 (1914).

624 A. Magnano Co. v. Hamilton, 292 U.S. 40 (1934).

625 Pittsburgh v. Alco Parking Corp., 417 U.S. 369 (1974).

626 Tanner v. Little, 240 U.S. 369 (1916).

627 Commonwealth Edison Co. v. Mont., 453 U.S. 609 (1981).

628 Salomon v. State Tax Com., 278 U.S. 484 (1929).

629 W. Union Tel. Co. v. Indiana, 165 U.S. 304 (1897).

630 Martin v. District of Columbia, 205 U.S. 135 (1907).

f. *Retroactivity*

Chapter V.D.3.b(4) generally addresses retroactive taxes. The principal state tax opinion on the subject distinguished the decisions finding retroactive federal tax changes to violate the Due Process Clause by stating they were: ". . . rested on the ground that the nature or amount of the tax could not reasonably have been anticipated by the taxpayer at the time of the particular voluntary act which the statute later made the taxable event."[631] But the event at issue in the case was receipt of a dividend, which taxpayer could not have avoided and so the tax adopted after the dividend was received was constitutional.

The Court did not consider a tax to have retroactive effect when a state taxing statute was enacted after the creation of a legal relationship that leads to the subject of taxation. For example, an inheritance tax could apply to the distribution of the personal property held by the executor after the enactment, even though the decedent died before the enactment.[632] Similarly, the power of appointment was created before the inheritance tax was adopted but the exercise occurred afterwards.[633] The inheritance tax law applied to the exercise of the power of appointment even though the will was executed before the law was enacted.[634] But when the gift was absolute and irrevocable prior to the enactment of the tax on such a gift, the application of the new tax to the gift violated Due Process.[635] An early opinion stated that the Fourteenth Amendment did not prohibit retrospective legislation as such and the state could apply a new collection law to taxes overdue when the law was enacted.[636] A state could require an estate to pay property taxes on estate property that the decedent had failed to pay, not as an administrative claim but a newly imposed penalty at a rate that differed from the rate that would have been paid.[637]

The United States can withdraw the permission for states to tax federal instrumentalities and render liens for prior taxes unenforceable, without violating Due Process, because the former permission was a gratuity or bounty.[638]

g. *Arbitrary*

Arbitrariness of state action is always a potential ultimate complaint under the Due Process Clause, and sometimes the Court bases a ruling on no more than that. The property tax assessor's failure to take account of the effect of the 1929

[631] Welch v. Henry, 305 U.S. 134 (1938) (considered retroactivity to be both an equal protection and due process issue). *See also* McKesson Corp. v. Division of Alcoholic Beverages & Tobacco, 496 U.S. 18 (1990) at footnote 23 (discussing retroactive taxation of other taxpayers to remedy a discrimination).

[632] Carpenter v. Pa., 58 U.S. 456 (1855) (although predated the 14th Amendment); Cahen v. Brewster, 203 U.S. 543 (1906) (estate still being administered when tax adopted).

[633] Orr v. Gilman, 183 U.S. 278 (1902).

[634] Chanler v. Kelsey, 205 U.S. 466 (1907).

[635] Coolidge v. Long, 282 U.S. 582 (1931).

[636] League v. Texas, 184 U.S. 156 (1902).

[637] Bankers Trust Co. v. Blodgett, 260 U.S. 647 (1923).

[638] Maricopa County v. Valley Nat'l Bank, 318 U.S. 357 (1943).

Crash on taxpayer's property values violated the Due Process clause.[639] A state could not tax a nonresident corporation on the number of its authorized but unissued shares even though it attempted to "apportion" that number to property in the state, because authorized shares is an arbitrary number;[640] even though that is true, the *Air-Way* opinion really was an early complaint about rationally relating the amount of tax to the amount of business done in the state.[641] The Court later ruled that it was not arbitrary to graduate a tax on domestic corporations on the basis of authorized stock, and on foreign corporations based on their authorized dollar capital because it reflected the potential to have capital.[642] The Court refused to choose among various method of valuing a railroad for property taxation, capitalization methods, interest rates, etc., in the absence of fraud by the assessor.[643]

h. *Husband-Wife*

A surprising early Supreme Court tax decision ruled that a state could not collect tax on a wife's income from the husband.[644] The Court ruled it violated Due Process as a taking of another person's property and also violated the Equal Protection Clause. Justice Holmes dissented, citing the thousand year understanding of the marriage couple as one. But *Kahn v. Shevin* allowed a state tax rule preferring widows to widowers.[645] A state can choose to impose an inheritance tax on the death of one spouse even though the survivor already owned an interest in the property.[646]

i. *Procedural Issues*

Legislative due process. Although a taking of property requires some prior notice and process, the enactment of tax laws by the state legislature is not a taking and does not require prior notice;[647] the legislature is presumed to have determined

---

[639] Great Northern Ry. Co. v. Weeks, 297 U.S. 135 (1936).

[640] Air-Way Electric Appliance Corp. v. Day, 266 U.S. 71 (1924) (also violated Commerce Clause); explained by Western Cartridge Co. v. Emmerson, 281 U.S. 511 (1930).

[641] *Air-Way* was decided at a time when any tax on a nonresident corporation that was found to engage in interstate commerce was likely to be viewed as a Commerce Clause violation. Even though the state court (but not the state statute) applied a sort of apportionment, the Court professed to believe that applying the proportion to a base that exceeded all of the actual capital would, in effect, tax values outside the state. It was as if the modern day apportionment formula was applied to four times the unitary business income.

[642] Roberts & Schaefer Co. v. Emmerson, 271 U.S. 50 (1926); Atlantic Refining Co. v. Virginia, 302 U.S. 22 (1937).

[643] Illinois C. R. Co. v. Greene, 244 U.S. 555 (1917).

[644] Hoeper v. Tax Com. of Wisconsin, 284 U.S. 206 (1931). *Cf.* Fernandez v. Wiener, 326 U.S. 340 (1945) (property of both spouses was estate taxed upon the termination of the interest of one spouse).

[645] Kahn v. Shevin, 416 U.S. 351 (1974).

[646] Moffitt v. Kelly, 218 U.S. 400 (1910).

[647] Carson v. Brockton Sewerage Com., 182 U.S. 398 (1901); Phillip Wagner, Inc. v. Leser, 239 U.S. 207 (1915) (special assessment for city enacted by legislature); Valley Farms Co. v. County of Westchester, 261 U.S. 155 (1923).

that the property included in the taxing district would benefit from the assessment.[648] The legislature could determine the amount of the assessments and no further process was due taxpayers.[649] That principle includes creation of an assessment district by a local agency to which the legislature delegated the power after defining the scope of the district and how the tax would be apportioned.[650] The legislative creation of the city charter with the taxing method defined was sufficient due process and *Norwood v. Baker* does not require prior notice in such cases.[651] And it included an order of the State Board of Equalization of Colorado increasing the valuation of all taxable property in the City of Denver forty percent.[652] But when a subsidiary agency creates the taxing district for special assessments an opportunity to be heard must be provided to the landowners.[653] The presumption of the legislature or its authorized body having provided due process did not extend to a special assessment district created under state law by petition of landowners, and dissenting landowners have a right to prior notice and right to object.[654]

Non-legislative due process. But when the amount of tax is not determined by the legislature, or built into a city charter that it adopted, a due process right to notice and hearing on the amount of tax due from a taxpayer can apply. This was fought out mostly in the context of local special assessment districts. Numerous taxpayers sued to stop street paving, sewer, irrigation, or similar public projects that not only affected their properties but also imposed on them the costs by way of special assessments; the Court almost always rejected those arguments, mostly made under the Due Process Clause, sometimes without even discussing the procedures.[655]

A property taxpayer must be provided an opportunity to object to the amount of the tax either in the process of valuing the property or levying the tax or in proceedings for its collection.[656] The hearing need relate only to the property owner's part of the assessment.[657] The post assessment proceeding may be a court action after a general notice.[658] The post assessment hearing cannot limit a non-filing taxpayer to complain about fraud or corruption of the property tax assess-

---

[648] Chesebro v. Los Angeles County Flood Control Dist., 306 U.S. 459 (1939); Hagar v. Reclamation Dist. No. 108, 111 U.S. 701 (1884).

[649] Breiholz v. Board of Supervisors, 257 U.S. 118 (1921).

[650] Hancock v. Muskogee, 250 U.S. 454 (1919); Withnell v. Ruecking Constr. Co., 249 U.S. 63 (1919) (because the assessment was provided for in the city charter, no hearing was needed).

[651] Withnell v. Ruecking Constr. Co., 249 U.S. 63 (1919); French v. Barber Asphalt Paving Co., 181 U.S. 324 (1901), rejecting applicability of Norwood v. Baker, 172 U.S. 269 (1898) as a unique case in which a single landowner was targeted for assessment.

[652] Bi-Metallic Inv. Co. v. State Board of Equalization, 239 U.S. 441 (1915).

[653] Fallbrook Irrigation Dist. v. Bradley, 164 U.S. 112 (1896).

[654] Browning v. Hooper, 269 U.S. 396 (1926).

[655] Cass Farm Co. v. Detroit, 181 U.S. 396 (1901).

[656] Winona & St. Peter Land Co. v. Minnesota, 159 U.S. 526 (1895); King v. Portland City, 184 U.S. 61 (1902).

[657] Voigt v. Detroit City, 184 U.S. 115 (1902).

[658] Hetrick v. Lindsey, 265 U.S. 384 (1924); Davidson v. New Orleans, 96 U.S. 97 (1877).

ment.[659] Notice of creation of a special taxing district for a street project satisfied due process;[660] and a drainage district.[661] And the fact that particular land would receive no direct benefit from the drainage district did not free if from the tax.[662] The land need not abut the street being built by the tax district ("back lying property owners").[663] And benefitted property could be omitted from the taxing district.[664] Ten days to protest an assessment after the last publication of notice was enough.[665]

Property owners should receive notice of a proposed assessment and the opportunity to object at some point, to their portion of the assessment;[666] the taxpayer did not have a right to a hearing on the propriety of the district, but only on his portion of the tax.[667] In one case where a relatively small number of landowners was affected, the Court invalidated a special assessment created by a local government in secret.[668]

Although no hearing was allowed when the special assessment was established, the taxpayer received due process by having the opportunity for a hearing on its liability when the tax was being enforced.[669] A hearing before sale of the property to pay the taxes was sufficient.[670] Notice by publication and not personal notice of annual property tax assessment was sufficient.[671] The due process that must be provided to the taxpayer was administrative, not judicial.[672]

These rulings reflect the general principle that Due Process is satisfied by either an opportunity to be heard in a pre-deprivation or post tax payment (post deprivation) process.[673] *McKesson* ruled that reasonable backward looking relief must be available if the taxpayer paid under duress. Oddly the Court had long assumed that paying taxes in accordance with the state statute might be "voluntary" and thus sort of an admission that the tax was owed, precluding refund.[674] However, any sort of penalty making pre-deprevation remedies painful, can

---

[659] Central of Georgia R. Co. v. Wright, 207 U.S. 127 (1907).

[660] Lent v. Tillson, 140 U.S. 316 (1891).

[661] Wurts v. Hoagland, 114 U.S. 606 (1885); Soliah v. Heskin, 222 U.S. 522 (1912).

[662] Miller & Lux, Inc. v. Sacramento & San Joaquin Drainage Dist., 256 U.S. 129 (1921).

[663] Cleveland, C., C. & S. L. R. Co. v. Porter, 210 U.S. 177 (1908).

[664] Butters v. Oakland, 263 U.S. 162 (1923).

[665] Bellingham Bay & B. C. R. Co. v. New Whatcom, 172 U.S. 314 (1899).

[666] St. Louis & Kansas City Land Co. v. Kansas City, 241 U.S. 419 (1916); Spencer v. Merchant, 125 U.S. 345 (1888).

[667] St. Louis & S. R. Co. v. Nattin, 277 U.S. 157 (928).

[668] Londoner v. Denver, 210 U.S. 373 (1908). See explanation in Bi-Metallic Inv. Co. v. State Board of Equalization, 239 U.S. 441 (1915).

[669] Embree v. Kansas City & Liberty Boulevard Road Dist., 240 U.S. 242 (1916).

[670] Chapman v. Zobelein, 237 U.S. 135 (1915).

[671] Glidden v. Harrington, 189 U.S. 255 (1903) (trustee's property assessed).

[672] Palmer v. McMahon, 133 U.S. 660 (1890).

[673] McKesson Corp. v. Div. of Alcoholic Bevs. & Tobacco, 496 U.S. 18 (1990). For an early decision, see McMillen v. Anderson, 95 U.S. 37 (1877) (a suit to enjoin the license tax was sufficient due process).

[674] Atchison v. O'Connor, 223 U.S. 280 (1912) (held that taxes paid in compliance with law were not voluntary in that sense).

trigger the requirement of post-depreviation remedies with backward looking relief.[675] See also Ch. IX.I on Remedies.

Waiver and estoppel. A taxpayer that did not pursue an appeal in the state could not complain of unequal treatment when its misclassification might have been remedied by the appeal.[676] The Court respected the state court's determination of such waiver.[677]

Details of procedures. An administrative appeal from an initial hearing of the taxpayer's objection to a special taxing district was not required by due process, and specifically there was no need for an appeal method that would insure all taxpayers got the same decision.[678] A special taxing district could levy a new tax after the completion of a project for which the original tax had been ruled illegal.[679] The tax collector could retain far more valuable property than the tax owed where the taxpayer did not pursue its remedies.[680] Property that had been undervalued could be reassessed at a higher value by a commission appointed by the governor.[681] The state did not have to give notice of the duty to pay business taxes to a business owner; as a result, even an unsuspecting landlord whose property became liable for the tenant's taxes.[682] The buyer of land at a tax sale was subject to the statutory right of redemption, without notice.[683] The preservation of evidence of notice of tax sales is a matter of lesser constitutional significance.[684] The Due Process Clause did not require naming the property owner on the property tax assessment roll as long as there was some procedure for the owner to contest.[685] Even though the state law only required notice be given to a resident executor of property taxation the out of state executor who received actual notice and appeared and contested could not avoid the tax by the argument that the notice statute treated him unequally; in any event he was an "official resident."[686] An assessment did not violate due process because it was informally made by entry "on a jacket," and the railroad exercising the franchise of a purchased road could be taxed.[687] The Due Process Clause did not prevent a state from distraining federal bonds held in the state by an out of state insurance company to collect tax owed on other property.[688]

---

675 Harper v. Va. Dep't of Taxation, 509 U.S. 86 (1993).
676 Bradley v. Richmond, 227 U.S. 477 (1913).
677 Harding v. Illinois, 196 U.S. 78 (1904).
678 Ohio ex rel. Bryant v. Akron Metropolitan Park Dist., 281 U.S. 74 (1930).
679 Lombard v. West Chicago Park Comm'rs, 181 U.S. 33 (1901).
680 Nelson v. City Of New York, 352 U.S. 103 (1956).
681 Weyerhaueser v. Minnesota, 176 U.S. 550 (1900).
682 Hodge v. Muscatine County, 196 U.S. 276 (1905).
683 Rusch v. John Duncan Land & Mining Co., 211 U.S. 526 (1909). And law of redemption could be changed after the person acquired an interest in the land. Violet Trapping Co. v. Grace, 297 U.S. 119 (1936).
684 Straus v. Foxworth, 231 U.S. 162 (1913).
685 Castillo v. McConnico, 168 U.S. 674 (1898).
686 Gallup v. Schmidt, 183 U.S. 300 (1902).
687 Illinois C. R. Co. v. Kentucky, 218 U.S. 551 (1910).
688 Scottish Union & Nat'l Ins. Co. v. Bowland, 196 U.S. 611 (1905).

The state can delegate to state officials the creation of methods and procedures for levying a tax on the sale of wild animal skins.[689]

Liens and tax sales. The Due Process Clause required personal service or mailed notice to the mortgagee of real property whose interests may be affected by a sale of a tax lien on the real property.[690] But after the property owner had received due process in the levying of property tax, the county could sell the property for the taxes by notice in the newspaper only.[691] A foreclosure notice provided due process even though it only generally described the property.[692]

Standing. Buyers of gasoline could not pursue a due process argument against license taxes imposed on the sellers of gasoline.[693]

Constitutional arguments. Although state DORs commonly refuse to recognize federal constitutional limits on state tax statutes, that is not always true and in one case the Court found that the state's courts interpreted state law to require such administrative observance of constitutional standards in application of the taxing laws.[694] Therefore, the state statute was not unconstitutional on its face because the tax officials could be assumed to apply the Constitution. But a state remedy for overpayment was not adequate when the body to which the taxpayer must complain had no authority to address constitutional issues and the taxpayer did not have a right to appeal to a court that had that power.[695] A state court denied the taxpayer's constitutional rights by refusing to consider federal constitutional claims.[696]

See generally Ch. V.D.3.b(1), and Ch. IX.H and I, below.

j. *Errors, Mistakes, and Malfeasance*

Errors and mistakes by tax administrative officials, particularly as to property valuation, that are not the product of a pattern and practice or intentional disregard of constitutional rights usually will not be corrected by the Supreme Court under the Due Process Clause or otherwise.[697] The Court ruled that simple noncompliance with state tax law by local officials was not a violation of due process.[698]

---

[689] Lacoste v. Department of Conservation, 263 U.S. 545 (1924).

[690] Mennonite Bd. of Missions v. Adams, 462 U.S. 791 (1983).

[691] Longyear v. Toolan, 209 U.S. 414 (1908).

[692] Ontario Land Co. v. Wilfong, 223 U.S. 543 (1912).

[693] Williams v. Riley, 280 U.S. 78 (1929).

[694] Wheeling Steel Corp. v. Fox, 298 U.S. 193 (1936) ("according to the facts and the applicable principles of law").

[695] Hillsborough v. Cromwell, 326 U.S. 620 (1946). The *Cromwell* case was an extremely unusual one in which the nonresident was assessed a tax hundreds of times greater than the county's budget and was represented by the sons of two former Supreme Court Justices and by a future Justice (Brennan).

[696] Lawrence v. State Tax Com., 286 U.S. 276 (1932).

[697] Kelly v. Pittsburgh, 104 U.S. 78 (1881) (admitting that the land might be worth less than its tax value).

[698] French v. Taylor, 199 U.S. 274 (1905).

k. *Initiative and Referendum; Republican Form of Government*

The Court rejected an attack on an Oregon corporate tax passed by an initiative.[699] In addition to the Due Process Clause, the taxpayer claimed that taxation by public ballot violated the republican form of government, which Congress was supposed to insure in the states. But the Court said it could not enforce that Clause.[700] A jury does not have legislative power to set a reasonable license tax when it finds the tax charged to be unreasonable.[701] However, a court has the power to reduce a property tax assessment after hearing on objection to the assessed amount and that is not usurping a legislative function.[702]

l. *Vagueness*

A telephone tax was not void for vagueness when it would not become effective against the taxpayer until an administrative officer clarified various uncertainties in tax forms and regulations, as authorized by the law.[703]

m. *Bill of Rights Issues*

Normal due process did not apply to a state's attempt to burden a tax exemption by requiring a pledge not to engage in certain speech.[704]

n. *Voting*

The 24th Amendment forbids poll taxes as a condition of voting. But poll taxes remain viable otherwise.[705] The Court applied the 14th Amendment to strike down a precondition of listing property for taxes to voting.[706]

o. *Miscellaneous Due Process Arguments (That Failed)*

A state did not tax something that did not exist by taxing the contingent remainder at the value of the corpus undiminished by the life estate, because it merely collected a deposit on that amount at the time of death, to be adjusted and rebated when the life estate ended.[707]

The Due Process Clause does not prevent the state from taxing the full value of real property in rem without reduction for the mortgage debt.[708] A tax on the "business" of oil production is not "fiat" by virtue of the fact that part of the tax falls on the landowner, who is not in business; it was clearly a tax on oil produc-

---

[699] Pacific States Tel. & Tel. Co. v. Oregon, 223 U.S. 118 (1912).

[700] Several opinions reject that argument as political. Ohio ex rel. Bryant v. Akron Metropolitan Park Dist., 281 U.S. 74 (1930).

[701] Postal Tel.-Cable Co. v. New Hope, 192 U.S. 55 (1904).

[702] Security Trust & Safety Vault Co. v. Lexington, 203 U.S. 323 (1906).

[703] Pac. Tel. & Tel. Co. v. Seattle, 291 U.S. 300 (1934).

[704] Speiser v. Randall, 357 U.S. 513 (1958).

[705] Harper v. Virginia State Bd. of Elections, 383 U.S. 663 (1966), stating that Breedlove v. Suttles, 302 U.S. 277 (1937) was not overruled as to poll taxes generally.

[706] Hill v. Stone, 421 U.S. 289 (1975).

[707] Salomon v. State Tax Com., 278 U.S. 484 (1929).

[708] Paddell v. New York, 211 U.S. 446 (1908).

tion and all engaged in it.[709] The choice of the subjects of taxation is up to the state and is not a Due Process issue.[710] A railroad was not denied due process of law when a state agency failed to follow a state law exempting part of its property from taxation, because the state supreme court had found that law to conflict with the state constitution.[711]

Because dogs can be regulated, a city could impose a dog license tax and require dogs to be listed and valued for personal property tax purposes; and if not listed, the owner could not recover in a tort suit for harm to the dog; Due Process Clause not violated.[712]

12. *Compact Clause*

The Multistate Tax Compact that created the Multistate Tax Commission and provides for coordinated audits of multistate taxpayers did not violate the Compact Clause.[713] An interstate compact establishing jurisdiction over waters did not cede taxing jurisdiction for the land under the waters.[714]

E. In Rem Property Taxation

1. *Real Property*

a. *General*

Local governments commonly tax real property as such and can collect the tax from the property located within their jurisdiction without resort to the owner; that is called in rem taxation.[715] As a practical matter, no state can attempt to impose in rem taxation on the value of property not located in the state in some fashion because it cannot easily enforce its tax. The Supreme Court has stated that the state where real property is located has exclusive jurisdiction to tax the real property under the Due Process Clause.[716] Real property includes personal property affixed to real property, such as trailers.[717]

Even though a state has power to tax the value of real property in the state on an in rem basis it did not have the power under the Due Process Clause to impose personal liability for the tax on the nonresident owner even though the

---

[709] Barwise v. Sheppard, 299 U.S. 33 (1936).

[710] Memphis & C. R. Co. v. Pace, 282 U.S. 241 (1931).

[711] Huntington v. Worthen, 120 U.S. 97 (1887). See discussion of Contracts Clause cases involving tax exemptions, above.

[712] Sentell v. New Orleans & C. R. Co., 166 U.S. 698 (1897).

[713] United States Steel Corp. v. Multistate Tax Comm'n, 434 U.S. 452 (1978).

[714] Central R. Co. v. Jersey City, 209 U.S. 473 (1908).

[715] Mennonite Bd. of Missions v. Adams, 462 U.S. 791 (1983); United States v. County of Allegheny, 322 U.S. 174 (1944) (personal liability of owner might also be imposed); Witherspoon v. Duncan, 71 U.S. 210 (1867).

[716] Curry v. McCanless, 307 U.S. 357 (1939); Miller Bros. Co. v. Maryland, 347 U.S. 340 (1954) (see footnote 11); Union Refrigerator Transit Co. v. Kentucky, 199 U.S. 194 (1905).

[717] Polar Tankers, Inc. v. City of Valdez, 557 U.S. 1 (2009).

nonresident owner appeared in the state to contest the tax;[718] but could do so in effect by collecting the tax from another parcel of real property owned by the same nonresident in the state.[719]

2. *Personal Property*

a. *Tangible*

The in rem taxation of tangible personal property is subject to the same Due Process Clause rules as for real property except for the practical differences that tangible personal property is less likely to be taxed in rem and can be moved among states during a taxing period. Because there do not seem to be any Supreme Court decisions on in rem tangible personal property taxation, that subject will be discussed in Ch. IX.F. and G. below as part of taxing the owners. The Court has recognized the in personam nature of the taxation of moveables by stating "that personal property may be separated from its owner; and he may be taxed, on its account, at the place where it is, although not the place of his own domicil, and even if he is not a citizen or a resident of the State which imposes the tax."[720]

b. *Intangible*

A state usually cannot as a practical matter impose in rem tax on intangible personal property because the state usually cannot get its hands on the intangible,[721] and the intangible usually cannot be dissociated from a person related to the intangible rights, although that relevant person may not necessarily be the owner of the intangible property.[722] Therefore taxation of intangible property also will be discussed below in connection with taxation of residents and non residents. An exception might be intangibles created by the state itself, such as franchises and licenses, which are taxed, but the tax in effect is always upon the grantee and its receipt of the right, with payment demanded from the person, not the state-created right.

F. Taxation of Residents

1. *Real Property Value*

a. *Due Process Clause*

This section addresses taxes imposed on resident persons who are required to list or report their real property for ad valorem taxation in a state. The Due

[718] Dewey v. Des Moines, 173 U.S. 193 (1899).
[719] Nickey v. Mississippi, 292 U.S. 393 (1934).
[720] Pullman's Palace Car Co. v. Pennsylvania, 141 U.S. 18 (1891).
[721] Union Refrigerator Transit Co. v. Kentucky, 199 U.S. 194 (1905).
[722] Curry v. McCanless, 307 U.S. 357 (1939).

Process Clause precludes state taxation of any part of the value of a resident's real property located out of state.[723]

A state did not have jurisdiction to tax income from land located outside the state and owned by the taxpayer through an interest in a trust because the Court viewed the income tax as a property tax and viewed the trust beneficiary as owning the land and not an intangible.[724]

A municipality had Due Process Clause jurisdiction to tax so much of a bridge owned by a resident and extending across a river to another state as lay within its boundaries, which included the area below the low water mark.[725]

b. *Commerce Clause*

It would seem that there could not be a Commerce Clause issue about taxes charged on a resident's local real property, because only one state can impose them. But the Court applied the Commerce Clause to strike down a tax on real property owned by a charity because the charity ran a camp for the benefit of nonresidents and the general exemption from the property tax for charities did not apply to one that dealt with nonresidents.[726] This ruling shows the brittleness of the Court's Commerce Clause jurisprudence: if a state tax hinges a benefit on a fact that touches on interstate commerce, such as nonresidency in general, it is most likely to be invalidated due to facial discrimination.

2. *Personal Property Ad Valorem*

a. *Tangible Personal Property*

(1) *Due Process Clause*

The Court has applied with respect to tangible personal property owned by a resident rules similar to that applied to the resident's real property: the Due Process Clause prevents a government from taxing the value of tangible personal property owned by a resident but that is exclusively outside its legal boundaries,[727] and it has exclusive jurisdiction to tax tangible personal property within its legal boundaries.[728] The difficult cases involve tangible property that moves among states, highly common in the transportation industry.

When the resident's tangible personal property has a tax situs in the domiciliary state and has obtained a less than exclusive tax situs in another state—meaning the other state has acquired Due Process Clause jurisdiction to tax some

---

[723] Curry v. McCanless, 307 U.S. 357 (1939) (dictum); Miller Bros. Co. v. Maryland, 347 U.S. 340 (1954) (see footnote 11); Union Refrigerator Transit Co. v. Kentucky, 199 U.S. 194 (1905). Conclusion is supported by Standard Oil Co. v. Peck, 342 U.S. 382 (1952).

[724] Senior v. Braden, 295 U.S. 422 (1935). New York ex rel. Cohn v. Graves, 300 U.S. 308 (1937) stated that *Senior* involved a property tax.

[725] Henderson Bridge Co. v. Henderson City, 173 U.S. 592 (1899).

[726] Camps Newfound/Owatonna v. Town of Harrison, 520 U.S. 564 (1997).

[727] *See* Union Refrigerator Transit Co. v. Kentucky, 199 U.S. 194 (1905).

[728] Curry v. McCanless, 307 U.S. 357 (1939).

portion of the value, but the property was not exclusively located there during the year—the power of the state of residence to tax all of the value (and thus potentially create double taxation for Due Process Clause purposes) is likely, but unclear, and probably of only theoretical importance since the Commerce Clause will require apportionment by the domiciliary state.[729]

The Court last addressed the subject in 1962 in *Central R. Co. v. Pennsylvania*.[730] The decision was 4:3 and Justice Black wrote a concurrence that disagreed with the reasoning of the opinion of the Court as to the Due Process Clause, but agreed that the Commerce Clause determined the result that the domiciliary state could only tax an apportioned part of the taxpayer's moveable tangible property (rail cars). Justice Black particularly pushed back against the notion that the Due Process Clause precluded double taxation by the states, which Due Process Clause rulings commonly allow. The opinion of the Court ruled that some of the taxpayer's rail cars had obtained a nonexclusive situs in other states and the state of residence could only tax part of their value. While not entirely clear it appears that the Court applied the Due Process Clause to determine a state's power to tax based on property situs in the state and the Commerce Clause to determine how much value could be taxed. The Court's opinions after 1962 have not altered that reading of the 1962 opinion.[731]

Some earlier Due Process opinions suggested that the domiciliary state must tax on an apportioned basis, but they can be explained not to stand for that proposition. *Standard Oil v. Peck* (1952) ruled that the domiciliary state could not tax all of the value of ships moving among the states, but the facts seemed to be that the ships had no tax situs at all in the domiciliary state and had at least some tax situs in other states, which should fall under the general rule that tangible property completely located outside the state of domicile cannot be taxed by it.[732]

---

[729] Central R. Co. v. Pennsylvania, 370 U.S. 607 (1962); Northwest Airlines v. Minnesota, 322 U.S. 292 (1944) (using the term "actual situs" to describe the sole foreign location), as explained in Braniff Airways, Inc. v. Nebraska State Bd. of Equalization & Assessment, 347 U.S. 590 (1954). *See also* New York ex rel. New York C. & H. R. R. Co. v. Miller, 202 U.S. 584 (1906) (which established the principle of the domiciliary state's primary taxing authority despite transitory absence of the tangible property from the state).

[730] Central R. Co. v. Pennsylvania, 370 U.S. 607 (1962).

[731] Japan Line, Ltd. v. County of Los Angeles, 441 U.S. 434 (1979) (declined to apply the "home port" rule for ships; the taxpayer did not rely on the Due Process Clause and Foreign Commerce Clause applied); R. J. Reynolds Tobacco Co. v. Durham County, 479 U.S. 130 (1986) (Due Process Clause did not prevent county from taxing evidently all of the value of tobacco stored long term in the county by a nonresident corporation with a commercial domicile in the state).

[732] Standard Oil Co. v. Peck, 342 U.S. 382 (1952). The taxpayer's boats and barges were registered from Ohio, the state of the taxpayer's domicile, and spent 1.27 percent of the total barrel miles in waters adjacent to Ohio but not in Ohio; the Supreme Court deemed those contacts insufficient to create a tax situs in Ohio. *See* Standard Oil Co. v. Glander, 155 Ohio St. 61 (1951).

The Court once held the domiciliary state could tax a ship that was never in the state, but that may have been an application of the "home port doctrine" that is no longer followed.[733]

Tax situs means the state could tax the property, whether it does so.[734] The Court has stated in dictum that taxing situs requires "substantial nexus," while indicating that a lower standard was required for violation of the Tonnage Clause: the ships were subject to tax simply by entering the port.[735] "Substantial nexus" presumably refers to Commerce Clause nexus, although the opinion did not say so. Eighteen stops per day by a nonresident's aircraft established tax situs.[736] Railroad cars had a tax situs in a state even though they ran irregular schedules.[737] Boats that spent 1.27 percent of the total barrel miles in waters adjacent to Ohio but not in Ohio did not acquire Ohio tax situs.[738] The state of the owner's residence could assume no tax situs elsewhere for property in the state sometimes unless the owner proved otherwise.[739]

The state could tax a resident on tangible personal property in his possession (liquor) even if not owned by him (agents, etc.).[740] The state did not have jurisdiction to tax out of state tangible personal property owned by a resident based solely on the resident holding within the state warehouse receipts for the goods.[741]

(2) *Commerce Clause*

The Commerce Clause precluded the domiciliary state from taxing the full value of tangible personal property with a taxing situs in the state, which also has a taxing status outside the state.[742] But the Court did not apply that principle to a resident's temporary holding of grain in his grain elevator in the state, prior to moving it out of state for sale, and allowed the state to tax the full value in an early Commerce Clause ruling.[743] That may have been based on the failure of the

---

733 Southern Pacific Co. v. Kentucky, 222 U.S. 63 (1911). The Court ruled the state could tax a resident on a ship even though it could not possibly be present in the state, when it was not shown to have an exclusive taxable situs in any other state. See discussion of home port doctrine in Japan Line, Ltd. v. County of Los Angeles, 441 U.S. 434 (1979).

734 Central R. Co. v. Pennsylvania, 370 U.S. 607 (1962).

735 Polar Tankers, Inc. v. City of Valdez, 557 U.S. 1 (2009) (a Tonnage Clause case analogizing Due Process tax situs).

736 Braniff Airways, Inc. v. Nebraska State Bd. of Equalization & Assessment, 347 U.S. 590 (1954).

737 American Refrigerator Transit Co. v. Hall, 174 U.S. 70 (1899).

738 Standard Oil Co. v. Peck, 342 U.S. 382 (1952); Standard Oil Co. v. Glander, 155 Ohio St. 61 (1951).

739 Central R. Co. v. Pennsylvania, 370 U.S. 607 (1962).

740 Carstairs v. Cochran, 193 U.S. 10 (1904); Hannis Distilling Co. v. Baltimore, 216 U.S. 285 (1910); City of Detroit v. Murray Corp., 355 U.S. 489 (1958); Thompson v. Kentucky, 209 U.S. 340 (1908).

741 Selliger v. Kentucky, 213 U.S. 200 (1909).

742 Central R. Co. v. Pennsylvania, 370 U.S. 607 (1962).

743 Bacon v. Illinois, 227 U.S. 504 (1913).

grain to obtain a tax situs in the other states while owned by the taxpayer (who was in the business of buying and selling grain).

b. *Intangible Personal Property*

(1) *Due Process Clause*

Because jurisdiction to tax intangible personal property is not based on its location in the state but is based on the relationship to the state of a person having a legal relationship to the intangible, the Due Process Clause allows each state with jurisdiction over such persons to tax such intangible personal property, creating the possibility for multiple taxation of the same intangible property value because multiple persons having interests in the same property can be resident in different states,[744] and because the same person may be domiciled in multiple states according to the differing laws of those states.[745]

The domiciliary state could tax a person's out of state bank account as property, and the other state also may tax it under the Due Process Clause.[746] The domiciliary state could tax the resident's seat on the New York Stock Exchange as intangible personal property.[747] A state could tax stock owned by residents in foreign corporations under the Due Process Clause.[748] All of the value of stock owned by residents could be taxed even though the corporation that issued the stock owns property out of state.[749] The domiciliary state could tax bonds held even though secured by out of state real property.[750]

All of the value of securities held in trust out of state by a resident trustee could be taxed in the state.[751] But the state of residence of the trust beneficiary did not have Due Process Clause jurisdiction to tax the intangible property held in trust by an out of state trustee.[752]

The domiciliary state could not tax a franchise issued to the resident by another state to run a ferry between the two states.[753] That holding is not out of step because the franchise was viewed as an incorporeal hereditament in the nature of real property and to have no taxable situs outside the granting State; it did not involve the taxation of intangible personal property.[754]

The domiciliary state could tax the tangible and intangible value of the property of a domiciliary corporation as reduced by the value of the out of state

---

[744] Curry v. McCanless, 307 U.S. 357 (1939) (both state of domicile of trust grantor and state of domicile of trustee).

[745] Texas v. Florida, 306 U.S. 398 (1939).

[746] Fidelity & Columbia Trust Co. v. Louisville, 245 U.S. 54 (1917).

[747] Citizens Nat'l Bank v. Durr, 257 U.S. 99 (1921).

[748] Hawley v. Malden, 232 U.S. 1 (1914).

[749] Klein v. Board of Tax Supervisors, 282 U.S. 19 (1930).

[750] Kirtland v. Hotchkiss, 100 U.S. 491 (1879).

[751] Greenough v. Tax Assessors of Newport, 331 U.S. 486 (1947).

[752] Safe Deposit & Trust Co. of Baltimore v. Virginia, 280 U. S. 83 (1929); Brooke v. Norfolk, 277 U. S. 27 (1928).

[753] Louisville & Jeffersonville Ferry Co. v. Kentucky, 188 U.S. 385 (1903).

[754] Citizens Nat'l Bank v. Durr, 257 U.S. 99 (1921).

tangible property and the proportion of the property (a bridge) in the state.[755] A franchise tax on the value of the stock of a domestic subsidiary of a nonresident corporation was a tax on the tangible and intangible personal property of the resident in the state because the value of its realty was deducted.[756] A state did not violate the Due Process Clause by taxing the intangible property of a resident railroad that only operated in the state by apportioning the intangible value to counties for taxation according to trackage in the county.[757]

Although receivables from business activity may obtain a tax situs at a state other than the state of domicile, a corporation's capital stock and surplus, when taxed as intangible property, did not obtain a tax situs in the state of commercial domicile and so could be taxed at 100 percent of value by the chartering state.[758] The Due Process Clause allowed a state to tax the value of a domiciled corporation's stock in excess of the value of its property even though the corporation's only business situs was out of state.[759] A state could impose a graduated franchise tax that capped out at $2500 on the franchise it issued to a domiciliary railroad that had substantial out of state operations; the Court did not view the tax as falling on out of state property even though indirectly measured by the value of the franchise.[760] Or the state could attempt to tax the actual value of the franchise by eliminating out of state tangible property from the value and apportioning the intangible value.[761]

But the state violated the Due Process Clause by including in the value of the corporate property used to value its capital stock the value of coal of the domestic corporation located out of state.[762] The state supreme court had interpreted the capital tax as being a tax on the corporate property.

(2) *Commerce Clause*

The Commerce Clause was violated by taxing the value of intangibles (stock) held by residents less because the corporation paid more tax to the state on its income (because it did more business in the state), as a matter of facial discrimination against interstate commerce.[763]

---

[755] Henderson Bridge Co. v. Kentucky, 166 U.S. 150 (1897). *See also* St. Louis & E. S. L. E. R. Co. v. Missouri, 256 U.S. 314 (1921) (another bridge case).

[756] Susquehanna Power Co. v. State Tax Comm'n, 283 U.S. 297 (1931).

[757] Baker v. Druesedow, 263 U.S. 137 (1923).

[758] *See* Newark Fire Ins. Co. v. State Bd. of Tax Appeals, 307 U.S. 313 (1939).

[759] Cream of Wheat Co. v. County of Grand Forks, 253 U.S. 325 (1920) (the exclusive location of the corporation out of state did not invoke the rule applied to tangible personal property that acquires an exclusive tax situs out of state).

[760] Kansas City, Ft. S. & M. R. Co. v. Botkin, 240 U.S. 227 (1916); Kansas City, M. & B. R. Co. v. Stiles, 242 U.S. 111 (1916) (also Commerce Clause).

[761] Schwab v. Richardson, 263 U.S. 88 (1923). The state tax formula apportioned the intangible value but the opinion did not say that was necessary for Due Process Clause purposes. Because it was a tax on the franchise granted by the state measured by intangible value, the Court did not find the tax to fall on interstate commerce.

[762] Delaware, L. & W. R. Co. v. Pennsylvania, 198 U.S. 341 (1905).

[763] Fulton Corp. v. Faulkner, 516 U.S. 325 (1996).

The Commerce Clause did not prevent the domiciliary state in which the principal office was located from taxing all of the net value of the corporation's receivables.[764] A state could impose a franchise tax on the value of the capital stock based on the proportion of the value of the corporation's property in the state of its commercial domicile.[765]

3. *Business and Employment Activities*

a. *Due Process Clause*

Individuals have one residence for state tax purposes called their domicile, and the state of domicile has Due Process Clause jurisdiction to tax all of their income.[766] The Due Process Clause allowed the state that chartered a corporation to tax all of its income, which included the income earned by a trust administered by a domiciled corporate trustee.[767] West Virginia could tax the gas production of a domiciliary subsidiary of Standard Oil on all the gas it produced in the state (a huge amount), regardless of export out of state (also Commerce Clause not violated).[768] The state could collect an excise tax on the issuance of a note by a domestic corporation even though it sent the notes out of state to a lending bank.[769]

b. *Commerce Clause*

The Court understood that the Constitution limited state taxation of interstate commerce, because the Constitution gave Congress power to regulate interstate commerce. The plaintiff in the first case considered attacked a flat state license tax on resident brokers who dealt in interstate debt and the Court upheld the tax.[770] The Court's second case found a violation.[771] The resident railroad was taxed on freight it carried by the ton, out of, into and through the state (although the particular road appears to have made only intrastate trips). Because the Court was concerned that replication of that tax in every state would result in multiple taxation of the carriage of freight across country, it ruled the tax unconstitutional.

If no other state can tax a domiciliary's business income, the state could tax it all without apportionment.[772] And even in the era when a state could not tax an interstate business, it could tax the gross receipts from purely intrastate

[764] Virginia v. Imperial Coal Sales Co., 293 U.S. 15 (1934).

[765] Atlantic Lumber Co. v. Commissioner of Corp. & Taxation, 298 U.S. 553 (1936).

[766] Lawrence v. State Tax Com., 286 U.S. 276 (1932).

[767] Hanson v. Denckla, 357 U.S. 235 (1958).

[768] Hope Natural Gas Co. v. Hall, 274 U.S. 284 (1927).

[769] Graniteville Mfg. Co. v. Query, 283 U.S. 376 (1931).

[770] Nathan v. Louisiana, 49 U.S. 73 (1850).

[771] Case of State Freight Tax, 82 U.S. 232 (1873) ("The State in not herself the owner of the roadways, nor of the motive power.").

[772] Western Live Stock v. Bureau of Revenue, 303 U.S. 250 (1938), as explained in Okla. Tax Comm'n v. Jefferson Lines, 514 U.S. 175 (1995).

transportation of the domiciliary steamboat company.[773] A property tax could be imposed on cattle bought by a resident at a local stock yard and held there temporarily for resale.[774]

In the "peddler cases" the Court repeatedly upheld license taxes applied to peddlers who in fact mostly sold out of state goods like sewing machines, when the law did not distinguish between resident and nonresident peddlers or turn on the source of the goods.[775] But an early ruling relieved an evidently local peddler from criminal punishment for nonpayment of a peddlers tax that applied only to goods made out of state (sewing machines);[776] and alcohol made out of state.[777] The peddler cases must be carefully evaluated to determine if they rested solely on an inability to tax interstate commerce under prior law.[778]

The state could impose a license tax on managers of packing houses so long as it did not distinguish between those that brought in goods from other states.[779]

A state income tax on all of the income earned by residents from providing a service that affects interstate commerce was fairly apportioned because all of the value of the service was provided in the state (stevedoring).[780] A state severance tax on residents producing coal in the state did not violate the Commerce Clause because it satisfied the *Complete Auto* tests, even though almost all of the coal was shipped out of state; apportionment was not an issue because only one state can tax severance of coal.[781] A state could tax all of the profits from a joint venture selling gas in the state when the partner had its commercial domicile in the state.[782]

A state tax on all of a resident's gross receipts from selling tangible personal property out of state, even if it produced the property in the state, violated the Commerce Clause, without apportionment.[783] The state must apportion the gross receipts tax base of a resident corporation to exclude taxation of sales in other states and foreign countries.[784] A state must apportion the gross receipts

---

[773] New York ex rel. Cornell S. B. Co. v. Sohmer, 235 U.S. 549 (1915).

[774] Minnesota v. Blasius, 290 U.S. 1 (1933).

[775] Emert v. Missouri, 156 U.S. 296 (1895). For similar drummer cases on nonresidents, see Ch. IX.G.3.b(5).

[776] Welton v. Mo., 91 U.S. 275 (1875); Webber v. Va., 103 U.S. 344 (1880) (not clear where salesman lived, but called "sample merchant" as contrasted with resident merchants).

[777] Tiernan v. Rinker, 102 U.S. 123 (1880).

[778] Tenn. Wine & Spirits Retailers Ass'n v. Thomas, 139 S. Ct. 2449 (2019) (see note 21).

[779] Kehrer v. Stewart, 197 U.S. 60 (1905).

[780] Department of Revenue v. Association of Washington Stevedoring Cos., 435 U.S. 734 (1978) (overruling earlier decisions); Department of Treasury v. Ingram-Richardson Mfg. Co., 313 U.S. 252 (1941). *See also* Ficklen v. Shelby County Taxing Dist., 145 U.S. 1 (1892) (city could tax commissions earned by local commission agents for foreign businesses).

[781] Commonwealth Edison Co. v. Mont., 453 U.S. 609 (1981).

[782] Memphis Natural Gas Co. v. Beeler, 315 U.S. 649 (1942).

[783] Evco v. Jones, 409 U.S. 91 (1972); Philadelphia & Southern Mail S. S. Co. v. Pennsylvania, 122 U.S. 326 (1887).

[784] J. D. Adams Mfg. Co. v. Storen, 304 U.S. 307 (1938).

tax base of a bus company that collects the receipts in state but carries the passengers out of state because the other states may impose a double tax.[785]

Where there was no dispute about the apportionment formula the state's taxation of a percentage of the domiciliary's domestic and foreign business income as the franchise tax base satisfied both the Commerce Clause and the Due Process Clause.[786]

A county violated the Commerce Clause by taxing all of the Subchapter S income passed through to a resident from his corporation that did business out of state.[787] Justice Ginsburg's dissent argued that the domiciliary state has power to tax all of the resident's income without apportionment, citing a Native American tax case,[788] but that principle seems now to be limited to the Due Process Clause and can be upset by the Commerce Clause.

The Court did not even consider the Equal Protection ground (on which the lower court had upheld the discrimination) when it struck down a Hawaii excise tax imposed on a resident's income from sales of liquor not produced on the islands, applying the Commerce Clause.[789] Similarly, a tax on resident milk buyers on both in and out of state milk purchases from producers violated the Commerce Clause because the tax collections were effectively paid out to the local milk producers, meaning that only the out of state milk bore the tax.[790] A state could not exclude locally produced agricultural goods, such as logs, from a general property tax and so invalidated the tax as to the resident lumber mill's out of state sourced logs.[791]

A state waste disposal surcharge imposed on resident waste haulers violated the Commerce Clause because it charged almost three times as much for out of state waste, a facial discrimination against interstate commerce that was per se invalid because the state did not advance a legitimate local purpose that cannot be adequately served by reasonable nondiscriminatory alternatives.[792]

A state's use tax on purchases by residents from out of state vendors violated the Commerce Clause because in practice it applied a higher rate than the sales tax charged on local sales.[793] But a tax on "receipts" by retailers of inventory purchased from out of state was in effect a use tax and did not violate the Commerce Clause.[794]

See discussion of *Complete Auto Transit* in Ch. IX.G.3.b(2).

---

[785] Central Greyhound Lines, Inc. v. Mealey, 334 U.S. 653 (1948).

[786] Matson Navigation Co. v. State Bd. of Equalization, 297 U.S. 441 (1936).

[787] Comptroller of the Treasury v. Wynne, 575 U.S. 542 (2015). This opinion cited as precedent *J. D. Adams* and Gwin, White & Prince, Inc. v. Henneford, 305 U.S. 434 (1939), and Central Greyhound Lines, Inc. v. Mealey, 334 U.S. 653 (1948).

[788] Okla. Tax Comm'n v. Chickasaw Nation, 515 U.S. 450 (1995).

[789] Bacchus Imps. v. Dias, 468 U.S. 263 (1984).

[790] West Lynn Creamery, Inc. v. Healy, 512 U.S. 186 (1994). The plaintiffs were residents but the discriminated against class was out of state milk producers that sold to the plaintiffs.

[791] I. M. Darnell & Son Co. v. Memphis, 208 U.S. 113 (1908).

[792] Or. Waste Sys. v. Dep't of Envtl. Quality, 511 U.S. 93 (1994).

[793] Associated Indus. v. Lohman, 511 U.S. 641 (1994).

[794] J. Bacon & Sons v. Martin, 305 U.S. 380 (1939).

4. *Investment Activities*

a. *Due Process Clause*

A state had Due Process Clause jurisdiction to tax the income earned by a domiciliary from property located out of state that the state could not tax as property.[795] A state could tax the income from an out of state trust received by a domestic beneficiary even though the state where the trustee was located may have taxed the income to the trustee.[796]

The domicile of a trust beneficiary in the state did not give that state Due Process Clause jurisdiction to tax an out of state trustee on trust income not paid to the domiciliary, in the absence of other contacts between the trustee and the state.[797] Without rights to demand the income, the minimum contacts requirement was not met. This opinion states that the minimum contacts test is "borrowed from" *International Shoe*, which involved jurisdiction of a court over a person, but does not state that the tests are the same.[798]

b. *Commerce Clause*

A state did not violate the Commerce Clause by taxing residents on income from out of state municipal bond interest but not the state's own bond interest.[799] The grounds of the opinion are not generally applicable but reflect a version of the market participant exception that allowed the Court to find that the exemption was a governmental function and not a regulation of interstate commerce.

The Commerce Clause precluded a state intangible property tax on residents that facially discriminated against corporations in which they invested by taxing more heavily the stocks of corporations doing less business.[800] There was no compensating tax defense due to the state corporate income taxes supposedly paid by the corporations doing more business in the state.

5. *Estate and Gift; Other Activities*

a. *Due Process Clause*

Curry v. McCanless is a frequently cited opinion that ruled the Due Process Clause allowed a state to apply its estate tax to a resident decedent's exercise of a power of appointment she created over intangible property held in trust out of the state.[801] The same conclusion applied even though an out of state relative

---

[795] New York ex rel. Cohn v. Graves, 300 U.S. 308 (1937).

[796] Guaranty Trust Co. v. Virginia, 305 U.S. 19 (1938); Maguire v. Trefry, 253 U. S. 129 (1920).

[797] N.C. Dep't of Revenue v. Kimberley Rice Kaestner 1992 Family Trust, 139 S. Ct. 2213 (2019).

[798] International Shoe Co. v. Washington, 326 U. S. 310 (1945).

[799] Dep't of Revenue v. Davis, 553 U.S. 328 (2009).

[800] Fulton Corp. v. Faulkner, 516 U.S. 325 (1996).

[801] Curry v. McCanless, 307 U.S. 357 (1939); Bullen v. Wisconsin, 240 U.S. 625 (1916).

created the out of state trust.[802] And the event of death of the grantor of an irrevocable trust was a sufficient event to allow imposition of the state inheritance tax.[803] The state of domicile had Due Process Clause jurisdiction to tax the transmission at death by the decedent of an interest in trust property held by an out of state trustee, which was transferred by failure to exercise a power of revocation.[804] Such tax could apply to the value at death even if the legal disposition of the property by the decedent occurred earlier.[805]

The Due Process Clause allowed the state of the decedent's domicile to tax as intangible property the death transfer of an interest in a partnership owning real property out of state, stocks and bonds physically located out of state, out of state bank accounts and insurance proceeds, even if taxable in the other state; but the state could not tax bank notes and coin kept by the decedent in a safe deposit box in another State, which are tangible property and not subject to transfer tax by the State of his domicile.[806] The out of state tangible property that was not subject to tax included the out of state portion of the value of the federal estate tax base for tangible property used by the state inheritance tax.[807]

But the Court applied a step transaction analysis to prevent the resident decedent from avoiding an estate tax on intangibles by transforming intangibles into Federal Reserve notes held out of state, in contemplation of death: the state of domicile had jurisdiction under the Due Process Clause to tax a gift in contemplation of death carried out by an out of state agent or fiduciary who held the intangibles gifted in the first step of the effort to turn the intangible property into tangible property out of state.[808]

In dictum the Court stated that the state of domicile of the decedent shareholder also may tax the transfer of stock in an out of state corporation, while the state where the corporation was domiciled also could tax the transfer of its stock at death; there is no constitutional prohibition against double taxation of the transfer of intangibles.[809]

The domiciliary state did not have Due Process Clause jurisdiction to tax the transfer at death of paintings (or other tangible property) owned by the decedent that had acquired an "actual situs" out of state.[810] The Due Process Clause was not violated by including in the decedent's tax base the value of property

---

[802] Graves v. Schmidlapp, 315 U.S. 657 (1942)

[803] Guaranty Trust Co. v. Blodgett, 287 U.S. 509 (1933).

[804] Graves v. Elliott, 307 U.S. 383 (1937).

[805] Central Hanover Bank & Trust Co. v. Kelly, 319 U.S. 94 (1943); Keeney v. Comptroller of New York, 222 U.S. 525 (1912).

[806] Blodgett v. Silberman, 277 U.S. 1 (1928).

[807] Treichler v. Wisconsin, 338 U.S. 251 (1949) (stating that it is a federal question whether property is tangible or intangible for purposes of estate taxation).

[808] Pearson v. McGraw, 308 U.S. 313 (1939).

[809] State Tax Comm'n v. Aldrich, 316 U.S. 174 (1942).

[810] Frick v. Pennsylvania, 268 U.S. 473 (1925); City Bank Farmers Trust Co. v. Schnader, 293 U.S. 112 (1934).

appointed under a power of appointment so that under a progressive estate tax other beneficiaries received less net of the tax.[811]

b. *Commerce Clause*

A state did not violate the Commerce Clause by requiring long distance telephone carriers to charge a tax on calls originating and terminating in the state, for which the residents could claim a credit for tax paid to other states.[812] Only one state could impose such a tax, which made it internally consistent, and it was fairly apportioned to the state because the state was where the call originated or terminated, making it "externally consistent," referring to properly related in amount. *Goldberg v. Sweet* does not, however, stand for a principle that it is not the purpose of the Commerce Clause to protect residents from the state's taxation.[813]

G. Taxation of Nonresidents

1. *Real Property Value*

a. *Due Process Clause*

The Due Process Clause allowed a state to tax the value of real property located in the state owned by a nonresident.[814] Taxation of a nonresident's real property not located in the state would violate the Due Process Clause even though the state had jurisdiction over the nonresident person.[815] But when a state taxed a nonresident railroad's real property (fences) located in the state, but which the state law did not authorize it to tax, the tax violated the Fourteenth Amendment because it exceeded the taxing jurisdiction of the state.[816]

b. *Commerce Clause*

The state could tax Western Union on the value of its property (mostly real property but some personal property) in the state by multiplying the value of

---

811 Whitney v. State Tax Com., 309 U.S. 530 (1940); Binney v. Long, 299 U.S. 280 (1936).

812 Goldberg v. Sweet, 488 U.S. 252 (1989).

813 Comptroller of the Treasury v. Wynne, 575 U.S. 542 (2015).

814 Savings & Loan Soc. v. Multnomah County, 169 U.S. 421 (1898) (treating a mortgage as real property); Alexander v. Alexandria, 9 U.S. 1 (1809) (interpreted statute to tax land in the city owned by nonresidents without considering constitution).

815 There is no direct citation but see dissent of Justice Roberts in Wisconsin v. J. C. Penney Co., 311 U.S. 435 (1940). Also the conclusion follows from Standard Oil Co. v. Peck, 342 U.S. 382 (1952).

816 Santa Clara County v. Southern P. R. Co., 118 U.S. 394 (1886). This was the important case that established by the Reporter's note that corporations were entitled to the rights of "persons." Also, the Court would not disaggregate the tax on the fences from the "unit" of business property taxed and apportioned to the counties. The Court has stricken a state tax for lack of taxing jurisdiction where the tax authority did not follow state law, without reference to a violation of the U.S. Constitution. Ogden City v. Armstrong, 168 U.S. 224 (1897).

its capital stock times the telegraph line mileage in the state over its total line mileage.[817]

2. *Personal Property Value*

a. *Tangible Personal Property*

(1) *Due Process Clause*

Unlike land, personal property generally can move across state lines and states often tax the value of such property located in the state on a particular day of the year. For example, the state where trees are cut had jurisdiction to tax the value of logs in the state owned by a nonresident prior to floating out of the state; this early opinion did not reference the Due Process Clause.[818]

Habitual though irregular employment of personal property in the state in the railroad business created Due Process Clause situs creating jurisdiction to tax an average number of cars computed to be in the state.[819] However, the Due Process Clause required the nondomiciliary state to tax tangible personal property not permanently located there on an apportioned basis.[820] As to ships, this rule replaced the home port doctrine.[821] But in such cases apportionment is required only if the tangible personal property also has taxing situs in some other state.[822] The Due Process Clause allowed states to tax the property of multistate railroad, telegraph and sleeping car companies, in their state on a unit basis, valuing the whole of the business property as a going concern (evidently including intangible value) and taxing the portion in the state.[823] Nonresidents could be required to list for taxation personal property sitused in the taxing state, and in the case of fungible property such as rail cars, the listing could be based on the average number regularly used in the state.[824]

But applying the percentage of track miles in the state as compared with total track miles times the total value of all of the company's property did not rationally approximate the value of the average number of rail cars in the state during the year and the tax violated the Due Process Clause (as well as the Commerce

---

[817] Western Union Tel. Co. v. Taggart, 163 U.S. 1 (1896).

[818] Coe v. Errol, 116 U.S. 517 (1886) (primarily addressing the argument that the property tax violated the Import-Export Clause).

[819] American Refrigerator Transit Co. v. Hall, 174 U.S. 70 (1899).

[820] Ott v. Mississippi Valley Barge Line Co., 336 U.S. 169 (1949) (the opinion appeared to apply both the Due Process Clause and the Commerce Clause); Norfolk & W. R. Co. v. Missouri State Tax Comm'n, 390 U.S. 317 (1968).

[821] *See* Japan Line, Ltd. v. County of Los Angeles, 441 U.S. 434 (1979), discussing Hays v. Pac. Mail S.S. Co., 58 U.S. 596 (1854).

[822] Braniff Airways, Inc. v. Nebraska State Bd. of Equalization & Assessment, 347 U.S. 590 (1954) (stating that tax situs is an issue for the Due Process Clause).

[823] Adams Express Co. v. Ohio State Auditor, 165 U.S. 194 (1897); Adams Express Co. v. Kentucky, 166 U.S. 171 (1897).

[824] Johnson Oil Refining Co. v. Oklahoma, 290 U.S. 158 (1933).

Clause), when it in effect taxed unrelated out of state property.[825] Nor was track mileage a proper method of apportionment of the tax base when the cost of building track was substantially different in and out of state.[826]

However apportionment of value alone did not render a state's taxation of the property of a foreign person constitutional when the property was owned by a resident of another country (see Foreign Commerce Clause).[827]

Because a nonresident's tangible personal property had an exclusive situs in the taxing state, that was the only state that could tax the property.[828] Taxation of a nonresident's tangible personal property not located in the state would violate the Due Process Clause even though the state had jurisdiction over the nonresident person.[829]

Rulings on corporate franchise taxes can be confusing because the Court has treated franchise taxes on nonresident corporations sometimes as taxes on the franchise as property, and sometimes as taxes on the property owned by the corporation by which the value of the franchise is measured.[830] To the extent the tax fluctuates with the value and the value reflects the corporate property, both the Due Process Clause and the Commerce Clause required the value be limited to some measure of the property in the state.[831]

(2) *Commerce Clause*

The Commerce Clause and the Due Process Clause both required apportionment of tangible personal property of a nonresident that moves in and out of a state (for example, rail cars),[832] and this principle seems to have originated as a Commerce Clause rule.[833] The Commerce Clause allowed property taxation of the average number of rail cars habitually used in the state by a nonresident railroad.[834] But the Commerce Clause allowed a state to tax the whole value of a nonresident's ships registered in another state because the ships were solely engaged in business in the taxing state.[835] And an early decision allowing the state to charge $3,000 ad valorem tax per Pullman car used in the state may still be valid.[836]

---

825 Union Tank Line Co. v. Wright, 249 U.S. 275 (1919); Fargo v. Hart, 193 U.S. 490 (1904).

826 Wallace v. Hines, 253 U.S. 66 (1920).

827 Japan Line, Ltd. v. County of Los Angeles, 441 U.S. 434 (1979).

828 Union Refrigerator Transit Co. v. Kentucky, 199 U.S. 194 (1905).

829 The conclusion follows from Standard Oil Co. v. Peck, 342 U.S. 382 (1952).

830 St. Louis S. R. Co. v. Arkansas, 235 U.S. 350 (1914) (franchise tax was tax on property of corporation in the state).

831 St. Louis S. R. Co. v. Arkansas, 235 U.S. 350 (1914).

832 Norfolk & W. R. Co. v. Missouri State Tax Comm'n, 390 U.S. 317 (1968) (rejected attempt to prove that track mileage was not the proper measure of apportionment).

833 Pullman's Palace Car Co. v. Pennsylvania, 141 U.S. 18 (1891); Cudahy Packing Co. v. Minnesota, 246 U.S. 450 (1918) (rail cars valued based on earnings apportioned to state).

834 Union Refrigerator Transit Co. v. Lynch, 177 U.S. 149 (1900).

835 Old Dominion S.S. Co. v. Virginia, 198 U.S. 299 (1905) (operated solely in state).

836 Allen v. Pullman's Palace Car Co., 191 U.S. 171 (1903).

The Commerce Clause allowed states to tax the property of multistate railroad, telegraph and sleeping car companies in their state on a unit basis, valuing the whole of the business property as a going concern (evidently including intangible value) and taxing the portion of value deemed to be in the state.[837] The portion could be based on the relative gross receipts of the nonresident railroad.[838] Or gross receipts times the percentage of track mileage in the state could be taxed as the value of railroad property in the state.[839]

The state where trees were cut had jurisdiction to tax the value of logs owned in the state by a nonresident prior to floating out of the state.[840] Logs floating through a state did not establish nexus, before *Complete Auto*.[841] The state could levy a property tax on coal in barges on the river even though the owner had paid a property tax in the same year to another state where the coal was mined; the opinion did not focus on the double property taxation but seemed to treat the two taxes as independent because the coal had obtained a taxing jurisdiction in each state.[842]

b. *Intangible Personal Property*

(1) *Due Process Clause*

A nondomiciliary state could tax intangible property that has acquired a business situs in the state; that could occur when the corporation had a commercial domicile in the state, meaning that the state could tax stock it owned in subsidiaries;[843] could tax notes and receivables from sale of goods, less only receivables taxed in other state where manufacturing plant was located;[844] but the state of commercial domicile could not impose a property tax on the capital and surplus of a nonresident corporation because that could not acquire a situs through the commercial domicile alone.[845] The Due Process Clause allowed a state of residence of insureds to tax the credits owed by the insured to the out of state insurance company.[846]

A nondomiciliary state that is not the commercial domicile also could acquire Due Process Clause taxing jurisdiction over intangible property that had

---

[837] Wells, Fargo & Co. v. Nevada, 248 U.S. 165 (1918).

[838] Pullman Co. v. Richardson, 261 U.S. 330 (1923); Great Northern Ry. Co. v. Minnesota, 278 U.S. 503 (1929); Illinois C. R. Co. v. Minnesota, 309 U.S. 157 (1940) (gross earnings).

[839] Great Northern Ry. Co. v. Minnesota, 278 U.S. 503 (1929).

[840] Diamond Match Co. v. Ontonagon, 188 U.S. 82 (1903) (Commerce Clause).

[841] Champlain Realty Co. v. Brattleboro, 260 U.S. 366 (1922).

[842] Pittsburgh & Southern Coal Co. v. Bates, 156 U.S. 577 (1895); Brown v. Houston, 114 U.S. 622 (1885). *See also* Edelman v. Boeing Air Transport, Inc., 289 U.S. 249 (1933) (airplane fuel brought into state and stored for use subject to use tax upon withdrawal).

[843] First Bank Stock Corp. v. Minnesota, 301 U.S. 234 (1937). As to commercial domicile, see Ch. IX.D.2.c.

[844] Wheeling Steel Corp. v. Fox, 298 U.S. 193 (1936).

[845] Newark Fire Ins. Co. v. State Bd. of Tax Appeals, 307 U.S. 313 (1939).

[846] Liverpool & London & Globe Ins. Co. v. Board of Assessors, 221 U.S. 346 (1911); Orient Ins. Co. v. Board of Assessors, 221 U.S. 358 (1911) (same when premiums in hands of local collectors).

acquired a business situs in the state by being held there for business purposes: mortgage notes secured by property in the state and collected by an agent in the state who deposited the collections in banks in the state;[847] an out of state insurance company's policy loans on policies written in the state were found to be intangible property subject to taxation in the state;[848] a state could tax the notes generated in the state by loans made through an agent there by a French bank.[849] Even though an out of state insurance company could be taxed on the value of its loans made in the state, a policy reserve withdrawal by the insured was not a true loan and was not taxable because the cash was not owned by the insurance company.[850]

The Due Process Clause prevented the domiciliary state of a corporate debtor from requiring it to collect a property tax on the bonds it had issued out of interest it paid to nonresident bondholders; the state was effectively trying to tax the intangible owned by the nonresidents.[851] But a state did not violate the Due Process Clause by requiring a domestic corporation to pay (or withhold) a property tax upon the value of its shares, which tax was viewed as a tax on the nonresident shareholders' intangible property in the state.[852] The difference between the debt and stock rulings perhaps can be explained by the fact that a debt owed by the corporation is not property owned by it, but its stock reflects the value of the corporate property.[853]

A state could tax the memberships in a local chamber of commerce at the site of the chamber as to nonresident members.[854] New York could tax a nonresident on the intangible value of a seat on the New York Stock Exchange, either because the right grows out of the actual transactions of a business there localized, or because its exercise is fixed there, exclusively or dominantly.[855]

The Court ruled that a state could not tax a nonresident corporation on the entire value of its authorized capital stock because that represented value beyond the jurisdiction of the state; the Court treated the taxes as property taxes although called excise or license taxes.[856] The Court struck down a tax on the going concern value of an interstate railroad even though the total earnings were

---

[847] New Orleans v. Stempel, 175 U.S. 309 (1899); Bristol v. Washington County, 177 U.S. 133 (1900) (nonresident individual had an agent in the state who lent money and held notes in state).

[848] Metropolitan Life Ins. Co. v. New Orleans, 205 U.S. 395 (1907) (even if the notes were temporarily removed from the office of the local agent).

[849] State Board of Assessors v. Comptoir Nat'l D'Escompte, 191 U.S. 388 (1903).

[850] Board of Assessors v. New York Life Ins. Co., 216 U.S. 517 (1910).

[851] Case of State Tax on Foreign-Held Bonds, 82 U.S. 300 (1872).

[852] Schuylkill Trust Co. v. Pennsylvania, 302 U.S. 506 (1938); Corry v. Baltimore, 196 U.S. 466 (1905).

[853] Texas v. New Jersey, 379 U.S. 674 (1965) (an escheat ruling).

[854] Rogers v. Hennepin County, 240 U.S. 184 (1916).

[855] New York ex rel. Whitney v. Graves, 299 U.S. 366 (1937).

[856] International Paper Co. v. Massachusetts, 246 U.S. 135 (1918); Western Union Tel. Co. v. Kansas, 216 U.S. 1 (1910); Looney v. Crane Co., 245 U.S. 178 (1917); Cudahy Packing Co. v. Hinkle, 278 U.S. 460 (1929). *Cf.* Hump Hairpin Mfg. Co. v. Emmerson, 258 U.S. 290 (1922) (based on authorized dollar capital and apportioned to business in state, did not violate Commerce Clause).

apportioned on a mileage basis because the railroad proved that its system in the state was substantially less profitable than the entire system.[857] But the state won on better facts in a later version of the same case: the state could tax the franchise, said to be on intangible value, measured by track miles in the state and average per mile income.[858]

A state lacked Due Process Clause jurisdiction to tax the value as property of stocks and bonds held by a nonresident trustee out of state even though the settlor and beneficiaries of the trust lived in state; they had no present right to the corpus or income.[859]

However, the Court declined to decide the Due Process Clause issue and struck down a property tax on a nonresident corporation's receivables on equal protection grounds because residents' receivables were not taxed.[860]

Congress could fix the location of national bank shares (intangible personalty) at the office of the national bank in a state, by statute.[861]

Franchise taxes charged nonresident corporations often began as small flat amounts per year, but later the states increased them and the increases attracted suits. Where Texas charged domestic and foreign corporations a franchise tax (that was not a property tax) on the value of its stock (surplus and undivided profits), the Court ruled the tax fell on out of state values in violation of the Due Process Clause.[862]

(2) *Commerce Clause*

A tax on the value of intangible personal property such as the value of corporate stock facially violated the Commerce Clause by providing a reduction of the taxed value that increased as the corporation's in state activities increased.[863] Although the tax was levied on a resident, nonresident corporations were indirectly the object of the discrimination.

3. *Business and Employment Activities*

a. *Due Process Clause*

The Due Process Clause imposes separate "whether" and "how much" limits on a state's power to tax a nonresident.

(1) *Whether*

The whether limit requires a minimal connection or "nexus" of the taxpayer with the taxing state, which generally means carrying on business, including any

---

[857] Southern R. Co. v. Kentucky, 274 U.S. 76 (1927).

[858] Southern R. Co. v. Kentucky, 284 U.S. 338 (1932).

[859] Safe Deposit & Trust Co. v. Virginia, 280 U.S. 83 (1929).

[860] Wheeling Steel Corp. v. Glander, 337 U.S. 562 (1949).

[861] Tappan v. Merchants' Nat'l Bank, 86 U.S. 490 (1873) (no federal constitutional ground cited).

[862] Looney v. Crane Co., 245 U.S. 178 (1917) (also violated Commerce Clause).

[863] Fulton Corp. v. Faulkner, 516 U.S. 325 (1996).

part of a unitary business' activities.[864] The requirement is rooted in the reach of a state's sovereign power: has it given anything for which it can ask a tax in return?[865] That explanation oddly turns on its head the general rule that a tax is not an assessment of benefits, but that rule looks at the issue from the taxpayer's "how much" perspective, rather than the state's "whether" perspective.

But the Due Process Clause nexus rulings also relate to individuals' employment. A state could require withholding on compensation paid to nonresidents physically working in the state but not on residents' compensation; and could confine deductions to those related to the in state income.[866] A state had Due Process Clause jurisdiction to tax income earned by a nonresident from property located in the state.[867]

A state did not have taxing jurisdiction under the Due Process Clause to require a nonresident seller of tangible personal property to remit sales or use tax on sales made in person in the nonresident's state to residents of the taxing state.[868] The fact that the out of state vendor was licensed to do business in the state and knew that the buyer would use the goods in the state did not change that result.[869] But if the sale occurs in the buyer's state, as shown by delivery by the seller in the state, the state has jurisdiction to impose a gross receipts and sales tax.[870] The state could not require the out of state issuer of bonds to collect the resident bondholders' property tax by withholding tax on interest it paid to the resident, even though the issuer did business in the state.[871]

A state had Due Process jurisdiction to tax the gross receipts earned by an out of state vendor that both was the consignee of the goods delivered into the state and had employees involved with the sale of the goods in the state.[872] The Court upheld a use tax despite the fact that all of the seller's in-state solicitation was performed by independent contractors.[873] The presence of only salesmen in the state without power to bind the vendor created Due Process nexus to require

[864] Exxon Corp. v. Dep't of Revenue, 447 U.S. 207 (1980).

[865] Wisconsin v. J. C. Penney Co., 311 U.S. 435 (1940).

[866] Travis v. Yale & Towne Mfg. Co., 252 U.S. 60 (1920) (commuter tax; also a Commerce Clause ruling).

[867] Shaffer v. Carter, 252 U.S. 37 (1920).

[868] Miller Bros. Co. v. Maryland, 347 U.S. 340 (1954) This opinion surveys the entirety of the Supreme Court's state tax jurisprudence as of 1954. The fact that the seller delivered some purchases into the taxing state by its trucks is questionable.

[869] American Oil Co. v. Neill, 380 U.S. 451 (1965) (nonresident oil wholesaler delivered oil to buyer that would use it in taxing state; had registered as an oil dealer in the state).

[870] International Harvester Co. v. Department of Treasury, 322 U.S. 340 (1944) (and Commerce Clause); State Tax Comm'n v. Pacific States Cast Iron Pipe Co., 372 U.S. 605 (1963) (title passed in the taxing state).

[871] New York, L. E. & W. R. Co. v. Pennsylvania, 153 U.S. 628 (1894) (the opinion did not mention the Due Process Clause but likely was based on general notions of jurisdiction to tax, as well as a Contracts Clause claim).

[872] Department of Treasury v. Wood Preserving Corp., 313 U.S. 62 (1941).

[873] Scripto, Inc. v. Carson, 362 U.S. 207 (1960); Tyler Pipe Indus. v. Washington State Dep't of Revenue, 483 U.S. 232 (1987).

collection of the use tax.[874] The state had power to require use tax collection because the out of state vendor had agents in the state for whom it supplied offices.[875] The nonresident vendor maintained stores in the state and so could be required to collect use tax on its mail order sales into the state.[876] The nonresident vendor maintained two offices in the state and could be required to collect use tax on mail order sales into the state;[877] the same was true for a gross receipts tax.[878] However, the principle of *National Geographic* (use tax collection can be required) does not apply to an excise tax on the out of state seller: the state could not tax a wholesaler that had qualified to do business in the state on sales of goods to be delivered by common carrier into the state where the sales were disassociated from the local activities.[879]

The Due Process Clause did not require the physical presence of an out of state vendor in the state to require it to collect the market state's use tax because the seller has sold into that state, purposefully availing itself of the market, and thereby established "minimum contacts" for Due Process purposes.[880]

A surprising early decision found that a state where a Chrysler car was bought by a local resident could tax an insurance company from a third state that had contracted with the Michigan based Chrysler company to provide insurance automatically to all auto purchasers.[881]

A state could tax a nonresident insurance company on business done in the state by taxing it on the premiums received from insured residents, whether collected in the state or through the mail; the company had qualified to do business in the state and employees conducted its business there.[882] But a state could not tax premiums when the foreign insurer was not doing any business in the state and the insured just lived there.[883] A state could not tax a nonresident insurance company doing business in the state on all of the gross premiums received at its home office for insurance having no connection with the state.[884] The Due Process Clause precluded state taxation of premiums paid by a nondomiciliary corporation from its out of state office to a foreign insurer for insurance on property located in the state; this may be a special rule for insurance companies.[885] A state could tax a nonresident insurance company on premiums paid by insureds

---

874 General Trading Co. v. State Tax Comm'n, 322 U.S. 335 (1944).

875 Felt & Tarrant Mfg. Co. v. Gallagher, 306 U.S. 62 (1939).

876 Nelson v. Sears, Roebuck & Co., 312 U.S. 359 (1941); Nelson v. Montgomery Ward & Co., 312 U.S. 373 (1941).

877 National Geographic Soc. v. California Bd. of Equalization, 430 U.S. 551 (1977) (also Commerce Clause).

878 Norton Co. v. Department of Revenue, 340 U.S. 534 (1951).

879 American Oil Co. v. Neill, 380 U.S. 451 (1965).

880 Quill Corp. v. N.D., 504 U.S. 298 (1992), overruled on other grounds by South Dakota v. Wayfair, Inc., 138 S. Ct. 2080 (2018).

881 Palmetto Fire Ins. Co. v. Conn., 272 U.S. 295 (1926).

882 Equitable Life Assurance Soc. v. Pennsylvania, 238 U.S. 143 (1915).

883 Provident Sav. Life Assurance Soc. v. Kentucky, 239 U.S. 103 (1915).

884 Connecticut General Life Ins. Co. v. Johnson, 303 U.S. 77 (1938).

885 State Bd. of Ins. v. Todd Shipyards Corp., 370 U.S. 451 (1962).

in the state, after the company withdrew from doing business in the state.[886] The state did not violate the Due Process Clause by imposing a use tax on items brought into the state by a railroad to be used in its rail cars that would later go out of state.[887]

(2) *How Much*

The Due Process "how much" limit may be applied in terms of identifying income from particular property or activities of the nonresident in the taxing state, as shown in some of the decisions above. For example a state could collect a gross receipts tax limited to gross receipts received by the nonresident from sales into the state.[888] Alternately, the nonresident taxpayer that did business in the taxing state could be required to pay tax on part of its income (or other tax base) that bore a rational relationship to the State and "the intrastate values of the enterprise."[889] In those cases the Due Process issues are (1) whether the nonresident does business in a state and other states, (2) whether the business done in the taxing state is part of a unitary business done in other states, (3) use of various formulas to apportion the unitary tax base to the state, and (4) exclusion from that apportionment of nonbusiness income or income of other businesses not partly operated in the state.[890]

The similarity of this formulary to Commerce Clause analysis is confusing and deceptive because they come from entirely different constitutional analyses. Tracing back the citations in *Exxon Corp.* to their sources reveals that the key Due Process concept applicable is irrationality, which is always a potential feature of Due Process analysis. In addition, the earliest case cites are to Commerce Clause cases.[891] The distinction is particularly important as it involves the issue of double taxation.[892] Double taxation by states is anathema to the Commerce Clause but not to the Due Process Clause. Rather the Due Process Clause is concerned with whether the state has taxing jurisdiction over activities, property, income, etc. That question came to be answered in terms of rational relationship of the state to those taxed items of nonresidents, which is not designed to avoid double taxation but to tax rationally and within the state's jurisdiction.

The requirements of nexus and of apportionment of the unitary business income of a nonresident corporation are particularly confused because they are imposed by both the Due Process Clause and the Commerce Clause,[893] and the

---

886 Continental Assurance Co. v. Tennessee, 311 U.S. 5 (1940).

887 Southern Pacific Co. v. Gallagher, 306 U.S. 167 (1939).

888 Standard Pressed Steel Co. v. Department of Revenue, 419 U.S. 560 (1979) (also Commerce Clause).

889 Exxon Corp. v. Dep't of Revenue, 447 U.S. 207 (1980).

890 Mobil Oil Corp. v. Comm'r of Taxes, 445 U.S. 425 (1980) (there might be a nontaxable out of state discrete business enterprise); Container Corp. of Am. v. Franchise Tax Bd., 463 U.S. 159 (1983) (overseas subsidiaries were not separate from unitary business).

891 Fargo v. Hart, 193 U.S. 490 (1904).

892 *See* Ch. IX.D.11.b.

893 Allied-Signal, Inc. v. Dir., Div. of Taxation, 504 U.S. 768 (1992); Northwestern States Portland Cement Co. v. Minnesota, 358 U.S. 450 (1959).

Court often does not differentiate them and presumably means its explanations to apply to both.[894]

The Court early upheld under the Due Process Clause an income tax on a multistate wholesaler to which the state applied a three factor apportionment formula.[895] But the Court invalidated evidently on Due Process Clause grounds a single factor formula that apportioned almost all of the profits of an out of state manufacturer because its only plant was in the state.[896] Outside of such facts the Court approved a franchise tax on issued stock par or deemed value, multiplied by assets employed within the state over total assets.[897] A state could apportion a railroad's net income to the state based on the proportion of track miles in the state where the railroad failed to prove that the tracks in the state were either more expensive or more productive than the average.[898]

A state's value added tax did not violate the Due Process Clause when applied to a nonresident corporation's unitary business in a way that satisfied *Complete Auto* (stating a Commerce Clause test).[899] Similarly, the Due Process Clause can be satisfied by various formularies designed to tax the value of the franchise exercised in the state, even though out of state activities are considered in the formula.[900]

The scope of the unitary business is limited to businesses in a unitary relationship and to operational functions that may not be in a unitary relationship,[901] but not investment functions.[902] The "hallmarks" of a unitary relationship have been described as functional integration, centralized management, and economies of scale.[903] Therefore, investment income can only be taxed by the state of commercial domicile (and presumably actual domicile).[904] The Due Process Clause does not preclude taxation of dividend income paid by non U. S. subsidiaries of the nonresident corporation doing business in the state, so long as the dividend paying subsidiaries are part of the taxpayer's unitary business.[905]

An early statement of the Due Process Clause apportionment rule allowed the state to condition the tax on nonresidents on transactions occurring outside its borders (declaration of the dividends paid, to be taxed), so long as the foreign corporation also engaged in business within the state and the tax was apportioned to in state earnings.[906] But out of state transactions were found not to be

---

[894] MeadWestvaco Corp. v. Ill. Dep't of Revenue, 553 U.S. 16 (2008).
[895] Butler Bros. v. McColgan, 315 U.S. 501 (1942).
[896] Hans Rees' Sons, Inc. v. North Carolina ex rel. Maxwell, 283 U.S. 123 (1931).
[897] New York v. Latrobe, 279 U.S. 421 (1929).
[898] Norfolk & W. R. Co. v. North Carolina, 297 U.S. 682 (1936).
[899] Trinova Corp. v. Mich. Dep't of Treasury, 498 U.S. 358 (1991).
[900] International Harvester Co. v. Evatt, 329 U.S. 416 (1947).
[901] MeadWestvaco Corp. v. Ill. Dep't of Revenue, 553 U.S. 16 (2008).
[902] Allied-Signal, Inc. v. Dir., Div. of Taxation, 504 U.S. 768 (1992).
[903] MeadWestvaco Corp. v. Ill. Dep't of Revenue, 553 U.S. 16 (2008).
[904] Asarco, Inc. v. Idaho State Tax Comm'n, 458 U.S. 307 (1982).
[905] Mobil Oil Corp. v. Comm'r of Taxes, 445 U.S. 425 (1980).
[906] Wisconsin v. J. C. Penney Co., 311 U.S. 435 (1940).

part of the unitary business where various aspects of business activities (retailing) were not functionally integrated.[907]

b. *Commerce Clause*

(1) *Nexus*

The Commerce Clause does not require the physical presence of an out of state vendor in the state to require it to collect the market state's sales tax.[908] Rather the "substantial nexus" it requires can be created by an "extensive virtual presence," which was created by a national internet retailer through the internet and other advertising into the state.

Previously the Court had found Commerce Clause nexus to require use tax collection on mail order sales into the state only when the seller also had offices or other tangible connections in the state.[909] The state had jurisdiction to impose sales tax on an out of state vendor that accepted orders out of state but had offices and salesmen in the state and delivered in the state.[910] But the state had no jurisdiction to impose its sales tax when the seller accepted the order out of state, the goods were shipped out of state on common carrier, and the vendor's only other contact was some salesmen solicitations in state; these rulings must be reevaluated in view of *Wayfair*.[911]

A state could apply a use tax to storage of aircraft fuel in the state prior to fueling planes to fly between states, but likely would violate the Commerce Clause by taxing the consumption of tax in flights over the state,[912] or of telephone signals passing through the state,[913] based on lack of Commerce Clause nexus.

Although not literally a nexus issue, even before *Complete Auto Transit*, the Court did not uniformly apply a complete exemption of interstate business from state taxation, by allowing franchise taxes on the nonresident corporation operating a gas pipeline through the state.[914] It must be recalled that Public Law 86-272 prevents income taxation of nonresidents in some cases where sales tax can be collected (when sales persons are in the state and conduct limited sales activities).

---

[907] F. W. Woolworth Co. v. Taxation & Revenue Dep't, 458 U.S. 354 (1982).

[908] South Dakota v. Wayfair, Inc., 138 S. Ct. 2080 (2018). *See* Cummings, *Judicial Activism and the Commerce Clause*, 89 State Tax Notes 889 (Aug. 27, 2018).

[909] National Geographic Soc. v. California Bd. of Equalization, 430 U.S. 551 (1977) (two offices); Nelson v. Sears, Roebuck & Co., 312 U.S. 359 (1941); Nelson v. Sears, Roebuck & Co., 312 U.S. 359 (1941).

[910] McGoldrick v. Felt & Tarrant Mfg. Co., 309 U.S. 70 (1940); McGoldrick v. Berwind-White Coal Mining Co., 309 U.S. 33 (1940); McGoldrick v. Compagnie Generale Transatlantique, 309 U.S. 430 (1940).

[911] McLeod v. J. E. Dilworth Co., 322 U.S. 327 (1944) (sales tax).

[912] United Air Lines v. Mahin, 410 U.S. 623 (1973), citing Helson & Randolph v. Kentucky, 279 U.S. 245 (1929) (state could not tax fuel on ferry in waters between states).

[913] Goldberg v. Sweet, 488 U.S. 252 (1989) (dictum referring to Commerce Clause nexus and citing with approval *Mahin*; evidently did not believe *Complete Auto* had changed this result).

[914] Colonial Pipeline Co. v. Traigle, 421 U.S. 100 (1975); Memphis Natural Gas Co. v. Stone, 335 U.S. 80 (1948).

(2) Complete Auto Transit *Test*

The four prong test for discrimination against interstate commerce encapsulated in the *Complete Auto Transit* opinion primarily addressed in Ch. IX.D.4.h, above, is not limited to taxes on business activities of nonresidents, but arose in that context. When the tax base of a taxpayer doing business in more than one state is apportionable, each such state, including the domiciliary state, must limit the portion of the tax base subject to its tax according to the four requirements briefly referred to in *Complete Auto Transit.*[915] This 1977 opinion is often viewed as a break point in the Supreme Court's treatment of state taxes on activities touching interstate commerce, and so opinions before 1977 must be carefully examined to determine their continuing validity. Many opinions on the issue that were once frequently cited do not even appear in this book.

(3) *Unitary Business*

In more complex cases when the tax base cannot be assigned to one geographic location with any precision,[916] the Commerce Clause apportionment is accomplished by the unitary business model, which creates a tax base of the taxpayer's entire unitary business income and applies certain factors to apportion the appropriate part of that base to the state for application of its tax. A state can apply the unitary business income method of taxing the income of a multinational group when the unitary group has foreign subsidiaries,[917] and when it has a foreign parent.[918]

A state's value added tax did not violate the Commerce Clause when applied to a nonresident corporation's unitary business because (1) the elements of the base that the taxpayer wanted to directly allocate out of state could not be disaggregated from the tax base, and (2) the three factor formula applied to the base (sales, payroll and property) was reasonable.[919]

The sale of a non-unitary subsidiary produced a capital gain that was not subject to apportionment in the state because it was not income from the unitary business.[920] The Court assumed without deciding that the corporate taxpayer's domiciliary state might tax 100 percent of its dividends received from non U.S. unitary subsidiaries, but ruled that other states could tax such dividends on an apportioned basis.[921] However, that assumption should be contrary to *Wynne*, holding that even the domicile must apportion business income.[922]

---

[915] Complete Auto Transit, Inc. v. Brady, 430 U.S. 274 (1977).

[916] Trinova Corp. v. Mich. Dep't of Treasury, 498 U.S. 358 (1991).

[917] Container Corp. of Am. v. Franchise Tax Bd., 463 U.S. 159 (1983).

[918] Barclays Bank Plc v. Franchise Tax Bd., 512 U.S. 298 (1994).

[919] Trinova Corp. v. Mich. Dep't of Treasury, 498 U.S. 358 (1991).

[920] Allied-Signal, Inc. v. Dir., Div. of Taxation, 504 U.S. 768 (1992); MeadWestvaco Corp. v. Ill. Dep't of Revenue, 553 U.S. 16 (2008).

[921] Mobil Oil Corp. v. Comm'r of Taxes, 445 U.S. 425 (1980).

[922] Comptroller of the Treasury v. Wynne, 575 U.S. 542 (2015).

The unitary business taxation method precluded allocating interest deductions first to nonunitary income that would not be taxed in the nondomiciliary state.[923]

(4) *Pre-*Complete Auto Transit *Rulings Still Valid*

Complete Auto Transit likely did not invalidate all earlier Commerce Clause rulings, particularly those depending on direct allocation of income to the only state that could tax it.[924] Also, early rulings approving apportionment formulas may still be valid. Prior rulings precluding all taxation "on" interstate commerce had waxed and waned over time; indeed *Complete Auto* pointed out that the "modern origin" of a strict preclusion began just 31 years earlier in 1946 and that the Court had quickly backtracked. The rulings listed here have not been overruled by the Supreme Court.

A state franchise tax based on the value of the nonresident corporation's property in the state used in its business (a pipeline) did not violate the Commerce Clause.[925] But a tax on gas gathered by a pipeline company was not on in state activities solely and ran the risk of multiple taxation by other states.[926] A tax on oil did not discriminate against interstate commerce just because no oil was produced in the state.[927] The state could impose a license tax on an electric plant even though much of the generated electricity went out of state.[928]

A state could require withholding on compensation paid to nonresidents physically working in the state but not on residents' compensation; and could confine deductions to those related to the in state income.[929] A state could tax the gross receipts of a nonresident railway company from transportation into, out of and within the state.[930] The state could tax the tolls (rent) charged by a nonresident railroad to other railroads running on its lines in the state.[931] The state did not violate the Commerce Clause by taxing an out of state manufacturer on its goods for sale in the state but not taxing an in state manufacturer on goods sold at its plant; there was no facial discrimination because local and out

---

[923] Hunt-Wesson, Inc. v. Franchise Tax Bd., 528 U.S. 458 (2000). The opinion applied to expense apportionment the approach it had applied to expenses incurred to carry exempt bonds in First Nat'l Bank v. Bartow County Bd. of Tax Assessors, 470 U.S. 583 (1985).

[924] Complete Auto Transit, Inc. v. Brady, 430 U.S. 274 (1977).

[925] Southern Natural Gas Corp. v. Alabama, 301 U.S. 148 (1937) (taxpayer argued pipeline used in interstate commerce should be entirely exempt); Coverdale v. Arkansas-Louisiana Pipe Line Co., 303 U.S. 604 (1938).

[926] Michigan-Wisconsin Pipe Line Co. v. Calvert, 347 U.S. 157 (1954). *See* Commonwealth Edison Co. v. Mont., 453 U.S. 609 (1981) (describing the case as failing *Complete Auto* fourth prong because the tax bore no relation to activities in the state).

[927] Texas Co. v. Brown, 258 U.S. 466 (1922).

[928] Utah Power & Light Co. v. Pfost, 286 U.S. 165 (1932).

[929] Travis v. Yale & Towne Mfg. Co., 252 U.S. 60 (1920) (commuter tax; also a Due Process ruling).

[930] Railway Express Agency v. Virginia, 358 U.S. 434 (1959). Fulton Corp. v. Faulkner, 516 U.S. 325 (1996) characterized *Railway* as a tax on interstate commerce that was "in lieu of" a tax on intrastate commerce and not facially discriminatory.

[931] New York, L. E. & W. R. Co. v. Pennsylvania, 158 U.S. 431 (1895).

of state vendors who did not manufacture in the state were taxed the same.[932] A tax on the receipts of a nonresident pipeline company for transporting oil out of state did not violate the Commerce Clause.[933] A tax on a multistate railroad but applied only to the sales of tickets for transit beginning and ending in the state did not violate the Commerce Clause;[934] same for telephone calls tax.[935] A tax on gross receipts of interstate gas sold in state did not violate the Commerce Clause.[936] The Pullman Company could be charged $100.25 per mile of track located in the state over which its cars ran.[937] A city license tax on manufacturing in the city could be based on sales of the manufactured goods, whether in or out of state.[938] A state could levy the general sales tax on fuel sold in the state to an airline that operated solely in interstate commerce.[939] Goods in a warehouse produced locally and held for sale elsewhere could be subject to local property tax.[940]

A single factor apportionment formula for a nonresident corporation passed muster (real and tangible personal property percentage applied to net profits);[941] (real and tangible and intangible personal property percentage applied to net income);[942] and is still permitted (sales).[943] Also sales and property could be the two apportionment factors.[944] But proof by other methods of the income earned in the state can show that the state's formula badly failed to identify profits in the state, so that the Court ruled the tax was arbitrary and violated the Due Process Clause and probably the Commerce Clause (tangible property percentage applied to net income).[945]

Because the Commerce Clause protects commerce and not persons, Maryland could not impose tax on ships bringing out of state goods into the Baltimore

---

[932] Armour & Co. v. Virginia, 246 U.S. 1 (1918); Caskey Baking Co. v. Virginia, 313 U.S. 117 (1941).

[933] Interstate Oil Pipe Line Co. v. Stone, 337 U.S. 662 (1949).

[934] Indeed many states wrote their tax laws that way to avoid Commerce Clause problems. Pacific Express Co. v. Seibert, 142 U.S. 339 (1892). *See also* New York ex rel. Pennsylvania R. Co. v. Knight, 192 U.S. 21 (1904) (actually the tax was on the New York cab rides of a cab company established by the Pennsylvania Railroad for passengers leaving the interstate travel).

[935] Pacific Tel. & Tel. Co. v. Tax Com. of Washington, 297 U.S. 403 (1936).

[936] East Ohio Gas Co. v. Tax Com. of Ohio, 283 U.S. 465 (1931).

[937] Pullman Co. v. Adams, 189 U.S. 420 (1903).

[938] American Mfg. Co. v. St. Louis, 250 U.S. 459 (1919).

[939] Eastern Air Transport, Inc. v. South Carolina Tax Com., 285 U.S. 147 (1932).

[940] Federal Compress & Warehouse Co. v. McLean, 291 U.S. 17 (1934).

[941] Underwood Typewriter Co. v. Chamberlain, 254 U.S. 113 (1920) (important early ruling allowing apportioned income taxation of multistate corporations).

[942] Bass, Ratcliff & Gretton, Ltd. v. State Tax Comm'n, 266 U.S. 271 (1924).

[943] Moorman Mfg. Co. v. Bair, 437 U.S. 267 (1978); Ford Motor Co. v. Beauchamp, 308 U.S. 331 (1939) (gross receipts). General Motors Corp. v. District of Columbia, 380 U.S. 553 (1965) found a single sale factor apportionment improper, but also found it to be required by a regulation that violated the statute.

[944] United States Glue Co. v. Oak Creek, 247 U.S. 321 (1918).

[945] Hans Rees' Sons, Inc. v. North Carolina ex rel. Maxwell, 283 U.S. 123 (1931). *Cf.* Horn Silver Mining Co. v. New York State, 143 U.S. 305 (1892) (early ruling that state could determine tax base of corporations by reference to capital employed in state; opinion purported to say that was not a federal question as long as there was no discrimination).

harbor while not taxing ships transporting local goods.[946] A tax on nonresident salesmen of liquor made out of state violated the Commerce Clause.[947]

A tax on foreign corporations could be based on authorized capital stock when apportioned to property and business done in the state, considerably before *Complete Auto*.[948]

(5) *Non-Facial Discrimination*

The decisions in this category can appear conflicting because the outcome depends on the willingness of the Court to find an indirect discrimination against interstate commerce. The hypersensitivity of the Court to facial discrimination sometimes transfers to the non-facial cases, and sometimes does not.

A nominally flat tax on the operation of all trucks used for business, from which resident trucks were effectively exempted through a complicated method of applying different taxes and fees to in and out of state truckers, violated the Commerce Clause when applied to nonresident owners, whether the tax was claimed to be a user fee or treated as a tax.[949] The state did not violate the Commerce Clause by charging a $100 per year tax on every truck making some purely intrastate pickups and deliveries, even though it could apply the same to a truck that is primarily used in interstate commerce and to a truck solely used in intrastate commerce; there was no facial discrimination.[950] An earlier decision held that a tax per gallon on gas brought into the state by interstate carriers violated the Commerce Clause because it bore no relation to the use of the roads;[951] and in a similar case the Court accepted the state court's interpretation that the tax was on the gas and not on the use of the roads (contrary to the Court's usual insistence on deciding the subject of the tax for purposes of constitutional analysis).[952]

A state's flat license tax on "transient photographers" did disproportionately affect out of state photographers.[953] Likewise a city tax on door to door solicitors discriminated against interstate commerce in practice.[954] And a disproportion-

[946] Guy v. Baltimore, 100 U.S. 434 (1879).

[947] Walling v. Michigan, 116 U.S. 446 (1886).

[948] Hump Hairpin Mfg. Co. v. Emmerson, 258 U.S. 290 (1922).

[949] American Trucking Ass'ns v. Scheiner, 483 U.S. 266 (1987) (overruling several earlier decisions). Aero Mayflower Transit Co. v. Bd. of R.R. Comm'rs, 332 U.S. 495 (1947) and Aero Mayflower Transit Co. v. Ga. Pub. Serv. Com., 295 U.S. 285 (1935) were not overruled but the Scheiner opinion stated that it would look for discriminatory effect (these earlier cases approved a levy for use of roads that was a small flat amount per truck and another levy measured only by miles traveled in state).

[950] Am. Trucking Ass'ns v. Mich. PSC, 545 U.S. 429 (2005). *See also* Osborne v. Florida, 164 U.S. 650 (1897) (flat license tax to operate express companies in the area); Capitol Greyhound Lines v. Brice, 339 U.S. 542 (1950); Kane v. New Jersey, 242 U.S. 160 (1916) (flat auto license fee applied alike to residents and nonresidents); Dixie Ohio Express Co. v. State Revenue Com., 306 U.S. 72 (1939).

[951] McCarroll v. Dixie Greyhound Lines, Inc., 309 U.S. 176 (1940).

[952] Bingaman v. Golden Eagle Western Lines, Inc., 297 U.S. 626 (1936).

[953] Dunbar-Stanley Studios, Inc. v. Alabama, 393 U.S. 537 (1969).

[954] Nippert v. Richmond, 327 U.S. 416 (1946) (criminal enforcement).

ately high annual license tax on persons who display samples in any hotel room or house rented or occupied temporarily for the purpose of securing retail orders violated the Commerce Clause.[955] But a wholesaler's license applied to out of state soft drink vendor as well as local vendors without discrimination was upheld.[956] A $60 per year license tax imposed on a nonresident telegraph company doing interstate business was upheld in the period when most taxes on interstate businesses were stricken.[957]

The "drummer cases" sometimes involved residents but more often nonresident salesmen sent into the state from the home office of a retailer or wholesaler. In many drummer cases the local taxing statute depended on the out of state character of the employer but in most it depends on not having a local place of business (like the transient photographers). In the principal drummer case the Court grounded the discrimination on two facts, the first of which was later rejected: (1) the inability of states to tax interstate commerce, and (2) the necessarily heavier taxation of drummers who had no local place of business and almost inevitably dealt in interstate commerce.[958] Although the Court later disclaimed the preclusion, it did not disclaim the potential for discriminatorily taxing only interstate commerce by indirection.

The Commerce Clause precluded a state's taxation of "first use" of natural gas passing through interstate pipelines in the state because the state allowed credits to local customers that largely offset the tax on the pipeline owners, and the tax did not compensate for a state tax on gas produced in state because the state had no right to compensation for gas produced on federal lands.[959]

The Commerce Clause did not prevent Ohio use tax jurisdiction over a nonresident's oil purchases in the state where the rate varied based on the degree of in state activities of the pipeline vendor; the state did not facially discriminate against interstate commerce and a reason other than interstate commerce explained the difference (the two types of pipelines served different markets).[960]

A licensee fee or tax on foreign corporations could increase in proportion to the authorized capital because it has nothing to do with business or property in or out of the state.[961]

Where discrimination does not appear on the face of the statute the Court usually will not investigate legislative history to find a sinister purpose.[962]

---

[955] Best & Co. v. Maxwell, 311 U.S. 454 (1940).

[956] Wagner v. Covington, 251 U.S. 95 (1919).

[957] Postal Telegraph-Cable Co. v. Fremont, 255 U.S. 124 (1921).

[958] Robbins v. Shelby County Taxing Dist., 120 U.S. 489 (1887); Stockard v. Morgan, 185 U.S. 27 (1902). See for peddler cases on residents, Ch. IX.F.3.b.

[959] Maryland v. Louisiana, 451 U.S. 725 (1981).

[960] GMC v. Tracy, 519 U.S. 278 (1997).

[961] Atlantic Refining Co. v. Virginia, 302 U.S. 22 (1937) (today the discriminatory entry fee would be unconstitutional but the principle that the size of authorized capital does not relate to the amount of commerce should stand).

[962] Ohio Tax Cases, 232 U.S. 576 (1914).

(6) *Facial Discrimination*

A tax on gross receipts of wholesalers that exempted local manufacturers facially discriminated against interstate commerce even though local wholesalers who did not manufacture paid the tax; the Court rejected the possibility that another tax paid by local manufacturers was a compensating tax.[963] Similarly, assessment of a manufacturing tax only on those products manufactured in Washington that are sold to out-of-state customers facially discriminated against interstate commerce when out of state manufacturers make wholesale sales in the state subject to the wholesale tax; the Court rejected the compensatory tax defense.[964]

The state could not require nonresident fishermen to dock in state and weigh fish caught within three miles of the state in order to be taxed prior to shipment of the catch out of state; the Commerce Clause was violated because the effect of the tax was the exclusion of nonresident fishers.[965]

A motor fuels tax imposed on a nonresident violated the Commerce Clause by facial discrimination against interstate commerce when it granted a credit for fuels containing ethanol produced in the state but not ethanol produced in another state; the result was not changed by a reciprocity rule allowing the credit if the other state allowed a similar credit for the taxing state's ethanol.[966] Similarly, the Commerce Clause was violated by allowing a franchise tax credit based on exports from the taxing state but not other states, which discriminated against commerce in other states.[967]

The Commerce Clause precluded charging more in a fee or tax for disposing of hazardous waste generated out of state than in state; the discrimination against interstate commerce was facial.[968]

A use tax facially discriminated against interstate commerce and could avoid violating the Commerce Clause only if the paired sales tax was at the same rate.[969] A tax on nonresident laundry trucks at a higher rate than for resident trucks discriminated against interstate commerce.[970]

The Commerce Clause precluded a state corporate franchise tax that facially discriminated against foreign corporations by requiring them to pay franchise tax on a tax base different from that used by domestic corporations, which domestic corporations could manipulate to be lower and which produced generally lower tax on domestic corporations, because the state failed to prove that the higher tax was compensatory to some state tax on domestic corporations that makes their tax burdens "roughly approximate."[971]

---

[963] Armco, Inc. v. Hardesty, 467 U.S. 638 (1984); Ashland Oil v. Caryl, 497 U.S. 916 (1990).
[964] Tyler Pipe Indus. v. Washington State Dep't of Revenue, 483 U.S. 232 (1987).
[965] Toomer v. Witsell, 334 U.S. 385 (1948).
[966] New Energy Co. v. Limbach, 486 U.S. 269 (1988).
[967] Westinghouse Elec. Corp. v. Tully, 466 U.S. 388 (1984).
[968] Chemical Waste Management v. Hunt, 504 U.S. 334 (1992).
[969] Associated Indus. v. Lohman, 511 U.S. 641 (1994).
[970] Memphis Steam Laundry Cleaner, Inc. v. Stone, 342 U.S. 389 (1952).
[971] S. Cent. Bell Tel. Co. v. Ala., 526 U.S. 160 (1999).

4. *Investment Activities*

a. *Due Process*

A state did not violate the Due Process Clause by requiring a nonresident corporation paying dividends to nonresident shareholders to withhold from the dividends a tax reflecting the amount of income of the corporation earned in the state (because the tax was on the corporation not the investor).[972] But it was beyond the jurisdiction of the state to require the local corporation issuing bonds to collect a property tax on the nonresident bondholder by withholding from interest paid.[973]

b. *Commerce Clause*

A New York tax on stock sales violated the Commerce Clause because of two features: (1) it reduced the tax if the sale was on the New York Stock Exchange, and (2) it capped the tax only if the tax was on the New York Stock Exchange.[974] The discrimination against interstate commerce (trading stock out of New York) was facial, although the opinion did not use that term.

5. *Estate and Gift; Other Activities*

a. *Due Process*

The Court ruled that as a matter of jurisdictional power, the state of domicile of the decedent could impose an inheritance tax on a nonresident heir.[975] The state of incorporation of a corporation not headquartered there has jurisdiction under the Due Process Clause to impose a transfer tax on the stock of that corporation held by a decedent domiciled in another state.[976] But the state of domicile of the shareholder also may tax the transfer and there is no constitutional prohibition against double taxation of the transfer of intangibles.[977] The state where a corporation's property is located did not have Due Process Clause jurisdiction to impose an inheritance tax on the transfer of its stock by a nonresident decedent to a nonresident beneficiary even though the nonresident corporation had substantial property (and perhaps a commercial domicile) in the state.[978]

---

[972] International Harvester Co. v. Wisconsin Dep't of Taxation, 322 U.S. 435 (1944).

[973] R.R. Co. v. Jackson, 74 U.S. 262 (1869).

[974] Boston Stock Exch. v. State Tax Comm'n, 429 U.S. 318 (1977).

[975] Mager v. Grima, 49 U.S. 490 (1850).

[976] State Tax Comm'n v. Aldrich, 316 U.S. 174 (1942), specifically overruling First Nat'l Bank v. Maine, 284 U.S. 312 (1932), and implicitly overruled its predecessors Farmers Loan & Trust Co. v. Minnesota, 280 U.S. 204 (1930) (state of residence of bond issuer could not tax transfer of bonds at death of nonresident owner), Beidler v. South Carolina Tax Comm'n, 282 U.S. 1 (1930), and Baldwin v. Missouri, 281 U.S. 586 (1930). The overruled decisions were based on the incorrect view that the Due Process Clause prevents double taxation. An earlier Holmes opinion allowing double estate taxation was temporarily overruled and should now be correct. Blackstone v. Miller, 188 U.S. 189 (1903); Cory v. White, 457 U.S. 85 (1982) at no. 6.

[977] State Tax Comm'n v. Aldrich, 316 U.S. 174 (1942).

[978] Rhode Island Hospital Trust Co. v. Doughton, 270 U.S. 69 (1926).

With respect to negotiable paper (mortgage notes and corporate bonds) a state could impose an inheritance tax based on their physical situs as permanently located in a safe deposit box in the state but owned by a nonresident decedent.[979] The Court applied a step transaction analysis to prevent a state from taxing notes treated as tangible property in the state for purposes of an inheritance tax because the decedent had put them there to avoid his own state's inheritance tax.[980]

The Due Process Clause allowed a state to tax the transfer at death of paintings located in museums on loan from the owner decedent who resided in another state because the painting had acquired an "actual situs" in the taxing state, which evidently meant something like domicile: they had been located there with no intent of their owner to move them back to his domicile.[981]

The state could tax a nonresident's exercise of power of appointment over intangible property held in trust by a trustee in the taxing state.[982] The Due Process Clause precluded taxation of the income of a nonresident trust whose only contact with the state was a beneficiary who did not receive any trust income in the year, did not have a right to demand a distribution and did not have a right to receive any defined amount of trust income.[983] However, the opinion indicated that if the beneficiary had those rights or powers the beneficiary rather than the nonresident trust would be subject to tax.

The state where property is located could impose an inheritance tax on the nonresident's property that can vary with the total size of the estate, which includes property outside the state.[984]

A state could impose a transfer tax on stock owned by a nonresident in a nonresident corporation when the seller delivered the physical shares in the state.[985]

H. Collection Issues

1. *Notice*

Due process required that a mortgagee must receive personal service or mailed notice—something more than indirect notice—of collection of in rem real property taxes from the property.[986] Moreover, when notice of a tax sale is mailed to the property owner and is returned unclaimed, the tax authority must take additional reasonable steps to attempt to provide notice to the property owner

---

[979] Wheeler v. Sohmer, 233 U.S. 434 (1914).

[980] Buck v. Beach, 206 U.S. 392 (1907), as explained by Wheeler v. Sohmer, 233 U.S. 434 (1914). *But see* Iowa v. Slimmer, 248 U.S. 115 (1918) (refused to allow domiciliary state to sue the other state in the Supreme Court to enjoin administration of the estate).

[981] City Bank Farmers Trust Co. v. Schnader, 293 U.S. 112 (1934).

[982] Curry v. McCanless, 307 U.S. 357 (1939).

[983] N.C. Dep't of Revenue v. Kimberley Rice Kaestner 1992 Family Trust, 139 S. Ct. 2213 (2019).

[984] Maxwell v. Bugbee, 250 U.S. 525 (1919).

[985] New York ex rel. Hatch v. Reardon, 204 U.S. 152 (1907).

[986] Mennonite Bd. of Missions v. Adams, 462 U.S. 791 (1983); *cf.* Leigh v. Green, 193 U.S. 79 (1904), which is presumably overruled.

before selling his property, if it is practicable to do so.[987] Although notice of a tax sale is required, the sheriff's return need not recite the notice.[988]

A state was not required to give the taxpayer notice of the assessment of a tax, or an opportunity to contest it, before the assessment; but the taxpayer must have a venue to assert available defenses before the command of the State to pay it becomes final and irrevocable.[989]

A state could enforce a lien on a vehicle acquired by the taxpayer after the tax lien arose and the state tax lien could have priority over the purchase money lien.[990]

2. *Collection*

A state could collect an in rem tax owed by a nonresident on one piece of real property from other real property owned by the same person located in the state.[991] A state court could begin a court proceeding to enforce the lien of a state tax on real property in a suit begun while a proceeding on the part of the United States to forfeit title to the same property was pending in a federal court.[992]

3. *Bankruptcy*

A state could shift the burden of proof of nonliability for a tax owed by a domiciliary corporation for use tax to the corporate officer who was in bankruptcy.[993] Congress could exempt the property of bankrupt estates from state tax, but it has not done so.[994]

I. Taxpayer Remedies

1. *Retroactivity*

When the Court rules a state taxpayer has paid a tax that was collected in violation of the United States Constitution, obviously the ruling applies to that taxpayer on the merits, but the Court usually allows the state courts to determine the remedy as a matter of comity; however, the applicability of the ruling on the merits to taxes paid prior to the ruling by others is a matter of retroactivity determined by federal law.[995] The Court has considered three facts in determining retroactivity of the ruling to others: (1) it asks whether the decision established a new principle of law; (2) it weighs the merits and demerits in each case by looking to the prior history of the rule in question, its purpose and effect, and whether retrospective operation will further or retard its operation; (3) it weighs

[987] Jones v. Flowers, 547 U.S. 220 (2006).

[988] Turpin v. Lemon, 187 U.S. 51 (1902).

[989] Nickey v. Mississippi, 292 U.S. 393 (1934); Pittsburgh, C., C. & S. L. R. Co. v. Backus, 154 U.S. 421 (1894).

[990] International Harvester Co. v. Goodrich, 350 U.S. 537 (1956).

[991] Nickey v. Mississippi, 292 U.S. 393 (1934).

[992] Motlow v. State, 295 U.S. 97 (1935).

[993] Raleigh v. Ill. Dep't of Revenue, 530 U.S. 15 (2000).

[994] Swarts v. Hammer, 194 U.S. 441 (1904).

[995] Am. Trucking Ass'ns v. Smith, 496 U.S. 167 (1990).

the inequity imposed by retroactive application.[996] When the Court announces a ruling it is presumably retroactive, giving the state its two choices for remedy discussed below.[997] But if the Court overruled clear past precedent or decided a wholly new issue of first impression, its ruling may not have retroactive effect.[998]

When the Court finds that a taxpayer has paid too much on account of a Equal Protection Clause or Commerce Clause discrimination, the Due Process Clause requires the state to eliminate the discrimination but the Court will not tell the state how to do that and usually will remand; the state may refund some or all of the discriminatory tax or may tax the favored class more, although the latter remedy usually is not possible on a retrospective basis and usually is not the one the plaintiff wants.[999]

The Equal Protection Clause plaintiff that wins should not have to carry the burden of pursuing an increase in the tax on others to create equality; it is up to the state to produce the remedy of equal treatment.[1000] The Due Process Clause (at least) does not prevent a state from retroactively increasing the tax on others, otherwise that alternative would be a meaningless remedy.[1001] A taxpayer group that was likely to win a constitutional attack on a state's highway use tax obtained an injunction requiring the state to escrow the taxes paid pending final determination of the merits.[1002]

A state need not provide retrospective relief for a retroactive ruling if the taxpayer that paid the tax could have avoided paying by obtaining meaningful prepayment review in the state.[1003] Even though pre-deprivation review may be available, if it subjects the taxpayer to penalties or other costs it may place the taxpayer under duress, which also means that the state must provide backward looking relief.[1004] The state violated the taxpayer's Due Process Clause rights by eliminating its post payment remedy for tax overpayment after taxpayer paid the tax ("bait and switch").[1005]

---

[996] Harper v. Va. Dep't of Taxation, 509 U.S. 86 (1993), citing Chevron Oil Co. v. Huson, 404 U.S. 97 (1971); applied in Ashland Oil v. Caryl, 497 U.S. 916 (1990) and National Mines Corp. v. Caryl, 497 U.S. 922 (1990).

[997] James B. Beam Distilling Co. v. Georgia, 501 U.S. 529 (1991).

[998] Ashland Oil v. Caryl, 497 U.S. 916 (1990).

[999] Associated Indus. v. Lohman, 511 U.S. 641 (1994); Harper v. Va. Dep't of Taxation, 509 U.S. 86 (1993); Iowa-Des Moines National Bank v. Bennett, 284 U.S. 239 (1931); Comptroller of the Treasury v. Wynne, 575 U.S. 542 (2015).

[1000] Allegheny Pittsburgh Coal Co. v. County Com., 488 U.S. 336 (1989); Hillsborough v. Cromwell, 326 U.S. 620 (1946).

[1001] McKesson Corp. v. Div. of Alcoholic Bevs. & Tobacco, 496 U.S. 18 (1990).

[1002] American Trucking Ass'ns v. Gray, 483 U.S. 1306 (1987).

[1003] Harper v. Va. Dep't of Taxation, 509 U.S. 86 (1993).

[1004] Harper v. Va. Dep't of Taxation, 509 U.S. 86 (1993).

[1005] Reich v. Collins, 513 U.S. 106 (1994); Newsweek, Inc. v. Fla. Dep't of Revenue, 522 U.S. 442 (1998).

2. *Injunctions*

A state can choose to provide a pre-deprivation remedy or a post tax payment remedy to taxpayers to satisfy Due Process.[1006] Before 1937 the Court applied principles of equity to not enjoin the enforcement of an allegedly unconstitutional state tax if the state provided the remedy to the taxpayer of paying the tax and suing for refund.[1007] The Court would not allow equitable relief where the taxpayer had failed to pursue administrative remedies,[1008] including the remedy complained of.[1009]

The Tax Injunction Act, enacted in 1937, states: "The district courts shall not enjoin, suspend or restrain the assessment, levy or collection of any tax under State law where a plain, speedy and efficient remedy may be had in the courts of such State."[1010] Thus it denies a remedy. The TIA also applies to declaratory relief.[1011]

The TIA did not bar a suit seeking prospective change to the application of a state tax law to other persons.[1012] The TIA did not bar a suit by retailers who objected to making certain reports with respect to purchases by prospective use tax taxpayers.[1013] When the plaintiff state taxpayer seeks to achieve equality of taxation based on an Equal Protection or Commerce Clause claim by being taxed less, the TIA is a bar to suit originally in the federal court; but when the remedy is to eliminate the preference enjoyed by a third party it does not bar, unless principles of comity require deference to the state to reorganize its taxing scheme.[1014] Although the TIA might not stop a suit by the United States, production credit associations were subject to it even though federal instrumentalities.[1015]

The TIA is premised on the existence of a "plain, speedy and efficient remedy," which appears to require a state-court remedy that meets certain minimal procedural criteria.[1016] Prior refusal of the state courts to consider certain grounds (Foreign Commerce Clause) might mean the remedy would be insufficient,

---

[1006] McKesson Corp. v. Div. of Alcoholic Bevs. & Tobacco, 496 U.S. 18 (1990).

[1007] Matthews v. Rodgers, 284 U.S. 521 (1932); Toomer v. Witsell, 334 U.S. 385 (1948); Kohn v. Central Distributing Co., 306 U.S. 531 (1939); Henrietta Mills v. Rutherford County, 281 U.S. 121 (1930); Indiana Mfg. Co. v. Koehne, 188 U.S. 681 (1903). But the Court allowed an injunction to preclude a multiplicity of suits by small taxpayers. Lee v. Bickell, 292 U.S. 415 (1934).

[1008] Gorham Mfg. Co. v. State Tax Com., 266 U.S. 265 (1924); Milheim v. Moffat Tunnel Improv. Dist., 262 U.S. 710 (1923). The same defense led to dismissal of a suit for refund in federal court. First Nat'l Bank v. Board of County Comm'rs, 264 U.S. 450 (1924). *See also* Pittsburgh Railway v. Board of Public Works, 172 U.S. 32 (1898).

[1009] Farncomb v. Denver, 252 U.S. 7 (1920).

[1010] Similar language is contained in 28 U.S.C. § 1342, called the Johnson Act, which does not relate to state taxes.

[1011] Cal. v. Grace Brethren Church, 457 U.S. 393 (1982). *See also* Great Lakes Dredge & Dock Co. v. Huffman, 319 U.S. 293 (1943) (exercising equitable power to decline declaratory judgment where state remedy existed).

[1012] Hibbs v. Winn, 542 U.S. 88 (2004).

[1013] Direct Mktg. Ass'n v. Brohl, 575 U.S. 1 (2015).

[1014] Levin v. Commerce Energy, Inc., 560 U.S. 413 (2010).

[1015] Ark. v. Farm Credit Servs., 520 U.S. 821 (1997).

[1016] Rosewell v. La Salle Nat'l Bank, 450 U.S. 503 (1981).

but the plaintiff did not prove that would be the result of a state contest; and shareholders have a remedy if their corporation has the remedy.[1017] Because the taxpayer could pay and sue to recover the tax it had an adequate remedy and equity would not intervene.[1018] But the remedy is not adequate when the body to which the taxpayer must complain has no authority to address constitutional issues and the taxpayer does not have a right to appeal to a court that has that power.[1019] A remedy was sufficient because it provided a prepayment appeal process; if the taxpayer lost it must pay and sue and after a normal litigation period may receive refund, but without interest.[1020] A remedy was sufficient where the taxpayer could raise constitutional claims by declaratory judgment and obtain a preliminary injunction.[1021]

As stated above, before the TIA the Court applied principles of equity to avoid enjoining state taxes.[1022] In that period a remedy was insufficient where the state required the taxpayer to pursue a proceeding in equity in the state court, purely judicial in character, to enjoin excessive assessment.[1023] In an equity case preceding the TIA the Court ruled that a remedy was not sufficient when it was not practically available to the taxpayer due to the state court's actions.[1024]The Court ordered an interlocutory injunction where the state provided no remedy to recover taxes being contest paid during the pendency of the action if the tax were held to violate equal protection.[1025] Also before the TIA a remedy to pay and sue for refund was insufficient because it was new and had not yet been construed by the state courts.[1026] And a state remedy was insufficient when it allowed for arbitration and the arbitrators could not agree.[1027] The Court was particularly sympathetic to railroads who might have to pay and sue in multiple counties,[1028] or the outcome would be doubtful, without interest, and might involve a multiplicity of suits.[1029] An early opinion actually ordered a local government to levy a tax to pay a creditor, as provided for in the state's laws.[1030] But when the legis-

---

[1017] Franchise Tax Bd. v. Alcan Aluminium, 493 U.S. 331 (1990).

[1018] Arkansas Bldg. & Loan Asso. v. Madden, 175 U.S. 269 (1899).

[1019] Hillsborough v. Cromwell, 326 U.S. 620 (1946). The *Cromwell* case was an extremely unusual one in which the nonresident was assessed a tax hundreds of times greater than the county's budget and was represented by the sons of two former Supreme Court Justices and by a future Justice (Brennan).

[1020] Rosewell v. La Salle Nat'l Bank, 450 U.S. 503 (1981).

[1021] Tully v. Griffin, Inc., 429 U.S. 68 (1976).

[1022] Boise Artesian Hot & Cold Water Co. v. Boise City, 213 U.S. 276 (1909).

[1023] Bohler v. Callaway, 267 U.S. 479 (1925).

[1024] Brinkerhoff-Faris Trust & Sav. Co. v. Hill, 281 U.S. 673 (1930).

[1025] Ohio Oil Co. v. Conway, 279 U.S. 813 (1929).

[1026] Atlantic C. L. R. Co. v. Doughton, 262 U.S. 413 (1923); Dawson v. Kentucky Distilleries & Warehouse Co., 255 U.S. 288 (1921).

[1027] Turner v. Wade, 254 U.S. 64 (1920). But where they could agree the remedy was constitutional. McGregor v. Hogan, 263 U.S. 234 (1923).

[1028] Union P. R. Co. v. Board of County Comm'rs, 247 U.S. 282 (1918).

[1029] Hopkins v. Southern California Tel. Co., 275 U.S. 393 (1928).

[1030] Memphis v. Brown, 94 U.S. 715 (1877). The ground of jurisdiction may have been diversity. *See* Bass v. Taft, 137 U.S. 458 (1890).

lature reduced the city's obligation to collect the tax the Court ruled it did not violate the obligation of contract because there was no contract.[1031] But more than an assertion of a state tax's illegality was required to invoke the Court's equity jurisdiction.[1032]

The Court rejected the state's contention that a three-judge panel should have been formed to hear the plaintiffs' suit for injunction.[1033]

3. *Section 1983 Actions*

Principles of comity can prevent pursuit of a section 1983 damages action for state taxes in federal court when a plain, speedy and efficient state remedy is available.[1034] Section 1983 can apply to Commerce Clause claims.[1035]

4. *State Court Applying Federal Constitution*

State courts must enforce the federal constitution,[1036] but a state court ruling may be based both on the federal constitution and on a state ground, including a state ground that appears to be the same as the federal ground, such as equal protection. The Supreme Court of the United States has jurisdiction to review such a ruling unless there is an adequate and independent state ground for the ruling;[1037] there was no such ground when the state and federal grounds are identical, as in the case of equal protection when the state follows federal precedent.[1038] When the state court did not find the facts related to a federal law claim the Supreme Court will examine the evidence.[1039]

5. *Meaning of State Law*

If the meaning of a state statute is unclear and the taxpayer has a remedy on remand to obtain a court ruling on the meaning, the Court can remand for that purpose.[1040] The Court usually defers to the highest state court's interpretation of the state's taxing statute to determine its meaning (for example what is the intended subject of the tax).[1041] When a federal constitutional issue might be avoided by a decision on state law the Court will remand for consideration by

---

1031 Louisiana ex rel. Folsom v. Mayor & Adm'rs, 109 U.S. 285 (1883).

1032 Pacific Steam Whaling Co. v. United States, 187 U.S. 447 (1903).

1033 Ex parte Williams, 277 U.S. 267 (1928).

1034 42 U.S.C. section 1983; Fair Assessment in Real Estate Ass'n v. McNary, 454 U.S. 100 (1981); Nat'l Private Truck Council v. Okla. Tax Comm'n, 515 U.S. 582 (1995).

1035 Dennis v. Higgins, 498 U.S. 439 (1993), reversing decisions such as Keokuk & Hamilton Bridge Co. v. Salm, 258 U.S. 122 (1922).

1036 Testa v. Katt, 330 U.S. 386 (1947) (applying the supremacy clause).

1037 Flournoy v. Wiener, 321 U.S. 253 (1944).

1038 Fitzgerald v. Racing Ass'n, 539 U.S. 103 (2003) (federal cases are not "being used only for the purpose of guidance" and instead are "compelling the result").

1039 Merchants' Nat'l Bank v. Richmond, 256 U.S. 635 (1921).

1040 Hillsborough v. Cromwell, 326 U.S. 620 (1946).

1041 United Air Lines v. Mahin, 410 U.S. 623 (1973); Michigan v. Michigan Trust Co., 286 U.S. 334 (1932); Crew Levick Co. v. Pennsylvania, 245 U.S. 292 (1917); Pullman Co. v. Knott, 235 U.S. 23 (1914); St. Louis S. R. Co. v. Arkansas, 235 U.S. 350 (1914); Yazoo & M. v. R. Co. v. Adams, 181 U.S. 580 (1901).

the state court.[1042] The Court accepted a state court ruling that a state statute that appeared to prefer local merchants did not apply to the plaintiff's case.[1043]

Where the state courts had not made the determination, the Court decided if the taxpayer plaintiff was subject to the state tax under state law; it found it was not, thus avoiding a federal constitutional issue.[1044] The Court has interpreted and applied a state constitution and statute to invalidate a tax or not.[1045] But the Court would not address a state law that might be, but had not in the case before it been, interpreted to apply in an unconstitutional matter.[1046] The Court ruled that a violation of the state constitution was not a violation of the 14th Amendment.[1047] When the state property tax evaluators failed to follow state law the Court decided for the taxpayer on that basis.[1048]

When the Singer Sewing Machine company complained of a state tax that did not tax its state store sales but did tax its traveling salesmen sales and might tax its mail order sales, the Court interpreted the statute to be constitutional and thus not to tax the mail order sales; and found no discrimination between its store and salesmen sales (in effect Singer argued that it was on both sides of the discrimination).[1049]

But the Court has reversed a state court's determination that the state tax violated the Constitution when it found that the state court misidentified the subject of the tax as one beyond the state's taxing power.[1050] See Ch. IX.C.2.

The Court ruled a state tax unconstitutional and later the state's supreme court reinterpreted the same statute not to apply in the unconstitutional matter and the Supreme Court approved that change of interpretation.[1051]

6. *Issues Reviewable*

A taxpayer cannot raise in the Supreme Court a constitutional issue not raised in the state court and not reflected in the record.[1052] The 11th Amendment did not preclude Supreme Court review of a state court decision on state taxation in a suit brought by nonresidents (not a diversity jurisdiction issue).[1053] The

---

[1042] Spector Motor Service, Inc. v. McLaughlin, 323 U.S. 101 (1944).

[1043] American Steel & Wire Co. v. Speed, 192 U.S. 500 (1904).

[1044] James v. United Artists Corp., 305 U.S. 410 (1939).

[1045] Atlantic C. L. R. Co. v. Doughton, 262 U.S. 413 (1923); St. Louis-San Francisco R. Co. v. Middlekamp, 256 U.S. 226 (1921); Dawson v. Kentucky Distilleries & Warehouse Co., 255 U.S. 288 (1921); Hopkins v. Southern California Tel. Co., 275 U.S. 393 (1928); Gilman v. Sheboygan, 67 U.S. 510 (1863); Johnson v. Wells Fargo & Co., 239 U.S. 234 (1915).

[1046] Edelman v. Boeing Air Transport, Inc., 289 U.S. 249 (1933).

[1047] Pullman Co. v. Knott, 235 U.S. 23 (1914).

[1048] Louisville & N. R. Co. v. Greene, 244 U.S. 522 (1917); Greene v. Louisville & I. R. Co., 244 U.S. 499 (1917).

[1049] Singer Sewing Machine Co. v. Brickell, 233 U.S. 304 (1914).

[1050] Wisconsin v. J. C. Penney Co., 311 U.S. 435 (1940).

[1051] Schuylkill Trust Co. v. Pennsylvania, 302 U.S. 506 (1938); Georgia R. & Electric Co. v. Decatur, 297 U.S. 620 (1936).

[1052] New York ex rel. Cohn v. Graves, 300 U.S. 308 (1937).

[1053] S. Cent. Bell Tel. Co. v. Ala., 526 U.S. 160 (1999).

Court could decide a taxpayer's constitutional claims on state law grounds.[1054] When it was not clear that the state court decided the issue on a federal constitutional ground, the Court remanded for clarification.[1055] The Supreme Court has reviewed a state declaratory judgment on state privilege license tax applied to railroad.[1056]

7. *Diversity Jurisdiction; 11th Amendment*

The 11th Amendment did not bar early suits for injunctions against state officials individually enforcing what the nonresident plaintiff claimed to be an unconstitutional state tax.[1057] An out of state taxpayer was allowed to sue the local tax collector in federal court claiming diversity jurisdiction; evidently the state did not object.[1058] But in later similar cases styled against the state tax authority or the official office, when the state objected the Court dismissed the suit, finding that it was actually a suit against the state, barred by the 11th Amendment, usually in suits seeking refund.[1059] Federal court did not have jurisdiction to remove tax cloud from property title without making state a party and 11th Amendment prevented making state a party.[1060]

8. *Powers of Ministerial Officers*

State ministerial officers can (and often do) refuse to decide constitutional issues and that is not a federal issue.[1061] However, it is a denial of constitutional rights for a state court to refuse to consider federal constitutional claims.[1062] A state tax collector could not ask the Court to decide that its own state's tax law was unconstitutional.[1063] The giving of wrong information to the taxpayer by a tax official did not estop the state from collecting the correct amount of tax due.[1064] While the Court suggested that concepts of improper delegation of legislative power to state agencies might not be held to the same standard as Congress, it found no problem with a statute directing officials how to compute a tax rate based on objective facts.[1065]

1054 Hillsborough v. Cromwell, 326 U.S. 620 (1946); Sturges v. Carter, 114 U.S. 511 (1885).

1055 Minnesota v. National Tea Co., 309 U.S. 551 (1940).

1056 Nashville, C. & S. L. Ry. v. Wallace, 288 U.S. 249 (1933).

1057 Gunter v. Atlantic C. L. R. Co., 200 U.S. 273 (1906).

1058 Hillsborough v. Cromwell, 326 U.S. 620 (1946); Illinois C. R. Co. v. Adams, 180 U.S. 28 (1901); Wheless v. St. Louis, 180 U.S. 379 (1901) (dismissed because insufficient amount at issue).

1059 Kennecott Copper Corp. v. State Tax Comm'n, 327 U.S. 573 (1946); Ford Motor Co. v. Department of Treasury, 323 U.S. 459 (1945), reversed in part as to waiver by state's attorney, by Lapides v. Bd. of Regents, 535 U.S. 613 (2002); Great Northern Life Ins. Co. v. Read, 322 U.S. 47 (1944).

1060 Chandler v. Dix, 194 U.S. 590 (1904).

1061 Smith v. Indiana, 191 U.S. 138 (1903).

1062 Lawrence v. State Tax Com., 286 U.S. 276 (1932).

1063 Columbus & G. R. Co. v. Miller, 283 U.S. 96 (1931).

1064 Thompson v. Kentucky, 209 U.S. 340 (1908).

1065 Michigan C. R. Co. v. Powers, 201 U.S. 245 (1906) (discussing many other decisions); Breiholz v. Board of Supervisors, 257 U.S. 118 (1921).

9. *United States as Plaintiff*

The federal government did not have a common law right to recover state taxes that the federal government economically bore under a contract obligation with a private taxpayer.[1066]

10. *Full Faith and Credit*

Although a state's courts may not be required to entertain a suit by another state to collect the other state's taxes, the Full Faith and Credit Clause prevents it from denying to the other state the right to sue on its judgment for taxes owed.[1067]

State sovereign immunity received close scrutiny in three opinions involving the same taxpayer Hyatt: first the Court ruled that Hyatt could sue California in Nevada courts for alleged intentional torts California committed in trying to enforce its tax laws by activities allegedly occurring in Nevada.[1068] So full faith and credit did not require giving credit to California's law on sovereign immunity. In 2016 the Court held that Nevada should apply to California the same $50,000 limit it would apply if such a suit were brought against Nevada in Nevada.[1069] Peculiarly, this time full faith and credit was applied, but it did not mean that Nevada must give credit to California law; rather, it meant that California should get the same treatment in Nevada courts that Nevada would have received. Then in 2019 the Court held that a state is protected by sovereign immunity from suit in the courts of another state based on alleged torts committed out of state in efforts to collect taxes, overruling *Nevada v. Hall.*[1070]

A state court judgment on the liability of landowners for a special assessment tax did not deny full faith and credit in refusing to respect a federal court judgment in a suit brought against the taxing district by its creditors, to which the landowners were not parties.[1071] New York could not accept the administration of an estate by New Jersey and also claim that the decedent was resident in New York for purposes of applying an estate tax to property not located in New York; New York failed to give full faith and credit to the New Jersey probate.[1072]

11. *Other Procedural Issues*

Taxpayers as such had no standing to assert Commerce Clause and other constitutional objections to a state tax credit scheme designed to attract investment.[1073] A vendor with nexus to the taxing state that prepaid a sales tax to be collected from his customer did not have standing to assert the unconstitution-

---

[1066] United States v. California, 507 U.S. 746 (1993).
[1067] Milwaukee County v. M. E. White Co., 296 U.S. 268 (1935).
[1068] Franchise Tax Board of California v. Hyatt, 538 U.S. 488 (2003).
[1069] Franchise Tax Board of California v. Hyatt, 136 S. Ct. 1277 (2016).
[1070] Franchise Tax Board v. Hyatt, 139 S. Ct. 1485 (2019), overruling Nevada v. Hall, 440 U.S. 410 (1979).
[1071] Kersh Lake Drainage Dist. v. Johnson, 309 U.S. 485 (1940).
[1072] Tilt v. Kelsey, 207 U.S. 43 (1907).
[1073] DaimlerChrysler Corp. v. Cuno, 547 U.S. 332 (2006).

ality of the tax for which he was only a collection agent and did not bear the burden of the tax.[1074] The Court dismissed as inappropriate a suit to enjoin a local tax exemption for a church parking lot that was rented out, after the city changed the statute.[1075] A taxpayer who petitioned for a special taxing district was estopped to object to the tax levied to pay the bonds used to fund the district's improvements.[1076] A taxpayer who failed to follow the reasonable procedures for contesting the special assessment district tax did not have a due process claim.[1077]

The Due Process Clause prevents binding taxpayers to an outcome in other litigation of which they had no notice.[1078]

When the Court rules part of a state taxing statute unconstitutional it allows the state courts to determine whether that part is severable from the rest of the statute.[1079]

Although a taxpayer cannot sue a state in federal court to contest its taxes, the tax collector may sue the taxpayers in federal court. One such taxing authority did that and lost and the appellate court said the taxpayers' costs should be paid by the tax collector and the Supreme Court ruled that the trial court had no say in the costs matter.[1080]

The successor of a sued state tax official may be substituted for the original defendant.[1081]

The taxpayer cannot complain of lack of hearing when it failed to file the report that would have set in motion the procedure for it to be heard.[1082] The Court ruled that one hearing on property assessment valuations was all a property owner was entitled to.[1083] It ruled that it would abide by the lower federal trial court's finding that the property of other taxpayers had not been systematically undervalued.[1084]

J. Native American Taxation

Taxation of and by Native Americans is a highly confused subject that intersects with state taxation and usually has constitutional implications due to the sovereignty of tribes and the supremacy of federal control over many aspects of Native American law. The standard treatise is 1 Cohen's Handbook of Federal

---

1074 Monamotor Oil Co. v. Johnson, 292 U.S. 86 (1934).

1075 Diffenderfer v. Central Baptist Church, Inc., 404 U.S. 412 (1972).

1076 Shepard v. Barron, 194 U.S. 553 (1904).

1077 Utley v. St. Petersburg, 292 U.S. 106 (1934).

1078 Richards v. Jefferson County, 517 U.S. 793 (1996).

1079 Hallanan v. Eureka Pipe Line Co., 261 U.S. 393 (1923); Schneider Granite Co. v. Gast Realty & Inv. Co., 245 U.S. 288 (1917).

1080 City of San Antonio v. Hotels.com, L. P., 141 S. Ct. 1628 (2021).

1081 Gorham Mfg. Co. v. Wendell, 261 U.S. 1 (1923). But at one time this depended on state law. Shaffer v. Howard, 249 U.S. 200 (1919).

1082 Pullman Co. v. Knott, 235 U.S. 23 (1914).

1083 Michigan C. R. Co. v. Powers, 201 U.S. 245 (1906).

1084 Michigan C. R. Co. v. Powers, 201 U.S. 245 (1906).

Indian Law § 8. See Ch. IX.C.2.b as to the relevance of the legal incidence of tax on Native Americans.

As "Native Americans" is the currently preferred term applied to the individuals that the Constitution and older court cases refer to as "Indians," this chapter will use the term "Native American" to refer to these individuals and their tribes, except when quoting the Constitution or older court cases.

1. *Power of Native American Tribes to Tax*

Native American tribes have inherent power as sovereigns to tax, including the power to tax activities of non-Natives on Native lands.[1085] But tribes have only circumscribed power to tax non-Natives on non-Native fee lands (reservation land that had been deeded out of tribal member ownership):[1086] "[a] tribe may regulate, through taxation, licensing, or other means, the activities of nonmembers who enter consensual relationships with the tribe or its members, through commercial dealing, contracts, leases, or other arrangements. [second, a tribe may exercise] civil authority over the conduct of non-Natives on fee lands within the reservation when that conduct threatens or has some direct effect on the political integrity, the economic security, or the health or welfare of the tribe."[1087] These rules have become known as the *Montana* exceptions.

The Court's opinions routinely refer to non-Native (owned) fee lands, without defining it. It refers to land that was originally part of reservations, which the federal government caused to be transferred from the hybrid tribal ownership to traditional "fee title" ownership by individuals in the late 1800s to early 1900s. The tribal ownership may be called a hybrid because the federal government has considered itself to hold the tribal lands "in trust" for the tribes.[1088] Some of the title owners were tribe members, who could transfer it to non members after a period, usually of 25 years; other lands were deeded by the United States directly to non-Natives. Because the original member owners almost always eventually sold to non-Natives, approximately 60 percent of Native lands passed out of the ownership of the tribes in this fashion.[1089]

[1085] Merrion v. Jicarilla Apache Tribe, 455 U.S. 130 (1982).

[1086] Atkinson Trading Co. v. Shirley, 532 U.S. 645 (2001). The decision ruled against a hotel occupancy tax imposed on a hotel owned by non-Natives on fee lands. It contrasted Buster v. Wright, 135 F. 947 (8th Cir. 1905), which upheld a Native American imposed license tax on traders owning "town lots." *Buster* relied on Morris v. Hitchcock, 194 U.S. 384 (1904), upholding a Native American tax on grazers on its lands.

[1087] Mont. v. United States, 450 U.S. 544 (1981).

[1088] Johnson v. M'Intosh, 21 U.S. 543 (1823) started the theory of dual interest in Native lands; the trust concept came later.

[1089] Jessica A. Shoemaker, *An Introduction to American Indian Land Tenure: Mapping the Legal Landscape*, 5 J.L. Prop. & Soc'y 1, 22 (2020). The article explains there currently are three types of land ownership: lands held in trust by the United States for individual Native Americans; tribal trust lands, being essentially all of the reservation lands not in the other two categories; and fee lands (whether held by Native Americans or non-Natives). Sometimes the allotted fee lands were called fee patents because a patent was issued when the Native American was determined to be "competent" to hold and sell the fee land. Also individual trust land can be transferred into fee status. So there are at least three sources of non-Native fee lands.

But such lands, non-Native (meaning not owned by Native Americans) fee lands (meaning held in traditional fee title rather than as tribal reservations), often lie inside reservations in a checkerboard or random pattern, or at least contiguous with reservations.[1090] The process of allotting tribal lands in 40 to 160 acre parcels to members had been intended to cause assimilation of Native Americans into the general population, a policy that came to be seen as deeply flawed and that ultimately failed, while also producing massive legal and practical problems for the administration and control of Native lands.

Certain former reservation lands in Alaska were conveyed to Native corporations in fee simple by the United States.[1091] The Court ruled that the tribe could not tax non members on the fee lands because they were not in Indian country, which the Court stated for this purpose meant "all dependent Indian communities within the . . . United States . . . ." 18 U.S.C. § 1151(b). "Dependent Indian communities" refers to a limited category of Native lands that are neither reservations nor allotments (the other categories of Indian country set forth in § 1151), and that satisfy two requirements—first, they must have been set aside by the Federal Government for the use of the Native Americans as Native land; second, they must be under federal superintendence.

Tribes' taxing powers are subject to limits not applicable to states because Congress can take away the power; when that has occurred the tribe must obtain the approval of the Secretary of the Interior before any tax on nonmembers can take effect.[1092] But the Court ruled that absent a particular requirement no such preliminary approval was required of the Navajo tribe to tax oil companies operating leases on its lands due to the inherent sovereign power to tax.[1093]

The Court has assumed that the Commerce Clause applies to Native American taxation, while indicating that when Congress legislates with respect to Native American taxation without mentioning the Commerce Clause, it might not be necessary for the Court to apply the negative Commerce Clause.[1094]

A tribe could tax the severance of oil and gas by non-residents but exclude the oil and gas that was paid in kind to the tribe as royalties and otherwise used for tribal purposes.[1095] As an attribute of sovereignty the tribe could impose its sales taxes on sales on the reservation to non-Natives, and may do so in tandem with state taxes on the same sales.[1096]

1090 Judith V. Royster, *The Legacy of Allotment*, 27 Ariz. St. L.J. 1 (1995).
1091 Alaska v. Native Village of Venetie Tribal Gov't, 522 U.S. 520 (1998).
1092 Merrion v. Jicarilla Apache Tribe, 455 U.S. 130 (1982).
1093 Kerr-McGee Corp. v. Navajo Tribe of Indians, 471 U.S. 195 (1985).
1094 Merrion v. Jicarilla Apache Tribe, 455 U.S. 130 (1982).
1095 Merrion v. Jicarilla Apache Tribe, 455 U.S. 130 (1982).
1096 Wash. v. Confederated Tribes of Colville Indian Reservation, 447 U.S. 134 (1980).

2. *State Taxation*

a. *On Native American Lands*

(1) *Of Non-Natives*

The grants of lands to tribes by Congress have been construed to consent to state taxation of non-Natives doing business on the Indian Lands, such as levy of a severance tax on non-Native businesses that contract to extract oil.[1097] A state could tax the property used by a non-Native oil drilling company on leased Indian fee land (against a claim that the tax indirectly fell on the federal government).[1098] The state could tax a construction company doing work on Native lands for the federal government.[1099] The state could tax lessees grazing cattle on Native lands.[1100] A territory could tax railroad property on land ceded by the tribe to the United States for the railroad.[1101]

The Indian Commerce Clause did not prevent a state from applying its general sales tax to tobacco products sold by Native Americans on Native lands to nonmembers, without credit for the tribe's tax on the same sales, absent a showing of substantial detriment to the Native American businesses.[1102] Unless prohibited by an act of Congress, states can tax activities of non-Indians on Indian lands without violating the Due Process Clause, the Indian Commerce Clause, or otherwise, even though the tax reduced the value received by the Native Americans.[1103] However, the Court struck down a state tax on non-Natives that was so high as to substantially affect the ability of the Native Americans to sell their products (oil extraction; there 32.9 percent).[1104]

The state could not tax a non-Native logging company with respect to use of roads on Native lands built by the tribe and federal government; this opinion contains a detailed explanation of the hybrid cases involving non-Native on Native lands and applied a test that balanced the interference of the state tax with the federal statutory scheme, finding the tax would negatively impact the purpose of tribes earning logging revenues.[1105] Similarly, the state could not apply its gross receipts tax to a non-Native construction company's receipts for building a school for Native Americans on Native lands.[1106]

[1097] British-American Oil Producing Co. v. Board of Equalization, 299 U.S. 159 (1936); Indian Territory Illuminating Oil Co. v. Board of Equalization, 288 U.S. 325 (1933).

[1098] Taber v. Indian Territory Illuminating Oil Co., 300 U.S. 1 (1937).

[1099] Ariz. Dep't of Revenue v. Blaze Constr. Co., 526 U.S. 32 (1999).

[1100] Thomas v. Gay, 169 U.S. 264 (1898); Foster v. Pryor, 189 U.S. 325 (1903); Montana Catholic Missions v. Missoula County, 200 U.S. 118 (1906) (even cattle owned by a Catholic mission).

[1101] Utah & N. Railway v. Fisher, 116 U.S. 28 (1885).

[1102] Wash. v. Confederated Tribes of Colville Indian Reservation, 447 U.S. 134 (1980); California State Bd. of Equalization v. Chemehuevi Indian Tribe, 474 U.S. 9 (1985).

[1103] Cotton Petroleum Corp. v. New Mexico, 490 U.S. 163 (1989); Oklahoma Tax Comm'n v. Texas Co., 336 U.S. 342 (1949) (overruling earlier decisions).

[1104] Cotton Petroleum Corp. v. New Mexico, 490 U.S. 163 (1989) (footnote 17).

[1105] White Mountain Apache Tribe v. Bracker, 448 U.S. 136 (1980).

[1106] Ramah Navajo Sch. Bd. v. Bureau of Revenue, 458 U.S. 832 (1982).

The Court has applied the Indian Trader statute, 25 U. S. C. § 261, to preclude state taxation of gross receipts from sale of tractors made on the reservation to the tribe.[1107]

(2) *Of Native Americans*

The Court applies two principles to state taxation of Native Americans: (1) the States may tax Native tribes and Natives in Native country only when Congress has manifested clearly its consent to such taxation,[1108] and (2) statutes and treaties are to be construed liberally in favor of Natives.[1109] A statute giving a state civil jurisdiction on the reservation did not give it taxing jurisdiction to apply a property tax to a mobile home on Native trust lands.[1110]

The definition of Native American country extends beyond formal reservations: "to be outside the State's taxing jurisdiction; it is enough that the member lives in 'Indian country.' Congress has defined "Indian country" broadly to include formal and informal reservations, dependent Indian communities, and Indian allotments, whether restricted or held in trust by the United States. See 18 U.S.C. § 1151."[1111]

The Court applied those principles to strike down state taxes on oil royalties, which taxes were paid to the State by the lessees and then deducted by the lessees from the royalty payments made to the tribe.[1112] The state could not apply its income tax to the wages of a tribe member earned on the Reservation, and a strict construction of the relevant treaty did not show that Congress had changed that general principle; this opinion clearly states the general rule that states cannot tax Native American reservation lands or Native American income from activities carried on within the boundaries of the reservation, absent congressional consent.[1113] However, the state could tax oil royalties paid by the federal government to Native Americans.[1114]

The state could not apply ad valorem taxation to Indian Lands (also called trust lands, both on and off the Reservation), even that held in severalty by individual Indians under treaties.[1115] The state could not tax land held by Native transferees of the Native Americans that originally were given the tax exemption by federal statute.[1116] However, Native lands deeded out of the tribes under the allotment

---

1107 Cent. Mach. Co. v. Ariz. State Tax Comm'n, 448 U.S. 160 (1980).

1108 Mescalero Apache Tribe v. Jones, 411 U.S. 145 (1973).

1109 Kansas Indians, 72 U.S. 737 (1867); Mont. v. Blackfeet Tribe of Indians, 471 U.S. 759 (1985). *See also* Carpenter v. Shaw, 280 U.S. 363 (1930) (tax exemptions secured to the Native Americans by agreement between them and the national government are to be liberally construed in favor of the Indians).

1110 Bryan v. Itasca County, 426 U.S. 373 (1976).

1111 Oklahoma Tax Comm'n v. Sac & Fox Nation, 508 U.S. 114 (1993).

1112 Mont. v. Blackfeet Tribe of Indians, 471 U.S. 759 (1985).

1113 McClanahan v. Arizona State Tax Comm'n, 411 U.S. 164 (1973).

1114 Leahy v. State Treasurer of Oklahoma, 297 U.S. 420 (1936) (although the taxpayer asserted intergovernmental immunity).

1115 Kansas Indians, 72 U.S. 737 (1867).

1116 Board of County Comm'rs v. Seber, 318 U.S. 705 (1943).

laws were in some cases taxable by the states under the federal statutes, including lands that Congress had allowed the tribe to sell to tribe members,[1117] and to non-Natives, but later reacquired from the non-Natives,[1118] and to non-Natives subject to a reversion right.[1119] These were called non-Native fee lands, which are Native lands that Congress allowed tribes to sell (usually to tribe members) so that the land became freely alienable; in one case the Court construed the statute to make such taxable status permanent, even if the land was reacquired by the tribe; but the consent to tax was limited to in rem taxation of the land and did not extend to excise taxation of transactions with respect to the land.[1120]

But many states tried to tax fee lands owned by Native Americans without congressional consent and the United States was quite aggressive (in some cases) and successful in recovering local taxes paid by Native Americans under protest.[1121]

The state cannot tax property or use of vehicles by Native Americans on tribal lands.[1122] The state cannot tax vehicles owned by the tribe or members and used on and off the reservation.[1123]

Native Americans' defense against a state tax may be based on an expansive reading of a treaty. In *Cougar Den*, the Court affirmed the holding of the Supreme Court of the state of Washington that the 1855 treaty between the United States and the Yakama Nation precludes the state from imposing a tax on fuel transported in the state outside the reservation, because it was a tax that burdened use of the highways and thus violated the treaty right of travel upon public highways "in common with citizens of the United States."[1124] The liberal interpretation applied in that case was similar to an early case preventing Oklahoma from taxing land patented to individual Native Americans under a federal law making the land tax exempt generally.[1125]

Because the state tax incidence falls on the Native American retailer the state could not tax gas sales on Native lands.[1126] The state could not tax tobacco products sold to Native Americans on the Native lands.[1127]

[1117] Goudy v. Meath, 203 U.S. 146 (1906).

[1118] Cass County v. Leech Lake Band of Chippewa Indians, 524 U.S. 103 (1998).

[1119] Choctaw, O. & G. R. Co. v. Mackey, 256 U.S. 531 (1921).

[1120] County of Yakima v. Confederated Tribes & Bands of the Yakima Indian Nation, 502 U.S. 251 (1992). See explanation of this ruling in Upper Skagit Indian Tribe v. Lundgren, 138 S. Ct. 1649 (2018).

[1121] Ward v. Board of County Comm'rs, 253 U.S. 17 (1920).

[1122] Washington v. Confederated Tribes of Colville Indian Reservation, 447 U.S. 134 (1980); Moe v. Confederated Salish & Kootenai Tribes of Flathead Reservation, 425 U.S. 463 (1976). *See generally*, Staff of the Joint Committee on Taxation, Overview of Federal Tax Provisions and Analysis of Selected Issues Relating to Native American Tribes and their Members, pp. 4-6, JCX-8-20 (Feb. 28, 2020).

[1123] Wash. v. Confederated Tribes of Colville Indian Reservation, 447 U.S. 134 (1980).

[1124] Washington State Department of Licensing v. Cougar Den Inc., 139 S. Ct. 1000 (2019). *See* Cummings, *The Supreme Court's 2018 Term in Tax*, 164 Tax Notes 1001 (Aug. 12, 2019).

[1125] Choate v. Trapp, 224 U.S. 665 (1912); English v. Richardson, 224 U.S. 680 (1912).

[1126] Okla. Tax Comm'n v. Chickasaw Nation, 515 U.S. 450 (1995).

[1127] Dep't of Taxation v. Milhelm Attea & Bros., 512 U.S. 61 (1994).

The immunity of Native Americans from state tax extends to activities on formal or informal reservations, allotted lands, or dependent Native communities.[1128] Generally states can impose an inheritance tax on tribal members, except as to the transfer of fee land that Congress has explicitly protected from state taxation even though held in fee.[1129]

The scope of Native lands was substantially expanded, at least its true extent was recognized, in 2020 in *McGirt*.[1130] However, the Court had ruled in 2005 that the tribe's reacquisition of land after 200 years could not preclude the county from imposing property taxes on the tribe's land.[1131]

The Court ruled that the tribe could not remove to federal court a state court action brought by the state to collect tax from the tribe's casino.[1132] The United States could sue a county to enforce the tribe's tax exemption.[1133] The United States in suing a state on behalf of a Native American is not limited to state procedures for tax disputes.[1134] State did not have to pay interest on property tax to be refunded to United States on behalf of a Native American who had been forced to take fee patent ownership of land, making it taxable, which Congress later revoked.[1135]

b. *Off Native American Lands*

States can tax real property owned by Native Americans off the reservation.[1136] A state could collect sales tax on oil sold to a non-Native oil distributor off the Reservation, which the distributor would deliver to the Reservation for sale by Native Americans mostly to non-Natives; the decision depended on the legal incidence, not the economic incidence, of the tax, and the Court found it was not imposed on the sales on the Reservation.[1137]

[1128] Oklahoma Tax Comm'n v. Sac & Fox Nation, 508 U.S. 114 (1993).

[1129] Oklahoma Tax Comm'n v. United States, 319 U.S. 598 (1943); West v. Okla. Tax Com., 334 U.S. 717 (1948).

[1130] McGirt v. Oklahoma, 140 S. Ct. 2452 (2020) (a criminal case denying power of criminal laws of Oklahoma over Native Americans on fee lands that had been deeded out of Tribal ownership a century ago). Nebraska v. Parker, 136 S. Ct. 1072 (2016), involved a Native tribe that tried to collect a liquor tax from businesses in a town over which the tribe had not asserted control for decades. The plaintiffs sought an order that the tribe had no authority in the town and lost because the 1882 legislation allowing non-Native settlement of the area did not clearly "diminish" the tribal lands. The plaintiffs did not raise laches as an objection to the tax, but the opinion noted they might have.

[1131] City of Sherrill v. Oneida Indian Nation, 544 U.S. 197 (2005).

[1132] Okla. Tax Comm'n v. Graham, 489 U.S. 838 (1989).

[1133] United States v. Rickert, 188 U.S. 432 (1903) (based on viewing the patent lands as still belonging to the United States).

[1134] United States v. Board of County Comm'rs, 251 U.S. 128 (1919).

[1135] Board of County Comm'rs v. United States, 308 U.S. 343 (1939).

[1136] Shaw v. Gibson-Zahniser Oil Corp., 276 U.S. 575 (1928).

[1137] Wagnon v. Prairie Band Potawatomi Nation, 546 U.S. 95 (2005). This opinion contains extensive analysis of White Mountain Apache Tribe v. Bracker, 448 U.S. 136 (1980) for determining a state's authority over non-Natives' conduct on a reservation.

Generally states can tax Native Americans off the reservation and off Indian Lands, being lands granted to Natives by Congress; Tribal business on such non-Native lands are not exempt from state taxation as federal instrumentalities, even if specifically authorized by the federal government (as by lease of lands to Native Americans), and the principle that absent clear statutory guidance, courts ordinarily will not imply tax exemptions, applies as well to Native Americans.[1138] As a result, the state could collect a gross receipts tax from a Native ski business on land leased from the United States, but could not collect a use tax on fixtures attached to the land because that would be a tax on the land, which the relevant statute forbade.[1139]

In *Cougar Den*, the Court ruled that the 1855 treaty between the United States and the Yakama Nation precludes the state from imposing a tax on a motor fuel company owned by a tribe member and transported into the state outside the reservation, because the fuel was to be sold on the reservation to tribe members and would, in effect, burden their use of the highways and thus violate the treaty right of travel upon public highways "in common with citizens of the United States."[1140]

c. *Tribal Sovereignty*

Although equating tribes with other sovereigns is at the root of most of the rules of Native American taxation, tribes do not necessarily share all attributes of sovereignty and so a state does not improperly discriminate when it exempts from sales tax sales to the federal government and other states but not to tribes.[1141]

Federal taxation of Native Americans is addressed by Ch. II.C.10.

[1138] Mescalero Apache Tribe v. Jones, 411 U.S. 145 (1973).

[1139] Mescalero Apache Tribe v. Jones, 411 U.S. 145 (1973).

[1140] Wash. State Dep't of Licensing v. Cougar Den, Inc., 139 S. Ct. 1000 (2019).

[1141] Wagnon v. Prairie Band Potawatomi Nation, 546 U.S. 95 (2005).

Ch. X. Conclusion

This book's conclusions are stated in Chapter I.A. Contrary to the warnings referenced in that Chapter that there is no lack of federal tax constitutional law, much less Supreme Court federal tax constitutional law; rather, there is an abundance of such law. Viewed in their entirety, the Court's federal tax constitutional decisions reflect a remarkably hands off approach to federal taxation so far as a potential finding of constitutional violation is concerned.[1]

That fact, however, has not dissuaded taxpayers from attacking federal taxes using the Constitution, in addition to every other means, because taxes are the primary governmental means of depriving persons of their property without just compensation. However, aside from certain targeted limits on federal taxation, such as the Export Clause, the willingness of the Court to rule for federal taxpayers on constitutional grounds is quite limited, though the potential is there, dependent largely on the Court's political leanings of the moment.

Indeed, the exceptions that prove the rule of the Court's hands off approach to federal taxation, are the decisions that flowed directly from the Court's conservative leanings during certain periods: for example, *Pollock* (1895), *Drexel Furniture* (1922), *Butler* (1936).[2] These were clustered between 1895 and 1936, with the majority between 1922 and 1936.

---

[1] *See* Cummings, *Why Taxes Almost Always Have Been Constitutional*, 172 Tax Notes Federal 789 (Aug. 2, 2021).

[2] *See* Ch. I.E.2.b.

In 2012 the Court decided the most important attack on a federal attack since 1936, in the health insurance tax case, *Sebelius*, discussed in detail in Chapter III.E.2.c. That decision, its holdings and most of the reasoning in the opinion of the Court, are entirely consistent with the thrust of the prior precedents supporting the federal taxing power. There is no need to begin an analysis of a federal tax attack with *Sebelius*, because it did not create any new law. It appropriately fits into the general authorities on the broad scope of the taxing power, the power of taxes to regulate, the definition of a tax, and the limited scope of direct taxes, all discussed at length throughout this book.

In contrast with the relative hands off treatment of federal taxation, the Supreme Court has played a much more active role in creating the constitutional law of state taxation from scratch. The number of its state tax opinions swamps its federal tax opinions because (1) multiple unhappy taxpayers attacked (2) multiple state and local jurisdictions' levies and (3) when they lost in state court had a right to Supreme Court review for many decades. Nevertheless, subject to its unique role in policing the Commerce Clause, the Court mostly found state taxes constitutional too. The 2018 *Wayfair* ruling allowing states to collect sales tax from vendors with no physical presence in the state even reflects some particular sympathy for state taxation. But attacks will continue because not paying taxes is the best way to make money without doing anything.

Table of Cases